Introduction to Information Systems: Supporting and Transforming Business

Tenth Edition

R. KELLY RAINER JR.

BRAD PRINCE

WILEY

Director – Portfolio Management: Lise Johnson
Editors: Jennifer Manias/Julia Chase
Senior Editorial Assistant: Campbell McDonald
Customer Insights Manager: Francesca Baratta
Sr. Manager, Course Content & Production: Ed Brislin

Sr. Course Content Developer: Wendy Ashenberg
Sr. Course Production Operations Specialist: Nicole Repasky
Sr. Creative Product Designer: Tom Nery
Cover Photo: MarsYu / iStock / Getty Images

This book was typeset in 9.5/11.5 STIX Two at Lumina Datamatics, Inc.

Wiley is a global leader in research and education, unlocking human potential by enabling discovery, powering education, and shaping workforces. For over 200 years, Wiley has fueled the world's knowledge ecosystem. Today, our high-impact content, platforms, and services help researchers, learners, institutions, and corporations achieve their goals in an ever-changing world. Visit us at Wiley.com.

EPUB ISBN: 978-1-394-16512-4

The inside back cover will contain printing identification and country of origin if omitted from this page.

In addition, if the ISBN on the cover differs from the ISBN on this page, the one on the cover is correct.

Library of Congress Cataloging-in-Publication Data

Names: Rainer, R. Kelly, Jr., 1949- author. | Prince, Brad, 1978- author.
Title: Introduction to information systems : supporting and transforming
  business / R. Kelly Rainer Jr., Brad Prince.
Description: Tenth edition. | Hoboken : Wiley, [2023] | Includes index. |
Identifiers: LCCN 2023026385 (print) | LCCN 2023026386 (ebook) | ISBN
  9781394165124 (epub) | ISBN 9781394165162 (adobe pdf) | ISBN 9781394165711
  (paperback) | ISBN 9781394165711q(paperback) | ISBN 9781394165162q(adobe
  pdf) | ISBN 9781394165124q(epub)
Subjects: LCSH: Information technology. | Computer networks. | Management
  information systems.
Classification: LCC T58.5 (ebook) | LCC T58.5 .R35 2023 (print) | DDC
  658.4/038011 23/eng/20230--dc02
LC record available at https://lccn.loc.gov/2023026385
LC record available at https://lccn.loc.gov/2023026386

Printed in the United States of America.

SKY10052210_073123

The entire focus of this book is to help students become informed users of information systems and information technology. In general, informed users receive increased value from organizational information systems and technologies. We hope to help students do just that.

What Do Information Systems Have to Do with Business?

This edition of Rainer and Prince's *Introduction to Information Systems* will answer this question for you. In every chapter, you will see how real global businesses use technology and information systems to increase their profitability, gain market share, develop and improve their customer relations, and manage their daily operations. In other words, you will learn how information systems provide the foundation for all modern organizations, whether they are public sector, private sector, for-profit, or not-for-profit. We have several goals for all business majors, particularly undergraduates. First, we want to teach you how to use information technology to help you master your current or future jobs to help ensure the success of your organizations. Second, we want you to become *informed users* of information systems and information technology. Third, we want you to understand the digital transformation that your organization will likely be undergoing. The digital transformation of organizations is the acceleration of existing business processes and the development of new processes and business models. In this way, organizations can capitalize on the capabilities and opportunities of various technologies to improve performance. Examples of these technologies include Big Data, cloud computing, artificial intelligence, the Internet of Things, mobile computing, and electronic commerce. We address each of these in our book. To accomplish these goals, we focus on not merely *learning* the concepts of information technology but also on *applying* those concepts to perform business more effectively and efficiently. We concentrate on placing information systems in the context of business so that you will more readily grasp the concepts we present in the text.

Pedagogical Structure

Various pedagogical features provide a structured learning system that reinforces the concepts through features such as chapter-opening organizers, section reviews, study aids, frequent applications, and hands-on exercises and activities.

Chapter-opening organizers include the following pedagogical features:

- **Chapter Outline:** Lists the major concepts covered in each chapter.
- **Learning Objectives:** Provide an overview of the key learning goals that students should achieve after reading the chapter.

- **Opening Cases:** Chapter-opening cases address a business problem faced by actual organizations and how they employ information systems and information technology to solve the issues. The cases generally consist of a description of the problem, an overview of the IS solutions implemented, and a presentation of the results of the implementation. Each case closes with discussion questions so that students can further explore the concepts presented in the case.

Study aids are provided throughout each chapter. These include the following:

- IT's About Business cases provide real-world applications, with questions that relate to concepts covered in the text. Icons relate these sections to the specific functional areas in the text.
- Highlighted examples interspersed throughout the text illustrate the use (and misuse) of IT by real-world organizations, thus making the conceptual discussion more concrete.
- Tables list key points or summarize different concepts.
- End-of-section reviews (Before You Go On...) prompt students to pause and test their understanding of basic concepts before moving on to the next section.

End-of-chapter study aids provide extensive opportunities for the reader to review:

- **What's in IT for Me?** is a unique chapter summary section that demonstrates the relevance of topics for different functional areas (accounting, finance, marketing, production/operations management, and human resources management).
- The chapter **Summary**, keyed to learning objectives listed at the beginning of the chapter, enables students to review the major concepts covered in the chapter.
- **Closing cases** in each chapter address a business problem faced by actual companies and how they used IS to solve these issues. The cases generally consist of a description of the problem, an overview of the IS solution implemented, and a presentation of the results of that implementation. Each case is followed by discussion questions so that students can further explore the concepts presented in the case.

Hands-on exercises and activities require the reader to do something with the concepts they have studied. These include the following:

- **Apply the Concept Activities:** This book's unique pedagogical structure is designed to keep students actively engaged with the course material. Reading material in each chapter subsection is supported by an "Apply the

Concept" activity that is directly related to a chapter objective. These activities include links to online videos and articles and other hands-on activities that require students to immediately apply what they have learned. Each Apply the Concept has the following elements:

- Background (places the activity in the context of relevant reading material)
- Activity (a hands-on activity that students carry out)
- Deliverable (various tasks for students to complete as they perform the activity)

- **Discussion Questions and Problem-Solving Activities:** Provide practice through active learning. These exercises are hands-on opportunities to apply the concepts discussed in the chapter.

Key Features

We have been guided by the following educational principles that we believe will enhance the teaching and learning experience.

What's in IT for Me?   We emphasize the importance of information systems by calling attention in every chapter to how that chapter's topic relates to each business major. Icons guide students to relevant issues for their specific functional area—accounting (ACC), finance (FIN), marketing (MKT), production/operations management (POM), human resources management (HRM), and management information systems (MIS). Chapters conclude with a detailed summary (titled "What's in IT for Me?") of how key concepts in the chapter relate to each functional area.

Active Learning   We recognize the need to actively involve students in problem solving, creative thinking, and capitalizing on opportunities. Therefore, we have included in every chapter a variety of hands-on exercises, activities, and mini-cases, including exercises that require students to use software application tools. Through these activities and an interactive website, we enable students to apply the concepts they learn.

Diversified and Unique Examples from Different Industries   Extensive use of vivid examples from large corporations, small businesses, and government and not-for-profit organizations enlivens the concepts from the chapter. The examples illustrate everything from the capabilities of information systems to their cost and justification and the innovative ways that corporations are using IS in their operations. Small businesses have been included to recognize the fact that many students will work for small- to mid-sized companies, and some will even start their own small business. In fact, some students may already be working at local businesses, and the concepts they are learning in class can be readily observed or put into practice in their jobs. Each chapter constantly highlights the integral connection between business and IS. This connection is especially evident in the chapter-opening and closing cases, the "IT's About Business" boxes, and the highlighted examples.

Successes and Failures   Many textbooks present examples of the successful implementation of information systems, and our book is no exception. However, we go one step beyond by also providing numerous examples of IS failures, and we do so in the context of lessons that can be learned from such failures. Misuse of information systems can be very expensive.

Global Focus   An understanding of global competition, partnerships, and trading is essential to success in a modern business environment. Therefore, we provide a broad selection of international cases and examples. We discuss the role of information systems in facilitating export and import, the management of international companies, and electronic trading around the globe.

Innovation and Creativity   In today's rapidly changing business environment, creativity and innovation are necessary for a business to operate effectively and profitably. Throughout our book, we demonstrate how information systems facilitate these processes.

Focus on Ethics   With corporate scandals appearing in the headlines almost daily, ethics and ethical questions have come to the forefront of businesspeople's minds. In addition to devoting an entire chapter to ethics and privacy (Chapter 3), we have included examples and cases throughout the text that focus on business ethics.

A Guide to Icons in This Book   As you read this book, you will notice a variety of icons interspersed throughout the chapters.

These icons highlight material relating to different functional areas. IS concepts are relevant to all business careers, not just careers in IT. The functional area icons help students of different majors quickly pick out concepts and examples of particular relevance to them. Below is a quick reference of these icons:

ACCT **For the Accounting Major** highlights content relevant to the functional area of accounting.

FIN **For the Finance Major** highlights content relevant to the functional area of finance.

MKT **For the Marketing Major** highlights content relevant to the functional area of marketing.

POM **For the Production/Operations Management Major** highlights content relevant to the functional area of production/operations management.

HRM **For the Human Resources Major** highlights content relevant to the functional area of human resources.

MIS **For the MIS Major** highlights content relevant to the functional area of Management Information Systems.

What's New in Rainer *Introduction to Information Systems*, 10e

The new edition includes all new or updated chapter opening cases, chapter closing cases, and IT's About Business cases. The cases all cover international examples, highlight new and exciting technologies and include top global corporations.

Highlights of Rainer 10e

Digital Transformation of Organizations
More than likely, students will go to work for companies that are undergoing digital transformation. We emphasize digital transformation and the information technologies that drive such transformations. The technologies that drive digital transformation include Big Data (see Chapter 5), broadband Internet access (see Chapter 6), wireless and mobile computing (see Chapter 8), the Internet of Things (see Chapter 8), social computing (see Chapter 9), business analytics (see Chapter 12), agile systems development methods (see Chapter 13), cloud computing (see Technology Guide 3), and artificial intelligence (see Chapter 14).

Artificial Intelligence
In Chapter 14, we address the critically important topic of artificial intelligence:

- We first carefully define AI in terms of the tasks that humans perform, rather than how humans think. We then compare the capabilities of natural intelligence and artificial intelligence.
- We differentiate between weak AI and strong AI.
- We define supervised machine learning, semi-supervised machine learning, reinforcement learning, unsupervised machine learning, and deep learning.
- We address bias in machine-learning systems.
- We define neural networks and how they function.
- We discuss various applications of AI, including computer vision, natural language processing, robotics, speech recognition, and intelligent agents.
- In IT's About Business 14.2, we address ChatGPT. We define ChatGPT as a large language model and discuss how developers build such models. We describe its capabilities, advantages, and disadvantages. We then turn our attention to areas where the system is making an impact. These areas include education, journalism, search engines, and software engineering. We close with a look at ChatGPT-4 and ChatGPT detector systems.
- We provide a thorough discussion of AI applications in the functional areas, including accounting, finance, marketing, production/operations management, human resource management, and MIS.

Business Analytics
In Chapter 12, we expanded our discussion of the difference between analytics and statistics, added real-world scenarios that allow students to apply the business analytics process (Figure 12.3), and added a discussion of Google Analytics.

Social Computing
In Chapter 9, we added a section called "Problems with Social Computing." We address three serious issues with social media platforms: First, they allow almost anyone to publish any content. Second, the platforms employ psychological measures to keep visitors on their sites longer. Third, third-party entities employ various means to spread their messages. Our discussion includes bots, cyborgs, trolls, troll farms, fake news, and deepfakes, as well as the infinite scroll and randomly scheduled rewards.

E-Business and E-Commerce
In Chapter 7, we provide an expanded discussion of blockchain technology. We provide examples of the use of blockchains, including cryptocurrencies such as Bitcoin, the energy grid, digital content creators (e.g., music and journalism), and along supply chains.

Telecommunications and Networking
In Chapter 6, we provide an expanded discussion of the evolution of the Web, from Web 1.0 to Web 5.0.

Hardware

- In Technology Guide 1, we added a new section addressing augmented reality (AR), virtual reality (VR), and mixed reality (MR). We provide numerous real-world examples of AR, VR, and MR.
- We added a brief discussion of why Moore's Law is slowing down.
- We also added brief discussions of graphics processing units and quantum computing.

Cloud Computing

- In Technology Guide 3, we added a new section comparing the "Big Three" cloud computing vendors: Amazon Web Services, Microsoft Azure, and the Google Cloud Platform.
- We also added a discussion of multi–cloud computing environments.

Instructor Resources

Introduction to Information Systems, Tenth Edition, is supported by a comprehensive learning package that assists the instructor in creating a motivating and enthusiastic learning environment.

Instructor's Manual
The Instructor's Manual includes a chapter overview, teaching tips and strategies, answers to all end-of-chapter questions, supplemental mini-cases with essay questions and answers, and experiential exercises that relate to particular topics.

Test Bank
The Test Bank is a comprehensive resource for test questions. It contains multiple-choice, true/false, short answer, and essay questions for each chapter. The multiple-choice and true/false questions are labeled according to difficulty: easy, medium, or hard.

Computerized Test Bank
Wiley provides complimentary software to generate print exams or to import test bank questions into standard LMS formats. The assessment items available in this software are a subset of those in the WileyPLUS question banks. See the assignment banks in WileyPLUS for the complete catalog of assessment items related to the text.

PowerPoint Presentations
The PowerPoint presentations consist of a series of slides for each chapter of the text, are designed around the text content, and incorporate key points from the text and all text illustrations as appropriate.

Weekly Updates
Weekly updates, harvested from around the Web by Professor David Firth of the University of Montana, provide you with the latest IT news and issues. These are posted every Monday morning throughout the year at http://wileyinformationsystemsupdates.com and include links to articles and videos as well as discussion questions to assign or use in class.

WileyPLUS

WileyPLUS helps instructors:

- Save time by automating grading of practice, homework, quizzes, and exams
- Create a focused and personalized course that reflects their teaching style
- Quickly identify and understand student learning trends to improve classroom engagement
- Improve their course year over year using WileyPLUS data

Instructor Resources include:

- Lecture Videos—The authors provide an extensive series of lecture videos, ranging in length from 3 minutes to 10 minutes. The videos explain key concepts throughout the book, with each clip addressing a single concept. In this way, the lecture videos reinforce key concepts in the text without being confusing to the students.
- Data Analytics & Business Module—With the emergence of data analytics transforming the business environment, Wiley has partnered with business leaders in the Business-Higher Education Forum (BHEF) to identify the competencies graduates need to be successful in their careers. As a result, WileyPLUS includes a new data analytics module with industry-validated content that prepares operations management students for a changing workforce.
- ESG Module—That encourages students to explore the relationships between contemporary business and larger social issues with our Environmental, Social, and Corporate Governance (ESG) Module authored by Peter Moreira and Rosalie E. Harms (Coauthors on our Boone and Kurtz Contemporary Business title). With various discussion questions and assessment, students are challenged to think critically about societal structures, lived experiences, and sustainability.
- Activity Links—Apply the Concept activities link out to the Web, providing videos for students to view and use in the activities. When appropriate, students are provided with links f to complete as part of the deliverable.
- Instructor's Manual—This guide contains detailed solutions to all questions, exercises, and problems in the textbook.
- Practice Quizzes—These quizzes give students a way to test themselves on course material before exams. Each chapter exam contains fill-in-the-blank, application, and multiple-choice questions that provide immediate feedback with the correct answer.
- Reading Quizzes—These quizzes reinforce basic concepts from the reading.
- Gradable Excel Questions—Students can learn and practice beginner and advanced Excel skills while working directly in Excel. Graded feedback is given on a cell by cell basis.

Student Resources include:

- Video Lectures—The authors are featured in these video lectures, which provide explanations of key concepts throughout the book.
- Application Videos—The course provides videos taken from real world events and reported on by Bloomberg and provides activities for discussion and assessment that can be applied to the topic of the chapter.
- Adaptive Practice—The adaptive component provides targeted and personalized opportunities for practice to effectively prepare for class or quizzes and exams.
- Practice Quizzes—These quizzes give students a way to test themselves on course material before exams. Each chapter exam contains fill-in-the-blank, application, and multiple-choice questions that provide immediate feedback with the correct answer.
- *Microsoft Office 2016/2019/2021 Lab Manual & Instructor Resources*—by Ed Martin, Queens College, CUNY is a thorough introduction to the Microsoft Office products of Word, Excel, Access, and PowerPoint with screenshots that show students step-by-step instructions on basic MS Office tasks.

Wiley Custom Services

This group's services allow you to:

- Adapt existing Wiley content and combine texts
- Incorporate and publish your own materials
- Collaborate with our team to ensure your satisfaction

Wiley Custom Select

Wiley Custom Select allows you to build your own course materials using selected chapters of any Wiley text and your own material if desired. For more information, contact your Wiley sales representative or visit **http://customselect.wiley.com**.

Brief Contents

Contents

CHAPTER 1

Introduction to Information Systems

CHAPTER OUTLINE	LEARNING OBJECTIVES
1.1 Why Should I Study Information Systems?	**1.1 Identify** the reasons why being an informed user of information systems is important in today's world.
1.2 Overview of Computer-Based Information Systems	**1.2 Describe** the various types of computer-based information systems in an organization.
1.3 How Does IT Impact Organizations?	**1.3 Discuss** ways in which information technology can affect managers and nonmanagerial workers.
1.4 Importance of Information Systems to Society	**1.4 Identify** positive and negative societal effects of the increased use of information technology.

Opening Case

MKT Pink Sauce Storm on TikTok

Social media consists of websites and mobile applications that enable users to create and share content for the purpose of social networking. Given the vast numbers of users, many networks end up being used as platforms for promoting products, ideas, businesses, political agendas, opinions, humor, and much more. TikTok (www.tiktok.com) is an extremely popular social media platform that allows users to post short videos and to like, comment on, and follow other users. It has become an ideal medium for launching viral videos, reaching millions of users. In fact, it can literally make a person into superstar overnight. The platform is now available in more than 150 markets worldwide in 75 languages.

TikTok's success, however, is not without controversy. In September 2020, the app was almost banned from the United States due to fears that the Chinese government would have access to private usage data and could use it for blackmail. Congressional debates continue to this day. Nonetheless, TikTok is known for enabling small businesses to go viral overnight, due to product recommendations that cause a specific shade of blush to sell out everywhere and convincing thousands of people to make salmon rice bowls for lunch every day.

Consider the case of Pii, a single mom with two children. Pii had been working as a private chef in Miami since 2017. Before TikTok became available, she posted dozens of YouTube videos that ranged from mukbangs (live-streamed videos of people eating large amounts of food) to weight-loss vlogs (video blogs), in which she discussed trendy diets with questionable nutritional value.

Then, in June 2022, Chef Pii posted a video on TikTok to promote her new product that she called Pink Sauce. At that time, Pii had fewer than 1,000 followers. The video attracted more than 80,000 followers and 3 million likes, and her Pink Sauce quickly became a craze.

At first glance, Chef Pii's decision to use TikTok might seem like an ideal strategy. In reality, however, it presented several major challenges. Some users shared widespread criticism, particularly due to safety concerns over the sauce's "secret" ingredients, packaging, and distribution. Customers have used TikTok to voice complaints regarding high prices and two-week shipping times, along with reports of leaky packages and spoiled products. Some customers have even called out Chef Pii for potentially violating food distribution laws.

Chef Pii addressed the backlash on TikTok in a video post that attracted more than 3.5 million views. She apologized for the shipping delays and explained that she had experienced major problems trying to keep up with the overwhelming demand. She acknowledged that she had not anticipated that her business would take off as quickly as it did, and she conceded that trying to meet this demand might have resulted in some rushed work that led to errors on the nutrition label and packaging, including misspelled words and misprinted serving sizes. Pii concluded by thanking her customers for their business and assuring them that she and her team were working to provide a replacement product with a corrected label in the near future.

The U.S. Food and Drug Administration (FDA, **www.fda.gov**) requires manufacturers of salad dressings and condiments to obtain food facility registration. This registration allows the FDA to identify and locate the source of potential bioterrorism or food-borne illness in case of an outbreak. Chef Pii did not initially apply for food facility registration.

In addition, the FDA has established standards for testing, manufacturing, and labeling of food products. In April 2022, the agency updated its guidelines for nutritional fact labels on food and drink products for the first time in 20 years. Accurate and reasonable serving size is among the new requirements for food labels. The FDA now requires this information to appear in a bigger and bolder font and to "better reflect the amount people typically eat and drink today."

Since Chef Pii had not registered her product, her labels were not subject to review or the FDA requirements. This led to mistakes that left her open to criticism on the same platform that had made her product so successful. Pii's lack of knowledge regarding commercial food production generated significant obstacles. Ultimately, Chef Pii paused production to submit to the FDA's regulations and inspection of her commercial kitchen, and she made label corrections.

Chef Pii tried to respond to her critics on TikTok, explaining that she was doing the best she could, providing information but not giving away her secret, apologizing for labeling errors, and addressing the issues around the lack of FDA approval. It seemed, however, that everything she posted was scrutinized, criticized, and publicized. TikTok was working both in her favor and to her detriment.

Millions of people had heard about Pink Sauce. The product had been featured on multiple media outlets including *Taste of Home*, *Today*, the *Los Angeles Times*, *Forbes*, and *USA Today*. In addition, the Pink Sauce story had been highlighted on Facebook, Twitter, Instagram, and LinkedIn. As a result of this widespread publicity, Chef Pii's product was "discovered" and pursued by a commercial operation.

In August 2022, Dave's Gourmet, which manufactures pasta sauces and hot sauces, reached an agreement with Chef Pii. Basically, the company would manage the production and delivery of Pink Sauce, while Chef Pii would continue to promote the product over social media. Dave's Gourmet's long history in the pasta and hot sauce markets has given Pink Sauce immediate credibility as a viable and safe food product. The company has been contacted by national restaurant chains that want this unique sauce in their stores as soon as possible. It has also begun talks with a few major retail chains regarding selling Pink Sauce through their channels.

In August 2022, Chef Pii posted a video in which she stated she was "so excited" to be developing Pink Sauce with Dave's Gourmet in accordance with all of the FDA's regulations. Ultimately, social media created a platform for a creative chef to promote and sell a unique product, manage the rapid growth in demand, and locate a business partner to help ensure the product's long-term success.

Questions

1. **Identify and discuss three ways in which social media helped Chef Pii achieve rapid success.**

2. **Identify and discuss three ways in which social media created challenges for Chef Pii.**

3. **How does the success of Pink Sauce challenge assumptions about successfully creating a successful business?**

Sources: Compiled from "Dave's Gourmet, Tiktok's Chef Pii Partner to Launch Pink Sauce," *SpecialtyFood.com*, August 17, 2022; "Dave's Gourmet Partners with Social Media Influencer Chef Pii to Launch the Pink Sauce," *PR NewsWire*, August 17, 2022; "Pink Sauce Goes Viral on TikTok: Why Has the FDA Jumped In?," *FirstPost.com*, August 4, 2022; B. Lee, "'F in FDA' Trends after Questions about Pink Sauce Emerge on TikTok," *Forbes*, July 26, 2022; B. Lee, "'Pink Sauce'' Goes Viral on TikTok, Here Are the Concerns with This Condiment," *Forbes*, July 24, 2022; A. Silberling, "'Pink Sauce Went Viral on TikTok. But Then It Exploded (Literally)," *TechCrunch*, July 22, 2022; S. Swain-Wilson, "The Viral 'Pink Sauce Chef' Finally Responded to the TikTok Controversy," *mashed.com*, July 22, 2022; M Sato, "Nobody Knows What's in Pink Sauce, TikTok's Latest Viral Product," *TheVerge.com*, July 21, 2022; https://www.fda.gov/food/food-industry/how-start-food-business, accessed 8/17/2022; and thepinksauce.com, accessed 8/17/2022.

Introduction

information technology (IT) Any computer-based tool that people use to work with information and support the information and information-processing needs of an organization.

Information technology (IT) refers to any computer-based tool that people use to work with information and support an organization's information and information-processing needs.

IT has far-reaching effects on individuals, organizations, and our planet. Although this text is largely devoted to the many ways in which IT is transforming modern organizations, you will also learn about the significant impacts of IT on individuals and societies, the global economy, and our physical environment. IT is making our world smaller, enabling more and more people to communicate, collaborate, and compete, thereby leveling the playing field.

COVID forced people to depend on IT in new ways and demonstrated how far-reaching technology can be. Specifically, IT has come to the forefront of electronic commerce, distance education, and politics (consider social media and the 2020 elections). As you will see, throughout this book we draw attention to the numerous ways IT enables us to adapt to life during and after the pandemic.

This text focuses on the successful applications of IT in organizations; that is, how organizations can use IT to make decisions, solve business problems and achieve competitive advantage in the marketplace. However, not all business problems can be solved with IT. Therefore, you must continue to develop your business skills!

When you graduate, either you will start your own business or you will work for an organization, whether it is public sector, private sector, for-profit, or not-for-profit. Your organization will have to survive and compete in an environment that has been radically transformed by information technology. This environment is global, massively interconnected, intensely competitive, 24/7/365, real time, rapidly changing, and information intensive. To compete successfully, your organization must use IT effectively.

As you read this chapter and this text, keep in mind that the information technologies you will learn about are important to businesses of all sizes. No matter which area of business you major in, which industry you work for, or the size of your company, you will benefit from learning about IT. Who knows? Maybe you will use the tools you learn about in this class to make your great idea a reality by becoming an entrepreneur and starting your own business!

The modern environment is intensely competitive not only for your organization but for you as well. You must compete with human talent from around the world. Therefore, you personally will have to make effective use of IT.

Accordingly, this chapter begins with a discussion of three reasons why you should become knowledgeable about IT. Next, it distinguishes among data, information, and knowledge, and it differentiates computer-based information systems from application programs. Finally, it considers the impacts of information systems on organizations and on society in general.

1.1 Why Should I Study Information Systems?

LEARNING OBJECTIVE

Identify the reasons why being an informed user of information systems is important in today's world.

WILEY PLUS

Author Lecture Videos are available exclusively in *WileyPLUS*.
Apply the Concept activities are available in the Appendix and in *WileyPLUS*.

No doubt, you have noticed that the title of this book is about information systems, not information technology. So, before we proceed, we will differentiate information technology from information systems. As previously defined, **information technology (IT)** refers to any computer-based tool that people use to work with information and support an organization's information and information-processing needs. An **information system (IS)** collects, processes, stores, analyzes, and disseminates information for a specific purpose. While we will discuss IT, the primary purpose of this text is to build your knowledge of the ways that modern organizations make use of IT and IS in their daily operations.

Your use of IT makes you part of the most connected generation in history: you have grown up online; you are, quite literally, never out of touch; you use more information technologies (in the form of digital devices) for more tasks; and you are bombarded with more information than any generation in history. The *MIT Technology Review* refers to you as *Homo conexus*. Information technologies are so deeply embedded in your lives that your daily routines would be almost unrecognizable to a college student just 20 years ago.

Essentially, you practice *continuous computing*, surrounded by a movable information network. This network is created by constant communication among the digital devices you carry and wear (e.g., laptops, tablets, smartphones, and wearables); the wired and wireless networks that you access as you move about; and Web-based tools for finding information and communicating and collaborating with other people. Your network enables you to pull information about virtually anything from anywhere at any time, and to push your own ideas back to the Web, from wherever you are, via a mobile device. Think of everything you do online, often with your smartphone: register for classes; take classes (not just at your university); access class syllabi, information, PowerPoints, and lectures; research class papers and presentations; conduct banking; pay your bills; research, shop, and purchase products from companies and other people; sell your "stuff"; search for, and apply for, jobs; make your travel reservations (hotel, airline, and/or rental car); create your own blog and post your own podcasts and videos to it; design your own page on Facebook and LinkedIn; make and upload videos to YouTube and TikTok; take, edit, and share your digital photographs; stream music and movies to your personal libraries; use RSS feeds to create your personal electronic newspaper; text and Tweet your friends and family throughout your day; send Snaps; order a ride from Uber or Lyft; track the location and arrival time of the next campus bus; select a place or room to rent on Airbnb; and many other activities. (*Note*: If any of these terms are unfamiliar to you, don't worry. You will learn about everything mentioned here in detail later in this text.)

Let's put the preceding paragraph in perspective. What would a typical day for you be like if you had no access to computing devices of any kind, including your phone? This scenario also means that you have no access to the Internet.

The Informed User—You!

So, the question is: Why should you learn about information systems and information technology? After all, you can comfortably use a computer (or other electronic devices) to perform many activities, you have been surfing the Web for your entire life, and you feel confident that you can manage any apps that your organization's MIS department installs. Let's look at three reasons why you should learn about ISs and IT.

informed user A person who is knowledgeable about information systems and information technology.

MIS The first reason to learn about information systems and information technology is to become an **informed user**; that is, a person knowledgeable about ISs and IT. In general, informed users obtain greater value from whichever technologies they use. You will enjoy many benefits from being an informed user of IT, including:

- You will benefit more from your organization's IT applications because you will understand what is "behind" those applications (see **Figure 1.1**). That is, what you see on your computer screen is brought to you by your MIS department, who are operating "behind" your screen.

USERS   MIS

Sławomir Fajer/Adobe Stock

FIGURE 1.1 MIS provides what users see and use on their computers.

- You will be aware of potential security issues and be more prepared to avoid them. IT's About Business 1.1 presents a scenario where social engineering was used to hack Uber in 2022. An informed user should not have made this mistake.

- Even as a new graduate, you will quickly be in a position to recommend—and perhaps to help select—which IT applications your organization will use. In essence, you will enhance the quality of your organization's IT applications with your input.

- Being an informed user will keep you abreast of both new information technologies and rapid developments in existing technologies. Remaining "on top of things" will help you to anticipate the impacts that "new and improved" technologies will have on your organization and to make recommendations regarding the adoption and use of these technologies.

- You will understand how using IT can improve your organization's performance and teamwork as well as your own productivity.

- If you have ideas of becoming an entrepreneur, then being an informed user will help you to utilize IT when you start your own business.

IT's About Business **1.1**

MIS Informed Users Are an Important Part of Security

Every organization is vulnerable to attack. In some ways, vulnerability is a business requirement because employees need access to data to do their jobs. Anytime access is granted, however, there is an opportunity for an unauthorized party to access that data and use it for malicious purposes.

But an organization's data assets are protected behind passwords, multifactor authentication, and other security protocols, right? (You will learn more about these topics in Chapter 4: Information Security.) Of course, they are protected! Unfortunately, sometimes it takes only a little old-fashioned trickery to access these assets. In the IT world, we refer to this trickery as social engineering.

Social engineering is an attempt to gain access that has not been granted to you. Specifically, social engineering techniques are intended to manipulate authorized employees into providing unauthorized parties with access to private information, for example, by sharing their passwords. These actions are the digital equivalent of stealing a master key from a security guard. You now have access, but it is not legal access. At this point, you can go anywhere with the keys, and you don't even have to break in.

Social engineering has been used to carry out several high-profile hacks in recent years. In 2020 alone, more than 100 prominent Twitter accounts—including Elon Musk, Barack Obama, Bill Gates, and Kanye West—were hacked and used to promote a bitcoin scam. These hacks were carried out by teenagers who managed to gain access to Twitter's internal networks by targeting a small number of employees. Significantly, social engineering doesn't require access to everything. Rather, just one open door is often sufficient.

Social engineering is one of the easier ways to hack an organization. If a hacker wants in, it is easier if someone hands over a password. Many experts believe that humans are the "weakest link" in cybersecurity because they can be easily deceived. That is why there has been a sharp rise in social engineering attacks. In 2021, the FBI received nearly 324,000 complaints regarding social engineering. That total is almost three times higher than in 2019.

Hackers stole approximately $2.4 billion through social engineering techniques between 2019 and 2021. Consider the following case.

MIS Uber Under Attack

In September 2022, Uber (www.uber.com) announced that its systems had been hacked. In response, it shut down several internal information systems until it could verify that the systems had not been compromised. A hacker socially engineered an Uber employee after discovering the employee's WhatsApp number. The intruder tricked the employee into logging in to a fake Uber site that captured the driver's username and password, thus giving the hacker access to the genuine Uber site.

However, simply obtaining the password was not sufficient. Uber also employs multifactor authentication, or MFA, which requires both a password and an "approval" on another device. In this case, the employee was prompted to push a button on a smartphone to verify that the login was legitimate. One attempt was not enough. So the hacker repeated the credentials into the site, repeatedly prompting the driver to approve the MFA. Finally, the employee, confused or tired, approved the login. With that, the attacker was inside.

Once inside Uber's system, the intruder uncovered administrative credentials that gave access to some of Uber's network resources. Uber quickly shut down parts of its internal systems while it investigated the extent of the breach.

How should companies prevent social engineering?

Companies can employ multiple strategies to prevent social engineering attacks. The first and most important strategy is to train your employees to become informed users of information technologies. Some experts recommend that organizations think beyond generic training and focus on training that is more specific to each user. For example, the riskiest employees—those with the most access—should receive more in-depth training to match the nature of their access rights. Specifically, they should be informed of the social engineering techniques they are most likely to encounter and what steps they should take in case something suspicious occurs.

One widely accepted best practice is to limit access privileges to those employees that actually need to fulfill their job duties. This practice seems logical and straightforward to implement. Keep in mind, however, that it is common for employees' roles to change, or for employees to change jobs to ones that require completely different levels of access. If access rights are not continuously updated to reflect these changes, then employees can access data they do not need. Further, implementing this strategy can be challenging due to the volume of identities, assets, access privileges, and the different identity and access management (IAM) structures used by each app and service. Limiting privileges cannot prevent social engineering. However, it can minimize the damage because the employee has access only to limited data.

In addition, outside contractors and consultants who do not work for an organization often have access to its data. These permissions should be strictly limited to data these parties need to perform their responsibilities. Further, they should be removed as soon as access is no longer needed.

Uber's Results

After conducting an internal investigation of the September 2022 breach, Uber reported it found "no evidence" that users' private information had been compromised. The company quickly restored all services, including Uber, Uber Eats, Uber Freight, and the Uber Driver app. It also brought back all the internal software tools it had taken down as a precaution following the attack.

Conclusions

According to a 2022 report, attacks that utilize insider threats and compromised user credentials continue to grow by 47 percent each year. Organizations must manage this risk through regular training, security awareness sessions, and cybersecurity techniques.

Human errors and failure to follow best practices will always be a constant. Security experts must remember that most people in an organization are not nearly as focused on preventing security breaches as the experts would like them to be. Ultimately, informed users who can recognize and spot a trick are your best defense.

Questions

1. **How did a hacker gain access to Uber's systems?**
2. **Define and discuss social engineering.**
3. **What steps should organizations take to better secure their systems against social engineering attacks?**

Sources: Compiled from R. Turner, "Meaningful Learnings from the Uber Breach," *Infosecurity Magazine*, September 27, 2022; S. Vaughan-Nichols, "Uber Hack: It's the Simple Things That Kill Your Security," *The New Stack*, September 27, 2022; B. Schneier, "The Uber Hack Exposes More Than Failed Data Security," *The New York Times*, September 26, 2022; S. Sabin, "Uber Hack Challenges Popular Login Security Practices," *axios.com*, September 23, 2022; D. Winder, "Likely Uber Hacking Suspect, 17, Arrested by City of London Police," *Forbes*, September 23, 2022; S. Ray, "Social Engineering: How a Teen Hacker Allegedly Managed to Breach Both Uber and Rockstar Games," *Forbes*, September 20, 2022; E. Gately, "Latest Uber Data Breach Caused by Hacker Tricking Worker," *Data Center Knowledge*, September 20, 2022; G. Avner, "3 Tips for Mitigating the Uber Hack," *Security Boulevard*, September 19, 2022; R. Lakshmanan, "Uber Claims No Sensitive Data Exposed in Latest Breach... But There's More to This," *The Hacker News*, September 17, 2022; D. Goodin, "Uber Was Breached to Its Core, Purportedly by an 18-year-old. Here's What's Known," *arstechnica.com*, September 16, 2022; and F. Siddiqui, and J. Menn, "Uber Suffers Computer System Breach, Alerts Authorities," *The Washington Post*, September 16, 2022.

The second reason to learn about ISs and IT is that the organization you join will undoubtedly be undergoing a digital transformation. In fact, digital transformation has become one of the most important strategies for organizations. A December 2019 survey by *Forbes* magazine noted that 70 percent of companies surveyed had a digital transformation strategy in place or were working on such a strategy, and 56 percent of companies are prioritizing digital transformation worldwide as of 2021.

digital transformation The business strategy that leverages IT to dramatically improve employee, customer, and business partner relationships; support continuous improvement in business operations and business processes; and develop new business models and businesses.

Digital transformation is the business strategy that leverages IT to dramatically improve employee, customer, and business partner relationships; to support continuous improvement in business operations and business processes; and to develop new business models and businesses. The information technologies that drive digital transformation include:

- Big Data (see Chapter 5);
- Business Analytics (see Chapter 12);
- Broadband Internet access (see Chapter 6);
- Mobile Computing (see Chapter 8);
- The Internet of Things (see Chapter 8);
- Social Computing (see Chapter 9);
- Agile Systems Development methods (see Chapter 13);
- Cloud Computing (see Technology Guide 3);
- Artificial Intelligence (see Chapter 14);

The third reason to learn about ISs and IT is that managing the IS function within an organization is no longer the exclusive responsibility of the IS department. Rather, users now play key roles in every step of this process. The overall objective in this text is to provide you with the necessary information to contribute immediately to managing the IS function in your organization. In short, our goal is to help you become a very informed user!

IT Offers Career Opportunities

MIS Because IT is vital to the operation of modern businesses, it offers many employment opportunities. The demand for traditional IT staff—programmers, business analysts, systems analysts, and designers—is substantial. In addition, many well-paid jobs exist in areas such as the Internet and electronic commerce (e-commerce), mobile commerce (m-commerce), network security, telecommunications, and multimedia design.

The IS field includes the people in various organizations who design and build information systems, the people who use those systems, and the people responsible for managing those systems. At the top of the list is the chief information officer (CIO).

The CIO is the executive in charge of the IS function. In most modern organizations, the CIO works with the chief executive officer (CEO), the chief financial officer (CFO), and other senior executives. Therefore, he or she actively participates in the organization's strategic planning process. In today's digital environment, the IS function has become increasingly strategic within organizations. As a result, although most CIOs still rise from the IS department, a growing number are coming up through the ranks in the business units (e.g., marketing, finance). Regardless of your major, you could become the CIO of your organization one day. This is another reason to be an informed user of information systems!

Table 1.1 provides a list of IT jobs, along with a description of each one. For further details about careers in IT, see **www.linkedin.com**, **www.indeed.com**, and **www.monster.com**.

TABLE 1.1   Information Technology Jobs

Position	Job Description
Chief Information Officer	Highest-ranking IS manager; responsible for all strategic planning in the organization
IS Director	Manages all systems throughout the organization and the day-to-day operations of the entire IS organization
Information Center Manager	Manages IS services such as help desks, hotlines, training, and consulting
Applications Development Manager	Coordinates and manages new systems development projects
Project Manager	Manages a particular new systems development project
Systems Analyst	Interfaces between users and programmers; determines information requirements and technical specifications for new applications
Operations Manager	Supervises the day-to-day operations of the data and/or computer center
Programming Manager	Coordinates all applications programming efforts
Social Media Manager	Coordinates all social media development efforts and all social media monitoring and response efforts
Business Analyst	Focuses on designing solutions for business problems; interfaces closely with users to demonstrate how IT can be used innovatively
Systems Programmer	Creates the computer code for developing new systems software or maintaining existing systems software
Applications Programmer	Creates the computer code for developing new applications or maintaining existing applications
Emerging Technologies Manager	Forecasts technology trends; evaluates and experiments with new technologies
Network Manager	Coordinates and manages the organization's voice and data networks
Database Administrator	Manages the organization's databases and oversees the use of database-management software
Auditing or Computer Security Manager	Oversees the ethical and legal use of information systems
Webmaster	Manages the organization's website
Web Designer	Creates websites and pages

Career opportunities in IS are strong and are projected to remain strong over the next 10 years. The U.S. *News & World Report* listed its "100 best jobs of 2022" and Glassdoor listed its "50 best jobs in America for 2022." Glassdoor (www.glassdoor.com) is a website where current and former employees anonymously review companies. Let's take a look at these rankings. (Note that the rankings differ because the magazine and Glassdoor used different criteria in their research.) As you can see, jobs suited for MIS majors appear in both lists, many of them quite high. The job rankings are as follows:

U.S. News & World Report (out of 100)

#1 Information Security Analysis	#32 Web Developer
#5 Software Developer	#38 Database Administrator
#6 Data Scientist	#48 Computer Network Architect
#11 IT Manager	#52 Computer System Administrator
#27 Computer Systems Analyst	#68 Computer Support Specialist

Glassdoor (out of 50)

#1 Enterprise Architect	#12 Cloud Engineer
#2 Full Stack Engineer	#15 Information Security Engineer
#3 Data Scientist	#24 UX Designer
#4 DevOps Engineer	#30 Systems Engineer
#7 Data Engineer	#32 Scrum Master
#8 Software Engineer	#32 Software Developer
#9 Java Developer	#35 Data Analyst
#11 Backend Engineer	#47 Database Architect

Not only do IS careers offer strong job growth, but the pay is excellent as well. The Bureau of Labor Statistics, an agency within the Department of Labor that is responsible for tracking and analyzing trends relating to the labor market, notes that the median salary in 2019 for "computer and information systems managers" was approximately $159,020, and predicted that the profession would grow by an average of 11 percent per year through 2030.

LinkedIn (www.linkedin.com) analyzed thousands of profiles of members who graduated between 2018 and 2019. LinkedIn collected salary information using the LinkedIn Salary tool. It discovered that of the 10 highest-paying entry-level jobs, seven were in the technology industry. These jobs include:

Job	Median Starting Salary
#1 Data Scientist	$95,000
#2 Software Engineer	$90,000
#6 User Experience Designer	$73,000
#7 IT Consultant	$72,000
#8 Java Developer	$72,000
#9 Systems Engineer	$70,000
#10 Software Developer	$68,600

According to a July 2022 Gartner survey of 128 CFOs and CEOs indicates that technology spending will remain strong, even if the economy does not. The survey found that 41 percent would cut mergers and acquisitions first, followed by sustainability, workforce training and talent development, capital expenditure for physical network expansion, and product innovation. "Improvements in technology for improved efficiency and scalability" was dead last overall, with just 23 percent of respondents identifying it as a top area for belt-tightening. What's more, around 45 percent of the executives identified the category as the last place they would seek cuts. This is great news for students looking for strong job opportunities.

Managing Information Resources

Managing information systems in modern organizations is a difficult, complex task. Several factors contribute to this complexity. First, information systems have enormous strategic value to organizations. Firms rely on them so heavily that, in some cases, when these systems are not working (even for a short time), the firm cannot function. (This situation is called "being hostage to information systems.") Second, information systems are very expensive to acquire, operate, and maintain.

A third factor contributing to the difficulty in managing information systems is the evolution of the management information systems (MIS) function within the organization. When businesses first began to use computers in the early 1950s, the MIS department "owned" the only computing resource in the organization: the mainframe. At that time, end users did not interact directly with the mainframe.

MIS In contrast, in the modern organization, computers are located in all departments, and almost all employees use computers in their work. This situation, known as *end user computing*, has led to a partnership between the MIS department and the end users. The MIS department now acts as more of a consultant to end users, viewing them as customers. In fact, the main function of the MIS department is to use IT to solve end users' business problems.

MIS As a result of these developments, the responsibility for managing information resources is now divided between the MIS department and the end users. This arrangement raises several important questions. Which resources are managed by whom? What is the role of the MIS department, its structure, and its place within the organization? What is the appropriate relationship between the MIS department and the end users? Regardless of who is doing what, it is essential that the MIS department and the end users work in close cooperation.

There is no standard way to divide responsibility for developing and maintaining information resources between the MIS department and the end users. Instead, that division depends on several factors: the size and nature of the organization, the amount and type of IT resources, the organization's attitudes toward computing, the attitudes of top management toward computing, the maturity level of the technology, the amount and nature of outsourced IT work, and even the countries in which the company operates. Generally speaking, the MIS department is responsible for corporate-level and shared resources, and the end users are responsible for departmental resources. Table 1.2 identifies both the traditional functions and various new, consultative functions of the MIS department.

So, where do the end users come in? Take a close look at Table 1.2. Under the traditional MIS functions, you will see two functions for which you provide vital input: managing systems development and infrastructure planning. Under the consultative MIS functions, in contrast, you exercise the primary responsibility for each function, while the MIS department acts as your advisor.

TABLE 1.2   The Changing Role of the Information Systems Department

Traditional Functions of the MIS Department

Managing systems development and systems project management
- As an end user, you will have critical input into the systems development process. You will learn about systems development in Chapter 13.

Managing computer operations, including the computer center

Staffing, training, and developing IS skills

Providing technical services

Infrastructure planning, development, and control
- As an end user, you will provide critical input about the IS infrastructure needs of your department.

TABLE 1.2   The Changing Role of the Information Systems Department

New (Consultative) Functions of the MIS Department

Initiating and designing specific strategic information systems

- As an end user, your information needs will often mandate the development of new strategic information systems.

You will decide which strategic systems you need (because you know your business needs and requirements better than the MIS department does), and you will provide input into developing these systems.

Incorporating the Internet and electronic commerce into the business

- As an end user, you will be primarily responsible for effectively using the Internet and electronic commerce in your business. You will work with the MIS department to accomplish these tasks.

Managing system integration, including the Internet, intranets, and extranets

- As an end user, your business needs will determine how you want to use the Internet, your corporate intranets, and extranets to accomplish your goals. You will be primarily responsible for advising the MIS department on the most effective use of the Internet, your corporate intranets, and extranets.

Educating non-MIS managers about IT

- Your department will be primarily responsible for advising the MIS department on how best to educate and train your employees about IT.

Educating the MIS staff about the business

- Communication between the MIS department and business units is a two-way street. You will be responsible for educating the MIS staff on your business, its needs and requirements, and its goals.

Partnering with business unit executives

- Essentially, you will be in a partnership with the MIS department. You will be responsible for seeing that this partnership is one "between equals" and ensuring its success.

Managing outsourcing

- Outsourcing is driven by business needs. Therefore, the outsourcing decision resides largely with the business units (i.e., with you). The MIS department, working closely with you, will advise you on technical issues such as communications bandwidth and security.

Proactively using business and technical knowledge to see innovative ideas about using IT

- Your business needs will often drive innovative ideas about how to effectively use information systems to accomplish your goals. The best way to bring these innovative uses of IS to life is to partner closely with your MIS department. Such close partnerships have amazing synergies!

Creating business alliances with business partners

- The needs of your business unit will drive these alliances, typically along your supply chain. Again, your MIS department will act as your advisor on various issues, including hardware and software compatibility, implementing extranets, communications, and security.

Before you go on...

1. Rate yourself as an informed user. (Be honest; this isn't a test!)
2. Explain the benefits of being an informed user of information systems.
3. Discuss the various career opportunities offered in the IT field.

1.2 | Overview of Computer-Based Information Systems

LEARNING OBJECTIVE

Describe the various types of computer-based information systems in an organization.

Organizations refer to their management information systems functional area by several names, including the MIS Department, the Information Systems (IS) Department, the Information Technology (IT) Department, and the Information Services Department. Regardless of the name, however, this functional area deals with the planning for—and the development, management, and use of—information technology tools to help people perform all the tasks related to information processing and management. Recall that information technology relates to any computer-based tool that people use to work with information and support the information and information-processing needs of an organization.

As previously stated, an **information system** collects, processes, stores, analyzes, and disseminates information for a specific purpose. The purpose of information systems has been defined as getting the right information to the right people, at the right time, in the right amount, and in the right format. Because information systems are intended to supply useful information, we need to differentiate between information and two closely related terms: data and knowledge (see **Figure 1.2**).

Data items refer to an elementary description of things, events, activities, and transactions that are recorded, classified, and stored but are not organized to convey any specific meaning. Data items can be numbers, letters, figures, sounds, and images. Examples of data items are collections of numbers (e.g., 3.11, 2.96, 3.95, 1.99, 2.08) and characters (e.g., B, A, C, A, B, D, F, C).

Information refers to data that have been organized so that they have meaning and value to the recipient. For example, a grade point average (GPA) by itself is data, but a student's name coupled with his or her GPA is information. The recipient interprets the meaning and draws conclusions and implications from the information. Consider the examples of data provided in the preceding paragraph. Within the context of a university, the numbers could be grade point averages, and the letters could be grades in an Introduction to MIS class.

Knowledge consists of data and/or information that have been organized and processed to convey understanding, experience, accumulated learning, and expertise as they apply to a current business problem. For example, suppose that a company recruiting at your school has found over time that students with grade point averages over 3.0 have experienced the greatest success in its management program. Based on this accumulated knowledge, that company may decide to interview only those students with GPAs over 3.0. This is an example of knowledge

information system
(IS) A system that collects, processes, stores, analyzes, and disseminates information for a specific purpose.

Data items An elementary description of things, events, activities, and transactions that are recorded, classified, and stored but are not organized to convey any specific meaning.

information Data that have been organized so that they have meaning and value to the recipient.

knowledge Data and/or information that have been organized and processed to convey understanding, experience, accumulated learning, and expertise as they apply to a current problem or activity.

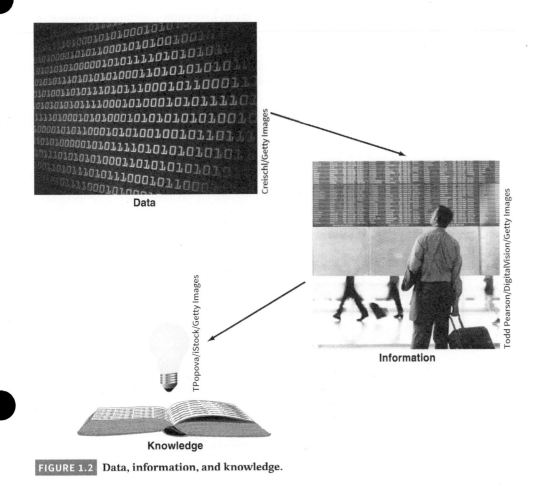

Data

Information

Knowledge

FIGURE 1.2 Data, information, and knowledge.

because the company utilizes information—GPAs—to address a business problem—hiring successful employees. As you can see from this example, organizational knowledge, which reflects the experience and expertise of many people, has great value to all employees.

Consider this example:

Data	Information	Knowledge
[No context]	[University context]	
3.16	3.16 + John Jones = GPA	* Job prospects
2.92	2.92 + Sue Smith = GPA	* Graduate school prospects
1.39	1.39 + Kyle Owens = GPA	* Scholarship prospects
3.95	3.95 + Tom Elias = GPA	

Data	Information	Knowledge
[No context]	[Professional baseball pitcher context]	
3.16	3.16 + Corey Kluber = ERA	
2.92	2.92 + Chris Sale = ERA	* Keep pitcher, trade pitcher, or send pitcher to minor leagues
1.39	1.39 + Clayton Kershaw = ERA	* Salary/contract negotiations
3.95	3.95 + Shane Bieber = ERA	

GPA = Grade point average (higher is better)
ERA = Earned run average (lower is better); ERA is the number of runs per nine innings that a pitcher surrenders.

You see that the same data items with no context can have entirely different meanings in different contexts.

Now that you have a clearer understanding of data, information, and knowledge, let's shift our focus to computer-based information systems. As you have seen, these systems process data into information and knowledge that you can use.

A **computer-based information system (CBIS)** is an information system that uses computer technology to perform some or all of its intended tasks. Although not all information systems are computerized, today most are. For this reason, the term "information system" is typically used synonymously with "computer-based information system." The basic components of computer-based information systems are listed below. The first four are called **information technology components. Figure 1.3** illustrates how these four components interact to form a CBIS.

- **Hardware** consists of devices such as the processor, monitor, keyboard, and printer. Together, these devices accept, process, and display data and information.
- **Software** is a program or collection of programs that enable the hardware to process data.
- A **database** is a collection of related files or tables containing data.
- A **network** is a connecting system (wireline or wireless) that enables multiple computers to share resources.
- **Procedures** are the instructions for combining the above components to process information and generate the desired output.
- *People* use the hardware and software, interface with it, or utilize its output.

Figure 1.4 illustrates how these components are integrated to form the wide variety of information systems found within an organization. Starting at the bottom of the figure, you see that the IT components of hardware, software, networks (wireline and wireless), and databases form the **information technology platform**. IT personnel use these components to

computer-based information system (CBIS) An information system that uses computer technology to perform some or all of its intended tasks.

information technology components Hardware, software, databases, and networks.

hardware A device such as a processor, monitor, keyboard, or printer. Together, these devices accept, process, and display data and information.

software A program or collection of programs that enable the hardware to process data.

database A collection of related files or tables containing data.

network A connecting system (wireline or wireless) that enables multiple computers to share resources.

Procedures The set of instructions for combining hardware, software, database, and network components in order to process information and generate the desired output.

information technology platform The name given to the combination of the IT components of hardware, software, networks (wireline and wireless), and databases.

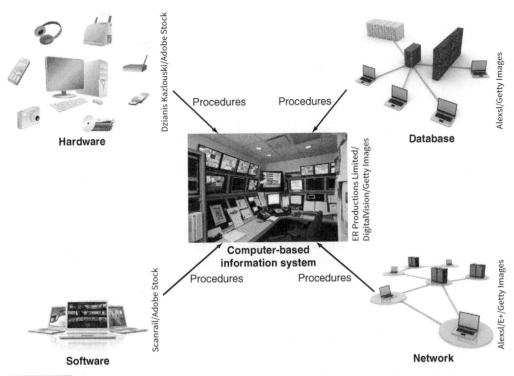

FIGURE 1.3 Computer-based information systems consist of hardware, software, databases, networks, procedures, and people.

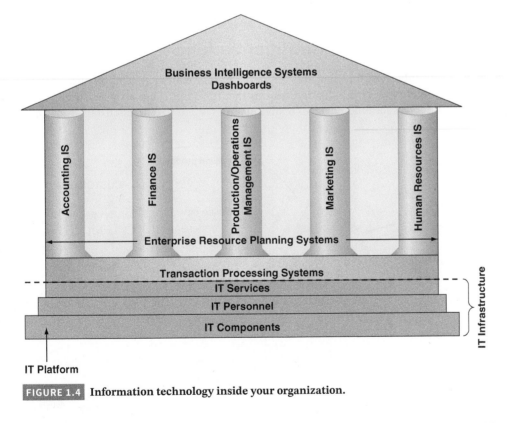

FIGURE 1.4 Information technology inside your organization.

develop information systems, oversee security and risk, and manage data. These activities cumulatively are called **information technology services**. The IT components plus IT services comprise the organization's **information technology infrastructure**. At the top of the pyramid are the various organizational information systems.

Computer-based information systems have many capabilities. **Table 1.3** summarizes the most important ones.

information technology services Activities performed by IT personnel using IT components; specifically, developing information systems, overseeing security and risk, and managing data.

information technology infrastructure IT components plus IT services.

TABLE 1.3 **Major Capabilities of Information Systems**

Perform high-speed, high-volume numerical computations.
Provide fast, accurate communication, and collaboration within and among organizations.
Store huge amounts of information in an easy-to-access yet small space.
Allow quick and inexpensive access to vast amounts of information worldwide.
Analyze and interpret vast amounts of data quickly and efficiently.
Automate both semiautomatic business processes and manual tasks.

application (or app) A computer program designed to support a specific task or business process.

departmental/functional information system ISs that support a particular functional area within the organization.

Information systems perform these various tasks via a wide spectrum of applications. An **application (or app)** is a computer program designed to support a specific task or business process. (A synonymous term is application program.) Each functional area or department within a business organization uses dozens of application programs. For instance, the human resources department sometimes uses one application for screening job applicants and another for monitoring employee turnover. The collection of application programs in a single department is usually referred to as a **departmental information system** (also known as a **functional area information system (FAIS)**). For example, the collection of application programs in the human resources area is called the human resources information system (HRIS). There are collections of application programs—that is, departmental information systems—in the other functional areas as well, such as accounting, finance, marketing, and production/operations.

The importance of information systems cannot be understated. In fact, a 2016 report from the Software Alliance shows that information systems added more than *$1 trillion of value* to the United States gross domestic product.

Types of Computer-Based Information Systems

Modern organizations employ many different types of information systems. Figure 1.4 illustrates the different types of information systems that function *within* a single organization, and **Figure 1.5** shows the different types of information systems that function *among* multiple

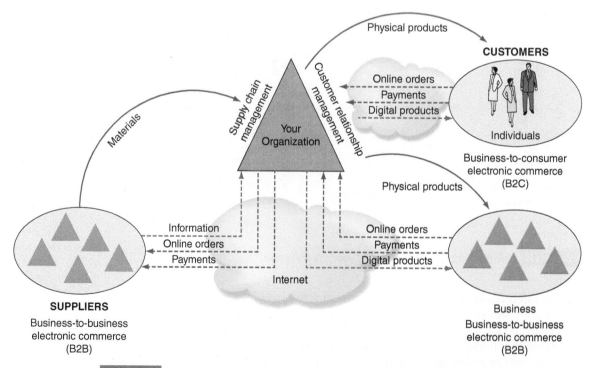

FIGURE 1.5 **Information systems that function among multiple organizations.**

organizations. You will study transaction processing systems, management information systems, and enterprise resource planning systems in Chapter 10. You will learn about customer relationship management (CRM) systems in Chapter 11 and supply chain management (SCM) systems in Chapter 11.

In the next section, you will learn about the numerous and diverse types of information systems employed by modern organizations. You will also read about the types of support these systems provide.

Breadth of Support of Information Systems

Certain information systems support parts of organizations, others support entire organizations, and still others support groups of organizations. This section addresses all of these systems.

Recall that each department or functional area within an organization has its own collection of application programs, or information systems. These functional area information systems are the supporting pillars for the information systems located at the top of Figure 1.4, namely, business intelligence systems and dashboards. As the name suggests, each FAIS supports a particular functional area within the organization. Examples are accounting IS, finance IS, production/operations management (POM) IS, marketing IS, and human resources IS.

ACCT **FIN** Consider these examples of IT systems in the various functional areas of an organization. In finance and accounting, managers use IT systems to forecast revenues and business activity, to determine the best sources and uses of funds, and to perform audits to ensure that the organization is fundamentally sound and that all financial reports and documents are accurate.

MKT In sales and marketing, managers use information technology to perform the following functions:

- *Product analysis*: Developing new goods and services
- *Site analysis*: Determining the best location for production and distribution facilities
- *Promotion analysis*: Identifying the best advertising channels
- *Price analysis*: Setting product prices to obtain the highest total revenues

Marketing managers also use IT to manage their relationships with their customers.

POM In *manufacturing*, managers use IT to process customer orders, develop production schedules, control inventory levels, and monitor product quality. They also use IT to design and manufacture products. These processes are called *computer-assisted design (CAD)* and *computer-assisted manufacturing (CAM)*.

HRM Managers in *human resources* use IT to manage the recruiting process, analyze and screen job applicants, and hire new employees. They also employ IT to help employees manage their careers, to administer performance tests to employees, and to monitor employee productivity. Finally, they rely on IT to manage compensation and benefits packages.

Two information systems that support the entire organization, **enterprise resource planning (ERP) systems** and transaction processing systems, are designed to correct a lack of communication among the functional area ISs. For this reason, Figure 1.4 shows ERP systems spanning the FAISs. ERP systems were an important innovation because organizations often developed the various functional area ISs as stand-alone systems that did not communicate effectively (if at all) with one another. ERP systems resolve this problem by tightly integrating the functional area ISs via a common database. In doing so, they enhance communications among the functional areas of an organization. For this reason, experts credit ERP systems with greatly increasing organizational productivity.

A **transaction processing system (TPS)** supports the monitoring, collection, storage, and processing of data from the organization's basic business transactions, each of which generates data. When you are checking out at Walmart, for example, a transaction occurs each time the cashier swipes an item across the bar code reader. Significantly, within an organization, different functions or departments can define a transaction differently. In accounting, for example, a transaction is anything that changes a firm's chart of accounts. The information system definition of a transaction is broader: a transaction is anything that changes the firm's database. The chart of accounts is only part of the firm's database. Consider a scenario in

enterprise resource planning (ERP) systems Information systems that take a business process view of the overall organization to integrate the planning, management, and use of all of an organization's resources, employing a common software platform and database.

transaction processing system (TPS) Information system that supports the monitoring, collection, storage, and processing of data from the organization's basic business transactions, each of which generates data.

which a student transfers from one section of an Introduction to MIS course to another section. This move would be a transaction to the university's information system but not to the university's accounting department (the tuition would not change).

The TPS collects data continuously, typically in *real time—that* is, as soon as the data are generated—and it provides the input data for the corporate databases. TPSs are considered critical to the success of any enterprise because they support core operations. Significantly, nearly all ERP systems are also TPSs, but not all TPSs are ERP systems. In fact, modern ERP systems incorporate many functions that previously were handled by the organization's functional area information systems. You study both TPSs and ERP systems in detail in Chapter 10.

ERP systems and TPSs function primarily within a single organization. Information systems that connect two or more organizations are referred to as **interorganizational information systems (IOSs)**. IOSs support many interorganizational operations, of which *supply chain management* is the best known. An organization's **supply chain** is the flow of materials, information, money, and services from suppliers of raw materials through factories and warehouses to the end customers.

interorganizational information systems (IOSs) Information systems that connect two or more organizations.

supply chain The flow of materials, information, money, and services from suppliers of raw materials through factories and warehouses to the end customers.

electronic commerce (e-commerce) systems A type of interorganizational information system that enables organizations to conduct transactions, called business-to-business (B2B) electronic commerce, and customers to conduct transactions with businesses, called business-to-consumer (B2C) electronic commerce.

Note that the supply chain in Figure 1.5 shows physical flows, information flows, and financial flows. Digitizable products are those that can be represented in electronic form, such as music and software. Information flows, financial flows, and digitizable products go through the Internet, whereas physical products are shipped. For example, when you order a computer from www.dell.com, your information goes to Dell via the Internet. When your transaction is completed (i.e., your credit card is approved and your order is processed), Dell ships your computer to you. (We discuss supply chains in more detail in Chapter 11.)

Electronic commerce (e-commerce) systems are another type of interorganizational information system. These systems enable organizations to conduct transactions, called business-to-business (B2B) electronic commerce, and customers to conduct transactions with businesses, called business-to-consumer (B2C) electronic commerce. Figure 1.5 illustrates B2B and B2C electronic commerce. Electronic commerce systems are so important that we discuss them in detail in Chapter 7, IT's About Business 1.2 presents the case of Zus Health, a company whose goal is to help the health care industry overcome some of its major electronic commerce challenges.

IT's About Business 1.2

MIS FIN Zus Health Digitally Revitalizing HealthCare

The Problem

Health care has historically been a local affair. You visit the doctors in your town, or perhaps you drive to the nearest metropolitan area to see a specialist. Regardless of the situation, however, your health care arrangements are typically limited by geography. Unfortunately, disease is not bound by geography, and patients who need specialized care might not be able to travel to the appropriate provider.

When COVID broke out, many providers shifted to virtual servicing, known as *telehealth*. In mid-2020, 52 percent of health-care visits were virtual. By 2022, when much of the economy had reopened, that number had dropped to 38 percent. However, that number is still higher than pre-COVID levels. Routine "urgent care" visits are often virtual, and mental and behavioral health treatments frequently have a virtual component.

Prior to the pandemic, many patients were suspicious of an "online doctor" and utilized virtual options only for extreme health conditions. However, fears of spreading or catching COVID during in-person medical visits led to a greater interest in and use of technology to provide and receive health care. Almost 75 percent of Americans surveyed reported that the pandemic has made them willing to try virtual care. Further, 25 percent of Americans over age 50 stated they had a virtual health care visit during the first three months of the pandemic, up from just 4 percent who had a remote visit in 2019.

Although they were simply trying to stay healthy during the pandemic, many patients and physicians came to recognize that telemedicine offers several advantages. Among them are cost savings, convenience, and the ability to provide care to people who have mobility limitations or who live in rural areas and don't have access to a local doctor or clinic.

Further, physicians realized that this new model would enable them to grow their practice into a niche specialization that is not limited by geography. They could expand their footprint, help more people, and focus on the area of medicine they truly enjoyed. Implementing this model, however, would require new business processes, new methods of sharing information, and a new technology infrastructure.

Jonathan Bush, CEO of Zus (www.zushealth.com), a company that creates digital health care technologies, became aware of this trend. He also recognized that this transition would encounter the same problems that marked the development of databases (see

Chapter 5). The key problems were *data inconsistency*, when data are stored in incompatible or inconsistent ways across systems, and *redundancy,* when data are unnecessarily duplicated across systems. Bush set out to address these problems.

The Solution

Bush wanted to create the health care industry's first shared development platform backed by a shared data record. A *shared development platform* is a set of standards that enable programmers to build software applications based on the appropriate technology. A *shared data record* is a central data repository that physicians can access so the data do not need to be duplicated in each system. According to the company website, "Zus offers the world's first industrial-strength, multi-tenant record infrastructure. It's an FHIR-native (Fast Healthcare Interoperability Resources), patient-centric source of truth, exhaustively maintained and never overwritten."

All doctors who want to practice medicine with a virtual component must collect and use the same personal and basic medical data on each visit. In addition, the flow of data within a medical practice is similar regardless of the type of care provided. Bush believed that a central repository would enable health care providers to share these data and workflows across practices to create greater efficiency in health care as a whole and not just for a single practice. This system would make it easier for providers to order and share labs, MRIs, X-rays, and numerous other tests across both geographical areas and information systems and therefore reduce health care costs.

The Results

Zus Health is in the process of building the "plumbing" that can become the standard for low-cost and interoperable components for every digital health care company. At the time of this writing, Zus's success has yet to be realized. Nevertheless, the concept has great appeal, as illustrated by the impressive amount of investment funding Zus has received. In 2021, the average funding received by private companies was $22.2 million. In contrast, Bush raised $34 million for Zus in one week. Since that time, Zus has built numerous partnerships within the health care industry. His goal is to provide a platform that will simplify the digitization of health care and solve one of society's biggest challenges—affordable, high-quality health care. The potential for platforms to unleash their power and improve a fragmented, broken health care system is undeniably great.

Questions

1. **What role did the pandemic play in moving health care toward virtual care?**
2. **How does a shift to virtual health care visits require an update in medical technology?**
3. **How and why does Jonathan Bush believe Zus will improve the health care industry?**

Sources: Compiled from M. Melchionna, "38 Percent of Patients Have Received Virtual Care in 2022," *MHealthIntelligence*—March 4, 2022; S. Joseph, "More Disruption, Please," *Forbes*, April 22, 2022; Z. Thomas (Host), "Health Tech Beyond the Pandemic," *WSJ Tech News Briefing* (podcast), May 25, 2022; S. Joseph, "Overcoming The "Cold Start" Problem in Healthcare," *Forbes*, July 11, 2022; J. O'Brien, "3 Questions for Jonathan Bush about Launch of Zus Health," *HealthLeadersMedia.com*, June 21, 2021; L. Lovett, "Health-Tech vet Jonathan Bush's New Venture Aims to Tackle Disjoined EHRs," *Mobihealthnew.com*, June 17, 2021; "Zus Health Closes $34M Series A Led by Andreessen Horowitz (a16z); Participation from F-Prime Capital, Maverick Ventures and Others," *Businesswire.com*, June 17, 2021; F. Pennic, "Jonathan Bush's Second Venture Zus Health Launches with $34M for Health Data Interoperability Platform," *HIT Consultant*, June 17, 2021; S. Watson, "Telehealth: The advantages and disadvantages," *Harvard Health Publishing*, October 12, 2020; https://corporatefinanceinstitute.com/resources/knowledge/trading-investing/series-a-financing/, Accessed on August 20, 2022; https://zushealth.com/ Accessed on 8/19/2022; https://www.fhir.org/ Accessed on 8/19/2022.

Support for Organizational Employees

So far, you have concentrated on information systems that support specific functional areas and operations. Now you will learn about information systems that typically support particular employees within the organization.

Clerical workers, who support managers at all levels of the organization, include bookkeepers, secretaries, electronic file clerks, and insurance claim processors. *Lower-level managers* handle the day-to-day operations of the organization, making routine decisions such as assigning tasks to employees and placing purchase orders. *Middle managers* make tactical decisions, which deal with activities such as short-term planning, organizing, and control.

Knowledge workers are professional employees such as financial and marketing analysts, engineers, lawyers, and accountants. All knowledge workers are experts in a particular subject area. They create information and knowledge, which they integrate into the business. Knowledge workers, in turn, act as advisors to middle managers and executives. Finally, *executives* make decisions that deal with situations that can significantly change the manner in which business is conducted. Examples of executive decisions are introducing a new product line, acquiring other businesses, and relocating operations to a foreign country.

Functional area information systems summarize data and prepare reports, primarily for middle managers, but sometimes for lower-level managers as well. Because these reports typically concern a specific functional area, report generators (RPGs) are an important type of functional area IS.

knowledge workers
Professional employees such as financial and marketing analysts, engineers, lawyers, and accountants, who are experts in a particular subject area and who create information and knowledge, which they integrate into the business.

TABLE 1.4   Types of Organizational Information Systems

Type of System	Function	Example
Transaction processing system	Processes transaction data from terminal	Walmart checkout point-of-sale business events
Enterprise resource planning	Integrates all functional areas of the organization	Oracle, SAP system
Functional area IS	Supports the activities within a specific functional area	System for processing payroll
Decision support system	Provides access to data and analysis tools	"What-if" analysis of changes in budget
Expert system	Mimics human expert in a particular area and makes decisions	Credit card approval analysis
Dashboards	Present structured, summarized information about aspects of business important to executives	Status of sales by product
Supply chain management system	Manages flows of products, services, and information among organizations	Walmart Retail Link system connecting suppliers to Walmart
Electronic commerce system	Enables transactions among organizations and between organizations and customers	www.dell.com

business analytics (BA) systems   See **business intelligence systems**.

business intelligence (BI) systems   Systems that provide computer-based support for complex, nonroutine decisions, primarily for middle managers and knowledge workers.

expert systems (ES)   An attempt to duplicate the work of human experts by applying reasoning capabilities, knowledge, and expertise within a specific domain.

dashboard   A business analytics presentation tool that provides rapid access to timely information and direct access to management reports.

Business analytics (BA) systems (also known as **business intelligence (BI) systems**) provide computer-based support for complex, nonroutine decisions, primarily for middle managers and knowledge workers. (They also support lower-level managers, but to a lesser extent.) These systems are typically used with a data warehouse, and they enable users to perform their own data analysis. You will learn about BA systems in Chapter 12.

Expert systems (ESs) attempt to duplicate the work of human experts by applying reasoning capabilities, knowledge, and expertise within a specific domain. They have become valuable in many application areas, primarily but not exclusively areas involving decision making. For example, navigation systems use rules to select routes, but we do not typically think of these systems as expert systems. Significantly, expert systems can operate as stand-alone systems or be embedded in other applications. We examine ESs in greater detail in Chapter 14.

Dashboards (also called **digital dashboards**) are a special form of IS that support all managers of the organization. They provide rapid access to timely information and direct access to structured information in the form of reports. Dashboards that are tailored to the information needs of executives are called *executive dashb*oards. Chapter 12 provides a thorough discussion of dashboards.

Table 1.4 provides an overview of the different types of information systems used by organizations.

Before you go on...

1. What is a computer-based information system?
2. Describe the components of computer-based information systems.
3. What is an application program?
4. Explain how information systems provide support for knowledge workers.
5. As we move up the organization's hierarchy from clerical workers to executives, how does the type of support provided by information systems change?

1.3 | How Does IT Impact Organizations?

LEARNING OBJECTIVE

Discuss ways in which information technology can affect managers and nonmanagerial workers.

WILEY PLUS

Author Lecture Videos are available exclusively in *WileyPLUS.*
Apply the Concept activities are available in the Appendix and in *WileyPLUS.*

Throughout this text, you will encounter numerous examples of how IT affects various types of organizations. These examples will make you aware of just how important IT actually is to organizations. In fact, for the vast majority of organizations, if their information systems fail, then they cease operations until the problems are found and fixed. Consider the following example.

On May 6, 2021, Colonial Pipeline, a provider that carries refined gasoline and jet fuel from Texas up the East Coast to New York, was forced to shut down after being hit by ransomware that left Colonial Pipeline unable to bill customers. Physically, the product could be delivered, but without an active billing system, the entire operation shut down, causing a major disruption in the fuel industry (over 10,000 gas stations were out of fuel for several days) until the ransom was paid and the system was restored. (You will learn more about this in the opening case for Technology Guide 3.)

This section provides an overview of the impact of IT on modern organizations. As you read this section, you will learn how IT will affect you as well.

IT Impacts Entire Industries

As of mid-2022, the technology required to transform industries through software had been developed and integrated and could be delivered globally. In addition, software tools and Internet-based services enabled companies in many industries to launch new software-powered startups without investing in new infrastructure or training new employees. For example, in 2000, operating a basic Internet application cost businesses approximately $150,000 per month. By mid-2022, operating that same application in Amazon's cloud could cost as little as $100 per month, depending on the amount of data traffic to and from the website. (We discuss cloud computing in Technology Guide 3.)

In essence, software is impacting every industry, and every organization must prepare for these impacts. Let's examine a few examples of software disruption across several industries. Many of these examples focus on two scenarios: (1) industries where software disrupted the previous market-leading companies and (2) industries where a new company (or companies) used software to achieve a competitive advantage.

The Book Industry In mid-2022, the largest book publisher and bookseller in the United States was Amazon, a software company. Amazon's core capability is its software engine, which can sell virtually anything online without building or maintaining any retail stores. Now even books themselves have become software products, known as electronic (or digital) books, or e-books. In 2020, physical books accounted for approximately 81 percent of total book sales, and electronic books accounted for approximately 19 percent of total book sales. Keep in mind that electronic book sales increased from 0 percent in 1994 when Amazon was founded to 19 percent 26 years later.

According to the 2018 Academic Student Ebook Experience Survey, 74 percent of respondents said that they preferred print books when reading for pleasure. Furthermore, 68 percent said that they preferred print books for assigned readings. In 2022, e-book sales were down 12 percent compared to the previous year. While some of this is attributed to the world reopening after the COVID-19 pandemic, the future is unknown yet is creating a continuous disruption in the book industry.

The Music Industry   Total U.S. album sales peaked at 785 million in 2000, which was the year after Napster was created. Napster was a service that allowed anyone with a computer and a reasonably fast Internet connection to download and trade music for free. From 2000 to 2018, the major music labels (companies) worked diligently to eliminate illegal downloading and sharing, begun by Napster in 2001. Despite these efforts, however, album sales continued to decline.

However, by 2019, music fans had shifted from illegal downloads to paid streaming platforms such as Spotify (**www.spotify.com**), Apple Music (**www.apple.com/apple-music/**), Amazon Prime (**www.amazon.com**), and Pandora (**www.pandora.com**), which generally charge $5 to $10 per month for unlimited access to millions of songs. Even though the record labels receive only about 0.3 cents each time a song is streamed, these small amounts are significant. In 2020, the global record industry reported revenues of $35.9 billion (up from $21.5 billion in 2019), with streaming generating $16.9 billion (up from $11.4 billion in 2019).

The Video Industry   Blockbuster—which rented and sold videos and ancillary products through its chain of stores—was the industry leader until it was disrupted by a software company, Netflix (**www.netflix.com**). By the first quarter, 2020, Netflix had the largest global subscriber base of any video service, with 167 million subscribers. Meanwhile, Blockbuster declared bankruptcy in February 2011 and was acquired by satellite television provider Dish Network (**www.dish.com**) a month later. In May 2022, only one Blockbuster store—located in Bend, Oregon—was still open.

MIS **The Software Industry**   Incumbent software companies such as Oracle and Microsoft are increasingly threatened by software-as-a-service (SaaS) products—for example, Salesforce (**www.salesforce.com**) and Android, an open-source operating system. (We discuss operating systems in Technology Guide 2 and SaaS in Technology Guide 3.)

The Video Game Industry   Today, the fastest growing entertainment companies are video game makers—again, software. Examples are Zynga (**www.zynga.com**), the creator of FarmVille; Rovio (**www.rovio.com**), the maker of Angry Birds; and Minecraft (**www.minecraft.net**), now owned by Microsoft (**www.microsoft.com**).

The Photography Industry   Software disrupted this industry years ago. Today it is virtually impossible to buy a mobile phone that does not include a software-powered camera. In addition, people can upload photos automatically to the Internet for permanent archiving and global sharing. Leading photography companies include Instagram (**www.instagram.com**), Shutterfly (**www.shutterfly.com**), Snapfish (**www.snapfish.com**), and Flickr (**www.flickr.com**). Meanwhile, Kodak, the longtime market leader—whose name was almost synonymous with cameras—declared bankruptcy in January 2012.

MKT **The Marketing Industry**   Today's largest direct marketing companies include Facebook (**www.facebook.com**), Google (**www.google.com**), and Amazon (**www.amazon.com**). All of these companies are using software to disrupt the retail marketing industry.

HRM **The Recruiting Industry**   LinkedIn (**www.linkedin.com**) is disrupting the traditional job-recruiting industry. For the first time, employees and job searchers can maintain their résumés on a publicly accessible website that interested parties can search in real time. Additionally, many companies are turning to recruitment automation through companies like Recruiter Flow (**www.recruiterflow.com**) to automate and expedite the applicant's experience.

FIN **The Financial Services Industry**   Software has transformed the financial services industry. Practically every financial transaction—for example, buying and selling stocks—is now performed by software. In fact, an entirely new name has been given to the merging of technology and financial services, FinTech (Financial Technologies). Also, many of the leading innovators in financial services are software companies. See our discussion of FinTech in Chapter 7.

The Motion Picture Industry   The process of making feature-length computer-generated films has become incredibly IT intensive. Studios require state-of-the-art information technologies, including massive numbers of servers, sophisticated software, and an enormous amount of storage (all described in **Technology Guide 1**).

Consider DreamWorks Animation (**www.dreamworks.com**), a motion picture studio that creates animated feature films, television programs, and online virtual worlds. For a single motion picture, the studio manages more than 500,000 files and 300 terabytes (a terabyte is 1 trillion bytes) of data, and it uses about 80 million central processing unit (CPU; described in **Technology Guide 1**) hours. As DreamWorks executives state, "In reality, our product is data that looks like a movie. We are a digital manufacturing company."

Software is also disrupting industries that operate primarily in the physical world. Consider these examples:

- *The Automobile Industry*: In modern cars, software is responsible for running the engine, controlling safety features, entertaining passengers, guiding drivers (and in some cases, responsible for fully autonomous driving) to their destinations, and connecting the car to mobile, satellite, and GPS networks. Other software functions include Wi-Fi receivers, which turn your car into a mobile hot spot; software, which helps maximize fuel efficiency; and ultrasonic sensors, which enable some models to parallel park automatically.

  The next step is to network all vehicles together, a necessary step toward the next major breakthrough: driverless cars. Google, Tesla (**www.tesla.com**), Apple, and all of the major automobile companies are now developing driverless vehicles.

- *The Agriculture Industry*: Agriculture is increasingly powered by software, including satellite analysis of soils linked to per-acre seed-selection software algorithms. In addition, precision agriculture makes use of automated, driverless tractors controlled by global positioning systems (GPS) and software. *Precision agriculture* is an approach to farm management that uses information technology to ensure that crops receive exactly what they need—for example, water, fertilizer, and pesticides—for optimum health and productivity.

- *The Fashion Industry*: Women have long "borrowed" special-occasion dresses from department stores, buying them and then returning them after wearing them for one evening. Now, Rent the Runway (**www.renttherunway.com**) has redefined the fashion business, making expensive clothing available to more women than ever before. The firm is also disrupting traditional physical retailers. After all, why buy a dress when you can rent one for a very low price? Some department stores feel so threatened by Rent the Runway that they have reportedly told vendors that they will remove floor merchandise if it ever shows up on that company's website.

- *The Legal Profession*: Today, electronic discovery (e-discovery) software applications can analyze documents in a fraction of the time that human lawyers would take, at a fraction of the cost. For example, UnitedLex (**www.unitedlex.com**) helped one company analyze 1.5 million documents for less than $100,000. That company estimated that the process would have cost $1.5 million had it been performed by lawyers.

IT Reduces the Number of Middle Managers

HRM   IT makes managers more productive, and it increases the number of employees who can report to a single manager. Thus, IT ultimately decreases the number of managers and experts. It is reasonable to assume, therefore, that in coming years organizations will have fewer managerial levels and fewer staff and line managers. If this trend materializes, promotional opportunities will decrease, making promotions much more competitive. Bottom line: pay attention in school!

IT Changes the Manager's Job

One of the most important tasks of managers is making decisions. A major consequence of IT has been to change the manner in which managers make their decisions. In this way, IT ultimately has changed managers' jobs.

IT often provides managers with near-real-time information, meaning that managers have less time to make decisions, making their jobs even more stressful. Fortunately, IT also provides many tools—for example, business analytics applications such as dashboards, search engines, and intranets—to help managers handle the volumes of information they must deal with on an ongoing basis.

So far in this section, we have been focusing on managers in general. Now let's focus on you. Due to advances in IT, you will increasingly supervise employees and teams who are geographically dispersed. Employees can work from anywhere at any time, and teams can consist of employees who are literally dispersed throughout the world. Information technologies such as telepresence systems (discussed in Chapter 6) can help you manage these employees even though you do not often see them face-to-face. For these employees, electronic or "remote" supervision will become the norm. Remote supervision places greater emphasis on completed work and less emphasis on personal contacts and office politics. You will have to reassure your employees that they are valued members of the organization, thereby diminishing any feelings they might have of being isolated and "out of the loop."

Will IT Eliminate Jobs?

One major concern of every employee, part-time or full-time, is job security. Relentless cost-cutting measures in modern organizations often lead to large-scale layoffs. Put simply, organizations are responding to today's highly competitive environment by doing more with less. Regardless of your position, then, you consistently will have to add value to your organization and make certain that your superiors are aware of this value.

Many companies have responded to difficult economic times, increased global competition, demands for customization, and increased consumer sophistication by increasing their investments in IT. In fact, as computers continue to advance in terms of intelligence and capabilities, the competitive advantage of replacing people with machines is increasing rapidly. This process frequently leads to layoffs. At the same time, however, IT creates entirely new categories of jobs, such as electronic medical record-keeping and nanotechnology.

HRM IT Impacts Employees at Work

Many people have experienced a loss of identity because of computerization. They feel like "just another number" because computers reduce or eliminate the human element present in noncomputerized systems.

The Internet threatens to exert an even more isolating influence than have computers and television. Encouraging people to work and shop from their living rooms could produce some unfortunate psychological effects, such as depression and loneliness.

HRM IT Impacts Employees' Health and Safety

Although computers and information systems are generally regarded as agents of "progress," they can adversely affect individuals' health and safety. In fact, the average American worker spends seven hours per day in front of some type of screen (consider laptops, tablets, smartphones, computers, and televisions). Let's consider two issues associated with IT: job stress and long-term use of the keyboard.

An increase in an employee's workload and/or responsibilities can trigger *job stress*. Although computerization has benefited organizations by increasing productivity, it also has created an ever-expanding workload for some employees. Some workers feel overwhelmed and have become increasingly anxious about their job performance. These feelings of stress and anxiety can actually diminish rather than improve workers' productivity while jeopardizing their physical and mental health. Management can help alleviate these problems by providing training, redistributing the workload among workers, and hiring more workers.

On a more specific level, the long-term use of keyboards can lead to *repetitive strain injuries* such as backaches and muscle tension in the wrists and fingers. *Carpal tunnel syndrome* is a particularly painful form of repetitive strain injury that affects the wrists and hands.

Andrey Popov/Adobe Stock

Media Bakery

Andrey Popov/Adobe Stock Photos

Media Bakery

FIGURE 1.6 Ergonomic products protect computer users.

Designers are aware of the potential problems associated with the prolonged use of computers. To address these problems, they continually attempt to design a better computing environment. The science of designing machines and work settings that minimize injury and illness is called *ergonomics*. The goal of ergonomics is to create an environment that is safe, well lit, and comfortable. Examples of ergonomically designed products are antiglare screens that alleviate problems of fatigued or damaged eyesight and chairs that contour the human body to decrease backaches. **Figure 1.6** displays some sample ergonomic products.

HRM IT Provides Opportunities for People with Disabilities

Computers can create new employment opportunities for people with disabilities by integrating speech-recognition and vision-recognition capabilities. For example, individuals who cannot type can use a voice-operated keyboard, and individuals who cannot travel can work at home.

Going further, adaptive equipment for computers enables people with disabilities to perform tasks they normally would not be able to do. For example, the Web and graphical user interfaces (GUIs; e.g., Windows) can be difficult for people with impaired vision to use. To address this problem, manufacturers have added audible screen tips and voice interfaces, which essentially restore the functionality of computers to the way it was before GUIs became standard.

Other devices help improve the quality of life in more mundane, but useful, ways for people with disabilities. Examples are a two-way writing telephone, a robotic page turner, a hair brusher, and a hospital-bedside video trip to the zoo or the museum. Several organizations specialize in IT designed for people with disabilities.

Before you go on...

1. Why should employees in all functional areas become knowledgeable about IT?
2. Describe how IT might change the manager's job.
3. Discuss several ways in which IT impacts employees at work.

1.4 | Importance of Information Systems to Society

LEARNING OBJECTIVE

Identify positive and negative societal effects of the increased use of information technology.

This section explains in greater detail why IT is important to society as a whole. Other examples of the impact of IT on society appear throughout the text.

IT Affects Our Quality of Life

IT has significant implications for our quality of life. The workplace can be expanded from the traditional nine-to-five job at a central location to 24 hours a day at any location. IT can provide employees with flexibility that can significantly improve the quality of leisure time, even if it doesn't increase the total amount of leisure time. Online meetings are now a fixture in our business life. These meetings have many advantages (easier to share documents, less travel, time savings). However, there are also many disadvantages when they are not coordinated properly. The Closing Case for this chapter discusses online and hybrid meetings and presents strategies to help them be successful.

While IT does bring significant improvements to quality of life, IT also can place employees on "constant call," which means they are never truly away from the office, even when they are on vacation. In fact, surveys reveal that the majority of respondents take their laptops and smartphones on their vacations, and 100 percent take their cell phones. Going further, the majority of respondents did some work while vacationing, and almost all of them checked their e-mail regularly. Boundaries are more important than ever because IT has made it easy to blur those lines.

The Robot Revolution Is Now Here

Once restricted largely to science fiction, robots that can perform practical tasks are now a reality. Two major types of robot are industrial robots and collaborative robots, or cobots.

An *industrial robot* is an automated, programmable machine used in manufacturing operations. Applications for industrial robots include welding, painting, assembly, disassembly, packaging and labeling, palletizing, and many others. *Collaborative robots*, or *cobots*, are machines designed to be used in collaborative applications where there are interactions with humans within a shared space. Applications for cobots include providing information in public spaces, transporting materials and products within a building, inspection of goods, patrolling perimeters, securing facilities, and many others. Now let's look at the differences between the two types.

POM Industrial robots versus cobots Cobots are designed to work alongside human employees, while industrial robots perform work in place of those employees. A cobot can assist employees with work that may be too dangerous, strenuous, or tedious for them to accomplish on their own. This assistance can create a safer, more efficient workplace without eliminating factory jobs. In contrast, industrial robots are used to automate the manufacturing process almost entirely without human help on the manufacturing floor. This process can free employees for more meaningful tasks that are less mundane and less prone to repetitive-motion injuries.

Cobots are also more easily programmable than industrial robots because they are capable of "learning" on the job. A factory worker can re-program a cobot simply by moving the cobot's arms along a desired path. At that point, the cobot will "remember" the new movement and be able to repeat it on its own. Industrial robots cannot be so easily reprogrammed and require an engineer to write new software for any changes in the process that the robot is to perform.

Industrial robots are designed for heavy manufacturing, while cobots are designed for light manufacturing. Industrial robots require safety cages to keep humans out of the workspace, while cobots are safe enough to function around people and do not require the same type of safety infrastructure that industrial robots require. Last but certainly not least, industrial robots are much more expensive ($100,000 to $150,000) than cobots ($35,000 to $50,000).

Cobots have become increasingly common on factory floors, in hospital corridors, and in farm fields. Amazon Robotics is an excellent example of cobots in a distribution center.

Traditionally, companies moved goods around their distribution centers with human-operated conveyors or with human-operated machines such as forklifts. That is, orders would enter the distribution center and humans would locate, pick, and pack the items for shipment.

Amazon Robotics, formerly Kiva Systems, reversed the process with cobots. In the new approach, the company stores items on portable storage units. When an order enters the company database, software locates the closest cobot to the item and directs it to retrieve that item. The cobots navigate around the distribution center by following bar code stickers on the floor. Each cobot has sensors that read the bar codes and prevent collisions. When the cobot reaches the correct storage unit, it slides underneath it and lifts it off the ground through a corkscrew action. The cobot then carries the storage units to a human operator who picks the item(s).

The bottom line with this system is that, rather than humans going to the items, the cobots bring the items to the humans. The system is much more efficient and accurate than the traditional one.

Drones   A *drone* is an unmanned aerial vehicle (UAV) (a flying robot, if you will) that either is controlled by pilots from the ground or autonomously follows a preprogrammed mission. Commercial drones function in a variety of business purposes, in contrast to drones used by hobbyists for recreational purposes.

An interesting use of drones is in the fight against deforestation. A good example of this process is in Yangon, Myanmar, where Dendra Systems (**www.dendra.io**) is working with a non-profit organization called Worldview International Foundation (**www.wif.foundation**) to plant mangrove saplings. Dendra, formerly BioCarbon Engineering, is a startup company that makes drones to plant trees and grasses.

Drones first fly over the area to be planted, map it, and collect data about the topography and soil conditions. Dendra integrates these data with satellite data of the area and determines the best locations to plant seeds. Once the company analyzes the data, drones fire biodegradable pods filled with germinated seeds and nutrients into the ground at the preselected locations. Over the next months, drones fly over the planted areas and monitor how the mangroves are growing.

Autonomous Vehicles   An autonomous, or self-driving, car (essentially a robot car) is a vehicle that is capable of sensing its environment and moving safely to its destination with little or no human input. When you think about autonomous vehicles, consider these statistics:

- Human error accounts for more than 90 percent of automobile accidents.
- Each year, more than 6 million vehicle accidents are reported to law enforcement.
- In 2011, a total of 42,915 Americans and 1.35 million people worldwide died in automobile accidents.
- The average car in the United States is used two hours per day, which is only 8 percent of the time. Therefore, a car owner owns a rapidly depreciating asset that is idle the vast majority of the time.

These statistics offer compelling reasons for autonomous vehicles, and the development of these vehicles is proceeding rapidly. Leading autonomous vehicle companies are Waymo (**www.waymo.com**), GM Cruise (**www.getcruise.com**), and Ford BlueCruise (**www.ford .com/technology/bluecruise**).

There is some bad news, however. Several fatalities have been reported with Tesla automobiles on full autopilot (self-driving mode). Whether these deaths were caused by the automobiles is under investigation.

It probably will be a long time before we see robots making decisions by themselves, handling unfamiliar situations, and interacting with people. Nevertheless, robots are extremely helpful in various environments, particularly those that are repetitive, harsh, or dangerous to humans.

The Emergence of Cognitive Computing: IBM Watson

MIS IBM Watson (www.ibm.com/watson) is a suite of enterprise-ready artificial intelligence services, applications, and software tools. Watson integrates advanced natural language processing, information retrieval, knowledge representation and reasoning, and machine learning technologies in order to answer open-domain (general) questions. IBM has labeled the type of processing demonstrated by Watson as *cognitive computing*. Watson has four primary capabilities:

- The ability to understand human language, with all of its nuance and ambiguity;
- The ability to learn and absorb information;
- The ability to formulate hypotheses;
- The ability to understand the context of a question.

By mid-2022, organizations in at least 20 industries were using Watson in a variety of applications. Some of these applications end up being sold to firms who can take these technical capabilities and refine and develop them for a specific industry. For example, in June of 2022, IBM sold the health division of Watson to Francisco Partners, a firm that specializes in health care technology and plans to establish a new company, Merative, that plans to invest heavily in the continued development of this tool. Merative's products will be organized into six product families to provide a variety of artificial intelligence insights to physicians and health care administrators. The opening case for Chapter 5, Data and Knowledge Management, presents a more detailed overview of the story of Watson Health.

IT Impacts Health Care

IT has brought about major improvements in health care delivery. Medical personnel use IT to make better and faster diagnoses and to monitor critically ill patients more accurately. IT has also streamlined the process of researching and developing new drugs. Expert systems now help doctors diagnose diseases, and machine vision is enhancing the work of radiologists. Surgeons use virtual reality to plan complex surgeries. They also employ surgical robots to perform long-distance surgery. Finally, doctors discuss complex medical cases via video-conferencing. New computer simulations re-create the sense of touch, allowing doctors-in-training to perform virtual procedures without risking harm to an actual patient.

Information technology can be applied to improve the efficiency and effectiveness of healthcare. Among the thousands of other health care applications, administrative systems are critically important. These systems perform functions ranging from detecting insurance fraud to creating nursing schedules to performing financial and marketing management.

The Internet contains vast amounts of useful medical information. Despite the fact that this information exists on the Internet, physicians caution against self-diagnosis. Rather, people should use diagnostic information obtained from Google and medical websites such as WebMD (www.webmd.com) only to ask questions of their physicians.

One of the earliest applications of IBM Watson was in the field of medicine. Watson is able to analyze vast amounts of medical data and provide insights.

Although some health data are structured—for example, blood pressure readings and cholesterol counts—the vast majority are unstructured. These data include textbooks, medical journals, patient records, and nurse and physician notes. In fact, modern medicine entails so much unstructured data that their rapid growth has surpassed the ability of health care practitioners to keep up. IBM emphasizes that Watson is *not* intended to replace health care professionals. Rather, its purpose is to assist them in avoiding medical errors and fine-tuning their medical diagnoses.

Before you go on...

1. What are some of the quality-of-life improvements made possible by IT? Has IT had any negative effects on our quality of life? If so, then explain, and provide examples.

2. Describe the robotic revolution, and consider its implications for humans. How do you think robotics will affect your life in the future?

3. Explain how IT has improved health care practices. Has the application of IT to health care created any problems or challenges? If so, then explain and provide examples.

What's in IT for Me?

In Section 1.2, we discussed how IT supports each of the functional areas of the organization. Here we examine the MIS function.

MIS For the MIS Major

The MIS function directly supports all other functional areas in an organization. That is, the MIS function is responsible for providing the information that each functional area needs in order to make decisions. The overall objective of MIS personnel is to help users improve performance and solve business problems using IT. To accomplish this objective, MIS personnel must understand both the information requirements and the technology associated with each functional area. Given their position, however, they must think "business needs" first and "technology" second.

Summary

1.1 Identify the reasons why being an informed user of information systems is important in today's world.

The benefits of being an informed user of IT include the following:

- You will benefit more from your organization's IT applications because you will understand what is "behind" those applications.

- You will be able to provide input into your organization's IT applications, thus improving the quality of those applications.

- You will quickly be in a position to recommend or to participate in the selection of IT applications that your organization will use.

- You will be able to keep up with rapid developments in existing information technologies, as well as the introduction of new technologies.

- You will understand the potential impacts that "new and improved" technologies will have on your organization. Consequently, you will be qualified to make recommendations concerning their adoption and use.

- You will play a key role in managing the information systems in your organization.

- You will be in a position to use IT if you decide to start your own business.

1.2 Describe the various types of computer-based information systems in an organization.

- Transaction processing systems (TPS) support the monitoring, collection, storage, and processing of data from the organization's basic business transactions, each of which generates data.

- Functional area information systems (FAISs) support a particular functional area within the organization.

- Interorganizational information systems (IOSs) support many interorganizational operations, of which supply chain management is the best known.

- Enterprise resource planning (ERP) systems correct a lack of communication among the FAISs by tightly integrating the functional area ISs via a common database.

- Electronic commerce (e-commerce) systems enable organizations to conduct transactions with other organizations (called business-to-business (B2B) electronic commerce), and with customers (called business-to-consumer (B2C) electronic commerce).

- Business intelligence (BI) systems provide computer-based support for complex, nonroutine decisions, primarily for middle managers and knowledge workers.

- Expert systems (ESs) attempt to duplicate the work of human experts by applying reasoning capabilities, knowledge, and expertise within a specific domain.

1.3 Discuss ways in which information technology can affect managers and nonmanagerial workers.

Potential IT impacts on managers:

- IT may reduce the number of middle managers.

- IT will provide managers with real-time or near-real-time information, meaning that managers will have less time to make decisions.

- IT will increase the likelihood that managers will have to supervise geographically dispersed employees and teams.

Potential IT impacts on nonmanagerial workers:

- IT may eliminate jobs.
- IT may cause employees to experience a loss of identity.
- IT can cause job stress and physical problems, such as repetitive stress injury.

1.4   List positive and negative societal effects of the increased use of information technology.

Positive societal effects:

- IT can provide opportunities for people with disabilities.
- IT can provide people with flexibility in their work (e.g., work from anywhere, anytime).
- Robots will take over mundane chores.
- IT will enable improvements in healthcare.

Negative societal effects:

- IT can cause health problems for individuals.
- IT can place employees on constant call.
- IT can potentially misinform patients about their health problems.

Key Terms

application (or app)   14
business analytics systems   18
business intelligence (BI) systems   18
computer-based information system
   (CBIS)   12
dashboard   18
data items   11
database   12
departmental information system   14
digital transformation   6
electronic commerce (e-commerce)
   systems   16

enterprise resource planning (ERP)
   systems   15
expert systems (ES)   18
functional area information systems
   (FAISs)   14
hardware   12
information   11
information system (IS)   11
information technology (IT)   2
information technology components   12
information technology infrastructure   13
information technology platform   12

information technology services   13
informed user   4
interorganizational information systems
   (IOSs)   16
knowledge   11
knowledge workers   17
network   12
procedures   12
software   12
supply chain   16
transaction processing system (TPS)   15

Discussion Questions

1. Would your university be a good candidate for digital transformation? Why or why not? Support your answer.

2. If you responded yes, then what types of digital initiatives should your university undertake to transform itself?

3. Describe a business that you would like to start. Discuss how information technology could: (a) help you find and research an idea for a business, (b) help you formulate your business plan, and (c) help you finance your business.

4. Your university wants to recruit high-quality high school students from your state. Provide examples of (a) the data that your recruiters would gather in this process, (b) the information that your recruiters would process from these data, and (c) the types of knowledge that your recruiters would infer from this information.

5. Can the terms data, information, and knowledge have different meanings for different people? Support your answer with examples.

6. Information technology makes it possible to "never be out of touch." Discuss the pros and cons of always being available to your employers and clients (regardless of where you are or what you are doing).

7. Robots have the positive impact of being able to relieve humans from working in dangerous conditions. What are some negative impacts of robots in the workplace?

8. Is it possible to endanger yourself by accessing too much medical information on the Web? Why or why not? Support your answer.

9. Describe other potential impacts of IT on societies as a whole.

10. What are the major reasons why it is important for employees in all functional areas to become familiar with IT?

11. Given that information technology is impacting every industry, what does this mean for a company's employees? Provide specific examples to support your answer.

12. Given that information technology is impacting every industry, what does this mean for students attending a college of business? Provide specific examples to support your answer.

13. Is the vast amount of medical information on the Web a good thing? Answer from the standpoint of a patient and from the standpoint of a physician.

Problem-Solving Activities

1. Visit some websites that offer employment opportunities in IT. Prominent examples are: www.linkedin.com, www.indeed.com, www.dice.com, www.monster.com, www.collegerecruiter.com, www.careerbuilder.com, www.jobcentral.com, www.job.com, www.career.com, www.simplyhired.com, and www.truecareers.com. Compare IT salaries to salaries offered to accountants, marketing personnel, financial personnel, operations personnel, and human resources personnel. For other information on IT salaries, check *Computerworld*'s annual salary survey.

2. Explore the role of the CIO in todays business world. Access www.cio.com and search through the resources listed under careers. What opportunities are available if you were graduating today?

3. Go to www.fedex.com.

    a. Find out what information is available to customers before they send a package.

    b. Find out about the "package tracking" system.

    c. Compute the cost of delivering a box, weighing 40 pounds, from your hometown to Long Beach, California (or to Lansing, Michigan, if you live in or near Long Beach). Compare the fastest delivery against the least cost. How long did this process take? Look into the business services offered by UPS. How do they make this process easier when you are a business customer?

4. Search the Web for information about the Department of Homeland Security (DHS). Examine the available information, and comment on the role of information technologies in the department.

5. Go to Twitter.com. Note the number of people on the platform daily and the number of tweets or posts in a 24-hour period. Check out your favorite clothing company and see how many of their customers are using the platform.

6. Access www.irobot.com, and investigate the company's Education and Research Robots. Surf the Web for other companies that manufacture robots, and compare their products with those of iRobot.

Closing Case

MIS POM Hybrid Work Means Hybrid Meetings

In the early months of the pandemic, most business meetings were entirely virtual. This reality created a level playing field when it came to virtual meetings in that everyone had to contend with the same videoconferencing issues. Everyone being online offered a similar meeting experience to each participant.

As the world adjusts to a new normal after COVID, it is clear that many people prefer hybrid work structures. In a 2021, Accenture Future of Work Study that surveyed over 9,000 workers from 11 countries and 13 industries, 83 percent of respondents said that a hybrid setup would be optimal for them. Hybrid work allows workers flexibility in setting their in-person hours, leaving scheduled meetings with a mix of some participants who are in-person while others are online, creating a hybrid meeting.

A *hybrid meeting* is an online meeting in which some participants attend from home and others from a conference room. This setup introduces various issues. For example, participants who are not in the office will likely feel left out. In addition, organizations need to ensure that their meetings are productive and beneficial for as many workers as possible, not just those in the office. Organizations want to empower staff to engage in every meeting. Yet, data show that roughly 70 percent of people who dial into meetings remotely feel disengaged.

Connected and Disconnected Participants

A 2022 study revealed that more than 50 percent of remote workers become distracted by e-mails or social media during meetings. Further, more than 20 percent even brought virtual meetings to bed. Finally, 10 percent admitted to coming up with fake excuses to leave meetings early. Overall, remote participants seem disconnected despite being directly connected to the meeting.

The key issue appears to be a real human connection. When asked about building rapport, 54 percent of respondents claimed they had fewer opportunities when they attended a meeting virtually. An additional 39 percent felt that their input would have greater value if they had participated in person. Finally, roughly 70 percent of respondents stated that collaboration between in-office and remote workers is challenging. Significantly, current IT tools—virtual meetings, group messaging, and file sharing—are intended to enhance productivity. However, these tools do not promote collaboration and connection.

In addition to these issues, there are some unintended consequences of hybrid meetings; for example, when people in the office focus on each other and fail to remember that there is an "invisible" person online, or when the online person fails to mute their microphone, creating a feedback problem for everyone in person. As another example, if the in-office microphone isn't sufficient to pick up everyone's voice, then online participants will miss out.

Solutions

Given all of these problems, we might ask, Can we make hybrid meetings work? Fortunately, the answer is yes. Below we present several recommendations on how to help make hybrid meetings successful.

Focus on collaboration, not just sharing. Although screen sharing is an effective strategy for conveying information, it does not promote knowledge sharing or collaboration. One study identified digital whiteboard tools as a potential solution that would be more collaborative and build team camaraderie.

Have everyone participate online through their laptop. To create equity, require that both in-person and remote participants use a computer with a webcam. Everyone is then visible through a webcam, everyone can chat, and everyone can contribute to the digital experience. This requirement effectively makes the hybrid meeting a "fully online" experience, while enabling some participants to build face-to-face relationships. One key suggestion: In-person participants in the same room should join the meeting audio through a single connection. Otherwise, the feedback will be terrible for the online participants.

Install multiple cameras in the conference room. One problem with using your laptop's webcam in the conference room is that you don't know where to look. At the webcam? At your colleague across the table, which gives everyone at home a nice view of your nostrils? At the wall? Installing multiple cameras around the conference room can eliminate this problem. You can look at and speak directly to your colleagues, the screen, and your notes. Today, the most popular videoconferencing platforms, including Zoom, Google Meet, and Microsoft Teams, use artificial intelligence (AI, see Chapter 14) to identify who is speaking and change camera views accordingly. These systems are more costly, but they are effective.

Set up high-quality audio for the in-person room. Ensure that the in-person meeting room is equipped with enough high-quality microphones so remote participants can hear everyone in the room. One microphone—or one cell phone set to speakerphone—in the middle of the room is insufficient. Online participants will not be able to hear everyone. Also, remind all participants to be aware of unnecessary noises. Opening a soda, typing loudly on the computer, and opening a piece of candy all create unnecessary noises, and the microphone hears everything.

Use extra-large screens to display online participants. An organization can set up a large screen in the middle of a room and then place two additional large monitors on each side of the room to display near-life-sized views of the remote participants. This practice can help to give online participants equal status.

Go all virtual into the metaverse. Virtual reality is creating new possibilities. Companies like Spacial offer software that enables users to develop near-real-life avatars. These avatars, driven by participants, sit around virtual tables, sip virtual coffees, and share information on virtual whiteboards. Although metaverse meetings currently are highly technical, the possibilities are endless. Moreover, they can make the meeting less expensive because the meeting "hardware"—think whiteboards—is simply computer code. There is no need for expensive cameras, microphones, or physical spaces. Rather, everything is contained in a virtual space that leaders can modify without expensive renovations.

Make use of AI. Cisco's Webex platform now uses AI to translate people's natural and nonverbal gestures into animated images. This technology enables users to perform simple actions like raising their hands or giving a thumbs-up without clicking a button. In addition, Webex features real-time closed-captioning and translation capabilities in more than 100 languages. Advanced noise cancellation features can filter out distracting environmental noises, especially during calls in shared spaces or home offices.

Conclusion

Hybrid meetings will remain a part of the working environment for the foreseeable future. Therefore, companies must continue to invest in solutions that work for all staff—regardless of whether they are in the office or hundreds of miles away. Maintaining employee engagement involves making everyone feel seen and heard in meetings. To accomplish this goal, organizations must consider the combination of behaviors and technologies that will create a healthy hybrid environment. When employees are committed and connected, then the entire business will benefit.

Questions

1. **What complications arise when some participants are in person and others are remote?**

2. **What role might AI play in making meetings more productive?**

3. **How can you use your computer to be better prepared for online meetings?**

Sources: Compiled from Staff Writer, "Cisco Tackles Video-Meeting Fatigue to Empower the Hybrid Work Model," *Tech Financials*, October 3, 2022; E. Roethler, "Yes, the Hybrid Workplace Can Work," *builtinchicago.com*, September 27, 2022; T. Bishop, "GeekWire Podcast: The New World of Hybrid Work, and the Next Generation of Smartphone Users," *GeekWire*, September 24, 2022; K. Errick, "Collaborative Tools Are More Needed Than Performance Tech in Remote Work, Study Says," *Nextgov.com*, September 23, 2022; J. McKendrick, "Remote and In-Person Work Balance Is Key, Even at the Most Virtual of Virtual Companies," *Forbes*, September 23, 2022; G. Kyvik, "Tackling Inequity in Hybrid Meetings: How Can Remote Workers Feel Seen and Heard?," *Telecom Reseller*, September 22, 2022; D. Martinus, "Over 50 Percent of Remote Workers Get Distracted by Emails or Social Media during Meetings," *Mashable SE Asia*, September 21, 2022; P. Goldstein, "How to Fine-Tune Meetings for Hybrid Work Settings," *BizTech*, September 20, 2022; L. Kolondy, "Tesla Struggles with Elon Musk's Strict Return-to-Office Policy," *CNBC.com*, September 14, 2022; S. Stern, "Hybrid Working: Why the Office-Home Balance Is Still a Challenge," *Financial Times*, September 4, 2022; B. Lovejoy, "Apple Return-to-Office Argument Rejected by Apple Together as It Petitions for Flexibility," *9to5Mac.com*, August 22, 2022; J. Stern, "Hybrid Work Meetings Are Hell. Tech Is Trying to Fix Them.," *The Wall Street Journal*, June 15, 2022; and https://www.accenture.com/us-en/insightsnew/future-workforce-index, accessed October 4, 2022.

CHAPTER 2

Organizational Strategy, Competitive Advantage, and Information Systems

CHAPTER OUTLINE	LEARNING OBJECTIVES
2.1 Business Processes	**2.1 Discuss** ways in which information systems enable business processes for a single functional area and cross-functional processes.
2.2 Business Process Reengineering, Business Process Improvement, and Business Process Management	**2.2 Differentiate** among business process reengineering, business process improvement, and business process management.
2.3 Business Pressures, Organizational Responses, and Information Technology Support	**2.3 Identify** effective IT responses to different kinds of business pressures.
2.4 Competitive Advantage and Strategic Information Systems	**2.4 Describe** the strategies that organizations typically adopt to counter Porter's five competitive forces.

Opening Case

MIS **HRM** **COVID Reshapes the Future of Work**

Many people have worked for the same organization in the same role since 2020, when the COVID-19 pandemic broke out. Still, they have probably experienced a great deal of change in how and where they perform their work and the tools they use, more than at any point in the history of the "office." Prior to the pandemic, the future of work was focused largely on digital transformation. *Digital transformation* includes investing in new ways to collaborate, using artificial intelligence (AI) to improve sales and marketing, and determining which channels were most effective for reaching their customers. However, as a result of COVID, that transformation had to expand to include how employees complete their work. *Hybrid working*, a term rarely heard before 2020, is now quite common. Hybrid working is defined by an arrangement that allows an employee to complete tasks from a location other than the office for a prescribed amount of time. Some employers require two to five days in the office, yet they allow the employee the flexibility to determine how and when to meet the requirement.

The transition from "office worker" to "hybrid worker" has been both exciting and extremely challenging for technology departments. Today, the future of work looks very different. Living rooms are used as offices, conference rooms are largely empty, and office hours are unpredictable. The entire concept of work has been turned upside down, and it seems unlikely to return to the pre-pandemic structure.

Organizations in the post-pandemic world are facing two significant pressures. First, the labor pool is smaller because baby boomers are retiring and the younger generations are decreasing in size. This shrinking labor pool is not a surprise. Rather, it reflects widely publicized population trends. However, these data did not predict the Great Resignation, which shrank the labor pool even further. The Great Resignation refers to a major trend that emerged during the pandemic. According to the U.S. Bureau of Labor Statistics (**www.bls.gov/**), in 2021 over 47 million Americans voluntarily retired or resigned from their jobs. About 50.5 million people quit their jobs in 2022, beating the prior record set in 2021. Researchers predict the great resignation will plateau by the end of 2023.

Second, many employees enjoyed the flexibility of remote work during the pandemic and now demand that flexibility in the current environment. This trend is especially common in the industries that successfully shifted to remote work. As a result, companies are under immense pressure to adjust their compensation, work hours, and work models to remain attractive to workers. Essentially, they must adopt remote work as a normal business practice.

Many companies are wrestling with integrating remote and hybrid work models into their culture. For more than two years during the pandemic, many knowledge workers enjoyed the freedom to spend weeks or months attending Zoom meetings (even while driving across the country) or filing reports from a lake house. In addition, the success of companies such as Dropbox, Twitter, and Slack demonstrates that it is possible to build a large and successful firm with hybrid workers if your business model allows it. However, not every role in every company can be performed remotely or on a hybrid basis. For example, certain health care activities can take place in a virtual environment, but others require in-person time. Still, organizations are sorting out how they can attract and retain employees in a labor market that is very much in favor of the employee.

According to the Microsoft 2022 Work Trends Index (**www.microsoft.com/en-us/worklab/work-trend-index**), 53 percent of employees prioritize health and well-being over work. Further, 47 percent are more likely to put family and their personal lives first. The Great Resignation indicates that employees are ready to find workplaces that match their priorities regarding how and where they want to work.

Trying to find an in-between ground has become more common than making an ultimatum about workers' in-person requirements, given the gap between employer expectations for employees to return to the office and what employees are actually doing. Gartner (**www.gartner.com**), a multinational advisory and research firm, published a survey from June 2022 reporting that, on average, HR executives and CEOs want knowledge workers in the office at least 60 percent of the time, but employees come in only about 35 percent of the time.

As companies survived the pandemic and planned to return to normal operations, they realized that "normal" would look different. Many companies had to rethink processes and evaluate what worked and what didn't. Today, employers are still searching for the optimal balance between their needs and those of their employees. Many employees who were able to shift to hybrid work have enjoyed the greater work/life flexibility—something they have no intention of giving up. According to the State of Remote Work report (**www.buffer.com/state-of-remote-work/2022**), based on data from over 2,000 remote workers around the world, 25 percent of employees would quit their jobs if they couldn't work remotely, and almost 50 percent would take a pay cut to continue to work remotely at least part-time. This trend is not going away.

Several companies have implemented solutions to this situation. For example, Amazon.com, Inc. went from planning to have employees in the office three days a week to letting directors of individual teams decide how frequently their workers must go in to the office. The company wants the majority of its employees to be able to travel easily to the office for a meeting on a day's notice. However, it is still reserving four weeks of remote work for almost all of its employees.

Apple Inc. (**www.apple.com**), which called its workers back to offices starting in April 2022, originally planned to offer two weeks of remote work each year. However, it added two more weeks to make it an entire month.

Yelp (**www.yelp.com**) promotes a remote-first, distributed workforce. Employees can choose to work from home and receive reimbursement for their Internet connection as well as $300 in office supplies to get started, or they can work from a nearby Yelp office with optional office days. Either way, the employee is in control of the decision of where to work. With so little in-person work, in July 2022, Yelp closed offices in New York, Washington, and Chicago and has plans to downsize its office in Phoenix.

What do these developments mean for the future of work? In mid-2022, Futurum Research and Microsoft collaborated on a study of 500 global business leaders to better understand the current state of the workplace. More than 70 percent of those surveyed reported that their workplace culture had improved. Employees have more voice in their companies' operations. In fact, 85 percent of respondents reported that decision-making processes had become more distributed, and almost 80 percent believed that collaboration has not been hindered by hybrid work. Many companies have been able to downsize workspaces while continuing to support hybrid and remote workers. Nearly 80 percent of those surveyed were able to restructure their offices to utilize unused conference space, and 75 percent were able to modify their lease or space costs. Gartner forecasts that 51 percent of US knowledge workers will work under hybrid arrangements by the end of 2023 and 20 percent will be fully remote.

These results appear to indicate the future of work is hybrid, more collaborative, and employee-led, and it will include less overhead and be more productive. That is a win for everyone involved.

Questions

1. **How did the transition to a hybrid workflow turn out and what do you make of future predictions?**

2. **What steps are employers taking to make the modern work environment friendlier for their employees?**

3. **How do you envision working throughout your career? Do you want to work in a hybrid environment? What would be the benefits and drawbacks to you?**

Sources: Compiled from A. Burton and P. Confino, "Why Yelp Chose to Shutter Its Offices While Others Opened Them," *Fortune*, September 2, 2022; R. Kulkarni, "65% Employees Are Unhappy Because of Work from Office Rule; May Resign in Next 6 Months (Survey Results)," *Trak.in*, August 29, 2022; V. Jha, "Does Hybrid Working Really Improve the Employee Experience?" *bluenotes. anz.com*, August 29, 2022; M. Pierce, "6 Key Trends That Will Change How You Do Business," *Entrepreneur*, August 27, 2022; D. Newman, "The Future of Work: More Hybrid, More Collaborative, More Automated," *Forbes*, July 31, 2022; K. Bindley, "Is Hybrid Work Killing Remote Summer? Yes, but It Doesn't Have To.," *Wall Street Journal*, July 24, 2022; K. Bindley, "Tech Workers Long Got What They Wanted. That's Over.," *Wall Street Journal*, July 15, 2022; Microsoft Work Trend Index, "Great Expectations: Making Hybrid Work Work," *microsoft.com*, March 16, 2022; J. Fuller and W. Kerr, "The Great Resignation Didn't Start with the Pandemic," *Harvard Business Review*, March 23, 2022; B. Andreatta, "The Great Resignation Is Quickly Becoming the Great Revolt: 5 Actions Leaders Should Take Now," *Entrepreneur*, December 6, 2021; S. Bhargava, "Solving the Labor Shortage for Small Businesses," *Entrepreneur*, October 4, 2021; and A. Suleman, "How to Avoid Drowning in Application Sprawl," *VentureBeat*, July 3, 2021.

Introduction

Organizations operate in the incredible complexity of the modern high-tech world. As a result, they are subject to myriad business pressures. Information systems help organizations respond to business pressures and to supporting organizations' global strategies. As you study this chapter, you will see that any information system can be *strategic*, meaning it can provide a competitive advantage if it is employed properly. The chapter-opening case, as well as the other cases in this chapter, illustrate how information technology (IT) can provide a competitive advantage to organizations.

Competitive advantage refers to any assets that provide an organization with an edge against its competitors in some measure such as cost, quality, or speed. A competitive advantage helps an organization control a market and accrue larger-than-average profits. Significantly, both strategy and competitive advantage take many forms.

Although many companies use technology in very expensive ways, an entrepreneurial spirit coupled with a solid understanding of what IT can do for you will provide competitive advantages to entrepreneurs just as it does for Wall Street CIOs. As you study this chapter, think of the small businesses in your area that are utilizing popular technologies in interesting and novel ways. Have any of them found an innovative use for Twitter? Facebook? Amazon? PayPal? Square? Zoom? If not, then can you think of any businesses that would benefit from employing these technologies?

This chapter is important for you for several reasons. First, the business pressures we address in the chapter will affect your organization. Just as important, however, they also will affect *you*. Therefore, you must understand how information systems can help you—and eventually your organization—respond to these pressures.

Acquiring a competitive advantage is also essential for your organization's survival. Many organizations achieve competitive advantage through the efforts of their employees. Therefore, becoming knowledgeable about strategy and how information systems affect strategy and competitive position will help you throughout your career.

This chapter encourages you to become familiar with your organization's strategy, mission, and goals and to understand its business problems and how it makes (or loses) money. It will help you understand how information technology contributes to organizational strategy. Furthermore, you likely will become a member of business or IT committees that decide (among many other things) how to use existing technologies more effectively and whether to adopt new ones. After studying this chapter, you will be able to make immediate contributions in these committees.

Essentially, organizations consist of a large number of diverse business processes. In this chapter, you will first learn about the different types of business processes and the support that information systems provide for all business processes.

The need for organizations to optimize their business processes has led to efforts such as business process improvement (BPI), business process reengineering (BPR), and business process management (BPM). You will learn how organizations address these important efforts and the key role that information systems play in supporting and enabling these efforts.

Next, you will see how information systems enable organizations to respond to business pressures. Finally, you will learn how information systems help organizations acquire competitive advantages in the marketplace.

competitive advantage
An advantage over competitors in some measure such as cost, quality, or speed; leads to control of a market and to larger-than-average profits.

2.1 Business Processes

LEARNING OBJECTIVE

Discuss ways in which information systems enable cross-functional business processes and business processes for a single functional area.

business process A collection of related activities that create a product or a service of value to the organization, its business partners, and its customers.

A **business process** is an ongoing collection of related activities that create a product or a service of value to the organization, its business partners, and its customers. The process involves three fundamental elements:

- *Inputs:* Materials, services, and information that flow through and are transformed as a result of process activities
- *Resources:* People and equipment that perform process activities
- *Outputs:* The product or a service created by the process

If the process involves a customer, then that customer can be either internal or external to the organization. A manager who is the recipient of an internal reporting process is an example of an internal customer. In contrast, an individual or a business that purchases the organization's products is the external customer of the fulfillment process.

Successful organizations measure their process activities to evaluate how well they are executing these processes. Two fundamental metrics that organizations employ in assessing their processes are efficiency and effectiveness. *Efficiency* focuses on doing things well in the process; for example, progressing from one process activity to another without delay or without wasting money or resources. *Effectiveness* focuses on doing the things that matter; that is, creating outputs of value to the process customer—for example, high-quality products.

Many processes cross functional areas in an organization. For example, product development involves research, design, engineering, manufacturing, marketing, and distribution. Other processes involve only a single functional area. **Table 2.1** identifies the fundamental business processes performed in an organization's functional areas.

Cross-Functional Processes

All the business processes in Table 2.1 fall within a single functional area of the company. However, many other business processes, such as procurement and fulfillment, cut across multiple functional areas; that is, they are cross-functional business processes, meaning that no single functional area is responsible for their execution. Rather, multiple functional areas collaborate to perform the process. For a cross-functional process to be successfully completed, each functional area must execute its specific process steps in a coordinated, collaborative way. To clarify this point, let's take a look at the procurement and fulfillment of **cross-functional processes**. We discuss these processes in greater detail in **Chapter 10**.

cross-functional processes No single functional area is responsible for a process's execution.

POM The *procurement process* includes all of the tasks involved in acquiring needed materials externally from a vendor. Procurement comprises five steps that are completed in three different functional areas of the firm: warehouse, purchasing, and accounting.

ACCT The process begins when the warehouse recognizes the need to procure materials, perhaps due to low inventory levels. The warehouse documents this need with a purchase requisition, which it sends to the purchasing department (step 1). In turn, the purchasing department identifies a suitable vendor, creates a purchase order based on the purchase requisition, and sends the order to the vendor (step 2). When the vendor receives the purchase order, it ships the materials, which are received in the warehouse (step 3). The vendor then sends an invoice, which is received by the accounting department (step 4). Accounting sends payment to the vendor, thereby completing the procurement process (step 5).

POM **ACCT** The *fulfillment process* is concerned with processing customer orders. Fulfillment is triggered by a customer purchase order that is received by the sales department. Sales then validates the purchase order and creates a sales order. The sales order communicates data related to the order to other functional areas within the organization, and it tracks the progress of the order. The warehouse prepares and sends the shipment to the customer. Once accounting is notified of the shipment, it creates an invoice and sends it to the customer. The customer then makes a payment, which accounting records.

TABLE 2.1   Examples of Business Processes

ACCT Accounting Business Processes

Managing accounts payable	Managing invoice billings
Managing accounts receivable	Managing petty cash
Reconciling bank accounts	Producing month-end close
Managing cash receipts	Producing virtual close

FIN Finance Business Processes

Managing account collection	Producing property tax assessments
Managing bank loan applications	Managing stock transactions
Producing business forecasts	Generating financial cash-flow reports
Applying customer credit approval and credit terms	

MKT Marketing Business Processes

Managing post-sale customer follow-up	Handling customer complaints
Collecting sales taxes	Handling returned goods from customers
Applying copyrights and trademarks	Producing sales leads
Using customer satisfaction surveys	Entering sales orders
Managing customer service	Training sales personnel

POM Production/Operations Management Business Processes

Processing bills of materials	Managing quality control for finished goods
Processing manufacturing change orders	Auditing for quality assurance
Managing master parts list and files	Receiving, inspecting, and stocking parts and materials
Managing packing, storage, and distribution	Handling shipping and freight claims
Processing physical inventory	Handling vendor selection, files, and inspections
Managing purchasing	

HRM Human Resources Business Processes

Applying disability policies	Producing performance appraisals and salary adjustments
Managing employee hiring	Managing resignations and terminations
Handling employee orientation	Applying training and tuition reimbursement
Managing files and records	Managing travel and entertainment
Applying health-care benefits	Managing workplace rules and guidelines
Managing pay and payroll	Overseeing workplace safety

MIS Management Information Systems Business Processes

Antivirus control	Applying electronic mail policy
Computer security issues incident reporting	Generating Internet use policy
Training computer users	Managing service agreements and emergency services
Computer user and staff training	Applying user workstation standards
Applying disaster recovery procedures	Managing the use of personal software

An organization's business processes can create a competitive advantage if they enable the company to innovate or to execute more effectively and efficiently than its competitors. They can also be liabilities, however, if they make the company less responsive and productive. Consider the airline industry. It has become a competitive necessity for all of the airlines to offer electronic ticket purchases through their websites. To provide competitive advantage, however, these sites must be highly responsive and they must provide both current and accurate information on flights and prices. An up-to-date, user-friendly site that provides fast answers to user queries will attract customers and increase revenues. In contrast, a site that provides outdated or inaccurate information, or has a slow response time, will hurt rather than improve business.

Clearly, good business processes are vital to organizational success. But how can organizations determine if their business processes are well designed? The first step is to document the process by describing its steps, its inputs and outputs, and its resources. The organization can then analyze the process and, if necessary, modify it to improve its performance.

To understand this point, let's consider the e-ticketing process involved in buying plane tickets. E-ticketing consists of four main process activities: searching for flights, reserving a seat, processing payment, and issuing an e-ticket. These activities can be broken down into more detailed process steps. The result may look like the process map in **Figure 2.1**. Note that different symbols correspond to different types of process steps. For example, rectangles (steps) are activities that are performed by process resources (reserve seats, issue e-ticket). Diamond-shaped boxes indicate decisions that need to be made (seats available?). Arrows are used as connectors between steps; they indicate the sequence of activities.

These symbols are important in the process flowchart (which is similar to a programming flowchart). Other symbols may be used to provide additional process details. For example, D-shaped boxes are used instead of rectangles when a waiting period is part of a process, ovals can show start and stop points, and process resources can be attached to activities with resource connector lines or included as an annotation or property for each activity box.

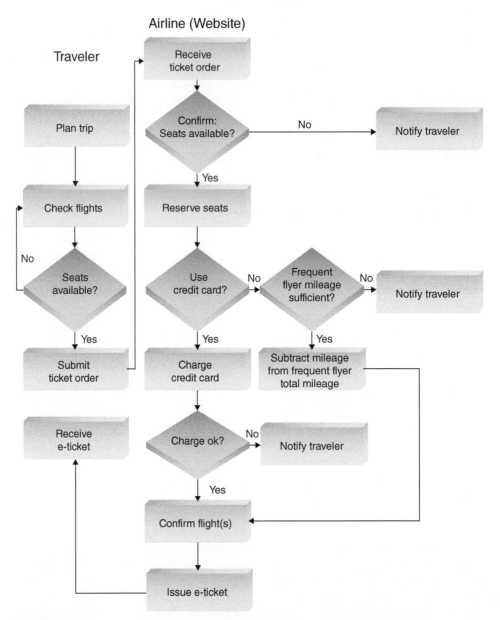

FIGURE 2.1   **Business process for ordering an e-ticket from an airline website.**

The customers of the process are travelers planning a trip, and the process output is an e-ticket. Travelers provide inputs to the process: the desired travel parameters to begin the search, the frequent flyer miles number, and their credit card information. Also, a computerized reservation system that stores information for many airlines provides some of the process inputs such as the seat availability and prices. The resources used in the process are the airline website, the computerized reservation system, and, if the customer calls the airline call center at any time during the process, the call center system and the human travel agents. The process creates customer value by efficiently generating an output that meets the customer search criteria—dates and prices. The performance of the process depends on efficiency metrics such as the time required to purchase an e-ticket, from the moment the customer initiates the ticket search until he or she receives the e-ticket. Effectiveness metrics include customer satisfaction with the airline website. Finally, the performance of the process may be affected if the quality or the timeliness of the inputs is low—for example, if the customer enters the wrong dates—or if the process resources are not available—for example, if the website crashes before the purchase is finalized.

Information Systems and Business Processes

MIS An information system (IS) is a critical enabler of an organization's business processes. Information systems facilitate communication and coordination among different functional areas, and allow easy exchange of, and access to, data across processes. Specifically, ISs play a vital role in three areas:

- Executing the process
- Capturing and storing process data
- Monitoring process performance

In this section, you will learn about each of these roles. In some cases, the role is fully automated—that is, it is performed entirely by the IS. In other cases, the IS must rely on the manager's judgment, expertise, and intuition.

MIS **Executing the Process**   An IS helps organizations execute processes efficiently and effectively. ISs are typically embedded into the processes, and they play a critical role in executing the processes. In other words, an IS and the processes are usually intertwined. If the IS does not work, the process cannot be executed. An IS helps execute processes by informing people when it is time to complete a task by providing the necessary data to complete the task and, in some cases, by providing the means to complete the task.

In the procurement process, for example, the IS generates the purchase requisitions and then informs the purchasing department that action on these requisitions is needed. The accountant will be able to view all shipments received to match an invoice that has been received from a supplier and verify that the invoice is accurate. Without the IS, these steps, and therefore the process, cannot be completed. For example, if the IS is not available, how will the warehouse know which orders are ready to pack and ship?

In the fulfillment process, the IS will inform people in the warehouse that orders are ready for shipment. It also provides them with a listing of what materials must be included in the order and where to find those materials in the warehouse.

MIS **Capturing and Storing Process Data**   Processes create data such as dates, times, product numbers, quantities, prices, and addresses, as well as who did what, when, and where. IS captures and stores these data, commonly referred to as *process data* or *transaction data*. Some of these data are generated and automatically captured by the IS. These are data related to who completes an activity, when, and where. Other data are generated outside the IS and must be entered into it. This data entry can occur in various ways, ranging from manual entry to automated methods involving data in forms such as bar codes and RFID tags that can be read by machines.

In the fulfillment process, for example, when a customer order is received by mail or over the phone, the person taking the order must enter data such as the customer's name, what the customer ordered, and how much he or she ordered. Significantly, when a customer order is received through the firm's website, then all customer details are captured by the IS. Data such as the name of the person entering the data (who), at which location the person is completing the task (where), and the date and time (when) are automatically included by the IS when it creates the order. The data are updated as the process steps are executed. When the order is shipped, the warehouse will provide data about which products were shipped and in what quantities, and the IS will automatically include data related to who, when, and where.

An important advantage of using an IS compared to a manual system or multiple functional area information systems is that the data need to be entered into the system only once. Furthermore, once they are entered, other people in the process can easily access them, and there is no need to reenter them in subsequent steps.

The data captured by the IS can provide immediate feedback. For example, the IS can use the data to create a receipt or to make recommendations for additional or alternative products.

MIS **Monitoring Process Performance**   A third contribution of IS is to help monitor the state of the various business processes. That is, the IS indicates how well a process is executing. The IS performs this role by evaluating information about a process. This information can be created at either the *instance level* (i.e., a specific task or activity) or at the *process level* (i.e., the process as a whole).

For example, a company might be interested in the status of a particular customer order. Where is the order within the fulfillment process? Was the complete order shipped? If so, when? If not, then when can we expect it to be shipped? Or, for the procurement process, when was the purchase order sent to the supplier? What will be the cost of acquiring the material? At the process level, the IS can evaluate how well the procurement process is being executed by calculating the lead time, or the time between sending the purchase order to a vendor and receiving the goods, for each order and each vendor over time.

Not only can the IS help monitor a process, but it can also detect problems with the process. The IS performs this role by comparing the information with a standard—that is, what the company expects or desires—to determine if the process is performing within expectations. Management establishes standards based on organizational goals.

If the information provided by the IS indicates that the process is not meeting the standards, then the company assumes that some type of problem exists. Some problems can be routinely and automatically detected by the IS, whereas others require a person to review the information and make judgments. For example, the IS can calculate the expected date that a specific order will be shipped and determine whether this date will meet the established standard. Or, the IS can calculate the average time taken to fill all orders over the past month and compare this information with the standard to determine if the process is working as expected.

POM   Monitoring business processes, then, helps detect problems with these processes. These problems are very often really symptoms of a more fundamental problem. In such cases, the IS can help diagnose the cause of the symptoms by providing managers with additional detailed information. For example, if the average time to process a customer order appears to have increased over the previous month, this problem could be a symptom of a more basic problem.

HRM   A manager can then drill down into the information to diagnose the underlying problem. To accomplish this task, the manager can request a breakdown of the information by type of product, customer, location, employees, day of the week, time of day, and so on. After reviewing this detailed information, the manager might determine that the warehouse has experienced an exceptionally high employee turnover rate over the last month and that the delays are occurring because new employees are not sufficiently familiar with the process. The manager might conclude that this problem will work itself out over time, in which case there is nothing more to be done. Alternatively, the manager could conclude that the new employees are not being adequately trained and supervised. In this case, the company must take actions to correct the problem. The following section discusses several methodologies that managers can use to take corrective action when process problems are identified.

Robotic Process Automation

Robotic process automation (RPA) is a system that enables enterprises to automate business processes and tasks that historically were carried out by employees. Companies that employ RPA develop software "robots"—known as *bots*—*that* automate the steps in a business process. Let's consider a variety of RPA scenarios.

MKT *Customer service:* Modern customers are accustomed to quick responses that solve their problems. Automated customer care bots can examine queries and route them to the correct customer care agent. Bots can also offer initial responses to customers without human intervention.

ACCT *Invoice processing:* RPA bots can automate the entire process from receipt to payment. The bots can automate receiving the invoice from the supplier, entering the invoice data, checking the invoice for correctness, and generating payments, thus minimizing human involvement.

POM *Sales orders:* RPA bots can automate tasks such as generating sales quotes and sales orders, monitoring the status of the order, generating invoices, generating payment terms and methods, monitoring returns, and generating refunds. Interestingly, RPA bots can monitor returns and generate refunds very quickly, which improves the customer experience and positively impacts the company's reputation.

HRM *Payroll:* RPA bots can verify that employee data are consistent across multiple systems, validate timesheets, load earnings and deductions in calculating the amount of payment, create the paycheck, administer benefits, and make any necessary reimbursements.

POM *Price comparison:* All businesses make purchases. In the purchasing process, companies perform research about pricing in order to make informed decisions. RPA bots compare prices from different vendors as well as product attributes and quality.

POM *Manage customer information:* In May 2020, Takeda Pharmaceuticals (www.takeda.com) was recruiting patients for a clinical trial of a COVID-19 treatment. It normally took the firm several weeks to collect the volunteers' information, determine who would be suitable for the trial, and prepare the paperwork. Takeda used RPA bots to create patient files, select data input fields, and cut and paste text. As a result, the firm finished each person's paperwork in days instead of weeks.

HRM *Processing HR information:* Businesses generate large amounts of employee data, which RPA bots can collect and organize. These data include employee history with the company, payroll, and level of training.

HRM *Recruitment:* RPA bots can source resumes from different platforms such as LinkedIn, assess candidate qualifications, and filter spam and unqualified applications.

Before you go on...

1. What is a business process?
2. Describe several business processes carried out at your university.
3. Define a cross-functional business process and provide several examples of such processes.
4. Pick one of the processes described in question 2 or 3 and identify its inputs, outputs, customer(s), and resources. How does the process create value for its customer(s)?
5. What is robotic process automation? Provide examples of its use in organizations.

2.2 Business Process Improvement, Business Process Reengineering, and Business Process Management

WILEY PLUS

Author Lecture Videos are available exclusively in *WileyPLUS.*
Apply the Concept activities are available in the Appendix and in *WileyPLUS.*

LEARNING OBJECTIVE

Differentiate between business process reengineering, business process improvement, and business process management.

Excellence in executing business processes is widely recognized as the underlying basis for all significant measures of competitive performance in an organization. Consider the following measures, for example:

- *Customer satisfaction:* The result of optimizing and aligning business processes to fulfill customers' needs, wants, and desires
- *Cost reduction:* The result of optimizing operations and supplier processes
- *Cycle and fulfillment time reduction:* The result of optimizing the manufacturing and logistics processes
- *Quality:* The result of optimizing the design, development, and production processes
- *Differentiation:* The result of optimizing the marketing and innovation processes
- *Productivity:* The result of optimizing each individual's work processes

The question is: How does an organization ensure business process excellence?

In their book *Reengineering the Corporation*, first published in 1993, Michael Hammer and James Champy argued that to become more competitive, American businesses needed to radically redesign their business processes to reduce costs and increase quality. The authors further asserted that information technology is the key enabler of such change. This radical redesign, called **business process reengineering (BPR)**, is a strategy for making an organization's business processes more productive and profitable. The key to BPR is for enterprises to examine their business processes from a "clean sheet" perspective and then determine how they can best reconstruct those processes to improve their business functions. BPRs popularity was propelled by the unique capabilities of information technology, such as automation and standardization of many process steps and error reduction due to improved communication among organizational information silos.

business process reengineering (BPR)
A radical redesign of a business process that improves its efficiency and effectiveness, often by beginning with a "clean sheet" (i.e., from scratch).

Although some enterprises have successfully implemented BPR, many organizations found this strategy too difficult, too radical, too lengthy, and too comprehensive. The impact on employees, on facilities, on existing investments in information systems, and even on organizational culture was overwhelming. Despite the many failures in BPR implementation, however, businesses increasingly began to organize work around business processes rather than individual tasks. The result was a less radical, less disruptive, and more incremental approach, called *business process improvement (BPI)*.

BPI focuses on reducing variation in the process outputs by searching for root causes of the variation in the process itself (e.g., a broken machine on an assembly line) or among the process inputs (e.g., a decline in the quality of raw materials purchased from a certain supplier). BPI is usually performed by teams of employees that include a process expert—usually the process owner (the individual manager who oversees the process)—as well as other individuals who are involved in the process. These individuals can be involved directly; for example, the workers who actually perform process steps. Alternatively, these individuals can be involved indirectly; for example, customers who purchase the outputs from the process.

Six Sigma is a popular methodology for BPI initiatives. Its goal is to ensure that the process has no more than 3.4 defects per million outputs by using statistical methods to analyze the process. (A defect is defined as a faulty product or an unsatisfactory service.) Six Sigma was developed by Motorola in the 1980s, and it is now used by companies worldwide, thanks in part to promotional efforts by early adopters such as GE. Six Sigma is especially appropriate for manufacturing environments, in which product defects can be easily defined and measured. Over the years, the methodology has been modified so that it focuses less on defects and more on customer value. As a result, it can now be applied to services as well as to products. Today, Six Sigma tools are widely used in financial services and health care institutions as components of process-improvement initiatives.

Regardless of the specific methodology you use, a successful BPI project generally follows five basic phases: define, measure, analyze, improve, and control (DMAIC). See **Figure 2.2**.

- In the *define phase*, the BPI team uses a graphical process diagram to document the existing "as is" process activities, process resources, and process inputs and outputs. The team also documents the customer requirements for the process output, together with a description of the problem to be addressed.

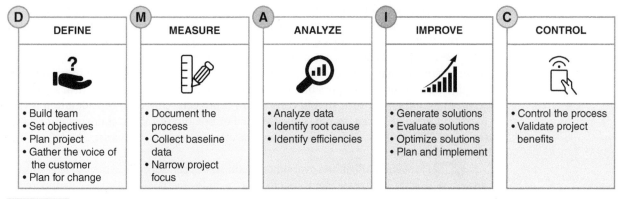

FIGURE 2.2 The Five Phases of BPI.

- In the *measure phase*, the BPI team identifies relevant process metrics, such as time and cost, to generate one output (product or service) and collects data to understand how metrics evolve over time. Sometimes the data already exist, in which case the team can extract them from the IS that supports the process. Other times, however, the BPI team must combine operational process data already stored in the company's IS systems with other data sources, such as customer and employee observations, interviews, and surveys.

- In the *analysis phase*, the BPI team examines the "as is" process diagram and the collected data to identify problems with the process (e.g., decreasing efficiency or effectiveness) and their root causes. If possible, the team should also benchmark the process; that is, compare its performance with that of similar processes in other companies, or other areas of the organization. The team can employ IT applications such as statistical analysis software or simulation packages in this phase.

  Using process simulation software during the analysis phase provides two benefits. First, it enables a process manager to quickly simulate a real situation (e.g., with a certain number of people undertaking activities) for a specific amount of time (e.g., a working day, a week, or a month). The manager can then estimate the process performance over time without having to observe the process in practice. Second, it allows the manager to create multiple scenarios; for example, using a different number of resources in the process or using a different configuration for the process steps. Process simulation software can also provide a number of outputs regarding a process, including the time used by all resources to execute specific activities, the overall cycle time of a process, the identification of resources that are infrequently used, and the bottlenecks in the process. Simulating a process provides a risk-free and inexpensive test of an improvement solution that does not need to be conducted with real resources.

- In the *improve phase*, the BPI team identifies possible solutions for addressing the root causes of the problem, maps the resulting "to be" process alternatives, and selects and implements the most appropriate solution. Common ways to improve processes are eliminating process activities that do not add value to the output and rearranging activities in a way that reduces delays or improves resource use. The organization must be careful, however, not to eliminate internal *process controls—those* activities that safeguard company resources, guarantee the accuracy of its financial reporting, and ensure adherence to rules and regulations.

- In the *control phase*, the team establishes process metrics and monitors the improved process after the solution has been implemented to ensure the process performance remains stable. An IS system can be very useful for this purpose.

Although BPI initiatives do not deliver the huge performance gains promised by BPR, many organizations prefer them because they are less risky and less costly. BPI focuses on delivering quantifiable results—and if a business case cannot be made, the project is not continued. All employees can be trained to apply BPI techniques in their own work to identify opportunities for improvement. Thus, BPI projects tend to be performed more from the bottom up, in contrast to BPR projects, which involve top-down change mandates. BPI projects take less time overall, and even if they are unsuccessful, they consume fewer organizational resources than BPR projects. However, if incremental improvements through BPI are no longer possible, or if significant changes occur in the firm's business environment, then the firm should consider BPR projects. One final consideration is that over time, employees can become overstretched or lose interest if the company undertakes too many BPI projects and does not have an effective system to manage and focus the improvement efforts.

POM To sustain BPI efforts over time, organizations can adopt **business process management (BPM)**, a management system that includes methods and tools to support the design, analysis, implementation, management, and continuous optimization of core business processes throughout the organization. BPM integrates disparate BPI initiatives to ensure consistent strategy execution.

business process management A management technique that includes methods and tools to support the design, analysis, implementation, management, and optimization of business processes.

Important components of BPM are process modeling and business activity monitoring. BPM begins with *process modeling*, which is a graphical depiction of all of the steps in a process. Process modeling helps employees understand the interactions and dependencies among the people involved in the process, the information systems they rely on, and the information they require to optimally perform their tasks. Process modeling software can support this activity.

Business activity monitoring (BAM) is a real-time approach for measuring and managing business processes. Companies use BAM to monitor their business processes, identify failures or exceptions, and address these failures in real time. Furthermore, because BAM tracks process operations and indicates whether they succeed or fail, it creates valuable records of process behaviors that organizations can use to improve their processes.

BPM activities are often supported by *business process management suites (BPMS)*. A BPMS is an integrated set of applications that includes a repository of process information such as process maps and business rules, tools for process modeling, simulation, execution, coordination across functions, and reconfiguration in response to changing business needs as well as process-monitoring capabilities.

Gartner (www.gartner.com), a leading IT research and advisory firm, states that companies need to focus on developing and mastering BPM skills throughout the organization. Gartner notes that high-performing companies use BPM technologies such as real-time process monitoring, visualization, analytics, and intelligent automated decision making to support intelligent business operations.

Another promising emerging trend is *social BPM*. This technology enables employees to collaborate using social media tools on wired and mobile platforms, both internally across functions and externally with stakeholders (such as customers or subject-area experts), to exchange process knowledge and improve process execution.

BPM initially helps companies improve profitability by decreasing costs and increasing revenues. Over time, BPM can create a competitive advantage by improving organizational flexibility—making it easy to adapt to changing business conditions and to take advantage of new opportunities. BPM also increases customer satisfaction and ensures compliance with rules and regulations. In all cases, the company's strategy should drive the BPM effort.

Before you go on...

1. What is business process reengineering?
2. What is business process improvement?
3. What is business process management?

2.3 Business Pressures, Organizational Responses, and Information Technology Support

---

LEARNING OBJECTIVE

Identify effective IT responses to different kinds of business pressures.

Modern organizations compete in a challenging environment. To remain competitive, they must react rapidly to problems and opportunities that arise from extremely dynamic conditions. In this section, you examine some of the major pressures confronting modern organizations and the strategies that organizations employ to respond to these pressures.

Business Pressures

The **business environment** is the combination of social, legal, economic, physical, and political factors in which businesses conduct their operations. Significant changes in any of these factors are likely to create business pressures on organizations. Organizations typically respond to these pressures with activities supported by IT. **Figure 2.3** illustrates the

business environment
The combination of social, legal, economic, physical, and political factors in which businesses conduct their operations.

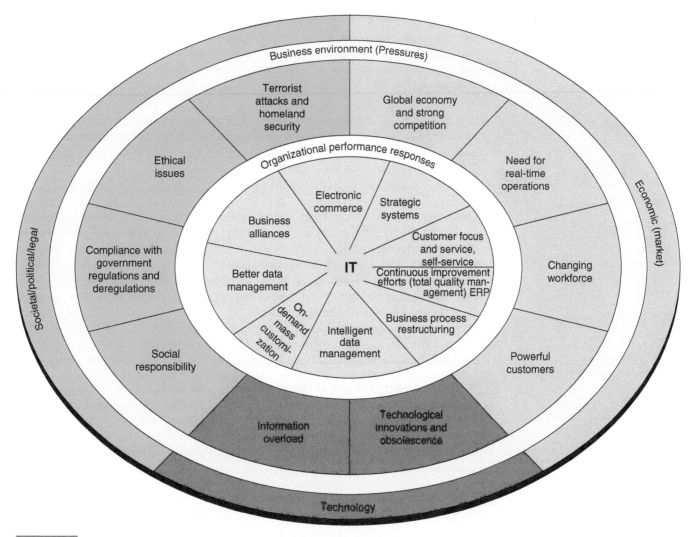

FIGURE 2.3 Business pressures, organizational performance and responses, and IT support.

relationships among business pressures, organizational performance and responses, and IT support. You will learn about three major types of business pressures: market, technology, and societal pressures.

MKT **Market Pressures** Market pressures are generated by the global economy, intense competition, the changing nature of the workforce, and powerful customers. Let's look more closely at each of these factors.

globalization The integration and interdependence of economic, social, cultural, and ecological facets of life, enabled by rapid advances in information technology.

Globalization Globalization is the integration and interdependence of economic, social, cultural, and ecological facets of life that have been made possible by rapid advances in information technology. Today, individuals around the world are able to connect, compute, communicate, collaborate, and compete everywhere and anywhere, any time, and all the time; to access limitless amounts of information, services, and entertainment; to exchange knowledge; and to produce and sell goods and services. People and organizations can now operate without regard to geography, time, distance, or even language barriers. The bottom line? Globalization is markedly increasing competition.

These observations highlight the importance of market pressures for you. Simply put, you and the organizations you join will be competing with people and organizations from all over the world.

Let's consider some examples of globalization:

- Multinational corporations operate on a global scale, with offices and branches located worldwide.
- Many automobile manufacturers use parts from other countries, such as a car being assembled in the United States with parts coming from Japan, Germany, or Korea.
- The World Trade Organization (WTO; www.wto.org) supervises international trade.
- Regional agreements such as the United States–Mexico–Canada Agreement (USMCA) have contributed to increased world trade and increased competition. In September 2018, the three countries reached an agreement to replace the North American Free Trade Agreement (NAFTA) with the USMCA. The three countries ratified the USMCA by March 2020.
- The European Union (EU) is an economic and political union of 27 countries that are located in Europe. Following general elections in 2017 and 2019, Parliament ratified the withdrawal agreement, and the United Kingdom left the European Union on January 31, 2020. The withdrawal was known as Brexit.
- The rise of India and China as economic powerhouses has increased global competition.

One important pressure that businesses in a global market must contend with is the cost of labor, which varies significantly among countries. In general, labor costs are higher in developed countries such as the United States and Japan than in developing countries such as Bangladesh and El Salvador. Also, developed countries usually offer greater benefits, such as health care, to employees, driving the cost of doing business even higher. Therefore, many labor-intensive industries have moved their operations to countries with low labor costs. IT has made such moves much easier to implement.

However, manufacturing overseas is no longer the bargain it once was, and manufacturing in the United States is no longer as expensive. For example, manufacturing wages in China have increased from $3.60 per hour in 2018 to $5.64 per hour in 2020, an increase of almost 60 percent.

HRM **The Changing Nature of the Workforce** The workforce, particularly in developed countries, is becoming more diversified. Increasing numbers of women, single parents, minorities, and persons with disabilities are now employed in all types of positions. IT is easing the integration of these employees into the traditional workforce. IT is also enabling people to work from home, which can be a major benefit for parents with young children and for people confronted with mobility or transportation issues.

MKT **Powerful Customers** Consumer sophistication and expectations increase as customers become more knowledgeable about the products and services they acquire. Customers can use the Internet to find detailed information about products and services, compare prices, and purchase items at electronic auctions.

Organizations recognize the importance of customers, and they have increased their efforts to acquire and retain them. Modern firms strive to learn as much as possible about their customers to better anticipate and address their needs. This process, called *customer intimacy*, is an important component of *customer relationship management (CRM)*, an organization-wide effort toward maximizing the customer experience. You will learn about CRM in Chapter 11.

MIS **Technology Pressures**   The second category of business pressures consists of those pressures related to technology. Two major technology-related pressures are technological innovation and information overload.

Technological Innovation and Obsolescence   New and improved technologies rapidly create or support substitutes for products, alternative service options, and superb quality. As a result, today's state-of-the-art products may be obsolete tomorrow. For example, how often are new versions of your smartphone being released? How quickly are electronic versions of books, magazines, and newspapers replacing traditional hard copy versions? These changes force businesses to keep up with consumer demands.

Consider the rapid technological innovation of the Apple iPad:

- Apple released its first iPad in April 2010.
- Apple released its iPad Mini in November 2012.
- Apple released its iPad Air in November 2013.
- Apple released its iPad Pro in November 2015.
- Apple released the latest version of its iPad Mini (6th generation) in 2021.
- Apple released the latest versions of its iPad (10th generation) and iPad Air (3rd generation) in 2022.
- Apple released the latest version of its iPad Air (5th generation) in March 2022.
- Apple released its iPad Pro (6th generation) with the M2 processor, the same chip they use in the Mac notebooks, in October 2022.

One manifestation of technological innovation is "bring your own device" (BYOD). BYOD refers to the policy of permitting employees to bring personally owned mobile devices (laptops, tablet computers, and smartphones) to the workplace and to use those devices to connect to the corporate network as well as for personal use. The academic version of BYOD involves students using personally owned devices in educational settings to connect to their school's network. **MIS** The rapid increase in BYOD represents a huge challenge for IT departments. Not only has IT lost the ability to fully control and manage these devices, but employees are now also demanding that they be able to conduct company business from multiple personal devices.

The good news is that BYOD has increased worker productivity and satisfaction. In fact, some employees with BYOD privileges actually work longer hours with no additional pay. The bad news is security concerns. Many companies with BYOD policies have experienced an increase in *malware* (malicious software, discussed in Chapter 4). Furthermore, there is an increased risk of losing sensitive proprietary information. Such information might not be securely stored on a personal mobile device, which can be lost or stolen.

Information Overload   The amount of information available on the Internet doubles approximately every year, and much of it is free. The Internet and other telecommunications networks are bringing a flood of information to managers. To make decisions effectively and efficiently, managers must be able to access, navigate, and use these vast stores of data, information, and knowledge. Information technologies such as search engines (discussed in Chapter 6) and data mining (Chapter 12) provide valuable support in these efforts.

Societal, Political, and Legal Pressures   The third category of business pressures includes social responsibility, government regulation/deregulation, spending for social programs, spending to protect against terrorism, and ethics. This section will explain how all of these elements affect modern businesses. We start with social responsibility.

Social Responsibility   Social issues that affect businesses and individuals range from the state of the physical environment, to company and individual philanthropy, to education. Some corporations and individuals are willing to spend time and money to address various social problems. These efforts are known as **organizational social responsibility**, or **individual social responsibility**.

One critical social problem is the state of the physical environment. A growing IT initiative, called *green IT*, addresses some of the most pressing environmental concerns. IT is instrumental in organizational efforts to "go green" in three areas:

1. *Facilities design and management.* Organizations are creating more environmentally sustainable work environments. Many organizations are pursuing Leadership in Energy and Environmental Design (LEED) certification from the U.S. Green Building Council, a nonprofit group that promotes the construction of environmentally friendly buildings. One impact of this development is that IT professionals are expected to help create green facilities.

2. *Carbon management.* As companies try to reduce their carbon footprints, they are turning to IT executives to develop the systems needed to monitor carbon throughout the organization and its supply chain, which can be global in scope. Therefore, IT employees need to become knowledgeable about embedded carbon and how to measure it in the company's products and processes.

3. *International and U.S. environmental laws.* IT executives must deal with federal and state laws and international regulations that impact everything from the IT products they buy, to how they dispose of them, to their company's carbon footprint.

IT's About Business 2.1 illustrates multiple ways in which various societal, economic, and technological pressures are affecting the rental car business. It then explores how Hertz has responded to these pressures to achieve a competitive advantage.

> **organizational social responsibility (also individual social responsibility)**   Efforts by organizations to solve various social problems.
>
> **individual social responsibility**   See **organizational social responsibility**.

IT's About Business 2.1

MIS **MKT** **FIN** **Renting Electric Vehicles for Competitive Advantage**

Like many other industries, the rental car industry was hit hard by the COVID-19 pandemic. In fact, by May 2020, Hertz Global Holdings, Inc. (www.hertz.com), a national car rental company that owns Dollar and Thrifty rentals, had filed for bankruptcy. The bankruptcy deal required Hertz to sell 180,000 vehicles from its fleet. By June 2021, as the economy began to recover from the pandemic, Hertz emerged from bankruptcy, and the car rental market was ready to move forward. Hertz, however, was in a difficult position. With its fleet reduced by 180,000 vehicles and demand returning, it had to determine what types of vehicles it should purchase to rebuild capacity.

To complicate matters, another major shift was occurring at that time. By the first quarter of 2022, electric vehicle (EV) sales accounted for more than 5 percent of new car sales in at least 19 countries. In the United States, more than 170,000 EVs were sold during this period. Many analysts believed this growth represented the "tipping point" for the EV industry. The *tipping point* is the point at which an evolving situation becomes irreversible. At this level of market saturation, EVs have shifted from a rare sighting, to a daily sighting, to "I think I might want one of those."

The dramatic expansion of the EV market has created several market pressures for the car rental industry. **Figure 2.2** presents three broad categories of outside forces and organizational

responses: societal/political/legal, economic, and technological pressures. Let's examine how these pressures impacted the rental car business.

Societal/Political/Legal Pressures

Reaching the tipping point doesn't immediately create customers. However, it highlights a moment when the general attitude toward a new development begins to swing toward a broader acceptance. Turo (www.turo.com), a car-sharing marketplace that allows peer-to-peer car rentals (similar to Airbnb [www.airbnb.com]) for living spaces) provides an excellent example of this societal change in attitude. The number of Teslas, a luxury EV manufactured by Tesla (www.tesla.com), listed for rent on Turo has exploded over the past few years. In 2014, Turo's marketplace listed fewer than 70 Teslas; by late 2021, that number exceeded 21,000. For all EVs, the number available to rent on Turo mushroomed from fewer than 200 to almost 27,000. Peer-to-peer rental is often considered a good measure of consumer interest due to its organic nature.

In a survey from Enterprise Holdings (www.enterprise holdings.com), the parent company of Enterprise Rent-A-Car, National Car Rental, and Alamo Rent-A-Car, more than 60 percent of their clients stated that a positive rental experience with a specific model made them consider purchasing one themselves. Having EVs on the lot for people to rent for an extended period allows customers to take a more substantial test drive. These extended rentals help customers answer many of their questions: Will the range work for me? Will I be able to find chargers? Do I enjoy the driving experience? This is crucial because many consumers are able to test an EV before making a purchase. Enterprise is not creating demand but instead is following the demand of the market to allow for more robust, personal tests of the EV concept.

Further, the increased demand for EVs is not restricted to the consumer market. Many corporations face political and legal pressures when determining the types of vehicles they pay for their employees to rent.

Often, corporations are accused of making decisions based exclusively on the bottom line. As we discuss later, renting EVs can offer financial benefits. In addition, however, many companies view renting EVs as a step toward achieving their environmental goals. EVs provide a quantifiable way for companies to reduce greenhouse gas (GHG) emissions, meet net-zero goals (human-caused emissions of carbon dioxide), and highlight their environmental, social, and governance (ESG) activities for sustainability investors and advocacy groups. Companies can employ these data to illustrate progress in implementing their green initiatives.

In August 2022, California announced that by 2035 it will prohibit the sale of new gasoline cars, signaling a state-mandated shift toward EVs. In addition, President Joe Biden has announced several initiatives to increase the number of EVs the U.S. government purchases. In addition, the administration's Bipartisan Infrastructure Law, which was signed into law in November 2021, allocated $5 billion to increase the number of EV charging stations. In September 2022, the U.S. Department of Transportation (www.transportation.gov/) announced that it had approved EV charging station plans for all 50 states, giving them access to the first $1.5 billion of the infrastructure money.

Politically, socially, and legally, the demand for EVs is growing across consumer, corporate, and political interests. It is no surprise that this demand has led Hertz to shift its fleet toward EVs.

Economic Pressures

In a typical year, the $56 billion U.S. rental industry purchases roughly 10 percent of manufacturers' new cars. This number, however, has declined significantly due to persistent supply-chain disruptions, particularly the shortage of essential computer chips. In 2021, the car rental industry bought 750,000 new cars, down from 2.1 million in 2019.

Given the economic pressures on Hertz, there are two primary reasons for the company to shift its fleet to EVs: cost reduction and premium pricing. EVs will have a direct economic impact on Hertz's overall profitability. In its 2021 annual report, Hertz signaled to its investors that its EVs would enhance the company's bottom line. Electricity is less expensive than fuel, maintenance costs for EVs are lower, and customers are willing to pay a premium for the rental. All of these benefits will expand the company's profit margin.

Technological Pressures

Technologically, Hertz is experiencing multiple pressures, some over which the company has no control. The most significant is renters' ability to charge their vehicles. Consumers who purchase an EV typically elect to have a charger installed at home, so they do not need the public charging grid. Renters, however, do not have this luxury. They require public charging access. This could be challenging for customers who rent an EV in a city with which they are unfamiliar and who have never charged or driven an EV. As we saw previously, the Bipartisan Infrastructure Law is allocating funds to increase the number of charging stations.

In addition, company agents and mechanics must be trained in EV technology. Currently, the industry has little standardization, so the learning curve is quite steep.

Hertz's Response

While Hertz was the first rental company to make a significant EV move, its two biggest rivals, Enterprise Holdings and Avis Budget Group, have since joined the race. Consumers benefit from having more rental companies offer EVs as part of their fleet because increased supply decreases costs. Currently, however, supply is not outpacing demand. Just as the full-scale adoption of EVs among U.S. drivers will take years, the rental car shift will be a marathon, not a sprint.

Hertz has made the most significant movements of any rental company in adding EVs to its fleet. In 2021, the company announced an order of 100,000 Teslas. In March 2022, they agreed to purchase 65,000 Polestar sedans. (Polestar is an EV manufacturer based in Sweden (www.polestar.com). Then, in September, they announced a deal to purchase 175,000 EVs from GMC (www.gmc.com).

These moves place Hertz far ahead of its competitors in the EV rental race. Several of their U.S. rivals claim to have big EV plans, but they have revealed few details.

Significantly, car rental companies have gambled on EVs in the past without success. For example, Hertz and Enterprise offered EVs from 2011 to 2017. Ultimately, however, they abandoned those efforts in the face of low gas prices and consumer confusion on the concept of the EV. The difference? The market had not yet reached the tipping point.

Questions

1. **Describe the political/social/legal pressures on Hertz.**
2. **Describe the technological pressures on Hertz.**
3. **Describe the economic pressures on Hertz.**
4. **How will EVs create a competitive advantage for Hertz?**

Sources: Compiled from E. Newburger, "All 50 States Get Green Light to Build EV Charging Stations Covering 75,000 Miles of Highways," *CNBC.com*, September 27, 2022; D. Ferris, "Hertz Places a Risky Wager on EVs," *eenews.net*, September 21, 2022; R. Bellan, "Biden to Announce $900M to Build EV Charging Stations," *TechCrunch*, September 14, 2022; C. Davenport, L. Friedman, and B. Plumer, "California to Ban the Sale of New Gasoline Cars," *New York Times*, August 24, 2022; S. Collie, "Hertz on Why Your Next Rental Car Might Be an EV," *carexpert.com.au*, August 11, 2022; T. Randall, "US Crosses the Electric-Car Tipping Point for Mass Adoption," *Bloomberg*, July 8, 2022; S. Segan, "Hertz Is Trying to Leave Gas Behind, but What's Standing in the Way?," *PC Magazine*, June 21, 2022; B. Woods, "How the Massive EV Transition Is Starting in the Car Rental Industry," *cnbc.com*, June 18, 2022; D. Shepardson and A. Sriram, "Hertz to Buy Up to 65,000 Electric Vehicles from Polestar," *reuters.com*, April 4, 2022; N. Naughton, "Hertz-Tesla Deal Signals Broad Shift to EVs for Rental-Car Companies," *Wall Street Journal*, November 27, 2021; L. Brown, "Hertz Buying 100,000 Teslas in $4.2 Billion Deal, Making EVs 20 Percent of Its Fleet," *Car and Driver*, November 2, 2021; A. Alamalhodaei, "Tesla's Deal with Hertz Opens a New Frontier for the EV maker," *techcrunch.com*, October 29, 2021; N. Bomey, "Hertz to Buy 100,000 Tesla Cars as Rental Car Company Pivots toward Electric Vehicles," *USA Today*, October 25, 2021; E. Schatzker, "Hertz Order for 100,000 EVs Sends Tesla Value to $1 Trillion," *Bloomberg*, October 25, 2021; and M. Gladwell, *The Tipping Point: How Little Things Can Make a Big Difference*, Back Bay Books, 2002.

Continuing our discussion of social responsibility, social problems all over the world may be addressed through corporate and individual philanthropy. In some cases, questions arise as to what percentage of contributions actually goes to the intended causes and recipients and what percentage goes to the charity's overhead. Another problem that concerns contributors is that they often exert little influence over the selection of the projects their contributions will support. The Internet can help address these concerns and facilitate generosity and connection. Consider the following examples:

- *PatientsLikeMe* (www.patientslikeme.com) or any of the thousands of message boards dedicated to infertility, cancer, and various other ailments: People use these sites and message boards to obtain information about health care decisions based on volunteered information, while also receiving much-needed emotional support from strangers.

- **FIN** *Kiva* (www.kiva.org): Kiva is a nonprofit enterprise that provides a link between lenders in developed countries and entrepreneurs in developing countries. Users pledge interest-free loans rather than tax-deductible donations. Kiva directs 100 percent of the loans to borrowers.

- *DonorsChoose* (www.donorschoose.org): DonorsChoose is an education-oriented website that functions entirely within the United States. Users make donations to public schools rather than loans. The website addresses the huge problem of underfunded public schools.

digital divide The gap between those who have access to information and communications technology and those who do not.

Still another social problem that affects modern business is the digital divide. The **digital divide** refers to the wide gap between those individuals who have access to information and communications technologies and those who do not. This gap exists both within and among countries.

One well-known project to narrow the divide is the One Laptop per Child (OLPC) project (www.laptop.org) OLPC is a nonprofit association dedicated to developing an inexpensive laptop aimed at revolutionizing how the world educates its children. In 2020, the price of OLPC's laptop remained approximately $230. (This price includes educational software loaded on the laptop.) However, there are many other costs associated with these laptops, including shipping, solar chargers, maintenance, and training. Some international users contend that the actual cost of one laptop is therefore approximately $450.

Compliance with Government Regulations Another major source of business pressures is government regulations regarding health, safety, environmental protection, and equal opportunity. Businesses tend to view government regulations as expensive constraints on their activities. In general, government deregulation intensifies competition.

In the wake of numerous corporate scandals, the U.S. government passed many new laws, including the Sarbanes-Oxley Act, the USA PATRIOT Act, the Gramm-Leach-Bliley Act, and the Health Insurance Portability and Accountability Act (HIPAA). Organizations must be in compliance with the regulations contained in these statutes. The process of becoming and remaining compliant is expensive and time consuming. In almost all cases, organizations rely on IT support to provide the necessary controls and information for compliance.

Protection against Terrorist Attacks Since September 11, 2001, organizations have been under increased pressure to protect themselves against terrorist attacks, both physical attacks and cyberattacks. Employees who are in the military reserves have also been called up for active duty, creating personnel problems. Information technology can help protect businesses by providing security systems and possibly identifying patterns of behavior associated with terrorist activities, including cyberattacks (discussed in Chapter 4). For a good example of a firm that provides this protection, see Palantir (www.palantir.com).

An example of protection against terrorism is the Department of Homeland Security's (DHS) Office of Biometric Identity Management (OBIM) program. (We discuss biometrics in Chapter 4.) OBIM (www.dhs.gov/obim) is a network of biometric screening systems such as fingerprint and iris and retina scanners that ties into government databases and watch lists to check the identities of millions of people entering the United States. The system is now operational in more than 300 locations, including major international ports of entry by air, sea, and land.

Ethical Issues   *Ethics* relates to general standards of right and wrong. *Information ethics* relates specifically to standards of right and wrong in information processing practices. Ethical issues are very important because, if handled poorly, they can damage an organization's image and destroy its employees' morale. The use of IT raises many ethical issues, ranging from monitoring e-mail to invading the privacy of millions of customers whose data are stored in private and public databases. Chapter 3 covers ethical issues in detail.

Unfortunately, not all organizations use information technology ethically. IT's About Business 2.2 provides an example of such a situation. It also illustrates how technology can be used to overcome unethical behavior.

IT's About Business 2.2

MIS   MLB Sign Stealing Stopped with Technology

The Problem

Sign stealing is a baseball practice in which one team tries to decipher its opponents' signs. Players, coaches, and managers use visible but disguised hand signals throughout each game. The team at bat exchanges signs among coaches, batters, and runners, and the team playing defense communicates on each play.

Determining what the opponent's signs mean can give a team a major competitive advantage. The most significant benefit is when a team steals the signs between the opposing catcher and pitcher. The batter can know if the next pitch will be a fastball or a breaking ball (curve or slider). If a batter knows which pitch is coming, then that knowledge negates the pitcher's most significant advantage; namely, the element of surprise.

Sign stealing has long been an accepted tradition in baseball. Accounts of sign stealing go back to the 1870s when the Hartford Dark Blues, a charter member of the National League, were accused of using a telegraph pole outside the ballpark to steal opponents' signs. The Blues allegedly hired a man to climb the pole and use binoculars to steal signs. From his perch, he would signal the Blues' bench as to what the next pitch would be.

Historically, players and coaches have attempted to steal their opponents' signs by watching the other team and trying to recognize patterns or sequences. Stealing signs is legal if teams do it visually. However, it is illegal if teams use cameras, binoculars, or electronic devices of any type.

Since the 2014 season, Major League Baseball (MLB; www. mlb.com) has allowed managers one chance per game to challenge a call on the field—but not balls and strikes—using a video replay system. Each team has a video replay review room. A center field camera generates the videos. Team replay assistants help notify managers when to challenge a call. Significantly, they have access only to the live game broadcast; they cannot access instant replay.

A major controversy erupted in November 2019 when Mike Fiers, a former pitcher for the Houston Astros, informed Ken Rosenthal and Evan Drellich of *The Athletic* that the Astros had been utilizing modern technologies to steal their opponents' signs in violation of MLB rules. The revelation led to an MLB investigation, which confirmed Fiers's accusations.

Here is how the scheme worked. At the beginning of the 2017 season, the Astros' video replay review room used the live game feed from the center field camera to decode the opposing team's sign sequences. Once they did so, a player in the room would act as a "runner" to relay the information to the dugout. The person in the dugout would notify the players in the dugout or signal the sign sequence to the runner on second base, who would decipher the catcher's sign and signal to the batter.

Eventually, Alex Cora, the Astros' bench coach, began to call the replay review room on the replay phone to obtain the sign information directly. On at least some occasions, the employees in the replay review room communicated the information by text message.

Two months into the 2017 season, a group of players discussed how the team could improve their system of decoding signs and sending the signals to the batter. Under the new system, Cora arranged for a video room technician to install a monitor displaying the center field camera feed immediately outside the Astros' dugout. One or more players watched the live feed. Then, after decoding the sign, a player would bang on a nearby trash can with a bat to communicate the upcoming pitch type to the batter. Generally, one or two bangs corresponded to certain off-speed pitches, while no bang corresponded to a fastball.

Was this scheme effective? Whether coincidentally or not, the Astros won the 2017 World Series, the first championship for the franchise, which entered the MLB in 1962.

The trash-can–banging practice ended before the 2018 season. However, the Astros' replay review room staff continued the sign-stealing scheme. The operation finally ended during the 2018 season when Astros players believed that other teams had discovered the practice and learned how to defeat it.

The Astros also deployed a computer software program called Codebreaker to steal signs from opposing catchers to pitchers. Using the center field camera, a staffer would log the stolen signs into a spreadsheet and then run an algorithm to determine an opponent's sign sequencing and what all the signs meant. Houston's front office joked that the program came from the team's "dark arts" department.

After the scheme became public, MLB commissioner Rob Manfred suspended A. J. Hinch and General Manager Jeff Luhnow for the 2020 season. Manfred also stripped the Astros of their first- and second-round selections in the 2020 and 2021 MLB drafts, and he fined the franchise $5 million. However, he declined to vacate the Astros' 2017 championship. Shortly after Hinch and Luhnow's suspensions were announced, Astros owner Jim Crane fired both men.

According to the MLB Commissioner's report, Alex Cora was the architect of the sign-stealing scheme. Significantly, Cora left the Astros after the 2017 season to manage the Boston Red Sox in 2018 and 2019. (The Red Sox won the championship in 2018.) However, in January 2020, after the scandal became public, he and the Red Sox "mutually agreed to part ways." In addition, Carlos Beltran, who had played for the Astros in 2017 and was hired to manage the New York Mets in November 2019, resigned his position on January 16, 2020.

These penalties, however, did not stop teams from trying to steal signs. It would take technology to accomplish that goal.

The Solution

Coaches, fielders, pitchers, catchers, batters, and runners must communicate while on the field. That part of the game will never go away. The method of communication, however, has changed drastically. Soon after the sign-stealing scandal went public, a technology product called PitchCom arrived that would allow pitchers, catchers, and select infielders to communicate via a small wearable keypad. This device has nine buttons plus a toggle for volume adjustment, a 6-inch soft receiver worn in a player's cap that employs a proprietary audio system using bone-conducting hearing technology, and, for catchers, a small tube-style earpiece attached to the catcher's mask.

Catchers can wear the receiver attached to a band on their wrist or, as most have now adopted, on their shin guard. The nine buttons are numbered and programmed by pitch types and locations. Catchers press their command for pitch type, followed by location, and the combination is then sent to the receivers via an encrypted channel.

The idea is simple enough. If baseball can eliminate old-fashioned pitch calling that relies on signs that the catcher flashes to the pitcher with his fingers, it will be harder for other teams to steal signs. As with any new technology, there have been a few hiccups. Periodically, devices did not operate, and pitchers could not hear the call. In addition, on at least one occasion, the ESPN network accidentally broadcasted the PitchCom over live TV. In general, however, all parties appear to agree that PitchCom is working.

Results

PitchCom was approved for use in the 2022 season and has been rapidly adopted. Four months into the season, all 30 MLB teams had employed the technology, and many teams had incorporated it into every game to replace the use of physical signs.

In response to the 2017 scandal, teams employed sign-switching methods that made it harder for opposing teams to decode signs. This strategy, however, made the game flow awkward and slow. The approval and adoption of PitchCom has not only virtually eliminated the possibility of sign stealing, but it has also reduced the average game time by six minutes compared to 2021. The technology has reduced the number of trips to the mound by managers and coaches to communicate with pitchers. As a result, the game now flows more smoothly and quickly.

Questions

1. Describe how the Astros used technology in the team's sign-stealing scheme.
2. Describe how the Astros used non-technological means in the team's sign-stealing scheme.
3. Information technologies, particularly wireless technologies, continue to improve rapidly. How has technology changed the game of baseball in the area of communication?

Sources: Compiled from C. Garcia, "After Four Months, PitchCom Is Changing MLB" *fansided.com*, August 16, 2022; S. Miller, "Baseball Buys In on the Digital Age. But at What Cost?," *The New York Times*, August 7, 2022; J. Lee, "PitchCom—Aimed at Foiling MLB's Would-Be Sign-Stealers—Is (Mostly) Winning over the Skeptics," *espn.com*, May 13, 2022; A. Castrovince, "MLB Informs Clubs PitchCom Is Approved for '22 Season," *mlb.com*, April 5, 2022; Baseball-reference.com, accessed September 6, 2022; S. Gardner, "Evan Gattis Admits 2017 Houston Astros 'Cheated Baseball and Cheated Fans,'" *USA Today*, April 2, 2020; N. Vigdor, "The Houston Astros Cheating Scandal Explained," *New York Times*, February 28, 2020; J. Bogage, "What Is Sign Stealing? Making Sense of Major League Baseball's Latest Scandal," *The Washington Post*, February 14, 2020; D. Sheinin, "Astros Say They Are Sorry but Draw a Line When It Comes to Questioning 2017 World Series Title," *The Washington Post*, February 13, 2020; M. Kennedy, "Houston Astros Apologize for Sign-Stealing, but Provide Fuel for Critics," *NPR.org*, February 13, 2020; "Everything You Need to Know about MLB's Sign-Stealing Scandal," *ESPN.com*, February 13, 2020; J. Diamond, "'Dark Arts' and 'Codebreaker': The Origins of the Houston Astros Cheating Scheme," *The Wall Street Journal*, February 7, 2020; L. Pope and T. Bannon, "8 Things to Know about the Astros' Sign-Stealing Scandal, Including a Former White Sox Pitcher's Early Suspicions," *Chicago Tribune*, January 17, 2020; J. Passan, "Astros' Jeff Luhnow, AJ Hinch Fired for Sign Stealing," *ESPN.com*, January 13, 2020; B. Nightengale, "MLB Hands Down Historic Punishment to Astros for Sign Stealing," *USA Today*, January 13, 2020; D. Waldstein, "Former Astros Pitcher Says Team Electronically Stole Signs in 2017," *New York Times*, November 12, 2019; M. Fiers and K. Rosenthal, "The Astros Stole Signs Electronically in 2017—Part of a Much Broader Issue for Major League Baseball," *The Athletic*, November 12, 2019; P. Dickson, *The Hidden Language of Baseball: How Signs and Sign Stealing Have Influenced the Course of Our National Pastime*, Lincoln: University of Nebraska Press, 2003; and www.mlb.com, accessed May 27, 2020.

Clearly, then, the pressures on organizations are increasing, and organizations must be prepared to take responsive actions if they are to succeed. You will learn about these organizational responses in the next section.

Organizational Responses

Organizations are responding to the various pressures just discussed by implementing IT such as strategic systems, customer focus, make-to-order and mass customization, and e-business. This section explores each of these responses.

Strategic Systems Strategic systems provide organizations with advantages that enable them to increase their market share and profits to better negotiate with suppliers and to prevent competitors from entering their markets. IT's About Business 2.3 provides an example of how strategically important information systems can be to an organization. As you will see, many information systems are so strategically important to organizations that if they are inadequate, or fail altogether, their organizations are at risk of failing as well.

IT's About Business **2.3**

MIS **MKT** NFL Stadiums Deploy Technology to Attract and Connect Fans

National Football League (**NFL**, www.nfl.com) teams and their stadiums compete with large, high-definition televisions (HDTVs) in fans' homes. Therefore, they must offer in-person attendees a better experience than that of fans watching the games from the comfort of their living room or den.

One vital area in which NFL teams must improve in order to attract fans is wireless connectivity within stadiums. Specifically, NFL stadiums must provide high-speed Wi-Fi connections (see Chapter 8) for fans who want to communicate with people inside and outside the stadiums. Fans also want to download information about the teams, the stadium, or the players to enhance their experience and share it with friends. Much of what is shared is pictures, and NFL stadiums must provide more network data capacity to accommodate fans using 12-megapixel cameras to capture images and videos that they upload to social media platforms.

Stadium visitors also engage with venue-specific apps and services. These services include ordering food from their seat, determining the length of the line to the closest bathroom, viewing instant replays, upgrading their seat location, and even viewing behind-the-scenes footage available only through the stadium app for fans physically present in the stadium.

To provide the services and functions that fans demand, stadiums typically have more than 2,000 Wi-Fi access points and Bluetooth beacons, as well as fiber-optic backbone networks (see Chapter 6) that provide almost 100 gigabits per second (Gbps) of available Internet bandwidth. In NFL stadiums, the Wi-Fi adoption rate by fans increased from 18 percent in 2013 to 45 percent in 2019. In addition, the average bandwidth transferred increased from 1.9 terabytes (TB, see Technology Guide 1) in 2015 to 4.6 TB in 2019.

Let's take a closer look at the technologies employed by NFL stadiums and teams. These technologies include wireless access points, mobile tickets, Wi-Fi 6, augmented reality, cashless transactions, biometric screening, and beacons.

Wireless Access Points. NFL stadium technology requires many wireless access points. A *wireless access point* (WAP, see Chapter 8) is a transmitter with an antenna that enables other Wi-Fi devices to connect to a wired local area network (WLAN, see Chapter 8) and the Internet. Some stadiums place these points under seats so they will be closer to users to provide stronger Wi-Fi signals. Under-seat access points are not always the best option, however, because they are more expensive to install and maintain. An alternative is to place access points on handrails and hide them under a sign or panel for aesthetic purposes. Access points improve connectivity by ensuring that each spot in the stadium has wireless coverage.

Wi-Fi 6. The NFL transitioned to Wi-Fi 6 for the 2022 season. Wi-Fi 6 is the next-generation standard for wireless fidelity. The biggest benefits of Wi-Fi 6 are its enhanced speed and its ability to support many devices and applications on a single network. Wi-Fi 6 speeds are estimated to be about 30 percent faster than Wi-Fi 5. SoFi Stadium, which opened in 2020, has more than 2,500 Wi-Fi 6 access points, providing four times more bandwidth than earlier versions of Wi-Fi and enabling everyone in the stadium to be on their phones simultaneously. During the 2022 Super Bowl, which was played at SoFi, more than 57,000 devices were connected to the stadium network, and many fans communicated with friends or family outside the stadium or at home.

Mobile Tickets. In the past, paper tickets were anonymous: A fan could buy a ticket and then give it to a friend. As a result, teams did not know who actually came to each game. To address this issue, during the 2019–2020 season, NFL stadiums introduced the digital mobile ticket. As one example, for the 2022–2023 season, SoFi Stadium, home of the Los Angeles Rams and Los Angeles Chargers, employed near field communication (NFC, see Chapter 8) technology to enable fans to enter the stadium more quickly. As fans approach stadium entries, they are greeted by the staff, who ensure that they comply with the NFL and SoFi Stadium's Clear Bag Policy (an efficient security measure used to ensure no prohibited items are brought into the stadium). Guests will be prompted to scan or tap their mobile tickets using one of the new hands-free pedestal scanners that are located at all entries. Fans entering with mobile tickets saved to their mobile wallet will pull up the ticket on their phone and then tap the back of their phone beneath the screen on the pedestal scanner. No barcode is needed because the entry will utilize NFC technology, which communicates a signal from the phone to the scanner. If the ticket is on the mobile Web or in a mobile app, then the ticket should have a rotating barcode. To enter, fans pull up their ticket and hold the barcode under the red light. All game attendees must have a valid mobile ticket on their phone that will turn the pedestal light green after it is scanned.

By putting mobile tickets on people's phones, stadiums have decreased the wait times at entrances. Further, they learn who is at the game. This knowledge enables them to market more effectively to the attendees and track their purchases. These data points are important for targeted marketing, such as personalized offers for merchandise.

Augmented Reality. The Dallas Cowboys utilize augmented reality (AR, see Technology Guide 1) in the team's "Pose with the Pros" app. Fans attending the game participate in an AR experience that lets them take photos with their favorite Cowboys players. A Samsung Galaxy S10 5G smartphone uses AR technology to superimpose the players' images into the shot. Then, a camera snaps a photo of the fan with the players. The app has gathered more than 50 million social media impressions. An *impression* occurs when somebody views a particular content on a social media website

Extended Reality. Fox NFL Sunday debuted a groundbreaking studio in 2022 that enables broadcasters to present new types of scenes for viewers. More than 5,000 square feet of LEDs surround the announcer's desk. Rather than using green screen technology (which requires a speaker to stand in front of a green screen so that their image can be overlaid on top of a background) to present reviews of plays, announcers can now stand in front of the LEDs with augmented reality displaying routes, plays, and outcomes. This technology will provide a much-improved viewer experience compared to the "chalkboard" Xs, Os, and arrows.

Cashless Transactions. In 2019, Mercedes-Benz Stadium, home of the Atlanta Falcons, began using a cashless system—for example, credit cards and phone apps—at most food and refreshment stands and kiosks. The Falcons contend that this system shortens lines and improves hygiene standards because staff no longer have to handle cash. Improved hygiene is of particular importance during the coronavirus pandemic.

Biometric Screening. Stadiums are beginning to use biometric screening (see Chapter 4) to shorten wait times in lines at the stadium entrances and concession stands. For example, Lumen Field (www.lumenfield.com/), home of the Seattle Seahawks, has begun using technology from CLEAR (www.clearme.com). Instead of traditional identification documents, CLEAR uses facial and finger-print recognition. Fans need to enroll only one time at a kiosk to be able to use "fast lanes" at stadium entrances and concession stands. As another example, for the 2022–23 season, SoFi Stadium contracted with Evolv to employ its weapons-detection security screen at all events. This system utilizes sensor technology to spot potential danger from weapons or other prohibited devices. Fans can walk through the detectors without removing anything from their pockets or clear bags.

Beacons. Beacons are small wireless transmitters that use low-energy Bluetooth technology to send signals to nearby devices (see Chapter 8). Stadiums and teams use beacons' accurate location capabilities to deliver targeted personalized messages, alerts, and offers on mobile devices. How do stadiums use beacons? Consider the following examples:

- Finding and upgrading seats: Beacons help fans find their seats quickly and easily. Stadiums can also target people who are waiting in line to go to cheaper seats, or they can offer fans on-the-spot discounted upgrades on better seating.

- Beacons situated next to refreshment stands can register how many people with the app are waiting in line. By making this information available, stadiums can direct fans to refreshment stands with shorter wait times.

- Beacons can create additional stadium revenue via mobile sales of merchandise or food. For instance, beacons enable fans to use the stadium app to order food from their seats.

Questions

1. Consider all the technologies discussed in this case. Taken together, are they strategically important to NFL stadiums and NFL teams? Why or why not? Provide specific examples to support your answer.

2. Have you experienced any of the technologies discussed in the case? Do you feel your experience was improved with the use of technology?

Sources: Compiled from P. Kurz, "'Fox NFL Sunday' to Debut Groundbreaking New XR/AR Studio," *tvtechnology.com*, September 9, 2022; B. Costa, "NFL Kickoff 2022: Fox Sports to Debut New Studio For Fox NFL Sunday," *Sports Video Group News*, September 9, 2022; S. Jackson, "New Food and Beverage, Entry Process, Fan Zones and Signage Coming to SoFi Stadium for 2022 Gamedays," *therams.com*, August 31, 2022; Z. Kerravala, "The NFL Knows a Lot about Deploying High-Capacity Wi-Fi Networks," *Network World*, February 11, 2020; T. Maddox, "Super Bowl 2020: How 5G Will Help Keep Fans Safe at the Game," *TechRepublic*, January 31, 2020; T. Maddox, "Super Bowl 54: 49ers and Chiefs Matchup Will Be the First 5G Super Bowl in History," *TechRepublic*, January 31, 2020; C. Reichert, "NFL's Biggest Stadium Will Open with Wi-Fi 6," *CNET*, November 1, 2019; S. Ogus, "Dallas Cowboys Use Augmented Reality in Popular New Fan Activation 'Pose with the Pros'," *Forbes*, September 13, 2019; "These Are the NFL Stadiums that Give Fans the Best and Worst Experiences," *Gameday News*, September 12, 2019; B. Fischer, "The More Fun League: NFL Aims for Better Fan Experience," *Sports Business Journal*, August 19, 2019; L. Bradley, "Top 5 Tech Trends Transforming In-Stadium Fan Experience," *Medium.com*, July 22, 2019; C. Arkenberg et al., "Redesigning Stadiums for a Better Fan Experience, *Deloitte*, June 27, 2019; T. Maddox, "Super Bowl 53 Is Poised to Make Digital History," *TechRepublic*, January 30, 2019; T. Maddox, "How Verizon and AT&T Are Preparing for Super Bowl 53," *TechRepublic*, January 31, 2019; M. Spencer, "How the NFL and Its Stadiums Became Leaders in Wi-Fi Technology and Monetizing Apps," *Chat Sports*, January 9, 2019; N. Mallik, "How Stadiums Can Use Beacons to Enhance Fans' Experiences," *beaconstac.com*, May 31, 2018; T. Maddox, "How the NFL and Its Stadiums Became Leaders in Wi-Fi, Monetizing Apps, and Customer Experience," TechRepublic, August 25, 2016; www.nfl.com, accessed May 30, 2020, https://www.extremenetworks.com/resources/infographic/nfl-superbowl-lvi-infographic/, accessed September 6, 2022; and https://www.therams.com/news/rams-sofi-stadium-entry-quicker-2022-season, accessed September 30, 2022.

MKT Customer Focus Organizational attempts to provide superb customer service can make the difference between attracting and retaining customers versus losing them to competitors. Numerous IT tools and business processes have been designed to keep customers happy. Recall that a *business process* is a collection of related activities that produce a product or a service of value to the organization, its business partners, and its customers. Consider Amazon, for example. When you visit Amazon's website any time after your first visit, the site welcomes you back by name, and it presents you with information about items that you might like, based on your previous purchases. In another example, Dell guides you through the process of purchasing a computer by providing information and choices that help you make an informed buying decision.

make-to-order The strategy of producing customized products and services.

POM Make-to-Order and Mass Customization Make-to-order is a strategy of producing customized (made to individual specifications) products and services. The business problem is how to manufacture customized goods efficiently and at a reasonably low cost. Part of the solution is to change manufacturing processes from mass production to mass customization. In mass production, a company produces a large quantity of identical items. An early example of mass production was Henry Ford's Model T, for which buyers could pick any color they wanted—as long as it was black.

Ford's policy of offering a single product for all of its customers eventually gave way to *consumer segmentation*, in which companies provide standard specifications for different consumer groups, or segments. Clothes manufacturers, for example, design their products in different sizes and colors to appeal to different customers. The next step was *configured mass customization*, in which companies offer features that allow each shopper to customize his or her product or service with a range of components. Examples are ordering a car, a computer, or a smartphone, for which the customer can specify which features he or she wants.

In the current strategy, known as **mass customization**, a company produces a large quantity of items, but it customizes them to match the needs and preferences of individual customers. Mass customization is essentially an attempt to perform make-to-order on a large scale. Examples are:

- NikeID (www.nikeid.com) allows customers to design their footwear.
- M&M candies: My M&M (www.mms.com) allows customers to add photos, art, and messages to candy.
- Dell (www.dell.com) and HP (www.hp.com) allow customers to exactly specify the computer they want.

mass customization
A production process in which items are produced in large quantities but are customized to fit the desires of each customer.

E-Business and E-Commerce   Conducting business electronically is an essential strategy for companies that are competing in today's business environment. *Electronic commerce (EC or e-commerce)* describes the process of buying, selling, transferring, or exchanging products, services, or information through computer networks, including the Internet. *E-business* is a somewhat broader concept. In addition to the buying and selling of goods and services, e-business also refers to servicing customers, collaborating with business partners, and performing electronic transactions within an organization. Chapter 7 focuses extensively on this topic. In addition, e-commerce applications appear throughout the text.

You now have a general overview of the pressures that affect companies in today's business environment and the responses that these companies choose to manage these pressures. To plan for the most effective responses, companies formulate strategies. In the new digital economy, these strategies rely heavily on information technology, especially strategic information systems. You examine these topics in the next section.

Before you go on...

1. What are the characteristics of the modern business environment?
2. Discuss some of the pressures that characterize the modern global business environment.
3. Identify some of the organizational responses to these pressures. Are any of these responses specific to a particular pressure? If so, then which ones?

2.4 Competitive Advantage and Strategic Information Systems

LEARNING OBJECTIVE

Describe the strategies that organizations typically adopt to counter Porter's five competitive forces.

WILEY PLUS

Author Lecture Videos are available exclusively in *WileyPLUS.*
Apply the Concept activities are available in the Appendix and in *WileyPLUS.*

A *competitive strategy* is a statement that identifies a business's approach to compete, its goals, and the plans and policies that will be required to carry out those goals (Porter, 1985).[1] A strategy, in general, can apply to a desired outcome, such as gaining market share. A competitive strategy focuses on achieving a desired outcome when competitors want to prevent you from

---
[1]Porter, M. E. (1985). *Competitive Advantage*, Free Press, New York.

reaching your goal. Therefore, when you create a competitive strategy, you must plan your own moves, but you must also anticipate and counter your competitors' moves.

Through its competitive strategy, an organization seeks a competitive advantage in an industry. That is, it seeks to outperform its competitors in a critical measure such as cost, quality, and time-to-market. Competitive advantage helps a company function profitably within a market and generate higher-than-average profits.

Competitive advantage is increasingly important in today's business environment, as you will note throughout the text. In general, the *core business* of companies has remained the same. That is, information technologies simply offer tools that can enhance an organization's success through its traditional sources of competitive advantage, such as low cost, excellent customer service, and superior supply chain management. **Strategic information systems (SISs)** provide a competitive advantage by helping an organization to implement its strategic goals and improve its performance and productivity. Any information system that helps an organization either achieve a competitive advantage or reduce a competitive disadvantage qualifies as a strategic information system.

> **Strategic information systems (SISs)** Systems that help an organization gain a competitive advantage by supporting its strategic goals and increasing performance and productivity.

Porter's Competitive Forces Model

The best-known framework for analyzing competitiveness is Michael Porter's **competitive forces model** (Porter, 1985). Companies use Porter's model to develop strategies to increase their competitive edge. Porter's model also demonstrates how IT can make a company more competitive.

> **competitive forces model** A business framework devised by Michael Porter that analyzes competitiveness by recognizing five major forces that could endanger a company's position.

Porter's model identifies five major forces that can endanger or enhance a company's position in a given industry. **Figure 2.4** highlights these forces. Although the Web has changed the nature of competition, it has not changed Porter's five fundamental forces. In fact, what makes these forces so valuable as analytical tools is that they have not changed for centuries. Every competitive organization, no matter how large or small, or which business it is in, is driven by these forces. This observation applies even to organizations that you might not consider competitive, such as local governments. Although local governments are not for-profit enterprises, they compete for businesses to locate in their districts, for funding from higher levels of government, for employees, and for many other things.

Significantly, Porter (2001)[2] concludes that the *overall* impact of the Web is to increase competition, which generally diminishes a firm's profitability. Let's examine Porter's five forces and the ways that the Web influences them.

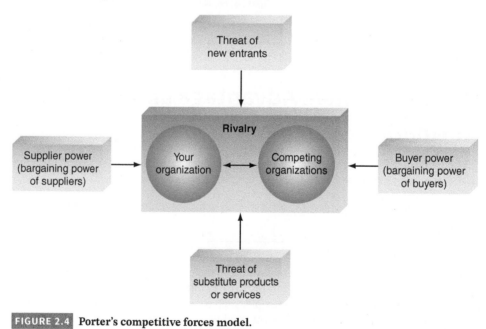

FIGURE 2.4 Porter's competitive forces model.

---

[2]Porter, M. E. (2001). "Strategy and the Internet," *Harvard Business Review*, March.

1. *The threat of entry of new competitors.* The threat that new competitors will enter your market is high when entry is easy and low when there are significant barriers to entry. An **entry barrier** is a product or service feature that customers have learned to expect from organizations in a certain industry. An organization that seeks to enter the industry must offer this feature to survive in the marketplace. There are many types of entry barriers. Consider, for example, legal requirements such as admission to the bar to practice law or obtaining a license to serve liquor, where only a certain number of licenses are available.

   Suppose you want to open a gasoline station. To compete in that industry, you would have to offer pay-at-the-pump service to your customers. Pay-at-the-pump is an IT-based barrier to entering this market because you must offer it for free. The first gas station that offered this service gained first-mover advantage and established barriers to entry. This advantage did not last, however, because competitors quickly offered the same service and thus overcame the entry barrier.

   For most firms, the Web *increases* the threat that new competitors will enter the market because it sharply reduces traditional barriers to entry, such as the need for a sales force or a physical storefront. Today, competitors frequently need only to set up a website. This threat of increased competition is particularly acute in industries that perform an *intermediation role*, which is a link between buyers and sellers (e.g., stock brokers and travel agents), as well as in industries in which the primary product or service is digital (e.g., the music industry). The geographical reach of the Web also enables distant competitors to compete more directly with an existing firm.

   In some cases, however, the Web increases barriers to entry. This scenario occurs primarily when customers have come to expect a nontrivial capability from their suppliers. For example, the first company to offer Web-based package tracking gained a competitive advantage from that service. Competitors were forced to follow suit.

   > **entry barrier** Product or service feature that customers expect from organizations in a certain industry; an organization trying to enter this market must provide this product or service at a minimum to be able to compete.

2. *The bargaining power of suppliers.* Supplier power is high when buyers have few choices from whom to buy and low when buyers have many choices. Therefore, organizations would rather have more potential suppliers so that they will be in a stronger position to negotiate price, quality, and delivery terms.

   The Internet's impact on suppliers is mixed. On the one hand, it enables buyers to find alternative suppliers and to compare prices more easily, thereby reducing the supplier's bargaining power. On the other hand, as companies use the Internet to integrate their supply chains, participating suppliers prosper by locking in customers.

3. *The bargaining power of customers (buyers).* Buyer power is high when buyers have many choices from whom to buy and low when buyers have few choices. For example, in the past, there were few locations where students could purchase textbooks (typically, one or two campus bookstores). In this situation, students had low buyer power. Today, the Web provides students with access to a multitude of potential suppliers as well as detailed information about textbooks. As a result, student buyer power has increased dramatically.

   In contrast, *loyalty programs* reduce buyer power. As their name suggests, loyalty programs reward customers based on the amount of business they conduct with a particular organization (e.g., airlines, hotels, car rental companies). Information technology enables companies to track the activities and accounts of millions of customers, thereby reducing buyer power. That is, customers who receive perks from loyalty programs are less likely to do business with competitors. (Loyalty programs are associated with customer relationship management, which you will study in **Chapter 11**.)

4. *The threat of substitute products or services.* If there are many alternatives to an organization's products or services, then the threat of substitutes is high. Conversely, if there are few alternatives, then the threat is low. Today, new technologies create substitute products very rapidly. For example, customers can purchase wireless telephones instead of landline telephones, Internet music services instead of traditional CDs, and ethanol instead of gasoline for their cars.

   Information-based industries experience the greatest threat from substitutes. Any industry in which digitized information can replace material goods (e.g., music, books, software) must view the Internet as a threat because the Internet can convey this information efficiently and at low cost and high quality.

Even when there are many substitutes for their products, however, companies can create a competitive advantage by increasing switching costs. *Switching costs* are the costs, in money and time, imposed by a decision to buy elsewhere. For example, contracts with smartphone providers typically include a substantial penalty for switching to another provider until the term of the contract expires (quite often, two years). This switching cost is monetary.

As another example, when you buy products from Amazon, the company develops a profile of your shopping habits and recommends products targeted to your preferences. If you switch to another online vendor, then that company will need time to develop a profile of your wants and needs. In this case, the switching cost involves time rather than money.

5. *The rivalry among existing firms in the industry.* The threat from rivalry is high when there is intense competition among many firms in an industry. The threat is low when the competition involves fewer firms and is not as intense.

In the past, proprietary information systems—systems that belong exclusively to a single organization—have provided strategic advantage to firms in highly competitive industries. Today, however, the visibility of Internet applications on the Web makes proprietary systems more difficult to keep secret. In simple terms, when I see my competitor's new system online, I will rapidly match its features to remain competitive. The result is fewer differences among competitors, which leads to more intense competition in an industry.

To understand this concept, consider the highly competitive grocery industry, in which Walmart, Kroger, Safeway, and other companies compete essentially on price. Some of these companies have IT-enabled loyalty programs in which customers receive discounts and the store gains valuable business intelligence on customers' buying preferences. Stores use this business intelligence in their marketing and promotional campaigns. (You will learn about business intelligence in Chapter 12.)

Grocery stores are also experimenting with RFID to speed up the checkout process, track customers through the store, and notify customers of discounts as they pass by certain products. Grocery companies also use IT to tightly integrate their supply chains for maximum efficiency and thus reduce prices for shoppers.

Established companies can also gain a competitive advantage by allowing customers to use data from the company's products to improve their own performance. For example, Babolat (www.babolat.com), a manufacturer of sports equipment, has developed its Babolat Play Pure Drive system. The system has sensors embedded into the handle of its tennis rackets. A smartphone app uses the data from the sensors to monitor and evaluate ball speed, spin, and impact location to give tennis players valuable feedback.

Competition is also being affected by the extremely low variable cost of digital products. That is, once a digital product has been developed, the cost of producing additional units approaches zero. Consider the music industry as an example. When artists record music, their songs are captured in digital format. Physical products, such as CDs or DVDs of the songs for sale in music stores, involve costs. The costs of a physical distribution channel are much higher than those involved in delivering the songs digitally over the Internet.

In fact, in the future, companies might give away some products for free. For example, some analysts predict that commissions for online stock trading will approach zero because investors can search the Internet for information to make their own decisions regarding buying and selling stocks. At that point, consumers will no longer need brokers to give them information that they can obtain themselves, virtually for free.

Porter's Value Chain Model

value chain A sequence of activities through which the organization's inputs, whatever they are, are transformed into more valuable outputs, whatever they are.

value chain model Model that shows the primary activities that sequentially add value to the profit margin; also shows the support activities.

Organizations use Porter's competitive forces model to design general strategies. To identify specific activities in which they can use competitive strategies for greatest impact, they use his value chain model (1985). A **value chain** is a sequence of activities through which the organization's inputs, whatever they are, are transformed into more valuable outputs, whatever they are. The **value chain model** identifies points for which an organization can use information technology to achieve a competitive advantage (see **Figure 2.5**).

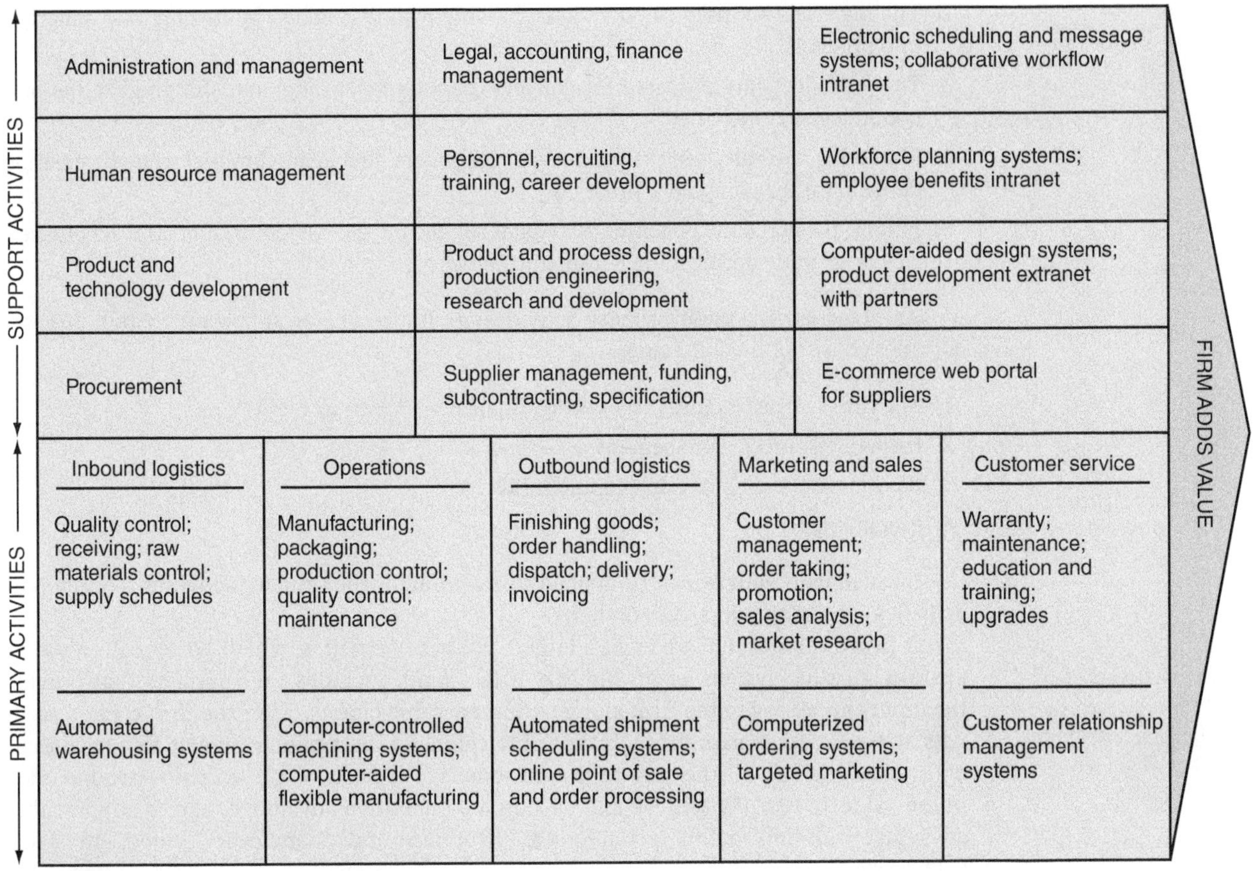

Administration and management	Legal, accounting, finance management	Electronic scheduling and message systems; collaborative workflow intranet
Human resource management	Personnel, recruiting, training, career development	Workforce planning systems; employee benefits intranet
Product and technology development	Product and process design, production engineering, research and development	Computer-aided design systems; product development extranet with partners
Procurement	Supplier management, funding, subcontracting, specification	E-commerce web portal for suppliers

Inbound logistics	Operations	Outbound logistics	Marketing and sales	Customer service
Quality control; receiving; raw materials control; supply schedules	Manufacturing; packaging; production control; quality control; maintenance	Finishing goods; order handling; dispatch; delivery; invoicing	Customer management; order taking; promotion; sales analysis; market research	Warranty; maintenance; education and training; upgrades
Automated warehousing systems	Computer-controlled machining systems; computer-aided flexible manufacturing	Automated shipment scheduling systems; online point of sale and order processing	Computerized ordering systems; targeted marketing	Customer relationship management systems

SUPPORT ACTIVITIES — *PRIMARY ACTIVITIES* (left axis) — *FIRM ADDS VALUE* (right axis)

FIGURE 2.5 **Porter's value chain model.**

According to Porter's value chain model, the activities conducted in any organization can be divided into two categories: primary activities and support activities. **Primary activities** relate to the production and distribution of the firm's products and services. These activities create value for which customers are willing to pay. The primary activities are buttressed by **support activities**. Unlike primary activities, support activities do not add value directly to the firm's products or services. Rather, as their name suggests, they contribute to the firm's competitive advantage by supporting the primary activities.

Next, you will see examples of primary and support activities in the value chain of a manufacturing company. Keep in mind that other types of firms, such as transportation, health care, education, retail, and others, have different value chains. The key point is that *every* organization has a value chain.

In a manufacturing company, primary activities involve purchasing materials, processing the materials into products, and delivering the products to customers. Manufacturing companies typically perform five primary activities in the following sequence:

1. Inbound logistics (inputs)
2. Operations (manufacturing and testing)
3. Outbound logistics (storage and distribution)
4. Marketing and sales
5. Services

As work progresses in this sequence, value is added to the product in each activity. Specifically, the following steps occur:

1. The incoming materials are processed (in receiving, storage, and so on) in activities called *inbound logistics.*

primary activities Those business activities related to the production and distribution of the firm's products and services, thus creating value.

support activities Business activities that do not add value directly to a firm's product or service under consideration but support the primary activities that do add value.

2. The materials are used in operations, in which value is added by turning raw materials into products.

3. These products are prepared for delivery (packaging, storing, and shipping) in the outbound logistics activities.

4. Marketing and sales sell the products to customers, increasing product value by creating demand for the company's products.

5. Finally, the company performs after-sales service for the customer, such as warranty service or upgrade notification, adding further value.

As noted earlier, these primary activities are buttressed by support activities. Support activities consist of the following:

1. The firm's infrastructure (accounting, finance, and management)

2. Human resources management

3. Product and technology development (R&D)

4. Procurement

Each support activity can be applied to any or all of the primary activities. The support activities can also support one another.

value system   A stream of activities that includes the producers, suppliers, distributors, and buyers, all of whom have their own value chains.

A firm's value chain is part of a larger stream of activities, which Porter calls a **value system**. A value system, or an *industry value chain*, includes the suppliers that provide the inputs necessary to the firm along with their value chains. After the firm creates products, these products pass through the value chains of distributors (which also have their own value chains), all the way to the customers. All parts of these chains are included in the value system. To achieve and sustain a competitive advantage, and to support that advantage with information technologies, a firm must understand every component of this value system.

Strategies for Competitive Advantage

Organizations continually try to develop strategies to counter the five competitive forces identified by Porter. You will learn about five of those strategies here. Before we go into specifics, however, it is important to note that an organization's choice of strategy involves trade-offs. For example, a firm that concentrates only on cost leadership might not have the resources available for research and development, leaving the firm unable to innovate. As another example, a company that invests in customer happiness (customer orientation strategy) will experience increased costs.

Companies must select a strategy and then stay with it, because a confused strategy cannot succeed. This selection, in turn, decides how a company will use its information systems. A new information system that can improve customer service but will increase costs slightly will be welcomed at a high-end retailer such as Nordstrom's, but not at a discount store such as Walmart. The following list presents the most commonly used strategies. **Figure 2.6** provides an overview of these strategies.

1. *Cost leadership strategy.* Produce products and services at the lowest cost in the industry. An example is Walmart's automatic inventory replenishment system, which enables the company to reduce inventory storage requirements. As a result, Walmart stores use floor space only to sell products and not to store them, thereby reducing inventory costs.

2. *Differentiation strategy.* Offer different products, services, or product features than your competitors. Southwest Airlines, for example, has differentiated itself as a low-cost, short-haul express airline. This has proved to be a winning strategy for competing in the highly competitive airline industry.

3. *Innovation strategy.* Introduce new products and services, add new features to existing products and services, or develop new ways to produce them. A classic example is the introduction of automated teller machines (ATMs) by Citibank. The convenience and

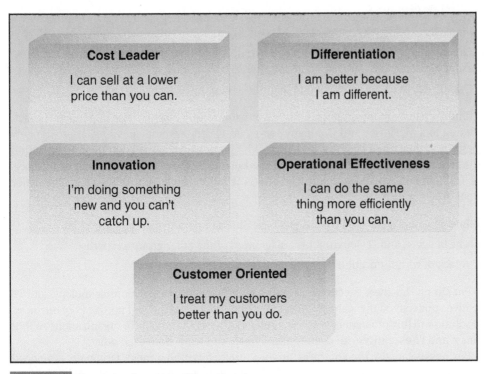

FIGURE 2.6 **Strategies for competitive advantage.**

cost-cutting features of this innovation gave Citibank a huge advantage over its competitors. Like many innovative products, the ATM changed the nature of competition in the banking industry. Today, an ATM is a competitive *necessity* for any bank. Another excellent example is Apple's rapid introduction of innovative products.

4. *Operational effectiveness strategy.* Improve the manner in which a firm executes its internal business processes so that it performs these activities more effectively than its rivals. Such improvements increase quality, productivity, and employee and customer satisfaction while decreasing time to market.

5. *Customer orientation strategy.* Concentrate on making customers happy. Web-based systems are particularly effective in this area because they can create a personalized, one-to-one relationship with each customer. Amazon (www.amazon.com), Apple (www.apple.com), and Starbucks (www.starbucks.com) are classic examples of companies devoted to customer satisfaction.

Business–Information Technology Alignment

The best way for organizations to maximize the strategic value of IT is to achieve business–information technology alignment. In fact, the holy grail of organizations is business–information technology alignment, or strategic alignment (which we will call simply *alignment*). **Business–information technology alignment (business–IT alignment)** is the tight integration of the IT function with the organization's strategy, mission, and goals. That is, the IT function directly supports the business objectives of the organization. There are six characteristics of excellent alignment:

1. Organizations view IT as an engine of innovation that continually transforms the business, often creating new revenue streams.

2. Organizations view their internal and external customers and their customer service function as supremely important.

3. Organizations rotate business and IT professionals across departments and job functions.

business–information technology alignment The tight integration of the IT function with the strategy, mission, and goals of the organization.

4. Organizations provide overarching goals that are completely clear to each IT and business employee.

5. Organizations ensure that IT employees understand how the company makes (or loses) money.

6. Organizations create a vibrant and inclusive company culture.

Unfortunately, many organizations fail to achieve this type of close alignment. In fact, according to a McKinsey and Company survey on IT strategy and spending, approximately 27 percent of the IT and business executives who participated agreed that their organization had adequate alignment between IT and the business. Given the importance of business and IT alignment, why do so many organizations fail to implement this policy? The major reasons are:

- Business managers and IT managers have different objectives
- The business and IT departments are ignorant of the other group's expertise
- A lack of communication

Put simply, business executives often know little about information technology, and IT executives understand the technology but may not understand the real needs of the business. One solution to this problem is to foster a collaborative environment in organizations so that business and IT executives can communicate freely and learn from each other.

Businesses can also use enterprise architecture to foster alignment. Originally developed as a tool to organize a company's IT initiatives, the enterprise architecture concept has evolved to encompass both a technical specification (the information and communication technologies and the information systems used in an organization) and a business specification (a collection of core business processes and management activities).

Before you go on...

1. What are strategic information systems?

2. According to Porter, what are the five forces that could endanger a firm's position in its industry or marketplaces?

3. Describe Porter's value chain model. Differentiate between Porter's competitive forces model and his value chain model.

4. What strategies can companies use to achieve competitive advantage?

5. What is business–IT alignment?

6. Provide examples of business–IT alignment at your university, regarding student systems. (*Hint:* What are the "business" goals of your university with regard to student registration, fee payment, grade posting, and so on?)

What's in IT for Me?

For All Business Majors

All of the functional areas of any organization are literally composed of a variety of business processes, as we can see from the examples discussed in this chapter. Regardless of your major, you will be involved in a variety of business processes from your first day on the job. Some of these processes you will perform by yourself; some will involve only your group, team, or department; and some will involve several (or all) functional areas of your organization.

It is important for you to be able to visualize processes, understand the inputs and outputs of each process, and know the "customer" of each process. If you can accomplish these things, then you will contribute to making processes more efficient and effective. This often means incorporating information technology in the process. It is also important for you to understand how each process fits into your organization's strategy.

In addition, all functional areas in any organization must work together in an integrated fashion for the firm to respond adequately to business pressures. These responses typically require each functional area to employ a variety of information systems to support, document, and manage cross-functional business processes. In today's competitive global marketplace, it is more critical than ever that these responses be timely and accurate.

It is also essential that all functional areas work together for the organization to achieve a competitive advantage in its marketplace. Again, the functional areas use a variety of strategic information systems to achieve this goal.

You have seen why companies must be concerned with strategic advantage. But why is this chapter so important for you? There are several reasons. First, the business pressures you have learned about have an impact on your organization, but they also affect you as an individual. So, it is critical that you understand how information systems can help you, and eventually your organization, to respond to these pressures.

Achieving a competitive advantage is also essential for your organization's survival. In many cases, you, your team, and all your colleagues will be responsible for creating a competitive advantage. Therefore, having general knowledge about strategy and about how information systems affect the organization's strategy and competitive position will help you in your career.

You also need a basic knowledge of your organization's strategy, mission, and goals, as well as its business problems and how it makes (or loses) money. You now know how to analyze your organization's strategy and value chain, as well as the strategies and value chains of your competitors. You also have acquired a general knowledge of how information technology contributes to organizational strategy. This knowledge will help you to do your job more effectively, to be promoted more quickly, and to contribute significantly to the success of your organization.

Summary

2.1 Discuss ways in which information systems enable cross-functional business processes and processes for a single functional area.

A business process is an ongoing collection of related activities that produce a product or a service of value to the organization, its business partners, and its customers. Examples of business processes in the functional areas are managing accounts payable, managing accounts receivable, managing after-sale customer follow-up, managing bills of materials, managing manufacturing change orders, applying disability policies, employee hiring, computer user and staff training, and applying Internet use policy. The procurement and fulfillment processes are examples of cross-functional business processes.

2.2 Compare and contrast business process reengineering and business process management to determine the different advantages and disadvantages of each.

Business process reengineering (BPR) is a radical redesign of business processes that is intended to improve the efficiency and effectiveness of an organization's business processes. The key to BPR is for enterprises to examine their business processes from a "clean sheet" perspective and then determine how they can best reconstruct those processes to improve their business functions. Because BPR proved difficult to implement, organizations have turned to business process management. Business process management (BPM) is a management technique that includes methods and tools to support the design, analysis, implementation, management, and optimization of business processes.

2.3 Identify effective IT responses to different kinds of business pressures.

- *Market pressures:* An example of a market pressure is powerful customers. Customer relationship management is an effective IT response that helps companies achieve customer intimacy.
- *Technology pressures:* An example of a technology pressure is information overload. Search engines and business intelligence applications enable managers to access, navigate, and use vast amounts of information.
- *Societal, political, and legal pressures:* An example of a societal, political, or legal pressure is social responsibility, such as the state of the physical environment. Green IT is one response that is intended to improve the environment.

2.4 Describe the strategies that organizations typically adopt to counter Porter's five competitive forces.

Porter's five competitive forces:

1. *The threat of entry of new competitors:* For most firms, the Web increases the threat that new competitors will enter the market by reducing traditional barriers to entry. Frequently, competitors need only to set up a website to enter a market. The Web can also increase barriers to entry, as when customers come to expect a nontrivial capability from their suppliers.

2. *The bargaining power of suppliers:* The Web enables buyers to find alternative suppliers and to compare prices more easily, thereby reducing suppliers' bargaining power. From a different perspective, as companies use the Web to integrate their supply chains, participating suppliers can lock in customers, thereby increasing suppliers' bargaining power.

3. *The bargaining power of customers (buyers):* The Web provides customers with incredible amounts of choices for products, as well as information about those choices. As a result, the Web increases buyer power. However, companies can implement loyalty programs in which they use the Web to monitor the activities of millions of customers. Such programs reduce buyer power.

4. *The threat of substitute products or services:* New technologies create substitute products very rapidly, and the Web makes information about these products available almost instantly. As a result, industries (particularly information-based industries) are in great danger from substitutes (e.g., music, books, newspapers, magazines, software). However, the Web also can enable a company to build in switching costs, so that it will cost customers time or money to switch from your company to that of a competitor.

5. *The rivalry among existing firms in the industry:* In the past, proprietary information systems provided strategic advantage for firms in highly competitive industries. The visibility of Internet applications on the Web makes proprietary systems more difficult to keep secret. Therefore, the Web makes strategic advantage more short-lived.

The five strategies are as follows:

1. *Cost leadership strategy*—Produce products and services at the lowest cost in the industry

2. *Differentiation strategy*—Offer different products, services, or product features

3. *Innovation strategy*—Introduce new products and services, put new features in existing products and services, or develop new ways to produce them

4. *Operational effectiveness strategy*—Improve the manner in which internal business processes are executed so that a firm performs similar activities better than its rivals

5. *Customer orientation strategy*—Concentrate on making customers happy

Key Terms

business environment   43
business process   34
business process management   42
business process reengineering
   (BPR)   40
business–information technology
   alignment   59
competitive advantage   33

competitive forces model   54
cross-functional processes   34
digital divide   48
entry barrier   55
globalization   44
individual social responsibility   46
make-to-order   52
mass customization   53

organizational social responsibility (also
   individual social responsibility)   46
primary activities   57
Strategic information systems (SISs)   54
support activities   57
value chain   56
value chain model   56
value system   58

Discussion Questions

1. Consider the student registration process at your university:

   a. Describe the steps necessary for you to register for your classes each semester.

   b. Describe how information technology is used (or is not used) in each step of the process.

2. Why is it so difficult for an organization to actually implement business process reengineering?

3. Explain why IT is both a business pressure and an enabler of response activities that counter business pressures.

4. What does globalization mean to you in your choice of a major? In your choice of a career? Will you have to be a "lifelong learner"? Why or why not?

5. What might the impact of globalization be on your standard of living?

6. Is IT a strategic weapon or a survival tool? Discuss.

7. Why might it be difficult to justify a strategic information system?

8. Describe the five forces in Porter's competitive forces model and explain how increased access to high-speed Internet has affected each one.

9. Describe Porter's value chain model. What is the relationship between the competitive forces model and the value chain model?

10. Describe how IT can be used to support different value chains for different companies.

11. Discuss the idea that an information system by itself can rarely provide a sustainable competitive advantage.

Problem-Solving Activities

1. Surf the Internet for information about the Department of Homeland Security. Examine the available information, and comment on the role of information technologies in the department.

2. Experience mass customization by designing your own shoes at www.nike.com, your car at www.jaguar.com, your business card at www.iprint.com, and your diamond ring at www.bluenile.com. Summarize your experiences.

3. Software can greatly enhance a business's successful BPM. Check out www.appian.com and summarize the tool's benefits.

4. Access www.go4customer.com. What does this company do, and where is it located? Who are its customers? Provide examples of how a U.S. company would use its services.

5. As a society, we are actively trying to reduce the digital divide. Go to www.internetsociety.org and read the blog titled "What is the Digital Divide?". Do you think community networks are the answer? Why or why not?

6. Access the website of Walmart China (www.walmartchina. com/english/index.htm). How does Walmart China differ from

your local Walmart (consider products, prices, services, and so on)? Describe these differences.

7. Apply Porter's value chain model to Costco (www.costco.com). What is Costco's competitive strategy? Who are Costco's major competitors? Describe Costco's business model. Describe the tasks that Costco must accomplish for each primary value chain activity. How would Costco's information systems contribute to Costco's competitive strategy, given the nature of its business?

8. Apply Porter's value chain model to Dell (www.dell.com). What is Dell's competitive strategy? Who are Dell's major competitors? Describe Dell's business model. Describe the tasks that Dell must accomplish for each primary value chain activity. How would Dell's information systems contribute to Dell's competitive strategy, given the nature of its business?

Closing Case

MIS POM MKT Pick n Pay Creates an Operational and Customer-Oriented Advantage with the Cloud

In 1967, Raymond Ackerman purchased four Pick n Pay (www.pnp .co.za) stores in Cape Town, South Africa. Today, there are more than 2,000 stores in the Pick n Pay Group in eight countries across southern Africa. In addition, the company owns a 49 percent investment in TM Supermarkets in Zimbabwe.

The Pick n Pay Group is a retail business in the consumer goods industry that is headquartered in Cape Town, South Africa. There are multiple store formats under three brands—Pick n Pay, Boxer, and TM Supermarkets. Pick n Pay operates one of the largest online grocery platforms in Sub-Saharan Africa. According to their mission, they serve customers to create an excellent place to shop. Customers inform everything from the range of products offered to how they design their stores. To keep customers their first priority, the company needs to understand their diverse and changing needs.

A huge organization like Pick n Pay stores terabytes (TB) of data in multiple locations. Sharing data and analytics quickly and efficiently is crucial to running an organization in a way to be able to quickly respond to the market. Pick n Pay needed a modernized enterprise resource planning (ERP) solution to enhance communication across the supply chain, divisions, and geographical and political boundaries. Pick n Pay already used SAP (www.sap .com), but it was locally installed and operated. A true enterprise version that would connect and share date across the numerous locations would need to be moved into the cloud (see Technology Guide 3).

In addition, at the time of this writing in 2022, SAP is planning to terminate support for its on-premise solutions by 2027, effectively requiring customers to migrate to the cloud. For Pick n Pay, upgrading to SAP S/4HANA and the cloud is the logical, strategic choice to create a competitive advantage.

Pick n Pay chose to implement SAP S/4HANA, installed on the Amazon Web Services (AWS) platform. To assist with the installation, they selected Lemongrass as their partner. Let's take a look at each piece of this solution.

SAP. SAP S/4HANA. SAP has been a household name in ERP for years. There are many known benefits to implementing SAP. Among the most important are the following:

- **Adaptability.** A cloud-based solution can more easily adapt to changing business needs. As one example, it is more robust at supporting a hybrid workforce.

- **Collaborations are easier.** A cloud-based solution makes it easier to collaborate with business partners and suppliers. It even simplifies the acquisition of new businesses by making it simpler to bring them into the environment.

- **Lower ownership costs.** Because the company's resources are stored in a central location and are often hosted by a third party, the overall ownership costs are lower.

- **Faster analytics insights.** Because S/4HANA runs on the HANA in-memory database, it increases performance exponentially. Instead of storing data in a data warehouse and waiting for it to load, the core ERP system now provides analytics and faster insights and can share them more readily.

- **More accurate forecasting.** AI and machine learning applications continue to evolve slowly but steadily in S/4HANA to improve modeling, predictive outcomes, and forecasting.

AWS. As mentioned above, SAP is often installed on a third-party solution. For more than 15 years, AWS has been the world's most comprehensive and broadly adopted cloud offering. AWS continually expands its services to support multiple cloud workloads. It now has more than 200 fully featured services supporting many basic operations such as computing, storage, databases, and networking, as well as more advanced functions such as analytics, machine learning and artificial intelligence (AI), Internet of Things (IoT), and virtual and augmented reality (VR and AR).

In 2004, AWS established a presence in Cape Town to pioneer technologies focused on networking, next-generation software for customer support, and software programs used by AWS, among other technologies. This proximity to a cloud provider was a key reason Pick n Pay selected AWS as their provider. While SAP S/4HANA functions without regard to geographic location, the implementation process benefits from a provider who operates in the same time zone, the same language, and within the same economic structure.

Lemongrass. Lemongrass (www.lemongras.com) is a software-enabled service provider focused on delivering superior, highly automated, managed services to enterprise-level customers. They are a premier consulting partner that enables customers like Pick n Pay to migrate their mission-critical SAP—including SAP S/4HANA—and non-SAP workloads to AWS while also managing these workloads with a high level of automation and agility (see Figure 2.7). They specialize in providing the experience, expertise, and best practices to assist their customers with an SAP transformation. Lemongrass helps engineer strategies and services that enable their customers to enjoy the benefits of scale and agility while controlling risks and uncertainties. Also,

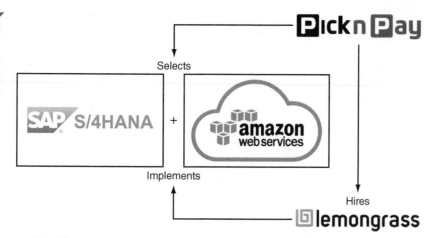

FIGURE 2.7   **Relationship Between Pick n Pay and Lemongrass**.

they have demonstrated the ability to migrate SAP systems to the cloud with almost no downtime. For Pick n Pay, the combination of SAP S/4HANA, running on AWS servers, with the migration led by Lemongrass, was the optimal solution.

Lemongrass designed a solution for Pick n Pay using its proven templates and patterns to migrate, operate, and automate their SAP workloads. Lemongrass supported moving the entire range of SAP and non-SAP workloads to the cloud.

Modernizing its SAP workloads with AWS enabled Pick n Pay to connect operations, sales, customer surveys, and loyalty data across its organization. The new SAP environment runs on AWS to support the company's online and physical sales, streamline its supply chain network, forecast inventory, and conduct detailed market analysis to offer the right retail mix merchandise.

With AWS, Pick n Pay can dynamically scale its operations to meet business demand during peak retail seasons. This feature helps Pick n Pay scale its online shopping services, which run on AWS, to serve thousands of South African customers during its busiest shopping periods and holidays. In addition, the combination of SAP running on the AWS platform has enabled Pick n Pay to perform market testing and develop viable products quickly and cost-effectively. This ability has helped the company remain at the forefront of retail innovation on the African continent.

Based on its collaborations with past clients, Lemongrass expects Pick n Play to realize a cost savings of 45 percent to 75 percent with the new cloud-based strategy. Moving to the cloud will enable Pick n Pay to streamline its operations and modernize the supply chain network for its stores, develop new digital customer experiences in grocery shopping, and expand into new areas of business.

Questions

1. **Why did Pick n Pay want to upgrade their enterprise solution to one that was hosted in the cloud?**

2. **Why did Pick n Pay use Lemongrass's services for this project?**

3. **How do AWS and SAP provide a competitive advantage to Pick n Pay and other retailers that use their products?**

Sources: Compiled from L. Monzon, "AWS Opens New Offices in Johannesburg, South Africa," *IT News Africa*, September 1, 2022; A. Payne, "Three Ideas to Challenge Your Thinking about Digital Procurement," *SupplyChainBrain*, September 1, 2022; M. Evatt, "AWS Sreamlines Operations for Pick n Pay," *ERP Today*, August 26, 2022; Staff Writer, "The Six Biggest Retail Technology News Stories of the Week," *Retail Technology Innovation Hub*, August 26, 2022; M. Wheatley, "South African Retailer Pick n Pay Migrates Its Entire IT Infrastructure to Amazon's Cloud," *SiliconANGLE*, August 25, 2022; P. Saunders, "Are ERP Projects Really the Stuff of Nightmares?" *Forbes*, June 28, 2022; C. Parizo, "9 Top SAP S/4HANA Benefits for Businesses," *TechTarget*, March 1, 2022; P. Rutten, F. Rosa, and R. Villars, "The Mighty Struggle to Migrate SAP to the Cloud May Be Over," *IDC White Paper*, February, 2022; P. Farbinger, "ERP Is Dead," *E-3 Magazine*, January 17, 2022; Lemongrass, "Fender Chooses Lemongrass to Lead Its SAP-to-Cloud Growth Initiative," news release, January 12, 2022, https://www.globenewswire.com/news release/2022/01/12/2365731/0/en/Fender-Chooses-Lemongrass-to-Lead-its-SAP-to-Cloud-Growth-Initiative.html; and J. O'Donnell, "Google-Lemongrass Partnership Boosts SAP on GCP," *TechTarget*, October 4, 2021, https://lemongrasscloud.com/.

CHAPTER 3

Ethics and Privacy

CHAPTER OUTLINE	LEARNING OBJECTIVES
3.1 Ethical Issues	**3.1 Define** ethics, and explain its three fundamental tenets and the four categories of ethical issues related to information technology.
3.2 Privacy	**3.2 Discuss** at least one potential threat to the privacy of the data stored in each of three places that store personal data.

Opening Case

MIS **Facial Recognition in India Raises Concerns**

The city of Hyderabad, India, experienced terror attacks in 2007 and 2013 when it was part of the state of Andhra Pradesh. The 2007 bomb blast killed at least 42 people, and the 2013 blast killed 18 people and injured 119 more. Pervasive police surveillance began after the blasts when authorities passed an amendment to the Public Safety Act that required all establishments with a gathering of more than 100 people to install closed-circuit television (CCTV) cameras and turn over the footage to the police when requested to do so.

In 2014, India created Telangana as a separate state from Andhra Pradesh with Hyderabad as its capital. By 2022, Telangana had installed 830,000 CCTV cameras. According to the Indian Ministry of Home Affairs, more than 60 percent of all police CCTV cameras across India are located in Telangana.

Using footage from the city's CCTV cameras, the Hyderabad Police Department has deployed facial recognition software. *Facial recognition systems* employ machine learning algorithms (see **Chapter 14**) to record specific, distinctive details of a person's face. These details, such as the distance between the eyes or the shape of the chin, are converted into a mathematical representation and compared to data on other faces in a facial recognition database. Telangana authorities have built a Command and Control Centre where all of the state's facial-recognition–capable cameras are monitored in real time.

Privacy advocates allege that the Hyderabad police department uses facial recognition for many questionable objectives, including cordon-and-search operations, profiling random people for narcotics, and unlawful phone-searching activities. Cordon-and-search operations involve sealing off a neighborhood, conducting door-to-door searches, and taking fingerprint scans and photographs of citizens. Activists contend that authorities usually carry out these operations in communities where Muslims, Dalits (untouchables—the lowest caste), and other socioeconomically marginalized populations live.

In another type of police operation, police officers randomly stop and search commuters and pedestrians, take their photos, and collect their biometric data (see **Chapter 4**). Police use an app on their smartphones called TSCOP. The app contains facial recognition technology that can run the images through India's national Crime and Criminal Tracking Networks and Systems in real time.

Telangana authorities are integrating numerous facial-recognition datasets into a "smart governance program" called Samagram. This program provides the state government with a 360-degree digital profile of every resident's life, including their name, address, phone number, marital status, children, birth and death details, and employment status. The profile also includes data from police records, as well as utility service data, tax payments, passports, and voter identification.

Telangana authorities claim that, when given a resident's name, their software can provide access to his or her entire digital footprint in seconds. The software is also useful in *family tree forensics*; that is, the use of DNA and family tree data to learn the identity of criminals.

Privacy advocates are protesting police use of facial recognition in Telangana. Amnesty International has called Hyderabad a "total surveillance city." Activists argue that taking photographs of random civilians violates their right to privacy. Further, there are no safeguards for the public. Specifically, civilians are not notified as to how the photographs are used, how long they are stored, or where they are stored and by whom. Further, they have no official redress mechanism. Though the Supreme Court of India recognized privacy as a fundamental right in 2017, there is still no legal framework to govern the issues related to personal data protection and privacy.

The Hyderabad Police Department responds that using technology for police work has lowered the crime rate and has also helped trace missing children. They further maintain that they are now able to apprehend 99 percent of suspects within 24 hours.

As a final note, the police's practice of photographing people and taking scans of their fingerprint to build a criminal database violates Indian law. India's Identification of Prisoners Act of 1920 prohibits police from taking photographs of people unless they are arrested or convicted of a crime. The 1920 Act also prohibits sharing such photographs with other law enforcement agencies. The practice continues despite the 1920 law because authorities are not enforcing that law.

Questions

1. Discuss the ethicality and legality of the Telangana authorities' capture and use of personal data, including photos and biometric data.

2. Discuss the ethicality and legality of the Telangana authorities' use of facial recognition software.

3. The Telangana police maintain that the department's use of technology has reduced the crime rate, enabled the police to quickly apprehend suspects, and helped find missing children. Discuss the trade-off between these advantages and the loss of privacy for citizens.

Sources: Compiled from Q. Inzamam and H. Qadri, "This Part of India Is on the Verge of Becoming a Complete Surveillance State," *Slate.com*, July 13, 2022; A. Ghosh, "Facial Recognition Is Out of Control in India," *Motherboard*, June 13, 2022; "Hyderabad: Command and Control Centre to Be Inaugurated by July," *India Today*, May 11, 2022; R. Sabha, "The Criminal Procedure (Identification) Bill," *PRS Legislative Research*, April 2022; R. Chandran, "India's Surveillance Hotspot, Facial Recognition Taken to Court," *Reuters*, January 19, 2022; H. Suresh, "Why Hyderabad Became India's Surveillance Capital," *The News Minute*, December 7, 2021; "India: Hyderabad 'on the brink of becoming a total surveillance city'," *Amnesty International*, November 9, 2021; A. Bokil et al., "Settled Habits, New Tricks: Casteist Policing Meets Big Tech in India," *tni.org*, May, 2021; V. Bansal, "The Hyderabad Model of CCTV Surveillance," *Livemint News*, November 10, 2020; J. Umanadh, "Telangana Cops Can Now Recognize an Offender in Real-Time," *Deccan Herald*, July 25, 2019; "A Centralized Database of Citizens in the State of Telangana Is under Consideration," *FirstPost Tech2*, January 31, 2017; D. Mathew, "Hyderabad Citizens under 360 Degree Police Scanner," *Telangana Today*, January 28, 2017; and "Hyderabad Blasts: 16 Killed, 119 Injured," *The Indian Express*, February 24, 2013.

Introduction

You will encounter numerous ethical and privacy issues in your career, many of which will involve IT in some manner. Ethics and privacy are closely related to each other and also to IT, and both raise significant questions involving access to information in the digital age. The answers to these questions are not straightforward. In fact, IT has made finding answers to these questions even more difficult.

Consider facial recognition apps in the chapter opening case. Are these apps legal? Are they ethical? In a further example, suppose your organization decides to adopt social computing technologies (which you will study in **Chapter 9**) to include business partners and customers in new product development. You will be able to analyze the potential privacy and ethical implications of implementing these technologies.

This chapter provides insights into how to respond to ethical and privacy issues. Further, it will help you to make immediate contributions to your company's code of ethics and its privacy policies. You will also be able to provide meaningful input concerning the potential ethical and privacy impacts of your organization's information systems on people within and outside the organization.

All organizations, large and small, must be concerned with ethics. In particular, small business (or start-up) owners face a very difficult situation when their employees have access to sensitive customer information. There is a delicate balance between access to information and the appropriate use of that information. This balance is best maintained by hiring honest and trustworthy employees who abide by the organization's code of ethics. Ultimately, this issue leads to another question: Does the small business, or a start-up, even have a code of ethics to fall back on in this type of situation?

WILEY PLUS

Author Lecture Videos are available exclusively in *WileyPLUS*.
Apply the Concept activities are available in the Appendix and in *WileyPLUS*.

3.1 Ethical Issues

LEARNING OBJECTIVE

Describe ethics, its three fundamental tenets, and the four categories of ethical issues related to information technology.

ethics The principles of right and wrong that individuals use to make choices to guide their behaviors.

Ethics refers to the principles of right and wrong that individuals use to make choices that guide their behavior. Deciding what is right or wrong is not always easy or clear-cut. Fortunately, there are many frameworks that can help us make ethical decisions.

Ethical Frameworks

There are many sources for ethical standards. Here we consider five widely used standards: the utilitarian approach, the rights approach, the fairness approach, the common good approach, and the deontology approach. There are many other sources, but these five are representative.

The *utilitarian approach* states that an ethical action is the one that provides the most good or does the least harm. The ethical corporate action would be the one that produces the greatest good and does the least harm for all affected parties—customers, employees, shareholders, the community, and the physical environment.

The *rights approach* maintains that an ethical action is the one that best protects and respects the moral rights of the affected parties. Moral rights can include the rights to make one's own choices about what kind of life to lead, to be told the truth, not to be injured, and to enjoy a degree of privacy. Which of these rights people are actually entitled to—and under what circumstances—is widely debated. Nevertheless, most people acknowledge that individuals are entitled to some moral rights. An ethical organizational action would be one that protects and respects the moral rights of customers, employees, shareholders, business partners, and even competitors.

The *fairness approach* posits that ethical actions treat all human beings equally, or, if unequally, then fairly, based on some defensible standard. For example, most people might believe it is fair to pay people higher salaries if they work harder or if they contribute a greater amount to the firm. However, there is less certainty regarding CEO salaries that are hundreds or thousands of times larger than those of other employees. Many people question whether this huge disparity is based on a defensible standard or whether it is the result of an imbalance of power and hence is unfair.

The *common good approach* highlights the interlocking relationships that underlie all societies. This approach argues that respect and compassion for all others are the basis for ethical actions. It emphasizes the common conditions that are important to the welfare of everyone. These conditions can include a system of laws, effective police and fire departments, healthcare, a public educational system, and even public recreation areas.

Finally, the *deontology approach* states that the morality of an action is based on whether that action itself is right or wrong under a series of rules, rather than on the consequences of that action. An example of deontology is the belief that killing someone is wrong, even if it was in self-defense.

If we combine these five standards, then we can develop a general framework for ethics (or ethical decision making). This framework consists of five steps:

1. Recognize an ethical issue:

   Could this decision or situation damage someone or some group?

   Does this decision involve a choice between a good and a bad alternative?

   Does this issue involve more than simply legal considerations? If so, then in what way?

2. Get the facts:

   What are the relevant facts of the situation?

   Do I have sufficient information to make a decision?

   Which individuals or groups have an important stake in the outcome?

   Have I consulted all relevant persons and groups?

3. Evaluate alternative actions:

   Which option will produce the most good and do the least harm? (the utilitarian approach)

   Which option best respects the rights of all stakeholders? (the rights approach)

   Which option treats people equally or proportionately? (the fairness approach)

   Which option best serves the community as a whole, and not just some members? (the common good approach)

4. Make a decision and test it:

   Considering all the approaches, which option best addresses the situation?

5. Act and reflect on the outcome of your decision:

How can I implement my decision with the greatest care and attention to the concerns of all stakeholders?

How did my decision turn out, and what did I learn from this specific situation?

Now that we have created a general ethical framework, we will focus specifically on ethics in the corporate environment.

Ethics in the Corporate Environment

code of ethics A collection of principles intended to guide decision making by members of an organization.

Many companies and professional organizations develop their own codes of ethics. A **code of ethics** is a collection of principles intended to guide decision making by members of the organization. For example, the Association for Computing Machinery (**www.acm.org**), an organization of computing professionals, has a thoughtful code of ethics for its members (see **www.acm.org/code-of-ethics**).

Keep in mind that different codes of ethics are not always consistent with one another. Therefore, an individual might be expected to conform to multiple codes. For example, a person who is a member of two large professional computing-related organizations may be simultaneously required by one organization to comply with all applicable laws and by the other organization to refuse to obey unjust laws.

Fundamental tenets of ethics include:

responsibility A tenet of ethics in which you accept the consequences of your decisions and actions.

accountability A tenet of ethics that refers to determining who is responsible for actions that were taken.

liability A legal concept that gives individuals the right to recover the damages done to them by other individuals, organizations, or systems.

- **Responsibility** means that you accept the consequences of your decisions and actions.
- **Accountability** refers to determining who is responsible for actions that were taken.
- **Liability** is a legal concept that gives individuals the right to recover the damages done to them by other individuals, organizations, or systems.

Before you go any further, it is critical that you realize that what is *unethical* is not necessarily *illegal*. For example, a bank's decision to foreclose on a home can be technically legal, but it can raise many ethical questions. In many instances, then, an individual or organization faced with an ethical decision is not considering whether to break the law. As the foreclosure example illustrates, however, ethical decisions can have serious consequences for individuals, organizations, and society at large. This chapter's **closing case** addresses the legality and ethicality of the actions of the Norwegian Telenor Group in Myanmar.

ACCT We have witnessed a large number of extremely poor ethical decisions, not to mention outright criminal behavior, at many organizations. During 2001 and 2002, three highly publicized fiascos occurred at Enron, WorldCom, and Tyco. At each company, executives were convicted of various types of fraud for using illegal accounting practices. These actions led to the passage of the Sarbanes–Oxley Act in 2002. Sarbanes–Oxley requires publicly held companies to implement financial controls and company executives to personally certify financial reports.

Then, the subprime mortgage crisis of 2008 exposed unethical lending practices throughout the mortgage industry. The crisis also highlighted pervasive weaknesses in the regulation of the U.S. financial industry as well as the global financial system. It ultimately contributed to a deep recession in the global economy. Along these same lines, financier Bernie Madoff was convicted in 2009 of operating a Ponzi scheme and sentenced to 150 years in federal prison. Several of Madoff's employees were also convicted in 2014.

FIN Unfortunately, ethical misbehavior continued. Consider Wells Fargo bank (**www.wellsfargo.com**). In 2016, authorities found that bank employees had created approximately 2 million fake customer checking and credit card accounts without their knowledge. Bank employees had created the accounts under pressure from supervisors to meet daily account quotas. The bank then charged customers at least $1.5 million in fees for the fake accounts. Not only were the bank's victims charged overdraft and maintenance fees, but their credit scores were lowered for not staying current on accounts that they did not even know about.

Wells Fargo fired some 5,300 employees. The bank was also ordered to pay $185 million in fines, which is a very small amount compared to the $5.6 billion that the bank earned in the second quarter of 2016. Furthermore, in October 2016, Wells Fargo CEO John Stumpf stepped down from his position.

In June 2018, Wells Fargo was again accused of misconduct by the Securities and Exchange Commission (SEC, www.sec.gov). The SEC said that the bank collected large fees by "improperly encouraging" brokerage clients to actively trade high-fee debt products that were intended to be held to maturity. The bank agreed to pay a $4 million penalty and to return to clients $930,377 of fees it gained from the transactions plus $178,064 of interest.

MIS Avast (www.avast.com) is a computer-security company based in the Czech Republic. Some 400 million people around the world use the firm's software. In 2019, researchers found that the company used browser extensions (small software programs that customize the browsing experience) to watch everything their customers did online. Avast then sold that data to corporate customers as "insights." Clients included Google, Microsoft, PepsiCo, and McKinsey.

In October 2021, whistleblower Frances Haugen went public after sharing sensitive internal documents from Meta Platforms (www.meta.com) regarding its Facebook platform with regulators and journalists. The documents noted that Meta prioritized profits over people, used its algorithms to foster social discord, and enabled drug cartels and human traffickers to openly conduct business on its platform.

In addition to Meta's questionable ethical practices, Haugen's freedom to walk away with the documents shows that the company has poor internal controls. Haugen said that she had spent months accessing internal documents she had no professional reason to access.

Meta evidently had no effective system to issue alerts when someone without proper credentials accessed sensitive documents, which is a serious problem for a company that was fined $5 billion by the Federal Trade Commission in 2019 for privacy violations.

Meta hired its first-ever chief compliance officer in January 2022. It remains to be seen how much independence and authority is given to the CCO.

Advancements in information technologies have generated a new set of ethical problems. Computer processing power doubles roughly every 18 months, meaning that organizations are more dependent than ever on their information systems. Organizations can store increasing amounts of data at decreasing costs. As a result, they can maintain more data on individuals for longer periods of time. Going further, computer networks, particularly the Internet, enable organizations to collect, integrate, and distribute enormous amounts of information on individuals, groups, and institutions. These developments have created numerous ethical problems concerning the appropriate collection and use of customer information, personal privacy, and the protection of intellectual property. As IT's About Business 3.1 illustrates, geofencing warrants are being closely scrutinized for their serious legal and ethical implications.

IT's About Business **3.1**

MIS **MKT** **Controversy over Geofencing**

A *geofence* is a virtual perimeter for a real-world, physical geographic area. *Geofencing* is the use of GPS, Wi-Fi, cellular data, or sensor technology (e.g., RFID tags) to create a virtual geographic boundary, enabling software to trigger a response when a mobile device enters or leaves a particular area.

Businesses have employed geofencing as a form of location-based marketing for years. When potential customers enter a geofence, a store can send them a text message, an in-app notification, or a social media advertisement.

An excellent example of this strategy is Burger King's Whopper Detour marketing campaign. In this case, Burger King (www.bk.com) offered its burger for just 1 cent, but only to customers who downloaded the Burger King app and then ordered through it, *while physically visiting a McDonald's restaurant*. Prior to the campaign, Burger King had collected data on thousands of McDonald's restaurants and then created geofences around every one of them to trigger the in-app promotion. The campaign enabled Burger King to capture market share and gain free publicity at the same time.

Controversy arises when authorities use geofencing in *geofence warrants*. These warrants are an investigative technique that collects data from any user's device that was in a specified area within a certain time range. Police requests for geofence warrants drastically increased from fewer than 1,000 in 2018 to more than 11,000 in 2020. Significantly, Google is the only technology company that is publicly known to release this data to law enforcement specifically in response to geofence warrants. It is not clear if, and how many, other companies do the same.

Geofence warrants work differently from typical search warrants. With typical search warrants, authorities identify a suspect or person of interest and then obtain a warrant from a judge to search that person's home or belongings. With geofence warrants, police start with a time and location that a suspected crime took place and then request data from Google for the devices surrounding that location at that time, usually within a one- or two-hour window. If Google complies, it supplies a list of anonymized data about the devices in the area. This data consists of GPS coordinates, the time stamps of when the devices were in the area, and an anonymized identifier, known as a *reverse location obfuscation identifier (RLOI)*. Because this list can include many devices, police conduct their own investigation—for example, by examining video footage or interviewing witnesses—to reduce the number of potential suspects. Google then provides more specific information, such as an e-mail address or the name of the account holder, for the users on the reduced list.

Authorities can and do serve warrants on phone companies. However, cell phone towers can locate phones only to within roughly three-quarters of a mile. Google's location technologies, which can leverage GPS, Wi-Fi, and Bluetooth signals, provide much more accurate locations.

Privacy advocates maintain that geofence warrants are essentially fishing expeditions, and they are calling for the technique to be banned. Specifically, because geofence warrants have an inherently wide scope, they can give police access to location data from people who have no connection to criminal activities. Thus, geofence warrants put innocent people at risk of wrongful arrest. For example, in 2019, a single geofence warrant in connection with an arson in Milwaukee, Wisconsin, resulted in nearly 1,500 device identifiers being sent to the Bureau of Alcohol, Tobacco, Firearms, and Explosives.

Civil liberties groups further argue that geofence warrants violate Fourth Amendment protections against unreasonable searches. Several cases around the United States are currently challenging the constitutionality of these warrants.

Even more alarming to privacy advocates, authorities are using geofence warrants to gather information on people who attend protests. For example, NBC News reported in 2019 that the University of North Carolina used geofencing to monitor the location and social media activity of antiracism protesters on campus.

Court documents also suggest that the FBI used geofence warrants to collect location data and account information on hundreds of devices inside the U.S. Capitol during the January 6, 2021, riot. News outlets and publications have reported numerous federal criminal cases that cite Google geolocation data to place suspects inside the Capitol on that day, including at least six cases where the identity of the suspect appears to have been unknown to the FBI prior to the warrant.

Privacy activists propose that, at a minimum, law enforcement should minimize search areas, delete any data they access as soon as possible, and provide much more robust justifications for their use of geofencing, similar to the requirements when the police request permission for a wiretap. For example, authorities should answer questions such as, "Why is this size of area necessary? Why this time? Why not use a narrower geographical area and a tighter time frame?"

Law enforcement authorities contend that geofence warrants are legal because Google users agree to have their location tracked. Authorities further claim that they request only anonymized data until they find a device that draws their suspicion. They maintain that evidence provided by a geofence warrant is not enough to charge someone with a crime.

Questions

1. **Discuss the ethicality and legality of the use of geofence warrants.**

2. **The fundamental tenets of ethics include responsibility, accountability, and liability. Discuss each of these tenets with respect to the use of geofence warrants.**

Sources: Compiled from "Burger King Found a Way to Offer Whoppers at McDonald's," *CBC Radio*, June 16, 2022; C. Seltzer, "Google Knows Where You've Been. Should It Tell the Police?," *Slate*, May 16, 2022; D. Mirshahi, "Geofence Warrants—How Police Use Your Phone's Location Data and a Recent Virginia Court Ruling," *WRIC*, April 5, 2022; J. Bambauer, "Letting Police Access Google Location Data Can Help Solve Crimes," *The Washington Post*, March 28, 2022; J. Schuppe, "Cellphone Dragnet Used to Find Bank Robbery Suspect Was Unconstitutional, Judge Says," *NBC News*, March 7, 2022; M. Harris, "How a Secret Google Geofence Warrant Helped Catch the Capital Riot Mob," *Wired*, September 30, 2021; S. Fussell, "An Explosion in Geofence Warrants Threatens Privacy across the U.S.," *Wired*, August 27, 2021; L. Barghouty, "What Are Geofence Warrants?" *The Markup*, September 1, 2020; A. Kemmis, "What Is Geofencing? Everything You Need to Know about Location-Based Marketing," *SmartBug*, January 8, 2020; A. Sen, "UNC Campus Police Used Geofencing Tech to Monitor Antiracism Protestors," *NBC News*, December 21, 2019; R. Levinson-Waldman, "Cellphones, Law Enforcement, and the Right to Privacy," Brennan Center For Justice at New York University School of Law, August, 2019; J. Valentino-DeVries, "Tracking Phones, Google Is a Dragnet for the Police," *The New York Times*, April 13, 2019; and A. Robertson, "Gap 'Geofencing' Campaign Puts Super-Localized Ads on Your Phone," *The Verge*, March 13, 2012.

Ethics and Information Technology

All employees have a responsibility to encourage ethical uses of information and information technology. Many of the business decisions you will face at work will have an ethical dimension. Consider the following decisions that you might have to make:

- **HRM** Should organizations monitor employees' Web surfing and email?
- **MKT** Should organizations sell customer information to other companies?
- **HRM** Should organizations audit employees' computers for unauthorized software or illegally downloaded music or video files?

The diversity and ever-expanding use of IT applications have created a variety of ethical issues. These issues fall into four general categories: privacy, accuracy, property, and accessibility.

1. *Privacy issues* involve collecting, storing, and disseminating information about individuals.
2. *Accuracy issues* involve the authenticity, fidelity, and correctness of information that is collected and processed.
3. *Property issues* involve the ownership and value of information.
4. *Accessibility issues* revolve around who should have access to information and whether they should pay a fee for this access.

Table 3.1 lists representative questions and issues for each of these categories. Online Ethics Cases also presents 14 scenarios that raise ethical issues. These scenarios will provide a context for you to consider situations that involve ethical or unethical behavior.

Many of the issues and scenarios discussed in this chapter involve privacy as well as ethics. In the next section, you will learn about privacy issues in more detail.

TABLE 3.1   A Framework for Ethical Issues

Privacy Issues

What information about oneself should an individual be required to reveal to others?

What kinds of surveillance can an employer use on its employees?

What types of personal information can people keep to themselves and not be forced to reveal to others?

What information about individuals should be kept in databases, and how secure is the information there?

Accuracy Issues

Who is responsible for the authenticity, fidelity, and accuracy of the information collected?

How can we ensure that the information will be processed properly and presented accurately to users?

How can we ensure that errors in databases, data transmissions, and data processing are accidental and not intentional?

Who is to be held accountable for errors in information, and how should the injured parties be compensated?

Property Issues

Who owns the information?

What are just and fair prices for its exchange?

How should we handle software piracy (illegally copying copyrighted software)?

Under what circumstances can one use proprietary databases?

Can corporate computers be used for private purposes?

How should experts who contribute their knowledge to create expert systems be compensated?

How should access to information channels be allocated?

Accessibility Issues

Who is allowed to access information?

How much should companies charge for permitting access to information?

How can access to computers be provided for employees with disabilities?

Who will be provided with the equipment needed for accessing information?

What information does a person or an organization have a right to obtain, under what conditions, and with what safeguards?

1. What does a code of ethics contain?
2. Identify and discuss the fundamental tenets of ethics.

privacy   The right to be left alone and to be free of unreasonable personal intrusions.

information privacy The right to determine when, and to what extent, personal information can be gathered by or communicated to others.

3.2 Privacy

LEARNING OBJECTIVE

Discuss at least one potential threat to the privacy of the data stored in each of three places that store personal data.

In general, **privacy** is the right to be left alone and to be free of unreasonable personal intrusions. **Information privacy** is the right to determine when, and to what extent, information about you can be gathered or communicated to others. Privacy rights apply to individuals, groups, and institutions. The right to privacy is recognized today in all the U.S. states and by the federal government, either by statute or in common law.

Privacy can be interpreted quite broadly. However, court decisions in many countries have followed two rules fairly closely:

1. The right of privacy is not absolute. Privacy must be balanced against the needs of society.
2. The public's right to know supersedes the individual's right of privacy.

These two rules illustrate why determining and enforcing privacy regulations can be difficult.

As we discussed earlier, rapid advances in information technologies have made it much easier to collect, store, and integrate vast amounts of data on individuals in large databases. On an average day, data about you are generated in many ways: surveillance cameras located on toll roads, on other roadways, in busy intersections, in public places, and at work; credit card transactions; telephone calls (landline and cellular); banking transactions; queries to search engines; and government records (including police records). These data can be integrated to produce a **digital dossier**, which is an electronic profile of you and your habits. The process of forming a digital dossier is called **profiling**. (See **IT's About Business 3.1** for an excellent example of profiling.)

Data aggregators, such as LexisNexis (**www.lexisnexis.com**) and Acxiom (**www.acxiom.com**), are prominent examples of profilers. These companies collect public data such as real estate records and published telephone numbers, in addition to nonpublic information such as Social Security numbers; financial data; and police, criminal, and motor vehicle records. They then integrate these data to form digital dossiers on most adults in the United States. They ultimately sell these dossiers to law enforcement agencies and companies that conduct background checks on potential employees. They also sell them to companies that want to know their customers better, a process called *customer intimacy.*

The problem with data aggregators, social media sites, marketing firms, and others is the methods they use to gather data on all of us. **IT's About Business 3.2** discusses some of these methods and then looks at how DuckDuckGo (**www.duckduckgo.com**) helps users avoid the most intrusive methods.

digital dossier   An electronic description of an individual and his or her habits.

profiling   The process of forming a digital dossier.

Electronic Surveillance

electronic surveillance Tracking people's activities with the aid of computers.

According to the American Civil Liberties Union (ACLU), tracking people's activities with the aid of information technology has become a major privacy-related problem. The ACLU notes that this monitoring, or **electronic surveillance**, is rapidly increasing, particularly with the

IT's About Business 3.2

MIS **MKT** **Data-Tracking Methods on the Web and DuckDuckGo**

Today, there are many ways that you are tracked as you navigate the Web. We first examine some of the most common data-tracking methods. We then take a look at how DuckDuckGo helps limit such tracking and the loss of privacy from it.

Data-Tracking Methods

Cookies are small amounts of text and computer code stored on your computer or phone that are sent to your browser from websites you visit. These files track and monitor your login information, the sites you visit, the items you click on these pages, and your location. Advertisers and data brokers use cookies to create a digital profile of each user in order to target advertisements to that user. There are several types of cookies.

First-party cookies, also known as persistent cookies, are stored directly on the website you visit. They help sites to remember your information and settings when you revisit those sites. First-party cookies cannot be used to track user activities on other websites; they track activities only on the original site where the cookie was placed.

Third-party cookies are placed on a website by some entity other than the owner of the website, and they collect user data for the third party. Marketing companies, social media websites, and data brokers use third-party cookies to track users between websites and display more relevant ads.

Web beacons, also known as Web bugs or tracking beacons, are very small, often transparent graphic images that are placed on websites or in e-mails to monitor the behavior of the user visiting the website or sending the e-mail. A third party typically uses them to monitor the activity on a website.

IP addresses uniquely identify all Internet-connected devices. When you visit a website, it might record and remember your IP address and use it to track your activity. IP addresses provide the city, zip code, or area code of your ISP, as well as your ISP's name.

Session replay scripts are programs that record a visitor's activity on a website, including their mouse movement, clicks, and scrolls. Significantly, session replay scripts can record how long visitors hover over a clickable link, even if they do not click on it.

Favicons are small, 16 × 16 pixel icons that serve as branding for your website. Favicons are found next to anything that identifies your website, such as bookmarks, tabs, toolbar apps, history results, and search bars. Their main purpose is to help visitors locate your page easier when they have multiple tabs open. The problem with favicons is that they can be used to track users because the favicon can store a unique identifier for a user that is readable in a browser's incognito mode. Further, users cannot remove the identifier by closing the browser, restarting the system, using a VPN, or installing AdBlockers.

Browser fingerprinting integrates information about your device—including its operating system, language preferences, and time zone—to create a unique identifier that is used to trace your online activity.

DuckDuckGo

Founded in 2008, DuckDuckGo (www.duckduckgo.com) began as an Internet search engine that emphasizes protecting searchers' privacy and avoiding personalized, precisely targeted search results. Simply put, DuckDuckGo guarantees its users that it does not track them at all.

According to DuckDuckGo's marketing research, the vast majority of people using the Web want more privacy. Illustrating how concerned users are regarding their lack of privacy, consider Apple's new App Tracking Transparency system. This system prompts iOS users to opt in to being tracked by third-party apps rather than handing over their data by default. Significantly, only 13 percent of users are choosing to allow tracking.

Like Google Search, DuckDuckGo makes money by selling ads based on people's search results. The difference is that the ads you see when you are searching on Google are generally targeted to you based on your past and present searches plus what Google knows about your behavior, a process called *behavioral targeting or advertising*. DuckDuckGo's ads are based only on your current search term, because DuckDuckGo does not know anything about you. It does not assign you an identifier or keep track of your search history in order to personalize your results. Therefore, DuckDuckGo employs *contextual targeting or advertising*.

DuckDuckGo's tracker prevention works differently from most other tracker-prevention products. The problem is that even allowing a tracker to load in the first place can enable it to gather highly specific data about a user, including their IP address. However, surveillance is so integral to the infrastructure of most websites that they will stop functioning if you block all cookies. For this reason, DuckDuckGo prevents the cookie from loading at all. To avoid the broken-site problem, DuckDuckGo replaces some trackers with a dummy that tricks the website into thinking that its cookie has loaded.

DuckDuckGo has enhanced its original search engine with free privacy-centric tools, including a browser extension, its Email Protection feature, a tool within its Android app that blocks third parties from tracking you through any other app on your phone, and DuckDuckGo's privacy browser.

Browser extension. In 2019, DuckDuckGo added a feature to its browser extension that directs users to encrypted versions of websites whenever possible, preventing hackers and Internet Service Providers from tracking you.

Email Protection feature. DuckDuckGo researchers found that roughly 70 percent of e-mails have some sort of tracker embedded in them. In more than 30 percent of those cases, the trackers are sending users' plaintext e-mail addresses over the Internet, potentially exposing them to any number of marketers, data brokers, and hackers.

In 2021, DuckDuckGo launched its Email Protection feature. This feature gives users a free "@duck.com" e-mail address. The tool stops tracking by forwarding messages through a DuckDuckGo e-mail address, which analyzes their contents for trackers and removes them before sending them to in-boxes. The company is also extending this feature by providing unique, disposable forwarding e-mail addresses, which can be easily generated in DuckDuckGo's mobile browser or its desktop browser extension.

The personal DuckDuckGo e-mail is meant to be given out to friends and contacts you know, while the disposable e-mail addresses should be used when signing up for free trials, newsletters, or any source you suspect might sell your address. If the disposable e-mail address is compromised, you can easily deactivate it and obtain another one.

Third-party blocking feature in Android mobile app. DuckDuckGo's new feature operates in the background, even when the app itself is not in use, to block third parties from tracking you through any other app on your phone. It uses the phone's VPN permission to route all traffic through DuckDuckGo so that it can block requests from anyone on its tracker list before they have an opportunity to gather any user data. This feature will not stop first-party data collection, meaning that the app you are using can still collect your data. However, that app will not be able to pass that data to other companies, including Facebook, which currently tracks users through a vast number of unrelated apps.

Privacy browser. In April 2022, DuckDuckGo launched its privacy browser, which uses DuckDuckGo's private search engine as the default option, blocks ad trackers on each site you visit, and shows how many trackers have been blocked. The browser includes a built-in option for saving passwords and incorporates the company's Email Protection feature.

The new browser also addresses cookie consent pop-ups. The first time you use the browser, you will be asked if you want to allow it to manage the pop-ups that appear. If you give it permission to do so, it will automatically set the cookie preferences on each site you visit and pick the option to "maximize privacy." In practice, you will not see cookie pop-ups.

Questions

1. **Discuss the ethicality and legality of the use of each tracking method.**

2. **The fundamental tenets of ethics include responsibility, accountability, and liability. Discuss each of these tenets with respect to the use of each tracking method.**

3. **Advertising companies defend tracking users on websites and across the Web because they enable advertisers to produce highly targeted ads. These companies maintain that targeted ads feel less "in your face" than traditional ads and are more personalized based on each** user's specific interests. The problem with this type of marketing is that users surrender their privacy. Are you willing to give up some of your privacy to be tracked and then shown personalized ads? Why or why not?

Sources: Compiled from Z. McAuliffe, "Forget Google Search: Here's Why You Should Switch to DuckDuckGo," *CNET*, July 31, 2022; C. Rao, "Data Privacy Concerns Trigger Restrictions on Google Chrome in Dutch Schools," *Android Police*, July 24, 2022; M. Burgess, "DuckDuckGo's Privacy Browser Finally Lands on Desktop," *Wired*, April 12, 2022; M. Burgess, "The Quiet Way Advertisers Are Tracking Your Browsing," *Wired*, February 26, 2022; C. Pilette, "Internet Tracking: How and Why We're Followed Online," *NortonLifeLock*, August 23, 2021; D. Gershgorn, "DuckDuckGo Launches New Email Protection Service to Remove Trackers," *The Verge*, July 20, 2021; G. Edelman, "DuckDuckGo's Quest to Prove Online Privacy Is Possible," *Wired*, June 16, 2021; C. Thompson, "Tech Companies Don't Need to Be Creepy to Make Money," *Wired*, May 14, 2021; David Nield, "What's Google FLoC? And How Does It Affect Your Privacy?" *Wired*, May 9, 2021; A. Barbaschow, "User 'Opt-In' Rate for Tracking across iOS Sitting at 13% Globally" *ZDNet*, May 9, 2021; "EFF Partners with DuckDuckGo to Enhance Secure Browsing and Protect User Information on the Web," *Electronic Frontier Foundation*, April 15, 2021; "1 in 5 Consumers Has Avoided Buying a Brand over Its Data Practices: Survey Finds Widespread Skepticism over How Companies Collect and Use Personal Data," *The Conference Board*, November 17, 2020; N. Perrin, "Search Marketing 2020," *eMarketer*, November 2, 2020; A. Sankin, "I Scanned the Websites I Visit with Blacklight, and It's Horrifying. Now What?," *The Markup*, September 22, 2020; David Nield, "All the Ways Facebook Tracks You—and How to Limit It," *Wired*, January 12, 2020; L. Newman, "DuckDuckGo Will Automatically Encrypt More Sites You Visit," *Wired*, November 19, 2019; David Nield, "All the Ways Google Tracks You—and How to Stop It," *Wired*, May 27, 2019; R. Nakashima, "Google Tracks Your Movements, Like It or Not," *AP News*, August 13, 2018; D. Goodin, "New Sites Can Fingerprint You Online Even When You Use Multiple Browsers," *Ars Technica*, February 13, 2017; and www.duckduckgo.com, accessed August 5, 2022.

emergence of new technologies. Electronic surveillance is conducted by employers, the government, and other institutions.

Americans today live with a degree of surveillance that would have been unimaginable just a few years ago. For example, surveillance cameras track you at airports, subways, banks, and other public venues. (See this chapter's opening case.) Inexpensive digital sensors are also now everywhere. They are incorporated into laptop webcams, video-game motion sensors, smartphone cameras, utility meters, passports, and employee ID cards. Step out your front door and you could be captured in a high-resolution photograph taken from the air or from the street by Google or Microsoft as they update their mapping services. Drive down a city street, cross a toll bridge, or park at a shopping mall, and your license plate can be recorded and time-stamped.

Technologies such as low-cost digital cameras, motion sensors, and biometric readers are helping to increase the monitoring of human activity. The costs of storing and using digital data are also rapidly decreasing. The result is an explosion of sensor data collection and storage.

A special problem arises with smartphones that are equipped with global positioning system (GPS) sensors. These sensors routinely *geotag* photos and videos, embedding images with the longitude and latitude of the location shown in the image. Thus, you could be inadvertently supplying criminals with useful intelligence by posting personal images on social networks or photo-sharing websites. These actions would show the criminals exactly where you live and when you are there. You could be providing government agencies with useful information as well.

MIS Another example of how new devices can contribute to electronic surveillance is facial recognition technology. Just a few years ago, this software worked only in very controlled settings such as passport checkpoints. However, this technology can now match faces even in regular snapshots and online images. This chapter's opening case provides an example of how advances in facial recognition technologies can negatively impact privacy.

Photo tagging is the process of assigning names to images of people. Facial recognition software then indexes facial features. Once an individual in a photo is tagged, the software searches for similar facial features in untagged photos. This process allows the user to quickly group photos in which the tagged person appears. Significantly, the individual is not aware of this process.

Why is tagging important? The reason is that once you are tagged in a photo, that photo can be used to search for matches across the entire Internet or in private databases, including databases fed by surveillance cameras. How could this type of surveillance affect you? As one example, a car dealer can take a picture of you when you step onto the car lot. He or she could then quickly profile you (find out information about where you live, your employment, etc.) on the Web to achieve a competitive edge in making a sale. Even worse, a stranger in a restaurant could photograph you with a smartphone and then go online to profile you for reasons of his or her own. One privacy attorney has asserted that losing your right to anonymity would have a chilling effect on where you go, whom you meet, and how you live your life.

Drones are presenting additional surveillance concerns. Low-cost drones with high-performance cameras can be used for persistent aerial surveillance. Since the beginning of modern aviation, landowners have had rights to the airspace above their property up to 500 feet. However, to regulate small, low-flying drones, the Federal Aviation Administration (FAA; www.faa.gov) has assumed authority all the way down to the ground.

Consider this example. You see a drone flying about 100 feet above your backyard and you suspect that it is spying on you. Who is flying it? Whom are you going to sue? And if you do sue, how are you going to prove that the drone was spying on you?

The FAA is responsible for addressing drone-related privacy concerns. The Federal Trade Commission (FTC; www.ftc.gov), the U.S. government's primary consumer privacy agency, is also exploring the drone privacy issue.

HRM The scenarios we just considered deal primarily with your personal life. However, electronic surveillance has become a reality in the workplace as well. In general, employees have very limited legal protection against surveillance by employers. The law supports the right of employers to read their employees' e-mail and other electronic documents and to monitor their employees' Internet use. Today, more than three-fourths of organizations routinely monitor their employees' Internet usage. Two-thirds of them also use software to block connections to inappropriate websites, a practice called *URL filtering*. Furthermore, organizations are installing monitoring and filtering software to enhance security by blocking malicious software and to increase productivity by discouraging employees from wasting time.

MIS In one organization, the chief information officer (CIO) monitored roughly 13,000 employees for three months to determine the type of traffic they engaged in on the network. He then forwarded the data to the chief executive officer (CEO) and the heads of the human resources and legal departments. These executives were shocked at the questionable websites the employees were visiting, as well as the amount of time they were spending on those sites. The executives quickly decided to implement a URL filtering product.

In general, surveillance is a concern for private individuals regardless of whether it is conducted by corporations, government bodies, or criminals. As a nation, the United States is still struggling to define the appropriate balance between personal privacy and electronic surveillance, especially in situations that involve threats to national security.

Personal Information in Databases

Modern institutions store information about individuals in many databases. Perhaps the most visible locations of such records are credit-reporting agencies. Other institutions that store personal information include banks and financial institutions; cable TV, telephone, and utility companies; employers; mortgage companies; hospitals; schools and universities; retail establishments; government agencies (Internal Revenue Service, your state, your municipality); and many others.

There are several concerns about the information you provide to these record keepers. Some of the major concerns are as follows:

- Do you know where the records are?
- Are the records accurate?
- Can you change inaccurate data?
- How long will it take to make a change?
- Under what circumstances will the personal data be released?
- How are the data used?
- To whom are the data given or sold?
- How secure are the data against access by unauthorized people?

Information on Internet Bulletin Boards, Newsgroups, and Social Networking Sites

Every day we see more and more *electronic bulletin boards*, *newsgroups*, and *electronic discussions* such as chat rooms and *social networking sites* (discussed in **Chapter 9**). These sites appear on the Internet, within corporate intranets, and on blogs. A *blog*, short for "weblog," is an informal, personal journal that is frequently updated and is intended for general public reading. How does society keep owners of bulletin boards from disseminating information that may be offensive to readers or simply untrue? This is a difficult problem because it involves the conflict between freedom of speech on the one hand and privacy on the other. This conflict is a fundamental and continuing ethical issue in the United States and throughout the world.

There is no better illustration of the conflict between free speech and privacy than the Internet. Many websites contain anonymous, derogatory information on individuals, who typically have little recourse in the matter. The vast majority of U.S. firms use the Internet in examining job applications, including searching on Google and on social networking sites. Consequently, derogatory information contained on the Internet can harm a person's chances of being hired.

Privacy Codes and Policies

privacy policies (or privacy codes) An organization's guidelines for protecting the privacy of customers, clients, and employees.

privacy codes See **privacy policies.**

opt-out model A model of informed consent that permits a company to collect personal information until the customer specifically requests that the data not be collected.

opt-in model A model of informed consent in which a business is prohibited from collecting any personal information unless the customer specifically authorizes it.

Privacy policies (or **privacy codes**) are an organization's guidelines for protecting the privacy of its customers, clients, and employees. In many corporations, senior management has begun to understand that when they collect vast amounts of personal information, they must protect it. Many organizations also give their customers some voice in how their information is used by providing them with opt-out choices. The **opt-out model** of informed consent permits the company to collect personal information until the customer specifically requests that the data not be collected. Privacy advocates prefer the **opt-in model** of informed consent, which prohibits an organization from collecting any personal information unless the customer specifically authorizes it.

One privacy tool available to consumers is the *Platform for Privacy Preferences* (P3P), a protocol that automatically communicates privacy policies between an electronic commerce website and visitors to that site. P3P enables visitors to determine the types of personal data that can be extracted by the sites they visit. It also allows visitors to compare a site's privacy policy to the visitors' preferences or to other standards, such as the Federal Trade Commission's (FTC) Fair Information Practices Standard or the European Directive on Data Protection.

Table 3.2 provides a sampling of privacy policy guidelines. The last section, "Data Confidentiality," refers to security, which we consider in **Chapter 4**. All of the good privacy intentions in the world are useless unless they are supported and enforced by effective security measures.

Despite privacy codes and policies, and despite opt-out and opt-in models, guarding whatever is left of your privacy is becoming increasingly difficult. This problem is illustrated in **IT's About Business 3.1** and **3.2**, as well as this chapter's **opening** and **closing cases.**

TABLE 3.2   Privacy Policy Guidelines: A Sampler

Data Collection

- Data should be collected on individuals only for the purpose of accomplishing a legitimate business objective.
- Data should be adequate, relevant, and not excessive in relation to the business objective.
- Individuals must give their consent before data pertaining to them can be gathered. Such consent may be implied from the individual's actions (e.g., applications for credit, insurance, or employment).

Data Accuracy

- Sensitive data gathered on individuals should be verified before they are entered into the database.
- Data should be kept current, where and when necessary.
- The file should be made available so that the individual can ensure that the data are correct.
- In any disagreement about the accuracy of the data, the individual's version should be noted and included with any disclosure of the file.

Data Confidentiality

- Computer security procedures should be implemented to ensure against unauthorized disclosure of data. These procedures should include physical, technical, and administrative security measures.
- Third parties should not be given access to data without the individual's knowledge or permission, except as required by law.
- Disclosures of data, other than the most routine, should be noted and maintained for as long as the data are maintained.
- Data should not be disclosed for reasons incompatible with the business objective for which they are collected.

International Aspects of Privacy

As the number of online users has increased globally, governments throughout the world have enacted a large number of inconsistent privacy and security laws. This highly complex global legal framework is creating regulatory problems for companies. Approximately 50 countries have some form of data protection laws. Many of these laws conflict with those of other countries, or they require specific security measures. Other countries have no privacy laws at all.

The absence of consistent or uniform standards for privacy and security obstructs the flow of information among countries (*transborder data flows*). The European Union (EU), for one, has taken steps to not only overcome this problem but also to protect the rights of individuals. The EU data protection laws are stricter than the U.S. laws and therefore could create problems for the U.S.-based multinational corporations, which could face lawsuits for privacy violations.

On May 25, 2018, the *General Data Protection Regulation* (GDPR), the world's strongest data protection laws, went into effect in the European Union. The GDPR modernizes laws that protect the personal information of individuals because previous data protection laws across Europe could not keep pace with rapid technological changes. The GDPR changes how businesses and public sector organizations manage the information of their customers. The regulation also increases the rights of individuals and gives them more control over their own information.

The GDPR covers both personal data and sensitive personal data. *Personal data* includes information that can be used to identify a person, such as a name, address, Internet Protocol (IP) address, and many other pieces of information. *Sensitive personal data* encompasses genetic data, racial information, information about religious and political views, sexual orientation, and trade union membership, among others.

The GDPR applies to *data controllers*, which are the organizations that have relationships with data subjects, and *data processors*, which are organizations that work for data controllers and process personal data on the controllers' behalf. The GDPR defines a *natural person* as a living human being and a *data subject* as a human being whose data an organization has or processes.

The GDPR states that data controllers and data processors should keep minimal data on each data subject, secure it properly, ensure that it is accurate, and retain the data for only as long as it is needed. The GDPR also covers individuals' rights, which include:

- The right to know what organizations are doing with their data
- The right to ask, at any time, for copies of all the data that organizations have about them
- The right to know an organization's justification why it has their data and how long it is planning to keep it
- The right to have their data corrected, if needed
- The right to have their data deleted. This provision is called the "right to be forgotten"

The GDPR provides the ability for regulators to fine businesses that do not comply with the regulation. Specifically, regulators can fine an organization:

- If it does not correctly process an individual's data
- If it experiences a security breach
- If it is required to have, but does not have, a data protection officer

The transfer of data into and out of a nation without the knowledge of either the authorities or the individuals involved raises a number of privacy issues. Whose laws have jurisdiction when records are stored in a different country for reprocessing or retransmission purposes? For example, if data are transmitted by a Polish company through a U.S. satellite to a British corporation, which country's privacy laws control the data, and at what points in the transmission? Questions like these will become more complicated and frequent as time goes on. Governments must make an effort to develop laws and standards to cope with rapidly changing information technologies to solve some of these privacy issues.

The United States and the European Union share the goal of protecting their citizens' privacy, but the United States takes a different approach. To bridge the different privacy approaches, the U.S. Department of Commerce, in consultation with the European Union, developed a "safe harbor" framework to regulate the way that the U.S. companies export and handle the personal data (e.g., names and addresses) of European citizens. In 2016, the European Commission and the U.S. Department of Commerce established the EU-US Privacy Shield, a new legal framework for transatlantic data flows, put in place to replace Safe Harbor.

Before you go on...

1. Describe the issue of privacy as it is affected by IT.
2. Discuss how privacy issues can impact transborder data flows.

What's in IT for Me?

ACCT **For the Accounting Major**

Public companies, their accountants, and their auditors have significant ethical responsibilities. Accountants now are being held professionally and personally responsible for increasing the transparency of transactions and assuring compliance with Generally Accepted Accounting Principles (GAAP). In fact, regulatory agencies such as the Securities and Exchange Commission (SEC) and the Public

Company Accounting Oversight Board (PCAOB) require accounting departments to adhere to strict ethical principles.

FIN **For the Finance Major**

As a result of global regulatory requirements and the passage of Sarbanes–Oxley, financial managers must follow strict ethical guidelines. They are responsible for full, fair, accurate, timely, and understandable disclosure in all financial reports and documents that their companies submit to the SEC and in all other public financial reports. Furthermore, financial managers are responsible for compliance with all applicable governmental laws, rules, and regulations.

MKT For the Marketing Major

Marketing professionals have new opportunities to collect data on their customers; for example, through business-to-consumer electronic commerce (discussed in **Chapter 7**). Business ethics clearly mandate that these data should be used only within the company and should not be sold to anyone else. Marketers do not want to be sued for invasion of privacy over data collected for their marketing database.

Customers expect their data to be properly secured. However, profit-motivated criminals want that data. Therefore, marketing managers must analyze the risks of their operations. Failure to protect corporate and customer data will cause significant public relations problems and outrage customers. Customer relationship management (discussed in **Chapter 11**) operations and tracking customers' online buying habits can expose unencrypted data to misuse or result in privacy violations.

POM For the Production/Operations Management Major

POM professionals decide whether to outsource (or offshore) manufacturing operations. In some cases, these operations are sent overseas to countries that do not have strict labor laws. This situation raises serious ethical questions. For example: Is it ethical to hire employees in countries with poor working conditions in order to reduce labor costs?

HRM For the Human Resource Management Major

Ethics is critically important to HR managers. HR policies define the appropriate use of information technologies in the workplace. Questions such as the following can arise: Can employees use the Internet, e-mail, or chat systems for personal purposes while at work? Is it ethical to monitor employees? If so, then how, how much, and how often? HR managers must formulate and enforce such policies while at the same time maintaining trusting relationships between employees and management.

MIS For the MIS Major

Ethics might be more important for MIS personnel than for anyone else in the organization, because these individuals have control of the organization's information assets. They also have control over a huge amount of employees' personal information. As a result, the MIS function must be held to the highest ethical standards.

Summary

3.1 Describe ethics, its three fundamental tenets, and the four categories of ethical issues related to information technology.

Ethics refers to the principles of right and wrong that individuals use to make choices that guide their behavior.

Fundamental tenets of ethics include responsibility, accountability, and liability. Responsibility means that you accept the consequences of your decisions and actions. Accountability refers to determining who is responsible for actions that were taken. Liability is a legal concept that gives individuals the right to recover the damages done to them by other individuals, organizations, or systems.

The major ethical issues related to IT are privacy, accuracy, property (including intellectual property), and access to information.

Privacy may be violated when data are held in databases or transmitted over networks. Privacy policies that address issues of data collection, data accuracy, and data confidentiality can help organizations avoid legal problems.

3.2 Discuss at least one potential threat to the privacy of the data stored in each of three places that store personal data.

Privacy is the right to be left alone and to be free of unreasonable personal intrusions. Threats to privacy include advances in information technologies, electronic surveillance, personal information in databases, Internet bulletin boards, newsgroups, and social networking sites. The privacy threat in Internet bulletin boards, newsgroups, and social networking sites is that you might post too much personal information that many unknown people can see.

Key Terms

accountability   68
code of ethics   68
digital dossier   72
electronic surveillance   72
ethics   66

information privacy   72
liability   68
opt-in model   76
opt-out model   76
privacy   72

privacy codes   76
privacy policies (or privacy codes)   76
profiling   72
responsibility   68

Discussion Questions

1. In 2008, the Massachusetts Bay Transportation Authority (MBTA) obtained a temporary restraining order barring three Massachusetts Institute of Technology (MIT) students from publicly displaying what they claimed to be a way to get "free subway rides for life." Specifically, the 10-day injunction prohibited the students from revealing vulnerabilities of the MBTA's fare card. The students were scheduled to present their findings in Las Vegas at the DEFCON computer hacking conference. Were the students' actions legal? Were their actions ethical? Discuss your answer from the students' perspective and then from the perspective of the MBTA.

2. Frank Abagnale, the criminal played by Leonardo DiCaprio in the motion picture *Catch Me If You Can*, ended up in prison. After he left prison, however, he worked as a consultant to many companies on matters of fraud.

   a. Why do these companies hire the perpetrators (if caught) as consultants? Is this a good idea?

   b. You are the CEO of a company. Discuss the ethical implications of hiring Frank Abagnale as a consultant.

3. Access various search engines to find information relating to the use of drones (unmanned aerial vehicles [UAVs]) for electronic surveillance purposes in the United States.

   a. Take the position favoring the use of drones for electronic surveillance.

   b. Take the position against the use of drones for electronic surveillance.

4. Research the Volkswagen "Diesel Dupe." The fundamental tenets of ethics include responsibility, accountability, and liability. Discuss each of these tenets as it applies to the Volkswagen scandal.

5. Research the Facebook–Cambridge Analytica scandal.

   a. Discuss the legality and the ethicality of Facebook in the Facebook–Cambridge Analytica incident.

   b. Discuss the legality and the ethicality of Cambridge Analytica in the Facebook–Cambridge Analytica incident.

   c. Describe how each of the fundamental tenets of ethics (responsibility, accountability, and liability) applies to Facebook and then to Cambridge Analytica in this incident.

6. Research Quizlet (**www.quizlet.com**).

   a. Discuss the ethicality of students' use of Quizlet (and similar apps) for exams.

   b. If students discover that the actual exam questions were on Quizlet, discuss the ethicality of them not telling the professor.

7. Do you feel that Americans have adequate privacy protections for their data? Why or why not? Does your answer change for Europeans?

Problem-Solving Activities

1. An information security manager routinely monitored Web surfing among her company's employees. She discovered that many employees were visiting the "sinful six" websites. (*Note*: The "sinful six" are websites with material related to pornography, gambling, hate, illegal activities, tastelessness, and violence.) She then prepared a list of the employees and their surfing histories and gave the list to management. Some managers punished their employees. Some employees, in turn, objected to the monitoring, claiming that they should have a right to privacy.

   a. Is monitoring of Web surfing by managers ethical? (It is legal.) Support your answer.

   b. Is employee Web surfing on the "sinful six" ethical? Support your answer.

   c. Is the security manager's submission of the list of abusers to management ethical? Why or why not?

   d. Is punishing the abusers ethical? Why or why not? If yes, then what types of punishment are acceptable?

   e. What should the company do in this situation? (*Note*: There are a variety of possibilities here.)

2. Access the Computer Ethics Institute's website at **www.cpsr.org/issues/ethics/cei**. The site offers the "Ten Commandments of Computer Ethics." Study these rules and decide whether any others should be added.

3. Access the Association for Computing Machinery's code of ethics for its members (**www.acm.org/code-of-ethics**). Discuss the major points of this code. Is this code complete? Why or why not? Support your answer.

4. The Electronic Frontier Foundation (**www.eff.org**) has a mission of protecting rights and promoting freedom in the "electronic frontier." Review the organization's suggestions about how to protect your online privacy, and summarize what you can do to protect yourself.

5. Access your university's guidelines for ethical computer and Internet use. Are there limitations as to the types of websites that you can visit and the types of material you can view? Are you allowed to change the programs on the lab computers? Are you allowed to download software from the lab computers for your personal use? Are there rules governing the personal use of computers and e-mail?

6. Access **www.albion.com/netiquette/corerules.html**. What do you think of this code of ethics? Should it be expanded? Is it too general?

7. Access **www.cookiecentral.com** Does this site provide information that helps you protect your privacy? If so, explain how.

8. Do you believe that a university should be allowed to monitor e-mail sent and received on university computers? Why or why not? Support your answer.

9. Go to www.google.com and research their privacy policy, Do you feel that it goes far enough? What changes in 2023 will help further protect your privacy?

10. Visit **www.xnspy.com** and look at all the different monitoring activities the software performs. All these activities are legal, but are they ethical? Using the ethical frameworks discussed in this chapter, explain your answer.

Closing Case

MIS **MKT** **FIN**   The Norwegian Telenor Group's Actions in Myanmar

Internet service in Myanmar (formerly Burma) has been available since 2000, but the military regime in control of the country heavily censored Internet usage. The majority of citizens accessed the outside world via Internet cafés.

Beginning in September 2011, the military regime in control of the country reduced Internet censorship and permitted international telecommunications companies to offer Internet service. In June 2013, the Myanmar government awarded Telenor Myanmar (TM, www.telenor.com.mm), a subsidiary of the Norwegian Telenor Group (NTG, www.telenor.com), a 15-year contract to develop telecommunications in the country. By October 2014, TM had provided mobile network operations for the entire country.

In 2015, Nobel Peace Prize winner and former political prisoner Aung San Suu Kyi led her National League for Democracy political party to a landslide victory in Myanmar's first openly contested election in 25 years. In 2020, her party again won an overwhelming victory.

During Suu Kyi's time in office, Myanmar's citizens gained social freedoms. The country also attracted foreign investment, which helped create an expanding middle class. The population rapidly moved online. SIM cards that had previously cost $1,000 became inexpensive and readily available. A SIM card, also called a *subscriber identification module*, is a small memory card that contains unique information that identifies it to a specific mobile network. The card also identifies the owner and enables them to communicate with a mobile network. SIM cards can store contact lists; text messages; who calls whom, when, and for how long; and other information used by the telecommunications company that supplied the card.

In February 2021, the military seized power in a coup, justifying its actions by alleging voter fraud during the November 2020 general election. Government officials arrested Suu Kyi, cut Internet services, and took news channels off the air.

Further, the military junta ordered TM to implement surveillance technology that would empower authorities to block Web content; spy on calls, messages, and Web traffic; and track users. The company refused. In May 2021, NTG, the parent company, wrote off the entire $783 million value of Telenor Myanmar. NTG then announced in July 2021 that it would leave Myanmar, selling 100 percent of the company to the M1 Group (www.m1group.com), a Lebanese investment group, for $105 million.

Although NTG intended to sell TM exclusively to the M1 Group, reports surfaced that military leaders would block the sale unless M1 awarded Shwe Byain Phyu an 80 percent controlling stake in TM. Shwe Byain Phyu is a Myanmar conglomerate with alleged close ties to the military junta. In May 2022, M1 completed the sale of Telenor Myanmar to Shwe Byain Phyu.

Prior to the sale of TM, political activists believed that their personal data was safe because they were using SIM cards from TM. They felt secure because TM was a subsidiary of a Norwegian company, and Norway had long been associated with democracy and human rights. The announcement of the sale alarmed the activists, who worried that the sale would empower the military regime to access the data of more than 18 million TM customers.

The military could use this data to map out the activists' association with family members and colleagues and use that information to target dissidents.

In response, more than 470 civil rights groups in Myanmar filed a legal complaint against TM's sale to M1. Specifically, they alleged that TM operations and data are subject to Europe's General Data Protection Regulation (GDPR) privacy law because TM is a subsidiary of a Norwegian company. The complaint claimed that NTG wanted to leave Myanmar as quickly as possible and thereby avoid its responsibility to its customers. This action was an attempt to compel Norway's Data Protection Authority to intervene and to prove that NTG has control over its subsidiary's data processing activities in Myanmar. In addition, some activists contacted NTG directly to request that the company delete their personal data. A law firm in Oslo, Norway, that was working on the case agreed with the activists that NTG was planning to leave Myanmar without safeguarding its customers' data.

NTG denied the activists' allegations. The company stated that it did not manage any Myanmar data in Norway or the European Union; therefore, the GDPR did not apply to TM's customer data. The company further argued that customers' phone call information would be transferred to M1—and ultimately to Shwe Byain Phyu—as part of the sales process to enable continued operations and avoid disrupting customer services.

The Norwegian government did not respond to requests for comment. A spokesperson for the Norwegian Telenor Group stated that the situation in Myanmar had "developed in a direction where we are in a conflict between local laws and our values, international law, and human rights principles. In the sales process, assessments of human rights, privacy, and the safety of our employees have been key considerations."

In June 2022, the United Nations condemned the Myanmar military junta's attempts to establish a "digital dictatorship" in the country by restricting Internet access, shutting down the Internet, and implementing online censorship, surveillance, and other barriers to Internet access. Reporters contend that serious human rights violations are taking place while the Internet is blacked out.

Questions

1. Discuss the ethicality and legality of the Norwegian Telenor Group's sale of Telenor Myanmar to M1.

2. The fundamental tenets of ethics include responsibility, accountability, and liability. Discuss each of these tenets with respect to the Norwegian Telenor Group's sale of Telenor Myanmar to M1.

3. Do you agree or disagree with the Norwegian Telenor Group's sale of Telenor Myanmar to M1? Why or why not? If you disagree, what do you think the Norwegian Telenor Group should have done instead?

Sources: Compiled from "Myanmar: UN Experts Condemn Military's 'Digital Dictatorship'," *United Nations Office of Human Rights*, June 7, 2022; N. Lusan and E. Fishbein, "Internet Blackouts Are Hiding an Ongoing Human Rights Catastrophe," *Rest of World*, April 26, 2022; "Military-Linked Company Shwe Byain Phyu

Has Taken Control of Telenor Myanmar," *Justice for Myanmar*, May 16, 2022; "Pro-Junta Militia Calls for Killing of Myanmar Reporters and Their Family Members," *Radio Free Asia*, May 3, 2022; "Telenor Completes Myanmar Business Sale, to Be Paid over 5 Years," *Reuters*, March 25, 2022; K. Zaw, "Myanmar Junta Cuts off Internet Access 'Indefinitely' to Resistance Stronghold of Sagaing," *Myanmar Now*, March 4, 2022; J. Greig, "Outrage over Telenor Myanmar Sale Grows as More Ties between Military and New Owner Revealed," *ZDNet*, February 14, 2022; "Shwe Byain Phyu's Military Links Exposed," *Justice for Myanmar*, February 13, 2022; "NUG Acting President Calls on Norway's Prime Minister to Prevent Sale of Telenor to Junta-Linked Company," *Myanmar Now*, February 11, 2022; "Telenor 'Rushing' to Get Junta Approval for Sale to Military-Linked Company by End of Week," *Myanmar Now*, February 9, 2022; T. Paing, "Myanmar Citizen Files Data Privacy Complaint against Telenor with Norwegian Government Agency," *Myanmar Now*, February 8, 2022; M. Meaker, "Myanmar's Fight for Democracy Is Now a Scrap over Phone Records," *Wired*, February 8, 2022; T. Paing, "Telenor Sale to Military-Linked Consortium to Be Complete in Mid-February," *Myanmar Now*, February 4, 2022; M. Bachelet, "'Urgent, Renewed Effort' Needed to Restore Civilian Rule in Myanmar," *United Nations News*, January 28, 2022; S. Reed, "TotalEnergies and Chevron Prepare to Leave a Critical Gas Field in Myanmar," *The New York Times*, January 21, 2022; "Aung San Suu Kyi: Myanmar Democracy Icon Who Fell from Grace," *BBC News*, December 6, 2021; "Myanmar: SOMO and 474 CSOs Submit Complaint to the OECD Norwegian NCP Concerning Telenor's 'Irresponsible' Disengagement from Myanmar," *Business & Human Rights Resource Center*, July 29, 2021; F. Potkin and P. McPherson, "How Myanmar's Military Moved in on the Telecoms Sector to Spy on Citizens," *Reuters*, May 18, 2021; "Telenor Posts First-Quarter Loss after Writing off Myanmar Business Following Coup," *CNBC*, May 4, 2021; H. Regan, "Why the Generals Really Took Back Power in Myanmar," *CNN*, February 8, 2021; A. Daga and S. Sonal, "3-CVC Buys Telecom Tower Firm in Myanmar's Second Biggest Deal, *Reuters*, December 11, 2020; www.telenor.com, www.telenor.com.mm, accessed July 26, 2022.

CHAPTER 4

Information Security

CHAPTER OUTLINE	LEARNING OBJECTIVES
4.1 Introduction to Information Security	**4.1 Identify** the five factors that contribute to the increasing vulnerability of information resources, and provide specific examples of each factor.
4.2 Unintentional Threats to Information Systems	**4.2 Compare** and contrast human mistakes and social engineering, and provide a specific example of each one.
4.3 Deliberate Threats to Information Systems	**4.3 Discuss** the 10 types of deliberate attacks.
4.4 What Organizations Are Doing to Protect Information Resources	**4.4 Describe** the three risk mitigation strategies, and provide an example of each one in the context of owning a home.
4.5 Information Security Controls	**4.5 Identify** the three major types of controls that organizations can use to protect their information resources, and provide an example of each one.

Opening Case

 **Supply Chain Attacks**

What if the legitimate hardware and software that make up an organization's supply chain network have been compromised at the source? This question is the focus of a supply chain attack.

A *supply chain attack* targets organizations by focusing on weaker links in that organization's supply chain. For example, a supply chain attack can enable hackers to compromise enterprise networks by attacking connected applications or services owned or used by business partners such as suppliers. A supply chain attack can begin several companies removed from the intended target, making the attack harder to detect.

Targeting a weak point in a supply chain increases the chances that an attack will succeed, because the attackers are taking advantage of the trust that firms have in third-party vendors. Supply chain attacks are difficult to detect because they frequently involve software that is both trusted and widely distributed.

Another reason supply chain attacks frequently succeed is that companies often do not consider the risk serious enough to protect themselves against it. Specifically, organizations typically do not have a dedicated group that is tasked with managing third-party vendors.

Supply chain attacks can occur when attackers insert malicious computer code into a company's software product or a malicious component into a company's hardware product. By compromising a single supplier, attackers can take over its distribution systems. Any application the company sells, any software update it pushes out, or the physical equipment it ships to customers can then be turned into Trojan horses. This type of supply chain attack impacted SolarWinds in 2019.

SolarWinds (www.solarwinds.com) is a software company that provides systems management tools for network and IT infrastructure monitoring, as well as other technical services, to thousands of organizations around the world. One of the company's products is an IT performance-monitoring system called Orion. As an IT monitoring system, Orion has high-level access to customers' IT systems.

The attackers gained access by compromising a digitally signed SolarWinds Orion network-monitoring component, thereby opening a backdoor into the networks of thousands of SolarWinds government and enterprise customers. Company executives pointed to an intern who created the weak password "solarwinds123," which then leaked online.

Basically, attackers inserted malicious computer code into the Orion system and delivered the backdoor malware as an update to the Orion software. A *backdoor* is a means to access a computer system or encrypted data that bypasses the system's customary security mechanisms. The malware could also access system files and blend in with legitimate SolarWinds activity without being detected, even by antivirus software. The hackers only had to install the malicious code into a new batch of software distributed by SolarWinds as an update or a patch.

In this attack, the hackers gained access to the networks, systems, and data of thousands of SolarWinds customers. Among the targets were many public and private organizations, including local, state, and federal agencies. The breadth of the hack was unprecedented. Overall, it was one of the largest successful attacks of its kind.

Going further, SolarWinds customers were not the only affected targets. Because the hack exposed the operations of Orion customers, the hackers could potentially gain access to the data and networks of Orion's customers and business partners as well. As a result, the number of affected victims increased exponentially.

The attackers first gained access to the SolarWinds systems in September 2019; however, the attack was not publicly discovered until December 2020. This time gap gave the attackers at least 14 months of undetected access.

The first victim to detect the breach was the cybersecurity company FireEye, a SolarWinds customer. FireEye realized they had been infected when they discovered the infection in their customers' systems. Microsoft subsequently reported that it found the malware in its systems and that the malware was affecting its customers as well. Note: In 2021, Symphony Technology Group (STG), an American private equity firm, bought McAfee Enterprise and FireEye, and merged the two companies under the name Trellix **www.trellix.com**).

To cut off the hackers from their customers' systems, Microsoft and FireEye cooperated to block and isolate versions of Orion known to contain the malware. They turned the domain used by the backdoor malware that was inserted into Orion into a kill switch. This action prevented the malware from operating further. Even with the kill switch in place, however, the hack continued. Investigators have enormous amounts of data to continue to study, because many companies that use the Orion software are not yet certain if they are free of the malware.

The purpose of the attack remains unknown. Federal investigators and cybersecurity experts believe a Russian espionage operation—most likely Russia's Foreign Intelligence Service—is behind the attack. The Russian government has denied any involvement.

Since the attack was discovered, SolarWinds has recommended that customers update their existing Orion platform. The company has released patches for the malware and other potential vulnerabilities discovered since the first attack. SolarWinds also recommended that customers who are unable to update Orion isolate SolarWinds servers and/or change passwords for accounts that have access to those servers.

The Orion breach could also lead to changes in the cybersecurity industry. Public- and private-sector organizations are learning that it is not enough to build a firewall and hope that it protects them. They must actively seek out vulnerabilities in their systems and either fix them or turn them into traps against these types of supply chain attacks.

These efforts can be extremely challenging, however, due to the nature of the cybersecurity industry. Specifically, developers build modern software applications from many components that can originate from multiple sources. Any one of these components could potentially represent a risk if it contains an unpatched vulnerability. For this reason, it is critical that developers, the organizations they work for, and the end users be aware of the myriad components that make up an application. This approach is known as a *software bill of materials* (SBOM). An SBOM is like a nutritional label found on packaged foods that clearly shows consumers what is inside a product.

In May 2021, the Biden administration issued an executive order mandating SBOMs in all government agencies. The order also instructs U.S. government agencies to purchase software only from vendors who provide SBOMs.

Questions

1. **Explain why it is so difficult to detect a supply chain attack.**

2. **Discuss how a software bill of materials (SBOM) could prevent some supply chain attacks.**

3. **Should SBOMs be mandatory for all software providers? Explain your answer.**

Sources: Compiled from S. Lyngaas, "Russian Hackers behind SolarWinds Breach Continue to Scour U.S. and European Organizations for Intel, Researchers Say," *CNN*, July 19, 2022; "Why Hackers Are Increasingly Targeting Digital Supply Chains," *CSO*, July 13, 2022; S. Oladimeji, "SolarWinds Hack Explained: Everything You Need to Know," *TechTarget*, June 29, 2022; S. Kerner, "Colonial Pipeline Hack Explained: Everything You Need to Know," *TechTarget*, April 26, 2022; L. Tung, "Supply Chain Attacks Are Getting Worse, and You Are Not Ready for Them," *ZDNet*, August 3, 2021; A. Greenberg, "Hacker Lexicon: What Is a Supply Chain Attack?" *Wired*, May 31, 2021; B. Fung and G. Sands, "Former SolarWinds CEO Blames Intern for 'solarwinds123' Password Leak," *CNN*, February 26, 2021; T. Thompson, "The SolarWinds Hack Was All but Inevitable," *The Conversation*, February 9, 2021; A. Scroxton, "SolarWinds Patches Two Critical CVEs in Orion Platform," *TechTarget*, February 3, 2021; R. McMillan and D. Volz, "Suspected Russian Hack Extends Far beyond SolarWinds Software, Investigators Say," *Wall Street Journal*, January 29, 2021; S. Ramakrishna, "New Findings from Our Investigation of Sunburst," *SolarWinds*, January 11, 2021; A. Scroxton, "SolarWinds Attack almost Certainly Work of Russian Spooks," *Computer Weekly*, January 6, 2021; A. Culafi, "The SolarWinds Attacks: What We Know So Far," *TechTarget*, January 6, 2021; A. Waldman, "SolarWinds Backdoor Infected Tech Giants, Impact Unclear," *TechTarget*, December 21, 2020; L. Newman, "How to Understand the Russian Hack Fallout," *Wired*, December 19, 2020; R. Wright, "Risk & Repeat: SolarWinds Backdoor Shakes Infosec Industry," *TechTarget*, December 18, 2020; A. Culafi, "Microsoft, FireEye Create Kill Switch for SolarWinds Backdoor," *TechTarget*, December 17, 2020; A. Waldman, "SolarWinds Breach Highlights Dangers of Supply Chain Attacks," *TechTarget*, December 16, 2020; R. Wright, "SolarWinds Backdoor Used in Nation-State Cyber Attacks," *TechTarget*, December 14, 2020; "Highly Evasive Attacker Leverages SolarWinds Supply Chain to Compromise Multiple Global Victims with Sunburst Backdoor," *Mandiant*, December 13, 2020; and www.solarwinds.com, accessed August 8, 2022.

Introduction

The cases in this chapter provide several lessons. First, it is difficult—if not impossible—for organizations to provide perfect security for their data. Second, there is a growing danger that countries are engaging in economic cyberwarfare. Third, it appears that it is impossible to secure the Internet. Information security impacts each and every one of us, and, unfortunately, our personally identifiable, private data are not secure.

The solutions for these and other related issues are not clear. As you learn about information security in the context of information technology, you will acquire a better understanding of these issues, their importance, their relationships, and their trade-offs. Keep in mind that the issues involved in information security impact individuals and small organizations as well as large enterprises.

Information security is especially important to small businesses. Large organizations that experience an information security problem have greater resources to both resolve and survive the problem. In contrast, small businesses have fewer resources and therefore can be more easily crippled by a data breach.

When properly used, information technologies can have enormous benefits for individuals, organizations, and entire societies. In Chapters 1 and 2, you read about diverse ways in which IT has made businesses more productive, efficient, and responsive to consumers. Unfortunately, bad actors can misuse information technologies, often with devastating consequences. Consider the following scenarios:

- Individuals can have their personal data and subsequently their identities stolen.
- Organizations can have customer information stolen, leading to financial losses, erosion of customer confidence, and legal actions.
- Countries face the threats of *cyberterrorism* and *cyberwarfare*, terms for Internet-based attacks. Cyberwarfare is a critical problem for the U.S. government. In fact, President Barack Obama signed a cyberwarfare directive in October 2012 that, for the first time, laid out specific ground rules for how and when the U.S. military can carry out offensive and defensive cyber operations against foreign threats. The directive emphasized the U.S. government's focus on cybersecurity as a top priority, a focus that continues to grow in importance.

Clearly, the misuse of information technologies has come to the forefront of any discussion of IT. In fact, according to security analysts, cybercrime will cost the world approximately $10.5 trillion per year by 2025.

With organizations facing the loss or theft of billions of records since the beginning of 2019, they must be aware of the full financial impact of a data breach. According to IBM Security's annual study of the financial impact of data breaches in organizations, the average cost of a breach in the United States in 2021 was $4.3 million. While less common, breaches of more than 1 million records cost companies an average of $42 million in losses, and breaches of 50 million records cost companies $401 million. The average amount of time for a company to identify a breach was 287 days after it occurred. It then took companies an additional 73 days to contain the breach.

FIN The direct costs of a data breach include hiring forensic experts, notifying customers, setting up telephone hotlines to field queries from concerned or affected customers, offering free credit monitoring, and providing discounts for future products and services. The more intangible costs include the loss of business from increased customer turnover—called *customer churn*—and diminished customer trust.

HRM Unfortunately, employee negligence causes many data breaches, meaning that organizational employees are a weak link in information security. It is therefore very important for you to learn about information security so that you will be better prepared when you enter the workforce.

4.1 | Introduction to Information Security

security The degree of protection against criminal activity, danger, damage, or loss.

information security Protecting an organization's information and information systems from unauthorized access, use, disclosure, disruption, modification, or destruction.

threat Any danger to which an information resource may be exposed.

exposure The harm, loss, or damage that can result if a threat compromises an information resource.

vulnerability The possibility that an information resource will be harmed by a threat.

LEARNING OBJECTIVE

Identify the five factors that contribute to the increasing vulnerability of information resources, and provide specific examples of each factor.

Security can be defined as the degree of protection against criminal activity, danger, damage, or loss. Following this broad definition, information security refers to all of the processes and policies designed to protect an organization's information and information systems (IS) from unauthorized access, use, disclosure, disruption, modification, or destruction. You have seen that information and information systems can be compromised by deliberate criminal actions and by anything that can impair the proper functioning of an organization's information systems.

Before continuing, let's consider these key concepts. Organizations collect huge amounts of information, and they employ numerous information systems that are subject to myriad threats. A threat to an information resource is any danger to which a system may be exposed. The exposure of an information resource is the harm, loss, or damage that can result if a threat compromises that resource. An information resource's vulnerability is the possibility that a threat will harm that resource.

Today, five key factors are contributing to the increasing vulnerability of organizational information resources, making it much more difficult to secure them:

1. Today's interconnected, interdependent, wirelessly networked business environment
2. Smaller, faster, cheaper computers and storage devices
3. Decreasing skills necessary to be a computer hacker
4. International organized crime taking over cybercrime
5. Lack of management support

The first factor is the evolution of the IT resource from mainframe-only to today's highly complex, interconnected, interdependent, wirelessly networked business environment. The Internet now enables millions of computers and computer networks to communicate freely and seamlessly with one another. Organizations and individuals are exposed to a world of untrusted networks and potential attackers. In general, a *trusted network* is any network within your organization, and an *untrusted network* is any network external to your organization. Also, wireless technologies enable employees to compute, communicate, and access the Internet anywhere and at any time. Significantly, wireless is an inherently unsecure broadcast communications medium.

The second factor reflects the fact that modern computers and storage devices—for example, thumb drives or flash drives—continue to become smaller, faster, cheaper, and more portable, with greater storage capacity. These characteristics make it much easier to steal or lose a computer or a storage device that contains huge amounts of sensitive information. Also, far more people are able to afford powerful computers and connect inexpensively to the Internet, thus raising the potential of an attack on information assets.

The third factor is that the computing skills necessary to be a hacker are *decreasing*. The reason is that the Internet contains information and computer programs called *scripts* that users with limited skills can download and use to attack any information system that is connected to the Internet. (Security experts can also use these scripts for legitimate purposes, such as testing the security of various systems.) IT's About Business 4.1 illustrates how a hacker used a publicly available script to successfully penetrate T-Mobile.

The fourth factor is that international organized crime is taking over cybercrime. Cybercrime refers to illegal activities conducted over computer networks, particularly the Internet. Consulting company Accenture (www.accenture.com) maintains that groups of well-organized criminal organizations have taken control of a global billion-dollar crime network. The network, powered by skillful hackers, targets known software security weaknesses.

cybercrime Illegal activities executed on the Internet.

These crimes are typically nonviolent; however, they are quite lucrative. Consider, for example, that losses from armed robberies average hundreds of dollars and those from white-collar crimes can average tens of thousands of dollars. In contrast, losses from computer crimes can average hundreds of thousands of dollars. Furthermore, computer crimes can be committed from anywhere in the world at any time, effectively providing an international safe haven for cybercriminals.

The fifth, and final, factor is lack of management support. For the entire organization to take security policies and procedures seriously, senior managers must set the tone. Unfortunately, senior managers often do not do so. Ultimately, however, lower-level managers may be even more important. These managers are in close contact with employees every day and are thus in a better position to determine whether employees are following security procedures.

IT's About Business 4.1

MIS MKT T-Mobile Experiences Multiple Breaches

In 2018, a breach impacted approximately two million T-Mobile customers in what the company referred to as an "unauthorized capture of data." The hackers did not steal any financial data. However, customers' personal information such as names, addresses, and birthdates were compromised.

In November 2019, T-Mobile (www.t-mobile.com) confirmed an attack that impacted some of its U.S. prepaid customers; that is, customers who fund their accounts in advance. The company announced that its cybersecurity team had "discovered and shut down malicious, unauthorized access to some of the information related to your T-Mobile wireless account."

In March 2020, T-Mobile experienced another breach when hackers compromised the company's e-mail vendor. The attack affected both customers and company employees. The stolen data included names, phone numbers, addresses, account numbers, rate plans and features, and billing information. For some individuals, their Social Security numbers, government identification numbers, and financial account information also might have been compromised.

In December 2020, a breach illegally accessed T-Mobile's customers' proprietary network information. The company reported that the attack impacted roughly 200,000 people.

In August 2021, T-Mobile suffered another successful attack in which data from more than 48 million people was compromised. Of this total, the vast majority—more than 40 million—were former or prospective customers who had applied for credit with the carrier. The remaining 7.8 million were current postpaid customers; that is, customers who are billed at the end of each month. These users had their names, dates of birth, Social Security numbers, IMEI numbers, and driver's license information stolen. IMEI stands for International Mobile Equipment Identity, which helps to identify a specific phone across all mobile networks and obtain information on that phone, including the model and where it was manufactured. An additional 850,000 prepaid customers had their names, phone numbers, and PINs exposed.

Later that month, 21-year-old John Binns, a native of Virginia who was living in Turkey, told the *Wall Street Journal* that he was behind the breach. Binns claimed he launched the attack to retaliate against alleged mistreatment by U.S. intelligence personnel. He reported that he first scanned the carrier's Internet addresses for weak spots using a publicly available tool (which he declined to name). He then broke through the T-Mobile defenses after discovering an unprotected router exposed on the Internet. From the compromised router, he moved to T-Mobile's local area network and then to the more than 100 mostly Oracle databases that contain user information. Binns claimed that he had access to T-Mobile systems for two to three weeks before the carrier noticed and repaired the problem.

In addition to identity theft, the stolen data made it easier for Binns or other bad actors to perpetrate SIM swap attacks, particularly against the prepaid customers who had their PINs and phone numbers exposed. In a *SIM swap*, attackers move your phone number to their own device, typically so that they can intercept SMS-based two-factor authentication codes, making it easier to break into your online accounts.

According to court documents unsealed in April 2022, T-Mobile hired a third party to pay Binns for exclusive access to the stolen data and therefore limit the data from leaking more widely. After the third party paid $200,000, however, the criminals continued to sell the data. This news highlights some of the controversial tactics that some companies use when they respond to data breaches, either to mitigate the leak of stolen information or to try to identify the attackers who breached their networks.

An important question is whether T-Mobile needed to store such sensitive information from 40 million people with whom it was not doing business at the time of the breach. Or, if the company was going to keep that data, why did it not take better precautions to protect it?

Privacy advocates have long emphasized *data minimization*, a practice that encourages companies to store as little information as necessary. Europe's General Data Protection Regulation (GDPR) has put that practice into law, requiring that personal data be "adequate, relevant, and limited to what is necessary to the purposes for which they are processed."

The United States, in contrast, has no equivalent law. U.S. privacy laws that mention data minimization generally do not require it but instead recommend it as a best practice. Until the United States adopts a privacy law similar to the GDPR, or state-level legislation such as the California Consumer Privacy Act, data minimization will be left to the organizations that capture and store consumer data. Further, because the United States does not have a comprehensive cybersecurity law, agencies such as the Federal Communications Commission (FCC) and Federal Trade Commission (FTC) have limited ability to apply pressure to organizations that do not maintain rigorous cybersecurity in protecting their data.

In July 2022, T-Mobile agreed to pay $350 million to customers to settle a class action lawsuit over the August 2021 data breach.

Questions

1. T-Mobile hired a third party to attempt to purchase the company's stolen data. Was this a good idea? Why or why not?

2. Discuss the principle of data minimization as it applies to the T-Mobile breach.

3. Should the United States have a data protection law similar to Europe's General Data Protection Regulation? Why or why not? Support your answer.

Sources: Compiled from M. Moon, "T-Mobile Will Pay $350 Million to Settle Lawsuits over Massive Data Breach," *Yahoo!News*, July 23, 2022; J. Cox, "T-Mobile Investigating Claims of Massive Customer Data Breach," *Motherboard*, August 15, 2021; J. Cox, "T-Mobile Secretly Bought Its Customer Data from Hackers to Stop Leak. It Failed," *Vice.com*, April 12, 2022; J. Cipriani, "T-Mobile Data Breach 2021: Here's What It Means for Securing Your Data," *CNET*, September 9, 2021; D. FitzGerald, "T-Mobile Hacker Who Stole Data on 50 Million Customers: 'Their Security Is Awful'," *Wall Street Journal*, August 27, 2021; N. Garfinkel, "T-Mobile Hacker Explains How He Breached Carrier's Security," *Axios*, August 26, 2021; L. Whitney, "T-Mobile Breach Exposed Personal Data of Almost 50 Million People," *TechRepublic*, August 19, 2021; Y. Reyes, "T-Mobile Says Hackers Stole Information on over 40 Million People," *Axios*, August 18, 2021; B. Barrett, "The T-Mobile Breach Is Much Worse than It Had to Be," *Wired*, August 18, 2021; B. Barrett, "The T-Mobile Breach Is One You Can't Ignore," *Wired*, August 16, 2021; and www.t-mobile.com, accessed August 10, 2022.

Before you go on...

1. Define information security.
2. Differentiate among a threat, an exposure, and a vulnerability.
3. Why are the skills needed to be a hacker decreasing?

4.2 Unintentional Threats to Information Systems

WILEY PLUS

Author Lecture Videos are available exclusively in *WileyPLUS*.
Apply the Concept activities are available in the Appendix and in *WileyPLUS*.

LEARNING OBJECTIVE

Compare and contrast human mistakes and social engineering, and provide a specific example of each one.

Information systems are vulnerable to many potential hazards and threats, as you can see in **Figure 4.1**. The two major categories of threats are unintentional threats and deliberate threats. This section discusses unintentional threats, and the next section addresses deliberate threats.

Unintentional threats are acts performed without malicious intent that nevertheless represent a serious threat to information security. A major category of unintentional threats is human error.

Human Errors

HRM Organizational employees span the breadth and depth of the organization, from mail clerks to the CEO, and across all functional areas. There are two important points to be made about employees. First, the higher the level of employee, the greater the threat he or she poses to information security. This is true because higher-level employees typically have greater access to corporate data, and they enjoy greater privileges on organizational information systems. Second, employees in two areas of the organization pose especially significant threats to information security: human resources and information systems. Human resources employees generally have access to sensitive personal information about all employees. Likewise, IS employees not only have access to sensitive organizational data, but they also frequently control the means to create, store, transmit, and modify those data. Consider these two examples.

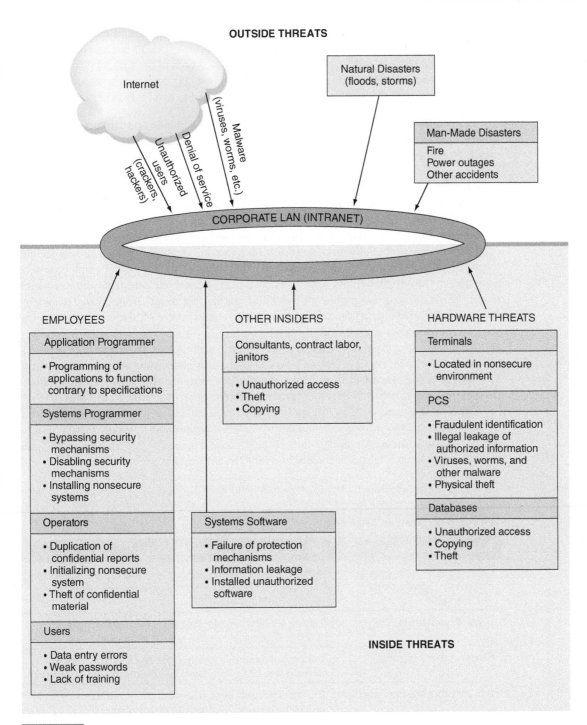

OUTSIDE THREATS

Internet

Malware (viruses, worms, etc.)

Unauthorized users (crackers, hackers)

Denial of service

Natural Disasters (floods, storms)

Man-Made Disasters

Fire
Power outages
Other accidents

CORPORATE LAN (INTRANET)

EMPLOYEES

Application Programmer

• Programming of applications to function contrary to specifications

Systems Programmer

• Bypassing security mechanisms
• Disabling security mechanisms
• Installing nonsecure systems

Operators

• Duplication of confidential reports
• Initializing nonsecure system
• Theft of confidential material

Users

• Data entry errors
• Weak passwords
• Lack of training

OTHER INSIDERS

Consultants, contract labor, janitors

• Unauthorized access
• Theft
• Copying

Systems Software

• Failure of protection mechanisms
• Information leakage
• Installed unauthorized software

HARDWARE THREATS

Terminals

• Located in nonsecure environment

PCS

• Fraudulent identification
• Illegal leakage of authorized information
• Viruses, worms, and other malware
• Physical theft

Databases

• Unauthorized access
• Copying
• Theft

INSIDE THREATS

FIGURE 4.1 **Information Security Threats**

- **MIS** **POM** For 10 years, a Siemens contractor created spreadsheets that the company used to manage equipment orders. The spreadsheets contained custom macros that enabled Siemens to automate inventory and order management. The contractor embedded logic bombs that would trigger after a certain date and crash the spreadsheets. Each time the spreadsheets would crash, Siemens would call him and he would "fix the problem" for a fee.

   The scheme fell apart when he was out of town and had to give his password for the spreadsheets to Siemens IT staff so that they could use the spreadsheets to fill an urgent order. They found the logic bombs and the police arrested the contractor.

- **MKT** A marketing and software company in the United Kingdom terminated an IT employee. After he left, he could still access the company's systems because he had stolen a fellow employee's login credentials. He then deleted each of the firm's 23 Amazon Web Services servers. As a result, the firm said that it lost "big contracts with some clients" totaling about $700,000. The perpetrator was sentenced to two years in prison.

Other relevant employees include contract labor, consultants, and janitors and guards. Contract labor, such as temporary hires, may be overlooked in information security arrangements. However, these employees often have access to the company's network, information systems, and information assets. Consultants, although technically not employees, perform work for the company. Depending on the nature of their work, they may also have access to the company's network, information systems, and information assets.

Finally, janitors and guards are the most frequently ignored people in information security systems. Companies frequently outsource their security and janitorial services. As with contractors, then, these individuals work for the company, although they technically are not employees. Moreover, they are usually present when most—if not all—other employees have gone home. They typically have keys to every office, and nobody questions their presence in even the most sensitive parts of the building. In fact, an article from *2600: The Hacker Quarterly* (www.2600.com) described how to get a job as a janitor for the purpose of gaining physical access to an organization.

Human errors or mistakes by employees pose a serious problem. These errors are typically the result of laziness, carelessness, or a lack of awareness concerning information security. This lack of awareness arises from poor education and training efforts by the organization. Human mistakes manifest themselves in many different ways, as illustrated in Table 4.1.

The human errors you have just studied, although unintentional, are committed entirely by employees. However, employees also can make unintentional mistakes in response to actions by an attacker. Attackers often employ social engineering to induce individuals to make unintentional mistakes and disclose sensitive information.

TABLE 4.1   **Human Mistakes**

Human Mistake	Description and Examples
Carelessness with computing devices (e.g., laptops, tablets, smartphones)	Losing or misplacing these devices, or using them carelessly so that malware is introduced into an organization's network
Opening questionable e-mails	Opening e-mails from someone unknown, or clicking on links embedded in e-mails (see *phishing attack* in Table 4.2)
Careless Internet surfing	Accessing questionable websites; can result in malware and alien software being introduced into the organization's network
Poor password selection and use	Choosing and using weak passwords (see *strong passwords* in the "Authentication" section later in this chapter)
Carelessness with one's workspace	Leaving desks and filing cabinets unlocked when employees go home at night; not logging off the company network when leaving the office for any extended period of time
Carelessness using unmanaged devices	Unmanaged devices are those outside the control of an organization's IT department and company security procedures. These devices include computers belonging to customers and business partners, computers in the business centers of hotels, and so on
Carelessness with discarded equipment	Discarding old computer hardware and devices without completely wiping the memory; includes computers, smartphones, BlackBerry® units, and digital copiers and printers
Careless monitoring of environmental hazards	These hazards, which include dirt, dust, humidity, and static electricity, are harmful to the operation of computing equipment

Social Engineering

Social engineering is an attack in which the perpetrator uses social skills to trick or manipulate legitimate employees into providing confidential company information such as passwords. The most common example of social engineering occurs when the attacker impersonates someone else on the telephone, such as a company manager or an IS employee. The attacker claims he forgot his password and asks the legitimate employee to give him a password to use. Other common ploys include posing as an exterminator, an air conditioning technician, or a fire marshal. Examples of social engineering abound.

In one company, a perpetrator entered a company building wearing a company ID card that looked legitimate. He walked around and put up signs on bulletin boards reading "The help desk telephone number has been changed. The new number is 555-1234." He then exited the building and began receiving calls from legitimate employees thinking they were calling the company's help desk. Naturally, the first thing the perpetrator asked for was each caller's username and password. He now had the information necessary to access the company's information systems.

Two other social engineering techniques are tailgating and shoulder surfing. *Tailgating* is a technique designed to allow the perpetrator to enter restricted areas that are controlled with locks or card entry. The perpetrator follows closely behind a legitimate employee and, when the employee gains entry, the attacker asks him or her to "hold the door." *Shoulder surfing* occurs when a perpetrator watches an employee's computer screen over the employee's shoulder. This technique is particularly successful in public areas such as in airports and on commuter trains and airplanes.

social engineering Getting around security systems by tricking computer users inside a company into revealing sensitive information or gaining unauthorized access privileges.

Before you go on...

1. What is an unintentional threat to an information system?
2. Provide examples of social engineering attacks other than the ones just discussed.

4.3 | Deliberate Threats to Information Systems

LEARNING OBJECTIVE

Discuss the 10 types of deliberate attacks.

WILEY PLUS

Author Lecture Videos are available exclusively in *WileyPLUS.*
Apply the Concept activities are available in the Appendix and in *WileyPLUS.*

There are many types of deliberate threats to information systems. We provide a list of 10 common types for your convenience:

1. Espionage or trespass
2. Information extortion
3. Sabotage or vandalism
4. Theft of equipment or information
5. Identity theft
6. Compromises to intellectual property
7. Software attacks
8. Alien software
9. Supervisory control and data acquisition (SCADA) attacks
10. Cyberterrorism and cyberwarfare

Espionage or Trespass

Espionage or trespass occurs when an unauthorized individual attempts to gain illegal access to organizational information. It is important to distinguish between competitive intelligence and industrial espionage. Competitive intelligence consists of legal information-gathering techniques, such as studying a company's website and press releases, attending trade shows, and similar actions. In contrast, industrial espionage crosses the legal boundary.

Information Extortion

Information extortion occurs when an attacker either threatens to steal, or actually steals, information from a company. The perpetrator demands payment for not stealing the information, for returning stolen information, or for agreeing not to disclose the information. An increasingly serious type of information extortion is ransomware.

ransomware (or digital extortion) Malicious software that blocks access to a computer system or encrypts an organization's data until the organization pays a sum of money.

Ransomware, or digital extortion, blocks access to a computer system or encrypts an organization's data until the organization pays a sum of money. Victims are told to pay the ransom, usually in Bitcoin. Attackers typically use the anonymizing Tor network (**www.torproject.org**).

Ransomware attacks are growing rapidly. In 2021, ransomware attacks extorted over $20 billion globally. As bad as these figures look, the reality is probably worse. Experts estimate that fewer than 25 percent of ransomware attacks are reported. Significantly, security analysts note that over half of the companies compromised by ransomware pay the ransom.

Methods of Attack Most commonly, ransomware attacks use spear phishing and whaling attacks. These e-mails are carefully tailored to look as convincing as possible, so they appear no different from any other e-mail the victim might receive.

Some ransomware developers distribute ransomware to any hacker who wants to use it. This process is called *ransomware-as-a-service*. In this type of ransomware, the original creators publish the software on the Dark Web, allowing other criminals to use the code in return for receiving 40 to 50 percent of each ransom paid.

Rather than threatening to delete encrypted data, some cybercriminals are beginning to threaten to release it to the public, a strategy known as *doxxing*. For organizations that deal with private and sensitive customer data, such as financial services, hospitals, and law firms, such attacks can have severe consequences. In addition to the impact to brand reputation, regulations such as the Health Information Portability and Accountability Act (HIPAA) require customer notifications and other activities that can quickly total hundreds of thousands of dollars. Compared to other industry segments, personal health information is 50 times more valuable than financial information on the Dark Web.

The Costs of Ransomware Direct costs are the ransom payment. Indirect costs include the cost of recovering files from backup and restoring encrypted systems, business interruption, loss of reputation, liability (lawsuits), loss of data, investments in additional cybersecurity software, additional staff training, and increased cyber insurance (particularly covering ransomware attacks).

Protection against Ransomware There are many steps that organizations can take to protect itself against ransomware infections.

- Perhaps most importantly, all organizations must provide education and training so that users are aware of phishing, spear phishing, and whaling attacks and do not click on any suspicious e-mails or links in e-mails.
- Organizations must install the latest versions of software and apply patches immediately.
- Organizations must back up crucial data and information often, preferably through an encrypted cloud-based storage company or an online backup service. Examples are iDrive (**www.idrive.com**) and Carbonite (**www.carbonite.com**). Important: the backup data storage must be connected to your system only when you are backing up the data.

- Organizations should employ *anti-ransomware software*. Packages such as Acronis Ransomware Protection (**www.acronis.com**) and Malwarebytes Anti-Ransomware Beta (**www.malwarebytes.com**) use two methods to defeat ransomware. First, they detect the digital signatures of known malware to recognize it going forward. This approach does not work if the software has not yet encountered a particular type of malware.

  Second, they detect malware by its behavior. These programs monitor the activity of apps, and they quarantine processes that perform suspicious actions, such as generating an encryption key or starting to encrypt files. This method is more effective at detecting and stopping ransomware than simply searching for malware signatures because it can detect new threats as well as known threats.

- Organizations should utilize the *No More Ransom* initiative (**www.nomoreransom.org**). The portal, founded by the National High Tech Crime Unit of the Netherlands' police, Europol's European Cybercrime Center, Kaspersky, and McAfee, launched in 2016 and today involves 188 partners across law enforcement, cybersecurity companies, academia, and others. The portal is available in 37 languages.

  As of August 2022, the portal offered 136 free ransomware decryption tools that can decrypt 165 ransomware families. No More Ransom has helped more than six million ransomware victims recover their encrypted files for free. To date, the portal has saved victims from paying over $1 billion.

  The portal also offers information and advice on how to avoid falling victim to ransomware as well as free decryption tools for various types of ransomware to help victims retrieve their encrypted data. The portal is updated as often as possible to ensure that tools are available to fight the latest forms of ransomware. The portal's Crypto Sheriff app allows users to upload encrypted files to help identify to which form of ransomware they have fallen victim and then directs them to a free decryption tool if one is available.

- Organizations should also be aware that individual security companies regularly release decryption tools to counter the ongoing evolution of ransomware. Many of these companies post updates about these tools on their company blogs as soon as they have cracked the malware's code.

IT's About Business 4.2 discusses a successful ransomware attack against Colonial Pipeline.

IT's About Business **4.2**

MIS POM The Colonial Pipeline Hack

On January 11, 2021, antivirus company Bitdefender (**www.bitedefender.com**) announced that it had discovered an error in the ransomware that an entity known as DarkSide was using to attack businesses in the United States and Europe. Bitdefender then provided companies facing ransom demands from DarkSide with a free tool they could download to avoid paying millions of dollars to the hackers.

Unfortunately, by publicizing its tool, Bitdefender alerted DarkSide to the error, which involved reusing the same digital keys to lock and unlock multiple victims. The next day, DarkSide announced that it had repaired the flaw, and they thanked Bitdefender for "helping us fix our issues."

The following May, DarkSide successfully attacked Colonial Pipeline (**www.colpipe.com**), the largest pipeline system for refined oil products in the United States. The pipeline is 5,500 miles long, and it can carry three million barrels of fuel per day, which is nearly half the fuel for the East Coast, between Texas and New York.

Attackers accessed Colonial's network through an exposed password for a VPN account. A Colonial employee likely used the same password for the VPN in another location. That password was somehow compromised as part of a different data breach. The attackers infected some of the company's digital systems, shutting down its pipeline for several days.

The Colonial hack is the largest publicly disclosed cyberattack against vital infrastructure in U.S. history. It consisted of multiple stages that targeted the company's IT systems. The attack began when DarkSide accessed the Colonial network. The attackers stole 100 gigabytes of data in two hours. They then infected the company's network with ransomware that impacted many computer systems, including billing and accounting. Fortunately, pipeline's operational technology systems that actually move the oil were not directly compromised.

To prevent the ransomware from spreading, Colonial shut down its pipeline. They then engaged cybersecurity firm Mandiant (**www.mandiant.com**) to investigate the attack. Colonial also alerted the FBI, Cybersecurity and Infrastructure Security Agency, U.S. Department of Energy, and Department of Homeland Security of the incident.

The attack caused significant and immediate impacts. For example, many carriers in the airline industry experienced a jet fuel shortage. Also, some airports, including Atlanta and Nashville, experienced disruptions.

In addition, fear of a gas shortage caused panic buying and long lines at gas stations in many states, particularly in the

Southeast. There was also a spike in prices at the gas pump. In some areas, panic buying led to shortages as consumers purchased more gasoline than usual. Finally, the attack was classified as a national security threat because the pipeline transports oil from refineries to industry markets. As a result, on May 9, President Biden declared a state of emergency.

In addition to its impacts on the nation's fuel supplies, the attack compromised the personal information of nearly 6,000 individuals, most of whom were current or former Colonial employees and their family members. The hackers gained access to records, including names, contact information, birth dates, Social Security numbers, driver's license and military ID numbers, and health insurance information. On May 7, DarkSide demanded a ransom of 75 bitcoin, which was worth approximately $4.4 million.

Colonial CEO Joseph Blount stated that when DarkSide issued the ransom demand, it was not clear how widespread the intrusion was or how long it would take Colonial to restore the compromised systems. Colonial paid the ransom in hopes of speeding up its recovery time. The company restarted its pipeline operations on May 12.

Bitcoin is a cryptocurrency that ransomware attackers commonly use due to the mistaken belief that it cannot be traced. In fact, users must have a digital wallet to hold bitcoin. The U.S. Department of Justice (DOJ) was able to find the digital address of the wallet that the attackers had used. It then obtained a court order to seize the bitcoin. In a June 7 press conference, Deputy Attorney General Lisa Monaco announced that the DOJ's Ransomware and Digital Extortion Task Force had traced the ransom paid by Colonial. The operation recovered 64 of the 75 bitcoin that Colonial had paid. At the time of the recovery, the 64 bitcoin were worth approximately $2.4 million.

Court documents released by the DOJ revealed that the FBI followed the bitcoin public ledger to an address that received two payments on May 8 totaling 75 bitcoin. From there, the FBI accessed the funds by using the private key linked to the bitcoin address. The FBI did not specify how it obtained the key or why the full ransom amount was not recovered.

After the attack, DarkSide announced on its website that future attacks "would avoid social consequences." Soon afterward, DarkSide publicly shut down their operations. They then reappeared under the name BlackMatter, which shut down as well. A new ransomware group, called BlackCat or ALPHV, then appeared. Authorities believe that BlackCat is operated by the same people who created DarkSide and BlackMatter.

Questions

1. Why has ransomware become such a serious global problem? (*Hint:* What is a so-called "victimless crime"?)

2. You are the CEO of a company that has just experienced a ransomware attack. Discuss all the variables you would consider in your decision whether to pay the ransom. (*Hints:* Amount and type of data stolen, amount of ransom demanded, etc.)

3. Would you consider the Colonial Pipeline attack to also be a SCADA attack? Why or why not? Support your answer. (*Hint:* Look ahead to SCADA attacks later in this section.)

4. Would you consider the Colonial Pipeline attack to also be a supply chain attack? Why or why not? Support your answer. (*Hint:* Review the chapter-opening case.)

Sources: Compiled from N. Wasson, "Ransomware Gang behind Colonial Pipeline Attack Claims Another Major Victim," *HotHardware*, August 2, 2022; M. Kapko, "Luxembourg Supplier Encevo Hit by Ransomware Attack," *Cybersecurity Dive*, August 1, 2022; S. Kerner, "Colonial Pipeline Hack Explained: Everything You Need to Know," *TechTarget*, April 26, 2022; U.S. Department of State, "Reward Offers for Information to Bring DarkSide Ransomware Variant Co-Conspirators to Justice," press release, November 4, 2021; B. Fung, "Colonial Pipeline Says Ransomware Attack Also Led to Personal Information Being Stolen," *CNN Business*, August 16, 2021; D. Uberti, "How the FBI Got Colonial Pipeline's Ransom Money Back," *Wall Street Journal*, June 11, 2021; A. Culafi, "Mandiant: Compromised Colonial Pipeline Password Was Reused," *TechTarget*, June 9, 2021; K. Benner and N. Perlroth, "U.S. Seizes Share of Ransom from Hackers in Colonial Pipeline Attack," *New York Times*, June 8, 2021; A. Waldman, "FBI Seized Colonial Pipeline Ransom Using Private Key," *TechTarget*, June 8, 2021; R. Dudley and D. Golden, "The Colonial Pipeline Ransomware Hackers Had a Secret Weapon: Self-Promoting Cybersecurity Firms," *Wired*, May 24, 2021; L. Manfredi, "Colonial Pipeline Hacker DarkSide Reaped $90M from 47 Victims," *Fox News*, May 18, 2021; K. Lyons, "Colonial Pipeline Says Operations Back to Normal Following Ransomware Attack," *The Verge*, May 15, 2021; L. Newman, "Colonial Pipeline Paid a $5M Ransom—and Kept a Vicious Cycle Turning," *Wired*, May 14, 2021; W. Englund and E. Nakashima, "Panic Buying Strikes Southeastern United States as Shuttered Pipeline Resumes Operations," *Washington Post*, May 12, 2021; S. Nichols, "Colonial Pipeline Runs Dry Following Ransomware Attack," *TechTarget*, May 10, 2021; M. Russon, "U.S. Fuel Pipeline Hackers 'Didn't Mean to Create Problems,'" *BBC News*, May 10, 2021; and www.colpipe.com, accessed August 7, 2022.

Sabotage or Vandalism

Sabotage and vandalism are deliberate acts that involve defacing an organization's website, potentially damaging the organization's image and causing its customers to lose faith. One form of online vandalism is a hacktivist or cyberactivist operation. These are cases of high-tech civil disobedience to protest the operations, policies, or actions of an organization or government agency. For example, on February 25, 2022, Twitter accounts associated with Anonymous, a decentralized hacktivist movement, stated that they had launched cyberoperations against the Russian Federation in retaliation for the invasion of Ukraine.

The group temporarily disabled the website of the Defense Ministry along with other state-owned websites. Anonymous also linked 200 gigabytes of e-mails from a Belarusian weapons manufacturer that provided logistical support for Russia in the invasion of Ukraine. Anonymous also hacked into Russian television channels and played Ukrainian music through them and showed uncensored news of events in Ukraine.

Theft of Equipment or Information

Computing devices and storage devices are becoming smaller yet more powerful with vastly increased storage. Common examples are laptops, iPads, smartphones, digital cameras, thumb drives, and iPods. As a result, these devices are becoming easier to steal and easier for attackers to use to steal information. In fact, not all attacks on organizations involve sophisticated software.

Table 4.1 points out that one type of human mistake is carelessness with laptops and other small computers such as tablets and, particularly, smartphones. In fact, many computing devices have been stolen because of such carelessness. The cost of a stolen device includes the loss of data, the loss of intellectual property, device replacement, legal and regulatory costs, investigation fees, and lost productivity.

One form of theft, known as *dumpster diving*, involves rummaging through commercial or residential trash to find discarded information. Paper files, letters, memos, photographs, IDs, passwords, credit cards, and other forms of information can be found in dumpsters. Unfortunately, many people never consider that the sensitive items they throw in the trash might be recovered and used for fraudulent purposes.

Dumpster diving is not necessarily theft, because the legality of this act varies. Because dumpsters are usually located on private premises, dumpster diving is illegal in some parts of the United States. Even in these cases, however, these laws are enforced with varying degrees of rigor.

Identity Theft

Identity theft is the deliberate assumption of another person's identity, usually to gain access to his or her financial information or to frame him or her for a crime. Techniques for illegally obtaining personal information include the following:

- Stealing personal data in computer databases
- Infiltrating organizations that store large amounts of personal data; for example, data aggregators such as Acxiom (**www.acxiom.com**)
- Impersonating a trusted organization in an electronic communication (phishing)
- Stealing mail or dumpster diving

Consider this identity-theft scheme in May 2020. With 40 million Americans filing for jobless benefits as a result of COVID, criminals targeted outdated computer systems in some state unemployment offices. A Nigerian crime ring called Scattered Canary used stolen password data and Social Security numbers to file false unemployment claims in Washington and several other states.

The criminals stole approximately $650 million from Washington. When the state detected the breach in June 2020, officials were able to recover $333 million of the money. The damage was so extensive that the state used its National Guard to examine nearly 200,000 claims for fraud.

Recovering from identity theft is costly, time consuming, and burdensome. Victims also report problems in obtaining credit and obtaining or holding a job, as well as adverse effects on insurance or credit rates. Victims also state that it is often difficult to remove negative information from their records, such as their credit reports.

Compromises to Intellectual Property

Protecting intellectual property is a vital issue for people who make their livelihood in knowledge fields. **Intellectual property** is the property created by individuals or corporations that is protected under *trade secret*, *patent*, and *copyright* laws.

A **trade secret** is an intellectual work, such as a business plan, that is a company secret and is not based on public information. An example is the formula for Coca-Cola. A **patent** is an official document that grants the holder exclusive rights on an invention or a process for a

---

identity theft Crime in which someone uses the personal information of others to create a false identity and then uses it fraudulently.

intellectual property The intangible property created by individuals or corporations, which is protected under trade secret, patent, and copyright laws.

trade secret Intellectual work, such as a business plan, that is a company secret and is not based on public information.

patent A document that grants the holder exclusive rights on an invention or process for a specified period of time, currently 20 years.

copyright A grant from a governmental authority that provides the creator of intellectual property with ownership of it for a specified period of time, currently the life of the creator plus 70 years.

specified period of time. **Copyright** is a statutory grant that provides the creators or owners of intellectual property with ownership of the property, also for a designated period. Current U.S. laws award patents for 20 years and copyright protection for the life of the creator plus 70 years. Owners are entitled to collect fees from anyone who wants to copy their creations. It is important to note that these are definitions under U.S. law. There is some international standardization of copyrights and patents, but it is far from total. Therefore, there can be discrepancies between U.S. law and other countries' laws.

The most common intellectual property related to IT deals with software. In 1980, the U.S. Congress amended the Copyright Act to include software. The amendment provides protection for the *source code* and *object code* of computer software, but it does not clearly identify what is eligible for protection. For example, copyright law does not protect fundamental concepts, functions, and general features such as pull-down menus, colors, and icons. However, copying a software program without making payment to the owner—including giving a disc to a friend to install on his or her computer—is a copyright violation. Not surprisingly, this practice, called **piracy**, is a major problem for software vendors. The BSA (**www.bsa.org**) Global Software Piracy Study found that the commercial value of software theft totals billions of dollars per year.

piracy Copying a software program (other than freeware, demo software, etc.) without making payment to the owner.

Software Attacks

malware Malicious software such as viruses and worms.

Software attacks have evolved from the early years of the computer era, when attackers used malicious software—called **malware**—to infect as many computers worldwide as possible, to the profit-driven, Web-based attacks of today. Modern cybercriminals use sophisticated, blended malware attacks, typically through the Web, to make money.

Software attacks target all Internet-connected devices, even smart televisions. As increasing numbers of Internet of Things devices (see Chapter 8) are installed, they provide billions of new targets for cybercriminals to target. As a result, hackers could hold your connected home or connected car hostage. There is even the potential that hackers could infect medical devices, thereby putting lives directly at risk.

Table 4.2 displays a variety of software attacks. These attacks are grouped into three categories: remote attacks requiring user action, remote attacks requiring no user action, and software attacks initiated by programmers during the development of a system.

Not all cybercriminals are sophisticated, however. For example, a student at a U.S. university was sentenced to one year in prison for using keylogging software (discussed later in this chapter) to steal 750 fellow students' passwords and vote himself and four of his fraternity brothers into the student government's president and four vice president positions. The five positions would have brought the students a combined $36,000 in stipends.

The student was caught when university security personnel noticed strange activity on the campus network. Authorities identified the computer used in the activity from its IP address. On this computer, which belonged to the student in question, authorities found a PowerPoint presentation detailing the scheme. Authorities also found research on his computer, with queries such as "how to rig an election" and "jail time for keylogger."

Once the university caught on to the scheme, the student reportedly turned back to hacking to try to get himself out of trouble. He created new Facebook accounts in the names of actual classmates, going as far as conducting fake conversations between the accounts to try to deflect the blame. Those actions contributed to the one-year prison sentence, which the judge imposed even after the student pleaded guilty and requested probation.

Consider another example. In July 2019, the FBI and the bank Capital One (**www.capital one.com**) announced a huge data breach. Data stolen in the breach included 106 million credit card applications and compromised data such as names, addresses, phone numbers, e-mail addresses, dates of birth, 140,000 Social Security numbers, 80,000 bank account numbers, and some credit scores. The breach affected over 100 million Americans and 6 million Canadians. The bank stated that responding to the incident would cost between $100 million and $150 million.

On July 17, 2019, an unidentified person notified Capital One that the data had been posted on a GitHub account. The FBI examined the account and discovered the account owner's full name and résumé. Not only that but the suspect posted about her actions on Slack and Twitter. A search of her bedroom found "files and items" that referenced Capital One. Authorities charged her with computer fraud and wire fraud.

TABLE 4.2   Types of Software Attacks

Type	Description
Remote Attacks Requiring User Action	
Virus	Segment of computer code that performs malicious actions by attaching to another computer program
Polymorphic virus	Segment of computer code that modifies itself (i.e., changes its computer code) to avoid detection by anti-malware systems, while keeping its same functionality
Worm	Segment of computer code that performs malicious actions and will replicate, or spread, by itself (without requiring another computer program)
Phishing attack	Attacks that use deception to acquire sensitive personal information by masquerading as official looking e-mails or instant messages
Spear phishing attack	Phishing attacks target large groups of people. In spear phishing attacks, the attackers find out as much information about an individual as possible to improve their chances that phishing techniques will be successful and obtain sensitive, personal information
Whaling attack	Phishing attack that targets high-value individuals such as senior executives in an attempt to steal sensitive information from a company such as financial data or personal details about employees
Smishing attack	Short for "voice phishing," these attacks attempt to defraud people over the phone
Vishing attack	A phishing attack carried out over mobile text message. Also known as Short Message Service phishing
Remote Attacks Needing No User Action	
Denial-of-service attack	An attacker sends so many information requests to a target computer system that the target cannot manage them successfully and typically ceases to function (crashes)
Distributed denial-of-service attack	An attacker first takes over many computers, typically by using malicious software. These computers are called *zombies* or **bots**. The attacker uses these bots—which form a **botnet**—to deliver a coordinated stream of information requests to a target computer, causing it to crash
Attacks by a Programmer Developing a System	
Trojan horse	Software programs that hide in other computer programs and reveal their designed behavior only when they are activated
Back door	Typically a password, known only to the attacker, that allows him or her to access a computer system at will, without having to go through any security procedures (also called a *trap door*)
Logic bomb	A segment of computer code that is embedded within an organization's existing computer programs and is designed to activate and perform a destructive action at a certain time or date

virus   Malicious software that can attach itself to (or "infect") other computer programs without the owner of the program being aware of the infection.

worm   Destructive programs that replicate themselves without requiring another program to provide a safe environment for replication.

phishing attack   An e-mail attack that uses deception to fraudulently acquire sensitive personal information by masquerading as an official looking e-mail.

spear phishing   An attack in which the perpetrators find out as much information about an individual as possible to improve their chances that phishing techniques will obtain sensitive, personal information.

distributed denial of service (DDoS) attack   A denial of service attack that sends a flood of data packets from many compromised computers simultaneously.

bot   A computer that has been compromised by, and under the control of, a hacker.

botnet   A network of computers that have been compromised by, and under control of, a hacker, who is called the botmaster.

Trojan horse   A software program containing a hidden function that presents a security risk.

logic bombs   Segments of computer code embedded within an organization's existing computer programs.

Alien Software

Many personal computers have alien software, or *pestware*, running on them that the owners are unaware of. **Alien software** is clandestine software that is installed on your computer through duplicitous methods. It typically is not as malicious as viruses, worms, or Trojan horses, but it does use up valuable system resources. It can also enable other parties to track your Web surfing habits and other personal behaviors.

The vast majority of pestware is **adware**—software that causes pop-up advertisements to appear on your screen. Adware is common because it works. According to advertising

alien software   Clandestine software that is installed on your computer through duplicitous methods.

adware   Alien software designed to help pop-up advertisements appear on your screen.

agencies, for every 100 people who close a pop-up ad, 3 click on it. This "hit rate" is extremely high for Internet advertising.

spyware Alien software that can record your keystrokes or capture your passwords.

Spyware is software that collects personal information about users without their consent. Three common types of spyware are stalkerware, keystroke loggers, and screen scrapers.

Stalkerware is spyware used to monitor people close to the perpetrator. Victims typically do not know the stalkerware is on their device unless they run an antivirus scan. Developers of stalkerware market their apps as child safety or anti-theft tools. However, these apps can easily be used for the purpose of spying on a partner.

This software has powerful surveillance functions which include keylogging; making screenshots; monitoring Internet activity; recording location; recording video and phone calls; and intercepting app communications made via Skype, Facebook, WhatsApp, and iMessage, as well as others. Most stalkerware apps are not available on official app stores. Installation does not necessarily require access to the victim's device. Rather, a perpetrator can send the intended victim an innocuous-seeming download, such as a picture.

Keystroke loggers, also called *keyloggers*, record both your individual keystrokes and your Web browsing history. The purposes range from criminal—for example, theft of passwords and sensitive personal information such as credit card numbers—to annoying—for example, recording your Internet search history for targeted advertising.

Companies have attempted to counter keyloggers by switching to other forms of identifying users. For example, at some point all of us have been forced to look at wavy, distorted letters and type them correctly into a box. That string of letters is called a *CAPTCHA*, and it is a test. The point of CAPTCHA is that computers cannot (yet) accurately read those distorted letters. Therefore, the fact that you can transcribe them means that you are probably not a software program run by an unauthorized person, such as a spammer. As a result, attackers have turned to *screen scrapers*, or *screen grabbers*. This software records a continuous "movie" of a screen's contents rather than simply recording keystrokes.

spamware Alien software that uses your computer as a launch platform for spammers.

spam Unsolicited e-mail.

Spamware is pestware that uses your computer as a launch pad for spammers. Spam is unsolicited e-mail, usually advertising for products and services. When your computer is infected with spamware, e-mails from spammers are sent to everyone in your e-mail address book, but they appear to come from you.

Not only is spam a nuisance, but it wastes time and money. Spam costs U.S. companies billions of dollars every year. These costs arise from productivity losses, clogged e-mail systems, additional storage, user support, and antispam software. Spam can also carry viruses and worms, making it even more dangerous.

A new tool from DoNotPay (**www.donotpay.com**) offers help in unsubscribing from e-mail lists. To use most subscription management tools, such as Unroll.me, you have to grant the service access to your e-mail account, so that it can analyze your messages.

DoNotPay's antispam service works differently. You just forward your spam e-mails to **spam@donotpay.com** and a bot (software robot) will automatically unsubscribe you from that mailing list. In that way, DoNotPay does not need access to your account and only sees e-mails that you want it to manage.

Going further, DoNotPay will check if there is currently a class action settlement against the organization that sent you the e-mail. If there is, you can instruct DoNotPay to automatically claim any compensation for which you are eligible on your behalf. If your claim is successful, you will receive payment. DoNotPay is not involved in the payment transaction.

cookies Small amounts of information that websites store on your computer, temporarily or more or less permanently.

Cookies are small amounts of information that websites store on your computer, temporarily or more or less permanently. In many cases, cookies are useful and innocuous. For example, some cookies are passwords and user IDs that you do not want to retype every time you access the website that issued the cookie. Cookies are also necessary for online shopping because merchants use them for your shopping carts. See **IT's About Business 3.2** for a thorough discussion of the different types of cookies and their impact on our privacy.

Tracking cookies, however, can be used to track your path through a website, the time you spend there, what links you click on, and other details that the company wants to record, usually for marketing purposes. Tracking cookies can also combine this information with your name, purchases, credit card information, and other personal data to develop an intrusive profile of your spending habits.

Most cookies can be read only by the party that created them. However, some companies that manage online banner advertising are, in essence, cookie-sharing rings. These companies can track information such as which pages you load and which ads you click on. They then share this information with their client websites, which may number in the thousands.

Supervisory Control and Data Acquisition (SCADA) Attacks

SCADA refers to a large-scale distributed measurement and control system. SCADA systems are used to monitor or to control chemical, physical, and transport processes such as those used in oil refineries, water and sewage treatment plants, electrical generators, and nuclear power plants. Essentially, SCADA systems provide a link between the physical world and the electronic world.

SCADA systems consist of multiple sensors, a master computer, and communications infrastructure. The sensors connect to physical equipment. They read status data such as the open/closed status of a switch or a valve, as well as measurements such as pressure, flow, voltage, and current. They control the equipment by sending signals to it, such as opening or closing a switch or a valve or setting the speed of a pump. The sensors are connected in a network, and each sensor typically has an Internet address (Internet Protocol, or IP, address, discussed in Chapter 6). If attackers gain access to the network, then they can cause serious damage, such as disrupting the power grid over a large area or upsetting the operations of a large chemical or nuclear plant. Such actions could have catastrophic results. Consider these examples.

- In April 2022, Russian hackers targeted the Ukrainian power grid and attempted to cause a blackout that would have affected two million people. The hackers attempted to destroy computers at a Ukrainian energy company, using malware specifically designed to destroy targeted systems by erasing key data and rendering them useless. Ukrainian officials said that they successfully handled the attack, which they stated was intended to support Russian military operations in eastern Ukraine.

- In October 2021, an employee of a water treatment plant in the city of Oldsmar, Florida, noticed that his mouse cursor was moving strangely and was not under his control. The cursor began clicking through the water treatment plant's controls. Within seconds, the intruder was attempting to change the water supply's levels of sodium hydroxide, also known as caustic soda, increasing the setting from 100 parts per million to 11,100 parts per million. In low concentrations, the chemical regulates the pH level of drinkable water. At high levels, it severely damages any human tissue that it touches. According to city officials, the operator quickly spotted the intrusion and returned the sodium hydroxide to normal levels.

- Another type of SCADA attack using hardware rather than software occurred in July 2020 when a drone approached a Pennsylvania power substation. Two 4-foot nylon ropes dangled from the drone, with a thick copper wire connected to the ends with electrical tape. The drone was stripped of any identifiable markings, as well as its onboard camera and memory card, in an effort by its owner to avoid detection. Its likely goal, according to the Department of Homeland Security, the FBI, and the National Counterterrorism Center, was to create a short circuit and disrupt operations of the utility. The drone crashed before it reached its target and the operator was not found.

Cyberterrorism and Cyberwarfare

Cyberterrorism and **cyberwarfare** refer to malicious acts in which attackers use a target's computer systems, particularly through the Internet, to cause physical, real-world harm or severe disruption, often to carry out a political agenda. These actions range from gathering data to attacking critical infrastructure, for example, through SCADA systems. We treat the two types of attacks as synonymous here, even though cyberterrorism is typically carried out by individuals or groups, whereas cyberwarfare is carried out by nation-states or non-state actors such as terrorists.

cyberterrorism
A premeditated, politically motivated attack against information, computer systems, computer programs, and data that results in violence against noncombatant targets by subnational groups or clandestine agents.

cyberwarfare War in which a country's information systems could be paralyzed from a massive attack by destructive software.

1. Why has the theft of computing devices become more serious over time?
2. What are the three types of software attacks?
3. Define alien software and explain why it is a serious problem.
4. What is a SCADA system? Why can attacks against SCADA systems have catastrophic consequences?

4.4 What Organizations Are Doing to Protect Information Resources

LEARNING OBJECTIVE

Describe the three risk mitigation strategies, and provide an example of each one in the context of owning a home.

Why is stopping cybercriminals such a challenge? Table 4.3 illustrates the many major difficulties involved in protecting information. Because organizing an appropriate defense system is so important to the entire enterprise, it is one of the major responsibilities of any prudent CIO as well as of the functional managers who control information resources. In fact, IT security is the business of *everyone* in an organization.

In addition to the problems listed in Table 4.3, another reason why information resources are difficult to protect is that the online commerce industry is not particularly willing to install safeguards that would make completing transactions more difficult or complicated. As one example, merchants could demand passwords or personal identification numbers for all credit card transactions. However, these requirements might discourage people from shopping online. For credit card companies, it is cheaper to block a stolen credit card and move on than to invest time and money prosecuting cybercriminals.

The final reason why information resources are difficult to protect is that it is extremely difficult to catch perpetrators. However, it is possible to catch attackers, albeit with great effort, time, and expense, as this chapter's closing case illustrates.

Organizations spend a great deal of time and money protecting their information resources. Before doing so, they perform risk management.

TABLE 4.3 Difficulties in Protecting Information Resources

Hundreds of potential threats exist.
Computing resources may be situated in many locations.
Many individuals control or have access to information assets.
Computer networks can be located outside the organization, making them difficult to protect.
Rapid technological changes make some controls obsolete as soon as they are installed.
Many computer crimes are undetected for a long period of time, so it is difficult to learn from experience.
People tend to violate security procedures because the procedures are inconvenient.
The amount of computer knowledge necessary to commit computer crimes is usually minimal. As a matter of fact, a potential criminal can learn hacking, free, from the Internet.
The costs of preventing hazards can be very high. Therefore, most organizations simply cannot afford to protect themselves against all possible hazards.
It is difficult to conduct a cost-benefit justification for controls before an attack occurs because it is difficult to assess the impact of a hypothetical attack.

A **risk** is the probability that a threat will impact an information resource. The goal of **risk management** is to identify, control, and minimize the impact of threats. In other words, risk management seeks to reduce risk to acceptable levels.

FIN The Enterprise Risk Management (ERM) framework guides risk management in the enterprise. ERM is a risk-based approach to managing an enterprise that integrates internal control, the Sarbanes–Oxley Act mandates, and strategic planning. ERM consists of several steps:

- Determine the relationship of risk to organizational goals.

- Differentiate between risks and opportunities.

- Assess risk, which involves three steps: (1) assess the value of each asset being protected, (2) estimate the probability that each asset will be compromised, and (3) compare the probable costs of the asset's being compromised with the costs of protecting that asset. The organization then considers how to mitigate the risk.

    Risk mitigation has two functions: (1) implementing controls to prevent identified threats from occurring and (2) developing a means of recovery if the threat becomes a reality. The three most common risk mitigation strategies are:

    Risk acceptance: Accept the potential risk, continue operating with no controls, and absorb any damages that occur.

    Risk transference: Transfer the risk by using other means to compensate for the loss, such as by purchasing insurance.

    Risk limitation: Limit the risk by implementing controls that minimize the impact of the threat.

- Implement controls.

- Evaluate the controls. Examine the costs of implementing adequate control measures against the value of those control measures. If the costs of implementing a control are greater than the value of the asset being protected, the control is not cost effective. Organizations evaluate controls through information systems auditing.

    Companies implement security controls to ensure that information systems function properly. These controls can be installed in the original system, or they can be added after a system is in operation. Installing controls is necessary but not sufficient to provide adequate security. People who are also responsible for security need to answer questions such as: Are all controls installed as intended? Are they effective? Has any breach of security occurred? If so, what actions are required to prevent future breaches?

    These questions must be answered by independent and unbiased observers. Such observers perform the task of *information systems auditing*. In an IS environment, an **audit** is an examination of information systems, their inputs, outputs, and processing.

Created by the International Systems Audit and Control Association (ISACA; www .isaca.org), COBIT 5 provides a framework for IT security and IT auditing. The framework's intent is to align IT with business objectives and manage risk. The COBIT 5 framework is based on five principles, the first three of which apply most directly to security issues.

1. Meeting stakeholder needs: A system should be in place that addresses enterprise information security requirements. The system should include metrics for the number of clearly defined key security roles and the number of security-related incidents reported.

2. Covering the enterprise end-to-end: A security plan should be accepted and communicated throughout the organization. This process includes the level of stakeholder satisfaction with the plan, the number of security solutions that are different from those in the plan, and the number of security solutions deviating from the enterprise security architecture that can lead to security gaps and possibly increase the time needed to resolve security or compliance issues.

3. Applying a single, integrated framework: Information security solutions are implemented throughout the organization. The solutions include the number of services and solutions that align with the security plan and security incidents caused by noncompliance with the security plan.

4. Enabling a holistic approach.

5. Separating governance from management.

risk   The likelihood that a threat will occur.

risk management   A process that identifies, controls, and minimizes the impact of threats, in an effort to reduce risk to manageable levels.

audit   An examination of information systems, their inputs, outputs, and processing.

1. Identify and discuss several reasons why it is difficult to protect information resources.
2. Compare and contrast risk management and risk analysis.

4.5 Information Security Controls

LEARNING OBJECTIVE

Identify the three major types of controls that organizations can use to protect their information resources, and provide an example of each one.

controls Defense mechanisms (also called *countermeasures*).

To protect their information assets, organizations implement **controls**, or defense mechanisms (also called *countermeasures*). These controls are designed to protect all of the components of an information system, including data, software, hardware, and networks. Because there are so many diverse threats, organizations use layers of controls, or *defense-in-depth*.

Controls are intended to prevent accidental hazards, deter intentional acts, detect problems as early as possible, enhance damage recovery, and correct problems. Before you study controls in more detail, it is important to emphasize that the single most valuable control is user education and training. Effective and ongoing education makes every member of the organization aware of the vital importance of information security.

In this section, you will learn about three major types of controls: physical controls, access controls, and communications controls. **Figure 4.2** illustrates these controls. In addition to applying controls, organizations plan for business continuity in case of a disaster, and they periodically audit their information resources to detect possible threats. You will study these topics in this section as well.

Physical Controls

physical controls Controls that restrict unauthorized individuals from gaining access to a company's computer facilities.

Physical controls prevent unauthorized individuals from gaining access to a company's facilities. Common physical controls include walls, doors, fencing, gates, locks, badges, guards, and alarm systems. More sophisticated physical controls include pressure sensors, temperature sensors, and motion detectors. One shortcoming of physical controls is that they can be inconvenient to employees.

Guards deserve special mention because they have very difficult jobs, for at least two reasons. First, their jobs are boring and repetitive and generally do not pay well. Second, if guards perform their jobs thoroughly, the other employees may harass them, particularly if they slow up the process of entering the facility.

Organizations also implement physical security measures that limit computer users to acceptable login times and locations. These controls also limit the number of unsuccessful login attempts, and they require all employees to log off their computers when they leave for the day. They also set the employees' computers to automatically log off the user after a certain period of disuse.

A basic security strategy for organizations is to be prepared for any eventuality. A critical element in any security system is a *business continuity plan*, also known as a *disaster recovery plan*.

business continuity The chain of events linking planning to protection and to recovery.

Business continuity is the chain of events linking planning to protection and to recovery. The purpose of the business continuity plan is to provide guidance to people who keep the business operating after a disaster occurs. Employees use this plan to prepare for, respond to, and recover from events that affect the security of information assets. The objective is to

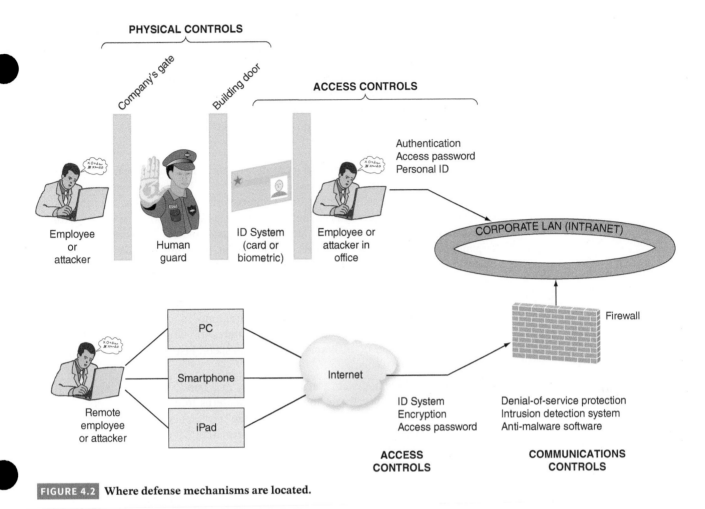

FIGURE 4.2 Where defense mechanisms are located.

restore the business to normal operations as quickly as possible following an attack. The plan is intended to ensure that critical business functions continue.

In the event of a major disaster, organizations can employ several strategies for business continuity. These strategies include hot sites, warm sites, and cold sites. A *hot site* is a fully configured computer facility with all of the company's services, communications links, and physical plant operations. A hot site duplicates computing resources, peripherals, telephone systems, applications, and workstations. A *warm site* provides many of the same services and options as the hot site. However, it typically does not include the actual applications the company needs. A warm site includes computing equipment such as servers, but it often does not include user workstations. A *cold site* provides only rudimentary services and facilities, such as a building or a room with heating, air conditioning, and humidity control. This type of site provides no computer hardware or user workstations.

Hot sites reduce risk to the greatest extent, but they are the most expensive option. Conversely, cold sites reduce risk the least, but they are the least expensive option.

Access Controls

Access controls restrict unauthorized individuals from using information resources. These controls involve two major functions: authentication and authorization. **Authentication** confirms the identity of the person requiring access. After the person is authenticated (identified), the next step is authorization. **Authorization** determines which actions, rights, or privileges the person has, based on his or her verified identity. Let's examine these functions more closely.

access controls   Controls that restrict unauthorized individuals from using information resources and are concerned with user identification.

authentication   A process that determines the identity of the person requiring access.

authorization   A process that determines which actions, rights, or privileges the person has, based on verified identity.

Authentication

To authenticate (identify) authorized personnel, an organization can use one or more of the following methods: something the user is, something the user has, something the user does, or something the user knows.

Something the user is, also known as **biometrics**, is an authentication method that examines a person's innate physical characteristics. There are many different types of biometrics, which include fingerprint scanning, palm prints, retinal scanning, iris scanning, analysis of heartbeats and body temperature, voice recognition, and facial recognition. Let's look at examples of how organizations use biometrics for authentication.

biometrics   The science and technology of authentication (i.e., establishing the identity of an individual) by measuring the subject's physiological or behavioral characteristics.

- **POM**   Your voice changes as you age, becoming a little rougher each year. Nuance Communications Gatekeeper (**www.nuance.com**), a voice biometrics tool, analyzes the caller's voice "roughness" and other "micro-characteristics" that humans cannot hear to confirm that an older person is calling. Nuance customer Telefonica (**www.telefonica.com/en**) used the tool to help with increased contact center volume during the COVID-19 pandemic. When the tool identifies an older person, the company routes them to priority customer service with shorter wait times and protocols to prevent fraudulent account takeover.

- **FIN**   At Barclays Bank (**www.barclays.co.uk**), over 65 percent of calls are now handled by voice recognition, providing enrolled customers much faster, easier access to account services. Rather than spending five minutes providing passwords, PINs, and answering security questions, Barclays' customers spend just 20 seconds verifying their identities with voice recognition.

- **FIN**   Security personnel were watching activity in a bank branch. Biometric sensors had detected unusual heartbeats and body heat patterns from new customers who had entered to open an account. It turns out that those "customers" had entered the United States days before as human cargo on a ship from another country. A criminal gang was using them to orchestrate financial fraud. The sensors had detected telltale signs of stress, alerting bank personnel to the attempted fraud.

Something the user has is an authentication mechanism that includes regular identification (ID) cards, smart ID cards, and tokens. *Regular ID cards*, or *dumb cards*, typically have the person's picture and often his or her signature. *Smart ID cards* have an embedded chip that stores pertinent information about the user. (Smart ID cards used for identification differ from smart cards used in electronic commerce, which you learn about in Chapter 7. Both types of card have embedded chips, but they are used for different purposes.) *Tokens* have embedded chips and a digital display that presents a login number that the employees use to access the organization's network. The number changes with each login.

Something the user does is an authentication mechanism that includes voice recognition, signature recognition, and keystroke dynamics. In *voice recognition*, the user speaks a phrase—for example, his or her name and department—that has previously been recorded under controlled conditions. The voice recognition system matches the two voice signals.

In *signature recognition*, the user signs his or her name, and the system matches this signature with one previously recorded under controlled, monitored conditions. Signature recognition systems also match the speed and the pressure of the signature.

Keystroke dynamics identifies an individual based on his or her typing pattern and the rhythm and speed of typing on a keyboard. This mechanism creates a baseline for users' typing and then uses that baseline to watch for abnormalities. Keystroke dynamics is also called, somewhat confusingly, behavioral biometrics. We place it here because the process is what a user does.

The main two measurements used for keystroke dynamics are dwell time and flight time. Dwell time is how long a key is pressed and flight time is the length of time between releasing one key and pressing the next key. Other measurements include frequent mistakes and which shift keys an individual uses for capitalization.

Something the user knows is an authentication mechanism that includes passwords and passphrases. **Passwords** are private combinations of characters that only the user should know. Passwords, which are often weak and repeated, present a huge information security problem to organizations and to our online lives. Security firms typically find the most popular passwords are "123456," "123456789," "qwerty," and "password."

password   A private combination of characters that only the user should know.

Most of us have to remember numerous passwords for different online services, and we typically must choose complicated strings of characters to make them harder to guess. Passwords must effectively manage the trade-off between convenience and security. For example, if passwords are 50 characters in length and include special symbols, they might keep your computer and its files safe, but they would be impossible to remember.

We have all bought into the idea that a password is sufficient to protect our data, as long as it is sufficiently elaborate. In reality, however, passwords by themselves can no longer protect us, regardless of how unique or complex we make them. In fact, security experts refer to passwords and PINs as a "double fail." First, they are easily stolen or hacked and easily forgotten. Second, they provide very poor security and a terrible customer experience at the same time.

Weak passwords leave users and organizations vulnerable to hacking. In fact, they are the number one target of cybercriminals, and some 80 percent of successful breaches involve weak or stolen passwords. Attackers employ many strategies to obtain our passwords, no matter how strong they are. They can guess them, steal them (with phishing or spear phishing attacks), crack them using brute force computation, guess them from information on social media profiles, or obtain them online. (*Brute force password cracking* means that a computer system tries all possible combinations of characters until a password is discovered.)

If you must use passwords, make them *strong passwords*, which are more difficult for hackers to discover. Strong passwords should be at least 12 characters long. The more characters your password has, the stronger it will be. Strong passwords should include a mix of uppercase and lowercase letters, a mix of letters and numbers, and special characters such as ! * & $ or #.

Many users have turned to passphrases. A **passphrase** is a series of characters that is longer than a password but is still easy to memorize. Examples of passphrases are "maytheforcebewithyoualways" and "thisisasgoodasitgets."

The problems with passwords and potentially passphrases remain. Given these problems, what are users and businesses supposed to do?

passphrase A series of characters that is longer than a password but is still easy to memorize.

- *Use password managers.*

    Rather than users creating, and then trying to remember, passwords and passphrases, security experts recommend the use of password managers. *Password managers* are software packages that provide users with the capability to generate unique, long, complex, easily changed passwords for their online accounts. These packages also offer the secure, encrypted storage of these passwords in either a local or cloud-based password vault. Users must provide a single master password to access the vault. By using a password manager, users do not have to memorize different passwords for all their online accounts.

    However, if hackers access the password to the vault, then they have access to all the user's accounts. Therefore, many password managers provide two-factor authentication for additional security.

- *Use multifactor authorization.*

    To identify authorized users more efficiently and effectively, organizations are implementing more than one type of authentication, a strategy known as *multifactor authentication*. This system is particularly important when users log in from remote locations.

    Single-factor authentication, which is notoriously weak, commonly consists simply of a password. Two-factor authentication consists of a password plus one type of biometric identification, such as a fingerprint. Three-factor authentication is any combination of three authentication methods.

    Multifactor authentication is useful for several reasons. For example, voice recognition is effective when a user calls from an office, but it is less optimal when calling from a crowded subway or busy street. Similarly, fingerprint and iris scanners are effective when users are not busy with other tasks, but they are less than optimal when users are driving.

    Multifactor authentication enables increasingly powerful security processes. For example, a quick fingerprint scan in a mobile banking app could enable a customer to access their account balance or perform other low-level functions. However, a request to transfer money, pay bills, or apply for a line of credit would trigger a request for voice or iris recognition. In most cases, the more factors the system uses, the more reliable it is.

However, stronger authentication is also more expensive, and, as with strong passwords, it can be irritating to users.

- *Use passwordless authentication.*

  Passwordless authentication is a means to verify a user's identity without using a password. Passwordless authentication decreases complexity while increasing security. This type of authentication can be achieved in several different ways:

- Use biometrics, including physical biometrics (see above), as well as behavioral biometrics.

- Use tokens. For example, consider the YubiKey from Yubico (**www.yubico.com**), which is a hardware-based security key. The key replaces passwords and passphrases with strong hardware-based authentication using private/public key (asymmetric) cryptography. In addition, a single security key can work across thousands of accounts.

- Use magic links. A user enters his or her e-mail address and the system sends them an e-mail. The e-mail contains a link, which when clicked, grants access to the user.

  Several initiatives are under way to improve the authentication process under the auspices of the Fast Identity Online (FIDO) alliance (**www.fidoalliance.org**). FIDO is an industry consortium that was created to address the inability of strong authentication devices to work together and the problems that users face in creating and remembering multiple usernames and passwords.

  FIDO2 is the latest specification of the FIDO Alliance. FIDO2 enables authentication where users identify themselves with cryptographic authenticators, such as biometrics, or external authenticators, such as FIDO keys (see passkeys below), tokens, or mobile devices. FIDO2 provides the option of using two-factor authentication.

  In May 2022, with the support of Google, Apple, and Microsoft, the FIDO Alliance announced a new type of authentication that uses FIDO2-based passkeys stored on your phone to unlock your online accounts without requiring a password or passphrase. The passkey will be encrypted to protect it from compromise and will be accessible only when you unlock your phone. When you try to sign into an app or website either on the phone itself, a nearby computer, or other device, the passkey will automatically log you in regardless of the operating system or browser and without you having to enroll or re-enroll your device. If you switch to a new phone, your passkey will transfer seamlessly to it.

- *Use Adaptive authentication.*

  The next step is to combine passwordless authentication with adaptive (behavioral) authentication. Adaptive authentication uses machine learning (see Chapter 14) to develop patterns of typical user behavior. Any time the system notices a deviation from the pattern, it regards the log-in attempt as risky and takes appropriate actions.

  For example, suppose a user logs in to the system via their laptop early in the morning every weekday. Over time, the system establishes that this is their typical log-in behavior. Then one day, the user logs in to the system on a Saturday.

  The user used the same laptop, it was early in the morning, and their geographical location remained the same. The system calculates a relatively higher risk score for this behavior, which warrants the use of a secondary authentication factor, such as a token.

  A few days later, the system notices a log-in attempt from the same user, originating from a different country and from a different device. The system calculates an exponentially higher risk score and blocks the user. It is later discovered that it was a log-in attempt from a cybercriminal who had spoofed the user's identity.

privilege A collection of related computer system operations that can be performed by users of the system.

least privilege A principle that users be granted the privilege for some activity only if there is a justifiable need to grant this authorization.

Authorization   After users have been properly authenticated, the rights and privileges to which they are entitled on the organization's systems are established in a process called *authorization*. A **privilege** is a collection of related computer system operations that a user is authorized to perform. Companies typically base authorization policies on the principle of **least privilege**, which posits that users be granted the privilege for an activity only if there is a justifiable need for them to perform that activity.

Communications Controls

Communications controls (also called **network controls**) secure the movement of data across networks. Communications controls consist of firewalls, anti-malware systems, whitelisting and blacklisting, encryption, virtual private networks (VPNs), transport layer security (TLS), and employee monitoring systems.

Firewalls A **firewall** is a system that prevents a specific type of information from moving between untrusted networks, such as the Internet, and private networks, such as your company's network. Put simply, firewalls prevent unauthorized Internet users from accessing private networks. All messages entering or leaving your company's network pass through a firewall. The firewall examines each message and blocks those that do not meet specified security rules.

Firewalls range from simple, for home use, to very complex for organizational use. **Figure 4.3(a)** illustrates a basic firewall for a home computer. In this case, the firewall is implemented as software on the home computer. **Figure 4.3(b)** shows an organization that has implemented an external firewall, which faces the Internet, and an internal firewall, which faces the company network. Corporate firewalls typically consist of software running on a computer dedicated to the task. A **demilitarized zone (DMZ)** is located between the two firewalls. Messages from the Internet must first pass through the external firewall. If they conform to the defined security rules, they are then sent to company servers located in the DMZ. These servers typically handle Web page requests and e-mail. Any messages designated for the company's internal network—for example, its intranet—must pass through the internal firewall, again with its own defined security rules, to gain access to the company's private network.

The danger from viruses and worms is so severe that many organizations are placing firewalls at strategic points *inside* their private networks. In this way, if a virus or worm does get through both the external and internal firewalls, then the internal damage may be contained.

Anti-malware Systems **Anti-malware systems**, also called *antivirus* or *AV* software, are software packages that attempt to identify and eliminate viruses and worms, and other malicious software. AV software is implemented at the organizational level by the IS department. Hundreds of AV software packages are currently available. Among the best known are Norton AntiVirus (www.broadcom.com), McAfee VirusScan (www.mcafee.com), and Trend Micro Maximum Security (www.trendmicro.com).

Anti-malware systems are generally reactive. Whereas firewalls filter network traffic according to categories of activities that are likely to cause problems, anti-malware systems

communications controls (also network controls) Controls that deal with the movement of data across networks.

network controls See **communications controls.**

firewall A system (either hardware, software, or a combination of both) that prevents a specific type of information from moving between untrusted networks, such as the Internet, and private networks, such as your company's network.

demilitarized zone (DMZ) A separate organizational local area network that is located between an organization's internal network and an external network, usually the Internet.

anti-malware systems (antivirus software) Software packages that attempt to identify and eliminate viruses, worms, and other malicious software.

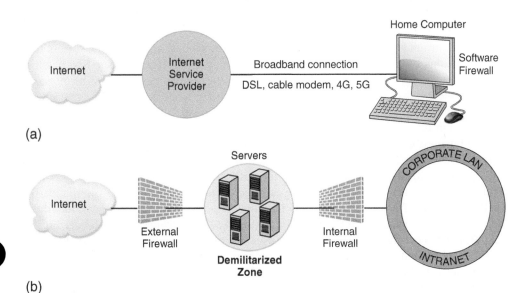

(a)

(b)

FIGURE 4.3 **(a) Basic firewall for a home computer. (b) Organization with two firewalls and a demilitarized zone.**

filter traffic according to a database of specific problems. These systems create definitions, or signatures, of various types of malware and then update these signatures in their products. The anti-malware software then examines suspicious computer code to determine whether it matches a known signature. If the software identifies a match, then it removes the code. For this reason, organizations regularly update their malware definitions.

Because malware is such a serious problem, the leading vendors are rapidly developing anti-malware systems that function proactively as well as reactively. These systems evaluate behavior rather than relying entirely on signature matching. In theory, therefore, it is possible to catch malware before it can infect systems.

It is important to note that organizations must not rely only on anti-malware systems. The reason is that new types of malware are appearing too rapidly for such systems to keep pace. Therefore, multifactor authentication is critically important.

Whitelisting and Blacklisting

A report by the Yankee Group (www.451research.com), a technology research and consulting firm, stated that 99 percent of organizations had installed anti-malware systems, but 62 percent still suffered malware attacks. As we have seen, anti-malware systems are usually reactive, and malware continues to infect companies.

One solution to this problem is whitelisting. Whitelisting is a process in which a company identifies the software that it will allow to run on its computers. Whitelisting permits acceptable software to run, and it either prevents any other software from running or lets new software run only in a quarantine environment until the company can verify its validity.

Whereas whitelisting allows nothing to run unless it is on the whitelist, blacklisting allows everything to run unless it is on the blacklist. A blacklist, then, includes certain types of software that are not allowed to run in the company environment. For example, a company might blacklist peer-to-peer file sharing on its systems. Besides software, people, devices, and websites can also be whitelisted and blacklisted.

Encryption

Organizations that do not have a secure channel for sending information use encryption to stop unauthorized eavesdroppers. Encryption is the process of converting an original message into a form that cannot be read by anyone except the intended receiver.

All encryption systems use a key, which is the code that scrambles and then decodes the messages. The majority of encryption systems use public-key encryption. Public-key encryption—also known as *asymmetric encryption*—uses two different keys: a public key and a private key (see Figure 4.4). The public key (locking key) and the private key (the unlocking key) are created simultaneously using the same mathematical formula or algorithm. Because the two keys are mathematically related, the data encrypted with one key can be decrypted by using the other key. The public key is publicly available in a directory that all parties can access. The private key is kept secret, never shared with anyone, and never sent across the Internet. In this system, if Hannah wants to send a message to Harrison, she first obtains Harrison's public key (locking key), which she uses to encrypt her message (put the message in the "two-lock box"). When Harrison receives Hannah's message, he uses his private key to decrypt it (open the box).

Although this arrangement is adequate for personal information, organizations that conduct business over the Internet require a more complex system. In these cases, a third party, called a certificate authority, acts as a trusted intermediary between the companies. The certificate authority issues digital certificates and verifies the integrity of the certificates. A digital certificate is an electronic document attached to a file that certifies that the file is from the organization it claims to be from and has not been modified from its original format. As you can see in Figure 4.5, Sony requests a digital certificate from VeriSign, a certificate authority, and it uses this certificate when it conducts business with Dell. Note that the digital certificate contains an identification number, the issuer, validity dates, and the requester's public key. For examples of certificate authorities, see www.entrust.com, www.verisign.com, www.cybertrust.com, www.secude.com, and www.thawte.com.

---

whitelisting A process in which a company identifies acceptable software and permits it to run, and either prevents anything else from running or lets new software run in a quarantined environment until the company can verify its validity.

blacklisting A process in which a company identifies certain types of software that are not allowed to run in the company environment.

encryption The process of converting an original message into a form that cannot be read by anyone except the intended recipient.

public-key encryption (also called *asymmetric encryption*) A type of encryption that uses two different keys: a public key and a private key.

certificate authority A third party that acts as a trusted intermediary between computers (and companies) by issuing digital certificates and verifying the worth and integrity of the certificates.

digital certificate An electronic document attached to a file certifying that the file is from the organization it claims to be from and has not been modified from its original format or content.

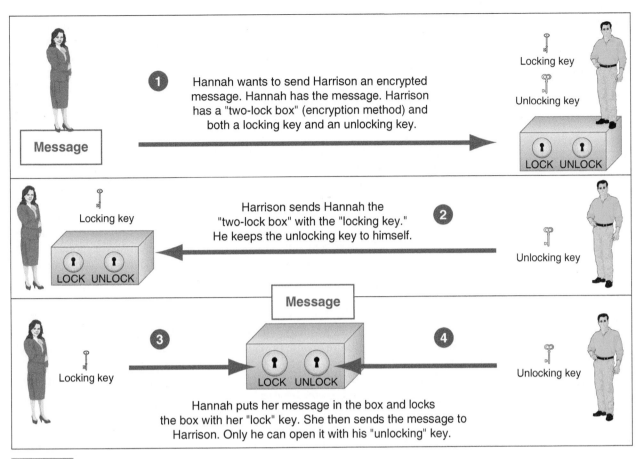

FIGURE 4.4   How public-key encryption works.

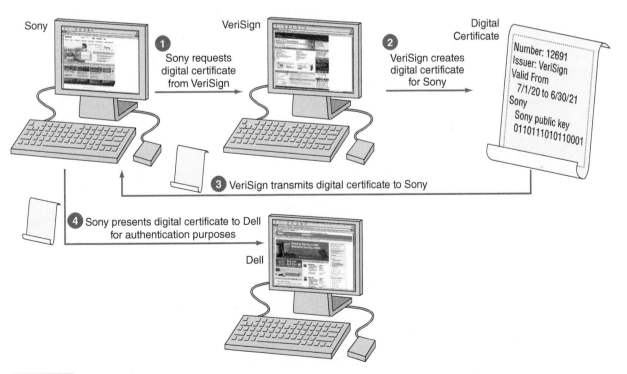

FIGURE 4.5   How digital certificates work. Sony and Dell, business partners, use a digital certificate from VeriSign for authentication.

virtual private network (VPN) A private network that uses a public network (usually the Internet) to securely connect users by using encryption.

Virtual Private Networking

A **virtual private network (VPN)** is a private network that uses a public network (usually the Internet) to connect users. VPNs essentially integrate the global connectivity of the Internet with the security of a private network and thereby extend the reach of the organization's networks. VPNs are called *virtual* because they have no separate physical existence. They use the public Internet as their infrastructure. They are created by using logins, encryption, and other techniques to enhance the user's *privacy*, which we defined in Chapter 3 as the right to be left alone and to be free of unreasonable personal intrusion.

VPNs have several advantages. First, they allow remote users to access the company network. Second, they provide flexibility. That is, mobile users can access the organization's network from properly configured remote devices. Third, organizations can impose their security policies through VPNs. For example, an organization may dictate that only corporate e-mail applications are available to users when they connect from unmanaged devices.

tunneling A process that encrypts each data packet to be sent and places each encrypted packet inside another packet.

To provide secure transmissions, VPNs use a process called *tunneling*. **Tunneling** encrypts each data packet to be sent and places each encrypted packet inside another packet. In this manner, the packet can travel across the Internet with confidentiality, authentication, and integrity. Figure 4.6 illustrates a VPN and tunneling.

Transport Layer Security

transport layer security (TLS) An encryption standard used for secure transactions such as credit card purchases and online banking.

Transport layer security (TLS), formerly called **secure socket layer (SSL)**, is an encryption standard used for secure transactions such as credit card purchases and online banking. TLS encrypts and decrypts data between a Web server and a browser end to end.

secure socket layer (SSL) See **transport layer security**.

TLS is indicated by a URL that begins with "https" rather than "http," and it often displays a small padlock icon in the browser's status bar. Using a padlock icon to indicate a secure connection and placing this icon in a browser's status bar are artifacts of specific browsers. Other browsers use different icons; for example, a key that is either broken or whole. The important thing to remember is that browsers usually provide visual confirmation of a secure connection.

HRM Employee Monitoring Systems

employee monitoring systems Systems that monitor employees' computers, e-mail activities, and Internet surfing activities.

Many companies are taking a proactive approach to protecting their networks against what they view as one of their major security threats, namely, employee mistakes. These companies are implementing **employee monitoring systems**, which scrutinize their employees' computers, e-mail activities, and Internet surfing activities. These products are useful to identify employees who spend too much time surfing on the Internet for personal reasons, who visit questionable websites, or who download music illegally. Vendors that provide monitoring software include Veriato (www.veriato.com) and Forcepoint (www.forcepoint.com).

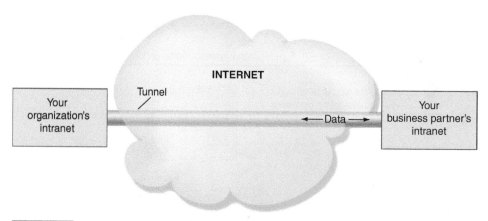

FIGURE 4.6 Virtual private network and tunneling.

Before you go on...

1. What is the single most important information security control for organizations?
2. Differentiate between authentication and authorization. Which of these processes is always performed first?
3. Compare and contrast whitelisting and blacklisting.
4. What is the purpose of a disaster recovery plan?

What's in IT for Me?

ACCT For the Accounting Major

Public companies, their accountants, and their auditors have significant information security responsibilities. Accountants are now being held professionally responsible for reducing risk, assuring compliance, eliminating fraud, and increasing the transparency of transactions according to Generally Accepted Accounting Principles (GAAP). The SEC and the Public Company Accounting Oversight Board (PCAOB), among other regulatory agencies, require information security, fraud prevention and detection, and internal controls over financial reporting. Forensic accounting, a combination of accounting and information security, is one of the most rapidly growing areas in accounting today.

FIN For the Finance Major

Because information security is essential to the success of organizations today, it is no longer the concern only of the CIO. As a result of global regulatory requirements and the passage of the Sarbanes–Oxley Act, responsibility for information security also lies with the CEO and CFO. Consequently, all aspects of the security audit, including the security of information and information systems, are a key concern for financial managers.

CFOs and treasurers are also increasingly involved with investments in information technology. They know that a security breach of any kind can have devastating financial effects on a company. Banking and financial institutions are prime targets for computer criminals. A related problem is fraud involving stocks and bonds that are sold over the Internet. Finance personnel must be aware of both the hazards and the available controls associated with these activities.

MKT For the Marketing Major

Marketing professionals have new opportunities to collect data on their customers; for example, through business-to-consumer electronic commerce. Customers expect their data to be properly secured. However, profit-motivated criminals want those data. Therefore, marketing managers must analyze the risk of their operations. Failure to protect corporate and customer data will cause significant public relations problems and make customers very angry. It can also lead to lawsuits, and it could cause companies to lose customers to competitors. CRM operations and tracking customers' online buying habits can expose data to misuse (if they are not encrypted) or result in privacy violations.

POM For the Production/Operations Management Major

Every process in a company's operations—inventory purchasing, receiving, quality control, production, and shipping—can be disrupted by an IT security breach either in the company or at a business partner. Any weak link in supply chain management or enterprise resource management systems puts the entire chain at risk. Companies may be held liable for IT security failures that impact other companies.

HRM For the Human Resource Management Major

HR managers have responsibilities to secure confidential employee data. They must also ensure that all employees explicitly verify that they understand the company's information security policies and procedures.

For the MIS Major

The MIS function provides the security infrastructure that protects the organization's information assets. This function is critical to the success of the organization, even though it is almost invisible until an attack succeeds. All application development, network deployment, and introduction of new information technologies have to be guided by IT security considerations. MIS personnel must customize the risk exposure security model to help the company identify security risks and prepare responses to security incidents and disasters.

Senior executives of publicly held companies look to the MIS function for help in meeting Sarbanes–Oxley Act requirements, particularly in detecting "significant deficiencies" or "material weaknesses" in internal controls and remediating them. Other functional areas also look to the MIS function to help them meet their security responsibilities.

Summary

4.1   Identify the five factors that contribute to the increasing vulnerability of information resources, and provide specific examples of each factor.

The five factors are the following:

- Today's interconnected, interdependent, wirelessly networked business environment
  - *Example*: The Internet
- Smaller, faster, cheaper computers and storage devices
  - *Examples*: Netbooks, thumb drives, iPads
- Decreasing skills necessary to be a computer hacker
  - *Example*: Information system hacking programs circulating on the Internet
- International organized crime taking over cybercrime
  - *Example*: Organized crime has formed transnational cyber-crime cartels. Because it is difficult to know exactly where cyberattacks originate, these cartels are extremely hard to bring to justice.
- Lack of management support
  - *Example*: Suppose that your company spent $10 million on information security countermeasures last year, and they did not experience any successful attacks on their information resources. Short-sighted management might conclude that the company could spend less during the next year and obtain the same results. Bad idea.

4.2   Compare and contrast human mistakes and social engineering, and provide a specific examples of each one.

Human mistakes are unintentional errors. However, employees can also make unintentional mistakes as a result of actions by an attacker, such as social engineering. *Social engineering* is an attack through which the perpetrator uses social skills to trick or manipulate a legitimate employee into providing confidential company information.

An example of a human mistake is tailgating. An example of social engineering is when an attacker calls an employee on the phone and impersonates a superior in the company.

4.3   Discuss the 10 types of deliberate attacks.

The 10 types of deliberate attacks are the following:

Espionage or trespass occurs when an unauthorized individual attempts to gain illegal access to organizational information.

Information extortion occurs when an attacker either threatens to steal, or actually steals, information from a company. The perpetrator demands payment for not stealing the information, for returning stolen information, or for agreeing not to disclose the information.

Sabotage and vandalism are deliberate acts that involve defacing an organization's website, possibly causing the organization to lose its image and experience a loss of confidence by its customers.

Theft of equipment and information is becoming a larger problem because computing devices and storage devices are becoming smaller yet more powerful with vastly increased storage, making these devices easier and more valuable to steal.

Identity theft is the deliberate assumption of another person's identity, usually to gain access to his or her financial information or to frame him or her for a crime.

Preventing *compromises to intellectual property* is a vital issue for people who make their livelihood in knowledge fields. Protecting intellectual property is particularly difficult when that property is in digital form.

Software attacks occur when malicious software penetrates an organization's computer system. Today, these attacks are typically profit-driven and Web-based.

Alien software is clandestine software that is installed on a computer through duplicitous methods. It is typically not as malicious as viruses, worms, or Trojan horses, but it does use up valuable system resources.

Supervisory control and data acquisition refers to a large-scale distributed measurement and control system. SCADA systems are used to monitor or control chemical, physical, and transport processes. A *SCADA attack* attempts to compromise such a system to cause damage to the real-world processes that the system controls.

With both *cyberterrorism* and *cyberwarfare*, attackers use a target's computer systems, particularly through the Internet, to cause physical, real-world harm or severe disruption, usually to carry out a political agenda.

4.4   Describe the three risk-mitigation strategies, and provide an example of each one in the context of owning a home.

The three risk-mitigation strategies are the following:

Risk acceptance, in which the organization accepts the potential risk, continues operating with no controls, and absorbs any damages that occur. If you own a home, you may decide not to insure it. Thus, you are practicing risk acceptance. Clearly, this is a bad idea.

Risk limitation, in which the organization limits the risk by implementing controls that minimize the impact of threats. As a homeowner, you practice risk limitation by putting in an alarm system or cutting down weak trees near your house.

Risk transference, in which the organization transfers the risk by using other means to compensate for the loss, such as by purchasing insurance. The vast majority of homeowners practice risk transference by purchasing insurance on their houses and other possessions.

4.5 Identify the three major types of controls that organizations can use to protect their information resources, and provide an example of each one.

Physical controls prevent unauthorized individuals from gaining access to a company's facilities. Common physical controls include walls, doors, fencing, gates, locks, badges, guards, and alarm systems. More sophisticated physical controls include pressure sensors, temperature sensors, and motion detectors.

Access controls restrict unauthorized individuals from using information resources. These controls involve two major functions: authentication and authorization. Authentication confirms the identity of the person requiring access. An example is biometrics. After the person is authenticated (identified), the next step is authorization. Authorization determines which actions, rights, or privileges the person has, based on his or her verified identity. Authorization is generally based on least privilege.

Communications (network) controls secure the movement of data across networks. Communications controls consist of firewalls, anti-malware systems, whitelisting and blacklisting, encryption, virtual private networking, secure socket layer, and vulnerability management systems.

Key Terms

access controls   103
adware   97
alien software   97
anti-malware systems (antivirus software)   107
audit   101
authentication   103
authorization   103
biometrics   104
blacklisting   108
bot   97
botnet   97
business continuity   102
certificate authority   108
communications controls (also network controls)   107
controls   102
cookies   98
copyright   96
cybercrime   86
cyberterrorism   99
cyberwarfare   99
demilitarized zone (DMZ)   107

denial-of-service attack   000
digital certificate   108
distributed denial of service (DDoS) attack   97
employee monitoring systems   110
encryption   108
exposure   86
firewall   107
identity theft   95
information security   86
intellectual property   95
least privilege   106
logic bombs   97
malware   96
network controls See communications controls   107
passphrase   105
password   104
patent   95
phishing attack   97
physical controls   102
piracy   96
privilege   106

public-key encryption (also called asymmetric encryption)   108
ransomware   92
risk   101
risk management   101
secure socket layer (SSL) See transport layer security.   110
security   86
social engineering   91
spam   98
spamware   98
spear phishing   97
spyware   98
threat   86
trade secret   95
transport layer security (TLS)   110
Trojan horse   97
tunneling   110
virtual private network (VPN)   110
virus   97
vulnerability   86
whitelisting   108
worm   97

Discussion Questions

1. Why are computer systems so vulnerable?

2. Why should information security be a prime concern to management?

3. Is security a technical issue? A business issue? Both? Support your answer.

4. Compare information security in an organization with insuring a house.

5. Why are authentication and authorization important to e-commerce?

6. Why is cross-border cybercrime expanding rapidly? Discuss possible solutions.

7. What types of user authentication are used at your university or place of work? Do these measures seem to be effective? What if a higher level of authentication were implemented? Would it be worth it, or would it decrease productivity?

8. Why are federal authorities so worried about SCADA attacks?

Problem-Solving Activities

1. A critical problem is assessing how far a company is legally obligated to go in order to secure personal data. Because there is no such thing as perfect security (i.e., there is always more that one can do), resolving this question can significantly affect cost.

   a. When are security measures that a company implements sufficient to comply with its obligations?

   b. Is there any way for a company to know if its security measures are sufficient? Can you devise a method for an organization to determine if its security measures are sufficient?

2. Enter www.scambusters.org. Find out what the organization does. Learn about e-mail scams and website scams. Report your findings.

3. Visit www.dhs.gov (Department of Homeland Security). Search the site for "National Strategy to Secure Cyberspace" and write a report on their agenda and accomplishments to date.

4. Enter www.alltrustnetworks.com and other vendors of biometrics. Find the devices they make that can be used to control access into information systems. Prepare a list of products and major capabilities of each vendor.

5. Visit www.embroker.com and read the blog titled Top 10 Cybersecurity Threats in 2023. Select one threat that you have experienced and write about what could be done to prevent it.

6. Software piracy is a global problem. Access the following websites: www.bsa.org and www.privacy.microsoft.com/en-US/. What can organizations do to mitigate this problem? Are some organizations dealing with the problem better than others?

7. Investigate the Sony PlayStation Network hack that occurred in April 2011.

   a. What type of attack was it?

   b. Was the success of the attack due to technology problems at Sony, management problems at Sony, or a combination of both? Provide specific examples to support your answer.

   c. Which Sony controls failed?

   d. Could the hack have been prevented? If so, how?

   e. Discuss Sony's response to the hack.

   f. Describe the damages that Sony incurred from the hack.

8. Investigate the Equifax hacks in 2017.

   a. What type of attack was it?

   b. What actions should Equifax have taken to prevent the breaches? Provide specific examples to support your answer.

   c. Place yourself as a victim in the Equifax breaches. What should you do when you are notified (or when you think) that your personal data has been compromised?

   d. In light of the Equifax breaches, should all consumers have the option to opt out of credit bureaus? Why or why not?

9. Checkout a password manager such as www.1password.com. What are the benefits and limitations to such a system? Would you use this product? Why or why not?

10. Visit www.cisa.gov/stopransomware. This is the U.S. Government's official one-stop location for resources to tackle ransomware more effectively. List three actions you can take to better protect yourself and your employer.

Closing Case

MIS   **Successful Operations against Cybercrime**

The An0m Phone Sting

An0m looked like any other smartphone. Purchasing it, however, was much more complicated. First, you had to "know a guy." Then, you had to pay $1,700 for the phone plus a $1,250 annual subscription. This was a large amount of money for a phone that could not make phone calls or browse the Internet.

Nevertheless, nearly 100,000 users around the world paid the money to gain access to a specific application installed on the phone. Users could open the phone's calculator to enter a specific sum that launched a secret messaging application. This app encrypted every message, which could be received only by another An0m user. Significantly, the app could not be downloaded from any app store. The only way to access the app was to buy a phone with the app preinstalled.

Most phones have the option to remotely wipe the device's data. To ensure that suspects could not delete their phones' data, authorities used Faraday bags, which are containers lined with metal that prevent a phone from sending and receiving a kill signal. The An0m phone came with a solution to Faraday bags. Users could set an option to wipe the phone's data if the device went offline for a specified amount of time. They could also set particularly sensitive messages to self-erase after the messages were opened. Finally, they could record and send voice memos in which the phone would automatically disguise the speaker's voice.

There was just one problem for users: The phone and messaging app had been built, marketed, and sold by the FBI and the Australian federal police. Authorities developed the An0m phone to make it attractive for criminals around the world who would want to take advantage of its features.

By 2021, roughly 9,000 police officers across 18 countries had collected approximately 20 million messages sent via the app since its launch in 2018. Using this data, on June 7, 2021, authorities arrested more than 800 people around the world. Their alleged crimes ranged from drug trafficking, to money laundering, to attempted murder. Seized evidence included almost 40 tons of drugs—cocaine, cannabis, and synthetic drugs—250 guns, 55 luxury cars, and more than $48 million in various currencies and cryptocurrencies.

DarkMarket Shut Down

DarkMarket was a website that authorities described as probably the largest illegal marketplace on the Dark Web. The website, which had 500,000 users and nearly 2,500 vendors, enabled anyone using a Tor browser and cryptocurrency to buy and sell drugs, forged money, forged or stolen credit cards, anonymous SIM cards, and malware. The site had processed more than 320,000 transactions, and approximately $170 million in Bitcoin and Monero cryptocurrencies had been exchanged.

In January 2021, international authorities shut down DarkMarket. The takedown of DarkMarket was a lengthy law-enforcement operation that involved German, the United States, Australian, British, Danish, Swiss, Ukrainian, and Moldovan authorities. The primary operator behind DarkMarket, a 34-year-old Australian man, was arrested in Germany. Authorities seized more than 20 servers in Moldova and Ukraine, along with the data contained on them. In October 2021, a joint operation of the U.S. Department of Justice (DOJ), Europol, and many other agencies arrested 150 people across eight countries and seized more than 230 kilograms (500 pounds) of drugs and $31.6 million in cash and cryptocurrency.

The Disruption of Emotet

The Emotet malware was originally designed to attack banks and evolved into one of the largest botnets in the world, targeting victims with data theft and ransomware. Emotet contains functionality that helps the malware escape detection by some anti-malware products. Emotet also has worm functions that enable the malware to replicate itself from one system to another. These functions have led the U.S. Department of Homeland Security to conclude that Emotet is one of the most costly and destructive types of malware, impacting government and private sectors, organizations, and individuals.

In January 2021, authorities launched Operation Ladybird, a global coalition of law enforcement agencies across the United States, Canada, the United Kingdom, the Netherlands, Germany, France, Lithuania, and Ukraine, along with private security researchers. The authorities simultaneously hijacked hundreds of Emotet command-and-control servers that were located in more than 90 countries, and they arrested at least two of the criminals behind the botnet.

To prohibit these servers from communicating with the botnet's owners, authorities placed their own computers at the IP addresses of those command-and-control computers. As a result, compromised machines could not communicate with the botnet. As a result, Emotet no longer worked, and the compromised machine no longer functioned as part of the botnet.

REvil

REvil is a Russian-speaking cybercriminal gang that has stolen millions of dollars from U.S. organizations. In addition to masterminding some of the most expensive ransomware attacks of 2020 and 2021, REvil also created the ransomware-as-a-service (RaaS) malware business model. The group openly sold its malware and other cybercriminal tools to third-party hackers to enable them to execute malicious attacks. In return, REvil received 20 percent of any ransomware payments any of their affiliate hackers obtained.

In an operation conducted by authorities in the United States and other countries, law enforcement and other cybercrime specialists hacked into REvil's computer network infrastructure and took control of at least some of the group's command-and-control servers. On November 8, 2021, the DOJ announced that it had indicted two REvil members for their involvement in the gang. In addition, they had recovered more than $6 million in alleged ransom payments, which they intended to restore to businesses and government entities who had paid REvil to unlock compromised data and applications.

For years, Russia had ignored and denied accusations that it had offered safe harbor to Russian ransomware hackers who were attacking Western targets. Then, in early 2022, at the request of the United States, the Federal Security Service of the Russian Federation announced a joint effort with the Ministry of Internal Affairs that led to the arrest of 14 people associated with the REvil group. However, it does not appear that any Russian members of the gang will be extradited to the United States. Europol also announced that Romanian law enforcement officials arrested two suspect REvil affiliates who allegedly perpetrated 5,000 ransomware attacks and extorted $600,000 from their victims.

Unfortunately, other members of REvil are continuing their attacks. The U.S. State Department continues to offer a $10 million reward for information leading to the identification or location of "any individual holding a key leadership position" in the REvil group.

Questions

1. Describe the various methods that authorities used in the vignettes discussed in this case to stop illegal cyber-activity and apprehend suspects.

2. Were these methods technical, behavioral, or a combination of both? Provide examples to support your answer.

3. Why is it critical to have the support of, and collaboration with, law enforcement agencies in different countries when pursuing cybercriminals?

Sources: P. O'Neill, "The U.S. Is Unmasking Russian Hackers Faster than Ever," *MIT Technology Review*, February 21, 2022; "REvil Ransomware Gang Arrested in Russia," *BBC News*, January 17, 2022; L. Whitney, "Russia Arrests REvil Ransomware Gang Members at Request of U.S. Officials," *TechRepublic*, January 14, 2022; L. Whitney, "U.S. Amps Up War on Ransomware with Charges against REvil Attackers," *TechRepublic*, November 9, 2021; L. Newman, "The Biggest Ransomware Bust Yet Might Actually Make an Impact," *Wired*, November 8, 2021; M. Chatterjee, "The Demise of White House Market Will Shake Up the Dark Web," *Wired*, November 1, 2021; B. Barrett, "Dark Web Drug Busts Lead to 150 Arrests," *Wired*, October 26, 2021; D. Palmer, "These Ransomware Criminals Lost Millions of Dollars in Payments when Researchers Secretly Found Mistakes in Their Code," *ZDNet*, October 26, 2021; L. Whitney, "REvil Ransomware Group Reportedly Taken Offline by Multi-Nation Effort," *TechRepublic*, October 25, 2021; S. Parkin," 'Every Message Was Copied to the Police': The Inside Story of the Most Daring Surveillance Sting in History," *The Guardian*, September 11, 2021; "AnOm: Hundreds Arrested in Massive Global Crime Sting Using Messaging App," *BBC News*, June 8, 2021; A. Greenberg, "Cops Disrupt Emotet, the Internet's 'Most Dangerous Malware'," *Wired*, January 27, 2021; L. Newman, "A Coordinated Takedown Targets 'OGUser' Account Thieves," *Wired*, February 4, 2021; and G. Butler, "The World's 'Largest Illegal Darknet Marketplace' Has Been Shut Down," *VICE*, January 12, 2021.

CHAPTER 5

Data and Knowledge Management

CHAPTER OUTLINE	LEARNING OBJECTIVES
5.1 Managing Data	5.1 **Discuss** ways that common challenges in managing data can be addressed using data governance.
5.2 The Database Approach	5.2 **Identify** and assess the advantages and disadvantages of relational databases.
5.3 Big Data	5.3 **Define** *Big Data*, and explain its basic characteristics.
5.4 Data Warehouses and Data Marts	5.4 **Explain** the elements necessary to successfully implement and maintain data warehouses.
5.5 Knowledge Management	5.5 **Describe** the benefits and challenges of implementing knowledge management systems in organizations.
5.6 Appendix: Fundamentals of Relational Database Operations	5.6 **Understand** the processes of querying a relational database, entity-relationship modeling, and normalization and joins.

Opening Case

MIS Elementary, Watson. Not quite so fast, IBM

In 2015, IBM (www.ibm.com) launched Watson Health, an artificial intelligence (AI) platform with the intended purpose of helping health care providers revolutionize cancer treatment. Sound ambitious? It was, even for a massive company like IBM. If anyone could accomplish great things, however, it was IBM. The company had already demonstrated Watson's remarkable ability to learn and make decisions. In 2011, Watson beat the world's best chess players.

Recognizing that technology can help provide better health care, the industry has identified AI as a potential source of deep insights and suggestions. AI can consume vast amounts of data, analyze and interpret those data, and provide insights to physicians. It can be applied to the most practical problems clinicians face every day and keep up with the latest information while treating each patient as a unique case.

For example, to provide better care, oncologists—doctors who treat cancers—could use AI to access information dealing with entire populations rather than rely on specific cases they had been able to review. However, physicians are not the only group interested in health care–related AI. Numerous stakeholders—patients, providers, hospitals, and insurers—could employ AI to address their distinctive needs.

Unfortunately, in the case of Watson Health, AI did not deliver the kind of progress IBM initially envisioned. In fact, the unit wasn't even profitable. In 2021, the *Wall Street Journal* reported that Watson Health had generated only $1 billion in revenue. This number was far less than the $4 billion that IBM had invested in the technology. Meanwhile, several IBM partners and clients had canceled or scaled back their oncology projects with Watson. Ultimately, in early 2022, IBM sold Watson Health to another company.

What Went Wrong?

In assessing Watson Health's lack of success, many analysts point to the sheer complexity of health care data. IBM apparently underestimated the complexity of health care records and overestimated Watson's ability to consume, compile, and interpret those records. Most people's healthcare records are still on paper and are recorded differently. Although Watson could quickly analyze data, it took an enormous amount of human effort to prepare the data points so that Watson could analyze them.

In addition, combining an individual's multiple data records into a single cohesive story was nearly impossible. For example, a patient could go to a hospital for lung cancer treatment yet also see a pulmonologist for breathing problems. Logically, the records are intertwined. From Watson's perspective, however, they are separate, unique stories.

Another problem is that the data entered into Watson's cancer diagnostic tool were not actual patient data. Recognizing how highly complex health care record data are, IBM decided to load hypothetical data, meaning that the original data sample contained diagnoses on fake cases to train the system to analyze real patient data. Medical providers, however, rely on real studies that are approved and recognized by the government and the medical profession and are published in professional journals. Therefore, many providers refused to accept the advice they received from Watson as viable. Other physicians expressed concerns about the recommendations that Watson was giving. They just were not relevant. Some physicians reported that Watson would suggest a treatment that was not available in the local area, did not comply with existing protocols, or simply was not effective.

Further, some location-specific patient needs are related to socioeconomic status. For example, one of the primary sources of diagnostic information was a group of experts at Memorial Sloan Kettering Cancer Center in New York. Although the hospital is considered one of the most renowned cancer institutions in the world, and the health care suggestions are highly viable, its patient list is biased toward a wealthy subset of patients. This tendency is called *AI bias*. It is a mounting concern, especially for demographic groups that are underrepresented in the data used to create the diagnostic tools.

To attempt to improve Watson's validity in the eyes of health care providers, IBM spent billions of dollars on data acquisitions. They bought Truven Health Analytics, Phytel, Explorys, and Merge Healthcare. Truven offered an insurance database with 300 million customer data points. Explorys provided clinical data of electronic health records kept by health systems representing roughly 50 million patients. Phytel provided additional physician data, and Merge offered a huge imaging database. IBM's plan was to make these vast data sources available to Watson, which could then identify patterns that physicians could never find.

Results

The health care industry is data rich but analysis deficient. Data are incompatible across practice, specializations, and groups, creating a vacuum where the industry can do better. A unified approach to data storage and sharing is required to make the intent of Watson Health a reality. Only when all data can be easily shared, accessed, and analyzed and the resulting reports shared with the community can the full breadth of AI truly impact health care.

In 2021, the U.S. government put many steps in place to require hospitals to provide access to population health data through the Fast Healthcare Interoperability Resources (FHIR, pronounced "fire"). FHIR provides a standardized way to structure clinical data and financial information. The federal government is mandating that the information kept inside various technology stacks be made accessible to other providers to improve outcomes and experiences for patients.

On the positive side, AI does perform certain health care tasks that can support the type of widespread improvements that Watson was created to implement. Two major examples are image classification and natural language processing (the ability for a computer to understand spoken commands and carry out a basic conversation). Computers can rapidly analyze thousands of images for correlations to aid in diagnostics. Unfortunately, health care data include much more than just image data.

The final result for Watson? In January 2022, IBM sold Watson Health to Francisco Partners, who changed the name to Merative and narrowed the scope of the system to more manageable expectations.

Questions

1. Why was Watson so much better at chess than at health care?

2. Identify and discuss three problems with the data that Watson was using to produce recommendations.

3. What would you recommend Francisco Partners do differently to realize success from the Merative platform?

Sources: Compiled from J. Glaser, M. O'Kane, B. Ryan, and E. Schneider, "How to Use Digital Health Data to Improve Outcomes," *Harvard Business Review,* September 12, 2022; L. Vespoli, "Where Watson Went Wrong," mmm-online.com, September 8, 2021; K. Gulen, "Artificial Intelligence as the Cornerstone of Emerging Technologies," dataconomy.com, September 6, 2022; E. Sweeney, "Experts Say IBM Watson's Flaws Are Rooted in Data Collection and Interoperability," Fierce Healthcare, September 6, 2017; eHealth Network, "How Are AI and ML Changing the Way Healthcare Is Delivered?," ehealth.eletsonline.com, August 31, 2022; J. Kagan, "IBM Watson Health Fails, Becomes Merative After Acquisition," equities.com, July 25, 2022; J. Gagon, "FHIR and the Coming Transformation of Healthcare Data," *Forbes,* August 15, 2022; D. Muoio, "Watson Health, Under New Investment Firm Ownership, Is Reborn as Merative," Fierce Healthcare, July 5, 2022; A. Sraders, "Data Sharing in Health Care Is Complicated. Industry Executives Discuss How They're Thinking About Improving and Using It," *Fortune,* May 12, 2022; P. Olson, "Too Much AI May Not Be Good for Your Health or the NHS," *Washington Post,* May 12, 2022; J. Gagnon, "IBM Watson Health's Challenges Tell Us More About Healthcare Data Than It Does About AI," *Forbes,* May 3, 2022; S. Durbhakula, "IBM Dumping Watson Health Is an Opportunity to Reevaluate Artificial Intelligence," medcitynews.com, March 27, 2022; S. Konam, "Where Did IBM Go Wrong with Watson Health?" qz.com, March 2, 2022; L. O'Leary, "How IBM's Watson Went from the Future of Health Care to Sold Off for Parts," slate.com, January 31, 2022; J. Davis, "Watson Health Sale Signals More Pragmatic AI for Healthcare," *Information Week,* January 27, 2022; M. Davis, S. Deveau, and J. Davalos, "IBM Sells Some Watson Health Assets for More Than $1 Billion," bloomberg.com, January 21, 2022; and R. Miller, "IBM Reportedly Shopping Watson Health Just as Healthcare Gets Hot," TechCrunch.com, January 7, 2022.

Introduction

Information technologies and systems support organizations in managing—that is, acquiring, organizing, storing, accessing, analyzing, and interpreting—data. As you noted in Chapter 1, when these data are managed properly, they become *information* and then *knowledge*. Information and knowledge are invaluable organizational resources that can provide any organization with a competitive advantage.

So, just how important are data and data management to organizations? From confidential customer information to intellectual property to financial transactions to social media posts, organizations possess massive amounts of data that are critical to their success. Of course, to benefit from these data, they need to manage it effectively. This type of management, however, comes at a huge cost. According to Symantec's (**www.symantec.com**) State of Information survey, digital information costs organizations worldwide more than $1 trillion annually. In fact, it makes up roughly *half* of an organization's total value. The survey found that large organizations spend an average of $40 million annually to maintain and use data, and small-to-medium-sized businesses spend almost $350,000.

This chapter examines the processes whereby data are transformed first into information and then into knowledge. Managing data is critical to all organizations. Few business professionals are comfortable making or justifying business decisions that are not based on solid information. This is especially true today, when modern information systems make access to that information quick and easy. For example, there are information systems that format data in a way that managers and analysts can easily understand. Consequently, these professionals can access these data themselves and then analyze the data according to their needs. The result is useful *information*. Managers can then apply their experience to use this information to address a business problem, thereby producing *knowledge*. Knowledge management, enabled by information technology, captures and stores knowledge in forms that all organizational employees can access and apply, thereby creating the flexible, powerful "learning organization."

Organizations store data in databases. Recall from Chapter 1 that a *database* is a collection of related data files or tables that contain data. We discuss databases in Section 5.2, focusing on the relational database model. In Section 5.6, we take a look at the fundamentals of relational database operations.

Clearly, data and knowledge management are vital to modern organizations. But, why should *you* learn about them? The reason is that you will play an important role in the development of database applications. The structure and content of your organization's database depend on how users (meaning you) define your business activities. For example, when database developers in the firm's MIS group build a database, they use a tool called *entity-relationship (ER) modeling*. This tool creates a model of how users view a business activity. When you understand how to create and interpret an ER model, then you can evaluate whether the developers have captured your business activities correctly.

Keep in mind that decisions about data last longer, and have a broader impact, than decisions about hardware or software. If decisions concerning hardware are wrong, then the equipment can be replaced relatively easily. If software decisions turn out to be incorrect, they can be modified, though not always painlessly or inexpensively. Database decisions, in contrast, are much harder to undo. Database design constrains what the organization can do with its data for a long time. Remember that business users will be stuck with a bad database design, while the programmers who created the database will quickly move on to their next projects.

Furthermore, consider that databases typically underlie the enterprise applications that users access. If there are problems with organizational databases, then it is unlikely that any applications will be able to provide the necessary functionality for users. Databases are difficult to set up properly and to maintain. They are also the component of an information system that is most likely to receive the blame when the system performs poorly and the least likely to be recognized when the system performs well. This is why it is so important to get database designs right the first time—and you will play a key role in these designs.

You might also want to create a small personal database using a software product such as Microsoft Access. If so, you will need to be familiar with at least the basics of the product.

After the data are stored in your organization's databases, they must be accessible in a form that helps users make decisions. Organizations accomplish this objective by developing *data warehouses*. You should become familiar with data warehouses because they are invaluable decision-making tools. We discuss data warehouses in Section 5.4.

You will also make extensive use of your organization's knowledge base to perform your job. For example, when you are assigned a new project, you will likely research your firm's knowledge base to identify factors that contributed to the success (or failure) of previous, similar projects. We discuss knowledge management in Section 5.5.

You begin this chapter by examining the multiple challenges involved in managing data. You then study the database approach that organizations use to help address these challenges. You turn your attention to Big Data, which organizations must manage in today's business environment. Next, you study data warehouses and data marts, and you learn how to use them for decision making. You conclude the chapter by examining knowledge management.

WILEY PLUS

Author Lecture Videos are available exclusively in *WileyPLUS*.
Apply the Concept activities are available in the Appendix and in *WileyPLUS*.

5.1 Managing Data

LEARNING OBJECTIVE

Discuss ways that common challenges in managing data can be addressed using data governance.

All IT applications require data. These data should be of high quality, meaning that they should be accurate, complete, timely, consistent, accessible, relevant, and concise. Unfortunately, the process of acquiring, keeping, and managing data is becoming increasingly difficult.

The Difficulties of Managing Data

Because data are processed in several stages and often in multiple locations, they are frequently subject to problems and difficulties. Managing data in organizations is difficult for many reasons.

1. The amount of data is increasing exponentially with time. Much historical data must be kept for a long time, and new data are added rapidly. For example, to support millions of customers, large retailers such as Walmart must manage many petabytes of data. (A petabyte is approximately 1,000 terabytes, or trillions of bytes; see Technology Guide 1.)

2. Data are also scattered throughout organizations, and they are collected by many individuals using various methods and devices. These data are frequently stored in numerous servers and locations and in different computing systems, databases, formats, and human and computer languages.

   MIS Organizations have developed information systems for specific business processes, such as transaction processing, supply chain management, and customer relationship management. The ISs that specifically support these processes impose unique requirements on data, which leads to repetition and conflicts across the organization. For example, the marketing function might maintain information on customers, sales territories, and markets. These data might be duplicated within the billing or customer service functions. This arrangement can produce inconsistent data within the enterprise. Inconsistent data prevent a company from developing a unified view of core business information—data concerning customers, products, finances, and so on—across the organization and its information systems. This situation refers to data silos.

   A **data silo** is a collection of data held by one group that is not easily accessible by other groups. Data silos hinder the process of gaining actionable insights from organizational data, create barriers to an overall view of the enterprise and its data, and delay

data silo A collection of data held by one group that is not easily accessible by other groups.

digital transformation efforts (see Chapter 1). One major method to remove data silos is through cloud data management (see Technology Guide 3 for a complete discussion of cloud computing).

3. Another problem is that data are generated from multiple sources: internal sources (e.g., corporate databases and company documents); personal sources (e.g., personal thoughts, opinions, and experiences); and external sources (e.g., commercial databases, government reports, and corporate websites).

   Some of these data sources are in the form of *data streams*, which are data that are continuously generated by point-of-sale systems, clickstream data, social media, and sensors. We take a brief look at these data streams here.

   - **POM** *Point-of-sale data.* Organizations capture data from each customer purchase with their POS systems. Clerks (or customers themselves using self-checkout) use bar code scanners to scan each item purchased. POS systems collect data in real time, such as the name, product identification number, and unit price of each item; the total amount of all items purchased; the sales tax on that amount; the payment method used; a time stamp of the purchase; and many other data points.

   - **MKT** *Clickstream data.* Clickstream data are those data that visitors and customers produce when they visit a website and click on hyperlinks (described in Chapter 6). Clickstream data include the terms that the visitor to the website entered into a search engine to reach that website, all links that users click, how long they spend on each page, if they click the "back" button, if they add or remove items from a shopping cart, and many other data points.

   - **MKT** *Social media data.* Social media data (also called social data) are the data collected from individuals' activity on social media websites, including Facebook, YouTube, LinkedIn, Twitter, and many others. These data include shares, likes and dislikes, ratings, reviews, recommendations, comments, and many other examples.

   - **MIS** *Sensor data.* The Internet of Things (IoT; see Chapter 8) is a system in which any object, natural or manmade, contains internal or external wireless sensor(s) that communicate with each other without human interaction. Each sensor monitors and reports data on physical and environmental conditions around it, such as temperature, sound, pressure, vibration, and movement. Sensors can also control physical systems, such as opening and closing a valve and adjusting the fuel mixture in your car. (See our discussion of supervisory control and data acquisition [SCADA] systems in Chapter 4.)

4. Adding to these problems is the fact that new sources of data such as blogs, podcasts, tweets, Facebook posts, YouTube videos, texts, and RFID tags and other wireless sensors are constantly being developed, and the data these technologies generate must be managed. Also, the data become less current over time. For example, customers move to new addresses or they change their names, companies go out of business or are bought, new products are developed, employees are hired or fired, and companies expand into new countries.

5. Data are also subject to *data rot*. Data rot refers primarily to problems with the media on which the data are stored. Over time, temperature, humidity, and exposure to light can cause physical problems with storage media and thus make it difficult to access data. The second aspect of data rot is that finding the machines needed to access the data can be difficult. For example, it is almost impossible today to find 8-track players to listen to music on. Consequently, a library of 8-track tapes has become relatively worthless, unless you have a functioning 8-track player or you convert the tapes to a more modern medium such as DVDs.

6. Data security, quality, and integrity are critical, yet they are easily jeopardized. Legal requirements relating to data also differ among countries as well as among industries, and they change frequently.

7. **ACCT** **FIN** Two other factors complicate data management. First, federal regulations— for example, the Sarbanes–Oxley Act of 2002—have made it a top priority for companies to better account for how they are managing information. Sarbanes–Oxley requires that (1) public companies evaluate and disclose the effectiveness of their internal financial controls and (2) independent auditors for these companies agree to this disclosure. The law also holds CEOs and CFOs personally responsible for such disclosures. If their companies

lack satisfactory data management policies and fraud or a security breach occurs, then the company officers could be held liable and face prosecution.

Second, companies are drowning in data, much of which are unstructured. As you have seen, the amount of data is increasing exponentially. To be profitable, companies must develop a strategy for managing these data effectively. (See IT's About Business 5.1.)

8. An additional problem with data management is Big Data. Big Data is so important that we devote Section 5.3 to this topic.

IT's About Business 5.1

MIS Data Governance Key to Unlocking Dark Data

The Business Problem

Organizations save vast amounts of data. However, their capacity for collecting data typically exceeds their ability to analyze the data. As a result, much of the data are not used to acquire knowledge or make decisions. We call these data *dark data* because they have not been brought to light and made useful to the organization.

A large majority of enterprise information is composed of dark data. According to a July 2022 report from the Enterprise Strategy Group (www.esg-global.com), an international research and consulting firm that focuses on technology, 20 percent of organizations state that more than 70 percent of their data are dark data. Significantly, much of this data is unstructured—for example, videos, images, and e-mails—making it challenging for any tool to analyze since the data does not fit neatly inside a database.

Why do organizations continue to collect dark data if they cannot utilize it? One reason is to comply with government regulations. Also, organizations fear they will need this information in the future, even though much of it is not currently helpful. For example, most companies maintain past employee files, financial information, transaction logs, confidential intelligence data, e-mails, internal presentations, downloaded attachments, and even surveillance video footage for which they have no current purpose. Instead, they save it "just in case" they might need it one day.

Dark data, then, can be anything and come from anywhere. It is generated by employees, customers, and business processes. It is created as log files by machines, applications, and security systems. It can be sensitive data that should never be saved but still is. It is any data generated by a user's daily digital interactions, such as instant messages or video meeting chats. It is often forgotten, unknown, and unused. It exists everywhere, spread across an organization's complete portfolio of data repositories, from databases to applications.

Although dark data is not used, it is potentially valuable information that organizations can employ to increase productivity and boost growth. For example, an organization installs sensors to identify the location of a gas leak. It then stores the data generated by the sensors. However, it never finishes the reporting structure. As a result, the organization has years of sensor data that it never uses. Now, imagine that a safety incident occurs. Information collected by those sensors could have prevented the incident if the organization had used it. Analyzing the available data could have both boosted profits by identifying the leak and avoided injuries. In addition, having the data and not utilizing it could lead to lawsuits or a public relations nightmare. Should the organization be liable for not using every bit of data at its disposal?

Given this scenario, should organizations stop collecting data they do not plan to use currently? The answer is, not necessarily. Let's look at potential paths forward.

IT Solution

Organizations must realize that what makes data "dark" is the fact that it is unstructured and unused. A logical starting point to utilizing dark data is to understand what data are available and what issues they might have.

This activity falls under data governance, which we define in Section 5.1 as an approach to managing information across an entire organization. Data governance involves a formal set of business processes and policies that are designed to ensure data are handled according to clearly defined practices. It is essential to determining what an organization has, what is valuable, what should be deleted, and what should be kept.

After identifying the valuable data, an organization has at least two paths forward. First, they can connect the dots between the dark data and good, operational data that are available inside individual business units. Identifying these relationships can create valuable insights that drive business decisions.

Second, companies can leave these data where they currently reside but add a metadata layer to index and search these data. Metadata, defined as data about data, can intelligently classify data by project, customer, work flow, status, or other criteria relating to critical organizational components. This approach takes the data out of the dark and makes them useful by organizing them. AI is designed to search through unstructured yet indexed data, and it could mine those data for insights.

Regardless of which path an organization chooses, the real advantage of bringing light to dark data is that the data can be used to benefit the business.

Questions

1. Define dark data.

2. Give examples of dark data.

3. What is the potential value of dark data to an organization?

Sources: Compiled from B. Lynch, "Three Keys to Securing Shadow Data," Security Boulevard, September 13, 2022; A. Sayed, "The Key to Business Growth? A Solid Data Strategy," *Fast Company*, September 12, 2022; T. Jones, "Mainframes Are Drowning in the Data Deluge," datacenterdynamics.com, September 9, 2022; N. Sonawane, "Strategies to Make the Most Out of Dark Data," *Enterprise Talk*, August 23, 2022; H. Selman, "If Only You Knew the Power of the Dark Data...," dataconomy.com, August 22, 2022; M. Korolov, "Unlocking the Hidden Value of Dark Data," *CIO*, August 11, 2022; and M. Labovich, "How Dark Data Can Unlock Real Value by Understanding Risk," pwc.com, May 3, 2022.

Data Governance

To address the numerous problems associated with managing data, organizations are turning to data governance. **Data governance** is an approach to managing information across an entire organization. It involves a formal set of business processes and policies that are designed to ensure that data are handled in a certain, well-defined fashion. That is, the organization follows unambiguous rules for creating, collecting, handling, and protecting its information. The objective is to make information available, transparent, and useful for the people who are authorized to access it, from the moment it enters an organization until it becomes outdated and is deleted.

One strategy for implementing data governance is master data management. **Master data management** is a process that spans all of an organization's business processes and applications. It provides companies with the ability to store, maintain, exchange, and synchronize a consistent, accurate, and timely "single version of the truth" for the company's master data.

Master data are a set of core data, such as customer, product, employee, vendor, and geographic location, that span the enterprise's information systems. It is important to distinguish between master data and transactional data. **Transactional data**, which are generated and captured by operational systems, describe the business's activities, or *transactions*. In contrast, master data are applied to multiple transactions, and they are used to categorize, aggregate, and evaluate the transactional data.

Let's look at an example of a transaction. You (Mary Jones) purchase one Samsung 42-inch LCD television, part number 1234, from Bill Roberts at Best Buy, for $2,000, on April 20, 2017. In this example, the master data are "product sold," "vendor," "salesperson," "store," "part number," "purchase price," and "date." When specific values are applied to the master data, then a transaction is represented. Therefore, transactional data would be, respectively, "42-inch LCD television," "Samsung," "Bill Roberts," "Best Buy," "1234," "$2,000," and "April 20, 2017."

An example of master data management is Dallas, Texas, which implemented a plan for digitizing the city's public and private records, such as paper documents, images, drawings, and video and audio content. The master database can be used by any of the 38 government departments that have appropriate access. The city is also integrating its financial and billing processes with its customer relationship management program. (You will learn about customer relationship management in Chapter 11.)

How will Dallas use this system? Imagine that the city experiences a water-main break. Before it implemented the system, repair crews had to search City Hall for records that were filed haphazardly. Once the workers found the hard-copy blueprints, they would take them to the site and, after examining them manually, would decide on a plan of action. In contrast, the new system delivers the blueprints wirelessly to the laptops of crews in the field, who can magnify or highlight areas of concern to generate a rapid response. This process reduces the time it takes to respond to an emergency by several hours.

Along with data governance, organizations use the database approach to efficiently and effectively manage their data. We discuss the database approach in Section 5.2.

As with all technology, being able to collect massive amounts of data from many different sources is a double-edged sword. IT's About Business 5.1 shows how a startup company helps organizations make sense of the vast amounts of data available to them.

data governance An approach to managing information across an entire organization.

master data management A process that provides companies with the ability to store, maintain, exchange, and synchronize a consistent, accurate, and timely "single version of the truth" for the company's core master data.

master data A set of core data, such as customer, product, employee, vendor, geographic location, and so on, that spans an enterprise's information systems.

transactional data Data generated and captured by operational systems that describe the business's activities, or transactions.

Before you go on...

1. What are some of the difficulties involved in managing data?
2. Define *data governance*, *master data*, and *transactional data*.

5.2 The Database Approach

WILEY PLUS

Author Lecture Videos are available exclusively in *WileyPLUS*.
Apply the Concept activities are available in the Appendix and in *WileyPLUS*.

LEARNING OBJECTIVE

Discuss the advantages and disadvantages of relational databases.

From the mid-1950s, when businesses first adopted computer applications, until the early 1970s, organizations managed their data in a *file management environment*. This environment evolved because organizations typically automated their functions one application at a time. Therefore, the various automated systems developed independently from one another, without any overall planning. Each application required its own data, which were organized in a data file.

data file (also table) A collection of logically related records.

A **data file** is a collection of logically related records. In a file management environment, each application has a specific data file related to it. This file contains all of the data records the application requires. Over time, organizations developed numerous applications, each with an associated application-specific data file.

For example, imagine that most of your information is stored in your university's central database. In addition, however, a club to which you belong maintains its own files, the athletics department has separate files for student athletes, and your instructors maintain grade data on their personal computers. It is easy for your name to be misspelled in one of these databases or files. Similarly, if you move, then your address might be updated correctly in one database or file but not in the others.

Using databases eliminates many problems that arose from previous methods of storing and accessing data, such as file management systems. Databases are arranged so that one set of software programs—the database management system—provides all users with access to all of the data. (You will study database management systems later in this chapter.) Database systems minimize the following problems:

- *Data redundancy*: The same data are stored in multiple locations.
- *Data isolation*: Applications cannot access data associated with other applications.
- *Data inconsistency*: Various copies of the data do not agree.

Database systems also maximize the following:

- *Data security*: Because data are "put in one place" in databases, there is a risk of losing a lot of data at one time. Therefore, databases must have extremely high security measures in place to minimize mistakes and deter attacks.
- *Data integrity*: Data meet certain constraints; for example, there are no alphabetic characters in a Social Security number field.
- *Data independence*: Applications and data are independent of one another; that is, applications and data are not linked to each other, so all applications are able to access the same data.

Figure 5.1 illustrates a university database. Note that university applications from the registrar's office, the accounting department, and the athletics department access data through the database management system.

A database can contain vast amounts of data. To make these data more understandable and useful, they are arranged in a hierarchy. We take a closer look at this hierarchy in the next section.

The Data Hierarchy

bit Short for *binary digit* (0s and 1s), the only data that a CPU can process.

Data are organized in a hierarchy that begins with bits and proceeds all the way to databases (see **Figure 5.2**). A **bit** (*binary digit*) represents the smallest unit of data a computer can process. The term *binary* means that a bit can consist only of a 0 or a 1. A group of eight bits,

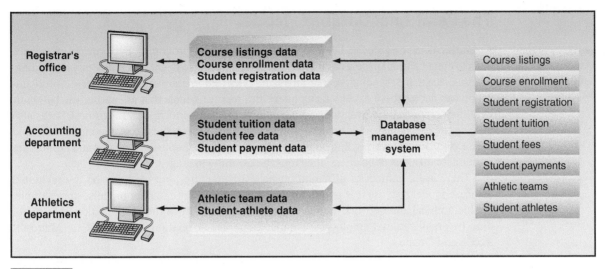

FIGURE 5.1 Database management system.

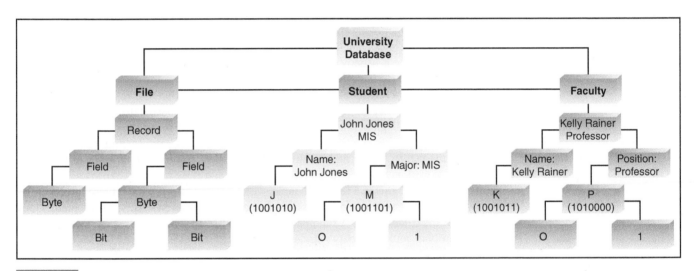

FIGURE 5.2 Hierarchy of data for a computer-based file.

called a **byte**, represents a single character. A byte can be a letter, a number, or a symbol. A logical grouping of characters into a word, a small group of words, or an identification number is called a **field**. For example, a student's name in a university's computer files would appear in the "name" field, and her or his Social Security number would appear in the "Social Security number" field. Fields can contain data other than text and numbers, such as an image, or any other type of multimedia. Examples are a motor vehicle department's licensing database that contains a driver's photograph, or a field that contains a voice sample to authorize access to a secure facility.

A logical grouping of related fields, such as the student's name, the courses taken, the date, and the grade, comprises a **record**. In the Apple iTunes Store, a song is a field in a record, with other fields containing the song's title, its price, and the album on which it appears. A logical grouping of related records is called a data file or a **table**. For example, a grouping of the records from a particular course, consisting of course number, professor, and students' grades, would constitute a data file for that course. Continuing up the hierarchy, a logical grouping of related files constitutes a *database*. Using the same example, the student course file could be grouped with files on students' personal histories and financial backgrounds to create a student database. In the next section, you will learn about relational database models.

byte   A group of eight bits that represents a single character.

field   A characteristic of interest that describes an entity.

record   A grouping of logically related fields.

table   A grouping of logically related records.

The Relational Database Model

database management system (DBMS) The software program (or group of programs) that provide access to a database.

A **database management system (DBMS)** is a set of programs that provide users with tools to create and manage a database. Managing a database refers to the processes of adding, deleting, accessing, modifying, and analyzing data that are stored in a database. An organization can access these data by using query and reporting tools that are part of the DBMS or by utilizing application programs specifically written to perform this function. DBMSs also provide the mechanisms for maintaining the integrity of stored data, managing security and user access, and recovering information if the system fails. Because databases and DBMSs are essential to all areas of business, they must be carefully managed.

There are a number of different database architectures, but we focus on the relational database model because it is popular and easy to use. Other database models—for example, the hierarchical and network models—are the responsibility of the MIS function and are not used by organizational employees. Popular examples of relational databases are Microsoft Access and Oracle.

Most business data—especially accounting and financial data—traditionally were organized into simple tables consisting of columns and rows. Tables enable people to compare information quickly by row or column. Users can also retrieve items rather easily by locating the point of intersection of a particular row and column.

relational database model Data model based on the simple concept of tables in order to capitalize on characteristics of rows and columns of data.

The **relational database model** is based on the concept of two-dimensional tables. A relational database generally is not one big table—usually called a *flat file*—that contains all of the records and attributes. Such a design would entail far too much data redundancy. Instead, a relational database is usually designed with a number of related tables. Each of these tables contains records (listed in rows) and attributes (listed in columns).

data model A diagram that represents entities in the database and their relationships.

entity Any person, place, thing, or event of interest to a user.

instance Each row in a relational table, which is a specific, unique representation of the entity.

To be valuable, a relational database must be organized so that users can retrieve, analyze, and understand the data they need. A key to designing an effective database is the data model. A **data model** is a diagram that represents entities in the database and their relationships. An **entity** is a person, a place, a thing, or an event—such as a customer, an employee, or a product—about which an organization maintains information. Entities can typically be identified in the user's work environment. A record generally describes an entity. An **instance** of an entity refers to each row in a relational table, which is a specific, unique representation of the entity. For example, your university's student database contains an entity called "student." An instance of the student entity would be a particular student. Thus, you are an instance of the student entity in your university's student database.

attribute Each characteristic or quality of a particular entity.

Each characteristic or quality of a particular entity is called an **attribute**. For example, if our entities were a customer, an employee, and a product, entity attributes would include customer name, employee number, and product color.

Consider the relational database example about students diagrammed in **Figure 5.3**. The table contains data about the entity called students. As you can see, each row of the table corresponds to a single student record. (You have your own row in your university's student database.) Attributes of the entity are student name, undergraduate major, grade point average, and graduation date. The rows are the records on Sally Adams, John Jones, Jane Lee, Kevin Durham, Juan Rodriguez, Stella Zubnicki, and Ben Jones. Of course, your university keeps much more data on you than our example shows. In fact, your university's student database probably keeps hundreds of attributes on each student.

primary key A field (or attribute) of a record that uniquely identifies that record so that it can be retrieved, updated, and sorted.

Every record in the database must contain at least one field that uniquely identifies that record so that it can be retrieved, updated, and sorted. This identifier field (or attribute) is called the **primary key**. For example, a student record in a U.S. university would use a unique student number as its primary key. (*Note:* In the past, your Social Security number served as the primary key for your student record. However, for security reasons, this practice has been discontinued.) In Figure 5.3, Sally Adams is uniquely identified by her student ID of 012345.

secondary key A field that has some identifying information, but typically does not uniquely identify a record with complete accuracy.

In some cases, locating a particular record requires the use of secondary keys. A **secondary key** is another field that has some identifying information but typically does not identify the record with complete accuracy. For example, the student's major might be a secondary key if a user wanted to identify all of the students majoring in a particular field of study. It should not be the primary key, however, because many students can have the same major. Therefore, it cannot uniquely identify an individual student.

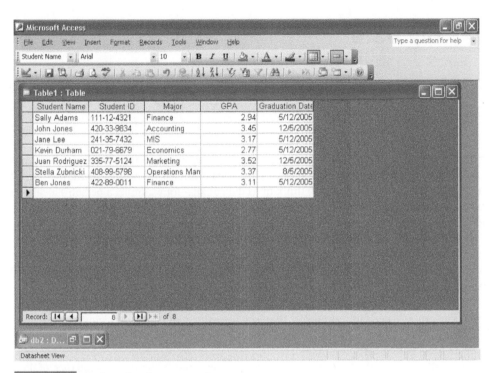

FIGURE 5.3 Student database example.

A **foreign key** is a field (or group of fields) in one table that uniquely identifies a row of another table. A foreign key is used to establish and enforce a link between two tables. We discuss foreign keys in Section 5.6.

Organizations implement databases to efficiently and effectively manage their data. There are a variety of operations that can be performed on databases. We look at three of these operations in detail in Section 5.6: query languages, normalization, and joins.

As we noted earlier in this chapter, organizations must manage huge quantities of data. Such data consist of structured and unstructured data and are called Big Data (discussed in Section 5.3). **Structured data** is highly organized in fixed fields in a data repository such as a relational database. Structured data must be defined in terms of field name and type (e.g., alphanumeric, numeric, and currency). **Unstructured data** refers to data that do not reside in a traditional relational database. Examples of unstructured data are e-mail messages, word processing documents, videos, images, audio files, PowerPoint presentations, Facebook posts, Tweets, Snaps, ratings and recommendations, and Web pages. Industry analysts estimate that 80 to 90 percent of the data in an organization are unstructured. To manage Big Data, many organizations are using special types of databases, which we also discuss in Section 5.3.

Because databases typically process data in real time (or near real time), it is not practical to allow users access to the databases. After all, the data will change while the user is looking at them! As a result, data warehouses have been developed to allow users to access data for decision making. You will learn about data warehouses in Section 5.4.

foreign key A field (or group of fields) in one table that uniquely identifies a row (or record) of another table.

structured data Highly organized data in fixed fields in a data repository such as a relational database that must be defined in terms of field name and type (e.g., alphanumeric, numeric, and currency).

unstructured data Data that do not reside in a traditional relational database.

Before you go on...

1. What is a data model?
2. What is a primary key? A secondary key?
3. What is an entity? An attribute? An instance?
4. What are the advantages and disadvantages of relational databases?

5.3   Big Data

LEARNING OBJECTIVE

Define Big Data and its basic characteristics.

We are accumulating data and information at an increasingly rapid pace from many diverse sources. In fact, organizations are capturing data about almost all events, including events that, in the past, firms never used to think of as data at all—for example, a person's location, the vibrations and temperature of an engine, and the stress at numerous points on a bridge—and then analyzing those data.

Organizations and individuals must process a vast amount of data that continues to increase dramatically. According to IDC (a technology research firm; **www.idc.com**), the world generates over one zettabyte (10^{21} bytes) of data each year. Furthermore, the amount of data produced worldwide is increasing by 50 percent each year.

As recently as the year 2000, only 25 percent of the stored information in the world was digital. The other 75 percent was analog; that is, it was stored on paper, film, vinyl records, and the like. By 2020, the amount of stored information in the world was more than 98 percent digital and less than 2 percent nondigital.

As we discussed at the beginning of this chapter, we refer to the superabundance of data available today as Big Data. **Big Data** is a collection of data that is so large and complex that it is difficult to manage using traditional database management systems. (We capitalize *Big Data* to distinguish the term from large amounts of traditional data.)

Essentially, Big Data is about predictions (see Predictive Analytics in Chapter 12). Predictions do not come from "teaching" computers to "think" like humans. Instead, predictions come from applying mathematics to huge quantities of data to infer probabilities. Consider these examples:

- The likelihood that an e-mail message is spam
- The likelihood that the typed letters "teh" are supposed to be "the"
- The likelihood that the direction and speed of a person jaywalking indicates that he will make it across the street in time, meaning that a self-driving car need only slow down slightly

Big Data systems perform well because they contain huge amounts of data on which to base their predictions. Moreover, these systems are configured to improve themselves over time by searching for the most valuable signals and patterns as more data are input.

Big Data   A collection of data so large and complex that it is difficult to manage using traditional database management systems.

Defining Big Data

It is difficult to define Big Data. Here we present two descriptions of the phenomenon. First, the technology research firm Gartner (**www.gartner.com**) defines Big Data as diverse, high-volume, high-velocity information assets that require new forms of processing in order to enhance decision making, lead to insights, and optimize business processes. Second, the Big Data Institute (TBDI; **www.bigdatainstitute.io**) defines Big Data as vast datasets that:

- Exhibit variety;
- Include structured, unstructured, and semistructured data;
- Are generated at high velocity with an uncertain pattern;
- Do not fit neatly into traditional, structured, relational databases; and
- Can be captured, processed, transformed, and analyzed in a reasonable amount of time only by sophisticated information systems.

Big Data generally consists of the following:

- Traditional enterprise data—for example, customer information from customer relationship management systems, transactional enterprise resource planning data, Web store transactions, operations data, and general ledger data.
- Machine-generated/sensor data—for example, smart meters; manufacturing sensors; sensors integrated into smartphones, automobiles, airplane engines, and industrial machines; equipment logs; and trading systems data.
- Social data—for example, customer feedback comments; microblogging sites such as Twitter; and social media sites such as Facebook, YouTube, and LinkedIn.
- Images captured by billions of devices located throughout the world, from digital cameras and camera phones to medical scanners and security cameras.

Let's take a look at a few specific examples of Big Data:

- Facebook's 2.45 billion users upload more than 350 million new photos every day. They also click a "like" button or leave a comment more than 5 billion times every day. Facebook's data warehouse stores more than 300 petabytes of data, and the platform receives 600 terabytes of incoming data per day.
- The 2 billion users of Google's YouTube service upload more than 300 hours of video per minute. Google itself processes on average more than 70,000 search queries per second.
- In July 2020 industry analysts estimated that Twitter users sent some 550 million tweets per day.
- Autonomous cars generate up to 20 terabytes of data per car per day.

Characteristics of Big Data

Big Data has three distinct characteristics: volume, velocity, and variety. These characteristics distinguish Big Data from traditional data:

1. *Volume*: We have noted the huge volume of Big Data. Consider machine-generated data, which are generated in much larger quantities than nontraditional data. For example, sensors in a single jet engine can generate 10 terabytes of data in 30 minutes. (See our discussion of the Internet of Things in Chapter 8.) With more than 25,000 airline flights per day, the daily volume of data from just this single source is incredible. Smart electrical meters, sensors in heavy industrial equipment, and telemetry from automobiles compound the volume problem.

2. *Velocity*: The rate at which data flow into an organization is rapidly increasing. Velocity is critical because it increases the speed of the feedback loop between a company, its customers, its suppliers, and its business partners. For example, the Internet and mobile technology enable online retailers to compile histories not only on final sales but also on their customers' every click and interaction. Companies that can quickly use that information—for example, by recommending additional purchases—gain competitive advantage.

3. *Variety*: Traditional data formats tend to be structured and relatively well described, and they change slowly. Traditional data include financial market data, point-of-sale transactions, and much more. In contrast, Big Data formats change rapidly. They include satellite imagery, broadcast audio streams, digital music files, Web page content, scans of government documents, and comments posted on social networks.

Irrespective of their source, structure, format, and frequency, Big Data are valuable. If certain types of data appear to have no value today, it is because we have not yet been able to analyze them effectively. For example, several years ago when Google began harnessing satellite imagery, capturing street views, and then sharing these geographical data for free, few people understood its value. Today, we recognize that such data are incredibly valuable because analyses of Big Data yield deep insights. We discuss analytics in detail in Chapter 12.

Issues with Big Data

Despite its extreme value, Big Data does have issues. In this section, we take a look at data integrity, data quality, and the nuances of analysis that are worth noting.

Big Data Can Come from Untrusted Sources

As we discussed earlier, one of the characteristics of Big Data is variety, meaning that Big Data can come from numerous, widely varied sources. These sources may be internal or external to the organization. For example, a company might want to integrate data from unstructured sources such as e-mails, call center notes, and social media posts with structured data about its customers from its data warehouse. The question is, how trustworthy are those external sources of data? For example, how trustworthy is a Tweet? The data may come from an unverified source. Furthermore, the data itself, reported by the source, may be false or misleading.

Big Data Is Dirty

Dirty data refers to inaccurate, incomplete, incorrect, duplicate, or erroneous data. Examples of such problems are misspelling of words and duplicate data such as retweets or company press releases that appear multiple times in social media.

Suppose a company is interested in performing a competitive analysis using social media data. The company wants to see how often a competitor's product appears in social media outlets as well as the sentiments associated with those posts. The company notices that the number of positive posts about the competitor is twice as great as the number of positive posts about itself. This finding could simply be a case of the competitor pushing out its press releases to multiple sources; in essence, blowing its own horn. Alternatively, the competitor could be getting many people to retweet an announcement.

Big Data Changes, Especially in Data Streams

Organizations must be aware that data quality in an analysis can change, or the data themselves can change, because the conditions under which the data are captured can change. For example, imagine a utility company that analyzes weather data and smart-meter data to predict customer power usage. What happens when the utility is analyzing these data in real time and it discovers that data are missing from some of its smart meters?

Managing Big Data

Big Data makes it possible to do many things that were previously much more difficult; for example, to spot business trends more rapidly and accurately, to prevent disease, to track crime, and so on. When Big Data is properly analyzed, it can reveal valuable patterns and information that were previously hidden because of the amount of work required to discover them. Leading corporations, such as Walmart and Google, have been able to process Big Data for years, but only at great expense. Today's hardware, cloud computing (see Technology Guide 3), and open-source software make processing Big Data affordable for most organizations.

For many organizations the first step toward managing data was to integrate information silos into a database environment and then to develop data warehouses for decision making. An *information silo* is an information system that does not communicate with other related information systems in an organization. After they completed this step, many organizations turned their attention to the business of information management—making sense of their rapidly expanding data. In recent years, Oracle, IBM, Microsoft, and SAP have spent billions of dollars purchasing software firms that specialize in data management and business analytics. (You will learn about business analytics in Chapter 12.)

In addition to existing data management systems, today many organizations employ NoSQL databases to process Big Data. Think of them as "not only SQL" (structured query language) databases. (We discuss SQL in Section 5.6.)

As you have seen in this chapter, traditional relational databases such as Oracle and MySQL store data in tables organized into rows and columns. Recall that each row is associated with a unique record, and each column is associated with a field that defines an attribute of that account.

In contrast, NoSQL databases can manipulate structured as well as unstructured data as well as inconsistent or missing data. For this reason, NoSQL databases are particularly useful when working with Big Data. Hadoop and MapReduce are particularly useful when analyzing massive databases.

Hadoop (www.hadoop.apache.org) is not a type of database. Rather, it is a collection of programs that allow people to store, retrieve, and analyze very large datasets using massively parallel processing. *Massively parallel processing* is the coordinated processing of an application by multiple processors that work on different parts of the application, with each processor utilizing its own operating system and memory. As such, Hadoop enables users to access NoSQL databases, which can be spread across thousands of servers, without a reduction in performance. For example, a large database application that could take 20 hours of processing time on a centralized relational database system might take only a few minutes when using Hadoop's parallel processing.

MapReduce refers to the software procedure of dividing an analysis into pieces that can be distributed across different servers in multiple locations. MapReduce first distributes the analysis (map) and then collects and integrates the results back into a single report (reduce).

Many products use NoSQL databases, including Cassandra (www.cassandra.apache.org), CouchDB (www.couchdb.apache.org), and MongoDB (www.mongodb.org). Let's take a look at how eHarmony uses Redis's (www.redis.io) in-memory NoSQL database. An in-memory database is a DBMS that primarily relies on main memory (see Technology Guide 1) for data storage, in contrast to DBMSs that use hard-drive storage.

The matchmaking site eHarmony (www.eharmony.com) uses Oracle's DBMS for cold data and Redis for hot data. *Cold data* refers to the storage of relatively inactive data that does not have to be accessed frequently or rapidly. *Hot data* refers to data that must be accessed frequently and rapidly. The eHarmony matching system applies analytics in near real time to quickly pair a candidate with a best-case potential match. Quickly serving up compatible matches requires rapid searches of personality trait data (i.e., Redis used with hot data). eHarmony's back-end business operations do not require high-speed access to data and therefore use Oracle with cold data.

Putting Big Data to Use

Modern organizations must manage Big Data and gain value from it. They can employ several strategies to achieve this objective.

Making Big Data Available
Making Big Data available for relevant stakeholders can help organizations gain value. For example, consider open data in the public sector. Open data are accessible public data that individuals and organizations can use to create new businesses and solve complex problems. In particular, government agencies gather vast amounts of data, some of which are Big Data. Making those data available can provide economic benefits. In fact, an Open Data 500 study at the GovLab at New York University discovered 500 examples of U.S.-based companies whose business models depend on analyzing open government data.

Enabling Organizations to Conduct Experiments
Big Data allows organizations to improve performance by conducting controlled experiments. For example, Amazon (and many other companies such as Google and LinkedIn) constantly experiments by offering slightly different looks on its website. These experiments are called A/B experiments, because each experiment has only two possible outcomes. Here is an example of an A/B experiment at Etsy (www.etsy.com), an online marketplace for vintage and handmade products.

When Etsy analysts noticed that one of its Web pages attracted customer attention but failed to maintain it, they looked more closely at the page and discovered that it had few "calls to action." (A call to action is an item, such as a button, on a Web page that enables a customer to do something.) On this particular Etsy page, customers could leave, buy, search, or click on two additional product images. The analysts decided to show more product images on the page.

Consequently, one group of visitors to the page saw a strip across the top of the page that displayed additional product images. Another group saw only the two original product images.

On the page with additional images, customers viewed more products and, significantly, bought more products. The results of this experiment revealed valuable information to Etsy.

Microsegmentation of Customers

Segmentation of a company's customers means dividing them into groups that share one or more characteristics. Microsegmentation simply means dividing customers up into very small groups, or even down to the individual customer.

For example, Paytronix Systems (www.paytronix.com) provides loyalty and rewards program software for thousands of different restaurants. Paytronix gathers restaurant guest data from a variety of sources beyond loyalty and gift programs, including social media. Paytronix analyzes this Big Data to help its restaurant clients microsegment their guests. Restaurant managers are now able to more precisely customize their loyalty and gift programs. Since they have taken these steps, they are noting improved profitability and customer satisfaction in their restaurants.

POM Creating New Business Models

Companies are able to use Big Data to create new business models. For example, a commercial transportation company operated a substantial fleet of large long-haul trucks. The company recently placed sensors on all of its trucks. These sensors wirelessly communicate sizeable amounts of information to the company, a process called *telematics*. The sensors collect data on vehicle usage—including acceleration, braking, cornering, and so on—in addition to driver performance and vehicle maintenance.

By analyzing this Big Data, the company was able to improve the condition of its trucks through near-real-time analysis that proactively suggested preventive maintenance. The company was also able to improve the driving skills of its operators by analyzing their driving styles.

The transportation company then made its Big Data available to its insurance carrier. Using this data, the insurance carrier was able to perform a more precise risk analysis of driver behavior and the condition of the trucks. The carrier then offered the transportation company a new pricing model that lowered its premiums by 10 percent due to safety improvements enabled by analysis of the Big Data.

Organizations Can Analyze More Data

In some cases, organizations can even process all of the data relating to a particular phenomenon, so they do not have to rely as much on sampling. Random sampling works well, but it is not as effective as analyzing an entire dataset. Random sampling also has some basic weaknesses. To begin with, its accuracy depends on ensuring randomness when collecting the sample data. However, achieving such randomness is problematic. Systematic biases in the process of data collection can cause results to be highly inaccurate. For example, consider political polling using landline phones. This sample tends to exclude people who use only cell phones. This bias can seriously skew the results because cell phone users are typically younger and more liberal than people who rely primarily on landline phones.

Big Data Used in the Functional Areas of the Organization

In this section, we provide examples of how Big Data is valuable to various functional areas in the firm.

HRM Human Resources

Employee benefits, particularly health care, represent a major business expense. Consequently, some companies have turned to Big Data to better manage these benefits. Caesars Entertainment (www.caesars.com), for example, analyzes health-insurance claim data for its 65,000 employees and their covered family members. Managers can track thousands of variables that indicate how employees use medical services, such as the number of emergency room visits and whether employees choose a generic or brand name drug.

Consider the following scenario. Data revealed that too many employees with medical emergencies were being treated at hospital emergency rooms rather than at less expensive urgent-care facilities. The company launched a campaign to remind employees of the high cost of emergency room visits, and they provided a list of alternative facilities. Subsequently, 10,000 emergencies shifted to less expensive alternatives, for a total savings of $4.5 million.

Big Data is also having an impact on *hiring*. An example is Catalyst IT Services (www. catalyte.io), a technology outsourcing company that hires teams for programming jobs. Traditional recruiting is typically too slow, and hiring managers often subjectively choose candidates who are not the best fit for the job. Catalyst addresses this problem by requiring candidates to fill out an online assessment. It then uses the assessment to collect thousands of data points about each candidate. In fact, the company collects more data based on *how* candidates answer than on *what* they answer.

For example, the assessment might give a problem requiring calculus to an applicant who is not expected to know the subject. How the candidate responds—laboring over an answer, answering quickly and then returning later, or skipping the problem entirely—provides insight into how that candidate might deal with challenges that he or she will encounter on the job. That is, someone who labors over a difficult question might be effective in an assignment that requires a methodical approach to problem solving, whereas an applicant who takes a more aggressive approach might perform better in a different job setting.

The benefit of this Big Data approach is that it recognizes that people bring different skills to the table and there is no one-size-fits-all person for any job. Analyzing millions of data points can reveal which attributes candidates bring to specific situations.

As one measure of success, employee turnover at Catalyst averages about 15 percent per year, compared with more than 30 percent for its U.S. competitors and more than 20 percent for similar companies overseas.

MKT **Product Development**   Big Data can help capture customer preferences and put that information to work in designing new products. For example, Ford Motor Company (www.ford.com) was considering a "three blink" turn indicator that had been available on its European cars for years. Unlike the turn signals on its U.S. vehicles, this indicator flashes three times at the driver's touch and then automatically shuts off.

Ford decided that conducting a full-scale market research test on this blinker would be too costly and time consuming. Instead, it examined auto-enthusiast websites and owner forums to discover what drivers were saying about turn indicators. Using text-mining algorithms, researchers culled more than 10,000 mentions and then summarized the most relevant comments.

The results? Ford introduced the three-blink indicator on the new Ford Fiesta in 2010, and by 2013 it was available on most Ford products. Although some Ford owners complained online that they have had trouble getting used to the new turn indicator, many others defended it. Ford managers note that the use of text-mining algorithms was critical in this effort because they provided the company with a complete picture that would not have been available using traditional market research.

POM **Operations**   For years, companies have been using information technology to make their operations more efficient. Consider United Parcel Service (UPS). The company has long relied on data to improve its operations. Specifically, it uses sensors in its delivery vehicles that can, among other things, capture the truck's speed and location, the number of times it is placed in Reverse, and whether the driver's seat belt is buckled. These data are uploaded at the end of each day to a UPS data center, where they are analyzed overnight. By combining GPS information and data from sensors installed on more than 46,000 vehicles, UPS reduced fuel consumption by 8.4 million gallons, and it cut 85 million miles off its routes.

MKT **Marketing**   Marketing managers have long used data to better understand their customers and to target their marketing efforts more directly. Today, Big Data enables marketers to craft much more personalized messages.

The United Kingdom's InterContinental Hotels Group (IHG; www.ihg.com) gathered details about the members of its Priority Club rewards program, such as income levels and whether members prefer family-style or business-traveler accommodations. The company then consolidated all this information with information obtained from social media into a single data warehouse. Using its data warehouse and analytics software, the hotelier launched a new marketing campaign. Where previous marketing campaigns generated, on average, between 7 and 15 customized marketing messages, the new campaign generated more than 1,500. IHG rolled out these messages in stages to an initial core of 12 customer groups, each of which is defined by 4,000 attributes. One group, for example, tends to stay on weekends, redeem reward points for gift cards, and register through IHG marketing partners. Using this information, IHG sent these customers a marketing message that alerted them to local weekend events.

The campaign proved to be highly successful. It generated a 35 percent higher rate of customer conversions, or acceptances, than previous similar campaigns.

POM Government Operations   Consider the United Kingdom. According to the INRIX Traffic Scorecard, although the United States has the worst congestion on average, London topped the world list for metropolitan areas. In London, drivers wasted an average of 101 hours per year in gridlock. Congestion is bad for business. The INRIX study estimated that the cost to the U.K. economy would be £307 billion between 2013 and 2030.

Congestion is also harmful to urban resilience, negatively affecting both environmental and social sustainability in terms of emissions, global warming, air quality, and public health. As for the livability of a modern city, congestion is an important component of the urban transport user experience (UX).

Calculating levels of UX satisfaction at any given time involves solving a complex equation with a range of key variables and factors: total number of transport assets (road and rail capacity, plus parking spaces), users (vehicles, pedestrians), incidents (roadwork, accidents, breakdowns), plus expectations (anticipated journey times and passenger comfort).

The growing availability of Big Data sources within London—for example, traffic cameras and sensors on cars and roadways—can help to create a new era of smart transport. Analyzing this Big Data offers new ways for traffic analysts in London to "sense the city" and enhance transport via real-time estimation of traffic patterns and rapid deployment of traffic management strategies.

Before you go on...

1. Define Big Data.
2. Describe the characteristics of Big Data.
3. Describe how companies can use Big Data to a gain competitive advantage.

5.4 Data Warehouses and Data Marts

LEARNING OBJECTIVE

Explain the elements necessary to successfully implement and maintain data warehouses.

Today, the most successful companies are those that can respond quickly and flexibly to market changes and opportunities. A key to this response is the effective and efficient use of data and information by analysts and managers. The challenge is to provide users with access to corporate data so they can analyze the data to make better decisions. Let's consider an example. If the manager of a local bookstore wanted to know the profit margin on used books at her store, then she could obtain that information from her database using SQL or query by example (QBE). However, if she needed to know the trend in the profit margins on used books over the past 10 years, then she would have to construct a very complicated SQL or QBE query. (Both SQL and QBE are defined in section 5.6.)

This example illustrates several reasons why organizations are building data warehouses and data marts. First, the bookstore's databases contain the necessary information to answer the manager's query, but the information is not organized in a way that makes it easy for her to find what she needs. Therefore, complicated queries might take a long time to answer, and they also might degrade the performance of the databases. Second, transactional databases are designed to be updated. This update process requires extra processing. Data warehouses and data marts are read-only. Therefore, the extra processing is eliminated because data already contained in the data warehouse are not updated. Third, transactional databases are designed to access a single record at a time. In contrast, data warehouses are designed to access large groups of related records.

To solve these problems, companies are using a variety of tools with data warehouses and data marts to make it easier and faster for users to access, analyze, and query data. You will learn about these tools in Chapter 12 on business analytics.

Describing Data Warehouses and Data Marts

In general, data warehouses and data marts support business analytics applications. As you will see in Chapter 12, business analytics encompasses a broad category of applications, technologies, and processes for gathering, storing, accessing, and analyzing data to help business users make better decisions. A **data warehouse** is a repository of historical data that are organized by subject to support decision makers within the organization.

Because data warehouses are so expensive, they are used primarily by large companies. A **data mart** is a low-cost, scaled-down version of a data warehouse that is designed for the end-user needs in a strategic business unit (SBU) or an individual department. Data marts can be implemented more quickly than data warehouses, often in less than 90 days. Furthermore, they support local rather than central control by conferring power on the user group. Typically, groups that need a single or a few business analytics applications require only a data mart rather than a data warehouse.

The basic characteristics of data warehouses and data marts include the following:

- *Organized by business dimension or subject.* Data are organized by subject—for example, by customer, vendor, product, price level, and region. This arrangement differs from transactional systems, where data are organized by business process such as order entry, inventory control, and accounts receivable.

- *Use online analytical processing.* Typically, organizational databases are oriented toward handling transactions. That is, databases use *online transaction processing* (OLTP), where business transactions are processed online as soon as they occur. The objectives are speed and efficiency, which are critical to a successful Internet-based business operation. In contrast, data warehouses and data marts, which are designed to support decision makers but not OLTP, use online analytical processing (OLAP), which involves the analysis of accumulated data by end users. We consider OLAP in greater detail in Chapter 12.

- *Integrated.* Data are collected from multiple systems and are then integrated around subjects. For example, customer data may be extracted from internal (and external) systems and then integrated around a customer identifier, thereby creating a comprehensive view of the customer.

- *Time variant.* Data warehouses and data marts maintain historical data; that is, data that include time as a variable. Unlike transactional systems, which maintain only recent data (such as for the last day, week, or month), a warehouse or mart may store years of data. Organizations use historical data to detect deviations, trends, and long-term relationships.

- *Nonvolatile.* Data warehouses and data marts are nonvolatile—that is, users cannot change or update the data. Therefore, the warehouse or mart reflects history, which, as we just saw, is critical for identifying and analyzing trends. Warehouses and marts are updated, but through IT-controlled load processes rather than by users.

data warehouse A repository of historical data that are organized by subject to support decision makers in the organization.

data mart A low-cost, scaled-down version of a data warehouse that is designed for the end-user needs in a strategic business unit (SBU) or a department.

- *Multidimensional.* Typically, the data warehouse or mart uses a multidimensional data structure. Recall that relational databases store data in two-dimensional tables. In contrast, data warehouses and marts store data in more than two dimensions. For this reason, the data are said to be stored in a **multidimensional structure**. A common representation for this multidimensional structure is the *data cube.*

multidimensional structure Storage of data in more than two dimensions; a common representation is the data cube.

The data in data warehouses and marts are organized by *business dimensions*, which are subjects such as product, geographic area, and time period that represent the edges of the data cube. If you look ahead to Figure 5.6 for an example of a data cube, you see that the product dimension is composed of nuts, screws, bolts, and washers; the geographic area dimension is composed of East, West, and Central; and the time period dimension is composed of 2016, 2017, and 2018. Users can view and analyze data from the perspective of these business dimensions. This analysis is intuitive because the dimensions are presented in business terms that users can easily understand.

A Generic Data Warehouse Environment

The environment for data warehouses and marts includes the following:

- Source systems that provide data to the warehouse or mart
- Data-integration technology and processes that prepare the data for use
- Different architectures for storing data in an organization's data warehouse or data marts
- Different tools and applications for the variety of users (You will learn about these tools and applications in Chapter 12.)
- **Metadata** (data about the data in a repository), data quality, and governance processes that ensure that the warehouse or mart meets its purposes

Figure 5.4 depicts a generic data warehouse or data mart environment. Let's drill down into the component parts.

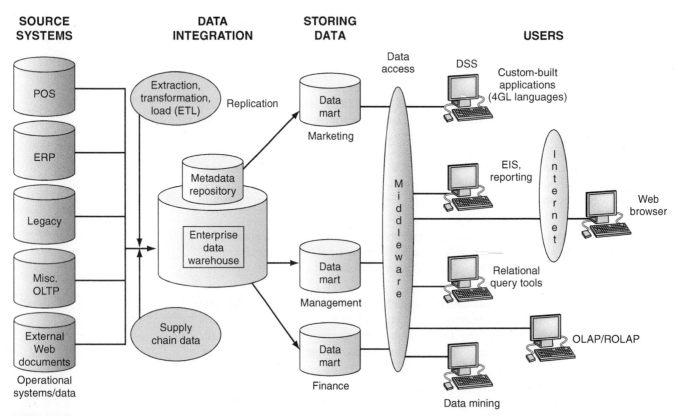

FIGURE 5.4 Data warehouse framework.

Source Systems   There is typically some "organizational pain point"—that is, a business need—that motivates a firm to develop its BI capabilities. Working backward, this pain leads to information requirements, BI applications, and requirements for source system data. These data requirements can range from a single source system, as in the case of a data mart, to hundreds of source systems, as in the case of an enterprise-wide data warehouse.

Modern organizations can select from a variety of source systems, including operational/transactional systems, enterprise resource planning (ERP) systems, website data, third-party data (e.g., customer demographic data), and more. The trend is to include more types of data (e.g., sensing data from RFID tags). These source systems often use different software packages (e.g., IBM, Oracle), and they store data in different formats (e.g., relational, hierarchical).

A common source for the data in data warehouses is the company's operational databases, which can be relational databases. To differentiate between relational databases and multidimensional data warehouses and marts, imagine your company manufactures four products—nuts, screws, bolts, and washers—and has sold them in three territories—East, West, and Central—for the previous three years—2019, 2020, and 2021. In a relational database, these sales data would resemble **Figure 5.5(a)** through **(c)**. In a multidimensional database, in contrast, these data would be represented by a three-dimensional matrix (or data cube), as depicted in **Figure 5.6**. This matrix represents sales *dimensioned by* products, regions, and year. Notice that Figure 5.5(a) presents only sales for 2016. Sales for 2017 and 2018 are presented in Figure 5.5(b) and (c), respectively. **Figure 5.7(a)** through **(c)** illustrates the equivalence between these relational and multidimensional databases.

Unfortunately, many source systems that have been in use for years contain "bad data"—for example, missing or incorrect data—and they are poorly documented. As a result, data-profiling software should be used at the beginning of a warehousing project to better understand the data. Among other things, this software can provide statistics on missing data, identify possible primary and foreign keys, and reveal how derived values—for example, column 3 = column 1 + column 2—are calculated. Subject area database specialists such as marketing and human resources personnel can also assist in understanding and accessing the data in source systems.

Organizations need to address other source systems issues as well. For example, many organizations maintain multiple systems that contain some of the same data. These enterprises need to select the best system as the source system. Organizations must also decide how granular, or detailed, the data should be. For example, does the organization need daily sales figures or data for individual transactions? The conventional wisdom is that it is best to store data at a highly granular level because someone will likely request those data at some point.

(a) 2019

Product	Region	Sales
Nuts	East	50
Nuts	West	60
Nuts	Central	100
Screws	East	40
Screws	West	70
Screws	Central	80
Bolts	East	90
Bolts	West	120
Bolts	Central	140
Washers	East	20
Washers	West	10
Washers	Central	30

(b) 2020

Product	Region	Sales
Nuts	East	60
Nuts	West	70
Nuts	Central	110
Screws	East	50
Screws	West	80
Screws	Central	90
Bolts	East	100
Bolts	West	130
Bolts	Central	150
Washers	East	30
Washers	West	20
Washers	Central	40

(c) 2021

Product	Region	Sales
Nuts	East	70
Nuts	West	80
Nuts	Central	120
Screws	East	60
Screws	West	90
Screws	Central	100
Bolts	East	110
Bolts	West	140
Bolts	Central	160
Washers	East	40
Washers	West	30
Washers	Central	50

FIGURE 5.5 **Relational databases.**

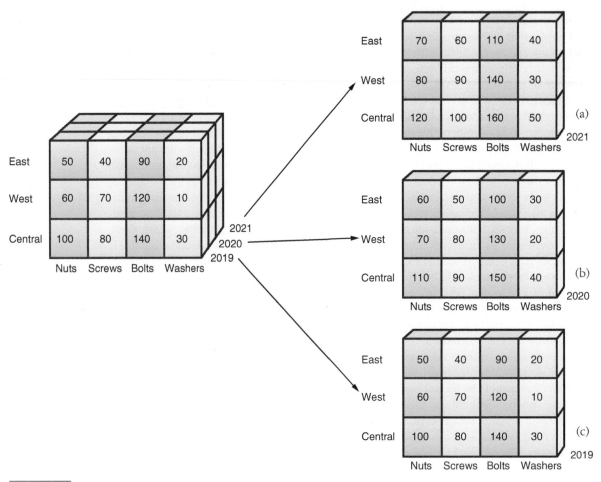

FIGURE 5.6 Data cube.

Data Integration   In addition to storing data in their source systems, organizations need to *extract* the data, *transform* them, and then *load* them into a data mart or warehouse. This process is often called ETL, although the term *data integration* is increasingly being used to reflect the growing number of ways that source system data can be handled. For example, in some cases, data are extracted, loaded into a mart or warehouse, and then transformed (i.e., ELT rather than ETL).

Data extraction can be performed either by handwritten code such as SQL queries or by commercial data-integration software. Most companies employ commercial software. This software makes it relatively easy to (1) specify the tables and attributes in the source systems that are to be used; (2) map and schedule the movement of the data to the target, such as a data mart or warehouse; (3) make the required transformations; and, ultimately, (4) load the data.

After the data are extracted, they are transformed to make them more useful. For example, data from different systems may be integrated around a common key, such as a customer identification number. Organizations adopt this approach to create a 360-degree view of all of their interactions with their customers. As an example of this process, consider a bank. Customers can engage in a variety of interactions: visiting a branch, banking online, using an ATM, obtaining a car loan, and more. The systems for these touch points—defined as the numerous ways that organizations interact with customers, such as e-mail, the Web, direct contact, and the telephone—are typically independent of one another. To obtain a holistic picture of how customers are using the bank, the bank must integrate the data from the various source systems into a data mart or warehouse.

Other kinds of transformations also take place. For example, format changes to the data may be required, such as using *male* and *female* to denote gender, as opposed to 0 and 1 or M

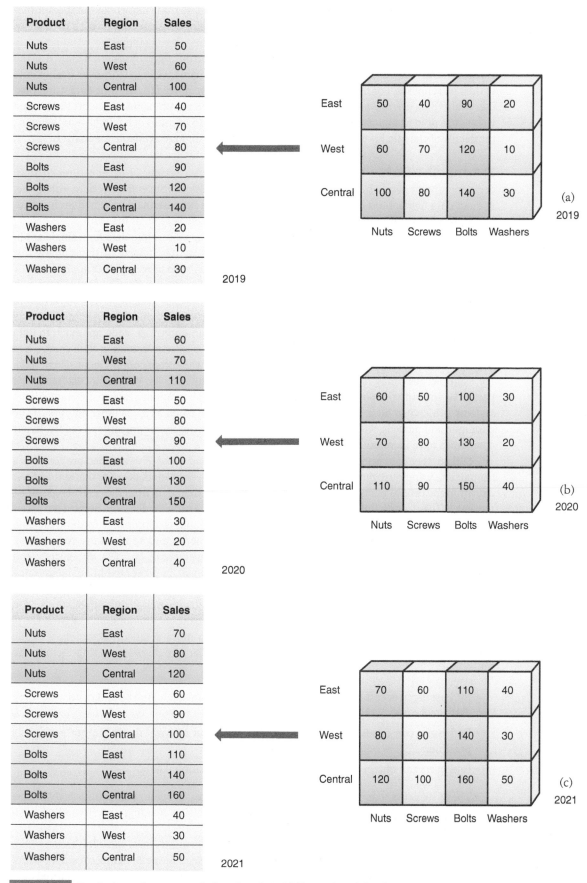

2019

Product	Region	Sales
Nuts	East	50
Nuts	West	60
Nuts	Central	100
Screws	East	40
Screws	West	70
Screws	Central	80
Bolts	East	90
Bolts	West	120
Bolts	Central	140
Washers	East	20
Washers	West	10
Washers	Central	30

2020

Product	Region	Sales
Nuts	East	60
Nuts	West	70
Nuts	Central	110
Screws	East	50
Screws	West	80
Screws	Central	90
Bolts	East	100
Bolts	West	130
Bolts	Central	150
Washers	East	30
Washers	West	20
Washers	Central	40

2021

Product	Region	Sales
Nuts	East	70
Nuts	West	80
Nuts	Central	120
Screws	East	60
Screws	West	90
Screws	Central	100
Bolts	East	110
Bolts	West	140
Bolts	Central	160
Washers	East	40
Washers	West	30
Washers	Central	50

FIGURE 5.7 Equivalence between relational and multidimensional databases.

and F. Aggregations may be performed, say on sales figures, so that queries can use the summaries rather than recalculating them each time. Data-cleansing software may be used to clean up the data; for example, eliminating duplicate records for the same customer.

Finally, data are loaded into the warehouse or mart during a specified period known as the "load window." This window is becoming smaller as companies seek to store ever-fresher data in their warehouses. For this reason, many companies have moved to real-time data warehousing, where data are moved using data-integration processes from source systems to the data warehouse or mart almost instantly. For example, within 15 minutes of a purchase at Walmart, the details of the sale have been loaded into a warehouse and are available for analysis.

Storing the Data   Organizations can choose from a variety of architectures to store decision-support data. The most common architecture is *one central enterprise data warehouse*, without data marts. Most organizations use this approach because the data stored in the warehouse are accessed by all users, and they represent the single version of the truth.

Another architecture is *independent data marts*. These marts store data for a single application or a few applications, such as marketing and finance. Organizations that employ this architecture give only limited thought to how the data might be used for other applications or by other functional areas in the organization. Clearly, this is a very application-centric approach to storing data.

The independent data mart architecture is not particularly effective. Although it may meet a specific organizational need, it does not reflect an enterprise-wide approach to data management. Instead, the various organizational units create independent data marts. Not only are these marts expensive to build and maintain, but they often contain inconsistent data. For example, they may have inconsistent data definitions such as: What is a customer? Is a particular individual a potential or a current customer? They might also use different source systems, which can have different data for the same item, such as a customer address (if the customer had moved). Although independent data marts are an organizational reality, larger companies have increasingly moved to data warehouses.

Still another data warehouse architecture is the *hub and spoke*. This architecture contains a central data warehouse that stores the data plus multiple dependent data marts that source their data from the central repository. Because the marts obtain their data from the central repository, the data in these marts still comprise the *single version of the truth* for decision-support purposes.

The dependent data marts store the data in a format that is appropriate for how the data will be used and for providing faster response times to queries and applications. As you have learned, users can view and analyze data from the perspective of business dimensions and measures. This analysis is intuitive because the dimensions are presented in business terms that users can easily understand.

Companies have reported hundreds of successful data-warehousing applications. You can read client success stories and case studies at the websites of vendors such as NCR Corp. (www.ncr.com) and Oracle (www.oracle.com). For a more detailed discussion, visit the Data Warehouse Institute (www.tdwi.org). The benefits of data warehousing include the following:

- End users can access needed data quickly and easily through Web browsers because these data are located in one place.
- End users can conduct extensive analysis with data in ways that were not previously possible.
- End users can obtain a consolidated view of organizational data.

These benefits can improve business knowledge, provide competitive advantage, enhance customer service and satisfaction, facilitate decision making, and streamline business processes.

Despite their many benefits, data warehouses and data marts have some limitations. Two emerging solutions are a data lake and a data lakehouse. **Figure 5.8** compares data warehouses and data lakes. You will notice that the data lake can handle more than structured data and employs artificial intelligence and machine learning to extract value from the data. IT's About Business 5.2 highlights some of these limitations and considers the emerging solution of data lakehouses.

Data Warehouses versus Data Lakes		
	Data Warehouse	**Data Lake**
Data Types	Structured, processed data from operational databases, applications, and transactional systems	Structured, semistructured, and unstructured data from sensors, apps, websites, etc.
Purpose	Predefined purpose for business intelligence, batch reporting, and data visualization	May not have a predefined purpose; typically used for artificial intelligence, machine learning, deep analysis, and discovery
Users	Data engineers, business analysts, data analysts	Data engineers and data scientists
Benefits	Categorized historical data stored in a single repository with ease of access for the end user	Data stored in its native format, allowing flexibility for data scientists to analyze and develop modes from diverse data sources

FIGURE 5.8 **Comparison of Data Warehouses and Data Lakes.**

data lake A central repository that stores all of an organization's data, regardless of their source or format.

IT's About Business **5.2**

MIS Data Lakes and Lakehouses

Most large organizations have an enterprise data warehouse (EDW) that contains data that have been cleaned and prepared for analysis through a process known as *extract, transform, and load* (ETL). It is crucial to execute this process accurately because analysis performed on inaccurate data will produce bad reports. With EDWs, organizations maintain the data using traditional databases, meaning that the EDW is built upon labeled rows and columns of data. EDWs are the primary mechanism in many organizations for performing analytics, reporting, and operations.

Despite their benefits to organizations, EDWs do have problems. Specifically, they require organizations to design the data model—called the *schema*—before they load any data into the EDW. A database schema defines the structure of the database and the data contained within that database. For example, in the case of relational databases, the schema specifies the tables and fields of the database. The schema also describes the content and structure of the physical data stored. These descriptions are called metadata, the data about the data that helps users understand the data contained in the database.

Because the structure of EDWs is defined by the schema, they are relatively inflexible and can answer only a limited number of questions. Further, EDWs are not designed to use unstructured data, such as streaming data from sensors (see the Internet of Things in Chapter 8) or social media data such as blog postings, product reviews, TikTok videos, Tweets, and photographs.

EDWs are also too rigid to be effective with Big Data due to the volume, variety, and velocity with which Big Data moves. As a result of these problems, organizations have realized that EDWs cannot meet all their business needs.

The emergence of systems such as Apache Hadoop (**www.hadoop.apache.org**) has enabled organizations to implement parallel searches on large data repositories to speed up data operations significantly. The ability to handle large, unstructured datasets provided the impetus for creating data lakes. A **data lake** is a central repository that stores all of an organization's data, regardless of the source or format of those data. Data lakes receive data in any form, from structured to unstructured. Structured data, such as POS transaction data, inventory data, and IoT data, can be easily analyzed by both data lakes and EDWs.

Unlike an EDW, however, a data lake can also analyze unstructured data such as social media posts, videos, pictures, and pdf files. A significant advantage to the data lake is that the data do not have to be consistent. For example, organizations might maintain the same type of information in different data formats, depending on where the data originate.

Organizations do not have to transform the data before entering them into the data lake as they would for an EDW. The data structure is unknown when the data are fed into the data lake. Instead, it is discovered only when the data are read, meaning that users do not model the data until they use it. This process is more flexible, making it easier for users to discover and enter new data sources. The artificial intelligence and machine learning capabilities of a data lake make it an excellent tool for providing much-needed organizational insights.

Data lakes provide many benefits for organizations:

- Organizations can derive value from unlimited types of data.
- Organizations have no limits on how they can query the data.
- Organizations do not create data silos. Instead, data lakes provide a unified view of data across the organization.

To load data into a data lake, organizations should take these steps:

- Define the incoming data from a business perspective.
- Document the context, origin, and frequency of the incoming data.
- Classify the incoming data's security level (public, internal, sensitive, restricted).
- Document the creation, usage, privacy, regulatory, and encryption business rules that apply to the incoming data.
- Identify the owner (sponsor) of the incoming data.
- Identify the data steward(s) who monitor and maintain the datasets.

After organizations follow these steps, they load all the data into a large table. Each data piece—a customer's name, a photograph, or a Facebook post—is placed in an individual cell. Metadata tags connect all the data in the data lake, so it does not matter where the data are located, where they came from, or the format. Organizations can add or change these tags as requirements evolve. Further, they can assign multiple tags to the same piece of data. Because the rules for storing the data do not need to be defined in advance, there is no need for expensive and time-consuming data modeling.

Organizations can also protect sensitive information by specifying who has access to the data in each cell and under what circumstances the data are loaded. For example, a retail operation might make cells containing customers' names and contact data available to sales and customer service. At the same time, however, it might make the cells having more sensitive, personally identifiable information or financial data available only to the finance department. In that way, when users run queries on the data, their access rights restrict which data they can view.

There are many examples of data lakes in practice. Let's consider how L'Oréal (www.lorealparisusa.com) employs its data lake.

POM **MKT** L'Oréal, a 100-year-old cosmetics industry leader, owns more than 40 brands. The company must analyze vast amounts of data, including 7 billion products manufactured annually, 50 million data points created daily, and 500 patents filed each year. The firm relies on scientists and marketing professionals to work together to create several thousand new formulas every year. The company must also ensure that its products are safe for humans. This process requires analyzing data about product formulas and raw materials as well as consumers' feelings toward the new formulas.

L'Oréal employed Talend (www.talend.com), a leading cloud-based data integration company, to create a data lake on Microsoft Azure. The platform integrates structured laboratory data with variable, often raw, unstructured data, such as images of models using L'Oréal cosmetics. The data are available in real time, and the data lake is refreshed several times daily.

ACCT L'Oréal developed its first application for the finance department to address the economic management of research. The application used data from their data lake to display performance indicators for research-related activities and their associated costs, such as tests for product certification.

L'Oréal's next application addressed research into the impact of its products on the human microbiome, which consists of the genetic material of all the microbes—bacteria, fungi, protozoa, and viruses—that live on and inside the human body. Another application involves products that can counter the effects of pollution on the skin.

These are complex, unstructured questions that require the type of analysis that data lakes offer. However, organizations continue to use EDWs in addition to data lakes because they have to ask both "small data" and "big data" questions. A small data question would be: "What is the total revenue for the Northeast region in 2020?" An EDW can easily and quickly answer this question because the data are well defined. A Big Data question would be: "Describe the detailed customer relationship over the past three years for a high-value customer who has moved her business to another firm." This question is more appropriate for a data lake because the variables are unclear and will probably include unstructured data such as e-mail messages and audio clips. It would be complicated or nearly impossible to answer with an EDW.

This approach requires that organizations maintain two systems for two types of data analysis. However, it is never recommended as a best practice to store data in two datasets in two formats. This disparity has given rise to a new concept called the *data lakehouse*. (Think of a lakehouse as a combination of the warehouse and the lake, not as a small structure that overlooks the lake.) The data lakehouse combines the structured query capabilities of an EDW and the unstructured AI and machine learning capabilities of the data lake. Essentially, it enables a single system to meet both operational and strategic needs.

Let's examine how Walgreens (www.walgreens.com) implemented a data lakehouse to support decision making regarding the distribution of the COVID-19 vaccine.

Walgreens' vision encompasses two major goals. The first is to ensure that the right medications are on the shelves when patients need them. The second is to help their pharmacists spend more time with patients and less time completing administrative tasks. However, their processes required a 48-hour turnaround, and their pharmacists could find only limited insights into the supply chain. The results were online and in-store order issues and miscalculated inventory levels. Walgreens needed a data solution that would provide accurate inventory insights and streamline operations so their pharmacists could focus on the patient rather than their systems.

Walgreens chose to complete its digital transformation with Microsoft Azure as their cloud provider and the Databricks Lakehouse Platform for its security, performance, and production scale. This combination of technologies migrated all of Walgreens' data into a lakehouse environment. It provided the pharmacists with data insights in near-instantaneous moments, not hours and days.

Since migrating to a lakehouse, Walgreens has optimized its supply chain by maintaining optimal inventory levels, thereby saving millions of dollars. The company is now processing 40,000 data events per second, and has realized an increase in pharmacists' productivity of 20 percent. As a result, pharmacists spend more time with patients, enabling them to improve their quality of care.

Questions

1. Discuss the advantages and disadvantages of enterprise data warehouses.

2. Describe the advantages and disadvantages of data lakes.

3. Why don't organizations use enterprise data warehouses to manage Big Data?

4. Describe the advantages and disadvantages of data lakehouses.

Sources: Compiled from S. Gibson, "The Rise of the Data Lakehouse: A New Era of Data Value," *CIO*, August 18, 2022; M. Segal, "Data Mart vs Data Warehouse vs Database vs Data Lake," zuar.com, December 28, 2021; A. Thusoo, "Data Lakes and Data Warehouses: The Two Sides of a Modern Cloud Data Platform," *Forbes*, July 7, 2020; C. Foot, "Key Factors for Successful Data Lake Implementation," TechTarget, July 6, 2020; V. Combs, "L'Oréal's New Data Lake Holds 100 Years of Product Development Research," *TechRepublic*, October 30, 2019; *Essential Guide to Data Lakes*, Matillion, 2019; S. Wooledge, "Data Lakes and Data Warehouses: Why You Need Both," Arcadia Data, October 11, 2018; T. King, "Three Key Data Lake Trends to Stay on Top of This Year," *Solutions Review*, May 11, 2018; T. Olavsrud, "6 Data Analytics Trends That Will Dominate 2018," *CIO*, March 15, 2018; P. Tyaqi and H. Demirkan, "Data Lakes: The Biggest Big Data Challenges," *Analytics Magazine*, September/October 2017; M. Hagstroem, M. Roggendorf, T. Saleh, and J. Sharma, "A Smarter Way to Jump into Data Lakes," McKinsey and Company, August 2017; P. Barth, "The New Paradigm for Big Data Governance," *CIO*, May 11, 2017; N. Mikhail, "Why Big Data Kills Businesses," *Fortune*, February 28, 2017; "Architecting Data Lakes," Zaloni, February 21, 2017; D. Kim, "Successful Data Lakes: A Growing Trend," The Data Warehousing Institute, February 16, 2017; L. Hester, "Maximizing Data Value with a Data Lake," Data Science Central, April 20, 2016; and https://www.databricks.com/customers/walgreens, accessed September 12, 2022.

Metadata   It is important to maintain data about the data, known as *metadata*, in the data warehouse. Both the IT personnel who operate and manage the data warehouse and the users who access the data require metadata. IT personnel need information about data sources; database, table, and column names; refresh schedules; and data-usage measures. Users' needs include data definitions, report and query tools, report distribution information, and contact information for the help desk.

Data Quality   The quality of the data in the warehouse must meet users' needs. If it does not, then users will not trust the data and ultimately will not use it. Most organizations find that the quality of the data in source systems is poor and must be improved before the data can be used in the data warehouse. Some of the data can be improved with data-cleansing software. The better, long-term solution, however, is to improve the quality at the source system level. This approach requires the business owners of the data to assume responsibility for making any necessary changes to implement this solution.

To illustrate this point, consider the case of a large hotel chain that wanted to conduct targeted marketing promotions using zip code data it collected from its guests when they checked in. When the company analyzed the zip code data, they discovered that many of the zip codes were 99999. How did this error occur? The answer is that the clerks were not asking customers for their zip codes, but they needed to enter something to complete the registration process. A short-term solution to this problem was to conduct the marketing campaign using city and state data instead of zip codes. The long-term solution was to make certain the clerks entered the actual zip codes. The latter solution required the hotel managers to assume responsibility for making certain their clerks entered the correct data.

Governance   To ensure that BI is meeting their needs, organizations must implement *governance* to plan and control their BI activities. Governance requires that people, committees, and processes be in place. Companies that are effective in BI governance often create a senior-level committee composed of vice presidents and directors who (1) ensure that the business strategies and BI strategies are in alignment, (2) prioritize projects, and (3) allocate resources. These companies also establish a middle management–level committee that oversees the various projects in the BI portfolio to ensure that these projects are being completed in accordance with the company's objectives. Finally, lower-level operational committees perform tasks such as creating data definitions and identifying and solving data problems. All of these committees rely on the collaboration and contributions of business users and IT personnel.

Users   Once the data are loaded in a data mart or warehouse, they can be accessed. At this point, the organization begins to obtain business value from BI; all of the prior stages constitute creating BI infrastructure.

There are many potential BI users, including IT developers; frontline workers; analysts; information workers; managers and executives; and suppliers, customers, and regulators. Some of these users are *information producers,* whose primary role is to create information for other users. IT developers and analysts typically fall into this category. Other users—including managers and executives—are *information consumers*, because they use information created by others.

Before you go on...

1. Differentiate between data warehouses and data marts.
2. Describe the characteristics of a data warehouse.
3. What are three possible architectures for data warehouses and data marts in an organization?
4. How might data lakes and data lakehouses reshape strategic planning for IT architecture?

| 5.5 | # Knowledge Management

WILEY PLUS

Author Lecture Videos are available exclusively in *WileyPLUS*.
Apply the Concept activities are available in the Appendix and in *WileyPLUS*.

LEARNING OBJECTIVE

Describe the benefits and challenges of implementing knowledge management systems in organizations.

As we have noted throughout this text, data and information are vital organizational assets. Knowledge is a vital asset as well. Successful managers have always valued and used intellectual assets. These efforts may not have been systematic, however, and they may not have ensured that knowledge was shared and dispersed in a way that benefited the overall organization. Moreover, industry analysts estimate that most of a company's knowledge assets are not housed in relational databases. Instead, they are dispersed in e-mail, word processing documents, spreadsheets, presentations on individual computers, and in people's heads. This arrangement makes it extremely difficult for companies to access and integrate this knowledge. The result frequently is less effective decision making.

Concepts and Definitions

knowledge management (KM) A process that helps organizations identify, select, organize, disseminate, transfer, and apply information and expertise that are part of the organization's memory and that typically reside within the organization in an unstructured manner.

Knowledge management (KM) is a process that helps organizations manipulate important knowledge that comprises part of the organization's memory, usually in an unstructured format. For an organization to be successful, knowledge, as a form of capital, must exist in a format that can be exchanged among persons. It must also be able to grow.

intellectual capital (or intellectual assets) Other terms for knowledge.

Knowledge

In the information technology context, knowledge is distinct from data and information. As you learned in Chapter 1, data are a collection of facts, measurements, and statistics; information is organized or processed data that are timely and accurate. Knowledge is information that is *contextual*, *relevant*, and *useful*. Simply put, knowledge is information in action. **Intellectual capital (or intellectual assets)** is another term for knowledge.

To illustrate, a bulletin listing all of the courses offered by your university during one semester would be considered *data*. When you register, you process the data from the bulletin to create your schedule for the semester. Your schedule would be considered *information*. Awareness of your work schedule, your major, your desired social schedule, and characteristics of different faculty members could be construed as *knowledge*, because it can affect the way you build your schedule. You see that this awareness is contextual and relevant (to developing an optimal schedule of classes) as well as useful (it can lead to changes in your schedule). The implication is that knowledge has strong experiential and reflective elements that distinguish it from information in a given context. Unlike information, knowledge can be used to solve a problem.

Numerous theories and models classify different types of knowledge. In the next section, we will focus on the distinction between explicit knowledge and tacit knowledge.

explicit knowledge The more objective, rational, and technical types of knowledge.

Explicit and Tacit Knowledge

Explicit knowledge deals with more objective, rational, and technical knowledge. In an organization, explicit knowledge consists of the policies, procedural guides, reports, products, strategies, goals, core competencies, and IT infrastructure of the enterprise. In other words, explicit knowledge is the knowledge that has been codified (documented) in a form that can be distributed to others or transformed into a process or a strategy. A description of how to process a job application that is documented in a firm's human resources policy manual is an example of explicit knowledge.

tacit knowledge The cumulative store of subjective or experiential learning, which is highly personal and hard to formalize.

In contrast, **tacit knowledge** is the cumulative store of subjective or experiential learning. In an organization, tacit knowledge consists of an organization's experiences, insights, expertise, know-how, trade secrets, skill sets, understanding, and learning. It also includes the organizational culture, which reflects the past and present experiences of the organization's people and processes, as well as the organization's prevailing values. Tacit knowledge is generally imprecise and costly to transfer. It is also highly personal. Finally, because it is unstructured, it is difficult to formalize or codify, in contrast to explicit knowledge. A salesperson who has worked with particular customers over time and has come to know their needs quite well would possess extensive tacit knowledge. This knowledge is typically not recorded. In fact, it might be difficult for the salesperson to put into writing, even if he or she were willing to share it.

Knowledge Management Systems

The goal of knowledge management is to help an organization make the most productive use of the knowledge it has accumulated. Historically, management information systems have focused on capturing, storing, managing, and reporting explicit knowledge. Organizations now realize they need to integrate explicit and tacit knowledge into formal information systems. **Knowledge management systems (KMSs)** refer to the use of modern information technologies—the Internet, intranets, extranets, and databases—to systematize, enhance, and expedite knowledge management both within one firm and among multiple firms. KMSs are intended to help an organization cope with turnover, rapid change, and downsizing by making the expertise of the organization's human capital widely accessible.

knowledge management systems (KMSs) Information technologies used to systematize, enhance, and expedite intra- and interfirm knowledge management.

Organizations can realize many benefits with KMSs. Most importantly, they make *best practices*—the most effective and efficient ways accomplishing business processes—readily available to a wide range of employees. Enhanced access to best-practice knowledge improves overall organizational performance. For example, account managers could make available their tacit knowledge about how best to manage large accounts. The organization could then use this knowledge when it trains new account managers. Other benefits include enhanced customer service, more efficient product development, and improved employee morale and retention.

At the same time, however, implementing effective KMSs presents several challenges. First, employees must be willing to share their personal tacit knowledge. To encourage this behavior, organizations must create a knowledge management culture that rewards employees who add their expertise to the knowledge base. Second, the organization must continually maintain and upgrade its knowledge base. Specifically, it must incorporate new knowledge and delete old, outdated knowledge. Finally, companies must be willing to invest in the resources needed to carry out these operations.

The KMS Cycle

A functioning KMS follows a cycle that consists of six steps (see **Figure 5.9**). The reason the system is cyclical is that knowledge is dynamically refined over time. The knowledge in an effective KMS is never finalized because the environment changes over time and knowledge must be updated to reflect these changes. The cycle works as follows:

1. *Create knowledge.* Knowledge is created as people determine new ways of doing things or develop know-how. Sometimes external knowledge is brought in.

2. *Capture knowledge.* New knowledge must be identified as valuable and be presented in a reasonable way.

3. *Refine knowledge.* New knowledge must be placed in context so that it is actionable. This is where tacit qualities (human insights) must be captured along with explicit facts.

4. *Store knowledge.* Useful knowledge must then be stored in a reasonable format in a knowledge repository so that other people in the organization can access it.

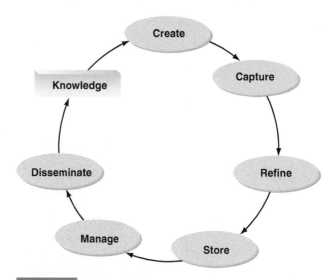

FIGURE 5.9 **The knowledge management system cycle.**

5. *Manage knowledge.* Like a library, the knowledge must be kept current. Therefore, it must be reviewed regularly to verify that it is relevant and accurate.

6. *Disseminate knowledge.* Knowledge must be made available in a useful format to anyone in the organization who needs it, anywhere and any time.

Before you go on...

1. What is knowledge management?
2. What is the difference between tacit knowledge and explicit knowledge?
3. Describe the knowledge management system cycle.

5.6 Appendix: Fundamentals of Relational Database Operations

WILEY PLUS

Author Lecture Videos are available exclusively in *WileyPLUS*.
Apply the Concept activities are available in the Appendix and in *WileyPLUS*.

LEARNING OBJECTIVE

Understand the processes of querying a relational database, entity–relationship modeling, and normalization and joins.

There are many operations possible with relational databases. In this section, we discuss three of these operations: query languages, normalization, and joins.

As you have seen in this chapter, a relational database is a collection of interrelated two-dimensional tables consisting of rows and columns. Each row represents a record, and each column (or field) represents an attribute (or characteristic) of that record. Every record in the database must contain at least one field that uniquely identifies that record so that it can be retrieved, updated, and sorted. This identifier field, or group of fields, is called the *primary key*. In some cases, locating a particular record requires the use of secondary keys. A secondary key is another field that has some identifying information, but typically does not uniquely identify the record. A foreign key is a field (or group of fields) in one table that matches the primary key value in a row of another table. A foreign key is used to establish and enforce a link between two tables.

These related tables can be joined when they contain common columns. The uniqueness of the primary key tells the DBMS which records are joined with others in related tables. This feature allows users great flexibility in the variety of queries they can make. Despite these features, however, the relational database model has some disadvantages. Because large-scale databases can be composed of many interrelated tables, the overall design can be complex, leading to slow search and access times.

Query Languages

structured query language
The most popular query language for requesting information from a relational database.

The most commonly performed database operation is searching for information. **Structured query language (SQL)** is the most popular query language used for interacting with a database. SQL allows people to perform complicated searches by using relatively simple statements or key words. Typical key words are SELECT (to choose a desired attribute), FROM (to specify the table or tables to be used), and WHERE (to specify conditions to apply in the query).

To understand how SQL works, imagine that a university wants to know the names of students who will graduate cum laude (but not magna or summa cum laude) in December 2005. (Refer to Figure 5.3 in this chapter.) The university IT staff would query the student relational database with an SQL statement such as:

SELECT Student_Name

FROM Student_Database

WHERE Grade_Point_Average > = 3.40 and Grade_Point_Average < 3.60.

The SQL query would return John Jones and Juan Rodriguez.

Another way to find information in a database is to use **query by example (QBE)**. In QBE, the user fills out a grid or template—also known as a *form*—to construct a sample or a description of the data desired. Users can construct a query quickly and easily by using drag-and-drop features in a DBMS such as Microsoft Access. Conducting queries in this manner is simpler than keying in SQL commands.

Entity–Relationship Modeling

Designers plan and create databases through the process of **entity–relationship modeling** using an **entity–relationship (ER) diagram**. There are many approaches to ER diagramming. You will see one particular approach here. The good news is that if you are familiar with one version of ER diagramming, then you will be able to easily adapt to any other version.

ER diagrams consist of entities, attributes, and relationships. To properly identify entities, attributes, and relationships, database designers first identify the business rules for the particular data model. **Business rules** are precise descriptions of policies, procedures, or principles in any organization that stores and uses data to generate information. Business rules are derived from a description of an organization's operations, and help to create and enforce business processes in that organization. Keep in mind that *you* determine these business rules, not the MIS department.

Entities are pictured in rectangles, and relationships are described on the line between two entities. The attributes for each entity are listed, and the primary key is underlined. The **data dictionary** provides information on each attribute, such as its name; if it is a key, part of a key, or a non-key attribute; the type of data expected (alphanumeric, numeric, dates, etc.); and valid values. Data dictionaries can also provide information on why the attribute is needed in the database; which business functions, applications, forms, and reports use the attribute; and how often the attribute should be updated.

ER modeling is valuable because it allows database designers to communicate with users throughout the organization to ensure that all entities and the relationships among the entities are represented. This process underscores the importance of taking all users into account when designing organizational databases. Notice that all entities and relationships in our example are labeled in terms that users can understand.

Relationships illustrate an association between entities. The *degree of a relationship* indicates the number of entities associated with a relationship. A *unary relationship* exists when an association is maintained within a single entity. A *binary relationship* exists when two entities are associated. A *ternary relationship* exists when three entities are associated. In this chapter, we discuss only binary relationships because they are the most common. Entity relationships may be classified as one-to-one, one-to-many, or many-to-many. The term *connectivity* describes the relationship classification.

Connectivity and cardinality are established by the business rules of a relationship. *Cardinality* refers to the maximum number of times an instance of one entity can be associated with an instance in the related entity. Cardinality can be mandatory single, optional single, mandatory many, or optional many. **Figure 5.10** displays the cardinality symbols. Note that there are four possible cardinality symbols: mandatory single, optional single, mandatory many, and optional many.

Let's look at an example from a university. An *entity* is a person, place, or thing that can be identified in the users' work environment. For example, consider student registration at a university. Students register for courses, and they also register their cars for parking permits. In this example, STUDENT, PARKING PERMIT, CLASS, and PROFESSOR are entities. Recall that an instance of an entity represents a particular student, parking permit, class,

query by example   To obtain information from a relational database, a user fills out a grid or template—also known as a *form*—to construct a sample or a description of the data desired.

entity–relationship (ER) modeling   The process of designing a database by organizing data entities to be used and identifying the relationships among them.

entity–relationship (ER) diagram   Document that shows data entities and attributes and relationships among them.

business rules   Precise descriptions of policies, procedures, or principles in any organization that stores and uses data to generate information.

data dictionary   A collection of definitions of data elements; data characteristics that use the data elements; and the individuals, business functions, applications, and reports that use these data elements.

relationships   Operators that illustrate an association between two entities.

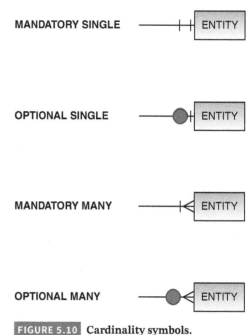

MANDATORY SINGLE

OPTIONAL SINGLE

MANDATORY MANY

OPTIONAL MANY

FIGURE 5.10 **Cardinality symbols.**

or professor. Therefore, a particular STUDENT (James Smythe, 8023445) is an instance of the STUDENT entity; a particular parking permit (91778) is an instance of the PARKING PERMIT entity; a particular class (76890) is an instance of the CLASS entity; and a particular professor (Margaret Wilson, 390567) is an instance of the PROFESSOR entity.

Entity instances have *identifiers*, or *primary keys*, which are attributes (attributes and identifiers are synonymous) that are unique to that entity instance. For example, STUDENT instances can be identified with Student Identification Number, PARKING PERMIT instances can be identified with Permit Number, CLASS instances can be identified with Class Number, and PROFESSOR instances can be identified with Professor Identification Number.

attribute Each characteristic or quality of a particular entity.

Entities have **attributes**, or properties, that describe the entity's characteristics. In our example, examples of attributes for STUDENT are Student Name and Student Address. Examples of attributes for PARKING PERMIT are Student Identification Number and Car Type. Examples of attributes for CLASS are Class Name, Class Time, and Class Place. Examples of attributes for PROFESSOR are Professor Name and Professor Department. (Note that each course at this university has one professor—no team teaching.)

Why is Student Identification Number an attribute of both the STUDENT and PARKING PERMIT entity classes? That is, why do we need the PARKING PERMIT entity class? If you consider all of the interlinked university systems, the PARKING PERMIT entity class is needed for other applications, such as fee payments, parking tickets, and external links to the state Department of Motor Vehicles.

Let's consider the three types of binary relationships in our example.

In a *one-to-one (1:1)* relationship, a single-entity instance of one type is related to a single-entity instance of another type. In our university example, STUDENT–PARKING PERMIT is a 1:1 relationship. The business rule at this university represented by this relationship is: students may register only one car at this university. Of course, students do not have to register a car at all. That is, a student can have only one parking permit but does not need to have one.

Note that the relationship line on the PARKING PERMIT side shows a cardinality of optional single. A student can have, but does not have to have, a parking permit. On the STUDENT side of the relationship, only one parking permit can be assigned to one student, resulting in a cardinality of mandatory single. See **Figure 5.11**.

The second type of relationship, *one-to-many (1:M)*, is represented by the CLASS–PROFESSOR relationship in **Figure 5.12**. The business rule at this university represented by this relationship is: at this university, there is no team teaching. Therefore, each class must have only one professor. On the other hand, professors may teach more than one class. Note that the relationship line on the PROFESSOR side shows a cardinality of mandatory single. In contrast, the relationship line on the CLASS side shows a cardinality of optional many.

The third type of relationship, *many-to-many (M:M)*, is represented by the STUDENT–CLASS relationship. Most database management systems do not support many-to-many relationships. Therefore, we use *junction* (or *bridge*) *tables*, so that we have two one-to-many relationships. The business rule at this university represented by this relationship is: students can register for one or more classes, and each class can have one or more students (see **Figure 5.13**). In this example, we create the REGISTRATION table as our junction table. Note that Student ID and Class ID are foreign keys in the REGISTRATION table.

Let's examine the following relationships:

- The relationship line on the STUDENT side of the STUDENT–REGISTRATION relationship shows a cardinality of optional single.

- The relationship line on the REGISTRATION side of the STUDENT–REGISTRATION relationship shows a cardinality of optional many.

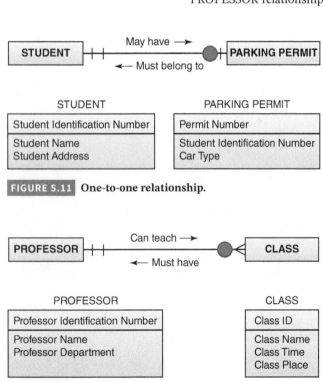

FIGURE 5.11 **One-to-one relationship.**

FIGURE 5.12 **One-to-many relationship.**

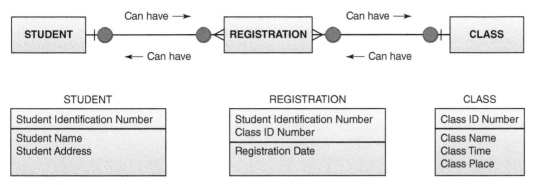

FIGURE 5.13 **Many-to-many relationship.**

- The relationship line on the CLASS side of the CLASS–REGISTRATION relationship shows a cardinality of optional single.
- The relationship line on the REGISTRATION side of the CLASS–REGISTRATION relationship shows a cardinality of optional many.

Normalization and Joins

To use a relational database management system efficiently and effectively, the data must be analyzed to eliminate redundant data elements. Normalization is a method for analyzing and reducing a relational database to its most streamlined form to ensure minimum redundancy, maximum data integrity, and optimal processing performance. Data normalization is a methodology for organizing attributes into tables so that redundancy among the non-key attributes is eliminated. The result of the data normalization process is a properly structured relational database.

Data normalization requires a list of all the attributes that must be incorporated into the database and a list of all of the defining associations, or functional dependencies, among the attributes. Functional dependencies are a means of expressing that the value of one particular attribute is associated with a specific single value of another attribute. For example, for Student Number 05345 at a university, exactly one Student Name, John C. Jones, is associated with it. That is, Student Number is referred to as the determinant because its value *determines* the value of the other attribute. We can also say that Student Name is functionally dependent on Student Number.

As an example of normalization, consider a pizza shop. This shop takes orders from customers on a form. Figure 5.14 shows a table of nonnormalized data gathered by the pizza shop. This table has two records, one for each order being placed. Because there are several

normalization A method for analyzing and reducing a relational database to its most streamlined form to ensure minimum redundancy, maximum data integrity, and optimal processing performance.

functional dependency A means of expressing that the value of one particular attribute is associated with, or determines, a specific single value of another attribute.

Order Number	Order Date	Customer ID	Customer F Name	Customer L Name	Customer Address	Zip Code	Pizza Code	Pizza Name	Quantity	Price	Total Price
1116	9/1/14	16421	Rob	Penny	123 Main St.	37411	P	Pepperoni	1	$11.00	$41.00
							MF	Meat Feast	1	$12.00	
							V	Vegetarian	2	$9.00	
1117	9/2/14	17221	Beth	Jones	41 Oak St.	29416	HM	Ham and Mushroom	3	$10.00	$56.00
							MF	Meat Feast	1	$12.00	
							TH	The Hawaiian	1	$14.00	

FIGURE 5.14 **Raw data gathered from orders at the pizza shop.**

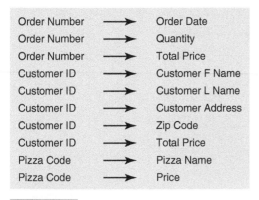

FIGURE 5.15 **Functional dependencies in pizza shop example.**

pizzas on each order, the order number and customer information appear in multiple rows. Several attributes of each record have null values. A null value is an attribute with no data in it. For example, Order Number has four null values. Therefore, this table is not in first normal form. The data drawn from that form is shown in Figure 5.14.

In our example, ORDER, CUSTOMER, and PIZZA are entities. The first step in normalization is to determine the functional dependencies among the attributes. The functional dependencies in our example are shown in **Figure 5.15**.

In the normalization process, we will proceed from nonnormalized data, to first normal form, to second normal form, and then to third normal form. (There are additional normal forms, but they are beyond the scope of this book.)

Figure 5.16 demonstrates the data in *first normal form*. The attributes under consideration are listed in one table and primary keys have been established. Our primary keys are Order Number, Customer ID, and Pizza Code. In first normal form, each ORDER has to repeat the order number, order date, customer first name, customer last name, customer address, and customer zip code. This data file contains repeating groups and describes multiple entities. That is, this relation has data redundancy, a lack of data integrity, and the flat file would be difficult to use in various applications that the pizza shop might need.

Consider the table in Figure 5.14 and notice the very first column (labeled Order Number). This column contains multiple entries for each order—three rows for Order Number 1116 and three rows for Order Number 1117. These multiple rows for an order are called *repeating groups*. The table in Figure 5.14 also contains multiple entities: ORDER, CUSTOMER, and PIZZA. Therefore, we move on to second normal form.

To produce second normal form, we break the table in Figure 5.16 into smaller tables to eliminate some of its data redundancy. Second normal form does not allow partial functional dependencies. That is, in a table in second normal form, every non-key attribute must be functionally dependent on the entire primary key of that table. **Figure 5.17** shows the data from the pizza shop in second normal form.

If you examine Figure 5.17, you will see that second normal form has not eliminated all the data redundancy. For example, each Order Number is duplicated three times, as are all customer data. In *third normal form*, non-key attributes are not allowed to define other non-key attributes. That is, third normal form does not allow transitive dependencies in which one non-key attribute is functionally dependent on another. In our example, customer information depends both on Customer ID and Order Number. **Figure 5.18** shows the data from the pizza shop in third normal form. Third normal form structure has these important points:

- It is completely free of data redundancy.
- All foreign keys appear where needed to link related tables.

Order Number	Order Date	Customer ID	Customer F Name	Customer L Name	Customer Address	Zip Code	Pizza Code	Pizza Name	Quantity	Price	Total Price
1116	9/1/14	16421	Rob	Penny	123 Main St.	37411	P	Pepperoni	1	$11.00	$41.00
1116	9/1/14	16421	Rob	Penny	123 Main St.	37411	MF	Meat Feast	1	$12.00	$41.00
1116	9/1/14	16421	Rob	Penny	123 Main St.	37411	V	Vegetarian	2	$9.00	$41.00
1117	9/2/14	17221	Beth	Jones	41 Oak St.	29416	HM	Ham and Mushroom	3	$10.00	$56.00
1117	9/2/14	17221	Beth	Jones	41 Oak St.	29416	MF	Meat Feast	1	$12.00	$56.00
1117	9/2/14	17221	Beth	Jones	41 Oak St.	29416	TH	The Hawaiian	1	$14.00	$56.00

FIGURE 5.16 **First normal form for data from pizza shop.**

Order Number	Order Date	Customer ID	Customer F Name	Customer L Name	Customer Address	Zip Code	Total Price
1116	9/1/14	16421	Rob	Penny	123 Main St.	37411	$41.00
1116	9/1/14	16421	Rob	Penny	123 Main St.	37411	$41.00
1116	9/1/14	16421	Rob	Penny	123 Main St.	37411	$41.00
1117	9/2/14	17221	Beth	Jones	41 Oak St.	29416	$56.00
1117	9/2/14	17221	Beth	Jones	41 Oak St.	29416	$56.00
1117	9/2/14	17221	Beth	Jones	41 Oak St.	29416	$56.00

Order Number	Pizza Code	Quantity
1116	P	1
1116	MF	1
1116	V	2
1117	HM	3
1117	MF	1
1117	TH	1

Pizza Code	Pizza Name	Price
P	Pepperoni	$11.00
MF	Meat Feast	$12.00
V	Vegetarian	$9.00
HM	Ham and Mushroom	$10.00
TH	The Hawaiian	$14.00

FIGURE 5.17 Second normal form for data from pizza shop.

ORDER

Order Number	Order Date	Customer ID	Total Price
1116	9/1/14	16421	$41.00
1117	9/2/14	17221	$56.00

CUSTOMER

Customer ID	Customer F Name	Customer L Name	Customer Address	Zip Code
16421	Rob	Penny	123 Main St.	37411
17221	Beth	Jones	41 Oak St.	29416

ORDER-PIZZA

Order Number	Pizza Code	Quantity
1116	P	1
1116	MF	1
1116	V	2
1117	HM	3
1117	MF	1
1117	TH	1

PIZZA

Pizza Code	Pizza Name	Price
P	Pepperoni	$11.00
MF	Meat Feast	$12.00
V	Vegetarian	$9.00
HM	Ham and Mushroom	$10.00
TH	The Hawaiian	$14.00

FIGURE 5.18 Third normal form for data from pizza shop.

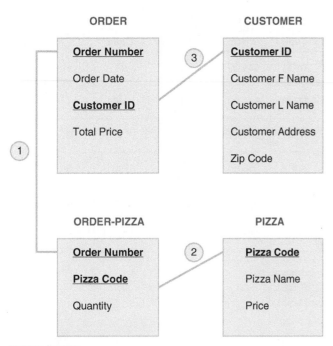

FIGURE 5.19 **The join process with the tables of third normal form to produce an order.**

join operation A database operation that combines records from two or more tables in a database.

Let's look at the primary and foreign keys for the tables in third normal form:

- *The ORDER relation:* The primary key is Order Number and the foreign key is Customer ID.
- *The CUSTOMER relation:* The primary key is Customer ID.
- *The PIZZA relation:* The primary key is Pizza Code.
- *The ORDER–PIZZA relation:* The primary key is a composite key, consisting of two foreign keys, Order Number and Pizza Code.

Now consider an order at the pizza shop. The tables in third normal form can produce the order in the following manner by using the join operation (see **Figure 5.19**). The **join operation** combines records from two or more tables in a database to obtain information that is located in different tables. In our example, the join operation combines records from the four normalized tables to produce an ORDER. Here is how the join operation works:

- The ORDER relation provides the Order Number (the primary key), Order Date, and Total Price.
- The primary key of the ORDER relation (Order Number) provides a link to the ORDER–PIZZA relation (the link numbered 1 in Figure 5.19).
- The ORDER–PIZZA relation supplies the Quantity to ORDER.
- The primary key of the ORDER–PIZZA relation is a composite key that consists of Order Number and Pizza Code. Therefore, the Pizza Code component of the primary key provides a link to the PIZZA relation (the link numbered 2 in Figure 5.19).
- The PIZZA relation supplies the Pizza Name and Price to ORDER.
- The Customer ID in ORDER (a foreign key) provides a link to the CUSTOMER relation (the link numbered 3 in Figure 5.19).
- The CUSTOMER relation supplies the Customer FName, Customer LName, Customer Address, and Zip Code to ORDER.

At the end of this join process, we have a complete ORDER. Normalization is beneficial when maintaining databases over a period of time. One example is the likelihood of having to change the price of each pizza. If the pizza shop increases the price of the Meat Feast from $12.00 to $12.50, this process is one easy step in Figure 5.19. The price field is changed to $12.50 and the ORDER is automatically updated with the current value of the price.

Before you go on...

1. What is structured query language?
2. What is query by example?
3. What is an entity? An attribute? A relationship?
4. Describe one-to-one, one-to-many, and many-to-many relationships.
5. What is the purpose of normalization?
6. Why do we need the join operation?

What's in IT for Me?

`ACCT` For the Accounting Major

The accounting function is intimately concerned with keeping track of an organization's transactions and internal controls. Modern databases enable accountants to perform these functions more effectively. Databases help accountants manage the flood of data in today's organizations so that they can keep their firms in compliance with the standards imposed by Sarbanes–Oxley.

Accountants also play a role in justifying the costs of creating a knowledge base and then auditing its cost-effectiveness. Also, if you work for a large CPA company that provides management services or sells knowledge, then you most likely will use some of your company's best practices, which are stored in a knowledge base.

`FIN` For the Finance Major

Financial managers make extensive use of computerized databases that are external to the organization, such as CompuStat and Dow Jones, to obtain financial data on organizations in their industry. They can use these data to determine if their organization meets industry benchmarks in return on investment, cash management, and other financial ratios.

Financial managers who produce the organization's financial status reports are also closely involved with Sarbanes–Oxley. Databases help these managers comply with the law's standards.

`MKT` For the Marketing Major

Databases help marketing managers access data from the organization's marketing transactions, such as customer purchases, to plan targeted marketing campaigns and to evaluate the success of previous campaigns. Knowledge about customers can make the difference between success and failure. In many databases and knowledge bases, the vast majority of information and knowledge concerns customers, products, sales, and marketing. Marketing managers regularly use an organization's knowledge base, and they often participate in creating that base.

`POM` For the Production/Operations Management Major

Production/operations personnel access organizational data to determine optimal inventory levels for parts in a production process. Past production data enable production/operations management (POM) personnel to determine the optimal configuration for assembly lines. Firms also collect quality data that inform them not only about the quality of finished products, but also about quality issues with incoming raw materials, production irregularities, shipping and logistics, and after-sale use and maintenance of the products.

Knowledge management is extremely important for running complex operations. The accumulated knowledge regarding scheduling, logistics, maintenance, and other functions is very valuable. Innovative ideas are critical for improving operations, and they can be supported by knowledge management.

`HRM` For the Human Resources Management Major

Organizations maintain extensive data on employees including gender, age, race, current and past job descriptions, and performance evaluations. HR personnel access these data to provide reports to government agencies regarding compliance with federal equal opportunity guidelines. HR managers also use these data to evaluate hiring practices and salary structures and to manage any discrimination grievances or lawsuits brought against the firm.

Databases help HR managers provide assistance to all employees as companies turn over more and more decisions about health care and retirement planning to the employees themselves. The employees can use the databases for help in selecting the optimal mix among these critical choices.

HR managers also need to use a knowledge base frequently to find out how past cases were handled. Consistency in how employees are treated not only is important, but it also protects the company against legal actions. In addition, training for building, maintaining, and using the knowledge system is sometimes the responsibility of the HR department. Finally, the HR department might be responsible for compensating employees who contribute their knowledge to the knowledge base.

`MIS` For the MIS Major

The MIS function manages the organization's data as well as the databases. MIS database administrators standardize data names by using the data dictionary. This process ensures that all users understand which data are in the database. Database personnel also help users access needed data and generate reports with query tools.

For All Business Majors

All business majors will have to manage data in their professional work. One way to manage data is through the use of databases and database management systems. It is likely that you will need to obtain information from your organization's databases. You will probably use structured query language to obtain this information. Further, as your organization plans and designs its databases, it will most likely use entity–relationship diagrams. You will provide much of the input to these diagrams. For example, you will describe the entities that you use in your work, the attributes of those entities, and the relationships among them. You will also help database designers as they normalize database tables by describing how the normalized tables relate to one another (e.g., through the use of primary and foreign keys). Finally, you will assist database designers as they plan their join operations to provide you with the information that you need when that information is stored in multiple tables.

Summary

5.1 Discuss ways that common challenges in managing data can be addressed using data governance.

The following are three common challenges in managing data:

- Data are scattered throughout organizations and are collected by many individuals using various methods and devices. These data are frequently stored in numerous servers and locations and in different computing systems, databases, formats, and human and computer languages.
- Data come from multiple sources.
- Information systems that support particular business processes impose unique requirements on data, which results in repetition and conflicts across an organization.

One strategy for implementing data governance is master data management. Master data management provides companies with the ability to store, maintain, exchange, and synchronize a consistent, accurate, and timely "single version of the truth" for the company's core master data. Master data management manages data gathered from across an organization, data from multiple sources, and data across business processes within an organization.

5.2 Discuss the advantages and disadvantages of relational databases.

Relational databases enable people to compare information quickly by row or column. Users also can easily retrieve items by finding the point of intersection of a particular row and column. However, large-scale relational databases can be composed of numerous interrelated tables, making the overall design complex, with slow search and access times.

5.3 Define Big Data and its basic characteristics.

Big Data is composed of high-volume, high-velocity, and high-variety information assets that require new forms of processing in order to enhance decision making, lead to insights, and optimize business processes. Big Data has three distinct characteristics that distinguish it from traditional data: volume, velocity, and variety.

- *Volume*: Big Data consists of vast quantities of data.
- *Velocity*: Big Data flows into an organization at incredible speeds.
- *Variety*: Big Data includes diverse data in differing formats.

5.4 Explain the elements necessary to successfully implement and maintain data warehouses.

To successfully implement and maintain a data warehouse, an organization must:

- Link source systems that provide data to the warehouse or mart.
- Prepare the necessary data for the data warehouse using data integration technology and processes.
- Decide on an appropriate architecture for storing data in the data warehouse or data mart.
- Select the tools and applications for the variety of organizational users.
- Establish appropriate metadata, data quality, and governance processes to ensure that the data warehouse or mart meets its purposes.

5.5 Describe the benefits and challenges of implementing knowledge management systems in organizations.

Organizations can realize many benefits with KMSs, including:

- Best practices are readily available to a wide range of employees
- Improved customer service
- More efficient product development
- Improved employee morale and retention

Challenges to implementing KMSs include:

- Employees must be willing to share their personal tacit knowledge.
- Organizations must create a knowledge management culture that rewards employees who add their expertise to the knowledge base.
- The knowledge base must be continually maintained and updated.
- Companies must be willing to invest in the resources needed to carry out these operations.

5.6 Understand the processes of querying a relational database, entity-relationship modeling, and normalization and joins.

The most commonly performed database operation is requesting information. *Structured query language* is the most popular query language used for this operation. SQL allows people to perform complicated searches by using relatively simple statements or key words. Typical key words are SELECT (to specify a desired attribute), FROM (to specify the table to be used), and WHERE (to specify conditions to apply in the query).

Another way to find information in a database is to use *query by example*. In QBE, the user fills out a grid or template—also known as a *form*—to construct a sample or a description of the data desired. Users can construct a query quickly and easily by using drag-and-drop features in a DBMS such as Microsoft Access. Conducting queries in this manner is simpler than keying in SQL commands.

Designers plan and create databases through the process of **entity–relationship modeling**, using an **entity–relationship diagram**. ER diagrams consist of entities, attributes, and relationships. Entities are pictured in boxes, and relationships are represented as lines. The attributes for each entity are listed, and the primary key is underlined.

ER modeling is valuable because it allows database designers to communicate with users throughout the organization to ensure that all entities and the relationships among the entities are represented. This process underscores the importance of taking all users into account when designing organizational databases. Notice that all entities and relationships in our example are labeled in terms that users can understand.

Normalization is a method for analyzing and reducing a relational database to its most streamlined form to ensure minimum redundancy, maximum data integrity, and optimal processing performance. When data are *normalized*, attributes in each table depend only on the primary key.

The *join operation* combines records from two or more tables in a database to produce information that is located in different tables.

Key Terms

attribute   148
Big Data   128
bit   124
business rules   147
byte   125
database management system
    (DBMS)   126
data dictionary   147
data file (also table)   124
data governance   123
data lake   141
data mart   135
data model   126
data silo   120
data warehouse   135

entity   126
entity–relationship (ER) diagram   147
entity–relationship (ER) modeling   147
explicit knowledge   144
field   125
foreign key   127
functional dependency   149
instance   126
intellectual capital (or intellectual
    assets)   144
join operation   152
knowledge management (KM)   144
knowledge management systems
    (KMSs)   145
master data   123

master data management   123
multidimensional structure   136
normalization   149
primary key   126
query by example   147
record   125
relational database model   126
relationships   147
secondary key   126
structured data   127
structured query language   146
table   125
tacit knowledge   144
transactional data   123
unstructured data   127

Discussion Questions

1. Is Big Data really a problem on its own, or are the use, control, and security of the data the true problems? Provide specific examples to support your answer.

2. What are the implications of having incorrect data points in your Big Data? What are the implications of incorrect or duplicated customer data? How valuable are decisions that are based on faulty information derived from incorrect data?

3. Explain the difficulties involved in managing data.

4. What are the problems associated with poor-quality data?

5. What is master data management? What does it have to do with high-quality data?

6. Explain why master data management is so important in companies that have multiple data sources.

7. Describe the advantages and disadvantages of relational databases.

8. Explain why it is important to capture and manage knowledge.

9. Compare and contrast tacit knowledge and explicit knowledge.

10. Draw the entity–relationship diagram for a company that has departments and employees. In this company, a department must have at least one employee, and company employees may work in only one department.

11. Draw the entity–relationship diagram for library patrons and the process of checking out books.

12. You are working at a doctor's office. You gather data on the following entities: PATIENT, PHYSICIAN, PATIENT DIAGNOSIS, and TREATMENT. Develop a table for the entity PATIENT VISIT. Decide on the primary keys and/or foreign keys that you want to use for each entity.

13. Read the article: S. Kliff and M. Sanger-Katz, "Bottleneck for U.S. Coronavirus Response: The Fax Machine," *New York Times*, July 13, 2020. Describe which of the problems in managing data (Section 5.1) are being emphasized by the COVID-19 pandemic.

Problem-Solving Activities

1. Access various employment websites (e.g., www.monster.com and www.dice.com) and find several job descriptions for a database administrator. Are the job descriptions similar? What are the salaries offered in these positions?

2. Access the websites of several real estate companies. Find the sites that take you through a step-by-step process for buying a home, that provide virtual reality tours of homes in your price range (say, $200,000 to $250,000) and location, that provide mortgage and interest

rate calculators, and that offer financing for your home. Do the sites require that you register to access their services? Can you request that an e-mail be sent to you when properties you might be interested in become available? How does the process outlined influence your likelihood of selecting this company for your real estate purchase?

3. There are many websites that provide demographic information. Access several of these sites and see what they offer. Do the sites differ in the types of demographic information they offer? If so, how? Do the sites require a fee for the information they offer? Would demographic information be useful to you if you wanted to start a new business? If so, how and why?

4. Search the Web for uses of Big Data in homeland security. Specifically, read about the spying by the U.S. National Security Agency (NSA). What role did technology and Big Data play in this questionable practice?

5. Visit www.bigcloud.global/5-brilliant-ted-talks-about-big-data. Watch one of the 5 talks and summarize the main points. Do you agree with the talk? Why or why not?

6. Search the Web for the article "Why Big Data and Privacy Are Often at Odds." What points does this article present concerning the delicate balance between shared data and customer privacy?

7. Access the websites of IBM (www.ibm.com), Microsoft (www.microsoft.com), and Oracle (www.oracle.com), and trace the capabilities of their latest data management products, including Web connections.

8. Access the website for the Gartner Group (www.gartner.com). Examine the company's research studies pertaining to data management. Prepare a report on the state of the art.

9. Diagram a knowledge management system cycle for a fictional company that sells customized T-shirts to students.

10. Visit www.databricks.com Explain how the platform provides solutions for the industry of your choice.

Closing Case

MIS **FIN** **ACCT** **Financial Data Aggregation and Sharing**

The Problem

Low-wage workers often have trouble accessing credit because they have poor or no credit scores. Modern freelance workers typically work for several companies and earn multiple small paychecks. This type of employment is referred to as the *gig economy*. Often, workers pick up separate gigs, have steady employment, and make a good living. However, they do not have many of the characteristics of a "credit-worthy" person. Because their income is sourced from so many places, lenders cannot access the data necessary to verify their ability to repay a loan. Therefore, gig workers, like low-wage workers, have difficulty securing traditional loan. The difference is that gig workers often have the income to avoid these loans, but there is no way to aggregate necessary data to share it with lenders.

When hard times come, many low-wage and gig workers turn to payday lenders, who offer short-term loans based on the anticipated upcoming paycheck and do not require a credit report. This trend was especially widespread in 2020, which was a challenging financial year, when many families were forced to seek financial assistance. That year, $9.5 billion in wages were taken early through payday loans, compared to $6.3 billion in 2019, an increase of 50 percent in one year.

Payday loans are popular and are sometimes necessary to make ends meet. However, these loans come with very high interest rates. Payday lenders justify this practice by arguing that they do not require a credit report, so the loans are risky.

Further, payday loans can trap borrowers in an endless cycle of ever-growing debt. How does this occur? Receiving your money before payday is always enticing. When you take your money early and hand over your paycheck, however, you don't receive as much money. For example, if Hayden expects a paycheck of $1,000, a payday lender might offer him $600 cash today in exchange for her $1,000 paycheck. As a result, Hayden has less money to make it to

the end of the month and will likely need another payday loan, further exacerbating the problem. A 2021 report found that more than 70 percent of pay advance users took out consecutive advances.

One reason people use payday loans is that they need money quickly, and payday loans are the most accessible loan they can get. It is significant to note that there are steps these individuals could take to lower their rate. For example, HR offices can provide employees with data such as a payslip and an employment certificate that could help them secure a lower rate. However, this process is bureaucratic, lengthy, and creates stacks of paper documentation. Gathering data is even more complicated for gig workers, who must go to multiple employers for documentation. Ultimately, many people who need money find it quicker and easier simply to take a high-interest payday loan.

Technology Solution to Data Sharing

In recent years, an industry has emerged that offers a technology-based solution to this data-sharing problem. One major industry player is Argyle (www.argyle.com), a self-described first mover in the workforce data industry. Argyle provides an application program interface (API) that retrieves data from workers' various employers and makes the data legible to potential lenders and other Fintech companies.

Argyle's primary niche is the gig economy. However, anyone can utilize their service. Argyle collects and organizes employee data records from multiple employers in a single location, creating comprehensive profiles for workers who previously did not have one. Argyle accesses customer-permissioned payroll data—that is, data that the customer gives permission to other entities to view— and routes those data to lenders. In turn, the lenders use the data to make decisions regarding loans.

Argyle's computerized payroll information processors provide a mechanism to aggregate these data. Specifically, they make records compiled from hundreds of thousands of payroll providers available to financial institutions. This direct access to payroll information can lower risks to lenders, who can then charge lower interest rates. It also allows for faster decision making and instant verification.

Concerns

Argyle's technology appears to address the problems of high risk for lenders and high interest rates for consumers. However, critics argue that users may pay a high price in terms of privacy. In 2021, Argyle attracted negative attention for paying workers to share their payroll log-in credentials so that the company could access their data and build the product. Argyle contends that it obtains worker consent in data gathering, as opposed to traditional players like Equifax that source data from employers.

Increasingly, customers want to know with whom their data are being shared and what they are being used for. Argyle extracts up to 140 data points per individual. These data can include shifts worked, time off, earnings and promotions history, health care, retirement contributions, and even reputational data such as on-time rate or a gig worker's customer star rating and deactivation history.

Advocates have raised concerns about the amount and the future use of the data that workers are handing over. Argyle's response is that they need the data to present "a holistic view of a worker's identity, including typical hours, work trajectory, reputation, and more." However, critics fear that this "holistic view" can be used in ways not currently intended. For example, an HR office could use these data to make hiring decisions rather than using references and applicant-provided information.

Future Considerations

Though the predatory loans are likely here to say, one way to avoid this situation is to use technology to provide daily payouts. Paperless technologies have largely eliminated the need for biweekly payouts. Workers who are paid on a daily basis are less likely to need to borrow money.

Gig workers can benefit from cash-advance apps and data aggregators like Argyle. These workers are not paid on a regular schedule. Although their overall income might be sufficient to pay their bills, the flow might not come at the right time. Data-driven cash-advance apps can offer them the option of a small loan to cover the financial gaps.

In addition, Argyle has entered into several partnerships to help expand the use of its data. For example, it has partnered with Highline Technologies, a payments FinTech, to bring payroll-linked lending and bill-pay capabilities to lenders nationwide. With payroll-linked lending, loans are automatically repaid through preset distributions directly from the borrower's paycheck. Payroll-linked lending and bill pay benefits consumers by providing them with access to lower-cost credit through more reputable, nonpredatory lenders. These services benefit lenders by decreasing missed payments by up to 66 percent and reducing default rates by more than 50 percent.

Argyle is also partnering with FinLocker, a fintech that stores personal credit, income, and other account data necessary to apply for mortgages. FinLocker uses these data to help consumers find appropriate real estate and loans. They also use the data to help mortgage lenders manage relationships with potential customers. Adding Argyle's aggregate employment data will shorten the underwriting process and simplify consumer mortgage applications. Because the data are verified by Argyle and FinLocker, lending institutions can make faster loan decisions while lowering overall costs.

Conclusion

Low-wage and gig workers have faced many financial challenges due to a lack of access to their financial data. When they needed short-term loans, they were limited to predatory lenders who are willing to take on risk in return for charging high interest rates. Today, however, data aggregation and sharing are paving the way for more options. These new options will make it easier for consumers to avoid predatory loans by receiving their pay immediately or by being able to secure safer loans.

Questions

1. **What is a data aggregator?**
2. **How can fintech companies connect payroll and billpay?**
3. **How can data sharing make it safer for consumers to obtain a loan?**

Sources: Compiled from E. Cardoza, "Highline and Argyle Partner to Bring Payroll-Linked Lending and Bill Pay Capabilities to Lenders," *IBS Intelligence*, August 30, 2022; "Highline Teams with Argyle to Drive Payroll-Linked Lending," pymnts.com, August 29, 2022; S. Fishman, "The Broken Connection Between Payroll Data and Financial Access," shmulikfishman.com, August 2, 2022; I. Ciutina, "How Atomic Uses Payroll Data to Unlock Opportunities for Banks, Fintechs and Their Customers," *Tearsheet*, July 1, 2022; S. Jeffery, "Argyle's Powering Complex Banking Decisions with Employment Data," *Tearsheet*, June 30, 2022; M. Shestack, "Can Fintech Put Payroll Data to Work for Workers?" *onlabor.org*, June 13, 2022; "Questions Loom about Payroll Data Provider Argyle's Motives to Pay Users for Login Details," *The Financial Revolutionist*, May 11, 2022; C. Harrington, "Workers Are Trading Staggering Amounts of Data for 'Payday Loans'," *Wired*, March 23, 2022; P. Centopani, "FinLocker and Argyle Partner for Employment, Income Verification," *National Mortgage News*, November 16, 2021; B. Bracken, "Gig Workers Being Paid $500 for Payroll Passwords," threatpost.com, May 12, 2021; and https://argyle.com/about, accessed October 20, 2022.

Telecommunications and Networking

Opening Case

MIS Still Trying to Close the Digital Divide

Broadband Internet has become increasingly necessary for Americans to do their jobs, participate in school, access health care, and stay connected. COVID brought these issues to prominence when many people were not able to work from home and their children could not attend online classes.

For decades, social analysts have used the term *digital divide* to refer to the gap between populations who have access to current information and communications technologies and those who do not. Today, the digital divide persists between people with broadband Internet access and those without. Research group BroadbandNow (www.broadbandnow.com) estimates that 42 million Americans have no broadband access. This problem is particularly serious in rural communities. Making matters worse, the United

States has the second-highest broadband costs among developed nations.

Most U.S. households have access to Internet download speeds of at least 100 megabits per second (Mbps) and upload speeds of 10 Mbps. However, despite the progress generated by programs sponsored by the Federal Communication Commission (FCC, www.fcc.gov), many rural Americans do not even have 4 Mbps download and 1 Mbps upload speeds.

The reason for this digital divide is straightforward: It is far more cost effective for Internet service providers (ISPs) to deliver broadband to high-density metropolitan areas than to low-density rural areas. As a result, rural areas traditionally have had low bandwidth or none at all.

To address this deficiency, the U.S. government has spent billions of dollars on programs to provide broadband Internet to underserved rural communities. However, flaws in the programs frequently prevented residents from obtaining this access.

FCC officials identify several reasons why previous programs have failed. First, the fact that many areas were targeted multiple times might be because one program ended and was replaced by a new one. For example, in one recent program, the 2020 Rural Digital Opportunity Fund, ISPs won rights to public funding in about 750,000 census blocks, covering every state except Alaska. An analysis found that more than half of those census blocks—areas with a combined population of 5.3 million—had been fully or partially covered by at least one previous federal broadband program.

Second, in an effort to upgrade as many people as possible with limited funds, the FCC subsidized incremental improvements. Many of those upgrades quickly became outdated as technology advanced and consumers wanted faster speeds.

Third, in certain cases, ISPs were allowed to choose which customers to upgrade. This process helped ensure that these companies would participate in these programs. However, it also enabled them to take public money while leaving large areas without broadband access.

The U.S. Census Bureau (**www.census.gov**) defines census blocks as statistical areas bounded by visible features such as roads, streams, and railroad tracks, as well as nonvisible boundaries such as property lines and city and county limits. The FCC's broadband maps are inaccurate because they rely on census blocks instead of address-by-address data. As a result, if ISPs report broadband service at just one home in a particular location, the FCC considers that entire census block to have full broadband access. This situation presents a very misleading picture of the penetration of broadband Internet in an area.

Fortunately, the FCC is updating its broadband penetration maps to reflect address-by-address data. In one specific example, the FCC is using a University of Georgia mapping program to determine on a house-by-house basis how many rural households in Northwest Georgia do not have broadband access.

On November 15, 2021, President Joe Biden signed the Bipartisan Infrastructure Law, which will deliver $65 billion to help ensure that every American has access to reliable high-speed Internet. Of this total, $42 billion was allocated for equipment and service deployments. The legislation will also help lower prices for Internet service and help close the digital divide. Finally, the law includes $14 billion in Internet subsidies for low-income Americans.

It is significant that this law mandates that companies receiving funds will have to provide service at faster speeds than they did under previous federal programs. Further, the money will be funneled through states rather than the FCC. Officials hope that the new mandates will help identify which areas are most in need of assistance and which providers can best serve those areas.

In many of these areas, a combination of physical and wireless networks would be cheaper and more practical than a single technology solution based on, for example, a region's geography and population density. Let's examine the various technologies that can provide broadband Internet access.

- *Fiber-optic cable* consists of thin strands of glass fibers that transmit information through pulses of light generated by lasers. Fiber-optics provide very high bandwidth connections.

- *Fixed wireless* (see Chapter 8) is the operation of wireless communication devices that connect two fixed locations with a wireless link. Fixed wireless networks use fiber backhauls. A *backhaul* is the transport of data from a wireless network to a wireline network.

- *5G home Internet* (see Chapter 8) is a type of fixed *wireless* Internet service. Providers install an indoor or outdoor 5G receiver at a house to pick up the wireless signal from a local wireless hub. A *wireless hub* is a site that provides wireless Internet access, for example, via Wi-Fi. An example of a wireless hub is a restaurant that offers free Wi-Fi to its customers. The hub is the Wi-Fi antenna itself. As of September 2022, the primary options for 5G home Internet were Starry (**www.starry.com**), T-Mobile (**www.t-mobile.com**), and Verizon (**www.verizon.com**).

- *Satellite Internet access* (see Chapter 8) can be provided via geostationary communication satellites that can deliver broadband Internet access to remote areas. New satellite constellations are being developed in low Earth orbit to enable low-latency (very little delay in transmission) Internet access.

- *Microsoft's Rural Airband initiative* involves the use of television white spaces (unused television frequencies) to deliver broadband Internet access over unused broadcast frequencies.

- Another solution is *do-it-yourself*. Let's consider two examples.

Jared Mauch built a fiber-to-the-home (FTTH) Internet provider in his home state of Michigan because existing Internet service providers (ISPs) did not provide sufficient bandwidth for his needs. He registered as a competitive access provider with the state government. While technically a phone company, Mauch provides only Internet service without any phone or TV offerings. *Competitive access providers* supply businesses with alternatives to local telephone companies in some markets. Competitive access providers use their own local infrastructure to route calls directly to and from the long-distance network, thus bypassing the local telephone companies' access charges.

When Mauch moved into his house in 2002, he had only a 1.5 Mbps Internet connection. As broadband technology improved, he expected that an ISP would eventually wire his house with cable or fiber. That did not happen. When he contacted a large cable company, they informed him that it would cost $50,000 to extend their cable network to his house. The company required those fees for line extensions when customers are outside their network area, even if the rest of the neighborhood already has service. Mauch then switched to a fixed wireless ISP that delivered about 50 Mbps.

Finally, Mauch created his own Internet provider—Washtenaw Fiber Properties, LLC—which now offers FTTH broadband to neighboring areas. By August 2022, he had 70 customers. Then, Mauch was awarded $2.6 million from the American Rescue Plan's Coronavirus State and Local Fiscal Recovery Funds. (The American Rescue Plan, which President Biden signed into law in March 2021, allocated nearly $2 trillion to help U.S. organizations and individuals deal with the pandemic.) At that time, Mauch's network had about 14 miles of fiber, and he planned to build another 38 miles to complete his project. His government contract requires him to extend his network from 70 homes to about 417. In fact, he plans to connect nearly 600 customers.

Under the contract terms, Mauch will provide 100 Mbps symmetrical Internet—*symmetrical* means the same download and upload speeds—with unlimited data for $55 per month, along with 1 gigabit per second (Gbps) with unlimited data for $79 per month. His installation fees are typically $199. Unlike many larger ISPs, Mauch provides simple bills that contain a single line item for Internet service and no extra fees.

Mauch has also purchased a whole-home backup generator to ensure that his customers will not lose connectivity in the case of a power outage. Many other potential customers want Mauch's service, having heard about it via word of mouth and local Facebook groups. Although he cannot provide service to all of them, he is advising people in other communities how to replicate his efforts.

Another do-it-yourself project is Elizabeth Bowles's company Aristotle Unified Communications LLC (**www.aristotle.net**). Aristotle plans to provide broadband access to households in rural Arkansas. Because fiber-optic cable is too expensive for the area, the company is using Citizens Broadband Radio Service, a wireless spectrum historically used by the U.S. Navy. The FCC has opened up part of this spectrum for commercial use, enabling Aristotle to beam fixed wireless broadband Internet access as far as six miles over signal stations installed on top of cell towers, barns, and even a prison.

Bowles understands that no single technology can solve the entire problem of broadband access in the area. As a result, she is also looking at the feasibility of Elon Musk's Starlink satellites (see Chapter 8) and 5G home Internet, depending on the geography of a particular region.

Questions

1. **List several reasons why it is so difficult to close the digital divide in the United States.**

2. **Should broadband Internet access be a fundamental right for all Americans? Why or why not? Support your answer.**

Sources: Compiled from J. Derobertis, "High-Speed Internet Access Coming to Some 500 Homes, Small Businesses in Livingston Parish," *The Advocate*, August 30, 2022; "Several Rural Communities to Benefit from Grants to Expand Broadband Internet Access," *WALA*, August 27, 2022; A. Wilkins, "Rural Broadband Access Aided by University of Georgia Mapping Program," *Chattanooga Times Free Press*, August 18, 2022; J. Brodkin, "This Man Built His Own ISP. Now He's Getting $2.6M to Expand It," *Ars Technica*, August 11, 2022; R. Tracy and A. DeBarros, "Why Rural Americans Keep Waiting for Fast Internet, Despite Billions Spent," *Wall Street Journal*, June 15, 2022; C. McNally, "What Is Fixed Wireless Internet?" Reviews.org, February 17, 2022; J. Brodkin, "ISPs Must Accept Gov't Subsidy on All Plans—No More Upselling, FCC Chair Says," *Ars Technica*, January 10, 2022; A. Carr, "Microsoft and an Army of Tiny Telecoms Are Part of a Plan to Wire Rural America," *Bloomberg Businessweek*, September 22, 2021; G. Tatter and M. Chakrabarti, "Rural Internet Access: How to Get Broadband across America," wbur.org, August 30, 2021; J. Brodkin, "Jared Mauch Didn't Have Good Broadband—So He Built His Own Fiber ISP," *Wired*, January 12, 2021; J. Brodkin, "FCC Data Fails to Count 21 Million People without Broadband, Study Finds," *Ars Technica*, February 6, 2020; M. Martin, "For the First Time, Census Bureau Data Show Impact of Geography, Income on Broadband Internet Access," www.census.gov, December 6, 2018; and www.census.gov, www.fcc.gov, accessed August 30, 2022.

Introduction

In addition to networks being essential in your personal lives, there are three fundamental points about network computing you need to know. First, in modern organizations, computers do not work in isolation. Rather, they constantly exchange data with one another. Second, this exchange of data—facilitated by telecommunications technologies—provides companies with many significant advantages. Third, this exchange can take place over any distance and over networks of any size.

Without networks, the computer on your desk would be merely another productivity-enhancement tool, just as the typewriter once was. The power of networks, however, turns your computer into an amazingly effective tool for accessing information from thousands of sources, thereby making both you and your organization more productive. Regardless of the type of organization (profit/not-for-profit, large/small, global/local) or industry (manufacturing, financial services, health care), networks in general, and the Internet in particular, have transformed—and will continue to transform—the way we do business.

Networks support new and innovative ways of doing business, from marketing to supply chain management to customer service to human resources management. In particular, the Internet and private *intranets*—networks located within a single organization that use Internet software and TCP/IP protocols—have enormous impacts on our lives, both professionally and personally.

For all organizations regardless of size, having a telecommunications and networking system is no longer simply a source of competitive advantage. Rather, it is necessary for survival.

Computer networks are essential to modern organizations, for many reasons. First, networked computer systems enable organizations to become more flexible so they can adapt to rapidly changing business conditions. Second, networks enable companies to share hardware, computer applications, and data across the organization and among different organizations. Third, networks make it possible for geographically dispersed employees and workgroups to share documents, ideas, and creative insights. This sharing encourages teamwork, innovation, and more efficient and effective interactions. Networks are also a critical link between businesses, their business partners, and their customers.

Clearly, networks are essential tools for modern businesses. But, why do *you* need to be familiar with networks? The simple fact is that if you operate your own business or you work in a business, then you cannot function without networks. You will need to communicate rapidly with your customers, business partners, suppliers, employees, and colleagues. Until about 1990, you would have used the postal service or the telephone system with voice or fax capabilities for business communication. Today, however, the pace of business is much faster—almost real time. To keep up with this incredibly fast pace, you will need to use computers, e-mail, messaging, the Internet, smartphones, and other mobile devices. Furthermore, all of these technologies will be connected through networks to enable you to communicate, collaborate, and compete on a global scale.

Networking and the Internet are the foundations for commerce in the 21st century. Recall that one key objective of this book is to help you become an informed user of information systems. Knowledge of networking is an essential component of modern business literacy.

We simply cannot overemphasize the global importance of the Internet. It has been said that the Internet is truly the nervous system of our world. A key point here is that people should have access to broadband Internet for the Internet to be truly useful in today's world. (See this chapter's opening case and the following example.)

Having fast (broadband) access to the Internet is a prerequisite for success for many people. In fact, the Federal Trade Commission (FTC), along with law enforcement agencies from six states, sued Internet service provider Frontier Communications (**www.frontier.com**), alleging that the company (a) failed to provide many consumers with Internet service at the speeds it promised them and (b) charged many of them for more expensive and higher-speed service than Frontier actually provided.

In May 2022, the FTC and the district attorney of Riverside, California, announced they had reached a settlement with Frontier. According to the settlement, Frontier must pay $50 to $60 million to deploy fiber-optics to 60,000 additional residential locations in California over the next four years. These locations currently have access only to the company's slower DSL network, which the FTC claims often failed to reach its advertised speeds. The order also forces Frontier to reform its practices nationwide. For example, the company can offer its DSL service to new customers only if it can provide the advertised speed. Another requirement bars Frontier from signing up new DSL subscribers in areas where congestion is already high due to too many existing users. Finally, Frontier must notify existing customers if their DSL Internet speeds are running slower than advertised and allow them to change or cancel the service at no additional charge.

You begin this chapter by learning what a computer network is and by identifying the various types of networks. You then study network fundamentals. You next turn your attention to the basics of the Internet and the World Wide Web. You conclude by examining the many network applications available to individuals and organizations—that is, what networks help you do.

WILEY PLUS

Author Lecture Videos are available exclusively in *WileyPLUS*.
Apply the Concept activities are available in the Appendix and in *WileyPLUS*.

computer network   A system that connects computers and other devices through communications media so that data and information can be transmitted among them.

bandwidth   The transmission capacity of a network, stated in bits per second.

broadband   The transmission capacity of a communications medium that is faster than 25 Mbps.

6.1 | What Is a Computer Network?

LEARNING OBJECTIVE

Compare and contrast the major types of networks.

A **computer network** is a system that connects computers and other devices (e.g., printers) through communications media so that data and information can be transmitted among them. Voice and data communication networks are continually becoming faster—that is, their bandwidth is increasing—and cheaper. **Bandwidth** refers to the transmission capacity of a network; it is stated in bits per second. Bandwidth ranges from narrowband (relatively low transmission capacity) to broadband (relatively high network capacity).

The telecommunications industry itself has difficulty defining the term *broadband*. The Federal Communications Commission's (FCC) rules define **broadband** as the transmission capacity of a communications medium (discussed later in this chapter) faster than 25 megabits per second (Mbps) for download—the transmission speed for material coming to you from an Internet server, such as a movie streamed from Netflix—and 3 Mbps for upload—the transmission speed for material that you upload to an Internet server such as a Facebook post or YouTube video.

Interestingly, some Federal Communications Commission (FCC; www.fcc.gov) members feel that the definition of broadband should be increased to 100 Mbps for download. The definition of broadband remains fluid, however, and it will undoubtedly continue to change to reflect greater transmission capacities in the future.

You are likely familiar with certain types of broadband connections such as *digital subscriber line (DSL)* and cable to your homes and dorms. DSL and cable fall within the range of transmission capacity mentioned here and are thus defined as broadband connections.

The various types of computer networks range from small to worldwide. They include (from smallest to largest) personal area networks (PANs), local area networks (LANs), metropolitan area networks (MANs), wide area networks (WANs), and the ultimate WAN, the Internet. PANs are short-range networks—typically a few meters—that are used for communication among devices close to one person. They can be wired or wireless. (You will learn about wireless PANs in Chapter 8.) MANs are relatively large networks that cover a metropolitan area. MANs fall between LANs and WANs in size. WANs typically cover large geographical areas; in some cases, they can span the entire planet and reach from Earth to Mars and beyond.

Local Area Networks

Regardless of their size, networks represent a compromise among three objectives: speed, distance, and cost. Organizations typically must select two of the three. To cover long distances, organizations can have fast communication if they are willing to pay for it, or inexpensive communication if they are willing to accept slower speeds. A third possible combination of the three trade-offs is fast, inexpensive communication with distance limitations. This is the idea behind local area networks.

A **local area network (LAN)** connects two or more devices in a limited geographical region, usually within the same building, so that every device on the network can communicate with every other device. Most LANs today use Ethernet (discussed later in this chapter). **Figure 6.1** illustrates an Ethernet LAN that consists of four computers, a server, and a printer, all of which connect through a shared cable. Every device in the LAN has a *network*

local area network (LAN) A network that connects communications devices in a limited geographic region, such as a building, so that every user device on the network can communicate with every other device.

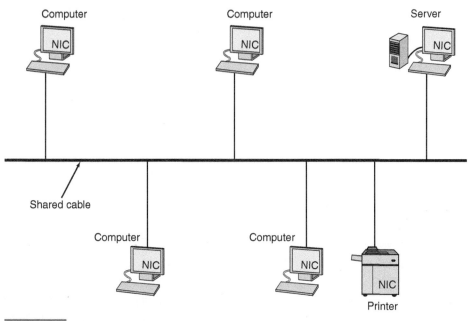

FIGURE 6.1 Ethernet local area.

interface card (NIC) that allows the device to physically connect to the LAN's communications medium. This medium is typically unshielded twisted-pair (UTP) wire.

Although it is not required, many LANs have a **file server** or **network server**. The server typically contains various software and data for the network. It also houses the LAN's network operating system, which manages the server and routes and manages communications on the network.

network server See **file server**.

file server (also called network server) A computer that contains various software and data files for a local area network as well as the network operating system.

Wide Area Networks

When businesses have to transmit and receive data beyond the confines of the LAN, they use wide area networks. The term *wide area network* did not even exist until local area networks appeared. Before that time, what we call a wide area network today was simply called a network.

A **wide area network (WAN)** is a network that covers a large geographical area. WANs typically connect multiple LANs. They are generally provided by common carriers such as telephone companies and the international networks of global communications services providers. Examples of these providers include AT&T (**www.att.com**) in the United States, Deutsche Telekom in Germany (**www.telekom.com**), and NTT Communications in Japan.

WANs have large capacities, and they typically combine multiple channels (e.g., fiber-optic cables, microwave, and satellite). WANs also contain **routers**—communications processors that route messages from a LAN to the Internet, across several connected LANs, or across a WAN such as the Internet. The Internet is an example of a WAN.

wide area network (WAN) A network, generally provided by common carriers, that covers a wide geographical area.

router A communications processor that routes messages from a LAN to the Internet, across several connected LANs, or across a wide area network such as the Internet.

Enterprise Networks

Organizations today have multiple LANs and may have multiple WANs. All of these networks are interconnected to form an **enterprise network**. Figure 6.2 displays a model of enterprise computing. Note that the enterprise network in the figure has a backbone network. Corporate **backbone networks** are high-speed central networks to which multiple smaller networks (such as LANs and smaller WANs) connect. The LANs are called *embedded LANs* because they connect to the backbone WAN.

Unfortunately, traditional networks can be rigid and lack the flexibility to keep pace with increasing business networking requirements. The reason for this problem is that the functions of traditional networks are distributed across physical routers and devices (i.e., hardware). Therefore, to implement changes, each network device must be configured individually. In some cases, devices must be configured manually. *Software-defined networks (SDN)* are an emerging technology that is becoming increasingly important to help organizations manage their data flows across their enterprise networks. With SDN, decisions that control how network traffic flows across network devices are managed centrally by software. The software dynamically adjusts data flows to meet business and application needs.

Think of traditional networks as the road system of a city in 1920. Data packets are the cars that travel through the city. A traffic officer (physical network devices) controls each intersection and directs traffic by recognizing the turn signals and the size and shape of the vehicles passing through the intersection. The officers can direct only the traffic at their intersection. They do not know the overall traffic volume in the city nor do they know traffic movement across the city. Therefore, it is difficult to control the city's traffic patterns as a whole and to manage peak-hour traffic. When problems occur, the city must communicate with each individual officer by radio.

enterprise network An organization's network, which is composed of interconnected multiple LANs and WANs.

backbone networks High-speed central networks to which multiple smaller networks (e.g., LANs and smaller WANs) connect.

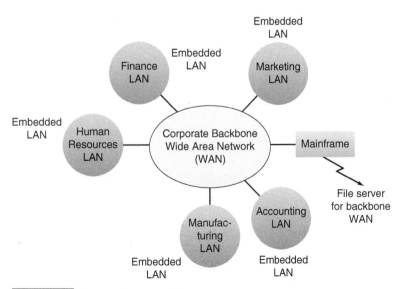

FIGURE 6.2 Enterprise network.

Now think of SDN as the road system of a modern city. Each traffic officer is replaced by a traffic light and a set of electronic vehicle counters, which are connected to central monitoring and control software. With this system, the city's traffic can be instantly and centrally controlled. The control software can direct traffic differently at various times of the day (say, rush hours). The software monitors traffic flow and automatically changes the traffic lights to help traffic flow through the city with minimal disruption.

Before you go on...

1. What are the primary business reasons for using networks?
2. What are the differences between LANs and WANs?
3. Describe an enterprise network.

6.2 Network Fundamentals

LEARNING OBJECTIVE

Describe the wireline communications media and transmission technologies.

In this section, you will learn the basics of how networks actually operate. You begin by studying wireline communications media, which enable computers in a network to transmit and receive data. You conclude this section by looking at network protocols and the types of network processing.

Today, computer networks communicate through *digital signals*, which are discrete pulses that are either on or off, representing a series of *bits* (0s and 1s). This quality allows digital signals to convey information in a binary form that can be interpreted by computers.

The U.S. public telephone system (called the "plain old telephone system" or POTS) was originally designed as an analog network to carry voice signals or sounds in an analog wave format. *Analog signals* are continuous waves that transmit information by altering the amplitude and frequency of the waves. POTS require *dial-up modems* to convert signals from analog to digital and vice versa. Dial-up modems are almost extinct in most parts of the developed world today.

Cable modems are modems that operate over coaxial cable—for example, cable TV. They offer broadband access to the Internet or to corporate intranets. Cable modem speeds vary widely. Most providers offer bandwidth between 1 and 6 million bits per second (Mbps) for downloads (from the Internet to a computer) and between 128 and 768 thousand bits per second (Kbps) for uploads. Cable modem services share bandwidth among subscribers in a locality. That is, the same cable line connects to many households. Therefore, when large numbers of neighbors access the Internet at the same time, cable speeds can decrease significantly.

DSL modems operate on the same lines as voice telephones and dial-up modems. DSL modems always maintain a connection, so an Internet connection is immediately available.

communications channel
Pathway for communicating data from one location to another.

Communications Media and Channels

Communicating data from one location to another requires some form of pathway or medium. A **communications channel** is such a pathway. It is comprised of two types of media: cable (twisted-pair wire, coaxial cable, or fiber-optic cable) and broadcast (microwave, satellite, radio, or infrared).

TABLE 6.1   **Advantages and Disadvantages of Wireline Communications Channels**

Channel	Advantages	Disadvantages
Twisted-pair wire	Inexpensive	Slow (low bandwidth)
	Widely available	Subject to interference
	Easy to work with	Easily tapped (low security)
Coaxial cable	Higher bandwidth than twisted-pair	Relatively expensive and inflexible
		Easily tapped (low to medium security)
	Less susceptible to electromagnetic interference	Somewhat difficult to work with
Fiber-optic cable	Very high bandwidth	Difficult to work with (difficult to splice)
	Relatively inexpensive	
	Difficult to tap (good security)	

wireless media   See **broadcast media**.

broadcast media (also called wireless media) Communications channels that use electromagnetic media (the "airwaves") to transmit data.

twisted-pair wire A communications medium consisting of strands of copper wire twisted together in pairs.

wireline media   See **cable media**.

cable media (also called wireline media) Communications channels that use physical wires or cables to transmit data and information.

coaxial cable   Insulated copper wire; used to carry high-speed data traffic and television signals.

Wireline media or **cable media** use physical wires or cables to transmit data and information. Twisted-pair wire and coaxial cables are made of copper, and fiber-optic cable is made of glass. The alternative is communication over **broadcast media** or **wireless media**. The key to mobile communications in today's rapidly moving society is data transmissions over electromagnetic media—the "airwaves." In this section, you will study the three wireline channels. Table 6.1 summarizes the advantages and disadvantages of each of these channels. You will become familiar with wireless media in Chapter 8.

Twisted-Pair Wire   The most prevalent form of communications wiring, **twisted-pair wire**, is used for almost all business telephone wiring. As the name suggests, it consists of strands of copper wire twisted in pairs (see Figure 6.3). Twisted-pair wire is relatively inexpensive to purchase, widely available, and easy to work with. However, it also has some significant disadvantages. Specifically, it is relatively slow for transmitting data, it is subject to interference from other electrical sources, and it can be easily tapped by unintended recipients to gain unauthorized access to data.

Coaxial Cable   Coaxial cable (Figure 6.4) consists of insulated copper wire. Compared with twisted-pair wire, it is much less susceptible to electrical interference, and it can carry much more data. For these reasons, it is commonly used to carry high-speed data traffic as well as television signals (thus the term *cable TV*). However, coaxial cable is more expensive and more difficult to work with than twisted-pair wire. It is also somewhat inflexible.

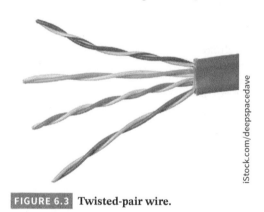

iStock.com/deepspacedave

FIGURE 6.3   **Twisted-pair wire.**

GIPhotoStock/Science Source

iStock.com/piotr_malczyk

Cross-section view   How coaxial cable looks to us

FIGURE 6.4   **Two views of coaxial cable.**

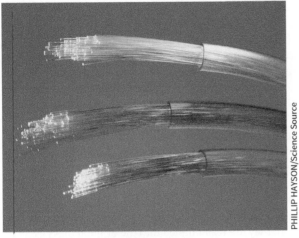

Cross-section view

PHILLIP HAYSON/Science Source

How fiber-optic cable looks to us

SPL/Science Source

FIGURE 6.5 **Two views of fiber-optic cable.**

Fiber Optics Fiber-optic cable (Figure 6.5) consists of thousands of very thin filaments of glass fibers that transmit information through pulses of light generated by lasers. The fiber-optic cable is surrounded by cladding, a coating that prevents the light from leaking out of the fiber.

Fiber-optic cables are significantly smaller and lighter than traditional cable media. They can also transmit far more data, and they provide greater security from interference and tapping. Fiber-optic cable is typically used as the backbone for a network, whereas twisted-pair wire and coaxial cable connect the backbone to individual devices on the network. As of August 2022, approximately 800,000 miles of 400 undersea fiber-optic cables carry over 98 percent of all transoceanic data. In 2022, Equiano, Google's latest subsea fiber-optic cable connecting Europe and Africa, became operational. Equiano is purported to be able to transmit data at 144 terabits (trillions of bits) per second between the two continents.

fiber-optic cable A communications medium consisting of thousands of very thin filaments of glass fibers, surrounded by cladding, that transmit information through pulses of light generated by lasers.

Network Protocols

Computing devices that are connected to the network must access and share the network to transmit and receive data. These devices are often referred to as *nodes* of the network. They work together by adhering to a common set of rules and procedures—known as a **protocol**—that enable them to communicate with one another. The two major protocols are the Ethernet and Transmission Control Protocol/Internet Protocol.

protocol The set of rules and procedures that govern transmission across a network.

Ethernet A common LAN protocol is **Ethernet**. Many organizations use 100-gigabit Ethernet through which the network provides data transmission speeds of 100 gigabits (100 billion bits) per second. As of September 2022, the categories of Ethernet cable are as follows:

ethernet A common local area network protocol.

- *Cat 5e* (*Cat 5 enhanced*) is the most common type of Ethernet cable. It is lowcost and supports up to 1,000 Mbps (1 Gbps). Further, Cat 5e reduces crosstalk, which is unwanted transfer of signal between the cables, for a more consistent connection.
- *Cat 6* supports the same speeds as Cat 5e but can provide shielding. Shielding is a thin protective barrier around the wires inside the Ethernet cable that further protects them from crosstalk and interference. Not all Cat 6 cables come with this feature.
- *Cat 6a* (*Cat 6 augmented*) supports speeds up to 10,000 Mbps (10 Gbps). All Cat 6a and higher cables feature shielding designed to eliminate crosstalk almost entirely.
- *Cat 7* and *Cat 7a* (*Cat 7 augmented*) only offer slightly higher bandwidth than Cat 6a.
- *Cat 8* supports speeds up to 40,000 Mbps (40 Gbps).

Transmission Control Protocol/Internet Protocol

Transmission Control Protocol/Internet Protocol (TCP/IP) A file transfer protocol that can send large files of information across sometimes unreliable networks with the assurance that the data will arrive uncorrupted.

The **Transmission Control Protocol/Internet Protocol (TCP/IP)** is the protocol of the Internet. TCP/IP uses a suite of protocols, the primary ones being the Transmission Control Protocol (TCP) and the Internet Protocol (IP). The TCP performs three basic functions: (1) it manages the movement of data packets (see further on) between computers by establishing a connection between the computers, (2) it sequences the transfer of packets, and (3) it acknowledges the packets that have been transmitted. The **Internet Protocol (IP)** is responsible for disassembling, delivering, and reassembling the data during transmission.

Internet Protocol (IP) A set of rules responsible for disassembling, delivering, and reassembling packets over the Internet.

Before data are transmitted over the Internet, they are divided into small, fixed bundles called *packets*. The transmission technology that breaks up blocks of text into packets is called **packet switching**. Each packet carries the information that will help it reach its destination—the sender's IP address, the intended recipient's IP address, the number of packets in the message, and the sequence number of the particular packet within the message. Each packet travels independently across the network and can be routed through different paths in the network. When the packets reach their destination, they are reassembled into the original message.

packet switching The transmission technology that divides blocks of text into packets.

It is important to note that packet-switching networks are reliable and fault tolerant. For example, if a path in the network is very busy or is broken, packets can be dynamically ("on the fly") rerouted around that path. Also, if one or more packets do not get to the receiving computer, then only those packets need to be resent.

Why do organizations use packet switching? The main reason is to achieve reliable end-to-end message transmission over sometimes-unreliable networks that may have short-acting or long-acting problems.

The packets use the TCP/IP protocol to carry their data. TCP/IP functions in four layers (see **Figure 6.6**). The *application layer* enables client application programs to access the other layers, and it defines the protocols that applications use to exchange data. One of these application protocols is the **Hypertext Transfer Protocol (HTTP)**, which defines how messages are formulated and how they are interpreted by their receivers. (We discuss hypertext in Section 6.3.) The *transport layer* provides the application layer with communication and packet services. This layer includes TCP and other protocols. The *Internet layer* is responsible for addressing, routing, and packaging data packets. The IP is one of the protocols in this layer. Finally, the *network interface layer* places packets on, and receives them from, the network medium, which can be any networking technology.

Hypertext Transfer Protocol (HTTP) The communications standard used to transfer pages across the www portion of the Internet; it defines how messages are formulated and transmitted.

Two computers using TCP/IP can communicate even if they use different hardware and software. Data sent from one computer to another proceed downward through all four layers, beginning with the sending computer's application layer and going through its network interface layer. After the data reach the receiving computer, they travel up the layers.

TCP/IP enables users to send data across sometimes-unreliable networks with the assurance that the data will arrive in uncorrupted form. TCP/IP is very popular with business organizations because of its reliability and the ease with which it can support intranets and related functions.

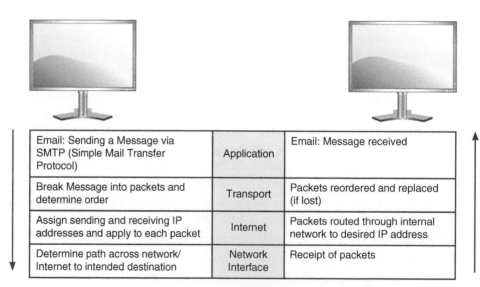

Email: Sending a Message via SMTP (Simple Mail Transfer Protocol)	Application	Email: Message received
Break Message into packets and determine order	Transport	Packets reordered and replaced (if lost)
Assign sending and receiving IP addresses and apply to each packet	Internet	Packets routed through internal network to desired IP address
Determine path across network/Internet to intended destination	Network Interface	Receipt of packets

FIGURE 6.6 **The four layers of the TCP/IP reference model.**

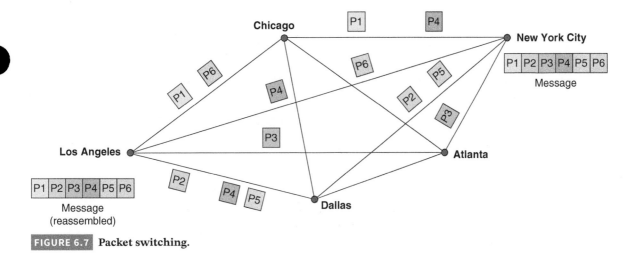

FIGURE 6.7 Packet switching.

Let's look at an example of packet switching across the Internet. **Figure 6.7** illustrates a message being sent from New York City to Los Angeles over a packet-switching network. Note that the different colored packets travel by different routes to reach their destination in Los Angeles, where they are reassembled into the complete message.

Types of Network Processing

Organizations typically use multiple computer systems across the firm. **Distributed processing** divides processing work among two or more computers. This process enables computers in different locations to communicate with one another through telecommunications links. A common type of distributed processing is client/server processing. A special type of client/server processing is peer-to-peer processing.

Client/Server Computing
Client/server computing links two or more computers in an arrangement in which some machines, called **servers**, provide computing services for user PCs, called **clients**. Usually, an organization performs the bulk of its processing or application and data storage on suitably powerful servers that can be accessed by less powerful client machines. The client requests applications, data, or processing from the server, which acts on these requests by "serving" the desired commodity.

Client/server computing leads to the ideas of "fat" clients and "thin" clients. As discussed in Technology Guide 1, *fat clients* have large storage and processing power and therefore can run local programs (such as Microsoft Office) if the network goes down. In contrast, *thin clients* may have no local storage and only limited processing power. Thus, they must depend on the network to run applications. For this reason, they are of little value when the network is not functioning.

Peer-to-Peer Processing
Peer-to-peer (P2P) processing is a type of client/server distributed processing in which each computer acts as *both* a client and a server. Each computer can access (as assigned for security or integrity purposes) all files on all other computers.

There are three basic types of peer-to-peer processing. The first type accesses unused CPU power among networked computers. An application of this type is SETI@home (**www.setiathome.ssl.berkeley.edu**). These applications are from open-source projects, and they can be downloaded at no cost.

The second form of peer-to-peer is real-time, person-to-person collaboration, such as Microsoft SharePoint Workspace. This product provides P2P collaborative applications that use buddy lists to establish a connection and allow real-time collaboration within the application.

The third peer-to-peer category is advanced search and file sharing. This category is characterized by natural language searches of millions of peer systems. It enables users to discover other users, not just data and Web pages. One example of this category is BitTorrent.

BitTorrent (**www.bittorrent.com**) is an open-source, free, peer-to-peer file-sharing application that simplifies the problem of sharing large files by dividing them into tiny pieces, or "torrents." BitTorrent addresses two of the biggest problems of file sharing: (1) downloading

distributed processing Network architecture that divides processing work between or among two or more computers that are linked together in a network.

client/server computing Form of distributed processing in which some machines (servers) perform computing functions for end-user PCs (clients).

servers Computers that provide access to various network services, such as printing, data, and communications.

clients Computers, such as users' personal computers, that use any of the services provided by servers.

peer-to-peer (P2P) processing A type of client/server distributed processing that allows two or more computers to pool their resources, making each computer both a client and a server.

bogs down when many people access a file at once and (2) some people leech, meaning they download content but refuse to share it. BitTorrent eliminates the bottleneck by enabling all users to share little pieces of a file at the same time—a process called *swarming*. The program prevents leeching because users must upload a file while they download it. Thus, the more popular the content, the more efficiently it travels over a network.

Before you go on...

1. Compare and contrast the three wireline communications channels.
2. Describe the various technologies that enable users to send high-volume data over any network.
3. Describe the Ethernet and TCP/IP protocols.

6.3 The Internet and the World Wide Web

WILEY PLUS

Author Lecture Videos are available exclusively in *WileyPLUS*.
Apply the Concept activities are available in the Appendix and in *WileyPLUS*.

Internet (the Net) A massive global WAN that connects approximately 1 million organizational computer networks in more than 200 countries on all continents.

Internet backbone The primary network connections and telecommunications lines that link the computers and organizational nodes of the Internet.

LEARNING OBJECTIVE

Describe the most common methods for accessing the Internet.

The **Internet** ("the Net") is a global WAN that connects approximately 1 million organizational computer networks in more than 200 countries on all continents. It has become so widespread that it features in the daily routine of some 5 billion people.

The computers and organizational nodes on the Internet can be of different types and makes. They are connected to one another by data communications lines of different speeds. The primary network connections and telecommunications lines that link the nodes are referred to as the **Internet backbone**. The Internet backbone is a fiber-optic network that is operated primarily by large telecommunications companies.

Many people mistakenly assume that Internet traffic (data transmissions) occurs wirelessly. However, only 1 percent of Internet traffic is carried by satellites. So, what does the Internet actually look like?

The Internet is quite tangible, consisting of underwater cables that total almost 750,000 miles in length. These cables, which range in thickness from a garden hose to about three inches in diameter, come onshore at cable landing points.

From these points, the cables are buried underground and make their way to large data centers. (We discuss data centers in Technology Guide 3.) In the United States, most of these underground cables are located along major roads and railways. In fact, one of the world's most concentrated hubs in terms of Internet connectivity is located in Lower Manhattan in New York City. IT's About Business 6.1 takes a detailed look at undersea fiber-optic cables being provided by technology companies, including Alphabet, Microsoft, Meta, and Amazon, as well as a group of Chinese enterprises.

IT's About Business 6.1

MIS **The Physical Structure of the Internet**

The actual physical Internet comprises approximately 400 underwater fiber-optic cables—called *subsea cables*—that link countries across the oceans. These cables carry roughly 98 percent of international Internet data and telephone traffic. Until recently, the vast majority of the undersea cables were installed, controlled, and used by telecommunications companies and governments.

Today, four giant technology companies—Microsoft, Alphabet, Meta, and Amazon—have become the dominant users of undersea cables. According to the subsea cable analysis firm TeleGeography (**www.telegeography.com**), by 2025 these four companies are on track to become the primary financiers and owners of more than 30 long-distance undersea cables that connect every continent except Antarctica.

These firms contend that they are laying these cables to increase bandwidth across the most developed parts of the world and to bring improved connectivity to underserved regions such as Africa. However, by building their own cable infrastructure, these companies are saving themselves money that they otherwise would have to pay other cable operators.

Subsea cabling is a challenging business, with multi-hundred-million-dollar capital costs, followed by continuous operational upgrades. Today, companies use two models to lay undersea cables: partnerships and sole ownership.

Partnerships. Meta (formerly Facebook) works with global and local partners, as well as with other technology companies such as Microsoft, on all of its subsea cables. Most of these tech-funded cables are collaborations among rivals. For example, the Marea cable, which extends more than 4,000 miles between Bilbao, Spain, and Virginia, is partly owned by Microsoft, Meta, and Telxius, a subsidiary of Telefónica, the Spanish telecommunications company.

Sharing bandwidth and cables among competitors helps ensure that each company has capacity on more cables. This redundancy is essential for keeping the world's Internet operating when a cable is severed or damaged, events that occur about 200 times per year. Sharing is also critical to ensuring that cloud services are available almost all the time, something that cloud vendors explicitly promise in their agreements with customers.

These deals also serve another purpose. Reserving some capacity for telecom carriers is a strategy to prevent regulators from classifying these U.S. technology firms as telecommunications companies. Tech companies have long argued that they are not common carriers like the telecoms because they do not sell any of their bandwidth to make money. If they were classified as telecoms, then they would have to adhere to the regulations governing the operations of these types of companies.

Sole ownership. In 2018, Google announced that it was planning wholly owned new transoceanic cables, becoming the first major non-telecom company to do so. By 2022, the company was the sole owner of three undersea cables. The market research firm TeleGeography predicts that Google will own six undersea cables by the end of 2023.

Google builds solely owned-and-operated undersea cables for two reasons. First, the company needs them to make its own services, such as Google Search and YouTube, fast and responsive. Second, Google wants to gain a competitive edge in the battle for customers for its cloud services.

Making landfall. The technology companies use partners for the landing parties in each country. (Google uses partners only for the landing parties in each country, while maintaining possession of the deepwater landing segments.) A *landing segment* is the location where an undersea cable makes landfall. A *landing party* is the terrestrial telecommunications company with which the undersea cable connects in a country. Partnering with foreign firms enables the technology companies to avoid being classified as landing parties, which are often subject to strict country-specific regulations. As a result, the companies concentrate most of their infrastructure investment on risk-free international waters.

The Internet companies are offering traditional telecoms an alternative business model: the opportunity to play middleman between their cables and inland users, who will continue to depend on terrestrial cables in the interior of a continent. In exchange for paying much of the capital costs, technology firms acquire direct links to the national and regional networks that connect the new subsea cables to their users.

Africa

Africa, home to 1.4 billion people, is the last relatively unconnected, populated continent. As a result, the technology companies are laying undersea cables to connect Africa with the rest of the world. The motivation for all of this activity is clear. The need for Internet content is rapidly increasing in Africa (and globally), and the existing cables are insufficient to deliver their products to their users. Further, with huge amounts of cash available, the tech companies are not waiting for telecom companies to lay new cables.

In 2008, almost all African data traffic originated outside the continent, hosted on servers in Europe, America, and Asia. In 2022, Google completed its undersea cable, called Equiano, linking Africa and Europe. Industry analysts predict that in the West African nation of Nigeria alone, the Equiano cable will improve download speeds by 600 percent, reduce retail data prices by 21 percent, and create economic activity that will indirectly create 1.6 million jobs and add $10 billion to the country's GDP. For South Africa, analysts forecast that by 2025 the cable will increase GDP by up to $7 billion and indirectly contribute to the creation of 180,000 jobs.

Meanwhile, Meta's 2Africa cable fully encircled the continent, connecting Africa, India, Pakistan, nearly all the Gulf States, and Europe. When the system is completed in 2024, it will be the longest undersea cable in the world, bringing Internet connectivity to 33 countries that are home to three billion people.

Equiano and 2Africa will connect Africa to the global Internet more robustly than ever. In addition to social media and Internet searches (and the ads that monetize them), they will carry the health, governance, and security data of entire countries. Because there are currently few large African data centers to store data regionally, these digital services will remain offshore.

Not to be outdone, in August 2022, Chinese companies completed the construction of an undersea fiber-optic cable known as Peace. The cable travels overland from China to Pakistan, where it submerges underwater and continues another 7,500 miles through the Red Sea. At that point, it branches north to France and south to South Africa. The cable will improve service for Chinese companies doing business in Europe and Africa.

The Big Question

The involvement of Alphabet, Microsoft, Meta, and Amazon in the cable-laying industry has driven down the cost of transmitting data across oceans for everyone—even their competitors—and helped increase the capacity to transmit data internationally by 41 percent in 2021 alone. Both Google and Meta emphasize the societal benefits of their cables. Google claims that its cables "interconnect humanity," and Meta contends that 2Africa will ensure "everyone can benefit from the economic, educational, and social advantages of a digitally connected world."

Despite these assertions, serious questions remain: Do we want the world's most powerful providers of Internet services and marketplaces to also own the infrastructure on which these services are delivered? Should big-tech firms be allowed to vertically integrate all the way down to the level of the physical infrastructure of the Internet? Once a cable is operational, could one company's network managers prioritize its own data traffic, ensuring the performance and reliability of their cloud services, while using that reliability as the services' key selling point? If Internet companies own their own fiber-optic networks, what kinds of public policy—if any—will keep the power of Internet companies in check?

Further, if Internet companies control the cables, they could effectively dictate Internet policy. The Internet's initial promise was to decentralize telecommunications, releasing consumers from the monopoly grip of telecom companies. In the near future, however, a small group of huge corporations could tighten their hold on our online activity while rebuilding the Internet itself. If the giants' cable building continues as planned, the future Internet will be less a network of interconnected networks, as it was originally conceived and has developed, and more like a *supranet*, dominated by a few mega networks operating upon their own global physical infrastructure.

Questions

1. **Do we want the world's most powerful providers of Internet services and marketplaces to also own the infrastructure on which these services are delivered? Why or why not? Support your answer.**

2. **If Internet companies own their own fiber-optic networks, what kinds of public policy will keep the power of Internet companies in check?**

Sources: Compiled from D. Henrick, "Equiano Cable to Add Billions to South Africa's GDP," cajnewssafrica.com, September 2, 2022; "PEACE Completed Construction from Pakistan to France," www.peacecable.net, August 19, 2022; T. Page, "Google Equiano: Internet Giant Bets Big on Africa with Latest Megaproject," *CNN*, August 8, 2022; "What Is Submarine Fiber Optic Cable? How Is It Laid?" kvcable.com, July 19, 2022; A. Blum and C. Baraka, "Sea Change," *Rest of World*, May 10, 2022; I. Haynes, "Linking China to Europe and Africa, Huawei Undersea Cable Ends in Kenya," techzine.eu, March 31, 2022; C. Mims, "Google, Amazon, Meta and Microsoft Weave a Fiber-Optic Web of Power," *Wall Street Journal*, January 15, 2022; H. Fouquet and T. Seal, "China's Undersea Cable Is Dividing the Internet," *Bloomberg Businessweek*, March 8, 2021; H. Fouquet, "China's 7,500-Mile Undersea Cable to Europe Fuels Feud," Bloomberg.com, March 4, 2021; and J. Griffiths, "The Global Internet Is Powered by Vast Undersea Cables. But They're Vulnerable." *CNN*, July 26, 2019.

As a network of networks, the Internet enables people to access data in other organizations and to communicate, collaborate, and exchange information around the world quickly, seamlessly, and inexpensively. Thus, the Internet has become a necessity for modern businesses. IT's About Business 6.2 illustrates how much the Internet has become a necessity not only for businesses but also for daily life.

IT's About Business **6.2**

MIS   The Afghanistan Sneakernet

When the Taliban—a strict Islamic fundamentalist group—last ruled Afghanistan between 1996 and 2001, the country remained analog. The Internet was effectively banned, along with music and other "modern concepts" such as women enjoying basic human rights. The result was that most Afghans were cut off from the emerging digital world. In August 2001, the Taliban regime was overthrown following a U.S.-led invasion in response to the 9/11 terrorist attacks. In 2021, they returned to power, and President Biden withdrew the remaining U.S. forces from the country.

Despite its negative approach to online life within its borders, the Taliban aggressively employed the Internet to spread its philosophy globally. The group has been on Twitter for a decade and has maintained an official website since 1998.

Even in a country with an Internet penetration of only 11.5 percent, Afghanistan's online presence and infrastructure are critical to its future. By 2021, Afghanistan had fewer than nine million Internet users, a number attributed to high costs and a lack of infrastructure across the country's mountainous areas. While the Taliban must decide what to do with the Internet in Afghanistan, the global companies that provide its infrastructure must decide what to do with the Taliban.

Today, five telecommunications companies operate in Afghanistan. Foreign countries primarily own or have invested in three of them. Because the Internet is centralized in a small number of service providers, most of which are based in the United States, everything from cloud vendors to social media could go offline if the international community decides to sanction the Taliban. Internet shutdowns would harm Afghan citizens, limiting their ability to access and share reliable information and putting them at risk of misinformation.

Let's look at how a small group of individuals is working with Internet technology under the Taliban. When the Taliban returned to power in 2021, one young entrepreneur had to make a number of decisions very quickly. He went to his shop and began to erase some of the sensitive data on his computer and moved the rest onto two hard drives. He then wrapped the drives in plastic and buried them underground.

It is significant that this individual had no state secrets on his computers. Instead, he is what is locally referred to as a *computer kar*, someone who sells digital content by hand in a country with spotty, intermittent Internet connections. Specifically, he sells movies, music, mobile applications, and iOS updates. Further, he helps other Afghans create Apple IDs and social media accounts, sets up and backs up their phones, and writes and sends e-mails for them.

Kars can sometimes download their information from the Internet when they are able to get a connection. When they cannot, they physically transport much of it on hard drives to neighboring cities and countries, forming a *sneakernet*.

Another kar commented that he uses his Wi-Fi at home to download music and other applications. However, the connection is not reliable. Therefore, every month he sends a 4-terabyte hard drive to Jalalabad—a city in eastern Afghanistan—where other kars fill the drive with content and return it within a week. The drive typically contains the latest Hollywood and Bollywood (Indian) movies, dubbed in Dari and Pashto, the Afghan national languages. The drive also contains Turkish TV dramas, video games, music, and applications. Filling the drive in Jalalabad costs him about $10.00. He contends that he can install more than 5 gigabytes of content on a customer's phone for just US$1.00. Most of his customers are men, but a few are women.

Afghanistan's kars admit that the Taliban takeover has hurt business. Their average earnings have decreased by 90 percent, from around $32 per day to $3.80. From that amount, they spend at least $1 per day for generator fuel, and they pay another $.50 per day to the city for the space they use as their offices.

In addition to policing their content, the Taliban have been cracking down on kars who have expanded their services to help Afghans fleeing persecution. Often, Afghans who are in hiding or who are waiting to be evacuated come to kars to help them back up their phone data on flash drives to avoid being caught by the Taliban, who examine phones at the checkpoints.

The kars find it very ironic that the Taliban are cracking down on them and their content now that they are in power, because the Taliban used the sneakernet themselves to recruit and radicalize followers when they were not in power. Despite the oppressive nature of the Taliban regime, the kars remain optimistic. During COVID lockdowns, demand increased for cartoon clips because children were locked in at home. Now, with the Taliban in power and widespread unemployment, people are also stuck at home. The kars hope that their customers will watch more movies.

Questions

1. **What is a sneakernet? Describe why kars had to form a sneakernet.**
2. **Discuss the irony of the Taliban repressing kars now that they are in power.**

Sources: Compiled from "The Taliban's Internet," HIP Consult, December 3, 2021; R. Kumar, "Can Afghanistan's Underground Sneakernet Survive the Taliban?" *MIT Technology Review*, November 26, 2021; S. Vavra and D. Falzone, "This Is Why the Taliban Keeps F*cking up the Internet," *Yahoo! News*, September 16, 2021; C. Stokel-Walker, "The Battle for Control of Afghanistan's Internet," *Wired*, September 7, 2021; O. Tangen, "What Happens to Afghans' Right to Internet under the Taliban?" *The Wire*, August 29, 2021; "Will the Taliban Restrict Internet Access in Afghanistan?," *MSN*, August 29, 2021; L. Cerulus, "Fears Loom over Afghanistan's Internet," *Politico*, August 25, 2021; N. Maranan, "Taliban and the Curtailment of Internet Freedoms," dailydoseofsocialmedia.blog, August 21, 2021; P. Mozur and Z. ur-Rehman, "How the Taliban Turned Social Media into a Tool for Control," *New York Times*, August 20, 2021; C. Winter et al., "The Taliban's Vast Propaganda Machine Has a New Target," *Wired*, August 20, 2021; "In Numbers: How Has Life Changed in Afghanistan in 20 Years?," *BBC News*, August 16, 2021; and K. Taneja, "From 'Night Letters' to the Internet: Propaganda, the Taliban and the Afghanistan Crisis," gnet-research. org, August 16, 2021.

The Internet grew out of an experimental project of the Advanced Research Project Agency (ARPA) of the U.S. Department of Defense. The project began in 1969 as the *ARPAnet*. Its purpose was to test the feasibility of a WAN over which researchers, educators, military personnel, and government agencies could share data, exchange messages, and transfer files.

Today, Internet technologies are being used both within and among organizations. An **intranet** is a network that uses Internet protocols so that users can take advantage of familiar applications and work habits. Intranets support discovery (easy and inexpensive browsing and search), communication, and collaboration inside an organization.

In contrast, an **extranet** connects parts of the intranets of different organizations. It also enables business partners to communicate securely over the Internet using virtual private networks (VPNs) (explained in Chapter 4). Extranets offer limited accessibility to the intranets of participating companies, as well as necessary interorganizational communications. They are widely used in the areas of business-to-business (B2B) electronic commerce (see Chapter 7) and supply chain management (SCM) (see Chapter 11).

No central agency manages the Internet. Instead, the costs of its operation are shared among hundreds of thousands of nodes. Thus, the cost for any one organization is small. Organizations must pay a small fee if they wish to register their names, and they need to install their own hardware and software to operate their internal networks. Organizations are obliged to move any data or information that enters their organizational network, regardless of the source, to their destination, at no charge to the senders. The senders, of course, pay the telephone bills for using either the backbone or regular telephone lines.

intranet A private network that uses Internet software and TCP/IP protocols.

extranet A network that connects parts of the intranets of different organizations.

Accessing the Internet

You can access the Internet in several ways. From your place of work or your university, you can use your organization's LAN. A campus or company backbone connects all of the various LANs and servers in the organization to the Internet. You can also log on to the Internet from your home or on the road, using either wireline or wireless connections.

Connecting through an Online Service
You can access the Internet by opening an account with an Internet service provider. An **Internet service provider (ISP)** is a company that provides Internet connections for a fee. Large ISPs include Comcast (**www.xfinity.com**), AT&T (**www.att.com**), Spectrum (**www.spectrum.com**), and Verizon (**www.verizon.com**).

ISPs connect to one another through **network access points (NAPs)**. NAPs are exchange points for Internet traffic. They determine how traffic is routed. NAPs are key

Internet service provider (ISP) A company that provides Internet connections for a fee.

network access points (NAPs) Computers that act as exchange points for Internet traffic and determine how traffic is routed.

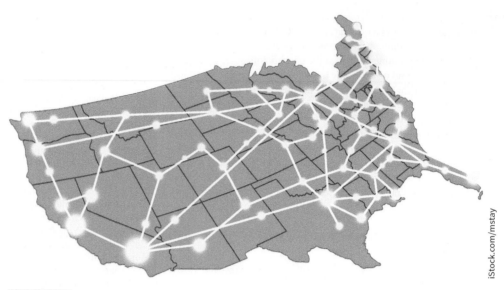

iStock.com/mstay

FIGURE 6.8 Internet (backbone in white).

components of the Internet backbone. Figure 6.8 displays a schematic of the Internet. The white links at the top of the figure represent the Internet backbone; the brown dots where the white links meet are the NAPs.

Connecting through Other Means   There have been several attempts to make access to the Internet cheaper, faster, and easier. For example, terminals known as Internet kiosks have been located in public places like libraries and airports (and even in convenience stores in some countries) for use by people who do not have their own computers. Accessing the Internet from smartphones and tablets is common, and fiber-to-the-home (FTTH) is growing rapidly. FTTH involves connecting fiber-optic cable directly to individual homes. Table 6.2 summarizes the various means of connecting to the Internet.

Connecting through Satellite   Satellite connections are worth noting in more detail. See our discussion in Section 8.1.

Google Fiber (FTTH)   Google Fiber (www.fiber.google.com) offers broadband services with both fiber-optic and fixed wireless technology. Google Fiber is available in 11 cities across 9 states. Google Fiber Webpass, a fixed wireless Internet that runs on Ethernet inside buildings, doesn't require a modem and is accessible in 15 metropolitan areas across the United States, but it is limited to apartments, condominiums, and businesses.

TABLE 6.2   Internet Connection Methods

Service	Description
Dial-up	Still used in the United States where broadband is not available
DSL	Broadband access through telephone companies
Cable modem	Access over your cable TV coaxial cable; can have degraded performance if many of your neighbors are accessing the Internet at once
Satellite	Access where cable and DSL are not available
Wireless	Very convenient, and WiMAX will increase the use of broadband wireless
Fiber-to-the-home (FTTH)	Expensive and usually placed only in new housing developments

Google Fiber features no contracts, no data caps, upload and download speeds of 1 Gbps, and 1 terabyte of free cloud storage. Google Fiber costs $70 per month for 1 Gbps plans and $100 per month for 2 Gbps plans.

Google Fiber Webpass features optional contracts, no data caps, and download speeds up to 1 Gbps, depending on individual building setup. Webpass customers have access to the 1 Gbps plan only, but they can receive a small discount for paying for a year of service up front ($62.50 per month or $750 due up front).

Addresses on the Internet   Each computer on the Internet has an assigned address, called the **Internet Protocol (IP) address** that distinguishes it from all other computers. The IP address consists of sets of numbers in four parts, separated by dots. For example, the IP address of one computer might be 135.62.128.91. You can access a website by typing this number in the address bar of your browser.

Currently, there are two IP addressing schemes. The first scheme, IPv4, was the most widely used. IP addresses using IPv4 consist of 32 bits, meaning that there are 2^{32} possibilities for IP addresses, or 4,294,967,295 distinct addresses. Note that the IP address in the preceding paragraph (135.62.128.91) is an IPv4 address. At the time that IPv4 was developed, there were not as many computers that needed addresses as there are today. Therefore, a new IP addressing scheme has been developed, IPv6, because we have run out of available IPv4 addresses.

IP addresses using IPv6 consist of 128 bits, meaning that there are 2^{128} possibilities for distinct IP addresses, which is an unimaginably large number. IPv6, which is replacing IPv4, will accommodate the rapidly increasing number of devices that need IP addresses, such as smartphones and devices that constitute the Internet of Things (see **Section 8.4**).

IP addresses must be unique so that computers on the Internet know where to find one another. The Internet Corporation for Assigned Names and Numbers (ICANN) (**www.icann.org**) coordinates these unique addresses throughout the world, working on behalf of an international "multistakeholder community" composed primarily of technology companies.

Because numeric IP addresses are difficult to remember, most computers have names as well. ICANN accredits certain companies called *registrars* to register these names, which are derived from the **domain name system (DNS)**. **Domain names** consist of multiple parts, separated by dots, that are read from right to left. For example, consider the domain name *business.auburn.edu*. The rightmost part (or zone) of an Internet name is its top-level domain (TLD). The letters *edu* in **business.auburn.edu** indicate that this is an educational site. The following are popular U.S. TLDs:

.com	commercial sites
.edu	educational sites
.mil	military government sites
.gov	civilian government sites
.org	organizations

To conclude our domain name example, *auburn* is the name of the organization (Auburn University), and *business* is the name of the particular machine (server) within the organization to which the message is being sent.

A TLD is the domain at the highest level in the hierarchical Domain Name System of the Internet. The TLD names are located in the root zone (rightmost zone) of the name. Management of most TLDs is delegated to responsible organizations by ICANN. ICANN operates the Internet Assigned Numbers Authority (IANA), which is in charge of maintaining the DNS root zone. Today, IANA distinguishes the following groups of TLDs:

- Country-code top-level domains (ccTLD): Two-letter domains established for countries or territories. For example, *de* stands for Germany, *it* for Italy, and *ru* for Russia.

- Internationalized country code top-level domains (IDN ccTLD): These are ccTLDs in non-Latin character sets (e.g., Arabic or Chinese).

- Generic top-level domains (gTLD): Top-level domains with three or more characters. gTLDs initially consisted of .gov, .edu, .com, .mil, .org, and .net. In late 2000, ICANN introduced .aero, .biz, .coop, .info, .museum, .name, and .pro.

Internet Protocol (IP) address   An assigned address that uniquely identifies a computer on the Internet.

domain name system (DNS)   The system administered by the Internet Corporation for Assigned Names (ICANN) that assigns names to each site on the Internet.

domain names   The name assigned to an Internet site, which consists of multiple parts, separated by dots, that are translated from right to left.

The Future of the Internet

Internet2 A new, faster telecommunications network that deploys advanced network applications such as remote medical diagnosis, digital libraries, distance education, online simulation, and virtual laboratories.

Researchers assert that if Internet bandwidth is not improved rapidly, then within a few years the Internet will be able to function only at a much-reduced speed. The Internet is sometimes too slow for data-intensive applications such as full-motion video files (movies) and large medical files (X-rays). The Internet is also unreliable and is not secure. As a result, Internet2 has been developed by many U.S. universities collaborating with industry and government. **Internet2** develops and deploys advanced network applications such as remote medical diagnosis, digital libraries, distance education, online simulation, and virtual laboratories. It is designed to be fast, always on, everywhere, natural, intelligent, easy, and trusted. Note that Internet2 is not a separate physical network from the Internet. For more details, see **www.internet2.edu**. IT's About Business 6.3 shows a possible future for the Internet, called the splinternet.

IT's About Business **6.3**

MIS The Splinternet

For most of its relatively short history, the Internet has had very limited centralized planning and governance. In general, the Internet today enables users to exchange ideas and information instantaneously and with minimal supervision, regardless of national boundaries.

The modern, open Internet also provides a platform that nations can use to undertake information warfare, manipulate one another's citizens, and/or project their interests past their own national borders. Many nations frame their Internet access policies to balance the destabilizing effects of the Internet against its benefits for economic development, trade, productivity, and intellectual and cultural exchange. Even democracies must strike a balance between a managed Internet and an open Internet. In Britain and South Korea, for example, Internet service providers (ISPs) are required by law to limit access to pornography.

As a result, a global splinternet is forming. The *splinternet*, also known as *Internet balkanization*, is a loosely connected set of national Internets. There are many reasons for the emergence of the splinternet.

Some countries are unhappy with the Western coalition that has traditionally controlled the Internet and its governance. For example, a wide variety of organizations conduct the actual operations of the Internet *domain name system* (DNS), but groups in the United States operate a majority of the "root servers" that function as the Internet's foundational layer. The DNS is basically an Internet phone book. For instance, when you type "google.com" into your browser, your computer uses the DNS to translate this domain name into an IP address, which identifies the correct server on the Internet to send your request.

Many countries are unhappy with the fact that the Internet was developed and engineered to ensure that no one can prevent anyone from sending anything to anyone. One reason is that those countries want to have more control over dissent. Another is that they are nervous about malicious software reaching military installations and critical power and water grids via the open Internet. (Recall our discussion of SCADA attacks in Chapter 4.)

Another catalyst for nations to develop national Internet control occurred in 2013 when Edward Snowden, a contractor with the U.S. National Security Agency (NSA), leaked a number of classified documents. These documents revealed that the NSA, through its PRISM program, had been collecting information from global users of Google, Facebook, Apple, Microsoft, and Yahoo!, including information about many national political leaders like Angela Merkel of Germany and Dilma Rousseff of Brazil. These revelations caused Brazil to pass the Marco Civil da Internet law, which requires global companies to comply with Brazilian laws concerning data protection. Other nations have taken similar actions.

Countries are using laws and regulatory powers within their jurisdictions to impose limits on digital activities. Specifically, many countries want to maintain sovereignty over their national data by implementing measures such as data privacy regulations and restrictions on data they deem inappropriate. As of August 2022, more than 30 regions or nations were imposing data sovereignty regulations, including the European Union (the General Data Protection Regulation or GDPR), Brazil, China, and India.

These policies particularly impact social media platforms such as Facebook and Twitter. These companies have users in almost every country, and governments are increasingly insisting that they comply with local laws and cultural norms regarding access and content. Let's take a closer look at the leading proponents of the splinternet.

China

China opted out of the open Internet by embedding a homegrown ISP and DNS infrastructure in the early 2000s. In addition, the country permitted very few entry and exit points to be built from the global Internet within its borders. China, therefore, has fewer digital borders to monitor.

China's Internet is enclosed by Golden Shield, a censorship and surveillance project operated by the country's Ministry of Public Security. One of the more notable components of Golden Shield is the Great Firewall of China, a series of legislative and technological actions that restrict citizens' access to foreign services like Google, Facebook, and the *New York Times*. China does not allow privately operated foreign Internet platforms, including many social media platforms that can promote dissent, opposition, or subversive ideas, to operate within its borders.

The firewall also selectively blocks certain Internet addresses, words, phrases, IP addresses, and so on, as defined by the government. Although formidable, the firewall is not perfect because virtual private networks (VPNs) and censorship avoidance software such as Tor can circumvent it.

Russia

Russia has developed a national Internet, known as RuNet, designed to be independent from the global Internet and easier to defend against attacks from abroad. However, outside observers contend that the move is part of Russia's long tradition of trying to control the flow of information among its citizens.

Russia will have many problems if it decides to actually implement RuNet.

- It will be very difficult for Russia to identify the myriad access points that its citizens use to get online, including their laptops, smartphones, and tablets. Some Russians will use servers abroad, such as Google's Public DNS, which Russia will not be able to duplicate. Therefore, the connection will fail when a Russian citizen tries to access these servers.

- If the authorities implement RuNet and require their ISPs to use it, Russian users might not notice that a website that is censored unless they actively try to access that site. For example, a user trying to connect to Facebook.com could be redirected to vk.com, a Russian social media service that strongly resembles Facebook. Russian users might not be pleased as they wonder how much the information on vk.com is censored by their government.

- The Internet is an essential component of the global economy. Therefore, disconnecting would seriously damage Russia's economy. For example, although many cloud vendors mirror (duplicate) their content in different regions, none of the major cloud services (Microsoft, Google, and Amazon Web Services) maintains data centers in Russia. As a result, Russia could have to create its own cloud service.

- Many Russian ISPs carry traffic on behalf of other ISPs, with reciprocal arrangements that these ISPs carry traffic for Russian ISPs. If Russia implements its disconnection project incorrectly, then a large amount of traffic going in and out of the country will simply be lost.

- The disconnection process will be technically difficult and very expensive.

- Even if a disaster does not occur—such as banking, hospital, or aviation facilities failing to connect—many websites could stop working. Most Web pages rely on multiple servers to function that may exist in different parts of the world. If Russia disconnects, then users may no longer have access to these servers.

- Other consequences have arisen with the Russian invasion of Ukraine. First, the European Union is trying to remove certain Russian outlets from the Internet. For instance, the EU is banning the state-owned RT television network and the Sputnik news agency, suggesting that not only should these sites be blocked, but also that search engines and social networks should hide or delete any post repeating content from these sites.

Second, in February 2022, the Ukrainian government called on ICANN to suspend Russia's access to the DNS system, effectively removing ".ru" sites from the Internet. ICANN rejected the proposal because ICANN has no legal power over the DNS system.

Currently, the question of whether the Kremlin intends to fully cut Russia off from the global Internet remained unresolved.

Other Countries

Not all countries fall completely into the category of the "global and open Internet" or a "sovereign and controlled Internet." Since 2015, several countries called digital deciders—Israel, Brazil, Ukraine, South Korea, and India, among others—have moved toward a more sovereign and controlled Internet. Their reasons vary, but several of those countries are in similar situations. Specifically, Ukraine, Israel, and South Korea, which exist in perpetual states of conflict, have discovered that their adversaries are weaponizing the Internet against them.

Further, an increasing number of Western countries are reconsidering what sovereignty on the Internet means. In the aftermath of election meddling in many countries, most notably the United States, and the well-documented practice by Russian operatives of creating discord on Western social media, many Western policymakers have become convinced that an open and free Internet can actually harm democracy itself.

Results

A future splinternet could take one of two forms. First, we could see a major splintering of the Internet that would involve technically incompatible protocols used by different countries. This type of splintering could be managed because technicians could probably find a way relatively quickly to bridge the different protocols.

The second form of splintering would be to continue using technically compatible protocols, but to have different governing bodies manage Internet services within their countries. Managing this type of splintering would involve politics rather than technology and could, therefore, be much more difficult than the first type.

The splinternet is already a threat to businesses that operate in multiple countries. If a business does nothing to respond, it may find its applications and services cut off from valuable customers in certain countries and regions. Further, firms will face large fines if they fail to comply with national and local Internet regulations.

To determine whether your company is at risk, consider these questions:

- Does the company have an international data strategy?

- Can the company manage data movement specific to certain regions, including the EU? India?

- Can the company quickly respond to important national or regional regulatory changes in various regions? China? Russia? Other regions?

- Can the company avoid being blocked from operating in other nations or regions by instantly changing its data management settings?

If firms cannot answer "yes" to each of these questions, then their international operations are at risk. Consequently, they must modernize their IT operations and data mobility strategy to align with the new splinternet reality.

Questions

1. **What are the advantages of the splinternet to a nation? Provide examples to support your answer.**

2. **What are the disadvantages of the splinternet to a nation? Provide examples to support your answer.**

3. What are the advantages of the splinternet to you as an individual? Provide examples to support your answer.

4. What are the disadvantages of the splinternet to you as an individual? Provide examples to support your answer.

Sources: Compiled from S. Bradley, "How Greater Online Regulation Is Prompting Fears of a 'Splinternet,'", *The Week*, May 25, 2023; M. Burgess, "Russia Is Quietly Ramping Up Its Internet Censorship Machine," *Wired*, July 25, 2022; A. Hetler, "The Splinternet Explained: Everything You Need to Know," *TechTarget*, June 7, 2022; "The Rise of Sovereign Internets," *BlueWing*, April 15, 2022; D. York, "What Is a Splinternet? And Why You Should Be Paying Attention," *Internet Society*, March 23, 2022; S. Mellow, "Experts Say Russia's War on Ukraine Is Accelerating the 'Splinternet.' But What Is the Splinternet?" *Fortune*, March 22, 2022; J. Ball, "Russia Is Risking the Creation of a 'Splinternet' – and It Could Be Irreversible," *MIT Technology Review*, March 17, 2022; F. Kenyon, "China's 'Splinternet' Will Create a State-Controlled Alternative Cyberspace," *The Guardian*, June 3, 2021; J. Sherman, "Russian and Iran Plan to Fundamentally Isolate the Internet, *Wired*, June 6, 2019.

The World Wide Web

Many people equate the Internet with the World Wide Web. However, they are not the same thing. The Internet functions as a transport mechanism, whereas the World Wide Web is an application that uses those transport functions. Other applications, such as e-mail, also run on the Internet.

World Wide Web (the Web or www)   A system of universally accepted standards for storing, retrieving, formatting, and displaying information through a client/server architecture; it uses the transport functions of the Internet.

The **World Wide Web (the Web or www)** is a system of universally accepted standards for storing, retrieving, formatting, and displaying information through a client/server architecture. The Web handles all types of digital information, including text, hypermedia, graphics, and sound. It uses graphical user interfaces (GUIs) (explained in Technology Guide 2), so it is very easy to navigate. Let's look at the different forms of the Web.

Surface Web. The *surface Web*—also known as the *visible Web*—is the collection of websites with which we are all familiar and use constantly. Surface websites are indexed by traditional search engines. They track user data, deploy cookies, and share Internet Protocol data. Examples of surface Web content are YouTube, Wikipedia, and basically everything that we can see on the results page of any search engine. Estimates are that the surface Web comprises 10–16 percent of the information on the Internet.

Deep Web. The *deep Web* refers to the collection of websites that traditional search engines cannot index. Deep Web content does not appear on the results pages of search engines because it exists behind passwords, firewalls, and paywalls and it requires credentials to access. Deep Web content includes databases, webmail pages, registration-required content, online banking pages, medical and financial records, personal files, and other forms of untracked Internet communication. Estimates are that the deep Web comprises 80–90 percent of information on the Internet.

Dark Web. The *Dark Web* is a network of websites, servers, forums, and communication tools that require encryption technologies to access and therefore cannot be indexed on traditional search engines. Compared to the surface Web and the deep Web, the Dark Web comprises a very small amount of information. Security experts estimate that there are between 10,000 and 100,000 active sites.

To access Dark Web sites, users must employ Tor, an acronym for The Onion Router. Tor is a free, open-source software that helps keep the source and destination of Internet traffic anonymous by sending each computer's IP address through a network of similarly encrypted IP addresses. Each computer knows only the immediate sender and the next recipient.

Users can also employ Tails, a portable and disposable Linux-based operating system that operates from a flash drive. Tails adds a layer of security to activities on the Dark Web. Despite Tor and Tails, however, there is no guarantee of complete anonymity on the Dark Web.

People and organizations use the Dark Web for both legitimate and criminal purposes. Criminals exploit the Dark Web's anonymity to sell guns, drugs, people (slavery), and stolen data.

On the positive side, organizations such as the United Nations, the Electronic Frontier Foundation, and news organizations use the Dark Web to protect dissidents, informants, and sources in oppressive countries. The Dark Web provides a safe haven for whistleblowers, activists, and journalists who need to share sensitive information but cannot do so publicly for fear of political persecution or retribution by their governments or employers.

Other legitimate Dark Web users include corporate IT departments and law enforcement agencies. Corporations monitor and search the Dark Web for stolen data and compromised accounts. Law enforcement agencies hunt criminals on the Dark Web. For example, the United Nations law enforcement department, the Office on Drugs and Crime, monitors the Dark Web and shares data with both the public and global police organizations such as Europol and the FBI.

Hypertext is the underlying concept defining the structure of the World Wide Web. Hypertext is the text displayed on a computer display or other electronic device with references, called *hyperlinks*, to other text that the reader can immediately access, or where text can be revealed progressively at additional levels of details. A **hyperlink** is a connection from a hypertext file or document to another location or file, typically activated by clicking on a highlighted word or image on the screen, or by touching the screen.

Organizations that wish to offer information through the Web must establish a *home page*, which is a text and graphical screen display that usually welcomes the user and provides basic information on the organization that has established the page. In most cases, the home page will lead users to other pages. All the pages of a particular company or individual are collectively known as a **website**. Most Web pages provide a way to contact the organization or the individual. The person in charge of an organization's website is its *webmaster*. (*Note: Webmaster* is a gender-neutral title.)

To access a website, the user must specify a **uniform resource locator (URL)** which points to the address of a specific resource on the Web. For example, the URL for Microsoft is **www.microsoft.com**. Recall that HTTP stands for *hypertext transport protocol*. The remaining letters in this URL—**www.microsoft.com**—indicate the domain name that identifies the Web server that stores the website.

Users access the Web primarily through software applications called browsers. **Browsers** provide a graphical front end that enables users to point and click their way across the Web, a process called *surfing*. Web browsers became a means of universal access because they deliver the same interface on any operating system on which they run. As of July 2019, Google Chrome was the leading browser, followed by Apple Safari, Firefox, Microsoft Internet Explorer, and Microsoft Edge.

The World Wide Web has evolved since Professor Tim Berners-Lee wrote the original computer code for it in 1999. Since that time, the Web has evolved from Web 0.0 to Web 3.0 today, with Web 4.0 and Web 5.0 still in the conceptual stage. We also address a new form of the Web developed by Professor Berners-Lee.

Each new version of the World Wide Web has transformed the ways in which users interact with data, information, organizations, and one another. The Web has also transformed the ways in which organizations conduct business. Let's examine how the Web has evolved since its invention in 1989.

Web 0.0: The Development of the Web (1989–1990). In 1989, Tim Berners-Lee, a British scientist at the European Organization for Nuclear Research (CERN), invented the World Wide Web—the first Web browser—and the fundamental protocols and algorithms that enabled the Web to expand globally. His original specifications of uniform resource locators (URLs), hypertext transport protocol (HTTP), and hypertext markup language (HTML) were the basic building blocks of the Web. The Web was introduced to the public in 1990.

Web 1.0: The Read-Only Web (1990–2000). Web 1.0 presented users with information, which typically was presented by organizations to users. For example, firms used static websites to display product information and directions to their closest brick-and-mortar store location.

This version of the Web was where users searched and found information. It was generally not interactive and users were basically content consumers.

Web 2.0: The Social (Read-Write) Web (2000–2010). Whereas Web 1.0 connected users with information, Web 2.0 connects people with people. With Web 2.0, users are able to create and upload content. Thus, Internet users are now participants and are able to interact with one another and with websites. They can collaborate on ideas, share information, and generate or create information that would be available to other users around the world.

Web 3.0: The Semantic (Read–Write–Execute) Web (2010–2020). Web 3.0 attempts to represent knowledge in a format that allows computers to automatically reach conclusions and make decisions utilizing certain reasoning capabilities. Two major applications underlie Web 3.0: semantic markup and Web services. *Semantic markup* is a method of structuring HTML so that HTML provides the meaning of the information in Web pages and Web applications rather than just its appearance. A *Web service* is an application designed to support machine-to-machine interaction over the Internet.

hypertext   Text displayed on a computer display with references, called hyperlinks, to other text that the reader can immediately access.

hyperlink   A connection from a hypertext file or document to another location or file, typically activated by clicking on a highlighted word or image on the screen or by touching the screen.

website   Collectively, all the Web pages of a particular company or individual.

uniform resource locator (URL)   The set of letters that identifies the address of a specific resource on the Web.

browsers   Software applications through which users primarily access the Web.

By combining semantic markup and Web services, Web 3.0 provides for machine-readable content, developed so that applications can directly interact with one another. Web applications can also interpret information for humans.

As we look at Web 4.0 and Web 5.0, keep in mind that we are speculating because these versions of the Web are still being developed.

Web 4.0: The Symbiotic Web (2020–2030). Web 4.0 is the open intelligent Web. The goal of the symbiotic Web is to enable humans and machines to interact in symbiosis. A *symbiotic relationship* between humans and machines is one in which humans and machines improve each other. Humans have capabilities such as compassion, intuition, and value judgement. Machines demonstrate learning, discovery, and fact checking. These capabilities complement and magnify each other.

Web 5.0 (2030 and beyond). Web 5.0, referred to as the *telepathic Web*, could emerge with technologies such as neural (brain) implants. These implants could give humans the ability to communicate with the Web through their thoughts. Web 5.0 could also see the emergence of intelligent virtual assistants that predict your needs from your behaviors without requiring many cues.

The Inrupt Project: A New Direction for Web Evolution. In 2018, Berners-Lee launched his Inrupt project (**www.inrupt.com**). While the Web will continue to evolve as advanced technologies such as artificial intelligence emerge, Berners-Lee is developing a new model for Web evolution.

Berners-Lee and other researchers designed Inrupt to decentralize the Web and take back power from platforms that have profited from centralizing it. As we have noted in previous chapters, the "bargain" with platforms such as Google and Amazon allows users to access the platforms' services in exchange for users' data. Inrupt is designed to redirect the balance of power from Web platforms to Web users.

Inrupt utilizes Solid, a decentralized Web platform built by Berners-Lee and other researchers at MIT (**www.mit.edu**). Inrupt differs from current versions of the Web in that all data that users access, create, or upload exist within each user's Solid pod. Each user will have a Solid identity and a Solid pod, that is, his or her personal online data store. The pods will provide users with control over their applications and data on the Web.

With Inrupt, users can allow access to particular elements of their data for particular services as they see fit and move their data from app to app instead of surrendering it. Inrupt could also use blockchain technology (see Chapter 7), which offers a means of independently verified personal identity. This verification respects privacy better than the accounts that users maintain on various platforms.

Before you go on...

1. Describe the various ways that you can connect to the Internet.
2. Identify each part of an Internet address.
3. Describe the difference between the Internet and the World Wide Web.
4. What are the functions of browsers?

6.4 Network Applications: Discovery

WILEY PLUS

Author Lecture Videos are available exclusively in *WileyPLUS.*
Apply the Concept activities are available in the Appendix and in *WileyPLUS.*

LEARNING OBJECTIVE

Explain the impact that discovery network applications have had on business and everyday life.

Now that you have a working knowledge of what networks are and how you can access them, the key question is: How do businesses use networks to improve their operations? In the next four sections of this chapter, we explore four network applications: discovery, communication, collaboration, and education. These applications, however, are merely a sampling of the many network applications that are currently available to users. Even if these applications formed an exhaustive list today, they would not do so tomorrow, when inevitably something new will be developed. Furthermore, placing network applications in categories is difficult because there will always be borderline cases. For example, telecommuting combines communication and collaboration.

The Internet enables users to access, or *discover information*, located in databases all over the world. By browsing and searching data sources on the Web, users can apply the Internet's discovery capability to areas ranging from education to government services to entertainment to commerce. Although having access to all this information is a great benefit, it is critically important to realize that there is no quality assurance for information on the Web. The Web is truly democratic in that *anyone* can post information to it. Therefore, the fundamental rule about information on the Web is "User beware!"

Think about discovery in 1960. How did you find information? You probably had to go to the library to check out a physical book. Contrast that process with how you would discover that information today. In fact, the overall trends in discovery have been as follows:

- In the past, you had to go to the information (the library). Today, the information comes to you through the Internet.

- In the past, only one person at a time could have the information (the book he or she checked out of the library). Today, the information is available to multiple users at the same time.

- In the past, you may not have been able to access the information you needed, for example, if the book was checked out. Today, the information is available to everyone simultaneously.

- In the past, you may have had to have your book translated if it were written in a different language. Today, automatic translation software tools are improving very rapidly.

However, there is a downside to the process of discovery. In June 2019 a crash outside Denver, Colorado, blocked the main access road to the Denver International Airport. Google Maps suggested a detour to many of the drivers trying to reach the airport.

The detour led some 100 drivers to a narrow dirt road near the airport. Unfortunately, the road ended up in a muddy, empty, privately owned field. Some cars in the front of the line became stuck in the mud. The narrow road only allowed passage of one car at a time, so cars at the back of the line had to turn around, one at a time, to untangle the mess.

Google's response? "While we always work to provide the best directions, issues can arise due to unforeseen circumstances."

Moral of the story: Don't follow discovery on the Web blindly!

The Web's major strength—the vast stores of information it contains—also presents a major challenge. The amount of information on the Web can be overwhelming, and it doubles approximately each year. As a result, navigating through the Web and gaining access to necessary information are becoming more and more difficult. To accomplish these tasks, people are increasingly using search engines, directories, and portals.

Search Engines and Metasearch Engines

A **search engine** is a computer program that searches for specific information by keywords and then reports the results. A search engine maintains an index of billions of Web pages. It uses that index to find pages that match a set of user-specified keywords. Such indexes are created and updated by *webcrawlers*, which are computer programs that browse the Web and create a copy of all visited pages. Search engines then index these pages to provide fast searches.

search engine A computer program that searches for specific information by keywords and reports the results.

In October 2022, four search engines accounted for almost all searches in the United States. They are, in order, Google (www.google.com), Bing (www.bing.com), Yahoo (www.yahoo.com), and DuckDuckGo (www.duckduckgo.com). The leading search engine in China is Baidu (www.baidu.com), which claims approximately 75 percent of the Chinese market.

Visual search uses real-world images (e.g., screenshots, Internet images, or photographs) as the basis for online searches. Modern visual search technology uses artificial intelligence (see Chapter 14) to understand the content and context of these images and return a list of related results. Approximately three-fourths of U.S. Internet users search for visual content prior to making a purchase. Leading visual search apps include Pinterest Lens, Google Lens, Bing Visual Search, Amazon Camera Search, eBay Image Search, and CamFind.

You can also use a metasearch engine. Metasearch engines search several engines at once and then integrate the findings to answer users' queries. Examples are Metacrawler (**www.metacrawler.com**), Mamma (**www.mamma.com**), KartOO (**www.kartoo.com**), and Dogpile (**www.dogpile.com**).

metasearch engine A computer program that searches several engines at once and integrates the findings of the various search engines to answer queries posted by users.

Publication of Material in Foreign Languages

The World Bank (**www.worldbank.org**) estimates that 80 percent of online content is available in only 1 of 10 languages: English, Chinese, Spanish, Japanese, Arabic, Portuguese, German, French, Russian, and Korean. Roughly 3 billion people speak one of these as their first language. However, more than 50 percent of all online content is written in English, which is understood by only 21 percent of the world's population. Consider India, whose citizens speak roughly 425 languages and dialects. Industry analysts estimate that less than 0.1 percent of all Web content is composed in Hindi, the first language of approximately 260 million people.

So not only is there a huge amount of information on the Internet, but it is also written in many languages. How, then, do you access this information? The answer is that you use an *automatic translation* of Web pages. Such translation is available to and from all major languages, and its quality is improving over time.

Companies invest resources to make their websites accessible in multiple languages as a result of the global nature of the business environment. That is, multilingual websites are now a competitive necessity. When companies are disseminating information around the world, getting that information correct is essential. It is not enough for companies to translate Web content. They must also localize that content and be sensitive to the needs of the people in local markets.

Translation services are expensive. Companies supporting 10 languages can spend $200,000 annually to localize information and another $50,000 to maintain their websites. Translation budgets for major multinational companies can total millions of dollars.

Some major translation products are Microsoft's Translator app (**www.translator .microsoft.com**), Google (**www.translate.google.com**) (see **Figure 6.9**), and Skype Translator (**www.skype.com/en/features/skype-translator/**), as well as products and services available at Trados (**www.sdltrados.com**) and Systran S.A. (**www.systransoft.com**). Google Translate and Microsoft Translator are free, based on machine learning (see Chapter 14), and instantly translate words, phrases, and Web pages between English and over 100 other languages.

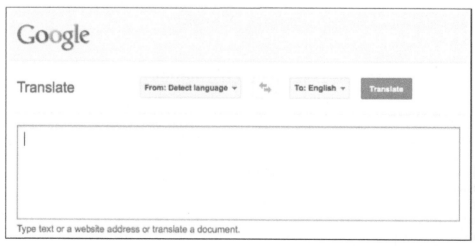

FIGURE 6.9 Google Translate. (Google and the Google logo are registered trademarks of Google Inc., used with permission).

Source: Google LLC

Portals

Most organizations and their managers encounter information overload. Information is scattered across numerous documents, e-mail messages, and databases at multiple locations and in multiple systems. Finding relevant and accurate information is often time consuming and may require users to access multiple systems.

MIS One solution to this problem is to use *portals*. A **portal** is a Web-based, personalized gateway to information and knowledge that provides relevant information from different IT systems and the Internet using advanced search and indexing techniques. After reading the next section, you will be able to distinguish among four types of portals: commercial, affinity, corporate, and industrywide. The four types of portals are differentiated by the audiences they serve.

A **commercial (public) portal** is the most popular type of portal on the Internet. It is intended for broad and diverse audiences, and it offers routine content, some of it in real time (e.g., a stock ticker). Examples are Lycos (**www.lycos.com**) and Microsoft Network (**www.msn.com**).

MKT In contrast, an **affinity portal** offers a single point of entry to an entire community of affiliated interests, such as a hobby group or a political party. Your university most likely has an affinity portal for its alumni. **Figure 6.10** displays the affinity portal for the University of West Georgia. Other examples of affinity portals are **www.informationweek.com** and **www.zdnet.com**.

MIS As the name suggests, a **corporate portal** offers a personalized, single point of access through a Web browser to critical business information located inside and outside an organization. These portals are also known as *enterprise portals*, *information portals*, and *enterprise information portals*. Besides making it easier to find needed information, corporate portals offer customers and employees self-service opportunities.

Whereas corporate portals are associated with a single company, an **industrywide portal** serves entire industries. An example is TruckNet (**www.trucknet.io**), a portal for the trucking industry and the trucking community, including professional drivers, owner/operators, and trucking companies.

portal A Web-based personalized gateway to information and knowledge that provides information from disparate information systems and the Internet, using advanced searching and indexing techniques.

commercial (public) portal A website that offers fairly routine content for diverse audiences. It offers customization only at the user interface.

affinity portal A website that offers a single point of entry to an entire community of affiliated interests.

corporate portal A website that provides a single point of access to critical business information located both inside and outside an organization.

industrywide portal A Web-based gateway to information and knowledge for an entire industry.

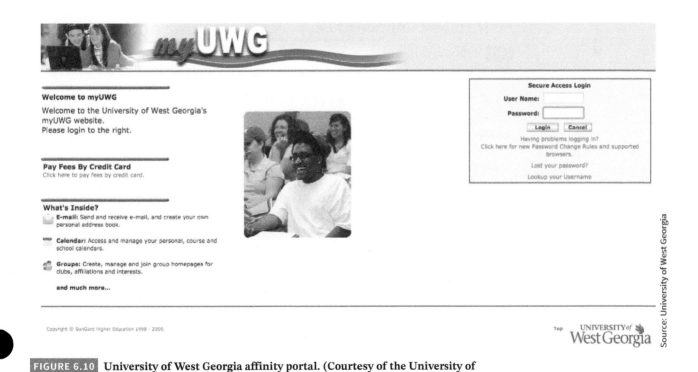

FIGURE 6.10 University of West Georgia affinity portal. (Courtesy of the University of West Georgia).

6.5   Network Applications: Communication

LEARNING OBJECTIVE

Explain the impact that communication network applications have had on business and everyday life.

The second major category of network applications is communication. There are many types of communication technologies, including e-mail, call centers, chat rooms, and voice. Furthermore, we discuss an interesting application of communication: telecommuting. (*Note*: You will read about other types of communication—blogging and microblogging—in Chapter 9.)

Electronic Mail

Electronic mail (e-mail) is the largest-volume application running over the Internet. Studies have found that almost all companies conduct business transactions through e-mail, and the vast majority confirm that e-mail is tied to their means of generating revenue. At the same time, however, the amount of e-mail that managers receive has become overwhelming. The problem is that too much e-mail can actually make a business less productive.

Web-Based Call Centers

MKT   Effective personalized customer contact is becoming an important aspect of Web-based customer support. Such service is provided through *Web-based call centers*, also known as *customer care centers*. For example, if you need to contact a software vendor for technical support, you will usually be communicating with the vendor's Web-based call center, using e-mail, a telephone conversation, or a simultaneous voice and Web session. Web-based call centers are sometimes located in foreign countries such as India. Such *offshoring* is an important issue for the U.S. companies. (We discuss offshoring in Chapter 13.)

Significantly, some U.S. companies are moving their call center operations back to the United States, for several reasons. First, they believe they have less control of their operations when the centers are located overseas. They must depend on the vendor company to uphold their standards, such as quality of service. A second difficulty is language differences, which can create serious communication problems. Third, companies that manage sensitive information risk breaching customer confidentiality and security. Finally, call center representatives typically work with many companies. As a result, they may not deliver the same level of customer services that each company requires.

Electronic Chat Rooms

Electronic chat refers to an arrangement in which participants exchange conversational messages in real time in a *chat room*. Chat programs allow you to send messages to people who are connected to the same channel of communication at the same time as you are. Anyone can join in the conversation. Messages are displayed on your screen as they arrive.

There are two major types of chat programs. The first type is Web based, which allows you to send messages to Internet users by using a Web browser and visiting a Web chat site. The second type is e-mail based (text only). It is called *Internet Relay Chat* (IRC). A business can use IRC to interact with customers, provide online experts for answers to questions, and so on.

Voice Communication

The plain old telephone service (POTS) has been largely replaced by Internet telephony. With **Internet telephony**, also known as **Voice-over-Internet Protocol** or **VoIP**, phone calls are treated as just another kind of data. That is, your analog voice signals are digitized, sectioned into packets, and then sent over the Internet.

Consider Skype (**www.skype.com**; now owned by Microsoft), which provides several VoIP services for free: voice and video calls to users who also have Skype; calls between Skype and landline and mobile phone numbers; wireless hotspot network access; instant messaging, text messaging, voice mail, one-to-one and group chats, and conference calls.

> **Internet telephony (Voice-over-Internet Protocol, or VoIP)**   The use of the Internet as the transmission medium for telephone calls.

Unified Communications

In the past, organizational networks for wired and wireless data, voice communications, and videoconferencing operated independently, and the IT department managed each network separately. This arrangement increased costs and reduced productivity.

Unified communications (UC) simplifies and integrates all forms of communications—voice, voice mail, fax, chat, e-mail, instant messaging, short message service, presence (location) services, and videoconferencing—on a common hardware and software platform. *Presence services* enable users to know where their intended recipients are and if they are available, in real time.

UC unifies all forms of human and computer communications into a common user experience. For example, UC allows an individual to receive a voice mail message and then read it in his or her e-mail inbox. In another example, UC enables users to seamlessly collaborate with another person on a project, regardless of where the user is located. One user could quickly locate the other user by accessing an interactive directory, determining whether that user is available, engaging in a text messaging session, and then escalating the session to a voice call or even a video call, all in real time.

> **unified communications** Common hardware and software platform that simplifies and integrates all forms of communications—voice, e-mail, instant messaging, location, and videoconferencing—across an organization.

Telecommuting

Knowledge workers are being called the distributed workforce, or "digital nomads." This group of highly prized workers is now able to work anywhere and anytime, a process called **telecommuting**. Distributed workers are those who have no permanent office at their companies, preferring to work in home offices, in airport lounges or client conference rooms, or even on a high school stadium bleacher. The growth of the distributed workforce is driven by globalization, extremely long commutes to work, ubiquitous broadband communications links (wireline and wireless), and powerful computing devices.

HRM Telecommuting offers a number of potential advantages for employees, employers, and society. For employees, the benefits include reduced stress and improved family life. Telecommuting also offers employment opportunities for housebound people such as single parents and persons with disabilities. Benefits for employers include increased productivity, the ability to retain skilled employees, and the ability to attract employees who do not live within commuting distance.

HRM However, telecommuting also has some potential disadvantages. For employees, the major disadvantages are increased feelings of isolation, possible loss of fringe benefits, lower pay (in some cases), no workplace visibility, lack of socialization, and the potential for slower promotions. In a 2013 study, researchers at Stanford University found that telecommuting employees are 50 percent less likely to receive a promotion than onsite workers. The researchers concluded that a lack of "face time" with bosses caused careers to stall.

> **telecommuting** A work arrangement whereby employees work at home, at the customer's premises, in special workplaces, or while traveling, usually using a computer linked to their place of employment.

Another problem is that telecommuting employees also often have difficulties "training" their families to understand that they are at work even though they are physically at home. Families have to understand that they should not disturb the telecommuter for anything that they would not disturb him or her about in a "real" office. The major disadvantages to employers are difficulties in supervising work and potential data security problems.

Before you go on...

1. Discuss the advantages and disadvantages of e-mail.
2. Why are many companies bringing their call centers back to the United States?
3. Describe Voice-over-Internet Protocol.
4. What are the advantages and disadvantages of telecommuting to you as an individual?

6.6 Network Applications: Collaboration

LEARNING OBJECTIVE

Explain the impact that collaboration network applications have had on business and everyday life.

collaboration   Mutual efforts by two or more individuals who perform activities to accomplish certain tasks.

workflow   The movement of information as it flows through the sequence of steps that make up an organization's work procedures.

virtual group (team) A workgroup whose members are in different locations and who meet electronically.

virtual collaboration The use of digital technologies that enable organizations or individuals to collaboratively plan, design, develop, manage, and research products, services, and innovative information systems and electronic commerce applications.

The third major category of network applications is collaboration. **Collaboration** refers to efforts by two or more entities—that is, individuals, teams, groups, or organizations—who work together to accomplish certain tasks. The term *workgroup* refers specifically to two or more individuals who act together to perform a task.

Workflow is the movement of information as it progresses through the sequence of steps that make up an organization's work procedures. Workflow management makes it possible to pass documents, information, and tasks from one participant to another in a way that is governed by the organization's rules or procedures. Workflow systems are tools for automating business processes.

If group members are working in different locations, they constitute a **virtual group (team)**. Virtual groups conduct *virtual meetings*—that is, they "meet" electronically. **Virtual collaboration** (or *e-collaboration*) refers to the use of digital technologies that enable organizations or individuals who are geographically dispersed to collaboratively plan, design, develop, manage, and research products, services, and innovative applications. Organizational employees frequently collaborate virtually with one another. Some organizations collaborate virtually with customers, suppliers, and other business partners to become more productive and competitive.

Collaboration can be *synchronous*, meaning that all team members meet at the same time. Teams may also collaborate *asynchronously* when team members cannot meet at the same time. Virtual teams, whose members are located throughout the world, typically must collaborate asynchronously.

Although a variety of software products are available to support all types of collaboration, many organizations feel that too many software tools are being used in collaborative efforts. These firms want a single place to know what was shared, who shared it with whom, and when. Firms also want smarter collaboration tools that are capable of anticipating workers' needs.

Collaborative software products include Google Drive (**www.drive.google.com**), Microsoft Teams (**www.microsoft.com/en-us/microsoft-teams/log-in**), Jive (**www.jive software.com**), RingCentral (**www.ringcentral.com**), Slack (**www.slack.com**), Atlassian (**www.atlassian.com**), and Meta's Workplace (**www.workplace.com**), as well as many others. In general, these products provide online collaboration capabilities, workgroup e-mail, distributed databases, electronic text editing, document management, workflow capabilities, instant virtual meetings, application sharing, instant messaging, consensus building, voting, ranking, and various application-development tools.

Consider multinational banking and financial services company BNY Mellon (**www.bnymellon.com**). The bank uses a proprietary, in-house-developed enterprise social networking tool called MySource Social to share ideas and expertise. The social network is integrated with BNY Mellon's communication and collaboration tools, such as e-mail, calendar, and instant messaging systems. MySource Social is an intranet site within which users can explore business partner groups featuring blogs and information from executives, special-interest groups, and ad hoc groups, such as those created for project teams. More than 90 percent of the 55,000 BNY Mellon employees worldwide have accessed the site in some way, and 40 percent are hands-on participants.

Crowdsourcing

One type of collaboration is **crowdsourcing**, in which an organization outsources a task to an undefined, generally large group of people in the form of an open call. Crowdsourcing provides many potential benefits to organizations. First, crowds can explore problems—and often resolve them—at relatively low cost, and often very quickly. Second, the organization can tap a wider range of talent than might be present among its employees. Third, by listening to the crowd, organizations gain firsthand insight into their customers' desires. Finally, crowdsourcing taps into the global world of ideas, helping companies work through a rapid design process. Let's look at some examples of crowdsourcing.

crowdsourcing A process in which an organization outsources a task to an undefined, generally large group of people in the form of an open call.

- **MIS** Crowdsourcing help desks: IT help desks are a necessary service on college campuses because students depend on their computers and Internet access to complete their schoolwork and attend class online. At Indiana University at Bloomington, IT help desks use crowdsourcing to alleviate the cost and pressure of having to answer so many calls. Students and professors post their IT problems on an online forum, where other students and amateur IT experts answer them.

- **MKT** Recruitment: Champlain College in Vermont developed a Champlain for Reel program, inviting students to share YouTube videos that recounted their experiences at the school and the ways they benefited from their time there. The YouTube channel serves to recruit prospective students, and it even updates alumni on campus and community events.

- **MKT** Scitable (**www.nature.com/scitable**) combines social networking and academic collaboration. Through crowdsourcing, students, professors, and scientists discuss problems, find solutions, and swap resources and journals. Scitable is a free site that lets each individual user turn to crowdsourcing for answers even while helping others.

- Violence broke out after the 2007 Kenyan elections. Within days, developers built a platform, Ushahidi (**www.ushahidi.com**), which means testimony or witness in Swahili. The platform crowdsourced 40,000 verified, firsthand reports of the violence via short-message service (SMS) and then sent alerts back to locals and to viewers around the world. By 2022, Ushahidi had evolved into an open-source, crisis-mapping platform accessible to anyone. To follow crises, Ushahidi analyzes millions of Tweets, hundreds of thousands of news articles, and geotagged, time-stamped data from a vast number of sources. Ushahidi has been used over 150,000 times in 160 countries, crowdsourcing more than 150 million reports.

Although crowdsourcing has numerous success stories, there are many questions and concerns about this system, including the following:

- Should the crowd be limited to experts? If so, then how would a company go about implementing this policy?

- How accurate is the content created by the nonexperts in the crowd? How is accuracy maintained?

- How is crowd-created content being updated? How can companies be certain the content is relevant?

- The crowd may submit too many ideas, with most of them being worthless. In this scenario, evaluating all of these ideas can be prohibitively expensive. For example, during the 2010 BP oil spill in the Gulf of Mexico, crowds submitted more than 20,000 suggestions on how to stem the flow of oil. The problem was very technical, so there were many poor suggestions. Nevertheless, despite the fact that BP was under severe time constraints, the company had to evaluate all of the ideas.

- Content contributors may violate copyrights, either intentionally or unintentionally.

- The quality of content (and therefore subsequent decisions) depends on the composition of the crowd. The best decisions may come if the crowd is made up of people with diverse opinions and ideas. In many cases, however, companies do not know the makeup of the crowd in advance.

Teleconferencing and Video Conferencing

teleconferencing   The use of electronic communication that allows two or more people at different locations to have a simultaneous conference.

Teleconferencing is the use of electronic communication technology that enables two or more people at different locations to hold a conference. There are several types of teleconferencing. The oldest and simplest is a telephone conference call, during which several people talk to one another from multiple locations. The biggest disadvantage of conference calls is that participants cannot communicate face-to-face, nor can they view graphs, charts, and pictures at other locations.

To overcome these shortcomings, organizations are increasingly turning to video teleconferencing, or videoconferencing. In a **videoconference**, participants in one location can see participants, documents, and presentations at other locations. The latest version of videoconferencing, called *telepresence*, enables participants to seamlessly share data, voice, pictures, graphics, and animation by electronic means. Conferees can also transmit data along with voice and video, which allows them to work together on documents and to exchange computer files.

videoconference   A virtual meeting in which participants in one location can see and hear participants at other locations and can share data and graphics by electronic means.

Telepresence systems range from on-premise, high-end systems to cloud-based systems. (We discuss on-premise computing and cloud computing in Technology Guide 3.) On-premise, high-end systems are expensive and require dedicated rooms with large high-definition screens to show people sitting around conference tables (see **Figure 6.11**). These systems have advanced audio capabilities that let everyone talk at once without canceling out any voices. These systems also require technical staff to operate and maintain. An example of a high-end system is Cisco's TelePresence system (**www.cisco.com**).

Having dedicated rooms where telepresence meetings take place is not particularly useful when so many employees work remotely. As a result, companies such as Fuze (**www.fuze.com**) and BlueJeans Network (**www.bluejeans.com**) offer telepresence systems that utilize

FIGURE 6.11 **Telepresence system.**

Jennifer Pottheiser/National Basketball Association/Getty Images cloud computing. (Verizon purchased BlueJeans in April 2020.) The cloud delivery model enables Fuze and BlueJeans to provide systems that are less expensive, more flexible, and require fewer in-house technical staff to operate and maintain. Fuze and BlueJeans can also deliver their telepresence systems to any device, including smartphones, tablets, and laptop and desktop computers.

Before you go on...

1. Describe virtual collaboration and why it is important to you.
2. Define crowdsourcing, and provide two examples of crowdsourcing not mentioned in this section.
3. Identify the business conditions that have made videoconferencing more important.

6.7 | Network Applications: Educational

LEARNING OBJECTIVE

Explain the impact that educational network applications have had on business and everyday life.

The fourth major category of network applications consists of education applications. In this section, we discuss e-learning, distance learning, and virtual universities.

E-Learning and Distance Learning

E-learning and **distance learning** are not the same thing, but they do overlap. E-learning refers to learning supported by the Web. It can take place inside classrooms as a support to conventional teaching, such as when students work on the Web during class. It also can take place in virtual classrooms, in which all coursework is completed online and classes do not meet face-to-face. In these cases, e-learning is a part of distance learning. Distance learning (DL) refers to any learning situation in which teachers and students do not meet face-to-face.

As a result of COVID, distance education became a critical necessity in March 2020. Distance learning increased dramatically in both K-12 and university classes in a matter of days and weeks.

According to the National Center for Education Statistics (NCES; **www.nces.ed.gov**), by April 2020, almost all K-12 schools had moved online and were employing distance education. The NCES also noted that by April 2020, 98 percent of colleges and universities had deployed distance education initiatives, moving the majority of their classes online.

Today, the Web provides a multimedia interactive environment for self-study. Web-enabled systems make knowledge accessible to those who need it, when they need it, anytime, anywhere. For this reason, e-learning and DL can be useful for both formal education and corporate training.

There are many benefits of e-learning. For example, online materials can deliver very current content that is of high quality (created by content experts) and consistent (presented the same way every time). It also gives students the flexibility to learn at any place, at any time, and at their own pace. In corporate training centers that use e-learning, learning time generally is shorter, which means that more people can be trained within a given time frame. This system reduces training costs and eliminates the expense of renting facility space.

Despite these benefits, e-learning has some drawbacks. For one, students must be computer literate. Also, they may miss the face-to-face interaction with instructors and fellow students. In addition, accurately assessing students' work can also be problematic because instructors really do not know who completed the assignments.

e-learning Learning supported by the Web; can be performed inside traditional classrooms or in virtual classrooms.

distance learning (DL) Learning situations in which teachers and students do not meet face-to-face.

E-learning does not usually replace the classroom setting. Rather, it enhances it by taking advantage of new content and delivery technologies. Advanced e-learning support environments, such as Blackboard (www.blackboard.com) or Canvas (www.instructure.com), add value to traditional learning in higher education.

A new form of distance learning has gained popularity, called *massive open online courses* or *MOOCs*. MOOCs are a tool for democratizing higher education. Several factors have contributed to the growth of MOOCs, including improved technology and the rapidly increasing costs of traditional universities. MOOCs are highly automated, complete with computer-graded assignments and exams.

MOOCs have not yet proved that they can effectively teach the thousands of students who enroll in them. They also do not provide revenues for universities. Furthermore, MOOCs can register a mixture of, for example, high school students, retirees, faculty, enrolled students, and working professionals. Designing a course that adequately meets the needs of such a diverse student population is quite challenging. Finally, although initial registrations for a MOOC might exceed 100,000 students, completion rates in any one MOOC tend to be less than 10 percent of that number. Nevertheless, despite these issues, hundreds of thousands of students around the world who lack access to universities are using MOOCs to acquire sophisticated skills and high-paying jobs without having to pay tuition or obtain a college degree.

In 2022, the world's top providers of MOOCs were l:

- Coursera (U.S.) is the largest MOOC platform in the world, with 97 million students and 8,250 courses.

- edX (U.S.) was acquired by 2U and stopped being a nonprofit. It is the second-largest MOOC in the world with 42 million students and 3,550 courses.

- XuetangX (China) is China's first and largest MOOC platform with over 80 million users and approximately 400 courses.

- FutureLearn (U.K.), now jointly owned by the Open University and the Australia- based SEEK Group, has 17 million students and 485 courses.

virtual universities Online universities in which students take classes on the Internet at home or at an offsite location.

Virtual Universities
Virtual universities are online universities in which students take classes on the Internet either at home or in an offsite location. A large number of existing universities offer online education of some form. Some universities, such as the University of Phoenix (www.phoenix.edu), Southern New Hampshire University (www.snhu.edu), California Virtual Campus (www.cvc.edu), and the University of Maryland Global Campus (www.umgc.edu), offer thousands of courses and dozens of degrees to students worldwide, all of them online. Other universities offer limited online courses and degrees, but they employ innovative teaching methods and multimedia support in the traditional classroom.

Before you go on...

1. Describe the differences between e-learning and distance learning.
2. What are virtual universities? Would you be willing to attend a virtual university? Why or why not?

What's in IT for Me?

ACCT For the Accounting Major

Accounting personnel use corporate intranets and portals to consolidate transaction data from legacy systems to provide an overall view of internal projects. This view contains the current costs charged to each project, the number of hours spent on each project by individual employees, and an analysis of how actual costs compare with projected costs. Finally, accounting personnel use Internet access to government and professional websites to stay informed on legal and other changes affecting their profession.

FIN For the Finance Major

Corporate intranets and portals can provide a model to evaluate the risks of a project or an investment. Financial analysts use two types of data in the model: historical transaction data from corporate databases through the intranet and industry data obtained through the Internet. Financial services firms can also use the Web for marketing and to provide services.

MKT For the Marketing Major

Marketing managers use corporate intranets and portals to coordinate the activities of the sales force. Sales personnel access corporate portals through the intranet to discover updates on pricing, promotion, rebates, customer information, and information about competitors. Sales staff can also download and customize presentations for their customers. The Internet, particularly the Web, opens a completely new marketing channel for many industries. Just how advertising, purchasing, and information dispensation should occur appears to vary from industry to industry, product to product, and service to service.

POM For the Production/Operations Management Major

Companies are using intranets and portals to speed product development by providing the development team with three-dimensional models and animation. All team members can access the models to explore ideas more quickly and to enhance feedback. Corporate portals, accessed through intranets, enable managers to carefully supervise their inventories as well as real-time production on assembly lines. Extranets are also proving valuable as communication formats for joint research and design efforts among companies. The Internet is also a great source of cutting-edge information for POM managers.

HRM For the Human Resources Management Major

Human resources personnel use portals and intranets to publish corporate policy manuals, job postings, company telephone directories, and training classes. Many companies deliver online training obtained from the Internet to employees through their intranets. Human resources departments use intranets to offer employees health care, savings, and benefit plans, as well as the opportunity to take competency tests online. The Internet supports worldwide recruiting efforts; it can also be the communications platform for supporting geographically dispersed work teams.

MIS For the MIS Major

As important as the networking technology infrastructure is, it is invisible to users (unless something goes wrong). The MIS function is responsible for keeping all organizational networks up and running all the time. MIS personnel, therefore, provide all users with an "eye to the world" and the ability to compute, communicate, and collaborate any time, anywhere. For example, organizations have access to experts at remote locations without having to duplicate that expertise in multiple areas of the firm. Virtual teaming allows experts physically located in different cities to collaborate on projects as though they were in the same office.

Summary

6.1   Compare and contrast the two major types of networks.

The two major types of networks are local area networks (LANs) and wide area networks (WANs). LANs encompass a limited geographical area and are usually composed of one communications medium. In contrast, WANs encompass a broad geographical area and are usually composed of multiple communications media.

6.2   Describe the wireline communications media and channels.

Twisted-pair wire, the most prevalent form of communications wiring, consists of strands of copper wire twisted in pairs. It is relatively inexpensive to purchase, widely available, and easy to work with. However, it is relatively slow for transmitting data, subject to interference from other electrical sources, and can be easily tapped by unintended recipients.

Coaxial cable consists of insulated copper wire. It is much less susceptible to electrical interference than is twisted-pair wire and it can carry much more data. However, coaxial cable is more expensive and more difficult to work with than twisted-pair wire. It is also somewhat inflexible.

Fiber-optic cables consist of thousands of very thin filaments of glass fibers that transmit information by way of pulses of light generated by lasers. Fiber-optic cables are significantly smaller and lighter than traditional cable media. They can also transmit far more data, and they provide greater security from interference and tapping. Fiber-optic cable is often used as the backbone for a network, whereas twisted-pair wire and coaxial cable connect the backbone to individual devices on the network.

6.3   Describe the most common methods for accessing the Internet.

Common methods for connecting to the Internet include dial-up, DSL, cable modem, satellite, wireless, and fiber to the home.

6.4   Explain the impact that discovery network applications have had on business and everyday life.

Discovery involves browsing and information retrieval and provides users the ability to view information in databases, download it, and process it. Discovery tools include search engines, directories, and portals. Discovery tools enable business users to efficiently find needed information.

6.5 Explain the impact that communication network applications have had on business and everyday life.

Networks provide fast, inexpensive *communications*, through e-mail, call centers, chat rooms, voice communications, and blogs. Communications tools provide business users with a seamless interface among team members, colleagues, business partners, and customers.

Telecommuting is the process whereby knowledge workers are able to work anywhere and any time. Telecommuting provides flexibility for employees, with many benefits and some drawbacks.

6.6 Explain the impact that collaboration network applications have had on business and everyday life.

Collaboration refers to mutual efforts by two or more entities (individuals, groups, or companies) that work together to accomplish tasks.

Collaboration is enabled by workflow systems. Collaboration tools enable business users to collaborate with colleagues, business partners, and customers.

6.7 Explain the impact that educational network applications have had on business and everyday life.

E-learning refers to learning supported by the Web. Distance learning refers to any learning situation in which teachers and students do not meet face-to-face. E-learning provides tools for business users to facilitate their lifelong learning aspirations.

Virtual universities are online universities in which students take classes on the Internet at home or an offsite location. Virtual universities make it possible for students to obtain degrees while working full-time, thus increasing their value to their firms.

Key Terms

affinity portal 183
backbone networks 164
bandwidth 162
broadband 162
broadcast media (also called wireless
   media) 166
browsers 179
cable media (also called wireline
   media) 166
client/server computing 169
clients 169
coaxial cable 166
collaboration 186
commercial (public) portal 183
communications channel 165
computer network 162
corporate portal 183
crowdsourcing 187
distance learning (DL) 189
distributed processing 169
domain name system (DNS) 175
domain names 175
e-learning 189
enterprise network 164

Ethernet 167
extranet 173
fiber-optic cable 167
file server (also called network server) 164
hyperlink 179
hypertext 179
Hypertext Transport Protocol (HTTP) 168
industrywide portal 183
Internet (the Net) 170
Internet backbone 170
Internet Protocol (IP) 168
Internet Protocol (IP) address 175
Internet service provider (ISP) 173
Internet telephony (Voice-over-Internet
   Protocol, or VoIP) 185
Internet2 176
intranet 173
local area network (LAN) 163
metasearch engine 182
network access points (NAPs) 173
network server 164
packet switching 168
peer-to-peer (P2P) processing 169
portal 183

protocol 167
router 164
search engine 181
servers 169
telecommuting 185
teleconferencing 188
Transmission Control Protocol/Internet
   Protocol (TCP/IP) 168
twisted-pair wire 166
unified communications 185
uniform resource locator (URL) 179
videoconference 188
virtual collaboration 186
virtual group (team) 186
virtual universities 190
Voice-over-Internet Protocol (VoIP) *See*
   Internet telephony.
website 179
wide area network (WAN) 164
wireless media 166
wireline media 166
workflow 186
World Wide Web (the Web or www) 178

Discussion Questions

1. What are the implications of having fiber-optic cable for everyone's home?

2. What are the implications of BitTorrent for the music industry? For the motion picture industry?

3. Discuss the pros and cons of P2P networks.

4. Should the Internet be regulated? If so, by whom?

5. Discuss the pros and cons of delivering this book over the Internet.

6. Explain how the Internet works. Assume you are talking with someone who has no knowledge of information technology (in other words, keep it very simple).

7. How are the network applications of communication and collaboration related? Do communication tools also support collaboration? Give examples.

8. Search online for the article from *The Atlantic:* "Is Google Making Us Stupid?" *Is* Google making us stupid? Support your answer.

9. Should businesses monitor network usage? Do you see a problem with employees using company-purchased bandwidth for personal use? Please explain your answer.

Problem-Solving Activities

1. Calculate how much bandwidth you consume when using the Internet every day. How many e-mails do you send daily and what is the size of each? (Your e-mail program may have e-mail file size information.) How many music and video clips do you download (or upload) daily and what is the size of each? If you view YouTube often, surf the Web to find out the size of a typical YouTube file. Add up the number of e-mail, audio, and video files you transmit or receive on a typical day. When you have calculated your daily Internet usage, determine if you are a "normal" Internet user or a "power" Internet user.

2. Compare the average bandwidth in Chicago IL and Hyden, KY. What is the difference and how do you think it affects the residents of each town?

3. Access several P2P applications, such as SETI@home. Describe the purpose of each application and indicate which ones you would like to join.

4. Access www.ipv6.com and list at least three advantages of IPv6.

5. Access www.icann.org and explain the organization's mission.

6. Set up your own website using your name for the domain name (e.g., KellyRainer).

    a. Explain the process for registering a domain.

    b. Which top-level domain will you use and why?

7. Access www.icann.org and obtain the name of an agency or company that can register a domain for the TLD that you selected. What is the name of that agency or company?

8. Access the website for that agency or company (in question 7) to learn the process that you must use. How much will it initially cost to register your domain name? How much will it cost to maintain that name in the future?

9. Create a chart or table describing the differences between a LAN and a WAN.

10. Visit www.ohmnilabs.com. Schedule a free demo of their new telepresence robot and write a paragraph explaining it.

11. Access the website of your university. Does the website provide high-quality information (the right amount, clear, accurate, etc.)? Do you think a high-school student who is thinking of attending your university would feel the same way as you?

12. Access the website of the Recording Industry Association of America (www.riaa.com). Discuss what you find there regarding copyright infringement (i.e., downloading music files). How do you feel about the RIAA's efforts to stop music downloads? List both the pros and cons to the organization stopping downloads.

13. Access the crowdsourcing website www.wazoku.com. Visit the challenge center and describe one challenge you would like to participate in.

14. Access various search engines other than Google. Search for the same terms on several of the alternative search engines and on Google. Compare the results on breadth (number of results found) and precision (results are what you were looking for).

15. Second Life (www.secondlife.com) is a three-dimensional, online world built and owned by its residents. Residents of Second Life are avatars who have been created by real people. Access Second Life, learn about it, and create your own avatar to explore this world. Learn about the thousands of people who are making "real-world" money from operations in Second Life.

16. Access Microsoft's Bing translator (www.bing.com/translator) or Google (www.translate.google.com) translation pages. Type in a paragraph in English and select, for example, English-to-French. When you see the translated paragraph in French, copy it into the text box, and select French-to-English. Is the paragraph that you first entered the same as the one you are looking at now? Why or why not? Support your answer.

17. Visit Coursera and list three courses you would be interested in taking. How do you think they could help you in your career development?

Closing Case

MIS   Internet Shutdowns

Internet shutdowns really began in December 2010 with the Arab Spring. As people across North Africa and the Middle East protested against authoritarian rulers, the Internet became a force for political mobilization. Protest movements gained traction in Facebook groups and on Twitter and YouTube. In response to one protest in January 2011, Egypt's President Hosni Mubarak shut down the Internet for five days.

According to AccessNow (www.accessnow.org), a digital rights advocacy group, in 2021, the number of Internet shutdowns rapidly increased to 182 across 34 countries. It is significant that most governments do not acknowledge that they initiated a shutdown. Rather, they attribute the disruption to technical problems or foreign cyberattacks, or they imply a lie that the government itself closed Internet access.

In most cases, governments want to control the Internet in order to control the political narrative. They view the Internet as a threat because it weakens their control of the information that is available to their citizens. They believe that social media, for instance, enable individuals and groups to produce and circulate alternative political narratives. It is significant that the United Nations has explicitly defined government-led Internet shutdowns and censorship as human rights violations.

Governments adopt four general approaches to controlling citizens' access to the Internet. The first, and most serious, is to completely block access to the Internet on all platforms. This approach incurs significant social, economic, and political costs.

Specifically, the financial costs can run into millions of dollars for each day that the Internet is blocked.

The second method is to block specific content, typically by restricting access to particular websites or applications. This strategy is the most common, and it usually targets social media platforms. Governments generally adopt this strategy because these sites have become platforms for various forms of political expression that they consider subversive.

The third strategy, usually carried out in secret, is *bandwidth throttling*. In this method, the government forces telecommunications operators or ISPs to lower the quality of their cell signals or Internet speed. This process makes the Internet and phones too slow to use. Throttling can also target certain online destinations such as social media sites.

Governments employ these strategies inside their countries. A fourth, more recent strategy is for a foreign government to cause Internet shutdowns in another country, while also employing the first three strategies in its own country. Russia is utilizing this strategy in its invasion of Ukraine (discussed below).

The strategies that governments adopt frequently depend on how much control they exercise over the telecommunications infrastructure in their country. The amount of control varies by country and over time. Unfortunately, some governments are considering laws that would increase that control.

Numerous examples exist of governments employing these methods to control Internet access. We consider several instances here.

Russia

Russia's strategy is to shut down internal websites that are presenting information opposing the government's invasion of Ukraine, while blocking Ukrainian government websites as well. For example, Russia's state communications and media monitor, Roskomnadzor, blocked several Russian and Ukrainian media outlet websites over their coverage of the invasion. As another example, the Kremlin blocked the Russian magazine *The New Times*, which has been openly critical of the invasion, for reporting details about Russian military casualties that the Russian Defense Ministry had not disclosed.

In addition, alleged Russian hackers brought down dozens of Ukrainian government websites immediately prior to the invasion. The attack crippled much of the government's public-facing infrastructure, including Diia, the most widely used site for managing government services online. The attack compromised the sites of the Cabinet of Ministers as well as the Ministries of Energy, Sports, Agriculture, Veterans' Affairs, and Ecology. Fortunately for Ukraine, the websites of the president and the Defense Ministry remained online.

India

India accounted for 85 percent of the world's Internet shutdowns in the first six months of 2022, according to Internet watchdog NetBlocks (https://netblocks.org). In just one example, police in the Indian state of Rajasthan, fearing outbreaks of religious violence, banned public gatherings and suspended Internet services a day after two Muslims posted a video claiming responsibility for killing a Hindu tailor in the city of Udaipur. Brandishing a meat cleaver, two bearded men announced in the video that they were avenging an insult to the prophet Mohammed attributed to the victim.

According to reports, the two suspects confronted the tailor earlier that month over a social media post in support of the Bharatiya Janata Party (BJP) that was traced to his mobile telephone. The BJP is known for its pro-Hindu policies. A police investigation ensued.

After being released, the tailor had told police that he was being threatened by some group but the police chose not to take action.

Authorities claimed they had suspended Internet services in several parts of Rajasthan to prevent the video from being circulated. The federal government asked social media platforms to immediately remove content that encouraged, glorified, or justified the killing. The Ministry of Electronics and Information Technology announced that the removal was necessary "to prevent any incitement and disruption of public order and to restore public peace and harmony."

Iran

On September 16, 2022, the Iranian Guidance Patrol, the religious morality police of Iran's government, arrested a 22-year-old Iranian woman named Mahsa Amini for not wearing the hijab in accordance with government standards. They accused her of wearing the hajib too loosely, showing some hair. Shortly after her arrest, she died in a Tehran hospital, under suspicious circumstances.

Police, after transferring her to a hospital, said that she had a heart attack at a police station. Eyewitnesses, including women detained with Amini, said police beat her severely and she died as a result of police brutality. These assertions, in addition to leaked medical scans, led independent observers to believe that Amini had had a cerebral hemorrhage.

Amini's death resulted in a series of protests, more widespread than the protests of 2009, 2017, and 2019. By October 2022, Iran Human Rights, an international nonprofit human rights organization with members inside and outside Iran, reported that security forces had killed at least 185 protesters.

In late September, Iranian authorities cut off Internet access in the country, stating that they would not restore access until calm was restored. The authorities hoped that by restricting the Internet they can control the protests. First, the government blocked Instagram and then WhatsApp. Several hours later, the local Internet, known as National Internet, replaced the global Internet, meaning that Iranians could only access local servers. These actions disrupt the process of sending videos, photos, and news from Iran to the world. Internet access in Iran is still not dependable and people are constantly vulnerable to future shutdowns.

Results

Even though Internet shutdowns continue, there is little evidence that they actually work. Let's consider three reasons they are not effective:

- Shutdowns frequently encourage dissent. They can create camaraderie among citizens that can inspire an even more powerful protest movement. In fact, observers have noted that Internet blackouts just drive people into the streets.

- Governments damage their economies when they shut down Internet applications and services. In just the first half of 2022, government-led Internet shutdowns cost the global economy $10 billion and technologically and economically impacted nearly two billion people.

- Consider the COVID-19 pandemic. During any pandemic, Internet blackouts seriously obstruct citizens' ability to access the most reliable data on infection counts, social distancing measures imposed in their area, current medical information, and corrections to circulating misinformation. Blackouts also hinder the public's ability to communicate with others and to call wirelessly for medical assistance. The bottom line is that Internet shutdowns cause tangible, physical harm.

Questions

1. Of the four strategies governments are using to control Internet access, which is the most effective at controlling Internet usage?

2. Of the four methods governments are using to control Internet access, which is the least effective?

3. In your opinion, is Internet access a fundamental human right? Why or why not? Support your answer. Be sure to include in your answer what your day would look like without Internet access of any kind.

Sources: Compiled from A. Kohli, "Here's What Has Happened in Iran since the Death of Mahsa Amini," *Yahoo! News*, October 8, 2022; A. Moshtaghian et al., "Young Iranians Are Rising Up against Decades of Repression – Arguably Bolder than Ever," *CNN*, September 25, 2022; A. MacDonald, "Mahsa Amini: Iran Shuts Down Internet as Death Toll from 'Bad Hijab' Protests Rises," *Middle East Eye*, September 22, 2022; V. Aggarwal, "Government-Imposed Internet Shutdowns Impacted 1.9 Billion People in First Half of 2022," *Network World*, August 4, 2022; A. Belanger, "Internet Shutdowns Cost Global Economy $10B so far in 2022," *Ars Technica*, July 6, 2022; "Killing of Indian Tailor Prompts Internet Shutdown over Unrest Fears," *Reuters*, June 30, 2022; "Internet Shutdowns: UN Report Details 'Dramatic' Impact on People's Lives and Human Rights," *United Nations Press Report*, June 23, 2022; K. Paul, "Russian Disinformation Surged on Social Media after Invasion of Ukraine, Meta Reports," *The Guardian*, April 7, 2022; "Russia Blocks Media Outlets, Others Hacked over Ukraine War," *Associated Press*, February 28, 2022; "Ukraine Struggles with Internet Blackout after Russian Invasion," *Business Standard*, February 25, 2022; T. Ryan-Moseley, "Why You Should Be More Concerned about Internet Shutdowns," *MIT Technology Review*, September 9, 2021; G. Volpicelli, "The Draconian Rise of Internet Shutdowns," *Wired*, September 2, 2021; S. Faleiro, "How India Became the World's Leader in Internet Shutdowns," *MIT Technology Review*, August 19, 2020; "End Internet Shutdowns to Manage COVID-19," *Human Rights Watch*, March 31, 2020; J. Sherman, "Democracies Can Become Digital Dictators," *Wired*, January 5, 2020; A. Ghoshal, "Indian Government Orders Mobile Internet to Be Suspended in the Capital, Says Airtel," *TheNextWeb*, December 19, 2019; D. Flamini, "The Scary Trend of Internet Shutdowns," Poynter.org, August 1, 2019; and "Shutting Down the Internet Doesn't Work—But Governments Keep Doing It," *The Conversation*, February 19, 2019.

CHAPTER 7

E-Business and E-Commerce

CHAPTER OUTLINE	LEARNING OBJECTIVES
7.1 Overview of E-Business and E-Commerce	**7.1 Describe** the eight common types of electronic commerce.
7.2 Business-to-Consumer (B2C) Electronic Commerce	**7.2 Describe** the various online services of business-to-consumer (B2C) commerce, along with specific examples of each one.
7.3 Business-to-Business (B2B) Electronic Commerce	**7.3 Describe** the three business models for business-to-business (B2B) electronic commerce.
7.4 Ethical and Legal Issues in E-Business	**7.4 Discuss** the ethical and legal issues related to electronic commerce, and provide examples.

Opening Case

MIS **MKT** **E-Commerce Is Transforming an Industry**

Carvana (www.carvana.com/), one of the largest used car retailers in the United States, was founded in 2012. It went public in 2017, and by 2021 it was named to the Fortune 500, one of the youngest companies ever to accomplish this feat. It is significant that it is one of few companies that offers an e-commerce-only approach to used-car sales.

Carvana and other online used-car dealerships benefit from popular dissatisfaction with the traditional car-buying experience. Complaints about the process included long hours, high pressure sales tactics and endless paperwork. In contrast, online dealerships offer easy browsing, home delivery, and no-contact pickup. Carvana's website includes an automotive "vending machine" that rolls out SUVs like 5,000-pound gumballs.

Because the online experience does not allow for a traditional test drive, however, Carvana's model could be considered a form of test ownership. For this reason, Carvana offers a seven-day risk-free return policy. This policy addresses customer fears regarding making a large purchase online. It offers customers an arguably better option than the typical test drive, which might last thirty minutes and cover ten miles. Customers can also trade in a vehicle. In that case, Carvana will deliver the "new" car and pick up the trade-in at the same time.

Carvana makes money in several ways. First, it earns a margin on each sale by selling the car for a markup above what the company paid. Second, it offers add-on options, the most critical being financing for the vehicle. Carvana packages the loans and sells them to other financial institutions at a premium. From 2014 to 2021, the company's gross profit per unit sold skyrocketed from $0 to $3,656.

Further, as with other e-commerce businesses, Carvana experienced a boom in sales during the pandemic, when shopping shifted largely to online and contact-free delivery. During 2020, Carvana sold more than 244,000 vehicles, an increase of 37 percent over 2019. In 2021, they sold more than 425,000 units, a 74 percent increase over 2020. However, this massive growth created severe headaches for Carvana. In fact, the company found itself in legal trouble in several states.

Growing Pains

Like any start-up that aims to reinvent old industries, Carvana suffered from some of the same problems as the system it was trying to replace. One major problem involved transferring titles. A car's title provides documentation of ownership. States have enacted laws for vehicle titles that deal with taxes, temporary and permanent tags, emissions, and insurance. Without a title, it is often difficult—if not impossible—to purchase insurance. It is also illegal to drive or sell the car if you do not have the proper paperwork.

Carvana's problems arose from both the volume of titles the company had to process and the variety of title processes. Regarding the first issue, the amount of title work inevitably exceeds the sales volume. Each sale requires a title transfer to the new owner.

Transactions that include a trade-in have multiple transfers that often include lien holders for the trade, adding another party to the process. Further, in many cases the vehicles are coming from or going to another state, thus adding another level of bureaucracy.

Compounding these difficulties, the variety of title processes is almost endless. Titles come from many owners or lien holders who handle titles differently. They come from different states that have distinctive processes, and they are held up at various points waiting for funds to transfer and clear the banks used. Carvana's backlog has led to many customers not receiving their titles in time to obtain insurance or tags and legally be able to operate their vehicles.

The Legal Woes

Carvana began to face legal action and fines after several customers did not receive their title and registration paperwork on time. During 2021–22, consumers filed numerous complaints against Carvana with state regulators and the Better Business Bureau. These complaints included incorrect paperwork, title and registration delays, incorrect financial transactions, incorrect vehicle pickup (sometimes Carvana picked up the wrong car when a trade-in was part of the transaction), and other troubles with the purchasing process.

Some customers claimed these delays prevented them from registering their cars for almost a year. In some cases, these customers were fined or received tickets. Other customers had to make monthly car payments on vehicles they couldn't insure or drive because the temporary tags had expired. One customer reported he had to return a car to Carvana after the company finally informed him it didn't possess the vehicle's title.

Multiple states have pending legal cases against Carvana. Specifically, Maryland, Arizona, Illinois, California, Pennsylvania, Texas, Michigan, North Carolina, and Florida have sued Carvana or restricted the company's ability to sell vehicles in the state. According to the Maryland Motor Vehicle Administration, between June 2021 and July 2022, Carvana was charged 386 late title fees totaling more than $17,000 in fines. In these cases, Carvana submitted paperwork 1 to 150 or more days after the 30-day deadline.

Carvana's Response

Carvana has admitted that their explosive growth created significant operational constraints in their system. Nevertheless, the company maintains that it is working to rectify each situation and it is being unfairly targeted. In response to the legal action filed by the state of Michigan against Carvana, in October 2022, Carvana filed a motion in the Michigan Court of Claims requesting the state stop its "illegal and irresponsible attempt to shut down a growing Michigan business with tens of thousands of customers over what amounts to technical paperwork violations involving title and transfer issues." The company has filed similar motions in other states as well for the same reason.

It is significant to note that despite these shortcomings, most Carvana customers receive their titles promptly and properly. The company wants to continue to serve those customers while correcting grievances for others.

Questions

1. **How has Carvana changed the used-car-buying experience?**

2. **How did the pandemic affect Carvana's operations?**

3. **Do you feel the states that have filed legal action against Carvana are helping or hurting their citizens?**

Sources: Compiled from B. Foldy and M. Colias, "Carvana Faces Government Scrutiny and Fines Following Consumer Complaints," *Wall Street Journal*, October 22, 2021; E. Shilling, "Good Luck With Your Carvana Purchase: Best Of Jalopnik," Jalopnik.com, October 22, 2021; J. LaReau, "Carvana Sues Michigan after Officials Suspended Its License to Sell Cars," *Detroit Free Press*, October 14, 2022; M. Sofastaii, "Maryland Joins Other States in Fining Carvana for Title Delays," wmar2news, October 11, 2022; S. Behnken, "Carvana Offers to Buy Back Vehicles after Failing for Months to Fork over Titles," wfla.com, October 7, 2021; C. Morris, "Carvana's Illinois Problems Continue. Startup Is Barred from Selling Cars in State for Second Time in under Three Months," *Fortune*, July 20, 2022; J. Adelman, "Carvana Sought to Disrupt Auto Sales. It Delivered Undriveable Cars." *Barron's*, June 24, 2022; B. Schafer, "Carvana Is Down 89% This Year—Time to Buy the Dip on This Pandemic Favorite?," *Motley Fool*, June 7, 2022; S. Rivers, "Carvana's Problems Pile Up after Losing License to Sell Cars in Illinois Over Title Issues," May 18, 2022; Carvana, "Carvana Announces Fourth Quarter and Full Year 2021 Results," press release, February 24, 2022; P. Aitken, "Carvana Allegedly Leaving Car Buyers on the Hook after Selling Cars without Title," February 16, 2022; M. Flinn, "Beware the Nationwide Used Car Dealer-Carvana and Vroom Title Issues," Georgia Consumer Lawyer, February 16, 2022; K. Stock, "Online Used-Car Dealers Thrive in Market Upended by Pandemic," *Bloomberg*, September 28, 2021; R. Furchgott, "Happy to Shun Showrooms, Millennials Storm the Car Market," *New York Times*, June 17, 2021; and Carvana, "Carvana Announces Fourth Quarter and Full Year 2020 Results," press release, February 25, 2021.

Introduction

electronic commerce (EC or e-commerce) The process of buying, selling, transferring, or exchanging products, services, or information through computer networks, including the Internet.

Electronic commerce (**EC** or **e-commerce**) is the process of buying, selling, transferring, or exchanging products, services, or information through computer networks, including the Internet. E-commerce is transforming all the business functional areas as well as their fundamental tasks, from advertising to paying bills. Its impact is so pervasive that it is affecting every modern organization. Regardless of where you land a job, your organization will be practicing electronic commerce.

Electronic commerce influences organizations in many significant ways. First, it increases an organization's *reach*: the number of potential customers to whom the company can market its products. In fact, e-commerce provides unparalleled opportunities for companies to expand worldwide at a small cost, to increase market share, and to reduce costs. By utilizing electronic commerce, many small businesses can now operate and compete in market spaces that were formerly dominated by larger companies.

Another major impact of electronic commerce has been to remove many of the barriers that previously impeded entrepreneurs seeking to start their own businesses. E-commerce offers amazing opportunities for you to open your own business.

As illustrated in the opening case, electronic commerce is also fundamentally transforming the nature of competition through the development of new online companies, new business models, and the diversity of EC-related products and services. Recall our discussion of competitive strategies in Chapter 2, particularly the impact of the Internet on Porter's five forces. You learned that the Internet can both endanger and enhance a company's position within a given industry.

It is important for you to have a working knowledge of electronic commerce because your organization almost certainly will be employing e-commerce applications that will affect its strategy and business model. This knowledge will make you more valuable to your organization, and it will enable you to quickly contribute to the e-commerce applications employed in your functional area. As you read "What's in IT for Me?" at the end of the chapter, envision yourself performing the activities discussed in your functional area.

Going further, you may decide to become an entrepreneur and start your own business. In this case, it is even more essential for you to understand electronic commerce, because e-commerce, with its broad reach, will more than likely be critical for your business to survive and thrive.

In this chapter, you will discover the major applications of e-business, and you will be able to identify the services necessary for its support. You will then study the major types of electronic commerce: business-to-consumer (B2C), business-to-business (B2B), consumer-to-consumer (C2C), business-to-employee (B2E), and government-to-citizen (G2C). You will conclude by examining several legal and ethical issues that impact e-commerce.

As you read this chapter, note that e-commerce can be performed wirelessly, as you will see in our discussion of mobile commerce in Chapter 8. E-commerce also has many social aspects, as you will see in our discussion of social commerce in Chapter 8. Finally, e-commerce can now be performed with texting and messaging.

7.1 | Overview of E-Business and E-Commerce

LEARNING OBJECTIVE

Describe the eight common types of electronic commerce.

WILEY PLUS

Author Lecture Videos are available exclusively in *WileyPLUS*.
Apply the Concept activities are available in the Appendix and in *WileyPLUS*.

Just how important is electronic commerce? Consider these statistics. Industry analysts estimated that U.S. retail sales in 2021 totaled approximately $6.6 trillion. Electronic commerce accounted for 13.2 percent of these sales, for a total of $870 billion. It is significant that e-commerce increased 14.2 percent in 2021 over 2020 and had a 50.5 percent increase over 2019. The increase in e-commerce has placed significant pressure on the retail industry. According to industry analysts, approximately 9,300 brick-and-mortar stores closed in 2019. Partially due to the pandemic, 12,200 stores closed in 2020. In 2021, there was a bit of recovery with just over 5,000 stores closing. Still, the average shift in just the past three years has been dramatic.

This section examines the basics of e-business and e-commerce. First, we define these two concepts. You then become familiar with pure and partial electronic commerce and examine the various types of electronic commerce. Next, you focus on e-commerce mechanisms, which are the ways that businesses and people buy and sell over the Internet. You conclude this section by considering the benefits and limitations of e-commerce.

electronic business (e-business) A broader definition of electronic commerce, including buying and selling of goods and services, and servicing customers, collaborating with business partners, conducting e-learning, and conducting electronic transactions within an organization.

Definitions and Concepts

Recall that electronic commerce describes the process of buying, selling, transferring, or exchanging products, services, or information through computer networks, including the Internet. **Electronic business (e-business)** is a somewhat broader concept. In addition to the buying and selling of goods and services, e-business refers to servicing customers, collaborating with business partners, and performing electronic transactions within an organization.

Electronic commerce can take several forms, depending on the degree of digitization involved. The *degree of digitization* is the extent to which the commerce has been transformed from physical to digital. This concept can relate to both the product or service being sold and the delivery agent or intermediary. In other words, the product can be either physical or digital, and the delivery agent can also be either physical or digital.

In traditional commerce, both dimensions are physical. Purely physical organizations are referred to as **brick-and-mortar organizations**. (You may also see the term *bricks-and-mortar*.) In contrast, in *pure EC* all dimensions are digital. Companies engaged only in EC are considered **virtual** (or **pure-play**) **organizations**. All other combinations that include a mix of digital and physical dimensions are considered *partial* EC (but not pure EC). **Click-and-mortar organizations** conduct some e-commerce activities, yet their primary business is carried out in the physical world. A common alternative to the term *click-and-mortar* is *clicks-and-bricks*. You will encounter both terms. Click-and-mortar organizations are examples of partial EC. E-commerce is now so well established that people generally expect companies to offer this service in some form.

Purchasing a shirt at Walmart Online or a book from Amazon.com is an example of partial EC because the merchandise, although bought and paid for digitally, is physically delivered by, for example, FedEx, UPS, or the U.S. Postal Service. In contrast, buying an e-book from Amazon.com or a software product from **Buy.com** constitutes pure EC because the product itself as well as its delivery, payment, and transfer are entirely digital. We use the term *electronic commerce* to denote both pure and partial EC.

There are a large number of e-commerce business models. **Table 7.1** describes several of these models. IT's About Business 7.1 presents an omnichannel strategy that seamlessly blends traditional brick-and-mortar stores into modern e-commerce.

brick-and-mortar organizations Organizations in which the product, the process, and the delivery agent are all physical.

virtual (or pure play) organizations Organizations in which the product, the process, and the delivery agent are all digital.

clicks-and-mortar organizations Organizations that do business in both the physical and digital dimensions.

TABLE 7.1   E-Commerce Business Models

Online direct marketing	Manufacturers or retailers sell directly to customers. Very efficient for digital products and services. Can allow for product or service customization (www.dell.com).
Electronic tendering system	Businesses request quotes from suppliers. Uses B2B with a reverse auction mechanism.
Name-your-own-price	Customers decide how much they are willing to pay. An intermediary tries to match a provider (www.priceline.com).
Find-the-best-price	Customers specify a need; an intermediary compares providers and shows the lowest price. Customers must accept the offer in a short time, or they may lose the deal (www.hotwire.com).
Affiliate marketing	Vendors ask partners to place logos (or banners) on partner's site. If customers click on a logo, go to a vendor's site, and make a purchase, then the vendor pays commissions to the partners.
Viral marketing	Recipients of your marketing notices send information about your product to their friends.
Group purchasing (e-coops)	Small buyers aggregate demand to create a large volume; the group then conducts tendering or negotiates a low price.
Online auctions	Companies run auctions of various types on the Internet. Very popular in C2C, but gaining ground in other types of EC as well (www.ebay.com).
Product customization	Customers use the Internet to self-configure products or services. Sellers then price them and fulfill them quickly (*build-to-order*) (www.jaguar.com).
Electronic marketplaces and exchanges	Transactions are conducted efficiently (more information to buyers and sellers; lower transaction costs) in electronic marketplaces (private or public).
Bartering online	Intermediary administers online exchange of surplus products or company receives "points" for its contribution, which it can use to purchase other needed items (www.bbubarter.com).
Deep discounters	Company offers deep price discounts. Appeals to customers who consider only price in their purchasing decisions.
Membership	Only members can use the services provided, including access to certain information, conducting trades, and so on.

IT's About Business 7.1

MIS **MKT** Omnichannel Target(ing)

The Business Problem

Target (www.target.com) is a general merchandise retailer that opened in 1962. In 1979, they surpassed $1 billion in annual sales. By 2018, the company had a store in every state, and an astounding 75 percent of the U.S. population now lives within ten minutes of a Target store. The retailer's tagline is "Expect More. Pay Less." This tagline reflects the company's positioning as a discount retailer that sells trendy essential items in areas such as homeware, toys, electronics, and sporting goods.

Since Target opened its first store, business models have changed dramatically. Perhaps it is most significant that the Internet has added a new channel to reach customers. Suddenly, Target found itself competing against Amazon—a store with no physical locations for customers to visit. Target responded by creating a website: Target.direct in 2000, which became Target.com in 2004. It seemed, however, as though there were two versions of Target—one physical, and one virtual. Customers couldn't always get the same products across these channels, and they couldn't return an online purchase to a physical store. Fast-forward to 2009, when Target introduced their mobile app, adding a third dimension to their channel mix. Again, however, the mobile app served one purpose, the website another, and the physical store a third. The question remained: Are you one customer of Target as a whole? Or, are you three distinct customers, depending on which medium you use to interact with the store?

Today, Target's customer interaction is far greater than in-store, online, or mobile. The company offers multiple platforms to interact with customers that include social media platforms, virtual assistants, the Web, and even the old-fashioned physical store aisle. Today's customers want businesses to be where they are. Problems don't always occur neatly within regular call center hours, nor do they happen only within a single channel. When customers need answers, they want those answers immediately. Research reveals that 40 percent of customers will give companies only a day to resolve their issues before they move to another channel or, worse, to a competitor. Even more imposing, 20 percent will give companies only a few minutes.

In addition to these changes, COVID has redefined the way millions of customers shop. Target has adjusted effectively to meet customers where they want to shop—whether online, in person, or both. However, Target's transformation wasn't a response to the pandemic. The company had begun preparations for a multi-platform strategy as early as 2016. The pandemic helped move customers along to appreciate the singularity of the experience regardless of their ability—or willingness—to visit a physical store.

Today, whether they are shopping via a mobile app, a website, social media, or in person, consumers expect a seamless and consistent experience when they interact with a brand. Today's empowered shoppers expect to be catered to; they expect convenience; they expect to be able to shop whenever and however they want.

The IT Solution

Target's actions, streamlining the customer experience across all platforms, are referred to as an *omnichannel customer experience strategy*. According to market experts, total sales from this type of strategy comprise approximately 46 percent of all e-commerce sales. The omnichannel experience involves marketing to, selling to, and serving customers on all channels to create an integrated and cohesive customer experience. The experience should be the same for customers regardless of which platform or method they choose.

As mentioned earlier, Target started down this strategic path in 2016. While many other retailers were trying to catch up with Amazon by shipping directly to a customer's home, Target chose a different path. The company built a fulfillment model using their existing store infrastructure to provide same-day service through their in-store pickup or drive-up services. Further, promising that orders would be ready in fewer than two hours with no minimum order was a game changer. In this way, Target differentiated itself from Amazon—which still struggles with same-day delivery—and Walmart—which requires a minimum order for drive-up service.

Today, customers can shop via the Target app and check inventory for an item in local stores. They can even learn in which aisle the item is located. They can also select in-store pickup, so the item is ready when they enter the store, or choose the drive-up to have someone bring it to their car. And, if they remember something else they need on their way to the store, they can seamlessly change the drive-up to a pickup in real time. Alternatively, they can choose to have the item shipped to their home. Finally, customers can mix buying online and in store and enjoy the same flexibility with returns.

Achieving the proper omnichannel mix between online and offline was a challenge. Since 2019, Target has invested $7 billion to build an integrated IT system that can provide real-time inventory, order updates across channels, and create picking logic (a guide for employees who are "picking" items from the shelf for same-day orders). Further, the company has overhauled the supply chain to reinvent and align the in-store, online, and mobile experience.

The Results

The key to Target's omnichannel strategy was to redefine the role of its store network. Using stores rather than warehouses and a host of delivery options to drive the same-day solution has made all the difference.

Unlike other retailers who built giant warehouses and a separate supply chain for their online stores, Target's model focused on its local stores. In fact, in 2020, the company's local stores fulfilled 95 percent of its total sales. Shipping from stores engages associates and makes inventory visible to both store associates and customers.

The strategic omnichannel innovations proved to be a winning combination. For 2021, Target's digital sales were up 31 percent, with omnichannel selling playing a significant role. More than ever, consumers are demanding options for obtaining their online orders. For many customers, waiting two or more days for an online order to be delivered is no longer an option.

Times have changed. Many of us walk around with phones in our pockets or purses that contain more than 100,000 times the processing power that took astronauts to the Moon. Customers with more information require a different approach. For now, the omnichannel strategy is working well for Target.

Questions

1. Is e-commerce a part of Target's brick-and-mortar strategy? Or, are Target's brick-and-mortar stores part of their e-commerce strategy?

2. **Have you experienced Target's Pick Up or Drive Up service? If so, what was it like for you?**

3. **How has Target differentiated itself with its omnichannel strategy?**

Sources: Compiled from A. Zaheer, "How to Develop a Seamless CS for the Omnichannel Shopper," *Total Retail*, August 31, 2022; B. Freedman, "The Retail Shift from Store to Home: Omnichannel Strategies That Are Here to Stay Post-Lockdown," *Forbes*, August 10, 2022; P. Tatevosian, "Can Target's Omnichannel Advantage Extend Record Profitability in 2022?," *Motley Fool*, May 11, 2022; M. Becker, "5 Successful Omnichannel Retailing Examples," emarsys.com, June 25, 2022; T. Harnett, "Why Omnichannel CX Succeeds When Channels Work Together," cmswire.com, March 17, 2022; C. Fontanella, "What is OmniChannel? 20 Top OmniChannel Experience Examples," *HubSpot*, February 1, 2022; Zacks Equity Research, "Target's (TGT) Omnichannel, Digitization Efforts Propel Sales," yahoo.com, January 24, 2022; D. Kline, "Target's Secret: Sharp Focus on Changing How People Shop," *TheStreet*, December 6, 2021; D. Ratliff, "Target Enhances Omnichannel Pickup and Payment Offerings for the Holidays," *Retail Touch Points*, October 27, 2021; R. Watson, "Building Out Omnichannel? Target Is the One to Watch," parcelindustry.com, September 27, 2021; S. Lauchlan, "How Target's Omni-Channel Leap of Faith 5 Years Ago Set It up for Retail's COVID Crisis and beyond," diginomica.com, March 3, 2021; F. Ali, "Omnichannel Fuels Target's 145% Growth in Ecommerce," digitalcommerce360.com, March 2, 2021; N. Botting, "Target: A Shining Example of Omnichannel Retail Success," blog.lengow.com, September 6, 2020; R. Redman, "Target Accelerates Omnichannel Game Plan," *Supermarket News*, March 3, 2020; and https://corporate.target.com/about/purpose-history/History-Timeline?era=2, accessed September 28, 2022.

Types of E-Commerce

E-commerce can be conducted between and among various parties. In this section, you will identify eight common types of e-commerce, and you will learn about three of them—C2C, B2E, and e-government—in detail. We discuss B2C and B2B in separate sections because they are very complex. We discuss mobile commerce in Chapter 8 and social commerce in Chapter 9.

- *Business-to-consumer electronic commerce (B2C)*: In B2C, the sellers are organizations, and the buyers are individuals. You will learn about B2C electronic commerce in Section 7.2.

- *Business-to-business electronic commerce (B2B)*: In B2B transactions, both the sellers and the buyers are business organizations. B2B comprises the vast majority of EC volume. You will learn more about B2B electronic commerce in Section 7.3. Look back to Figure 1.5 for an illustration of B2B electronic commerce.

- *Consumer-to-consumer electronic commerce (C2C)*: In C2C (also called customer-to-customer), an individual sells products or services to other individuals. The major strategies for conducting C2C on the Internet are auctions and classified ads. Most auctions are conducted by C2C intermediaries such as eBay (**www.ebay.com**). Let's take a look at Movate (**www.movate.com**). Movate is a B2C customer experience platform that facilitates C2C interactions.

MKT Many companies use Movate to facilitate the resolution of customer questions and complaints by knowledgeable customers themselves. Movate clients first enroll a group of knowledgeable customers, called answerers. Some client companies test their customers' writing skills and product knowledge before asking them to participate and become answerers. Movate's software has an artificial intelligence component that matches answerers with questions that it thinks they will be able to answer well, sending customer queries to them via the Movate app.

HRM Movate answerers have gig jobs, similar to Amazon's Mechanical Turk and Uber. A gig job is one in which an organization contracts with independent workers for short-term engagements where the worker is paid for each engagement. Movate pays answerers 70 percent of the fee for each customer query they resolve. Answerers have reputation scores; those with higher scores receive more questions and may be asked to contribute to collections of stock answers to common questions (known as frequently asked questions or FAQs).

Reputation scores, the flexibility of the work, and Movate's artificial intelligence component provide a competitive advantage over rivals such as InSided (**www.insided.com**) and IAdvize (**www.iadvize.com**) in the $4.3 billion customer self-service software market. An average Movate representative makes about $200 per week and the top 5 percent earn more than $2,000 per week. Movate has experienced very rapid growth.

- **HRM** *Business-to-employee (B2E):* In B2E, an organization uses EC internally to provide information and services to its employees. For example, companies allow employees to manage their benefits and to take training classes electronically. Employees can also buy discounted insurance, travel packages, and tickets to events on the corporate intranet. They can also order supplies and materials electronically. Finally, many companies have electronic corporate stores that sell the company's products to its employees, usually at a discount.

- *E-government:* E-government is the use of Internet technology in general and e-commerce in particular to deliver information and public services to citizens (called *government-to-citizen,* or *G2C EC*) and to business partners and suppliers (called *government-to-business,* or *G2B EC*). G2B EC is much like B2B EC, usually with an overlay of government procurement regulations. That is, G2B EC and B2B EC are conceptually similar. However, the functions of G2C EC are different from anything that exists in the private sector (e.g., B2C EC).

  E-government is also an efficient way of conducting business transactions with citizens and businesses and within the governments themselves. E-government makes government more efficient and effective, especially in the delivery of public services. An example of G2C electronic commerce is electronic benefits transfer, in which governments transfer benefits, such as Social Security and pension payments, directly to recipients' bank accounts.

- *Mobile commerce (m-commerce):* The term *m-commerce* refers to e-commerce that is conducted entirely in a wireless environment. An example is using cell phones to shop over the Internet.

- *Social commerce:* Social commerce refers to the delivery of electronic commerce activities and transactions through social computing.

- *Conversational commerce:* Conversational commerce is a type of electronic commerce using natural language processing (see Chapter 14) to engage in various means of conversation, such as online chat with messaging apps, chatbots on messaging apps or websites, and voice assistants.

  Messaging apps include Facebook Messenger (**www.messenger.com**), WhatsApp (**www.whatsapp.com**), Kik (**www.kik.com**), and WeChat (**www.wechat.com**). Customers can chat with company representatives, access customer support, ask questions, receive personalized recommendations, and click to purchase, all from within messaging apps. They have the options of interacting with a human representative, a chatbot, or a combination of the two. Facebook Messenger and WeChat are among the largest messaging apps in the world.

  Some 1.3 billion individuals use Facebook Messenger. Facebook's objective is to drive Messenger users to the more than 40 million businesses with an official brand Facebook page. For example, to shop for a T-shirt on Facebook Messenger, users can send a text to Messenger to start a chat with the mobile shopping app Spring. The app will request information concerning the buyer's budget and then display several possible T-shirts. If the customer does not like any of these choices, then Spring will present more options.

  Messenger also has a **chatbot**-building capability. In September 2022, there were approximately 300,000 active messenger bots on the app. These bots can process purchases without directing shoppers to a third party. To process transactions in Messenger, Facebook is collaborating with leading companies in the payments industry, including electronic payment leaders Stripe and PayPal Braintree, as well as credit card giants Visa, MasterCard, and American Express.

  Some 1.24 billion people use WeChat, China's massive social media site. They can utilize bots on the app to chat with friends about an upcoming concert, purchase tickets to the event, book a restaurant, split the check, and call a taxi. In addition to the individual WeChat users, 10 million Chinese businesses have an account. In fact, for some firms the WeChat bot completely replaces an Internet site.

Each type of EC is executed in one or more business models. A **business model** is the method by which a company generates revenue to sustain itself. **Table 7.1** summarizes the major EC business models.

chatbot A computer program that uses artificial intelligence and natural language processing to simulate human conversation, either by voice or text communication.

business model The method by which a company generates revenue to sustain itself.

Major E-Commerce Mechanisms

MKT Businesses and customers can buy and sell on the Internet through a number of mechanisms, including electronic catalogs and electronic auctions. Businesses and customers use electronic payment mechanisms to digitally pay for goods and services.

Catalogs have been printed on paper for generations. Today, they are also available over the Internet. *Electronic catalogs* consist of a product database, a directory and search capabilities, and a presentation function. They are the backbone of most e-commerce sites.

An **auction** is a competitive buying and selling process in which prices are determined dynamically by competitive bidding. Electronic auctions (e-auctions) generally increase revenues for sellers by broadening the customer base and shortening the cycle time of the auction. Buyers generally benefit from e-auctions because they can bargain for lower prices. They also do not have to travel to an auction at a physical location.

The Internet provides an efficient infrastructure for conducting auctions at lower administrative costs and with a greater number of involved sellers and buyers. Both individual consumers and corporations can participate in auctions.

There are two major types of auctions: forward and reverse. In **forward auctions**, sellers solicit bids from many potential buyers. Usually, sellers place items at sites for auction, and buyers bid continuously for them. The highest bidder wins the items. Both sellers and buyers can be either individuals or businesses. The popular auction site eBay.com is a forward auction site.

In **reverse auctions**, one buyer, usually an organization, wants to purchase a product or a service. The buyer posts a request for a quotation (RFQ) on its website or on a third-party site. The RFQ provides detailed information on the desired purchase. Interested suppliers study the RFQ and then submit bids electronically. Everything else being equal, the lowest-price bidder wins the auction. The reverse auction is the most common auction model for large purchases (in regard to either quantities or price). Governments and large corporations frequently use this approach, which may provide considerable savings for the buyer.

Auctions can be conducted from the seller's site, the buyer's site, or a third party's site. For example, eBay, the best-known third-party site, offers hundreds of thousands of different items in several types of auctions. Overall, more than 300 major companies, including **Amazon.com** and **Dellauction.com**, sponsor online auctions.

An *electronic storefront* is a website that represents a single store. An *electronic mall*, also known as a *cybermall* or an *e-mall*, is a collection of individual shops consolidated under one Internet address. Electronic storefronts and electronic malls are closely associated with B2C electronic commerce. You will study each one in more detail in Section 7.2.

An **electronic marketplace** (*e-marketplace*) is a central, virtual market space on the Web where many buyers and many sellers can conduct e-commerce and e-business activities. Electronic marketplaces are associated with B2B electronic commerce. You will learn about electronic marketplaces in Section 7.3.

Electronic Payment Mechanisms

MIS **ACCT** Implementing EC typically requires electronic payments. **Electronic payment mechanisms** enable buyers to pay for goods and services electronically, rather than writing a check or using cash. Payments are an integral part of doing business, whether in the traditional manner or online. Traditional payment systems have typically involved cash or checks.

In most cases, traditional payment systems are not effective for EC, especially for B2B. Cash cannot be used because there is no face-to-face contact between buyer and seller. Not everyone accepts credit cards or checks, and some buyers do not have credit cards or checking accounts. Finally, contrary to what many people believe, it may be *less* secure for the buyer to use the telephone or mail to arrange or send payments, especially from another country, than to complete a secured transaction on a computer. For all of these reasons, a better method is needed to pay for goods and services in cyberspace. This method is electronic payment systems. Let's take a closer look at electronic checks, electronic cards, and digital, online

---

auction A competitive process in which either a seller solicits consecutive bids from buyers or a buyer solicits bids from sellers, and prices are determined dynamically by competitive bidding.

forward auctions Auctions that sellers use as a selling channel to many potential buyers; the highest bidder wins the items.

reverse auctions Auctions in which one buyer, usually an organization, seeks to buy a product or a service, and suppliers submit bids; the lowest bidder wins.

electronic marketplace A virtual market space on the Web where many buyers and many sellers conduct electronic business activities.

electronic payment mechanisms Computer-based systems that allow customers to pay for goods and services electronically, rather than writing a check or using cash.

payments. We discuss the blockchain and various cryptocurrencies such as Bitcoin later in this chapter, and then discuss digital wallets in Chapter 8.

ACCT **Electronic Checks**   *Electronic checks (e-checks),* which are used primarily in B2B, are similar to regular paper checks. A customer who wishes to use e-checks must first establish a checking account with a bank. Then, when the customer buys a product or a service, he or she e-mails an encrypted electronic check to the seller. The seller deposits the check in a bank account, and the funds are transferred from the buyer's account into the seller's account.

Like regular checks, e-checks carry a signature (in digital form) that can be verified (see **www.authorize.net**). Properly signed and endorsed e-checks are exchanged between financial institutions through electronic clearinghouses.

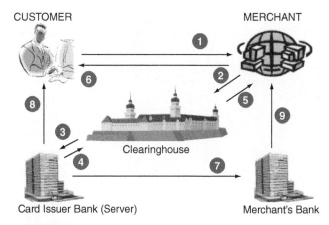

FIGURE 7.1 **How e-credit cards work. (The numbers 1–9 indicate the sequence of activities.)**

FIN **ACCT** **Electronic Cards**   There are a variety of electronic cards, and they are used for different purposes. The most common types are electronic credit cards, purchasing cards, stored-value money cards, and smart cards.

Electronic credit cards allow customers to charge online payments to their credit card account. These cards are used primarily in B2C and in shopping by small-to-medium enterprises (SMEs). Here is how e-credit cards work (see **Figure 7.1**).

1. When you purchase a book from Amazon, for example, your credit card information and purchase amount are encrypted in your browser. This procedure ensures the information is safe while it is "traveling" on the Internet to Amazon.

2. When your information arrives at Amazon, it is not opened. Rather, it is transferred automatically (in encrypted form) to a *clearinghouse*, where it is decrypted for verification and authorization.

3. The clearinghouse asks the bank that issued you your credit card (the card issuer bank) to verify your credit card information.

4. Your card issuer bank verifies your credit card information and reports this to the clearinghouse.

5. The clearinghouse reports the result of the verification of your credit card to Amazon.

6. Amazon reports a successful purchase and amount to you.

7. Your card issuer bank sends funds in the amount of the purchase to Amazon's bank.

8. Your card issuer bank notifies you (either electronically or in your monthly statement) of the debit on your credit card.

9. Amazon's bank notifies Amazon of the funds credited to its account.

Purchasing cards are the B2B equivalent of electronic credit cards (see **Figure 7.2**). In some countries, purchasing cards are the primary form of payment between companies. Unlike credit cards, where credit is provided for 30 days (for free) before payment is made to the merchant, payments made with purchasing cards are settled within a week.

Stored-value money cards allow you to store a fixed amount of prepaid money and then spend it as necessary. Each time you use the card, the amount is reduced by the amount you spent. **Figure 7.3** illustrates a New York City MetroCard (for the subway and bus).

Finally, *EMV smart cards* contain a chip that can store a large amount of information as well as a magnetic stripe for backward compatibility (see **Figure 7.4**). EMV stands for Europay, MasterCard, and Visa, the three companies that originally created the standard. EMV is a technical standard for

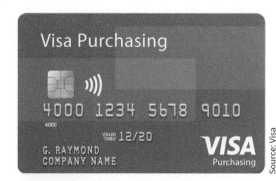

FIGURE 7.2 **Example of a purchasing card.**

Source: Visa

FIGURE 7.3 **The New York City MetroCard.**

Clarence Holmes Photography/ Alamy Stock Photo

FIGURE 7.4 **Smart cards are frequently multipurpose.**

smart payment cards. EMV cards can be physically swiped through a reader, inserted into a reader, or read over a short distance using near-field communications. EMV cards are also called "chip and PIN" or "chip and signature" depending on the authentication methods employed by the card issuer.

ACCT **MIS** **Digital, Online Payments** The rapid growth of electronic commerce necessitated a fast, secure method for customers to pay online using their credit cards. Traditionally, to process online credit card payments, merchants set up Internet merchant accounts and payment gateway accounts. The merchants obtained their merchant accounts through a bank.

A payment gateway is an application that authorizes payments for e-businesses, online retailers, bricks-and-clicks businesses, or traditional brick-and-mortar businesses. It is the virtual equivalent of a physical point of sale terminal located in retail outlets.

Payment gateways link, on one hand, to credit card accounts belonging to online customers and to Internet merchant accounts on the other. Payment gateways interact with the card issuer's bank to authorize the credit card in real time when a purchase is made. The funds received flow into the merchant account.

The leading providers of payment gateway accounts are PayPal (www.paypal.com), Authorize.net (www.authorize.net), Cybersource (www.cybersource.com), and Verisign (www.verisign.com). These providers help merchants set up merchant accounts and payment gateways in one convenient package. Let's look at how Stripe is disrupting the payments industry.

FIN **MIS** Founded in 2011, Stripe (www.stripe.com) is an electronic payment software solution in the financial technology (Fintech) industry whose goal is to transform e-payment systems. Stripe allows individuals and businesses to accept payments over the Internet. Stripe focuses on providing the technical, fraud prevention, and banking infrastructure required to operate online payment systems.

Using Stripe, merchants can integrate payment processing into their websites without having to register and maintain a merchant account. For online credit card transactions, merchants create a Stripe account and insert a few lines of JavaScript into their website's source code. When shoppers provide their credit card information, it is collected directly by Stripe's servers, so merchants do not need to handle sensitive data. Stripe processes the transaction, scans for signs of fraud, and charges a fee of 2.9 percent plus 30 cents per transaction. Stripe deposits the funds from the sale into the vendor's bank account a week later.

In the fall of 2018, Stripe moved into brick-and-mortar retail when the firm deployed a new product called Stripe Terminal. Terminal is Stripe's payments solution for fast-growing Internet businesses that sell products and services in person as well as online. For example, digital-first brands such as Warby Parker (eyeglasses; www.warbyparker.com) and Glossier (skin care and beauty products; www.glossier.com) use Terminal for in-person payments.

One of Stripe's main competitors is Adyen (www.adyen.com), a European service. Adyen offers merchants the ability to use one payment solution to globally track all online and brick-and-mortar sales.

Stripe says that it is targeting different customers than Adyen. Specifically, Stripe targets fast-growing, digital-first companies that have only recently begun expanding into physical retail. Ayden, however, targets large traditional brands such as L'Oréal and Burberry, although it does business with large Internet platforms such as eBay and Etsy.

Stripe also believes its technology differentiates it from Adyen. The firm states that Stripe Terminal will make it easy for stores to customize what shoppers see on the checkout screen, whether that is a discount offer or other messaging. Merchants will also be able to manage and send updates to all of their checkout equipment from one online account. Pricing for Stripe Terminal begins at a 2.7 percent fee, plus 5 cents for each transaction.

Beyond consumer product businesses, Stripe Terminal also targets business-to-business software platforms whose own customers operate brick-and-mortar chains. For instance, Mindbody (www.mindbodyonline.com), which makes software for wellness businesses like yoga studios and spas, is a Stripe customer.

Benefits and Limitations of E-Commerce

Few innovations in human history have provided as many benefits to organizations, individuals, and society as e-commerce has. E-commerce benefits organizations by making national and international markets more accessible and by lowering the costs of processing, distributing, and retrieving information. Customers benefit by being able to access a vast number of products and services around the clock. The major benefit to society is the ability to easily and conveniently deliver information, services, and products to people in cities, rural areas, and developing countries.

Despite all these benefits, EC has some limitations, both technological and nontechnological, that have restricted its growth and acceptance. One major technological limitation is the lack of universally accepted security standards. Also, in less-developed countries, telecommunications bandwidth is often insufficient, and accessing the Web is expensive. The remaining nontechnological limitation is the perception that EC is nonsecure.

Before you go on...

1. Define e-commerce and distinguish it from e-business.
2. Differentiate among B2C, B2B, C2C, and B2E electronic commerce.
3. Define e-government.
4. Discuss forward and reverse auctions.
5. Discuss the various online payment mechanisms.
6. Identify some benefits and limitations of e-commerce.

7.2 Business-to-Consumer (B2C) Electronic Commerce

LEARNING OBJECTIVE

Describe the various online services of business-to-consumer (B2C) commerce, along with specific examples of each.

WILEY PLUS

Author Lecture Videos are available exclusively in *WileyPLUS.*
Apply the Concept activities are available in the Appendix and in *WileyPLUS.*

B2B ecommerce is much larger than B2C ecommerce by volume, but B2C ecommerce is more complex. The reason is that B2C involves a large number of buyers making millions of diverse transactions per day from a relatively small number of sellers. As an illustration, consider Amazon, an online retailer that offers thousands of products to its customers. Each customer purchase is relatively small, but Amazon must manage every transaction as if that customer were its most important one. The company needs to process each order quickly and efficiently, and ship the products to the customer in a timely manner. It also has to manage returns. Multiply this simple example by millions, and you get an idea of how complex B2C ecommerce can be.

Overall, B2B complexities tend to be more business related, whereas B2C complexities tend to be more technical and volume related. As you noted in the previous section of this chapter, one of the complexities of B2C involves digital, online payments.

This section addresses the primary issues in B2C ecommerce. We begin by studying the two basic mechanisms that customers utilize to access companies on the Web: electronic storefronts and electronic malls. In addition to purchasing products over the Web, customers access online services, such as banking, securities trading, job searching, and travel. Companies engaged in B2C ecommerce must "get the word out" to prospective customers, so we turn our attention to online advertising. Finally, the complexity of B2C ecommerce creates two major challenges for sellers: channel conflict and order fulfillment, which we examine in detail.

Electronic Storefronts and Malls

electronic retailing (e-tailing) The direct sale of products and services through storefronts or electronic malls, usually designed around an electronic catalog format and auctions.

For several generations, home shopping from catalogs, and later from television shopping channels, has attracted millions of customers. **Electronic retailing (e-tailing)** is the direct sale of products and services through electronic storefronts or electronic malls, usually designed around an electronic catalog format and auctions.

E-commerce enables you to buy from anywhere, at any time. EC offers a wide variety of products and services, including unique items, often at lower prices. The name given to selling unique items is "the long tail." The *long tail* describes the retailing strategy of selling a large number of unique items in small quantities.

Shoppers can also gain access to very detailed supplementary product information. They can also easily locate and compare competitors' products and prices. Finally, buyers can find hundreds of thousands of sellers. Two popular online shopping mechanisms are electronic storefronts and electronic malls.

electronic storefront The website of a single company, with its own Internet address, at which orders can be placed.

As we saw earlier in the chapter, an **electronic storefront** is a website that represents a single store. Each storefront has a unique uniform resource locator (URL), or Internet address, at which buyers can place orders.

electronic mall A collection of individual shops under one Internet address; also known as a *cybermall* or an *e-mall*.

An **electronic mall**, also known as a *cybermall*, or an *e-mall*, is a collection of individual shops grouped under a single Internet address. Electronic malls may include thousands of vendors. For example, Microsoft Bing shopping, (**www.bing.com/shop**) includes tens of thousands of products from thousands of vendors, as does Amazon (**www.amazon.com**).

Online Service Industries

In addition to purchasing products, customers access needed services on the Web. Selling books, toys, computers, and most other products on the Internet can reduce vendors' selling costs by 20 to 40 percent. Further reduction is difficult to achieve because the products must be delivered physically. Only a few products, such as software and music, can be digitized and then delivered online for additional savings. In contrast, services such as buying an airline ticket and purchasing stocks or insurance can be delivered entirely through e-commerce, often with considerable cost reduction.

disintermediation Elimination of intermediaries in electronic commerce.

One of the most pressing EC issues relating to online services (as well as in marketing tangible products) is **disintermediation**. Intermediaries, also known as *middlemen*, have two functions: (1) they provide information, and (2) they perform value-added services such as consulting. The first function can be fully automated and most likely will be assumed by e-marketplaces and portals that provide information for free. When this development occurs, the intermediaries who perform only (or primarily) this function are likely to be eliminated. The process whereby intermediaries are eliminated is called *disintermediation*.

In contrast to simply providing information, performing value-added services requires expertise. Unlike the information function, then, this function can be only partially automated. Intermediaries who provide value-added services are thriving. The Web helps these employees in two situations: (1) when the number of participants is enormous, as with job searches, and (2) when the information that must be exchanged is complex.

In this section, you will examine some leading online service industries: banking, trading of securities (stocks, bonds), job matching, travel services, and advertising.

FIN **MIS** **Financial Technology (Fintech)**   Traditional banks have massive, entrenched, and inefficient legacy infrastructures: brick-and-mortar buildings and information technology infrastructures. These legacy infrastructures make it difficult for traditional banks to upgrade their systems or to be agile and flexible. Furthermore, their infrastructures are making banks' customer experience outdated. Customers now expect their financial experiences to be mobile, personalized, customizable, and accessible.

Responding to customer expectations, **Fintech** is an industry composed of companies that use technology to compete in the marketplace with traditional financial institutions and intermediaries in the delivery of financial services, which include banking, insurance, real estate, and investing. (Fintech is also a blanket term for disruptive technologies that are affecting the financial services industry.) Let's take a closer look at the many services that Fintech companies are offering.

FIN **Lending**   An alternative source of financing, person-to-person (P2P) lending platforms use machine learning technologies and algorithms to save individuals and businesses time and money and help them access a line of credit. P2P lending platforms provide borrowers with an easy, fast, simple, and lower-cost service that most traditional banks cannot match. The leading companies in this area are Lending Tree (**www.lendingtree.com**), Lending Club (**www.lendingclub.com**), Prosper (**www.prosper.com**), and Zopa (**www.zopa.com**).

FIN **Trading and Investing**   New automated financial advisors and wealth management services are making an impact on the industry. *Robo-advisors* create relatively straightforward asset allocation portfolios based on customers' ages and risk tolerance. Basically, they tell clients what percentage of stocks, bonds, and cash they should have. They then monitor the portfolio and reallocate funds as needed. *Robo-analysts* use sophisticated algorithms to make trading and investing a more automated online experience. Often in conjunction with human advisors, these platforms provide savings to users and offer financial research and planning services that are normally reserved for wealthy investors. They are also enabling users with small amounts of capital to begin investing. The leading companies in this area are Wealthfront (**www.wealthfront.com**), Betterment (**www.betterment.com**), etoro (**www.etoro.com**), and Robinhood (**www.robinhood.com**).

FIN **ACCT** **Personal Finance**   Fintech companies are trying to make personal finance more transparent and more affordable. Mobile apps and online platforms are now helping individuals and businesses develop a budget, find a loan, file their taxes, and invest. These platforms are also using technology to track daily expenditures and to help users analyze their financial status in real time. Leading companies in this area are Acorns (**www.acorns.com**), Learnvest (**www.learnvest.com**), Mint (**www.mint.com**), Nerdwallet (**www.nerdwallet.com**), and Billguard (**www.crunchbase.com/organizations/billguard**).

FIN **Funding**   Equity and crowdfunding platforms provide alternate sources of investment for individuals who want to start a business. Online crowdfunding platforms raise money from a large number of individuals who collectively fund projects that typically would not attract funding from traditional banks and venture capital firms. The leading companies in this area are Kickstarter (**www.kickstarter.com**), indiegogo (**www.indiegogo.com**), and gofundme (**www.gofundme.com**).

FIN **Currency Exchange and Remittances**   Transferring and exchanging money internationally can be a time-consuming and expensive process. Fintech companies are developing innovative platforms that make this process simpler, faster, and less expensive. These companies range from P2P currency exchanges that reduce the costs of exchanging currencies to mobile phone–based money transfers and remittance platforms that provide a cost-effective method for people to transfer small amounts of money overseas. The leading companies in this area are Wise (**www.wise.com**), Xoom (**www.xoom.com**), WeSwap (**www.weswap.com**), WorldRemit (**www.worldremit.com**), and mPesa.

FIN **Mobile Banking**   Mobile banking refers to the service that banks and other financial institutions provide to their customers that enables them to conduct a range of transactions by using an app on their mobile devices. The apps allow customers to remotely access and transact with their accounts. In the United States, approximately 72 percent of consumers use digital channels to open checking accounts.

FIN **Internet Banking (also called e-banking or online banking)**
Internet banking is closely related to mobile banking. However, instead of using an app,

Fintech   An industry composed of companies that use technology to compete in the marketplace with traditional financial institutions and intermediaries in the delivery of financial services, which include banking, insurance, real estate, and investing.

customers use the Internet. All of the transactions are conducted through the website of the financial institution. Several Internet-only banks have emerged including Ally (www.ally.com), TIAA Bank (www.tiaabank.com), and Axos Bank (www.axosbank.com/Personal).

FIN **ACCT** **Payments**   Casual payments that people make every day, such as $75 for domestic help or $40 to split a lunch check with friends, have long been a problem for the U.S. banking system. Today, new payment technologies are changing the ways that consumers bank, transfer money, and pay for goods and services.

With P2P services, consumers link a bank account, credit card, or debit card to a smartphone app and can then send money to anyone else with only the recipient's e-mail address or phone number. In the near future, many consumers will not carry a physical wallet filled with cash and credit cards, but only use a smartphone. The leading companies in this area are Venmo (www.venmo.com; subsidiary of PayPal), PayPal (www.paypal.com), Square (www.squareup.com), Apple Pay (www.apple.com/apple-pay), Google Pay (www.pay.google.com), and Facebook Messenger (www.messenger.com).

In June 2017, more than 30 major banks, including Bank of America, Citibank, JPMorgan Chase, and Wells Fargo, teamed up to introduce Zelle (www.zellepay.com), a digital payments network that allows consumers to send money instantly through participating banks' mobile apps. Consumers who utilize this network do not have to download a separate app.

ACCT **MIS** **Blockchain**   A *ledger* records a business's summarized financial information as debits and credits and displays their current balances. A blockchain is a decentralized, distributed, encrypted, secure, anonymous, tamper-proof, unchangeable, and often public digital ledger (a database, if you will) consisting of transactions bundled into *blocks*. Blocks contain details such as transaction timestamps and a link to the previous block. These links form the blockchain.

The blockchain records transactions across many computers so that blocks cannot be altered retroactively without the alteration of all subsequent blocks. This process allows all participants to independently verify and audit transactions. We now take a closer look at how blockchains function.

Nodes are the computers that support a blockchain network and keep it operating smoothly. Nodes are operated by individuals or groups of people who contribute money toward buying powerful computer systems. There are two types of nodes: full nodes and lightweight nodes. *Full nodes* keep a complete copy of the blockchain ledger, which is a record of every single transaction that has ever occurred. *Lightweight nodes* only download a fraction of the blockchain. Lightweight nodes are used by most people as a Bitcoin wallet for Bitcoin transactions.

A *miner* is a type of node that creates blocks in the blockchain. Miners bundle pending transactions into a block, verify that block, and add it to the blockchain.

To be able to add a block to the blockchain, a miner must compete to be the first to complete the Proof-of-Work (PoW) mining algorithm. Miners append a nonce, which is a random whole number, to the hashed contents of the block. (Note: The contents of the block are hashed when they are encrypted by a mathematical formula.) With the nonce appended to the block, miners rehash the contents to try to produce a hash value lower than or equal to the value set by the network. A *hash value* is a series of numbers and letters that is generated by the hash function. Miners keep trying different nonces until they obtain the correct hash value.

The miner who finds the correct hash value broadcasts the correct solution to the network. Receiving nodes validate the transactions in the block and accept it only if all are valid. Once a majority of nodes agree that all transactions in the recent past are unique (i.e., not double spent), the transactions in the block are cryptographically sealed into the block. Each new block is linked to previously sealed blocks to create a chain of accepted history, thereby preserving a verified record of every transaction.

The new block is then added to the blockchain and the winning miner receives 12.5 Bitcoin by the blockchain for its success. The winning miner also receives all of the fees from Bitcoin transactions that were included in that block.

The central problem in electronic cash is called *double spend*. Because electronic money consists of data, nothing stops a currency holder from trying to spend it twice.

Blockchain technology allows for the tracking of digital assets so that they can be verified as authentic and cannot be copied without permission. This capability makes blockchain ideal for financial transactions but also for other kinds of digital content such as contracts, and verified assets such as property deeds and election votes.

Blockchain technology does present problems, with the most significant being hacking. For instance, in 2019 an attacker gained control of more than half of Ethereum Classic (a cryptocurrency exchange) and was rewriting its transaction history. This attack is called a 51-percent attack. Between 2017 and 2019, industry analysts note that hackers had stolen nearly $2 billion in cryptocurrency, mostly from exchanges, and that is just what had been publicly revealed.

Another problem is that some blockchains allow for anonymity. As a result, cybercriminals use these blockchains for illegal purposes. Recall ransomware (see Chapter 4) where attackers typically require ransoms to be paid in cryptocurrency.

There are a variety of uses for blockchain technology. The most well-known is cryptocurrencies. We look at Bitcoin next and then examine other applications.

MIS Bitcoin

Blockchain is not Bitcoin but is the technology underlying Bitcoin. Bitcoin is the digital token and blockchain is the ledger to keep track of who owns the digital tokens. *Bitcoin* is a decentralized cryptocurrency, which is a digital form of currency that uses blockchain and cryptography for validation. The blockchain records every bitcoin and every transaction related to it.

The Bitcoin network is a peer-to-peer payment network that operates with encryption. Users send and receive Bitcoins, units of digital currency, by sending digitally signed messages to the network using Bitcoin cryptocurrency wallet software.

Let's look at an example of a simple Bitcoin transaction. Jim wants to send one Bitcoin to Sally.

Jim and Sally both have Bitcoin wallets. Each wallet contains two pieces of information. One is the public key, which is that person's Bitcoin address. The other is the private key, which is that person's Bitcoin password.

If someone loses their private key, they lose access to their Bitcoin wallet and their Bitcoin. No centralized entity exists that can recover private keys. In fact, if someone else has your private key, they can take your Bitcoin.

Sally sends Jim her public key. Jim opens his Bitcoin wallet, enters the instruction to send one Bitcoin to Sally's public address, and enters his private key to authorize the transaction. The Bitcoin network examines the proposed transaction. It checks to see that Jim has enough Bitcoin in his account and if the address Sally provided is valid.

After Jim and Sally's transaction passes these two tests, miners bundle it with other pending transactions into a block. The winning miner verifies the block and after consensus is reached, adds it to the blockchain. The blockchain processes the transaction and updates the database. Jim's balance is decreased by one Bitcoin and Sally's is credited by one Bitcoin.

POM Energy Grid

Power companies manage and control modern electrical grids. The power companies, as trusted intermediaries between producers and consumers, buy and sell power at the prices they set because they control the infrastructure.

However, rapid improvements in renewable energy sources and batteries are leading to innovations like microgrids in communities. A *microgrid* is a self-sufficient energy system that serves a discrete area, such as a college campus or a neighborhood. For instance, if homeowners generate more power than they need, they can sell the excess power to neighbors or businesses at market value. The peer-to-peer process of selling and buying energy can operate with blockchain technology, saving money because there is no intermediary in each transaction. The process also saves energy by keeping it local, because the farther that energy travels, the more that is wasted.

MKT POM Digital Content Creators

A major problem in the digital content space today is the lack of transparency regarding royalty payments and rights management. For the creators of digital content and virtual property, blockchain means enforceable copyrights, transparency around royalty payments, and payments made securely without an intermediary. Blockchain technology can provide evidence of ownership of content in both digital media and music. Further, with smart contracts on the blockchain, copyright becomes more enforceable. A *smart contract* is a self-executing contract with the terms of agreement between buyer and seller directly written into the software. The software and the agreements in the contract exist on a blockchain network.

Blockchains could eliminate the middlemen and enable musicians and other digital content creators to get paid directly by their audience. As the market shifts to blockchain over time, consumers could see lower prices for content, while content creators could see increased returns.

ACCT **The Music Industry**   The digitization of the music industry and the rise of streaming services such as iTunes, Spotify, and Pandora have transformed the way people buy and listen to music. As the industry has transitioned into a streaming model, issues with rights management, copyright enforcement, and royalty payments have led to new challenges that will force the music industry to rethink how payments are made to artists and creators.

For example, royalty payments are often difficult to calculate when there are multiple collaborators on a single track. Record companies, publishers, and streaming service providers also operate with siloed databases, making it difficult to keep track of music rights and who is owed what money.

With blockchain, each song file can have its royalty and licensing rights contained in the file. Each download can automatically trigger micropayments to the artist and he or she can get paid first instead of last.

Artist Imogen Heap was among the first musicians to start experiments with blockchain. In 2015, she used the Ethereum blockchain-based Ujo platform to launch the song "Tiny Human" for $0.60 per download. Heap has also founded her own blockchain-based offering, Mycelia, that aims to give artists more control over how their music is sold and circulated.

ACCT **Journalism**   Similar to the music industry, blockchain-verified micropayments could change the revenue system for journalism. Stories could have their rights embedded in each file and readers could be charged a small amount of Bitcoin for each piece of content that they actually consumed. Specifically, accessing an article would automatically send a micropayment to a smart contract that has been originally coded to transparently pay all of the parties involved in the creation and publication of that article with the appropriate payment percentages. The result could be that readers think about which material is worth consuming, leading to the best journalism being funded.

POM **Supply Chains**   Blockchain technology could help track and monitor raw materials as they pass through supply chains, adding transparency and the ability to trace materials to their source. In logistics, blockchain could help keep track of each stage of a transport container's journey from point to point, creating a clear record of who authorized its movement, who moved it, and when.

- Diamond conglomerate De Beers has deployed its blockchain-backed platform, Tracr, to track diamonds throughout their journey from mines to stores. With Tracr, diamonds are given a Global Diamond ID that records carat, color, clarity, and other attributes. The ID number is used to track the diamond through the supply chain.

  A company called Everledger (www.everledger.io) combines blockchain technology with machine learning, the Internet of Things, and nanotechnology to create a digital twin of each diamond. This process ensures traceability of each diamond in a secure, unchangeable, and private platform. The unique identity of each diamond enables stakeholders to buy and sell with confidence and establishes trust all along the supply chain, from mine to customer.

- According to the World Health Organization (www.who.int), 400,000 people die each year from contaminated food. IBM said that many of the critical issues affecting food safety, such as cross-contamination, the spread of food-borne illness, unnecessary waste, and the cost of recalls, are magnified by a lack of transparency and traceability along the supply chain, encompassing growers, suppliers, processors, distributors, retailers, regulators, and consumers. As a result, it can take weeks to identify the precise point of contamination, causing further illness, lost revenue, and wasted product.

Walmart, Wegmans, Nestle, and four other major food providers joined with IBM to create the IBM Food Trust Network. Before this network was created, it would take Walmart at least seven days to catch an E-coli outbreak. With blockchain and the IBM network, it takes 2.2 seconds for Walmart to trace any of their food products back to the exact farm of origin. In another example, one major fast food retailer uses blockchain to track the temperature of meat in near real time as it moves along the supply chain from farm to restaurant.

FIN **Online Securities Trading**   Millions of Americans use computers to trade stocks, bonds, and other financial instruments. In fact, several well-known securities companies, including E*Trade, Ameritrade, and Charles Schwab, offer only online trading because it is cheaper than a full-service or discount broker. On the Web, investors can find a considerable amount of information regarding specific companies or mutual funds in which to invest (e.g., www.cnn.com/business and www.bloomberg.com).

HRM **The Online Job Market**   Job seekers use online job market sites such as www.monster.com, www.indeed.com, www.simplyhired.com, and www.linkedin.com to help them find available positions. In many countries (including the United States), governments must advertise job openings on the Internet. (See our discussion on LinkedIn and "how to find a job" in Chapter 9.)

MKT **Travel Services**   The Internet is an ideal place to plan, explore, and arrange almost any trip economically. Online travel services allow you to purchase airline tickets, reserve hotel rooms, and rent cars. Most sites also offer a fare-tracker feature that sends e-mail messages about low-cost flights. Examples of comprehensive online travel services are www.expedia.com, www.travelocity.com, and www.orbitz.com. Online services are also provided by all major airline vacation services, large conventional travel agencies, car rental agencies, hotels (e.g., www.hotels.com), and tour companies. In a variation of this process, www.priceline.com allows you to set a price you are willing to pay for an airline ticket or hotel accommodations. It then attempts to find a vendor that will match your price.

One costly problem that e-commerce can cause is "mistake fares" in the airline industry. For example, in January 2019 Cathay Pacific (www.cathaypacific.com) offered business class flights from Vietnam to several U.S. cities for $675. This price was incorrect; the actual price would have been about $4,000. The U.S. Department of Transportation no longer requires airlines to honor mistake fares, but Cathay honored the tickets purchased before the airline fixed the erroneous price.

MKT **Online Advertising**   *Advertising* is the practice of disseminating information to attempt to influence a buyer–seller transaction. Traditional advertising on TV or in newspapers involves impersonal, one-way mass communication. In contrast, direct response marketing, or telemarketing, contacts individuals by direct mail or telephone and requires them to respond in order to make a purchase. The direct response approach personalizes advertising and marketing. At the same time, however, it can be expensive, slow, and ineffective. It can also be extremely annoying to the consumer.

Online advertising has redefined the advertising process, making it media rich, dynamic, and interactive. It improves on traditional forms of advertising in a number of ways. First, online ads can be updated any time at minimal cost and therefore can be kept current. These ads can also reach very large numbers of potential buyers all over the world. Furthermore, they are generally cheaper than radio, television, and print ads. Finally, online ads can be interactive and targeted to specific interest groups or individuals.

Online advertising is responsible in large part for the profit margins of content creators, and it plays a critical role in keeping online content free. In 2020, online advertising spending worldwide totaled $336 billion. Also that year, online advertising spending in the United States ($151 billion) exceeded spending on traditional advertising ($107 billion).

The predominant business model for content creators, as well as platforms such as Google and Facebook, has always involved the income from online advertising. Advertising is sold based on *impressions*, or the number of times that people view an ad. Consequently, content creators are placing more—and more intrusive—ads on each Web page, thus irritating users even more. Such ads include banners, pop-up ads, pop-under ads, and e-mail. Although cost effective, e-mail advertising is often misused, causing consumers to receive a flood of unsolicited e-mail, or *spam*. **Spamming** is the indiscriminate distribution of electronic ads without the permission of the recipient. Unfortunately, spamming is becoming worse over time.

spamming Indiscriminate distribution of e-mail without the recipient's permission.

Today, online advertising is facing a crisis because content creators have been placing more and more intrusive ads. As a result, users have become irritated with videos that automatically start playing when they load a Web page and full-screen takeovers that force them to find and then click on a tiny "x" before they can read the content that they wanted in the first place. They are also concerned with cookies that track every Web page they visit and every click they make, thus enabling advertisers to target them with increasing frequency and precision.

MIS **MKT** As a result of these problems with online advertising, many Web users are employing ad-blocking software—called *ad blockers*—to prevent online advertising. According to the Global Ad-Blocking Behavior Report by GlobalWebIndex (**www.globalwebindex. com**), approximately 47 percent of users worldwide used an ad blocker in 2020. Industry analysts estimate that the global revenue loss to content creators in 2020 ranged from $16 billion to $78 billion, depending on how actively the content creators adopted ad blocking countermeasures. There are several types of ad blockers:

- Ad blockers that will stop almost every ad and tracker; for example, Privacy Badger (**www. privacybadger.org**), which is operated by the nonprofit Electronic Frontier Foundation.

- Ad blockers that are for-profit businesses. The most popular ad blocker is Adblock Plus (**www.adblockplus.org**), with more than 100 million users worldwide. The tool blocks ads, banners, pop-ups, and video ads, and stops tracking services.

- Ad blockers that collect data. Ghostery (**www.ghostery.com**) monitors Web servers that are being accessed from a particular Web page and matches them with its library of known trackers. Ghostery then shows that tracker to users.

- Ad blockers that use the freemium model. Blockers such as Disconnect (**www.dis connect.me**) and 1Blocker (**www.1blocker.com**) are free apps for mobile users, who then have to pay if they want to use features such as being able to simultaneously block more than one ad or tracker.

- Ad blockers that are a function of operating systems. For example, Google Chrome will block ads from sites that engage in particularly annoying behavior. Apple's latest operating systems enable owners of Apple devices to download Web browser extensions that block ads. Brave (**www.brave.com**) is a free, open-source Web browser that blocks ads and website trackers.

Not surprisingly, content creators are fighting back against ad-blocking software. For example, about 30 percent of the Internet's top 10,000 websites use software designed to subvert browser-level ad blocking. In addition, they have begun using ad-block detectors. This type of software tool looks for ad blockers and then asks the user to disable them. It might even deny access to content until they do.

It is very important to realize that all of the "free" content on the Web must be paid for in some manner. If online ads are no longer viable, then content on the Web will be displayed only behind paywalls. That is, users will have to pay (e.g., subscriptions) to view content. And the results? The battles between content creators and ad blockers continue.

Issues in E-Tailing

Despite e-tailing's increasing popularity, many e-tailers continue to face serious issues that can restrict their growth. Three significant issues are channel conflict, order fulfillment, and personalized pricing.

channel conflict The alienation of existing distributors when a company decides to sell to customers directly online.

MKT **POM** **Channel Conflict** Clicks-and-mortar companies may face a conflict with their regular distributors when they sell directly to customers online. This situation, known as **channel conflict**, can alienate distributors. Channel conflict has forced some companies to avoid direct online sales. For example, Walmart, Lowe's, and Home Depot would rather have customers come to their stores. Therefore, although all three companies maintain e-commerce websites, their sites place more emphasis on providing information—products, prices, specials, and store locations—than on online sales.

Channel conflict can arise in areas such as pricing and resource allocation—for example, how much money to spend on advertising. Another potential source of conflict involves the logistics services provided by the offline activities to the online activities. For example, how should a company handle returns of items purchased online? Some companies have completely separated the "clicks" (the online portion of the organization) from the "mortar" or "bricks" (the traditional bricks-and-mortar part of the organization). However, this approach can increase expenses, reduce the synergy between the two organizational channels, and alienate customers. As a result, many companies are integrating their online and offline channels, a process known as **multichanneling**.

Multichanneling has created the opportunity for showrooming. *Showrooming* occurs when shoppers visit a brick-and-mortar store to examine a product in person. They then conduct research about the product on their smartphones. Often, they then purchase the product from the website of a competitor of the store they are visiting. Showrooming is causing problems for brick-and-mortar retailers, such as Target, Best Buy, and others. At the same time, showrooming benefits Amazon, eBay, and other online retailers.

multichanneling A process in which a company integrates its online and offline channels.

POM Order Fulfillment   The second major issue confronting e-commerce is *order fulfillment*, which can create problems for e-tailers. Anytime a company sells directly to customers, it is involved in various order-fulfillment activities. It must perform the following activities: quickly find the products to be shipped; pack them; arrange for the packages to be delivered speedily to the customer's door; collect the money from every customer, either in advance, by COD, or by individual bill; and handle the return of unwanted or defective products.

It is very difficult to accomplish these activities both effectively and efficiently in B2C, because a company has to ship small packages to many customers and do it quickly. For this reason, companies involved in B2C activities can experience difficulties in their supply chains.

In addition to providing customers with the products they ordered and doing it on time, order fulfillment provides all related customer services. For example, the customer must receive assembly and operation instructions for a new appliance. If the customer is unhappy with a product, the company must also arrange for an exchange or a return.

MKT Personalized Pricing   The third major issue in e-commerce is personalized pricing. In the relationship between buyers and sellers, price has traditionally been a meeting point. The practice of setting a fixed price for a good or service, which appeared in the 1860s, eliminated haggling. Each party surrendered something in this relationship. Buyers were forced to accept, or not accept, the fixed price on the price tag. In return, retailers gave up the ability to exploit customers' varying willingness to pay more for a particular good or service. That is, retailers surrendered the ability to make more profit.

Today, consumers are accustomed to *standardized pricing*, which means that when a product is sold through multiple channels, the cost should not vary by more than the difference in shipping, taxation, and distribution costs. If the price is higher for a product at a certain retailer, then customers can easily use the Internet to compare prices and features among a huge number of retailers to purchase that product from another retailer, a process known as showrooming. There is even a website, **www.camelcamelcamel.com**, that tracks Amazon prices for specific products and alerts consumers when a price drops below a preset threshold.

In theory, charging all consumers the same price is ineffective for merchants, because some customers would have been willing to pay more, and others who opted not to buy would have bought at a lower price. Economic theory states that personalized pricing can save companies this lost revenue.

Personalized pricing is the practice of pricing items at a point determined by a particular customer's perceived ability to pay. The optimal outcome of personalized pricing *for the merchant* is maximizing the price that each customer will pay. Merchants are now able to approximate the maximum price that each customer will pay. How do merchants do this?

personalized pricing Personalized pricing is the practice of pricing items at a point determined by a particular customer's perceived ability to pay

They analyze the data that consumers generate when they place items in shopping carts; swipe their rewards cards at store registers; "like" something on Facebook; provide ratings, reviews, and recommendations; and perform many other actions. They also virtually assess each customer who visits their website. Specifically, when a customer accesses a retailer's site, the merchant may know where the customer is located based on his or her Internet Protocol address. Merchants also may know the customer's ZIP code. In that case, they can determine the customer's socioeconomic status based on data from the most recent federal census.

As a result of analyzing this Big Data, retailers are developing increasingly sophisticated personalized pricing algorithms. That is, retailers can find the optimal, profit-maximizing price of a good or a service for a particular customer. As a result, prices can fluctuate hour-to-hour and even minute-to-minute. For example, the price of a can of soda in a vending machine can now vary with the outside temperature.

When merchants combine these data with cookies (see Chapter 4), they can learn a significant amount about individual customers. Based on these data, merchants can predict which products a customer is interested in purchasing, when he or she is likely to purchase them, and, critically, the price he or she would be willing to pay. That is, a merchant can estimate a customer's *reservation price*—the maximum amount they would be willing to pay for a specific product, before they had "reservations" about buying it—and then charge them that amount.

Furthermore, with e-commerce, merchants can easily adjust prices for different customers simply by changing them in the system in real time. They therefore avoid the expense of physically changing the prices on thousands of products.

For example, Delta Airlines (**www.delta.com**) uses personalized pricing to raise ticket prices for frequent flyers. The rationale is that these customers probably have to travel frequently, usually for business. They therefore are willing (however unenthusiastically) to pay more than infrequent travelers.

Companies such as Wiser (**www.wiser.com**), Dunnhumby (**www.dunnhumby.com**), and Blue Yonder (**www.blueyonder.com**; now owned by JDA Software) offer personalized pricing solutions to retailers. Blue Yonder claims it can optimize prices not only according to the region but also according to the channel in which the customer is interacting with the retailer.

Most companies hesitate to utilize personalized pricing because it remains to be seen whether consumers will accept the practice. Typically, when consumers hear about the practice, they react negatively, and companies employing the practice experience customer dissatisfaction.

A valuable source of data for companies in personalizing prices is what competitors are charging. Brick-and-mortar retailers can send mystery shoppers to their competitors' stores to note prices, but online merchants use software to scan rival websites and collect data, a process called scraping that is carried out by software called scraping bots.

Large companies have internal teams dedicated to scraping, whereas smaller companies use retail price optimization firms such as Competera (**www.competera.net**) and Price2Spy (**www.price2spy.com**). These firms scrape pricing data from websites and use machine-learning algorithms to help their customers decide how much to charge for different products.

Retailers want to see rivals' prices but they also want to prevent rivals from spying on them. Retailers also want to protect intellectual property like product photos and descriptions, which can be scraped and reused by competitors. So, many retailers show different prices to people than to scraping bots. The question is: How do retailers detect bots?

If a website visitor makes hundreds of requests per minute, it is probably a bot. Another method is to look for human behavior. Specifically, when humans tap a button on their phones, they move the phone very slightly. This movement can be detected by the phone's accelerometer and gyroscope. These movements predict that the site visitor is a human and the absence of such movements predicts that the user is probably a bot.

Keep in mind that retailers must allow some, but not all, bots to scrape a website. If websites blocked bots entirely, then they would not show up on search results. Furthermore, retailers generally want their pricing and items to appear on shopping comparison websites such as Google and Price Grabber (**www.pricegrabber.com**). IT's About Business 7.2 presents a recent story where variable (dynamic) pricing created a problem for Bruce Springsteen.

IT'S About Business 7.2

MKT **Dynamic Pricing and The Boss**

Background

In the age before digital tickets, it was common to go to a ticketed event and see someone selling tickets on the street corner. People would purchase tickets on their way into the event, often negotiating the price on the spot. This practice, known as *scalping*, was common for sporting events, concerts, and any other events where the demand for tickets is far greater than the supply.

Bruce Springsteen, who is known for standing up for working-class people, has always been viewed as offering an excellent deal. His concerts were priced fairly, and his performances were outstanding, often lasting longer than three hours. As with other popular events, however, tickets were sometimes scalped for a premium price, far above their face value. This activity is generally criticized as unfair, unethical, and potentially fraudulent (by scalping fake tickets). In some cases, it is illegal.

StubHub.com (www.stubhub.com) has built an entire business allowing individuals to resell tickets, often at a higher price. In some cases, a customer purchases tickets and then cannot attend. In these cases, it makes sense to resell the tickets. In other cases, however, a person purchases the best seats for an event with the express intent of reselling them for a large premium. In these cases, the scalpers pocket the price increase (minus the StubHub fees), and none of the extra revenue goes to the artist or the venue.

There are other issues with StubHub as well. When events are canceled and people request a refund, they likely will receive the face value from the venue and not the amount they paid through StubHub.

Clearly, then, the practice of buying tickets through a reselling portal like StubHub poses a risk for consumers. In addition, performers stand to lose money. Artists and teams receive a portion of the revenue from each ticket sale. However, if a $100 ticket sells on StubHub for $1,000, then the artist does not receive the extra royalty. In general, when tickets are priced below what customers are willing to pay, then scalpers stand to make more money from ticket sales than the performers.

The IT Solution

What is an appropriate solution? For the customer, a better process where the customer who purchases the tickets is the customer who will attend the concert would lower their risk. For the venue and the artist, a pricing strategy prices tickets according to what customers are willing to pay. Such a strategy could help the artists and venues—rather than the scalpers—to receive most of the profits.

As early as 2011, llanjubegan to employ a strategy called *dynamic pricing*. The company uses data analytics to adjust the price of a percentage of tickets according to demand. In theory, this strategy would allow promoters to sell the most sought-after tickets at a higher price, while filling up the least desirable seats by charging less. To succeed, the algorithm needs to take into account many factors such as time since tickets went on sale, time until the event, seat location, remaining seats in that location, total number of seats remaining, and the number of times a person has visited the site.

Ticketmaster (www.ticketmaser.com) utilizes these factors to respond to real-time supply and demand, sometimes in a matter of minutes. It is significant to note that companies in other areas also employ dynamic pricing. For example, Amazon updates prices every ten minutes. If you want to experience this system, simply place an item in your cart. Then, check back every day or so. You might see a note informing you that the price for that item has changed. Similarly, airlines continually adjust pricing for their seats; hotels adjust pricing based on demand, supply, and availability; ride-sharing platforms charge more for peak times; and so on. A 2018 report from Deloitte (www.deloitte.com) and Salesforce (www.salesforce.com) found that 40 percent of brands that utilize artificial intelligence to personalize the customer experience also employ dynamic pricing. Further, the proportion of businesses that employ this strategy will continue to increase.

At face value, dynamic pricing appears to be logical and ethical. Data help to set the price where it needs to be to sell the most tickets at the highest prices. However, the process of dynamic pricing should be employed carefully such as not to offend loyal customers who are accustomed to certain ticket prices.

For years, people would camp out for days to be in line to get the best seats. These customers would sacrifice their time and convenience, but not their money. Once ticket sales went online, however, it was about who could refresh their page and get the tickets in their cart first. Now that dynamic pricing is in play, it isn't always about the race to be first for the best seats. It is now about whether you are willing to pay a far higher price for them.

Some people feel that now the artists are scalping their own tickets. Others, however, feel that fans need to be realistic: Sometimes the best seats are worth more than other seats. Premium pricing, adjusted dynamically, reflects that belief, and it attempts to capture more revenue for the artist and the venue.

The Results

Bruce Springsteen, born in 1949, is likely nearing the end of his career. He vowed never to have a "farewell tour," so fans assume that each tour could be the last. His next tour, scheduled for 2023, will be his first in seven years. For some fans, the long break between shows, and the fact that this could be his final tour, makes the concert more valuable. Dynamic pricing algorithms tapped into this reality and priced the tickets accordingly.

Springsteen is not alone in using dynamic pricing. Taylor Swift, Drake, Paul McCartney, and Harry Styles have embraced dynamic pricing. Currently, artists such as The Weeknd, Alicia Keys, and Carrie Underwood also are offering their best seats—often dubbed "Platinum Tickets"—through this system. None of these artists, however, has built their careers on the working-class platform.

Nearly 90 percent of tickets were sold at a face value between $59.50 to $399, with an average price of $202. Only 1.3 percent of tickets across all shows sold for more than $1,000. So, the number of seats that were "Springsteen scalped" is minimal. Nevertheless, many fans were outraged because Springsteen always touted himself as a working-class hero, yet near the end of his career he shifted from traditional pricing to dynamic pricing—a move that cut many of his working-class fans out of the chance to get the best seats.

Questions

1. **Who do you feel for the most in this situation: artists who are losing revenue from scalped tickets or customers who are overpaying for their tickets?**

2. **What alternatives to dynamic pricing could Bruce Springsteen have employed?**

3. **Should Springsteen's image as an advocate for working-class people have affected the pricing decision?**

Sources: Compiled from S. Bhattacharyya, "Retailers Double Down on Dynamic Pricing to Protect Margins," *CFO Dive*, September 1, 2022; M. CavaSpringsteen Tickets for $4,000? How Dynamic Pricing Works and How You Can Beat the *System*." *USA Today*, August 17, 2022; A. Stewart, "Bruce Springsteen Fans Face $5,000 Tickets—And a 'Crisis of Faith'," *Washington Post*, August 3, 2022; J. Sparrow, "Dynamic Ticketing: Springsteen's Manager Defends Pricing," musically.com, July 29, 2022; W. Gittins, "What Is Dynamic Pricing and Why Are Bruce Springsteen Concert Tickets So Expensive?" as.com, July 28, 2022; A. Mahdawi, "Springsteen Tickets Are Going for a Whopping $4,000—What Else Are We Paying Dynamic Prices For?" *The Guardian*, July 27, 2022;

R. Ho, "Bruce Springsteen Fans Outraged over 'Dynamic Pricing' of Concert Tickets with Prices Hitting $5,000," *Atlanta Journal Constitution*, July 27, 2022; R. Neubecker, "The Case of the $5,000 Springsteen Tickets," *New York Times*, July 26, 2022; M. Spear, "Ticketmaster's 'Dynamic Ticket Pricing' Has Bruce Springsteen Tickets Going For $4,000," cbsnews.com, July 22, 2022; C. Brooks, "What Is Dynamic Pricing, and How Does It Affect E-commerce?," business.com, June 29, 2022; B. Sisario, "Ticketmaster Plans to Use a Variable Pricing Policy," *New York Times*, April 18, 2011; and R. Friedman, "StubHub: Adele Fans Won't Get Money Back Until Singer Reschedules Shows, Can't Resell Tickets Now," showbiz411.com, January 21, 2022.

Before you go on...

1. Describe electronic storefronts and malls.
2. Discuss various types of online services, such as securities trading, job searches, travel services, and so on.
3. Discuss online advertising, its methods, and its benefits.
4. Identify the major issues related to e-tailing.
5. What are spamming, permission marketing, and viral marketing?

7.3 Business-to-Business (B2B) Electronic Commerce

LEARNING OBJECTIVE

Describe the three business models for business-to-business (B2B) electronic commerce.

In business-to-business (B2B) e-commerce, the buyers and sellers are business organizations. B2B comprises about 85 percent of EC volume. It covers a broad spectrum of applications that enable an enterprise to form electronic relationships with its distributors, resellers, suppliers, customers, and other partners. B2B applications use any of several business models. The major models are sell-side marketplaces, buy-side marketplaces, and electronic exchanges.

Sell-Side Marketplaces

sell-side marketplace B2B model in which organizations sell to other organizations from their own private e-marketplace or from a third-party site.

In the **sell-side marketplace** model, organizations sell their products or services to other organizations electronically from their own private e-marketplace website or from a third-party website. This model is similar to the B2C model in which the buyer is expected to come to the seller's site, view catalogs, and place an order. In the B2B sell-side marketplace, however, the buyer is an organization.

The key mechanisms in the sell-side model are forward auctions and electronic catalogs that can be customized for each large buyer. Sellers such as Dell Computer (**www.dellrefurbished.com**) use auctions extensively. In addition to conducting auctions from their own websites, organizations can use third-party auction sites like eBay to liquidate items. Companies such as SAP Ariba (**www.ariba.com**) help organizations to auction old assets and inventories.

The sell-side model is used by hundreds of thousands of companies. The seller can be either a manufacturer (e.g., Dell or IBM), a distributor (e.g., www.avnet.com), or a retailer (e.g., www.bigboxx.com). The seller uses EC to increase sales, reduce selling and advertising expenditures, increase delivery speed, and lower administrative costs. The sell-side model is especially suitable to customization. Many companies allow their customers to configure their orders online. For example, at Dell (www.dell.com), you can determine the exact type of computer that you want. You can choose the type of chip, the size of the hard drive, the type of monitor, and so on. Similarly, the Jaguar website (www.jaguar.com) allows you to customize the Jaguar you want. Self-customization greatly reduces any misunderstandings concerning what customers want, and it encourages businesses to fill orders more quickly.

Buy-Side Marketplaces

`POM` *Procurement* is the overarching function that describes the activities and processes needed to acquire goods and services. Distinct from purchasing, procurement involves the activities necessary to establish requirements, sourcing activities such as market research and vendor evaluation, and negotiation of contracts. *Purchasing* refers to the process of ordering and receiving goods and services. It is a subset of the procurement process.

The **buy-side marketplace** is a model in which organizations attempt to procure needed products or services from other organizations electronically. A major method of procuring goods and services in the buy-side model is the reverse auction.

The buy-side model uses EC technology to streamline the procurement process. The goal is to reduce both the costs of items procured and the administrative expenses involved in procuring them. EC technology can also shorten the procurement cycle time.

Procurement by using electronic support is referred to as **e-procurement**. E-procurement uses reverse auctions, particularly group purchasing. In **group purchasing**, multiple buyers combine their orders so that they constitute a large volume and therefore attract more seller attention. When buyers place their combined orders on a reverse auction, they can also negotiate a volume discount. Typically, the orders of small buyers are aggregated by a third-party vendor.

buy-side marketplace B2B model in which organizations buy needed products or services from other organizations electronically, often through a reverse auction.

e-procurement. Purchasing by using electronic support.

group purchasing The aggregation of purchasing orders from many buyers so that a volume discount can be obtained.

Electronic Exchanges

Private exchanges have one buyer and many sellers. Electronic marketplaces (e-marketplaces), called **public exchanges** or just **exchanges**, are independently owned by a third party, and they connect many sellers with many buyers. Public exchanges are open to all business organizations. Public exchange managers provide all of the necessary information systems to the participants. Thus, buyers and sellers merely have to "plug in" in order to trade. B2B public exchanges are often the initial point of contacts between business partners. Once the partners make contact, they may move to a private exchange or to private trading rooms provided by many public exchanges to conduct their subsequent trading activities.

Electronic exchanges deal in both direct and indirect materials. *Direct materials* are inputs to the manufacturing process, such as safety glass used in automobile windshields and windows. *Indirect materials* are items, such as office supplies, that are needed for maintenance, operations, and repairs (MRO).

There are three basic types of public exchanges: vertical, horizontal, and functional. All three types offer diversified support services, ranging from payments to logistics.

Vertical exchanges connect buyers and sellers in a given industry. Examples of vertical exchanges are www.plasticsnet.com in the plastics industry and www.papersite.com in the paper industry. Vertical e-marketplaces offer services that are particularly suited to the community they serve. Vertical exchanges are frequently owned and managed by a *consortium*, a term for a group of major players in an industry. For example, Marriott and Hyatt own a procurement consortium for the hotel industry, and Chevron owns an energy e-marketplace.

public exchanges (or exchanges) Electronic marketplaces in which there are many sellers and many buyers, and entry is open to all; frequently owned and operated by a third party.

exchanges See **public exchanges.**

Horizontal exchanges connect buyers and sellers across many industries. They are used primarily for MRO materials. Examples of horizontal exchanges are TradersCity (**www.traderscity.com**), Globalsources (**www.globalsources.com**), and Alibaba (**www. alibaba.com**).

HRM Finally, in *functional exchanges*, needed services such as temporary help or extra office space are traded on an "as-needed" basis. For example, in April 2020 a group of chief human resources officers (CHROs) led by Accenture launched a new functional exchange, called People + Work, to connect companies laying off employees due to the COVID-19 pandemic with companies looking to fill positions. The platform gathers non-confidential workforce information by location, experience, and current job title. It gives organizations with open positions a view into the people available to fill those jobs. There is no cost for employers to submit information or to search for potential employees.

Before you go on...

1. Briefly differentiate between the sell-side marketplace and the buy-side marketplace.
2. Briefly differentiate among vertical exchanges, horizontal exchanges, and functional exchanges.

7.4 Ethical and Legal Issues in E-Business

LEARNING OBJECTIVE

Discuss the ethical and legal issues related to electronic commerce, along with examples.

Technological innovation often forces a society to reexamine and modify its ethical standards. In many cases, the new standards are incorporated into law. In this section, you will learn about two important ethical considerations—privacy and job loss—as well as various legal issues arising from the practice of e-business.

Ethical Issues

Many of the ethical and global issues related to IT also apply to e-business. Here you will learn about two basic issues: privacy and job loss.

By making it easier to store and transfer personal information, e-business presents some threats to privacy. To begin with, most electronic payment systems know who the buyers are. It may be necessary, then, to protect the buyers' identities. Businesses frequently use encryption to provide this protection.

Another major privacy issue is tracking. For example, individuals' activities on the Internet can be tracked by cookies (discussed in Chapter 4). Cookies store your tracking history on your personal computer's hard drive, and anytime you revisit a certain website, the server recognizes the cookie. In response, antivirus software packages routinely search for potentially harmful cookies.

In addition to compromising individual privacy, the use of EC may eliminate the need for some of a company's employees, as well as brokers and agents. The manner in which these unneeded workers, especially employees, are treated can raise ethical issues. How should the company handle the layoffs? Should companies be required to retrain employees for new positions? If not, how should the company compensate or otherwise assist the displaced workers? The Closing Case for this chapter presents an opposition to EC changing the way we buy cars. One of the arguments against it is the number of autoworkers (primarily at the local dealerships) who would lose their jobs.

Another interesting ethical/legal question involves national governments. What if a government limited electronic commerce from foreign companies to favor local companies? Should customers have access to the best products or to the companies that will best support their local industry?

Legal and Ethical Issues Specific to E-Commerce

Many legal issues are related specifically to e-commerce. A business environment in which buyers and sellers do not know one another and cannot even see one another creates opportunities for dishonest people to commit fraud and other crimes. These illegal actions range from creating a virtual bank that disappeared along with the investors' deposits to manipulating stock prices on the Internet. Unfortunately, fraudulent activities on the Internet are increasing.

Fraud on the Internet   Internet fraud has grown even faster than Internet use itself. In one case, stock promoters falsely spread positive rumors about the prospects of the companies they touted in order to boost the stock price. In other cases, the information provided might have been true, but the promoters did not disclose that they were paid to talk up the companies. Stock promoters specifically target small investors who are lured by the promise of fast profits.

Stocks are only one of many areas in which swindlers are active. Auctions are especially conducive to fraud, by both sellers and buyers. Other types of fraud include selling bogus investments, setting up phantom business opportunities, and fraudulent affiliate marketing.

MIS **MKT** **Fraudulent Affiliate Marketing**   *Affiliate marketing* involves a merchant paying a commission to other online entities, known as affiliates, for referring new business to the merchant's website. Affiliates are paid only when their marketing efforts actually result in a transaction, such as a customer registration, a completed lead form, a new free trial user, a new newsletter subscriber, or product sale.

Affiliates do promote legitimate businesses, such as Amazon.com and eBay, but they are also behind many of the misleading and fraudulent ads that appear on Facebook, Instagram, Twitter, Google, and the rest of the Internet. *Affiliate fraud* refers to false or unscrupulous activity conducted to generate commissions from an affiliate marketing program. Consider the following example.

A manufacturer of a fake nutritional supplement wants to sell it and does not care how the sales actually take place. The vendor approaches an affiliate network and offers to pay a commission per customer sign-up. The network spreads the word to affiliates, who design often misleading ads and pay to place them on various websites in hopes of earning commissions. The affiliates take the risk, paying to run ads without knowing if they will work. However, if even a small percentage of the people who see the ads become buyers, the profits could be substantial.

Affiliates once had to guess what kind of person might fall for their ads, targeting users by age, geography, or interests. Today, Facebook's analytics tools perform the targeting for them automatically.

Facebook tracks who clicks on ads as well as who buys the product, then starts targeting others whom its algorithms predict should be shown the ads because they are likely to buy. Affiliates typically lose money for a few days as Facebook gathers data through trial and error, and then their sales rapidly increase.

A software program called Voluum enables affiliates to track their campaigns and defeat the ad networks' defenses. The software can track marketing campaigns across multiple platforms, such as Facebook, Google, Twitter, and other websites. Voluum enables affiliates to tailor the content they deliver according to a number of factors, including the location or IP address associated with a user. The feature is useful for ad targeting—for example, showing Spanish speakers a message in their native language.

Facebook must police a $40 billion annual ad platform that malicious players are constantly trying to subvert. Facebook reviewers examine ads that users or Facebook algorithms have flagged as questionable and ban accounts that break the rules. However, Voluum makes it easy for affiliates to identify the addresses of Facebook's ad reviewers and program campaigns to show them, and only them, legitimate content. This process is called *cloaking*. Interestingly, Google has banned Voluum based on cloaking concerns but not Facebook.

Affiliates who are caught and banned can easily circumvent this problem. They simply open new Facebook accounts under different names. Some affiliates buy clean profiles from "farmers." Others rent accounts from strangers or make deals with underhanded advertising agencies to find other solutions.

The U.S. Federal Trade Commission (FTC; **www.ftc.gov**) regularly publishes examples of scams that are most likely to be spread by e-mail or to be found on the Web. Let's look at some ways in which consumers and sellers can protect themselves from online fraud.

Tips for safe electronic shopping:

- Look for reliable brand names at sites such as Walmart Online, Disney Online, and Amazon. Before purchasing, make sure that the site is authentic by entering the site directly and not from an unverified link.

- Search any unfamiliar selling site for the company's address and phone and fax numbers. Call and quiz the employees about the seller.

- Check out the vendor with the local Chamber of Commerce or Better Business Bureau (**www.bbbonline.org**). Look for seals of authenticity such as TRUSTe.

- Investigate how secure the seller's site is by examining the security procedures and by reading the posted privacy policy.

- Examine the money-back guarantees, warranties, and service agreements.

- Compare prices with those in regular stores. Too-low prices are too good to be true and some catch is probably involved.

- Ask friends what they know. Find testimonials and endorsements on community websites and well-known bulletin boards.

- Find out what your rights are in case of a dispute. Consult consumer protection agencies and the National Consumer League's Fraud Center (**www.fraud.org**).

- Check Consumerworld (**www.consumerworld.org**) for a collection of useful resources.

- For many types of products, **www.resellerratings.com** is a useful resource.

Domain Names Another legal issue is competition over domain names. Domain names are assigned by central nonprofit organizations that check for conflicts and possible infringement of trademarks. Obviously, companies that sell goods and services over the Internet want customers to be able to find them easily. In general, the closer the domain name matches the company's name, the easier the company is to locate.

A domain name is considered legal when the person or business who owns the name has operated a legitimate business under that name for some time. Companies such as Christian Dior, Nike, Deutsche Bank, and even Microsoft have had to fight or pay to acquire the domain name that corresponds to their company's name. Consider the case of Delta Air Lines. Delta originally could not obtain the Internet domain name delta.com because Delta Faucet had already purchased it. Delta Faucet had been in business under that name since 1954, so it had a legitimate business interest in using the domain name. Delta Air Lines had to settle for delta-airlines.com until it bought the domain name from Delta Faucet. Delta Faucet is now at **deltafaucet.com**.

Cybersquatting *Cybersquatting* refers to the practice of registering or using domain names for the purpose of profiting from the goodwill or the trademark that belongs to someone else. The Anti-Cybersquatting Consumer Protection Act (1999) permits trademark owners in the United States to sue for damages in such cases.

However, some practices that could be considered cybersquatting are not illegal, although they may well be unethical. Perhaps the more common of these practices is "domain tasting." Domain tasting lets registrars profit from the complex money trail of pay-per-click advertising. The practice can be traced back to the policies of the organization responsible for regulating

Web names, the Internet Corporation for Assigned Names and Numbers (ICANN) (www.icann.org). In 2000, ICANN established the five-day "Add Grace Period" during which a company or person can claim a domain name and then return it for a full refund of the registry fee. ICANN implemented this policy to allow someone who mistyped a domain to return it without cost. In some cases, companies engage in cybersquatting by registering domain names that are very similar to their competitors' domain names in order to generate traffic from people who misspell Web addresses.

Domain tasters exploit this policy by claiming Internet domains for five days at no cost. These domain names frequently resemble those of prominent companies and organizations. The tasters then jam these domains full of advertisements that come from Yahoo! and Google. Because this process involves zero risk and 100 percent profit margins, domain tasters register millions of domain names every day—some of them over and over again. Experts estimate that registrants ultimately purchase less than 2 percent of the sites they sample. In the vast majority of cases, they use the domain names for only a few days to generate quick profits.

FIN **ACCT** **Taxes and Other Fees**   In offline sales, most states and localities tax business transactions that are conducted within their jurisdiction. The most obvious example is sales taxes. Federal, state, and local authorities are working on taxation policy for e-businesses. This problem is particularly complex for interstate and international e-commerce. For example, some people claim that the state in which the *seller* is located deserves the entire sales tax (in some countries, it is a value-added tax [VAT]). Others contend that the state in which the *server* is located should also receive some of the tax revenues.

In addition to the sales tax, there is a question about where—and in some cases, whether—electronic sellers should pay business license taxes, franchise fees, gross receipts taxes, excise taxes, privilege taxes, and utility taxes. Furthermore, how should tax collection be controlled? Legislative efforts to impose taxes on e-commerce are opposed by an organization named the Internet Freedom Fighters.

Even before electronic commerce over the Internet emerged, the basic law in the United States was that as long as a retailer did not have a physical presence in the state where the consumer was shopping, that retailer did not have to collect a sales tax. Shoppers were supposed to track such purchases and then pay the taxes owed in their annual tax filings. Few people, however, did this or were even aware of their obligation. The result was that online retailers were able to undercut the prices of their non-Internet (e.g., brick-and-mortar stores) competitors for years.

In December 2013, the U.S. Supreme Court declined to get involved in state efforts to force Web retailers such as Amazon to collect sales tax from customers even in places where the companies do not have a physical presence. In light of the court's decision to stay out of the issue, in July 2019 45 states and the District of Columbia had passed legislation requiring online retailers to collect sales taxes from their customers. (Alaska, Delaware, Montana, New Hampshire, and Oregon do not have state sales taxes.)

Copyright   Recall from Chapter 4 that intellectual property is protected by copyright laws and cannot be used freely. This point is significant because many people mistakenly believe that once they purchase a piece of software, they have the right to share it with others. In fact, what they have bought is the right to *use* the software, not the right to *distribute* it. That right remains with the copyright holder. Similarly, copying material from websites without permission is a violation of copyright laws. Protecting intellectual property rights in e-commerce is extremely difficult, however, because it involves hundreds of millions of people in 200 countries with differing copyright laws who have access to billions of Web pages.

Before you go on...

1. List and explain some ethical issues in EC.
2. Discuss the major legal issues associated with EC.
3. Describe buyer protection and seller protection in EC.

What's in IT for Me?

ACCT For the Accounting Major

Accounting personnel are involved in several EC activities. Designing the ordering system and its relationship with inventory management requires accounting attention. Billing and payments are also accounting activities, as are determining cost and profit allocation. Replacing paper documents with electronic ones will affect many of the accountant's tasks, especially the auditing of EC activities and systems. Finally, building a cost-benefit and cost-justification system to determine which products and services to take online and creating a chargeback system are critical to the success of EC.

FIN For the Finance Major

The worlds of banking, securities and commodities markets, and other financial services are being reengineered because of EC. Online securities trading and its supporting infrastructure are growing more rapidly than any other EC activity. Many innovations already in place are changing the rules of economic and financial incentives for financial analysts and managers. Online banking, for example, does not recognize national boundaries, and it may create a new framework for financing global trades. Public financial information is now accessible in seconds. These innovations will dramatically transform the manner in which finance personnel operate.

MKT For the Marketing Major

EC has brought about a major revolution in marketing and sales. Perhaps its most obvious feature is the transition from a physical to a virtual marketplace. Equally important, however, is the radical transformation to one-on-one advertising and sales and to customized and interactive marketing. Marketing channels are being combined, eliminated, or recreated. The EC revolution is creating new products and markets while significantly altering existing ones. Digitization of products and services also has implications for marketing and sales. The direct producer-to-consumer channel is expanding rapidly and is fundamentally redefining the nature of customer service. As the battle for customers intensifies, marketing and sales personnel are becoming the most critical success factor in many organizations. Online marketing can be a blessing to one company and a curse to another.

POM For the Production/Operations Management Major

EC is transforming the manufacturing system from product-push mass production to order-pull mass customization. This transformation requires a robust supply chain, information support, and reengineering of processes that involve suppliers and other business partners. Suppliers can use extranets to monitor and replenish inventories without having to constantly reorder. The Internet and intranets also help reduce cycle times. Many production/operations problems that have persisted for years, such as complex scheduling and excess inventories, are being solved rapidly with the use of Web technologies. Companies can now use external and internal networks to find and manage manufacturing operations in other countries much more easily. Also, the Web is reengineering procurement by helping companies conduct electronic bids for parts and subassemblies, thus reducing costs. All in all, the job of the progressive production/operations manager is closely tied in with e-commerce.

HRM For the Human Resource Management Major

HR majors need to understand the new labor markets and the impacts of EC on old labor markets. Also, the HR department can use EC tools for such functions as procuring office supplies. Moreover, becoming knowledgeable about new government online initiatives and online training is critical. HR personnel must also become familiar with the major legal issues related to EC and employment.

For the MIS Major

The MIS function is responsible for providing the information technology infrastructure necessary for electronic commerce to function. This infrastructure includes the company's networks, intranets, and extranets. The MIS function is also responsible for ensuring that e-commerce transactions are secure.

Summary

7.1   Describe the eight common types of electronic commerce.

In *business-to-consumer (B2C)* electronic commerce, the sellers are organizations and the buyers are individuals.

In *business-to-business (B2B)* electronic commerce, the sellers and the buyers are businesses.

In *consumer-to-consumer (C2C)* electronic commerce, an individual sells products or services to other individuals.

In *business-to-employee (B2E)* electronic commerce, an organization uses EC internally to provide information and services to its employees.

E-government is the use of Internet technology in general and e-commerce in particular to deliver information and public services to citizens (called government-to-citizen or G2C EC) and business partners and suppliers (called government-to-business or G2B EC).

Mobile commerce refers to e-commerce that is conducted entirely in a wireless environment.

Social commerce refers to the delivery of electronic commerce activities and transactions through social computing.

Conversational commerce refers to electronic commerce using messaging and chat apps to offer a daily choice, often personalized, of a meal, product, or service.

We leave the examples of each type to you.

7.2 Describe the various online services of business-to-consumer (B2C) commerce, along with specific examples of each.

Fintech is an industry composed of companies that use technology to compete in the marketplace with traditional financial institutions and intermediaries in the delivery of financial services, which include banking, insurance, real estate, and investing.

Online securities trading involves buying and selling securities over the Web.

Online job matching over the Web offers a promising environment for job seekers and for companies searching for hard-to-find employees. Thousands of companies and government agencies advertise available positions, accept résumés, and take applications on the Internet.

Online travel services allow you to purchase airline tickets, reserve hotel rooms, and rent cars. Most sites also offer a fare-tracker feature that sends you e-mail messages about low-cost flights. The Internet is an ideal place to economically plan, explore, and arrange almost any trip.

Online advertising over the Web makes the advertising process media-rich, dynamic, and interactive.

We leave the examples to you.

7.3 Describe the three business models for business-to-business electronic commerce.

In the *sell-side marketplace* model, organizations attempt to sell their products or services to other organizations electronically from their own private e-marketplace website or from a third-party website. Sellers such as Dell Computer (**www.dellrefurbished.com**) use sell-side auctions extensively. In addition to auctions from their own websites, organizations can use third-party auction sites, such as eBay, to liquidate items.

The *buy-side marketplace* is a model in which organizations attempt to buy needed products or services from other organizations electronically.

E-marketplaces, in which there are many sellers and many buyers, are called *public exchanges*, or just exchanges. Public exchanges are open to all business organizations. They are frequently owned and operated by a third party. There are three basic types of public exchanges: vertical, horizontal, and functional. *Vertical exchanges* connect buyers and sellers in a given industry. *Horizontal exchanges* connect buyers and sellers across many industries.

In *functional exchanges*, needed services such as temporary help or extra office space are traded on an as-needed basis.

7.4 Discuss the ethical and legal issues related to electronic commerce, along with examples.

E-business presents some threats to privacy. First, most electronic payment systems know who the buyers are. It may be necessary, then, to protect the buyers' identities with encryption. Another major privacy issue is tracking, through which individuals' activities on the Internet can be tracked by cookies.

The use of EC may eliminate the need for some of a company's employees, as well as brokers and agents. The manner in which these unneeded workers, especially employees, are treated can raise ethical issues. How should the company handle the layoffs? Should companies be required to retrain employees for new positions? If not, how should the company compensate or otherwise assist the displaced workers?

We leave the examples up to you.

Key Terms

auction   204
brick-and-mortar organizations   200
business model   203
buy-side marketplace   219
channel conflict   214
chatbots   203
clicks-and-mortar organizations   200
disintermediation   208
electronic business (e-business)   199

electronic commerce (EC or
   e-commerce)   3
electronic mall   208
electronic marketplace   204
electronic payment mechanisms   204
electronic retailing (e-tailing)   208
electronic storefront   208
e-procurement   219
exchanges   219

Fintech   209
forward auctions   204
group purchasing   219
multichanneling   215
public exchanges (or exchanges)   219
reverse auctions   204
sell-side marketplace   218
spamming   214
virtual (or pure play) organizations   200

Discussion Questions

1. Discuss the major limitations of e-commerce. Which of these limitations are likely to disappear? Why?

2. Discuss the reasons for having multiple EC business models.

3. Distinguish between business-to-business forward auctions and buyers' bids for RFQs.

4. Discuss the benefits to sellers and buyers of a B2B exchange.

5. What are the major benefits of G2C electronic commerce?

6. Discuss the various ways to pay online in B2C. Which method(s) would you prefer and why?

7. Why is order fulfillment in B2C considered difficult?

8. Discuss the reasons for EC failures.

9. Should Mr. Coffee sell coffeemakers online? *Hint*: Take a look at the discussion of channel conflict in this chapter.

10. In some cases, individuals engage in cybersquatting so that they can sell the domain names to companies expensively. In other cases, companies engage in cybersquatting by registering domain names that are very similar to their competitors' domain names in order to generate traffic from people who misspell Web addresses. Discuss each practice in regard to its ethical nature and legality. Is there a difference between the two practices? Support your answer.

11. Do you think information technology has made it easier to do business? Or has it only raised the bar on what is required to be able to do business in the twenty-first century? Support your answer with specific examples.

12. With the rise of electronic commerce, what do you think will happen to those without computer skills, Internet access, computers, smartphones, and so on? Will they be able to survive and advance by hard work?

Problem-Solving Activities

1. Assume you are interested in buying a car. You can find information about cars at numerous websites. Access five websites for information about new and used cars, financing, and insurance. Decide which car you want to buy. Configure your car by going to the car manufacturer's website. Finally, try to find the car from www.autobytel.com. What information is most supportive of your decision-making process? Write a report about your experience.

2. Compare the various electronic payment methods. Specifically, collect information from the vendors cited in this chapter and find additional vendors using Google. Pay attention to security level, speed, cost, and convenience.

3. Conduct a study on selling diamonds and gems online. Access such sites as www.bluenile.com, www.jtv.com, www.tiffany.com, and www.jewleryexchange.com.

   a. What features do these sites use to educate buyers about gemstones?

   b. How do these sites attract buyers?

   c. How do these sites increase customers' trust in online purchasing?

   d. What customer service features do these sites provide?

4. Access www.nacha.org. What is NACHA? What is its role? What is the ACH? Who are the key participants in an ACH e-payment? Describe the "pilot" projects currently under way at ACH.

5. Access www.espn.com. Identify at least five different ways the site generates revenue.

6. Access www.queendom.com. Examine its offerings and try some of them. What type of electronic commerce is this? How does this website generate revenue?

7. Access www.ediets.com. Prepare a list of all the services the company provides. Identify its revenue model.

8. Access www.theknot.com. Identify the site's revenue sources.

9. Access www.mint.com. Identify the site's revenue model. What are the risks of giving this website your credit and debit card numbers, as well as your bank account number?

10. Enter www.alibaba.com. Identify the site's capabilities. Look at the site's private trading room. Write a report. How can such a site help a person who is making a purchase?

11. Enter www.grubhub.com. Explore the site. Why is the site so successful? How does it compare to doordash? Which is better?

12. Enter www.dell.com, go to "Desktops," and configure a system. Register to "My Cart" (no obligation). What calculators are used there? What are the advantages of this process as compared with buying a computer in a physical store? What are the disadvantages?

13. Enter www.chime.com and www.ally.com to identify their services. Prepare a report.

14. Access various travel sites such as www.travelocity.com, www.orbitz.com, www.expedia.com, and www.kayak.com. Compare these websites for ease of use and usefulness. Note differences among the sites. If you ask each site for the itinerary, which one gives you the best information and the best deals?

15. Visit ULTA Beauty at www.ulta.com. Describe their makeup try on tools. Do you think this is an effective tool for making purchasing decisions? Why or why not?

16. Read The Future Of E-Commerce: Trends To Watch In 2023 at www.forbes.com. Pick one trend and describe how a business you know is using that trend.

Closing Case

MIS **FIN** **MKT** **Direct Electric Vehicle (EV) Sales via E-Commerce**

Amazon taught us that many of the sales channels to which we were accustomed were unnecessary. Removing the middleman—that is, the local store—was possible for thousands of products. And, customers still made an educated purchase. Online merchants could reach customers far separated from them geographically while lowering costs and increasing profits. It is interesting that a similar development occurred around the turn of the 19th century when Sears & Roebuck introduced their mail-order catalog system. Suddenly, customers had access to thousands of products within a few weeks.

It is significant that the cover of the Fall 1900 Sears & Roebuck catalog contained the following quote: "This book tells just what your storekeeper at home pays for everything he buys ~ and will prevent him from overcharging you on anything you buy from him." Apparently, the company believed they could increase their profits while decreasing costs to the consumer.

A similar scenario is emerging today in the automotive industry. Electric vehicle (EV) manufacturers want to sell directly to consumers to reduce costs, perhaps as much as $2,000 per vehicle. Still, several factors are hindering this move to e-commerce for the entire industry. Perhaps the major factor is opposition from the middlemen—in this case, local dealerships.

It isn't that the industry hasn't embraced e-commerce. Customers regularly shop online for new and used vehicles, schedule appointments with sales and service personnel, and order parts. Companies like Carvana and Vroom even allow customers to order used vehicles online and have them shipped directly to their address. However, auto manufacturers cannot utilize e-commerce to sell directly to consumers. Most state laws require manufacturers to sell to dealerships who then sell to the customer. Most EV companies want to fully embrace e-commerce and bypass the dealer to work directly with the customer.

Let's examine this issue from the following perspectives:

1. Understanding the industry's history will provide the context for current laws and regulations that hinder the shift to e-commerce.

2. Examining examples will help determine if direct, manufacturer-to-consumer purchases are possible and, if so, are preferred.

3. Presenting some concluding thoughts will explore the future of e-commerce in the EV industry.

Industry History and Politics

Early in the automotive era, three manufacturers—General Motors, Ford, and Chrysler—were so dominant that their market control allowed them to impose unfair conditions. These companies had allowed independent dealers to carry their vehicles, while they simultaneously developed corporate-owned dealerships, which enabled them to sell directly to customers. These corporate-owned dealerships could beat the independent dealers on price because sales were direct, effectively making more money for the manufacturer.

In response, car dealerships urged state lawmakers to pass laws preventing the manufacturers from creating corporate-owned dealership networks that would control the market. Lawmakers passed laws to protect the dealerships by making direct sales illegal. Although these measures protected the dealerships, they did not benefit the customers, who would have benefited from the lower prices. It is significant that many of these laws are still in effect. Unlike nearly every other consumer good, you can't visit an auto manufacturer's website, customize a car, and have it delivered. Instead, a dealership is legally required to act as a middleman.

For many years, dealerships were a kind of local monopoly. You went to your one local Ford dealer if you wanted a Ford truck. Dealerships became influential in their communities by sponsoring everything from local baseball teams to fundraisers and, of course, by donating to local and statewide politicians. It is no surprise that they utilized this influence to lobby against attempts to change the legal protection they enjoyed. For example, Ford attempted to establish a retail network in the late 1990s, but they abandoned the effort after running into strong resistance from independent dealerships. Ultimately, the independent dealerships

won and direct, manufacturer-to-consumer auto sales have been illegal for many years.

Today, start-up vehicle manufacturers—primarily EV manufacturers like Tesla and Rivian—are lobbying states to repeal these laws. For example, consider the case of Georgia, which is home to a $5 billion Rivian plant. In 2022, a bill to allow EV manufacturers to sell directly to consumers never made it out of committee. Opponents argued that the economic benefits these companies would obtain will not stay in the states that generate the sales, as they do with franchised dealers. The Automobile Dealers Association of Georgia (gada.com) stated: "Ultimately, direct sales by manufacturers will mean dealerships closing and a loss of jobs for hard-working Georgians." Advocates for the bill responded that consumer choice and free-market values should take priority over the interests of dealerships and state tax dollars. Despite their efforts, however, Georgia consumers still cannot purchase a Rivian directly.

In a similar scenario, the United Service Workers Union (USWU) and United Auto Workers (UAW), who represent automotive workers, urged state lawmakers in New York to reject a 2022 proposal to allow manufacturers to sell EVs direct-to-consumer. They also cited concerns that this bill would undercut a traditional business model that benefited manufacturers, dealers, and workers.

Selling Directly to the Consumer

Consumers are the ones who seem to lose. EV manufacturers do not sell the volume of vehicles like traditional gas- or diesel-powered vehicles. Customers have to drive to pick up their vehicle or pay shipping from the states that allow the sale (some states allow sales if the manufacturer has a physical presence in the state).

Despite the challenges, Rivian sells most of its vehicles online from five company-owned stores that serve as showrooms and warranty service locations. The company processes its online transactions in Illinois, the site of its first factory, and ships vehicles directly to the buyer.

Tesla sells its EVs directly to consumers through their website or through their network of showrooms. The purchase is still direct with the manufacturer, but the experience can include a local facility.

Despite the history, politics, and changing business models required to make direct EV sales a reality, change is happening. Consumers are voting with their wallets in spite of the additional cost associated with picking up or having their vehicle delivered. In 2020, 80 percent of electric vehicles were sold through direct sales.

As the market moves forward, more consumers may become comfortable with buying a vehicle sight unseen. Still, a majority will always want the chance to sit in a vehicle and test drive it before making a major purchasing decision.

The Future

Independent auto dealers have been a fixture of American life since the early 20th century. They did the complex and expensive work of finding customers, advertising in specific markets, and servicing customers. When you work hard to establish a system, you are wary of introducing fundamental changes to that system.

When your business methods work, even your competitors will copy you. For example, General Motors is expanding in China, following Tesla's playbook. Rather than negotiate with the

Chinese government for dealership protection, the company plans to launch a direct-sales platform named Durant Guild.

General Motors plans for Durant Guild to operate just as Tesla does. It will sell directly to buyers but through showroom events. Durant Guild's purpose is not necessarily to sell large volumes of vehicles. Rather, it is intended to generate interest in GM's cars.

What does the future hold for the automotive market? One thing seems inevitable. Whether they are purchased online and received as a delivery, partially online and picked up at a dealer, or across a state line, it seems that direct-sales of EVs are the future.

Questions

1. Analysts believe that manufacturers selling directly to consumers could lower overall costs by $2,000 per vehicle. In your opinion, do these savings justify such a dramatic shift in the industry?

2. List and explain the factors that have protected dealerships for so many years.

3. What reasons do the dealerships and unions give for opposing the direct sales of EVs through e-commerce? Are these reasons valid? Support your answer.

4. Can you think of an omnichannel approach to EV sales that would make use of the brick-and-mortar dealerships?

Sources: D. Mihalascu, "Three-Quarters Of EV Shoppers Prefer to Buy at Dealerships: Survey," InsideEVs.com, September 27, 2022; J. Zurschmeide, "Buying an EV May Be New, but Customers Cling to Tradition," *The Detroit Bureau*, September 26, 2022; D. Kenny, "Banning of Direct Electric Vehicle Sales Only Helps Car Dealers," *Real Clear Markets*, September 23, 2022; J. Lancaster, "Ford's EV Charger Mandate Shows How Broken Dealership Laws Are," Reason.com, September 20, 2022; S. McLain, "The Man from Rivian Who Wants to Change How We Buy Cars," *Wall Street Journal*, September 17, 2022; S. Loveday, "GM to Launch Tesla-Style Direct Sales Model In China," InsideEVs.com, September 9, 2022; R. Walker, "GM Copies Tesla; To Set Up Direct-To-Consumer Sales Channel in China," *Drive Tesla Canada,* September 8, 2022; L. Lowery, "State Support Not Unanimous as EV OEM Sales & Repair Sites Expand," *Repairer Driven News*, June 22, 2022; F. Lambert, "Tesla Is Aiming to Improve Service and Make Majority of Appointments Same-Day Repairs," June 6, 2022;N. Reisman, "UAW Workers: Reject Expansion of Direct Sales for Electric Vehicle Makers," *Spectrum News 1*, May 11, 2022; T. Spigolon, "Legislation for Direct Sales of EVs Faces Rough Road in General Assembly," *Covington News*, March 23, 2022; J. Crider, "Georgia Tells Rivian: You Can't Sell Electric Trucks Here," CleanTechnica.com, March 21, 2022; P. Stenquist, "Why You Might Buy Your Next Car Online," *New York Times*, June 21, 2022; https://www.history.com/news/sears-catalog-houses-hubcaps, accessed September 29, 2022; and https://www.mackinac.org/archives/2021/The%20Case%20for%20Direct%20Sales%20–%20March%202021%20Update.pdf, accessed September 29, 2022.

CHAPTER 8

Wireless, Mobile Computing, and Mobile Commerce

CHAPTER OUTLINE	LEARNING OBJECTIVES
8.1 Wireless Technologies	**8.1 Identify** the advantages and disadvantages of each of the four main types of wireless transmission media.
8.2 Wireless Computer Networks and Internet Access	**8.2 Explain** how businesses can use short-range, medium-range, and long-range wireless networks.
8.3 Mobile Computing and Mobile Commerce	**8.3 Provide** a specific example of how each of the five major m-commerce applications can benefit a business.
8.4 The Internet of Things	**8.4 Describe** the Internet of Things, and provide examples of how organizations can use the Internet of Things.

Opening Case

MIS Putting Satellites to Work

Education in Remote Areas

Sotomo is a small village in remote southern Chile that can be accessed only by boat. Only twenty families live there, and they survive by catching mussels and fish to sell at market, a five-hour round trip by boat. SpaceX (www.spacex.com) —a company that designs and manufactures spacecraft and rockets—selected Sotomo as one of two locations in Chile to conduct a pilot project to receive free Internet access for a year. The other location is Caleta Sierra, a small fishing village close to Chile's northern deserts.

Diego is a seven-year-old living in Sotomo whose father takes him to school by boat. Using tablets provided by the education ministry, the school's seven pupils can now access online learning materials, watch films, make virtual museum visits, and make video calls to children in other schools as a result of the SpaceX project. Their only teacher at Sotomo's John F. Kennedy School uses the Internet for professional development.

The teacher and his students receive signals via a satellite dish installed on the school's roof that transmits via a Wi-Fi device to most of the school's facilities and its outdoor patio. Ultimately, the plan is to extend Internet access to the rest of the hamlet. Internet access in the village is available only from noon to midnight because Sotomo has only a limited supply of diesel to run the generator that supplies power to the village. Internet access via SpaceX is a significant advance over the patchy Internet signal that residents previously received on their phones by leaning out of windows or paddling out into the bay.

Diego loves to go out on his father's fishing boat. His father, however, has more ambitious plans for Diego, and he hopes that the new Internet connection will broaden his son's horizons.

Early Warning for Natural Disasters

In July 2020, a massive landslide struck Hunan province in southern China. Twelve days before the landslide, the village received an orange alert citing data anomalies that pointed to accelerating surface sliding following days of heavy rain. All 33 inhabitants in one village were evacuated in time, thanks to early warnings by advanced positioning technologies that provide more accurate readings than were previously possible.

These positioning technologies are powered by China's Bei-Dou GPS system and its ground-based stations. The satellites' position sensors can detect subtle changes of a few meters in real time in the land's surface in landslide-prone regions across the country.

More Accurate Hurricane Predictions

A major challenge in dealing with hurricanes involves predicting the track the storm will take, how intense the storm will be, and where it will make landfall. Although geostationary satellites have some value, their effectiveness ends at cloud tops because the satellites provide only visible and infrared images that cannot pierce cloud cover.

Scientists need to collect data about the interior of a storm, its motion, temperature, and moisture content. To obtain these data, they plan to use the TROPICS (Time-Resolved Observations of Precipitation structure and storm Intensity with a Constellation of Smallsats) system (www.tropics.ll.mit.edu), a nanosatellite project that will ultimately consist of seven polar-orbiting satellites that will monitor the Earth's tropical zones where hurricanes form.

Polar satellites have 500-mile-high orbits, much lower than geostationary satellites, which orbit at 22,300 miles. These lower orbits enable polar satellites to gather data that enable scientists to monitor what is happening within a storm.

The TROPICS satellite constellation will provide a detailed look into a storm every 30 to 40 minutes. The data these satellites gather are transmitted to the National Weather Service and the National Hurricane Center as input into weather-prediction models.

A virtual pretest of the TROPICS system demonstrated that a forecast of a hurricane's track improved by 15 percent. The pretest also revealed a consistent improvement in temperature and wind forecasts up to five days before landfall as well as more accurate humidity forecasts up to 36 hours before landfall.

Limiting Deforestation

Proponents of satellite imagery and machine learning want to solve major problems. One of the most important of these problems is deforestation, an activity that impacts the entire Earth.

However, stopping deforestation begins with identifying the problem from space. Although a Brazilian government program helped reduce deforestation by 80 percent from 2004 to 2012, when Jair Bolsonaro was elected president in 2019, he weakened enforcement and encouraged opening the rainforest to industry and cattle ranching. As a result, deforestation in the Amazon reached the highest levels seen in more than a decade.

The Brazil-based nonprofit Imazon (www.imazon.org.br) protects the Amazon rainforest using satellite imagery. In the early 2000s, Imazon scientists understood that 90 percent of deforestation occurs within three miles of newly created roads. Although satellites have long been able to track road expansion, Imazon scientists initially had to label satellite images by hand, creating what eventually became training data. When researchers fed that training data into a machine learning system, it revealed 13 times more roads than previously identified.

Imazon has signed cooperation agreements with public prosecutors who are gathering evidence of environmental crimes in four Brazilian states that border the Amazon rainforest. Their objective is to share information that can help prioritize enforcement resources. Imazon and the prosecutors are aware that when they prosecute people who have deforested protected lands, the damage has already been done. Therefore, Imazon wants to use machine learning to stop deforestation before it happens by integrating road-detection models with models designed to predict which communities bordering the rainforest are at the highest risk of deforestation within the next year.

Monitoring Illegal Fishing

Spire Global (www.spire.com), which operates a low-earth-orbit constellation of 140 small satellites, specializes in tracking maritime, aviation, and weather patterns. Its satellites are designed to pick up radio signals sent out by boats around the world. The primary use of these signals is to prevent vessels from crashing into one another. However, listening for these signals is also a useful strategy to track illegal maritime activity.

Spire notes that boats move in a distinct way when they are fishing. The company can predict what kind of fishing equipment boats are using by their speed, direction, and the way they turn. Of the 60,000 vessels that emit such signals, Spire asserts that 5,000 have been found conducting illegal activities, including fishing at restricted times or offloading hauls of protected fish to other vessels to avoid checks at ports.

In 2020, Japanese authorities found that fishing boats kept washing up on their shores with dead North Koreans onboard. They could not explain the appearance of these ships.

Using Spire satellites, a nonprofit organization called Global Fishing Watch (www.globalfishingwatch.org) discovered that China was fishing illegally in North Korean waters. Competition from modern, larger Chinese fishing trawlers forced smaller North Korean wooden boats to sail north to fish in Russian waters. The North Korean boats were severely underequipped for the long-distance travel necessary to reach the Russian fishing grounds. As a result, more than 500 of these boats washed ashore on Japanese coasts. These incidents frequently involved starvation and deaths of the North Koreans on board. When China was presented the evidence, it halted its illegal fishing activities.

Monitoring Illegal Logging and Poaching

Rainforest Connection (www.rfcx.org), based in Texas, uses Swarm Technologies (www.swarm.space; acquired by SpaceX in August 2021) satellites to track illegal logging and poaching in more than 30 countries. In areas where loggers or poachers might operate, Rainforest Connection places solar-powered acoustic (sound) sensors called Guardians high in treetops. These sensors are designed to blend in with the tree from the ground. The Guardians contain software that can detect the sounds of illegal activities, such as chainsaws and gunshots, up to a mile away. When they detect these activities, they send a signal to one of Swarm's satellites, which in turn relays the information back to a ground station. Rainforest Connection then alerts law enforcement to the suspected illegal activity.

Prior to working with Swarm, Rainforest Connection relied on cellular networks to transmit data. Although this arrangement was quicker, the networks could monitor only regions that were close to populated areas. Swarm has doubled Rainforest Connection's detection capabilities.

Monitoring Russian Destruction of Ukrainian Archaeological Sites

Scientists at University College of London's Institute of Archaeology use imagery from a Planet Labs (www.planet.com) constellation to track Russia's shelling of archaeological sites in Ukraine. Planet's satellites provide images of the entire Earth every day. This imagery has enabled the scientists, working with the Global Heritage Fund, to identify more than 165 sites that have been damaged or destroyed by Russian artillery. Scientists catalog these sites in hopes that some of them can be at least partially restored after the conflict ends.

Questions

1. **What are the advantages of employing low-earth-orbit satellites for so many uses?**

2. **What are the disadvantages of employing low-earth-orbit satellites for so many uses?**

3. **Describe additional uses of low-earth-orbit satellites for "social good."**

Sources: Compiled from J. O'Callaghan, "Swarms of Satellites Are Tracking Illegal Fishing and Logging," *Wired*, August 30, 2022; "Global Heritage Fund Leveraging Planet SkySat to Protect the Cultural Fabric of Ukraine," *planet.com*, August 18, 2022; K. Johnson, "Satellites and AI Can Help Solve Big Problems – If Given the Chance," *Wired*, June 5, 2022; J. Spring, "Brazil's Amazon Deforestation Sets First-Quarter Record despite March Dip," *Reuters*, April 8, 2022; N. Patel, "Who Is Starlink Really For?" *MIT Technology Review*, September 6, 2021; J. McDonald, "How Sandwich-Sized Satellites Are Helping Transmit Data from Remote Locations," *Emerging Technologies Morning Brew*, August 25, 2021; P. Sanhueza,

"Elon Musk's Satellites Beam Internet into Remote Chilean Fishing Hamlet," *Reuters*, August 19, 2021; M. Herbst, "Tiny Satellites Could Help Warn of the Next Big Hurricane," *Wired*, June 25, 2021; L. Xin, "Hyper-Accurate Positioning Is Rolling Out Worldwide," *MIT Technology Review*, February 24, 2021; J. Park et al., "Illuminating Dark Fishing Fleets in North Korea," *Science Advances*, July 22, 2020; M. Sandy, "'The Amazon Is Completely Lawless': The Rainforest after Bolsonaro's First Year," *The New York Times*, December 5, 2019; and I. Demir and R. Raskar, "Addressing the Invisible: Street Address Generation for Developing Countries with Deep Learning," *arxiv.org*, November 10, 2018.

Introduction

The traditional working environment that required users to sit at a wired computer is ineffective and inefficient. Today, workers have access to computers that are small enough to carry or wear and that can communicate through wireless networks; that is, your computing device now comes with you. Wireless computing is convenient and enables you to be more productive.

Wireless computing is critical to the success of both individuals and organizations. However, in some parts of the world, broadband wireless connections are intermittent, have poor quality (low bandwidth), and are expensive. IT's About Business 8.1 illustrates how citizens of Zimbabwe obtain wireless Internet access and citizens of South Africa use wireless to acquire information about riots and unrest.

IT's About Business **8.1**

MIS Wireless Internet Access in Africa

Zimbabwe

At the end of 2020, Econet (www.econet.co.zw) and NetOne (www.netone.co.zw) had a combined 94.5 percent market share for providing Internet access to the African nation of Zimbabwe. Analysts contend that the lack of competition, combined with the high costs of operating a telecommunications business in the country—due to import tariffs on communications equipment, foreign currency risk, and weak electricity infrastructure—has kept prices high for consumers. According to the Alliance for Affordable Internet (AAI; www.a4ai.org), an Internet-access advocacy nonprofit, Zimbabwe is one of the most expensive places in Africa to access mobile Internet, relative to people's income.

On Econet, the country's largest telecommunications carrier, 1.4 gigabytes of data retails for 2,000 Zimbabwean dollars ($15), which is more than twice AAI's benchmark of 2 percent of average monthly income. Further, outside big cities such as Harare and Bulawayo, signal strength is often weak. The high cost of Internet access has discouraged individuals and businesses from adopting digital services and prevented Zimbabweans from accessing educational materials and health services online.

Zimbabweans living near the border with Mozambique have discovered a solution. Traders cross the border on foot or on motorbikes and purchase SIM cards in bulk from Movitel (www.movitel.co.mz), Mozambique's largest mobile network. They then return to border towns such as Chimanimani, where they distribute the SIM cards to supermarkets and corner shops. There, stores sell the SIM cards with a markup of more than 50 percent.

Many people in these border towns rely on this black-market trade, where 2 gigabytes of data from Movitel can cost as little as 200 meticais ($3). They can access the Web at lower prices and faster speeds, thanks to Movitel wireless signals that extend across the border. Chimanimani's inexpensive foreign broadband access has enabled the town to avoid the fate of other rural districts in Zimbabwe and across Africa, where young workers, including those in vital roles, relocate to cities in search of better opportunities.

The availability of cheaper data and faster access has turned Chimanimani into a remote working hub for people who need to be online for work. For example, consider one environmentalist working for Environmental Buddies (www.ebztrust.org), a charity based in Harare that promotes sustainable forests and waste management across Zimbabwe. He uses Zoom, WhatsApp, and Skype from Movitel's broadband signals to conduct daily electronic meetings about his work in Chimanimani, a place where hurricanes often damage ecosystems. As another example, the founder of the nongovernment organization (NGO) Orphans Dreams, which provides free math lessons to orphaned children, has been able to stay in the region because cheap Internet access enables him to connect to free educational apps such as Khan Academy and Buzzmath that he can use in the classroom.

Some entrepreneurs have moved to Chimanimani to take advantage of the lower costs of online service. For example, a former nurse moved from Harare to set up a Chinese medicine business. She needs broadband Internet access to communicate via Zoom or WhatsApp with a medical doctor located in Harare before giving out prescribed dosages of herbs.

Similarly, a bookkeeper relocated from Harare in search of lower Internet costs and a more affordable small-town lifestyle. She receives plenty of business from townspeople who file their taxes electronically and from local entrepreneurs who need to prepare car imports for customs.

South Africa

Zello (www.zello.com) is a voice-first "walkie-talkie" app that is faster than typing and requires no literacy skills. Zello was originally designed to help people communicate and organize after natural disasters. Users subscribe to channels to talk to one another, using Wi-Fi to send live audio files that are accessible to anyone listening in on the channel. Users employ Zello to broadcast their location, share tips, and communicate with rescuers or survivors in the aftermath of a hurricane, flood, or other emergency. Taxi drivers, ambulance workers, and delivery personnel also use Zello when they want to send hands-free voice messages.

In South Africa, which lacks a formal emergency response system like 911 in the United States, people increasingly are using Zello to coordinate ad hoc ambulances and neighborhood patrols. One channel, South Africa Community Action Network, has 11,600 paying members who give donations for emergency services such as ambulances, along with more than 33,000 nonpaying members. Today, people in areas of unrest are using Zello to connect and communicate.

For example, in 2021, former South African president Jacob Zuma was sentenced to 15 months in prison for corruption during his presidency. Zuma had a loyal following but also many detractors. His arrest caused protests and widespread looting, particularly in his home city of Durban. The violence led to more than 200 deaths and 2,500 arrests.

For many South Africans, keeping track of what was happening was difficult. WhatsApp chats were flooded with confusing and often contradictory reports. As a result, 180,000 people turned to Zello to find reliable reports concerning the unrest. One user asserted that some people were using Zello to identify houses and storefronts that were ripe for looting, while others were tuning in to determine whether they should flee or stay where they were. Another user claimed that live communications over Zello enabled his family to know the whereabouts of looters and that Zello was much faster than the news channels on television and radio.

Questions

1. **What steps should the Zimbabwean government take to make Internet access more affordable in that country? Why would greater Internet access be so important to Zimbabwe?**

2. **All technologies are double-edged swords; that is, they can be used for good reasons or bad reasons. Other than the examples noted in this case, provide additional examples where Zello was used to actually help rioters.**

Sources: Compiled from P. Awesu, "The Rise of Internet Access in Africa," *The Circular*, April 26, 2022; N. Bhobo, "Black Market SIM Cards Turned a Zimbabwean Border Town into a Remote Work Hub," *Rest of World*, April 6, 2022; L. Monzon, "The Challenges in Getting Internet Access to All South Africans," *IT News Africa*, March 22, 2022; E. Roux, "Did Looters Use This App to Coordinate Actions and Find 'Weak Points'?," *The South African*, August 20, 2021; "Internet Access and Affordability in Zimbabwe," *zimbabwe.misa.org*, July 28, 2021; S. Smith, "The Reason behind the Riots in South Africa," *yr.media*, July 23, 2021; T. Basu, "How Zello Keeps People Connected during South Africa's Unrest," *MIT Technology Review*, July 20, 2021; U. Chioma, "Mobile Phone Users Turn to Black Market for SIM Cards," *The Nigeria Lawyer*, April 26, 2021; V. Muhamba, "Are We Any Closer to Universal Internet Access in Zimbabwe?" *techzim.co.zw*, June 9, 2020; and F. Mudzingwa, "Why Is Internet Access in Zimbabwe so Expensive?" *techzim.co.zw*, November 8, 2018.

The ability to communicate anytime and anywhere provides organizations with a strategic advantage by increasing productivity and speed and improving customer service. We use the term **wireless** to describe telecommunications in which electromagnetic waves, rather than some form of wire or cable, carry the signal between communicating devices such as computers, smartphones, and iPads.

wireless Telecommunications in which electromagnetic waves carry the signal between communicating devices.

Before you continue, it is important to distinguish between the terms *wireless* and *mobile*—they can mean different things. The term *wireless* means exactly what it says: without wires. In contrast, *mobile* refers to something that changes its location over time. Some wireless networks, such as MiFi (discussed later in this chapter), are also mobile. Others, however, are fixed. For example, microwave towers form *fixed wireless* networks.

Wireless technologies enable individuals and organizations to conduct mobile computing, mobile commerce, and the Internet of Things. We define these terms here, and then we discuss each one in detail later in the chapter.

Mobile computing refers to a real-time, wireless connection between a mobile device and other computing environments, such as the Internet or an intranet. *Mobile commerce*—also known as *m-commerce*—refers to e-commerce (EC) transactions (see Chapter 7) conducted with a mobile device. The *Internet of Things* means that virtually every object contains embedded sensors and has processing power with either wireless or wired connections to a global network.

Wireless technologies and mobile commerce are spreading rapidly, replacing or supplementing wired computing. Almost all (if not all) organizations use wireless computing. Therefore, when you begin your career, you will likely be assigned a company smartphone and a wirelessly enabled computer. Clearly, then, it is important for you to learn about wireless computing not only because you will be using wireless applications but also because wireless computing will be important to your organization. In your job, you will be involved with customers who conduct wireless transactions, with analyzing and developing mobile commerce applications, and with wireless security. And the list goes on.

Simply put, an understanding of wireless technology and mobile commerce applications will make you more valuable to your organization. When you look at "**What's in IT for Me?**" at the end of the chapter, envision yourself performing the activities discussed in your functional area. For those of you who are inclined to be entrepreneurs, an understanding of wireless technology can also help you start and grow your own business.

The wireless infrastructure upon which mobile computing is built is reshaping the entire IT field. The technologies, applications, and limitations of mobile computing and mobile commerce are the focus of this chapter. You begin the chapter by learning about wireless devices, wireless transmission media, and wireless security. You continue by examining wireless computer networks and wireless Internet access. You then look at mobile computing and mobile commerce, which are made possible by wireless technologies. Next, you turn your attention to the Internet of Things.

8.1   Wireless Technologies

LEARNING OBJECTIVE

Identify the advantages and disadvantages of each of the four main types of wireless transmission media.

WILEY PLUS

Author Lecture Videos are available exclusively in *WileyPLUS*. **Apply the Concept activities are available in the Appendix and in** *WileyPLUS*.

Wireless technologies include both wireless devices, such as smartphones, and wireless transmission media, such as microwave, satellite, and radio. These technologies are fundamentally changing the ways organizations operate.

Individuals are finding wireless devices convenient and productive to use, for several reasons. First, people can make productive use of time that was formerly wasted—for example, while commuting to work on public transportation. Second, because people can take these devices with them, their work locations are becoming much more flexible. Third, wireless technology enables people to schedule their working time around personal and professional obligations.

Wireless Devices

Wireless devices provide three major advantages to users:

1. They are small enough to easily carry or wear.
2. They have sufficient computing power to perform productive tasks.
3. They can communicate wirelessly with the Internet and other devices.

Modern smartphones exhibit a process called *dematerialization*. Essentially, dematerialization occurs when the functions of many physical devices are included in one other physical device. Consider that your smartphone includes the functions of digital cameras for images and video, radios, televisions, Internet access through Web browsers, recording studios, editing suites, movie theaters, GPS navigators, word processors, spreadsheets, stereos, flashlights, board games, card games, video games, an entire range of medical devices, maps, atlases, encyclopedias, dictionaries, translators, textbooks, watches, alarm clocks, books, calculators, address books, credit card swipers, magnifying glasses, money and credit cards, car keys, hotel keys, cellular telephony, Wi-Fi, e-mail access, text messaging, a full QWERTY keyboard, and many, many other things. **Figure 8.1** illustrates the process of dematerialization with smartphones.

Our smartphones have come a long, long way in a short period of time. Compare these smartphone capabilities (as of September 2022):

- Apple's first iPhone (2007) had a 3.5-inch screen, a 2-megapixel camera, 16 gigabytes of storage, and it did not support third-party apps.

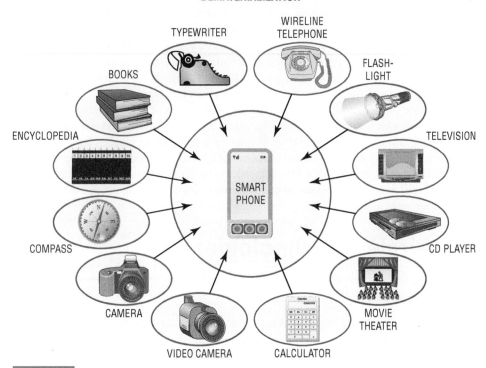

FIGURE 8.1 **Dematerialization with smartphones.**

- The Apple iPhone 14 Pro (2022) has a 6.1-inch screen, three 48-megapixel cameras (wide angle, ultra-wide angle, and telephoto), one 12-megapixel selfie camera, and up to 512 gigabytes of storage. It also provides biometrics for security and supports a vast array of apps.

One downside of smartphones is that people can use them to copy and pass on confidential information. For example, if you were an executive at Intel, would you want workers snapping pictures of their colleagues with your secret new technology in the background? After all, one of the functions of a smartphone is that of a digital camera that can transmit wirelessly. New jamming devices are being developed to counter the threat. Some companies, such as Samsung (www.samsung.com), have recognized the danger and have banned these devices from their premises altogether.

Another downside of smartphones is the increasing number of scam calls. According to First Orion (www.firstorion.com), a company that provides call management and protection for wireless carriers, approximately 45 percent of U.S. mobile traffic consisted of scam calls in the first half of 2022. Regardless of any disadvantages, however, cell phones, and particularly smartphones, have had a far greater impact on human society than most of us realize.

In July 2019, the Federal Communications Commission passed a provision that forces network operators to implement SHAKEN/STIR, the new industry standard for verifying the source of phone calls. As of September 2022, here is what the major wireless carriers were doing about spam calls.

- Verizon (www.verizon.com) offers free tools to its mobile and home customers. For mobile, Call Filter is a free app that screens and automatically blocks incoming spam calls based on risk level and allows customers to report spam.
- T-Mobile (www.t-mobile.com) offers Scam Shield to every customer, which provides free scam identification and blocking.
- AT&T (www.att.com) Call Protect is a free service that automatically provides screen alerts for spam calls and blocks them.

Despite the shortcomings of smartphones, they have the ability to literally change lives, particularly because they provide users with Internet access. IT's About Business 8.2 illustrates how smartphones are impacting women in India.

IT's About Business 8.2

MIS Indian Women Use Smartphones to Close the Gender Gap

Historically, the majority of India's smartphone users have been men. According to one analysis, in 2020 more than 40 percent of men but only 25 percent of women owned a smartphone. One report noted that millions of Indian women are prevented from owning a smartphone by their fathers and husbands.

Not having access to a smartphone has worsened an already deep gender gap for women in India. This gap blocks women from accessing increasingly important ways of communicating and learning, making it more difficult for them to find work, upgrade their skills, and assert their political rights. As a result, Indian women are less likely than men to be literate or employed in India's formal workforce. Further, because India has more than 30 official languages, it is difficult for many women to access the Internet using English keyboards.

Fortunately, three changes occurred in 2016 that significantly increased the number of Indian women who have access to smartphones. First, the Chinese manufacturer Xiaomi (www.mi.com) began to produce smartphones in India. In particular, they introduced entry-level models that cost less than $100. Second, the Indian telecommunications company Reliance Jio (www.jio.com) launched a new wireless service that offered free nationwide voice and data for the first year. About 100 million people subscribed to the network in its first six months. From 2016 to 2022, the average cost for accessing 1 gigabyte of data dropped from $3.10 to $.09. Third, WhatsApp enabled users to communicate using sounds and images.

These three changes have enabled increasing numbers of Indian women to access the Internet. They can access information, build networks, and participate in the economy.

Let's take a closer look at two Indian women: Diya and Meera. Diya is a member of a nomadic tribe in southern India. Like 200 million other women in India, she is illiterate and has never attended school. She can sign her name and understand where a bus is going or what a road sign says, but not much more. She never owned a full-feature smartphone because it was too expensive. And, even if she could have afforded one, she could not read or write well enough to use it.

As a result of the three changes just discussed, however, Diya finally could afford to purchase a smartphone and use it both visually and orally. This development changed Diya's life. Her access to the Internet was no longer blocked by written words. She now uses photographs and audio memos to communicate with friends and family, and she employs voice commands to search for videos. Before Diya purchased her phone, she had to travel by foot over mountains to the city of Madurai, where people she knew were her only contacts with the outside world.

Illegal logging is an ongoing problem in forests near Diya's home. So, Diya joined a WhatsApp group in which she creates videos and photographs of her local forest. She notes that sometimes teak and sandalwood trees "go missing." She takes pictures and compares them to older photographs to document the missing trees. She then shares the photos with rangers and forest officials. In the event of a confrontation with illegal loggers, her husband videotapes the situation to protect her. They then send the video, along with a voice message, to journalists.

Meera always wanted to have her own shop. Her family, however, would not allow her to have money of her own. Instead, she would earn money by sewing dresses in her village and give the money to her family.

Fortunately for Meera, Google and Tata Trusts (www.tatatrusts.org) have been working with local Indian organizations to make it easier for women to access the Internet. The two companies operate the Internet Saathi, or Internet Friend, program, which trains rural women to be digital pioneers. In particular, the women learn to use smartphones with voice commands in local languages. The program has trained more than 90,000 women to be Saathis. In turn, the Saathis have helped more than 35 million women to learn to use smartphones to access the Internet.

After Meera became a Saathi, she began to use YouTube to look up new fashion trends and to learn to stitch different designs. She searches for high-quality cloth in the market in a neighboring town to use to sew dresses that sell for a premium. In her village, Meera earned 200 rupees (about $3.00) per dress. In the market, her dresses sell for 450 to 750 rupees ($6 to $10) each.

During the COVID pandemic lockdown, Meera created a WhatsApp group of friends and acquaintances. She shared interesting fashion videos with the group and took preorders for dresses. She created a visual catalog and she built inventory in anticipation of a future increase in demand.

Wireless service in rural India can be intermittent. Diya often has to go to specific spots in the forest to use her phone, and Meera frequently must wait for videos to load. The Indian government is working to upgrade wireless networks, which will make it even easier for additional women (and men) to access the Internet.

Questions

1. We have discussed the difficulties that Indian women experience in obtaining smartphones. What difficulties might they encounter as they continue to use their phones?

2. Other than those discussed in this case, what advantages can Indian women realize from Internet access?

Sources: Compiled from "75 Years, 75% Literacy: India's Long Fight against Illiteracy," *The Times of India*, August 14, 2022; "Tribal Women Have a Significant Role in India's Transformation," *Hindustan Times*, August 9, 2022; S. Sun, "Share of Mobile Phone Owners in India in 2020, by Gender and Type," *Statista*, April 20, 2022; A. Malhotra, "5G Rollout in India in 2022: Things You Should Know," *The Mobile Indian*, December 28, 2021; N. Panda, "Upgrading Networks for the Next Era of Connectivity," *Fortune India*, July 8, 2021; R. Srivastava and A. Nagaraj, "Smartphones Give Rural Women in India a Lifeline," *BusinessDay*, June 22, 2021; Y. Sampathkumar, "In India, Smartphones and Cheap Data Are Giving Women a Voice," *Wired*, January 4, 2021; R. Agarwal, *India Connected: How the Smartphone Is Transforming the World's Largest Democracy*," Oxford University Press, 2018; "Women and Mobile in India: Realising the Opportunity," *gsma.com*, October 24, 2016; "The Smartphone Is Hurting India's Women," *PYMNTS*, October 13, 2016; and E. Bellman and A. Malhotra, "Why the Vast Majority of Women in India Will Never Own a Smartphone," *Wall Street Journal*, October 13, 2016.

TABLE 8.1   Advantages and Disadvantages of Wireless Media

Channel	Advantages	Disadvantages
Microwave	High bandwidth Relatively inexpensive	Must have unobstructed line of sight Susceptible to environmental interference
Satellite	High bandwidth Large coverage area	Expensive Must have unobstructed line of sight Signals experience propagation delay Must use encryption for security
Radio	High bandwidth Signals pass through walls Inexpensive and easy to install	Creates electrical interference problems Susceptible to snooping unless encrypted

Wireless Transmission Media

Wireless media, or broadcast media, transmit signals without wires. The major types of wireless media are microwave, satellite, and radio. Table 8.1 lists the advantages and disadvantages of each type.

microwave transmission A wireless system that uses microwaves for high-volume, long-distance, point-to-point communication.

Microwave   **Microwave transmission** systems transmit data through electromagnetic waves. These systems are used for high-volume, long-distance, line-of-sight communication. *Line-of-sight* means that the transmitter and receiver are in view of each other. This requirement creates problems because the Earth's surface is curved. For this reason, microwave towers usually cannot be spaced more than 30 miles apart.

Clearly, then, microwave transmissions offer only a limited solution to data communications needs, especially over very long distances. Microwave transmissions are also susceptible to environmental interference during severe weather such as heavy rain and snowstorms. Although long-distance microwave data communications systems are still widely used, they are being replaced by satellite communications systems.

TABLE 8.2   Three Basic Types of Telecommunications Satellites

Type	Characteristics	Orbit	Number	Use
GEO	Satellites stationary relative to point on Earth Few satellites needed for global coverage Transmission delay (approximately 0.25 second) Most expensive to build and launch Longest orbital life (many years)	22,300 miles	8	TV signal
MEO	Satellites move relative to point on Earth Moderate number needed for global coverage Requires medium-powered transmitters Negligible transmission delay Less expensive to build and launch Moderate orbital life (6 to 12 years)	6,434 miles	10 to 12	GPS
LEO	Satellites move rapidly relative to point on Earth Large number needed for global coverage Requires only low-power transmitters Negligible transmission delay Least expensive to build and launch Shortest orbital life (as low as 5 years)	400 to 700 miles	Many	Telephone

Satellite   **Satellite transmission** systems make use of communication satellites. Currently, there are three types of satellites circling Earth: geostationary-earth-orbit (GEO), medium-earth-orbit (MEO), and low-earth-orbit (LEO). Each type has a different orbit, with GEO being farthest from Earth and LEO being the closest. In this section, you examine the three types of satellites and then discuss three satellite applications: global positioning systems, Internet transmission through satellites, and commercial imaging. Table 8.2 compares and contrasts the three types of satellites.

As with microwave transmission, satellites must receive and transmit data through line of sight. However, the enormous *footprint*—the area of Earth's surface reached by a satellite's transmission—overcomes the limitations of microwave data relay stations. That is, satellites use *broadcast* transmission, which sends signals to many receivers at one time. So, even though satellites are line-of-sight, like microwave, they are high enough for broadcast transmission, thus overcoming the limitations of microwave.

The most basic rule governing footprint size is simple: the higher a satellite orbits, the larger its footprint. Thus, medium-earth-orbit satellites have a smaller footprint than geostationary satellites, and low-earth-orbit satellites have the smallest footprint of all. Figure 8.2 compares the footprints of the three types of satellites.

Types of Orbits   *Geostationary-earth-orbit satellites* orbit 22,300 miles directly above the equator. These satellites maintain a fixed position above Earth's surface because, at their altitude, their orbital period matches the 24-hour rotational period of Earth. For this reason, receivers on Earth do not have to track GEO satellites. GEO satellites are excellent for sending television programs to cable operators and for broadcasting directly to homes.

One major limitation of GEO satellites is that their transmissions take a quarter of a second to send and return. This brief pause, one kind of **propagation delay**, makes two-way telephone conversations difficult. Also, GEO satellites are large and expensive, and they require substantial amounts of power to launch.

Medium-earth-orbit satellites are located about 6,000 miles above Earth's surface. MEO orbits require more satellites to cover Earth than GEO orbits because MEO footprints are smaller. MEO satellites have two advantages over GEO satellites: they are less expensive and they do not have an appreciable propagation delay. However, because MEO satellites move with respect to a point on Earth's surface, receivers must track these satellites. (Think of a satellite dish slowly turning to remain oriented to a MEO satellite.)

Low-earth-orbit satellites are located 400 to 700 miles above Earth's surface. Because LEO satellites are much closer to Earth, they have little, if any, propagation delay. Like MEO satellites, however, LEO satellites move with respect to a point on Earth's surface and therefore must be tracked by receivers. Tracking LEO satellites is more difficult than tracking MEO satellites because LEO satellites move much more quickly relative to a point on Earth.

Unlike GEO and MEO satellites, LEO satellites can pick up signals from weak transmitters. This feature makes it possible for satellite telephones to operate through LEO satellites, because they can operate with less power using smaller batteries. Another advantage of LEO satellites is that they consume less power and cost less to launch.

At the same time, however, the footprints of LEO satellites are small, which means that many satellites are needed to cover the planet. For this reason, a single organization often produces multiple LEO satellites, known as *LEO constellations*. Many companies have deployed LEO constellations to provide global voice and data communications. Two of the oldest are Iridium (**www.iridium.com**) and Globalstar (**www.globalstar.com**).

Global Positioning Systems   The **global positioning system (GPS)** is a wireless system that uses satellites to enable users to determine their position anywhere on Earth. GPS is supported by MEO satellites that are shared worldwide. As of September 2022, the world had four international GPS systems: United States' GPS, Russia's *GLONASS,* China's BeiDou, and the European Union's *Galileo.* In addition, India's NAVIC (seven satellites) and Japan's QZSS (four satellites) are regional GPS systems.

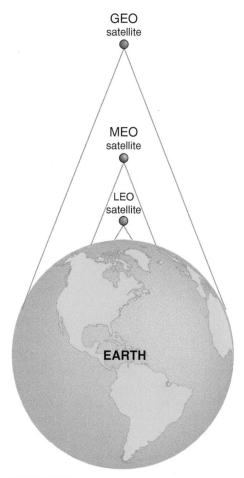

FIGURE 8.2   **Comparison of satellite footprints.**

satellite transmission   A wireless transmission system that uses satellites for broadcast communications.

propagation delay   Any delay in communications from signal transmission time through a physical medium.

global positioning system (GPS)   A wireless system that uses satellites to enable users to determine their position anywhere on Earth.

FIGURE 8.3 **Drivers can obtain GPS information from their automobile.**

AP Images/Jeffchiu

All GPS satellites have an extremely accurate clock. The exact position of each satellite is always known because the satellite continuously broadcasts its position along with a time signal. By using the known speed of the signals and the distance from three satellites (for two-dimensional location) or four satellites (for three-dimensional location), it is possible to find the location of any receiving station or user. GPS software can also convert the user's latitude and longitude to an electronic map.

Most of you are probably familiar with GPS in automobiles, which "talks" to drivers when giving directions. **Figure 8.3** illustrates a driver obtaining GPS information in a car.

Commercial use of GPS for activities such as navigating, mapping, and surveying has become widespread, particularly in remote areas. Cell phones in the United States now must have a GPS embedded in them so that the location of a person making an emergency call—for example, 911, known as *wireless 911*—can be detected immediately.

It is almost impossible to overstate how much the world's economy depends on the GPS system. There are some 7 billion GPS receivers in use around the world. In fact, a study by research firm RTI International (**www.rti.org**) estimated that the loss of GPS service globally would cost private sector organizations approximately $1 billion per day.

The telecommunications industry, banks, airlines, electric utilities, cloud computing businesses, television networks, emergency services, and the military require constantly precise GPS timing. In fact, the U.S. Department of Homeland Security has designed 16 sectors of infrastructure as critical, and 14 of them depend on GPS.

Prior to 2020, the GPS II system could provide locations that were accurate to within five to ten meters. The GPS III system will become fully operational in 2023 and will be three times more accurate than the GPS II system. As a result, GPS reception is accurate to one to three meters and more reliable, even indoors and in dense urban areas. Further, GPS III signals are eight times more resistant to jamming.

NASA is working on developing international compatibility and interoperability for GPS satellites. A United Nations committee is proposing a common set of definitions for GPS signals from the United States, Europe, Russia, China, Japan, and India. When finished, GPS receivers will be able to access all GPS satellites, which in turn will lead to positioning within inches.

Europe's Galileo satellite navigation system was out of service for one week beginning on July 11, 2019. The incident took down all of the system's timing and navigation features other than Search and Rescue, which helps people in remote areas.

Navigation systems that relied on Galileo could not function. However, these systems were able to seamlessly transition to the United States GPS system rather than taking flawed data and using it to calculate inaccurate positions and routes. The lengthy outage is a serious reminder of the modern world's reliance on GPS systems.

In September 2022, the eastern Mediterranean region, including Israel, was experiencing an increase in GPS jamming. The GPS interference was observed mostly along Turkey's southern coast, Syria, Lebanon, Cyprus, and Israel. In past occurrences, authorities thought that Russian military systems in Syria were the cause of the disruptions, but it is also possible that Israeli systems have contributed to the effect as well.

The jamming of the satellite-based GPS mostly affects passenger planes and not ground-based systems in vehicles. The European Organization for the Safety of Air Navigation said it is likely that the jamming comes from the use of anti-drone systems.

MIS **Internet over Satellite**   In many regions of the world, Internet over satellite (IoS) is the only option available for Internet connections because installing cables is either too expensive or physically impossible. IoS enables users to access the Internet from GEO satellites on a dish mounted on the side of their homes. Although IoS makes the Internet available to many people who otherwise could not access it, it has its drawbacks. Not only do GEO satellite transmissions involve a propagation delay, but they can also be disrupted by environmental influences such as thunderstorms. Many companies are entering this market.

- OneWeb (**www.oneweb.world**) has deployed a LEO constellation to bring Internet access to all corners of the globe. The firm is targeting rural markets, emerging markets, and in-flight Internet services on airlines. As of September 2022, OneWeb was approaching its goal of a 648-satellite LEO constellation.

- SpaceX's (www.spacex.com) LEO constellation, Starlink, provides long-distance Internet traffic for people in sparsely populated areas. As of September 2022, SpaceX had launched just over 2,000 satellites. The company is planning for 12,000 satellites in total.
- Project Kuiper is Amazon's LEO constellation and is planned to consist of 3,236 satellites. On April 5, 2022, Amazon announced a set of launch contracts with three launch providers over the next decade. As of September 2022, Project Kuiper had not launched any satellites.

Commercial Imaging   Another satellite application is commercial images from orbit, using very small satellites, called *nanosatellites*. Several companies are involved in launching nanosatellites for scientific and commercial purposes. Let's look at some of these companies here.

- Planet Labs (Planet; www.planet.com) takes pictures of the Earth more frequently than traditional satellites and at a small fraction of the cost. The company's LEO constellation, called Dove, helps entire industries obtain images anywhere on the earth. Planet can also capture video that can be used to develop three-dimensional models of any area that is imaged.

    Planet is able to image every location on the entire planet every day. Planet has deployed a platform, Queryable Earth, that customers can use to track, planes, ships, roads, buildings, and forests worldwide.

    A farm software business in the agriculture division of DowDuPont (www.dupont.com), called Corteva (www.corteva.com), uses Planet's satellites to access daily images of the Earth, as well as some of Planet's archive of images. Granular analyzes the images to provide information to farmers. For example, farmers use Granular's analyses to develop crop and field plans, delegate duties to employees, track inventory, and predict yield and revenue.

- **FIN** The World Bank (www.worldbank.org) monitors high-risk urban development by integrating satellite imaging data from NASA's Landsat satellites and the European Space Agency's Sentinel satellites with census data.

- **POM** Spire's (www.spire.com) LEO constellation locates objects. For example, more than 250,000 ships broadcast an automatic identification signal. Spire satellites pick up these signals and provide frequent updates of the ships' positions without the vessels having to use expensive dedicated satellite communications.

- **POM** Ursa Space Systems (www.ursaspace.com) analyzes satellite imaging data to estimate the amount of oil in 10,000 oil storage tanks worldwide by focusing on the heights of the lids to measure fluctuation in the oil levels of the tanks. The company estimates oil stockpiles and oil demand.

- **POM** Orbital Insight (www.orbitalinsight.com) also has an oil storage tracker and performs daily automobile counts for 80 U.S. retailers.

- **POM** EarthCast Technologies (www.earthcastdemo.com) provides in-flight forecasts to pilots. Pilots have long had access to basic weather information for their departure and arrival airports, but EarthCast gives them the ability to map out conditions along a particular flight path.

- ICEYE Oy (www.iceye.com) is planning to launch a constellation of 18 satellites that will allow it to capture images of almost any spot on Earth every three hours.

- **POM** SpaceKnow (www.spaceknow.com) uses image data from about 200 public and private satellites to track everything from planes at airports, to shipping containers in ports, to cars at amusement parks. The company's clients are particularly interested in infrastructure development; for example, whether there are new mines in the cobalt-rich Democratic Republic of Congo, which could impact that mineral's prices.

- Imazon (www.imazon.org.br) uses image data from the European Space Agency's Sentinel satellites to police the deforestation of the Amazonian basin in Brazil. The organization focuses on providing data to local governments in the region through its "green municipalities" program, which trains officials to identify deforestation.

- **POM** Indigo Ag Inc. (www.indigoag.com) analyzes image data from NASA and European Space Agency satellites to track global crops, such as wheat, rice, and others.
- Global Fishing Watch (GFW; www.globalfishingwatch.org) analyzes satellite ship-tracking image data to help identify where and when vessels are fishing illegally. The organization was jointly founded by three companies: SkyTruth (www.skytruth.org), which uses satellites to monitor natural resource extraction and promote environmental protection; Oceana (www.oceana.org), an international ocean conservation organization; and Google, which provides data analytics.

radio transmission Uses radio-wave frequencies to send data directly between transmitters and receivers.

Radio Radio transmission uses radio wave frequencies to send data directly between transmitters and receivers. Radio transmission has several advantages. First, radio waves travel easily through normal office walls. Second, radio devices are fairly inexpensive and easy to install. Third, radio waves can transmit data at high speeds. For these reasons, radio increasingly is being used to connect computers to both peripheral equipment and local area networks (LANs; discussed in Chapter 6). (Note: Wi-Fi and cellular also use radio frequency waves.)

As with other technologies, however, radio transmission has its drawbacks. First, radio media can create electrical interference problems. Also, radio transmissions are susceptible to snooping by anyone who has similar equipment that operates on the same frequency.

satellite radio (or digital radio) A wireless system that offers uninterrupted, near CD-quality sound that is beamed to your radio from satellites.

Another problem with radio transmission is that when you travel too far away from the source station, the signal breaks up and fades into static. Most radio signals can travel only 30 to 40 miles from their source. However, satellite radio overcomes this problem. Satellite radio, or *digital radio*, offers uninterrupted, near CD-quality transmission that is beamed to your radio, either at home or in your car, from space. In addition, satellite radio offers a broad spectrum of stations, including many types of music, news, and talk. Sirius XM (www.siriusxm.com) is a leading satellite radio company whose listeners subscribe to its service for a monthly fee.

Internet Blimps Altaeros (www.altaeros.com) makes the SuperTower, which is a tethered blimp that floats at about 800 feet altitude. Each blimp acts like a regular cell tower but with a footprint of up to 4,000 square miles. Altaeros claims that one SuperTower will replace 15 land-based cell towers and cut the cost of delivering wireless service by 60 percent. There are many types of use cases for Altaeros SuperTowers:

- Seamlessly expand your 4G footprint with wide-area coverage from an aerial cell tower.
- Easily upgrade to 5G by simply swapping the payload equipment from their platform on the ground.
- Deliver broadband speeds to spread-out rural communities and businesses.
- Completely cover a remote worksite with uninterrupted coverage with a single ST-Flex unit to enhance safety and productivity on the job site and outside the gate.

Wireless Security

Clearly, wireless networks provide numerous benefits for businesses. However, they also present a huge challenge to management—namely, their inherent lack of security. Wireless is a broadcast medium, and transmissions can be intercepted by anyone who is close enough and has access to the appropriate equipment. There are four major threats to wireless networks: rogue access points, war driving, eavesdropping, and radio frequency jamming.

A *rogue access point* is an unauthorized access point into a wireless network. The rogue could be someone in your organization who sets up an access point meaning no harm but fails to inform the IT department. In more serious cases, the rogue is an "evil twin"—someone who wishes to access a wireless network for malicious purposes.

In an *evil twin attack*, the attacker is in the vicinity with a Wi-Fi-enabled computer and a separate connection to the Internet. Using a *hotspotter*—a device that detects wireless networks and provides information on them—the attacker simulates a wireless access point with the same wireless network name, or SSID, as the one that authorized users expect. If the signal is strong enough, then users will connect to the attacker's system instead of the real access point. The attacker can then serve them a Web page asking for them to provide confidential information such as usernames, passwords, and account numbers. In other cases, the attacker simply captures wireless transmissions. These attacks are more effective with public hotspots (e.g., McDonald's and Starbucks) than with corporate networks.

War driving is the act of locating WLANs while driving (or walking) around a city or elsewhere. To war drive or walk, you simply need a Wi-Fi detector and a wirelessly enabled computer. If a WLAN has a range that extends beyond the building in which it is located, then an unauthorized user might be able to intrude into the network. The intruder can then obtain a free Internet connection and possibly gain access to important data and other resources.

Eavesdropping refers to efforts by unauthorized users to access data that are traveling over wireless networks. Finally, in *radio frequency (RF) jamming*, a person or a device intentionally or unintentionally interferes with your wireless network transmissions.

To protect wireless networks, we encrypt our transmissions. Developed by the Wi-Fi Alliance, WPA2 is a type of encryption used to secure the vast majority of Wi-Fi networks. A WPA2 network provides unique encryption keys for each wireless client that connects to it. WPA3 is the latest implementation of WPA2.

Before you go on...

1. Describe the most common types of wireless devices.
2. Describe the various types of transmission media.
3. Describe four threats to the security of wireless transmissions.

8.2 Wireless Computer Networks and Internet Access

LEARNING OBJECTIVE

Explain how businesses can use short-range, medium-range, and long-range wireless networks.

You have learned about various wireless devices and how these devices transmit wireless signals. These devices typically form wireless computer networks, and they provide wireless Internet access. In this section, you will study wireless networks, which we organize by their effective distance: short range, medium range, and wide area.

Short-Range Wireless Networks

Short-range wireless networks simplify the task of connecting one device to another. They also eliminate wires, and they enable users to move around while they use their devices. In general, short-range wireless networks have a range of 100 feet or less. In this section, you consider three basic short-range networks: Bluetooth, ultra-wideband (UWB), and near-field communications (NFC).

Bluetooth   Bluetooth (www.bluetooth.com) is an industry specification used to create small personal area networks. A **personal area network** is a computer network used for

Bluetooth Chip technology that enables short-range connection (data and voice) between wireless devices.

personal area network A computer network used for communication among computer devices close to one person.

communication among computer devices (e.g., telephones, personal digital assistants, smartphones) located close to one person. Bluetooth is a very successful wireless technology with more than 40 billion device shipments.

Bluetooth uses low-power, radio-based communication. Bluetooth 5.2 can transmit up to approximately 50 megabits per second (Mbps) up to 400 meters (roughly 1300 feet). These characteristics mean that Bluetooth 5 will be important for Internet of Things (discussed in Section 8.4) applications. Advantages of Bluetooth include low power consumption and the fact that it uses radio waves that are emitted in all directions from a transmitter. For this reason, you do not have to point one Bluetooth device at another to create a connection.

Bluetooth low energy, marketed as *Bluetooth Smart*, enables applications in the health care, fitness, security, and home entertainment industries. Compared to "classic" Bluetooth, Bluetooth Smart is less expensive and consumes less power, although it has a similar communication range. Bluetooth Smart is fueling the "wearables" (wearable computer) development and adoption.

Bluetooth is widely used to address the increasing demand for high-speed, highly accurate indoor location services, which enable the tracking of people and objects within a set space. These services allow organizations to understand the movement of people and reduce the loss of revenue from lost or stolen assets.

Bluetooth continues to be extremely useful regarding COVID. Bluetooth health-monitoring applications on wearables (e.g., Fitbit and Apple Watch) track body temperature, heart rate, respiratory rate, and other biometric measurements in real time to help diagnose COVID quickly.

Other applications of Bluetooth include the following:

- Mobile payments for frictionless checkout at retail outlets
- Smart Tags to keep track of traveler luggage and belongings
- Remote monitoring of patients suffering from chronic heart diseases or other ailments
- Real-time connectivity for manufacturing and industrial uses; assistance in improving quality and predicting maintenance
- Vehicles with intelligent seats and steering wheels, remote keyless entry systems, infotainment systems, and intelligent proximity reporting
- Home automation systems with sensors for tracking water leakages, fire breakouts, and motion in case of unauthorized entry
- Real-time player-tracking systems used by European professional hockey leagues so that coaches can analyze their play

ultra-wideband (UWB)
A high-bandwidth wireless technology with transmission speeds in excess of 100 Mbps that can be used for applications such as streaming multimedia from, say, a personal computer to a television.

Ultra-Wideband   Ultra-wideband (UWB) is a high-bandwidth wireless technology with transmission speeds in excess of 100 Mbps. Let's take a closer look at Humatics (www.humatics.com), a leading company in UWB technologies. The firm offers several microlocation systems that use UWB technology, including the Humatics Rail Navigation System and the Milo Microlocation System.

The Humatics Milo Microlocation System (www.humatics.com) uses sensors embedded within products, equipment, or robots to provide real-time, reliable, ultra-precise (less than one millimeter) location data so that organizations know exactly where objects and equipment are and where they are going. For example, companies are using the Milo system to precisely control the movements of not only industrial robot arms, but also the movements of cobots.

Other interesting ultra-wideband applications include:

- Mobile robotics: Enable robots to navigate autonomously indoors and in other GPS-denied environments and to guide drones as they fly
- **POM** Heavy equipment industries such as manufacturing and mining: Precisely position the arm of a crane and track forklifts moving indoors and outdoors
- Defense and security: Low false alarm rate, wireless perimeter fences, and indoor mapping and through-wall surveillance

A laptop equipped with UWB can recognize that its owner is sitting in front of it by listening to the signal from their smartphone or smartwatch. The laptop could then automatically log in to any service that person is authorized to use, in another step toward the elimination of usernames and passwords (see Chapter 4).

Near-Field Communication   Near-field communication (NFC) has the smallest range of any short-range wireless network. It is designed to be embedded in mobile devices such as cell phones and credit cards. For example, using NFC, you can wave your device or card within a few centimeters of POS terminals to pay for items. NFC can also be used with mobile wallets (discussed in Section 8.3).

near-field communication (NFC)   The smallest of the short-range wireless networks that is designed to be embedded in mobile devices like cell phones and credit cards.

Medium-Range Wireless Networks

Medium-range wireless networks are the familiar wireless local area networks (WLANs). The most common type of medium-range wireless network is Wireless Fidelity, or Wi-Fi. WLANs are useful in a variety of settings, some of which may be challenging.

Wireless Fidelity is a medium-range WLAN, which is a wired LAN but without the cables. In a typical configuration, a transmitter with an antenna, called a wireless access point (see Figure 8.4), connects to a wired LAN or to satellite dishes that provide an Internet connection. A wireless access point provides service to a number of users within a small geographical perimeter (up to approximately 300 feet), known as a hotspot. Multiple wireless access points are needed to support a larger number of users across a larger geographical area. To communicate wirelessly, mobile devices, such as laptop PCs, typically have a built-in wireless network interface capability.

Wi-Fi provides fast and easy Internet or intranet broadband access from public hotspots located at airports, hotels, Internet cafés, universities, conference centers, offices, and homes. Users can access the Internet while walking across a campus, to their office, or through their homes. Users can also access Wi-Fi with their laptops, desktops, or PDAs by adding a wireless network card. Most PC and laptop manufacturers incorporate these cards into their products.

The Institute of Electrical and Electronics Engineers (IEEE) has established a set of standards for wireless computer networks. The IEEE standard for Wi-Fi is the 802.11 family. Fortunately, the Wi-Fi Alliance (www.wi-fi.org) decided to rename Wi-Fi generations with simple version numbers. Therefore, Wi-Fi 802.11ac, deployed in 2013, was renamed Wi-Fi 5 and Wi-Fi 802.11ax, deployed in 2019, is Wi-Fi 6.

Wi-Fi 6 advantages include faster speeds (eventually up to 10 gigabits per second), lower latency (delay in transmissions), much better battery life, improved security, and support for multiuser environments. As a result of these improvements, Wi-Fi 6 will be beneficial for Internet of Things applications.

The major benefits of Wi-Fi are its low cost and its ability to provide simple Internet access. It is the greatest facilitator of wireless Internet—that is, the ability to connect to the Internet wirelessly.

Corporations are integrating Wi-Fi into their strategies. For example, Starbucks, McDonald's, Panera, and Barnes & Noble offer customers Wi-Fi in many of their stores, primarily for Internet access. To illustrate the value of Wi-Fi, consider Meter's (www.meter.com) business model.

Installing an office network is more difficult than it might appear. The process has traditionally required a company to buy its own complicated equipment and then manage that equipment along with a relationship with one of more Internet service providers.

Meter charges customers a monthly fee of 15 cents per square foot of office space to completely set up a wireless network and connect it to the Internet. A customer sends Meter a floor plan and Meter determines the equipment the office will need. Meter contends that it is uniquely equipped to do this because it makes all its own hardware and software and sets up the connections through its relationship with Internet providers.

Because companies generally manage their own office networking, handing control to a start-up has sometimes been a tough sell. However, companies are realizing that giving the office networking job to Meter is less expensive and less time-consuming. For example, real estate companies such as Tishman Speyer have begun partnering with Meter so tenants who

wireless local area network (WLAN)   A computer network in a limited geographical area that uses wireless transmission for communication.

Wireless Fidelity (Wi-Fi)   A set of standards for wireless local area networks based on the IEEE 802.11 standard.

wireless access point   An antenna connecting a mobile device to a wired local area network.

hotspot   A small geographical perimeter within which a wireless access point provides service to a number of users.

FIGURE 8.4 **Wireless access point.**

Roman Samokhin/Shutterstock

move into a new office can simply say that they would like Internet service as part of their contract and have it turned on right away.

In September 2022, Meter said it was managing millions of square feet of office space for a variety of companies. However, going forward it will probably find it difficult to convince larger companies to buy its service because those companies have already made large networking investments.

Wi-Fi Direct   Until late 2010, Wi-Fi could operate only if the hotspot contained a wireless antenna. Because of this limitation, organizations have typically used Wi-Fi for communications of up to about 800 feet. For shorter, peer-to-peer connections, they have used Bluetooth.

This situation changed following the introduction of a new iteration of Wi-Fi known as Wi-Fi Direct. *Wi-Fi Direct* enables peer-to-peer communications so devices can connect directly. It enables users to transfer content among devices without having to rely on a wireless antenna. Devices with Wi-Fi Direct can broadcast their availability to other devices just as Bluetooth can. Finally, Wi-Fi Direct is compatible with the more than 1 billion Wi-Fi devices currently in use.

Wi-Fi Direct will probably challenge the dominance of Bluetooth in the area of device-to-device networking. It offers a similar type of connectivity but with greater range and much faster data transfer.

MiFi   *MiFi* is a small, portable wireless device that provides users with a permanent Wi-Fi hotspot wherever they go. Thus, users are always connected to the Internet. The range of the MiFi device is about 10 meters (roughly 30 feet). Developed by Novatel, the MiFi device is also called an *intelligent mobile hotspot*. Accessing Wi-Fi through the MiFi device allows up to five persons to be connected at the same time, sharing the same connection. MiFi also allows users to use Voice-over-Internet-Protocol technology (discussed in Chapter 6) to make free (or inexpensive) calls, both locally and internationally.

MiFi provides broadband Internet connectivity at any location that offers 3G cellular network coverage. One drawback is that MiFi is expensive both to acquire and to use.

Li-Fi   *Light Fidelity* (Li-Fi) is a technology for wireless communication among devices using light to transmit data and position. Li-Fi is a visible communications system that can transmit data at high speeds over the visible light spectrum, ultraviolet, and infrared radiation.

In terms of users, Li-Fi is similar to Wi-Fi. The key difference is that Wi-Fi uses electromagnetic waves at radio frequencies to transmit data. Using light to transmit data allows Li-Fi to offer several advantages over Wi-Fi:

- Li-Fi provides far greater bandwidth capacity.
- Li-Fi provides very high peak data transmission rates (theoretically up to 200 Gbps).
- Li-Fi enables communications among 100 times more devices on the Internet of Things.
- Li-Fi provides enhanced security for wireless communications due to reduced interception of signals.
- Li-Fi is more effective in areas susceptible to electromagnetic interference, such as aircraft cabins and hospitals.

Super Wi-Fi   The term *Super Wi-Fi* was coined by the U.S. Federal Communications Commission (FCC) to describe a wireless network proposal that creates long-distance wireless Internet connections. (Despite the name, Super Wi-Fi is *not* based on Wi-Fi technology.) Super Wi-Fi uses the lower-frequency "white spaces" between broadcast TV channels. These frequencies enable the signal to travel farther and penetrate walls better than normal Wi-Fi frequencies. Super Wi-Fi is in use in over 100 countries.

Paris Brothers (**www.parisbrothers.com**) provides specialized logistics services across a variety of business sectors in addition to their specialty food manufacturing and distribution business. The company operates a 1.5 million-square-foot underground industrial space established in an old limestone mine called The SubTropolis in Kansas City, Missouri.

The underground facility offers low-cost storage and office space. Wi-Fi connectivity is mission critical to the firm's operations and coverage lapses directly impact its bottom line.

However, rows of large stone pillars present line-of-sight challenges for wireless technology. In addition, the refrigeration units and large electric motors cause electrical interference with wireless signals. Further, sustained sub-zero temperatures in some areas impact wireless equipment such as routers. These problems have resulted in equipment failures with Wi-Fi equipment as well as spotty coverage. The company successfully deployed Super Wi-Fi because it provides long-range signals and advanced interference resistance.

Wide-Area Wireless Networks

Wide-area wireless networks connect users to the Internet over a geographically dispersed territory. These networks typically operate over the licensed spectrum—that is, they use portions of the wireless spectrum that are regulated by the government. In contrast, Bluetooth, Wi-Fi, and Super Wi-Fi operate over the unlicensed spectrum and are therefore more prone to interference and security problems. In general, wide-area wireless network technologies fall into two categories: cellular radio and wireless broadband.

Cellular Radio   **Cellular telephones (cell phones)** provide two-way radio communications over a cellular network of base stations with seamless handoffs. Cellular telephones differ from cordless telephones, which offer telephone service only within a limited range through a single base station attached to a fixed landline—for example, within a home or an office.

The cell phone communicates with radio antennas, or towers, placed within adjacent geographic areas called *cells* (see **Figure 8.5**). A telephone message is transmitted to the local cell—that is, the antenna—by the cell phone and is then passed from cell to cell until it reaches the cell of its destination. At this final cell, the message either is transmitted to the receiving cell phone or it is transferred to the public switched telephone system to be transmitted to a wireline telephone. This is why you can use a cell phone to call other cell phones as well as standard wireline phones.

Cellular technology is quickly evolving, moving toward higher transmission speeds, richer features, and lower latencies (delays). This rapid evolution is necessary because more people are using mobile phones and tablets and data traffic is exploding. Cellular technology has progressed through a number of stages:

- *First generation (1G)* cellular networks, introduced in 1982, used analog signals and had low bandwidth (capacity).

- *Second generation (2G)* networks, introduced in 1992, used digital signals primarily for voice communication and provided data communication up to 10 kilobits per second (Kbps).

- *2.5G* used digital signals and provided voice and data communication up to 144 Kbps.

- *Third generation (3G)* networks, introduced in 2001, used digital signals and could transmit voice and data up to 384 Kbps when the device was moving at a walking pace, 128 Kbps when it was moving in a car, and up to 2 Mbps when it was in a fixed location. 3G supported video, Web browsing, and instant messaging.

- *Fourth generation (4G)* networks, introduced in 2012, are not one defined technology or standard. The International Telecommunications Union (ITU) has specified speed requirements for 4G: 100 Mbps (million bits per second) for high-mobility communications such as cars and trains and 1 Gbps (billion bits per second) for low-mobility communications such as pedestrians. 4G systems provide a secure mobile broadband system to all types of mobile devices. See IT's Personal for more information.

cellular telephones (cell phones) Phones that provide two-way radio communications over a cellular network of base stations with seamless handoffs.

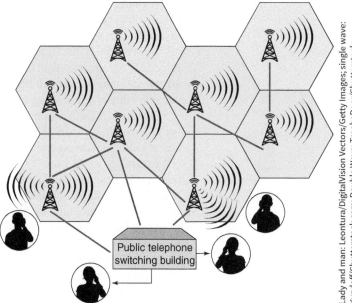

Lady and man: Leontura/DigitalVision Vectors/Getty Images; single wave: Kyryloff/Shutterstock.com; Double Wave: TroobaDoor/Shutterstock; Cell phone tower: Kaissa/Shutterstock.com

FIGURE 8.5   **A cellular network and the public switched telephone system.**   Sources: Image Source; © Engine **Images-Fotolia.com**; © AP/ Wide World Photos

- *Long-term evolution* (*LTE*) is a wireless broadband technology designed to support roaming Internet access through smartphones and handheld devices. LTE is approximately 10 times faster than 3G networks.

  XLTE (advanced LTE) is designed to handle network congestion when too many people in one area try to access an LTE network. XLTE is designed to provide access for all users with no decrease in bandwidth.

- *Fifth generation (5G)* is the latest cellular standard. After an early experiment at the 2018 Winter Olympics, 5G began more widespread deployment in 2019. We discuss 5G in detail in the next section.

Fifth-generation (5G) cellular networks

By September 2022, some 70 countries had 5G networks, reaching 1 billion users. There are three types of 5G technology: low-band, middle-band, and high-band.

Low-band 5G, the baseline level, is best for nationwide coverage but has the most limited performance compared to the other two types of 5G. Low-band 5G's signal can penetrate obstacles and travel long distances. One low-band 5G tower, transmitting on the same frequency that was once used for TV broadcasts, can serve customers within hundreds of square miles, also covering more rural locations. This baseline tier is already approximately 20 percent faster than 4G LTE networks.

Mid-band 5G is about six times faster than 4G LTE and is likely to be more available in major metropolitan areas of the United States. Mid-band 5G offers service within smaller areas compared to low-band 5G. For everyday users, mid-band 5G may prove to be the ideal tier in terms of performance and proximity to a tower.

High-band 5G, also called millimeter wave 5G, is characterized by extremely low latency and is approximately 10 times faster than 4G LTE networks. High-band 5G enables messages to transmit almost immediately, but it requires close proximity to a tower. High-band 5G enables higher capacity for transferring data, quicker downloads, better communications, and improved access to information, making businesses more efficient and powering applications across vehicle technologies, smart cities, education, and more. High-band 5G is largely limited to line-of-sight transmission and can be easily interrupted by weather, structural interference, and distance.

To recap the characteristics of 5G spectrum bands, think of each band and its capabilities as beams of light. Low-band is similar to a floodlight. It casts an illuminating beam across a wide area but may not be the most concentrated, high-performing light. Mid-band closely resembles the beam of a flashlight that is more precise with a smaller cast radius. High-band is like a laser pointer with ultimate precision but a small scope of illumination.

All three 5G bands are alike in that they all serve enhanced mobile broadband and Internet of Things capabilities. However, the three types of 5G also have exclusive use cases adapted to their unique spectrum bands.

Low-band 5G has numerous applications, including public transportation and first responder connectivity, fleet tracking, IoT monitoring, and kiosks. Improvements in low-band 5G transmission speeds will broaden fixed wireless use cases and increase the performance and reliability of applications like pop-up stores and mobile command centers.

Mid-band 5G will continue to add to the performance and capabilities of applications that typically run in low-band 5G. For example, a first responder who previously was only able to access multiple wireless applications from their police cruiser would be able to utilize mobile HD streaming in mid-band 5G. Similarly, a surveillance camera network in low-band 5G may offer a multi-camera viewing experience, but when operating in mid-band 5G, the surveillance may include HD visual-recognition features. Mid-band 5G will also handle augmented reality for commerce and public safety.

High-band 5G is best for applications requiring the highest performance, including artificial intelligence (AI) video recognition, wireless robotics, and wireless fiber replacements. In addition to facilitating remote surgeries and enabling factories to perform preventive self-maintenance, high-band 5G provides business continuity through large-site failover and can accommodate sporting events or large conventions.

There are many uses for 5G. We consider several of them here.

- *Enhanced agricultural productivity*. Smart farming (also called precision agriculture) is underway. 5G is enhancing the data collection and transmission from Internet of Things sensors. 5G also extends the geographic reach of precision agriculture to rural areas.

- *Improved remote education.* Pandemic-era restrictions that led to remote learning high-lighted the vulnerabilities of current networks. 5G networks will provide higher speeds, higher capacities, and greater reliability, all of which will enhance remote education.

- **POM** *Expanded intelligent logistics.* The logistics field, including transportation, has been expanding its use of the Internet of Things to monitor shipments in movement. 5G will enable more IoT sensors, all of which will have faster transmission speeds and greater data-gathering capacities.

- *Advanced health care.* Health care organizations can use 5G in many ways, such as ana-lytics, patient monitoring, remote diagnostics, and robot-assisted telesurgery.

- *Improved manufacturing operations.* 5G promises more flexibility than wired networks, while retaining the high capacity, high reliability, and low latency that manufacturing needs, particularly robotics.

Wireless Broadband, or WiMAX   Worldwide Interoperability for Microwave Access, popularly known as WiMAX, is the name for IEEE Standard 802.16. WiMAX has a wireless access range of up to 31 miles, compared to 300 feet for Wi-Fi. WiMAX also has a data transfer rate of up to 75 Mbps. It is a secure system, and it offers features such as voice and video. WiMAX antennas can transmit broadband Internet connections to antennas on homes and businesses located miles away. For this reason, WiMAX can provide long-distance broad-band wireless access to rural areas and other locations that are not currently being served.

Consider this example of the«««« use of WiMAX. On April 1, 2015, a fire broke out in the underground electrical cable ducts in a tunnel under a major highway in London. The fire burned for 36 hours and caused major disruptions to broadband service in the area. With fiber optic, broadband access to the Internet not available, businesses turned to WiMAX from the telecom-munications company Luminet (**www.luminet.co.uk**). One business owner noted that Luminet helped his company get its main office back online in less than 24 hours. Furthermore, Luminet's broadband service helped the company quickly move its staff back from its disaster recovery site.

IT's Personal: Wireless and Mobile

What the GSM3GHSDPA+4GLTE?   This chapter explains the many mobile plat-forms that are available to you as a consumer. Specifically, it discusses cellular, Bluetooth, Wi-Fi, satellite, and other wireless options. Within the cellular area, however, things get con-fusing because telecommunications companies use so many acronyms. Have you ever won-dered if Verizon 3G was equivalent to AT&T 3G? What about 4G and 4G LTE? Of course, most people assume that 4G is faster than 3G, but by how much?

To appreciate this confusion, consider that when Apple released one update to its mobile operating system (iOS), AT&T suddenly began to display 4G rather than 3G on the iPhone—despite the fact that the phone had not been upgraded! Pretty nice, right? Wrong. In this instance, the "upgrade" simply consisted of a new terminology for the existing technology. The speed of the 3G/4G network had *not* changed. (Note: AT&T "4G LTE" is a different tech-nology that does offer significantly higher speeds than AT&T 3G or 4G.)

Actual connection speeds are described in bit rates, meaning how many bits (1s or 0s) a device can transmit in 1 second. For example, a speed listed as 1.5 Mbps translates to 1.5 million bits per second. That sounds like a tremendous rate. Knowing the bits per second, however, is only part of understanding the actual speed. In reality, connection speed is not the same as *throughput*, which is the amount of bandwidth actually available for you to use. Throughput will always be less than the connection speed.

To understand this point, consider how your car operates. It is probably capable of driving more than 100 mph. However, you are "throttled down" by various speed limits, so you never reach this potential speed. Your actual speed varies, depending on the route you take, the speed limits imposed along that route, the weather, the amount of traffic, and many other fac-tors. In the same way, even though AT&T, Verizon, Sprint, and other companies boast incred-ible wireless speeds ("Up to 20 Mbps!"), they will always say "up to" because they know that you will never actually download a file at that rate.

The best method for determining the actual speeds of the various networks is to go to your local wireless store and run a speed test using the demo model they have on display. This test will give you firsthand experience of the actual throughput speed you can expect from their network. The result is much more realistic than terms such as 3G, 4G, and 4G LTE.

Here is how to perform the test. First, make certain the unit is connected only to a cellular network (not Wi-Fi). Then go to **www.speedtest.net**, and click "Begin Test." I ran this test from my iPhone 4S on AT&T's 4G (not 4G LTE) network. My download speed was 3.80 Mbps, and my upload speed was 1.71 Mbps. These numbers are more informative than any name they are given (3G, 4G, etc.) because they indicate exactly what I can expect from my wireless connection. Run this test at competing stores (AT&T, Verizon, Sprint, T-Mobile, etc.), and you will have real data to compare. As names change, you can always run a test to find the facts.

Before you go on...

1. What is Bluetooth? What is a WLAN?
2. Describe Wi-Fi, cellular service, and WiMAX.

8.3   Mobile Computing and Mobile Commerce

WILEY PLUS

Author Lecture Videos are available exclusively in *WileyPLUS.*
Apply the Concept activities are available in the Appendix and in *WileyPLUS.*

LEARNING OBJECTIVE

Provide a specific example of how each of the five major m-commerce applications can benefit a business.

In the traditional computing environment, users come to a computer, which is connected with wires to other computers and to networks. Because these networks need to be linked by wires, it is difficult or even impossible for people on the move to use them. In particular, salespeople, repair people, service employees, law enforcement agents, and utility workers can be more effective if they can use IT while in the field or in transit. Mobile computing was designed for workers who travel outside the boundaries of their organizations as well as for anyone traveling outside his or her home.

mobile computing A real-time connection between a mobile device and other computing environments, such as the Internet or an intranet.

Mobile computing refers to a real-time connection between a mobile device and other computing environments, such as the Internet or an intranet. This innovation is revolutionizing how people use computers. It is spreading at work and at home; in education, health care, and entertainment; and in many other areas.

Mobile computing has two major characteristics that differentiate it from other forms of computing: mobility and broad reach. *Mobility* means that users carry a device with them and can initiate a real-time contact with other systems from wherever they happen to be. *Broad reach* refers to the fact that when users carry an open mobile device, they can be reached instantly, even across great distances.

Mobility and broad reach create five value-added attributes that break the barriers of geography and time: ubiquity, convenience, instant connectivity, personalization, and localization of products and services. A mobile device can provide information and communication regardless of the user's location (*ubiquity*). With an Internet-enabled mobile device, users can access the Web, intranets, and other mobile devices quickly and easily, without booting up a PC or placing a call through a modem (*convenience* and *instant connectivity*). A company can customize information and send it to individual consumers as a short message service (SMS) (*customization*). Further, knowing a user's physical location helps a company advertise its products and services (*localization*). Mobile computing provides the foundation for mobile commerce (m-commerce), to which we now turn.

Mobile Commerce

Besides affecting our everyday lives, mobile computing is also transforming the ways organizations conduct business by enabling businesses and individuals to engage in mobile commerce. As you saw at the beginning of this chapter, **mobile commerce** (or *m-commerce*) refers to electronic commerce (EC) transactions that are conducted in a wireless environment, especially on the Internet. Like regular EC applications, m-commerce can be transacted on the Internet, private communication lines, smart cards, and other infrastructures. M-commerce creates opportunities for businesses to deliver new services to existing customers and to attract new customers. The development of m-commerce is driven by the widespread availability of mobile devices, the declining prices of such devices, and rapidly improving wireless bandwidth.

Mobile computing and m-commerce include many applications, which result from the capabilities of various technologies. You will examine these applications and their impact on business activities in the next section.

mobile commerce (or m-commerce) Electronic commerce transactions that are conducted with a mobile device.

Mobile Commerce Applications

Mobile commerce applications are many and varied. The most popular applications include location-based applications, financial services, intrabusiness applications, accessing information, and telemetry. The rest of this section examines these various applications and their effects on the ways people live and do business.

FIN **ACCT** **Financial Services** Mobile financial applications include banking, wireless payments and micropayments, money transfers, mobile wallets, and bill payment services. The bottom line for mobile financial applications is to make it more convenient for customers to transact business regardless of where they are or what time it is.

Web shoppers have historically preferred to pay with credit cards. Because credit card companies typically charge fees on transactions, however, credit cards are an inefficient way to make very small purchases. The growth of relatively inexpensive digital content, such as music (e.g., iTunes), ringtones, and downloadable games, is driving the growth of *micropayments*—that is, very small purchase amounts, usually less than $10—as merchants seek to avoid paying credit card fees on small transactions.

A **mobile wallet**, also called a digital wallet, is an app that people use to make financial transactions. These apps can be downloaded on users' desktops or on their smartphones. When the app is on a smartphone, it becomes a mobile wallet. Mobile wallets replace the need to carry physical credit and debit cards, gift cards, and loyalty cards, as well as boarding passes and other forms of identification. Mobile wallets may also store insurance and loyalty cards, drivers' licenses, ID cards, website passwords, and login information. Furthermore, mobile wallets eliminate having to enter shipping, billing, and credit card data each time a user makes a purchase at a website. The data are encrypted in the user's phone, tablet, or computer, and the wallet contains a digital certificate that identifies the authorized cardholder.

mobile wallet (m-wallet) A technology that allows users to make purchases with a single click from their mobile devices.

FIN To use a mobile wallet, consumers wave their phones a few inches above a payment terminal instead of swiping a plastic card. This process uses near-field communication. There are a number of mobile wallets and payment apps from which to choose.

- *Google Wallet* is a mobile wallet that uses near-field communications to allow its users to store debit cards, credit cards, loyalty cards, and gift cards on their smartphones. With Google Wallet, users launch an app and then type in a PIN so Google can access their stored card credentials. Google Wallet also provides a peer-to-peer payment system that can send money to a real, physical Google Wallet card.

- *Google Pay* (a different app from Google Wallet) allows users to tap and pay in stores and use and redeem loyalty cards, gift cards, and offers in stores.

- *Starbucks mobile pay app* launched before the other three top payments apps—Apple Pay, Google Pay, and Samsung Pay. The app lets users pay with their phones and earn credits toward future purchases. The Starbucks app is available on both iOS and Android, whereas Apple Pay, Google Pay, and Samsung Pay users are restricted by the type of phone they have.

- *Samsung Pay* is a mobile payment app and digital wallet that lets users make payments using compatible phones. The service supports contactless payments using near-field communications and also supports magnetic stripe–only payment terminals. In countries like India, the service supports bill payments.

- *MasterCard's Contactless, American Express's ExpressPay*, and *Visa's PayWave* are EMV-compatible, contactless payment features. EMV—which stands for Europay, MasterCard, and Visa, the three companies that originally created the standard—is a technical standard for smart payment cards. EMV cards are smart cards that store their data on chips rather than on magnetic stripes. They can be either contact cards that must be physically inserted into a reader or contactless cards that can be read over a short distance using radio-frequency identification (RFID) technology. (We discuss RFID in Section 8.4.) EMV cards are also called chip-and-pin cards.

- PayPal, Venmo, and Zelle all offer mobile wallet functionality. All three apps can be downloaded on both iOS and Android devices.

- PayPal is a digital payments platform that allows users to send and receive money online, as well as make purchases at online retailers.

- Venmo is a peer-to-peer mobile payment service that allows users to send and receive money from friends and family. It also has a social component that allows users to see and comment on their friends' transactions.

- Zelle is a digital payments network that allows users to send and receive money directly from their bank accounts.

- *Apple Pay* is a mobile wallet that uses near-field communications to enable users to make payments using various Apple devices. Apple Pay does not require Apple-specific contactless payment terminals; rather, it will work with Visa's PayWave, MasterCard's PayPass, and American Express's ExpressPay terminals. The wallet is similar to other wallets with the addition of two-factor authentication. Users hold their authenticated Apple device to the point-of-sale system. iPhone users authenticate by holding their fingerprint to the phone's Touch ID sensor, and Apple Watch users authenticate by double-clicking a button on the device.

- *Amazon Pay* is a service that lets customer use the payment methods already associated with their Amazon accounts to make payment for goods and services on third-party websites. Amazon Pay Places allows users to order ahead and pay for goods in-store via the Amazon app.

- *Alipay Wallet* (https://global.alipay.com/platform/site/ihome) is a mobile and online payment platform from the Ant Financial Services Group, an affiliate company of the Chinese Alibaba Group (www.alibabagroup.com). Alipay provides numerous payment services. The platform operates with Visa and MasterCard to provide payment services for Taobao (a Chinese online shopping website) and Tmall (a Chinese-language website for B2C online retail spun off from Taobao), as well as almost 500,000 online and local Chinese businesses.

  Users can employ the app to pay for local in-store purchases, credit card bills, bank account management, person-to-person money transfers, train tickets, food orders, ride hailing, taxi fees, water and electricity utility bills, cable television fees, tuition fees, and traffic fines.

- *WeChat* (www.web.wechat.com) is a Chinese messaging, social media, and mobile payment app developed by Tencent (www.tencent.com). WeChat Pay is a digital wallet service incorporated into WeChat. Users who have provided bank account information can use the app to pay bills, order goods and services, transfer money to other users, and pay in stores.

- *Huawei Pay*: Huawei (www.huawei.com), the Chinese mobile phone manufacturer, partnered with UnionPay, China's state-operated card network, to launch the Huawei Pay mobile wallet in September 2016. The wallet uses NFC and biometrics to make in-store payment through Huawei phones.

- *Peru Digital Payments*, a company owned and operated by that country's leading financial institutions, launched BIM in 2016. BIM is a mobile payment program that consolidates all of their online customer interfaces in a single system. The software is the first of its kind. Although there are 255 mobile money programs in 89 countries, no other program includes all of a country's banks. Furthermore, all three major Peruvian wireless carriers will offer users access to BIM.

- *Brazil Pix* is an instant payment platform created and managed by the Central Bank of Brazil. Pix allows fast money transfers over smartphones. To send cash to someone, a customer must have a bank account and can set up his or her Pix account with a simple key, such as an e-mail address or phone number. Like Zelle (**www.zellepay.com**) in the United States, Pix works through multiple apps from banks and other digital wallet services.

  For instance, the owner of a small cat-sitting business notes that before Pix, she had to have accounts in many different banks so that her clients would not have to pay the fee to send money to another bank. Those fees could be 30 percent of the cost of her service. With Pix, she needs just one account. Further, she often works on weekends and holidays when pet owners are traveling. She is able to receive payment immediately without having to wait for banks to open.

  Using Pix does have risks. A common crime in Brazil is "express kidnapping," where criminals grab victims, take them to an ATM, and force them to withdraw the maximum amount possible. Now criminals skip the trip to an ATM and simply force people to transfer their savings via the Pix app. Although Pix transactions are traceable, criminals may use accounts in other people's names. Brazilian banking authorities have added protections such as limiting the amount a customer can transfer at night, when such assaults are more common.

The stakes in this competition are enormous because the small fees generated every time consumers swipe their cards add up to tens of billions of dollars annually in the United States alone. The potential for large revenue streams is real because mobile wallets have clear advantages. For example: Which are you more likely to have with you at any given moment—your phone or your physical wallet? Also, keep in mind that if you lose your phone, it can be located on a map and remotely deactivated. Plus, your phone can be password protected. Your physical wallet, however, cannot perform these functions.

Location-Based Applications and Services

M-commerce B2C applications include location-based services and location-based applications. Location-based mobile commerce is called **location-based commerce** (or L-commerce).

location-based commerce (L-commerce) Mobile commerce transactions targeted to individuals in specific locations, at specific times.

Location-based services provide information that is specific to a given location. For example, a mobile user can (1) request the nearest business or service, such as an ATM or a restaurant; (2) receive alerts, such as a warning of a traffic jam or an accident; and (3) locate a friend. Wireless carriers can provide location-based services such as locating taxis, service personnel, doctors, and rental equipment; scheduling fleets; tracking objects such as packages and train boxcars; finding information such as navigation, weather, traffic, and room schedules; targeting advertising; and automating airport check-ins.

MKT Consider, for example, how location-based advertising can make the marketing process more productive. Marketers can use this technology to integrate the current locations and preferences of mobile users. They can then send user-specific advertising messages concerning nearby shops, malls, and restaurants to consumers' wireless devices.

MKT Mobile Advertising

Mobile advertising is a form of advertising through cell phones, smartphones, or other mobile devices. Analysts estimate that mobile advertising revenue will reach approximately $7 billion by 2020.

Intrabusiness Applications

Although business-to-consumer (B2C) m-commerce receives considerable publicity, most of today's m-commerce applications actually are used *within* organizations. In this section, you will see how companies use mobile computing to support their employees.

POM Mobile devices are increasingly becoming an integral part of workflow applications. For example, companies can use non-voice mobile services to assist in dispatch functions—that is, to assign jobs to mobile employees, along with detailed information about the job. Target areas for mobile delivery and dispatch services include transportation (delivery of food, oil, newspapers, cargo; courier services; tow trucks; taxis), utilities (gas, electricity, phone, water); field service (computers, office equipment, home repair); health care (visiting nurses, doctors, social services); and security (patrols, alarm installation).

mobile portal A portal that
aggregates and provides content
and services for mobile users.

voice portal A website with an
audio interface.

telemetry The wireless
transmission and receipt of data
gathered from remote sensors.

Accessing Information Another vital function of mobile technology is helping users obtain and use information. Two types of technologies—mobile portals and voice portals—are designed to aggregate and deliver content in a form that will work within the limited space available on mobile devices.

A **mobile portal** aggregates and provides content and services for mobile users. These services include news, sports, and e-mail; entertainment, travel, and restaurant information; community services; and stock trading. Major players around the world are i-mode from NTT DoCoMo, Vodafone, O2, T-Mobile, Yahoo!, AOL, and MSN.

A **voice portal** is a website with an audio interface. Voice portals are not websites in the normal sense because they can also be accessed through a standard phone or a cell phone. A phone number connects you to a website on which you can request information verbally. The system finds the information, translates it into a computer-generated voice reply, and tells you what you want to know. Most airlines use voice portals to provide real-time information on flight status.

Another example of a voice portal is Nuance (**www.nuance.com**), a leader in the voice portal marketspace. The company's AI-enabled, interactive voice response (IVR) solutions provide conversational, automated experiences between company representatives and customers. These IVR solutions accelerate rapid resolution of customer inquiries.

POM **Telemetry Applications** Telemetry refers to the wireless transmission and receipt of data gathered from remote sensors. Telemetry has numerous mobile computing applications. For example, technicians can use telemetry to identify maintenance problems in equipment, and doctors can monitor patients and control medical equipment from a distance. Car manufacturers use telemetry applications for remote vehicle diagnosis and preventive maintenance. For example, drivers of many General Motors cars use its OnStar system (**www.onstar.com**) in numerous ways.

An interesting telemetry application for individuals is an iPhone app called Find My iPhone. Find My iPhone is a part of the Apple iCloud (**www.apple.com/icloud**). This app provides several very helpful telemetry functions. If you lose your iPhone, for example, it offers two ways to find its approximate location on a map. First, you can sign in to the Apple iCloud from any computer. Second, you can use the Find My iPhone app on another iPhone, iPad, or iPod Touch.

If you remember where you left your iPhone, you can write a message and display it on your iPhone's screen. The message might say, "Left my iPhone. Please call me at 301-555-1211." Your message appears on your iPhone, even if the screen is locked. And if the map indicates that your iPhone is nearby—perhaps in your office under a pile of papers—you can tell Find My iPhone to play a sound that overrides the volume or silent setting.

If you left your iPhone in a public place, you may want to protect its contents. You can remotely set a four-digit passcode lock to prevent people from using your iPhone, accessing your personal information, or tampering with your settings. Going further, you can initiate a remote wipe (erase all contents) to restore your iPhone to its factory settings. If you eventually find your phone, then you can connect it to your computer and use iTunes to restore the data from your most recent backup.

If you have lost your iPhone and you do not have access to a computer, you can download the Find My iPhone app to a friend's iPhone, iPad, or iPod Touch and then sign in to access all the Find My iPhone features.

Before you go on...

1. What are the major drivers of mobile computing?
2. Describe mobile portals and voice portals.
3. Describe wireless financial services.
4. Discuss some of the major intrabusiness wireless applications.

8.4 The Internet of Things

WILEY PLUS

Author Lecture Videos are available exclusively in *WileyPLUS*.
Apply the Concept activities are available in the Appendix and in *WileyPLUS*.

LEARNING OBJECTIVE

Describe the Internet of Things and provide examples of how organizations can use the Internet of Things.

The **Internet of Things (IoT)** refers to the billions of animate (living) and inanimate objects that are equipped with embedded sensors and connected wirelessly to the Internet. Each object has a unique identity (i.e., its own IP address) and is able to send and receive data over the Internet without human interaction. Because the IoT generates huge amounts of data, it is a significant driver of analytics (see Chapter 12) and machine learning systems (see Chapter 14).

There are two types of IoT: consumer IoT and industrial IoT. *Consumer IoT* devices range from smartwatches, smartphones, wearable devices, smart home speakers, lightbulbs, electrical outlets, thermostats, door locks, doorbells, appliances, and other smart home products. For consumers, the smart home is where they most likely come into contact with the consumer IoT.

The *Industrial Internet of Things (IIoT)*, also called the fourth industrial revolution, Industry 4.0, or machine-to-machine (M2M), all refer to the use of IoT technology in a business setting. The basic concept for the IIoT is to use a combination of sensors, wireless networks, Big Data, AI, and analytics to measure and optimize industrial processes. The IIoT refers to the billions of industrial devices—anything from machines in a factory to the engines on an airplane—that are equipped with sensors, connected to wireless networks, and gather and share data.

Security and privacy are two of the biggest problems with the IoT. Privacy is critically important because sensors are collecting our extremely sensitive data—for example, what you say in your own home or your personal medical data.

The IoT's security track record has been extremely poor. Many IoT devices are small and inexpensive and do not contain the necessary built-in security features to counter threats. Even worse, the majority of IoT transmissions are not encrypted. Therefore, these devices are permanently at risk.

Hackers are now targeting IoT devices because their inherent lack of security makes them easy to compromise and become part of botnets. In 2016, attackers used the Mirai worm to compromise hundreds of thousands of IoT devices to form a massive botnet. They then used their botnet to conduct distributed denial-of-service attacks to take down major websites.

Connecting industrial machinery into IIoT networks increases the risk of hackers attacking these devices. Industrial espionage or a destructive SCADA attack (see Chapter 4) are potential risks.

Three technologies have been essential factors in the rapid deployment of the IoT: IPv6 (discussed in Chapter 6), which created a vast number of IP addresses; 5G technologies, which provide a vastly improved communications infrastructure for the IoT; and wireless sensors.

A **wireless sensor** is an autonomous device that monitors its own condition as well as physical and environmental conditions around it, such as temperature, sound, pressure, vibration, and movement. Sensors can also control physical systems, such as opening and closing a valve and adjusting the fuel mixture in your car (see SCADA systems in Chapter 4).

Wireless sensors contain processing, storage, and radio-frequency antennae for sending and receiving messages. Each sensor "wakes up" or activates for a fraction of a second when it has data to transmit. It then relays those data to its nearest neighbor. So, rather than every sensor transmitting its data to a remote computer, the data travel from sensor to sensor until they reach a central computer, where they are stored and analyzed. An advantage of this process is that if one sensor fails, then another one can pick up the data. This process is efficient and reliable, and it extends the battery life of the sensor.

Radio-frequency identification tags are one type of wireless sensor. **Radio-frequency identification (RFID)** technology allows manufacturers to attach tags containing antennae

Internet of Things (IoT) A scenario in which objects, animals, and people are provided with unique identifiers and the ability to automatically transfer data over a network without requiring human-to-human or human-to-computer interaction.

wireless sensor An autonomous device that monitors its own condition as well as physical and environmental conditions around it, such as temperature, sound, pressure, vibration, and movement.

radio-frequency identification (RFID) technology A wireless technology that allows manufacturers to attach tags with antennae and computer chips on goods and then track their movement through radio signals.

Oehoeboeroe/E+/Getty Images

← QR code

ra-photos/Getty Images

← RFID tag

Stoked/Stockbyte/Media Bakery/
Getty Images

← Barcode

FIGURE 8.6 Barcodes, RFID tags, and QR codes.

Ecken, Dominique/
Keystone Pressedienst/
Zuma Press

FIGURE 8.7 Small RFID reader and RFID tag.

and computer chips on products. The tags contain enough data to uniquely identify each item. As RFID tags are decreasing in size and cost, they are replacing bar codes and QR codes.

Bar codes are cheap but do not provide as much data as an RFID chip. Quick response (QR) codes were also developed to replace bar codes. A *QR code* is a two-dimensional code, readable by dedicated QR readers and camera phones. QR codes store much more information than bar codes because they store information horizontally and vertically. Figure 8.6 illustrates bar codes, QR codes, and an RFID tag. Figure 8.7 shows a small RFID reader and RFID tag.

There are numerous examples of how the Internet of Things is being deployed. We discuss just a few of them here.

The smart home. In a *smart home*, your home computer, television, lighting and heating controls, smart speakers, home security systems (including smart window and door locks), thermostats, and appliances have embedded sensors and can communicate with one another through a home network. You control these networked objects through your smartphone, television, home computer, and even your automobile. Appropriate service providers and homeowners can access the devices for which they are authorized. Smart home technology can be applied to any building, turning it into a smart building.

POM *Smart stores.* A smart store is a brick-and-mortar retail establishment that has deployed smart shelves and smart products. Smart shelves contain embedded weight sensors that automatically keep track of inventory. Smart products have embedded sensors such as RFID tags that uniquely identify each item. Smart stores also use cameras to track shoppers and products. A current example of smart store is Amazon Go, the cashierless checkout grocery store. Some smart stores have deployed smart mirrors, where customers can virtually try on as many pieces of clothing as they want without needing a fitting room.

POM *Smart cities.* A smart city is an urban area that uses a variety of IoT sensors to analyze data collected from citizens, devices (e.g., smart streetlight, traffic signals, environmental monitoring sensors, surveillance cameras), buildings, and other assets. City employees use the insights to manage assets, resources, and services efficiently to improve city operations. Examples of these operations include monitoring and managing traffic and transportation systems, power plants, utilities, water supply networks, waste systems, crime detection and prevention, libraries, hospitals, and other community services.

The *Array of Things* is a modular network of interactive sensor boxes (called nodes) that collect and process urban data in real time to citizens, scientists, and policy makers. Each node contains high-resolution cameras and microphones, along with sensors to measure humidity, vibration, magnetic fields, temperature, air pollution, barometric pressure, sound, wind speed and direction, and amount of rain. Each node also has an Nvidia graphics processing unit to perform computations on images out in the field and send only processed data to the network, a form of edge computing.

The Array of Things brings a new depth to the information available on a city's environment and its transportation networks. This process in turn supports more informed, data-driven policy decisions around a range of complex challenges, including flooding, air quality, public health, pedestrian traffic, and road conditions.

The Array of Things is expanding through a project called Semi-Automatic Ground Environment (SAGE). Unlike other urban sensing systems, which tend to be proprietary, SAGE allows anyone to write software for its nodes. The library of open-source applications developed for the nodes is available on GitHub. It is growing constantly and includes programs for identifying birds by their songs and classifying funnel clouds from images.

Automotive. Modern cars have many sensors that monitor functions such as engine operation, tire pressure, fluid levels, and many others. Cars can warn drivers of impending mechanical or other problems and automatically summon roadside assistance or emergency services when necessary. Furthermore, sensors provide advanced driver assistance such as automatic parking, monitoring blind spots, detecting driver drowsiness, forward collision warning, and many other functions.

The next evolution in the automotive space is autonomous vehicles. These vehicles must communicate with one another instantaneously many times per second to avoid collisions and operate correctly. 5G's high-bandwidth transmission speed, low latency, low battery consumption, high reliability, and ability to support huge numbers of connected devices are all critically important characteristics that will help to make autonomous vehicles a viable technology.

POM *Smart factories.* A smart factory is a flexible system that optimizes performance across an interconnected network of automated machines, robots, and humans. It can adapt to, and learn from, new conditions in real or near-real time and autonomously operate entire production processes. A network of IoT sensors monitors equipment and flags potential and current issues. For example, sensors using AI may recognize sounds or note other conditions that signal a problem with equipment. These sensors can reduce human site inspections, improve site inspection productivity as problem areas are predicted, reduce safety risks on the production floor, and increase productivity.

POM *Digital twins.* A digital twin is a virtual (digital) representation of a real-world (physical) product or service. With physical entities, such as engines, modeled in software and analyzing real-time sensor data, engineers can find potential problems before they actually occur as well as perform simulations to optimize performance.

Consider the Siemens Internet of Trains project, which has enabled the manufacturer to move from only selling trains to offering a guarantee that its trains will arrive on time. In this project, Siemens embedded sensors in trains and railroad tracks in select locations in Spain, Russia, and Thailand. The firm then used that data to train machine-learning models (the digital twin) to discover signs that tracks or trains may be having problems. Having detailed insights into which parts of the rail network are most likely to fail and when has allowed repairs to be targeted where they are most needed, a process called predictive maintenance. That process, in turn, has enabled Siemens to start selling what it calls *outcome as a service*, which is a guarantee that trains will arrive on time close to 100 percent of the time.

One of the first companies to integrate IoT sensor data with machine learning models was ThyssenKrupp, which operates 1.1 million elevators worldwide and has been feeding data collected by sensors in its elevators into machine-learning models (the digital twin) for years. These models provide real-time updates on the status of elevators and predict which are likely to fail and when, allowing the company to perform preventive maintenance where it is needed. This process reduces elevator outages and saves money on unnecessary servicing.

MKT *Customer service.* The NTT Indycar Series (www.indycar.com) consists of five races, including the Indianapolis 500. The organization is using a combination of a digital twin process, analytics, and machine learning to give fans access to in-depth, real-time insights.

NTT creates a digital twin for every car in the series by using historical data as a foundation. Each car is equipped with more than 140 sensors that collect millions of data points during each race to feed the digital twin. The data include variables such as speed, oil pressure, tire wear, and g-forces. NTT uses machine learning and predictive analytics on the digital twin data to deliver insights to fans that previously would have been available only to race team engineers. Such insights include race predictions, pit-stop performance impact, and the effects of fuel levels and tire wear.

MKT Cushman & Wakefield (www.cushmanwakefield.com), a commercial real estate company with 400 offices across 60 countries, uses digital twins to improve the process of listing and renting commercial properties for both landlords and tenants. The firm scans each property in three dimensions, producing more than 1,000 digital twins of buildings, comprising 33 million square feet. The firm is now able to show these properties to prospective tenants and buyers in a virtual, three-dimensional environment.

The user is able to "walk through" each property at their own pace in their own time as if they were on-site in person. Viewing the digital twins saves clients time, effort, and money. Cushman & Wakefield views the technology as complementary to in-person visits, rather than a replacement for them.

POM *Supply chain management.* The IoT can make a company's supply chain much more transparent. A company can now track, in real time, the movement of raw materials and parts through the manufacturing process to finished products delivered to the customer. Sensors in fleet vehicles (e.g., trucks) can monitor the condition of sensitive consignments (e.g., the temperature of perishable food). They can also trigger automatic security alerts if a container is opened unexpectedly.

POM *Energy management.* Sensors can be integrated into all forms of energy-consuming devices, for example, switches, power outlets, lightbulbs, and televisions. They will be able to communicate directly with utility companies through smart meters to balance power generation and energy usage. Another valuable application of sensors is to use them in smart electrical meters, thereby forming a *smart grid.*

POM *Transportation.* Sensors placed on complex transportation machines such as jet engines and locomotives can provide critical information on their operations. Consider General Electric (GE; www.ge.com), which embeds "intelligence" in the form of 250 sensors in each of its giant locomotives. The sensors produce 9 million data points every hour. How can these sensors improve the performance of such a huge machine?

One of the biggest problems on locomotives is faulty bearings. If a bearing fails, then an axle might freeze, leaving a train marooned on the tracks. To avoid this type of scenario, GE embeds one sensor inside each locomotive's gear case that transmits data on oil levels and contaminants. By examining these data, GE can predict the conditions that cause bearings to fail and axles to freeze. GE data analysts claim that sensors that predict part failures before they occur translate into billions of dollars of savings for GE's rail customers.

POM In another example, Rolls-Royce has deployed digital twin technology to monitor its jet engines. The company can monitor each engine in real time, the conditions in which it is flying, and how the pilot uses it. The manufacturer is tailoring its maintenance programs to ensure that it is optimizing for the life an engine has, not the life that the manual says it has.

The company has been offering engine monitoring as a service to its customers for years, but its digital twin capability has enabled it to tailor its service for each specific engine. Digital twins have helped Rolls-Royce extend the time between maintenance for some engines by up to 50 percent, dramatically reducing its inventory of parts and spares. The technology has also helped Rolls-Royce improve the efficiency of its engines, reducing 22 million tons of carbon emissions to date.

Health care. In a hospital in Gujarat, India, a patient had a tiny balloon inserted into a blood vessel in his heart. He then had a stent placed in the vessel to keep in wide open. While performing these two procedures, the surgeon was 20 miles away. The surgeon used augmented reality, high-definition video, and real-time data readings from medical sensors. The surgeon received precise three-dimensional data from X-rays sent to his augmented reality headset, which he used to control the remote robotic surgical tool. This process is called *telesurgery*.

Many patients reside and receive care outside traditional hospitals and clinics, such as assisted living facilities or their homes. Patients with non-life-threatening conditions can either wear sensors or have them implanted—for example, to monitor blood pressure or glucose levels. These sensors are monitored by medical staff. In many cases, the patients can be shown how to interpret the sensor data themselves. Also, consumer-oriented sensors such as the Fitbit and Apple iWatch can monitor patients' activity levels and overall health.

POM *Agriculture.* Sensors monitor, in real time, air temperature, humidity, soil temperature, soil moisture, leaf wetness, atmospheric pressure, solar radiation, trunk/stem/fruit diameter, wind speed and direction, and rainfall. The data from these sensors are used in precision agriculture. *Precision agriculture* is a farming technique based on observing, measuring, and responding to inter- and intra-field variability in crops.

POM *Animal husbandry.* Dairy cattle are largely "produced" by artificial insemination but only if the procedure occurs when a cow is in estrus. Cows are only in estrus about once every 21 days and estrus lasts only 12 to 18 hours. Unfortunately, estrus usually occurs between 10:00 p.m. and 8:00 a.m., when farmers are sleeping. Further, estrus is difficult to predict as it relies on farmers' experience. In fact, farmers only get it right statistically about 55 percent of the time.

Japanese dairy farmers wanted to know how to increase their percentage of successful artificial inseminations and they turned to data scientists at Fujitsu. To gather data, the scientists inserted sensors into the cows' first stomach, which measured the number of steps a cow takes. After data collection, the scientists found that the onset of estrus could be detected because the cows took significantly more steps (measured by the sensor). When the number of steps for a particular cow increased in that manner, estrus began 16 hours later.

Significantly, if artificial insemination took place in the first 2 hours of estrus, there was a much higher probability of producing a female. If the procedure took place later in estrus, there was a higher probability of producing a male. Furthermore, the scientists claimed that, using the number of steps a cow takes, it is possible to detect as many as ten different diseases! Using this application of the Internet of Things, Japanese farmers were able to significantly increase their herd size and the health of their cows.

Hospitality. The Royal Park Hotel in Detroit, Michigan, has integrated smart hotel technology to improve its guests' experience. The hotel first installed 160 wireless access points, one in each of the 143 guest rooms, and others across the property. The access points in each guest room contain an IoT module with a unique address.

The first application involved smart room locks. After a guest makes a reservation, that guest's phone or smart device can access their room once they arrive during the period of time that the reservation is valid. The connected locks enable management to monitor when doors are open or closed, locked or unlocked. If a guest has a reservation for a room and is also renting a meeting room, the app will provide seamless access to both.

Smart locks provide increased security for guests. If someone attempts to open a door with a device that is not associated with it, the smart lock will notify management through a "wandering intruder" feather. The key on the intruder's app will not work. With mapping capabilities, the IoT system will alert management of the intruder's location so security staff can investigate.

The hotel's IoT system also provides increased security for staff members. Wireless beacons on staff lanyards send alerts when pushed, notifying managers and security staff of the employee's exact location and that a potential situation could be occurring.

The hotel added beacons to carts, trays, and other hotel equipment such as rollaway beds. This process helps manage inventory in storage, hallways, and guest rooms, as well as notify staff when items, such as food carts or trays, should be picked up. A geofencing feature also alerts management when assets leave the property.

The hotel's lighting and HVAC (heating, ventilation, and air conditioning) systems are connected via the IoT. Therefore, each room has a smart thermometer to monitor room temperatures and the room can be "put to sleep" when there are no occupants in it. This process saves energy and lowers the carbon footprint of the hotel.

Before you go on...

1. Define the Internet of Things and RFID.

2. Provide two examples (other than those mentioned in this section) of how the Internet of Things benefits organizations (public sector, private sector, for-profit, or not-for-profit).

3. Provide two specific business uses of RFID technology.

What's in IT for Me?

ACCT For the Accounting Major

Wireless applications help accountants count and audit inventory. They also expedite the flow of information for cost control. Price management, inventory control, and other accounting-related activities can be improved with the use of wireless technologies.

FIN For the Finance Major

Wireless services can provide banks and other financial institutions with a competitive advantage. For example, wireless electronic payments, including micropayments, are more convenient (anywhere, anytime) than traditional means of payment, and they are less expensive. Electronic bill payment from mobile devices is becoming more popular, increasing security and accuracy, expediting cycle time, and reducing processing costs.

MKT For the Marketing Major

Imagine a whole new world of marketing, advertising, and selling, with the potential to increase sales dramatically. Such is the promise of mobile computing. Of special interest for marketers are location-based advertising as well as the new opportunities resulting from the Internet of Things and RFID. Finally, wireless technology also provides new opportunities in sales force automation (SFA), enabling faster and better communications with both customers (CRM) and corporate services.

Wireless technologies offer many opportunities to support mobile employees of all kinds. Wearable computers enable offsite employees and repair personnel working in the field to service customers faster, better, and less expensively. Wireless devices can also increase productivity within factories by enhancing communication and collaboration as well as managerial planning and control. Mobile computing technologies can also improve safety by providing quicker warning signs and instant messaging to isolated employees.

Mobile computing can improve HR training and extend it to any place at any time. Payroll notices can be delivered as SMSs. Wireless devices can also make it even more convenient for employees to select their own benefits and update their personal data.

MIS personnel provide the wireless infrastructure that enables all organizational employees to compute and communicate anytime, anywhere. This convenience provides exciting, creative, new applications for organizations to reduce expenses and improve the efficiency and effectiveness of operations (e.g., to achieve transparency in supply chains). Unfortunately, as you read earlier, wireless applications are inherently insecure. This lack of security is a serious problem with which MIS personnel must contend.

Summary

8.1 Identify the advantages and disadvantages of each of the four main types of wireless transmission media.

Microwave transmission systems are used for high-volume, long-distance, line-of-sight communication. One advantage is the high volume. A disadvantage is that microwave transmissions are susceptible to environmental interference during severe weather such as heavy rain and snowstorms.

Satellite transmission systems make use of communication satellites, and they receive and transmit data through line-of-sight. One advantage is that the enormous footprint—the area of Earth's surface reached by a satellite's transmission—overcomes the limitations of microwave data relay stations. Like microwaves, satellite transmissions are susceptible to environmental interference during severe weather.

Radio transmission systems use radio-wave frequencies to send data directly between transmitters and receivers. An advantage is that radio waves travel easily through normal office walls. A disadvantage is that radio transmissions are susceptible to snooping by anyone who has similar equipment that operates on the same frequency.

8.2 Explain how businesses can use short-range, medium-range, and long-range wireless networks.

Short-range wireless networks simplify the task of connecting one device to another, eliminating wires, and enabling people to move around while they use the devices. In general, short-range wireless networks have a range of 100 feet or less. Short-range wireless networks include Bluetooth, ultra-wideband, and near-field communications. A business application of ultra-wideband is the PLUS Real-Time Location System from Time Domain. Using PLUS, an organization can locate multiple people and assets simultaneously.

Medium-range wireless networks include Wi-Fi networks. *Wi-Fi* provides fast and easy Internet or intranet broadband access from public hotspots located at airports, hotels, Internet cafés, universities, conference centers, offices, and homes.

Wide-area wireless networks connect users to the Internet over geographically dispersed territory. They include cellular telephones and wireless broadband. *Cellular telephones* provide two-way radio communications over a cellular network of base stations with seamless handoffs. *Wireless broadband* has a wireless access range of up to 31 miles and a data transfer rate of up to 75 Mbps. WiMAX can provide long-distance broadband wireless access to rural areas and remote business locations.

8.3 Provide a specific example of how each of the five major m-commerce applications can benefit a business.

Location-based services provide information specific to a location. For example, a mobile user can (1) request the nearest business or service, such as an ATM or restaurant, (2) receive alerts, such as a warning of a traffic jam or an accident, and (3) find a friend. With *location-based advertising*, marketers can integrate the current locations and preferences of mobile users. They can then send user-specific advertising messages about nearby shops, malls, and restaurants to wireless devices.

Mobile financial applications include banking, wireless payments and micropayments, money transfers, wireless wallets, and bill payment services. The bottom line for mobile financial applications is to make it more convenient for customers to transact business regardless of where they are or what time it is.

Intrabusiness applications consist of m-commerce applications that are used *within* organizations. Companies can use nonvoice mobile services to assist in dispatch functions—that is, to assign jobs to mobile employees, along with detailed information about the job. When it comes to *accessing information*, mobile portals and voice portals are designed to aggregate and deliver content in a form that will work within the limited space available on mobile devices. These portals provide information anywhere and anytime to users.

Telemetry is the wireless transmission and receipt of data gathered from remote sensors. Company technicians can use telemetry to identify maintenance problems in equipment. Car manufacturers use telemetry applications for remote vehicle diagnosis and preventive maintenance.

8.4   Describe the Internet of Things and provide examples of how organizations can use the Internet of Things.

The Internet of Things (IoT) is a system in which any object, natural or manmade, has a unique identity (using IPv6) and the ability to send and receive information over a network (i.e., the Internet) without human interaction.

We leave the examples of various uses of the IoT up to the student.

Key Terms

Bluetooth   241
cellular telephones (cell phones)   245
global positioning system (GPS)   237
hotspot   243
Internet of Things (IoT)   253
location-based commerce
   (L-commerce)   251
microwave transmission   236
mobile commerce (or m-commerce)   249
mobile computing   248

mobile portal   252
mobile wallet (m-wallet)   249
near-field communication (NFC)   243
personal area network   241
propagation delay   237
radio-frequency identification (RFID)
   technology   253
radio transmission   240
satellite radio (or digital radio)   240
satellite transmission   237

telemetry   252
ultra-wideband (UWB)   242
voice portal   252
wireless   232
wireless access point   243
Wireless Fidelity (Wi-Fi)   243
wireless local area network (WLAN)   243
wireless sensor   253

Discussion Questions

1. Given that you can lose a cell phone as easily as a wallet, which do you feel is a more secure way of carrying your personal data? Support your answer.

2. If mobile computing is the next wave of technology, would you ever feel comfortable with handing a waiter or waitress your cell phone to make a payment at a restaurant the way you currently hand over your credit or debit card? Why or why not?

3. What happens if you lose your NFC-enabled smartphone or it is stolen? How do you protect your personal information?

4. In your opinion, is the mobile (or digital) wallet a good idea? Why or why not?

5. Discuss how m-commerce can expand the reach of e-business.

6. Discuss how mobile computing can solve some of the problems of the digital divide.

7. Explain the benefits that wireless commerce provides to consumers and the benefits that wireless commerce provides to merchants.

8. Discuss the ways in which Wi-Fi is being used to support mobile computing and m-commerce. Describe the ways in which Wi-Fi is affecting the use of cellular phones for m-commerce.

9. You can use location-based tools to help you find your car or the closest gas station. However, some people see location-based tools as an invasion of privacy. Discuss the pros and cons of location-based tools.

10. Discuss the benefits of telemetry in health care for everyone during the COVID-19 pandemic.

11. Discuss how wireless devices can help people with disabilities.

12. Which of the applications of the Internet of Things do you think are likely to gain the greatest market acceptance over the next few years? Why?

Problem-Solving Activities

1. Investigate commercial applications of voice portals. Visit several vendors, for example, Microsoft and Nuance. What capabilities and applications do these vendors offer?

2. Examine how new data-capture devices such as RFID tags help organizations accurately identify and segment their customers for activities such as targeted marketing. Browse the Web and develop five potential new applications not listed in this chapter for RFID technology. What issues would arise if a country's laws mandated that such devices be embedded in everyone's body as a national identification system?

3. Investigate commercial uses of GPS. Start with **www.neigps.com**. Can some of the consumer-oriented products be used in industry? Prepare a report on your findings.

4. Access **www.bluetooth.com**. Examine the types of products being enhanced with Bluetooth technology. Present two of these products to the class and explain how they are enhanced by Bluetooth technology.

5. Explore **www.qualcomm.com** Prepare a summary of the types of mobile services and applications Qualcomm currently supports and plans to support in the future.

6. Enter www.ibm.com. Search for "wireless e-business." Research the resulting stories to determine the types of wireless capabilities and applications IBM's software and hardware support. Describe some of the ways these applications have helped specific businesses and industries.

7. Enter www.onstar.com. What types of *fleet* services does OnStar provide? Are these any different from the services OnStar provides to individual car owners? (Play the movie.)

8. Access www.ericsson.com. Read their page on the Internet of Things and watch the video on Connected Mangroves. What do you think of this idea? What other ideas do you have?

9. Visit your cell provider's website and compare their 5G plans. Which 5G capable phone would you choose? Would you change from what you have right now or are you already on a 5G plan?

Closing Case

MIS **Bringing Broadband Access to Underserved Populations in New York City**

As in most cities, residents of wealthier neighborhoods in New York City have more options for Internet service than people in underserved areas. Internet providers in affluent areas have more incentive to compete on service and price. On some blocks on the Upper West Side of Manhattan, for example, residents can choose among four carriers.

In contrast, in one area of Brooklyn, residents had to choose between Altice or Optimum, which is owned by Altice. While fiber connections are the best option for Internet access, fixed wireless options (that you see below) can deliver a signal strong enough for most residential uses and are usually much faster and cheaper to deploy than fiber.

Consider residents of one apartment building in Brooklyn who had become tired and irritated with the take-it-or-leave-it pricing for the intermittent, poor-quality service that Internet providers offered in their neighborhood. They turned to NYC Mesh (www.nycmesh.net), a nonprofit community Wi-Fi initiative.

Ted, a NYC Mesh volunteer, installed a router on the building's rooftop that would deliver inexpensive Wi-Fi. NYC Mesh has a subsidized option for installations. Plus, members pay a suggested monthly donation of $20 to $60. The installation took two hours and cost $240 to cover the equipment, plus a $50 tip for Ted. After the installation was complete, an app on Ted's phone indicated that the strength of the broadband connection was sufficient for members' needs.

NYC Mesh has no paid employees. A team of 30 to 40 volunteers, about one-third of them women, install the equipment and maintain the network. NYC Mesh utilizes the online platform Slack to organize projects. The initiative documents its work on Slack's public channels for the benefit of other groups who are interested in starting community Wi-Fi projects.

New York City has many fixed-wireless organizations. They range from community-owned models such as Community Tech NY (www.communitytechny.org) and People's Choice (www.peopleschoice.coop) to for-profits such as Starry (www.starry.com). NYC Mesh covers more neighborhoods than the others; it is the largest community network in the city. It includes more than 1,000 active member nodes throughout the five boroughs of New York City with users concentrated in lower Manhattan and central Brooklyn.

Brian Hall, the founder of NYC Mesh, plans to expand the organization because 46 percent of households living in poverty, representing 1 million New Yorkers, do not have broadband. Hall hopes to encourage New York residents to view the Internet as a utility that everyone should be able to access.

NYC Mesh has installed its first supernode in downtown Manhattan and another on the Brooklyn waterfront. The supernodes serve as central computers that handle data flows and connections for the organization's neighborhood hubs and nodes.

In 2006, Mayor Michael Bloomberg entered a franchise agreement with Verizon that allowed the company to bury fiber-optic cable under city streets in exchange for installing high-speed Fios in every neighborhood. However, Verizon failed to provide broadband in many low-income neighborhoods. In 2020, the city reached a settlement with Verizon, requiring it to connect an additional 500,000 households, with at least 125,000 in underserved neighborhoods, by 2023.

In January 2020, Mayor Bill de Blasio's office released its Internet Master Plan, a new vision of the city's broadband infrastructure. The plan offered free use of the rooftops of public buildings and streetlight poles to providers to build out their network infrastructures. The plan favored organizations such as NYC Mesh, whose technology depends on rooftop access, versus the larger providers, who must either bury their cable or string it from telephone poles.

As a result of Mayor de Blasio's plan, NYC Mesh began negotiating with the New York City Housing Authority (NYCHA) to put a hub on a 24-story tower in Bedford–Stuyvesant (Bed–Stuy), a neighborhood in the northern part of Brooklyn. This hub would extend the nonprofit's coverage area to low-income sections of Brooklyn. As a result, hundreds of buildings within a two-mile radius of the hub could get broadband Internet access, and it would not cost the city anything.

NYC Mesh received approval to install the hub, along with hubs in two other developments in the Bronx and Queens. As part of Phase One of the Internet Master Plan, NYC Mesh installed free public hot spots around the exterior grounds of the three projects. The city selected four other providers to wire up 10 other NYCHA developments. The other companies must provide residents with access to Wi-Fi in their apartments for no more than $20 per month.

NYC Mesh has applied to establish hubs on an additional 163 public buildings as part of Phase Two. If successful, this project would allow NYC Mesh to cover much of the city in the next five to seven years. Because each router installation comes with a free public Wi-Fi hot spot, NYC Mesh could help make broadband Internet universal throughout New York City.

The Internet does sometimes go down. NYC Mesh volunteers pride themselves on resolving service issues quickly. However, as the organization expands, it will need more volunteers to maintain the system.

NYC Mesh faces difficulties expanding in certain areas. First, not all renters can put routers on the roofs of their buildings. Second, some people are suspicious of free Internet and will not use the hot spots. One NYC Mesh member suggested that if the government really wants to help, it should fund training for volunteers, subsidize hardware costs, and pay for network education so that community members would understand the hubs they enjoy.

Questions

1. **Are nonprofit organizations such as NYC Mesh a competitive threat to incumbent Internet providers in New York City? Why or why not? Support your answer.**

2. **Describe potential problems that NYC Mesh will face as it expands. Be sure to include in your answer the potential responses of incumbent Internet providers in New York City.**

Sources: Compiled from J. Kim, "A Complete Timeline of the Internet Master Plan under Mayor Bill de Blasio," *Technology Law NYC*, January 7, 2022; "New York City to Close Digital Divide for 1.6 Million Residents, Advance Racial Equity," *nyc.gov*, October 28, 2021; R. Deffenbaugh, "New Broadband Provider Takes Aim at Digital Divide in NYCHA," *Crain's New York Business*, September 3, 2021; Z. Ludwig, "NYC Mesh: Volunteers Take on the Internet Industry," *Philanthropy4Technology*, August 19, 2021; B. Broyard, "Welcome to the Mesh Brother: Guerilla Wi-Fi Comes to New York," *The New York Times*, July 16, 2021; J. Edwards, "Sick of Traditional Internet Providers, BK Neighbors Are Setting up Their Own WiFi with NYC Mesh," *bkreader.com*, May 10, 2021; "Recovery for All of Us: New York City Announces Free and Low-Cost Broadband Access for 13 NYCHA Developments, Serving up to 30,000 Residents," *nyc.gov*, May 6, 2021; N. Hicks and N. Musumeci, "NYC Gets Verizon to Expand Fios Broadband to 500K More Households," *New York Post*, November 24, 2020; L. Yang, "The Volunteers Blanketing Cities with Wireless Internet," *MIT Technology Review*, October 21, 2020; and "New York City's Digital Divide: 500,000 Households Have No Internet Access When It Is More Important than Ever Before," *Citizens' Committee for Children*, April 24, 2020.

CHAPTER 9

Social Computing

CHAPTER OUTLINE	LEARNING OBJECTIVES
9.1 Web 2.0	**9.1 Describe** six Web 2.0 tools and two major types of Web 2.0 sites.
9.2 Fundamentals of Social Computing in Business	**9.2 Describe** the benefits and risks of social commerce to companies.
9.3 Social Computing in Business: Shopping	**9.3 Identify** the methods used for shopping socially.
9.4 Social Computing in Business: Marketing	**9.4 Discuss** innovative strategies to use social networking sites for advertising and market research.
9.5 Social Computing in Business: Customer Relationship Management	**9.5 Explain** how social computing improves customer service.
9.6 Social Computing in Business: Human Resource Management	**9.6 Discuss** different ways that human resource managers make use of social computing.

Opening Case

[MIS] **[MKT]** **Continuing Problems with Online Reviews**

Problems with online reviews have existed since the first review was posted in 1999. Review problems fall into three major categories. First, etailers and their customers must deal with an increasing number of fake reviews. Second, online sellers are unethically and perhaps illegally contacting customers who leave negative reviews. Third, bad actors are weaponizing reviews as instruments of extortion. Let's take a closer look at each type of issue and see how companies are dealing with these issues.

Amazon Fake Reviews

Thousands of fake reviews push products across Amazon's (www .amazon.com) global digital storefront every day. In fact, the huge etailer has experienced problems for years with fake reviews that artificially boost product ratings.

Making matters worse, a thriving cottage industry sells fake reviews on Amazon. Sellers court Amazon shoppers on Facebook across dozens of networks, including Amazon Review Club and Amazon Reviewers Group, to provide positive feedback in exchange for money or other compensation. Another group, which calls itself "Amazon Product Review," boasted more than 40,000 members until Facebook removed it early in 2022. That group evaded detection through the algorithm-eluding strategy of swapping a few letters in phrases that would cause it to be detected by Amazon's recognition systems.

Amazon reported more than 1,000 review-selling groups to social media platforms in the first quarter of 2022, three times the number from the same period the previous year. It is significant to note that Amazon is placing the responsibility for the prevalence of fake reviews on social media companies for their failure to monitor and remove those groups.

In 2022, Amazon filed a lawsuit against the administrators of more than 10,000 Facebook groups that coordinate cash or goods for buyers who are willing to post fake product reviews. In addition to the United States, these groups recruit fake reviewers and operate in Amazon's online storefronts in the United Kingdom, France, Germany, Spain, Italy, and Japan.

Sellers Respond Unethically to Negative Reviews on Amazon

Some Amazon sellers are contacting unhappy buyers directly to revise or delete their negative reviews in exchange for refunds or gift cards. As the number of unhappy shoppers declines, the overall average star rating of products increases.

In fact, sellers who ship products via Amazon are not supposed to contact customers directly. To do so violates the terms to which the sellers agree on Amazon's platform. These terms specify that both sellers and brands—which can be distinct from sellers—are permitted to communicate with buyers only through Amazon's messaging platform, which hides the customer's e-mail address. They also prohibit sellers and brands from requesting that a customer remove a negative review or post a positive one. Sellers who fulfill orders themselves receive customer names and mailing addresses. However, for orders that Amazon fulfills, customer data is supposed to be hidden from sellers and brands.

Consider one Amazon customer, Joan, who purchased a bottle of household cleaning fluid based on almost 1,000 excellent Amazon reviews. The product did not work as advertised, so Joan left a negative review. One week later, she received an e-mail from someone claiming to be from the customer service team of the household cleaner's brand. That person offered her a refund to remove her negative review. The person continued by saying if they did not receive a response, they would assume that Joan did not see their e-mail and would continue to send e-mails.

Joan requested a refund, but she did not want to delete her review. Another representative e-mailed her the next day and declined to issue her a refund. Instead, the person offered to refund her twice what she paid for the product if she would remove her review. Joan declined.

The company continued to e-mail Joan about removing her negative review. Joan contacted Amazon twice about the matter, but the e-mails continued. However, when a writer for a well-known technology magazine contacted Amazon to comment on the situation, the listing for the product disappeared, and the e-mails stopped.

Sellers and brands can find ways to reach customers despite Amazon's regulations. In Joan's case, she believes that a free gift insert in the cleaning fluid's packaging, which prompted her to enter her e-mail address and order ID number, enabled the brand to link her review with her e-mail address. An Amazon spokesperson stated that such inserts violate company policy.

The seller might also have been able to look up Joan's name and mailing address in sales records provided by Amazon and then use that information to find her e-mail address. Amazon has since stopped including names and mailing addresses in records of most Amazon-fulfilled purchases. Sellers now typically see only a buyer's city, state, and zip code.

Compounding the problem are third-party companies that take customers' shipping information and match it to known e-mail addresses, a practice that also violates Amazon's rules. One company offers an e-mail extraction service for Amazon sellers. The company uses Google and social media sites to match buyers' names with contact information. Another company provides e-mail addresses of reviewers for up to $60 each. Making matters worse, Amazon employees have been accused of accepting bribes in exchange for information that benefitted third-party sellers.

What can we do to prevent sellers from targeting us based on our reviews?

- Do not use your name in Amazon reviews.
- Go to Your Account on Amazon. Under "Ordering and Shipping Preferences," click on your Amazon profile. Click "Edit your public profile," then "Edit privacy settings" to manage what information appears on your profile. You can also choose to hide all activity.
- Save all of your communications. If you receive any questionable e-mails, make screenshots of them, and forward the screenshots to Amazon customer service.
- Block the seller's e-mail address. By replying to a seller or a brand, you could be confirming that your e-mail address belongs to a legitimate customer.

Google Reviews Used in Extortion

In a new attack strategy, criminals are leaving negative ratings on restaurants' Google pages in an attempt to extort digital gift cards. Restauranteurs first notice a rapid increase in one-star ratings on Google, with no description or photos, from people who have never eaten at their restaurants. Soon after the reviews are posted, they receive e-mails from a person claiming responsibility and requesting a $75 Google Play gift card to remove the negative ratings. The e-mails, from several Gmail accounts, request payment to a Proton e-mail account. If the criminals do not receive the gift card, then more bad ratings will follow.

One chef and owner stated that Google removed her one-star ratings after she tweeted the company to complain. Another restaurant owner claimed that her one-star ratings were taken down after her customers raised an outcry on social media. Some restauranteurs, however, contend that it has been difficult to reach someone at Google to help them. Specifically for one restaurant, Google ruled that one of the recent one-star ratings that the owner reported as fake did not violate the platform's policies and would not be removed.

Law enforcement officials have urged restaurant owners to contact Google if they are targeted and to report the crimes to local police departments, the FBI, and the Federal Trade Commission (FTC). One security consultant recommended that, after contacting the authorities, restaurants should inform their customers about the fake reviews, perhaps on social media, in an effort to mitigate the damage. One final note: A Google spokesperson reported that teams of analysts as well as automated systems monitor reviews for such abuses.

Questions

1. **What steps should Amazon take to remove fake reviews from the platform?**

2. **Although not specifically covered in this case, what are the possible impacts of fake reviews on buyers? On sellers?**

3. **Is it even possible for Amazon to remove fake reviews from its huge, dynamic, real-time, platform? Why or why not?**

4. **How can companies protect themselves from reviewers trying to extort them? How can companies protect themselves from reviewers trying to extort them?**

Sources: Compiled from "Study Examines the Impact of Fake Online Reviews on Sales," phys.org, September 9, 2022; A. Friedman, "Study Reveals That You Can't Trust 70% of the Amazon Reviews for This Current iPhone Model," phonearena.com, September 7, 2022;

"The Curious Case of Fake Reviews: How Businesses Are Battling Negative Feedback Online," *Economic Times*, September 6, 2022; A. Hern, "Amazon Delays the Rings of Power Ratings to Combat Fake Reviews," *Guardian*, September 4, 2022; C. Morales, "Restaurants Face an Extortion Threat: A Bad Rating on Google," *New York Times*, July 11, 2022; T. Hatmaker, "Amazon Sues Admins from 10,000 Facebook Groups over Fake Reviews," *TechCrunch*, July 18, 2022; N. Nguyen, "When Amazon Customers Leave Negative Reviews, Some Sellers Hunt Them Down," *Wall Street Journal*, August 8,

2021; M. Grossman, "Six Charged with Bribing Amazon Employees to Boost Third-Party Sellers," *Wall Street Journal*, September 18, 2020; D. Lee and H. Murphy, "Facebook Groups Trading Fake Amazon Reviews Remain Rampant," *Financial Times*, August 12, 2020; J. Emont, L. Stevens, and R. McMillan, "Amazon Investigates Employees Leaking Data for Bribes," *Wall Street Journal*, September 16, 2018; and E. Dwoskin and C. Timberg, "How Merchants Use Facebook to Flood Amazon with Fake Reviews," *Washington Post*, April 23, 2018.

Introduction

Humans are social beings. Therefore, human behavior is innately social. Humans typically orient their behavior around other members of their community. As a result, people are sensitive to the behavior of people around them, and their decisions are generally influenced by their social context.

Traditional information systems support organizational activities and business processes, and they concentrate on cost reductions and productivity increases. A variation of this traditional model, **social computing**, is a type of IT that combines social behavior and information systems to create value. Social computing focuses on improving collaboration and interaction among people and on encouraging user-generated content.

Significantly, in social computing, social information is not anonymous. Rather, it is important precisely because it is linked to particular individuals, who in turn are linked to their own networks of individuals.

Social computing makes socially produced information available to everyone. This information may be provided directly, as when users rate a movie (e.g., at Rotten Tomatoes), or indirectly (as with Google's PageRank algorithm, which sequences search results). This information may not be accurate, as you see in this chapter's opening case.

In social computing, users, rather than organizations, produce, control, use, and manage content via interactive communications and collaboration. As a result, social computing is transforming power relationships within organizations. Employees and customers are empowered by their ability to use social computing to organize themselves. Thus, social computing can influence people in positions of power to listen to the concerns and issues of "ordinary people." Organizational customers and employees are joining this social computing phenomenon, with serious consequences for most organizations.

Significantly, most governments and companies in modern developed societies are not prepared for the new social power of ordinary people. Today, managers, executives, and government officials can no longer control the conversation around policies, products, and other issues.

In the new world of business and government, organizational leaders will have to demonstrate authenticity, even-handedness, transparency, good faith, and humility. If they do not, then customers and employees may distrust them, to potentially disastrous effects. For example, customers who do not like a product or service can quickly broadcast their disapproval. Another example is that prospective employees do not have to take their employers at their word for what life is like at their companies—they can find out from people who already work there. A final example is that employees now have many more options to start their own companies, which could compete with their former employers.

As you see from these examples, the world is becoming more democratic and reflective of the will of ordinary people, enabled by the power of social computing. On the one hand, social power can help keep a company vital and can enable customers and employee activists to become a source of creativity, innovation, and new ideas that will move a company forward. On the other hand, companies that show insensitivity toward customers or employees quickly find themselves on a downward slide.

When a series of brushfires caused serious damage in Tasmania, SellItOnline offered to donate generators to Tasmanians impacted by the fires. While the message appeared gracious at first, the company clarified that the number of generators they donated would be

social computing A type of information technology that combines social behavior and information systems to create value.

completely dependent on how many new fans their Facebook page received. The response was highly negative as SellItOnline looked to be trying to grow their Facebook fanbase in response to a tragedy.

Organizations today are using social computing in a variety of innovative ways, including marketing, production, customer relationship management, and human resource management. In fact, so many organizations are competing to use social computing in as many new ways as possible that an inclusive term for the use of social computing in business has emerged: *social commerce*. Because social computing is facilitated by Web 2.0 tools and sites, you begin this chapter by examining these technologies. You then turn your attention to a diverse number of social commerce activities, including shopping, advertising, market research, customer relationship management, and human resource management.

When you complete this chapter, you will have a thorough understanding of social computing and the ways in which modern organizations use this technology. You will be familiar with the advantages and disadvantages of social computing as well as the risks and rewards it can bring to your organization. For example, most of you already have pages on social networking sites, so you are familiar with the positive and negative features of these sites. This chapter will enable you to apply this knowledge to your organization's efforts in the social computing arena. You will be in a position to contribute to your organization's policies on social computing. You will also be able to help your organization create a strategy to utilize social computing. Finally, social computing offers incredible opportunities for entrepreneurs who want to start their own businesses.

9.1 | Web 2.0

WILEY PLUS

Author Lecture Videos are available exclusively in *WileyPLUS*.
Apply the Concept activities are available in the Appendix and in *WileyPLUS*.

Web 2.0 Websites that emphasize user-generated content, ease of use, participatory culture, and compatibility with other products, systems, and devices for end users.

tag A keyword or term that describes a piece of information.

LEARNING OBJECTIVE

Describe six Web 2.0 tools and two major types of Web 2.0 sites.

The World Wide Web, which you learned about in Chapter 6, first appeared in 1990. Web 1.0 was the first generation of the Web. We did not use this term in Chapter 6 because there was no need to say "Web 1.0" until Web 2.0 emerged.

The key developments of Web 1.0 were the creation of websites and the commercialization of the Web. Users typically had minimal interaction with Web 1.0 sites. Rather, they passively received information from those sites.

Web 2.0 refers to websites that emphasize user-generated content, ease of use, participatory culture, and compatibility with other products, systems, and devices for end users. These websites enrich the user experience by encouraging social interaction, collaboration, and user-centered design. Web 2.0 sites often harness collective intelligence (e.g., wikis); deliver functionality as services, rather than packaged software (e.g., Web services); and feature remixable applications and data (e.g., mashups).

In the following sections, we discuss six Web 2.0 information technology tools: tagging, Really Simple Syndication, blogs, microblogs, wikis and social networking sites. We then turn our attention to the two major types of Web 2.0 sites: social networking sites and mashups.

Tagging

A **tag** is a keyword or term that describes a piece of information, for example, a blog, a picture, an article, or a video clip. Users typically choose tags that are meaningful to them. Tagging allows users to place information in multiple, overlapping associations rather than in rigid categories. For example, a photo of a car might be tagged with "Corvette," "sports car," and "Chevrolet." Tagging is the basis of *folksonomies*, which are user-generated classifications that use tags to categorize and retrieve Web pages, photos, videos, and other Web content.

One specific form of tagging, known as *geotagging*, refers to tagging information on maps. For example, Google Maps allows users to add pictures and information, such as restaurant or hotel ratings, to maps. Therefore, when users access Google Maps, their experience is enriched because they can see pictures of attractions, reviews, and things to do, posted by everyone, and all related to the map location they are viewing.

Really Simple Syndication

Really Simple Syndication (RSS) is a Web 2.0 feature that allows you to receive the information you want (customized information), when you want it, without having to surf thousands of websites. RSS allows anyone to syndicate (publish) his or her blog, or any other content, to anyone who has an interest in subscribing to it. When changes to the content are made, subscribers receive a notification of the changes and an idea of what the new content contains. Subscribers can then click on a link that will take them to the full text of the new content.

For example, **www.cnn.com** provides RSS feeds for each of its main topic areas, such as world news, sports news, technology news, and entertainment news. NBC uses RSS feeds to allow viewers to download the most current version of shows such as *Meet the Press* and *NBC Nightly News.* **Figure 9.1** illustrates how to search an RSS and locate RSS feeds.

To use RSS, you can utilize a special newsreader that displays RSS content feeds from the websites you select. Many such readers are available, several of them for free (see Feedspot; **www.feedspot.com**). In addition, most browsers have built-in RSS readers. For an excellent RSS tutorial, visit **www.mnot.net/rss/tutorial.**

> **Really Simple Syndication (RSS)** A technology that allows users to receive the information they want, when they want it, without having to surf thousands of websites.

Blogs

A **weblog** (**blog** for short) is a personal website, open to the public, in which the site creator expresses his or her feelings or opinions via a series of chronological entries. *Bloggers*—people who create and maintain blogs—write stories, convey news, and provide links to other articles and websites that are of interest to them. The simplest method of creating a blog is to

> **blog (weblog)** A personal website, open to the public, in which the site creator expresses his or her feelings or opinions with a series of chronological entries.

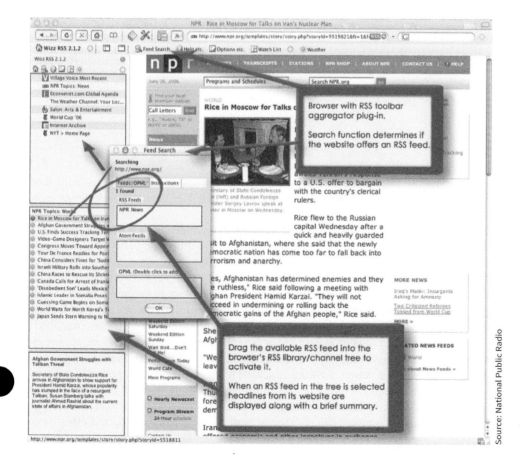

Source: National Public Radio

FIGURE 9.1 The website of National Public Radio (NPR) with RSS toolbar aggregator and search function.

blogosphere The term for the millions of blogs on the Web.

sign up with a blogging service provider, such as www.blogger.com (now owned by Google), www.xanga.com, or www.movabletype.com. The **blogosphere** is the term for the millions of blogs on the Web.

MKT Many companies listen to consumers in the blogosphere who express their views on the companies' products. Marketers refer to these views as *consumer-generated media*. For example, Nielsen (www.nielsen.com) "mines" the blogosphere to provide information for its clients in several areas. Nielsen helps clients find ways to serve potential markets, ranging from broad-based to niche markets. The company also helps clients detect false rumors before these rumors appear in the mainstream media, and it gauges the potency of a marketing push or the popularity of a new product.

Blogs often provide incredibly useful information, often before the information becomes available in traditional media outlets (e.g., television, newspapers). Although blogs can be very useful, they also have shortcomings. Perhaps the primary value of blogs is their ability to bring current, breaking news to the public in the fastest time possible. Unfortunately, in doing so, bloggers sometimes cut corners, and their blogs can be inaccurate. Regardless of their various problems, however, blogs have transformed the ways in which people gather and consume information.

Microblogging

microblogging A form of blogging that allows users to write short messages (or capture an image or embedded video) and publish them.

Microblogging is a form of blogging that allows users to write short messages (or capture an image or embedded video) and publish them. These messages can be submitted via text messaging from mobile phones, instant messaging, e-mail, or simply over the Web. The content of a microblog differs from that of a blog because of the limited space per message. A popular microblogging service is Twitter, which allows 280 characters per tweet. In addition to text, Twitter users can include links, photos, and videos.

Twitter A free microblogging service that allows its users to send messages and read other users' messages and updates.

Twitter (www.twitter.com) is a free microblogging service that allows its users to send messages and read other users' messages and updates, known as **tweets**. Tweets are displayed on the user's profile page and delivered to other users who have signed up to receive them.

tweet Messages and updates posted by users on Twitter.

MKT Twitter is becoming a very useful business tool. It allows companies to quickly share information with people interested in their products, thereby creating deeper relationships with their customers. Businesses also use Twitter to gather real-time market intelligence and customer feedback. As an individual user, you can use Twitter to inform companies about your experiences with their business, offer product ideas, and learn about great offers.

Microblogging is very popular in China, with Weibo (www.weibo.com) being the most popular microblogging service in that country. Weibo has over 200 million monthly active members.

Wikis

wiki A website on which anyone can post material and make changes to other material.

A **wiki** is a website made up entirely of content posted by users. Wikis have an "edit" link on each page that allows any user to add, change, or delete material, thus fostering easy collaboration.

Wikis take advantage of the combined input of many individuals. Consider Wikipedia (www.wikipedia.org), an online encyclopedia that is the largest existing wiki. Wikipedia contains about 6.5 million articles in English (as of November 2022), which attract some 500 million views every day. Wikipedia relies on volunteer administrators who enforce a neutral point of view, and it encourages users to delete copy that displays a clear bias. Nevertheless, there are still major debates over the reliability of Wikipedia articles. Many educators will not allow students to cite references from Wikipedia because Wikipedia content is of uncertain origin. Moreover, Wikipedia does not provide any quality assessment or fact checking by experts. Therefore, academics and other professionals have major concerns about the accuracy of user-provided content.

POM **MKT** Organizations use wikis in several ways. In project management, for example, wikis provide a central repository for capturing constantly updated product features and specifications, tracking issues, resolving problems, and maintaining project histories. In addition, wikis enable companies to collaborate with customers, suppliers, and other business partners on projects. Wikis are also valuable in knowledge management. For example, companies use wikis to keep enterprise-wide documents, such as guidelines and frequently asked questions, accurate and current.

Social Networking Websites

A **social network** is a social structure composed of individuals, groups, or organizations linked by values, visions, ideas, financial exchange, friendship, kinship, conflict, or trade. **Social networking** refers to activities performed using social software tools (e.g., blogging) or social networking features (e.g., media sharing). Social networking allows convenient connections to those of similar interest.

A social network can be described as a map of all relevant links or connections among the network's members. For each individual member that map is his or her **social graph**. Mark Zuckerberg of Facebook originally coined this term to refer to the social network of relationships among Facebook users. The idea was that Facebook would take advantage of relationships among individuals to offer a richer online experience.

Social networks can also be used to determine the social capital of individual participants. **Social capital** refers to the number of connections a person has within and between social networks.

Participants congregate on *social networking websites*, where they can create their own profile page for free and on which they can write blogs and wikis; post pictures, videos, or music; share ideas; and link to other Web locations they find interesting. Social networkers chat using instant messaging and Twitter, and they tag posted content with their own key words, making content searchable and facilitating interactions and transactions. Social network members converse, collaborate, and share opinions, experiences, knowledge, insights, and perceptions with one another. They also use these websites to find like-minded people online, either to pursue an interest or a goal or just to establish a sense of community among people who may never meet in the real world.

Participants who post on social networking sites tend to reveal a great deal of personal information. As a result, if they are not careful, their information could be stolen.

Table 9.1 displays the variety of online social networking platforms. Social networking websites allow users to upload their content to the Web in the form of text, voice, images, and videos.

These social networking sites collect a massive amount of data, some of it uploaded by their users and some generated from monitoring user activity on the sites. The vast amount of data gathered by social networks has led to well-documented problems, which became prominent with the Facebook–Cambridge Analytica scandal in 2018.

social network A social structure composed of individuals, groups, or organizations linked by values, visions, ideas, financial exchange, friendship, kinship, conflict, or trade.

social networking Activities performed using social software tools (e.g., blogging) or social networking features (e.g., media sharing).

social graph A map of all relevant links or connections for one member of a social network.

social capital The number of connections a person has within and between social networks.

TABLE 9.1 Categories of Social Networking Websites

Socially oriented: Socially focused public sites, open to anyone:
- Facebook (www.facebook.com)
- Instagram (www.instagram.com)
- Hi5 (www.hi5.com)
- *TikTok* (www.tiktok.com)

Messaging apps:
- *WhatsApp* (www.whatsapp.com, owned by Meta)
- *Facebook Messenger* (www.messenger.com)
- *Snapchat* (www.snapchat.com)
- *WeChat* (www.wechat.com), the leading messenger app in China
- *Viber* (www.viber.com), the leading app in countries such as Kyrgyzstan, Ukraine, Belarus, Armenia, Azerbaijan, and Bosnia–Herzegovina
- *Moya Messenger* (www.moya.app), a leading app in South Africa

Professional networking: Focused on networking for business professionals:
- LinkedIn (www.linkedin.com)

(continued)

TABLE 9.1 Categories of Social Networking Websites *(continued)*

Media sharing:

- *Netcasting* includes podcasting (audio) and videocasting (audio and video). For example, educational institutions use netcasts to provide students with access to lectures, lab demonstrations, and sports events. In 2007, Apple launched iTunes U, which offers free content provided by major U.S. universities such as Stanford and MIT.
- Web 2.0 media sites allow people to come together and share user-generated digital media, such as pictures, audio, and video.
- Video (Amazon Video on Demand, YouTube, Hulu, Facebook)
- Music (Amazon MP3, Last.fm, Rhapsody, Pandora, Facebook, iTunes)
- Photographs (Photobucket, Flickr, Shutterfly, Picasa, Facebook)

Communication:

- Blogs: Blogger, LiveJournal, TypePad, WordPress, Vox, Xanga
- Microblogging/Presence applications: Twitter, Tumblr, Yammer

Collaboration: Wikis (Wikimedia, PBworks, Wetpaint)

Social bookmarking (or *social tagging*): Focused on helping users store, organize, search, and manage bookmarks of Web pages:

- Mendeley (www.mendeley.com)
- Mix (https://mix.com)
- EndNote (www.endnote.com)

Social news: Focused on user-posted news stories that are ranked by popularity based on user voting:

- Digg (www.digg.com)
- Reddit (www.reddit.com)

Events: Focused on alerts for relevant events, people you know nearby, etc.:

- Eventful (www.audacy.com/eventful)
- Meetup (www.meetup.com)
- Foursquare (www.foursquare.com)

Virtual meeting place: Sites that are essentially three-dimensional worlds, built and owned by the residents (the users):

- Second Life (www.secondlife.com)

Discovery:

- Foursquare (www.foursquare.com) helps its members discover and share information about businesses and attractions around them.
- Angie (www.angie.com) provides verified reviews of local contractors for home improvement projects and makes it easy to get quotes and connect with local pros.

Online marketplaces for microjobs: Sites that unemployed, underemployed or gig workers use to connect to opportunities. Workers choose their jobs and negotiate their rates.

- TaskRabbit (www.taskrabbit.com) enables people to farm out chores to a growing number of temporary personal assistants. The part-time or full-time tasks are especially popular with stay-at-home moms, retirees, and students.
- Fiverr (www.fiver.com) is a global online marketplace for freelance services. *Fiverr* connects businesses with freelancers offering digital services in 500+ categories.

Problems with Social Networks: Fake News, Deepfakes, Bots, Cyborgs, Trolls, Content Moderation, and Dark Patterns

Recall our discussions of how social media platforms make money: they offer free services in exchange for users' data. They then analyze the data in order to target advertisements to each user. The more data they collect, the more accurate their targeting, the more likely that visitors will click on an ad, the higher the rates that advertisers will pay the platforms, and the more money the platforms will make.

The platforms pay the most attention to two metrics: the number of unique visitors to their websites and the length of time that each visitor spends on the sites. The more visitors to the site and the longer the time they spend on the site, the more money the platform can charge the advertising companies.

To attract more users, platforms offer a wide array of free services. For example, consider the large number of free services that Facebook and Google provide.

Engagement is the process of keeping users on websites as long as possible. Platforms program their algorithms to push (emphasize) content that results in high engagement. Not surprisingly, this content is often sensationalized. Consider the phrase, "If it bleeds, it leads." This phrase means that the more sensational the content, the greater the number of people who will read it or watch it. For instance, if a large passenger airliner crashes, the news rapidly spreads globally on news networks, on social media, and in print. In contrast, we do not see content covering the fact that Atlanta Hartsfield International Airport handled 2,500 flights successfully and safely on a particular day.

There are three serious issues associated with social media platforms. First, they allow almost anyone to publish almost any content. Unfortunately, content on these platforms can consist of false information such as fake news and deepfakes. Second, the platforms employ psychological measures to keep visitors on the sites longer. Third, various third-party entities such as marketing agencies, governments, political parties, and publicity managers employ various means in conjunction with social media platforms to spread their messages, both true and false. Let's take a closer look at each of these issues.

False Information   There are two kinds of *fake news*: content that is entirely untrue and content that has some truth but is not totally accurate. Unfortunately, it can be difficult for readers to identify fake content. Fortunately, however, there are strategies that you can use to identify fake news.

- Consider the source of the content. Who or what organization is responsible for the content? Is there even a source listed? If so, then can you check these sources to determine whether they are legitimate?

- Read beyond the headline. If a piece of content has a provocative headline, then read the entire piece before you decide whether to believe it or to pass it along.

- Check the date. Some content is not completely fake, but it distorts real events. Fake news can claim that something that happened in the past is actually a current event.

- Check the facts. Access FactCheck.org (www.factcheck.org), Snopes.com (www.snopes.com), the *Washington Post* Fact Checker (www.washingtonpost.com/news/fact-checker), and PolitiFact.com (www.politifact.com). It is likely that at least one of these sites has already fact-checked the latest viral content that appears in your news feed.

Deepfakes are videos that have been digitally created with artificial intelligence to make it appear something happened that did not. They are an emerging threat because improvements in video-editing software make it possible for bad actors to create increasingly realistic footage of, for example, former U.S. President Barack Obama delivering a speech he never made, in a place he never visited. Deepfakes are expensive and difficult to create. However, advancing technologies are making them easier, faster, and less expensive to create.

In contrast, *shallowfakes*—also called *cheapfakes*—are videos that have been altered with more basic techniques, such as slowing down or speeding up footage or cutting and splicing it. Because shallowfakes are easy and inexpensive to create, they are dangerous as well.

An example of a shallowfake is the altered May 2019 video of Speaker Nancy Pelosi speaking at a conference. The video appeared to have sections cut out and having been slowed down to make her speech sound continually garbled. The video had more than 2.5 million views on Facebook. Significantly, the social platform did not take down the video, despite its fact-checkers flagging it as "partly false."

Psychological Measures   Remember that a primary function of social media platforms is to hold visitors' attention as long as possible. To accomplish this goal, the sites employ the infinite scroll and randomly scheduled rewards.

Infinite scroll is a design technique that loads content continuously as the user scrolls down the page, eliminating the need to keep clicking to load additional content. *Doomscrolling* refers specifically to an infinite scroll of bad news.

Randomly scheduled rewards is a strategy in which the platforms give visitors a "reward" at irregular intervals because someone liked a post or a photo that they uploaded, sent them a text, retweeted one of their tweets, or any number of other actions. When a visitor receives a reward, his or her brain releases a neurotransmitter called dopamine. Dopamine creates feelings of pleasure that motivates a visitor to repeat behaviors such as continuing to click on links or continuing to scroll on social media platforms. The irregularity and unpredictably of the rewards are what make these platforms so addictive.

Third-Party Entities

A variety of entities use an assortment of methods to spread their agendas around the world via social media. These methods include social bots, cyborgs, and troll factories.

Social bots are a type of chatbot (see Chapter 7) that automatically produce content on social media. This content can be either in support of or in opposition to campaigns, brands, politicians, and issues. For example, social bots can be programmed to leave supportive comments on a politician's Facebook page, target journalists with a number of angry tweets, or engage with a post to artificially inflate its popularity. Social bots are typically programmed to conceal that they are bots so that they appear to be humans.

Some social bots are programmed to follow people, resulting in millions of *fake followers* for Internet influencers, politicians, and the platforms themselves. For example, researchers contend that bot software automatically operates nearly 50 million Twitter accounts. On Facebook, social bots are used to automate group pages and spread political advertisements.

Marketing agencies, governments, political parties, publicity managers, and other entities pay humans to create hundreds of fake accounts, operated by bots, that disseminate ambiguous or false information to influence and manipulate public opinion on social media, especially Facebook and Twitter. The humans and the bots they create are called *cyborgs*. Although it is not ethical or legal to use cyborgs to manipulate public opinion, the practice is widespread around the world.

A *troll* is a person who intentionally initiates online conflict or offends other users to distract or create divisions by posting inflammatory or off-topic posts in an online community or on a social media platform. The goal is to provoke others and derail discussions. A *troll farm* is a group of Internet trolls who interfere with the political process in various countries. One study revealed that 30 governments worldwide paid trolls in troll farms to spread propaganda and attack critics.

A combination of social bots, cyborgs, and trolls are very effective at manipulating public discussion on social media. Here is how the process works:

- Any one, or combination, of social bots, cyborgs, or trolls begins the conversation, seeding new ideas and driving discussion in online communities.

- Another type of social bot called amplifier bots escalate the importance of the new ideas by repurposing, retweeting, and republishing them.

- Yet another type of social bot, approval bots engage with specific tweets or comments, "liking," "retweeting," or "replying" to make the ideas appear more credible and legitimate.

- Along with the first three functions, in hotly contested topic areas other social bots harass and attack individuals and organizations in an attempt to push them out of the conversation.

In the most successful bot- and cyborg-aided campaigns, real human social media users are influenced to the point that they willingly participate in sharing fake or inflammatory content with their own social groups. This process often leads to mainstream media coverage, which provides additional legitimacy to the ideas even when the media coverage is intended to debunk false or misleading information.

A very serious problem of social networks is their difficulty moderating the content on their sites. IT's About Business 9.1 addresses how Facebook is trying to manage this issue.

IT's About Business 9.1

MIS **MKT** **Moderating the Content on Facebook**

For years, Facebook has been under scrutiny and widely criticized for the violent and hateful content that appears on the platform. Facebook CEO Mark Zuckerberg has repeatedly pledged to clean up the platform. He has also promoted the use of machine learning algorithms (see Chapter 14) to remove toxic posts, and he has announced efforts to hire thousands of content moderators to remove the messages that the algorithms do not catch.

Rather than hiring content moderators itself, Facebook has contracted with outside companies to assume that responsibility. Since 2012, Facebook has hired at least ten consulting and staffing companies worldwide to moderate its content.

The consulting firm Accenture (www.accenture.com) has become Facebook's largest partner in moderating content. Accenture's contract with Facebook is worth $500 million per year. The firm employs more than 5,000 of the 15,000 people Facebook claims to have hired to inspect content on the platform.

Unfortunately, Accenture has absorbed the worst facets of moderating content and made Facebook's content issues its own. The relationship between Facebook and Accenture highlights Facebook's effort to distance itself from the most damaging, toxic part of its business. In short, Accenture must manage the mental health issues that its workers have developed from reviewing Facebook content. Those issues are intensified by Facebook's performance goals and the numerous changes Facebook makes in its content policies.

Much of Facebook's work with Accenture goes back to the nudity problem. In 2007, millions of users were joining the platform every month, and many of them posted nude photos. Facebook reached a settlement that year with New York State Attorney General Andrew Cuomo that required the company to take down pornographic posts flagged by users within 24 hours.

As a result of that settlement, Facebook employees who policed content were quickly overwhelmed by the volume of work. Facebook executives pushed the moderation team to find automated solutions for inspecting the content. Facebook also looked to outsource content moderation, which was cheaper than hiring employees, provided tax and regulatory benefits, and gave Facebook the flexibility to grow or shrink quickly in regions where the company did not have offices or language expertise.

In 2012, Accenture signed on as a contractor to moderate content, particularly outside the United States. That year, Facebook sent employees to Manila, Philippines, and Warsaw, Poland, to train Accenture employees to inspect content. The Accenture workers learned to use a Facebook software system as well as the platform's guidelines for leaving content up, taking it down, or sending the content to a manager for review.

In 2016, federal authorities discovered that Russian operatives had used Facebook to spread divisive posts to American voters for the presidential election. In response, the company hired more than 3,000 people, in addition to the 4,500 employees it already had, to police the platform.

Moderating content is challenging, to say the least. Although algorithms remove more than 90 percent of objectionable material on Facebook and Instagram, outsourced moderators must decide what to do with posts that the algorithms do not catch. These workers receive a performance score that is based on correctly reviewing posts that violate Facebook's policies. If they make mistakes more than 5 percent of the time, they can be fired.

However, Facebook's rules about what was acceptable changed constantly, creating confusion and stress. For instance, when people used a gas station emoji as slang for selling marijuana, workers deleted the posts for violating the company's content policy on drugs. Facebook then told moderators not to remove the posts, but later reversed its policy.

For years, tensions had mounted within Accenture. Moderators worked eight-hour shifts examining Facebook's most noxious posts, trying to prevent them from spreading online. Some of the moderators reported that they had begun experiencing depression, anxiety, and paranoia. Accenture responded by hiring mental health counselors.

In 2018, Accenture introduced new policies regarding the health of their content moderators. The company changed the counselors' titles to "wellness coaches" and instructed them not to offer psychological assessments or diagnoses. Instead, they were to provide "short-term support" such as suggesting moderators take walks or listen to calming music. Mental health counselors responded that these policies limited their ability to treat workers.

By 2019, the moderation situation was deteriorating. That year, another technology consulting company hired to moderate Facebook content, Cognizant (www.cognizant.com), said that it was leaving content moderation after the technology site *The Verge* described the low pay and mental health effects on Cognizant workers at an Arizona office. Cognizant said that its decision would cost the company at least $240 million in revenue and lead to 6,000 job cuts.

In 2019, Julie Sweet was named CEO of Accenture. She quickly ordered a review of the firm's moderation business and subsequently implemented several changes. In December 2019, Accenture created a two-page legal disclosure to inform moderators about the risks of the job. The document stated that the work had "the potential to negatively impact your emotional or mental health." In October 2020, Accenture listed content moderation for the first time as a risk factor in its annual report, asserting that it could leave the firm vulnerable to media scrutiny and legal troubles.

In 2020, U.S. moderators filed a class-action suit against Facebook. Facebook argued that it was not liable because the workers were employed by contractors such as Accenture. Regardless, in May, Facebook reached a $52 million settlement with the moderators.

In August 2022, Accenture terminated 60 of its content moderators without providing them with an explanation. The company informed the workers during a video call in which Accenture representatives claimed the workers had been selected at random via an algorithm. The representatives reportedly told the workers that they could reapply and interview for new positions in the company.

Questions

1. How should Accenture handle the negative impacts of reviewing toxic Facebook content on its moderators? Is the company doing enough to help these workers with their mental health? Why or why not? Support your answer.

2. Refer to Chapter 14. With enough data, which Facebook certainly has, is it possible to train its machine-learning algorithms to catch more than 90 percent of toxic content on the site? Why or why not? Support your answer.

Sources: Compiled from "Artificial Intelligence Is Now Used to Track Down Hate Speech," *ABC News*, September 9, 2022; K. Bell, "Dozens of Facebook Contractors Lost Their Jobs after an Algorithm Reportedly Chose Them 'at Random'," *Engadget*, August 18, 2022; A. Satariano and M. Isaac, "The Silent Partner Cleaning up Facebook for $500 Million a Year," *New York Times*, August 31, 2021; H. Messenger and K. Simmons, "Facebook Content Moderators Say They Receive Little Support, Despite Company Promises," *NBC News*, May 10, 2021; C. Newton, "Facebook Will Pay $52 Million in Settlement with Moderators Who Developed PTSD on the Job," *The Verge*, May 12, 2020; Q. Wong, "Facebook Content Moderation Is an Ugly Business."

Here's Who Does It," *CNET*, June 19, 2019; C. Newton, "The Trauma Floor," *The Verge*, February 25, 2019; S. Frenkel and K. Benner, "To Stir Discord in 2016, Russians Turned Most Often to Facebook," *New York Times*, February 17, 2018; N. Hopkins, "Facebook Moderators: A Quick Guide to Their Job and Challenges," *Guardian*, May 21, 2017; A. Newitz, "Will Facebook Actually Hire 3,000 Content Moderators, or Will They Outsource?," *Ars Technica*, May 4, 2017; V. Goel, "Facebook Scrambles to Police Content Amid Rapid Growth," *New York Times*, May 3, 2017; "Good Question: How Does Facebook Monitor Its Content?," *CBS News*, April 18, 2017; and "Facebook Settles New York Child Safety Probe," *Reuters*, October 16, 2007.

Another negative aspect of social networks is their use of dark patterns. IT's About Business 9.2 discusses dark patterns in detail.

IT's About Business 9.2

MIS Dark Patterns

Dark patterns, which existed in the physical world long before the advent of the Internet, began as deceptive marketing practices. Recall the mail-order music club Columbia House's deal to buy 12 CDs for just one penny, plus shipping and handling. Customers who signed on were automatically opted in to a CD-a-month club that was almost impossible to cancel.

Unfortunately, the Internet has made dark patterns much more widespread and powerful. A *dark pattern*—also known as a *deceptive design pattern*— is a user interface design that manipulates or influences users to make certain choices, such as buying overpriced insurance with their purchase or signing up for recurring bills.

As one example, Instagram users may see a pop-up asking if they want the service to "use your app and website activity" to "provide a better ads experience." Two boxes appear at the bottom of the pop-up: In one box, with a slightly darker shade of black than the pop-up background, users can choose to "Make ads less personalized." The other box, which is bright blue, urges users to "Make ads more personalized." Instagram uses terms such as *activity* and *personalized* instead of *tracking* and *targeting*, so users might not realize what they are actually giving the app permission to do; that is, allow Instagram to use their data to more precisely target them with ads. A "better experience" sounds positive, so Instagram makes the option it wants users to select much more prominent and attractive than the one it hopes users will avoid.

For years, dark patterns have been influencing users into giving up their data, money, and time. Let's look at several more examples.

Privacy Zuckering. Named after Facebook CEO Mark Zuckerberg, this practice involves making it difficult for users to find opt-out features but easy for them to provide more information than they intended. Another facet of this dark pattern involves a site having a complex, often obscure Terms and Conditions and Privacy Policy, which "zuckers" users into giving away their information.

Bait and switch. These patterns, which originated with brick-and-mortar stores, advertise a product or service for free or at a greatly reduced price that is not available or is stocked only in small quantities. After announcing that the product is unavailable, the website presents similar products with higher prices or lesser quality.

Confirmshaming: This pattern uses shame to drive users to act. Companies attempt to guilt users into a particular behavior, such as signing up for a newsletter or receiving a free guide. For example, one offer featured the "Yes, I want it" action in a bright green box, while the harder-to-see "no" option read "I don't want smarter email." Another business seeking to sign up potential customers provided users with these two boxes: "Heck yeah" and "Nope, I'm rich."

Misdirection: Many software installation programs have a button that resembles a typical confirmation button. The dark pattern displays a prominent "I accept these terms" button that asks the user to accept the terms of a program unrelated to the one they are trying to install. Because the user will typically accept the terms by habit, they can unwittingly install the unrelated program. The button for the alternative action in the installer, which allows the user to skip installing the unrelated program, is much less prominently displayed or seems counterintuitive (such as declining the terms of service).

Some websites use misdirection to request information that is not required. For example, a user enters a username and password on one page, which offers a prominent "Next" button as an option. When the user clicks that button, the page asks the user for their e-mail address. The page displays a small, hard-to-see link that enables the user to go to the next page without providing their e-mail address. Most users do not notice this link and will therefore provide their e-mail address.

Websites also employ confusing wording to trick users into formally accepting an option that they believe has the opposite meaning. For example, a personal data processing consent button might display the label "Don't sell my personal information."

Roach motel. This dark pattern provides an obvious path to enter but a difficult path to exit. Prominent examples are businesses that require subscribers to print and mail their opt-out or cancellation request. Another example involves tricking consumers into signing up for subscriptions and making it difficult for them to cancel. Yet another tactic is to force users to check a nearly hidden box to decline an action that they did not want in the first place.

Trick questions: Companies exploit the fact that users tend to scan Web pages quickly by embedding checkboxes that feature actions that are the opposite of what they expect. One example is forcing users to opt out of a newsletter or recurring charge.

Disguised ads. Disguised ads often appear on free websites that let users convert or download audio or video files. After users enter the file or URL, the most prominent button on the page reads "download now," which, in fact, opens another page that is completely unrelated to what users are doing on the site. Some downloading sites force users to click the ad at least once before serving the link that they are actually looking for.

Sneak into basket. This dark pattern, which often occurs with hosting services, adds unnecessary upgrades immediately before checkout. If users do not notice that they have to uncheck a box to *not* pay for extra features, they will experience a higher-than-expected price. For example, although some businesses are upfront about the fact that users will get a deal if they agree to a subscription, others automatically sign up users. Because they have the users' credit card information, users might not discover this problem until an unrequested product arrives in the mail, along with an unexpected credit card charge.

Cookie consent pop-ups. Websites will inform users that they use cookies and then ask them to "accept" the cookies, usually by clicking on a big, prominent, brightly colored icon. However, if consumers want to refuse the cookies, they have to search for, and click through, to a menu of settings and disable them manually. Most people do not have the time or desire to do this for every website they visit, if they even understand what is being requested in the first place.

Other dark patterns include the following:

- Users sign up for a trial streaming service, only to be automatically charged when the trial expires.

- Users cannot see how to opt out of an app's interstitial ad because the "X" at the upper-right corner is too small and faint to see. (*Interstitial ads* are ads that cover the entire screen of an app or a website page.)

- An ad where the "X" is so small that the user accidentally clicks on the ad itself and is redirected to the ad's website.

Privacy advocates, regulators, and lawmakers are considering legislation to outlaw the use of dark patterns so consumers can use the Internet without constantly being manipulated. In March 2021, California adopted amendments to the California Consumer Privacy Act that prohibit the use of deceptive user interfaces that have "the substantial effect of subverting or impairing a consumer's choice to opt-out." Banned dark patterns include forcing users to click through multiple screens, to scroll through lengthy privacy policies, urging users not to opt out, and using confusing language.

Questions

1. **Why do companies use dark patterns?**

2. **The fundamental tenets of ethics include responsibility, accountability, and liability. Discuss each of these tenets with respect to dark patterns. (Refer to Chapter 3.)**

Sources: Compiled from D. Beres, "5 Dark Patterns That Exploit Your Attention—and Could Steal Your Money," *eco.com* (blog), September 6, 2022; T. Kenney, "Credit Karma Said Users Were 'Pre-Approved' for Credit Cards, Feds Say. They Weren't," *Miami Herald*, September 2, 2022; K. Adams and S. Fernandez, "Thought You Unsubscribed? Digital Tactics That Deceive Consumers Are Often Designed to Be Sneaky," Marketplace.org, August 29, 2022; S. Lichti, "Demystifying Dark Patterns: A Practical Primer," transcend.io, August 26, 2022; J. Lake, "What Are Dark Patterns and How Do They Violate Your Privacy?," comparitech.com, June 14, 2022; "Australia Fines Expedia Group's Trivago $33 Million on Misleading Hotel Room Rates," Reuters, April 21, 2022; S. Morrison, "Dark Patterns, the Tricks Websites Use to Make You Say Yes, Explained," *Vox*, April 1, 2021; J. Vincent, "California Bans 'Dark Patterns' That Trick Users into Giving Away Their Personal Data," *The Verge*, March 16, 2021; T. Simonite, "Lawmakers Take Aim at Insidious Digital 'Dark Patterns,'" *Wired*, January 29, 2021; S. Human and F. Cech, "A Human-Centric Perspective on Digital Consenting: The Case of GAFAM," Human Centred Intelligent Systems, *Smart Innovation, Systems and Technologies*, vol. 189 (Springer: Singapore, May 30, 2020) 139–59; and A. Mathur et al., "Dark Patterns at Scale: Findings from a Crawl of 11K Shopping Websites," *Proceedings of the ACM Human-Computer Interaction* 3, no. 81 (November, 2019).

Enterprise Social Networks

MIS **HRM** Business-oriented social networks can be public, such as **www.linkedin.com**. As such, they are owned and managed by an independent company.

However, an increasing number of companies have created in-house, private social networks for their employees, former employees, business partners, and/or customers. Such networks are "behind the firewall" and are often referred to as *corporate social networks*. Employees utilize these networks to create connections that allow them to establish virtual teams, bring new employees up to speed, improve collaboration, and increase employee retention by creating a sense of community. Employees are able to interact with their coworkers on a level that is typically absent in large organizations or in situations where people work remotely.

Corporate social networks are used for many processes, including:

- Networking and community building, both inside and outside an organization
- *Social collaboration*: Collaborative work and problem-solving using wikis, blogs, instant messaging, collaborative office, and other special-purpose Web-based collaboration platforms

- *Social publishing*: Employees and others creating, either individually or collaboratively, and posting content—photos, videos, presentation slides, and documents—into a member's or a community's accessible-content repository such as YouTube, Flickr, and SlideShare

- Social views and feedback

- *Social intelligence and social analytics*: Monitoring, analyzing, and interpreting conversations, interactions, and associations among people, topics, and ideas to gain insights. Social intelligence is useful for examining relationships and work patterns of individuals and groups and for discovering people and expertise.

Mashups

mashup A website that takes different content from a number of other websites and mixes them together to create a new kind of content.

A **mashup** is a website that takes different content from a number of other websites and mixes them together to create a new kind of content. The launch of Google Maps is credited with providing the start of mashups. A user can take a map from Google, add his or her data, and then display a map mashup on his or her website that plots crime scenes, cars for sale, or anything else (see **Figure 9.2**). There are many examples of mashups:

- An excellent example of a mashup is **www.wikimapia.org** which combines a wiki with Google Maps that allows users to contribute information about geographical places.

- Craigslist developed a dynamic map of all available apartments in the United States that are listed on their website (**www.housingmaps.com**).

- Everyblock.com is a mashup of Web services that integrates content from newspapers, blogs, and government databases to inform citizens of cities such as Chicago, New York, and Seattle about what is happening in their neighborhoods. This information includes criminal activities, restaurant inspections, and local photos posted on Flickr.

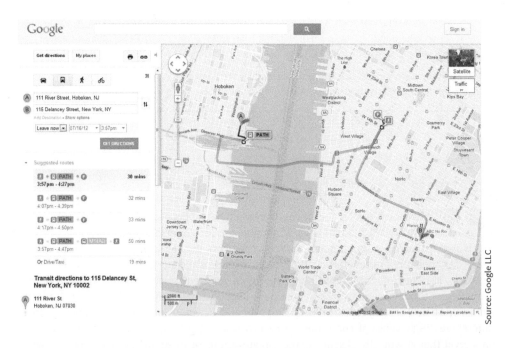

FIGURE 9.2 **Google Maps (www.google.com/maps) is a classic example of a mashup. In this case, Google Maps is pulling in information from public transportation websites to provide the customer with transit directions.**

Source: Google LLC

Before you go on...

1. Differentiate between blogs and wikis.
2. Differentiate between social networking websites and corporate social networks.

9.2 Fundamentals of Social Computing in Business

LEARNING OBJECTIVE

Describe the benefits and risks of social commerce to companies.

Social computing in business, or **social commerce**, refers to the delivery of electronic commerce activities and transactions through social computing. Social commerce also supports social interactions and user contributions, allowing customers to participate actively in the marketing and selling of products and services in online marketplaces and communities. With social commerce, individuals can collaborate online, obtain advice from trusted individuals, and find and purchase goods and services. A few examples of social commerce include:

- **POM** Disney allows people to book tickets on Facebook without leaving the social network.
- **MKT** PepsiCo provides a live notification when its customers are close to physical stores (grocery, restaurants, gas stations) that sell Pepsi products. The company then uses Foursquare to send them coupons and discount information.
- **MKT** Mountain Dew attracts video game lovers and sports enthusiasts via DEWmocracy contests. The company also encourages the most dedicated community members to contribute ideas on company products.
- **MKT** Levi's advertises on Facebook by enabling consumers to populate a "shopping cart" based on what their friends think they would like.

Benefits and Risks of Social Commerce

Social commerce offers numerous benefits to both customers and vendors, as described in Table 9.2. Despite all of its benefits, social commerce does involve risks. It is problematic,

WILEY PLUS

Author Lecture Videos are available exclusively in *WileyPLUS.*
Apply the Concept activities are available in the Appendix and in *WileyPLUS.*

social commerce The delivery of electronic commerce activities and transactions through social computing.

TABLE 9.2   Potential Benefits of Social Commerce

Benefits to Customers

- Better and faster vendor responses to complaints, because customers can air their complaints in public (on Twitter, Facebook, YouTube)
- Customers can assist other customers (e.g., in online forums)
- Customers' expectations can be met more fully and quickly
- Customers can easily search, link, chat, and buy while staying on a social network's page

Benefits to Businesses

- Can test new products and ideas quickly and inexpensively
- Learn a lot about their customers
- Identify problems quickly and alleviate customer anger
- Learn about customers' experiences via rapid feedback
- Increase sales when customers discuss products positively on social networking sites
- Create more effective marketing campaigns and brand awareness
- Use low-cost user-generated content, for example, in marketing campaigns
- Obtain free advertising through viral marketing
- Identify and reward influential brand advocates

for example, to advertise a product, brand, or company on social computing websites where content is user generated and is not edited or filtered. Companies that employ this strategy must be willing to accept negative reviews and feedback. Of course, negative feedback can be some of the most valuable information that a company receives, if it utilizes this information properly.

Companies that engage in social computing are always concerned with negative posts. For example, when a company creates a Facebook business page, by default the site allows other members of the website—potentially including disgruntled customers or unethical competitors—to post notes on the firm's Facebook page and to comment on what the firm has posted.

Going further, if the company turns off the feature that lets other users write on its page, people may wonder what the company is afraid of. The company will also be eliminating its opportunity to engage in customer conversations, particularly conversations that could market the firm's products and services better than the company could do itself. Similarly, the company could delete posts. However, that policy only encourages the post author to scream even louder about being censored.

Another risk is the 20–80 rule of thumb, which posits that a minority of individuals (20 percent) contribute most of the content (80 percent) to blogs, wikis, social computing websites, and so on. For example, in an analysis of thousands of submissions to the news voting site Digg over a three-week time frame, the *Wall Street Journal* reported that roughly 33 percent of the stories that made it to Digg's homepage were submitted by 30 contributors (out of 900,000 registered members).

Other risks of social computing include:

- Information security concerns
- Invasion of privacy
- Violation of intellectual property and copyright
- Employees' reluctance to participate
- Data leakage of personal information or corporate strategic information
- Poor or biased quality of users' generated content
- Cyberbullying/cyberstalking and employee harassment

MKT Consider Rosetta Stone (www.rosettastone.com), which produces software for language translation. To obtain the maximum possible mileage out of social computing and limit the firm's risks on social media, Rosetta Stone implemented a strategy to control its customer interaction on Facebook. The strategy involves both human intervention and software to help monitor the firm's Facebook presence. Specifically, the software helps to monitor Wall posts and respond to them constructively.

Another risk of social commerce occurs when social networks disrupt existing businesses. For example, Craigslist (www.craigslist.org) began the disruption of local newspapers, and Nextdoor (www.nextdoor.com) is continuing that disruption, as you see in this chapter's closing case.

A new business model has emerged, enabled by social computing and environmental concerns. This business model is called *collaborative consumption*.

Collaborative Consumption

collaborative consumption
An economic model based on sharing, swapping, trading, or renting products and services, enabling access over ownership.

Collaborative consumption is an economic model based on sharing, swapping, trading, or renting products and services, enabling access over ownership. The premise of collaborative consumption is that having access to goods and services is more important than owning them. This new model is transforming social, economic, and environmental practices.

Collaborative consumption is a broad term that includes many practices, such as collaborative production, crowdfunding, peer-to-peer lending, and others. In collaborative production, users sell the extra power generated from their solar panels back to the utility company's grid to help power someone else's home. Crowdfunding is the practice of funding a project by raising money from a large number of people, typically via the Internet. Peer-to-peer lending is the practice of lending money to unrelated individuals without using a traditional financial institution such as a bank.

Collaborative consumption is a very old concept. We have been bartering and cooperating throughout human history. If we did not have money, we traded time, meals, favors, or personal belongings, and many cultures today do the same. On the Web, the peer-to-peer model started with eBay (www.ebay.com) in 1995. Then Craigslist (www.craigslist.com) began in the late 1990s, followed by Zipcar (www.zipcar.com) in 2000, and Airbnb (www.airbnb.com) in 2007.

Trust is the greatest concern of this new economic model. Sharing works well only when the participants' reputations are involved. Most sharing platforms try to address this issue by creating a self-policing community. Almost all platforms require profiles of both parties, and they feature community rating systems.

Startups such as TrustCloud (www.trustcloud.com) are trying to become the portable reputation system of this new economy. The company has developed an algorithm that collects (if you choose to opt in) your online "data exhaust"—the trail you leave as you engage with others on Facebook, LinkedIn, Twitter, commentary-filled sites like TripAdvisor, and others. It then calculates your reliability, consistency, and responsiveness. The result is a contextual badge that you carry to any website, a trust rating similar to the credit rating you have in the "offline" world.

Collaborative consumption does have advantages. Participants cite advantages that include self-management, variety, and the flexibility that comes from being able to set one's own schedules. The model can be beneficial for part-time workers, young people such as students, the unemployed, stay-at-home parents, and retired persons. The model allows people to share their underused assets and earn income.

For example, over half of Airbnb hosts in San Francisco said that the service helps them pay their rent, and the average RelayRides member makes an extra $250 per month. PricewaterhouseCoopers estimates that the sharing economy (i.e., collaborative consumption) will reach $355 billion globally by 2025.

Collaborative consumption has positive environmental impacts. As our population grows, we are using valuable resources—water, food, oil—in a way that is not sustainable. The new model helps us to utilize our natural resources more wisely by sharing, not owning.

On the other hand, collaborative consumption does have disadvantages. Law and regulatory agencies are trying to keep abreast of the rapidly growing companies in this economy. Consider these examples:

- Without a permit, residents in San Francisco are prohibited from renting for under 30 days (although the practice still occurs).
- New York City passed an "illegal hotel law" in 2010 that prevents people from subletting apartments for less than 29 days, which is preventing Airbnb from expanding its market in the city.
- Uber and Lyft often function as taxi companies, but do not have to follow worker regulations or laws that apply to existing taxi companies because the services consider their employees to be independent contractors rather than employees.

People working for collaborative consumption services often work seven-day weeks, performing a series of one-off tasks. They have little recourse when the services for which they work change their business models or pay rates. To reduce the risks, workers typically sign up for multiple services. Another disadvantage is that the pay may be less than expected when participants factor in the time spent, expenses, insurance costs, and taxes on self-employment earnings.

Participants have no basic employee benefits or protections. As independent contractors, they do not quality for employee benefits such as health insurance, disability insurance, payroll deductions for Social Security, retirement savings plans, or unemployment benefits. They do not have the right to organize into a union, meaning that they do not have access to union-based collective bargaining processes. They also do not have the right to due process should a service remove them from its platform. As of September 2022, Uber continues to face class-action lawsuits regarding whether its drivers should be classified as employees or independent contractors.

There are numerous, diverse companies in the collaborative consumption market including:

- Uber (**www.uber.com**) operates the Uber mobile app, which allows consumers with smartphones to submit a trip request that is sent to Uber drivers who use their own cars.
- Airbnb (**www.airbnb.com**) is a website for people to list, find, and rent lodgings.
- Zipcar (**www.zipcar.com**) and Turo (**www.turo.com**) are car-sharing services.
- Swimply (**www.swimply.com**) lets swimming pool owners rent out their pools.
- Skillshare (**www.skillshare.com**) provides access to top-class tutors very cheaply.
- Tradesy (**www.tradesy.com**) lets users sell and buy used clothes from well-known brands. The service takes 9 percent of profits.
- Bla Bla Car (**www.blablacar.com**) lets you rent out extra seats in your car when you go on a trip.
- Olio (**www.olioapp.com**) is an app where users can find leftover food to share. This service is important in the United States, where we waste some 30 percent of our food.
- Marriott International (**www.marriott.com**) offers meeting spaces on LiquidSpace (**www.liquidspace.com**). LiquidSpace is an online marketplace that allows people to rent office space by the hour or the day. Hundreds of Marriott hotels now list meeting spaces, and the program has expanded the company's reach by attracting local business-people from surrounding areas.
- FLOOW2 (**www.floow2.com**), based in the Netherlands, calls itself a "business-to-business sharing marketplace where companies and institutions can share equipment, as well as the skills and knowledge of personnel." The company lists more than 25,000 types of equipment and services in industries such as construction, agriculture, transportation, real estate, and health care.

Companies are engaged in many types of social commerce activities, including shopping, advertising, market research, customer relationship management, and human resource management. In the next sections of this chapter, you will learn about each social commerce activity.

Before you go on...

1. Briefly describe the benefits of social commerce to customers.
2. Briefly describe the risks of social commerce to businesses.
3. What are the benefits of collaborative consumption to customers?
4. What are the benefits and risks of collaborative consumption to participants (i.e., workers)?

WILEY PLUS

Author Lecture Videos are available exclusively in *WileyPLUS.*

Apply the Concept activities are available in the Appendix and in *WileyPLUS.*

social shopping A method of electronic commerce that takes all of the key aspects of social networks (friends, groups, voting, comments, discussions, reviews, etc.) and focuses them on shopping.

9.3 | Social Computing in Business: Shopping

LEARNING OBJECTIVE

Identify the methods used for shopping socially.

Social shopping is a method of electronic commerce that takes all of the key aspects of social networks—friends, groups, voting, comments, discussions, reviews, and others—and focuses them on shopping. Social shopping helps shoppers connect with one another based on taste, location, age, gender, and other selected attributes.

The nature of shopping is changing, especially shopping for brand-name clothes and related items. For example, popular brands such as Gap, Shopbop, InStyle, and Lisa Klein are joining communities on Stylehive (www.stylehive.com) to help promote the season's latest fashion collections. Shoppers are using sites like ThisNext (www.thisnext.com) to create profiles and blogs about their favorite products in social communities. Shoppers can tag each item, so that all items become searchable. Moreover, searching within these websites can yield results targeted specifically to individual customers.

There are several methods to shop socially. You will learn about each of them in the next section.

Ratings, Reviews, and Recommendations

MKT Prior to making a purchase, customers typically collect information such as what brand to buy, from which vendor, and at what price. Online customers obtain this information via shopping aids such as comparison agents and websites. Today, customers also use social networking to guide their purchase decisions. They are increasingly utilizing ratings, reviews, and recommendations from friends, fans, followers, and experienced customers. Significantly, this chapter's opening case illustrates how common fake reviews are and how careful we must all be when considering reviews about a product or a service.

Ratings, *reviews*, and *recommendations* are usually available in social shopping. In addition to seeing what is already posted, shoppers have an opportunity to contribute their own ratings and reviews and to discuss ratings and reviews posted by other shoppers (see Figure 9.3). The ratings and reviews come from the following sources:

- *Customer ratings and reviews*: Integrated into the vendor's Web page, a social network page, a customer review site, or in customer feeds (e.g., Amazon, iTunes, Buzzillions, Epinions)
- *Expert ratings and reviews*: Views from an independent authority (e.g., Metacritic)
- *Sponsored reviews*: Paid-for reviews (e.g., SponsoredReviews, PayPerPost)
- *Conversational marketing*: Individuals converse via e-mail, blog, live chat, discussion groups, and tweets. Monitoring these conversations yields rich data for market research and customer service

MKT As one example, Maui Jim (www.mauijim.com), the sunglasses company, employed favorable word-of-mouth marketing as a key sales driver. The company uses Bazaarvoice's Ratings & Reviews to allow customers to contribute five-point ratings and

NetPhotos/Alamy Stock Photo

FIGURE 9.3 Yelp (www.yelp .com) users submit reviews of local business within a local metropolitan area. Some communities have pages that feature a Review of the Day.

authentic product reviews on the company's entire line of sunglasses and accessories. In effect, Maui Jim extended customers' word-of-mouth reviews across the Web.

Maui Jim encourages its customers to share their candid opinions on the style, fit, and performance of all of its sunglasses models. To accomplish this goal, the company integrates customer reviews into its website's search function to ensure that shoppers who are interested in a particular product will see that product's rating in the search results. Customer response to this rating system has been overwhelmingly positive.

Social recommendation websites such as Zinrelo (**www.zinrelo.com**), and Yelp (**www.yelp.com**) encourage conversations about purchases. The product recommendations are submitted by users' friends and acquaintances and arguably are more trustworthy than reviews posted by strangers.

ThisNext (**www.thisnext.com**) is a website where people recommend their favorite products to others. The site blends two powerful elements of real-world shopping: word-of-mouth recommendations from trusted sources and the ability to browse products in a way that naturally leads to discovery.

We must be careful when our search results reflect only our thinking on a subject. This process forms a filter bubble (coined by Eli Pariser). A *filter bubble* is a result of a personalized search where a website algorithm predicts what information or product a user would like based on the user's location and past searches on the website. As a result, users receive only information that reflects their past choices and reinforces their viewpoints.

Examples of such website algorithms are Google Personalized Search results, Amazon's A9 search engine, and Facebook's personalized news stream. For example, if you search Amazon only for books in the science fiction category, you may miss out on outstanding books in other genres because Amazon will primarily recommend science fiction titles.

As another example, one user who searched Google for "BP" received investment news for British Petroleum. Another user searched for that exact term and received information about the Deepwater Horizon oil spill, a catastrophe that occurred in 2010 when an oil rig that belonged to BP exploded, killing 11 workers and releasing four million barrels of oil into the Gulf of Mexico.

Filter bubbles can isolate us, leading to many problems. IT's About Business 9.3 discusses how to break out of filter bubbles.

IT's About Business 9.3

MIS **How to Break Out of Filter Bubbles**

A *filter bubble* is a state of intellectual isolation that can result from personalized searches when a website's machine learning algorithm (see Chapter 14) selectively predicts what information a user would like to see based on information about the user, such as location, past click behavior, and search history. As a result, users are not presented with information that disagrees with their viewpoints, effectively isolating them in their own cultural or ideological bubbles. Essentially, the content that appears in your filter bubble depends on who you are and what you do. However, you do not decide what information gets into the bubble. More important, you do not see what gets edited out.

Filter bubbles can lead to problems. They may cause our views to become stagnant and unchanging, even for harmless issues like our taste in movies. They may stop us from being exposed to new experiences or ideas. They may prevent us from sharing and understanding other points of view. In short, they may decrease, or even eliminate, conversations with people who have different points of view. Filter bubbles, then, can lead to extremist views, both social and political.

Many people have been attempting to break out of their filter bubbles by looking beyond their usual news and information sources. Fortunately, they have options. Let's take a closer look at some of them.

AllSides. AllSides (**www.allsides.com**) assesses the political bias of prominent media outlets and presents different versions of similar news stories from sources on the political right, left, and center. Their goal is to expose readers to news outside their filter bubbles.

The Flip Side. The Flip Side (**www.theflipside.io**) wants to help bridge the gap between liberals and conservatives. The site summarizes conservative and liberal news concerning one policy issue each day. The goal is to become a news source for liberals, moderates, independents, conservatives, and people with no strong political leanings.

Ground News. Ground News (**www.ground.news**) was created to be a news destination for everyone, regardless of political ideology. The site curates/aggregates news stories from numerous sources and labels each source by bias rating.

Essentially, Ground News publishes a summary of a news story and then provides links to other sources that report on the same news. Each link is assigned a bias rating along a spectrum: Far Left, Left, Leans Left, Center, Leans Right, Right, Far Right. It is significant to note that Ground News does not determine bias ratings itself. Rather, it relies on authoritative bias raters such as Media Bias Fact Check (www.mediabiasfactcheck .com), AllSides (www.allsides.com), and Ad Fontes Media (www.adfontesmedia.com).

TheirTube. On an average day, people around the world watch 1 billion hours of video on YouTube. Roughly 70 percent of these videos are recommended by YouTube's machine learning recommendation system (see Chapter 14.) These recommendations attempt to maximize user engagement and thus maximize ad revenue by predicting what a viewer will watch. As a result, these recommendations tend to reinforce the same points of view, creating a filter bubble for each user.

TheirTube is a YouTube filter bubble simulator that demonstrates how YouTube's recommendations can drastically shape users' experiences on the platform and, as a result, shape their worldview. It does this by demonstrating how the YouTube home page would appear for six different personas, each of which is located inside a separate filter bubble. Each persona simulates the viewing environment of real YouTube users who are inside that persona's filter bubble by re-creating a YouTube account with a similar viewing history.

Visitors to sites like these seek out diverse views and enjoy discussing issues from diverse viewpoints. Many of the visitors are trying to understand friends and acquaintances who hold differing political stances. Use of these sites is growing. However, their numbers are tiny compared with other social media sites.

Other experiments are trying to shift the social media experience away from extreme content (see IT's About Business 9.1). For instance, what if a person's status on social media depended on traits such as open-mindedness? The Flip Side and Duke University's Polarization Lab are working on social platforms that are based on this concept. The Flip Side's version will raise posts read by people with diverse ideologies. For example, the more likes by conservatives that a liberal's post receives, the more often it will be displayed to other users.

Reddit (www.reddit.com) hosts a forum called Change My View (www.reddit.com/r/changemyview). In this forum, people share opinions and award points to other users whose replies help them think differently.

Finally, Stanford University's Center for Deliberative Democracy brings together registered voters with different political beliefs in groups of 8 to 15 to discuss difficult issues. Participants are selected randomly and are polled on their views before and after the discussions. Before the meetings, participants are assigned readings summarizing arguments for and against the policies to be discussed.

Questions

1. **Think about the content you consume from various social media sites. Are you in a filter bubble? Why or why not? How would you know? Provide examples to support your answer.**

2. **What are the advantages of breaking out of your filter bubble? Consider both social advantages and political advantages in your answer.**

Sources: Compiled from N. Weiss-Blatt, "Don't Be So Certain That Social Media Is Undermining Democracy," *Daily Beast*, August 11, 2022; E. Volokh, "Filter Bubbles, Polarization, and Social Media Platform Restrictions," *Reason*, October 24, 2021; M. Fuchs, "How Some Americans Are Breaking out of Political Echo Chambers," *Wired*, June 14, 2021; D. Mees, "The Dangers of Filter Bubbles and Echo Chambers," *Medium*, March 16, 2021; "How Different Are Americans' Facebook Feeds?" *The Markup*, March 11, 2021; L. Dormehl, "Filter Bubbles Are Ruining the Internet. This Algorithm Pops Them," *Digital Trends*, January 26, 2021; W. Gould, "Are You in a Social Media Bubble? Here's How to Tell," *NBC News*, October 21, 2019; E. Shearer and E. Grieco, "Americans Are Wary of the Role Social Media Sites Play in Delivering the News," Pew Research Center, October 2, 2019; "What Does Filter Bubble Mean?," *Techopia*, May 17, 2018; K. Allred, "The Causes and Effects of 'Filter Bubbles' and How to Break Free," *Medium*, April 13, 2018; and M. Brenders, "Filter Bubbles vs. Democracy in the Age of Social Media," *Medium*, March 23, 2018.

Group Shopping

Group shopping websites such as Groupon (www.groupon.com) and LivingSocial (www .livingsocial.com), see **Figure 9.4**) offer major discounts or special deals during a short time frame. Group buying is closely associated with special deals (flash sales).

People who sign up with LivingSocial receive e-mails that offer deals at, for example, a restaurant, a spa, or an event in a given city. They can click on either "Today's Deal" or "Past Deal" (some past deals can still be active). They can also click on an icon and receive the deal the next day. Customers who purchase a deal receive a unique link to share with their friends. If a customer convinces three or more people to buy that specific deal using his or her link, then the customer's deal is free.

Individuals can also shop together virtually in real time. In this process, shoppers log on to a website and then contact their friends and family. Everyone then shops online at the same time. Some real-time shopping providers, such as DoTogether (www.dotogether.com) and Wet Seal (www.wetseal.com), have integrated their shopping service directly into Facebook. Customers log in to Facebook, install the firm's app, and then invite their friends to join them on a virtual retail shopping experience.

FIGURE 9.4 LivingSocial (www.livingsocial.com) is a popular example of a group shopping website.

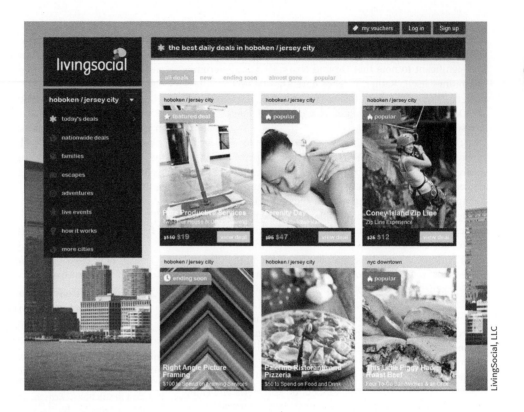

Shopping Communities and Clubs

MKT Shopping clubs host sales for their members that last just a few days and usually feature luxury brands at heavily discounted prices. Club organizers host three to seven sales per day, usually via e-mail messages that entice club members to shop at more than 70 percent off retail—but quickly, before supplies run out.

Luxury brands effectively partner with online shopping clubs to dispose of special-run, sample, overstock, or liquidation goods. These clubs are rather exclusive, which prevents the brands' images from being diminished. Examples are Beyond the Rack (**www.beyondtherack .com**), Gilt (**www.gilt.com**), Rue La La (**www.ruelala.com**), and One King's Lane (**www .onekingslane.com**).

Kaboodle (**www.kaboodle.com**) is another example of a shopping community. Kaboodle is a free service that lets users collect information from the Web and store it on a Kaboodle list that they can share with other shoppers. Kaboodle simplifies shopping by making it easier for people to find items they want in a catalog and by allowing users to share recommendations with one another using Kaboodle lists and groups. People can also use Kaboodle lists for planning vacations, sharing research for work and school, sharing favorite bands with friends, and basically everything else they might want to collect and share information about.

Social Marketplaces and Direct Sales

social marketplaces Websites that act as online intermediaries that harness the power of social networks for introducing, buying, and selling products and services.

MKT **Social marketplaces** act as online intermediaries that harness the power of social networks for introducing, buying, and selling products and services. A social marketplace helps members market their own creations (see Etsy in **Figure 9.5**). Other examples are as follows:

- Craigslist (**www.craigslist.com**) provides online classifieds in addition to supporting social activities such as meetings and events.
- Art Mavens (**www.artmavens.io**) is a social network and freelancer marketplace for the arts community.
- Flipsy (**www.flipsy.com**) can be used by anyone to list, buy, and sell books, music, movies, and games.

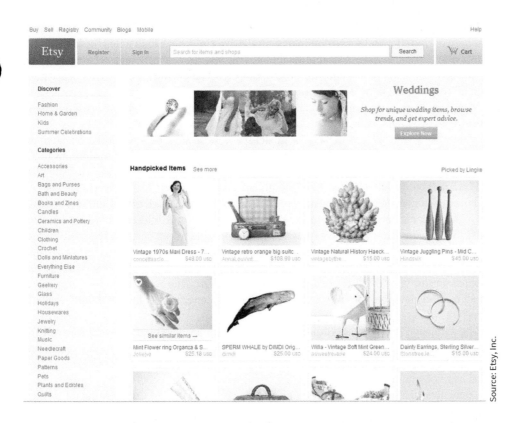

Source: Etsy, Inc.

FIGURE 9.5 Etsy (www.etsy .com) **is a social marketplace for all handmade or vintage items.**

Before you go on...

1. Prior to making a purchase, why are ratings, reviews, and recommendations so important to potential customers?
2. Define collaborative consumption, and describe how collaborative consumption is a "green" phenomenon.

9.4 Social Computing in Business: Marketing

LEARNING OBJECTIVE

Discuss innovative ways to use social networking sites for advertising and market research.

MKT *Marketing* can be defined as the process of building profitable customer relationships by creating value for customers and capturing value in return. There are many components to a marketing campaign, including (1) define your target audience; (2) develop your message (i.e., how you will solve their problem); (3) decide on how you will deliver your message (e.g., e-mail, snail mail, Web advertising, social networks); and (4) follow up.

Advertising

MKT **Social advertising** refers to advertising formats that make use of the social context of the user viewing the ad. Social advertising is the first form of advertising to leverage forms of social influence such as peer pressure and friend recommendations and likes.

> **WILEY PLUS**
>
> **Author Lecture Videos are available exclusively in** *WileyPLUS.*
> **Apply the Concept activities are available in the Appendix and in** *WileyPLUS.*

> **social advertising** Advertising formats that make use of the social context of the user viewing the ad.

Many experts believe advertising is the solution to the challenge of making money from social networking sites and social commerce sites. Advertisers have long noted the large number of visitors on social networks and the amount of time they spend there. As a result, they are willing to pay to place ads and run promotions on social networks. Advertisers now post ads on all major social networking websites.

Most ads in social commerce consist of branded content paid for by advertisers. These ads belong to two major categories: *social advertisements* (or *social ads*) and *social apps*. Social advertisements are ads placed in paid-for media space on social media networks. Social apps are branded online applications that support social interactions and user contributions (e.g., Nike+).

Viral marketing—that is, word-of-mouth advertising—lends itself especially well to social networking. For example, consider the Dove Real Beauty Sketch campaign (**www.dove.com**). The campaign employed a forensic sketch artist who would draw two different sketches of the same person. One sketch was drawn in the way people would describe themselves, and the other sketch was drawn in the way that an acquaintance would describe that other person.

The result was an emotional sensation, showing how harshly people view themselves compared to the favorable way strangers view each other. The campaign video has more than 69 million views on YouTube, and the campaign received more than four billion media impressions.

The campaign was so successful because it played to people's emotions and was worthy of sharing with friends. This viral marketing campaign is one of the many reasons consumers associate the Dove brand with self-love and body positivity. Not only was it viral, but it also landed as the brand intended it to.

There are other innovative methods to advertise in social media. Consider the following:

- Use a company Facebook page, including a store that attracts fans and lets them "meet" other customers. Then, advertise in your Facebook store.
- Tweet business success stories to your customers.
- Integrate ads into YouTube videos.
- Use native advertising. *Native advertising* is a sales pitch that fits into the flow of the information being shown. Many publishers view native advertising as risky because it has the potential to erode the public's trust.

Market Research

MKT Traditionally, marketing professionals used demographics compiled by market research firms as one of their primary tools to identify and target potential customers. Obtaining this information was time-consuming and costly because marketing professionals had to ask potential customers to provide it. Today, however, members of social networks provide this information voluntarily on their pages! (Think about all the information that you provide on your favorite social networking websites.) Because of the open nature of social networking, merchants can easily find their customers, see what they do online, and learn who their friends are.

This information provides a new opportunity to assess markets in near real time. Word of mouth has always been one of the most powerful marketing methods—more often than not, people use products that their friends like and recommend. Social media sites can provide this type of data for numerous products and services.

Companies are utilizing social computing tools to obtain feedback from customers. This trend is referred to as *conversational marketing*. These tools enable customers to supply feedback via blogs, wikis, online forums, and social networking sites. Again, customers are providing much of this feedback to companies voluntarily and free. Social computing not only generates faster and cheaper results than traditional focus groups but also fosters closer customer relationships.

Retailers are aware that customers, especially younger ones, not only want to be heard but also want to know whether other customers agree with them. Consequently, retailers are increasingly opening up their websites to customers, allowing them to post product reviews, ratings, and, in some cases, photos and videos.

As a result of this strategy, customer reviews are emerging as prime locations for online shoppers to visit. Approximately half of consumers consult reviews before making an online purchase, and almost two-thirds are more likely to purchase from a site that offers ratings and reviews.

Using social computing for market research is not restricted to businesses. Customers also enjoy the capabilities that social computing offers when they are shopping.

Conducting Market Research Using Social Networks

MKT Customer sentiment expressed on Twitter, Facebook, and similar sites represents an incredibly valuable source of information for companies. Customer activities on social networking sites generate huge amounts of data that must be analyzed, so that management can conduct better marketing campaigns and improve their product design and their service offerings. The monitoring, collection, and analysis of socially generated data, and the resultant strategic decisions are combined in a process known as **social intelligence** (also called *social listening*).

social intelligence   The monitoring, collection, and analysis of socially generated data and the resultant strategic decisions.

MKT An example of social intelligence comes from Gillette (www.gillette.com), which launched the Gillette TREO in 2018. The TREO was the first razor specifically designed to shave someone else, in response to comments shared by caregivers on social media. Through social media listening, Gillette realized that there was a need for such a product because many people shave another person daily.

With the increase in awareness around high sodium intake, fast food customers were showing hesitance about some foods. Wendy's (www.wendys.com) wanted to keep the favorability toward their french fries at a high level. Through social intelligence, Wendy's discovered that "sea salt" was mentioned much more positively than salt or sodium. The chain added sea salt into the marketing and advertising for their french fries, which helped improve their sales.

Luxury automobile brands such as BMW (www.bmw.com) are interested in which vehicle features that drivers like the most. The automaker measured sentiment levels to understand how consumers felt with new features of its cars. With social intelligence, BMW found that their new laser-guided headlights had high conversation volume and favorability levels. The firm began to emphasize the headlights in their advertising as an exciting new feature.

Social networks provide excellent sources of valuable information for market research. In this section you will see illustrative examples of how to use Facebook, Twitter, and LinkedIn for market research.

Using Facebook for Market Research

There are several ways to use Facebook for market research. Consider the following examples:

- Obtain feedback from your Facebook fans (and their friends if possible) on advertising campaigns, market research, and so on. It is the equivalent of holding a free focus group.
- Test-market your messages. Provide two or three options, and ask fans which one they prefer and why.
- Use Facebook for survey invitations (i.e., to recruit participants). Essentially, turn Facebook into a giant panel, and ask users to participate in a survey. Facebook offers a self-service model for displaying ads, which can function as invitations to take a survey. Facebook also allows you to target your audience very specifically based on traditional demographic criteria such as age and gender.

Using Twitter for Market Research

Your customers, your prospects, and industry thought leaders all use Twitter, making it a rich source of instantly updated information. Consider the following examples:

- Visit Twitter Search (www.twitter.com/search). Enter a company's Twitter name. Not only can you follow what the company is saying, you can also follow what everyone is saying to them. Monitoring replies to your competitors and their employees will help you develop your own Twitter strategy by enabling you to observe (a) what your competitors are doing and, more important, (b) what people think about them. You can also follow the company's response to this feedback.

- Take advantage of the tools that enable you to find people in the industries in which they operate. Use search.twitter.com to monitor industry-specific keywords.

- An increasing number of companies are utilizing Twitter to solicit information from customers and to interact with them. Examples are Dell (connecting with customers), JetBlue (learning about customers), Teusner Wines (gathering feedback, sharing information), and Pepsi (rapid response time in dealing with complaints).

Using LinkedIn for Market Research   Post a question (e.g., solicit advice) regarding the topic or issue you are interested in. You may obtain a better result if you go to a specific LinkedIn group.

Before you go on...

1. Is social advertising more effective than advertising without a social component? Why or why not?
2. Describe how marketing professionals use social networks to perform marketing research.

9.5 Social Computing in Business: Customer Relationship Management

LEARNING OBJECTIVE

Describe how social computing improves customer service.

The customer service profession has undergone a significant transformation, both in the ways that customer service professionals conduct business and in the ways that customers adapt to interacting with companies in a newly connected environment. Social computing has vastly altered both the expectations of customers and the capabilities of corporations in the area of customer relationship management. (We discuss customer relationship management in detail in Chapter 11.)

Customers are now incredibly empowered. Companies are closely monitoring social computing not only because they are mindful of the negative comments posted by social network members but also because they perceive an opportunity to involve customers proactively to reduce problems through improved customer service.

Consider this example. Papa John's Pizza (**www.papajohns.com**) fired a cashier at one of its New York restaurants and apologized to an Asian-American customer for a receipt that identified her as "lady chinky eyes." Minhee Cho, a communications manager at the non-profit investigative journalism group ProPublica, posted a photo of the receipt on her Twitter account, and it was viewed almost 200,000 times in a single day. John Schnatter, chairman and CEO of Papa John's, immediately posted an apology on Facebook. In his apology, he asserted that he had apologized personally to Ms. Cho as well.

Empowered customers know how to use the wisdom and power of crowds and communities to their benefit. These customers choose how they interact with companies and brands, and they have elevated expectations concerning their experiences with a company. They are actively involved with businesses, not just as purchasers but also as advocates and influencers. As a result, businesses must respond to customers quickly and appropriately. Fortunately, social computing provides many opportunities for businesses to do just that, thereby offering them the opportunity to turn disgruntled customers into champions for the firm.

> **Before you go on...**
>
> 1. Discuss why social computing is so important in customer relationship management.
> 2. Describe how social computing improves customer service.

9.6 Social Computing in Business: Human Resource Management

LEARNING OBJECTIVE

Discuss different ways in which human resource managers make use of social computing.

WILEY PLUS

Author Lecture Videos are available exclusively in *WileyPLUS.*
Apply the Concept activities are available in the Appendix and in *WileyPLUS.*

HRM Human resource (HR) departments in many organizations use social computing applications outside their organizations (recruiting) and inside their organizations (employee development). For example, Deloitte Touche Tohmatsu (**www.deloitte.com**) created a social network to assist its HR managers in downsizing and regrouping teams.

Recruiting

HRM Both recruiters and job seekers are moving to online social networks as recruiting platforms. Enterprise recruiters are scanning online social networks, blogs, and other social resources to identify and find information about potential employees. If job seekers are online and active, there is a good chance that they will be seen by recruiters. In addition, on social networks there are many passive job seekers—people who are employed but would take a better job if one appeared. So, it is important that both active and passive job seekers maintain online profiles that accurately reflect their background and skills. Closing Case 1 takes a look at the rewards and the difficulties inherent in the online recruiting process. It also provides some tips to assist you in a job search.

One HR director uses the HR social media management software Bullhorn Reach (**www .bullhorn.com**), which allows her to post jobs to eight different social networks simultaneously. Bullhorn Reach also enables her to analyze metrics that measure the effectiveness of her social recruiting efforts.

Onboarding

HRM *Onboarding* is how new employees acquire the necessary knowledge, skills, and behaviors to become effective members of the organization. Through the use of social media, new hires can learn what to expect in their first few days on the job and find answers to common questions. Because they are available inside the company's firewall, these social communities can provide detailed information about corporate policies, as well as giving employees the opportunity to complete necessary forms online. These communities also provide introductory training, such as workplace safety information and how to use enterprise applications.

Employee Development

HRM Human resource managers know that the best strategy to enable, encourage, and promote employee development is to build relationships with employees. To this end, a number of HR professionals are using enterprise social tools such as Chatter (**www.salesforce. com/chatter**) and Yammer (**www.yammer.com**) to tap in to the wisdom of every employee.

These tools help connect employees to work efficiently across organizations and to collaborate on sales opportunities, campaigns, and projects. They help companies simplify workflows and capture new ideas. They enable HR managers to find subject matter experts within the organization, recommending relevant people for every project team, sales team, and other functions.

As HR managers learn more about employees' skills, expertise, and passions through such tools, they can better motivate them, thereby helping them become more engaged and excited about their work. Employees can then be better rewarded for their expertise.

Another area of employee development is training. A large percentage of the time and expense of employee education and learning management can be minimized by utilizing e-learning and interactive social learning tools. These tools help create connections among learners, instructors, and information. Companies find that these tools facilitate knowledge transfer within departments and across teams. Examples of these tools are Moodle (www.moodle.com), Joomla (www.joomla.org), and Bloomfire (www.bloomfire.com).

In 2015, LinkedIn acquired Lynda.com, an online education company offering thousands of video courses in software, creative, and business skills. The company produces video tutorials taught by industry experts. Members of Lynda have unlimited access to watch the videos.

With this acquisition, LinkedIn plans to incorporate job certifications and training into its offerings. One LinkedIn executive noted that a LinkedIn user could be looking for a job, immediately see the skills necessary for that job, and then be prompted to take the relevant and accredited course on Lynda that will help him or her acquire those skills and land the job.

Finding a Job

The other side of organizational recruiting are those people looking for jobs. Let's say you want to find a job. Like the majority of job hunters, you will probably conduct at least part of your search online because the vast majority of entry-level positions in the United States are now listed only online. Job sites are the fastest, least expensive, and most efficient method to connect employers with potential employees.

Today, job searchers use traditional job sites and social networks such as LinkedIn. Applicants like you have helped LinkedIn raise its market share in job searches from 4.7 percent in 2010 to more than 12 percent by early 2015.

To find a job, your best bet is to begin with LinkedIn (www.linkedin.com), which has roughly 165 million members. You should definitely have a profile on LinkedIn, which, by the way, is free. (See the bulleted list that follows for mistakes to avoid on your LinkedIn profile.)

LinkedIn's success comes from its ability to accurately identify its market segment. The company's automated approach does not lend itself well to the upper tier of the job market—for example, CEO searches—where traditional face-to-face searches continue to be the preferred strategy. At the other end of the spectrum—that is, low-paying, low-skill jobs such as cashiers and truck drivers—job boards provide faster results. LinkedIn targets the vast sweet spot between these two extremes, helping to fill high-skill jobs that pay anywhere from $50,000 to $250,000 or more per year. This is the spot you will likely occupy when you graduate.

A number of job-search companies are competing with LinkedIn. These companies are trying to create better-targeted matching systems that leverage social networking functionality. These companies include Indeed (www.indeed.com), Monster (www.monster.com), SimplyHired (www.simplyhired.com), Career Builder (www.careerbuilder.com), Jobvite (www.jobvite.com), Dice Open Web (www.dice.com), and many others.

The most important secret to making online job search sites work for you is to use them carefully. Job coaches advise you to spend 80 percent of your day networking and directly contacting the people in charge of jobs you want. Devote another 10 percent to headhunters. Spend only the remaining 10 percent of your time online.

Here is how to make your time online count. To start with, as you saw above, you should have a profile on LinkedIn. The following list makes suggestions for maximizing your online profile and shows you the mistakes NOT to make on your LinkedIn profile.

- Do have a current, professional picture. (No dogs, no spouses, no babies, etc.)
- Do make certain your LinkedIn Status is correct and current.

- Do join groups related to your field of study or even to your personal interests.
- Do list an accurate skill set. Do not embellish.
- Do not use the standard connection request. Do some research on that person and tailor your connection request to that person.
- Do not neglect LinkedIn's privacy settings. When you have a job and are looking for another one, you will want to be discreet. You can set your privacy settings so that your boss does not see that you are looking for opportunities.
- Do not skip the summary. The summary is a concise way of selling yourself. Write it in the first person.
- Do not eliminate past jobs or volunteer work.
- Do not say you have worked with someone when you have not.

Next, access the job sites such as those listed above. These sites list millions of jobs and they make it easy to narrow your search using filters. These filters include title, company name, location, and many others. Indeed allows you to search within a specific salary range. SimplyHired lets you sort for friendly, socially responsible, and even dog-friendly workplaces.

These sites have advanced search options. Try plugging in the name of a company you might want to work for or an advanced degree that qualifies you for specialized work. For example, you could enter "CFA" if you are a certified financial analyst or "LEED" if you are a building engineer with expertise in environmental efficiency.

SimplyHired has a useful tool called "Who do I know?" If you have a LinkedIn profile, then this tool will instantly display your LinkedIn contacts with connections to various job listings. "Who do I know?" also syncs with Facebook.

One more trick to using the aggregators: configure them to deliver listings to your inbox. Set up an e-mail alert that delivers new job postings to you every day.

You should also search for niche sites that are specific to your field. For technology-related jobs, for instance, Dice (www.dice.com) has a strong reputation. For nonprofit jobs, try Idealist (www.idealist.org). For government jobs, the U.S. government's site is an excellent resource: www.usajobs.gov.

One more great online resource is Craigslist (www.craigslist.com). It is one site the aggregators do not tap. Craigslist focuses on local listings, and it is especially useful for entry-level jobs and internships.

Beyond locating listings for specific jobs, career coaches contend that job sites can be a resource for keywords and phrases that you can pull from job descriptions and include in your résumé, cover letters, and e-mails. Use the language from a job description in your cover letter.

Websites like Vault, Monster, and CareerBuilder provide some helpful career tips. Vault, in particular, offers very useful career guides.

The bottom line: it is critical to extend most of your efforts *beyond* an online search.

Before you go on...

1. Explain why LinkedIn has become so important in the recruiting process.
2. If you are looking for a job, what is the major problem with restricting your search to social networks?

What's in IT for Me?

ACCT For the Accounting Major

Audit teams use social networking technologies internally to stay in touch with team members who are working on multiple projects. These technologies serve as a common channel of communications.

For example, an audit team manager can create a group, include his or her team members as subscribers, and then push information regarding projects to all members at once. Externally, these technologies are useful in interfacing with clients and other third parties for whom the firm and its staff provide services.

FIN For the Finance Major

Many of the popular social networking sites have users who subscribe to finance-oriented subgroups. Among these groups are finance professionals who collaborate and share knowledge as well as nonfinancial professionals who are potential clients.

MKT For the Marketing Major

Social computing tools and applications enable marketing professionals to become closer to their customers in a variety of ways, including blogs, wikis, ratings, and recommendations. Marketing professionals now receive almost real-time feedback on products.

POM For the Production/Operations Management Major

Social computing tools and applications enable production personnel to "enlist" business partners and customers in product development activities.

HRM For the Human Resource Management Major

Social networks offer tremendous benefits to human resource professionals. HR personnel can perform a great deal of their recruiting activities by accessing such sites as LinkedIn. They can also check out potential new hires by accessing a large number of social networking sites. Internally, HR personnel can utilize private, internal social networks for employee expertise and experience in order to find the best person for a position or project team.

MIS For the MIS Major

The MIS department is responsible for two aspects of social computing usage: (1) monitoring employee usage of social computing applications while at work, both time and content, and (2) developing private, internal social networks for company employees and then monitoring the content of these networks.

Summary

9.1   Describe six Web 2.0 tools and two major types of Web 2.0 sites.

A *tag* is a keyword or term that describes a piece of information (e.g., a blog, a picture, an article, or a video clip).

Really Simple Syndication allows you to receive the information you want (customized information), when you want it, without having to surf thousands of websites.

A *weblog* (*blog* for short) is a personal website, open to the public, in which the site creator expresses his or her feelings or opinions with a series of chronological entries.

Microblogging is a form of blogging that allows users to write short messages (or capture an image or embedded video) and publish them. A *wiki* is a website on which anyone can post material and make changes to already posted material. Wikis foster easy collaboration and harness the collective intelligence of Internet users.

Social networking websites allow users to upload their content to the Web in the form of text (e.g., blogs), voice (e.g., podcasts), images, and videos (e.g., videocasts).

A *mashup* is a website that takes different content from a number of other websites and mixes them together to create a new kind of content.

9.2   Describe the benefits and risks of social commerce to companies.

Social commerce refers to the delivery of electronic commerce activities and transactions through social computing.

Benefits of social commerce to customers include the following: better and faster vendors' response to complaints; customers can assist other customers; customers' expectations can be met more fully and quickly; customers can easily search, link, chat, and buy while staying in the social network's page.

Benefits of social commerce to vendors include the following: can test new products and ideas quickly and inexpensively; learn much about their customers; identify problems quickly and alleviate anger; learn from customers' experiences with rapid feedback; increase sales when customers discuss products positively on social networking site; create better marketing campaigns and brand awareness; use low-cost user-generated content, for example, in marketing campaigns; get free advertising through viral marketing; identify influential brand advocates and reward them.

Risks of social computing include information security concerns; invasion of privacy; violation of intellectual property and copyright; employees' reluctance to participate; data leakage of personal information or corporate strategic information; poor or biased quality of users' generated content; cyberbullying or cyberstalking and employee harassment.

9.3   Identify the methods used for shopping socially.

Social shopping is a method of electronic commerce that takes all of the key aspects of social networks—friends, groups, voting, comments, discussions, reviews, and others—and focuses them on shopping.

Methods for shopping socially include what other shoppers say, group shopping, shopping communities and clubs, social marketplaces and direct sales, and peer-to-peer shopping.

9.4   Discuss innovative ways to use social networking sites for advertising and market research.

Social advertising represents advertising formats that employ the social context of the user viewing the ad.

Innovative ways to advertise in social media include the following: create a company Facebook page; Tweet business success stories to your customers; integrate ads into YouTube videos; add a Facebook "Like" button with its sponsored story to your product; use sponsored stories.

- *Using Facebook for market research*: Get feedback from your Facebook fans (and their friends if possible) on advertising campaigns, market research, etc.; test-market your messages; use Facebook for survey invitations.
- *Using Twitter for market research*: Use Twitter Search; use Twellow; look at the chart on TweetStats.
- *Using LinkedIn for market research*: Post a question (e.g., solicit advice) regarding the topic or issue you are interested in.

9.5 Describe how social computing improves customer service.

Customers are now incredibly empowered. Companies are closely monitoring social computing not only because they are mindful of the negative comments posted by social network members but also because they see an opportunity to involve customers proactively to reduce problems by improved customer service.

Empowered customers know how to use the wisdom and power of crowds and communities to their benefit. These customers choose how they interact with companies and brands, and they have elevated expectations. They are actively involved with businesses, not just as purchasers but also as advocates and influencers. As a result, businesses must respond to customers quickly and accurately. Fortunately, social computing provides many opportunities for businesses to do just that, thereby giving businesses the opportunity to turn disgruntled customers into champions for the firm.

9.6 Discuss different ways in which human resource managers make use of social computing.

- *Recruiting*: Both recruiters and job seekers are moving to online social networks as new recruiting platforms. Enterprise recruiters are scanning online social networks, blogs, and other social resources to identify and find information about potential employees. If job seekers are online and active, there is a good chance that they will be seen by recruiters. In addition, on social networks there are many passive job seekers—people who are employed but would take a better job if it appeared. So, it is important that both active and passive job seekers maintain profiles online that truly reflect them.
- *Onboarding*: The use of social media to help new employees acquire the necessary knowledge, skills, and behaviors to become effective members of the organization.
- *Employee development*: HR managers are using social tools to build relationships with employees. As HR managers learn more about employees, they can help them become more engaged and excited about their work.

Key Terms

blog (weblog) 267
blogosphere 268
collaborative consumption 278
mashup 276
microblogging 268
Really Simple Syndication (RSS) 267
social advertising 285

social capital 269
social commerce 277
social computing 265
social graph 269
social intelligence 287
social marketplaces 284
social network 269

social networking 269
social shopping 280
tag 266
tweet 268
Twitter 268
Web 2.0 266
wiki 268

Discussion Questions

1. How would you describe Web 2.0 to someone who has not taken a course in information systems?

2. If you were the CEO of a company, would you pay attention to blogs about your company? Why or why not? If yes, would you consider some blogs to be more important or more reliable than others? If so, which ones? How would you find blogs relating to your company?

3. Do you have a page on a social networking website? If yes, why? If no, what is keeping you from creating one? Is there any content that you definitely would not post on such a page?

4. How can an organization best employ social computing technologies and applications to benefit its business processes?

5. What factors might cause an individual, an employee, or a company to be cautious in the use of social networks?

6. Why are advertisers so interested in social networks?

7. What sorts of restrictions or guidelines should firms place on the use of social networks by employees? Are social computing sites a threat to security? Can they tarnish a firm's reputation? If so, how? Can they enhance a firm's reputation? If so, how?

8. Why are marketers so interested in social networks?

9. Why are human resource managers so interested in social networks?

Problem-Solving Activities

1. Visit www.wikihow.com. Explain the process for creating a new wiki.

2. Go to Amazon's Mechanical Turk website (www.mturk.com). View the available Human Intelligence Tasks (HITs). Are there any HITs that you would be interested in to make some extra money? Why or why not?

3. Access Pandora (www.pandora.com). Why is Pandora a social networking site?

4. Access ChatRoulette (www.chatroulette.com). What is interesting about this social networking site?

5. Using a search engine, look up the following:

   • *Most popular or most visited blogs.* Pick two and follow some of the posts. Why do you think these blogs are popular?

   • *Top10Best Blogsites* (www.top10best-blogsites.com). Pick two and consider why they might be the "best blogs."

6. Research how to be a successful blogger. What does it take to be a successful blogger? What time commitment might be needed? How frequently do successful bloggers post?

7. Explain how www.citibikenyc.com allows for collaborative consumption. How has this affected related industries such as public transportation?

8. Go to www.shopify.com. Describe the shopping experience. How does it compare to www.amazon.com?

9. Visit www.yelp.com. Look up your favorite restaurant. Do you agree with the reviews? Why or why not?

10. Create an account on www.linkedin.com if you do not already have an account. Describe the methods you can use for updating your profile and how you think this can help you in a future career search?

Closing Case

MIS **Nextdoor**

Between 2005 and 2020, the United States lost more than 25 percent of its local newspapers. In many neighborhoods, Nextdoor (www.nextdoor.com) has begun to assume the roles those newspapers once filled. Nextdoor is becoming the platform for people to discuss local news and events. It provides a hyperlocal social networking service for neighborhoods. *Hyperlocal* refers to information oriented around a well-defined community, with its primary focus directed to the population of that community.

Nextdoor was designed as a site to trade gardening tips, offer babysitting services, or complain about a homeowner who does not clean up after their dog. It is significant that Nextdoor requires users to submit their real names and addresses to the service. This policy ensures that users know who is providing information or posting complaints.

Nextdoor makes money by charging businesses to place ads among the posts that appear in users' feeds. In general, the platform focuses on local advertisers, including many of the same ones who previously sustained local newspapers.

Nextdoor operates in 268,000 neighborhoods in 11 countries. The app became much more popular during the COVID pandemic. In the first two weeks of March 2020 alone, user engagement increased by 80 percent as neighbors searched for advice on where to find toilet paper and masks, and stay-at-home orders hindered in-person interactions. The app also became an important tool for local authorities to communicate information regarding shutdown measures, mask mandates, and testing sites.

As with all social media sites, Nextdoor has both positive and negative features. Let's consider both aspects here.

Positive aspects. Nextdoor's algorithm that ranks posts does not seem to be as aggressive as those of large social media sites. Nextdoor has no followers, so there is little incentive for users to post clickbait or engagement bait. *Clickbait* or *engagement bait* is deceptive, sensationalized, or misleading content, such as a headline or link, that is designed to attract attention and to entice users to read, view, or listen to the content. Because each user is identified by their real first name, last initial, and neighborhood of residence, Nextdoor can feel more like actually talking to your neighbors. In addition, good news, which can be difficult to find on local television newscasts or newspapers, often features prominently on Nextdoor.

Negative aspects. Nextdoor is fundamentally opaque. Users cannot view posts from outside their location, and there are no public analyses about what types of posts perform well or poorly. In addition, several of the app's design features tend to direct users toward the "noisiest" posts, sometimes at the expense of the truth.

Further, Nextdoor seems to be most effective at amplifying the quality-of-life concerns of the more affluent residents. For example, by requiring a verified mailing address at sign-up, the platform systematically excludes homeless populations. Also, although the platform's user guidelines discourage users from discussing national politics, Nextdoor has drawn scrutiny for its role in promoting discussions of race, social class, and crime. For example, posts warning of crime and "suspicious" people appear in Nextdoor feeds without the context that a competent local reporter might add, such as putting local crime rates in historical perspective or noting root causes of crimes such as unemployment or cuts to social services.

Further, Nextdoor can make it difficult for users to distinguish between truth and misinformation. Users can post an image, but the majority of posts are text-only. Posts that include a link to another website do not display any preview of the headline or image to encourage readers to click through, as do Facebook and Twitter. As a result, "facts" cited in support of users' opinions often appear without citations to verify them. Although the app is growing in popularity, it shows few signs that it is capable of developing the accountability that local newspapers often demonstrated.

Unlike the leading social platforms, which prioritize original posts over replies and comments, reply threads on Nextdoor form the core of its content, a feature the app shares with Reddit. However, Nextdoor does not have Reddit's upvoting and downvoting mechanism for raising some replies over others. Instead, Nextdoor tends to surface and even send push notifications for the posts that receive the largest volume of replies. As a result, controversial comments that elicit many angry rebuttals are amplified instead of buried.

Compounding these issues is the fact that Nextdoor relies entirely on unpaid volunteer moderators who are not always well equipped to handle these problems. These moderators can decide whether to take posts down or leave them up and to close discussions or leave them open. However, they have few in-between options.

Let's consider an example of how Nextdoor influences local politics. A school district was holding a referendum regarding an increase in school funding. As the date for the vote approached, opponents' posts on Nextdoor claimed that the district was wasting money, that its administrators were corrupt, and that it already spent more money per student than certain other districts with higher test scores. The last claim was correct, but it omitted the context that the district was home to both the state's school for the deaf and its largest autism program.

Advocates of the referendum wanted to post counterarguments on Nextdoor but were hindered by the app's decentralized structure. Some district officers, for instance, could not access the posts and discussions happening in some areas of the district because they were visible only to that neighborhood's residents, and the officers lived in other neighborhoods. (*Note*: The school district included several Nextdoor neighborhoods.)

In the referendum, moderators noted that people on both sides of the issue chose only those statistics that supported their position. Further, nobody was empowered to review the evidence and state which statistics were valid.

After the referendum failed, some proponents pointed to misinformation on Nextdoor as a factor in its defeat. One month after the vote, the school board eliminated 63 jobs, with the alternative being bankruptcy and a bid for a state bailout. Some parents who had supported the referendum moved to other areas with better-funded schools. Others placed their children in private schools, furthering the trends that had put the district in difficult financial shape to begin with.

The school district promptly began to plan for a follow-up referendum the next year. That time, the district provided supporters in all neighborhoods with facts and counterarguments to post whenever they encountered criticism on various Nextdoor neighborhoods around the district. As the election approached, Nextdoor threads examined the district's finances, budget, administrator salaries, and what the consequences would be if the referendum passed or failed.

Voter turnout nearly doubled for the second referendum. The result was a landslide, with 70 percent of voters approving all funding requests. Exactly what role Nextdoor played in the second referendum is difficult to assess. However, proponents believed that the informal Nextdoor information campaign certainly made a difference in the outcome.

Questions

1. **Should Nextdoor rank the importance of posts as Reddit does? Why or why not? Support your answer.**

2. **Is it a good idea for Nextdoor to require a user's real name and address to upload a post and consume the content from the user's neighborhood? Why or why not? Support your answer.**

3. **Should people in one neighborhood (as defined by Nextdoor) be permitted to read content from an adjoining neighborhood? Why or why not? Support your answer.**

Sources: Compiled from A. Rutledge and T. Francisco, "Verizon and Nextdoor Connecting Neighborhoods," wgntv.com, September 7, 2022; "Small-Town Newspapers Struggling to Survive," *Yahoo! News*, December 23, 2021; "With Local News Struggling, the Nextdoor App Is Shaping Local Politics," NPR.org, February 4, 2021; J. Low, "Nextdoor App Is Replacing Local Newspapers with Gossip, Innuendo, and Rumor," *The Lowdown*, January 27, 2021; W. Oremus, "Nextdoor Is Quietly Replacing the Small-Town Paper," *OneZero*, January 27, 2021; R. Heilweil, "The Messy Politics of Nextdoor," *Vox*, October 26, 2020; M. Kelly, "Inside Nextdoor's 'Karen Problem'," *The Verge*, June 8, 2020; R. Paulas, "On Nextdoor, the Homeless Are the Enemy," *OneZero*, September 30, 2019; J. Fallows, "There's Hope for Local Journalism," *Atlantic*, September 18, 2019; "Many Small Newspapers Struggle to Survive, but a Few Are Thriving," *Daily Universe*, April 18, 2019; A. Robinette, "Small Town Newspapers Swimming against the Social Media Wave," *Delta Business Journal*, June 15, 2018; and https://nextdoor.com, accessed September 9, 2022.

CHAPTER 10

Information Systems within the Organization

CHAPTER OUTLINE	LEARNING OBJECTIVES
10.1 Transaction Processing Systems	**10.1 Explain** the purpose of transaction processing systems.
10.2 Functional Area Information Systems	**10.2 Explain** the types of support that information systems can provide for each functional area of the organization.
10.3 Enterprise Resource Planning (ERP) System	**10.3 Identify** advantages and drawbacks to businesses implementing an enterprise resource planning (ERP) system.
10.4 ERP Support for Business Processes	**10.4 Describe** the three main business processes supported by ERP systems.

Opening Case

MIS Composable Business

Background

Modern organizations must be able to adapt quickly to changing customer expectations and industry regulations and respond to competitive pressures. Technology has flattened competition and, in some ways, turned it upside down. Large organizations that have invested significant time and money in their information systems often struggle to respond to market changes as quickly as smaller, more agile organizations. To compete, organizations must offer an experience that differentiates them from the competition, while also matching customers' expectations.

For example, imagine that you were working in the banking industry in the early 1990s. For most banks, the status quo for the customer experience had changed little in more than a decade. Banks had invested millions of dollars and countless person-hours to implement internal systems to support the existing customer experience. These systems consisted of technology that was tightly integrated and very rigid.

Often, a single vendor provided these systems, meaning that one company provided an entire suite of software options. There were no options for outside integrations. These single-vendor technology stacks are referred to as "monolithic." The term *monolithic* refers to a single large block of stone. It was applied

to single-vendor systems because these systems are single, large, "heavy," and difficult to upgrade. For many years, monolithic systems were sufficient because the user experience had not changed. Bank customers would visit the physical location to deposit, transfer, and withdraw money. They also kept personal records to maintain their account balance and reconcile their account with a monthly statement, just as they had for almost a century.

During the early 1990s, however, bank administrators might have heard about offering online services to their customers. Still, this service was not yet imminent enough for banks to consider updating their systems. Further, any upgrades depended on the resources and policies of their current technology provider. For most banks, switching the entire technology stack to offer additional tools was simply not practical.

The situation began to change rapidly at the turn of the 21st century. Amazon (www.amazon.com) was six years into changing how we shop, and, in 2004, Facebook (www.facebook.com) began to transform how we connect. These developments led customers to demand more from their banking experience. Specifically, they wanted to access their bank accounts online just as they accessed their store accounts, library cards, and work information. The first banks to offer online banking were able to capitalize on the innovative differentiator. But other banks responded, and by 2006, more than 80 percent offered some version of online banking. Customers could now log in to their accounts and check for their current (or pending) balance. These websites and applications, however, functioned only on computers. They did not work on mobile, tablet, or any other app-related platforms.

In 2007, Apple (www.apple.com) introduced the iPhone, and consumer habits began to shift to a mobile-first mindset. Similar to online banking, mobile banking was initially a differentiator. Within a few years, however, being able to log in to your account through a mobile app had become a mainstream customer expectation that no longer conferred a competitive advantage.

Since that time, the banking industry has undergone many dramatic changes. The monolithic technology stacks of the past can no longer support the rate of change necessary for banks to remain relevant. Modern-day commerce requires much more agility than a monolithic system can accommodate. Increasingly, leading bankers are shifting away from these monolithic systems to keep up with the speed of change, fluctuating customer demands, and disruptive trends. Research suggests that almost half (47 percent) of consumers across all generational segments would switch banks to access better digital capabilities.

The IT Solution

Banks often consider basic technology changes only when their current technology no longer can address their unique needs or their customers' expectations. They realize they are limited to their platform's current offerings or future features roadmap, which might not align with the bank's needs or strategies. Not only does this problem impact elements like their day-to-day decisions or ongoing operations, but it also limits future growth opportunities.

The solution to this problem, which we discuss below, is called a composable system. Creating this type of system requires an entirely new mindset. The monolithic mindset was based on the belief that IT systems are complicated and the safest way to build them is to go with a single vendor where everything is designed to work together seamlessly. But, what if customers want a feature—for example, Alexa integration—and the existing system doesn't have a mechanism for integrating this feature? Should a bank change to a new monolithic system that will support Alexa? If they do, then which features they currently have will they lose?

Now, imagine a technology that would enable the bank to add new features to any system regardless of whether the same provider built them. What if businesses could seamlessly interchange components, systems, and options without touching backbone systems? This flexibility would enable banks to implement new features, rapid updates, and better customer service. By utilizing this type of technology, known as a *composable system*, banks can add, remove, and change features without upsetting the entire system.

The most important component of a composable system is the application programming interface (API), which is a set of instructions that enable two applications to speak to each other. Banks can employ APIs to provide access in multiple languages, support customers with visual impairments, and enhance their customer interfaces with graphics, support chatbots, artificial intelligence, and more. Customers can access all their information through whichever tool they prefer. In essence, APIs allow for an endless degree of customization.

Composable banking gives organizations the option to pick and choose. Gartner (www.gartner.com) describes the choices as "packaged business capabilities" that any vendor can provide. Further, composable commerce enables banks to develop a commerce suite using the best vendors for each job—from promotions to transfers to account setup. Composable commerce architectures operate within an open ecosystem of vendors.

In contrast to monolithic systems, which require extensive, risky upgrades every few years, a composable architecture favors constant development. Because composable architectures leverage the cloud, banks can instantly roll out updates for their customers without system downtime for maintenance. As a result, they can swap out components as their needs or preferences change, reducing—or even eliminating—the need for a dreaded platform change. Further, composable architecture tools enable bankers to choose the exact components they need to configure new products with limited IT involvement.

The Results

As an industry, banks are still transitioning to a composable platform. It took years to move into the monolithic systems, and change doesn't happen overnight. Some banks, however, have taken major steps toward implementing a composable system. For example, in 2019, Banca Mediolanum Group (www.bancamediolanum.it), an Italian Commercial Banking group, created a new, digital-first bank called Flowe (www.flowe.com) from the bottom up. In the past, this system would have taken years to build. But using a composable platform, Flowe was able to go live in 2020. In just five months, Flowe grew to 600,000 customers.

Bancorp (www.thebancorp.com) created an entirely mobile bank called Varo Bank (www.varomoney.com). Developing a new bank in a monolithic platform would have taken years. Varo, however, obtained its charter in July 2020, and by August 2021, it had attracted four million new accounts. Varo was designed to be agile by leveraging a cloud-banking platform, enabling the bank to quickly compose solutions built from best-of-breed capabilities. Varo boasts lower operational costs—estimated at 25 percent of traditional costs—that not only improve business margins but also enable the bank to launch more competitive solutions, thereby creating opportunities with which other banks cannot compete.

Questions

1. **Define a monolithic platform and identify its major advantages and disadvantages.**

2. **Define a composable system and identify its major advantages and disadvantages.**

3. **How has technology changed the information systems used in the banking industry?**

Sources: Compiled from P. Varadhan, "Why the Future of Banking Is Composable," finextra.com, September 30, 2022; J. Cottrell, "Three Composable Commerce Myths," *Forbes*, September 27, 2022; D. Mistry, "Making Composable Banking Work," *Fintech Futures*, September 23, 2022; D. Swanson, "The Future of Commerce: Going Headless," *Total Retail*, September 22, 2022; A. Denizeri, "Making Supply Chain Planning Agile with Modular Planning Technologies," *Logistics Viewpoints*, September 20, 2022; S. Govindu, "From Cacophony to Symphony: Composable Enterprise and the Customized Experience," *Forbes*, September 16, 2022; S. Remekie, "Composable: The Marketer's Perspective and Roadmap," cnswire.com, September 14, 2022; R. Harbols, "Outpace the Competition with Composable Commerce," *Forbes*, September 6, 2022; J. Jarmon, "Introducing the Composable Business: How Customer-Centered APIs Are Empowering Executives to Open New Markets," *Forbes*, June 15, 2022; J. England, "Technology in Fintech and the Story of Online Banking," *FinTech*, June 8, 2022; R. Shevlin, "Which Bank

Has the Best Mobile Banking App?" *Forbes*, June 6, 2022; J. Cottrell, "Why Composable Commerce Is Gaining Traction," *Forbes*, March 31, 2022; P. Varadhan, "Why Composability Is the Future of Banking," *International Banker*, May 30, 2022; S. Zimberg, "How Banks Can Catch Up to the Speed and Scale of Fintechs," *The Financial Brand*, May 27, 2022; B. Nixon, "How CIOs Can 'Tune Up' for the IT Composability Paradigm," *Forbes*, February 22, 2022; V. Afshar,

"Next Generation Business Applications Are Scalable, Composable and Intelligent," zdnet.com, June 23, 2021; K. Panetta, "Gartner Keynote: The Future of Business Is Composable," *Gartner*, October 19, 2020; S. Perez, "Mobile Banking Startup Varo Is Becoming a Real Bank," techcrunch.com, August 3, 2020; and S. Mahalingam, "Composable Banking Platform through Open Bank APIs," finextra .com, February 16, 2016.

Introduction

The opening case illustrates the importance of agility in today's fast-paced, volatile market. Businesses must be able to adapt their systems to customers' changing needs and demands. Although this case focuses on the impact of technology on the banking industry, the application of composable architecture reaches almost all industries.

It is important to note that "systems within organizations" do not have to be owned by the organization itself. Instead, organizations can deploy very productive ISs that are owned by an external vendor. The key point is that "systems within an organization" are intended to support internal processes, regardless of who actually owns the systems.

It is important for you to have a working knowledge of ISs within your organization for a variety of reasons. First, your job will require you to access corporate data that are supplied primarily by your firm's transaction processing systems and enterprise resource planning systems. Second, you will have a great deal of input into the format and content of the reports that you receive from these systems. Third, you will use the information contained in these reports to perform your job more productively.

This chapter will teach you about the various information systems that modern organizations employ. We begin by considering transaction processing systems, the most fundamental organizational information systems. We continue with the functional area management information systems, and we conclude with enterprise resource planning systems.

10.1 | Transaction Processing Systems

WILEY PLUS

Author Lecture Videos are available exclusively in *WileyPLUS*.
Apply the Concept activities are available in the Appendix and in *WileyPLUS*.

LEARNING OBJECTIVE

Explain the purpose of transaction processing systems.

Millions (sometimes billions) of transactions occur in large organizations every day. A **transaction** is any business event that generates data worthy of being captured and stored in a database. Examples of transactions are a product manufactured, a service sold, a person hired, and a payroll check generated. In another example, when you are checking out of Walmart, each time the cashier swipes an item across the bar code reader, that is one transaction.

A transaction processing system (TPS) supports the monitoring, collection, storage, and processing of data from the organization's basic business transactions, each of which generates data. The TPS collects data continuously, typically in *real time*—that is, as soon as the data are generated—and it provides the input data for the corporate databases. TPSs are critical to the success of any enterprise because they support core operations.

In the modern business world, TPSs are inputs for the functional area information systems and business intelligence systems, as well as business operations such as customer relationship management, knowledge management, and e-commerce. TPSs have to efficiently handle both high volumes of data and large variations in those volumes (e.g., during periods of peak processing). They must also avoid errors and downtime, record results accurately and

transaction Any business event that generates data worth capturing and storing in a database.

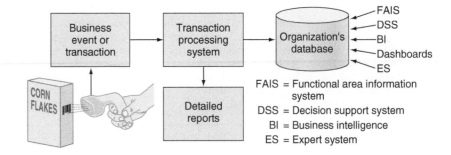

FIGURE 10.1 How transaction processing systems manage data.

securely, and maintain privacy and security. Figure 10.1 illustrates how TPSs manage data. Consider these examples of how TPSs handle the complexities of transactional data:

- When more than one person or application program can access the database at the same time, the database has to be protected from errors resulting from overlapping updates. The most common error is losing the results of one of the updates.

- When processing a transaction involves more than one computer, the database and all users must be protected against inconsistencies arising from a failure of any component at any time. For example, an error that occurs at some point in an ATM withdrawal can enable a customer to receive cash, although the bank's computer indicates that he or she did not. (Conversely, a customer might not receive cash, although the bank's computer indicates that he or she did.)

- **ACCT** It must be possible to reverse a transaction in its entirety if it turns out to have been entered in error. It is also necessary to reverse a transaction when a customer returns a purchased item. For example, if you return a sweater that you have purchased, then the store must credit your credit card for the amount of the purchase, refund your cash, or offer you an in-store credit to purchase another item. The store must also update its inventory.

- **ACCT** It is frequently important to preserve an audit trail. In fact, for certain transactions an audit trail may be legally required.

These and similar issues explain why organizations spend millions of dollars on expensive mainframe computers. In today's business environment, firms must have the dependability, reliability, and processing capacity of these computers to handle their transaction processing loads.

Regardless of the specific data processed by a TPS, the actual process tends to be standard, whether it occurs in a manufacturing firm, a service firm, or a government organization. As the first step in this procedure, people or sensors collect data, which are entered into the computer through any input device. Generally speaking, organizations try to automate the TPS data entry as much as possible because of the large volume involved, a process called *source data automation* (discussed in Technology Guide 1).

batch processing Transaction processing system (TPS) that processes data in batches at fixed periodic intervals.

online transaction processing (OLTP) Transaction processing system (TPS) that processes data after transactions occur, frequently in real time.

Next, the system processes data in one of two basic ways: batch processing and online processing. In **batch processing**, the firm collects data from transactions as they occur, placing them in groups, or *batches*. The system then prepares and processes the batches periodically (say, every night).

In **online transaction processing (OLTP)**, business transactions are processed online as soon as they occur. For example, when you pay for an item at a store, the system records the sale by reducing the inventory on hand by one unit, increasing sales figures for the item by one unit, and increasing the store's cash position by the amount you paid. The system performs these tasks in real time by means of online technologies.

Before you go on...

1. Define TPS.
2. List the key functions of a TPS.

Functional Area Information Systems

LEARNING OBJECTIVE

Explain the types of support that information systems can provide for each functional area of the organization.

Each department or functional area within an organization has its own collection of application programs, or information systems. Each of these **functional area information systems (FAIS)** supports a particular functional area by increasing its internal efficiency and effectiveness. FAISs often convey information in a variety of reports, which you will see later in this chapter. Examples of FAISs are accounting IS, finance IS, production/operations management (POM) IS, marketing IS, and human resources (HR) IS.

Before we present each functional area, we consider a historical debate among organizations: Should IT exist as its own centralized functional area? Or, should IT support be decentralized within each functional area? The pendulum has swung both ways over the years. Today, however, cloud technology brings a new consideration. IT's About Business 10.1 presents this debate.

functional area information systems (FAIS) Systems that provide information to managers (usually mid-level) in the functional areas to better support managerial tasks of planning, organizing, and controlling operations.

IT's About Business 10.1

MIS IT: Centralized vs. Decentralized

Who should IT workers report to? They work *with* everyone in an organization, but do they work *for* everyone in the organization? Should there be an IT area in each department to handle the technology needs of that department? Or, should IT be centralized in a single department to which everyone goes for all technology issues?

The dilemma of designing the IT department has been around since the 20th century. Technology was generally expensive and complex. Further, most workers did not grow up using technology in their daily lives. As a result, there was a need for experts to build and maintain the technology. This need led most organizations to establish a centralized, company-wide technology department. Throughout the 1980s and 1990s, this arrangement was the "correct" way to deploy and manage technology. Now, fast-forward to the 21st century. Most organizations continue to maintain centralized technology departments, even though younger, tech-savvy generations are entering the workforce.

The centralized IT department provided organizational direction and standardization. IT departments became "Dell shops" or "Oracle shops" based on the hardware and software decisions made by leadership. This standardization and consistency reduced costs and streamlined maintenance. Decentralized IT, on the other hand, is an organizational structure in which daily operations and decision-making responsibilities are delegated to respective business units.

Many expensive and complex areas like cybersecurity have benefitted from centralized management. For other areas, however, having a single point of responsibility created a bottleneck because organizations' IT needs outgrew the capability of the department. Some IT departments have reported being 18 months behind on fulfilling system or application updates.

When a department is 18 months behind, people begin to look elsewhere for solutions. Today, according to a 2022 ManageEngine (a provider of enterprise software systems) study, "IT at Work: 2022 and Beyond" (**www.manageengine.com/survey/it-at-work-2022/us-canada.html**), an increasing number of IT-related decisions are being made outside the formal IT department. In addition, the cloud has changed the business requirements of the IT Department because the amount of on-premise hardware is significantly reduced. Further, tech-savvy employees can participate in DevOps, an interdepartmental effort between an IT development group and business operations, regardless of the departmental structure.

In some ways, the department designed to foster innovation and business success has hindered the services it is intended to provide. As a result, some IT experts have called for the end of the traditional IT department. For example, a November 2021 article in the *Wall Street Journal* asserted that it is time for the IT department to "shape up or ship out." Of course, this article elicited a lot of feedback.

In the following section, we examine the advantages of both a centralized and decentralized structure. We then consider how the changing nature of IT decision making, the cloud, and a more tech-savvy workforce might change the design of the IT department.

Centralized IT Departments

The benefits of a centralized structure are often associated with increased purchasing power, improved information flow among IT team members, and a watchful view of the enterprise's technical infrastructure from both an operational network and a security perspective. Specifically, consider the following benefits.

- A centralized IT Department can help to lower hardware costs by keeping all servers and networking equipment in one place. However, this benefit applies only if your employees are centralized or can securely connect to the local servers. Today, a cloud-based solution can provide most of the functions local servers and mainframes provide, almost eliminating this advantage.

- A centralized structure can lower initial and ongoing software costs. It is easier to negotiate the pricing of software licenses and support contracts for an entire company than for individual departments. For this reason, a centralized IT structure will increase purchasing power. This power can result in better contract terms and better support. A centralized design also gives the IT staff better oversight and makes routine tasks easier. Regular maintenance, such as software installations, updates, and security patches, can be accomplished from one location, thereby lowering the overall cost of ownership. In decentralized IT setups, completing these tasks would require staff to manage each area separately, which can drive up costs and decrease productivity. As with hardware, however, a cloud-based solution removes the need to maintain separate sites, thus reducing this advantage.

- Centralized IT can more readily comply with industry regulations. Some industries have specific rules. For example, healthcare providers must comply with HIPAA standards, and financial companies must provide annual data security reporting to meet Sarbanes–Oxley requirements. However, modern, cloud-based solutions often satisfy these regulations for their customers, eliminating this advantage.

In sum, then, a centralized IT department provides several advantages. These advantages, however, have changed as technology has increasingly shifted to the cloud. Now, let's consider the advantages of a decentralized IT department.

Decentralized IT Departments

As stated earlier, decentralized IT is an organizational structure in which daily operations and decision-making responsibilities are delegated to respective business units. This structure offers several advantages. It is especially practical when the various departments or business units have distinctive IT needs and strategies.

- When all departments have decision-making authority, they can choose and configure IT resources to match their specific needs. Decision making is quick and does not require a chain of approvals.

- Decentralization creates greater organizational redundancy and a more resilient IT structure. If all departments maintain individual servers, then one server can go down and the others will not be affected. Further, one server can function as a backup for another department during a network failure.

- Less bureaucracy enables an organization to respond more quickly to IT trends. Departments can make independent decisions, so it is easier for them to leverage new technologies. Quicker responses to emerging technology trends can be a competitive advantage.

These benefits aside, in the 2022 ManageEngine Survey, 99 percent of respondents reported that their organization faces challenges due to IT decentralization. Most notable are maintaining IT security (more than 50 percent), overall quality maintenance (more than 40 percent), and the reliability of ongoing support (37 percent).

Conclusion

How to decide? Large organizations with multiple legacy systems are very often moving elements of their IT department away from a centralized system. The reason is that the role of the IT department is changing (see **Table 1.2**: The Changing Role of the Information Systems Department). In turn, the organizational structure must adapt to these changes.

Companies that need to respond quickly to new IT developments are less likely to establish a centralized IT management structure. As-a-service solutions enable organizations to build and deliver a unique customer experience much faster than centralized structures.

The way forward is most likely a hybrid structure that will offer the benefits of both approaches. The aspects of IT management that provide an advantage at an overarching level—for example, security, compliance, and API standards—are centralized. However, a department can make purchases directly if it meets the established standards. Overall, hybrid IT models will support but not control the technology decisions the various departments make.

Changing business processes to adopt a hybrid system will not be easy. Start-ups have an advantage because they can build modern technological possibilities into their organizational structure from the ground up. In contrast, established companies must determine how to reallocate and redeploy IT resources in a new, decentralized world to meet the constantly changing needs of various departments.

Questions

1. Describe a centralized IT department and discuss its advantages.

2. Describe a decentralized IT department and discuss its advantages.

3. How does the cloud change the advantages you discussed in these questions?

4. Describe a hybrid IT structure.

Sources: Compiled from J. Peppard, "Get Rid of the IT Department? Some People Think Otherwise," *Wall Street Journal*, September 18, 2022; D. Weldon, "Centralized vs. Decentralized Data Systems—Which Choice Is Best?" *VentureBeat*, September 12, 2022; J. Erolin, "Is It Time for Decentralized IT?" BairesDev.com, May 13, 2022; C. Betz, and W. McKeon-White, "3 Reasons the IT Department Is Here to Stay," *CIO Dive*, December 13, 2021; J. Peppard, "It's Time to Get Rid of the IT Department," *Wall Street Journal*, November 27, 2021; J. Chapel, "How Cloud Has Affected the Centralization vs. Decentralization of IT," Dataversity.net, August 9, 2021; R. Kumar, "Your IT Organizational Structure: Should You Centralize or Decentralize?" SoftwareAdvice.com, May 20, 2020; and https://www.manageengine.com/survey/it-at-work-2022/us-canada.html, accessed October 10, 2022.

As illustrated in Figure 10.1, the FAIS access data from the corporate databases. The following sections discuss the support that FAISs provide for these functional areas.

`ACCT` `FIN` Information Systems for Accounting and Finance

A primary mission of the accounting and finance functional areas is to manage money flows into, within, and out of organizations. This mission is very broad because money is involved in all organizational functions. Therefore, accounting and finance information systems are very diverse and comprehensive. In this section, you focus on certain selected activities of the accounting and finance functional area.

Financial Planning and Budgeting   Appropriate management of financial assets is a major task in financial planning and budgeting. Managers must plan for both acquiring and using resources. For example:

- *Financial and economic forecasting*: Knowledge about the availability and cost of money is a key ingredient for successful financial planning. Cash flow projections are particularly important because they inform organizations what funds they need, when they need them, and how they will acquire them.

  Funds for operating organizations come from multiple sources, including stockholders' investments, bond sales, bank loans, sales of products and services, and income from investments. Decisions concerning funding for ongoing operations and for capital investment can be supported by decision support systems and business analytics applications (discussed in Chapter 12). Numerous software packages for conducting economic and financial forecasting are also available. Many of these packages can be downloaded from the Internet, some of them free.

- *Budgeting*: An essential component of the accounting and finance function is the annual budget, which allocates the organization's financial resources among participants and activities. The budget allows management to distribute resources in the way that best supports the organization's mission and goals.

  Several software packages are available to support budget preparation and control and to facilitate communication among participants in the budget process. These packages can reduce the time involved in the budget process. Furthermore, they can automatically monitor exceptions for patterns and trends.

Managing Financial Transactions   Many accounting and finance software packages are integrated with other functional areas. For example, Sage 50cloud Accounting by Sage (https://www.sage.com/en-us/products/sage-50cloud/) offers a sales ledger, a purchase ledger, a cash book, sales order processing, invoicing, stock control, a fixed assets register, and more.

Companies involved in electronic commerce need to access customers' financial data (e.g., credit line), inventory levels, and manufacturing databases (to determine available capacity and place orders). For example, Microsoft Dynamics GP (now www.dynamics .microsoft.com—formerly Great Plains Software) offers 50 modules that meet the most common financial, project, distribution, manufacturing, and e-business needs.

Organizations, business processes, and business activities operate with, and manage, financial transactions. Consider these examples:

- *Global stock exchanges*: Financial markets operate in global, 24/7/365, distributed electronic stock exchanges that use the Internet both to buy and sell stocks and to broadcast real-time stock prices.

- *Managing multiple currencies*: Global trade involves financial transactions that are carried out in different currencies. The conversion ratios of these currencies are constantly in flux. Financial and accounting systems use financial data from different countries, and they convert the currencies from and to any other currency in seconds. Reports based on these data, which formerly required several days to generate, can now be produced in only seconds. In addition to currency conversions, these systems manage multiple languages.

- *Virtual close*: Companies traditionally closed their books (accounting records) quarterly, usually to meet regulatory requirements. Today, many companies want to be able to close their books at any time, on very short notice. Information systems make it possible to close the books quickly in what is called a *virtual close*. This process provides almost real-time information on the organization's financial health.

- *Expense management automation*: Expense management automation (EMA) refers to systems that automate the data entry and processing of travel and entertainment expenses. EMA systems are Web-based applications that enable companies to quickly and consistently collect expense information, enforce company policies and contracts, and reduce unplanned purchases as well as airline and hotel expenses. They also allow companies to reimburse their employees more quickly because expense approvals are not delayed by poor documentation.

Investment Management   Organizations invest large amounts of money in stocks, bonds, real estate, and other assets. Managing these investments is a complex task for several reasons. First, organizations have literally thousands of investment alternatives dispersed throughout the world to choose from. These investments are also subject to complex regulations and tax laws, which vary from one location to another.

Investment decisions require managers to evaluate financial and economic reports provided by diverse institutions, including federal and state agencies, universities, research institutions, and financial services firms. Thousands of websites also provide financial data, many of them free.

To monitor, interpret, and analyze the huge amounts of online financial data, financial analysts employ two major types of IT tools: Internet search engines and business intelligence and decision support software.

Control and Auditing   One major reason why organizations go out of business is their inability to forecast or secure a sufficient cash flow. Underestimating expenses, overspending, engaging in fraud, and mismanaging financial statements can lead to disaster. Consequently, it is essential that organizations effectively control their finances and financial statements. Let's examine some of the most common forms of financial control.

- *Budgetary control*: After an organization has finalized its annual budget, it divides those monies into monthly allocations. Managers at various levels monitor departmental expenditures and compare them against the budget and the operational progress of corporate plans.

- *Auditing*: Auditing has two basic purposes: (1) to monitor how the organization's monies are being spent and (2) to assess the organization's financial health. *Internal audits* are performed by the organization's accounting and finance personnel. These employees also prepare for periodic *external audits* by outside CPA firms.

- *Financial ratio analysis*: Another major accounting and finance function is to monitor the company's financial health by assessing a set of financial ratios, including liquidity ratios (the availability of cash to pay debt), activity ratios (how quickly a firm converts noncash assets to cash assets), debt ratios (measure the firm's ability to repay long-term debt), and profitability ratios (measure the firm's use of its assets and control of its expenses to generate an acceptable rate of return).

MKT Information Systems for Marketing

It is impossible to overestimate the importance of customers to any organization. Therefore, any successful organization must understand its customers' needs and wants and then develop its marketing and advertising strategies around them. Information systems provide numerous types of support to the marketing function. Customer-centric organizations are so important that we cover this topic in detail in Chapter 11.

POM Information Systems for Production/Operations Management

The production/operations management (POM) function in an organization is responsible for the processes that transform inputs into useful outputs as well as for the overall operation of the business. The POM function is responsible for managing the organization's supply chain. Because supply chain management is vital to the success of modern organizations, we address this topic in detail in Chapter 11. Because of the breadth and variety of POM functions, we discuss only four here: in-house logistics and materials management, planning production and operation, computer-integrated manufacturing (CIM), and product life cycle management (PLM).

Blockchain (see Chapter 7) is radically transforming manufacturing. IT's About Business 10.2 presents several ways that blockchain has impacted, and will continue to impact, manufacturing.

IT's About Business 10.2

MIS POM Blockchain and Manufacturing

Blockchain. What a strange word. It brings to mind an image of a very impractical tool. What could you do with a chain made of blocks? In the digital world, the answer is, quite a lot!

What exactly is blockchain (see Chapter 7)? Perhaps it would help to explain how things work without blockchain. Imagine that you work for a local hardware store, and a customer returns a can of spray paint because it was the wrong color. The packaging indicates the paint is blue, but when the customer used it, the paint was red. Your supervisor tasked you with calling the distributor to inform them and to find out how many other items might have this same problem.

You start by examining your shipments to see when they were delivered and in which order. You need to know how many other items in that order might be incorrectly labeled. Armed with this information, you call your distributor. They take your order numbers and delivery dates, and they begin to match that information with their records. They find that the order originated from a single supplier. Now, with the information about the supplier, the products, and the orders, they reach out to the supplier.

The supplier takes all the information from the hardware store and the distributor and matches this information to theirs. They identify the incorrectly labeled batch, and they discover that it was produced and labeled by one of their partners. They reach out to the partner with the information from the hardware store, distributor, and supplier to determine the extent of the incorrect labeling. They have to wait five business days for a response because the partner was sick with COVID. Overall, it takes two weeks for each party to collect their information and communicate with the other parties.

This scenario illustrates the challenges that result when each company keeps an independent list of product information. These lists are called *ledgers*. Sometimes ledgers are kept on paper or there is only one digital copy, and they are not easy to access and share. Researching the incorrectly labeled spray paint took several phone calls and extensive employee time.

What if there were a better way? This is where blockchain technology comes in. Blockchain is an open, shared, encrypted, and redundant digital ledger. It is everywhere—at least for people who have access—and is available 24/7.

Put simply, blockchain enables organizations to keep track of transactions and records in a way that is fast, secure, and highly reliable. Because the blockchain is shared, all information is transparent and accessible to everyone with access. Clearly, then, a blockchain would have significantly reduced the work required for the hardware store employee to research the improperly labeled spray paint. Rather than requiring multiple phone calls to gather data, blockchain would have answered the questions in a matter of seconds. Further, the hardware store could have viewed the entire path of that particular can and identified the source of the incorrect labeling. The hardware manager would have known the extent of the problem and could have taken corrective action.

Who Is Using Blockchain?

Several industries are making use of blockchain. One prominent example is the supply chain industry. A 2021 industry report revealed that 10 percent of companies surveyed planned to invest in blockchain by 2024. Further, 12 percent had implemented blockchain, and 41 percent predicted they will be using it by 2026.

Blockchain is also the technology behind cryptocurrency. Cryptocurrency doesn't exist without blockchain. However, blockchain will impact many other businesses. Companies like Home Depot and IBM have already adopted blockchain to improve supplier relationships. These companies have reported that vendor disputes have declined significantly and transaction times are shorter.

In addition, blockchain has gained a footing in the grocery industry, where knowing the source of a product literally can be a matter of life or death. The technology is enabling retailers to quickly pinpoint the source of outbreaks of pathogens like *E. coli*. Blockchain-based traceability will reduce the time required to resolve scandals surrounding food safety or quality and outbreaks of foodborne illnesses. Moreover, it will help companies comply with government regulations, and it will enhance consumer confidence. Finally, allowing consumers to access blockchain via a QR code can provide a competitive advantage.

Walmart, which employs IBM's blockchain platform, claims that it used to take at least six days to trace the source of mangos. Now, blockchain can trace the origin of mangos in 2.2 seconds.

How Will Blockchain Transform Manufacturing?

Manufacturing is as much about managing product flows as it is about producing goods. Tracking items along the supply chain, managing inventory, securing data, and ensuring payments are critical to a manufacturer's success. Let's examine how blockchain can help manufacturers carry out each of these functions.

Improved traceability. Blockchain is a decentralized ledger, meaning that each person associated with the manufacturer's supply chain can effectively store and share information. This information can include the origin of materials, shipping status, compliance measures, and other details. All members have access to these data. Greater traceability creates greater transparency. When there is greater transparency in operations, there is greater transparency in the product, and the customer has an enhanced purchase experience.

Optimized inventory management. Inventory management is where blockchain is proving to be a game changer for manufacturers. With distributed blockchain ledgers, manufacturers can track the location of supplies throughout all stages of assembly. Furthermore, monitoring supplies and processed goods in real time enables manufacturers to make more accurate delivery commitments to their customers.

Enhanced data security. Blockchain solutions keep data more secure through encryption and nearly uneditable data. With the integration of blockchain solutions, manufacturers do not have to worry about a breach of large volumes of client and supplier data. Blockchains are distributed, duplicated, and synchronized, providing several layers of data security. This security instills trust in the shared data among partners.

Automated payments with smart contracts. Because blockchain records are nearly perfect, members can make payments quickly and automatically. When smart contracts are run on a blockchain, companies can automatically make a payment when the prerequisite conditions are met. In addition, blockchain eliminates many—or most—of the human errors in transactions.

Conclusion

Manufacturers are searching for ways to reduce costs in today's global supply chain. Customers want to know where their products were sourced. Government agencies want to quickly identify the source of product recalls to limit the societal impact. Businesses want data that are secure and easily accessible. Blockchain addresses these needs and solves many problems with its open, secure, distributed ledger platform.

Questions

1. What is a ledger?
2. What is a digital ledger?
3. Describe three ways blockchain will improve manufacturing processes.

Sources: Compiled from J. Speakman, "How Blockchain and IoT Are Changing the World for the Better," blockzeit.com, October 4, 2022; R. Kohil, A. Srivastava, and C. Varshneya, "Industry 5.0: The Next Paradigm Shift in Manufacturing," zinnov.com, September 30, 2022; A. Tuncturk, "Blockchain 101—The Ultimate Guide for Beginners," coincodex.com, September 29, 2022; K. Adams, "Blockchain Technology: The Future of the Manufacturing Industry," *TechTarget*, August 30, 2022; K. Miller, "5 Ways Blockchain Can Revolutionize the Manufacturing Industry," *ReadWrite*, August 27, 2022; E. Boer et al., "Transforming Advanced Manufacturing through Industry 4.0," McKinsey & Company, June 27, 2022; D. Edwards, "The Real-World Use Cases for Blockchain Technology," *Robotics & Automation News*, May 20, 2022; J. Miller, "Blockchain Drives Transparency in the Supply Chain," *Supply Chain Dive*, March 22, 2022; M. del Castillo, and M. Schifrin (eds.), "Forbes Blockchain 50 2022," *Forbes*, February 8, 2022; D. Turpitka, "Blockchain in the Automotive Sector: Three Use Cases and Three Challenges," *Forbes*, December 22, 2021; and W. Henry, L. Pawczuk, "Blockchain: Ready for Business," Deloitte .com, December 7, 2021.

In-House Logistics and Materials Management Logistics management deals with ordering, purchasing, inbound logistics (receiving), and outbound logistics (shipping) activities. Related activities include inventory management and quality control.

Inventory Management As the name suggests, inventory management determines how much inventory an organization should maintain. Both excessive inventory and insufficient inventory create problems. Overstocking can be expensive because of storage costs and the costs of spoilage and obsolescence. However, keeping insufficient inventory is also expensive because of last-minute orders and lost sales.

Operations personnel make two basic decisions: when to order and how much to order. Inventory models, such as the economic order quantity (EOQ) model, support these decisions. Many commercial inventory software packages are available that automate the application of these models.

Many large companies allow their suppliers to monitor their inventory levels and ship products as they are needed. This strategy, called *vendor-managed inventory (VMI)*, eliminates the need for the company to submit purchasing orders. We discuss VMI in Chapter 11.

Quality Control Quality control systems used by manufacturing units provide information about the quality of incoming material and parts, as well as the quality of in-process semifinished and finished products. These systems record the results of all inspections and then compare these results with established metrics. They also generate periodic reports that contain information about quality—for example, the percentage of products that contain defects or that need to be reworked. Quality control data, collected by Web-based sensors, can be interpreted in real time. Alternatively, they can be stored in a database for future analysis.

Planning Production and Operations
In many firms, POM planning is supported by IT. POM planning has evolved from material requirements planning (MRP) to manufacturing resource planning (MRP II) to enterprise resource planning (ERP). We briefly discuss MRP and MRP II here, and we examine ERP in detail later in this chapter.

Inventory systems that use an EOQ approach are designed for items for which demand is completely independent—for example, the number of identical personal computers a computer manufacturer will sell. In manufacturing operations, however, the demand for some items is interdependent. Consider, for example, a company that makes three types of chairs, all of which use the same screws and bolts. In this case, the demand for screws and bolts depends on the total demand for all three types of chairs and their shipment schedules. The planning process that integrates production, purchasing, and inventory management of interdependent items is called *material requirements planning (MRP)*.

MRP deals only with production scheduling and inventories. More complex planning also involves allocating related resources, such as money and labor. For these cases, more complex, integrated software, called *manufacturing resource planning (MRP II)*, is available. MRP II integrates a firm's production, inventory management, purchasing, financing, and labor activities. Thus, MRP II adds functions to a regular MRP system. In fact, MRP II has evolved into *enterprise resource planning (ERP)*.

Computer-Integrated Manufacturing
Computer-integrated manufacturing (CIM) (also called *digital manufacturing*) is an approach that integrates various automated factory systems. CIM has three basic goals: (1) to simplify all manufacturing technologies and techniques, (2) to automate as many of the manufacturing processes as possible, and (3) to integrate and coordinate all aspects of design, manufacturing, and related functions through computer systems.

> **computer-integrated manufacturing (CIM)** An information system that integrates various automated factory systems; also called *digital manufacturing*.

Product Life Cycle Management
Even within a single organization, designing and developing new products can be expensive and time consuming. When multiple organizations are involved, the process can become very complex. *Product life cycle management (PLM)* is a business strategy that enables manufacturers to share product-related data that support product design and development and supply chain operations. PLM applies Web-based collaborative technologies to product development. By integrating formerly disparate functions, such as a manufacturing process and the logistics that support it, PLM enables these functions to collaborate, essentially forming a single team that manages the product from its inception through its completion, as shown in **Figure 10.2**.

HRM Information Systems for Human Resource Management

Initial human resource information system (HRIS) applications dealt primarily with transaction processing systems such as managing benefits and keeping records of vacation days. As organizational systems have moved to intranets and the Web, so have HRIS applications.

Many HRIS applications are delivered through an HR portal. (See our discussion of LinkedIn in Chapter 9.) For example, numerous organizations use their Web portals to advertise job openings and to conduct online hiring and training. In this section, you consider how organizations are using IT to perform some key HR functions: recruitment, HR maintenance and development, and HR planning and management.

Recruitment
Recruitment involves finding potential employees, evaluating them, and deciding which ones to hire. Some companies are flooded with viable applicants; others have difficulty finding the right people. IT can be helpful in both cases. IT can also assist in related activities such as testing and screening job applicants.

With millions of résumés available online (in particular, LinkedIn), it is not surprising that companies are trying to find appropriate candidates on the Web, usually with the help of specialized search engines. Companies also advertise hundreds of thousands of jobs on the Web. Online recruiting can reach more candidates, which

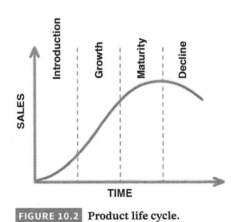

FIGURE 10.2 Product life cycle.

may bring in better applicants. The costs of online recruitment are also usually lower than traditional recruiting methods such as advertising in newspapers or in trade journals.

Human Resources Development

After employees are recruited, they become part of the corporate human resources pool, which means they must be evaluated and developed. IT provides support for these activities. Throughout their career, they have access to various internal resources, and IT helps to manage their access levels.

Most employees are periodically evaluated by their immediate supervisors. In some organizations, peers or subordinates also evaluate other employees. Evaluations are typically digitized, and they are used to support many decisions, ranging from rewards to transfers to layoffs.

IT also plays an important role in training and retraining. Some of the most innovative developments are taking place in the areas of intelligent computer-aided instruction and the application of multimedia support for instructional activities. For example, companies conduct much of their corporate training over their intranet or on the Web.

Human Resources Planning and Management

Managing human resources in large organizations requires extensive planning and detailed strategy. IT support is particularly valuable in the following three areas:

1. *Payroll and employees' records*: The HR department is responsible for payroll preparation. This process is typically automated, meaning that paychecks are printed or money is transferred electronically into employees' bank accounts.

2. *Benefits administration*: In return for their work contributions to their organizations, employees receive wages, bonuses, and various benefits. These benefits include health care and dental care, pension contributions (in a decreasing number of organizations), 401(k) contributions, wellness centers, and child care centers.

   Managing benefits is a complex task because organizations typically offer multiple options, allowing employees to choose and trade off their benefits. In many organizations, employees can access the company portal to self-register for specific benefits.

3. *Employee relationship management*: In their efforts to better manage employees, companies are developing *employee relationship management* (ERM) applications, for example, a call center for employees to discuss problems.

Table 10.1 provides an overview of the activities that the FAIS support. Figure 10.3 identifies many of the information systems that support these five functional areas.

TABLE 10.1 Activities Supported by Functional Area Information Systems

ACCT FIN Accounting and Finance

Financial planning and cost of money

Budgeting—allocates financial resources among participants and activities

Capital budgeting—financing of asset acquisitions

Managing financial transactions

Handling multiple currencies

Virtual close—the ability to close the books at any time on short notice

Investment management—managing organizational investments in stocks, bonds, real estate, and other investment vehicles

Budgetary control—monitoring expenditures and comparing them against the budget

Auditing—ensuring the accuracy of the organization's financial transactions and assessing the condition of the organization's financial health

Payroll

MKT Marketing and Sales

Customer relations—knowing who customers are and treating them appropriately

Customer profiles and preferences

Salesforce automation—using software to automate the business tasks of sales, thereby improving the productivity of salespeople

(continued)

TABLE 10.1   Activities Supported by Functional Area Information Systems *(continued)*

POM   Production/Operations and Logistics

Inventory management—when to order new inventory, how much inventory to order, and how much inventory to keep in stock

Quality control—controlling for defects in incoming materials and goods produced

Materials requirements planning (MRP)—planning process that integrates production, purchasing, and inventory management of interdependent items

Manufacturing resource planning (MRP II)—planning process that integrates an enterprise's production, inventory management, purchasing, financing, and labor activities

Just-in-time systems (JIT)—a principle of production and inventory control in which materials and parts arrive precisely when and where needed for production

Computer-integrated manufacturing—a manufacturing approach that integrates several computerized systems, such as computer-assisted design (CAD), computer-assisted manufacturing (CAM), MRP, and JIT

Product life cycle management—business strategy that enables manufacturers to collaborate on product design and development efforts, using the Web

HRM   Human Resource Management

Recruitment—finding employees, testing them, and deciding which ones to hire

Performance evaluation—periodic evaluation by superiors

Training

Employee records

Benefits administration—retirement, disability, unemployment, and so on

Profitability Planning	Financial Planning	Employment Planning, Outsourcing	Product Life Cycle Management	Sales Forecasting, Advertising Planning	**STRATEGIC**
Auditing, Budgeting	Investment Management	Benefits Administration, Performance Evaluation	Quality Control, Inventory Management	Customer Relations, Sales Force Automation	**TACTICAL**
Payroll, Accounts Payable, Accounts Receivable	Manage Cash, Manage Financial Transactions	Maintain Employee Records	Order Fulfillment, Order Processing	Set Pricing, Profile Customers	**OPERATIONAL**
ACCOUNTING	**FINANCE**	**HUMAN RESOURCES**	**PRODUCTION/ OPERATIONS**	**MARKETING**	

FIGURE 10.3   **Examples of information systems supporting the functional areas.**

Reports

All information systems produce reports: transaction processing systems, functional area information systems, ERP systems, customer relationship management systems, business intelligence systems, and so on. We discuss reports here because they are so closely associated with FAIS and ERP systems. These reports generally fall into three categories: routine, ad hoc (on-demand), and exception.

routine reports Reports produced at scheduled intervals.

Routine reports are produced at scheduled intervals. They range from hourly quality control reports to daily reports on absenteeism rates. Although routine reports are extremely valuable to an organization, managers frequently need special information that is not included in these reports. At other times, they need the information that is normally included in routine reports, but at different times ("I need the report today, for the last three days, not for one week").

Such out-of-the routine reports are called **ad hoc (on-demand) reports**. Ad hoc reports can also include requests for the following types of information:

ad hoc (on-demand) reports Nonroutine reports that often contain special information that is not included in routine reports.

- **Drill-down reports** display a greater level of detail. For example, a manager might examine sales by region and decide to "drill down" by focusing specifically on sales by store and then by salesperson.

drill-down reports Reports that show a greater level of details than is included in routine reports.

- **Key indicator reports** summarize the performance of critical activities. For example, a chief financial officer might want to monitor cash flow and cash on hand.

key indicator reports Reports that summarize the performance of critical activities.

- **Comparative reports** compare, for example, the performances of different business units or of a single unit during different times.

comparative reports Reports that compare performances of different business units or times.

Some managers prefer exception reports. **Exception reports** include only information that falls outside certain threshold standards. To implement *management by exception*, management first establishes performance standards. The company then creates systems to monitor performance (through the incoming data about business transactions such as expenditures), to compare actual performance to the standards, and to identify exceptions to the standards. The system alerts managers to the exceptions through exception reports.

exception reports Reports that include only information that exceeds certain threshold standards.

MKT Let's use sales as an example. First, management establishes sales quotas. The company then implements a FAIS that collects and analyzes all of the sales data. An exception report would identify only those cases in which sales fell outside an established threshold—for example, more than 20 percent short of the quota. It would *not* report expenditures that fell *within* the accepted range of standards. By leaving out all "acceptable" performances, exception reports save managers time, thus helping them focus on problem areas.

Before you go on...

1. Define a functional area information system and list its major characteristics.
2. How do information systems benefit the finance and accounting functional area?
3. Explain how POM personnel use information systems to perform their jobs more effectively and efficiently.
4. What are the most important HRIS applications?
5. Compare and contrast the three basic types of reports.

WILEY PLUS

Author Lecture Videos are available exclusively in *WileyPLUS*.
Apply the Concept activities are available in the Appendix and in *WileyPLUS*.

10.3 Enterprise Resource Planning Systems

LEARNING OBJECTIVE

Identify advantages and drawbacks to businesses implementing an enterprise resource planning system.

Historically, functional area information systems were developed independent of one another, resulting in *information silos*. These silos did not communicate well with one another, and this lack of communication and integration made organizations less efficient. This inefficiency was particularly evident in business processes that involve more than one functional area, such as procurement and fulfillment.

Enterprise resource planning (ERP) systems are designed to correct a lack of communication among the FAISs. ERP systems resolve this problem by tightly integrating the

FAIS through a common database. For this reason, experts credit ERP systems with greatly increasing organizational productivity. ERP systems adopt a business process view of the overall organization to integrate the planning, management, and use of all of an organization's resources, employing a common software platform and database.

The major objectives of ERP systems are to tightly integrate the functional areas of the organization and to enable information to flow seamlessly across them. Tight integration means that changes in one functional area are immediately reflected in all other pertinent functional areas. In essence, ERP systems provide the information necessary to control the business processes of the organization.

It is important to understand that ERP systems are an evolution of FAIS. That is, ERP systems have much the same functionality as FAIS, and they produce the same reports.

Although some companies have developed their own ERP systems, most organizations use commercially available ERP software. The leading ERP software vendor is SAP (www. sap.com). Other major vendors include Oracle (www.oracle.com).

ERP II Systems

ERP systems were originally deployed to facilitate business processes associated with manufacturing, such as raw materials management, inventory control, order entry, and distribution. However, these early ERP systems did not extend to other functional areas, such as sales and marketing. They also did not include any customer relationship management (CRM)

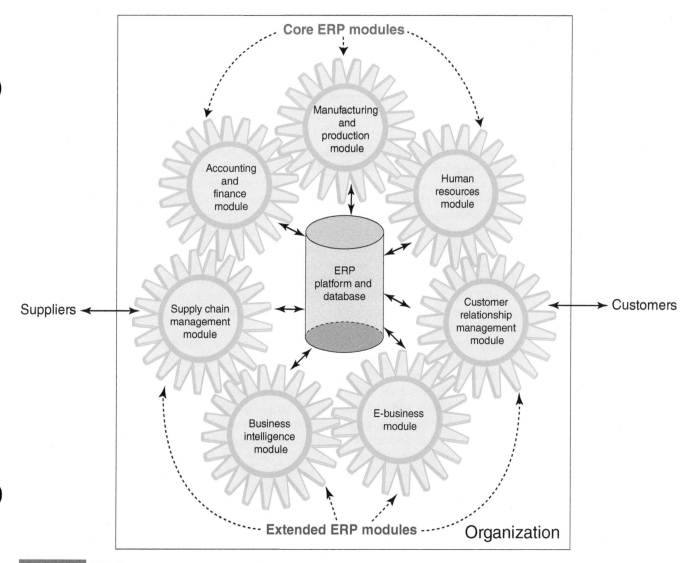

FIGURE 10.4 ERP II system.

TABLE 10.2   **ERP Modules**

Core ERP Modules

ACCT **FIN** **Financial Management.** These modules support accounting, financial reporting, performance management, and corporate governance. They manage accounting data and financial processes such as general ledger, accounts payable, accounts receivable, fixed assets, cash management and forecasting, product-cost accounting, cost-center accounting, asset accounting, tax accounting, credit management, budgeting, and asset management.

POM **Operations Management.** These modules manage the various aspects of production planning and execution such as demand forecasting, procurement, inventory management, materials purchasing, shipping, production planning, production scheduling, materials requirements planning, quality control, distribution, transportation, and plant and equipment maintenance.

HRM **Human Resource Management.** These modules support personnel administration (including workforce planning, employee recruitment, assignment tracking, personnel planning and development, and performance management and reviews), time accounting, payroll, compensation, benefits accounting, and regulatory requirements.

Extended ERP Modules

MKT **Customer Relationship Management.** (Discussed in detail in Chapter 11.) These modules support all aspects of a customer's relationship with the organization. They help the organization to increase customer loyalty and retention, and thus improve its profitability. They also provide an integrated view of customer data and interactions, helping organizations to be more responsive to customer needs.

POM **Supply Chain Management.** (Discussed in detail in Chapter 11.) These modules manage the information flows between and among stages in a supply chain to maximize supply chain efficiency and effectiveness. They help organizations plan, schedule, control, and optimize the supply chain from the acquisition of raw materials to the receipt of finished goods by customers.

MIS **Business Analytics.** (Discussed in detail in Chapter 12.) These modules collect information used throughout the organization, organize it, and apply analytical tools to assist managers with decision making.

MIS **E-Business.** (Discussed in detail in Chapter 7.) Customers and suppliers demand access to ERP information, including order status, inventory levels, and invoice reconciliation. Furthermore, they want this information in a simplified format that can be accessed on the Web. As a result, these modules provide two channels of access into ERP system information—one channel for customers (B2C) and one for suppliers and partners (B2B).

---

capabilities that enable organizations to capture customer-specific information. Finally, they did not provide Web-enabled customer service or order fulfillment.

Over time, ERP systems evolved to include administrative, sales, marketing, and human resources processes. Companies now employ an enterprise-wide approach to ERP that uses the Web and connects all facets of the value chain. (You might want to review our discussion of value chains in Chapter 2.) These systems are called ERP II.

ERP II systems

Interorganizational ERP systems that provide Web-enabled links among key business systems (e.g., inventory and production) of a company and its customers, suppliers, distributors, and others.

ERP II systems are interorganizational ERP systems that provide Web-enabled links among a company's key business systems—such as inventory and production—and its customers, suppliers, distributors, and other relevant parties. These links integrate internal-facing ERP applications with the external-focused applications of supply chain management and customer relationship management. **Figure 10.4** illustrates the organization and functions of an ERP II system.

The various functions of ERP II systems are now delivered as e-business suites. The major ERP vendors have developed modular, Web-enabled software suites that integrate ERP, customer relationship management, supply chain management, procurement, decision support, enterprise portals, and other business applications and functions. Examples are Oracle's e-Business Suite and SAP's mySAP. The goal of these systems is to enable companies to execute most of their business processes using a single Web-enabled system of integrated software rather than a variety of separate e-business applications.

ERP II systems include a variety of modules that are divided into core ERP modules—financial management, operations management, and human resource management—and extended ERP modules—customer relationship management, supply chain management, business intelligence, and e-business. If a system does not have the core ERP modules, then it is not a legitimate ERP system. The extended ERP modules, in contrast, are optional. Table 10.2 describes each of these modules.

Benefits and Limitations of ERP Systems

ERP systems can generate significant business benefits for an organization. The major benefits fall into the following three categories:

1. *Organizational flexibility and agility*: As you have seen, ERP systems break down many former departmental and functional silos of business processes, information systems, and information resources. In this way, they make organizations more flexible, agile, and adaptive. The organizations can therefore respond quickly to changing business conditions and capitalize on new business opportunities.

2. *Decision support*: ERP systems provide essential information on business performance across functional areas. This information significantly improves managers' ability to make better, more timely decisions.

3. *Quality and efficiency*: ERP systems integrate and improve an organization's business processes, generating significant improvements in the quality of production, distribution, and customer service.

Despite all of their benefits, however, ERP systems do have drawbacks. The major limitations of ERP implementations include the following:

- The business processes in ERP software are often predefined by the best practices that the ERP vendor has developed. *Best practices* are the most successful solutions or problem-solving methods for achieving a business objective. As a result, companies may need to change their existing business processes to fit the predefined business processes incorporated into the ERP software. For companies with well-established procedures, this requirement can create serious problems, especially if employees do not want to abandon their old ways of working and resist the changes.

- At the same time, however, an ERP implementation can provide an opportunity to improve and in some cases completely redesign inefficient, ineffective, or outdated procedures. In fact, many companies benefit from implementing best practices for their accounting, finance, and human resource processes, as well as other support activities that companies do not consider a source of competitive advantage.

   Recall from Chapter 2, however, that different companies organize their value chains in different configurations to transform inputs into valuable outputs and achieve competitive advantages. Therefore, although the vendor's best practices, by definition, are appropriate for most organizations, they might not be the "best" one for your company if they change those processes that give you a competitive advantage.

- ERP systems can be extremely complex, expensive, and time consuming to implement. (We discuss the implementation of ERP systems in detail in the next section.) In fact, the costs and risks of failure in implementing a new ERP system are substantial. Quite a few companies have experienced costly ERP implementation failures. Specifically, they have suffered losses in revenue, profits, and market share when core business processes and information systems failed or did not work properly. In many cases, orders and shipments were lost, inventory changes were not recorded correctly, and unreliable inventory levels caused major stock outs. Companies such as Hershey Foods, Nike, A-DEC, and Connecticut General sustained losses in amounts up to hundreds of millions of dollars. In the case of FoxMeyer Drugs, a $5 billion pharmaceutical wholesaler, the ERP implementation was so poorly executed that the company had to file for bankruptcy protection.

In almost every ERP implementation failure, the company's business managers and IT professionals underestimated the complexity of the planning, development, and training that were required to prepare for a new ERP system that would fundamentally transform their business processes and information systems. The following are the major causes of ERP implementation failure:

- Failure to involve affected employees in the planning and development phases and in change management processes
- Trying to accomplish too much too fast in the conversion process

- Insufficient training in the new work tasks required by the ERP system
- Failure to perform proper data conversion and testing for the new system

Implementing ERP Systems

Companies can implement ERP systems by using either on-premise software or software-as-a-service (SaaS). We differentiate between these two methods in detail in Technology Guide 3.

On-Premise ERP Implementation   Depending on the types of value chain processes managed by the ERP system and a company's specific value chain, there are three strategic approaches to implementing an on-premise ERP system:

1. *The vanilla approach*: In this approach, a company implements a standard ERP package using the package's built-in configuration options. When the system is implemented in this way, it will deviate only minimally from the package's standardized settings. The vanilla approach can enable the company to perform the implementation more quickly. However, the extent to which the software is adapted to the organization's specific processes is limited. Fortunately, a vanilla implementation provides general functions that can support the firm's common business processes with relative ease, even if they are not a perfect fit for those processes.

2. *The custom approach*: In this approach, a company implements a more customized ERP system by developing new ERP functions designed specifically for that firm. Decisions concerning the ERP's degree of customization are specific to each organization. To use the custom approach, the organization must carefully analyze its existing business processes to develop a system that conforms to the organization's particular characteristics and processes. Customization is also expensive and risky because computer code must be written and updated every time a new version of the ERP software is released. Going further, if the customization does not perfectly match the organization's needs, then the system can be very difficult to use.

3. *The best-of-breed approach*: This approach combines the benefits of the vanilla and customized systems while avoiding the extensive costs and risks associated with complete customization. Companies that adopt this approach mix and match core ERP modules as well as other extended ERP modules from different software providers to best fit their unique internal processes and value chains. Thus, a company may choose several core ERP modules from an established vendor to take advantage of industry best practices—for example, for financial management and human resource management. At the same time, it may also choose specialized software to support its unique business processes—for example, for manufacturing, warehousing, and distribution. Sometimes companies arrive at the best-of-breed approach the hard way. For example, Dell wasted millions of dollars trying to customize an integrated ERP system from a major vendor to match its unique processes before it realized that a smaller, more flexible system that integrated well with other corporate applications was the answer.

Software-as-a-Service ERP Implementation   Companies can acquire ERP systems without having to buy a complete software solution (i.e., on-premise ERP implementation). Many organizations are using software-as-a-service (SaaS) (discussed in Chapter 13 and Technology Guide 3) to acquire cloud-based ERP systems. (We discuss cloud computing in Technology Guide 3.)

In this business model, the company rents the software from an ERP vendor who offers its products over the Internet using the SaaS model. The ERP cloud vendor manages software updates and is responsible for the system's security and availability.

Cloud-based ERP systems can be a perfect fit for some companies. For example, companies that cannot afford to make large investments in IT, yet already have relatively structured business processes that need to be tightly integrated, might benefit from cloud computing.

The relationship between the company and the cloud vendor is regulated by contracts and by service level agreements (SLAs). The SLAs define the characteristics and quality of service; for example, a guaranteed uptime, or the percentage of time that the system is available. Cloud vendors that fail to meet these conditions can face penalties.

The decision about whether to use on-premise ERP or SaaS ERP is specific to each organization, and it depends on how the organization evaluates a series of advantages and disadvantages. The following are the three major advantages of using a cloud-based ERP system:

1. The system can be used from any location that has Internet access. Consequently, users can work from any location using online shared and centralized resources (data and databases). Users access the ERP system through a secure virtual private network (VPN) connection (discussed in Chapter 4) with the provider.

2. Companies using cloud-based ERP avoid the initial hardware and software expenses that are typical of on-premise implementations. For example, to run SAP on-premise, a company must purchase SAP software as well as a license to use SAP. The magnitude of this investment can hinder small- to medium-sized enterprises (SMEs) from adopting ERP.

3. Cloud-based ERP solutions are scalable, meaning it is possible to extend ERP support to new business processes and new business partners (e.g., suppliers) by purchasing new ERP modules.

There are also disadvantages to adopting cloud-based ERP systems that a company must carefully evaluate. The following are the three major disadvantages of using a cloud-based ERP system:

1. It is not clear whether cloud-based ERP systems are more secure than on-premise systems. In fact, a survey conducted by North Bridge Venture Partners indicated that security was the primary reason why organizations did not adopt cloud-based ERP.

2. Companies that adopt cloud-based ERP systems sacrifice their control over a strategic IT resource. For this reason, some companies prefer to implement an on-premise ERP system, using a strong in-house IT department that can directly manage the system.

3. A direct consequence of the lack of control over IT resources occurs when the ERP system experiences problems; for example, if some ERP functions are temporarily slow or are not available. In such cases, having an internal IT department that can solve problems immediately rather than dealing with the cloud vendor's system support can speed up the system recovery process.

    This situation is particularly important for technology-intensive companies. In such companies, IT is crucial to conduct any kind of business with customers. Examples are e-commerce companies, banks, and government organizations that manage emergencies or situations that might involve individual and national security (e.g., health care organizations, police, the homeland security department, antiterrorism units, and others).

Finally, slow or unavailable software from a cloud-based ERP vendor creates business continuity problems for the client. (We discuss business continuity in Chapter 4.) That is, a sudden system problem or failure makes it impossible for the firm to operate. Companies lose money when they lose business continuity because customers cannot be serviced and employees cannot do their jobs. A loss of business continuity also damages the company's reputation because customers lose trust in the firm.

Enterprise Application Integration

For some organizations, integrated ERP systems are not appropriate. This situation is particularly true for companies that find the process of converting from their existing system too difficult or time consuming.

Such companies, however, may still have isolated information systems that need to be connected with one another. To accomplish this task, these companies can use enterprise application integration. An **enterprise application integration (EAI) system** integrates existing systems by providing software, called *middleware*, that connects multiple applications. In essence, the EAI system allows existing applications to communicate and share data, thereby enabling organizations to existing applications while eliminating many of the problems caused by isolated information systems. EAI systems also support implementation of best-of-breed ERP solutions by connecting software modules from different vendors.

enterprise application integration (EAI) system A system that integrates existing systems by providing layers of software that connect applications together.

Before you go on...

1. Define ERP and describe its functions.
2. What are ERP II systems?
3. Differentiate between core ERP modules and extended ERP modules.
4. List some drawbacks of ERP software.
5. Highlight the differences between ERP configuration, customization, and best-of-breed implementation strategies.

10.4 | ERP Support for Business Processes

WILEY PLUS

Author Lecture Videos are available exclusively in *WileyPLUS.*
Apply the Concept activities are available in the Appendix and in *WileyPLUS.*

cross-departmental process A business process that originates in one department and ends in another department or originates and ends in the same department while involving other departments.

LEARNING OBJECTIVE

Describe the three main business processes supported by ERP systems.

ERP systems effectively support a number of standard business processes. In particular, ERP systems manage end-to-end, cross-departmental processes. A **cross-departmental process** is one that (1) originates in one department and ends in a different department or (2) originates and ends in the same department but involves other departments.

The Procurement, Fulfillment, and Production Processes

The following are the three prominent examples of cross-departmental processes:

1. The *procurement process*, which originates in the warehouse department (need to buy) and ends in the accounting department (send payment)
2. The *fulfillment process*, which originates in the sales department (customer request to buy) and ends in the accounting department (receive payment)
3. The *production process*, which originates and ends in the warehouse department (need to produce and reception of finished goods) but involves the production department as well

These three processes are examined in more detail in the following sections, focusing on the steps that are specific to each one.

procurement process A cross-functional business process that originates when a company needs to acquire goods or services from external sources, and it concludes when the company receives and pays for them.

POM **ACCT** **The Procurement Process** The **procurement process** originates when a company needs to acquire goods or services from external sources, and it concludes when the company receives and pays for them. Let's consider a procurement process in which the company needs to acquire physical goods (see **Figure 10.5**). This process involves three main departments—Warehouse, Purchasing, and Accounting—and it consists of the following steps:

1. The process originates in the warehouse department, which generates a purchase requisition to buy the needed products.
2. The warehouse forwards the requisition to the purchasing department, which creates a purchase order (PO) and forwards it to a vendor. Generally, companies can choose from a number of vendors, and they select the one that best meets their requirements in regard to convenience, speed, reliability, and other characteristics.
3. After the company places the order, it receives the goods in its warehouse department, where someone physically checks the delivery to make certain that it corresponds to what

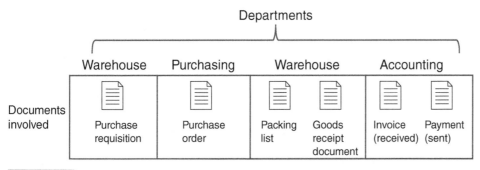

FIGURE 10.5 Departments and documents flow in the procurement process.

the company ordered. He or she performs this task by comparing a packing list attached to the shipment against the PO.

4. If the shipment matches the order, then the warehouse issues a goods receipt document.

5. At the same time or shortly thereafter, the accounting department receives an invoice from the vendor. Accounting then checks that the PO, the goods receipt document, and the invoice match. This process is called the *three-way match*.

6. After Accounting verifies the match, it processes the payment and sends it to the vendor.

The Order Fulfillment Process   In contrast to procurement, in which the company purchases goods from a vendor, in the **order fulfillment process**, also known as the *order-to-cash process*, the company sells goods to a customer. Fulfillment originates when the company receives a customer order, and it concludes when the company receives a payment from the customer.

The fulfillment process can follow two basic strategies: sell-from-stock and configure-to-order. *Sell-from-stock* involves fulfilling customer orders directly using goods that are in the warehouse (stock). These goods are standard, meaning that the company does not customize them for buyers. In contrast, in *configure-to-order*, the company customizes the product in response to a customer request.

MKT **POM** **ACCT**   A fulfillment process involves three main departments: Sales, Warehouse, and Accounting. This process includes the following steps:

1. The sales department receives a customer inquiry, which essentially is a request for information concerning the availability and price of a specific good. (We restrict our discussion here to fulfilling a customer order for physical goods rather than services.)

2. After Sales receives the inquiry, it issues a quotation that indicates availability and price.

3. If the customer agrees to the price and terms, then Sales creates a customer purchase order (PO) and a sales order.

4. Sales forwards the sales order to the warehouse. The sales order is an interdepartmental document that helps the company keep track of the internal processes that are involved in fulfilling a specific customer order. It also provides details of the quantity, price, and other characteristics of the product.

5. The warehouse prepares the shipment and produces two other internal documents: the picking document, which it uses to remove goods from the warehouse, and the packing list, which accompanies the shipment and provides details about the delivery.

6. At the same time, Accounting issues an invoice for the customer.

7. The process concludes when Accounting receives a payment that is consistent with the invoice.

Figure 10.6 shows the fulfillment process. Note that it applies to both sell-from-stock and configure-to-order because the basic steps are the same for both strategies.

order fulfillment process   A cross-functional business process that originates when the company receives a customer order, and it concludes when it receives a payment from the customer.

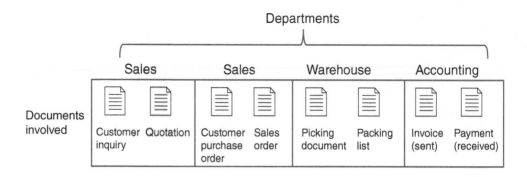

FIGURE 10.6 **Departments and documents flow in the fulfillment process.**

production process   A cross-functional business process in which a company produces physical goods.

POM   The Production Process   The **production process** does not occur in all companies because not all companies produce physical goods. In fact, many businesses limit their activities to buying (procurement) and selling products (e.g., retailers).

The production process can follow two different strategies: make-to-stock and make-to-order. (See the discussion of the pull model and the push model in Chapter 11.) *Make-to-stock* occurs when the company produces goods to create or increase an *inventory*; that is, finished products that are stored in the warehouse and are available for sales. In contrast, *make-to-order* occurs when production is generated by a specific customer order.

Manufacturing companies that produce their own goods manage their interdepartmental production process across the production and warehouse departments. The production process involves the following steps:

1. The warehouse issues a planned order when the company needs to produce a finished product, either because the warehouse has insufficient inventory or because the customer placed a specific order for goods that are not currently in stock.

2. Once the planned order reaches Production, the production controller authorizes the order and issues a production order, which is a written authorization to start the production of a certain amount of a specific product.

3. To assemble a finished product, Production requires a number of materials (or parts). To acquire these materials, Production generates a material withdrawal slip, which lists all of the needed parts, and forwards it to the warehouse.

4. If the parts are available in the warehouse, then the warehouse delivers them to Production. If the parts are not available, then the company must purchase them through the procurement process.

5. After Production has created the products, it updates the production order specifying that, as planned, a specific number of units of product now can be shipped to the warehouse.

6. As soon as the warehouse receives the finished goods, it issues a goods receipt document that certifies how many units of a product it received that are available for sales.

This overview of the production process is a highly simplified one. In reality, the process is very complex, and it frequently involves additional steps. ERP systems also collect a number of other documents and pieces of information such as the bill of materials (a list of all materials needed to assemble a finished product), the list of work centers (locations where the production takes place), and the product routing (production steps). All of these topics require an in-depth analysis of the production process and are therefore beyond the scope of our discussion here. **Figure 10.7** illustrates the production processes.

A number of events can occur that create exceptions or deviations in the procurement, fulfillment, and production processes. Deviations may include the following:

- A delay in the receipt of products
- Issues related to an unsuccessful three-way match regarding a shipment and its associated invoice (procurement)
- Rejection of a quotation

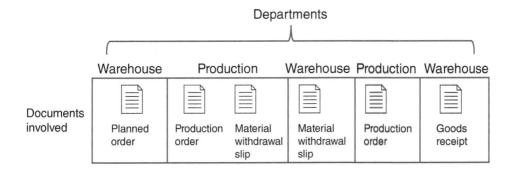

FIGURE 10.7 **Departments and documents flow in the production process.**

- A delay in a shipment
- A mistake in preparing the shipment or in invoicing the customer (fulfillment)
- Overproduction of a product
- Reception of parts that cannot be used in the production process
- Unavailability of certain parts from a supplier

Companies use ERP systems to manage procurement, fulfillment, and production because these systems track all of the events that occur within each process. Furthermore, the system stores all of the documents created in each step of each process in a centralized database, where they are available as needed in real time. Any exceptions or mistakes made during one or more interdepartmental processes are handled right away by simply querying the ERP system and retrieving a specific document or piece of information that needs to be revised or examined more carefully. Therefore, it is important to follow each step in each process and to register the corresponding document into the ERP system.

Figure 10.8 portrays the three cross-functional business processes we just discussed. It specifically highlights the integration of the three processes, which is made possible by ERP systems.

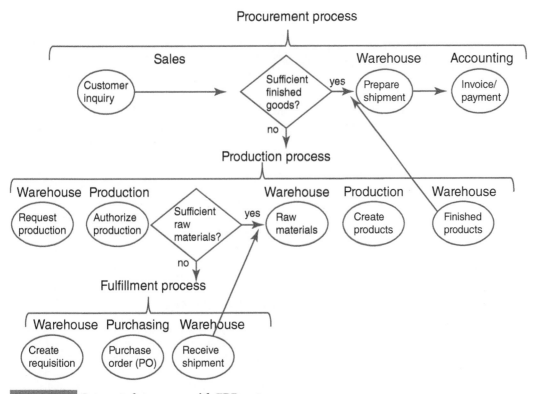

FIGURE 10.8 **Integrated processes with ERP systems.**

Interorganizational Processes: ERP with SCM and CRM

Although the procurement and the fulfillment processes involve suppliers and customers, they are considered (together with the production process) intraorganizational processes because they originate and conclude within the company. However, ERP systems can also manage processes that originate in one company and conclude in another company. These processes are called *interorganizational processes*, and they typically involve supply chain management (SCM) and customer relationship management (CRM) systems. (You can find a more detailed description of CRM and SCM in Chapter 11). Here, we focus on the integration of these processes within a firm's industry value chain.

SCM and CRM processes help multiple firms in an industry coordinate activities such as the production-to-sale of goods and services. Let's consider a chain of grocery stores whose supply chain must properly manage perishable goods. On the one hand, store managers need to stock only the amount of perishable products that they are reasonably sure they will sell before the products' expiration dates. On the other hand, they do not want to run out of stock of any products that customers need.

ERP SCM systems have the capability to place automatic requests to buy fresh perishable products from suppliers in real time. That is, as each perishable product is purchased, the system captures data on that purchase, adjusts store inventory levels, and transmits these data to the grocery chain's warehouse as well as the products' vendors. The system executes this process by connecting the point-of-sale barcode scanning system with the warehouse and accounting departments, as well as with the vendors' systems. SCM systems also use historical data to predict when fresh products need to be ordered before the store's supply becomes too low.

ERP CRM systems also benefit businesses by generating forecasting analyses of product consumption based on critical variables such as geographical area, season, day of the week, and type of customer. These analyses help grocery stores coordinate their supply chains to meet customer needs for perishable products. Going further, CRM systems identify particular customer needs and then use this information to suggest specific product campaigns. These campaigns can transform a potential demand into sales opportunities and convert sales opportunities into sales quotations and sales orders. This process is called the *demand-to-order* process.

Before you go on...

1. What are the three main intraorganizational processes that are typically supported by ERP systems?
2. Why is it important that all steps in each process generate a document that is stored in the ERP system?
3. What is the difference between intraorganizational and interorganizational processes?
4. What are the two main ES systems that support interorganizational processes?

What's in IT for Me?

ACCT For the Accounting Major

Understanding the functions and outputs of TPSs effectively is a major concern of any accountant. It is also necessary to understand the various activities of all functional areas and how they are interconnected. Accounting information systems are a central component in any ERP package. In fact, all large CPA firms actively consult with clients on ERP implementations, using thousands of specially trained accounting majors.

FIN For the Finance Major

IT helps financial analysts and managers perform their tasks better. Of particular importance is analyzing cash flows and securing the financing required for smooth operations. Financial applications can also support such activities as risk analysis, investment management, and global transactions involving different currencies and fiscal regulations.

Finance activities and modeling are key components of ERP systems. Flows of funds (payments), at the core of most supply chains, must be executed efficiently and effectively. Financial arrangements are especially important along global supply chains, where currency conventions and financial regulations must be considered.

MKT For the Marketing Major

Marketing and sales expenses are usually targets in a cost-reduction program. Also, sales force automation improves not only salespeoples' productivity (and thus reduces costs) but also customer service.

POM For the Production/Operations Management Major

Managing production tasks, materials handling, and inventories in short time intervals, at a low cost, and with high quality is critical for competitiveness. These activities can be achieved only if they are properly supported by IT. IT can also greatly enhance interaction with other functional areas, especially sales. Collaboration in design, manufacturing, and logistics requires knowledge of how modern information systems can be connected.

HRM For the Human Resource Management Major

Human resources managers can increase their efficiency and effectiveness by using IT for some of their routine functions. Human resources personnel need to understand how information flows between the HR department and the other functional areas. Finally, the integration of functional areas through ERP systems has a major impact on skill requirements and scarcity of employees, which are related to the tasks performed by the HRM department.

MIS For the MIS Major

The MIS function is responsible for the most fundamental information systems in organizations: the transaction processing systems. The TPSs provide the data for the databases. In turn, all other information systems use these data. MIS personnel develop applications that support all levels of the organization (from clerical to executive) and all functional areas. The applications also enable the firm to do business with its partners.

Summary

10.1 Explain the purpose of transaction processing systems.

TPSs monitor, store, collect, and process data generated from all business transactions. These data provide the inputs into the organization's database.

10.2 Explain the types of support that information systems can provide for each functional area of the organization.

The major business functional areas are production/operations management, marketing, accounting/finance, and human resources management. Table 10.1 provides an overview of the many activities in each functional area supported by FAIS.

10.3 Identify advantages and drawbacks to businesses implementing an ERP system.

Enterprise resource planning (ERP) systems integrate the planning, management, and use of all of the organization's resources. The major objective of ERP systems is to tightly integrate the functional areas of the organization. This integration enables information to flow seamlessly across the various functional areas.

The following are the major benefits of ERP systems:

- Because ERP systems integrate organizational resources, they make organizations more flexible, agile, and adaptive. The organizations can therefore react quickly to changing business conditions and capitalize on new business opportunities.

- ERP systems provide essential information on business performance across functional areas. This information significantly improves managers' ability to make better, more timely decisions.

- ERP systems integrate organizational resources, resulting in significant improvements in the quality of customer service, production, and distribution.

The following are the major drawbacks of ERP systems:

- The business processes in ERP software are often predefined by the best practices that the ERP vendor has developed. As a result, companies may need to change existing business processes to fit the predefined business processes of the software. For companies with well-established procedures, this requirement can be a huge problem.

- ERP systems can be extremely complex, expensive, and time consuming to implement. In fact, the costs and risks of failure in implementing a new ERP system are substantial.

10.4 Describe the three main business processes supported by ERP systems:

The *procurement process* that originates in the warehouse department (need to buy) and ends in the accounting department (send payment).

The *fulfillment process* that originates in the sales department (customer request to buy) and ends in the accounting department (receive payment).

The *production process* that originates and ends in the warehouse department (need to produce and reception of finished goods) but involves the production department as well.

We leave the details of the steps in each of these processes up to you.

Key Terms

ad hoc (on-demand) reports   310
batch processing   300
comparative reports   310
computer-integrated manufacturing
    (CIM)   307
cross-departmental
    process   316

drill-down reports   310
enterprise application integration (EAI)
    system   315
ERP II systems   312
exception reports   310
functional area information systems
    (FAIS)   301

key indicator reports   310
online transaction processing (OLTP)   300
order fulfillment process   317
procurement process   316
production process   318
routine reports   310
transaction   299

Discussion Questions

1. Why is it logical to organize IT applications by functional areas?

2. Describe the role of a TPS in a service organization.

3. Describe the relationship between TPS and FAIS.

4. Discuss how IT facilitates the budgeting process.

5. How can the Internet support investment decisions?

6. Describe the benefits of integrated accounting software packages.

7. Discuss the role that IT plays in support of auditing.

8. Investigate the role of the Web in human resources management.

9. What is the relationship between information silos and enterprise resource planning?

Problem-Solving Activities

1. Visit www.immagic.com and look up the report titled Transaction Processing: Use Cases from Higher Education. Describe experiences you have had at your university with any one of the use cases.

2. Enter www.sas.com and access *revenue optimization*. Explain how the software helps in optimizing prices.

3. Watch the demo for IBM Sterling Management System at www.ibm.com. Describe the benefits of this type of fulfillment system.

4. Examine the capabilities of the following (and similar) financial software packages: Financial Analyzer (from Oracle) and CFO Vision (from SAS Institute). Prepare a report comparing the capabilities of the software packages.

5. Surf the Net and find free accounting software. (Try www.cnet.com and www.tucows.com.) Download the software and try it. Compare the ease of use and usefulness of each software package.

6. Examine the capabilities of the following financial software packages: Financial Analyzer (from www.oracle.com) and Financial Management (from www.sas.com). Prepare a report comparing the capabilities of the software packages.

7. Find Simply Accounting Basic from Sage Software (www.sage.com/us/sage-50-accounting). Why is this product recommended for small businesses?

8. Enter www.cornerstoneondemand.com and www.sap.com. Examine their software products and compare them.

9. Visit www.netsuite.com and read the article titled 5 Benefits of ERP for Businesses in 2022. Summarize the effects ERP has on global businesses.

10. Read one of the latest articles at www.erpfocus.com. Summarize what you learned.

Closing Case

 MIS **POM** **J&J ERP's Successful Failure**

By some estimates, between 55 percent and 75 percent of ERP implementation attempts fail. "Failure," however, does not necessarily mean that the implementation was not complete or operational. It could mean that the process cost more money or took more time than was estimated, or it didn't achieve the efficiency level it was supposed to provide.

Consider the following statistics: Sixty percent of customers are unhappy with their new system. Ninety percent feel that the system fails to deliver any measurable return on the investment (ROI). Fifty-seven percent contend that the implementation took longer than expected. Fifty-four percent of implementations exceeded their project budget, and 40 percent caused unintended operational disruptions. Each of these responses would likely be categorized as an implementation failure, even though the ERP system was functioning properly.

If implementing an ERP system is so problematic, then why do companies take on the task? Put simply, something in the business has changed. Current information systems are not providing the necessary support to operate in today's fast-paced, agile environment. In some cases, business partners update their systems, which requires companies that work with them to do the same. Or, on-premise hardware could be at the end of its life, requiring updates. Regardless of the reason, many companies begin ERP transformation projects, and the majority are unhappy with the results.

Consider the case of J&J Snack Foods (www.jjsnack.com), producer of several snack food beverages (such as ICEE frozen drinks), baked goods (such as Super Pretzel soft pretzels), and retail goods (such as Sour Patch Kids). In February 2022, J&J began an upgrade to its JD Edwards ERP system to strengthen its supply chain in two ways. First, they were preparing to add capacity, improve operational efficiency, accelerate growth potential, and increase margins. The new system would enable the company to offer benefits to customers in the form of better products and lower prices and to shareholders in the form of increased profits and dividends.

Second, J&J was aligning their enterprise platforms. Their frozen beverage division was already on the JD Edwards system. J&J hoped the transition would bring the entire organization into alignment. Specifically, it would provide a seamless, integrated process for their operation, from raw materials to manufacturing to order fulfillment. The single system across all divisions would provide a unified view of the entire operation.

J&J scheduled its transition during what is typically its slowest quarter. Nevertheless, the process created several operational, manufacturing, and supply chain challenges. At the end of the second quarter of 2022, the company reported losing $20 million in sales and $4.5 million in profits. From this perspective, the implementation appeared to be a failure.

What could have gone wrong? Many companies do not disclose the specifics of their system implementation failures. However, industry experts who study ERP implementations have identified many common problems. Below, we summarize these obstacles to success, and we also present suggestions for successful system implementations.

Implementation management is the first—and likely the most significant—ERP system challenge. ERP systems are modular and cannot be deployed in a single phase in any firm. Rather, implementation occurs in stages. Each stage is critical, because you must complete each step flawlessly before you can move on to the next phase. Good communication is essential, because management wants to hear from staff about any challenges they are experiencing with the new system throughout and after the implementation.

Planning is vital to ensure that the transition accounts for unanticipated delays and expenses to keep the project on schedule. A primary task that often causes projects to go over budget and fail to meet deadlines is data preparation. It is essential, therefore, to delete duplicate records, add missing information, and validate data before the data are migrated to the ERP system.

Data integration is perhaps the most significant benefit of ERP software. Therefore, data migration from the old systems to the new ones is crucial. Once the data are prepared for integration, proper data migration must be thoroughly planned and handled with great care.

Managing the budget is critical because ERP projects frequently exceed their estimated costs. This problem occurs because organizations underestimate the time required to transition to the new system. In addition, predicting business disruptions that will extend the implementation time is extremely difficult. Therefore, companies should allocate extra funds at the start of the project to create flexibility for unforeseen circumstances.

Finally, perpetual improvement requires continual monitoring and upgrading. Although an organization might implement ERP once, the system must be adaptable and scalable so that it can evolve with the business. After the application is deployed, the project team is responsible for addressing bugs and adding new functionality as required. Because the goal is to continue utilizing ERP systems for years after they are implemented, it is critical to audit or review them periodically to ensure they are aligned.

Results

So, how did J&J's new ERP system perform? Recall that the implementation dragged down the company's results in the second quarter of 2022. By the end of the third quarter, however, J&J reported the best sales quarter in its history. In their Frozen Beverages division, for example, sales grew by 23.5 percent compared to the same quarter in 2021. In the Food Services division, sales increased by 16 percent over the same period. These record quarterly sales and significant improvements resulted in an improved gross margin of 28.7 percent.

What initially appeared to be an ERP implementation failure was, in fact, simply not yet complete. The J&J team worked tirelessly to rebound from the challenges reported in the second quarter. The company has stated that it does not expect any further negative impacts from the system implementation.

Although successful ERP implementations are difficult to deploy, they are possible. It is easy to become overwhelmed by a project as large and complex as an ERP implementation. Still, with a thoughtful planning process and steadfast follow-through, you can make yours a success.

Questions

1. **What were J&J's goals when they implemented the new ERP system?**

2. **What are the common challenges of implementing ERP?**

3. **Discuss two or three ways you can better prepare for an ERP upgrade.**

Sources: Compiled from J. Schrader, "Why ERP Implementations Fail: How to Avoid the 7 Pitfalls," crestwood.com, April 25, 2022; E. Schroeder, "J&J Snack Profit off on ERP System Implementation," *Food Business News*, May 4, 2022; S. Zimmerman, "ERP Implementation Woes Cost J&J Snack Foods Estimated $20M," *Supply Chain Dive*, May 10, 2022; S. Mishra, "How to Overcome the Challenges in ERP Implementation," *Enterprise Talk*, May 11, 2022; E. St-Jean, "8 Ways to Avoid Business Disruption from a New ERP System," *TechTarget*, May 26, 2022; E. Hallstrom, "ERP Growing Pains Hurt J&J Snack Foods," *Food Processing*, May 11, 2022; J&J Snack Foods Corp., "J & J Snack Foods' Fiscal Third Quarter Revenue Increases by 17.2% to an All Time Quarterly Record of $380.2M," *GlobeNewsWire*, press release, August 2, 2022; C. Crail and K. Main, "8 ERP System Examples," *Forbes*, October 6, 2022; S. Simon, "ERP Implementation: The 5-Step Methodology You Need to Go Live without a Hitch," *Boston Business Journal*, October 1, 2022; R. Carlton, "Ten ERP Failure Statistics That Highlight the Importance of Getting It Right First Time Round," erpfocus.com, August 22, 2019; and https://jjsnack.com/about/, accessed October 12, 2022.

CHAPTER 11

Customer Relationship Management and Supply Chain Management

Opening Case

  MIS **POM** **Robots to the Rescue**

Background

Our highly interconnected global supply chain faces serious challenges with no obvious solutions. Many of these challenges can be traced to the outbreak of COVID-19 in 2020. When the world shut down to slow down the spread of the pandemic, many people began to work from home or became unemployed. Meanwhile, purchasing patterns shifted to items needed at home. Demand for home office furniture, toilet paper, and small appliances skyrocketed. Supplies of these items were limited, and manufacturing, warehousing, and delivery workers were at home or working limited shifts.

Further, everyone needed medical supplies such as masks, gowns, and hand sanitizer. It is significant to note that most of these goods were produced in China. China ramped up production of these items and shipped them out. Unfortunately, this increased production did not resolve the problems. Instead, we came to realize that we had a global shipping problem. The one thing China needed to ship out the supplies was the one thing they did not have—shipping containers.

Shipping containers were unevenly distributed around the world because thousands of them sat on ships waiting to be unloaded or in ports waiting to be picked up and transported. This trend continued during 2021 and 2022. There were multiple reports of ships in daylong queues waiting to make it to port and ports that were backlogged and almost at full capacity. Further, when products finally made it to warehouses, there were not enough workers to pick them up and prepare them for delivery.

The crisis revealed how a shift in the global supply chain can have a cascading effect on global commerce. An October 2022 report revealed that the following goods were in short supply: various food items, automotive backup cameras, carbon dioxide for beer, baby formula, computer chips, and tampons. Overall, almost every industry has felt the squeeze of supply chain issues.

It is significant that many of these factors are beyond the control of the distribution companies. The global labor shortage is a challenge at every stage of the supply chain. Regarding warehouses, for example, the new generation of the labor force strongly prefers to work in offices. Warehouse work is dirty, tiring, monotonous, and dangerous. To address this worker shortage, many warehouses are turning to robots.

Robotics and automation are not new to warehousing. Conveyor belts, scanners, and other innovations have been transforming the industry for decades. However, these techniques created a hybrid system where technology augmented human activity. In contrast, in modern hybrid systems, human labor augments the robotic technology.

The ultimate goal of robotic technology is to create an operation in which robots are capable of replacing humans. Robots are not subject to fatigue, illness, or injury, and they do not form unions or demand benefits. Training robots is as easy as updating the software that directs the robot. Some experts, however, estimate that we are years away from implementing fully automated warehousing.

The Technology Response

The robots in use today, known as *autonomous mobile robots* (AMRs), are capable of understanding and moving autonomously within their environment. Previous generations of robots were capable only of performing repetitive tasks such as moving pallets along predetermined paths. In contrast, today's robots can employ artificial intelligence (AI) to travel autonomously and handle goods of various sizes and shapes.

AMRs can quickly and accurately deliver parts and tools to the skilled workers who need them. They can also handle potentially dangerous materials, thereby eliminating the risk for human workers. Further, AMRs can take over time-consuming and redundant tasks to relieve pressure on human workers while at the same time avoiding supply chain congestion by quickly and safely moving goods and clearing backlogged goods from warehouses and other storage spaces.

Robots bring multiple advantages to warehousing. For starters, they are highly proficient at performing repetitive operations such as sorting, picking, and putting products in their designated places. Further, the software that powers these robots can enhance inventory management.

Also, robots can reduce high labor costs. Robots never get sick, not even during a pandemic. They never stay home to attend to their children. Unlike human workers, robots can be easily scaled up and cut back, eliminating the need to hire and train temporary employees.

Another benefit of utilizing robots is improved workplace safety. Monotonous tasks cause both mental and physical fatigue, which reduces productivity and increases the risk of injury. AI-enabled robots can alleviate the mental strain by reducing the chances of errors and enabling human workers to focus on more fruitful tasks such as quality and safety.

For these and other reasons, warehousing companies are pursuing automation and are eager to embrace robots as an alternative to human workers.

The Results

An October 2022 report by BlueWeave Consulting (**www.blueweaveconsulting.com**), a firm that focuses on providing data analytics and market intelligence, predicted that the global AMR market will grow steadily owing to the increasing popularity of e-commerce across the world. The report estimated that the global AMR market, which totaled $2.37 billion in 2021, will reach nearly $9.5 billion by 2028. Clearly, AMRs are becoming an essential element of the warehousing industry.

Walmart (**www.walmart.com**) is accelerating its investment in warehouse automation. Walmart has hired Symbotic (**www.symbotic.com**), a robotics and automation-based company, to automate its 42 U.S. distribution centers. In October 2022, the company acquired e-grocery automation firm Alert Innovation (**www.alertinnovation.com**), which produces custom-built inventory-handling technology. Walmart has worked with Alert since 2016 to customize automation for its grocery micro-fulfillment operation. In 2019, it began piloting Alert's Alphabot system, which is designed to store, retrieve, and dispense orders by using robots that move in multiple directions without lifts or conveyors. The retail giant claims the Alphabot technology will enable it to leverage its massive store footprint—4,700 stores located within 10 miles of 90 percent of the U.S. population—to modernize grocery product storage and fulfillment. The acquisition of Alert is part of Walmart's plan to expand technology throughout its operations and create the "next generation of fulfillment centers."

Walgreens (**www.walgreens.com**) is opening new robotic micro-fulfillment centers to pack prescription medications. These centers use robotic technology to automate tasks such as picking and packing, reducing the need for manual labor and enabling more inventory to fit into a smaller space. For example, their Dallas center fills 35,000 prescriptions for 500 stores every day. The robotic technology reduces their pharmacists' workload by 25 percent while producing cost savings of roughly $1 billion per year.

As the volume of prescriptions has risen during COVID, a national shortage of pharmacists has forced Walgreens to reduce pharmacy hours and offer signing bonuses as high as $75,000 in select markets. The company expects to open 22 micro-fulfillment centers nationally by 2025. At that point, as much as 50 percent of its total prescription volume could be filled automatically. Human pharmacists will continue to manually fill orders that involve controlled substances or are time sensitive. Chief Walgreens rival CVS is also utilizing micro-fulfillment centers for some orders.

Other organizations will soon see the benefits of deploying robots in their warehouses or picking and packaging, but there will be easier ways to start using robots—robots-as-a-service (RaaS). The benefits of RaaS became clear in 2020, when manufacturing, distribution, and warehousing organizations had to adapt quickly to evolving conditions to survive.

RaaS allows organizations to support shifts to their supply chains, providing scalability and reliability as conditions change rapidly. Among the financial advantages of RaaS is that there are no upfront costs. Instead, the funds come out of a company's operating expense line. This arrangement eliminates the need for capital expense approvals, which can delay the implementation of new technology and require investments that can drain budgets. Finally, because RaaS typically utilizes a cloud-based architecture, deployment can be completed within weeks. In general, a cloud-based RaaS model can provide companies with the infrastructure for greater operational resilience, a necessity in today's unpredictable industrial landscape.

Conclusions

The modern warehouse runs on robots. The past few decades have seen significant advancements in robotics and logistics, enabling futuristic warehouses to take shape. Within the walls of these facilities, robots automate nearly every function—from shelving and packing to distribution and cleaning. These robots have improved efficiency during a period of ever-rising customer demand, helping businesses not only to meet their goals but also to grow and improve.

Questions

1. **What are autonomous mobile robots? How do they differ from previous generations of robots?**

2. **What advantages do robots bring to warehousing?**

3. **Do you think warehouses will ever be fully automated? Why or why not?**

Sources: Compiled from G. Mitra, "Powering the Next Generation of Robotic Workers...without Wires," *Smart Industry*, October 14, 2022; R. Goodman, "How COVID-19 Opened the Door to Robots in the Warehouse," *Supply Chain Brain*, video, October 13, 2022; M. Romain, "Robots Could Be Replacing People in Warehouses as Workers Disappear," *Village Free Press*, October 9, 2022; Blue Weave Consulting, "Global Autonomous Mobile Robots Market Size to Surge Fast USD 9.4 Billion by 2028 | BlueWeave Consulting," *GlobeNewsWire*, October 10, 2022; P. Seitz, "Labor Shortage Spurs Drive to Automate Warehouses," *Investor's Business Daily*, October 7, 2022; M. Ruggles, "Walmart Acquires Automated Grocery Firm to Bolster Fulfillment," *Supply Chain Dive*, October 6, 2022; R. Aggarwal, "Disrupt the Disruptions: Industry 4.0-Driven Nearshoring to Bolster Your Supply Chain," *Forbes*, October 6, 2022; R. Michel, "Robots Edge into Packaging," *Modern Materials Handling*, October 4, 2022; D. Berthiaume, "Walgreens to Reportedly Use Robots in Pharmacy Supply Chain," *Drug Store News*, October 3, 2022; S. Kumar, "AI-Powered Robots Have Become Nice to Necessity for Warehousing Automation," *Entrepreneur*, September 29, 2022; DC Velocity Staff, "Warehouse Management: Top Trends to Watch," *DC Velocity*, September 19, 2022; J. Douglas, "China's Factories Accelerate Robotics Push as Workforce Shrinks," *Wall Street Journal*, September 18, 2022; P. Goodman, "The Supply Chain Broke. Robots Are Supposed to Help Fix It." *New York Times*, September 7, 2022; P. Sisson, "Robots Aren't Done Reshaping Warehouses," *New York Times*, July 12, 2022; L. Gamio and P. Goodman, "How the Supply Chain Crisis Unfolded," *New York Times*, December 5, 2021; and P. Goodman, "'It's Not Sustainable': What America's Port Crisis Looks Like Up Close," *New York Times*, October 14, 2021.

Introduction

In Chapter 10, you learned about information systems that support activities within the organization. In this chapter, you study information systems that support activities that extend outside the organization to customers and suppliers. The first half of this chapter addresses customer relationship management (CRM) systems and the second half addresses supply chain management systems (SCM).

Organizations are emphasizing a customer-centric approach to their business practices because they realize that long-term customer relationships provide sustainable value that extends beyond an individual business transaction. Organizations are also integrating their strategy and operations with supply chain partners because tight integration along the supply chain also leads to sustainable business value. Significantly, customer relationship management and supply chain management are critically important for all enterprises, regardless of size.

The chapter opening case *points out how important the innovative use of robots is to overcoming supply chain pressures. Businesses are able to automate repetitive process in hot and sometimes dangerous environments where human exhaustion can present a problem. Not only are they able to operate in difficult environments, they assist in the efficiency and accuracy of the supply chain.*

Supply chain management is equally important for organizations to successfully compete in the marketplace. Today, supply chain management is an integral part of all organizations and can improve customer service and reduce operating costs. Let's look at these two areas in more detail.

- **POM** *Improve the fulfillment process.* Customers expect to receive the correct products as quickly as possible. Therefore, products must be on hand in the correct locations. Furthermore, follow-up support after a sale must be effective and efficient.

- **FIN** *Reduce operating costs.* For example, retailers depend on their supply chains to quickly distribute expensive products so that they will not have the inventory carrying costs for costly, depreciating products.

Delays in production are costly. Supply chains must ensure the reliable delivery of materials to assembly plants to avoid expensive delays in manufacturing.

At this point, you might be asking yourself: Why should *I* learn about CRM and SCM? The answer, as you will see in this chapter, is that customers and suppliers are supremely important to *all* organizations. Regardless of your job, you will have an impact, directly or indirectly, on managing your firm's customer relationships and its supply chain. When you read the What's in IT for Me? section at the end of this chapter, you will learn about opportunities to make immediate contributions on your first job. Therefore, it is essential that you acquire a working knowledge of CRM, CRM systems, supply chains, SCM, and SCM systems.

11.1 Defining Customer Relationship Management

WILEY PLUS

Author Lecture Videos are available exclusively in *WileyPLUS.*
Apply the Concept activities are available in the Appendix and in *WileyPLUS.*

LEARNING OBJECTIVE

Identify the primary functions of both customer relationship management (CRM) and collaborative CRM strategies.

Before the supermarket, the mall, and the automobile, people purchased goods at their neighborhood store. The owners and employees recognized customers by name and knew their preferences and wants. For their part, customers remained loyal to the store and made repeated purchases. Over time, however, this personal customer relationship became impersonal as people moved from farms and small towns to cities, consumers became mobile, and supermarkets and department stores achieved economies of scale through mass marketing. Although prices were lower and products were more uniform in quality, the relationship with customers became nameless and impersonal.

The customer relationship has become even more impersonal with the rapid growth of the Internet and the World Wide Web. In today's hypercompetitive marketplace, customers are increasingly powerful; if they are dissatisfied with a product or a service from one organization, a competitor is often just one mouse click away. Furthermore, as more and more customers shop on the Web, an enterprise does not even have the opportunity to make a good first impression *in person.*

Customer relationship management returns to personal marketing. That is, rather than market to a mass of people or companies, businesses market to each customer individually. By employing this approach, businesses can use information about each customer—for example, previous purchases, needs, and wants—to create highly individualized offers that customers are more likely to accept. The CRM approach is designed to achieve *customer intimacy.*

Customer relationship management is a customer-focused and customer-driven organizational strategy. That is, organizations concentrate on assessing customers' requirements for products and services and then provide a high-quality, responsive customer experience. CRM is not a process or a technology per se; rather, it is a customer-centric way of thinking and acting. The focus of modern organizations has shifted from conducting business transactions to managing customer relationships. In general, organizations recognize that customers are the core of a successful enterprise, and the success of the enterprise depends on effectively managing relationships with them.

The CRM approach is enabled by information technology in the form of various systems and applications. However, CRM is not only about the software. Sometimes the problem with managing relationships is simply a lack of time or information. Old systems may contain the needed information, but this information may take too long to access and may not be usable across a variety of applications or devices. The result is that companies have less time to spend with their customers.

In contrast, modern CRM strategies and systems build sustainable long-term customer relationships that create value for the company as well as for the customer. That is, CRM helps companies acquire new customers and retain and expand their relationships with profitable

customer relationship management (CRM) A customer-focused and customer-driven organizational strategy that concentrates on addressing customers' requirements for products and services, and then providing high-quality, responsive services.

existing customers. Retaining customers is particularly important because repeat customers are the largest generator of revenue for an enterprise. Also, organizations have long understood that winning back a customer who has switched to a competitor is vastly more expensive than keeping that customer satisfied in the first place.

Figure 11.1 depicts the CRM process. The process begins with marketing efforts, through which the organization solicits prospects from a target population of potential customers. A certain number of these prospects will make a purchase and thus become customers. A certain number of these customers will become repeat customers. The organization then segments its repeat customers into low- and high-value repeat customers. An organization's overall goal is to maximize the *lifetime value* of a customer, which is that customer's potential revenue stream over a number of years.

Over time all organizations inevitably lose a certain percentage of customers, a process called *customer churn*. The optimal result of the organization's CRM efforts is to maximize the number of high-value repeat customers while minimizing customer churn.

CRM is a fundamentally simple concept: treat different customers differently because their needs differ and their value to the company may also differ. A successful CRM strategy not only improves customer satisfaction but also makes the company's sales and service employees more productive, which in turn generates increased profits. Researchers at the National Quality Research Center at the University of Michigan discovered that a 1 percent increase in customer satisfaction can lead to as much as a 300 percent increase in a company's *market capitalization*, defined as the number of shares of the company's stock outstanding multiplied by the price per share of the stock. Put simply, a minor increase in customer satisfaction can generate a major increase in a company's overall value.

Up to this point, you have been looking at an organization's CRM strategy. It is important to distinguish between a CRM *strategy* and CRM *systems*. Basically, CRM systems are information systems designed to support an organization's CRM strategy. For organizations to pursue excellent relationships with their customers, they need to employ CRM systems that provide the infrastructure needed to support those relationships. Because customer service

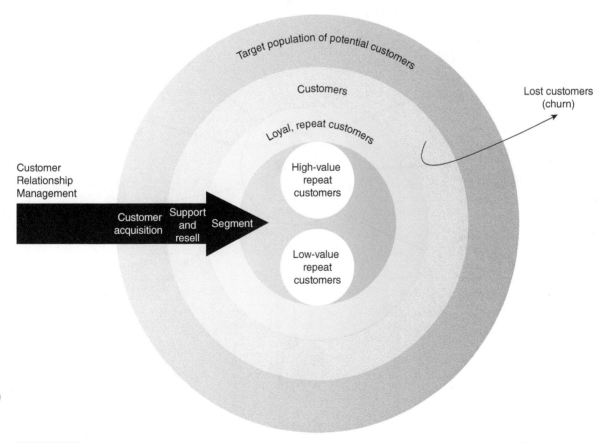

FIGURE 11.1 **The customer relationship management process.**

and support are essential to a successful business, organizations must place a great deal of emphasis on both their CRM strategy and their CRM systems.

Broadly speaking, CRM systems lie along a continuum, from *low-end CRM systems*—designed for enterprises with many small customers—to *high-end CRM systems*—for enterprises with a few large customers. An example of a low-end system is Amazon, which uses its CRM system to recommend products to returning customers. An example of a high-end system is Boeing, which, for example, uses its CRM system to coordinate staff activities in a campaign to sell its new 787 aircraft to Delta Airlines. As you study the cases and examples in this chapter, consider where on the continuum a particular CRM system would fall.

Although CRM varies according to circumstances, all successful CRM policies share two basic elements: (1) the company must identify the many types of customer touch points, and (2) it needs to consolidate data about each customer. Let's examine these two elements in more detail.

Customer Touch Points

customer touch point Any interaction between a customer and an organization.

Organizations must recognize the numerous and diverse interactions they have with their customers. These interactions are referred to as *customer touch points*. Traditional customer touch points include telephone contact, direct mailings, and actual physical interactions with customers during their visits to a store. Organizational CRM systems, however, must manage many additional customer touch points that occur through the use of popular personal technologies. These touch points include e-mail, websites, and communications through smartphones (see **Figure 11.2**).

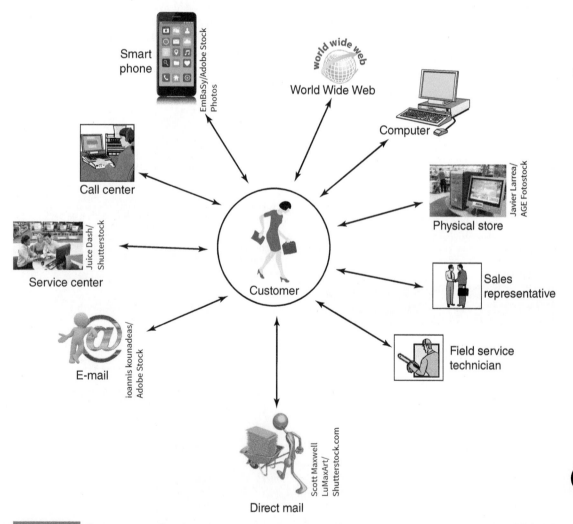

FIGURE 11.2 **Customer touch points.**

The business–customer relationship is constantly evolving. As personal technology usage changes, so too must the methods that businesses use to interface with their customers. It is now possible to physically locate customers through their smartphones. As a result, location information can now provide another customer touch point. IT's About Business 11.1 discusses the changing expectations of customers and how modern CRMs must be adaptable to changing business needs.

IT's About Business **11.1**

MIS **MKT** Customizable CRM Brings Speed and Agility

Business Problem

Customer relationship management is at the heart of every business. Businesses need loyal customers who return and who encourage new customers, which enables the business to expand its customer base and business network.

In the fifth edition of the "State of the Connected Customer" report, Salesforce (www.salesforce.com) stated that 71 percent of customers switched brands at least once during 2021. Almost 50 percent of those customers were looking for better customer service. In addition, 83 percent of customers expect to interact with someone immediately when they contact a company, and 78 percent use multiple communication channels.

Further, 56 percent stated they are more likely to buy from a brand that offers a loyalty program. Customers want to feel an emotional connection to brands. They also want to be treated personally at every step in the purchasing process. The report also states that 75 percent of customers expect businesses to understand their unique needs and expectations, and 66 percent expect companies to anticipate their future needs.

Switching brands for better customer service? Expecting loyalty programs? Anticipating being known and treated personally at every step? Having personal needs anticipated? Managing customers is complicated because relationships are not numbers, conversions, metrics, data, or cost centers. Rather, they are human, and they are based on personal experiences. Customers expect businesses to become more personal. If they don't, then customers are willing to walk away.

The challenge is that organizations are *not* human. They are numbers, metrics, and cost centers. To maintain loyal customers, however, the business must empower its humans—its employees—to behave toward other humans—its customers—in ways that feel relational. Meeting this challenge involves more than becoming customer focused. It also involves the operations, data, processes, and people necessary to anticipate and deliver the experiences customers want and the engagement that builds relationships in real time. To address this need, companies implement customer relationship management tools.

The Technology Solution

Monday.com (www.monday.com) is a customizable workflow management system that had more than 150,000 customers at the end of 2021. It is primarily designed to implement custom-built workflows within an organization. Monday.com is a platform that enables users to drag, drop, and build tools to help nonhuman organizations show their employees how to react humanly to their customers.

Further, Monday.com, can be programmed to respond automatically to customers on behalf of the organization. For example, several tasks happen automatically when a customer's payment status changes from "pending" to "cleared." First, a personalized e-mail updates the customer that the payment has cleared, and the supply room receives information for product packaging, with a customized thank-you note to add to the shipping box. Accounting records are updated, and the sales team receives congratulations from management.

Each of these behaviors—and infinitely more—is programmed to behave the way the organization has defined when interacting with a customer. To perform this task, however, organizations require a customizable, simple, and accessible tool. The need for this level of customization is where Monday.com comes in.

Initially, Monday.com was designed to enable automated communication within the organization. Employees use the platform to organize workflow, communicate, share files, update teams, track progress, view dashboards, and more. With more than 150,000 customers worldwide, it is no surprise that customers began building workflows that would automate the customer relationship activities that are vital to organizational success. Monday.com recognized this and decided to add their own CRM functionality to their platform to better serve their customers.

Monday.com's CRM product enables users to automate tedious tasks, to close more deals faster, and to fully customize the program to suit the company's work processes. Organizations can sync Gmail/Outlook to send and receive e-mails or automatically keep a log of their sent e-mails, all within Monday.com. In addition, the platform automatically notifies businesses when a lead opens or replies to an e-mail so they can follow up immediately. Finally, when sales are completed, Monday.com will help manage post-sale activities.

In addition to providing the necessary tools for sales leads and deals, Monday.com's CRM platform offers a comprehensive and flexible database for the entire customer journey. The platform automates the process of adding new clients to the system, providing representatives with all the data related to a specific account. This shared workflow enables the company to transition seamlessly from prospective customers to confirmed accounts regardless of which representatives interact on behalf of the organization. Automations enable customer data to sync across departments, ensuring that organizations manage every account efficiently and effectively.

Monday.com enables organizations to automate behavior throughout the customer's journey. Sales representatives used to manage this process themselves. Calling in to check on customers and maintaining relationships was a purely human activity that was not supported by organizations' information systems. Further, the best sales representatives built strong relationships that often followed them when they changed organizations. Customers typically were loyal primarily to the representative. Monday.com's CRM platform is designed to shift this relationship to the organization.

Results

Monday.com is built on an easy-to-understand, low-code/no-code framework and can be implemented within minutes. However, the customization will take time, and it likely will never be finished because it will constantly adapt to customers' changing needs. The platform does not require a dedicated administrator. It saves companies time and money, increasing revenue by as much as 30 percent. It enables business owners and sales teams to manage every aspect of their sales cycle and customer data in one centralized location.

Ray White (www.raywhite.com) is Australia's most prominent real estate franchise. The company operates more than 880 offices worldwide, generating more than $6.6 billion annually in sales. They wanted to implement a CRM platform, but they could not find one that fit their needs. Eventually, the company was introduced to Monday.com and they customized their CRM with almost 1,300 automations and integrations. This automation enabled them to plan their workflow two to three years in advance.

Utilizing Monday.com, Ray White now plans customer contact points for tax time, holidays, scheduled inspections, and other important events. These regular contact points give the impression that the company is personally keeping up with a relationship that has already been established when an agent was present in person with the customer. The ability to automatically do this and other work for more than 2,000 clients has helped Ray White increase its efficiency in performing administrative tasks by 70 percent.

In a recent review by Business.com (www.business.com), Monday.com was selected as the most customizable CRM solution available on the market today. This customization ability enables organizations and sales managers to make the software their own and to align it perfectly with the customer journey.

Questions

1. What are some advantages of an easily customizable CRM?
2. How does a CRM establish a customer relationship with an organization rather than a particular sales representative?
3. How does Monday.com's platform support the customer journey that an organization desires to create for its customers?

Sources: Compiled from B. Solis, "Reinforcing the 'R' in CRM," *Destination CRM*, October 3, 2022; S. Jajoo, "Customer Relationship Management: It's More Than Just Conversions," *Entrepreneur*, September 22, 2022; A. Rudder and K. Main, "Pipedrive vs Monday.com (2022 Comparison)," *Forbes Advisor*, September 5, 2022; A. Drapkin, "Monday.com Rolls Out Brand New CRM for Sales Teams," tech.co, August 8, 2022; D. Taylor, "7 CRM Features of Monday.com That Can Help You Build Your Business," *Ascent*, August 5, 2022; D. MacRae, "Monday.com Launches Monday Sales CRM," *Marketing Tech*, August 3, 2022; C. Trueman, "Monday.com Launches New CRM Tool," *ComputerWorld*, August 3, 2022; https://www.business.com/reviews/monday-crm/, accessed October 17, 2022; and https://www.youtube.com/watch?v=TX4kk4OlQfY&t=38s, accessed October 18, 2022.

Businesses recognize this, but they have not moved all of their touch points in sync and this has led to several channel conflicts. For example, have you ever placed an online order only to get to the store and find out that they never received your order? Or do you have to wait because they didn't prepare it when it was promised by the online system? What about when you try to return something you purchased online only to find out that you have to ship it back rather than dropping it off at the local brick-and-mortar version of the same store?

Today, effective marketing makes use of all of these channels (touch points) in sync with one another. We call this omni-channel marketing (*omni* meaning all). Omni-channel marketing refers to an approach to customers that creates a seamless experience regardless of the channel (or device) used to "touch" the business. Many businesses are creating omni-channel strategies to drive this cohesive experience for their customers. To accomplish this goal, businesses must utilize information systems (specifically CRM) because the need for data consistency across channels is more apparent now than ever.

Data Consolidation

MIS Data consolidation is also critical to an organization's CRM efforts. The organization's CRM systems must manage customer data effectively. In the past, customer data were stored in isolated systems (or silos) located in different functional areas across the business—for example, in separate databases in the finance, sales, logistics, and marketing departments. Consequently, data for individual customers were difficult to share across the various functional areas.

As you saw in Chapter 5, modern interconnected systems built around a data warehouse now make all customer-related data available to every unit of the business. This complete dataset on each customer is called a *360° view* of that customer. By accessing this view, a company can enhance its relationship with its customers and ultimately make more productive and profitable decisions.

Data consolidation and the 360º view of the customer enable the organization's functional areas to readily share information about customers. This information sharing leads to collaborative CRM. **Collaborative CRM systems** provide effective and efficient interactive communication with the customer throughout the entire organization. That is, they integrate communications between the organization and its customers in all aspects of marketing, sales, and customer support. Collaborative CRM systems also enable customers to provide direct feedback to the organization. As you read in Chapter 9, social media applications such as social networks, blogs, microblogs, and wikis are very important to companies that value customer input into their product and service offerings, as well as into new product development.

The most recent push for consolidated data is called **customer identity management**. Large businesses with several divisions and brands need to understand who their customers are across the business and how their relationship has changed over time. Much the way databases and data warehouses centralize data within a division (meaning all functional areas share data), a customer identity management platform within a CRM will help a company create the 360° view across an entire organization and not just within a division.

Recall that an organization's CRM system contains two major components: operational CRM systems and analytical CRM systems. You will learn about operational CRM systems in the next section. We provide a brief overview of analytical CRM systems at the end of Section 11.2, and discuss these systems in more detail in Chapter 12.

collaborative CRM system A CRM system in which communications between the organization and its customers are integrated across all aspects of marketing, sales, and customer support processes.

customer identity management A marketing technology intended to complete a 360° view of a customer across an organization.

Before you go on...

1. What is the definition of customer relationship management?
2. Why is CRM so important to an organization?
3. Define and provide examples of customer touch points.

11.2 Operational Customer Relationship Management Systems

LEARNING OBJECTIVE

Describe how businesses might use applications of each of the two major components of operational CRM systems.

Operational CRM systems support front-office business processes. **Front-office processes** are those that directly interact with customers; that is, sales, marketing, and service. The two major components of operational CRM systems are customer-facing applications and customer-touching applications (discussed further on). Operational CRM systems provide the following benefits:

- Efficient, personalized marketing, sales, and service
- A 360º view of each customer
- The ability of sales and service employees to access a complete history of customer interaction with the organization, regardless of the touch point

An example of an operational CRM system involves Caterpillar, Inc. (**www.cat.com**), an international manufacturer of industrial equipment. Caterpillar uses its CRM tools to accomplish the following objectives:

- Improve sales and account management by optimizing the information shared by multiple employees and by streamlining existing processes (e.g., taking orders using mobile devices)

WILEY PLUS

Author Lecture Videos are available exclusively in *WileyPLUS.* **Apply the Concept activities are available in the Appendix and in** *WileyPLUS.*

operational CRM system The component of CRM that supports the front-office business processes that directly interact with customers (i.e., sales, marketing, and service).

front-office processes Those processes that directly interact with customers; that is, sales, marketing, and service.

- Form individualized relationships with customers, with the aim of improving customer satisfaction and maximizing profits
- Identify the most profitable customers and provide them with the highest level of service
- Provide employees with the information and processes necessary to know their customers
- Understand and identify customer needs, and effectively build relationships among the company, its customer base, and its distribution partners

Customer-Facing Applications

customer-facing CRM applications Areas in which customers directly interact with the organization, including customer service and support, sales force automation, marketing, and campaign management.

customer interaction center (CIC) A CRM operation in which organizational representatives use multiple communication channels to interact with customers in functions such as inbound teleservice and outbound telesales.

sales force automation (SFA) The component of an operational CRM system that automatically records all the aspects in a sales transaction process.

In **customer-facing CRM applications**, an organization's sales, field service, and customer interaction center representatives interact directly with customers. These applications include customer service and support, sales force automation, marketing, and campaign management.

MKT Customer Service and Support Customer service and support refers to systems that automate service requests, complaints, product returns, and requests for information. Today, organizations have implemented **customer interaction centers (CIC)**, in which organizational representatives use multiple channels such as the Web, telephone, fax, and face-to-face interactions to communicate with customers.

One of the best-known customer interaction centers is the *call center*, a centralized office set up to receive and transmit a large volume of requests by telephone. Call centers enable companies to respond to a large variety of questions, including product support and complaints.

MIS Sales Force Automation Sales force automation (SFA) is the component of an operational CRM system that automatically records all of the components in a sales transaction process. SFA systems include a *contact management system*, which tracks all communications between the company and the customer, the purpose of each communication, and any necessary follow-up. This system eliminates duplicated contacts and redundancy, which in turn reduces the risk of irritating customers. SFA also includes a *sales lead tracking system*, which lists potential customers or customers who have purchased related products; that is, products similar to those that the salesperson is trying to sell to the customer.

Other elements of an SFA system can include a *sales forecasting system*, which is a mathematical technique for estimating future sales, and a *product knowledge system*, which is a comprehensive source of information regarding products and services. More-developed SFA systems also have online product-building features, called *configurators*, that enable customers to model the product to meet their specific needs. For example, you can customize your own running shoe at Nike By You (**www.nike.com/nike-by-you**). Finally, many current SFA systems enable salespeople in the field to connect remotely with customers and the home office through Web-based interfaces on their smartphones.

MKT Marketing Thus far, you have focused primarily on how sales and customer service personnel can benefit from CRM systems. However, CRM systems have many important applications for an organization's marketing department as well. For example, they enable marketers to identify and target their best customers, to manage marketing campaigns, and to generate quality leads for sales teams. CRM marketing applications can also sift through volumes of customer data—a process known as *data mining* (discussed in Chapter 12)—to develop a *purchasing profile*; that is, a snapshot of a consumer's buying habits that may lead to additional sales through cross-selling, upselling, and bundling.

Cross-selling is the marketing of additional related products to customers based on a previous purchase. This sales approach has been used very successfully by banks. For example, if you have a checking and savings account at your bank, then a bank officer will recommend other products for you, such as certificates of deposit (CDs) or other types of investments.

Upselling is a strategy in which the salesperson provides customers with the opportunity to purchase related products or services of greater value in place of, or along with, the consumer's initial product or service selection. For example, if a customer goes into an electronics store to buy a new television, a salesperson may show him a pricey 1080i HD LED television placed next to a less expensive LCD television in the hope of selling the more expensive set (assuming that the customer is willing to pay more for a sharper picture). Other common examples of upselling are warranties on electronics merchandise and the purchase of a car wash after buying gas at a gas station.

Finally, *bundling* is a form of cross-selling in which a business sells a group of products or services together at a lower price than their combined individual prices. For example, your cable company might bundle cable TV, broadband Internet access, and telephone service at a lower price than you would pay for each service separately.

MKT **Campaign Management**   *Campaign management applications* help organizations plan campaigns that send the right messages to the right people through the right channels. Organizations manage their campaigns very carefully to avoid targeting people who have opted out of receiving marketing communications. Furthermore, companies use these applications to personalize individual messages for each particular customer.

Customer-Touching Applications

Corporations have used manual CRM systems for many years. In the mid-1990s, for example, organizations began to use the Internet, the Web, and other electronic touch points (e.g., e-mail, point-of-sale terminals) to manage customer relationships. In contrast with customer-facing applications, through which customers deal with a company representative, customers who use these technologies interact directly with the applications themselves. For this reason, these applications are called **customer-touching CRM applications** or **electronic CRM (e-CRM)** applications. Customers typically can use these applications to help themselves. There are many types of e-CRM applications. Let's examine some of the major ones.

customer-touching CRM applications (also called electronic CRM or e-CRM) Applications and technologies with which customers interact and typically help themselves.

electronic CRM (e-CRM) See customer-touching CRM applications.

Search and Comparison Capabilities   It is often difficult for customers to find what they want from the vast array of products and services available on the Web. To assist customers, many online stores and malls offer search and comparison capabilities, as do independent comparison websites (see www.mysimon.com).

Technical and Other Information and Services   Many organizations offer personalized experiences to induce customers to make purchases or to remain loyal. For example, websites often allow customers to download product manuals. One example is General Electric's website (www.ge.com), which provides detailed technical and maintenance information and sells replacement parts to customers who need to repair outdated home appliances. Another example is Goodyear's website (www.goodyear.com), which provides information about tires and their use.

Customized Products and Services   Another customer-touching service that many online vendors use is mass customization, a process through which customers can configure their own products. For example, Dell (www.dell.com) allows customers to configure their own computer systems. The Gap (www.gap.com) enables customers to "mix and match" an entire wardrobe. Websites such as) and Apple's iTunes (www.apple.com/itunes) allow customers to pick individual music titles from a library and customize a CD, a feature that traditional music stores do not offer.

Customers now also view account balances or check the shipping status of orders at any time from their computers or smartphones. If you order books from Amazon, for example, you can look up the anticipated arrival date. Many other companies, including FedEx and UPS, provide similar services (see www.fedex.com and www.ups.com).

Personalized Web Pages   Many organizations permit their customers to create personalized Web pages. Customers use these pages to record purchases and preferences, as well as problems and requests. For example, American Airlines (www.aa.com) generates personalized Web pages for each of its registered travel-planning customers.

FAQs   Frequently asked questions (FAQs) are a simple tool for answering repetitive customer queries. Customers may find the information they need by using this tool, thereby eliminating the need to communicate with an actual person.

E-mail and Automated Response   The most popular tool for customer service is e-mail. Inexpensive and fast, companies use e-mail not only to answer customer inquiries but also to disseminate information, send alerts and product information, and conduct correspondence on any topic.

loyalty program   Programs that offer rewards to customers to influence future behavior.

Loyalty Programs   Loyalty programs recognize customers who repeatedly use a vendor's products or services. Loyalty programs are appropriate when two conditions are met: a high frequency of repeat purchases and limited product customization for each customer.

Although loyalty programs are frequently referred to as "rewards programs," their actual purpose is not to reward *past* behavior, but rather to influence *future* behavior. Significantly, the most profitable customers are not necessarily those whose behavior can be most easily influenced. As one example, most major U.S. airlines provide some "elite" benefits to anyone who flies 25,000 miles with them and their partners over the course of a year. Customers who fly first class pay much more for a given flight than those who fly in economy class.

Nevertheless, these customers reach elite status only 1.5 to 2 times faster than economy-class passengers. Why is this true? The reason is that, although first-class passengers are far more profitable than discount seekers, they also are less influenced by loyalty programs. Discount flyers respond much more enthusiastically to the benefits of frequent flyer programs. Therefore, airlines award more benefits to discount flyers than to first-class flyers (relative to their spending).

The airlines' frequent flyer programs are probably the best-known loyalty programs. Other popular loyalty programs are casino players' clubs, which reward frequent players, and supermarkets, which reward frequent shoppers. Loyalty programs use a database or data warehouse to maintain a record of the points (or miles) a customer has accrued and the rewards to which he or she is entitled. The programs then use analytical tools to mine the data and learn about customer behavior.

Analytical CRM Systems

analytical CRM system   CRM system that analyzes customer behavior and perceptions in order to provide actionable business intelligence.

Analytical CRM systems provide business intelligence by analyzing customer behavior and perceptions. (We discuss analytics in detail in Chapter 12.) For example, analytical CRM systems typically provide information concerning customer requests and transactions, as well as customer responses to the organization's marketing, sales, and service initiatives. These systems also create statistical models of customer behavior and the value of customer relationships over time, as well as forecasts about acquiring, retaining, and losing customers.

Important technologies in analytical CRM systems include data warehouses, data mining, decision support, and other business intelligence technologies. After these systems have completed their various analyses, they supply information to the organization in the form of reports and digital dashboards.

Analytical CRM systems analyze customer data for a variety of purposes, including:

- Designing and executing targeted marketing campaigns
- Increasing customer acquisition, cross-selling, and upselling
- Providing input into decisions relating to products and services (e.g., pricing and product development)
- Providing financial forecasting and customer profitability analysis

Figure 11.3 illustrates the relationship between operational CRM systems and analytical CRM systems.

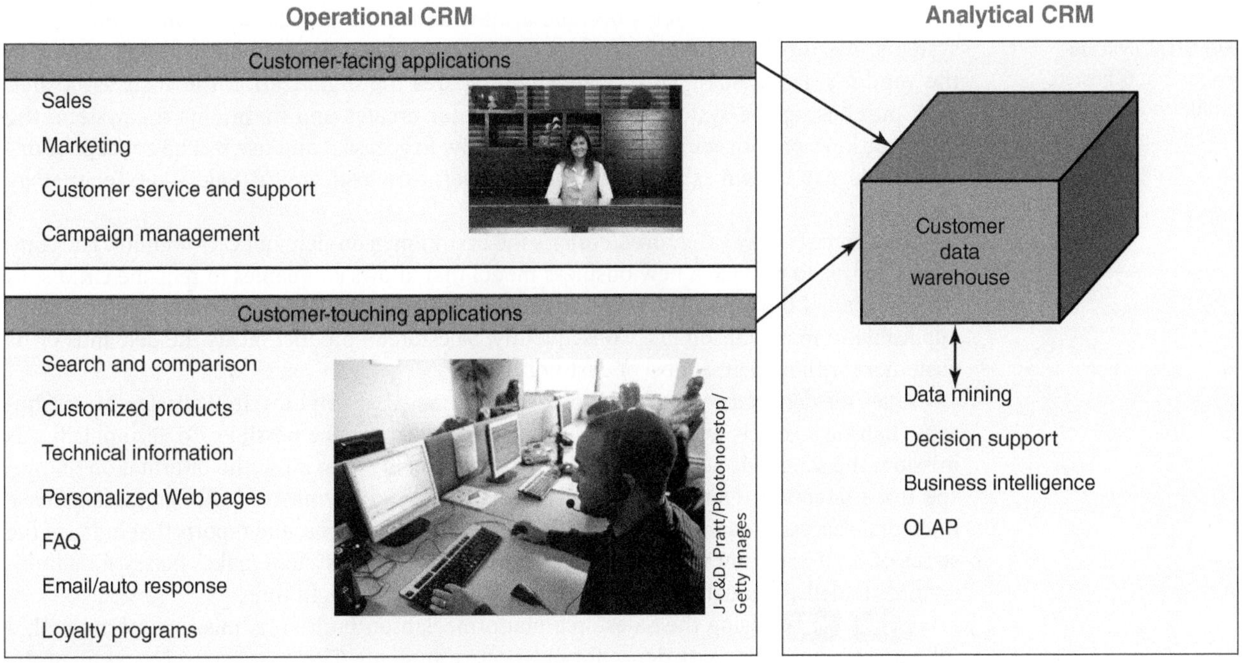

FIGURE 11.3 The relationship between operational CRM and analytical CRM.

Before you go on...

1. Differentiate between customer-facing applications and customer-touching applications.
2. Provide examples of cross-selling, upselling, and bundling (other than the examples presented in the text).

11.3 Other Types of Customer Relationship Management Systems

LEARNING OBJECTIVE

Explain the advantages and disadvantages of mobile CRM systems, on-demand CRM systems, open-source CRM systems, social CRM systems, and real-time CRM systems.

WILEY PLUS

Author Lecture Videos are available exclusively in *WileyPLUS.*
Apply the Concept activities are available in the Appendix and in *WileyPLUS.*

Now that you have examined operational and analytical CRM systems, let's shift our focus to other types of CRM systems. Five exciting developments in this area are on-demand CRM systems, mobile CRM systems, open-source CRM systems, social CRM, and real-time CRM.

On-Demand CRM Systems

Customer relationship management systems may be implemented as either *on-premise* or *on-demand*. Traditionally, organizations used on-premise CRM systems, meaning that they purchased the systems from a vendor and then installed them on site. This arrangement was expensive, time consuming, and inflexible. Some organizations, particularly smaller ones, could not justify the costs of these systems.

on-demand CRM system
A CRM system that is hosted by an external vendor in the vendor's data center.

On-demand CRM systems became a solution for the drawbacks of on-premise CRM systems. An **on-demand CRM system** is one that is hosted by an external vendor in the vendor's data center. This arrangement spares the organization the costs associated with purchasing the system. Because the vendor creates and maintains the system, the organization's employees also need to know how to access it and use it. The concept of on-demand is also known as *utility computing* or *software-as-a-service* (SaaS) (see Technology Guide 3).

Salesforce (www.salesforce.com) is the best-known on-demand CRM vendor. The company's goal is to provide a new business model that allows companies to rent the CRM software instead of buying it. The secret to their success is that CRM has common requirements applicable to many customers. Consequently, Salesforce's product meets the demands of its customers without a great deal of customization.

One Salesforce customer is Babson College (www.babson.edu) in Wellesley, Massachusetts. Babson's goal is to deliver the best applicant experience possible. To accomplish this mission, the school decided to use Salesforce to bring together all of the information on prospective students in a single location. All personnel who are involved with admissions have immediate access to candidate contact information, applications, and reports that indicate the status of each applicant within the enrollment process. This system makes it easy for administrators to deliver valuable information to applicants at the right time.

POM **MKT** Using the Salesforce platform, Babson built an admissions portal with a fully personalized user experience for prospective students. The portal consolidates all of the information that potential students need. Furthermore, it displays different information to students at different points in the application process.

MKT The Bespoke Collection (www.bespokecollection.com) is a wine producer and lifestyle brand based in Yountville, California. The company comprises two wine labels and two art galleries. The firm is noted for its commitment to fine wines, elegant art experiences, and unique customer experiences. Bespoke builds deep customer relationships with its loyalty programs and memberships.

As Bespoke's customer base grew, managing customer data became a challenge. By employing the Salesforce CRM, the company was able to offer their customers the kind of personal attention that defined their organization. As just one example, when a customer makes a purchase, the next morning at 10:00 a.m. they automatically receive a personalized e-mail.

Salesforce enables Bespoke to concentrate on relationship-based rather than transaction-based sales. The company was able to increase customer retention, customer satisfaction, referrals, and order value.

Despite their benefits, on-demand CRM systems have potential problems. First, the vendor could prove to be unreliable, in which case the client company would have no CRM functionality at all. Second, hosted software is difficult or impossible to modify, and only the vendor can upgrade it. Third, vendor-hosted CRM software may be difficult to integrate with the organization's existing software. Finally, giving strategic customer data to vendors always carries security and privacy risks.

Mobile CRM Systems

mobile CRM system An interactive CRM system in which communications related to sales, marketing, and customer service activities are conducted through a mobile medium for the purpose of building and maintaining customer relationships between an organization and its customers.

A **mobile CRM** system is an interactive system that enables an organization to conduct communications related to sales, marketing, and customer service activities through a mobile medium for the purpose of building and maintaining relationships with its customers. Mobile CRM systems involve interacting directly with consumers through portable devices such as smartphones. Mobile CRM systems help to create personalized customer relationships that may be accessed anywhere and at any time. In fact, the opportunities offered by mobile marketing are so rich that many companies are employing mobile CRM systems in their marketing activities. An excellent example of a mobile CRM system is Walt Disney's Magic Band.

Open-Source CRM Systems

As explained in Technology Guide 2, the source code for open-source software is available at no cost. **Open-source CRM systems**, therefore, are CRM systems whose source code is available to developers and users.

open-source CRM system
CRM software whose source code is available to developers and users.

Open-source CRM systems provide the same features or functions as other CRM software, and they may be implemented either on-premise or on-demand. Leading open-source CRM vendors include SugarCRM (www.sugarcrm.com), and Vtiger (www.vtiger.com). Let's look at an example.

MKT Larsen Jewellery (www.larsenjewellery.com.au), founded by Lars Larsen, is an Australian jeweler. He has created a niche in custom-made fine jewelry, focusing on special experiences, lifetime customer relationships, and personal service.

Interestingly, Larsen operates as a face-to-face retailer without a traditional store. He has established studio workshops where customers work with jewelers to participate in the creation of their own unique pieces of jewelry.

Traditionally, Larsen recorded and managed its customer information entirely on paper, including customer inquiries, payments, production, and servicing. This process worked when the firm had a low volume of high-value sales. However, Larsen wanted to expand his locations, which meant that manual processes would no longer be feasible.

Because all customer details were maintained manually, capturing, finding, and using this data took time. Larsen needed to keep all customer information such as contact details, purchases, and design sketches in an easily accessible central repository.

Larsen also could not effectively analyze manual data. He wanted to know how many of the people who visited his studios actually became customers. He also wanted to understand the products and experiences that people were interested in so he could shape his strategy and marketing efforts accordingly.

In addition to transitioning away from manual processes, Larsen had to contend with pressure from online jewelers. These firms operate high-volume, low-margin businesses, which impact customer attitudes and lower their price expectations.

While Larsen does offer value for the money, the brand is not the cheapest. Larsen's value is based on personal service with customers helping to create their own jewelry and then returning regularly to have their jewelry cleaned and maintained.

Larsen had three problems. First, brands that focus on value rather than price must set themselves apart through service and customer experience. Second, the firm had to automate its business processes. Third, with plans to open branches around Australia, Larsen needed to ensure that the business had efficient and repeatable processes. As a result, Larsen needed a CRM package that would help the jeweler solve these problems.

Larsen chose SugarCRM (www.sugarcrm.com). The CRM software, enhanced with Flexidocs, lets staff easily capture information and use it to enhance the customer experience. Customer details are all in one place, along with their jewelry certificates, payment histories, and service records. Flexidocs (www.flexidocs.co) allows users to generate documents with a single click using data from CRM systems. Firms can then e-mail the documents to customers, ready for electronic signing.

Larsen implemented SugarCRM over a six-month period. The jeweler first deployed the package in its Sydney branch so problems could be worked out before extending it to Melbourne.

The benefits became clear very quickly. SugarCRM provided Larsen with checks, balances, and automated prompts to ensure that the company's processes became more efficient and human errors were minimized. The package also provided a central repository for all customer information that makes it easy for users to access for analysis.

The benefits of open-source CRM systems include favorable pricing and a wide variety of applications. These systems are also easy to customize. This is an attractive feature for organizations that need CRM software that is designed for their specific needs. Finally, updates and bug (software error) fixes for open-source CRM systems are rapidly distributed, and extensive support information is available free of charge.

Like all software, however, open-source CRM systems have certain risks. The most serious risk involves quality control. Because open-source CRM systems are created by a large community of unpaid developers, there is sometimes no central authority responsible for overseeing the quality of the product. (We discuss open-source software in Technology Guide 2.) Furthermore, for best results, companies must have the same IT platform in place as the one on which the open-source CRM system was developed.

Social CRM

social CRM The use of social media technology and services to enable organizations to engage their customers in a collaborative conversation in order to provide mutually beneficial value in a trusted and transparent manner.

Social CRM is the use of social media technology and services to enable organizations to engage their customers in a collaborative conversation in order to provide mutually beneficial value in a trusted and transparent manner. Social CRM is the company's response to the customers' ownership of this two-way conversation. In social CRM, organizations monitor services such as Facebook, Twitter, and LinkedIn (among many others) for relevant mentions of their products, services, and brand, and they respond accordingly.

MKT *Example.* When organic tea brand Steaz (www.steaz.com) began posting on Facebook and Twitter about the importance of teas being organic, consumers paid attention and sales doubled. When Steaz offered downloadable coupons on the two social media sites, in one hour 250,000 coupons were downloaded and 2,830 tweets about the offer were recorded.

MKT *Example.* General Motors (www.gm.com) launched Fastlane, one of the first blogs personally written by senior executives. Customer feedback through the blog save the company $180,000 per year versus traditional focus group research. The blog also generated enormous goodwill from company executives responding to consumers.

MKT *Example.* H&R Block (www.hrblock.com) used Facebook and Twitter to provide immediate access to a tax professional in the tax preparation firm's Get It Right social media campaign. The effort resulted in 1.5 million unique visitors and answered 1 million questions for a 15 percent increase in business versus the prior year.

Social media are also providing methods that customers are using to obtain faster, better customer service. Morton's Steakhouse certainly put social media to good use in surprising a customer.

MKT A corporate manager was in meetings all day, and he had to take a later flight home that caused him to miss his dinner. So, he jokingly tweeted Morton's Steakhouse (www.mortons.com) and requested that the restaurant show up with a steak when he landed.

Morton's saw the Tweet, discovered that the tweeter was a frequent customer (and frequent tweeter—he had 100,000 Twitter followers), pulled data on what he typically ordered, identified the flight he was on, and then sent a delivery person to Newark Airport (New Jersey) to serve him his dinner. When he got to the reception lobby at the airport, he noticed a man in a tuxedo holding a card with his name. The man was also carrying a bag that contained a Porterhouse steak, shrimp, potatoes, bread, two napkins, and silverware.

The nearest Morton's restaurant was 24 miles from the airport, and the manager's flight took only two hours. This scenario says a lot about both Morton's customer service and the speed of social media. Admittedly, the entire scenario was a publicity stunt that went explosively viral over the Internet. This is not the point, however. The questions that businesses should be asking themselves are: Would your company even consider doing something like this? If not, why not?

Real-Time CRM

real-time CRM system A CRM system enabling organizations to respond to customer product searches, requests, complaints, comments, ratings, reviews, and recommendations in near real time, 24/7/365.

Organizations are implementing real-time customer relationship management to provide a superior level of customer satisfaction for today's always-on, always-connected, more knowledgeable, and less loyal customers. **Real-time CRM systems** help organizations to respond to customer product searches, requests, complaints, comments, ratings, reviews, and recommendations in near real-time, 24/7/365. Southwest Airlines provides an excellent example of real-time CRM.

POM **MKT** A passenger was in her seat on a Southwest Airlines flight about to take off when the plane turned back to the gate. A flight attendant asked her to get off the plane. When she checked with the Southwest agent at the desk inside the terminal, he told her that her son was in a coma after suffering a head injury and to call her husband.

Even before she had disembarked, Southwest had rebooked her on the next nonstop flight to her son's city—free of charge. The airline offered her a private waiting area, rerouted her luggage, allowed her to board first, and packed a lunch for her. Moreover, the airline delivered her luggage to where she was going to stay and called her to ask about her son. The woman said that her son was recovering and that she could not be more grateful for the way she was treated.

Southwest Airlines went above and beyond their responsibilities after they learned of the son's accident. Details were not available about how the airline learned of the son's accident, but it is clear that Southwest brought customer relationship management to a new level.

Before you go on...

1. Describe on-demand CRM.
2. Describe mobile CRM.
3. Describe open-source CRM.
4. Describe social CRM.
5. Describe real-time CRM.

11.4 | Supply Chains

LEARNING OBJECTIVE

Describe the three components and the three flows of a supply chain.

Modern organizations are increasingly concentrating on their core competencies and on becoming more flexible and agile. To accomplish these objectives, they rely on other companies rather than on companies they own to supply the goods and services they need. Organizations recognize that these suppliers can perform these activities more efficiently and effectively than they can. This trend toward relying on an increasing number of suppliers has led to the concept of supply chains. A supply chain is the flow of materials, information, money, and services from raw material suppliers, through factories and warehouses, to the end customers. A supply chain also includes the *organizations* and *processes* that create and deliver products, information, and services to the end customers.

Supply chains enhance trust and collaboration among supply chain partners, thus improving supply chain visibility and inventory velocity. **Supply chain visibility** refers to the ability of all organizations within a supply chain to access or view relevant data on purchased materials as these materials move through their suppliers' production processes and transportation networks to their receiving docks. Organizations can also access or view relevant data on outbound goods as they are manufactured, assembled, or stored in inventory and then shipped through their transportation networks to their customers' receiving docks. The more quickly a company can deliver products and services after receiving the materials required to make them—that is, the higher the *inventory velocity*—the more satisfied the company's customers will be. In addition, supply chain visibility promotes quick responses to problems or changes along the supply chain by enabling companies to shift products to where they are needed.

Supply chain information has historically been obtained by manual, labor-based tracking and monitoring, but is now increasingly being generated by sensors, RFID tags, meters, GPS, and other devices and systems. How does this transformation affect supply chain managers? For one thing, they now have real-time information on all products moving through their supply chains. Supply chains will therefore rely less on labor-based tracking and monitoring,

supply chain visibility The ability of all organizations in a supply chain to access or view relevant data on purchased materials as these materials move through their suppliers' production processes.

because the new technology will allow shipping containers, trucks, products, and parts to report on their own status. The overall result is a vast improvement in supply chain visibility.

Supply chains are a vital component of the overall strategies of many modern organizations. To use supply chains efficiently, a business must be tightly integrated with its suppliers, business partners, distributors, and customers. A critical component of this integration is the use of information systems to facilitate the exchange of information among the participants in the supply chain.

The Structure and Components of Supply Chains

POM The term *supply chain* comes from a picture of how the partnering organizations are linked. **Figure 11.4** illustrates a typical supply chain. (Recall that **Figure 1.5** also illustrated a supply chain, in a slightly different way.) Note that the supply chain involves three segments:

1. *Upstream*, where sourcing or procurement from external suppliers occurs.

    In this segment, supply chain managers select suppliers to deliver the goods and services the company needs to produce its product or service. Furthermore, SC managers develop the pricing, delivery, and payment processes between a company and its suppliers. Included here are processes for managing inventory, receiving and verifying shipments, transferring goods to manufacturing facilities, and authorizing payments to suppliers.

2. *Internal*, where packaging, assembly, or manufacturing takes place.

    SC managers schedule the activities necessary for production, testing, packaging, and preparing goods for delivery. They also monitor quality levels, production output, and worker productivity.

3. *Downstream*, where distribution takes place, frequently by external distributors.

    In this segment, SC managers coordinate the receipt of orders from customers, develop a network of warehouses, select carriers to deliver products to customers, and implement invoicing systems to receive payments from customers.

The flow of information and goods can be bidirectional. For example, damaged or unwanted products can be returned, a process known as *reverse flows* or *reverse logistics*. In the retail clothing industry, for example, reverse logistics involves clothing that customers return, either because the item had defects or because the customer did not like the item.

Tiers of Suppliers   Figure 11.4 shows several tiers of suppliers. As the diagram indicates, a supplier may have one or more subsuppliers, a subsupplier may have its own subsupplier(s), and so on. For an automobile manufacturer, for example, Tier 3 suppliers produce basic products such as glass, plastic, and rubber; Tier 2 suppliers use these inputs to make windshields, tires, and plastic moldings; and Tier 1 suppliers produce integrated components such as dashboards and seat assemblies.

The Flows in the Supply Chain   There are typically three flows in the supply chain: material, information, and financial. *Material flows* are the physical products, raw materials,

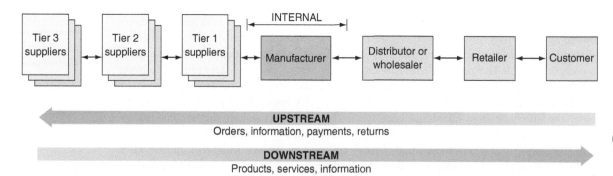

FIGURE 11.4 Generic supply chain.

supplies, and so forth that flow along the chain. Material flows also include the reverse flows discussed earlier. A supply chain thus involves a *product life cycle* approach, from "dirt to dust."

Information flows consist of data related to demand, shipments, orders, returns, and schedules, as well as changes in any of these data. Finally, *financial flows* involve money transfers, payments, credit card information and authorization, payment schedules, e-payments, and credit-related data.

Significantly, different supply chains have different numbers and types of flows. For example, in service industries, there may be no physical flow of materials, but there is frequently a flow of information, often in the form of documents (physical or electronic copies). For example, the digitization of software, music, and other content can create a supply chain without any physical flow. Notice, however, that in such a case there are two types of information flows: one that replaces materials flow (digitized software) and another that provides the supporting information (orders, billing, and so on). To manage the supply chain, an organization must coordinate all three flows among all of the parties involved in the chain, a topic we turn to next.

Before you go on...

1. What is a supply chain?
2. Describe the three segments of a supply chain.
3. Describe the flows in a supply chain.

11.5 Supply Chain Management

LEARNING OBJECTIVE

Identify popular strategies to solving different challenges of supply chains.

The function of **supply chain management (SCM)** is to improve the processes a company uses to acquire the raw materials it needs to produce a product or service and then deliver that product or service to its customers. That is, supply chain management is the process of planning, organizing, and optimizing the various activities performed along the supply chain. There are five basic components of SCM:

1. *Plan*: Planning is the strategic component of SCM. Organizations must have a strategy for managing all the resources that are involved in meeting customer demand for their product or service. Planning involves developing a set of metrics (measurable deliverables) to monitor the organization's supply chain to ensure that it is efficient and it delivers high quality and value to customers for the lowest cost.

2. *Source*: In the sourcing component, organizations choose suppliers to deliver the goods and services they need to create their product or service. Supply chain managers develop pricing, delivery, and payment processes with suppliers, and they create metrics to monitor and improve their relationships with their suppliers. They also develop processes for managing their goods and services inventory, including receiving and verifying shipments, transferring the shipped materials to manufacturing facilities, and authorizing supplier payments.

3. *Make*: This is the manufacturing component. Supply chain managers schedule the activities necessary for production, testing, packaging, and preparation for delivery. This component is the most metric-intensive part of the supply chain, in which organizations measure quality levels, production output, and worker productivity.

WILEY PLUS

Author Lecture Videos are available exclusively in *WileyPLUS.*
Apply the Concept activities are available in the Appendix and in *WileyPLUS.*

supply chain management (SCM) An activity in which the leadership of an organization provides extensive oversight for the partnerships and processes that compose the supply chain and leverages these relationships to provide an operational advantage.

4. *Deliver*: This component, often referred to as logistics, is in which organizations coordinate the receipt of customer orders, develop a network of warehouses, select carriers to transport their products to their customers, and create an invoicing system to receive payments.

5. *Return*: Supply chain managers must create a responsive and flexible network for receiving defective, returned, or excess products back from their customers, as well as for supporting customers who have problems with delivered products.

Like other functional areas, SCM uses information systems. The goal of SCM systems is to reduce the problems, or friction, along the supply chain. Friction can increase time, costs, and inventories and decrease customer satisfaction. SCM systems, therefore, reduce uncertainty and risks by decreasing inventory levels and cycle time while improving business processes and customer service. These benefits make the organization more profitable and competitive.

Various circumstances can cause problems with global supply chains, including hurricanes, tornados, and other weather events. However, the COVID-19 pandemic has had a far greater impact than these other phenomena. The pandemic was totally unforeseen, it had global impacts, and it did not give supply chain planners much time to react.

POM Supply chains also lead to increased sales and profits. Consider Adidas (**www .adidas.com**), the leading sports shoe brand in Russia, with more than 1,200 stores in that country. As part of its strategy to optimize the customer experience, Adidas built the supply chain infrastructure needed to enable initiatives such as RFID chips (see Chapter 8), ship from store, click and collect, and endless aisle.

- *Ship from store*: Goods ordered online are delivered from a physical store.

- *Click and collect*: Customers buy products online and collect the products at a physical store or warehouse. By October 2018 some 70 percent of Adidas online sales were through click and collect.

- *Endless aisle*: Using in-store kiosks, customers can order products not in stock in their local store but available in another store. Products are then delivered using the ship from store process or click and collect process.

Russia is, physically, the largest country in the world. Shipping goods from one end of Russia to the other can take up to 15 days using traditional delivery systems. With its three supply chain initiatives, Adidas reduced delivery times and costs while increasing sales and profits. Here is the reason why. Consumers typically return 50 percent of the products they buy online if delivery is made within 24 hours. However, if delivery takes 3 days, consumers may return 70 percent of products. Therefore, because these three processes increase the speed of delivery, customers return fewer goods, which leads to higher completed sales and increased profits.

Significantly, SCM systems are a type of interorganizational information system. In an **interorganizational information system (IOS)**, information flows among two or more organizations. By connecting the IS of business partners, IOSs enable the partners to perform a number of tasks.

interorganizational information system (IOS) An information system that supports information flow among two or more organizations.

- Reduce the costs of routine business transactions

- Improve the quality of the information flow by reducing or eliminating errors

- Compress the cycle time involved in fulfilling business transactions

- Eliminate paper processing and its associated inefficiencies and costs

- Make the transfer and processing of information easier for users

push model A business model in which the production process begins with a forecast, which predicts the products that customers will want as well as the quantity of each product. The company then produces the amount of products in the forecast, typically by using mass production, and sells, or "pushes," those products to consumers.

The Push Model Versus the Pull Model

Many SCM systems employ the **push model**. In this model, also known as *make-to-stock*, the production process begins with a forecast, which is simply an educated guess as to customer demand. The forecast must predict which products customers will want and in what quantities. The company then produces the amount of products in the forecast, typically by using mass production, and sells, or "pushes," those products to consumers.

Unfortunately, these forecasts are often incorrect. Consider, for example, an automobile manufacturer that wants to produce a new car. Marketing managers conduct extensive research, including customer surveys and analyses of competitors' cars, and then provide the results to forecasters. If the forecasters' predictions are too high—that is, if they predict that customers will purchase a certain number of these new cars but actual demand falls below this amount—then the automaker has excess cars in inventory and will incur large carrying costs (the costs of storing unsold inventory). Furthermore, the company will probably have to sell the excess cars at a discount.

From the opposite perspective, if the forecasters' predictions are too low—that is, actual customer demand exceeds expectations—then the automaker probably will have to run extra shifts to meet the demand, thereby incurring substantial overtime costs. Furthermore, the company risks losing business to its competitors if the car that customers want is not available. Thus, using the push model in supply chain management can cause problems, as you will see in the next section.

To avoid the uncertainties associated with the push model, many companies now employ the pull model of supply chain management, using Web-enabled information flows. In the **pull model**, also known as *make-to-order*, the production process begins with a customer order. Therefore, companies make only what customers want, a process closely aligned with mass customization (discussed in Chapter 1).

POM A prominent example of a company that uses the pull model is Dell Computer (**www.dell.com**). Dell's production process begins with a customer order. This order not only specifies the type of computer the customer wants but also alerts each Dell supplier as to the parts of the order for which that supplier is responsible. That way, Dell's suppliers ship only the parts that Dell needs to produce the computer.

Not all companies can use the pull model. Automobiles, for example, are far more complicated and more expensive to manufacture than computers, so automobile companies require longer lead times to produce new models. Automobile companies do use the pull model, but only for specific automobiles that some customers order (e.g., Rolls-Royce, Bentley, and other extremely expensive cars).

> **pull model**   A business model in which the production process begins with a customer order and companies make only what customers want, a process closely aligned with mass customization.

Problems Along the Supply Chain

As you saw earlier, friction can develop within a supply chain. One major consequence of friction is poor customer service. In some cases, supply chains do not deliver products or services when and where customers—either individuals or businesses—need them. In other cases, the supply chain provides poor quality products. Other problems associated with supply chain friction are high inventory costs and revenue loss.

The problems along the supply chain arise primarily from two sources: (1) uncertainties and (2) the need to coordinate multiple activities, internal units, and business partners. A major source of supply chain uncertainties is the *demand forecast*. Demand for a product can be influenced by numerous factors such as competition, price, weather conditions, technological developments, overall economic conditions, and customers' general confidence. Another uncertainty is delivery times, which can be affected by numerous factors ranging from production machine failures to road construction and traffic jams. Quality problems in materials and parts can also create production delays, which also generate supply chain problems.

One major challenge that managers face in setting accurate inventory levels throughout the supply chain is known as the bullwhip effect. The **bullwhip effect** refers to erratic shifts in orders up and down the supply chain (see **Figure 11.5**). Basically, the variables that affect customer demand can become magnified when they are viewed through the eyes of managers at each link in the supply chain. If each distinct entity that makes ordering and inventory decisions places its interests above those of the chain, then stockpiling can occur at as many as seven or eight locations along the chain. Research has revealed that in some cases this type of hoarding has led to as much as a 100-day supply of inventory that is waiting "just in case," versus the 10- to 20-day supply manufacturers normally keep at hand.

> **bullwhip effect**   Erratic shifts in orders up and down the supply chain.

FIGURE 11.5 The bullwhip effect.

Solutions to Supply Chain Problems

Supply chain problems can be very costly. Therefore, organizations are motivated to find innovative solutions. During the oil crises of the 1970s, for example, Ryder Systems, a large trucking company, purchased a refinery to control the upstream part of the supply chain and to ensure it had sufficient gasoline for its trucks. Ryder's decision to purchase a refinery is an example of vertical integration. **Vertical integration** is a business strategy in which a company purchases its upstream suppliers to ensure that its essential supplies are available as soon as the company needs them. Ryder later sold the refinery because it could not manage a business it did not understand and because oil became more plentiful.

Ryder's decision to vertically integrate was not the best method for managing its supply chain. In the remainder of this section, you will look at some other possible solutions to supply chain problems, many of which are supported by IT.

vertical integration Strategy of integrating the upstream part of the supply chain with the internal part, typically by purchasing upstream suppliers, so as to ensure timely availability of supplies.

Using Inventories to Solve Supply Chain Problems   Undoubtedly, the most common solution to supply chain problems is *building inventories* as insurance against supply chain uncertainties. As you have learned, holding either too much or too little inventory can be very costly. Thus, companies make major attempts to optimize and control inventories.

One widely used strategy to minimize inventories is the **just-in-time (JIT)** inventory system. Essentially, JIT systems deliver the precise number of parts, called *work-in-process* inventory, to be assembled into a finished product at precisely the right time.

Although JIT offers many benefits, it has certain drawbacks as well. To begin with, suppliers are expected to respond instantaneously to requests. As a result, they have to carry more inventory than they otherwise would. In this sense, JIT does not *eliminate* excess inventory; rather, it simply *shifts* it from the customer to the supplier. This process can still reduce the overall inventory size if the supplier can spread the increased inventory over several customers. However, that is not always possible.

JIT also replaces a few large supply shipments with a large number of smaller ones. In terms of transportation, then, the process is less efficient.

just-in-time (JIT) An inventory system in which a supplier delivers the precise number of parts to be assembled into a finished product at precisely the right time.

Information Sharing   Another common approach to solving supply chain problems, and especially to improving demand forecasts, is *sharing information* along the supply chain. Information sharing can be facilitated by electronic data interchange and extranets, topics you will learn about in the next section.

One notable example of information sharing occurs between large manufacturers and retailers. For example, Walmart provides Procter & Gamble (P&G) with access to daily sales information from every store for every item that P&G makes for Walmart. This access enables P&G to manage the *inventory replenishment* for Walmart's stores. By monitoring inventory levels, P&G knows when inventories fall below the threshold for each product at any Walmart store. These data trigger an immediate shipment.

Information sharing between Walmart and P&G is executed automatically. It is part of a vendor-managed inventory strategy. **Vendor-managed inventory (VMI)** occurs when the supplier, rather than the retailer, manages the entire inventory process for a particular product or group of products. Significantly, P&G has similar agreements with other major retailers. The benefit for P&G is accurate and timely information on consumer demand for its products. Thus, P&G can plan production more accurately, minimizing the bullwhip effect.

A problem that has been exacerbated by the pandemic is the increasing numbers of products that customers are returning. IT's About Business 11.2 presents an overview of shoppers' changing attitudes and expectations regarding product returns.

vendor-managed inventory (VMI)   An inventory strategy where the supplier monitors a vendor's inventory for a product or group of products and replenishes products when needed.

IT's About Business **11.2**

`MKT` `MIS` `POM`   **Return Problems**

Customers love free returns. They make online shopping less risky, and they allow customers to "bracket" their purchases. *Bracketing* refers to the practice in which customers buy multiple sizes or colors of the same item and then return the items they don't want. According to the National Retail Federation (www.nrf.com), in 2020, shoppers sent back roughly $100 billion worth of merchandise. In 2021, that amount more than doubled to $218 billion. This trend is not sustainable.

Ironically, although customers are returning far more items than ever before, many shoppers consider this process to be too complicated. According to Shopify (www.shopify.com), 58 percent of shoppers state they are "not satisfied" with the ease of making returns. Customers further claim they are willing to abandon brands if the brands do not offer easy return policies. Further, 72 percent of shoppers are willing to spend more money and order more frequently from online stores that offer a customer-friendly return process. In sum, customers increasingly are making their purchasing decisions based on how simple it is to "undo" those decisions.

Return policies became even more important following the COVID outbreak. The world was unprepared for the pandemic. Retailers were not prepared for the surge in online shopping. They were even less prepared for the huge volumes of returns. Before the pandemic, many retailers considered returns as a standard cost of doing business. In contrast, today the return process has become a vital component of the customer experience.

Easy and free returns have become the expectation. However, this practice has reinforced consumers' treatment of purchases more as risk-free discoveries for size and style than as end-of-shopping journeys. Retailers report that this reality is especially true for select categories such as women's shoes and dresses.

Although shoppers appreciate free shipping and free returns, it is not free for retailers to take those items back. One estimate found that processing a return costs a company 66 percent of the sales price of the product. The costs to the retailer include ground shipping and the labor involved in processing, sorting, and preparing those goods to be resold. These added processing costs are causing retailers to lose, on average, millions of dollars every year.

For many retailers, 2022 was a challenging year financially. In response, some companies are adjusting their return policies in an attempt to decrease loss associated with returns. Managing returns, however, has been a relatively neglected problem. Any lag time in returns in a fashion-based business (or any business where trends and seasons impact pricing) can lead to significant markdowns for reselling the merchandise. Brands that sell returns at wholesale prices face an added challenge. Retail returns often arrive all at once at the end of a selling season, making the resell market more difficult because of the short shelf life of the item relative to the season. Also, marking down prices too much can lead to value erosion relative to competing retailers. For example, if customers become accustomed to a particular brand cutting prices by 50 percent, they may begin to associate the value at 50 percent of the manufacturer's suggested retail price. Finally, there is the environmental impact: An estimated 10 percent of all returns end up in a landfill.

One relatively unpopular approach to this problem is to charge customers for returns. In theory, this practice would force customers to make better, more final purchasing decisions to avoid paying the return fee. For example, fashion retailer Zara (www.zaar.com) added a fee of $3.95. JCPenney (www.jcpenney.com), Abercrombie & Fitch (www.abercrombie.com), and J.Crew (www.jcrew.com) charge roughly $8 for returns. Of course, the unintended outcome may be that customers shop elsewhere.

Other companies are offering free returns only to their most loyal shoppers. For example, shoe retailer DSW (www.dsw.com) charges customers $8.50 to return an item unless they are members of the VIP rewards programs. To become members, customers must spend at least $200 each year.

A different strategy to reduce the number of returns is to provide more information to help customers make better purchasing decisions. In the apparel industry, retailers need to help shoppers understand how clothes will fit them before they make a purchase. In the past, retailers employed supermodels to promote their products. Today, they use a variety of people with different skin tones, heights, and weights to help shoppers better understand what they are buying.

Other retailers provide in-depth customer feedback on their competitors' brands as well as their own products. This feedback helps customers to decide between brands rather than bracket their order with multiple brands with the intention of returning unwanted items.

Looking further ahead, several companies are investing in augmented-reality technology to support the customer in their buying process. Nike (www.nike.com), for example, launched a digitally focused store in China that offers a foot-scanning technology. They are not alone in this. Several shoe stores have scanning tools to help customers make more informed decisions about the shoes they will purchase. This tool helps customers to determine their best-fit size for different sneakers and styles. Similarly, Sephora's Virtual Artist (www.sephora.my/pages/virtual-artist)

enables customers to "try on" makeup products through the app or in-store screens.

Moving beyond apparel and makeup, Amazon employs augmented reality to enable customers to "see" items in their own space. For example, customers can see how a painting will look in their room or how a different-sized TV will fit on the wall. Warby Parker allows customers to virtually "try on" hundreds of pairs of glasses.

Despite these efforts, however, customers will continue to return items. Knowing this is the case, businesses can deploy strategies to help reduce the cost of returns to the company.

One strategy is to simplify the process by encouraging customers to return items directly to a store. For example, Nordstrom (www.nordstrom.com) offers contactless curbside return and return kiosks. Not only is this process simple and convenient, but customers also don't have to interact with a sales associate who asks why they don't want the item.

Some retailers have established stores known as *return consolidation centers* that are dedicated entirely to returns. These centers operate based on clear guidelines as to how to manage returns. Data inform employees whether an item should be discarded or retained and resold. Decisions are based on the profit margin from the initial sale, seasonality, item condition, packaging condition, and other product-specific considerations.

Another strategy to make returns more convenient is to outsource the process to a third party that specializes in this area. Companies like Happy Return (www.happyreturns.com) and Narvar (www.corp.narvar.com) operate thousands of drop-off locations nationwide. Retailers can outsource this service and receive cleaned, prepped, and sorted returns without having to manage the reverse logistics.

The timely return of resalable inventory is crucial in categories that are season sensitive. For example, a customer purchases summer apparel near the end of the season and returns it within the 45-day window. That item might not have a place on the shelves after the store has switched to fall products. There might not be anything physically wrong with the product or the packaging. However, the window of time to sell the product at the same price has closed. Third-party companies that quickly process returns before they go out of season help reduce this loss.

Finally, some retailers will use return cost analytics to determine whether the cost of the return is higher than the liquidation/resale value. If this is the case, then they would consider letting the customer keep the item.

The Future of Online Returns

Online shopping and free returns have transformed the buying process. It is easy to hold, feel, try on, and discover items before purchasing them when you are shopping in a physical store. In contrast, online customers must "buy" the right to physically see the product. They then decide whether to keep or return it. For this reason, returns are a requirement in online shopping. The level of convenience and transparency in the returns experience is critical to consumer retention. This difference in the process underscores the importance of clear, consistent communication on return options, processes, and status for retailers.

For some retailers, the return dilemma has inspired acquisitions and new approaches. Walmart (www.walmart.com) bought a virtual fitting room start-up, Zeekit, to help customers see themselves in apparel before making a purchase. Best Buy has a separate store to sell returned items rather than putting them back on the shelf. These items are covered by warranty, and product descriptions let purchasers know if all parts are available or something is missing. Some other companies, including Amazon (www.amazon.com), provide refunds but let consumers keep unwanted items rather than deal with the hassle and cost of a low-value return. These "refund and keep" decisions are driven by analysis and awareness of the growing return problem. Regardless of the strategies ahead, companies must deal with the issue of returns.

Questions

1. How has online shopping increased the volume of returns?

2. Discuss how technology can be used to lessen the number of returns by helping customers make informed decisions.

3. How can businesses utilize technology to better manage returns?

Sources: Compiled from A. Hartmans, "The Era of Free Returns May Be Coming to an End. Here's Why Retailers Have Started Charging Return Fees—and How You Can Avoid Them." *Business Insider*, October 14, 2022; G. Petro, "'Desperation in the Air' as the Great Retail Destocking Picks Up Steam," *Forbes*, October 14, 2022; M. Corkery, "Retail's 'Dark Side': As Inventory Piles Up, Liquidation Warehouses Are Busy," *New York Times*, July 30, 2022; M. Repko, "A More Than $761 Billion Dilemma: Retailers' Returns Jump as Online Sales Grow," *CNBC*, January 25, 2022; M. Simoncic and A. Lozano, "Returns Are the New Growth Strategy," *Retail Dive*, December 23, 2021; E. Dopson, "The Plague of Ecommerce Return Rates and How to Maintain Profitability," shopify.com, August 25, 2021; G. Jezerc, "Returning to Normal: How Retail Can Beat the Returns Challenge," *First Insight*, August 13, 2021; J. Mitchell, "How Online Returns Will Impact the Post-Covid Customer Experience," *Supply Chain Brain*, July 15, 2021; J. Ader et al., "Returning to Order: Improving Returns Management for Apparel Companies," *McKinsey & Company*, May 25, 2021; and "$428 Billion in Merchandise Returned in 2020," National Retail Foundation, press release, January 11, 2021.

Before you go on...

1. Differentiate between the push model and the pull model.

2. Describe various problems that can occur along the supply chain.

3. Discuss possible solutions to problems along the supply chain.

11.6 Information Technology Support for Supply Chain Management

LEARNING OBJECTIVE

Explain the utility of each of the three major technologies that support supply chain management.

WILEY PLUS

Author Lecture Videos are available exclusively in *WileyPLUS*.
Apply the Concept activities are available in the Appendix and in *WileyPLUS*.

Clearly, SCM systems are essential to the successful operation of many businesses. As you have seen, these systems—and IOSs in general—rely on various forms of IT to resolve problems. Three technologies, in particular, provide support for IOSs and SCM systems: electronic data interchange, extranets, and Web services. You will learn about Web services in Technology Guide 3. In this section, you examine the other two technologies.

Electronic Data Interchange (EDI)

Electronic data interchange (EDI) is a communication standard that enables business partners to exchange routine documents, such as purchasing orders, electronically. EDI formats these documents according to agreed-upon standards (e.g., data formats). It then transmits messages over the Internet using a converter, called a *translator*.

EDI provides many benefits that are not available with a manual delivery system. To begin with, it minimizes data entry errors, because each entry is checked by the computer. The length of the message can also be shorter, and the messages are secured. EDI also reduces cycle time, increases productivity, enhances customer service, and minimizes paper usage and storage. **Figure 11.6** contrasts the process of fulfilling a purchase order with and without EDI.

EDI does have some disadvantages. Business processes must sometimes be restructured to fit EDI requirements. Also, there are many EDI standards in use today, so one company might have to use several standards to communicate with multiple business partners.

In today's world, in which every business has a broadband connection to the Internet and where multi-megabyte design files, product photographs, and PDF sales brochures are routinely e-mailed, the value of reducing a structured e-commerce message from a few thousand XML bytes to a few hundred EDI bytes is negligible. As a result, EDI is being replaced by XML-based Web services. (You will learn about XML in Technology Guide 3.)

electronic data interchange (EDI) A communication standard that enables business partners to transfer routine documents electronically.

Extranets

To implement IOSs and SCM systems, a company must connect the intranets of its various business partners to create extranets. **Extranets** link business partners over the Internet by providing them access to certain areas of each other's corporate intranets (see **Figure 11.7**).

The primary goal of extranets is to foster collaboration between and among business partners. A business provides extranet access to selected B2B suppliers, customers, and other partners. These individuals access the extranet through the Internet. Extranets enable people located outside a company to collaborate with the company's internal employees. They also allow external business partners to enter the corporate intranet, through the Internet, to access data, place orders, check the status of those orders, communicate, and collaborate. Finally, they make it possible for partners to perform self-service activities such as checking inventory levels.

Extranets use virtual private network (VPN) technology to make communication over the Internet more secure. The major benefits of extranets are faster processes and information flow, improved order entry and customer service, lower costs (e.g., for communications, travel, and administrative overhead), and overall improved business effectiveness.

extranets Networks that link business partners over the Internet by providing them access to certain areas of each other's corporate intranets.

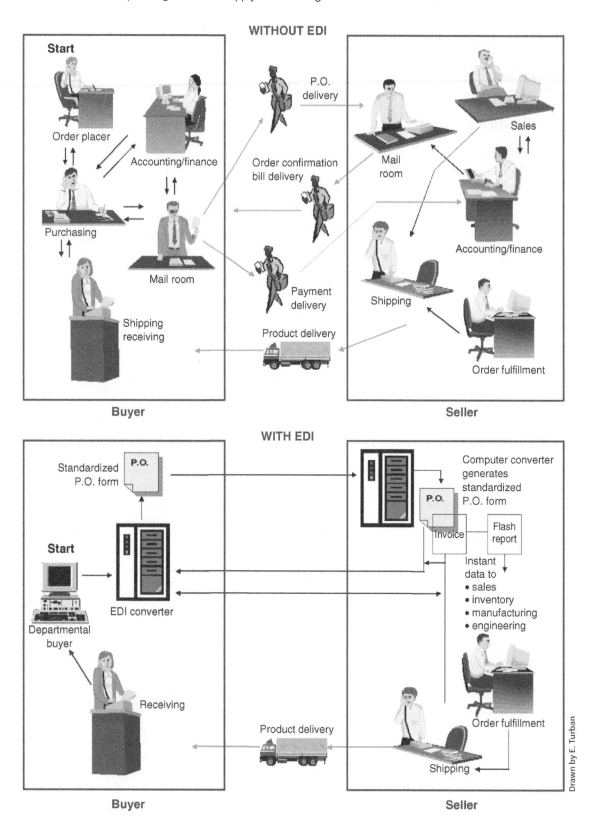

WITHOUT EDI

Start
Order placer
Accounting/finance
Purchasing
Mail room
Shipping receiving

Buyer

P.O. delivery
Order confirmation bill delivery
Payment delivery
Product delivery

Mail room
Sales
Accounting/finance
Shipping
Order fulfillment

Seller

WITH EDI

Standardized P.O. form
P.O.
Start
EDI converter
Departmental buyer
Receiving

Buyer

Computer converter generates standardized P.O. form
P.O.
Invoice
Flash report
Instant data to
• sales
• inventory
• manufacturing
• engineering
Order fulfillment
Product delivery
Shipping

Seller

Drawn by E. Turban

FIGURE 11.6 Comparing purchase order (PO) fulfillment with and without EDI.

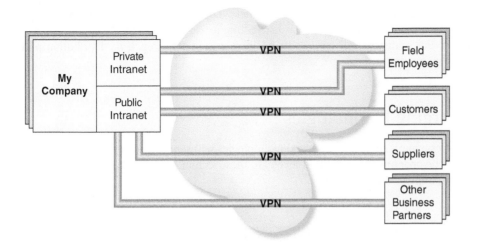

FIGURE 11.7 **The structure of an extranet.**

There are three major types of extranets. The type that a company chooses depends on the business partners involved and the purpose of the supply chain. We present each type next, along with its major business applications.

A Company and Its Dealers, Customers, or Suppliers   This type of extranet centers on a single company. An example is the FedEx extranet, which allows customers to track the status of a delivery. Customers use the Internet to access a database on the FedEx intranet. Enabling customers to monitor deliveries saves FedEx the cost of hiring human operators to perform that task over the phone.

An Industry's Extranet   Just as a single company can set up an extranet, the major players in an industry can team up to create an extranet that will benefit all of them. For example, OpenText (www.opentext.com) enables companies to collaborate effectively through a network that provides a secure global medium for B2B information exchange. This network is used for mission-critical business transactions by leading international organizations in aerospace, automotive, chemical, electronics, financial services, health care, logistics, manufacturing, transportation, and related industries. It offers customers a reliable extranet as well as VPN services.

Joint Ventures and Other Business Partnerships   In this type of extranet, the partners in a joint venture use the extranet as a vehicle for communication and collaboration. An example is Bank of America's (www.bankofamerica.com) extranet for commercial loans. The partners involved in making these loans include a lender, a loan broker, an escrow company, and a title company. The extranet connects lenders, loan applicants, and the loan organizer, Bank of America. A similar case is Lending Tree (www.lendingtree.com), a company that provides mortgage quotes for homeowners and also sells mortgages online. Lending Tree uses an extranet for its business partners (e.g., the lenders).

Portals and Exchanges

As you saw in Chapter 6, corporate portals offer a single point of access through a Web browser to critical business information in an organization. In the context of B2B supply chain management, these portals enable companies and their suppliers to collaborate very closely.

There are two basic types of corporate portals: procurement (sourcing) portals for a company's suppliers (upstream in the supply chain) and distribution portals for a company's customers (downstream in the supply chain). **Procurement portals** automate the business processes involved in purchasing or procuring products between a single buyer and multiple suppliers. For example, Boeing has deployed the Boeing Supplier Portal through

procurement portals
Corporate portals that automate the business processes involved in purchasing or procuring products between a single buyer and multiple suppliers.

distribution portals
Corporate portals that automate the business processes involved in selling or distributing products from a single supplier to multiple buyers.

which it conducts business with its suppliers. **Distribution portals** automate the business processes involved in selling or distributing products from a single supplier to multiple buyers. For example, Dell services its business customers through its distribution portal at **www.premier.dell.com**.

Emerging Technologies

Logistics experts predict that several technologies will significantly impact supply chains by 2025. The opening case presented several of these technologies and the impact they will have on the supply chain.

Before you go on...

1. Define EDI, and list its major benefits and limitations.
2. Define an extranet, and explain its infrastructure.
3. List and briefly define the major types of extranets.
4. Differentiate between procurement portals and distribution portals.

What's in IT for Me?

ACCT For the Accounting Major

Customer Relationship Management

CRM systems can help companies establish controls for financial reporting related to interactions with customers in order to support compliance with legislation. For example, Sarbanes–Oxley requires companies to establish and maintain an adequate set of controls for accurate financial reporting that can be audited by a third party. Other sections (302 and 401(b)) have implications for customer activities, including the requirements that sales figures reported for the prior year be correct. Section 409 requires companies to report material changes to financial conditions, such as the loss of a strategic customer or significant customer claims about product quality.

CRM systems can track document flow from a sales opportunity to a sales order, to an invoice, to an accounting document, thus enabling finance and accounting managers to monitor the entire flow. CRM systems that track sales quotes and orders can be used to incorporate process controls that identify questionable sales transactions. CRM systems can provide exception-alert capabilities to identify instances outside defined parameters that put companies at risk.

Supply Chain Management

The cost accountant will play an important role in developing and monitoring the financial accounting information associated with inventory and cost of goods sold. In a supply chain, much of the data for these accounting requirements will flow into the organization from various partners within the chain. It is up to the chief accountant, the comptroller or CFO, to prepare and review these data.

Going further, accounting rules and regulations and the cross-border transfer of data are critical for global trade. IOSs can facilitate such trade. Other issues that are important for accountants are taxation and government reports. Creating information systems that rely on EDI also requires the attention of accountants. Finally, detecting fraud in global settings (e.g., transfers of funds) can be facilitated by appropriate controls and auditing.

FIN For the Finance Major

Customer Relationship Management

CRM systems allow companies to track marketing expenses, collecting appropriate costs for each individual marketing campaign. These costs then can be matched to corporate initiatives and financial objectives, demonstrating the financial impact of the marketing campaign.

Pricing is another key area that impacts financial reporting. For example, what discounts are available? When can a price be overridden? Who approves discounts? CRM systems can put controls into place for these issues.

Supply Chain Management

In a supply chain, the finance major will be responsible for analyzing the data created and shared among supply chain partners. In many instances, the financial analyst will recommend actions to improve supply chain efficiencies and cash flow. This may benefit all of the partners in the chain. These recommendations will be based on financial models that incorporate key assumptions such as supply chain partner agreements for pricing. Through the use of extensive financial modeling, the financial analyst helps to manage liquidity in the supply chain.

Many finance-related issues exist in implementing IOSs. For one thing, establishing EDI and extranet relationships involves structuring payment agreements. Global supply chains may involve complex financial arrangements, which can have legal implications.

MKT For the Marketing Major

Customer Relationship Management

CRM systems are an integral part of every marketing professional's work activities. CRM systems contain the consolidated customer data that provides the foundation for making informed marketing decisions. Using these data, marketers develop well-timed and targeted sales campaigns with customized product mixes and established price points that enhance potential sales opportunities and therefore increase revenue. CRM systems also support the development of forecasting models for future sales to existing clients through the use of historical data captured from previous transactions.

Supply Chain Management

A tremendous amount of useful sales information can be derived from supply chain partners through the supporting information systems. For example, many of the customer support activities take place in the downstream portion of the supply chain. For the marketing manager, an understanding of how the downstream activities of the supply chain relate to prior chain operations is critical.

Furthermore, tremendous amounts of data are fed from the supply chain supporting information systems into the CRM systems that are used by marketers. The information and a complete understanding of its genesis are vital for mixed-model marketing programs.

POM For the Production/Operations Management Major

Customer Relationship Management

Production is heavily involved in the acquisition of raw materials, conversion, and distribution of finished goods. However, all of these activities are driven by sales. Increases or decreases in the demand for goods will increase or decrease a company's need for raw materials. Integral to a company's demand is forecasting future sales, an important feature of CRM systems. Sales forecasts are created from the historical data stored in CRM systems.

This information is critical to a production manager who is placing orders for manufacturing processes. Without an accurate future sales forecast, production managers can face inventory problems (discussed in detail in this chapter). The use of CRM systems for production and operational support is critical to efficiently managing the company's resources.

Supply Chain Management

The production/operations management major plays an important role in the supply chain development process. In many organizations, the production/operations management staff may even lead the supply chain integration process because of their extensive knowledge of the organization's manufacturing components. Because the production/operations staff are in charge of procurement, production, materials control, and logistical handling, they must possess a comprehensive understanding of SCM techniques.

The downstream segment of supply chains is where marketing, distribution channels, and customer service are conducted. An understanding of how downstream activities are related to the other segments is critical. Supply chain problems can reduce customer satisfaction and negate marketing efforts. It is essential, then, that marketing professionals understand the nature of such problems and their solutions. Also, learning about CRM, its options, and its implementation is important for designing effective customer services and advertising.

As competition intensifies globally, finding new global markets becomes critical. IOSs provide an opportunity to improve marketing and sales. Understanding the capabilities of these technologies as well as their implementation issues will enable the marketing department to excel.

HRM For the Human Resources Major

Customer Relationship Management

Companies trying to enhance their customer relationships must recognize that employees who interact with customers are critical to the success of CRM strategies. Essentially, the success of CRM is based on the employees' desire and ability to promote the company and its CRM initiatives. In fact, research analysts have found that customer loyalty is based largely on employees' capabilities and their commitment to the company.

As a result, human resource managers know that a company that desires valued customer relationships needs valued relationships with its employees. Therefore, HR managers are implementing programs to increase employee satisfaction and are training employees to execute CRM strategies.

Supply Chain Management

Supply chains require the employees of partners in the chain to interact effectively. These interactions are the responsibility of the human resources manager, who must be able to address supply chain issues that relate to staffing, job descriptions, job rotations, and accountability. All of these areas are complex within a supply chain, and they require the HR function to understand the relationships among partners as well as the movement of resources.

Preparing and training employees to work with business partners (frequently in foreign countries) requires knowledge about how IOSs operate. Sensitivity to cultural differences and extensive communication and collaboration can be facilitated with IT.

MIS For the MIS Major

Customer Relationship Management

The IT function in the enterprise is responsible for the corporate databases and data warehouse, as well as the correctness and completeness of the data stored in them. That is, the IT department provides the data used in a 360° view of the customer. Furthermore, IT personnel provide the technologies underlying the customer interaction center.

Supply Chain Management

The MIS staff will be instrumental in the design and support of information systems—both internal organizational and interorganizational—that will underpin the business processes that are part of the supply chain. In this capacity, the MIS staff must have a concise knowledge of the business, the systems, and the points of intersection between the two.

Summary

11.1   Identify the primary functions of both customer relationship management (CRM) and collaborative CRM.

Customer relationship management (CRM) is an organizational strategy that is customer focused and customer driven. That is, organizations concentrate on assessing customers' requirements for products and services and then on providing high-quality, responsive services. CRM functions include acquiring new customers, retaining existing customers, and growing relationships with existing customers.

Collaborative CRM is an organizational CRM strategy in which data consolidation and the 360º view of the customer enable the organization's functional areas to readily share information about customers. The functions of collaborative CRM include integrating communications between the organization and its customers in all aspects of marketing, sales, and customer support processes and enabling customers to provide direct feedback to the organization.

11.2   Describe how businesses might use applications of each of the two major components of operational CRM systems.

Operational CRM systems support the front-office business processes that interact directly with customers (i.e., sales, marketing, and service). The two major components of operational CRM systems are customer-facing applications and customer-touching applications.

Customer-facing CRM applications include customer service and support, sales force automation, marketing, and campaign management. *Customer-touching applications* include search and comparison capabilities, technical and other information and services, customized products and services, personalized Web pages, FAQs, e-mail and automated response, and loyalty programs.

11.3   Explain the advantages and disadvantages of mobile CRM systems, on-demand CRM systems, open-source CRM systems, social CRM systems, and real-time CRM systems.

On-demand CRM systems are hosted by an external vendor in the vendor's data center. Advantages of on-demand CRM systems include lower costs and a need for employees to know only how to access and use the software. Drawbacks include possibly unreliable vendors, difficulty in modifying the software, and difficulty in integrating vendor-hosted CRM software with the organization's existing software.

Mobile CRM systems are interactive systems through which communications related to sales, marketing, and customer service activities are conducted through a mobile medium for the purpose of building and maintaining customer relationships between an organization and its customers. Advantages of mobile CRM systems include convenience for customers and the chance to build a truly personal relationship with customers. A drawback could be difficulty in maintaining customer expectations; that is, the company must be extremely responsive to customer needs in a mobile, near-real-time environment.

Open-source CRM systems are those whose source code is available to developers and users. The benefits of open-source CRM systems include favorable pricing, a wide variety of applications, easy customization, rapid updates and bug (software error) fixes, and extensive free support information. The major drawback of open-source CRM systems is quality control.

Social CRM is the use of social media technology and services to enable organizations to engage their customers in a collaborative conversation to provide mutually beneficial value in a trusted and transparent manner.

Real-time CRM means that organizations are able to respond to customer product searches, requests, complaints, comments, ratings, reviews, and recommendations in near real-time, 24/7/365.

11.4   Describe the three components and the three flows of a supply chain.

A *supply chain* is the flow of materials, information, money, and services from raw material suppliers, through factories and warehouses, to the end customers. A supply chain involves three segments: upstream, where sourcing or procurement from external suppliers occurs; internal, where packaging, assembly, or manufacturing takes place; and downstream, where distribution takes place, frequently by external distributors.

There are three flows in the supply chain: *material flows*, which are the physical products, raw materials, supplies, and so forth; *information flows*, which consist of data related to demand, shipments, orders, returns, and schedules, as well as changes in any of these data; and *financial flows*, which involve money transfers, payments, credit card information and authorization, payment schedules, e-payments, and credit-related data.

11.5   Identify popular strategies to solving different challenges of supply chains.

Two major challenges in setting accurate inventory levels throughout a supply chain are the *demand forecast* and the *bullwhip effect*. Demand for a product can be influenced by numerous factors such as competition, prices, weather conditions, technological developments, economic conditions, and customers' general confidence. The *bullwhip effect* refers to erratic shifts in orders up and down the supply chain.

The most common solution to supply chain problems is *building inventories* as insurance against SC uncertainties. Another solution is the *just-in-time* (JIT) inventory system, which delivers the precise number of parts, called *work-in-process inventory*, to be assembled into a finished product at precisely the right time. The third possible solution is *vendor-managed inventory* (VMI), which occurs when the vendor, rather than the retailer, manages the entire inventory process for a particular product or group of products.

11.6   Explain the utility of each of the three major technologies that support supply chain management.

Electronic data interchange (EDI) is a communication standard that enables the electronic transfer of routine documents, such as purchasing orders, between business partners.

Extranets are networks that link business partners over the Internet by providing them access to certain areas of each other's corporate intranets. The main goal of extranets is to foster collaboration among business partners.

Corporate portals offer a single point of access through a Web browser to critical business information in an organization. In the context of business-to-business supply chain management, these portals enable companies and their suppliers to collaborate very closely.

Key Terms

analytical CRM system   336
bullwhip effect   345
collaborative CRM system   333
customer-facing CRM applications   334
customer interaction center (CIC)   334
customer identity management   333
customer relationship management
   (CRM)   328
customer-touching CRM applications
   (also called electronic CRM or
   e-CRM)   335
customer touch point   330

distribution portals   352
electronic CRM (e-CRM)   335
electronic data interchange (EDI)   349
extranets   349
front-office processes   333
interorganizational information system
   (IOS)   344
just-in-time (JIT)   346
loyalty program   336
mobile CRM system   338
on-demand CRM system   338
open-source CRM system   339

operational CRM system   333
procurement portals   351
pull model   345
push model   344
real-time CRM system   340
sales force automation (SFA)   334
social CRM   340
supply chain management (SCM)   343
supply chain visibility   341
vendor-managed inventory (VMI)   347
vertical integration   346

Discussion Questions

1. How do customer relationship management systems help organizations achieve customer intimacy?

2. What is the relationship between data consolidation and CRM systems?

3. Discuss the relationship between CRM and customer privacy.

4. Distinguish between operational CRM systems and analytical CRM systems.

5. Differentiate between customer-facing CRM applications and customer-touching CRM applications.

6. Explain why Web-based customer interaction centers are critical for successful CRM systems.

7. Why are companies so interested in e-CRM applications?

8. Discuss why it is difficult to justify CRM applications.

9. You are the CIO of a small company with a rapidly growing customer base. Which CRM system would you use: an on-premise CRM

system, an on-demand CRM system, or an open-source CRM system? Remember that open-source CRM systems may be implemented either on-premise or on-demand. Discuss the pros and cons of each type of CRM system for your business.

10. List and explain the important components of a supply chain.

11. Explain how a supply chain approach may be part of a company's overall strategy.

12. Explain the important role that information systems play in supporting a supply chain strategy.

13. Would Rolls-Royce Motorcars (**www.rolls-roycemotorcars.com**) use a push model or a pull model in its supply chain? Support your answer.

14. Why is planning so important in supply chain management?

Problem-Solving Activities

1. Access **www.ups.com** and **www.fedex.com**. Examine some of the IT-supported customer services and tools provided by the two companies. Compare and contrast the customer support provided on the two companies' websites.

2. Enter **www.anntaylor.com**, **www.hermes.com**, and **www.tiffany.com**. Compare and contrast the customer service activities offered by these companies on their websites. Do you see marked similarities? Differences?

3. Access your university's website. Investigate how your university provides for customer relationship management. (*Hint:* First decide who your university's customers are.)

4. Access **www.sugarcrm.com**, and take the interactive tour. Prepare a report on SugarCRM's functionality to the class.

5. Visit **www.crmside.com/apple-crm-case-study/**. List three things you learned about Apple's success with CRM.

6. Compare Starbucks' (**www.starbucks.com**) loyalty program with Dunkin Donuts (**www.dunkindonuts.com**).

7. Enter **www.apics.org**, **www.cio.com**, **www.findarticles.com**, and **www.google.com**, and search for recent information on supply chain management.

8. Surf the Web to find a procurement (sourcing) portal, a distribution portal, and an exchange (other than the examples presented in this chapter). List the features they have in common and those features that are unique.

9. Visit **www.boomi.com/platform/b2b-management/** and view their demo. Describe the benefits this type of software provides to businesses.

10. Describe the current career opportunities available in supply chain management after visiting **www.ascm.org**

Closing Case

MIS POM MKT **Customers and Supply in the Food Delivery Industry**

The COVID-19 pandemic changed the way the world eats. Before 2020, restaurant-quality meal delivery was limited largely to cuisines such as pizza and Chinese food. Today, food delivery is a global market worth more than $150 billion, having tripled since 2017. The market more than doubled in the United States during the COVID-19 pandemic.

There was a reason most restaurants did not focus on delivery prior to the pandemic: Delivery is a major challenge. To begin with, it is expensive. Restaurants either must hire drivers or use third-party providers like DoorDash and Uber Eats, which charge a fee that cuts into the restaurants' already narrow margins. Also, delivery is stressful for employees, who must balance taking care of in-store customers while filling increasing numbers of to-go and delivery orders. Finally, when deliveries go wrong, the restaurants take the blame, whether or not it is their fault.

Before the pandemic, food delivery apps like DoorDash and Uber Eats were niche services that were popular primarily in big cities. Then, during the lockdown, these apps earned staggering amounts of money. For example, Uber Eats reported $4.8 billion in revenue in 2020, a 152 percent increase over 2019. DoorDash's revenue jumped 268 percent from 2019 to 2020. From January through September 2020, the company recorded 543 million orders, compared to 181 million during the same period in 2019. Customers appreciated the convenience of being able to order food and have it delivered to their homes.

For restaurants, the shift to delivery through these apps provided a much-needed revenue source while the lockdown was in effect. Further, for people who lost their jobs and students who were sent home from college, a part-time job as a food delivery driver offered an opportunity to earn money.

By 2023, the pandemic was over, and dine-in restrictions in most places had ended. Customers, however, had become accustomed to food delivery, and they continued to utilize the service. However, the industry is dealing with a number of issues:

- Delivery companies are losing money.
- Restaurants must deal with operational changes.
- Restaurants face delivery driver issues.
- Customers are often dissatisfied.

We discuss each of these issues below.

Delivery companies are losing money

Given the volume of orders, it is hard to believe that delivery companies are not profitable. In fact, they earn only a small percentage of each food order. DoorDash and Uber Eats actually spend more money on advertising and technology than they earn from deliveries.

The delivery companies make money by charging restaurants a fee for each order placed through their app. The standard fee is 30 percent. The apps also charge a service fee to the customer.

According to experts, the average DoorDash order during the pandemic was for $36. The company's 30 percent fee would equal $10.80, plus another $2 or so for the service fee. That might sound like a lot of money, especially when we multiply it by hundreds of millions of orders. However, that $12.80 is gross revenue. DoorDash has to pay its drivers, fund its advertising and promotional campaigns, deal with returns and refunds, and cover all of its operational expenses. When those costs are considered, DoorDash is left with net earnings of 2.5 percent of the customer's overall bill. That is a meager $0.90 for every $36 order. This slim margin has not been sufficient to make DoorDash and Uber Eats profitable, even though they take in billions of dollars in revenue.

Restaurants must deal with operational changes

Many restaurants quickly adjusted to full-time delivery and take-out orders during the pandemic. They repurposed spaces to accommodate the new workflow, and they closed dining rooms. Today, however, restaurants must balance in-person, take-out, and delivery food options that were not part of the business prior to the pandemic.

Unfortunately, the current model of employing food delivery companies does not appear to be working. If customers choose delivery over in-person dining, then restaurants lose too much money to the companies' commissions. Even when lawmakers in Seattle capped the apps' commission at 15 to 20 percent during the pandemic, restaurants in that area still struggled to turn a profit on each order.

In addition, delivery services found and posted old restaurant menus. Many restaurants had added menu items and removed others. Suddenly, they received orders for meals they no longer provided. Even restaurants that did not contract with DoorDash and Uber Eats were unwillingly forced into the delivery ecosystem when their menus were posted on apps without their consent.

Restaurants face delivery driver issues

Meal deliveries became more challenging after the pandemic. Many drivers who previously could ride a regular bike now have to ride an electric bike to move faster and cover longer distances. They must work longer hours, make more deliveries, and compete in a more saturated market.

According to some reports, ten delivery cyclists died in the first nine months of 2021. That number includes one driver who died after a hit-and-run and another driver who was stabbed. Many drivers have lobbied for protection from local and federal governments.

Customers are often dissatisfied

According to a 2021 survey, food delivery errors are fairly common. In fact, roughly 90 percent of customers have had a food delivery order go wrong. In these cases, 50 percent of customers requested a refund. However, 40 percent ordered from a different restaurant rather than taking the refund. In addition, these customers frequently complained to the delivery service or to the actual driver.

Solutions

From restaurants to drivers to app companies, the math of food delivery does not seem to add up. Nonetheless, food delivery is here to stay. Let's examine how some restaurants, drivers, delivery companies, and government entities have responded to the issues we just discussed. We begin with the restaurants.

Restaurants

One way to make food delivery profitable is to charge consumers more for the convenience. In 2020, for example, Chipotle (www .chipotle.com), the popular Mexican food chain, sold nearly 50 percent of its food orders via delivery. To recoup the cost of the delivery companies' commissions, Chipotle charges 17 percent more for delivery than for in-store purchases.

Other restaurants have set up online-only concepts explicitly designed for delivery. Online-only brands enable restaurants to promote products that travel well for delivery, such as sandwiches and wings. This strategy can transform the service from a burden into a competitive advantage. As one example, Applebee's (www.applebees.com) launched an online-only brand, Cosmic Wings (www.cosmicwings.com), which serves Cheeto-flavored chicken wings. Brinker International (EAT), the owner of Chili's (www.chilis.com) and Maggiano's Little Italy (www.maggia-nos.com), has two virtual brands: It's Just Wings (www.itsjust-wings.com) and Maggiano's Italian Classics (www.facebook .com/maggianosclassics/).

Fast-casual and fast-food restaurants, which were already designed to get people out the door quickly, have refined their drive-thrus and incentives. Their goal is to move customers away from delivery. Several chains have added "express" drive-thru lanes for customers who order through the app. The goal is to make it easier for someone to swing by the fast drive-thru lane than to wait on a delivery.

Chipotle calls their drive-thru Chipotlane. It is significant that as the number of customers who use Chipotlane has increased, the volume of delivery orders has decreased. Further, Chipotle reported that the best margin is found when customers place app orders before they arrive. This approach helps to manage the workload and reduces the stress on their delivery system of parking lot congestion, drivers' stress with traffic, and food quality upon receipt.

When chains cannot convince customers to use speedier drive-thrus, they try other incentives. One approach is to offer a small bonus to customers who skip delivery. For example, in August 2022, Domino's (DPZ) began to offer a $3 credit toward the next purchase for customers who pick up their pizza rather than have it delivered. The chain also promised to deliver the pizza to customers in fewer than two minutes—but only if those customers drove themselves to a Domino's location and parked in the assigned spot.

Using a mobile app and reward programs appears to be the best strategy. This approach enables restaurants to offer personalized deals while making more money from each sale. At McDonald's, for instance, customers can receive a free order of large fries and 1,500 bonus points for downloading the company's app and signing up for its rewards program. Customers enjoy rewards; the restaurants benefit from more data, a more manageable order process, and loyal customers. An app on a person's home screen is like a personal billboard. And, if the user enables notifications, then the app can speak to customers with reminders, rewards, and suggestions.

Finally, some restaurant chains have simply stopped employing delivery services. For example, EatWell DC, whose restaurants include Logan Tavern, Commissary, Grillfish, and The Pig, has ended its relationships with all delivery apps for two reasons: First, they claimed that rising fees benefit only the delivery companies. Second, the restaurants want customers to enjoy their food at its peak, and they have no control over the quality, timeliness, or condition of the meals when customers receive their orders.

Delivery Companies

The most notable strategies employed by the delivery companies are to serve as an intermediary between restaurants and delivery customers and expand the use of their delivery systems to other industries. For example, Grubhub pivoted to become an online marketing partner for restaurants. They still deliver food, but their platform is also used to help restaurants promote their store and their products.

Meanwhile, companies like DoorDash and Uber Eats plan to become more profitable by expanding into other sectors such as groceries, pharmacies, and alcohol. DoorDash drivers are already fulfilling deliveries for big box stores like Walmart and Petco. This strategy will enable them to capitalize on their core service of providing customer convenience for stores that do not offer a delivery service.

Drivers

Delivery drivers are often the forgotten players in the delivery system. Restaurants have reputations to uphold, and the delivery driver is responsible for transporting purchased meals safely and swiftly. Drivers, however, must contend with many factors that are beyond their control, including traffic, accidents, and the accuracy of GPS map instructions. As a result, drivers are often treated poorly by restaurants, customers, and even their employer.

Delivery drivers are vulnerable. They were repeatedly exposed to COVID-19 while customers stayed home safely, enjoying their food. They endure extreme weather, violent attacks, and traffic accidents while covering all their travel expenses and bringing home what often amounts to less than the minimum wage. They often wear clothes to designate that they work for a delivery company, which means to everyone else that they have food with them, making them a target for theft.

In New York City, a rise in robberies and injuries led delivery drivers to form a group called Los Deliveristas Unidos (United Delivery People) to organize the city's delivery workers around the common cause of better protection and safety. The group successfully lobbied the city council to establish minimum salaries and require restaurants to permit drivers to use their bathrooms, which was previously not allowed. They also requested that the city install better lighting on dark bridges and that the police take crimes against delivery workers more seriously. In May 2021, members of Los Deliveristas Unidos marched through Times Square to call attention to their situation.

The Government Response

Some municipalities are taking aggressive actions against presumed price gouging for delivery services. For example, in 2021, Seattle imposed a 15 percent cap on the commission that third-party, app-based services can charge to deliver food. The city also required third-party meal-delivery apps to obtain written consent from restaurants before listing their menus or taking orders. Delivery services could be fined $250 per violation.

Government entities are still wrestling with tips for people in the delivery area. Should restaurant employees who prepare to-go orders receive a regular wage or a tipped wage for their work? Or, imagine that a customer orders a meal and adds a tip. Does the tip go to the driver who delivered the food? Or, should the restaurant worker who prepared the meal for delivery receive part of the tip? And, because the restaurant employee and the driver work for different employers, who will manage the split?

Conclusion

The post-pandemic food delivery industry represents a radical shift in customer relationship management and the supply chain for ready-to-eat meals. This industry has become a basic part of our culture. Several issues need to be addressed, however, for this practice to become profitable.

Questions

1. **Describe the issues that restaurants face regarding food delivery. How have they responded?**

2. **Discuss the issues and responses for delivery companies.**

3. **Discuss the issues and responses for delivery drivers.**

4. **What policies have governments adopted to protect delivery drivers and customers? Can you think of additional actions they could take? Explain your answer.**

Sources: Compiled from J. Rudisuela, "Province Pushing to Make Restaurant Food Delivery Fee Cap Permanent," *Capital Daily*, October 7, 2022; F. Phillips, "Food Delivery Apps Can Be Both a Blessing and a Curse for Restaurants: 5 Tips to Avoid a Tip Credit Landmine," *JD Supra*, October 4, 2022; I. Krietzberg, "Higher Prices, Skimpier Portions and Apps—How Fast-Food Chains Are Changing Value Deals," *CNBC*, August 6, 2022; K. Beaton, "Consumer Survey: Delivery Apps Often Fail to Deliver," The Food Institute, June 29, 2022; L. Held, "The Next Frontier of Labor Organizing: Food-Delivery Workers," *Civil Eats*, May 4, 2022; J. Clabaugh, "Big DC Restaurant Owner Cuts All Ties with Food Delivery Apps," *WTOP News*, May 4, 2022; H. Reinblatt, "How Spoiled Are Consumers with On-Demand Delivery?," *CircuitBlog*, study, April 28, 2022; R. Wile, "Food-Delivery Apps Lose Steam as People Return to In-Person Dining," *NBC News*, April 23, 2022; N. Gabrielle, "Food Delivery Apps Are Convenient, but You're Probably Overpaying," *Motley Fool*, March 24, 2022; T. Carroll, "How Are Food Delivery Apps Addressing Rising Gasoline Prices?" *InsideHook*, March 19, 2022; D. Weiner-Bronner, "Your Delivery Orders Are Making Restaurants Mad. Now They're Fighting Back," CNN Business, February 23, 2022; D. Roos, "Who (If Anyone) Makes Money Off Food Delivery Apps, Like Uber Eats?" howstuffworks.com, December 16, 2021; B. Allyn, "Ordering Food on an App Is Easy. Delivering It Could Mean Injury and Theft," NPR, November 3, 2021; K. Ahuja et al., "Ordering In: The Rapid Evolution of Food Delivery," McKinsey, September 22, 2021; T. Vinh, "Seattle Cracks Down on Food Delivery Apps with One of the Strictest Laws in Country," *Seattle Times*, September 9, 2021; D. Weiner-Bronner, "Spending More on DoorDash and UberEats? This Fee May Be Why," CNN Business, January 23, 2021; and J. Castrodale, "Cities Are Capping Delivery App Fees to Protect Restaurants during the COVID-19 Crisis," *Food & Wine*, April 28, 2020.

Business Analytics

Opening Case

MIS Zillow

Founded in 2006, Zillow (www.zillow.com) is a U.S. online real estate platform that helps home buyers (or landlords) connect with sellers (or renters). Zillow developed an estimate for a home, called a Zestimate, based on a range of publicly available information, including the multiple listing service (MLS) database, user-submitted details, and market trends. The MLS data allow Zillow to analyze the sales of comparable houses in a neighborhood, given property features ranging from the basic (e.g., square footage, number of bedrooms and bathrooms) to the particular (e.g., fireplace, stainless steel appliances, original wood floors). The resulting Zestimate is, in theory, an accurate estimate of a home's market value. And, it is freely available to anyone who is interested.

Zillow made money in four ways, discussed below. The company has employed the first three methods since its founding. Zillow entered its fourth money-making practice—the iBuyer marketplace—in 2018 and exited it in 2021.

Premier Agent branding. Zillow offers Premier Agent branding on their website, which includes searches of multiple listing services, client reviews, past sales, biographies of these agents,

photos, and videos. Real estate agents can also purchase advertising with Zillow. Zillow targets ads at users in agents' local markets to help them attract new clients who are buying or selling homes. Finally, Premier Agent provides agents with a customer relationship management system that helps them track Zillow users who have expressed interest in working with an agent. Zillow's iBuyer program provided more income than its Premier Agent services for a time, but today Premier Agent remains Zillow's primary source of revenue.

Advertising for property management companies. Zillow charges property management companies to advertise their listings on the Zillow Rental Manager, which includes websites from Zillow, Trulia, and Hotpads. Zillow directs prospective renters to these advertisers.

Advertising for other businesses. Zillow also sells advertising space on its site to mortgage lenders and other businesses that want to reach Zillow customers, including interior designers, home organization retailers, and general contractors. Most of these advertisers are in the real estate industry, but some sell telecommunications services, automotive products and services, insurance, and consumer products.

Instant Buyer. Instant Buyer (iBuyer), also called *digital real estate flipping*, is a real estate transaction model in which companies purchase residential properties directly from private sellers with the goal of reselling them, hopefully for a profit. Companies use algorithms to quickly value, buy, and sell homes. These firms estimate the price at which they think they can sell a property; this then informs their offers to buy. They tend to offer lower prices than traditional buyers. However, they attract sellers by promising faster, all-cash deals.

Zillow joined the iBuying business in 2018 with the launch of Zillow Offers. The company planned to use its Zestimates algorithm to predict what a home would be worth in a few months and then offer a cash sum to the seller that would provide the company with a small profit while covering the costs of repairs. Zillow trained its algorithm (see Chapter 14) on millions of home valuations across the country before employing it to estimate the price of properties that the company itself had purchased.

Zillow hoped to profit on each "flip" and use the transaction and home improvement data to improve future Zestimates. Home sellers could get the benefit of a near-instant cash offer, cutting out real estate agents, listings, and showings. Zillow intended to make no more than a 2 percent profit so that homeowners would not feel lowballed, a problem that could discourage future sellers. The business model followed the assumption that Zillow's algorithm, fed by the company's massive amounts of data, would be able to predict home prices with high accuracy.

Let's take a closer look at Zillow's experience with iBuying.

First quarter, 2021. In the first quarter of 2021, Zillow's home-sale profits were more than twice as high as anticipated. Zillow had expected to make money primarily from transaction fees and from services such as title insurance—not from making large profits on the flips. However, the company's algorithm, which was supposed to predict housing prices, did not seem to understand the market.

In addition, Zillow was on track to significantly miss its annual target for the number of homes it wanted to buy. It was also falling behind its top competitor, Opendoor. To address this problem, the company decided to speed up the pace and volume of its home purchases by offering prices well above what its algorithm and analysts had calculated as the market value.

Second quarter, 2021. In the second quarter of 2021, Zillow Offers purchased more than 3,800 homes, more than twice as many as the previous quarter. The company was buying so many homes that its staff began to fall behind on closings and renovations. Zillow struggled to find contractors and renovation materials in the middle of a broader labor and supply shortage. As a result, Zillow had to keep homes longer, which increased their insurance and interest payments. In addition, the company would have to sell many of the homes it had purchased during the summer in the winter, when the housing market is usually weaker.

Third quarter, 2021. By the summer of 2021, Zillow was paying too much money for homes and buying too many of them, just when price increases were starting to slow. During this quarter, the company purchased nearly 10,000 homes.

To keep up with those purchases, Zillow overworked its staff while it disregarded internal concerns that it was paying too much for homes. Analysts who confirmed that the company was overpaying were routinely overruled.

In addition, the company hired more than 100 pricing analysts to double-check the algorithm's predictions by examining comparable sales. That process reduced the risk of overpaying, but also made it more difficult to flip many homes quickly and cheaply.

The median price Zillow was paying for homes in Phoenix—one of the largest iBuyer markets—rose from \$351,000 in May to \$475,000 in September. By then, competitors were purchasing fewer homes and reducing their prices. In contrast, Zillow continued to pay \$65,000 more than the median home price. It is significant that during the third quarter, Zillow sold homes for 5 to 7 percent less than it had forecast.

Fourth quarter, 2021. In early October 2021, Zillow recorded its most active week buying homes in Phoenix as part of its goal to buy 5,000 homes per month by 2024. An October analysis of Zillow listings revealed that two-thirds of its homes were on the market at prices lower than what Zillow had paid for them, with the average discount on those homes being 4.5 percent. That month, Zillow halted home purchases for the remainder of the year.

In November 2021, Zillow closed Zillow Offers, which was responsible for the majority of the company's revenue (surpassing the company's Premier Agent service) but none of its profits. Zillow also cut about 2,000 jobs, and it wrote down losses of more than \$500 million on the value of its remaining homes. Also in November, Zillow announced the sale of 2,000 of its leftover homes to Pretium Partners, a New York-based investment firm that planned to operate the homes as rentals. That sale still left Zillow with thousands more homes to sell.

The reason for closing Zillow Offers was that, in the face of tremendous variability in home demand and prices, Zillow's algorithm could not accurately forecast home prices three to six months in advance. The algorithm had experienced some of the limits of technology in a business still driven by intangible factors such as emotional attachments and personal tastes.

These variables make it difficult to predict home prices months in advance because they are difficult to capture or quantify with algorithms. For instance, the system may capture that a home has three bedrooms, but does it note whether they are laid out in a way that makes sense? Also, what is the impact of an abandoned, run-down home in the neighborhood? It is interesting that some Zillow competitors factor other variables into their algorithms such as neighborhood noise, road noise, proximity to transportation, school data, crime data, and proximity to power lines.

As we noted previously, Zillow's business model followed the assumption that its algorithm, fed by the company's massive amount of data, would be able to predict home prices with high accuracy. When Zillow employed its algorithm to buy and sell homes, the algorithm badly misread the market. It appears that the algorithm could not account for the unexpected increase in home prices and sales during COVID. These increases came from the following factors:

- Mortgage rates reached a historic low in January 2021 and stayed low throughout the pandemic. America's largest generation in history aged into their prime home-buying years.

- Roughly 30 percent of jobs, mostly high-paying, could be performed remotely, meaning that people spent more time at home.

- People wanted to move to suburban environments, opting for yards and the extra space needed to accommodate simultaneous work and school.

Bottom line: It appears that the Zestimate algorithm functions appropriately when it is used as originally intended; that is, as a reasonably accurate estimation of a home's market value. However, it is not suited for accurately predicting house prices three to six months in the future.

Questions

1. Describe Zillow's business problem(s). Keep in mind that there may be more than one.

2. Describe the various types of data that Zillow utilizes in this case.

3. Describe the descriptive analytics applications that Zillow employs.

4. Describe the predictive analytics applications that Zillow employs.

5. In the case, Zillow applied its Zestimates algorithm to a new task: to accurately predict house prices three to six months in the future. Where in the Business Analytics Process (see Figure 12.3) does this change fit? Support your answer.

Sources: Compiled from D. Wallace, "Zillow Slapped with First Federal Lawsuit from Shareholders over Home-Flipping Business Flop," *Fox Business*, November 18, 2021; R. Lenihan, "Zillow Concealed Problems with Home-Flipping Business, Lawsuit Says," *The Street*, November 17, 2021; W. Parker and K. Putzier, "What Went Wrong with Zillow? A Real-Estate Algorithm Derailed Its Big Bet," *Wall Street Journal*, November 17, 2021; M. Blake, "A Zillow Problem....or an iBuying Problem?" *Housing Wire*, November 15, 2021; C. Stokel-Walker, "Why Zillow Couldn't Make Algorithmic House Pricing Work," *Wired*, November 11, 2021; N. Friedman, "Homes Now Typically Sell in a Week, Forcing Buyers to Take Risks," *Wall Street Journal*, November 11, 2021; N. Friedman and W. Parker, "Opendoor, Offerpad Report Record Revenue for Third Quarter," *Wall Street Journal*, November 10, 2021; W. Parker, "Zillow Sells 2,000 Homes in Dismantling Its House-Flipping Business," *Wall Street Journal*, November 10, 2021; S. Gandel, "Zillow, Facing Big Losses, Quits Flipping Houses and Will Lay off a Quarter of Its Staff," *New York Times*, November 2, 2021; L. Lambert, "Zillow Closes Troubled Home-Flipping Business Amid a 'Decelerating' Housing Market," *Fortune*, November 2, 2021; W. Parker and N. Friedman, "Zillow Quits Home-Flipping Business, Cites Inability to Forecast Prices," *Wall Street Journal*, November 2, 2021; H. Frishberg, "Zillow's Flips Flop, Hurting Profits but Benefitting Some Homeowners," *New York Post*, October 28, 2021; M. DelPrete, "iBuying Is Hard: Zillow Pauses New Purchases," www.mikedp.com, October 19, 2021; A. Bahney, "Zillow Slams the Brakes on Home Buying as It Struggles to Manage Its Backlog of Inventory," CNN, October 19, 2021; P. Clark, "Zillow Caught up in TikTok Drama over Big-Money Role in Housing," *Bloomberg*, September 24, 2021; A. Campo-Flores et al., "The Pandemic Changed Where Americans Live," *Wall Street Journal*, April 27, 2021; J. Demsas, "Covid-19 Caused a Recession. So Why Did the Housing Market Boom?," *Vox*, February 5, 2021; G. Buchak et al., "Why Is Intermediating Houses So Difficult? Evidence from iBuyers," SSRN, June 24, 2020; V. Fuhrmans, "Zillow Sees a Future in House Flipping," *Wall Street Journal*, May 10, 2019; and www.zillow.com, accessed August 15, 2022.

Introduction

The chapter's opening case illustrates the importance and far-reaching nature of business analytics applications. **Business analytics (BA)** is the process of developing actionable decisions or recommendations for actions based on insights generated from historical data. Business analytics examines data with a variety of tools; it formulates descriptive, predictive, and prescriptive analytics models; and it communicates these results to organizational decision makers. This definition distinguishes between business analytics and statistics. Essentially, the business analytics process uses statistical procedures to accomplish its goals.

Business analytics can answer questions such as what happened, how many, how often, where is the problem, what actions are needed, why is this happening, what will happen if these trends continue, what will happen next, what is the best (or worst) that can happen, and what actions should the organization take to achieve various successful business outcomes?

There is also some confusion between the terms *business analytics* and *business intelligence*. **Business intelligence (BI)** has been defined as a broad category of applications, technologies, and processes for gathering, storing, accessing, and analyzing data to help business users make better decisions. Many experts argue that the terms should be used interchangeably. We agree and, for simplicity, we use the term *business analytics (BA)* throughout this chapter.

This chapter describes information systems (ISs) that support *decision making*. Essentially all organizational information systems support decision making (refer to Figure 1.4). Fundamental organizational ISs such as transaction processing systems, functional area information systems, and enterprise resource planning systems provide a variety of reports that help decision makers. This chapter focuses on business analytics systems, which provide critical support to the vast majority of organizational decision makers.

The chapter begins by reviewing the manager's job and the nature of modern managerial decisions. This discussion will help you to understand why managers need computerized support. The chapter then introduces the business analytics process and addresses each step in that process in turn.

business analytics (BA)
The process of developing actionable decisions or recommendations for actions based on insights generated from historical data.

business intelligence (BI)
A broad category of applications, technologies, and processes for gathering, storing, accessing, and analyzing data to help business users make more informed decisions.

It is impossible to overstate the importance of business analytics within modern organizations. Recall from Chapter 1 that the essential goal of information systems is to provide the right information to the right person, in the right amount, at the right time, in the right format. In essence, BA achieves this goal. Business analytics systems provide actionable business results that decision makers can act on in a timely fashion.

It is also impossible to overstate the importance of your input into the BA process within an organization, for several reasons. First, you will use your organization's BA applications, probably from your first day on the job, *regardless of your major field of study*. You will decide how you want to analyze the data by using analytics models and statistical tools. We refer to this process as *user-driven analysis*. You will use BA presentation applications such as dashboards to present your findings succinctly and understandably. You will work closely with your MIS department to ensure that these applications meet your needs.

In general, there are three types of analytics users: business users, business analysts, and data scientists. The *business user* accesses analytics applications to perform their jobs. The *business analyst* typically manages, cleans, abstracts, and aggregates data as well as conducts a range of analytical and statistical procedures on that data. The *data scientist* builds upon the core competencies of the business analyst with additional mathematics, modeling, algorithmic, programming, and machine-learning skills.

As we proceed from business users to business analysts to data scientists, technical skill requirements increase. For example, business users would typically be majors (other than business analytics majors) who take the introductory course(s) in analytics in colleges of business. Business analysts typically major in business analytics in colleges of business and data scientists typically major in mathematics, statistics, or computer science.

Much of this chapter is concerned with large-scale BA applications. You should keep in mind, however, that smaller organizations, and even individual users, can implement small-scale BA applications as well.

After you finish this chapter, you will have a basic understanding of decision making, the BA process, and the incredibly broad range of BA applications that are employed in modern organizations. This knowledge will enable you to immediately and confidently provide input into your organization's BA processes and applications. Furthermore, this chapter will help you use your organization's BA applications to effectively analyze data and thus make better decisions. We hope that this chapter will help you "ask the next question." Enjoy!

12.1   Managers and Decision Making

WILEY PLUS

Author Lecture Videos are available exclusively in *WileyPLUS*.
Apply the Concept activities are available in the Appendix and in *WileyPLUS*.

management   A process by which organizational goals are achieved through the use of resources.

productivity   The ratio between the inputs to a process and the outputs from that process.

LEARNING OBJECTIVE

Use a decision support framework to demonstrate how technology supports managerial decision making at each phase of the decision-making process.

Management is a process by which an organization achieves its goals through the use of resources (people, money, materials, and information). These resources are considered to be *inputs*. Achieving the organization's goals is the *output* of the process. Managers oversee this process in an attempt to optimize it. A manager's success is often measured by the ratio between the inputs and outputs for which he or she is responsible. This ratio is an indication of the organization's **productivity**.

The Manager's Job and Decision Making

To appreciate how information systems support managers, you must first understand the manager's job. Managers do many things, depending on their position within the organization, the type and size of the organization, the organization's policies and culture, and the personalities of the managers themselves. Despite these variations, however, all managers perform three basic roles (Mintzberg, 1973):

1. *Interpersonal roles:* figurehead, leader, liaison
2. *Informational roles:* monitor, disseminator, spokesperson, analyzer
3. *Decisional roles:* entrepreneur, disturbance handler, resource allocator, negotiator

Early information systems primarily supported the informational roles. In recent years, however, information systems have been developed that support all three roles. In this chapter you will focus on the support that IT can provide for decisional roles.

A **decision** refers to a choice among two or more alternatives that individuals and groups make. Decisions are diverse and are made continuously. Decision making is a systematic process. Economist Herbert Simon (1977) described decision making as composed of three major phases: intelligence, design, and choice. Once the choice is made, the decision is implemented. **Figure 12.1** illustrates this process, highlighting the tasks that are in each phase. Note that there is a continuous flow of information from intelligence to design to choice (bold lines). At any phase, however, there may be a return to a previous phase (broken lines).

This model of decision making is quite general. Undoubtedly, you have made decisions in which you did not construct a model of the situation, validate your model with test data, or conduct a sensitivity analysis. The model we present here is intended to encompass *all* of the conditions that might occur when making a decision. For some decisions, some steps or phases may be minimal, implicit (understood), or completely absent.

The decision-making process starts with the *intelligence phase*, in which managers examine a situation and then identify and define the problem or opportunity. In the *design phase*, decision makers construct a model for addressing the situation. They perform this task by making assumptions that simplify reality and by expressing the relationships among all of the relevant variables. Managers then validate the model by using test data. Finally, decision makers set criteria for evaluating all of the potential solutions that are proposed. The *choice*

decision A choice that individuals and groups make among two or more alternatives.

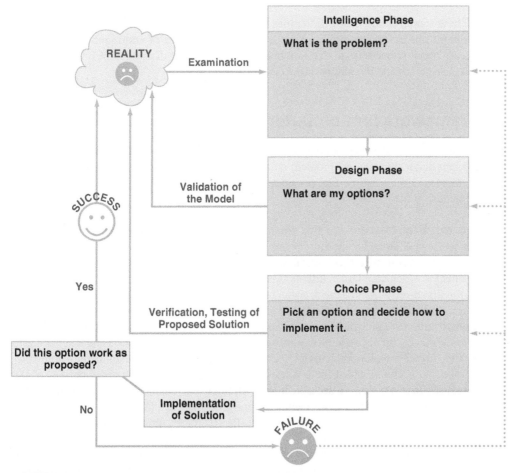

FIGURE 12.1 The process and phases in decision making.

phase involves selecting a solution or course of action that seems best suited to resolve the problem. This solution (the decision) is then implemented. Implementation is successful if the proposed solution solves the problem or seizes the opportunity. If the solution fails, then the process returns to the previous phases. Computer-based decision support assists managers in the decision-making process.

Why Managers Need IT Support

Making good decisions is very difficult without solid information. Information is vital for each phase and activity in the decision-making process. Even when information is available, however, decision making is difficult because of the following trends:

- The *number of alternatives* is constantly *increasing* because of innovations in technology, improved communications, the development of global markets, and the use of the Internet and e-business. A key to good decision making is to explore and compare many relevant alternatives. The greater the number of alternatives, the more a decision maker needs computer-assisted searches and comparisons.

- Most decisions must be made *under time pressure.* It is often not possible to manually process information fast enough to be effective.

- Because of increased uncertainty in the decision environment, decisions are becoming more complex. It is usually necessary to *conduct a sophisticated analysis* to make a good decision.

- It is often necessary to rapidly access remote information, consult with experts, or conduct a group decision-making session, all without incurring major expenses. Decision makers, as well as the information they need to access, can be situated in different locations. Bringing everything together quickly and inexpensively represents a serious challenge.

These trends create major difficulties for decision makers. Fortunately, as you will see throughout this chapter, computerized decision support can be of enormous help. Next you will learn about two aspects of decision making that place our discussion of BA in context—problem structure and the nature of the decisions.

A Framework for Computerized Decision Analysis

To better understand business analytics, note that various types of decisions can be placed along two major dimensions: problem structure and the nature of the decision (Gorry and Scott Morton, 1971). **Figure 12.2** provides an overview of decision making along these two dimensions.

Problem Structure   The first dimension is *problem structure*, in which decision-making processes fall along a continuum ranging from highly structured to highly unstructured (see the left column in **Figure 12.2**). *Structured decisions* deal with routine and repetitive problems for which standard solutions exist, such as inventory control. In a structured decision, the first three phases of the decision process—intelligence, design, and choice—are laid out in a particular sequence, and the procedures for obtaining the best (or at least a good enough) solution are known. These types of decisions are candidates for decision automation.

At the other extreme of complexity are *unstructured decisions.* These decisions are intended to deal with "fuzzy" complex problems for which there are no cut-and-dried solutions. An unstructured decision is one in which there is no standardized procedure for carrying out any of the three phases. In making such a decision, human intuition and judgment often play an important role. Typical unstructured decisions include planning new service offerings, hiring an executive, and choosing a set of research and development (R&D) projects for the coming year. Although BA cannot make unstructured decisions, it can provide information that assists decision makers.

Located between structured and unstructured decisions are *semistructured* decisions, in which only some of the decision-process phases are structured. Semistructured decisions require a combination of standard solution procedures and individual judgment. Examples of

	Operational Control	Management Control	Strategic Planning	IS Support
Structured	Accounts receivable, order entry `1`	Budget analysis, short-term forecasting, personnel reports, make-or-buy analysis `2`	`3`	MIS, statistical models (management science, financial, etc.)
Semistructured	Production scheduling, inventory control `4`	Credit evaluation, budget preparation, plant layout, project scheduling, reward systems design `5`	Building a new plant, mergers and acquisitions, planning (product, quality assurance, compensation, etc.) `6`	Decision support systems, business intelligence
Unstructured	`7`	Negotiating, recruiting an executive, buying hardware, lobbying `8`	New technology development, product R&D, social responsibility planning `9`	Decision support systems, expert systems, enterprise resource planning, neural networks, business intelligence, Big Data

FIGURE 12.2 Decision-support framework.

semistructured decisions are evaluating employees, setting marketing budgets for consumer products, performing capital acquisition analysis, and trading bonds.

The Nature of Decisions   The second dimension of decision support deals with the *nature of decisions.* All managerial decisions fall into one of three broad categories:

1. *Operational control:* Executing specific tasks efficiently and effectively
2. *Management control:* Acquiring and using resources efficiently in accomplishing organizational goals
3. *Strategic planning:* The long-range goals and policies for growth and resource allocation

These categories are displayed along the top row of **Figure 12.2.**

The Decision Matrix   The three primary classes of problem structure and the three broad categories of the nature of decisions can be combined in a decision-support matrix that consists of nine cells, as diagrammed in **Figure 12.2.** Lower-level managers usually perform the tasks in cells 1, 2, and 4. The tasks in cells 3, 5, and 7 are usually the responsibility of middle managers and professional staff. Finally, the tasks in cells 6, 8, and 9 are generally carried out by senior executives.

Today, it is difficult to state that certain organizational information systems support certain cells in the decision matrix. The fact is that the increasing sophistication of ISs means that essentially any information system can be useful to any decision maker, regardless of their level or function in the organization. As you study this chapter, you will see that business analytics is applicable across all cells of the decision matrix.

Before you go on...

1. Describe the decision-making process proposed by Simon.
2. You are registering for classes next semester. Apply the decision-making process to your decision about how many and which courses to take. Is your decision structured, semistructured, or unstructured? Support your answer.
3. Consider your decision-making process when registering for classes next semester. Explain how information technology supports (or does not support) each phase of this process.

12.2 | The Business Analytics Process

LEARNING OBJECTIVE

Describe each phase of the business analytics process.

As previously defined, *business analytics* is the process of developing actionable decisions or recommendations for actions based on insights generated from historical data. Business analytics encompasses not only applications, but also technologies and processes. It includes both "getting data in" (to a data mart or warehouse) and "getting data out" (through BA applications).

The use of BA in organizations varies considerably. In smaller organizations, BA may be limited to Excel spreadsheets. In larger ones, BA is enterprise-wide, and it includes a wide variety of applications. The importance of BA to organizations continues to grow, to the point where it is now a requirement for competing in the marketplace. That is, BA is a competitive necessity for organizations.

Although BA has become a common practice across organizations, not all organizations use BA in the same way. For example, some organizations employ only one or a few applications, whereas others use enterprise-wide BA. In general, there are three specific analytics targets that represent different levels of change. These targets differ in regard to their focus; scope; level of sponsorship, commitment, and required resources; technical architecture; impact on personnel and business processes; and benefits.

- *The development of one or a few related analytics applications.* This target is often a point solution for a departmental need, such as campaign management in marketing. Sponsorship, approval, funding, impacts, and benefits typically occur at the departmental level. For this target, organizations usually create a data mart to store the necessary data. Organizations must be careful that the data mart—an "independent" application—does not become a "data silo" that stores data that are inconsistent with, and cannot be integrated with, data used elsewhere in the organization.

- *The development of infrastructure to support enterprise-wide analytics.* This target supports both current and future analytics needs. A crucial component of analytics at this level is an enterprise data warehouse. Because it is an enterprise-wide initiative, senior management often provides sponsorship, approval, and funding. The impacts and benefits are also felt throughout the organization.

  MKT **MIS** An example of this target is the 3M Corporation (www.3m.com). Historically, 3M's various divisions had operated independently, using separate decision-support platforms. Not only was this arrangement costly, it prevented 3M from integrating the data and presenting a "single face" to its customers. For example, sales representatives did not know whether or how business customers were interacting with other 3M divisions. The solution was to develop an enterprise data warehouse that enabled 3M to operate as an integrated company. As an added benefit, the costs of implementing this system were offset by savings resulting from the consolidation of the various platforms.

- *Support for organizational transformation.* With this target, a company uses business analytics to fundamentally transform the ways it competes in the marketplace. Business analytics supports a new business model, and it enables the business strategy. Because of the scope and importance of these changes, critical elements such as sponsorship, approval, and funding originate at the highest organizational levels. The impact on personnel and processes can be significant, and the benefits accrue across the organization.

  MKT Harrah's Entertainment (a brand of Caesars Entertainment; www.caesars .com) provides a good example of this analytics target. Harrah's developed a customer loyalty program known as Total Rewards. To implement the program, Harrah's created a data warehouse that integrated data from casino, hotel, and special event systems—for example, wine-tasting weekends—across all of the various customer touchpoints, such as slot machines, table games, and the Internet. Harrah's used these data to reward loyal customers and to reach out to them in personal and appealing ways, such as through promotional offers. These efforts helped the company to become a leader in the gaming industry.

Regardless of the scope of BA, all organizations employ a BA process, which Figure 12.3 depicts. Let's look at each step of Figure 12.3 in turn, from left to right.

The Business Analytics Process

The entire BA process begins with a business problem, often called *pain points* by practicing managers. When organizations face business problems, they often turn to business analytics, through the process illustrated in Figure 12.3, to help solve those problems. Before we begin our discussion of the BA process, let's emphasize the importance of the technologies that underlie the entire process (see Figure 12.3). These technologies are all improving very rapidly.

MIS Microprocessors (or chips) are becoming increasingly powerful (see Technology Guide 1). In particular, graphics processing units (GPUs) are essential to neural networks, another underlying technology of the BA process. (We discuss neural networks in Chapter 14.)

Advances in digital storage capacity and access speed are driving the cost of storage down, meaning that organizations are able to store and analyze huge amounts of data. Transmission speed (bandwidth; see Chapter 6) in computer networks, particularly the Internet, is also rapidly increasing. As a result, decision makers are able to collaborate on difficult, time-sensitive decisions regardless of their locations. Other underlying technologies include machine learning and deep learning, which we discuss in Chapter 14.

Now let's examine the BA process in detail. To illustrate each step in the BA process, we look at Fandango as an example. The BA process begins with defining the business problem.

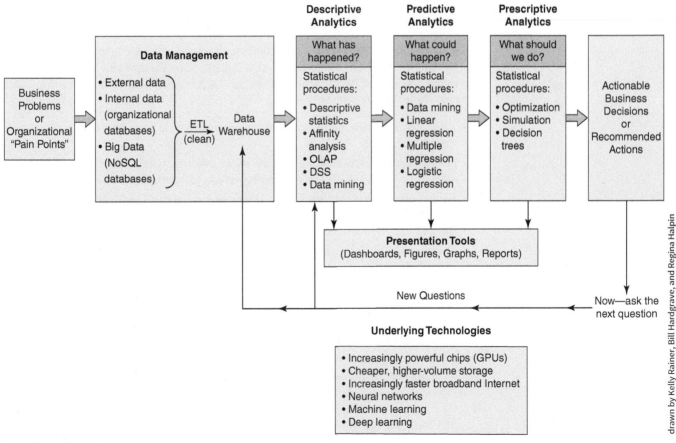

FIGURE 12.3 The Business Analytics Process.

Define the Business Problem

The first, an arguably most important, issue that you will face in the BA process is to define the business problem that you want to address. Defining the business problem is not always easy, but these questions can provide you with guidance:

- What is the organization trying to accomplish?
- What are the organization's goals?
- What business process is the organization trying to improve? Recall that a *business process* (see Chapter 2) is an ongoing collection of related activities that create a product or service of value to the organization, its business partners, and its customers.
- How would improving this business process contribute to making the organization more successful?
- Other, more specific, questions include:
  - Why have profits decreased?
  - Which customers are moving to our competitors and why?
  - Why has demand for a particular product decreased and why?

Recall that we are using Fandango to illustrate each step in the BA process. Here we discuss Fandango's business problem. Fandango (**www.fandango.com**) is the leading online (website and mobile) ticket seller for movie theaters. The company sells millions of tickets to approximately 20,000 movie theaters across the United States. Customers can print their tickets at home with bar codes scanned at the theater or they can have their tickets printed out upon arrival at the theater. Fandango charges a premium over the ticket price to use its services but does enable people to procure tickets to popular movies without having to stand in long lines.

Because Fandango receives a premium for each movie ticket sold, the company's business problem is how to best target the movies that their customers most likely want to see, advertise those movies on Fandango's website, and offer promotions to those movies. In that way, customers will buy more tickets, increasing Fandango's revenue.

MIS Data Management

After defining the business problem, we consider the data that we have for analysis. As we have noted, organizations are now able to analyze rapidly increasing amounts of data. As you learned in Chapter 5, these data can come from data streams. These streams include:

- *Point-of-sale (POS) data.* Organizations capture data from each customer purchase with their POS systems.
- *Clickstream data.* Clickstream data are those data that visitors and customers produce when they visit a website and click on hyperlinks (described in Chapter 6).
- *Social media data.* Social media data (also called social data) are the data collected from individuals' activity on social media websites. These data include shares, likes and dislikes, ratings, reviews, recommendations, comments, and many other examples.
- *Sensor data.* The Internet of Things (IoT; see Chapter 8) is a system in which any object, natural or manmade, contains internal or external wireless sensor(s) that communicate with each other without human interaction. Each sensor monitors and reports data on physical and environmental conditions around it, such as temperature, sound, pressure, vibration, and movement.

As noted in Chapter 5, these four data streams, together with data in organizational databases, comprise Big Data. We defined Big Data as diverse, high-volume, high-velocity information assets that require new forms of processing in order to enhance decision making, lead to insights, and optimize business processes. Essentially, Big Data is the heart of the analytics process.

At this point, organizations integrate and "clean" these data into data marts and data warehouses (see Chapter 5) through a process called *extract, transform, and load (ETL)*. The data in the data warehouse are now available to be analyzed by business users, business analysts, and data scientists.

MIS Fandango   Recall that we are using Fandango to illustrate each step in the BA process. Here we discuss Fandango's data management. Fandango captures data about customers, movie theaters, ticket sales, and show times. For each customer, Fandango collects data on the movies they see, how often they go to movie theaters, their favorite movie genre, the day of the week they go to theaters, and many other variables. Fandango collects Big Data from its website (clickstream data), social media sites (social data), promotions, and other sources.

Descriptive Analytics, Predictive Analytics, and Prescriptive Analytics
Organizations perform three types of analytics applications: descriptive analytics, predictive analytics, and prescriptive analytics. We discuss these analytics applications in Sections 12.3, 12.4, and 12.5, respectively.

At the end of Section 12.4, we present an example (with summarized data) that illustrates how a decision maker proceeds through the BA process. In our example, we address only descriptive analytics and predictive analytics. We do not include prescriptive analytics in this example because this type of analytics is not yet widespread in industry.

Presentation Tools
All three types of analytics produce results, which must be communicated to decision makers in the organization. In general, data scientists perform these analyses. Many organizations have employees who "translate" the results of these analyses into business terms for the decision makers. These employees often use presentation tools in the form of dashboards to communicate the message visually. We discuss dashboards and other presentation tools in Section 12.6.

Ask the Next Question
What is critically important about the analytics process is that once the results are obtained and presented, decision makers must be ready to "ask the next question." Everyone involved in the BA process must use his or her creativity and intuition at this point. In addition, the results of the BA process will almost always lead to new, unanswered questions.

Business Analytics Tools

A variety of BA tools are available to analyze data. They include Excel, multidimensional analysis (also called online analytical processing, or OLAP), data mining, and decision-support systems. BA also employs numerous statistical procedures, which include descriptive statistics; affinity analysis; linear, multiple, and logistic regression; as well as many others.

Other than Excel, we discuss BA tools and statistical procedures in the context of the analytics application for which they are most appropriate. We discuss Excel here because it is the most popular and common BA tool. Furthermore, Excel incorporates the functionality of many of the other BA tools and statistical procedures. For example, analysts can use Excel to provide descriptive statistics and to perform regression analyses.

BA vendors typically design their software so that it interfaces with Excel. How does this process work? Essentially, users download plug-ins that add functionality—for example, the ability to list the top 10 percent of customers, based on purchases—to Excel. Excel then connects to the vendor's application server, which provides additional data analysis capabilities, which in turn connects to a backend database, a data mart, or a data warehouse. This arrangement gives Excel users the functionality and access to data that are typical of sophisticated BA products while allowing them to work with a familiar tool.

In the next three sections, we address descriptive analytics, predictive analytics, and prescriptive analytics, respectively. Each section begins by defining the type of analytics, continues with a discussion of the BA tools and statistical procedures that are appropriate to that type of analytics, and closes with examples of that type of analytics.

12.3 Descriptive Analytics

LEARNING OBJECTIVE

Provide a definition and a use case example for descriptive analytics.

descriptive analytics
A type of business analytics that summarize what has happened in the past and allow decision makers to learn from past behaviors.

Organizations must analyze huge amounts of raw data to make sense of them. This overall process is known as *data reduction*. Data reduction is the conversion of raw data into a smaller amount of more useful information. Descriptive, predictive, and prescriptive analytics are essentially steps in data reduction.

Descriptive analytics is the first step in data reduction. Descriptive analytics summarizes what has happened in the past and enables decision makers to learn from past behaviors. Organizations employ descriptive analytics to generate information such as total stock in inventory, average dollars spent per customer, and year-over-year change in sales. Common examples of descriptive analytics are reports that provide historical insights regarding an organization's production, financials, operations, sales, finance, inventory, and customers.

BA Tools in Descriptive Analytics

BA tools in descriptive analytics applications include online analytical processing, data mining, decision-support systems, and a variety of statistical procedures. Examples of such statistical procedures are descriptive statistics, affinity analysis, and many others (see **Figure 12.3**). We take a closer look at these tools here.

online analytical processing (OLAP) (or multidimensional data analysis) A set of capabilities for "slicing and dicing" data using dimensions and measures associated with the data.

multidimensional data analysis See **online analytical processing (OLAP)**.

Online Analytical Processing Some BA applications include online analytical processing (OLAP), also referred to as multidimensional analysis capabilities. OLAP involves "slicing and dicing" the data that are stored in a dimensional format, "drilling down" the data to greater detail, and "rolling up" the data to greater summarization (less detail).

Consider our example from **Chapter 5**. Recall **Figure 5.6**, which illustrates the data cube. The product is on the *x*-axis, geography is on the *y*-axis, and time is on the *z*-axis. Now, suppose you want to know how many nuts the company sold in the Western region in 2017. You would slice and dice the cube, using *nuts* as the specific measure for product, *West* as the measure for geography, and *2017* as the measure for time. The value or values that remain in the cell(s) after our slicing and dicing is (are) the answer to our question. As an example of drilling down, you might also want to know how many nuts were sold in January 2017. Alternatively, you might want to know how many nuts were sold from 2017 through 2019, which is an example of aggregation, also called "roll up."

data mining The process of searching for valuable business information in a large database, data warehouse, or data mart.

Data Mining Data mining refers to the process of searching for valuable business information in a large database, data warehouse, or data mart. Data mining can perform two basic operations: (1) identifying previously unknown patterns and (2) predicting trends and behaviors. The first operation is a descriptive analytics application, and the second is a predictive analytics application.

In descriptive analytics, data mining can identify previously hidden patterns in an organization's data. For example, a descriptive analytics application can analyze retail sales data to discover seemingly unrelated products that people often purchase together. A classic example is beer and diapers (even though it is an urban legend). Data mining found that young men tend to buy beer and diapers at the same time when shopping at convenience stores. This type of analysis is called affinity analysis or market basket analysis.

POM **MKT** *Affinity analysis* is a data mining application that discovers co-occurrence relationships among activities performed by specific individuals or groups. In retail, affinity analysis is used to perform *market basket analysis*, in which retailers seek to understand the purchase behavior of customers. Retailers use this information for the purposes of cross-selling, up-selling, sales promotions, loyalty programs, store design (physical location of products), and discount offers. An example of cross-selling with market basket analysis is Amazon's use of "customers who bought book A might also like to buy book B."

In another example, market basket analysis could inform a retailer that customers often purchase shampoo and conditioner together. Therefore, putting both items on promotion at the same time would not create an increase in revenue, whereas a promotion involving just one of the items would likely drive sales of the other.

Decision-Support Systems   Decision-support systems (DSSs) combine models and data to analyze semistructured problems and some unstructured problems that involve extensive user involvement. *Models* are simplified representations, or abstractions, of reality. Decision-support systems enable business managers and analysts to access data interactively, to manipulate these data, and to conduct appropriate analyses.

DSSs can enhance learning, and they can contribute to all levels of decision making. They also employ mathematical models. Finally, they have the related capabilities of sensitivity analysis, what-if analysis, and goal-seeking analysis, which you will learn about next. Keep in mind that these three types of analysis are useful for any type of decision-support application. Excel, for example, supports all three.

POM **MKT** To learn about DSSs and the three types of analysis, let's look at an example. Blue Nile (www.bluenile.com) is an online retailer of certified diamonds. The firm's website has a built-in decision-support system to help customers find the diamond that best meets their needs. Blue Nile's DSS provides an excellent example of sensitivity analysis, what-if analysis, and goal-seeking analysis.

Access the Blue Nile website, and click on "Diamonds" in the upper left corner. On the drop-down box, you will see "View all diamonds." Keep in mind that when you experiment with the Blue Nile DSS, the number of round diamonds available will vary from what we obtained when we accessed the DSS and performed the analyses. The reason is that the Blue Nile website is updated in near-real time as the company sells its diamonds.

There are many types of diamonds, but for this example click on "Round." You will see:

- The number of round diamonds available for sale, again in the upper left corner. When we accessed the Blue Nile DSS, the firm offered 112,333 round diamonds for sale.

- Five slide bars labeled Price, Carat, Cut, Color, and Clarity. Each slide bar represents a variable in Blue Nile's DSS.

- A list of each diamond accompanied by a value for each of the five variables. This list constitutes the data—that is, all round diamonds available for sale—for your analyses.

Sensitivity Analysis   Sensitivity analysis examines how sensitive an output is to any change in an input while keeping other inputs constant. Sensitivity analysis is valuable because it enables the system to adapt to changing conditions and to the varying requirements of different decision-making situations. Let's perform *two sensitivity analyses* on the data:

- First, adjust the slide bars for the Carat variable, so that you will see only those round diamonds between 1.00 and 1.50 carats. Keep all of the other slide bars in their fully open position. In that way, you keep the other variables constant. Note that the number of round diamonds available decreases dramatically. When we followed this procedure, the number of round diamonds for sale dropped to 14,009.

- Second, adjust the slide bars for the Color variable, so that you will see only those round diamonds of D, E, and F color. Be sure to open the slide bars for Carat and to keep the other slide bars in their fully open position. When we followed this procedure, the number of round diamonds available for sale dropped to 58,993.

decision-support systems (DSSs)   Business intelligence systems that combine models and data in an attempt to solve semistructured and some unstructured problems with extensive user involvement.

Comparing the results of these two sensitivity analyses, we can say that the number of round diamonds for sale is more sensitive to changes in Carat than to changes in Color, if we keep the other variables constant.

What-If Analysis   A model builder must make predictions and assumptions regarding the input data, many of which are based on the assessment of uncertain futures. The results depend on the accuracy of these assumptions, which can be highly subjective. *What-if analysis* attempts to predict the impact of changes in the assumptions—that is, the input data—on the proposed solution.

Let's perform a *what-if analysis* on the data. A young man's fiancée has decided that she would like her engagement ring to be between one and two carats, at least a Very Good cut, an F color or better, and a clarity of at least VVS2 (VVS2 means "two very, very small imperfections"). Adjust the slide bars for all four of the variables at the same time. When we followed this procedure, the number of round diamonds available for sale dropped to 3,830.

Goal-Seeking Analysis   *Goal-seeking analysis* represents a "backward" solution approach. Goal seeking attempts to calculate the value of the inputs necessary to achieve a desired level of output.

Let's perform a *goal-seeking analysis* on the data. When the young man in our example looked at the list of 3,830 diamonds (using the scroll bar on the right side of the list), he noticed that the prices ranged from $6,356 to $10,117. He told his fiancée that he had only $5,000 to invest in a diamond. They consequently opened up the slide bars for the Carat, Cut, Color, and Clarity variables and adjusted the slide bar for the Price variable to be between $4,500 and $5,000. When we followed this procedure, the number of round diamonds available for sale increased to 3,874.

The couple now had the problem of examining the list of diamonds to decide which combination of the four variables would be suitable. They did this by performing several what-if analyses:

- They decided that they really wanted a diamond between one and two carats. After adjusting the Carat slide bar, the number of round diamonds available dropped to 2,035.
- then decided that they wanted a D, E, or F color. After adjusting the Color slide bar, the number of round diamonds available dropped to 424.
- Next, they chose a Cut that was at least Very Good. After adjusting the Cut slide bar, the number of round diamonds available dropped to 266.
- The couple noticed that all 266 diamonds had a Clarity variable of either SI1 (one small imperfection) or SI2 (two small imperfections). At this point they either could decide that this level of clarity is acceptable or they could perform additional what-if analyses on other variables.

Examples of Descriptive Analytics Applications

We present several examples of descriptive analytics in this section. Keep in mind that descriptive analytics applications often immediately suggest predictive analytics applications. Let's look at your class attendance, Fandango, and OptumRx.

MKT Fandango   Recall that we are using Fandango to illustrate each step in the BA process. Here we discuss examples of Fandango's descriptive analytics applications. Fandango analyzes the historical movie preferences of its customers and historical data from movie titles. Using these data, Fandango analysts investigate the total sales for different genres of movies; for example, comedy, drama, action, and others. Using a sample of moviegoers, the company calculates the average ticket sales for a week for each movie and each genre, the most popular movie, the distribution of customers among the movie genres and specific titles, the busiest hours of the day and most popular day of the week for each movie theater, and many other analyses. These descriptive analyses help Fandango set ticket prices; offer discounts for certain movies, certain show times, and certain days of the week; set budgets for promotions and advertising; and many other possible actions.

FIN **HRM** **OptumRx** Pharmacy care service company OptumRx (www.optumrx
.com) was analyzing a client company's prescription-drug claims when the firm noticed that
the client's spending on acne medicine seemed high compared with other clients' spending
on the medication. Analyzing the data, OptumRx found that employees had been prescribed
newer brand-name acne drugs that were largely combinations of older generic medicines.
OptumRx informed the client, a 60,000-employee company, who then began to require patients
to begin treatment with the cheaper medicines and to use the more expensive medicines only
if the others did not work. Within six months, the company had saved more than $70,000.

POM **HRM** In another case, OptumRx noted that at one of its client companies, drugs
for attention deficit hyperactivity disorder (ADHD) were being overprescribed to adults. Some
of these employees were using the drug to improve their performance at work. The firm's
benefit manager formulated stricter rules concerning reimbursement for ADHD prescriptions
and saved the 19,000-worker company $110,000.

HRM OptumRx also uses descriptive analytics to improve patient health. For instance,
the company can analyze how frequently asthma sufferers are refilling their prescriptions to
discover whether they are taking too many puffs on their inhalers. This could indicate that
these employees require a different drug. Switching patients to more effective medicines is
worthwhile even if these drugs are more expensive, because they can help reduce costly hospitalizations and visits to emergency rooms.

The emergence of technology for capturing, storing, and using real-time data (e.g., the
Internet of Things, see Chapter 8) has enabled real-time BA users to employ analytics to analyze data in real time. Real-time BA also helps organizations to make decisions and to interact
with customers in new, innovative ways. Real-time BA is closely related to descriptive analytics because the focus of decisions is real time rather than some point in the future. Google
Analytics is an excellent example of real-time BA of clickstream data.

Google Analytics is one of the most popular Web analytics services. The service is free,
and it is an application under the Google Marketing Platform. *Web analytics* is the collection
and analysis of clickstream data to measure Web traffic, to assess and improve the performance of a website, and to perform market research. Google Analytics offers many benefits to
organizations, including the following:

- Automatic data collection: A company sets up its Google Analytics account and places
  computer code on its website. This code enables Google Analytics to immediately begin
  collecting data.

- Users can choose from many reports that Google has created or build their own customized reports using the drag-and-drop interface.

- Users can link their Google Ads account seamlessly with Google Analytics. *Google Ads*
  is an online advertising platform that is triggered every time a user performs a keyword
  search. Through auctions, advertisers bid to display advertisements, service offerings,
  product listings, and videos to users.

- Users can track internal website searches to reveal what goods and services potential customers are looking for after they arrive on the website. Users can also track the number of
  unique visitors to a website, the pages they view, the number of views per page, the length
  of time viewers spend per page, and many other variables. With these insights, uses can
  make necessary changes or additions to their website navigation and their product and
  service offerings.

- Users can determine how visitors reached their websites. That is, they can find out which
  keywords visitors employed to find the user's website.

- *Bounce rate* is the percentage of visitors who leave a website after visiting only one page.
  Google Analytics provides detailed reports of any pages on users' websites that experience a high bounce rate. These data enable users to identify the reasons for this problem
  and fix them.

- The Audience section of Google Analytics provides data about visitors to websites, including their age, gender, interests, devices, language used, and location (country and city).

- Users can see how much traffic to their websites is driven by social media platforms.
  Google Analytics also indicates the conversion rate of website visitors from each social

platform. *Conversion rate* is the percentage of visitors who take a desired action, such as making a purchase. This information enables users to allocate their advertising budget efficiently across various social media platforms.

- Users can perform A/B testing without having to write any code. A/B testing is a user experience research method that compares two versions of, for instance, a website. The method compares user responses to each version to determine which version is more effective. For example, on version A of its website, a company places the buy button at the top right of a page. On version B, the company places the buy button at the bottom right of that page. Other than the placement of the buy button, the pages are identical. The company analyzes the data from Web visitors to determine which version leads to the most purchases.

Let's look at how several companies use Google Analytics:

- General Electric (www.ge.com) tracks the country of origin for visitors to its website. This information provides GE with insights into market demand as well as strategies to improve its website to manage multiple languages and cultures.
- AccuWeather (www.accuweather.com) obtains a complete picture of its online and offline marketing campaign effectiveness and captures insights into the behavior of its mobile audience.
- Nissan (www.nissan-global.com) gains a better understanding of its target audience's product preferences.
- Barnes and Noble (www.barnesandnoble.com) learns how different author layouts, chapter snippets, and reviews impact the ways that visitors navigate content on the site. The bookseller also receives valuable data on the most viewed titles and the characteristics of visitors who purchased certain titles.
- The Four Seasons (www.fourseasons.com) gains insights into the travel patterns and habits of its guests and potential guests. Integrating these data into the company's strategy helps the hotelier to market to customers and to decide which other sites to partner with for advertising.

Before you go on...

1. Describe the purpose of descriptive analytics.
2. Discuss the BA tools that are commonly used in descriptive analytics.

---

predictive analytics
A type of business analytics that examines recent and historical data in order to detect patterns and predict future outcomes and trends.

12.4 Predictive Analytics

LEARNING OBJECTIVE

Provide a definition and a use case example for predictive analytics.

Predictive analytics examines recent and historical data to detect patterns and predict future outcomes and trends. Predictive analytics provides estimates about the likelihood of a future outcome.

The purpose of predictive analytics is *not* to tell decision makers what will happen in the future. Predictive analytics can only forecast what *might* happen in the future, based on probabilities. Predictive analytics applications forecast customer behavior and purchasing patterns, identify trends in sales activities, and forecast demand for inputs from suppliers.

BA Tools in Predictive Analytics

Organizations use a variety of BA tools and statistical procedures in performing predictive analytics. The tools include data mining, and the statistical procedures include linear regression, multiple regression, and logistic regression. Recall that data mining can perform two basic operations: (1) identifying previously unknown patterns and (2) predicting trends and behaviors. The first operation is a descriptive analytics application, and the second is a predictive analytics application. There are many other tools and statistical procedures that are used in predictive analytics.

Examples of Predictive Analytics Applications

In this section we present numerous examples of predictive analytics. Keep in mind that descriptive analytics applications often immediately suggest predictive analytics applications. Let's continue with the examples of class attendance and Fandango.

Should I Go to Class?   If I go to class today, will my attendance positively impact my grade? Conversely, if I do not go to class today, will my absence negatively impact my grade?

MKT **Fandango**   Recall that we are using Fandango to illustrate each step in the BA process. Here we discuss examples of Fandango's predictive analytics applications. How does the ticket seller know when to send e-mails to its members with discount offers for a specific movie on a specific day? Consider John Jones. Predictive analytics tools analyze terabytes of data to determine that although John likes science fiction movies, he has not seen the latest science fiction movie, which has been in theaters since the previous Friday. Consequently, Fandango could send him a discount offer for this movie.

MKT **Marketing Examples**

- Using predictive analytics, organizations can employ targeted marketing, where firms classify customer demographics to predict which customers will respond to a mailing or buy a particular product. Further, firms can use data from past promotional mailings to identify those prospects who are most likely to respond favorably to future mailings.

- Predictive analytics drives the coupons you receive at the grocery cash register. United Kingdom grocery giant Tesco (www.tesco.com) predicts which discounts customers will redeem so it can better target more than 100 million personalized coupons annually at cash registers in 13 countries. This process increased coupon redemption rates by 360 percent over previous methods.

- Websites predict which ads you will click so they can instantly choose which ad to show you, a process that drives millions of dollars in new revenue.

- Wireless carriers predict how likely you are to cancel and defect to a competitor—a process called *churn*—possibly before you have decided to do so. These predictions are based on factors such as dropped calls, your phone usage, your billing information, and whether your contacts have already defected.

- Leading online dating companies Match (www.match.com), OkCupid (www.okcupid.com), and eHarmony (www.eharmony.com) predict which prospect on your screen will be the most compatible with you.

POM **Production and Operations Management Examples**

- Predictive analytics can enable organizations to determine correct inventory levels and distribution schedules among outlets.

- The difference between *preventive maintenance* and *predictive maintenance* is that preventive maintenance is scheduled at regular intervals, while predictive maintenance occurs as needed based on conditions of the asset. Because predictive maintenance occurs only when needed, it reduces labor and material costs.

In 2015, ThyssenKrupp launched a predictive maintenance service based on data from sensors that measure a variety of operating conditions on the firm's 120,000 elevators around the world. Based on predictive analytics of the sensor data, if a condition falls outside normal limits the company dispatches an engineer. The goal is to get an engineer to the site before the elevator breaks down. Often when the engineer arrives, the system has already done much of the diagnostic work.

- Car maker BMW (www.bmw.com) is using predictive analytics to address vulnerabilities early in its production cycle. The manufacturer analyzes data from its global warranty, diagnostics, and repair units to optimize the design and production of new vehicles. By analyzing multiple data sources, BMW can find patterns that will help it to pinpoint potential design flaws.

- Tyson Foods (www.tysonfoods.com) is using predictive analytics to predict the potential of the coronavirus to impact its meat processing plants. The company's insights-as-a-service unit integrates COVID-19 testing data from counties where its plants are located, data about areas where Tyson employees live, and public data such as county population density and socioeconomic data to predict COVID-19 outbreaks in (and around) its plants.

FIN Finance Examples

- Banks use predictive analytics to forecast levels of bad loans, to predict credit card spending by new customers, to determine which kinds of customers will best respond to (and qualify for) new loan offers, and to forecast bankruptcy and other forms of default.

  Banks also use predictive analytics to detect fraudulent credit card transactions. Over time, a pattern emerges of the typical ways that you use your credit card, the amounts you spend, and so on. If a thief steals your card and uses it fraudulently, then that usage typically varies noticeably from your established pattern and the charges are denied.

- Financial services firms employ predictive analytics to produce credit scores. They use these scores to determine the probability that customers will make future credit payments on time.

- Retailers such as AAFES (stores on military bases) use Fraud Watch from SAP (www.sap.com) to combat fraud by employees in the company's 1,400 stores.

- Simpa Networks ((www.facebook.com/simpanetworks)) sells solar-as-a-service to poor households and small businesses in India. Simpa partnered with DataKind (www.datakind.org), whose data scientists analyzed Simpa's historical customer data to help Simpa assess the credit worthiness of potential customers.

HRM Human Resource Management Examples

- Credit Suisse (www.credit-suisse.com) uses predictive analytics to determine who might leave the company and why. Analysts provided this information anonymously to managers so that they could address the issues raised for all employees. In this way, no employee was singled out. This analysis reduced turnover risk factors and increased employee retention. The company saves approximately $70 million per year through reduced employee turnover.

- An engaged employee is one who is enthusiastic about his or her work and takes positive action to further the organization's goals. Shoe retailer Clarks (www.clarksusa.com) used predictive analytics to examine the relationship between employee engagement and the company's financial performance. The results indicated that every 1 percent improvement in engagement led to a 0.4 percent in business performance.

- United Kingdom-based KPMG (www.kpmg.com/uk)) developed a proprietary system, Workplace Analytics, to implement retention solutions as soon as an employee is identified as considering leaving a firm. The system analyzes hundreds of behaviors such as e-mail use, phone use, travel habits, commute times, and paid time off, while considering unemployment and opportunity in the surrounding geographic area, to provide individuals' retention scores. If that score changes, an employer can take appropriate actions to counter the likelihood that the individual will quit. For example, the employer can promote workplace flexibility, adjust workloads to prevent burnout, or offer perks.

Insurance Examples

- Allstate Insurance (www.allstate.com) tripled the accuracy of predicting bodily injury liability from car crashes based on the characteristics of the insured vehicle. That is, the insurer adjusted the rates based on the vehicle. This process resulted in approximately $40 million in annual savings.

- Insurers use predictive analytics to forecast claim amounts and medical coverage costs, classify the most important elements that affect medical coverage, and predict which customers will buy new insurance policies.

Government Examples

- In his FiveThirtyEight blog (www.fivethirtyeight.com), Nate Silver famously analyzed polling and economic data to predict the results of the 2008 presidential election, calling 49 out of 50 states correctly. He then correctly predicted all 50 states in the 2012 presidential election. In contrast, Silver failed to correctly predict that Donald Trump would win the 2016 presidential election. Bouncing back, he did correctly predict that Joe Biden would win the 2020 presidential election.

- Officials in some states are using predictive analytics to assess the risk that a convict will offend again.

Health Care Examples

- Health care organizations correlate demographics of patients with critical illnesses and develop more accurate insights on how to identify and treat symptoms and their causes. For example, Microsoft and Stanford University analyzed the search data of millions of users to successfully identify previously unreported side effects of certain medications.

- Stanford University data scientists used predictive analytics to diagnose breast cancer better than human physicians by discovering an innovative method that takes into account additional contributing factors in tissue samples.

Other Examples

- The National Weather Service (www.weather.gov) predicts weather with increasing accuracy and precision by analyzing a myriad of variables, including past and present atmospheric conditions, location, temperature, air pressure, wind speed, and many others.

- Sentiment analysis is another type of predictive analysis. *Sentiment analysis* is the process of analyzing opinions expressed in a piece of text (e.g., a Tweet) or in a speech to determine whether the writer's or listener's attitude toward a particular topic, product, or service is positive, negative, or neutral. The output of sentiment analysis is a sentiment score, which can be positive or negative. Further, this score can also be any number between –1 and +1, indicating the degree of positivity or negativity.

Unintended Consequences of Predictive Analytics

Predictive analytics clearly provides organizations with numerous advantages. In fact, one could say that predictive analytics is critically important for an organization's success. However, predictive analytics applications can produce questionable, or even harmful, results for organizations. For example, we look at unintended consequences of predictive analytics for Target, Uber, and the Los Angeles Police Department.

MKT *Target.* Target (www.target.com) identified 25 products that, when purchased together, indicate that a woman is likely pregnant. The value of these data was that Target could send coupons to the pregnant woman at a habit-forming period of her life. Unfortunately, Target's algorithms led to a public-relations problem.

A man walked into a Target outside Minneapolis, Minnesota, and demanded to see the manger. He had coupons that had been sent to his daughter, and he was quite angry. He told the manager that his daughter was a teenager, and he wanted to know if Target was trying to encourage her to become pregnant.

The manager did not know what the man was talking about. He noted that the mailer was addressed to the man's daughter and it contained advertisements for maternity clothing, nursery furniture, and pictures of smiling infants. The manager apologized and then called the man a few days later to apologize again. However, the father was embarrassed. He told the manager that his daughter was indeed pregnant and that he owed the manager an apology.

POM *Uber* (www.uber.com). In December 2016, Uber's algorithm automatically raised rates (surge pricing) in Sydney, Australia, as people tried to get away from a downtown restaurant where an armed man was holding 17 people hostage. Three people, including the gunman, died. Uber later apologized for raising fares, which reportedly quadrupled, and then offered refunds.

Problems are most likely to arise when algorithms make things happen automatically, without human intervention or oversight. Uber is now working on a global policy to prevent price increases in times of disaster or emergency.

Example of Descriptive Analytics and Predictive Analytics

Let's consider the following example to demonstrate how descriptive and predictive analytics are used to bridge the gap between data management and actionable business decisions.

POM Weather data can be used to make predictions relating to certain business problems. Suppose you are the northeast district manager for the American Automobile Association (AAA; www.aaa.com), and your district covers multiple offices in several states. You need to create a work schedule for your employees, who receive and dispatch service calls. Your goal is to provide optimal coverage in your offices, reduce unnecessary salary expenses, and provide excellent customer service by reducing customers' wait time. Therefore, you decide to predict the number of service calls your offices receive per day during normal business hours based on the daily low temperature measured in degrees.

Data Management: To investigate this business problem, you collect data on service calls for the past year from the AAA locations within your district. You first "clean" the data by adjusting for outliers and missing values, resulting in a final sample of 3,219 service calls.

You are now ready to build a regression model using temperature as the independent variable to predict the number of customer service calls received in any given day; this is the dependent variable. You will use the results to predict how many employees should be available to receive and dispatch customer service calls.

Descriptive Analytics: For this example, the correlation between daily low temperature and the number of service calls was found to be –0.84, with an average of 48 service calls per day. The correlation is negative because as the temperature decreases, the data indicate that the number of service calls increases.

The square of this correlation, $R^2 = .71$, is the predictive power of the model. That is, the model, using low daily temperature, explains approximately 71 percent of the variation in the number of calls received each day. Therefore, 1 minus R^2 means that 29 percent of the variance in the dependent variable is due to extraneous or unexplained variables.

Predictive Analytics: The manager has decided to use linear regression for his predictive analysis. To do so, certain reasonable assumptions must be met:

- He must have at least 30 data points.
- The relationship between the independent and dependent variables must be linear. The linearity assumption can best be tested with scatter plots.

- Even though the data are assumed to be normally distributed, he should check this assumption.

The sample size of 3,219 satisfies the first assumption. The manager then used Excel to test the second assumption, producing a scatterplot to determine if the plot of each ordered pair of data (independent variable, dependent variable) produced a linear pattern. The scatterplot for the data did exhibit a linear pattern. Therefore, linear regression is an acceptable statistical procedure for these data.

To check for normality, the manager calculated the correlation between the data and the normal scores of the data. If the value is near 1, then the sample dataset is likely to be normal. This dataset met the normality assumption.

Now that the three linear regression assumptions have been met, the next step is to define the linear regression model between these two variables using Excel or a similar statistical package. The linear regression model is:

$$\text{Number of calls received} = 124.79 - 1.5 \times (\text{daily low temperature})$$

These results indicate that for every one degree of increase in the daily low temperature, the predicted daily number of calls received will decrease by 1.5. That is, AAA will expect to receive fewer calls on warmer days and more calls on colder days. At a temperature of 0 degrees ($x = 0$), the expected number of calls will be approximately 125.

Actionable Business Decision: Based on the linear regression, the district manager is able to use the projected daily low temperature for up to 10 days in advance to predict how many service calls the offices will receive each day. (The Weather Channel provides reasonably accurate daily temperatures on a 10-day outlook.) Therefore, he can predict how many employees will be needed to manage the expected number of service calls in order to ensure low wait times for the customers.

Now, ask the next question: At this point, the manager can return to the data management stage with new input variables. For the AAA data in this example, it is feasible to consider another business problem with the appropriate inputs or to expand the analysis by considering other variables relevant to the business question in the example. For example, the manager might want to include the actual time of day, by hour, so that he could more accurately decide on staffing levels. He also might want to examine the location of his AAA branches as a variable. Adding these variables would require the use of new regression models.

You also want to recall that our example is for the northeast district, where temperatures are cooler than in some other regions of the country. Therefore, if we were to use data from the southwest, then we would have to perform the analyses again. Otherwise, if we used the northeast regression model for the southwest, what would be the result for a 100-degree day? The answer is that the number of calls received would be negative!

Our example proceeds from data management to descriptive analytics to predictive analytics (through a simple linear regression model). We address how the results of predictive analytics often lead to additional questions that include additional variables, which would require a multiple linear regression model.

From a statistical perspective, we might ask: Aren't there many different analytical approaches to solving the same problem? The answer is yes. But a more important question to ask is: Which one approach is the best? The answer to this question is—none! The best approach depends on the kind of data you are working with. And because data come in all shapes and sizes, there cannot be one best approach for all problems. Therefore, selecting the best model for the particular data is always an important exercise in data analytics.

Before you go on...

1. Describe the purpose of predictive analytics.
2. Discuss the BA tools that are commonly used in predictive analytics.

prescriptive analytics
A type of business analytics that recommends one or more courses of action, showing the likely outcome of each decision.

12.5 Prescriptive Analytics

LEARNING OBJECTIVE

Provide a definition and a use case example for prescriptive analytics.

Prescriptive analytics goes beyond descriptive and predictive models by recommending one or more courses of action and by identifying the likely outcome of each decision. Predictive analytics does not predict one possible future; rather, it suggests multiple future outcomes based on the decision maker's actions. Prescriptive analytics attempts to quantify the effect of future decisions in order to advise on possible outcomes before the decisions are actually made.

Some companies are successfully using prescriptive analytics to optimize production, scheduling, and inventory along the supply chain to ensure they deliver the right products at the right time so they can optimize the customer's experience.

Prescriptive analytics requires predictive analytics with two additional components: actionable data and a feedback system that tracks the outcome produced by the action taken. Because prescriptive analytics is able to predict the possible consequences based on different choices of action, it can also recommend the best course of action to achieve any prespecified outcome.

BA Tools in Prescriptive Analytics

Organizations use a variety of BA tools and statistical procedures to perform prescriptive analytics. Statistical procedures include optimization, simulation, and others. A discussion of these procedures is beyond the scope of this text.

Examples of Prescriptive Analytics Applications

We present numerous examples of prescriptive analytics in this section. Let's begin by returning once again to our examples of class attendance and Fandango.

Should I Go to Class?   Based on my predictive analytics results, I will set the alarm on my phone and check the transit bus schedule. If I decide to drive my car, I may have to get up earlier in order to find a parking place.

POM Fandango   Recall that we are using Fandango to illustrate each step in the BA process. Here we discuss examples of Fandango's prescriptive analytics applications. Fandango uses prescriptive analytics so it can change ticket price offerings every hour. The company has identified the most desirable movie times by analyzing millions of show times instantaneously. The company then uses these data to set an optimal price for any given time, based on the supply of show times and the demand for movie tickets. This process maximizes profits. The data from each show indicate how much each ticket price contributes to profits.

MIS Waymo (Google) Driverless Car   During every trip, the car makes multiple decisions about what to do based on predictions of future outcomes. For example, when approaching an intersection, the car must determine whether to go left, right, or straight ahead. Based on its destination, it makes a decision. Additionally, the car must anticipate what might be coming in regard to vehicular traffic, pedestrians, bicyclists, and so on. The car must also analyze the impact of a possible decision before it actually makes that decision.

POM The Oil and Gas Industry   Companies in this industry analyze a variety of structured and unstructured data, including video, image, and sound data, to optimize hydraulic fracturing (fracking) operations. One prescriptive analytics application optimizes the materials and equipment necessary to pump oil out of the ground. It further optimizes scheduling, production, inventory, and supply chain design to ensure that the right products are delivered in the right amount to the right customers at the right time in the most efficient manner.

UPS provides an outstanding example of how an enterprise can employ all three analytics applications. IT's About Business 12.1 details how UPS has progressed from descriptive analytics to predictive analytics and finally to prescriptive analytics.

Augmented analytics is a rapidly emerging type of analytics that integrates artificial intelligence (AI) and machine learning (ML) (see Chapter 14) into the traditional analytics process (see Figure 12.3). IT's About Business 12.2 discusses augmented analytics and provides examples of how organizations are using this type of analytics today.

augmented analytics
A type of analytics platform that integrates artificial intelligence (AI) and machine learning (ML) into the traditional analytics process to automate the selection and preparation of data, the generation of insights, and the communication of those insights.

IT's About Business **12.1**

POM United Parcel Service Uses Three Types of Analytics

The Problem

United Parcel Service (UPS, www.ups.com) is a global organization with 424,000 employees and nearly 100,000 vehicles. UPS drivers deliver roughly 21 million packages per day and far more in December, typically making between 120 and 175 "drops" per day. Between any two drops, drivers can take a number of possible paths. With 55,000 routes in the United States alone, the total number of possible routes is inconceivably vast. Clearly, it is in the best interest of UPS and its drivers to find the most efficient routes. Therefore, any tiny amount of efficiency that can be gained in daily operations yields significant improvements to the company's bottom line. Essentially, "little" things matter a great deal to UPS.

In addition, the rapid increase in electronic commerce, or e-commerce, has shifted an increasing number of UPS's delivery stops from retailers to private residences. (We discussed e-commerce in Chapter 7.) In fact, half of UPS's total deliveries in 2021 were to residences. Historically, drivers would drop off multiple packages at a retailer. Today, they must make scattered stops to drop off packages at individual homes. This scenario involves more routes and is more time consuming.

In addition, UPS must manage a low-margin business as well as a unionized workforce that is compensated at the high end of the industry scale. It is significant to note that rival FedEx (www.fedex.com) uses independent contractors for its ground network. Consequently, FedEx does not have the burden of expensive employee benefits packages. UPS also faces intense competition from Amazon with its low-cost package delivery service, called the Delivery Service Partner program.

To address these challenges, UPS is deploying analytics applications. Since 2016, UPS has been collecting and analyzing roughly 1 billion data points per day as the company tracks the real-time status of each package as it moves across the UPS shipping network. Analytics is critical to UPS because their customers have very complex supply chains and are demanding to be informed more precisely as to when their packages will be delivered.

To improve its analytics processes, UPS has implemented the Enhanced Dynamic Global Execution (EDGE) programs, which include DIADs, package placement on UPS vans, routing outbound packages, handling undeliverable packages, and the Package Flow Technologies system. UPS has also developed its Harmonized Enterprise Analytics Tool (HEAT). The two programs are saving the company hundreds of millions of dollars per year.

The Solution

For decades UPS has been using three types of analytics to produce efficiencies:

- Descriptive analytics asks, "Where are we today?"
- Predictive analytics asks, "With our current trajectory, where *will* we be tomorrow?"
- Prescriptive analytics asks, "Where *should* we be tomorrow?"

As UPS has moved from descriptive to predictive to prescriptive analytics, its data needs have expanded, the skill set of its employees has improved, and the business impact of analytics has increased. We consider these developments next.

Descriptive Analytics

DIADs. UPS implemented descriptive analytics in the 1990s when the company provided its drivers with hand-held computers, called Delivery Information Acquisition Devices (DIADs). The DIADs enabled UPS to capture detailed data that measured the company's current status. For example, the company measured driving variables in hundredths of a second. Their reasoning was that reducing one mile per driver per day in the United States alone would add up to $50 million to the bottom line annually.

Package placement on delivery vans. In 2017, UPS began equipping its delivery trucks with Bluetooth receivers to reduce the number of incorrectly loaded packages. The receivers emit a loud beep if a worker puts a package into a vehicle that is not going to the package's destination. When workers enter the correct truck, a different beep confirms that they are in the right place. The system works by transmitting wireless signals between the Bluetooth receivers and the scanning devices that workers wear on their hips and hands to read the labels on UPS packages.

When UPS workers scan packages in the morning, the data update the service that the company has deployed to send customers progress e-mails about their shipments. Customers who have signed up for the free service then receive a message that their package will arrive that day, along with an estimated delivery time.

Routing outbound packages. Another project informs seasonal workers where to direct the outbound packages that UPS vehicles pick up throughout the day and bring to the company's sorting facilities. UPS hires nearly 100,000 of these workers from November through January. In the winter of 2018, UPS outfitted roughly 2,500 of these workers with scanning devices and $8 Bluetooth headphones that issue one-word directions, such as "Green," "Red," or "Blue." These colors correspond to specific conveyor belts, which then transport the packages to other parts of the building for further processing.

Undeliverable packages. UPS does make mistakes with some deliveries. In the past, UPS managers relied on historical data and radio conversations with drivers to estimate how many undeliverable packages they would need to handle each night. To streamline this process, the company has initiated a project that informs managers how many returned packages will arrive at their processing center and when. Managers can then assemble the appropriate number of workers to reroute the packages.

Predictive Analytics

One EDGE project was the UPS Package Flow Technologies system, which was designed to provide predictive analytics. With this system, drivers started the day with a DIAD that detailed the packages they were to deliver and the order in which they were to deliver those packages. Essentially, the DIAD became the drivers' assistant. The system enabled UPS to reduce total delivery driving globally by 85 million miles per year. That process saved the firm 8.5 million gallons of fuel, and it prevented 85,000 metric tons of carbon dioxide from entering the atmosphere.

However, drivers had to provide different services from the same vehicle—for example, deferred service and premium service. Some packages had to be delivered by 10:30 a.m., others by noon, and still others by 2:00 p.m. Drivers had to decide how they were going to service those customers. With so many variables to consider, it was practically impossible for drivers to optimize their routes.

To better manage the enormous amounts of data it captures, UPS created its Harmonized Enterprise Analytics Tool (HEAT). HEAT has the capacity to analyze billions of data points per day, which include customer data, operational data, and planning data. In addition, it can add new events as they occur in the delivery of a package.

HEAT leverages predictive analytics, machine learning, and multi-model forecasting with seasonality growth factors (e.g., the Christmas season) to support forecasting, operations visibility, optimization, and reporting. In short, HEAT creates a digital twin of the entire UPS shipping network. HEAT's ability to help UPS adjust to severe, unexpected events was tested in February 2021, when a massive winter storm impacted much of North America, leaving almost 10 million people without power. HEAT enabled UPS managers to dynamically redistribute its transportation network assets—for example, trucks and regional shipping facilities—to move packages around the hardest-hit areas. The system also enabled UPS to recover quickly after the storm and return operations to normal.

Prescriptive Analytics

Despite these innovations, UPS realized that it needed to take analytics to the next level. So, in mid-2012, the company began deploying its On-Road Integrated Optimization and Navigation (ORION) system. ORION reorganizes the drivers' routes based on today's customers, today's needs, and today's packages, and it designs deliveries in a very specific, optimized order. ORION takes into account UPS business rules, maps, the times that drivers need to be at specific locations, and customer preferences. ORION can alter delivery routes dynamically based on changing weather conditions and accidents. The system can also examine the deliveries that still need to be completed and continue to optimize the remaining route.

At first, ORION used publicly available maps. However, these maps were not detailed enough. Therefore, UPS drew their own maps, which displayed features, such as a customer's half-mile driveway or a back alley, that save time getting to a receiving dock. ORION needed these data points in order to optimize package delivery.

Unfortunately, analytics algorithms cannot anticipate every variable. For example, a business customer typically receives one package per day. If ORION knows that the package is not tied to a certain delivery time, then the algorithm might suggest dropping it off in the morning one day but in the afternoon the next day, depending on that day's tasks. That process might be the most efficient approach for UPS, but customers would not know when to expect deliveries. This can be a problem because customers typically do not like that amount of uncertainty.

When UPS drivers are on the road, they usually travel at speeds of 20 to 25 miles per hour. Therefore, every mile reduced equates to a savings of two to three minutes. By shortening routes by seven to eight miles per day, ORION enables UPS to deliver more packages.

ORION enhances UPS customer service with more efficient routing, and it enables UPS to offer innovative services and customized solutions. An example of this type of service is UPS My Choice, which is a free system that allows residential customers to decide "how, where, and when home deliveries occur." UPS's chatbot, called UPS Bot, is integrated with the UPS My Choice system, so customers are able to obtain information about their incoming packages and deliveries without providing a tracking number.

UPS Bot mimics human conversation, and it can respond to customer queries such as, "Where is the nearest UPS location?" In addition, it can track packages and provide shipping rates. Customers can ask the bot questions through text or voice commands, mobile devices, social media channels, and virtual assistants such as Alexa and Google Assistant. UPS Bot is able to recognize these requests and take the appropriate steps to respond to them.

Another UPS project, Network Planning Tool (NPT), optimizes the flow of packages in the UPS network from loading docks to sorting to the final destination. NPT enables UPS engineers to view activity at UPS facilities around the world and route shipments to the ones with the most capacity. NPT creates forecasts about package volume and weight based on an analysis of historical data.

NPT enables UPS to organize packages by destination and move them at the lowest possible cost while still meeting delivery dates. It helps engineers group all outbound packages into the smallest number of trailers or cargo planes. NPT can also schedule truck and plane trips so those drivers and pilots always pick up parcels on their return trips and therefore do not return home with empty vehicles.

NPT provides a single cloud-based platform where UPS engineers can view data and run simulations to help create their plans and schedules. NPT's algorithms understand the distribution of all the packages in the UPS logistics system, and they can determine the best way to bypass a problematic facility while meeting deadlines and not overwhelming other UPS facilities.

The Results

In April 2016, UPS won the prestigious Edelman Prize for excellence in analytics and operations research for its ORION project. UPS completed the deployment of ORION at the end of 2016.

The results from ORION have been outstanding. UPS is realizing savings of between $300 and $400 million per year in driver productivity and fuel economy. Furthermore, with ORION, UPS drivers have saved 100 million miles in driving, decreasing carbon emissions by 100,000 metric tons per year. ORION will generate further environmental benefits and cost reductions when UPS equips its vehicles outside the United States with this technology.

UPS continues to look into the future. As a major example, ORION provides a natural transition to driverless vehicles. The company need only integrate ORION with the software of autonomous delivery vehicles, and those vehicles will take optimal routes to get UPS personnel where they need to go to deliver packages.

Finally, UPS is using drone deliveries for some applications, including dropping essential supplies in Rwanda and demonstrating how medicines could be delivered to islands. In rural areas, where drones have the space to execute deliveries and the distance between stops makes efficient deliveries challenging, drones launched from the roofs of UPS trucks provide a solution to reduce costs and improve service. On October 1, 2019, UPS received the Federal Aviation Administration's first full approval for the company's drone airline, called UPS Flight Forward.

Questions

1. Explain how DIADs were a descriptive analytics solution for UPS.

2. Explain how the Package Flow Technologies system was a predictive analytics solution for UPS.

3. Explain how the ORION system was a prescriptive analytics solution for UPS.

4. Describe another potential application for the UPS ORION system. That is, what is the next question that UPS managers might ask of ORION?

5. Is UPS's Network Planning Tool a descriptive analytics application, a predictive analytics application, a prescriptive analytics application, or some combination? Support your answer with examples.

Sources: Compiled from T. Olavsrud, "UPS Delivers Resilience, Flexibility with Predictive Analytics," *CIO*, August 6, 2021; "UPS Flight Forward Attains FAA's First Full Approval for Drone Airline," UPS, press release, October 1, 2019; P. High, "UPS's Chief Information and Engineering Officer Champions Prescriptive Analytics," *Forbes*, July 15, 2019; E. Woyke, "How UPS Uses AI to Deliver Holiday Gifts in the Worst Storms," *MIT Technology Review*, November 21, 2018; N. Shields, "UPS Is Turning to Predictive Analytics," *Business Insider*, July 20, 2018; S. Schwartz, "UPS Working to Consolidate Data Points on Single Platform with Analytics, Machine Learning," *CIO Dive*, July 19, 2018; B. Marr, "The Brilliant Ways UPS Uses Artificial Intelligence, Machine Learning and Big Data," *Forbes*, June 15, 2018; S. Rosenbush, "UPS Expands Role of Predictive Analytics," *Wall Street Journal*, April 26, 2018; E. Woyke, "How UPS Delivers Faster Using $8 Headphones and Code That Decides When Dirty Trucks Get Cleaned," *MIT Technology Review*, February 16, 2018; "How UPS Delivers Predictive Analytics," *CIO*, September 28, 2016; T. Davenport, "Prescriptive Analytics Project Delivering Big Dividends at UPS," *DataInformed*, April 19, 2016; C. Powers, "How UPS Augments Its Drivers' Intuition with Predictive Analytics," *ASUG News*, June 9, 2015; E. Siegel, "Predictive Analytics Driving Results, ROI at UPS," *Data Informed*, June 1, 2015; E. Siegel, "Wise Practitioner—Predictive Analytics Interview Series: Jack Levis of UPS," *Predictive Analytics World*, April 28, 2015; J. Berman, "UPS Is Focused on the Future for Its ORION Technology," *Logistics Management*, March 3, 2015; S. Rosenbush and L. Stevens, "At UPS, the Algorithm Is the Driver," *Wall Street Journal*, February 16, 2015; J. Dix, "How UPS Uses Analytics to Drive Down Costs," *Network World*, December 1, 2014; and K. Noyes, "The Shortest Distance between Two Points? At UPS, It's Complicated," *Fortune*, July 25, 2014; www.ups.com, accessed August 14, 2022.

IT's About Business 12.2

MIS   Augmented Analytics

Global organizations are collecting exponentially larger volumes of structured and unstructured data, a total that will reach 175 zettabytes by 2025. (One *zettabyte* is approximately equal to 1 billion terabytes.) To utilize all of these data in their decision making, businesses will have to employ augmented analytics.

Definition and capabilities of augmented analytics. **Augmented analytics** integrates artificial intelligence (AI) and machine learning (ML) (see Chapter 14) into traditional analytics (see Figure 12.3) to automate the processes of selecting and preparing data and then generating and communicating insights based on those data.

Augmented analytics brings analytical capabilities, including recommendations, insights, or guidance on a query, to more people; that is, organizations can *democratize use of data*. Thus, business users can make decisions based on data without requiring the services of data scientists or IT professionals.

Augmented analytics solutions come with prebuilt models and algorithms, so companies do not need a data scientist to do this work. Leading augmented analytics platforms feature intuitive interfaces that employ natural language processing (NLP). Therefore, nontechnical users can easily ask questions from datasets using standard business terminology. The system will then utilize *natural language generation* (NLG) to find and query the correct dataset and provide easy-to-understand results and recommendations using data visualization tools such as dashboards.

Let's examine these capabilities more closely:

- Recommend, prepare, and enrich data: With traditional analytics, users have to decide which datasets to query. In contrast, an augmented analytics solution will (a) recommend which datasets to include in user analyses, (b) alert users when those datasets are updated, and (c) suggest new datasets if users are not receiving the results they expect.

- Create dashboards and reports: Augmented analytics helps interpret and communicate results in an easily understandable context, thereby enabling users to quickly make business decisions.

- Provide natural language interfaces: Augmented analytics allows users to query datasets using natural language. The system can also provide these results using everyday business language.

- Forecast trends and cluster data: The augmented system provides accurate forecasts and predictions based on historical data.

- Use proactive, personalized analytics with mobile applications: The augmented system provides a personalized assistant that understands individual users. For example, it can determine which charts to present to a client at an offsite sales meeting based on the client's location.

Differences between traditional analytics and augmented analytics. You are familiar with the traditional analytics process. Let's differentiate between this process and augmented analytics.

The traditional analytics process typically relies on dashboards. These dashboards are based on business questions that are defined in advance. Answering these questions requires accessing a database or data warehouse. Answering a new question requires time (days or weeks) and the technical skills of data scientists or analytics specialists.

In contrast, the augmented analytics process is continuous. With augmented analytics, the AI and ML are built into the product. Model building and analyses are always working in the background to continuously learn and help users make more accurate decisions. Keep in mind that data continuously flow into organizations (see Data Streams in **Chapter 5**). AI and ML process these data in near realtime to provide increasingly accurate predictions, insights, and recommendations.

Traditional analytics uses a publisher/consumer model in which a few data scientists or analytics specialists create reports and dashboards for potentially thousands of users. As noted above, augmented analytics provides results for all users and enables them to access and analyze datasets on their own.

Now that we understand how augmented analytics differs from traditional analytics, let's consider several examples of augmented analytics in action.

POM *Firefighting.* For some time, firefighters have relied on traditional analytics to predict the possible behavior of fires, using data ranging from weather patterns to satellite footage of potential fire fuels and historical fire behavior.

Today, firefighters are using augmented analytics to contain and extinguish forest fires. For instance, in the summer of 2021, a team was trying to control a wildfire that had jumped over a firebreak; that is, an area of cleared land that prevents a fire from spreading. As the captain was driving to the fire, he received an e-mail containing a statistical analysis from a researcher. The analysis predicted that the location of the firebreak had only a 10 percent chance of containing the blaze. The researcher had used the Suppression Difficulty Index (SDI), an augmented analytics tool that integrates machine learning, big data, and forecasting. The captain was frustrated with the analysis because his team had spent time and effort building that firebreak. He promptly had his team create a new firebreak where the tool indicated would be the most successful in slowing the fire.

Another popular augmented analytics tool, which is used in half of our national forests, is the potential operational delineations (PODs) package. PODs integrate the data sources used in traditional analytics with firefighter knowledge, advanced spatial analytics, and other statistical models, including the SDI, to help teams predict the most likely places for a fire to break out. It can also help them plan an attack on a fire before it even breaks out. PODs superimpose these integrated data sources over a map of a region to deliver visual insights.

An even more advanced augmented analytics tool, the potential control locations (PCLs) algorithm, uses machine learning to suggest where firefighters should place their control lines—for example, firebreaks—during a blaze. In addition to all the data sources we have mentioned, the PCLs algorithm integrates data such as distances from roads, the locations of ridges and flat ground, what kind of fuel is present on the ground, and historical fire perimeters.

Firefighters are also presenting the results of their analyses to communities prior to the fire season. They want to educate the residents as well as have the residents map local priorities. That is, the residents note which locations must be defended at all costs and which areas can be exposed to the fire to help thin out the landscape to ensure that future fires are less intense.

POM *PepsiCo.* The food and beverage company PepsiCo (**www.pepsico.com**) includes Frito-Lay, Gatorade, Pepsi-Cola, Quaker, Tropicana, and SodaStream. Prior to COVID, PepsiCo had developed its augmented analytics Sales Intelligence Platform, which integrates retailer data with PepsiCo supply chain data. The platform predicts out-of-stock items and alerts retailers to replenish those items.

When the pandemic struck, the platform encountered unusual supply chain signals as consumers purchased larger-than-normal amounts of staples during global lockdowns. For instance, customers wanted as much oatmeal as possible, along with paper towels and toilet paper. As a result, thousands of retailers experienced out-of-stocks. PepsiCo used its Sales Intelligence Platform to predict many of these out-of-stocks. The company's salespeople then alerted retailers so they could replenish the items.

POM *Agriculture.* The Climate Corporation (**www .climate.com**) is a digital agriculture company that helps farmers to determine which crops to plant and where and when to plant them. The company's seed advisor service collects historical data such as past crop yields and soil samples. It then combines that data with other data sources—including weather data—and runs it through thousands of augmented analytics models. In turn, these models provide recommendations regarding which seeds to plant and when, how deep to plant the seeds, and how far apart to space the rows. The company asserted that farmers who used this information were able to increase their yields by more than nine bushels per acre.

MKT *Retail.* Retailers employ augmented analytics to automatically analyze customer data and identify trends. If you can anticipate which products customers are likely to buy, then you can make better decisions about product assortment, pricing, and promotions.

POM *Manufacturing.* Managers use augmented analytics to automatically analyze sensor and machine data to identify issues and optimize production. Consider factories where managers know the exact state of every assembly line, the output of each human worker, and even the power usage of individual machines. These managers are able to predict bottlenecks before they occur and take measures to prevent them.

FIN *Financial services.* Augmented analytics platforms analyze huge amounts of financial data to help banks prevent fraud by recognizing patterns. Consider, for example, your credit card transactions. Over time, your credit card company's augmented analytics platform captures data on each transaction and creates a profile of how and where you typically spend money. As you put more transactions on your card, the analytics platform refines its profile of you. In that way, when a transaction does not fit your profile, you will automatically receive a query, "Did you make this purchase?" In some cases, the platform will cancel your card and notify you that your credit card company is sending you a new card.

Questions

1. Describe why it is necessary to integrate artificial intelligence and machine learning into traditional analytics packages.

2. Identify and discuss the differences between traditional analytics and augmented analytics.

Sources: Compiled from D. Drai, "Five Ways Augmented Analytics Is Protecting Business Revenue," *Information Age*, August 18, 2022; Q. Larson, "What Is Augmented Analytics? A Definition and Example Use Cases," freecodecamp.org, April 4, 2022; R. Kaur, "Augmented Analytics 101: A Starter's Guide," *SelectHub*, April 2, 2022; "Augmented Analytics Explained: Definition Use Cases, Benefits, Features, and More," Tableau.com, 2022; T. Olavsrud, "PepsiCo Tackles Supply Chain with Data," *CIO*, November 30, 2017; B. Petrova, "Augmented Analytics Guide: Definition, Examples, & Use Cases," revealbi.io, November 17, 2021; "Augmented Analytics," *Technopedia*, July 19, 2021; "Introducing Augmented Analytics & How It Benefits Businesses," *Monkey Learn*, February 16, 2021; L. Massey, "Fighting Fires with Advanced Analytics and Innovative Tech," iianalytics.com, September 22, 2020; E. Chickowski, "5 Augmented Analytics Examples in the Enterprise," *TechTarget*, August 20, 2019; "Augmented Analytics Guide: The What, Why, and How," *AnswerRocket*, February 8, 2019; and P. Ghosh, "Augmented Analytics Use Cases," *Dataversity*, June 20, 2018.

Before you go on...

1. Describe the purpose of prescriptive analytics.
2. Discuss the BA tools that are commonly used in prescriptive analytics.

12.6 Presentation Tools

LEARNING OBJECTIVE

Describe two examples of presentation tools.

WILEY PLUS

Author Lecture Videos are available exclusively in *WileyPLUS*. **Apply the Concept activities are available in the Appendix and in** *WileyPLUS*.

As you saw in **Figure 12.3**, organizations use presentation tools to display the results of analyses to users in visual formats such as charts, graphs, figures, and tables. This process, known as *data visualization*, makes the results more attractive and easier to understand. Organizations can present the results after they have performed descriptive analytics, predictive analytics, and prescriptive analytics. A variety of visualization methods and software packages that support decision making are available. Dashboards are the most common BA presentation tool. We discuss them next. We also consider geographic information systems, another valuable data visualization tool.

Dashboards

Dashboards evolved from executive information systems, which were designed specifically for the information needs of top executives. Today, however, many employees, business partners, and customers use digital dashboards.

A dashboard provides easy access to timely information and direct access to management reports. It is user friendly, it is supported by graphics, and, most important, it enables managers to examine exception reports and drill down into detailed data. **Table 12.1** summarizes the various capabilities that are common to many dashboards. Some of the capabilities discussed in this section have been incorporated into many BA products, as illustrated in **Figure 12.4**.

One outstanding example of a dashboard is Bloomberg LP (**www.bloomberg.com**), a privately held company that provides a subscription service that sells financial data, software to analyze these data, trading tools, and news (electronic, print, TV, and radio). All of this

TABLE 12.1 The Capabilities of Dashboards

Capability	Description
Drill down	The ability to go to details, at several levels; it can be done by a series of menus or by clicking on a drillable portion of the screen.
Critical success factors (CSFs)	The factors most critical for the success of business. These can be organizational, industry, departmental, or for individual workers.
Key performance indicators (KPIs)	The specific measures of CSFs.
Status access	The latest data available on a KPI or some other metric, often in real time.
Trend analysis	Short-, medium-, and long-term trends of KPIs or metrics, which are projected using forecasting methods.
Exception reporting	Reports highlight deviations larger than defined thresholds. Reports may include only deviations.

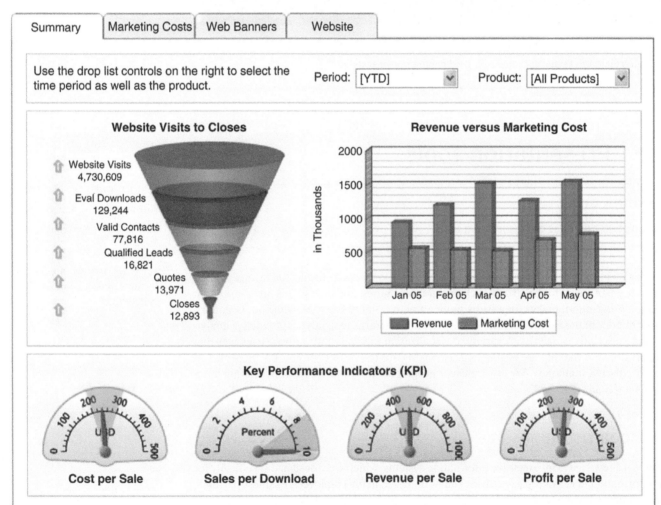

Source: Dundas Data Visualization, Inc.

FIGURE 12.4 Sample performance dashboard.

information is accessible through a color-coded Bloomberg keyboard that displays the desired information on a computer screen, either the user's screen or one that Bloomberg provides. Users can also set up their own computers to access the service without a Bloomberg keyboard. The subscription service plus the keyboard is called the Bloomberg Terminal. It is literally a do-it-yourself dashboard because users can customize their information feeds as well as the look and feel of those feeds (see Figure 12.5).

Carlos Osorio/Toronto Star/Zuma Press

FIGURE 12.5 Bloomberg Terminal.

A unique and interesting application of dashboards to support the informational needs of executives is the Management Cockpit. Essentially, a Management Cockpit is a strategic management room containing an elaborate set of dashboards that enable top-level decision makers to pilot their businesses better. The goal is to create an environment that encourages more efficient management meetings and boosts team performance through effective communication. To help achieve this goal, the dashboard graphically displays KPIs and information relating to critical success factors on the walls of a meeting room called the *Management Cockpit Room* (see Figure 12.6). The cockpit-like arrangement of instrument panels and displays helps managers visualize how all of the different factors in the business interrelate.

The Management Cockpit is a registered trademark of SAP, created by Professor Patrick M. Georges.

FIGURE 12.6 Management Cockpit.

Within the room, the four walls are designated by color: Black, Red, Blue, and White. The Black Wall displays the principal success factors and financial indicators. The Red Wall measures market performance. The Blue Wall projects the performance of internal processes and employees. Finally, the White Wall indicates the status of strategic projects. The Flight Deck, a six-screen, high-end PC, enables executives to drill down to detailed information. External information needed for competitive analyses can easily be imported into the room.

Board members and other executives hold meetings in the Management Cockpit Room. Managers also meet there with the comptroller to discuss current business issues. The Management Cockpit can implement various what-if scenarios for this purpose. It also provides a common basis for information and communication. Finally, it supports efforts to translate a corporate strategy into concrete activities by identifying performance indicators.

Geographic Information Systems

geographic information system (GIS) A computer-based system for capturing, integrating, manipulating, and displaying data using digitized maps.

A **geographic information system (GIS)** is a computer-based system for capturing, integrating, manipulating, and displaying data using digitized maps. Its most distinguishing characteristic is that every record or digital object has an identified geographical location. This process, called *geocoding*, enables users to generate information for planning, problem solving, and decision making. The graphical format also makes it easy for managers to visualize the data. There are countless applications of GISs to improve decision making in both the public and private sectors.

POM As one example, Children's National Health System offers injury prevention advice to the community. Clinicians have found that using geospatial data helps them accomplish this mission. The health care center integrated its existing electronic health records system with GIS software from ESRI (www.esri.com) to display health data with geospatial coordinates. One of the integrated system's first projects focused on pediatric burn cases.

GIS mapping enabled the clinic to identify on a map the hotspots where injuries were occurring. That map allowed staff members to develop prevention programs tailored to the demographics of areas with high rates of injuries. For example, if the system identifies a cluster of children with burns in a particular neighborhood, then the staff will work with community groups to provide parents with Spanish translations of information about safety.

The new system has produced results. The clinic is seeing fewer burn patients overall and fewer patients requiring high-level burn care. Children's National Health System is now using its system to map concentrations of other medical conditions such as obesity and asthma.

Before you go on...

1. Discuss why presentation tools are so valuable in the business analytics process.
2. What is a dashboard? Why are dashboards so valuable to an organization's decision makers?

What's in IT for Me?

ACCT **For the Accounting Major**

BA is used extensively in auditing to uncover irregularities. It also is used to uncover and prevent fraud. CPAs use BA for many of their duties, ranging from risk analysis to cost control.

FIN **For the Finance Major**

People have been using computers for decades to solve financial problems. Innovative BA applications have been created for activities such as making stock market decisions, refinancing bonds, assessing debt

risks, analyzing financial conditions, predicting business failures, forecasting financial trends, and investing in global markets.

MKT **For the Marketing Major**

Marketing personnel utilize BA in many applications, from planning and executing marketing campaigns, to allocating advertising budgets, to evaluating alternative routings of salespeople. New marketing approaches such as targeted marketing and database marketing depend heavily on IT in general and on data warehouses and business intelligence applications in particular.

POM **For the Production/Operations Management Major**

BA supports complex operations and production decisions from inventory control, to production planning, to supply chain integration.

HRM **For the Human Resources Management Major**

Human resources personnel employ BA for many of their activities. For example, BA applications can find résumés of applicants posted on the Web and sort them to match needed skills and to support management succession planning.

MIS **For the MIS Major**

MIS provides the data infrastructure used in BA. MIS personnel are also involved in building, deploying, and supporting BA applications.

Summary

12.1 Use a decision-support framework to demonstrate how technology supports managerial decision making at each phase of the decision-making process.

When making a decision, either organizational or personal, the decision maker goes through a three-step process: intelligence, design, and choice. When the choice is made, the decision is implemented. In general, it is difficult to state which information systems support specific decision makers in an organization. Modern information systems, particularly business analytics systems, are available to support everyone in an organization.

12.2 Describe each phase of the business analytics process.

Business analytics is the process of developing actionable decisions or recommendations for actions based on insights generated from historical data. The phases in the business analytics process are shown in Figure 12.3 and include data management, descriptive analytics (with associated analytics tools and statistics procedures), predictive analytics (with associated analytics tools and statistical procedures), prescriptive analytics (with associated analytics tools and statistical procedures), and presentation tools. The results of the business analytics process are actionable business decisions.

12.3 Provide a definition and a use case example for descriptive analytics.

Descriptive analytics summarizes what has happened in the past and allows decision makers to learn from past behaviors. We leave the example to you.

12.4 Provide a definition and a use case example for predictive analytics.

Predictive analytics examines recent and historical data in order to detect patterns and predict future outcomes and trends. We leave the example to you.

12.5 Provide a definition and a use case example for prescriptive analytics.

Prescriptive analytics goes beyond descriptive and predictive models by recommending one or more courses of action and identifying the likely outcome of each decision. We leave the example to you.

12.6 Describe two examples of presentation tools.

A dashboard provides easy access to timely information and direct access to management reports. It is user friendly, it is supported by graphics, and, most important, it enables managers to examine exception reports and drill down into detailed data.

A geographic information system (GIS) is a computer-based system for capturing, integrating, manipulating, and displaying data using digitized maps. Its most distinguishing characteristic is that every record or digital object has an identified geographical location.

Key Terms

augmented analytics 381
business analytics (BA) 361
business intelligence (BI) 361
data mining 370
decision 363

decision-support systems (DSSs) 371
descriptive analytics 370
geographic information system (GIS) 388
management 362
multidimensional data analysis 370

online analytical processing (OLAP) (or multidimensional data analysis) 370
predictive analytics 374
prescriptive analytics 380
productivity 362

Discussion Questions

1. Your company is considering opening a new factory in China. List several typical activities involved in each phase of the decision (intelligence, design, and choice).

2. Recall that a market basket analysis (a type of data mining) of convenience store purchases revealed that customers tended to buy beer and diapers at the same time when they shopped. Now that the analysis uncovered this relationship exists, provide a rationale for it. Note: You will have to decide what the next question is.

3. American Can Company announced that it was interested in acquiring a company in the health maintenance organization (HMO) field. Two decisions were involved in this act: (1) the decision to acquire an HMO and (2) the decision of which HMO to acquire. How can the use of BA assist the company in this endeavor?

4. Discuss the strategic benefits of business analytics.

5. In early 2012, the *New York Times* reported the story of a Target data scientist who was able to predict if a customer was pregnant based on her pattern of previous purchases.

   a. Describe the business analytics models that the data scientist used.

   b. Refer to Chapter 3 and discuss the ethics of Target's analytics process.

   c. Research the story and note the unintended consequences of Target's analytics process.

6. Consider the admissions process at your university. Your university's admissions process involves the analysis of many variables to decide whom to admit to each year's freshman class. Contact your admissions office and gather information on the variables used in the admissions process. As you recall from applying at your university, typical variables would include high school attended, high school grade point average, standardized test scores such as ACT or SAT, and many others. (Do not be surprised if there are variables that your admissions office cannot provide.)

   a. Provide an example of how your admissions office uses descriptive analytics in the admissions process. Use the variables you have found in your example.

   b. Provide an example of how your admissions office uses predictive analytics in the admissions process. Use the variables you have found in your example.

   c. Provide an example of how your admissions office uses prescriptive analytics in the admissions process. Use the variables you have found in your example.

Problem-Solving Activities

1. Consider a large city, which has placed sensors in all its trash dumpsters. The sensors measure how full each dumpster is.

   a. Describe a descriptive analytics application using this sensor data.

   b. Describe a predictive analytics application using this sensor data.

   c. Describe a prescriptive analytics application using this sensor data.

2. Consider General Electric's latest-generation LEAP aircraft engine (www.geaerospace.com). Sensors in this engine measure vibration and several different temperatures (depending on the location of the sensor).

   a. Describe a descriptive analytics application using this sensor data.

   b. Describe a predictive analytics application using this sensor data.

   c. Describe a prescriptive analytics application using this sensor data.

3. You are a business analyst for a chain of grocery stores. You analyze retail sales data, perform a descriptive analytics application, and discover that bread and milk are the two products that are purchased together more often than any other pair of products.

   a. Describe a predictive analytics application using these data.

   b. Describe a prescriptive analytics application using these data.

4. Consider Rent the Runway (RTR; www.renttherunway.com). RTR buys designer dresses wholesale and rents them over the Web,

charging only a fraction of the price of the dress. When RTR merchandisers decide whether to buy a new dress, they follow a list of 40 data points such as fabric, zippers, stitching, and shape to determine whether the dress will hold up to the rigors of multiple rentals. The longer the lifespan, the higher the return on capital. In mid-2017, RTR was averaging more than 30 turns (rentals) per dress.

With every dress it rents, RTR's analytics algorithms learn more about effective strategies to track the location of each item, forecast demand, select shipping methods, set prices, and control inventory. RTR's algorithms also examine customer reviews to learn which dresses women are renting for certain occasions. They then forecast demand to determine whether the prepaid shipping label that goes with a dress should require the customer to return the dress overnight or whether a three-day return, which costs less, is sufficient.

   a. Describe a descriptive analytics application using this sensor data.

   b. Describe a predictive analytics application using this sensor data.

   c. Describe a prescriptive analytics application using this sensor data

5. Visit www.marketingplatform.google.com. Describe the different types of analytics Google provides for businesses. Which of these tools would you use for predictive analytics? Which for prescriptive analytics?

6. Visit www.ibm.com/topics/predictive-analytics. Describe one of IBM's use cases.

7. Check out www.tableau.com. Describe the different types of visualizations they have for the different types of analytics.

Closing Case

MIS **Google's Earth Engine**

Google Earth (www.earth.google.com) is a platform that presents a three-dimensional representation of Earth based on a 70-petabyte database that contains satellite imagery, aerial photography, Street View imagery, and geographical information systems (GIS) data. The program maps the Earth by superimposing these data onto a three-dimensional globe, enabling users to view cities and landscapes from various angles. Today, Google Earth covers more than 97 percent of the world, and it includes 10 million miles of Street View imagery. (Google Street View provides interactive panoramas from positions along many streets in the world.) As just one interesting example of the data that Google Earth collects every day, users can analyze detailed information on the soil composition more than one foot underground and the amount of water vapor rising from farmland.

An important application of Google Earth is the Google Earth Engine. The Google Earth Engine (GEE, www.earthengine.google.com) is a cloud computing platform that enables users to analyze Google Earth's database by providing a data catalog of images, computational power, and data analysis software necessary to analyze the data. The GEE allows scientists to collaborate using data, algorithms, and visualizations.

For example, GEE allows users to observe dynamic changes in agriculture, natural resources, and climate using geospatial data from the Landsat and Sentinel-2 satellite programs. Landsat satellites pass over the same places on Earth every 16 days, and Sentinel-2 satellites every 10 days.

Public Use (Pro Bono) Applications

GEE scientists analyze massive datasets to answer critical questions for a number of pro bono clients that include conservation groups, city agencies, community advocates, and researchers. Let's consider several examples:

- In the Ferlo region of the West African nation of Senegal, climate change is making it more difficult for herders to find water for their cattle. GEE scientists alert the farmers via radio to the best place to locate water.
- Via a shared website, GEE scientists target locations in Los Angeles where planting trees would be most helpful in lowering surface temperatures.
- *State of Hawaii*. The State of Hawaii faces many challenges as the climate crisis worsens, including landslides, wildfires, storm surges, flooding, lava flows, rock falls, and cliff erosion. These problems cause serious problems not only for the state's infrastructure and systems but also for the health, safety, and economic opportunities of the state's citizens.

To address these problems, Hawaii used GEE to build a public-facing mapping tool to help policymakers and the public decide where to invest resources as the state seeks to combat climate change. The tool provides an easier, more visual way for residents, public officials, and lawmakers to see where the risks are. The map is coded with green, yellow, and red, mapped across the islands, identifying low- to high-risk areas. The various constituencies can use the map to determine in which areas to place resources and the amount of resources to place in each area.

- Researchers at the University of Maryland used the GEE to survey the extent, loss, and gain of global tree cover over the course of more than a decade. The study analyzed nearly all global land, excluding only Antarctica and some Arctic islands. The result was the first map of global forest change. The researchers noted that it would have taken them 15 years to complete their study on a single computer. In contrast, the GEE platform enabled them to complete the study in only 15 days.
- Using the GEE platform, the Map of Life (www.mol.org) biodiversity team has developed an interactive map to view and analyze habitat ranges and to assess the security of individual species. The GEE enables the team to refine their predictions for the locations of at-risk species. Users can adjust the parameters—for example, a decrease in the amount of water in a particular area—and GEE updates the map dynamically, immediately displaying the impact on the species range and the amount of protected habitat.
- Global Forest Watch (www.globalforestwatch.org), an initiative of the World Resources Institute, is a dynamic online forest monitoring system designed to enhance forest management and conservation. Global Forest Watch uses GEE to measure and visualize changes to the world's forests. Users can analyze data from over the past decade or receive alerts about possible new threats in near real time. Corporations, nonprofits, governments, and indigenous groups use the system to protect against illegal logging and make supply chains more transparent. For example, GEE places bright pink dots on interactive maps that inform the Indigenous people of Peru about the locations of illegal logging activity.
- Scientists in the Global Health Group at the University of California, San Francisco, are using GEE to predict malaria outbreaks. Local health workers can use the UCSF tool to upload their information about known cases of malaria. The platform will then integrate this information with real-time satellite data to predict where new cases are likely to occur.
- The European Commission's Joint Research Center (JRC) uses GEE to develop high-resolution maps of global surface water occurrence, change, seasonality, recurrence, and transitions. The study analyzes both permanent and seasonal water bodies. Understanding these changes is vital to ensure the security of our global water supply for agriculture, industry, and human consumption; to assess water-related disaster reduction and recovery; and to study waterborne pollution and the spread of disease.

Unfortunately, the insights GEE provides sometimes come with risks. Consider, for example, the case of Cloud to Street, a company that maps drought and flood zones in communities at risk from climate change. In South Sudan, Cloud to Street was warned not to make its maps public after locals worried that gangs of marauders from rebel factions in the ongoing civil war might use them to target vulnerable villages.

Commercial Applications

GEE developers have also been working on commercial applications. In October 2021, the company announced a for-profit version of the service. Customers included Unilever Plc and Swiss Re AG.

- *Unilever*. Unilever is using GEE to ensure that its palm oil, a key ingredient in many consumer goods, does not come from illegal logging in tropical forests. The company is trying to meet its pledge to keep its supply chain free of deforestation. It monitors 42 million acres of farms and tracks the images of agriculture and traffic through 77,000 small villages to assess which of its 1,900 mills might be receiving palm oil from illegal farms.

- *Regrow*. Sydney, Australia, start-up Regrow Ag uses GEE to measure agricultural *carbon sequestration*—the process of capturing, securing, and storing carbon dioxide from the atmosphere—and its clients' crop yields. The goal is to identify opportunities to reduce emissions and improve yields. Regrow analyzes data such as shortwave infrared imaging that reveals the health of plants, the proportion of green cover to soil in a field, and the amount of crop residue left over after harvest. Farmers can use these data to adjust their inputs or crop types and to calculate the amount of carbon their farming practices emit or sequester.

Based on the information Regrow provides, farmers now often reduce field cultivations and plant cover crops rather than leaving their fields bare. Cover crops are noncash crops that are planted to cover the soil rather than for the purpose of being harvested and sold. The fewer times farmers till a field, the less carbon they release into the atmosphere. If they plant cover crops, the plants prevent the soil from eroding over the winter. In that way, Regrow can provide the farmers with some knowledge of what they will be paid for adopting these practices and taking part in the carbon market.

Questions

1. **Describe the various types of data that Google Earth Engine uses.**

2. **Provide an example of a descriptive analytics application that Google Earth Engine employs.**

3. **Provide an example of a predictive analytics application that Google Earth Engine employs.**

Sources: Compiled from A. Dalton, "Sydney Start-Up Regrow Ag First to Harness Google Earth Engine," *Sydney Morning Herald*, August 2, 2022; D. du Perez, "Hawaii Maps Investment Priorities to Tackle Climate Crisis Using Google Cloud," *Diginomica*, July 6, 2022; "Google's Earth Observation Data Now Accessible to Businesses, Governments Worldwide," *Business Review Live*, June 28, 2022; N. Mott, "Google Expands Availability of Earth Engine to 'Restore a Livable Planet'," *PC Magazine*, June 28, 2022; L. Kaufman, "Google Wants to Save the Planet with Satellite Images," *Bloomberg BusinessWeek*, November 10, 2021; N. Gorelick, "The Nature of Water: Unveiling the Most Detailed View of Water on Earth," *Google Blog*, December 7, 2016; A. Joshi et al., "Tracking Changes and Preventing Loss in Critical Tiger Habitat," *Science Advances*, April 1, 2016; M. Gunther, "Google-Powered Map Helps Fight Deforestation," *Guardian*, March 10, 2015; W. Jetz, "Map of Life: A Preview of How to Evaluate Species Conservation with Google Earth Engine," *Google Blog*, January 8, 2015; L. Kurtzman, "UCSF, Google Earth Engine Making Maps to Predict Malaria," ucsf.edu, September 10, 2014; M. Hansen, et al., "High-Resolution Global Maps of 21st Century Forest Cover Change," *Science*, November 15, 2013; https://earthengine.google.com; and www.globalforestwatch.org, accessed August 14, 2022.

CHAPTER 13

Acquiring Information Systems and Applications

CHAPTER OUTLINE	LEARNING OBJECTIVES
13.1 Planning for and Justifying IT Applications	**13.1 Explain** the different cost–benefit analyses that companies must consider when they formulate an IT strategic plan.
13.2 Strategies for Acquiring IT Applications	**13.2 Discuss** the four business decisions that companies must make when they acquire new applications.
13.3 Traditional Systems Development Life Cycle	**13.3 List** and explain the primary tasks and the importance of each of the six processes involved in the systems development life cycle.
13.4 Alternative Methods and Tools for Systems Development	**13.4 Describe** alternative development methods and the tools that augment these methods.

Opening Case

MIS Southwest Airlines Meltdown Due to Technical Debt

In December 2022, a winter storm dropped multiple feet of snow across much of the United States, leading to widespread flight cancellations over the holiday season. Most airlines returned to normal operations within two to four days. There was one major exception: Southwest Airlines (www.southwest.com).

Southwest's meltdown began on December 21 and lasted through the end of the year. The airline cancelled nearly 17,000 flights and reported a net loss of $220 million for the fourth quarter of 2022. By comparison, they reported a profit of $68 million for the same period in 2021.

Why did Southwest perform so poorly? The company's IT systems were adequate to operate under normal operations, where schedules and assignments were created and executed. Their systems proved inadequate, however, when major problems arose. Multiple departments had to manually readjust flight schedules and reassign crews. Under this system, Southwest could manage a maximum of roughly 300 changes. In fact, the epic nature of the storm created more than 2,500 changes as well as continued cancellations and issues involving employees' time.

It is significant to note that executives at Southwest were aware of these issues prior to the storms. In 2016, the Southwest Airlines Pilots Association (SWAPA) unanimously approved a vote of no confidence in then-CEO Gary Kelly. Their main issue was his refusal to invest in updating their critically outdated IT infrastructure and flight operations. Meltdowns had begun—although on a much smaller scale—as early as 2014. In November 2022, SWAPA President Casey Murray (www.swapa.org) again encouraged executives to invest in their IT, fearing a significant meltdown if a catastrophic event occurred. That event occurred a month later.

Southwest experienced many challenges during this time. First, their process for reassigning pilots and crew members could not operate on a national level. When a flight was canceled, crew members had to report their location and receive their next assignment by phone. Due to the number of cancellations, the phone system was overloaded. There were not enough lines or agents to keep up with the demand. Some crew members reported waiting on hold for as long as 17 hours to receive their new assignment.

Compounding this problem, Southwest flies primarily point-to-point rather than moving passengers through a hub with connecting flights. Again, this model is efficient and cost effective when operations are normal. It is not resilient, however, when challenges arise. Because many Southwest flights are short and need to be rescheduled very quickly, one flight delay immediately causes numerous other delays and disrupts the overall schedule.

Further complicating matters is the fact that the Federal Aviation Administration (FAA) enforces a timeout period. Flight crews consisting of one pilot cannot be on duty more than 8 hours, and crews with two pilots cannot be on duty more than 10 hours. So, while crews are sitting on the ramp waiting for flight instructions or for flight attendants to be scheduled, they are technically on duty. If their remaining duty time is insufficient to complete the planned flight, then the flight must be canceled.

Southwest, then, faced multiple challenges: the nearly nationwide weather patterns, their outdated rescheduling system, insufficient phone support, and FAA regulations. It is no wonder their system melted down and they could function only at a minimal capacity.

The Problem—Technical Debt

Southwest relied on old, deficient software that the company failed to update, despite repeated requests from their pilots. When organizations choose not to keep their systems up to date and capable of delivering in all business needs, they incur technical debt. *Technical debt* refers to a gap between what the software needs to be and what it actually is. Expenditures to update software are considered debt. In effect, the organization "owes money" to the system. Further, the longer organizations wait to update their information systems, the more "interest" they accrue, and the more expensive the update will be. Meltdowns, such as the one experienced by Southwest, result from this technical debt.

Technical debt is often a necessary part of the development process and is accumulated intentionally. For example, imperfect but stable sections of code might be left alone—especially if other, more important program features are urgently needed. However, in all cases, organizations must be aware that some technical debt exists and will need to be managed. Further, investing in software and systems that aren't directly visible to the customer is not appealing. It sometimes takes away from the "very appealing" bottom line. You don't see many press releases touting investments that do little more than maintain the status quo.

How Systems Development Addresses Technical Debt

System maintenance is a vital component of the systems development life cycle (SDLC). Periodic maintenance is essential for security purposes and for keeping the system compatible with the latest hardware devices that will access the system. However, an updated system might not be able to scale to meet the organization's current needs, leaving an organization with a functioning system that cannot manage capacity requirements. System maintenance also addresses the critical issue of keeping the system in alignment with current business needs, operations, and disaster planning.

Few companies will ever experience a systems failure as massive or as widely publicized as Southwest did. However, many companies make the same mistake; that is, they neglect investments that impact both the customer and employee experiences. Sometimes, as in the case of Southwest, improvements occur only when the situation reaches a breaking point.

Southwest neglected its systems, building up massive technical debt. How great was this debt? The airline announced plans to spend $1.3 billion on IT infrastructure during 2023. This sum represents 30 percent of their planned capital spending for the entire year. Further, it does not include lost revenue during the fourth quarter of 2022 or the future lost revenue when 2 million customers use the 25,000 frequent flier miles they received as compensation for the inconvenience the meltdown may have caused. Finally, it does not take into account the vast amounts of negative publicity and the devastating impact to the airline's reputation.

Many CEOs are evaluated based on the bottom line, and investments must be justified by the potential return they bring to the organization. This focus on the bottom line makes it easy to push maintenance to the side. However, the technical debt still must be repaid. The question is whether to pay it now or to postpone it until a catastrophe occurs.

Questions

1. What is technical debt, and how is it repaid?
2. Why did Southwest incur so much technical debt?
3. How can organizations better manage systems development to avoid technical debt?

Sources: Compiled from: T. Brown, "A Look at Technical Debt," *IT Chronicles*, April 4, 2022; D. Meyer, "Southwest Airlines' Post-Christmas Meltdown Thanks to 'Outdated IT' Systems, Poor Scheduling," nypost.com, December 27, 2022; D. Goldman, "Why Southwest Is Melting Down," CNN.com, December 28, 2022; N. Chau, "What Caused Southwest's Holiday Meltdown? It Wasn't Just Weather, Pilots Say, cbsnews.com, December 29, 2022; Z. Tufekci, "The Shameful Open Secret Behind Southwest's Failure," *New York Times*, December 31, 2023; R. Jennings, "Southwest Airlines: 'Shameful' Technical Debt Bites Back," devops.com, January 5, 2023; R. Dooley, "Southwest's $825 Million Loss Signals Why Companies Shouldn't Put Off Internal Investments," *Forbes*, January 6, 2023; D. Cameron, "Southwest Airlines Earnings Hit by $220 Million Loss After Holiday Meltdown," *Wall Street Journal*, January 26, 2023, https://thestack.technology/southwest-airlines-technical-debt-meltdown-warnings/, accessed January 25, 2023; and https://www.productplan.com/glossary/technical-debt/, accessed January 25, 2023.

Introduction

Competitive organizations move as quickly as they can to acquire new information technologies or modify existing ones when they need to improve efficiencies and gain strategic advantage. As you learned from the chapter opening case, some organizations create "technical debt" when they neglect the need to upgrade and update systems.

Today, acquisition goes beyond building new systems in-house, and IT resources involve far more than software and hardware. The old model in which firms built their own systems is being replaced with a broader perspective of IT resource acquisition that provides companies with a number of options. Now companies must decide which IT tasks will remain in-house, and even whether the entire IT resource should be provided and managed by outside organizations. Regardless of which approach an organization chooses, however, it must be able to manage IT projects adeptly.

In this chapter, you learn about the process of acquiring IT resources from a managerial perspective. This means from *your* perspective, because you will be closely involved in all aspects of acquiring information systems and applications in your organization. In fact, when we mention "users" in this chapter, we are talking about you. You also study the available options for acquiring IT resources and how to evaluate those options. Finally, you learn how organizations plan and justify the acquisition of new information systems.

13.1 | Planning for and Justifying IT Applications

LEARNING OBJECTIVE

Discuss the different cost–benefit analyses that companies must take into account when formulating an IT strategic plan.

Organizations must analyze the need for applications and then justify each purchase in regard to costs and benefits. The need for information systems is usually related to organizational planning and to the analysis of its performance vis-à-vis its competitors. The cost–benefit justification must consider the wisdom of investing in a specific IT application versus spending the funds on alternative projects. This chapter focuses on the formal processes of large organizations. Smaller organizations employ fewer formal processes, or no processes at all. It is important to note, however, that even if a small organization does not have a formal process for planning and justifying IT applications, the steps of a formal process exist for a reason, and they have value. At the very least, decision makers in small organizations should consider each step when they are planning changes in their information systems.

When a company examines its needs and performance, it generates a prioritized list of both existing and potential IT applications, called the **application portfolio**. These are the applications that have to be added or modified if they already exist.

application portfolio The set of recommended applications resulting from the planning and justification process in application development.

IT Planning

The planning process for new IT applications begins with an analysis of the *organizational strategic plan*, which is illustrated in **Figure 13.1**. The organization's strategic plan identifies the firm's overall mission, the goals that follow from that mission, and the broad steps required to reach these goals. The strategic planning process modifies the organization's objectives and resources to match its changing markets and opportunities.

The organizational strategic plan and the existing IT architecture provide the inputs in developing the IT strategic plan. The *IT architecture* delineates the way an organization should utilize its information resources to accomplish its mission. It encompasses both the technical and the managerial aspects of information resources. The technical aspects include hardware and operating systems, networking, data management systems, and applications software. The managerial aspects specify how the IT department will be managed, how the functional area managers will be involved, and how IT decisions will be made.

FIGURE 13.1 The information systems planning process.

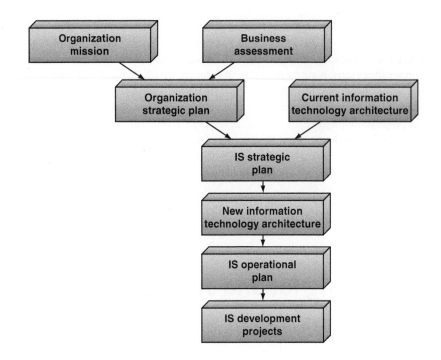

FIGURE 13.1 The information systems planning process.

IT strategic plan   A set of long-range goals that describe the IT infrastructure and major IT initiatives needed to achieve the goals of the organization.

The **IT strategic plan** is a set of long-range goals that describe the IT infrastructure and identify the major IT initiatives needed to achieve the organization's goals. The IT strategic plan must meet three objectives:

1. *It must be aligned with the organization's strategic plan.* This alignment is critical because the organization's information systems must support the organization's strategies. (Recall the discussion of organizational strategies and information systems in Chapter 2.)

    Consider the example of Nordstrom (**www.nordstrom.com**) versus Walmart (**www.walmart.com**). An application that improves customer service at a small cost would be considered favorably at Nordstrom, but it would be rejected at Walmart. The reason is that the application would fit in favorably (i.e., align) with Nordstrom's service-at-any-cost strategy. However, it would not fit in well with Walmart's low-cost strategy. You see two department stores, same application, same cost and benefits—but different answers to the question, "Should we develop the application?"

2. *It must provide for an IT architecture that seamlessly networks users, applications, and databases.*

3. *It must efficiently allocate IS development resources among competing projects so that the projects can be completed on time and within budget and still have the required functionality.*

The existing IT architecture is a necessary input into the IT strategic plan because it acts as a constraint on future development efforts. It is not an absolute constraint, however, because the organization can change to a new IT architecture. Companies prefer to avoid this strategy, however, because it is expensive and time consuming.

Consider this example. You have a Mac (Apple) system, and you need a new software application. You search and find several such packages for both Mac and MS Windows. Unfortunately, the best package runs only on Windows. How much better would this package have to be for you to justify switching from Mac to Windows?

IT steering committee A committee composed of a group of managers and staff representing various organizational units that is set up to establish IT priorities and to ensure that the MIS function is meeting the needs of the enterprise.

One critical component in developing and implementing the IT strategic plan is the **IT steering committee**. This committee, comprised of a group of managers and staff who represent the various organizational units, is created to establish IT priorities and to ensure that the MIS function is meeting the organization's needs. The committee's major tasks are to link corporate strategy with IT strategy, to approve the allocation of resources for the MIS function, and to establish performance measures for the MIS function and ensure they are met. The IT steering committee is important to you because it ensures that you get the information systems and applications that you need to do your job.

After a company has agreed on an IT strategic plan, it next develops the **IS operational plan**. This plan consists of a clear set of projects that the IS department and the functional area managers will execute in support of the IT strategic plan. A typical IS operational plan contains the following elements:

- *Mission:* The mission of the IS function (derived from the IT strategy).
- *IS environment:* A summary of the information needs of the individual functional areas and of the organization as a whole.
- *Objectives of the IS function:* The best current estimate of the goals of the IS function.
- *Constraints on the IS function:* Technological, financial, personnel, and other resource limitations on the IS function.
- *The application portfolio:* A prioritized inventory of present applications and a detailed plan of projects to be developed or continued during the current year.
- *Resource allocation and project management:* A listing of who is going to do what, how, and when.

IS operational plan Consists of a clear set of projects that the IS department and the functional area managers will execute in support of the IT strategic plan.

Evaluating and Justifying IT Investment: Benefits, Costs, and Issues

Developing an IT plan is the first step in the acquisition process. Because all companies have limited resources, they must justify investing resources in some areas, including IT, rather than in others. Essentially, justifying IT investment involves calculating the costs, assessing the benefits (values), and comparing the two. This comparison is frequently referred to as cost–benefit analysis. Cost–benefit analysis is not a simple task.

Assessing the Costs   Calculating the dollar value of IT investments is not as simple as it may seem. One of the major challenges that companies face is to allocate fixed costs among different IT projects. *Fixed costs* are those costs that remain the same regardless of any change in the company's activity level. Fixed IT costs include infrastructure costs and the costs associated with IT services and IT management. For example, the salary of the IT director is fixed, and adding one more application will not change it.

Another complication is that the costs of a system do not end when the system is installed. Rather, costs for maintaining, debugging, and improving the system can accumulate over many years. This is a critical point because organizations sometimes fail to anticipate these costs when they make the investment.

A dramatic example of unanticipated expenses was the Year 2000 (Y2K) reprogramming projects, which cost organizations worldwide billions of dollars. In the 1960s, computer memory was very expensive. To save money, programmers coded the "year" in the date field 19_ _, instead of _ _ _ _. With the "1" and the "9" hard-coded in the computer program, only the last two digits varied, so computer programs needed less memory. However, this process meant that when the year 2000 rolled around, computers would display the year as 1900. This programming technique could have caused serious problems with financial applications, insurance applications, and countless other apps.

Programmers who wanted to avoid the Y2K bug had two options: entirely rewrite the code or adopt a quick fix called windowing, which would treat all dates from 00 to 20 as from the 2000s rather than the 1900s. As estimated 80 percent of computers fixed in 1999 used the quicker, cheaper option. The theory was that these systems would no longer be in use in 2020, but many are still operational.

The Year 2020 bug (Y2020) is a lingering side effect of attempts to fix the Y2K, or millennium bug. Programmers chose 1920 to 2020 as the standard window because of the significance of the midpoint, 1970. Many programming languages and systems manage dates and times as seconds from 1970/01/01, also called Unix time.

As of January 1, 2020, the systems that used the quick fix have rolled back to 1920. Utility company bills have reportedly been produced with the erroneous date of 1920, while tens of thousands of parking meters in New York City have declined credit card transactions.

Thousands of cash registers manufactured by Polish firm Novitus have been unable to print receipts due to a problem with the register's clock. *WWE 2K20*, a professional wrestling videogame, stopped working at midnight on January 1, 2020. Within 24 hours, the game's developers, 2K, issued a downloadable fix.

The Y2K and the Y2020 examples illustrate the point that database design choices tend to affect the organization for a long time. As the twenty-first century approached, no one was still using hardware or software from the 1960s (other than a few legacy applications). Database design choices made in the 1960s, however, were often still in effect decades after the companies implemented them.

Assessing the Benefits   Evaluating the benefits of IT projects is typically even more complex than calculating their costs. Benefits may be more difficult to quantify, especially because many of them are intangible (e.g., improved customer or partner relations and improved decision making). As an employee, you will probably be asked for input about the intangible benefits that an IS provides for you.

The fact that organizations use IT for multiple purposes further complicates benefit analysis. To obtain a return from an IT investment, the company must also implement the technology successfully. In reality, many systems are not implemented on time, within budget, or with all of the features originally envisioned for them. Also, the proposed system may be "cutting edge." In these cases, there may be no precedent for identifying the types of financial payback the company can expect.

Conducting the Cost–Benefit Analysis   After a company has assessed the costs and benefits of IT investments, it must compare them. You have studied, or will study, cost–benefit analyses in more detail in your finance courses. The point is that real-world business problems do not come in neatly wrapped packages labeled "this is a finance problem" or "this is an IS problem." Rather, business problems span multiple functional areas.

There is no uniform strategy for conducting a cost–benefit analysis. Rather, an organization can perform this task in several ways. Here you see four common approaches: (1) net present value, (2) return on investment, (3) breakeven analysis, and (4) the business case approach.

1. Analysts use the *net present value (NPV)* method to convert future values of benefits to their present-value equivalent by "discounting" them at the organization's cost of funds. They can then compare the present value of the future benefits with the cost required to achieve those benefits to determine whether the benefits exceed the costs.

2. *Return on investment (ROI)* measures management's effectiveness in generating profits with its available assets. ROI is calculated by dividing the net income generated by a project by the average assets invested in the project. ROI is a percentage, and the higher the percentage return, the better.

3. *Breakeven analysis* determines the point at which the cumulative dollar value of the benefits from a project equals the investment made in the project.

4. In the *business case approach*, system developers write a business case to justify funding one or more specific applications or projects. IS professionals will be a major source of input when business cases are developed because these cases describe what you do, how you do it, and how a new system could better support you.

Before you go on...

1. What are some problems associated with assessing the costs of IT?
2. Why are the intangible benefits from IT so difficult to evaluate?
3. Describe the NPV, ROI, breakeven analysis, and business case approaches.

13.2 Strategies for Acquiring IT Applications

WILEY PLUS

Author Lecture Videos are available exclusively in *WileyPLUS*.
Apply the Concept activities are available in the Appendix and in *WileyPLUS*.

LEARNING OBJECTIVE

Discuss the four business decisions that companies must make when they acquire new applications.

After a company has justified an IT investment, it must then decide how to pursue it. As with cost–benefit analyses, there are several options for acquiring IT applications. To select the best option, companies must make a series of business decisions. The fundamental decisions are the following:

- *How much computer code does the company want to write?* A company can choose to use a totally prewritten application (write no computer code), customize a prewritten application (write some computer code), or custom write an entire application (write all new computer code).
- *How will the company pay for the application?* Once the company has decided how much computer code to write, it must decide how to pay for it. With prewritten applications or customized prewritten applications, companies can buy them or lease them. With totally custom applications, companies use internal funding.
- *Where will the application run?* The next decision is whether to run the application on the company's platform or on someone else's platform. In other words, the company can employ either a software-as-a-service vendor or an application service provider. (You will examine these options later in this chapter.)
- *Where will the application originate?* Prewritten applications can be open-source software or they can come from a vendor. The company may choose to customize prewritten open-source applications or prewritten proprietary applications from vendors. Furthermore, it may customize applications in-house, or it can outsource the customization. Finally, it can write totally custom applications in-house, or it can outsource this process.

In the following sections, you will find more details on the variety of options that companies looking to acquire applications can select from. A good rule of thumb is that an organization should consider all feasible acquisition methods in light of its business requirements. You will learn about the following acquisition methods:

- Purchase a prewritten application
- Customize a prewritten application
- Lease the application
- Use application service providers and software-as-a-service vendors
- Use open-source software
- Use outsourcing
- Employ continuous development
- Employ custom development

Purchase a Prewritten Application

Many commercial software packages contain the standard features required by IT applications. Therefore, purchasing an existing package can be a cost-effective and time-saving strategy compared with custom-developing the application in-house. Nevertheless, a company should carefully consider and plan the buy option to ensure that the selected package contains

TABLE 13.1   Advantages and Limitations of the Buy Option

Advantages

Many different types of off-the-shelf software are available.

The company can try out the software before purchasing it.

The company can save time by buying rather than building.

The company can know what it is getting before it invests in the product.

Purchased software may eliminate the need to hire personnel specifically dedicated to a project.

Disadvantages

Software may not exactly meet the company's needs.

Software may be difficult or impossible to modify, or it may require huge business process changes to implement.

The company will not have control over software improvements and new versions.

Purchased software can be difficult to integrate with existing systems.

Vendors may discontinue a product or go out of business.

The software is controlled by another company with its own priorities and business considerations.

The purchasing company lacks intimate knowledge about how and why the software functions as it does.

all of the features necessary to address the company's current and future needs. Otherwise, these packages can quickly become obsolete. Before a company can perform this process, it must decide which features a suitable package must include.

In reality, a single software package can rarely satisfy all of an organization's needs. For this reason, a company must sometimes purchase multiple packages to fulfill different needs. It then must integrate these packages with one another as well as with its existing software. Table 13.1 summarizes the advantages and limitations of the buy option.

Customize a Prewritten Application

Customizing existing software is an especially attractive option if the software vendor allows the company to modify the application to meet its needs. However, this option may not be attractive in cases when customization is the *only* method of providing the necessary flexibility to address the company's needs. It is also not the best strategy when the software is either very expensive or likely to become obsolete in a short time. Furthermore, customizing a prewritten application can be extremely difficult, particularly for large, complex applications.

Lease the Application

Compared with the buy option and the option to develop applications in-house, the lease option can save a company both time and money. Of course, leased packages (like purchased packages) may not exactly fit the company's application requirements. However, as noted, vendor software generally includes the features that are most commonly needed by organizations in a given industry. Again, the company will decide which features are necessary.

Interested companies commonly apply the 80/20 rule when they evaluate vendor software. Put simply, if the software meets 80 percent of the company's needs, then the company should seriously consider modifying its business processes so that it can use the remaining 20 percent. Many times, this is a better long-term solution than modifying the vendor software. Otherwise, the company will have to customize the software every time the vendor releases an updated version.

Leasing can be especially attractive to small and medium-sized enterprises (SMEs) that cannot afford major investments in IT software. Large companies may also prefer to lease packages to test potential IT solutions before committing to major investments. A company that does not employ sufficient IT personnel with the appropriate skills for developing custom IT applications may also choose to lease instead of develop the software it needs in-house. Even those companies that employ in-house experts may not be able to afford the long wait for strategic applications to be developed in-house. Therefore, they lease (or buy) applications from external resources to establish a quicker presence in the market.

Leasing can be executed in one of three ways. The first way is to lease the application from a software developer, install it, and run it on the company's platform. The vendor can assist with the installation and will frequently offer to contract for the support and maintenance of the system. Many conventional applications are leased this way.

The other two options involve leasing an application and running it on the vendor's platform. Organizations can accomplish this process by using an application service provider or a software-as-a-service vendor.

Application Service Providers and Software-as-a-Service Vendors

An **application service provider (ASP)** is an agent or a vendor who assembles the software needed by enterprises and then packages it with services such as development, operations, and maintenance. The customer then accesses these applications through the Internet. **Figure 13.2** illustrates the operation of an ASP. Note that the ASP hosts both an application and a database for each customer.

Software-as-a-service (SaaS) is a method of delivering software in which a vendor hosts the applications and provides them as a service to customers over a network, typically the Internet. Customers do not own the software. Rather, they pay for using it. SaaS eliminates the need for customers to install and run the application on their own computers. Therefore, SaaS customers save the expense (money, time, IT staff) of buying, operating, and maintaining the software. For example, Salesforce (**www.salesforce.com**), a well-known SaaS provider for customer relationship management (CRM) software solutions, provides these advantages for its customers. **Figure 13.3** displays the operation of a SaaS vendor. Note that the vendor hosts an application that multiple customers can use. The vendor also hosts a database that is partitioned for each customer to protect the privacy and security of each customer's data.

At this point, companies have made the first three decisions and must now decide where to obtain the application. Recall that in general, for prewritten applications, companies can use open-source software or obtain the software from a vendor. For customized prewritten applications, they can customize open-source software or customize vendor software. For totally customized applications, they can write the software in-house, or they can outsource the process.

application service provider (ASP) An agent or vendor who assembles the software needed by enterprises and packages them with outsourced development, operations, maintenance, and other services.

software-as-a-service (SaaS) A method of delivering software in which a vendor hosts the applications and provides them as a service to customers over a network, typically the Internet.

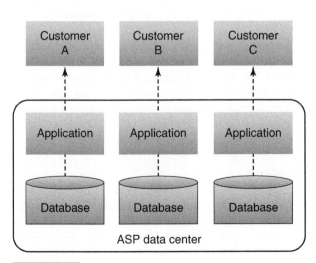

FIGURE 13.2 Operation of an application service provider.

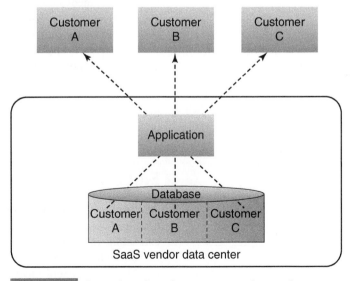

FIGURE 13.3 Operation of a software-as-a-service vendor.

Use Open-Source Software

Organizations obtain a license to implement an open-source software product and either use it as is, customize it, or develop applications with it. Unless the company is one of the few that want to tinker with their source code, open-source applications are basically the same as a proprietary application except for licensing, payment, and support. Open-source software is really an alternative source of applications rather than a conceptually different development option. (We discuss open-source software in Technology Guide 2.)

Outsourcing

outsourcing Use of outside contractors or external organizations to acquire IT services.

Acquiring IT applications from outside contractors or external organizations is called **outsourcing**. Companies can use outsourcing in many situations. For example, they might want to experiment with new IT technologies without making a substantial up-front investment. They also might use outsourcing to obtain access to outside experts. One disadvantage of outsourcing is that companies must frequently place their valuable corporate data under the control of the outsourcing vendor.

Several types of vendors offer services for creating and operating IT systems, including e-commerce applications. Many software companies, from IBM to Oracle, offer a range of outsourcing services for developing, operating, and maintaining IT applications. IT outsourcers, such as EDS, offer a variety of services. Also, the large CPA companies and management consultants—for example, Accenture—offer outsourcing services.

For example, Philip Morris International (the non-U.S. operation of Philip Morris) outsourced its IT infrastructure management to Indian services firm Wipro. The companies concluded a five-year contract in which Wipro manages the tobacco company's applications and IT using Wipro's cloud-based management platform. (We discuss cloud computing in Technology Guide 3.) The contract is reported to be worth some $35 million.

Some companies outsource offshore, particularly in India and China. *Offshoring* can save money, but it includes risks as well. The risks depend on which services are being offshored. If a company is offshoring application development, then the major risk is poor communication between users and developers. In response to these risks, some companies are bringing outsourced jobs back in-house, a process called *reverse outsourcing*, or *insourcing*.

Continuous Development

Continuous application development automates and improves the process of software delivery. In essence, a software development project is not viewed as having a defined product, with development stopped when the product is implemented. Rather, a software development project is viewed as constantly changing in response to changing business conditions and in response to user acceptance.

continuous application development The process of steadily adding new computer code to a software project when the new computer code is written and tested.

Continuous application development is the process of steadily adding new computer code to a software project when the new computer code is written and tested. Each development team member submits new code when it is finished. Automated testing is performed on the code to ensure that it functions within the software project. Continuous code submission provides developers with immediate feedback from users and status updates for the software on which they are working.

Employ Custom Development

Another option is to custom build an application. Companies can either perform this operation in-house or outsource the process. Although custom development is usually more time consuming and costly than buying or leasing, it often produces a better fit with the organization's specific requirements.

The development process starts when the IT steering committee (discussed previously in this chapter), having received suggestions for a new system, decides it is worth exploring.

These suggestions come from users (you in the near future). Understanding this process will help you obtain the systems that you need. Conversely, not understanding this process will reduce your chances, because other people who understand it better will make suggestions that use up available resources.

As the company goes through the development process, its mindset changes. In systems investigation (the first stage of the traditional systems development life cycle), the organization is trying to decide whether to build something. Everyone knows it may or may not be built. In the later stages of the development process, the organization is committed to building the application. Although a project can be canceled at any time, this change in attitude is still important.

The basic, backbone methodology for custom development is the systems development life cycle (SDLC), which you will read about in the next section. Section 14.4 examines the methodologies that complement the SDLC: prototyping, joint application development, integrated computer-assisted systems development tools, and rapid application development. You will also consider four other methodologies: agile development, end-user development, component-based development, and object-oriented development.

Before you go on...

1. Describe the four fundamental business decisions that organizations must make when they acquire information systems.

2. Discuss each of the seven development methods in this section with regard to the four business decisions that organizations must make.

13.3 Traditional Systems Development Life Cycle

LEARNING OBJECTIVE

Enumerate the primary tasks and the importance of each of the six processes involved in the systems development life cycle.

WILEY PLUS

Author Lecture Videos are available exclusively in *WileyPLUS.*
Apply the Concept activities are available in the Appendix and in *WileyPLUS.*

systems development life cycle (SDLC) Traditional structured framework, used for large IT projects, that consists of sequential processes by which information systems are developed.

The **systems development life cycle (SDLC)** is the traditional systems development method that organizations use for large-scale IT projects. The SDLC is a structured framework that consists of sequential processes by which information systems are developed. For our purposes (see **Figure 13.4**), we identify six processes, each of which consists of clearly defined tasks:

1. Systems investigation
2. Systems analysis
3. Systems design
4. Programming and testing
5. Implementation
6. Operation and maintenance

Alternative SDLC models contain more or fewer stages. The flow of tasks, however, remains largely the same. When problems occur in any phase of the SDLC, developers often must go back to previous phases.

Systems development projects produce desired results through team efforts. Development teams typically include users, systems analysts, programmers, and technical specialists.

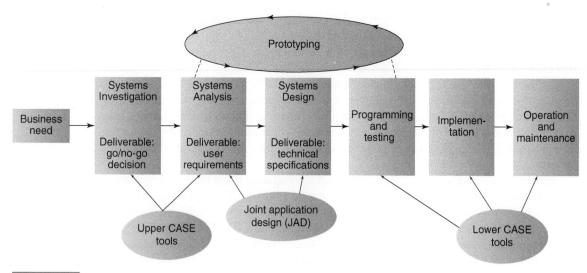

FIGURE 13.4 A six-stage systems development life cycle with supporting tools.

systems analysts
IS professionals who specialize in analyzing and designing information systems.

programmers IS professionals who modify existing computer programs or write new computer programs to satisfy user requirements.

technical specialists Experts on a certain type of technology, such as databases or telecommunications.

systems stakeholders
All people who are affected by changes in information systems.

systems investigation The initial stage in the traditional SDLC that addresses the business problem (or business opportunity) by means of the feasibility study.

Users are employees from all functional areas and levels of the organization who interact with the system, either directly or indirectly. **Systems analysts** are IS professionals who specialize in analyzing and designing information systems. **Programmers** are IS professionals who either modify existing computer programs or write new programs to satisfy user requirements. **Technical specialists** are experts on a certain type of technology, such as databases or telecommunications. The **systems stakeholders** include everyone who is affected by changes in a company's information systems—for example, users and managers. All stakeholders are typically involved in systems development at various times and in varying degrees.

Figure 13.5 indicates that users have high involvement in the early stages of the SDLC, lower involvement in the programming and testing stage, and higher involvement in the later stages. Table 13.2 discusses the advantages and disadvantages of the SDLC.

Systems Investigation

The initial stage in a traditional SDLC is systems investigation. Systems development professionals agree that the more time they invest in (1) understanding the business problem to be solved, (2) specifying the technical options for the systems, and (3) anticipating the problems they are likely to encounter during development, the greater the chances of success. For these reasons, **systems investigation** addresses *the business problem* (or business opportunity) by means of the feasibility study.

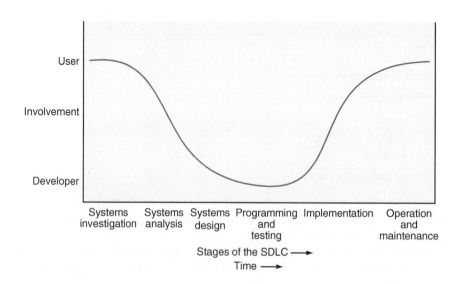

FIGURE 13.5 Comparison of user and developer involvement over the SDLC.

TABLE 13.2   Advantages and Disadvantages of System Acquisition Methods

Traditional Systems Development (SDLC)

Advantages	Disadvantages
• Forces staff to systematically go through every step in a structured process • Enforces quality by maintaining standards • Has lower probability of missing important issues in collecting user requirements	• May produce excessive documentation • Users may be unwilling or unable to study the approved specifications • Takes too long to progress from the original ideas to a working system • Users have trouble describing requirements for a proposed system

Prototyping

Advantages	Disadvantages
• Helps clarify user requirements • Helps verify the feasibility of the design • Promotes genuine user participation • Promotes close working relationship between systems developers and users • Works well for ill-defined problems • May produce part of the final system	• May encourage inadequate problem analysis • Is not practical with large number of users • User may not want to give up the prototype when the system is completed • May generate confusion about whether the system is complete and maintainable • System may be built quickly, which can result in lower quality

Joint Application Design

Advantages	Disadvantages
• Involves many users in the development process • Saves time • Generates greater user support for the new system • Improves the quality of the new system • The new system is easier to implement • The new system has lower training costs	• Difficult to get all users to attend the JAD meeting • The JAD approach is subject to all of the problems associated with any group meeting

Integrated Computer-Assisted Software Engineering

Advantages	Disadvantages
• Can produce systems with a longer effective operational life • Can produce systems that closely meet user requirements • Can speed up the development process • Can produce systems that are more flexible and adaptable to changing business conditions • Can produce excellent documentation	• Systems are often more expensive to build and maintain • The process requires more extensive and accurate definition of user requirements • It is difficult to customize the end product

Rapid Application Development

Advantages	Disadvantages
• Can speed up systems development • Users are intensively involved from the start • Improves the process of rewriting legacy applications	• Produces functional components of final systems, but not the final systems themselves

End-User Development

Advantages	Disadvantages
• Bypasses the IS department and avoids delays • User controls the application and can change it as needed • Directly meets user requirements • Promotes increased user acceptance of new system • Frees up IT resources	• May eventually require maintenance from IS department • Documentation may be inadequate • Leads to poor quality control • System may not have adequate interfaces to existing systems • May create lower-quality systems

Object-Oriented Development

Advantages	Disadvantages
• Objects model real-world entities • New systems may be able to reuse some computer code	• Works best with systems of more limited scope (i.e., with systems that do not have huge numbers of objects)

feasibility study Investigation that gauges the probability of success of a proposed project and provides a rough assessment of the project's feasibility.

The primary task in the systems investigation stage is the feasibility study. Organizations have three basic solutions to any business problem relating to an information system: (1) do nothing and continue to use the existing system unchanged, (2) modify or enhance the existing system, or (3) develop a new system. The feasibility study analyzes which of these three solutions best fits the particular business problem. It also provides a rough assessment of the project's technical, economic, and behavioral feasibility.

- *Technical feasibility* determines whether the company can develop or otherwise acquire the hardware, software, and communications components needed to solve the business problem. Technical feasibility also determines whether the organization can use its existing technology to achieve the project's performance objectives.

- *Economic feasibility* determines whether the project is an acceptable financial risk and, if so, whether the organization has the necessary time and money to successfully complete the project. You have already learned about the commonly used methods to determine economic feasibility: NPV, ROI, breakeven analysis, and the business case approach.

- *Behavioral feasibility* addresses the human issues of the systems development project. You will be heavily involved in this aspect of the feasibility study.

After the feasibility analysis is completed, a go/no-go decision is reached by the steering committee if there is one or by top management in the absence of a committee. The go/no-go decision does not depend solely on the feasibility analysis. Organizations often have more feasible projects than they can fund. Therefore, the firm must prioritize the feasible projects and pursue those with the highest priority. Unfunded feasible projects may not be presented to the IT department at all. These projects therefore contribute to the *hidden backlog*, which are projects that the IT department is not aware of.

If the decision is no-go, then the project is either put on the shelf until conditions are more favorable or it is discarded. If the decision is go, then the project proceeds, and the systems analysis phase begins.

Systems Analysis

systems analysis The examination of the business problem that the organization plans to solve with an information system.

Once a development project has the necessary approvals from all participants, the systems analysis stage begins. Systems analysis is the process whereby systems analysts examine the business problem that the organization plans to solve with an information system.

The primary purpose of the systems analysis stage is to gather information about the existing system to determine the requirements for an enhanced system or a new system. The end product of this stage, known as the *deliverable*, is a set of *system requirements*.

Arguably, the most difficult task in systems analysis is to identify the specific requirements that the system must satisfy. These requirements are often called *user requirements*, because users (meaning you) provide them. When the systems developers have accumulated the user requirements for the new system, they proceed to the systems design stage.

Systems Design

systems design Describes how the new system will resolve the business problem.

Systems design describes how the system will resolve the business problem. The deliverable of the systems design phase is the set of *technical system specifications*, which specify the following:

- System outputs, inputs, and user interfaces
- Hardware, software, databases, telecommunications, personnel, and procedures
- A blueprint of how these components are integrated

scope creep Adding functions to an information system after the project has begun.

When the system specifications are approved by all participants, they are "frozen." That is, they should not be changed. Adding functions after the project has been initiated causes scope creep, in which the time frame and expenses associated with the project expand beyond the agreed-upon limits. Scope creep endangers both the project's budget and its schedule. Because scope creep is expensive, successful project managers place controls on changes requested by users. These controls help to prevent runaway projects.

Programming and Testing

If the organization decides to construct the software in-house, then programming begins. Programming involves translating the design specifications into computer code. This process can be lengthy and time consuming, because writing computer code is as much an art as it is a science. Large-scale systems development projects can involve hundreds of computer programmers who are charged with creating hundreds of thousands of lines of computer code. These projects employ programming teams. The teams often include functional area users, who help the programmers focus on the business problem.

Thorough and continuous testing occurs throughout the programming stage. Testing is the process that assesses whether the computer code will produce the expected and desired results. It is also intended to detect errors, or bugs, in the computer code.

programming The process of writing or coding software programs.

Implementation

Implementation (or *deployment*) is the process of converting from an old computer system to a new one. The conversion process involves organizational change. Only end users can manage organizational change, not the MIS department. The MIS department typically does not have enough credibility with the business users to manage the change process. Organizations use three major conversion strategies: direct, pilot, and phased.

In a direct conversion, the old system is cut off and the new system is turned on at a certain point in time. This type of conversion is the least expensive. It is also the riskiest because if the new system does not work as planned, there is no support from the old system. Because of these risks, few systems are implemented using direct conversion.

A pilot conversion introduces the new system in one part of the organization, such as in one plant or one functional area. The new system runs for a period of time and is then assessed. If the assessment confirms that the system is working properly, then the system is implemented in other parts of the organization.

A phased conversion introduces components of the new system, such as individual modules, in stages. Each module is assessed. If it works properly, then other modules are introduced until the entire new system is operational. Large organizations commonly combine the pilot and phased approaches. That is, they execute a phased conversion using a pilot group for each phase. A fourth strategy is *parallel conversion*, in which the old and new systems operate simultaneously for a time. This strategy is seldom used today. One reason is that parallel conversion is totally impractical when both the old and new systems are online. Imagine that you are completing an order on Amazon, only to be told, "Before your order can be entered here, you must provide all the same information again, in a different form, and on a different set of screens." The results would be disastrous for Amazon. Regardless of the type of implementation process that an organization uses, the new system may not work as advertised. In fact, the new system may cause more problems than the old system that it replaced.

implementation The process of converting from an old computer system to a new one.

direct conversion
Implementation process in which the old system is cut off and the new system is turned on at a certain point in time.

pilot conversion
Implementation process that introduces the new system in one part of the organization on a trial basis. When the new system is working properly, it is introduced in other parts of the organization.

phased conversion
Implementation process that introduces components of the new system in stages, until the entire new system is operational.

Operation and Maintenance

After the new system is implemented, it will operate for a period of time, until (like the old system it replaced) it no longer meets its objectives. Once the new system's operations are stabilized, the company performs audits to assess the system's capabilities and to determine if it is being used correctly.

Systems require several types of maintenance. The first type is *debugging* the program, a process that continues throughout the life of the system. The second type is *updating* the system to accommodate changes in business conditions. An example is adjusting to new governmental regulations, such as changes in tax rates. These corrections and upgrades usually do not add any new functions. Instead, they simply help the system continue to achieve its objectives. In contrast, the third type of maintenance *adds new functions* to the existing system without disturbing its operation.

Before you go on...

1. Describe the feasibility study.
2. What is the difference between systems analysis and systems design?
3. Describe structured programming.
4. What are the four conversion methods?

13.4 Alternative Methods and Tools for Systems Development

LEARNING OBJECTIVE

Describe alternative development methods and the tools that augment these methods.

Alternative methods for systems development include joint application design, rapid application development, agile development, and end-user development.

Joint Application Design

joint application design (JAD) A group-based tool for collecting user requirements and creating system designs.

Joint application design (JAD) is a group-based tool for collecting user requirements and creating system designs. It is most often used within the systems analysis and systems design stages of the SDLC. JAD involves a group meeting attended by the analysts and all of the users that can be conducted either in person or through the computer. During this meeting, all users jointly define and agree on the systems requirements. This process saves a tremendous amount of time. Table 13.2 lists the advantages and disadvantages of the JAD process.

Rapid Application Development

rapid application development (RAD) A development method that uses special tools and an iterative approach to rapidly produce a high-quality system.

Rapid application development (RAD) is a systems development method that can combine JAD, prototyping, and integrated computer-assisted software engineering (ICASE) tools (discussed later in this section) to rapidly produce a high-quality system. In the first RAD stage, developers use JAD sessions to collect system requirements. This strategy ensures that users are intensively involved early on. The development process in RAD is iterative; that is, requirements, designs, and the system itself are developed and then undergo a series, or sequence, of improvements. RAD uses ICASE tools to quickly structure requirements and develop prototypes. As the prototypes are developed and refined, users review them in additional JAD sessions. RAD produces the functional components of a final system rather than prototypes. To understand how RAD functions and how it differs from SDLC, see **Figure 13.6**. Table 13.2 highlights the advantages and disadvantages of the RAD process.

Agile Development

agile development A software development methodology that delivers functionality in rapid iterations, measured in weeks, requiring frequent communication, development, testing, and delivery.

Agile development is a software development methodology that delivers functionality in rapid iterations, which are usually measured in weeks. To be successful, this methodology requires frequent communication, development, testing, and delivery. Agile development focuses on rapid development and frequent user contact to create software that addresses the needs of business users. This software does not have to include every possible feature the user

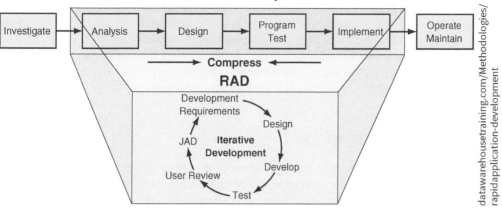

FIGURE 13.6   A rapid prototyping development process versus SDLC.

will require. Rather, it must meet only the user's more important and immediate needs. It can be updated later to introduce additional functions as they become necessary. The core tenet of agile development is to do only what you have to do to be successful right now.

One type of agile development uses the *scrum approach*. A key principle of scrum is that during a project, users can change their minds about what they want and need. Scrum acknowledges that a development problem cannot be fully understood or defined from the start. Therefore, scrum focuses on maximizing the development team's ability to deliver iterations quickly and to respond effectively to additional user requirements as they emerge.

Scrum contains sets of practices and predefined roles. The primary roles are:

- *Scrum master:* Maintains the processes (typically replaces a project manager)
- *Product owner:* Represents the business users and any other stakeholders in the project
- *Team:* A cross-functional group of about seven people who perform the actual analysis, design, coding, implementation, testing, and so on

Scrum works this way: during each *sprint*—typically a two- to four-week period—the team creates a potentially shippable product increment, such as working and tested software. The set of features that goes into each sprint comes from the product backlog, which is a prioritized set of high-level work requirements to be completed.

The sprint planning meeting determines which backlog items will be addressed during a sprint. During this meeting, the product owner informs the team of the items in the product backlog that he or she wants to be completed. The team members then determine how many of these projects they can commit to during the next sprint, and they record this information in the sprint backlog.

During a sprint, no one is allowed to change the sprint backlog, which means that the requirements are frozen for the sprint. Each sprint must end on time. If the requirements are not completed for any reason, then they are left out and returned to the product backlog. After each sprint is completed, the team demonstrates how to use the software.

An interesting type of agile development is a methodology called *minimum viable product (MVP)* development. Applications developed using MVP methodology have just the required amount of functionality to operate successfully. On the other hand, MVP applications do not have so much functionality (i.e., too many features) that the development process takes too long and costs too much.

DevOps

DevOps (a combination of "development" and "operations") is a practice that was first presented in 2009 and has really gained traction in the last few years. DevOps is a form of software development that brings the developers and the users (operations) together throughout the entire process with the goal of reducing the time to deployment, increasing the usability of the finished product, and lowering the cost of new app development.

There are several factors that have increased the applications of DevOps methodology. First, organizations have less time to develop and deploy applications, there is less room for error, and the number of applications being developed is on the rise. In fact, a recent study showed that most organizations plan to release 17 applications each year. The DevOps framework is a solid response to the business pressures organizations face today.

End-User Development

end-user development
Approach in which the organization's end users develop their own applications with little or no formal assistance from the IT department.

shadow IT   Technology implemented by end-users without receiving proper approvals from the organizational IT department.

End-user development is an approach in which the organization's end users develop their own applications with little or no formal assistance from the IT department. Table 13.2 lists the advantages and disadvantages of end-user development. Sometimes this form of IT development or acquisition is called **Shadow IT** (also known as *Stealth IT* or *Rogue IT*). While the end users bypassing the IT department might make it easier for them to adopt the tools that they want to work with, this process also bypasses the security measures that the IT department is trying to enforce. These shadow IT systems can open systems to vulnerabilities and create avenues for criminals to access private company and customer data. As an employee, it is important to carefully consider adopting something that has not been approved by your organization. If your shadow IT creates a vulnerability that allows a breach, you will probably lose your job!

Tools for Systems Development

Several tools can be used with various systems development methods. These tools include prototyping, integrated computer-assisted software engineering, component-based development, and object-oriented development.

Design Thinking   Design thinking is a user-centered approach to application development. As you saw in the discussion of the SDLC, users' needs are considered at the very beginning of the process. And users are considered in all development methodologies. Unfortunately, development teams often move away from users' needs as they move toward the technical development of applications, integrations, implementations, and other considerations. Design thinking is an approach that, when used in conjunction with other development methodologies, will keep the user's needs front and center, increasing the chances of a successful adoption of the project. There are five steps to the design-thinking process:

Empathize: Empathy is the ability to see how a situation could feel to another person. Empathy does not mean you agree with the feeling, problem, or situation. Rather, you simply learn to see it as the other person does. In the design process, this helps designers and managers to set aside their own assumptions and feelings in order to see the situation as the person who will be the recipient of the final product. This is critical to successful IT projects and the reason why so many projects today include users in the entire process.

Define: In the Define stage, the problem is defined from the perspective of the user that the developers empathized with in the first stage. The problem is not stated in terms of systems, managerial goals, or corporate strategy. Rather, the focus is kept on the user and how the outcome of the project will change the way they accomplish their tasks.

Ideate: Brainstorming comes in many forms and methods. The important thing at this stage is that ideas are based on stages 1 and 2. Ideas are more likely to move the team toward a successful outcome when they are generated from a well-formed, empathy-based problem statement. There is no magic potion, except that all ideas have to stay aligned with the first two stages.

Prototype and Test: Stages 4 and 5 of design thinking can incorporate any of the development tools discussed below and any of the methods presented above. SDLC, RAD, JAD, and Agile all include users, but not to the extent or in the fashion of the design thinking process.

Design thinking is presented here as a linear process, but in practice, it is very nonlinear. The goal is to keep these considerations at the top of your mind during the entire project. For example, as you prototype and test a program, you will likely deepen your empathy for the users which can improve ideas and future iterations of the application.

Prototyping

The **prototyping** approach defines an initial list of user requirements, builds a model of the system, and then refines the system in several iterations based on users' feedback. Developers do not try to obtain a complete set of user specifications for the system at the outset, and they do not plan to develop the system all at once. Instead, they quickly develop a smaller version of the system known as a **prototype**. A prototype can take two forms. In some cases, it contains only the components of the new system that are of most interest to the users. In other cases, it is a small-scale working model of the entire system.

Users make suggestions for improving the prototype based on their experiences with it. The developers then review the prototype with the users and use their suggestions to refine it. This process continues through several iterations until the users approve the system or it becomes apparent that the system cannot meet the users' needs. If the system is viable, then the developers can use the prototype to build the full system. One typical use of prototyping is to develop screens that a user will see and interact with. Table 13.2 describes the advantages and disadvantages of the prototyping approach.

A practical problem with prototyping is that a prototype usually looks more complete than it actually is. That is, it may not use the real database, it usually does not have the necessary error checking, and it almost never includes the necessary security features. Users who review a prototype that resembles the finished system may not recognize these problems. Consequently, they might have unrealistic expectations about how close the actual system is to completion.

Integrated Computer-Assisted Software Engineering Tools

Computer-aided software engineering (CASE) refers to a group of tools that automate many of the tasks in the SDLC. The tools that are used to automate the early stages of the SDLC (systems investigation, analysis, and design) are called **upper CASE tools**. The tools used to automate later stages in the SDLC (programming, testing, operation, and maintenance) are called **lower CASE tools**. CASE tools that provide links between upper CASE and lower CASE tools are called **integrated CASE (ICASE) tools**. Table 13.2 lists the advantages and disadvantages of ICASE tools.

Component-Based Development

Component-based development uses standard components to build applications. Components are reusable applications that generally have one specific function, such as a shopping cart, user authentication, or a catalog. Compared with other approaches, component-based development generally involves less programming and more assembly. Component-based development is closely linked with the idea of Web services and service-oriented architectures, which you will study in Technology Guide 3.

Many startup companies are pursuing the idea of component-based application development. One example is Ning (**www.ning.com**), which allows organizations to create, customize, and share their own social network.

Object-Oriented Development

Object-oriented development is based on a different view of computer systems than the perception that characterizes traditional development approaches. Traditional approaches can produce a system that performs the original task but may not be suited for handling other tasks. This limitation applies even when these other tasks involve the same real-world entities. For example, a billing system will handle billing, but it probably cannot be adapted to handle mailings for the marketing department or to generate leads for the sales force. This is true even though the billing, marketing, and sales functions all use similar data, including customer names, addresses, and purchases. In contrast, an *object-oriented (OO) system* begins not with the task to be performed, but with the aspects of the real world that must be modeled to perform that task. Therefore, in our example, if the firm has a good model of its customers and its interactions with them, then it can use this model equally well for billings, mailings, and sales leads.

The development process for an object-oriented system begins with a feasibility study and an analysis of the existing system. Systems developers identify the *objects* in the new system—the fundamental elements in OO analysis and design. Each object represents a tangible, real-world entity such as a customer, bank account, student, or course. Objects have *properties*, or *data values*. For example, a customer has an identification number, a name, an address, an account number(s), and so on. Objects also contain the *operations* that can

prototyping An approach that defines an initial list of user requirements, builds a prototype system, and then improves the system in several iterations based on users' feedback.

prototype A small-scale working model of an entire system or a model that contains only the components of the new system that are of most interest to the users.

computer-aided software engineering (CASE) Development approach that uses specialized tools to automate many of the tasks in the SDLC. Upper CASE tools automate the early stages of the SDLC and lower CASE tools automate the later stages.

upper CASE tools Tools that are used to automate the early stages of the SDLC (systems investigation, analysis, and design).

lower CASE tools Tools used to automate later stages in the SDLC (programming, testing, operation, and maintenance).

integrated CASE (ICASE) tools CASE tools that provide links between upper CASE and lower CASE tools.

component-based development A software development methodology that uses standard components to build applications.

object-oriented development A systems development methodology that begins with aspects of the real world that must be modeled to perform a task.

be performed on their properties. For example, operations that can be performed on the customer object may include obtain-account-balance, open-account, withdraw-funds, and so on. Operations are also referred to as *behaviors*.

This approach enables OO analysts to define all the relevant objects needed for the new system, including their properties and operations. The analysts then model how the objects interact to meet the objectives of the new system. In some cases, analysts can reuse existing objects from other applications (or from a library of objects) in the new system. This process saves the analysts the time they otherwise would spend coding these objects. In most cases, however, even with object reuse, some coding will be necessary to customize the objects and their interactions for the new system.

containers A method of developing applications that run independently of the base operating system of the server.

Containers   Containers are a method of developing applications that run independently of the base operating system of the server. Containers allow application providers to develop, test, and deploy technology that will always run in practice exactly like it does in testing. This would allow software to be developed more rapidly. Primarily, they provide a level of portability that has brought about one of the biggest shifts in application development in years

To better understand containers, imagine that your vehicle is a container. You only interact with the environment inside the vehicle (the container). Your vehicle can travel on different types of terrain (platforms), but you do the same things inside (gas, brakes, lights, signals, etc.). The vehicle (container) has features built in to help manage the external environment (tires, shocks, windshield wipers, etc.). Containers have begun to revolutionize the speed of development because developers can focus on the container rather than the environments.

Application developers have always been plagued with platform challenges. (A platform is an underlying computer system on which application programs can run. On personal computers, Windows and Mac OS X are examples of platforms.) As one example, if a developer built an application in a Windows environment, then it might not run properly if it were deployed after a Windows update. In addition, it probably would not work in a Linux environment. Further, multiple versions of an application need to be developed to run on different environments, and they have to be continuously tested on platform updates.

One solution for this problem is to build and test applications on a virtual machine and then implement them on an identical virtual machine for customers. A *virtual machine* is a self-contained operating environment that behaves as if it were a separate physical computer. Building and testing on a virtual machine ensures that an application developed on one platform will run on a different platform. But what if you could develop an application that included its own environment and would run as it was developed regardless of the operating system on which it was deployed? That is exactly the idea behind a container.

Containers are not new; in fact, they have been tested since 2005. However, they were not widely embraced by mainstream IT leaders until 2014. The increased popularity of containers is largely due to Docker, an open-source project by Docker, Inc. (www.docker.com). Docker is a Linux-based product that enables applications to be developed and deployed in a container. Docker-created apps will run on any platform.

Low-Code/No-Code Development Platform   Low-Code Development Platforms (LCDPs) make use of visual interfaces to develop applications rather than traditional procedural hand-coding. LCDPs were first discussed as "no-code" but it was not practical because any integration with other existing systems relied on code. The amount of code necessary was reduced, but not removed, so the name "low-code" was adopted for this tool. This method allows for more rapid app development (because it reduces the amount of code that has to be written), and an expansion of those who can contribute to a project. LCDPs allow nontechnical users to provide input and efforts into app development. LCDPs will help to extend end-user development by making it easier to produce new programs with less formal training.

Apple has introduced a new enterprise development platform with low-code/no-code capabilities. Their product, called Claris Connect, allows users with little to no programming experience stitch together apps by connecting components of popular online services such as Trello, Slack, DocuSign, and Box, among others. Claris Connect uses a drag-and-drop interface for users to create workflows. Similarly, on the consumer side, Apple has created an app called "Shortcuts" that is drag-and-drop development that also stitches together apps that are installed on users' devices. It creates automation, reminders, and triggers to create workflows across apps saving users time and effort.

No-code is exactly that. There is no code required by the programmer. Visual tools are used to drop and drag components to design functional apps. Both low-code and no-code are discussed with applications in the closing case.

One example of no-code is Robotic Process Automation (RPA). This emerging technology is discussed in IT's About Business 13.1.

You have studied many methods that can be used to acquire new systems. Table 13.2 provides an overview of the advantages and disadvantages of each of these methods.

IT's About Business **13.1**

MIS Robotic Process Automation

When people hear the term *robotic*, they might think of R2D2 from *Star Wars*. The term *process* might create images of workflow, steps, procedures, and directions. *Automation* likely brings to mind an assembly line with robots performing repetitive tasks.

But, what is robotic process automation (RPA) within the context of digital computer technology? To answer this question, we first need to define a robot as any technology that can be programmed to complete a repetitive task independent of outside user interaction. We then need to define automation within the context of any physical or intellectual workflow.

Let's consider one example before we define RPA: Think about a smartphone. It does many things for you. These actions are referred to as *shortcuts*. Further, you can customize many of these shortcuts to match your specific needs. For example, your phone can send a command to turn your home lights on or off when you reach a specific location. You can also install shortcuts to communicate your arrival time, identify music, compare prices, create GIFs, and more. The possibilities are almost endless. These shortcuts are designed to automate a series of tasks. You only have to trigger the shortcut. It will then open the app and navigate through the steps for you.

Within this context, we will now define RPA. RPA is an emerging technology that replaces human effort by programming computers to perform repetitive, mundane tasks. Computers can perform these tasks more consistently and quickly than humans. RPA mimics human actions within digital systems just as assembly-line robots mimic human activities on a physical product. This technology enables organizations to automate manual, rule-based, repetitive tasks by building shortcuts that accurately complete mundane work for their business operations.

Why Are Companies Investing in Automation?

Many CIOs are turning to RPA to streamline enterprise operations and reduce costs by improving efficiency and accuracy. RPA also frees employees from routine, repetitive tasks so they can focus on higher-value work.

RPA operates in three ways: attended, unattended, and hybrid. We define each of these and then present applications and examples.

Attended RPA is a method that an employee triggers. For example, imagine an employee who is copying product information from the sales system into the inventory system. This process involves more than 10 steps. With RPA, the employee can run a program to perform the same process. However, the employee has to start the process. It is not automatic.

Unattended RPA is an event-based method that does not require human interaction to run. When a specific event occurs, the RPA launches a sequence of tasks. The trigger is typically time based, enabling unattended RPA to run according to a predetermined schedule. However, it can also be based on other events.

Hybrid RPA is the most common type of RPA. An end-to-end workflow generally employs attended and unattended RPA that work together to complete a task. For example, an unattended RPA could analyze data and present the output to a user. After considering the insights, the user identifies a solution and utilizes attended automation to execute the next series of actions. Together, these activities make up a hybrid RPA process.

Applications

Now that we understand what RPA is and how it functions, we examine several applications where RPA has impacted and will continue to impact daily routines.

Returns processing has traditionally been a costly manual process (see IT's About Business 11.2). With RPA, companies can manage returns more rapidly and at a reduced cost. RPA software can manage the bulk of the process, which includes a series of repetitive steps. Each organization's process is unique, but most systems perform the same basic actions: (a) send a message confirming receipt of the return, (b) update the inventory, (c) make a payment adjustment to the customer, and (d) ensure that the internal billing system is updated. RPA can easily automate these tasks.

Customer service agents deal with situations that vary from routine to highly unique. However, the process of gathering the necessary information is the same. When a customer contacts customer service with a question or problem, several pieces of data are necessary to identify the customer and the order. Many organizations have turned to RPA-driven chatbots to gather information and direct customers to the correct agent. RPA enables organizations to resolve problems more quickly, thereby enhancing customer satisfaction.

Manufacturing has utilized RPA to automate accounts payable, invoice processing, and supply chain management. In addition, RPA can order standardized inventory, report inventory levels, send automated reports to management, file invoices, drive sales, and handle data management for better reporting standards. Employing RPA to execute these processes improves the consistency and accuracy of the data.

Healthcare involves numerous manual tasks, each of which affects patient satisfaction. A single appointment to a medical facility involves invoice processing, claim management, appointment scheduling, billing, and many other activities. Today, RPA performs all these functions. In addition, it contributes to a faster patient check-out experience.

Cybersecurity employs RPA to improve security within applications, secure networks, and enhance threat prevention. RPA can also minimize potential attacks and threats by providing continuous protection. It can perform routine audits and eliminate unauthorized access. If a security breach occurs, RPA can quickly lock down the system and contact the appropriate individual or group. Without this rapid intervention, a breach can develop into a large-scale attack.

Benefits of RPA

RPA can increase a team's work capacity by 35 to 50 percent. Simple, repetitive tasks such as copying and pasting information between business systems can be accelerated by 30 to 50 percent when completed using RPA. In addition, organizations reported improved compliance (92 percent), better accuracy and quality (90 percent), enhanced productivity (86 percent), and cost reduction (59 percent). According to a 2022 Forrester research report, the market for RPA software solutions is expected to reach $22 billion by 2025.

RPA is growing in popularity and application. It streamlines workflows, which makes organizations more profitable, flexible, and responsive. It also increases employee satisfaction, engagement, and productivity by freeing them from mundane tasks. RPA can be rapidly deployed, and it can accelerate digital transformation. It is a growing field with a bright future.

And why shouldn't it be? After all, we like shortcuts on our phones. Why should we not have them for work?

Questions

1. **What is RPA?**
2. **Identify and explain the three types of RPA.**
3. **Why are organizations so interested in RPA initiatives?**

Sources: Compiled from A. Singh, "What Is Robotic Process Automation and How Can It Save You Time?," makeuseof. com, October 22, 2022; L. Raj, "Leveraging AI to Empower Your Knowledge Workforce," *Forbes*, October 18, 2022; J. Duez, "Surviving the Perfect Storm," *Forbes*, October 17, 2022; C. Basu Mallick, "What Is Robotic Process Automation (RPA)? Meaning, Working, Software, and Uses," *Spiceworks*, October 11, 2022; E. Ajao, "RPA Vendor Automation Anywhere Aims at Process Discovery," *TechTarget*, October 4, 2022; J. Bloomberg, "How UiPath Hopes to Reinvent Enterprise Automation," *SiliconANGLE*, October 1, 2022; J. Edwards, "Is Robotic Process Automation (RPA) the Next Big Thing in Automation?" readwrite.com, July 16, 2022; T. Olavsrud and C. Boulton, "What Is RPA? A Revolution in Business Process Automation," *CIO*, June 29, 2022; D. Edwards, "How Is Robotic Process Automation Revolutionising Businesses around the World?," April 20, 2022; L. Joseph and B. Schaffrik, "The RPA Market Will Grow to $22 Billion by 2025," Forrester, February 22, 2022; K. Casey, "4 Robotic Process Automation (RPA) Trends to Watch in 2022," *The Enterprisers Project*, January 6, 2022; S. Pritchard, "How Robotic Process Automation Is Getting Smarter as It Evolves," *ComputerWeekly*, April 12, 2021; K. Casey, "How to Explain Robotic Process Automation (RPA) in Plain English," *The Enterprisers Project*, July 30, 2020; and https://www.microsoft.com/en-us/worklab/work-trend-index/, accessed October 24, 2022.

Before you go on...

1. Describe the tools that augment the traditional SDLC.
2. Describe the alternate methods that can be used for systems development other than the SDLC.

What's in IT for Me?

ACCT For the Accounting Major

Accounting personnel help perform cost–benefit analyses on proposed projects. They may also monitor ongoing project costs to keep them within budget. Accounting personnel undoubtedly will find themselves involved with systems development at various points throughout their careers.

FIN For the Finance Major

Finance personnel are frequently involved with the financial issues that accompany any large-scale systems development project (e.g., budgeting). They also are involved in cost–benefit and risk analyses. To perform these tasks, they need to stay abreast of the emerging techniques used to determine project costs and ROI. Finally, because they must manage vast amounts of information, finance departments are also common recipients of new systems.

MKT For the Marketing Major

In most organizations, marketing, like finance, involves massive amounts of data and information. Like finance, then, marketing is also a hotbed of systems development. Marketing personnel will increasingly find themselves participating in systems development teams. Such involvement increasingly means helping to develop systems, especially Web-based systems that reach out directly from the organization to its customers.

POM For the Production/Operations Management Major

Participation in development teams is a common role for production/operations people. Manufacturing is becoming increasingly computerized and integrated with other allied systems, from design to logistics to customer support. Production systems interface frequently with marketing, finance, and human resources. They may also be part of a larger enterprise-wide system. Also, many end users in POM either develop their own systems or collaborate with IT personnel on specific applications.

HRM For the Human Resources Management Major

The human resources department is closely involved with several aspects of the systems acquisitions process. Acquiring new systems may require hiring new employees, changing job descriptions, or terminating employees. Human resources staff perform all of these tasks. Furthermore, if the organization hires consultants for the

development project, or outsources it, the human resources department may handle the contracts with these suppliers.

MIS For the MIS Major

Regardless of the approach that the organization adopts for acquiring new systems, the MIS department spearheads it. If the organization chooses either to buy or to lease the application, the MIS department leads in examining the offerings of the various vendors and in negotiating with the vendors. If the organization chooses to develop the application in-house, then the process falls to the MIS department. MIS analysts work closely with users to develop their information requirements. MIS programmers then write the computer code, test it, and implement the new system.

Summary

13.1 Discuss the different cost–benefit analyses that companies must take into account when formulating an IT strategic plan.

The four common approaches to cost–benefit analysis are the following:

1. *The net present value* method converts future values of benefits to their present-value equivalent by discounting them at the organization's cost of funds. They can then compare the present value of the future benefits with the cost required to achieve those benefits to determine whether the benefits exceed the costs.

2. *Return on investment* measures management's effectiveness in generating profits with its available assets. ROI is calculated by dividing net income attributable to a project by the average assets invested in the project. ROI is a percentage, and the higher the percentage return, the better.

3. *Breakeven analysis* determines the point at which the cumulative dollar value of the benefits from a project equals the investment made in the project.

4. In the *business case approach*, system developers write a business case to justify funding one or more specific applications or projects.

13.2 Discuss the four business decisions that companies must make when they acquire new applications.

- *How much computer code does the company want to write?* A company can choose to use a totally prewritten application (write no computer code), to customize a prewritten application (write some computer code), or to customize an entire application (write all new computer code).

- *How will the company pay for the application?* Once the company has decided how much computer code to write, it must decide how to pay for it. With prewritten applications or customized prewritten applications, companies can buy them or lease them. With totally custom applications, companies use internal funding.

- *Where will the application run?* Companies must decide where to run the application. The company may run the application on its own platform or run the application on someone else's platform (use either a software-as-a-service vendor or an application service provider).

- *Where will the application originate?* Prewritten applications can be open-source software or come from a vendor. Companies may choose to customize prewritten open-source applications or prewritten proprietary applications from vendors. Companies may customize applications in-house or outsource the customization. They also can write totally custom applications in-house or outsource this process.

13.3 Enumerate the primary tasks and the importance of each of the six processes involved in the systems development life cycle.

The six processes are the following:

1. *Systems investigation:* Addresses the business problem (or business opportunity) by means of the feasibility study. The main task in the systems investigation stage is the feasibility study.

2. *Systems analysis:* Examines the business problem that the organization plans to solve with an information system. Its main purpose is to gather information about the existing system to determine the requirements for the new system. The end product of this stage, known as the "deliverable," is a set of system requirements.

3. *Systems design:* Describes how the system will resolve the business problem. The deliverable is the set of technical system specifications.

4. *Programming and testing:* Programming translates the design specifications into computer code; testing checks to see whether the computer code will produce the expected and desired results and detects errors, or bugs, in the computer code. A deliverable is the new application.

5. *Implementation:* The process of converting from the old system to the new system through three major conversion strategies: direct, pilot, and phased. A deliverable is a properly working application.

6. *Operation and maintenance:* Types of maintenance include debugging, updating, and adding new functions when needed.

13.4 Describe alternative development methods and tools that augment development methods.

These are the *alternative methods:*

- *Joint application design* is a group-based tool for collecting user requirements and creating system designs.
- *Rapid application development* is a systems development method that can combine JAD, prototyping, and ICASE tools to rapidly produce a high-quality system.
- *Agile development* is a software development methodology that delivers functionality in rapid iterations, which are usually measured in weeks.
- *DevOps* is a software development methodology that includes employees from the IT *DEV*elopment group and the user *OP*erations group. The goal is to keep users involved in the entire development process.
- *End-user development* refers to an organization's end users developing their own applications with little or no formal assistance from the IT department.

These are the *tools:*

- *Design thinking* directs developers to create a deep understanding of users' needs by empathizing with their needs and defining the problem from the user perspective. Ideas and prototypes are generated to address this problem. The testing phase reveals a deeper appreciation for the user, clarifying empathy, and directing future revisions to the project.
- The *prototyping* approach defines an initial list of user requirements, builds a model of the system, and then improves the system in several iterations based on users' feedback.
- *Integrated computer-aided software engineering* combines upper CASE tools (automate systems investigation, analysis, and design) and lower CASE tools (programming, testing, operation, and maintenance).
- *Component-based development* uses standard components to build applications. Components are reusable applications that generally have one specific function, such as a shopping cart, user authentication, or a catalog.
- *Object-oriented development* begins with the aspects of the real world that must be modeled to perform that task. Systems developers identify the objects in the new system. Each object represents a tangible, real-world entity such as a customer, bank account, student, or course. Objects have *properties*, or *data values*. Objects also contain the *operations* that can be performed on their properties.

Table 13.2 shows advantages and disadvantages of alternative methods and tools.

Key Terms

agile development   408
application portfolio   395
application service provider (ASP)   401
component-based development   411
computer-aided software engineering
   (CASE)   411
containers   412
continuous application development   402
direct conversion   407
end-user development   410
feasibility study   406
implementation   407
integrated CASE (ICASE) tools   411

IS operational plan   397
IT steering committee   396
IT strategic plan   396
joint application design (JAD)   408
lower CASE tools   411
object-oriented development   411
outsourcing   402
phased conversion   407
pilot conversion   407
programmers   404
programming   407
prototype   411
prototyping   411

rapid application development (RAD)   408
scope creep   406
shadow IT   410
software-as-a-service (SaaS)   401
systems analysis   406
systems analysts   404
systems design   406
systems development life cycle
   (SDLC)   403
systems investigation   12
systems stakeholders   404
technical specialists   404
upper CASE tools   411

Discussion Questions

1. Discuss the advantages of a lease option over a buy option.

2. Why is it important for all business managers to understand the issues of IT resource acquisition?

3. Why is it important for everyone in business organizations to have a basic understanding of the systems development process?

4. Should prototyping be used on every systems development project? Why or why not?

5. Discuss the various types of feasibility studies. Why are they all needed?

6. Discuss the issue of assessing intangible benefits and the proposed solutions.

7. Discuss the reasons why end-user–developed information systems can be of poor quality. What can be done to improve this situation?

Problem-Solving Activities

1. Access www.ecommerceguide.com. Find the product review area. Read reviews of three software payment solutions. Assess them as possible components.

2. Use an Internet search engine to obtain information on CASE and ICASE tools. Select several vendors and compare and contrast their offerings.

3. Access www.ning.com. Observe how the site provides components for you to use to build applications. Build a small application at the site.

4. Enter www.ibm.com/software. Find its WebSphere product. Read recent customers' success stories. What makes this software so popular?

5. Enter the websites of Gartner (www.gartner.com), 451 Research (www.451research.com), and CIO (www.cio.com). Search for recent material about ASPs and outsourcing, and prepare a report on your findings.

6. StoreFront (www.storefront.net) is a vendor of e-business software. At its site, the company provides demonstrations illustrating the types of storefronts that it can create for shoppers. The site also provides demonstrations of how the company's software is used to create a store.

    a. Run the StoreFront demonstration to see how this is done.

    b. What features does StoreFront provide?

    c. Does StoreFront support smaller or larger stores?

    d. What other products does StoreFront offer for creating online stores? What types of stores do these products support?

7. Visit www.forbes.com and read the article titled "Build Vs. Buy: Why Most Businesses Should Buy Their Next Software Solution". Do you agree with the author? Why or why not?

8. Visit www.trustradius.com/agile-development. Select one of the featured tools and describe its benefits.

Closing Case

Low-Code/No-Code Development

The Business Problem

Most companies are not in the business of writing computer code to build software applications. All companies, however, employ software applications to run their business. Further, all software applications need to be regularly monitored and updated. Most organizations hire employees to perform this task. However, what do they do when the system needs a programming update, a new integration, or an extra feature added to support customers? Going further, what does an organization do when it needs to acquire an entirely new system?

Most organizations look to their IT department to address these scenarios. Today, however, the rate of change is quickly outpacing the availability of professional programmers. As a society, we are facing a developer shortage. Moreover, as the supply of programmers decreases relative to the increased demand, prices—in this case, salaries—will also increase. As a result, many businesses cannot afford the wages that programmers can earn. At the same time, the demand for software is increasing, and most companies cannot keep up with that demand. As a result, many IT projects remain unfinished, lost somewhere in the pending file.

The Technology Solution

What if advances in technology could help resolve this problem? Specifically, what if software designers and programmers could build programs that enable less technologically skilled workers to create programs with minimal or no coding required? This idea has been in development for many years. Recently, it seems to be gaining traction. It is referred to as *low-code/no-code* software development. Low-code/no-code applications enable employees who do not have software backgrounds to automate parts of their day-to-day responsibilities. At the same time, the IT group maintains oversight of security and access rights.

Although low-code and no-code are closely related, they are not the same, and it is important to know the difference. Let's take a closer look.

Low-Code. Low-code is a rapid application development technique that utilizes visual building blocks, such as point-and-click, drag-and-drop, and pull-down menu options. This automation enables users to focus on what makes their software unique rather than repeat the same code used in other applications.

For example, low-code might offer a drag-and-drop function that enables the user to upload files. This function would be a pre-written option: The user would simply drag-and-drop the "upload file" option into the application. They would not write the code that would access the file browser and upload and store the identified file. This function is standard and does not create a competitive advantage.

However, what the user does with that file might create a competitive advantage. For example, they could customize the file by scanning it for data, editing it, adding it to other files, or time stamping it. In contrast to the upload feature, these custom pieces need to be coded. This technique is referred to as *low-code* because only part of the process needs to be coded.

Although low-code development has limitations, it is effective when users are reorganizing workflows and updating interfaces. According to Gartner, the most common uses of low-code development are forms, workflows, and tools that replace paper, e-mail, or spreadsheets.

From a skills perspective, low-code development lies in the middle of the app development spectrum. "Pro-code," the traditional model, lies at one extreme, and "no-code" lies at the other.

No-Code. No-code development operates just as it sounds: It does not require any coding. No-code tools typically focus on a relatively narrow set of solutions or operations such as mobile app and chatbot builders, workflow automation, and website-design tools.

In contrast to low-code environments where developers might be involved in scripting and manual coding, the no-code approach depends entirely on visual tools. In this situation, a user can point-and-click and drag-and-drop, but there is no direct access to the code. No-code development opens the world of technology to a whole new audience of users who are not technical experts.

No-code tools can perform a broad range of functions. For example, they can create custom user interfaces for the Web or mobile applications. They can also create dashboards for analytics, display key performance indicators, and more. No-code methods increase process automation and implement decision authorizations.

Jack Welch, former CEO of General Electric, once observed, "If the rate of change on the outside exceeds the rate of change on the inside, the end is near." This assertion is valid only if there are no adjustments to the inside rate of change. Low-code/no-code is a technology response to accelerate development to ensure that the rate of change on the inside matches the outside.

Success Stories

Intercom (www.intercom.com) provides an engagement OS; that is, it offers a unified solution for all customer-facing areas such as sales, customer support, and marketing to collaborate. Their product enables businesses to connect with customers across the customer journey. Intercom's engagement OS is a low-code/no-code platform that empowers customer support professionals to develop automation themselves rather than wait for someone in the IT group to build it.

In an October 2022 product update, Intercom released their next-generation messenger, which enables customers to completely customize the platform with their colors, fonts, and styling to match their brand. More important, it allows for multiple feature configurations so the company can enable different levels of communications for different accounts. Other improvements include spaces such as "home," "help," or "news," Web and mobile messengers, content suggestions based on machine learning, and checklists.

Infragistics designs development tools that enable their customers to develop meaningful user interfaces and user experiences. In a July 2022 toolkit release, the company added low-code features to their product to accelerate the transition from the design for an application to the code production. This innovation will enable clients to build their customers' journeys more effectively. Modifications are easy, so Infragistics can build and test multiple options before they fully implement an update to their clients. This process is iterative, and it enables the company to engage in user-informed development until the customer experience is perfected.

Flow Designer is a low-code solution offered by Service-Now. ServiceNow is a platform that empowers companies to break down silos and share data across the entire organization. They are focused on developing their platform with a low-code/no-code process at its core. Their next goal is to create an ERP tool. With their focus on easy integrations and low-code development, ServiceNow will be primed to provide enterprise connectivity and the necessary agility to work in today's environment.

Conclusions

Modern organizations are searching for tools and strategies to overcome the gap between their software development needs and the availability of skilled programmers. Using low-code/no-code platforms empowers organizations to increase the speed of deployment while decreasing their reliance on professional programmers.

The number of tools and platforms designed to move development from the IT professionals to employees in other departments will continue to grow. However, there will always be a need for skilled programmers. Thousands of legacy systems are not prepared to work on modern information systems. Further, low-code/no-code systems do not build themselves. Someone must do the hard work of developing the systems.

Today, low-code/no-code development solutions are incorporated into rapid application development as a vast improvement to traditional development processes. They empower businesses to transform software development as we know it. Low-code/no-code development makes technology easier to build and utilize, boosts business agility, simplifies connections between people and data points, and increases the organization's overall efficiency.

Questions

1. What is low-code programming?
2. What is no-code programming?
3. How will low-code/no-code programming shift the labor needs in IT?
4. How will organizations benefit from the use of low-code/no-code platforms?

Sources: Compiled from R. Wood, "How to Balance Risk and Empowerment with Low-Code/No-Code Apps," *Acceleration Money*, October 20, 2022; K. Mullican, "How Low-Code/No-Code Addresses Custom Software Development Challenges," Acceleration Economy, October 20, 2022; G. Hulbert, "Low-Code, Not Low Tech," *Forbes*, October 18, 2022; J. Torres, "The Software Developer's Fate in Low-Code/No-Code World," *CMSWire*, October 12, 2022; Intercom, Inc., "Intercom Announces Major Updates to its Most Used Product: the Intercom Messenger," press release, prnewswire.com, October 12, 2022; P. Britt, "Low-Code and No-Code Making Inroads in Financial Services," *CMSWire*, October 4, 2022; S. Clark, "How Low-Code/No-Code Are Changing CX Design," *CMSWire*, September 21, 2022; A. Beatty, "Banking Gets Up to Code: Low-Code and No-Code Development That Is...," *Finextra*, August 29, 2022; Infragistics, "Infragistics Adds Low-Code Features & UI/UX Controls for Major Frameworks in Ultimate 22.1 Toolkit Release," press release, globenewswire.com, July 14, 2022; R. Cameron, "Why Low-Code Development Is a Game Changer," *Forbes*, July 7, 2022; V. Kruse, "Co-Code—Is This How We Deliver Value for Both IT and Business?," diginomica.com, June 10, 2022; D. Preez, "CEO Bill McDermott's Next Play Will See ServiceNow Go After ERP Modernization," diginomica.com, May 11, 2022; V. Aiyer, "Are No-Code Platforms Making Developers Redundant?," *Forbes*, March 14, 2022; K. Bhasin, "6 Technologists Discuss How No-Code Tools Are Changing Software Development," *TechCrunch*, March 10, 2022; V. Takru, "The Fundamentals of Mobile Application Development: Five Things to Consider," *Forbes*, November 29, 2021; D. Binunsky, "How Low-Code and No-Code Solutions Compare to RAD," DevOps.com, July 24, 2019; and R. Sheldon, "What Are the Advantages of Rapid Application Development?," *Tech Target*, January 5, 2018.

Artificial Intelligence

Opening Case

MIS **POM** **Artificial Intelligence in Amazon Fulfillment Centers**

The Good News

Amazon fulfillment centers are behind every same-day delivery that we enjoy. These centers process millions of items per day, three times more than what was possible at Amazon's warehouses only a decade ago. Constantly improving technology helps Amazon remain ahead of Walmart, Target, and many other retailers, which are now adopting many of the practices that Amazon pioneered years ago. One of these technologies is machine learning, which includes robots, computer vision systems, and productivity-

tracking systems. Let's begin our discussion of Amazon's use of artificial intelligence by examining the company's fulfillment center operations.

At the fulfillment centers, workers unload inventory items from trucks and place them on conveyor belts. The system automatically scans incoming items, lists them for sale on Amazon.com, and generates payments to suppliers. Other workers remove products from the conveyor belts and place the items on shelves, standing beside chain-link fences that separate them from the robots. In the past, these workers physically scanned bar codes to determine where an item should go. Today, video cameras automatically identify the items that workers take from bins, and green light beams illuminate the places on the shelves where workers should place each item.

In 2012, Amazon purchased Kiva Systems, which developed and produced warehouse robots. Previously, when a customer placed an order, workers had to walk through warehouse aisles to retrieve products from shelves, sometimes using hard copies of orders to locate certain items. In contrast, today the Kiva robots bring shelves of products to waiting employees, who pick the necessary items from each shelf to fulfill the order, place them in a bin, and send them along the assembly line to be packed and shipped.

Managers once used Excel spreadsheets to determine the number of workers needed at each station to keep up with customer orders. To automate this process, Amazon spreadsheet experts met with software engineers to develop the firm's warehouse management system, which is based on machine learning.

At first, this system was error-prone and slow. It overreacted to small changes in demand, sending workers hurrying to new stations, only to send them back to their previous positions after a couple of hours, a time-consuming and wasteful process. In another example, one early recommendation placed half an employee at one station and half an employee at another. However, the system learned from experience and improved over time.

Today, Amazon fulfillment center managers rely on the warehouse management system's recommendations. It is significant to note that they can override the system if they notice a problem. For the most part, however, they follow the system's recommendations. Also, rather than have a manager at each fulfillment center monitor the system, Amazon performs that task from a central location where managers monitor multiple warehouses simultaneously.

Today at Amazon fulfillment centers, managers watch multiple computer screens to monitor the operations. Blue dots represent robots moving products around the facility, and yellow figures indicate the humans who load and unload the robots' shelves. Green lines show conveyor belts moving orders to stations and eventually to delivery trucks.

The Bad News

Another machine learning application is Amazon's productivity-tracking system. This system can measure the number of seconds it takes a worker to complete a particular task. The system instructs workers what to do on the warehouse floor, sets productivity targets, and identifies employees who fail to meet those targets. Amazon has acknowledged that its system is not perfect, but it claims that most processes in its facilities allow managers to intervene when they feel it is necessary.

Unfortunately, Amazon's productivity-tracking technology has placed intense pressure on its employees. Workers contend that the pace of work pushes them to skirt safety rules and skip rest breaks. In fact, Amazon workers in the United States and the United Kingdom stated that they skipped bathroom breaks for fear of being disciplined for idling and ultimately losing their jobs. Workers also contend that Amazon's rules create an unsafe working environment. In fact, investigations have found that the rate of serious injuries at Amazon fulfillment centers has been almost double the industry average.

Similarly, employees at an Alabama warehouse complained they were being held to unreasonable productivity goals. Specifically, taking seconds longer than the average time to complete a task could lead to a warning about job performance. In 2020, these workers tried, unsuccessfully, to form a union.

Like their employees, Amazon managers also work under recommendations from the company's machine learning systems. One manager claimed that he took naps in his car after 12-hour shifts so that he could feel fresh enough to drive home.

On September 22, 2021, California Governor Gavin Newsome signed a bill into law that prohibits companies from imposing production quotas that prevent workers from complying with health and safety laws or from taking breaks to rest or use the bathroom. That same year, regulators in Washington State fined Amazon for its conduct at one warehouse, asserting that there was a direct connection between the fast pace of work and injuries at the facility. Amazon, which was appealing the fine, claimed that it was modifying its productivity-tracking tools to better identify problems that its employees are facing.

Amazon has adopted the long-term goal of building fully automated fulfillment centers that would minimize, if not eliminate, human intervention. This idea remains in the future, however. First, the company must develop a technology to teach robotic arms and hands to grasp objects of different sizes and textures.

Questions

1. **Describe the benefits that Amazon realizes from its use of ML applications in its fulfillment centers.**

2. **Discuss the human resource problems that Amazon is encountering with its use of ML applications in its fulfillment centers. Describe possible technology solutions to help Amazon workers. Now, propose management solutions to help Amazon workers.**

3. **From an Amazon customer's perspective, do the advantages of ML applications to Amazon outweigh worker problems in the company's warehouses? Why or why not? Support your answer.**

4. **If Amazon warehouse employees continue to attempt to unionize, what will be the likely response from Amazon? Explain your answer.**

Sources: Compiled from J. Peters, "Amazon Warehouse Workers in Albany Have Filed to Unionize," MSN.com, August 16, 2022; P. Moorhead, "Amazon Increased Output in 2021 Orders of Magnitude More than Carbon Emissions," *Forbes*, August 5, 2022; M. Watson, "Emerging Trend: Four Ways Amazon and Others Are Using AI to Personalize Work Schedules," Field Technologies Online, July 25, 2022; T. Bishop, "With New Warehouse Robots, Amazon Looks to Invent Its Way out of Its Safety Problems," *GeekWire*, June 22, 2022; R. Spiegel, "AI Comes Alive in Industrial Automation," *Design News*, December 14, 2021; N. Scheiber, "California Senate Passes Bill Reining in Amazon Labor Model," *New York Times*, October 21, 2021; M. Day, "When the Boss's Boss Is a Machine," *Bloomberg BusinessWeek*, September 27, 2021; J. Diaz, "A New Law in California Aims to Protect Workers at Retail Warehouses like Amazon's," NPR, September 23, 2021; C. Harrington, "California Senate Passes Warehouse Workers Bill, Taking Aim at Amazon," *Ars Technica*, September 11, 2021; "Meet the Robots inside Amazon's Fulfillment Centers," *CBS News*, June 13, 2021; "New Technologies to Improve Amazon Worker Safety," Amazon.com, June 13, 2021; A. Stanley, "Amazon Unveils Fleet of Cutesy-Named Robots to Make Its Warehouses Less of a Hazardous Hellscape," *Gizmodo*, June 13, 2021; J. Morse, "Amazon Announces New Employee Tracking Tech, and Customers Are Lining Up," *Mashable*, December 1, 2020; A. Farinacci, "AI, Robots, and Humans: Inside an Amazon Fulfillment Center," ny1.com, June 26, 2019; B. Ames, "Amazon Unveils Xanthus and Pegasus Fulfillment Robots," DC Velocity, June 6, 2019; M. Coyle, "New Robots, New Jobs," Amazon.com, June 5, 2019; S. Herget, "Amazon Uses AI

to Track and Fire Its Warehouse Workers," *NextPit*, May 1, 2019;
N. Statt, "Amazon Says Fully Automated Shipping Warehouses
Are at Least a Decade Away," *The Verge*, May 1, 2019; L. Dormehl,
"Amazon Is Using Smart Technology to Track Warehouse Worker
Productivity," *Digital Trends*, April 29, 2019; C. Jee, "Amazon's
System for Tracking Its Warehouse Workers Can Automatically Fire
Them," *MIT Technology Review*, April 26, 2019; S. Liao, "Amazon
Warehouse Workers Skip Bathroom Breaks to Keep Their Jobs, Says
Report," *The Verge*, April 16, 2018; and www.amazon.com, accessed
August 26, 2022.

Introduction

This chapter introduces you to artificial intelligence (AI) and machine learning (ML), emphasizing the wide diversity of AI and ML applications. We begin by defining artificial intelligence, differentiating between strong AI and weak AI, and contrasting the capabilities of natural intelligence and artificial intelligence. We continue by defining machine learning and discussing the differences between conventional programming and machine learning. We continue by defining supervised, semi-supervised, unsupervised, reinforcement learning, and deep learning. We conclude the chapter with a discussion of neural networks.

It is impossible to overstate the importance of AI and ML in today's organizations. It is also impossible to overstate the importance of your input into the development and use of AI and ML applications within an organization.

Consider the three main types of organizational employee involved with AI and ML application and development: business professionals, business analysts, and data scientists. Business professionals are responsible for identifying business opportunities that can be addressed with AI and ML applications and use those applications in performing their jobs. On one hand, business analysts work with business professionals to identify and define the business requirements for new AI and ML products, services, or processes. On the other hand, they work with data scientists to develop AI and ML models to ensure that business requirements are met. Data scientists are responsible for designing and implementing AI and ML models that can analyze large data sets to make predictions.

As we proceed from business professionals, to business analysts, to data scientists, technical skill requirements increase. For example, business users would include any university major. This point is critically important and emphasizes the fact that AI and ML applications impact everyone in an organization. In fact, we predict that introductory courses in artificial intelligence and machine learning will spread throughout universities in the near future! Business analysts would include any university major who takes several elective courses in AI and ML. For example, these courses could include an introductory course in AI and ML, a course in deep learning, and a course in data visualization. Data scientists typically major in computer science, management information systems, mathematics, or statistics.

So, the question is: Why should you learn about AI and ML? Let's look at reasons why it is so important that you learn about these topics. First, let's look at an organizational perspective. AI and ML are revolutionizing the way businesses operate. From automating repetitive tasks to optimizing decision-making, these technologies are changing the way companies operate and compete. In fact, companies that are early adopters of AI and ML have a significant competitive advantage over those that are slower to adopt. In addition, AI and ML can help businesses make better decisions by providing insights and predictions based on vast amounts of data.

Now let's take a personal perspective. In organizations today, working with AI and ML applications is no longer the exclusive responsibility of technical professionals. Business professionals now play key roles in developing and using AI and ML applications. Therefore, it is critically important that you become an informed user; that is, a person knowledgeable about AI and ML.

As a business professional, you are a domain expert. That is, you have knowledge, skills, and experience in a particular area of endeavor. This expertise includes knowledge of specific tools, business processes, and the range of systems and applications that your business function and organization use. Domain experts prioritize the why rather than the how of AI and ML model development. For example, an accountant would be an expert in the domain of accountancy. In college, you are developing domain expertise in your major field of study. As you gain experience in your career, your domain expertise will deepen. You will use your domain expertise in working with business analysts and data scientists to design, develop, implement, maintain, oversee, and work alongside any AI and ML app that the organization deploys.

Unfortunately, today there is a widespread lack of AI literacy among business professionals. This problem creates a serious barrier to the successful implementation of AI and ML projects. As a result, it would be extremely helpful for business professionals to know how to work with (or use) AI and ML applications, interpret their recommendations, rely on their outputs (or question those outputs), and oversee their functioning.

In addition, data scientists often lack business expertise, meaning that these professionals may not understand what their organization actually does or what each business function does. In short, data scientists "may not know what they don't know" about the business.

As a result, there can be a communication problem between business professionals and data scientists. That is, the two groups struggle to find a common language. They find it difficult to prioritize the right initiatives, ask the right questions, and align around a common and informed set of expectations. Finding this common language between data science teams and business domain experts is often the most important determinant of successful AI projects.

There are two solutions to this communication problem. First, as we noted above, business professionals should have a basic knowledge of AI and ML. In that way, business professionals can communicate with business analysts and data scientists. Second, because business analysts have organizational expertise as well as knowledge of AI and ML, they can act as "translators" between business professionals and data scientists. They can translate business requirements to data scientists and explain AI and ML models to business professionals.

After you finish this chapter, you will have a basic understanding of artificial intelligence and machine learning, and the incredibly broad range of AI and ML applications that are employed in modern organizations. This knowledge will enable you to immediately and confidently provide input into your organization's AI and ML application development and use. In essence, you will be on your way to becoming an informed user of AI and ML applications, and on your way to developing a common language to communicate with business analysts and data scientists.

14.1 Artificial Intelligence

WILEY PLUS

Author Lecture Videos are available exclusively in *WileyPLUS*.

Apply the Concept activities are available in the Appendix and in *WileyPLUS*.

artificial intelligence (AI)
A subfield of computer science concerned with studying the thought processes of humans and recreating the effects of those processes with machines such as computers.

LEARNING OBJECTIVE

Explain the potential value and the potential limitations of artificial intelligence.

Artificial intelligence (AI) is a subfield of computer science that studies the thought processes of humans and recreates the effects of those processes through information systems. We define **artificial intelligence** as the theory and development of information systems that are capable of performing tasks that normally require human intelligence. That is, we define AI in terms of the tasks that humans perform, rather than how humans think.

This definition raises the question, "What is *intelligent behavior*?" The following capabilities are considered to be signs of intelligence: learning or understanding from experience, making sense of ambiguous or contradictory messages, and responding quickly and successfully to new situations.

The ultimate goal of AI is to build machines that mimic human intelligence. A widely used test to determine whether a computer exhibits intelligent behavior was designed by Alan Turing, a British AI pioneer. The *Turing test* proposes a scenario in which a man and a computer both pretend to be human, and a human interviewer has to identify which is real. Based on this standard, the intelligent systems exemplified in commercial AI products are far from exhibiting any significant intelligence.

We can better understand the potential value of AI by contrasting it with *natural (human) intelligence*. AI has several important commercial advantages over natural intelligence, but it also displays some limitations. The strengths and limitations are outlined in Table 14.1.

Before we proceed, it is important to distinguish between strong artificial intelligence and weak artificial intelligence. **Strong AI**—also known as *artificial general intelligence*—is *hypothetical* artificial intelligence that matches or exceeds human intelligence. In other words, it refers to the intelligence of a machine that could successfully perform any intellectual task that a human being can. Strong AI, therefore, could be considered to have consciousness or

strong AI Hypothetical artificial intelligence that matches or exceeds human intelligence and could perform any intellectual task that humans can.

TABLE 14.1   The Capabilities of Natural Versus Artificial Intelligence

Capabilities	Natural Intelligence	Artificial Intelligence
Preservation of knowledge	Perishable from an organizational point of view	Permanent
Duplication and dissemination of knowledge in a computer	Difficult, expensive, time consuming	Easy, fast, and inexpensive
Total cost of knowledge	Can be erratic and inconsistent, incomplete at times	Consistent and thorough
Documentation of process and knowledge	Difficult, expensive	Fairly easy, inexpensive
Creativity	Can be very high	Low, uninspired
Use of sensory experiences	Direct and rich in possibilities	Must be interpreted first; limited
Recognizing patterns and relationships	Fast, easy to explain	Machine learning still not as good as people in most cases, but in some cases better than people
Reasoning	Making use of a wide context of experiences	Good only in narrow, focused, and stable domains

sentience. **Weak AI**—also called **narrow AI**—performs a useful and specific function that once required human intelligence to perform, and it does so at human levels or better. Common examples are character recognition, speech recognition, machine vision, robotics, data mining, medical informatics, and automated investing.

Today, systems that are labeled "artificial intelligence" are typically weak AI. However, weak AI is already powerful enough to make a dramatic difference in human life. Weak AI applications enhance human endeavors by complementing what people can do. For example, when you call your bank and talk to an automated voice, you are probably talking to a weak AI program. Researchers at universities and companies around the world are building weak AI applications that are rapidly becoming more capable.

Consider chess, which weak AI systems now play better than any human. In 1997, IBM's Deep Blue system beat the world chess champion, Garry Kasparov, for the first time. Since that time, chess-playing systems have become significantly more powerful.

In December 2017, Alphabet (Google's parent corporation) introduced AlphaZero, a deep reinforcement learning system (discussed later in this chapter). AlphaZero began with no knowledge of chess beyond the basic rules of the game. It then played against itself millions of times and learned from its mistakes. In a matter of hours, AlphaZero became the world's best chess player.

Interestingly, the advent of AI did not diminish the performance of purely human chess players. Instead, the opposite occurred. Cheap, highly functional chess programs have inspired more people than ever to play chess. Further, the players have become better than ever. In fact, today there are more than twice as many grandmasters as there were when Deep Blue beat Kasparov.

Similar to chess players, physicians who are supported by AI will have an enhanced ability to spot cancer in medical images; speech recognition algorithms running on smartphones will bring the Internet to millions of illiterate people in developing countries; digital assistants will suggest promising hypotheses for academic research; and image classification algorithms will enable wearable computers to layer useful digital information onto people's views of the real, physical world.

Despite these impressive results, however, AI does present challenges. For example, consider the power that AI brings to national security agencies in both autocracies and democracies. The capacity to monitor billions of conversations and to pick out every citizen from the crowd by his or her voice or face poses serious threats to privacy and liberty. Also, many individuals could become unemployed when AI develops the capabilities to perform their jobs.

Weak AI has become so powerful that scientists from University College London (UCL; www.ucl.ac.uk) compiled a list of AI-enabled crimes based on academic papers, news stories, popular culture, and a discussion with several dozen experts.

weak AI   (also called **narrow AI**) Performs a useful and specific function that once required human intelligence to perform and does so at human levels or better.

- *AI-enabled crimes of high concern:* Deepfakes, driverless vehicles as a weapon, spear phishing and whaling, AI-controlled systems (see SCADA systems in Chapter 4), large-scale ransomware, and AI-authored fake news.
- *AI-enabled crimes of moderate concern:* Misuse of military robots, autonomous attack drones, tricking facial recognition systems, manipulating financial or stock markets, and data poisoning. *Data poisoning* is an attack that tries to manipulate the training dataset of a machine learning system to control the predictive behavior of a trained model such that the model will label malicious examples into a desired class (e.g., labeling spam e-mails as safe).
- *AI-enabled crimes of low concern:* AI-authored fake reviews, AI-assisted stalking, forgery of content such as art and music, and burglar bots. *Burglar bots* are very small robots that can enter a home through a letter slot or a pet door and then send information to the thief about what is inside the home and whether anyone is at home.

Several technological advancements have led to enhancements of artificial intelligence. We take a brief look at each of them here:

- *Advancements in chip technology:* AI systems employ graphics processing units (called GPU chips; discussed in Technology Guide 1), which were developed to meet the visual and parallel processing demands of video games. GPU chips facilitate parallel processing in neural networks, which are the primary information architecture of AI software. (We discuss neural networks later in this chapter.)
- *Big Data:* As we discussed in Chapter 5, Big Data consists of diverse, high-volume, high-velocity information assets that require new types of processing that enhance decision making, insight discovery, and process optimization. Big Data is now being used to train *deep learning* software. (We discuss deep learning later in this chapter.)
- *The Internet and cloud computing:* The Internet (discussed in Chapter 6) and cloud computing (discussed in Technology Guide 3) make Big Data available to AI systems, specifically neural networks, and provide the computational capacity needed for AI systems.
- *Improved algorithms:* An **algorithm** is a problem-solving method expressed as a finite sequence of steps. Researchers are rapidly improving the capabilities of AI algorithms. AI algorithms also run much faster on GPU chips.

algorithm   A problem-solving method expressed as a finite sequence of steps.

Before you go on...

1. What is artificial intelligence?
2. Differentiate between artificial intelligence and human intelligence.
3. Differentiate between strong AI and weak AI.

WILEY PLUS

Author Lecture Videos are available exclusively in *WileyPLUS.*
Apply the Concept activities are available in the Appendix and in *WileyPLUS.*

machine learning systems   The ability of information systems to accurately perform new, unseen tasks, built on known properties learned from training or historical data that are labeled.

14.2 Machine Learning and Deep Learning

LEARNING OBJECTIVE

Differentiate among supervised, semi-supervised, unsupervised, reinforcement, and deep learning.

Machine learning (ML) is an application of artificial intelligence that provides systems with the ability to automatically learn and improve from experience without being explicitly programmed. Machine learning focuses on the development of computer programs that can access data and use those data to learn from themselves.

First, we discuss how machine learning differs from traditional computer programming and expert systems. We then discuss problems inherent to developing ML systems. We close this section with a discussion of several types of machine learning: supervised, semi-supervised, unsupervised, and reinforcement.

Traditional Programming versus Machine Learning

Fundamentally, traditional programming is a structured combination of data and a computer algorithm (computer program) that produces answers. In supervised machine learning, developers train the system with labeled input data and the expected output results. After the system is trained, developers feed it with unlabeled input data and examine the accuracy of the output data. Let's look at an example of the difference between traditional programming and supervised machine learning.

Traditional Programming   Let's say that we want to know the product of two numbers. The first column is **a** and the second column is **b**. With traditional programming, we create an algorithm (computer code), or $c = a \times b$. The results are 24, 15, and 18.

a	b	$c = a \times b$
6	4	24
3	5	15
9	2	18

Supervised Machine Learning   Let's use the same numbers as our example above as labeled input data to train a supervised machine learning system. We feed the system with these relationships:

6 and 4 are related to 24

3 and 5 are related to 15

We want to know how these numbers relate, so we let the system evaluate the relationships of known values and check its accuracy.

$6 ? 4 = 24$

$3 ? 5 = 15$

The system determines that the relationship between each pair is "multiply." If we say that the question mark is multiply and check our results, we find that they are correct.

So, if we then feed 9 and 2 into the system, it will tell us that the relationship is $9 \times 2 = 18$.

When the machine learning algorithm is trained on large amounts of labeled training data, it produces predictions for additional examples.

Expert Systems versus Machine Learning

Expert systems (ESs) are computer systems that attempt to mimic human experts by applying expertise in a specific domain. Essentially, an ES transfers expertise from a human domain expert (or other source) to the system. This knowledge is then stored in the system, typically in the form of IF-THEN rules. The more complex ESs are comprised of thousands of these rules.

ESs can make inferences and arrive at conclusions. Then, like a human expert, they offer advice or recommendations. Also like human experts, they can explain the logic behind the advice.

Expert systems do present problems. For instance, transferring domain expertise from human experts to the expert system can be difficult because humans cannot always explain *how* they know what they know. In addition, even if the domain experts can explain their entire reasoning process, automating that process might not be possible. The process might be either too complex or too vague, or it might require too many rules. Essentially, it is very difficult to program all the possible decision paths into an expert system.

There are significant differences between expert systems and machine learning systems. First, ESs require human experts to provide the knowledge for the system. In contrast, ML systems do not require human experts. Further, much like traditional programming, expert systems must be formally structured in the form of rules. By contrast, machine learning algorithms learn from ingesting vast amounts of data and by adjusting hyperparameters and parameters (discussed below).

Bias

Designers must consider the many types of bias when developing machine learning systems. The types of bias include underspecification, how developers approach a problem, and the data used to train the system.

Machine Learning Bias (Also Called Algorithm Bias)

Designers must consider the many types of bias when developing machine learning systems. The sources of bias include underspecification, how developers approach a problem, and the data used to train the system.

Underspecification   The training process for a machine learning system can produce multiple models, all of which pass the testing phase. However, these models will differ in small, arbitrary ways, depending on things such as the random values given to the nodes in a neural network before training starts, the number of training runs, and others (see Section 14.3). Developers typically overlook these differences if they do not impact how an ML model performs on its test. Unfortunately, these differences can lead to huge variations in how the model performs in the real world. Essentially, even if a training process can produce a good model, it could still ultimately produce a poor model. The process will not know the difference, and neither will the developers, until the model is employed in the real world.

How Developers Approach a Problem   Let's look at a simple example that illustrates how you might frame a problem. Consider the following numbers: 4, 9, 3, 6, 11, and 5. What is the next number in this series? Your answer to this problem is a product of how you intuitively see the problem and how you frame it. If you think in arithmetic terms, you may try some combination of addition and subtraction based on a pattern that you think exists. If you are a statistician, you may try to perform regression on the numbers to determine what the next one would be. There are many possible approaches.

The "answer" here is that there is no right answer because we picked these numbers at random. The critical point is how you chose to approach the problem. Your approach reveals your bias as to how you would try to solve the problem.

This simple example illustrates an essential issue in the field of AI. How developers approach or frame a problem determines how they set up the process of building the AI system and, ultimately, how the algorithm learns and produces answers.

How Data Can Bias an ML System   The third type of bias comes from the data that are used to train the system. This bias, known as *data shift*, comes from a mismatch between the data used to train and test the system and the data the system actually encounters in the real world. For example, an ML system trained only with current customers might not be able to predict the behaviors of new customers who are not represented in the training data.

When trained on some data, ML will likely pick up the same biases that already exist in society. For instance, ML systems used for criminal risk assessment have been found to be biased against people of color.

As a result, machine learning raises many ethical questions. ML systems trained on datasets collected from biased samples can exhibit these biases when they used, a problem called *algorithmic bias.* For example, using job hiring data from a firm with biased hiring policies could cause an ML system to duplicate this bias by scoring job applicants accordingly. Clearly, collecting the data and documenting the algorithmic rules used by an ML system in a responsible manner is a critical component of developing ML systems.

False Positives

Another challenging problem when building AI systems or evaluating outputs is seeing conditions where none actually exist, which is called a false positive. A *false positive* is a result that indicates that a given condition exists when it in fact does not. An example of a false positive is convicting an innocent person, identifying an e-mail as spam when it is not, flagging a legitimate transaction as fraudulent, and many others.

Analyzing complex datasets can be difficult. However, by being aware of false positives, AI practitioners can assess data objectively and not be misled by apparent, but erroneous, conditions.

We now turn our attention to the various types of machine learning: supervised, semi-supervised, unsupervised, reinforcement, and deep. **Figure 14.1** provides a visual look at how these types differ.

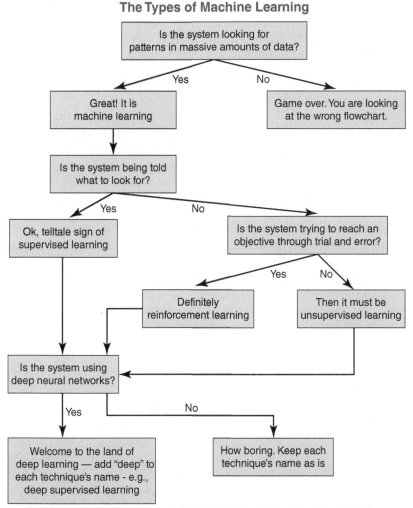

Source: K. Hao, "What Is Machine Learning?" MIT Technology Review, November 17, 2018.

FIGURE 14.1 The types of **machine learning.**

Supervised Learning

supervised learning　A type of machine learning where the system is given labeled input data and the expected output results.

As we discussed in the previous section, **supervised learning** is a type of machine learning in which the system is given labeled input data and the expected output results. Developers input massive amounts of data during the training phase as well as what output should be obtained from each specific input value. Developers then input unlabeled, never-been-seen data values to verify that the model is accurate.

Classification and regression analysis are important techniques for supervised learning. Classification algorithms are used when the outputs are restricted to a limited set of values; regression algorithms are used when the outputs can have any numerical value within a certain range.

Classification refers to a predictive modeling problem in which the system generates a class label for a given set of input data. There are four types of classification:

- *Binary classification* refers to classification problems that have only two class labels. Examples are e-mail spam detection (spam or not), churn prediction (churn or not), and conversion prediction (buy or not).

- *Multiclass classification* refers to classification problems with more than two class labels. Examples are news article categories, plant species classification, and optical character recognition.

- *Multilabel classification* refers to classification problems that have two or more class labels, where one or more class labels can be predicted from each example. Consider the example of photo classification, where a given photo may have multiple objects in the scene. The classification model may predict the presence of multiple known objects in the photo, such as an automobile, a person, a stop sign, and so on.

- *Imbalanced classification* refers to classification problems in which the number of classes in each class is unequally distributed. Typically, imbalanced classification problems are binary classification problems in which the majority of data points in the training data belong to one class and a minority to another class. Examples are fraud detection, outlier detection, and medical diagnostic tests.

Linear regression is a supervised machine learning algorithm in which the predicted output is continuous and has a constant slope. This algorithm is used to predict continuous variables such as sales or price, rather than classifying them into categories with a classification algorithm. There are two main types of linear regression: simple and multiple.

In *simple linear regression*, a single independent variable is used to predict the value of a dependent variable. For example, the Italian clothing company Benetton is examining its annual sales and the amount the firm is spending on advertising. Benetton uses simple linear regression, using advertising as the independent (predictor) variable to predict the dependent variable, sales.

In *multiple linear regression*, two or more independent variables are used to predict the value of a dependent variable. Suppose that Benetton wants to analyze the impact of product price, product advertising expense, store location, and season of the year on product sales. The firm would conduct a multiple linear regression, with price, advertising expense, store location, and season as the independent variables predicting the dependent variable, product sales.

Semi-Supervised Learning

semi-supervised learning　A type of machine learning that combines a small amount of labeled data with a large amount of unlabeled data during training.

Semi-supervised learning is a type of machine learning that combines a small amount of labeled data with a large amount of unlabeled data during training. For example, semi-supervised learning is an excellent text document classifier because it is very difficult to find a large amount of labeled text documents. The reason is that it is not efficient to have a human read through entire text documents to classify and label them. In this case, the algorithm learns from a small amount of labeled text documents while still being able to classify large amounts of unlabeled text documents in the training data.

Unsupervised Learning

Unsupervised learning is a type of machine learning that searches for previously unde-tected patterns in a dataset with no pre-existing labels and with minimal human supervision. The best time to use unsupervised learning is when an organization does not have data on desired outcomes. An example is when the firm wants to determine a target market for an entirely new product that it has never before sold.

Cluster analysis is one of the primary techniques in unsupervised learning. Cluster anal-ysis groups, or segments, data points to identify common characteristics. It then reacts based on whether each new piece of data exhibits these characteristics.

Example: Finding customer segments. Clustering is an unsupervised ML technique in which the goal is to find groups or clusters in input data. Developers use clustering to deter-mine customer segments in marketing data using variables such as gender, location, age, edu-cation, income bracket, and many others.

Example: Feature selection. Assume that developers want to predict how capable an appli-cant is of repaying a loan from the perspective of a bank. The goal is to provide loans to appli-cants who can repay them. Banks analyze large amounts of data about each application to make these predictions, including the applicant's average monthly income, average monthly debt payments, credit history, age, and many other variables.

Because banks typically collect more data than they use in making loan decisions, not all of the variables are relevant for predicting an applicant's ability to repay a loan. For instance, does an applicant's age make any difference in deciding whether he or she can repay the loan? Is the applicant's gender important? For this reason, eliminating unnecessary variables is an essential part of training an ML system. In feature selection, developers try to eliminate a sub-set of the original set of features (variables).

unsupervised learning A type of machine learning that looks for previously undetected patterns in a dataset with no pre-existing labels and with a minimum of human supervision.

Reinforcement Learning

Reinforcement learning is a type of machine learning in which the system learns to achieve a goal in an uncertain, potentially complex environment. In reinforcement learning, the sys-tem faces a game-like situation where it employs trial and error to find a solution to a problem. The developer awards penalties or rewards to the system for the actions it performs so that it will do what the developer wants. The system's goal is to maximize the total reward.

Although the designers set the reward policy—that is, the rules of the game—they give the model no hints or suggestions for how to solve the problem. The system must determine how to perform the task to maximize the reward, beginning with totally random trials and finishing with sophisticated tactics.

There are numerous examples of reinforcement learning applications. Some of these are:

reinforcement learning A type of machine learning where the system learns to achieve a goal in an uncertain, potentially complex environment.

- Recommendation systems
- Automated ad bidding and buying
- Dynamic resource allocation in wind farms, HVAC (heating and air conditioning) sys-tems, and computer clusters in data centers
- Automated calibration of engines and other machines
- Robotic control
- Autonomous vehicles such as self-driving cars
- Supply chain optimization

Deep Learning

Deep learning is a subset of machine learning in which artificial neural networks learn from large amounts of data. When supervised, semi-supervised, unsupervised, and reinforcement learning systems use neural networks, we add the term *deep* to each one, resulting in deep supervised learning, deep semi-supervised learning, and so on.

deep learning A subset of machine learning where artificial neural networks learn from large amounts of data.

Deep learning systems can solve complex problems even when they utilize a dataset that is very diverse and unstructured. These systems can discover new patterns without being exposed to labeled historical or training data. Widely used examples of deep learning are automatic speech recognition, image recognition, natural language processing, customer relationship management, recommendation systems, and drug discovery.

IT's About Business 14.1

POM HRM AI in the Global Shipping Industry

The Global Shipping Industry

The shipping industry is undergoing changes to increase efficiency and safety at ports and at sea. From small boats to huge container ships, shipping vessels are integral components of the global economy. According to the United Nations, ships transport approximately 90 percent of all worldwide commerce.

Maritime companies are leveraging machine learning and other technologies to design smart ports. In addition, they are developing the next generation of autonomous ships. At times, transforming a port involves updating an existing technical infrastructure comprising less-sophisticated components. For example, historically some ports have relied on low-tech, manual solutions. In these ports, workers physically visit a vessel with ropes that they use to measure the length and width of the ship. Then they decide which dock the ship should enter.

Smart ports. In contrast, smart ports employ advanced, innovative technologies to monitor and improve their operations. These technologies frequently take the form of digital twins. A *digital twin* is a digital representation of a physical system that maps that entity into a three-dimensional, virtual system. Digital twins integrate and analyze multiple data sources, including sensors on port equipment and vessels, inbound and outbound maritime traffic, port size, live weather conditions, and many other variables. Digital twins also enable port authorities to improve mooring and casting off, and to remotely control cranes and other equipment.

For example, in shallow water, the tides play a major role in scheduling loading and unloading operations, especially for larger vessels. Buoys equipped with sensors monitor tidal changes, water temperature, and other variables. These metrics provide a clearer picture of real-time conditions. Instead of sending out a crew to check the buoys, the buoys transmit their information to the port in real time.

When ships are arriving or leaving the dock, they must be loaded and unloaded efficiently and safely. To do so, ports use industrial cranes to transfer containers to and from each ship and around the port. Moving tons of cargo as winds blow through a port can compromise the structural integrity of these cranes over time. At times, this fatigue can lead to the catastrophic collapse of the crane itself. By monitoring the crane's structure and the meteorological environment at the port, operators can adjust docking and crane operations to increase safety. Cranes are equipped with cameras, an anemometer—an instrument that measures wind velocity—and other sensors to monitor the stress on the crane's structure while it is operating. Machine learning can then analyze these data to monitor trends and predict failures before they occur.

When a ship arrives and is unloading, port authorities must have the necessary number and types of trucks and trains waiting to receive the containers. The authorities monitor GPS sensors on the trucks and trains to precisely determine their locations, thus increasing the efficiency of transferring the containers.

Once the various sensors, ships, and port systems are integrated, machine learning systems can then optimize maritime scheduling. The system can answer such questions as: Which dock should we send the ship to? Which train or trucks should be waiting as the ship offloads its cargo? Where should the trains or trucks be positioned in the port when a ship is ready to load? These insights help to reduce bottlenecks and prevent accidents.

The largest port in Europe, the Port of Rotterdam (Netherlands) (www.portofrotterdam.com/en), has embraced digitization. Through its Smart Infrastructure program, it aims to have ships autonomously enter and leave the port by 2030. Further, the port operates an unmanned container terminal that utilizes autonomous cranes.

The second-largest port in Europe is the Port of Antwerp (Belgium) (www.portofantwerpbruges.com/en), which has also been digitized. The port utilizes a digital three-dimensional map that contains actionable real-time information as its digital twin. Smart cameras and computer vision are integrated into the map to produce an "intelligent wharf" which ensures that ships are safely and properly moored while also reducing wait times. The cameras have automatic image-recognition capabilities that increase security around the port and enable authorities to analyze and optimize equipment movements.

Ports are also addressing human operator fatigue. In the past, crane operators had to work under difficult conditions with narrow margins for error. They would sit for hours in a cockpit 10 to 12 stories high and watch several monitors while they controlled a giant crane. They also had to constantly take wind pressure into account. This job was stressful and caused fatigue.

In contrast, crane operators can now utilize sensor data to control their cranes remotely from buildings on the ground. This process reduces both operator fatigue and the risk of error during loading and unloading operations.

Smart ships. The shipping industry is reimagining the way cargo moves at sea. Smart ships use a number of sensors such as GPS, cameras, radar, and LIDAR for operations. (LIDAR is a system that measures distance to a target by illuminating the target with laser light and measuring the reflected light with a sensor.) Sensors enable these ships to operate with reduced crew sizes. Because the system reduces the number of crew members, the ship can be constructed without the life-support systems necessary to accommodate human crew members such as galleys, housing compartments, food storage, and restrooms. In turn, reducing ship size can minimize construction costs and fuel consumption and leave more room for storage. Put simply, a smaller autonomous ship can carry roughly the same amount of cargo as a much larger crewed vessel.

Smart ships must provide for control of the vessel and have the capacity to monitor the condition of each component of the vessel. Therefore, these ships typically contain redundant systems that prevent the system from failing in the event of a malfunction. Machine learning systems can analyze trends in data to predict operational failures in advance as well as notify ship owners as to necessary maintenance.

Questions

1. **Which type of machine learning applies to the following applications in this case? Support your answer for each application.**
   - **Port operations**
   - **Crane operations**
   - **Predicting preventive maintenance on port equipment**
   - **Optimizing the loading and unloading of ships**

2. **What are the advantages to ship owners of implementing ML applications? Support your answer.**

3. **What are the disadvantages to ship owners of implementing ML applications? Support your answer.**

4. **What are the advantages to crew members of implementing ML applications on ships? Support your answer.**

Sources: Compiled from "What Is Smart Shipping, and How Can It Change Art Logistics?," *Fine Art Shippers*, August 12, 2022; C. Cole, "Creating a Digital Twin: The Key to Building a Smart Vessel," *Siemens.com blog*, January 27, 2022; "Smart Shipping for the Supply Chain," Sobel Network Shipping Company, Inc., December 21, 2021; N. Joshi, "Why AI Adoption Is Lagging in International Shipping," *BBN Times*, December 7, 2021; M. Ball, "New AI-Powered Smart Shipping Solutions," *Unmanned Systems Technology*, November 5, 2021; A. Inam, "5 Ways AI Can help Mitigate the Global Shipping Crisis," *TechCrunch*, August 9, 2021; J. Donnelly, "How Can Digital Twins Help Ports?," *Port Technology*, July 20, 2021; J. Donnelly, "Digital Twin Shortens Playing Field for Expansive Belfast Harbor," *Port Technology*, May 21, 2021; J. Donnelly, "Measure, Optimize Terminal Machinery to Truly Greenify Ports," *Port Technology*, April 1, 2021; J. Donnelly, "AIDrivers Emphasises Digital Twin in PSA Singapore Project," *Port Technology*, March 19, 2021; N. Joshi, "Charting the Role of Artificial Intelligence in Shipping," *BBN Times*, October 7, 2020; A. Oriel, "Decoding the Future of Global Shipping with Artificial Intelligence," *Industry Wired*, August 28, 2020; J. Jackson, "What Are Smart Ports and How Will They Change the Shipping Industry?," *Searates*, August 21, 2020; R. Adams, "AI on the High Seas: Digital Transformation Is Revolutionizing Global Shipping," *TechRepublic*, August 19, 2020; F. Martin, "How AI & Automation Has Overhauled the Shipping Industry," *Analytics India Magazine; and* G. Spencer, "AI and Cargo Shipping: Full Speed Ahead for Global Maritime Trade," Microsoft.com, April 23, 2018.

Before you go on...

1. What is the difference between traditional computer programming and machine learning systems?
2. What is the difference between expert systems and machine learning systems?
3. Describe three types of bias that can negatively impact the development of machine learning systems.
4. Refer back to IT's About Business 3.3. Why are false positives so important in evaluating the output of machine learning systems in the case of facial recognition?
5. Differentiate between supervised learning, semi-supervised learning, unsupervised learning, reinforcement learning, and deep learning.

14.3 Neural Networks

LEARNING OBJECTIVE

Describe the structure of a neural network and discuss how that structure contributes to the purpose of neural networks in machine learning.

An artificial neural network, also known as a **neural network (NN)**, is a set of *virtual neurons*, or *nodes*, that work in parallel to simulate the way the human brain works, although in a greatly simplified form. Improvements in algorithms and increasingly powerful computer

WILEY PLUS

Author Lecture Videos are available exclusively in *WileyPLUS*.
Apply the Concept activities are available in the Appendix and in *WileyPLUS*.

neural network A set of virtual neurons, placed in layers, which work in parallel in an attempt to simulate the way the human brain works, although in a greatly simplified form.

chips and storage are enabling developers to create neural networks with billions of neurons. As a result, developers are training them to learn, recognize patterns, and make decisions in a humanlike way.

Neural networks consist of nodes, synapses (connections between nodes), weights, biases, and functions. A **node** in a neural network consists of software that has one or more weighted input connections, a bias function, an activation function, and one or more output connections.

The nodes are arranged in several layers: one input layer, one or more hidden layers, and one output layer (see **Figure 14.2**). The hidden layers are called "hidden" simply because they are located between the input and output layers. See **Figure 14.3** for an example of a generic neural network with one hidden layer. Note that a *deep neural network* contains multiple hidden layers.

node Software unit in a neural network that has one or more weighted connections, a transfer function that combines the inputs in some way, and an output connection.

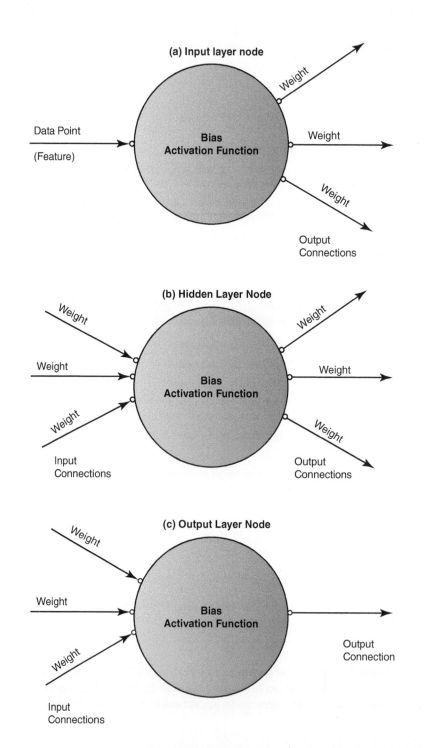

FIGURE 14.2 **Various types of nodes in neural networks.**

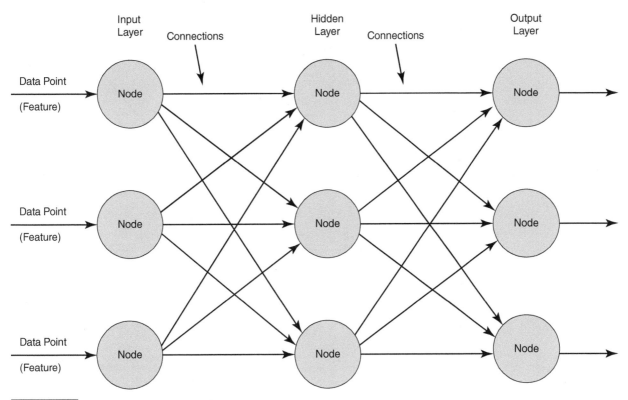

FIGURE 14.3 **A generic neural network.**

Neural network developers choose the network's *hyperparameters*, which include the number of hidden layers, the number of nodes in each layer, the learning rate (how much the system is allowed to change the parameters after each training iteration), and the activation functions in each node.

The *activation functions (AFs)* that reside at each node define the output of that node given an input or a set of inputs. (See **Figure 14.4** for an example of an activation function). AFs are a critical component of neural network design, and their selection is crucial for efficient and accurate performance. There are dozens of activation functions available to developers. These functions process incoming data in different ways, and developers chose them to provide the best model for the data. The key is to match the correct activation function with the data and the desired output predictions. For example, some activation functions are better suited for binary classification, while others perform best with continuous data.

Weights and biases are examples of *parameters* in a neural network. For the first training iteration, developers set weights and biases to some neutral value, such as 0 or 0.5, depending on the particular application. In subsequent iterations, weights and biases are adjusted by the loss function of the network with the goal of minimizing system inaccuracies.

Training Neural Networks

NNs learn best from large datasets. Developers randomly separate the data into *training*, *validation*, and *test* datasets. Typically, developers use approximately 60 percent of the overall dataset for training, 10 percent for validation, and the remaining 30 percent for testing. During training, developers use the validation data to evaluate how well the training process is progressing and to adjust the hyperparameters to better tune the network. When training is completed, developers use the test data to measure the performance of the NN to determine whether it is optimally trained and is a viable system that the organization can deploy.

FIGURE 14.4 **Swish activation function.**

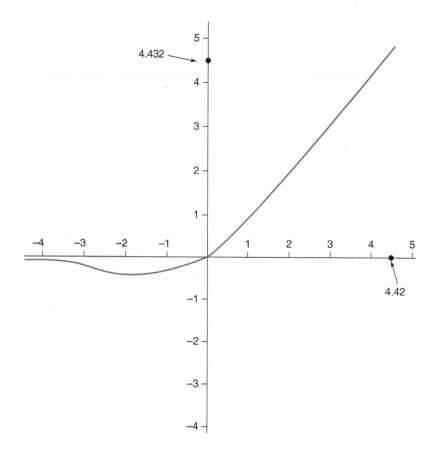

During the learning or training process, developers feed the numeric values of the training data into the input layer of nodes. Developers feed one feature, or variable, into each input node. For example, if developers are training an NN to predict house values, they might use the house's square footage, its age, the zip code, and the number of bedrooms and bathrooms. Each of those five variables is a feature, and there will be an input node for each feature. Therefore, the input layer will consist of five nodes. Because the goal of the NN is to predict a home's value, the output layer will consist of a single node, the predicted price. The NN will consist of one or more hidden layers (a decision made by the developers), each of which has one or more nodes.

Input nodes apply the bias (a mathematical change) to the input data value, producing a new value. The input node then applies the activation function to this new value, producing another new value. The input node then sends this new value to the next layer of nodes; that is, the first hidden layer. Along the pathways to the next layer, additional adjustments, known as *weights*, are applied to the data values.

As the weight-adjusted data arrive at the hidden-layer node from previous nodes, they are summed and the hidden-layer node applies another bias and an activation function to the summed data, producing a new value. The node then sends this value along the pathways to the next layer of nodes. The process in which biases, activation functions, and weights change the data values continues through to the last layer of nodes, the output layer. In the nodes of the output layer, the data undergo their final adjustments from the bias and activation function, and a loss function compares the just-processed data to the expected output value.

The difference between the derived data value and the expected value—that is, the loss function—initiates the process of back propagation. In this process, the values of the weights of each pathway and the bias values of each node are slightly changed in anticipation that the next iteration of data flowing through the neural network will result in a smaller error, or loss, upon output. After the adjustments by back propagation, the next data values begin their journey through the NN.

This process—new data, vast numbers of slight adjustments, the systems adjustments by back propagation—continues over and over until the training data are exhausted. At this point—if the loss function reveals that there are little to no required adjustments—developers consider the NN to be trained.

This chapter's Appendix shows an example of how neural networks function. While this example is highly simplified, it provides a look into the steps that neural networks take to learn the patterns that may exist among the large amounts of data they process.

Neural Networks for Specific Applications

Recurrent Neural Networks (RNNs)   A recurrent neural network is designed to access previous data such as sequential data or time series data during iterations of input. RNNs are used in applications where the RNN's decision must be based on previous output such as moving a robotic arm, reading a sentence, predicting time series, and composing music.

Convolutional Neural Networks (CNNs)   A convolutional neural network is designed to separate areas of image inputs by extracting features to identify edges, curves, and color density and then recombine these inputs for classification and prediction. CNNs are highly effective for image and pattern recognition applications such as facial recognition, video analysis, natural language processing, drug discovery, and anomaly detection. Let's take a closer look at how CNNs process images.

> **convolutional neural network**   A type of neural network designed to separate areas of image inputs by extracting features to identify edges, curves, and color density and then recombine these inputs for classification and prediction.

Each layer of the CNN manages a different level of abstraction. To process an image, the first layer is fed with raw images. That layer notes aspects of the images such as the brightness and colors of individual pixels and how those properties are distributed across the image. The next layer takes the first layer's observations and places them into more abstract categories such as identifying edges, shadows, and so on. The next layer analyzes those edges and shadows, searching for combinations that signify features such as eyes, lips, and ears. The final layer combines these observations into a representation of a face.

To train a CNN to learn facial recognition, developers will input millions of images. Some images will contain faces, and some will not. Each image will be labeled by a human, for example, through Amazon's Mechanical Turk. The images act as inputs to the neural network, and the labels—"face" or "not face"—are the outputs. The network's task is to develop a statistical rule, operationalized through the weights between processors, that correlates inputs with correct outputs.

To accomplish this task, the network will search for those features that are common to the images that display faces. Once these correlations are strong enough—that is, the weights, or strength of the connections between processors, are high enough—the network will be able to reliably differentiate faces from not-faces in its training set. The next step is to feed the neural network with a fresh set of unlabeled images to determine whether the facial recognition algorithms that the network has developed actually function with the new data.

NNs can also make mistakes. For example, developers trained a CNN to differentiate between images of wolves and Husky dogs. The researchers trained the CNN with numerous examples of photographs, and the CNN eventually achieved an accuracy rate of about 90 percent. The researchers then examined the inner workings of the CNN, focusing on which features contributed to correct classifications. They found that the CNN had learned based on the backgrounds of the training images—wolves were generally photographed on snow, and the dogs were photographed on grass. Therefore, the CNN tended to misclassify a photograph of a dog on a snowy background as being a wolf and to misclassify a wolf standing on a grassy field as a dog. The excellent performance of the CNN was misleading, and the CNN was unreliable for the purpose for which it was trained.

Generative Adversarial Networks (GANs)   A generative adversarial network consists of two neural networks that compete with each other in a zero-sum game in an effort to segregate real data from synthetic data. GANs separate real data from noise. They perform well in applications where filling in missing or incomplete data may be required. For example,

GANs are used for improving deep-space photography, for inpainting, and in other applications where completing missing digital data is required. (Note: *Inpainting* is a conservation process where damaged, deteriorating, or missing pars of an artwork are filled in to present a complete image.) GANs can also be used for creating deepfakes ranging from image manipulation to news embellishments.

Before you go on...

1. Describe the structure of a neural network.
2. Describe how a neural network operates. That is, describe how developers train neural networks.

14.4   Artificial Intelligence Applications

LEARNING OBJECTIVE

Provide use case examples of computer vision, natural language processing, robotics, image recognition, and intelligent agents.

The field of artificial intelligence has many applications. Note that these applications use machine learning, deep learning, and neural networks. In this section, we discuss computer vision, natural language processing, robotics, speech recognition, and intelligent agents. In Section 14.5, you will see numerous examples of these applications in use in all functional areas of organizations. These examples will emphasize how important artificial intelligence is to you, *regardless of your major.*

Computer Vision

computer vision   The ability of information systems to identify objects, scenes, and activities in images.

Computer vision refers to the ability of information systems to identify objects, scenes, and activities in images. Computer vision has diverse applications, including medical imaging to improve predicting, diagnosing, and treating diseases; facial recognition; and autonomous vehicles. Let's take a closer look at examples of computer vision at Amazon, Descartes Labs, and eBay.

POM *Amazon.* Amazon (www.amazon.com) has deployed an ML-based system in its fulfillment centers that enables workers to skip one manual item-scanning step per order. The system impacts Amazon's *stowing process*, which lets workers store items that have arrived from distributors and manufacturers anywhere on a warehouse's shelves, as long as each item's location is recorded in a computer so that it can be found again on the first try. This method requires workers to take an item out of a box, scan its bar code, place it on a shelf, and then scan the bar code on the shelf. The two scans provide the exact location of the item.

Computer vision enables workers to pick up an item, slide it under a scanner mounted nearby, and place it on a shelf. Amazon has trained the system to recognize where the worker places the item, and it records that location for future reference. The worker no longer has to scan the shelf. Eliminating this step improves efficiency. Given the hundreds of millions of items stored in its fulfillment centers, the system is providing large cost savings to Amazon.

POM *Descartes Labs.* Descartes Labs (www.descarteslabs.com), which uses artificial intelligence to analyze satellite imagery, launched its wildfire detector in the United States in July 2019. The company's system analyzes images that come in every five minutes from two U.S. government weather satellites.

The system uses several ML algorithms to determine whether a fire has begun. One algorithm examines spatial context, assessing whether the suspected fire is hotter than its surroundings. A second algorithm looks back in time to see what the area normally looks like when there is no fire. A third algorithm searches for areas that are unexpectedly hot compared to historical temperatures. Still another algorithm checks for the presence of smoke. Descartes claims that its system can detect a fire faster than firefighters or civilians. In fact, the company states that it can detect fires when they are only 10 acres in size.

MKT **POM** *eBay.* eBay's ML platform, Krylov helps users locate items based on taking a picture of an object or an image. Users can take a photo of an item they are searching for and then upload the image to the eBay app. Within milliseconds, the platform presents items that match the image.

Natural Language Processing

Natural language processing refers to the ability of information systems to work with text the way that humans do. For example, these systems can extract the meaning from text, and they can generate text that is readable, stylistically natural, and grammatically correct.

Because context is critical, the practical applications of natural language processing typically address relatively narrow areas such as analyzing customer feedback about a particular product or service, automating discovery in civil litigation or government investigations (e-discovery), and automating the writing of formulaic stories on topics such as corporate earnings and sports. We take a closer look at two examples of natural language processing, Google and eBay.

Google. In November 2020, Google (**www.google.com**) open-sourced an ML model called MT5 that the company claims can achieve state-of-the-art results on a range of English natural language processing tasks. Google trained the model on a dataset that covers 101 languages.

POM *eBay.* In addition to computer vision, eBay's ML platform, Krylov, provides ML-powered language translation services. The company has trained Krylov with vast amounts of data from its 1.4 billion listings for 183 million users in 190 markets.

Cross-border trade makes up nearly 60 percent of eBay's international revenue. Therefore, accurate, instantaneous translation is critical. eBay offered automatic translation prior to developing Krylov. However, the platform has significantly improved eBay's translation accuracy, which in turn has helped to increase the company's international sales by 11 percent.

natural language processing The ability of information systems to work with text the way that humans do.

Robotics

Integrating computer vision with tiny, high-performance sensors and actuators, a new generation of robots can work alongside people and flexibly perform multiple tasks in unpredictable environments. Examples are unmanned aerial vehicles; cooperative robots, called *cobots*, that share jobs with humans on the factory floor; robotic vacuum cleaners; and so on.

POM Amazon Robotics—formerly Kiva Systems, acquired by Amazon in March 2012 is an excellent example of cobots working in distribution centers. Rather than human inventory pickers selecting items for order fulfillment, Amazon's cobots bring the items to a human who fills the orders. Section 14.7 provides additional examples of the use of robots.

Speech Recognition

Speech recognition focuses on automatically and accurately transcribing human speech. This technology must manage diverse accents, dialects, and background noise. Furthermore, it must distinguish between homophones and work at the speed of natural speech. A *homophone* is a word that is pronounced the same as another word but differs in meaning;

speech recognition The ability of information systems to automatically and accurately transcribe human speech.

for example, "break" and "brake." Applications include medical dictation, hands-free writing, voice control of information systems, and telephone customer service applications. For example, popular voice-based digital assistants, such as Apple Siri, Microsoft Cortana, Google Assistant, Amazon Alexa, and Samsung Bixby, can understand our words, analyze our questions, and point us in the general direction of the right answer.

Chatbots

A chatbot is a computer program that uses artificial intelligence and natural language processing to simulate human conversation, either by voice or text communication. Organizations use chatbots, rather than a human, to solve a variety of problems such as the following:

- **MKT** **MIS** Customer service and support: Customers interact first with a chatbot that can help with routine problems. If the customer query requires human intervention, the chatbot directs the customer to customer-care agents. This process allows human agents to concentrate on more complex customer problems.

    For example, insurance company USAA (**www.usaa.com**) uses IBM Watson Assistant, a chatbot that enables its customers who are leaving military service to ask questions about, for example, college tuition reimbursement or changes to their health benefits. USAA executives note that the chatbot augments employees' expertise rather than replacing it. Watson Assistant helps shorten service calls, offers more context to incoming calls, and reduces the amount of paperwork around customer interactions.

- **HRM** **MIS** Organizational support: Chatbots can answer common employee questions regarding any part of the business. With additional training, chatbots can become employees' personal digital agents, improving their overall working experience.

    For example, chatbots can search websites for updated information on topics of your choice, such as price changes on desired products (e.g., airline tickets). Chatbots can monitor Internet sites, discussion groups, and mailing lists for stock manipulations, insider trading, and rumors that might affect stock prices.

    MIS IT services support: Chatbots can troubleshoot the most common problems employees face when using IT services. Such problems include outage alerts, password updates, periodic scans, and others. For example, Allstate uses chatbots to monitor its computer networks 24/7/365. These agents can predict a system crash 45 minutes before it happens and can detect electronic attacks to help prevent them.

IT's About Business 14.2 provides more detail on ChatGPT, a chatbot developed by OpenAI.

IT's About Business **14.2**

MIS ChatGPT

OpenAI (**www.openai.com**) is a nonprofit artificial intelligence research company whose goal is to advance artificial intelligence to benefit humanity as a whole. OpenAI developed the language model, ChatGPT, to perform a wide variety of tasks very accurately and quickly. *Language models* are statistical models that predict the probability of a sequence of words in a language. They are a key component in various natural language processing (NLP) tasks such as text generation, machine translation, and text classification. *Natural language processing* enables computers to understand, interpret, and generate human language in a useful and meaningful way.

Developers train language models on large amounts of text data to learn the patterns and relationships among words, thus providing these models with a vast text knowledge base. Once trained, the models can be used to generate new text by sampling words based on their predicted probabilities or to perform other NLP tasks by making predictions based on the input text.

OpenAI believes that ChatGPT technology can transform numerous industries and improve the quality of life for people around the world. The development of ChatGPT was also motivated by an increasing demand for conversational AI systems and the need for more advanced language models that could be used to develop those systems.

A *conversational AI system* is a type of AI that allows people to interact with computers using NLP. The goal of these systems is to improve the user experience and automate tasks that would otherwise require human intervention. These systems use machine learning algorithms and NLP to understand and respond to user input, allowing for more intuitive and humanlike interactions.

OpenAI released ChatGPT-3 in prototype form on November 30, 2022. Amazingly, the system gained over 1 million users in 5 days! It was the largest and most advanced language model to date, with more than 175 billion parameters.

ChatGPT is designed to mimic human conversation and is quite versatile. The most common applications of ChatGPT are the following:

- Build conversational AI systems: ChatGPT can be used for customer service and support such as answering frequently asked questions as well as building virtual assistants and other chatbots.

- Manage text:

  - Text generation: ChatGPT can generate creative writing, such as articles, stories, blog entries, song lyrics, poetry, fairy tales, and student essays and papers. The tool can also generate business strategies, summaries, captions, headlines, gift ideas, blog topics and blog entries, and vacation ideas, among many others. Interestingly, ChatGPT can also compose music.

  - Text classification: ChatGPT can classify text into different categories such as spam, fake news, and social media posts.

  - Text summarization: ChatGPT can reduce the length of text while preserving its key information.

  - Text completion: ChatGPT can predict the next word or sentence based on the content of the text.

- Answer questions: ChatGPT can answer questions by inferring context derived from a vast amount of text training data. For example, the system can answer test questions, including true-false and multiple-choice questions, short-answer questions, and essay questions.

- Analyze sentiments: ChatGPT can classify reviews and social media posts into positive, negative, or neutral sentiments.

- Translate communication from one language to another.

- Initiate technology: ChatGPT can write and debug computer programs.

ChatGPT provides users with many advantages. Here are the most significant:

- ChatGPT can generate text that is similar to human writing in terms of coherence and fluency.

- ChatGPT can understand the context of a given question or prompt and generate text accordingly.

- With its large amount of training data, ChatGPT achieves high accuracy in various NLP tasks.

- ChatGPT is very flexible. Users are able to fine-tune their questions for specific tasks and domains, allowing for customization to fit specific needs.

ChatGPT does have disadvantages and limitations. Here are the most notable:

- Bias: Like other AI models, ChatGPT may have biases in its training data that can affect the accuracy and fairness of its outputs.

- Lack of common sense: ChatGPT does not have a deep understanding of the world and may generate nonsensical or inappropriate responses.

- Misuse potential: ChatGPT's ability to generate humanlike text can be used for malicious purposes, such as spreading misinformation or propaganda.

- Limitations in handling words not in its vocabulary: ChatGPT may struggle to generate accurate responses for rare or unseen words.

- Limitations in understanding sarcasm or irony: ChatGPT may struggle to recognize and generate sarcastic or ironic language.

- Ethical and societal implications: The development and use of large language models like ChatGPT have raised ethical and societal concerns, such as the potential for biased results, privacy issues, and the impact on employment.

Let's now take a look at areas where ChatGPT is making an impact.

Education

ChatGPT has raised difficult questions in education about the definition of plagiarism and academic integrity. *Plagiarism* is taking another's ideas, writings, artistic designs, and so forth and presenting them as one's own, without attribution. More specifically, plagiarism includes taking parts of another's work and publishing them as one's own, either word for word or in substance. On the other hand, *academic integrity* means being honest when you research and use the work and contributions of others. Difficulties arise when the work is generated by *something* (such as ChatGPT) rather than *someone*.

Students may see ChatGPT as just another tool, such as spell-checkers or calculators. Unfortunately, some students are using ChatGPT to answer test questions and generate entire works, such as essays and term papers, and presenting them as their own work.

ChatGPT is causing teachers at all levels to change testing methods to keep up with the rapidly improving tool. For example, some teachers are requiring students to take exams in the classroom, where, for students using their computers, teachers are using lockdown browsers. Students not using computers answer the questions manually on bluebooks. A *lockdown browser* such as Respondus is installed on student computers and it disables the use of other browsers, applications, and desktop functions such as search. Students can move out of the lockdown browser once they complete the test and submit it.

Some public school systems, such as New York City's, have banned the use of ChatGPT on school devices and networks to diminish cheating. However, most universities have been reluctant to follow suit because it is not clear in all cases whether ChatGPT is a research tool or a plagiarism engine. The answer remains debatable.

Journalism

In January 2023, technology news outlet *CNET* (www.cnet.com) admitted it used ChatGPT to write over 70 articles after experts discovered the site's three-month-long "experiment with automation." *CNET*'s use of ChatGPT was unveiled when marketing expert Gael Breton tweeted that he had found a total of 75 finance articles published on the site that had been generated by ChatGPT. The articles carried the byline "CNET Money Staff" despite being generated by ChatGPT. Another technology site, *Futurism*, found that some CNET stories contained some "very dumb errors." The *Washington Post* noted that CNET only admitted to using ChatGPT after the site was called out by Breton, other experts, and other sites.

CNET began adding lengthy corrections to some of its AI-generated articles. The problem here is twofold: First, *CNET* tried to use ChatGPT to write articles, but the quality and accuracy left much to be desired. Second, *CNET* did not inform its readers that the site was using ChatGPT to write some of its articles.

Search Engines

Shortly after ChatGPT was released, industry analysts stated the tool would disrupt search engines because the tool can provide information in clear, simple sentences rather than just providing a list of Internet links. That is, ChatGPT can explain concepts in ways that people can easily understand. The system can also save users time as they do not necessarily need to visit the sites listed by a search engine to obtain the information for which they are searching and then integrate it. ChatGPT is designed to perform these two functions.

Software Engineering

ChatGPT can create simple software programs. Essentially, ChatGPT can write the computer code, tailored to a user's request and parameters, to build websites and other computer programs. Not only that, but ChatGPT can also correct software errors.

ChatGPT-4

ChatGPT-4, scheduled for release in 2023, will be the most advanced artificial intelligence system developed by OpenAI. The upcoming version of Chapter GPT-4 could have 1 trillion parameters, compared to 175 billion parameters for ChatGPT-3.

ChatGPT-4 will have the same capabilities as ChatGPT-3 but will produce much more accurate responses at a much faster rate and should be less expensive as well. ChatGPT-4 should enable humans to communicate in a more natural and accurate manner.

ChatGPT Detectors

Edward Tian, a senior at Princeton University, designed GPTZero (www.gptzero.me), a tool to help educators detect writing generated by ChatGPT. In early February 2023, the tool had a false-positive rate of less than 2 percent. (False positive means that the tool would identify that a portion of text was written by ChatGPT when it was not.) Educators can sign up to be on an e-mail list for updates about the next version of the technology. If a detector tool flags a student's writing as produced by ChatGPT, many teachers see that as a starting point for a conversation, rather than a clear case of academic dishonesty. For example, students may have used ChatGPT as a starting point for generating ideas in much the same way that students may use a tool such as Grammarly, which may rewrite sentences to make them more coherent and/or grammatically correct.

Questions

1. As a student, do you consider that ChatGPT enables research or enables plagiarism?

2. Do you think that ChatGPT might cause you to reconsider your choice of major? Why or why not?

3. Do you think that ChatGPT will disrupt your choice of profession? Why or why not?

4. Which professions do you think ChatGPT is least likely to disrupt? Support your answer.

(*Hint:* For questions 2, 3, and 4, take a look at Section 14.5.)

Sources: Compiled from B. Nolan, "ChatGPT Has Been Around for 2 Months and Is Causing Untold Chaos," *Business Insider*, January 28, 2023; J. Jolly, "What Is ChatGPT? Everything to Know about OpenAI's Free A.I. Essay Writer and How It Works," msn.com, January 28, 2023; E. Ofgang, "What Is GPTZero? The ChatGPT Detection Tool Explained by Its Creator," Techlearning.com, January 27, 2023; J. Bongiorno, "New AI Chatbot Can Do Students' Homework for Them," CBC News, January 27, 2023; A. Klein, "Can Digital Tools Detect ChatGPT-Inspired Cheating?," *EducationWeek*, January 27, 2023; L. Tung, "ChatGPT Can Write Code. Now Researchers Say It's Good at Fixing Bugs Too," *ZDNet*, January 26, 2023; S. Kelly, "ChatGPT Passes Exams from Law and Business Schools," CNN Business, January 26, 2023; A. Mitchell, "ChatGPT Could Make These Jobs Obsolete: 'The Wolf Is at the Door'," msn.com, January 25, 2023; M. Milano, "CNET Uses ChatGPT to Write Articles, Runs into Major Issues," *WebProNews*, January 19, 2023; D. Gewirtz, "Can AI Detectors Save Us from ChatGPT?," *ZDNet*, January 13, 2023; S. Svrluga, "Was That Essay Written by AI? A Student Made an App that Might Tell You," *Washington Post*, January 12, 2023; T. Barrabi, "NYC Schools Block Access to ChatGPT over Cheating Concerns," *New York Post*, January 5, 2023; L. Ocelot, "ChatGPT-4, the Newest and Most Advanced AI System, Might Prompt a Major Shift in the Way We Communicate," Medium.com, January 1, 2023; I. Khan, "ChatGPT Caused 'Code Red' at Google, Report Says," CNET, December 22, 2022; K. Rosenblatt, "An AI Chatbot Went Viral. Some Say It's Better than Google; Others Worry It's Problematic," NBC News, December 2, 2022; and https://openai.com, accessed February 2, 2023.

Before you go on...

1. Describe the advantages of computer vision, natural language processing, and speech recognition.

2. What are cobots?

3. Discuss how you might use information agents and monitoring and surveillance agents.

14.5 Artificial Intelligence in the Functional Areas

LEARNING OBJECTIVE

Provide use case examples of artificial intelligence applications in accounting, finance, marketing, production and operations management, human resource management, and management information systems.

ACCT AI in Accounting

By the end of 2020, machine learning systems were performing routine functions, freeing accountants to focus on performing judgment-intensive tasks and communicating with clients. Machine learning requires huge amounts of data to provide accurate results. Not surprisingly, then, the largest accounting firms are leading the industry in developing ML applications. The Big Four are Ernst & Young (www.ey.com), PwC (www.pwc.com), Deloitte (www.deloitte.com), and KPMG (www.kpmg.com). Consider these examples:

- KPMG uses IBM Watson, an ML system, to help leasing companies comply with the IFRS 16 lease accounting standard.

- Argus, an ML tool developed by Deloitte, reviews documents for key accounting information. The tool works with many types of documents, including but not limited to sales, leasing and derivatives contracts, employment agreements, invoices, client meeting minutes, legal letters, and financial statements. Deloitte has also deployed a service that monitors risk associated with ML algorithms. This service can help early adopters use machine learning tools with reduced fear of adverse effects.

- Suppose an accounting clerk is processing a transaction but is unsure whether to post the expense in this month's financials or the next month. Without an ML system, the clerk decides how to record that transaction. However, this decision might not be correct. If the entry is incorrect, it might go unchecked and uncorrected. This problem is one of the reasons why many companies are not confident in the accuracy of their most recent close and have had to reopen their books after close to correct errors.

  To help with such problems, Flexi (www.flexi.com), a provider of enterprise financial management software, has deployed an ML system that helps organizations avoid errors and accelerate the financial close process. Specifically, the system offers suggestions on how to correctly record transactions based on accounting rules.

Taxes   ML systems use knowledge of the tax code to process clients' tax information through a set of rules and calculate the amount of taxes they owe. In 2017, for example, H&R Block (www.hrblock.com) incorporated IBM Watson to help deliver the best outcome for each unique tax situation.

Tax preparation involves massive volumes of data, encompassing thousands of pages of the federal tax code, as well as state tax codes and local tax codes, all of which impact a client's tax outcome. H&R Block and IBM trained Watson using data from the more than 750 million returns that H&R Block had filed since 1955. H&R Block tax experts then validated Watson's conclusions and first applied Watson to the thousands of client questions and topics discussed with clients during the return filing process.

H&R Block uses Watson to understand context, interpret client intent, and draw connections between clients' statements and relevant areas of their returns. H&R Block professionals can then identify additional areas of possible tax implications to maximize client refunds or reduce their tax liabilities. The client can also follow along with the tax preparation process on a dedicated client companion screen that highlights areas for deductions, making the preparation process more transparent and understandable.

Here is how the process works. A customer enters an H&R Block office and sits down in front of a screen. A tax professional begins the usual interview, asking about life events, potential deductions, and possible credits, entering data as the client watches the screen. Throughout the process, Watson references 600 million data points, the entire U.S. tax code, and state and local tax codes, to outline areas with potential savings. After the customer interview, Watson displays a chart of all possible deductions and credits. The tax professional then goes through the chart with the customer, explaining all the different ways to increase a refund or reduce liabilities.

Auditing

An *audit* is an independent examination of the financial information of organizations to determine whether their financial statements are accurate. Let's look at examples where organizations use ML systems in auditing and compliance.

- *Problem:* Most enterprises audit only a fraction of their invoices, meaning they could miss errors, fraud, and contract violations. Machine learning systems validate all invoices against contract terms and assign a risk score based on errors, anomalies, and noncompliance with contract terms.

    Requirement: Automatically audit all invoices and flag high-risk invoices for manual review.

    Solution: ML systems will enable auditors to examine 100 percent of companies' financial transactions. ML algorithms will process and review the data, recognize anomalies, and compile a list of outliers for auditors to check. Instead of spending most of their time checking data, auditors can focus specifically on the reasons behind a pattern or anomaly. If auditors can check every transaction, then their financial information will be more accurate, and they can provide better advice to their clients. ML systems automatically approve low-risk invoices so they can proceed to payment, and they flag high-risk invoices for manual review.

- *Problem:* Accounting teams typically audit invoices after they have been paid. As time passes, it can become increasingly difficult for companies to recover erroneous or fraudulent spend. Even if a company can eventually recover the spend, there is a cost to not having that cash on hand.

    Requirement: Streamline the audit process to ensure that review of all spend happens prior to payment.

    Solution: ML systems streamline the manual review process to efficiently audit all spend prior to payment.

- *Problem:* Procurement teams may spend large amounts of time negotiating contract terms only to have vendor invoices violate them. Contract violations may relate to payment terms, volume discounts, and pricing mismatches.

    Requirement: Make sense of all contract terms and validate invoices against them to ensure that the invoice adheres to the contract.

    Solution: ML systems integrate with contract management systems and repositories to extract all contract terms. ML systems use semantic analysis to make sense of those terms in business contexts. Further, they are trained to identify invoices whose details do not comply. *Semantic analysis* is the process of drawing meaning from text; it is related to natural language processing.

- *Problem:* With thousands of invoices being processed every month, it is very difficult to examine each one. Fake invoices, shell companies, and vendor impersonation are only some of the methods that criminals use to target companies.

    Requirement: Identify suspect fraud in invoices.

    Solution: ML systems review invoices in relation to data in contracts, business systems, online sources, and other invoices to identify suspected fraud.

- *Problem:* Companies could be paying the same bill twice—once via expense reimbursement and again via invoice. If invoice and expense automation systems do not communicate, then duplicate spend can go unnoticed.

    Requirement: Detect duplicate spend across both invoice and expense automation systems.

Solution: ML systems remember all of the invoice- and expense-based spend that they process, regardless of when the spend occurs and what the receipts and invoices look like. Therefore, ML systems ensure that companies do not pay the invoice when they have already reimbursed the employee for the same spend, or vice versa.

- *Problem:* Duplicate invoices can occur. In rare cases, vendors send duplicate invoices on purpose. In the majority of cases, however, they are a mistake. They can also be a case of fraud by an employee. Invoice automation systems can catch duplicates, generally when those invoices have the same invoice number. If a vendor is sending a separate monthly or quarterly summary invoice, then duplicates can be even more difficult to catch.

  Requirement: Identify all duplicate invoices, regardless of when they are received, how they are grouped, and whether they have the same invoice number.

  Solution: ML systems do not forget data that they have ingested. They catch duplicate invoices—even ones sent at different times, broken up into smaller pieces, or having different invoice numbers—by matching individual line items and other data, and flag them for review prior to payment.

- *Problem:* An organization's reputation can be damaged by its vendor associations. Therefore, firms should consider reputation risks and monetary penalties arising from vendor misconduct, such as violation of the Foreign Corrupt Practices Act, the United Kingdom Bribery Act, and payments to companies with which a board member has a relationship.

  Requirement: Limit your exposure to vendor misconduct such as regulatory violations and conflicts of interest.

  Solution: ML systems check the names of vendors, politically exposed employees, and board members and their associations against online databases, flagging high-risk organizations and people.

- *Problem:* Companies receive thousands of invoices every month, making keeping abreast of associated discount opportunities very difficult.

  Requirement: Validate invoice amounts against early payment contract terms, and flag those that do not include these savings.

  Solution: ML systems extract and understand contract terms related to early payment. When an invoice payment deadline approaches, these systems flag savings opportunities associated with early payments.

- *Problem:* A minor delay in a firm's invoice automation system can result in paying invoices twice. The system may hold the invoice because an approver is on vacation or the invoice failed a two-way match for a minor reason. A business partner who would like to have the invoice paid might intervene to get the invoice paid manually. Afterward, the system may clear the hold and process the invoice, meaning that the firm has double-paid. The vendor might not realize it, and the firm will not discover the problem until it has audited the spend.

  Requirement: Flag all duplicate invoices as high risk if they have already been paid, even if payment occurred outside the normal process.

  Solution: ML systems remember all invoices and their payments, and they are trained to search for duplicate spend regardless of when invoices are paid, by whom, and under what circumstances.

- *Problem:* Many vendors are required to maintain insurance policies that protect them and your company. How does your company ensure that those policies provide sufficient coverage?

  Requirement: Ensure that your vendors are properly insured and that all policies are current.

  Solution: ML systems extract and make sense of the various insurance requirements in a firm's contracts, as well as their expiration dates. This process validates that all required insurance policies are current and meet a firm's coverage criteria. It also alerts the firm when coverage limits are insufficient or certificates need to be updated.

- *Problem:* Most companies employ contractors in a variety of departments such as janitorial services, temporary workers, systems integrators, and consultants. Firms generally trust their contractors to bill them for the hours they actually work. But how can the firms verify that they were billed correctly?

Requirement: Ensure that contractors are working the hours they claim in their invoices.

Solution: ML systems integrate with relevant business systems such as time tracking, card access, and e-mail and messaging. The systems build a profile of access and work activity for different types of contractors. When the system audits an invoice for a contractor who is inconsistent with the profile, it will flag the invoice as high risk.

- *Problem:* A three-way match refers to the three components—purchase order, receipt of goods, and supplier invoice—that must match within agreed-upon tolerance levels to ensure a proper and timely payment. This method is limited to price and units across invoices, receipts, and purchase orders. As a business becomes more sophisticated, it needs to validate not just price and units, but also volume discounts, payment terms, delivery times, transport conditions, chain of custody, service level agreements, and whatever else is meaningful to the business, based on data from any of the business systems.

  Requirement: Automatically match data elements from any of your business systems.

  Solution: ML systems recognize the content of invoices and match those data with data from enterprise systems such as contract management and enterprise resource planning to ensure that transactions are accurate.

- *Problem:* Businesses might have to make a conscious choice to pay more to ensure quality and timeliness in a supply chain. At the same time, however, businesses might want the lowest price, or at least the market rate, for goods and services. It is important for a firm to know how much it is paying and what the market rate is when it renegotiates contracts or chooses future business partners.

  Requirement: Have visibility into what you pay for goods and services versus market rate.

  Solution: ML systems gather information from thousands of online sources to understand market pricing and other details for goods and services. When an invoice price exceeds a certain threshold over the market price, the system will flag the invoice for review. By keeping track of overcharges over time, the firm will have improved insights into what suppliers are doing. These insights empower the company to have stronger negotiations at a later time.

- *Problem:* When a company renegotiates a contract for volume discounts, it should review vendors' invoices to ensure that they follow agreed-upon terms.

  Requirement: Ensure that invoices reflect the volume discounts specified in your contracts.

  Solution: ML systems make sense of the volume discounts in the firm's contracts and keep track of the firm's purchase volume. When the system audits an invoice that does not comply with the price for the firm's current volume, it will flag it for review.

- *Problem:* A small percentage of vendors might try to cheat a company's system. For example, they can send the firm a stream of fraudulent invoices that fall just below the review threshold, break up large invoices into smaller amounts, or slowly add extras and surcharges to each new invoice in hopes that the company will not notice. These anomalies can go unnoticed in many business systems.

  Requirement: Firm must be alerted to suspicious invoice activity before they make payment.

  Solution: ML systems use a combination of computer vision and semantic analysis to build a profile of what "good" invoices look like and uncover unusual patterns that humans might not notice.

- *Problem:* Company employees are often bogged down with invoice reviews and contract checks, forcing them to waste time on outdated, manual processes. Employees are responsible for validating invoices and work under the assumption that the service the firm is being billed for was delivered.

  Requirement: Ensure that invoices are for the correct amounts, are being paid to the correct vendors, and match the negotiated contract terms. This process removes employees from manual approvals so they can focus on more important tasks.

Solution: ML systems gather information from digital sensors such as an office key fob system and supplier contract terms, cross-matching them with invoices and enforcing compliance across the process. A *key fob* is a small, programmable device that provides access to a physical object. The device can be used to provide one-device, one-factor authentication to objects such as doors or automobiles.

How ChatGPT Impacts Accounting

1. Automation of routine tasks: ChatGPT can perform routine tasks such as data entry and financial statement preparation, freeing up accountants' time to focus on higher-value tasks.
2. Improved accuracy and efficiency: ChatGPT can assist accountants in generating reports and financial statements with improved accuracy and efficiency.
3. Enhanced data analysis: ChatGPT can assist accountants in analyzing large amounts of financial data, providing insights and recommendations for decision making.
4. Fraud detection: ChatGPT can be used to detect anomalies and patterns in financial data that may indicate fraud.
5. Improved customer service: ChatGPT can be used to respond to customer inquiries, freeing up time for accountants to focus on more complex tasks.

FIN AI in Finance

Machine learning systems have been in use for years in the financial sector. Here we look at four areas where these systems are widely used: process automation, security, insurance and risk management, and algorithmic training.

Process Automation   ML systems enable organizations to replace manual work, automate repetitive tasks, and increase productivity.

- *Chatbots.* ML-driven chatbots provide access to all of a customer's data. They communicate with customers to provide account information, send notifications to customers, track spending habits, provide credit scores, set and manage budgets, suggest how to save money, pay bills, and help them reset their passwords. Chatbots can also enable customer to search their account history for a specific transaction with a specific merchant, avoiding the hassle of searching their bank statements. The bots can also compute total amounts of credit and debt, a task that customers previously had to perform manually.

  Chatbots also assist in call centers. Organizations train the chatbots with data from previous customer interactions. The chatbots then interact directly with customers. If a chatbot cannot answer a query, it refers the customer to a human. For instance, Privatbank, a Ukrainian bank, has deployed chatbots across its mobile and Web platforms. The chatbots resolve general customer queries quickly, thereby enabling the bank to decrease the number of human assistants. Examples of chatbots are Bank of America's Erica, Capital One's Eno, Ally Bank's Ally Assist, USAA's Clinc, and HSBC's Amy.

  Robo-advisors are a special type of chatbot that analyze each customer's portfolio, risk tolerance, and previous investment decisions to offer advice to financial advisors on portfolio management and investment rebalancing decisions. For example, ForwardLane (**www.forwardlane.com**) provides advisors with personalized investment advice and quantitative modeling that used to be available only to extremely wealthy clients. The advisors can then pass along the information to their clients.

  Traditionally, human investment advisors have been responsible for managing financial portfolios. Today, financial institutions use ML to manage client portfolios and optimize clients' assets. Customers enter their present financial assets and goals. A robo-advisor then allocates the current assets across investment opportunities based on the customer's risk preferences and goals, taking into account real-time market dynamics.

- *Paperwork automation.* JPMorgan Chase & Co. (**www.jpmorganchase.com**) is a U.S. multinational investment bank and financial services company. The firm has implemented an ML system called Contract Intelligence (COiN) that leverages natural language processing and image recognition. COiN analyzes legal documents and extracts important data points and clauses. Before the bank deployed COiN in 2016, their lawyers spent 360,000 hours each year manually reviewing 12,000 commercial loan agreements. With COiN, the task is completed in seconds, saving huge amounts of time and expense

Security   Banks are introducing ML systems into their fraud detection systems. The banks have two objectives: (a) to detect real incidents of fraud quickly and accurately and (b) to prevent false positives. Banks do not want to abolish existing fraud detection rules, many of which were implemented to comply with government regulations. Rather, they want to augment their existing systems with new ML systems. Consider the following examples:

- *Monitoring.* Banks use ML systems to monitor thousands of transaction variables for every account in real time. These systems examine each action that a cardholder takes and then determine whether an attempted activity is characteristic of that individual. Significantly, they identify fraudulent behavior with high accuracy in real time. When they identify suspicious account behavior, they can request additional identification from the customer to validate the transaction. Alternatively, they can block the transaction.

    Consider rogue trading, which is a serious problem for banks around the world. Losses and fines since 2010 for the top 13 global banks have totaled more than $10 billion.

    In an attempt to stop rogue trading, banks have deployed ML systems that attempt to predict which traders are likely to go rogue. They monitor traders and their communications. For example, they search for obvious phrases and keywords such as "Let's take this conversation offline." They also monitor traders' credit scores, human resources reviews, court convictions, sizable divorce settlements, and many other variables to make their predictions more accurate.

    These ML systems make it more difficult for a trader to make the kind of enormous bets that led to one-off losses of as much as $6 billion in JPMorgan Chase and Co.'s "London Whale" scandal. In April and May 2012, $2 billion in trading losses occurred at the firm, based on transactions booked through their London branch. Trader Bruno Iksil, nicknamed the London Whale, accumulated enormous credit default swap (CDS) positions in the market. A *credit default swap* is a financial contract that allows an investor to swap or offset his or her credit risk with that of another investor.

- *Finding false positives.* False positives, which are legitimate transactions that are wrongly rejected due to suspected fraud, account for more than $100 billion in annual losses for global retailers, in addition to lost customers. ML systems, such as Mastercard's Decision Intelligence technology, analyze various data points to identify fraudulent transactions that human analysts might miss, while improving real-time approval accuracy and decreasing false positives. Using ML to spot unusual patterns and improve general regulatory compliance workflows helps financial organizations to be more efficient and accurate in their processes.

    The Nasdaq stock market is an attractive target for criminals. As the world's largest stock exchange by volume, it must be constantly monitored for attempts to illicitly beat the system. These attempts can include manipulations to inflate a stock's closing price; rapidly buying and selling stocks to give the false impression that a lot of activity has occurred; and spoofing, which is placing a large buy or sell order with no intention of actually executing it to create artificially high demand.

    The legacy Nasdaq surveillance system issued around 1,000 alerts per day for human analysts to investigate. Only a fraction of those cases were subsequently confirmed as fraud, which resulted in heavy fines. An ML system is now helping to monitor Nasdaq, augmenting the existing system to flag any signs of market abuse. The ML system also works with human analysts to monitor more than 17.5 million trades per day.

    The ML system was trained to detect particular types of abuse by learning from historical examples. Every time it detects similar suspicious activity, it alerts a human analyst, who possesses the appropriate expertise. After investigating the case, the analyst enters the outcome back into the ML system. In that way, the system learns and becomes better at catching instances of attempted abuse.

- *Image recognition.* Using image recognition, Onfido's platform plugs into various publicly available databases to provide employers with rapid identity verification and background checks for issues such as driving and criminal records.

Insurance and Risk Management   Consider usage-based insurance models, which are based on ML systems that utilize data from telematics and IoT sensors. The transformation from legacy fixed premium insurance models to modern pay-as-you-go models is the result of leveraging ML systems and driving data to more accurately profile driver and trip specifics in order to offer accurate micro-insurance premiums.

- *Client behavioral modeling.* Consider this hypothetical scenario from the near future. Suppose that a customer is driving a car on the highway on a long and tiring trip. The ML system in the car uses computer vision to note that his eyes are droopy. The system's sensors gather data that shows the way he is driving—for example, speed, handling, and braking—is different from the way he normally operates his car. The system then uses natural language processing over the car's speakers to tell him to park his car and get some rest. He resists, thinking that he does not need a break. The system tells him that after analyzing the number of hours that he has been driving, the speed at which the car is running, and his head movements, it feels that he must take at least a small break. On the automobile's digital screen, the system then offers to buy a coffee for him from the next coffee shop on the highway. He accepts the offer. In the near future, if he does not accept the offer, then the system will be able to slow the car and pull it gently off the highway.

- *Claim settlement.* ML systems are also impacting claim settlement. By leveraging computer vision and natural language processing in ML systems, insurance assessors can gather real-time information related to accidents and settle claims faster.

  The system takes charge of the entire process, walking the customer through it, step-by-step, in a conversational format. It gathers all the information required for processing the claim, including videos or photos of the damage, and uploads that information into a database. Next, the system examines the application for fraud, searching for anomalies and noncompliant data. It then accesses the insurer's adjustment model, where it examines a range of values for payout. Finally, it calculates and proposes payout amounts, based on a payout predictor model it has been trained on.

- *Compliance issues, regulatory issues, and risk management.* ML-powered systems help lenders lower compliance and regulatory costs by providing robust credit scoring and lending applications. These applications help lenders achieve faster and more accurate risk assessment by factoring in the applicant's character and repayment capacity. For example, Underwrite.ai (https://www.underwrite.ai) applies ML to provide lenders with dynamic models of credit risk. Significantly, these models outperform traditional approaches to lending.

  Banks use ML systems to stay in compliance and to identify fraud. For example, IPSoft's Amelia uses natural language processing to scan legal and regulatory text for compliance issues.

Algorithmic Trading   ML systems help to make better algorithmic trading decisions. ML algorithms monitor thousands of data sources in real time, including the news and trading results, to detect patterns that could force stock prices to go up or down. These systems can then act to sell, hold, or buy stocks according to its predictions.

How ChatGPT Impacts Finance

1. Automation of routine tasks: ChatGPT can be trained to perform routine tasks such as data entry, portfolio analysis, and financial statement preparation, freeing up finance professionals' time to focus on higher-value tasks.

2. Improved accuracy and efficiency: ChatGPT can assist finance professionals in generating reports and financial statements with improved accuracy and efficiency.

3. Enhanced data analysis: ChatGPT can assist finance professionals in analyzing large amounts of financial data, providing insights and recommendations for decision making.

4. Improved risk management: ChatGPT can be used to analyze financial data and identify potential risks, helping finance professionals make informed decisions about investments and risk management strategies.

5. Customer service: ChatGPT can be used to respond to customer inquiries and provide financial advice, freeing up time for finance professionals to focus on more complex tasks.

MKT AI in Marketing

Improved Lead Scoring Accuracy   Lead scoring helps enterprises rank prospective customers on a scale that represents their value to the firm. Improving lead scoring accuracy helps the company prioritize its lead generation strategies.

Marketing managers use ML systems to monitor customer behavior in order to obtain data for these calculations. For example, the systems track websites visited, e-mails opened, downloads, clicks, and many other variables. They also consider a customer's behavior on social media platforms, such as accounts they follow, posts they like and dislike, ads they engage with, and many other variables.

Easier to Predict Customer Churn   *Customer churn*, also known as customer turnover, is the number of customers who ended their relationship with a business. The *churn rate* is the percentage of customers who leave a business within a specified period of time.

Companies want to know how customers engage with a product, service, or mobile app. Churn rates are an indicator of customer satisfaction with the firms' products and services. Firms need to be able to predict their churn rate in order to minimize it.

To predict churn rates, companies are using ML systems to monitor customer behavior. For example, they ask when was the last time a customer signed in to their profile on the firm's website, how long they stayed on the website, and when was their last purchase. The answers to such questions, and many others, can predict that a customer will end their relationship with this company. ML systems can analyze such customer behavior at huge scale, enabling firms to better predict that certain customers might leave.

Profitable Dynamic Pricing Models   A *dynamic pricing* strategy allows businesses to offer flexible prices for the product and services they offer. Essentially, this strategy helps companies segment prices based on customer choices. Dynamic pricing is common in the hospitality, travel, and entertainment industries. The retail industry is now employing ML systems to implement this strategy as well.

Dynamic pricing is related to *real-time pricing*, which occurs when the value of goods is based on specific market conditions. For example, purchasing an airline ticket depends on how far in advance the customer purchases it, the number of tickets already purchased on that particular flight, and the location of the seat on the aircraft. Another example of real-time pricing is surge pricing on Uber and Lyft.

ML systems make it easier for companies to implement and improve their dynamic pricing models by analyzing vast amounts of data. These data include historical prices for each service or product, customer demand, and external factors such as industry trends, seasonality, weather, and location. ML systems also analyze customer information such as search and/or booking history, demographic features, income, and many other variables.

Sentiment Analysis   Companies that implement e-commerce cannot have face-to-face relationships with their customers. As a result, it is difficult to understand how customers are feeling. For instance, with face-to-face conversations, you can make judgments based on facial expressions, tone, and body language. You can then use these judgments to determine whether the person with whom you are speaking is happy, satisfied, or excited.

Companies that employ e-commerce need to know how customers are feeling in order to respond properly. ML systems can help in this area by analyzing text to determine whether the sentiment expressed by customers is positive or negative, a process called *sentiment analysis*.

ML systems read all digital communications and classify them as positive or negative. They then alert marketing managers, who can respond to negative comments and trends. ML systems can also identify happy and satisfied customers to help companies find social influencers and brand ambassadors.

Improve Website Experiments

A/B testing is an excellent method to improve the features of a company's website, mobile app, and e-mail marketing content. *A/B testing* is the process of showing two versions of, for example, the same Web page to different segments of website visitors at the same time and comparing which version drives more purchases or signups. ML systems analyze the results of thousands of A/B tests every day. Companies then use these data to improve their content to increase visitor engagement.

Consider Google RankBrain, an ML-based search engine algorithm that helps Google learn from users' search results to provide more relevant search results in the future. For example, if two people search for the same term on Google at the same time, they are most likely to see different search results based on the results of Google's A/B testing.

Prioritize Ad Targeting and Customer Personalization

ML systems are helping marketing managers target their ads more effectively. A company might produce excellent ads, but they will not be effective if the correct audiences are not viewing them. ML systems can help ensure that companies reach their target audience.

ML systems can also help personalize the customer experience. ML algorithms can predict which type of content will be the most popular with each unique visitor. ML systems can:

- Recommend content on a company's website based on users' history and preferences
- Remarket company's content across desktop, laptop, mobile, and social interfaces
- Personalize branded content in e-mails based on users' history across other channels
- Drive new, targeted users to relevant content

Product discovery. Product discovery is the first, and, arguably, the most important component of the shopping process. Retailers employ visual and voice search to help customers find what they are looking for.

ML-powered *visual search* systems enable customers to upload images and find similar products based on colors, shapes, and patterns. For example, American Eagle's (www.ae.com) ML-powered image-recognition system uses visual search to help people find the same or similar clothes as the image they have uploaded. The system also suggests other items that would go well with the product they buy.

Neiman Marcus uses ML-based intelligent visual search in its Snap. Find. Shop. app. Customers "snap" pictures of their favorite items. The app then searches inventory to find similar products. Customers who use this app can shop more efficiently.

Walmart, Tesco, Kohl's, Costco, and many other companies use Google or Amazon ML-powered voice-recognition technology and natural language processing to provide customers with simple and quick *voice search*. For instance, customers can ask Amazon's Alexa for a desired item and its delivery status without typing anything.

Alibaba (www.alibaba.com) is a Chinese multinational technology company that specializes in e-commerce. Alibaba's ML system chooses which items to display to customers when they visit the website and search for products. The system builds a customized page view for every visitor, displaying items they will be interested in. It is significant that the system also dynamically prices items based on its knowledge of the customer's past spending habits. By monitoring customer actions—whether they make a purchase, browse to a different item, or leave the site—the system learns in real time to make adjustments to these page views to increase the probability that the visit will end with the customer making a purchase.

Alibaba has deployed automated content generation to make it easier to write descriptions for items it sells. Its ML-driven copywriter uses natural language processing algorithms to produce 20,000 lines of copy in one second. The copywriter creates multiple versions of advertisements and runs them through algorithms trained on customer behavior data. The system finds which combination of words is most likely to result in customers clicking on them. It then uses those words to create its copy.

Product categorization. Love the Sales (www.lovethesales.com) is a fashion e-commerce aggregator that allows consumers to shop all sale items from multiple brands and retailers in a single online destination. The website uses ML systems to classify more than 1 million items from more than 500 brands and retailers. These systems tag items and sort them in different categories for customers.

Computer Vision for Product Recognition

ML systems help brands recognize their products in online images and videos. For instance, Miller Lite (www.millerlite.com) used an ML system to scan through user-generated content on social media. ML algorithms searched for images to find posts related to the brand. The systems tracked information about competing brands and influencers. In addition, it collected data about users who posted on social media about Miller Lite. The ML systems found 1.1 million posts associated with the brand, and they identified 575 Miller Lite promoters.

Amazon's Just Walk Out technology integrates machine learning with cameras and sensors in its Amazon Go cashierless stores. This technology automatically detects when products are taken from or returned to shelves. In addition, it keeps track of the items in a customer's virtual cart. When customers are finished shopping, they simply leave the store. Amazon then sends them a digital receipt and charges their Amazon accounts.

Other physical stores can use Amazon's Dash Cart, which is an ML-powered shopping cart that allows shoppers to skip the checkout line. Shoppers use a QR code in the Amazon app that enables them to easily sign in and begin using the cart. The cart has a screen where shoppers can access their Alexa Shopping Lists to check off items and view their subtotals and coupon scanners so shoppers can apply store coupons as they shop.

The cart uses a combination of computer vision algorithms and sensors to identify items that shoppers put in their carts. When shoppers exit through the store's Amazon Dash Cart line, sensors automatically identify the cart, and their payment is processed using the credit card on their Amazon account.

Relevant Recommendation Systems

ML systems in the form of intelligent personalization software can identify user preferences as well as people who know them best. For example, if users have multiple profiles on their Netflix account, they know that each time they launch the platform, it asks "Who is watching"? Then it provides "recommendations for you" based on shows, movies, and documentaries the user have already watched. These recommendations improve the customer experience.

ML systems help marketing managers discover which types of products consumers want based on their browsing histories and shopping behaviors. Relevant product suggestions increase conversions.

Monitoring Customer Satisfaction

ML systems such as facial recognition can detect customers' moods while they are shopping. Walmart has installed cameras at each checkout lane. If a customer looks annoyed, then a store representative will talk to them to resolve any potential problems.

Chatbots

Live chat enjoys a very high customer satisfaction rating. In fact, industry analysts assert that more than 60 percent of customers are more likely to return to a website if it offers a live chat feature.

Chatbots can help firms improve their live chat feature because ML systems improve chatbots' capabilities. For example, these systems use sentiment analysis to judge the mood of a customer message. When paired with social media, ML systems can gather more information about customers to apply when a chatbot receives a new message. That is, ML systems enable chatbots to personalize the customer experience. As a result, chatbots keep customers on pages for longer periods of time. They also decrease wait times for customers because they can handle simple, routine queries without human assistance.

Improved Audience Insights

With ML systems, companies can learn valuable information about their customers. This information provides more accurate data that firms can use to build more comprehensive, targeted customer profiles to increase customer engagement. For example, Affinio (www.affinio.com) helps companies discover various aspects of customer behavior, such as which customers are foodies, which ones watch a particular television show, and which ones have traveled to similar places.

Discover Trends   ML systems are capable of monitoring social media to inspire fresh product and content ideas that directly respond to customers' preferences. As one example, ice cream giant Ben & Jerry's (www.benjerry.com) launched a range of breakfast-flavored ice creams, including Fruit Loot, Frozen Flakes, and Cocoa Loco. The company introduced these products after it had employed ML systems to help its Insight division listen to what was being talked about in the public sphere. For instance, at least 50 songs within the public domain had mentioned "ice cream for breakfast" at one point. Discovering the popularity of this phrase across various platforms revealed the value of ML systems in identifying emerging trends.

Intelligent Marketing Campaigns   AdGreetz (www.adgreetz.com) is a marketing services company that has developed a ML-based advertising platform that can quickly generate thousands or millions of personalized ads.

The first campaign that AdGreetz conducted for Flipkart, giant Indian e-commerce vendor, reached 200 million people across multiple social media platforms. The audience, spread across different regions of India, was extremely diverse, consisting of people who live in different cities, speak different languages, and have different motivations and different relationships with Flipkart.

To give the ads a more significant impact, AdGreetz and Flipkart created about a million *creatives*, or ad banners and other forms of created online advertising. Each creative targeted different groups based on data collected from social media and Flipkart's e-commerce platform. These ads varied dramatically, including different colors, voices, and languages, depending on the target audience. Flipkart has subsequently used AdGreetz to produce an additional 40 campaigns.

How ChatGPT Impacts Marketing

1. Content creation: ChatGPT can be trained to generate written and visual content, freeing up time for marketers to focus on other tasks.

2. Customer service: ChatGPT can be used to respond to customer inquiries, freeing up time for marketers to focus on more strategic tasks.

3. Data analysis: ChatGPT can assist marketers in analyzing large amounts of data, providing insights into customer behavior and preferences and enabling informed decision making.

4. Personalization: ChatGPT can generate personalized marketing messages and recommendations based on customer data, improving customer engagement and increasing conversions.

5. Ad optimization: ChatGPT can be used to analyze ad performance and generate recommendations for optimization, improving the efficiency and effectiveness of marketing campaigns.

POM AI in Production/Operations Management

In the Factory   The *smart factory* is a highly digitized operation that continuously collects and shares data through connected machines, devices, and production systems. Smart factories use Big Data analytics (see Chapter 12), the industrial Internet of Things (see Chapter 8), machine learning, and robotics.

- *Production.* Volkswagen (www.volkswagen.com) is using computer vision to increase its production by 30 percent by 2025. The automaker deployed its first application in its Porsche Leipzig plant. Workers attach several labels to each vehicle they produce. These labels contain vehicle information. Many of the labels contain country-specific information and are written in the customer's language. The computer vision system ensures that the labels are applied properly.

At the Leipzig plant, an employee on the production line now scans the vehicle identification number (VIN) to ensure that the vehicle is identified correctly. The employee also takes photos of each label attached to each car. The computer vision app checks the images in real time to ensure that the labels have the correct content and are written in the appropriate language. This process saves several minutes per vehicle.

Another application of computer vision comes from Volkswagen's Ingolstadt plant, where Audi uses it for quality testing. The system detects the smallest cracks on the vehicle as well as defects in vehicle components.

- *Quality control.* Quality control is critical because customers expect products with zero defects. Defects damage the reputation of the manufacturer and its brand.

  Industry analysts have noted that ML systems increase defect detection rates up to 90 percent. These systems can also check for defects on all products in a production process rather than simply examining samples.

- *Predictive maintenance.* Equipment maintenance is a critical feature of every asset-reliant production operation. Unplanned downtime is expensive. Predictive maintenance techniques help determine the condition of in-service equipment to estimate when maintenance should be performed. This approach saves money and time over routine or time-based preventive maintenance because maintenance is performed only when needed.

  ML-based predictive maintenance systems are trained with data from sensors on the equipment. These systems search for patterns and anomalies in various equipment. They can help to reduce costs, enhance predictability, and make certain that equipment is available when needed. As an additional benefit, they can increase the length of the remaining useful life (RUL) of equipment.

  Consider smart locomotives manufactured by General Electric (GE; www.ge.com). GE has equipped its locomotive with sensors and cameras that gather data for the locomotives' ML system. GE improved its speed and accuracy in detecting problems in these giant, complex machines, which in turn reduced locomotive failure by 25 percent.

- *Robotics.* Smart factories are deploying increasing numbers of robots, which are driven by ML systems. An excellent example is Amazon's Kiva robots in the firm's distribution centers (see the chapter opening case).

In Transportation

An *autonomous vehicle* (automobile, bus, tractor, combine, boat, forklift, etc.) is a vehicle capable of sensing its environment and moving safely with little or no human input. These vehicles are powered by ML systems.

An early application of autonomous vehicles is in public transportation. For instance, Olli is an autonomous electric shuttle bus that operates around the world.

Another application involves autonomous delivery robots. For instance, Nuro delivery robots are delivering groceries and pizza from Domino's. These vehicles are geofenced, meaning that they can operate only inside a predetermined virtual perimeter overlaid on a real-world geographic area.

Another transportation-related application of ML systems is to resolve traffic control and traffic optimization problems using traffic sensors and cameras. Consider Surtrac from Rapid Flow Technologies (www.rapidflowtech.com). Surtrac is an ML-based traffic optimization system that responds in real time to changing traffic conditions by optimizing traffic flows. The system coordinates traffic flows on complex grids, not just on main streets. Surtrac also optimizes for many modes of travel, keeping vehicles, cyclists, pedestrians, and public transportation moving and safe.

Surtrac was first tested in Pittsburgh with a network of nine traffic signals on the city's major roads. The system reduced travel time by 25 percent, wait times at signals by 40 percent, stops by 30 percent, and vehicle emissions by 20 percent.

Along Supply Chains

AI in supply chains helps to deliver optimization capabilities required for more accurate capacity planning, improved productivity, higher quality, lower costs, and greater output, while promoting safer working conditions.

Supply chain optimization. ML systems contribute to solving complex constraint, cost, and delivery problems that companies face today. ML systems can provide supply chain managers with significant insights into how they can improve supply chain performance, anticipating anomalies in logistics costs and performance before they occur. Here are some of the ways in which ML systems help optimize supply chains.

- ML systems use data from Internet of Things sensors, telematics, intelligent transport systems, and traffic data.
- ML systems can improve the accuracy of demand forecasting.
- ML systems can reduce logistics costs by identifying patterns in track-and-trace data captured by IoT sensors. Track-and-trace apps provide real-time data on the location and status of items as they move through a supply chain.
- ML-based planning and optimization systems can reduce lost sales that result when products are not available. Further, these systems can reduce inventory along the supply chain.
- ML systems can optimize capacity utilization along the supply chain.
- ML systems can detect and act on inconsistent supplier quality levels and deliveries. These systems provide visibility into inbound deliveries and delays, and they enable firms to monitor the status of critical orders, including multicomponent orders, in near real time. They also alert companies when a late delivery will impact a customer order.

  When a supply chain disruption does occur, an ML system generates an alert and automatically brings together the right members of the supply chain team to resolve the issue. The system provides the team with the most relevant information, including insights into the orders that are being affected and the potential financial impacts. The system learns from each resolution, thereby improving its performance for the next disruption.

- ML systems use data from automated inspections to reduce the risk and the potential for fraud, while improving product and process quality. Inspectorio (**www.inspectorio. com**), an ML company, is addressing the many problems that a lack of inspection and supply chain visibility creates. Because there can be a time lag to receive handwritten factory inspections, Inspectorio digitizes those inspections and uses machine learning that enables retailers to monitor their supply chains in real time. This process enables retailers to quickly find and address problems in quality and compliance.
- ML systems provide end-to-end supply chain visibility as well as predictive and prescriptive insights into supply chain operations.
- ML systems help companies find and stop privileged credential abuse, which is the leading cause of security breaches across global supply chains. By using the least privilege access approach (see Chapter 4), firms can minimize attacks. Firms know that if a privileged user has entered the correct credentials but the request comes from a risky context, then stronger verification is needed to permit access. Zero Trust Privilege is a framework for verifying who is requesting access, the context of the request, and the risk of the access environment (see O'Reilly Media; **www.oreilly.com**). Centrify (**www.delinea. com/centrify**) a leader in this area.

Security   There are numerous examples of organizations applying ML systems to various aspects of security.

- In 2020, Facebook took down almost 6 billion fake accounts. Criminals use such accounts to spread spam, phishing links, and malware.

  Facebook distinguishes between two types of fake accounts: user-misclassified accounts and violating accounts. User-misclassified accounts are personal profiles for businesses that are meant to be Pages. Facebook simply converts these accounts to Pages.

  Violating accounts are more serious. These are personal profiles that engage in nefarious activities and violate the platform's terms of service. These activities can include using a fake name, impersonating someone, contacting other people to harass them, and many others. Facebook wants to remove violating accounts as quickly as possible without involving legitimate accounts (false positives).

  Facebook uses hand-coded rules and ML to block a fake account either before it is created or before it becomes active. After a fake account has gone live, detection is more difficult. At this point, Facebook's ML system, called Deep Entity Classification (DEC), becomes involved.

Facebook has trained DEC to differentiate fake and real users by their connection patterns across the network. The company calls these patterns *deep features*. They include average age or gender distribution of the user's friends, among thousands of others. In fact, Facebook uses more than 20,000 deep features to characterize each account, providing a snapshot of how each profile behaves.

DEC can identify one of four types of fake profiles:

- Illegitimate accounts that are not representative of the person
- Compromised accounts of real users that attackers have taken over
- Spammers who repeatedly send revenue-generating messages
- Scammers who manipulate users into divulging personal information

Since Facebook implemented DEC, it has limited the volume of fake accounts on the platform to roughly 5 percent of monthly active users. Unfortunately, Facebook has approximately 2.7 billion monthly active users, meaning that 135 million Facebook accounts are still fake!

- Amazon, which has long tried to eliminate counterfeit products from its site, is using machine learning to automatically monitor its website for fake items. The system uses data from Amazon sellers, which give Amazon their logos, trademarks, and other important data about their brands. Amazon's system then scans product listings every day searching for fake items before they are purchased.

  Previously, brands had to report counterfeit items to Amazon. In 2019, Amazon deployed ML-powered Project Zero, which allows brands to take down counterfeit items on their own without Amazon's help.

- In 2018, Walmart began using ML-powered computer vision from Irish startup Everseen (www.everseen.com) to deter theft and losses at its checkouts and self-checkouts in more than 1,000 of its stores. The system, called Missed Scan Detection, notifies attendants if an item moves past a scanner without being scanned, giving them a chance to correct the situation. Walmart maintains that *shrinkage rates*—the loss of goods to theft and accidents—have decreased at stores that employ the system.

  However, a group of Walmart employees who call themselves the Concerned Home Office Associates have claimed that the computer vision system often misidentifies innocuous behavior as theft (false positives) and often fails to stop actual instances of stealing. The group created a video that purports to show the technology failing to flag items that not being scanned in three Walmart stores. Their primary concern is false positives at self-checkouts, which frustrates customers and store associates and leads to longer checkout lines.

How ChatGPT Impacts Production/Operations Management

1. Automation of routine tasks: ChatGPT can be trained to perform routine tasks such as data entry and report generation, freeing up time for supply chain professionals to focus on higher-value tasks.

2. Improved accuracy and efficiency: ChatGPT can assist supply chain professionals in generating reports and analyzing data with improved accuracy and efficiency.

3. Enhanced data analysis: ChatGPT can assist supply chain professionals in analyzing large amounts of data, providing insights into supply chain performance and enabling informed decision making.

4. Inventory optimization: ChatGPT can be used to analyze inventory data and generate recommendations for optimization, improving the efficiency of supply chain operations.

5. Customer service: ChatGPT can be used to respond to customer inquiries, freeing up time for supply chain professionals to focus on more complex tasks.

HRM AI in Human Resources

Recruiting   Recruiting refers to the overall process of identifying, screening, and interviewing suitable candidates for available positions within an organization.

- *Candidate identification and screening.* Finding the right talent is a major problem for virtually all organizations. To assist with this process, AI companies are developing tools to scan résumés, online job profiles, and job queries much more quickly than humans can. These tools automate the candidate search process and move the best candidates to the top of the list.

  Consider DBS Bank (**www.dbs.com**). The DBS Talent Acquisition team created Jobs Intelligence Maestro (JIM), a virtual recruitment bot powered by artificial intelligence. The bank uses JIM to screen candidates applying to be wealth planning managers, a high-value job in the consumer bank.

  After DBS introduced JIM in 2018, the firm was able to shorten the screening time from 32 minutes per candidate to 8 minutes, improve the completion rate of job applications from 85 percent to 97 percent, and respond to 96 percent of all candidate queries through JIM. As a result, recruiters were able to spend more time personally sharing the culture and values of DBS with candidates.

  CareerBuilder (**www.careerbuilder.com**) is an employment website founded in 1995. In 2019 the company launched its Talent Discovery platform. CareerBuilder claims that the machine-learning tool finds potential employees faster and increases job applications. The company trained the tool with data that include 2.3 million job postings, 680 million unique profiles, 310 million unique résumés, 10 million job titles, and 1.3 billion skills.

  Talent Discovery provides a candidate appeal score that helps companies understand how effective a job posting will be at attracting candidates. It also offers recommendations to increase the posting's appeal. Further, it provides a map that displays similar competing jobs in a geographic area and the salaries those jobs are offering. Talent Discovery uses machine learning to help companies create job descriptions that are gender-neutral and tone-neutral to save time and help increase diversity.

- *Promoting diversity and inclusion.* Job descriptions can contain subtle messages about company culture, including its inclusiveness or lack thereof. An AI tool that helps identify problems with the language employed in job descriptions is Textio (**www.textio.com**). The tool analyzes writing for gender bias and other unintentional messages. It suggests alternative wording, serving as a writing coach on diversity and inclusion. Textio has a number of customers, including Expedia (**www.expedia.com**) and Zillow (**www.zillow.com**). Interestingly, Zillow has seen an 11 percent increase in female applicants since it began to use the tool.

- *Video interview analysis.* Because companies want to spend less time on the interviewing process, video interviewing software is becoming increasingly popular. For example, HireVue's video interviewing system employs voice and facial recognition technology, along with an ML ranking algorithm, to evaluate candidates.

Onboarding   *Onboarding* is the process by which new employees acquire the knowledge, skills, and behaviors they need to become effective organizational members.

As companies strive to retain talented employees, mentoring is becoming increasingly important. Consider the AI-driven app Ellen from Next Play. Ellen helps to (a) connect mentees with mentors at their company, (b) expand the mentee's network within the company, and (c) foster a sense of belonging at the workplace. Ellen also nudges mentors and mentees to engage in high-quality conversations. According to Next Play, more than 90 percent of Ellen matches stay in contact beyond their first three mentor/mentee meetings.

IBM is creating a system that answers new employees' most pressing or job-critical questions to help get them up to speed quickly. The system offers training suggestions and provides the names, locations, and contact information for people the employee should connect with very early in their employment.

Career Pathing   AI technology is helping HR professionals in the role of career pathing to enhance employee satisfaction and retention, succession planning, workforce planning, and overall company productivity and profitability. AI systems can efficiently match employees to suitable next-step positions based on their profiles and experience. This process is similar to the way these systems align external candidates to recommended positions within the company.

There are limitations of career pathing ML systems. Along with these systems, employees must be motivated to acquire, apply, and refine their skills to make the most of ML-recommended career paths. Further, more senior employees must help the employee progress through mentorship, project-based work, and vertical and lateral moves. Finally, if an employee wants a complete career overhaul or change, AI systems are not independently creative enough to design an entirely unique career path.

Identifying Employees Who Might Be Leaving the Organization

Veriato's (www.veriato.com) ML platform is designed to identify employees who might be considering leaving the organization. The tool tracks employee computer activity, such as e-mails, keystrokes, and Internet browsing, and stores the information for one month. It then analyzes these data to determine a baseline of normal activity patterns within the organization. Finally, it flags outliers by detecting changes in the overall tone of employees' communications, and it reports them to the employee's supervisor.

Monitoring Employees

Consider employee monitoring at Outback Steakhouse (www.outback.com). Casual dining chains are experimenting with surveillance technology designed to maximize employee efficiency and performance. One Outback location is testing a computer vision tool called Presto Vision (www.presto.com).

Presto Vision uses surveillance cameras that many restaurants already have installed. The system uses machine learning to analyze video footage of restaurant staff at work, particularly their interactions with guests. It provides metrics such as how often servers tend to their tables and how long it takes for food to come out of the kitchen and reach each table. At the end of a shift, managers receive an e-mail of the compiled statistics. They can then use these data to identify problems and determine whether servers, hostesses, and kitchen staff are adequately doing their jobs.

Presto Vision can also be used to correct employee performance in near real time. For instance, managers could be sent text messages when the number of people waiting for a table reaches a certain threshold. In another example, the system could detect when a guest's drink is almost empty and prompt servers to offer them a refill.

Significantly, Presto Vision's software does not identify individual diners, and it does not employ facial recognition technology. The company maintains that it does not collect any personal information and it deletes all video within three days of collection.

Such employee monitoring is a double-edged sword. Industry analysts note that workplace surveillance can have negative effects on employees, such as increased stress and lower job satisfaction.

Monitoring and Improving Employees' Health

Physically or mentally toxic work environments can negatively impact employees' health, resulting in organizational losses up to $300 billion annually. Analysts note further that 60 percent of working Americans experience chronic work-related stress.

To deal with these problems, many firms are asking their employees to opt in to company exercise and diet plans. For example, companies provide their employees with wearables such as the Fitbit and Apple Watch. In return, employees agree to share the data from their wearables with the company in return for a reduction in their health-care premiums. Let's look at how the National Football League (NFL; www.nfl.com) is using sensors to improve the health of players.

Research has highlighted the health risks associated with playing U.S. football. For example, in 2017 researchers from the Veterans Administration Boston Healthcare System and the Boston University School of Medicine published a study in the *Journal of the American Medical Association* that indicated that football players are at a high risk for developing long-term neurological conditions. The study, which did not include a control group, examined the brains of high school, college, and professional football players. Of the 111 NFL-level football players the researchers examined, all but 1 had some form of degenerative brain disease.

As a result, the NFL adopted Amazon Web Services (AWS; www.aws.amazon.com) and Amazon's machine learning products and services to better simulate and predict player injuries, with the goal of improving player health and safety. The partnership uses Next Gen

Stats (**www.nextgenstats.nfl.com**), an existing NFL and AWS agreement that enables the NFL to capture and process data on its players.

Sensors on player equipment and the football itself capture real-time location, speed, and acceleration data of players and the football. The data are then fed into AWS data analytics and machine learning tools to provide fans, broadcasters, and NFL teams with live and on-screen statistics and predictions, such as expected catch rates and pass completion probabilities. Using those data, as well as data from other sources such as video footage, equipment choice, playing surfaces, player injury data, type of play (run or pass), type, frequency, and angle of impact, the speed the players are running, as well as environmental factors (temperature, rain, wind, etc.), the NFL and AWS partnership creates a digital twin of each player.

Typically used in manufacturing to predict machine outputs and potential breakdowns, a *digital twin* is a virtual, digital model of a machine or a person created from real-time and historical data. Using machine learning and predictive analytics, a digital twin can be placed in any number of virtual scenarios, enabling data scientists to see how the digital twin's real-life counterpart would react. These scenarios do not risk the health and safety of real players. Further, data collected from these scenarios provide insights into changes to game rules, player equipment, and other factors that could make football a safer game.

How ChatGPT Impacts Human Resources

1. Automation of routine tasks: ChatGPT can be trained to perform routine tasks such as data entry, resume screening, and candidate correspondence, freeing up time for HR professionals to focus on higher-value tasks.

2. Improved accuracy and efficiency: ChatGPT can assist HR professionals in generating reports and analyzing data with improved accuracy and efficiency.

3. Enhanced data analysis: ChatGPT can assist HR professionals in analyzing large amounts of data, providing insights into HR performance and enabling informed decision making.

4. Improved candidate selection: ChatGPT can be used to analyze candidate data and generate recommendations for selection, improving the efficiency and effectiveness of the recruitment process.

5. Employee engagement: ChatGPT can be used to respond to employee inquiries, providing quick and accurate information and improving employee engagement.

MIS AI in Management Information Systems

Organizational information technology groups use machine learning in many areas. We consider several examples here.

Security   Organizations store vast amounts of customer, strategic, and other forms of data, which must be secured at all times. ML algorithms help identify potential threats and data breaches while also providing solutions to eliminate or mitigate such threats.

Server Optimization   Company servers frequently receive millions of requests per day. The servers, in turn, are required to open Web pages requested by users. Servers can become unresponsive if the number of requests exceeds their processing capacity. ML algorithms can optimize server processing to help meet this demand. In a server farm, ML algorithms allocate user requests among multiple servers to optimally meet demand.

Service Management   IT service management encompasses the activities performed by an IT team to design, deliver, operate, and control information technology services offered to organizational users. ML systems can assist the IT service team in several ways:

- Chatbots can recognize, categorize, and prioritize underlying problems in employee requests. In live chat, chatbots can use natural language processing to answer common questions without human intervention.

- Service desk teams have different skill sets. Some are better at resolving different types of requests than others. ML algorithms can automatically send requests to appropriate employees.

- Many IT requests require humans to perform a complex set of steps to fulfill the requests. In the case of employee onboarding, ML algorithms learn from a historical database of requests that cover a range of actions taken based on the type of employment and the employee's role and department. The algorithms can suggest what types of hardware and software an employee needs as well as the amount of access to organizational applications the employee should receive.

- Based on the historical database of requests and current user behavior patterns, ML algorithms can forecast and fulfill users' requests.

Software Development   Software development is the process of conceiving, specifying, designing, programming, documenting, testing, and error correcting involved in creating and maintaining applications:

- *DevOps* is the combination of cultural philosophies, practices, and tools that increase an organization's ability to quickly develop and deliver applications. Key functions within DevOps projects include continuous integration and continuous delivery. *Continuous integration* is the practice of combining computer code from multiple contributors on a single software project. *Continuous delivery* refers to a situation in which a version of the final software package is always ready to be released but is not sent to production before the decision is made to release it. *DevOps bots*, which are still under development, will be ML-powered bots that assist in all stages of the software development process. Let's take a closer look at bots' potential contributions to the process.

    Requirements gathering. Gathering user requirements remains an art form. DevOps bots will listen in on stakeholder interviews. As stakeholders define their requirements, the bots could conduct a real-time sentiment analysis. They could then determine which requirements the stakeholders considered important and which ones they were uncertain about. The bots could also flag any requirement with a history of negative project outcomes, proactively alert the project manager, and suggest improvements and alternative approaches.

    Users often do not comprehend the risk and cost implications of requested features. The bots will make the DevOps process more transparent to these users. This feature would help business users make more informed choices, particularly if they have a limited software development budget.

    The bots will also make the users aware of the different cost/risk profiles of alternative technologies. For example, if a development team proposes to introduce NoSQL databases into the existing IT environment, stakeholders need to know the operational impact of adding this type of database and the financial return they might expect.

    In the end, the bots could provide a list of prioritized project requirements, risk elements, and technology alternatives. The technology alternative would be in the form of a *DevOps toolchain*, which is a set of tools that help in the development, delivery, and management of software applications. Finally, the bots could provide a list of development project resources, including the appropriate developer skills, business experience, and availability.

    Writing the code. If developers are writing new computer code, then ML algorithms could examine its structure and syntax to help programmers write better code, find and repair software errors, save time, and improve productivity.

    If the developers are working with legacy (existing) code, they might find that this code is poorly documented. If the code was not fully documented, then developers typically begin their improvement efforts somewhere in the legacy code without being certain of the proper entry point. DevOps bots should automatically document the legacy code as well as the code developed by the new team. The bots should also assist the developers in finding the right entry points for enhancing the legacy code.

    Software testing and quality assurance. Software developers use ML algorithms to automatically find and repair errors and other issues within applications during development cycles. For example, tools such as Bugspots can be used to ensure that all software bugs are eliminated without human intervention. Bugspots is a Python implementation of the bug prediction algorithm used at Google.

Application deployment. Software versioning, a form of continuous deployment, is a strategy to categorize the unique states of computer software as it is developed and released. For example, Apple's iOS 14 is a version of Apple's mobile operating system. Software versioning is a critical component of application development and deployment. ML algorithms are useful in predicting problems that can occur in deployment.

AIOps   AIOps, the application of artificial intelligence to IT operations, gives IT professionals a real-time understanding of the issues that affect the availability and performance of the organization's information systems. AIOps learns from data sources such as traditional IT monitoring, logs, application and performance anomalies, and many others.

AIOps provides organizations with an overview across the entire IT environment—computation, network, storage, physical, virtual, and cloud. Specialized algorithms focus on specific tasks. For example, algorithms can pick out significant alerts from an event stream, identify correlations between alerts from different sources, assemble the correct team of human specialists to diagnose and resolve a situation, propose probable root causes and possible solutions based on past experiences, and learn from feedback to improve continuously over time.

Common uses of AIOps include:

- Predictive analytics to prevent system failure or disruption
- Event correlation and root cause analysis
- Optimization of infrastructure utilization
- Capacity planning and forecasting
- IT service management

How ChatGPT Impacts Management Information Systems

1. Automation of routine tasks: ChatGPT can be trained to perform routine tasks such as data entry and report generation, freeing up time for MIS professionals to focus on higher-value tasks.

2. Improved accuracy and efficiency: ChatGPT can assist MIS professionals in generating reports and analyzing data with improved accuracy and efficiency.

3. Enhanced data analysis: ChatGPT can assist MIS professionals in analyzing large amounts of data, providing insights into business performance and enabling informed decision making.

4. Improved decision making: ChatGPT can be used to analyze business data and generate recommendations for decision-making, improving the efficiency and effectiveness of business processes.

5. Improved customer service: ChatGPT can be used to respond to customer inquiries and provide technical support, freeing up time for MIS professionals to focus on more complex tasks.

Before you go on...

1. Look at the functional area that corresponds to your major.
   a. Discuss potential impacts of ML applications on your profession.
   b. Describe additional ML applications not discussed in the text.

14.6 Appendix

LEARNING OBJECTIVE

Understand the process by which a neural network transforms data values from the input node to the output node, and then calculates the loss function to initiate the back propagation process.

Consider a neural network designed to predict salaries based on the GPA of graduating seniors. We have data from four recent graduates and will use three of them to train the NN (see below). We have an input node for the GPA, two nodes in the hidden layer and an output node for predicting salaries. The output salaries are in thousands of dollars. We randomly select 3.42, 2.63, and 4.00 as our training data and we use the 3.70 GPA to test our NN.

GPA	Starting Salary (000)
3.42	$78.250
2.63	$49.200
4.00	$83.250
3.70	$79.800

For simplicity in our NN, we use Google's Swish activation function for all nodes. See Figure 14.4. Keep in mind that today's NNs typically use the same activation function for each layer of nodes, meaning that different layers can have different activation functions.

In **Figure 14.5**, the first GPA value, 3.42, enters the neural network at its input node. The input node bias (+1.00) shifts the GPA to 4.42 and the input node activation function shifts the 4.42 GPA to a value of 4.432. Look back to Figure 14.4, where you will see the Swish activation function shifting the value of 4.42 on the x-axis to the value of 4.432 on the y-axis. The value of 4.432 now moves to the hidden layer nodes.

Along the way, the data value of 4.432 is shifted by the upper pathway weight ($w_1 = 3.43$) to 15.202 and the lower pathway weight ($w_2 = 0.875$) to 3.878. Note: For the upper pathway, $4.432 \times 3.43 = 15.202$. For the lower pathway, $4.432 \times 0.875 = 3.878$.

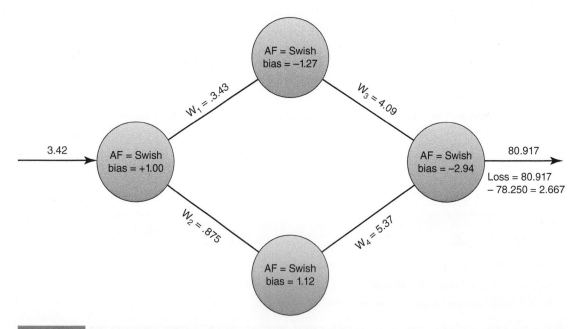

FIGURE 14.5 First iteration of neural network.

The upper pathway node bias ($b_1 = -1.27$) shifts the data value to 13.932 (15.202 – 1.27) while the lower pathway bias ($b_2 = 1.12$) shifts the data value to 4.998 (3.878 + 1.12).

Then, the hidden layer activation functions model the respective values to 13.932 (upper pathway) and 5.005 (lower pathway).

Next, weights ($w_3 = 4.09$, upper; $w_4 = 5.37$, lower) shift the data values to 56.981 and 26.876. Note: For the upper pathway, $13.932 \times 4.29 = 56.981$. For the lower pathway, $5.005 \times 5.37 = 26.876$.

Those two values are summed (56.981 + 26.876) to yield a value of 83.857 and then the last bias, $b_4(-2.94)$, shifts the value to 80.917 (83.857 – 2.94 = 80.917). The output node activation function performs the final calculation and produces an output value of 80.917. The NN's loss function compares the output value, 80.917, to the input salary value associated with the 3.42 GPA, 78.250, and determines a difference, a loss value, of 2.667.

The loss function uses the difference of 2.667 to recalculate the weights and biases throughout the neural network in the back propagation process. These weights and biases will be applied during the second iteration. See **Figure 14.6**.

The next GPA, 2.63, enters the neural network at the input node. The input node bias (+1.00) shifts the GPA to 3.63 and the input node activation function shifts the 3.63 GPA to a value of 3.657, which then moves to the hidden layer nodes.

Along the way, the data value of 3.657 is shifted by the upper pathway weight ($w_1 = 2.27$) to 8.300 and the lower pathway weight ($w_2 = 0.908$) to 3.320. Note: For the upper pathway, $3.657 \times 2.27 = 8.300$. For the lower pathway, $3.657 \times 0.908 = 3.32$.

The upper pathway node bias ($b_1 = -1.08$) shifts the data value to 7.220 (8.300 – 1.08) while the lower pathway bias, ($b_2 = 1.21$) shifts the data value to 4.530 (3.320 + 1.21).

Then, the hidden layer activation functions model the respective values to 7.221 (upper pathway) and 4.541 (lower pathway).

Next, weights ($w_3 = 3.94$, upper; $w_4 = 5.31$, lower) shift the data values to 28.451 and 24.112. Note: For the upper pathway, $7.221 \times 3.94 = 28.451$. For the lower pathway, $4.541 \times 5.31 = 24.112$).

Those two values are summed (28.451 + 24.112) to yield a value of 52.563 and then the last bias, $b_4(-1.28)$, shifts the value to 51.283 (52.563 – 1.28 = 51.283). The output node activation function performs the final calculation and produces an output value of 51.283. The NN's loss function compares the output value, 51.283, to the input salary value associated with the 2.63 GPA, 49.200, and determines a difference, a loss value, of 2.083.

The loss function uses that difference, 2.083, to recalculate the weights and biases throughout the neural network in the back propagation process. These weights and biases will be applied during the third iteration. See **Figure 14.7**.

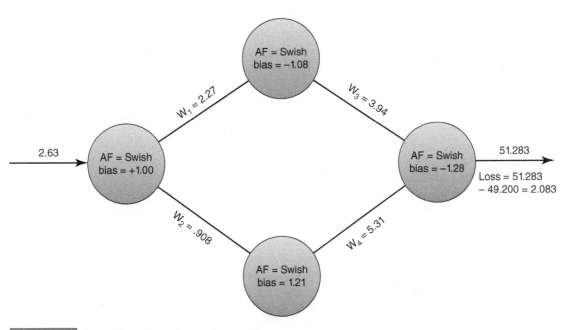

FIGURE 14.6 Second iteration of neural network.

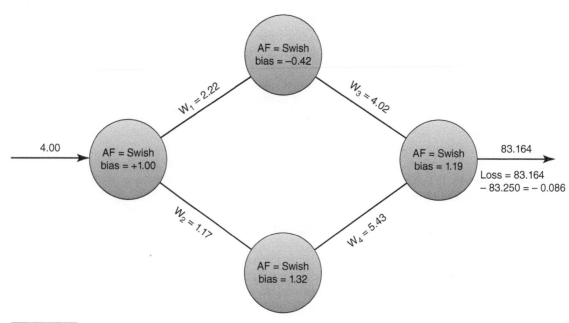

FIGURE 14.7 Third iteration of neural network.

The next GPA, 4.00, enters the neural network at the input node. The input node bias (+1.00) shifts the GPA to 5.00 and the input node activation function shifts the 5.00 GPA to a value of 5.007, which then moves to the hidden layer nodes.

Along the way, the data value of 5.007 is shifted by the upper pathway weight ($w_1 = 2.22$) to 11.115 and the lower pathway weight ($w_2 = 1.17$) to 5.858. Note: For the upper pathway, $5.007 \times 2.22 = 11.115$. For the lower pathway, $5.007 \times 1.17 = 5.858$.

The upper pathway node bias ($b_1 = -0.42$) shifts the data value to 10.695 (11.115 – 0.42) while the lower pathway bias, ($b_2 = 1.32$) shifts the data value to 7.178 (5.858 + 1.32).

Then, the hidden layer activation functions model the respective values to 10.695 (upper pathway) and 7.179 (lower pathway).

Next, weights ($w_3 = 4.02$, upper; $w_4 = 5.43$, lower) shift the data values to 42.994 and 38.980. Note: For the upper pathway, $10.695 \times 4.02 = 42.994$. For the lower pathway, $7.179 \times 5.43 = 38.980$.

Those two values are summed (42.994 + 38.980) to yield a value of 81.974 and then the last bias, b_4 (1.19), shifts the value to 83.164 (81.974 + 1.19 = 83.164). The output node activation function performs the final calculation and produces an output value of 83.164. The NN's loss function compares the output value, 83.164, to the input salary value associated with the 4.00 GPA, 83.250, and determines a difference, a loss value, of –0.086.

The loss function uses that difference, –0.086, to recalculate the weights and biases throughout the neural network in the back propagation process. These weights and biases will be applied during the third iteration. See Figure 14.8.

Now we check to see if the neural network is performing accurately for test data. Therefore, we enter the GPA of 3.70.

The GPA 3.70 enters the neural network at the input node. The input node bias (+1.00) shifts the GPA to 4.70 and the input node activation function shifts the 4.70 GPA to a value of 4.709, which then moves to the hidden layer nodes.

Along the way, the data value of 4.709 is shifted by the upper pathway weight ($w_1 = 2.22$) to 10.454 and the lower pathway weight ($w_2 = 1.17$) to 5.510. Note: For the upper pathway, $4.709 \times 2.22 = 10.454$. For the lower pathway, $4.709 \times 1.17 = 5.510$.

The upper pathway node bias ($b_1 = -0.42$) shifts the data value to 10.034 (10.454 – 0.42) while the lower pathway bias, ($b_2 = 1.32$) shifts that value to 6.830 (5.510 + 1.32).

Then, the hidden layer activation functions model the values to 10.034 (upper pathway) and 6.831 (lower pathway).

Next, weights ($w_3 = 4.13$, upper; $w_4 = 5.40$, lower) shift the data values to 41.441 and 36.886. Note: For the upper pathway, $10.034 \times 4.13 = 44.041$. For the lower pathway, $6.831 \times 5.40 = 36.886$.

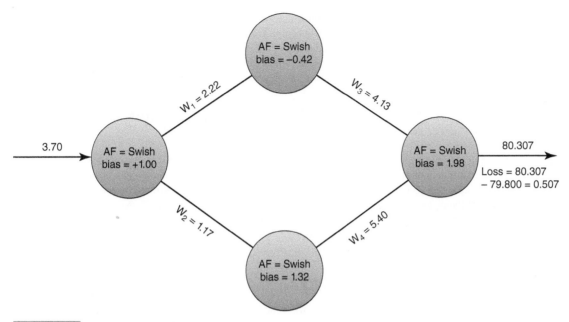

FIGURE 14.8 **Fourth iteration of neural network.**

Those two values are summed (41.441 + 36.886) to yield a value of 78.327 and then the last bias, b_4 (1.98), shifts the value to 80.307 (78.327 + 1.98). The output node activation function performs the final calculation and produces an output value of 80.307. The NN's loss function compares the output value, 80.307, to the input salary value associated with the 3.70 GPA, 79.800, and determines a difference, a loss value, of 0.507.

Our neural network predicted a salary of 80.307, or $80,307. The actual salary of the individual who had the 3.70 GPA was $79,800. Our network is off by $507 (approximately 99.3 percent accurate), an excellent result.

As you see in this example, the neural network continually shifts the system's weights and biases based on the magnitude of the difference between the computed salary and the actual salary (the loss) in an effort to match the pattern between GPAs and starting salaries of graduates from the sample data. The shifts in these values are usually small and occur over thousands of input values and iterations of the neural network.

Our example is very simplified because it involves only three sample values for training. However, it should convey how a neural network is trained by this continual shifting of parameters. When the differences between computed and actual salaries minimize over large amounts of data, the system is said to be trained.

Now imagine entering millions of data points into hundreds of input nodes that feed more than a dozen hidden layers comprised of hundreds of nodes each, and outputting dozens of discrete, computed data points to be compared to the actual data values. Then imagine the thousands of adjustments to the weights and biases throughout the network to accommodate the next data inputs. This is how complex and sophisticated machine learning can be.

What's in IT for Me?

The sections below provide a quick summary of artificial intelligent applications in each functional area of the organization. You will find detailed discussions of AI systems in the functional areas in Section 14.5.

control. Accounting personnel also use intelligent agents for mundane tasks such as managing accounts and monitoring employees' Internet use.

ACCT For the Accounting Major

AI systems are used extensively in auditing to uncover irregularities. They are also used to uncover and prevent fraud. Today's CPAs use AI systems for many of their duties, ranging from risk analysis to cost

FIN For the Finance Major

People have been using computers for decades to solve financial problems. Innovative AI systems have been developed for activities such as making stock market decisions, refinancing bonds, assessing debt risks, analyzing financial conditions, predicting business failures, forecasting financial trends, and investing in global markets. AI systems can often facilitate the use of spreadsheets and other computerized systems used in finance. Finally, AI systems can help reduce fraud in credit cards, stocks, and other financial services.

MKT For the Marketing Major

Marketing personnel use AI systems in many applications, from allocating advertising budgets to evaluating alternative routings of salespeople. New marketing approaches such as targeted marketing and marketing transaction databases are heavily dependent on IT in general and on AI systems in particular. AI systems are especially useful for mining customer databases and predicting customer behavior. Successful AI applications appear in almost every area of marketing and sales, from analyzing the success of one-to-one advertising to supporting customer help desks. With customer service becoming increasingly important, the use of intelligent agents is critical for providing fast response.

POM For the Production/Operations Management Major

AI systems support complex operations and production decisions, from inventory to production planning. AI systems in the production/operations management field manage tasks ranging from diagnosing machine failures and prescribing repairs to complex production scheduling and inventory control. Some companies, such as DuPont and Kodak, have deployed hundreds of AI systems in the planning, organizing, and control of their operational systems.

HRM For the Human Resources Management Major

Human resources personnel employ AI systems for many applications. For example, recruiters use these systems to find applicants' resumes on the Web and sort them to match needed skills. HR managers also use AI systems to evaluate candidates (e.g., tests, interviews). HR personnel use AI systems to train and support employees in managing their fringe benefits and to predict employee job performance and future labor needs.

MIS For the MIS Major

The MIS function develops (or acquires) and maintains the organization's various AI systems, as well as the data and models that these systems use. MIS staffers also interact frequently with subject area experts to capture the expertise used in AI systems.

Summary

14.1   Explain the potential value and the potential limitations of artificial intelligence.

Table 14.1 differentiates between artificial and human intelligence on a number of characteristics.

14.2   Differentiate among supervised, semi-supervised, unsupervised, reinforcement, and deep learning.

- *Supervised learning* is a type of machine learning in which the system is given labeled input data and the expected output results.
- *Semi-supervised learning* is a type of machine learning that combines a small amount of labeled data with a large amount of unlabeled data during training.
- *Unsupervised learning* is a type of machine learning that looks for previously undetected patterns in a dataset with no pre-existing labels and with minimal human supervision.
- *Reinforcement learning* is a type of machine learning in which the system learns to achieve a goal in an uncertain, potentially complex environment.
- *Deep learning* is a subset of machine learning in which artificial neural networks learn from large amounts of data.

14.3   Describe the structure of a neural network, and discuss how that structure contributes to the purpose of neural networks in machine learning.

A neural network is a set of nodes, or virtual neurons, that work in parallel in an attempt to simulate the way the human brain works, although in a greatly simplified form. Neural networks consist of several layers of nodes, called the input layer, hidden layers, and the output layer. Current neural networks are able to simulate billions of neurons. In this way, developers can train a neural network to learn, recognize patterns, and make decisions in a humanlike way.

14.4   Provide use case examples (in addition to the ones in the text) of computer vision, natural language processing, robotics, image recognition, and intelligent agents.

We leave the additional examples to you. You can search the Web to find numerous examples of each machine learning application.

14.5   Provide use case examples (in addition to the ones in the text) of artificial intelligence applications in accounting, finance, marketing, production and operations management, human resource management, and management information systems.

We leave the additional examples to you. You can search the Web to find numerous examples of numerous examples of machine learning applications in each functional area.

14.6   Understand the process by which a neural network transforms data values from the input node to the output node, and then calculates the loss function to initiate the back propagation process.

Key Terms

algorithm   424
artificial intelligence (AI)   422
computer vision   436
convolutional neural network   435
deep learning   429
machine learning systems   424

narrow AI   423
natural language processing   437
neural network   431
node   432
reinforcement learning   429
semi-supervised learning   428

speech recognition   437
strong AI   422
supervised learning   428
unsupervised learning   429
weak AI   423

Discussion Questions

1. What are the pros and cons of facial recognition as a business policy? As a public policy?

2. Consider your health care provider's data.
   - Who owns those data?
   - Who profits from analyzing them?
   - What are they used for?
   - Provide an example of an ML system that uses your data.

3. You are a passenger in a rented, autonomous vehicle that hits a pedestrian. Who or what has the liability for the accident? Support your conclusions.

4. You are a passenger in an autonomous vehicle that you own. While you are riding in the vehicle and reading a report for a business meeting, your vehicle hits a pedestrian. Who or what has the liability for the accident? Support your conclusions.

5. Suppose that your insurance company decides to price your car insurance premium based on data about your driving habits collected by sensors in your car that the firm inputs into an ML system.

   a. Would you be in favor of this new process? Why or why not?

   b. Would the cost of your new policy be in your favor? Why or why not? For example, what if you were speeding?

6. Suppose that your health care company decides to price your insurance premiums based on data about your health (e.g., blood pressure, glucose in your blood) and health habits (eating, exercising, sleeping, etc.) obtained from Fitbit sensors, smart watches, and intelligent scales in your bathroom.

   a. Would you be in favor of this new process? Why or why not?

   b. Would the cost of your new policy be in your favor? Why or why not? For example, what if you were under stress at your job and your blood pressure increased?

Problem-Solving Activities

1. Which machine learning algorithm would you use to predict admittance to your university's freshman class? Describe your algorithm by including your input data and output data.

2. Which machine learning algorithm would you use to identify an image as a dog or a cat? Describe your algorithm by including your input data and output data.

3. Which machine learning algorithm would you use to predict the weather? *Hint*: First define what "predicting the weather" means. Describe your algorithm by including your input data and output data.

4. Ask ChatGPT to write a letter to your professor convincing him or her to give you an A in the class. Were you happy with the results? What would you have done differently?

5. Visit www.pewresearch.org and examine their March 2022 research titled "How Americans think about artificial intelligence". Describe your stance.

6. Visit www.foreseemed.com/artificial-intelligence-in-healthcare and summarize how your healthcare will change in the future as a result of AI.

7. Go to www.zapier.com/blog/ai-job-search/. Pick one of the 9 tools listed and describe how it willimpact your future job search.

Closing Case

MIS **POM** **MKT** **AI in the Car Repair Industry**

The car repair business has four major players: the customer, the customer's insurance company, the claims adjuster, and the car repair shop (also known as a body shop). In addition, there are two types of claims adjusters: staff adjusters and independent adjusters. Staff adjusters, who are also known as company adjusters or employee adjusters, work for an insurance company as W-2 salaried employees. In contrast, independent adjusters are contracted through a third-party claims-handling company. The insurance company outsources the claim to one of these companies, which, in turn, assigns it to an independent adjuster.

The traditional car repair process. If a customer has an accident, a claims adjuster examines the damage and estimates the cost to repair the automobile and provides an appraisal. The goal of an appraisal is to determine the fair market value of the vehicle. In certain cases, the repair can cost more than the car is worth. In these cases, the insurance company will typically pay the customer what the car is worth as determined by the appraisal.

The first step in the appraisal process is to report the accident to the insurance company. Traditionally, claims adjusters had to travel to the scene of the wreck to appraise the vehicle. An appraisal expert would interview the customer to determine the circumstances of the accident before examining the vehicle itself.

During an appraisal, the adjuster determines the extent of the damage and the overall condition of the car itself. It is significant that appraisers have specific criteria to follow and standards to apply to determine how much the repair will cost. The amount of coverage under the customer's car insurance policy determines how much money the customer receives toward the car's repairs. The damage to the vehicle may be so severe that the adjuster writes off the car as a total loss.

At roughly the same time, the customer brings the vehicle to a repair shop. The shop performs diagnostics on the vehicle and estimates the cost of repairs, according to the vehicle's original equipment manufacturer's (OEM's) repair procedures.

Body shop owners maintain that they must follow precise OEM repair procedures. In contrast, insurance companies are trying to save money. The shop owners contend that claims adjusters, paid by insurance companies, typically want to pay less for repairs than the repair shop owners' estimates. Adjusters decide what the insurance companies will pay, which means that customers may have to pay for repair expenses not covered by their insurance policies.

One body shop owner explained that his shop had a difficult relationship with adjusters until one adjuster showed him the specific insurance company parameters that adjusters must meet. If adjusters approve repairs outside these parameters, they could lose their jobs. In turn, the owner began to educate adjusters about what it takes to safely repair a vehicle. Further, he began to provide a photo and supporting documentation, such as OEM repair procedures, for every line item on the vehicle repair plan.

Today's car repair process. Since the COVID-19 pandemic, shop owners see fewer appraisers. Instead, insurance companies are deploying machine learning systems that use digital photographs. Claims adjusters employ these systems to make virtual estimates of repair costs.

Virtual estimates are estimates where an adjuster does not physically inspect a damaged car. Instead, the insurance company instructs drivers who have been in an accident to download an app. The app directs them to take photos of their cars at certain angles and in a certain light. Using just those photos, a claims adjuster estimates how much it will cost to fix the car.

Virtual estimates save time and money for insurance companies. In person, adjusters can travel to and inspect 3 to 8 vehicles per day. With photos, adjusters save travel time and gasoline expense and can complete 15 to 20 estimates per day.

When insurance companies employ machine learning to analyze digital photos, the process becomes even faster and more efficient. Automobiles are excellent candidates for image-based machine learning. Cars have a consistent form: doors, windshields, bumpers, and so on. Many things can go wrong with the 30,000 parts in an average car, but the most common parts generally look a certain way. Therefore, insurers train their machine learning algorithms in classifying images using millions of photos of damaged cars of every make and model.

The system can then analyze a photo taken by a policyholder and draw conclusions about what needs to be fixed or whether a human inspection is required. Using data from local parts suppliers and repairers, the system then estimates the cost. Finally, the system guides the adjuster through the estimate process, and the adjuster double-checks the system's estimate.

Virtual estimates seem to be very accurate at quickly differentiating vehicles that can be fixed from vehicles that should be totaled. Experts contend they are also accurate at evaluating minor vehicle damage and crashes in which no one is hurt. It is significant to note that these types of accidents comprise the majority of accidents.

In fact, Tractable (https://tractable.ai), a company that uses computer vision and machine learning to develop algorithms for insurance companies, claims that 25 percent of its estimates are so accurate that they do not require human intervention. The company plans to increase that figure to 75 percent over time.

Insurance companies acknowledge that their systems do make errors. However, they emphasize that these systems constantly evolve and will continue to become more precise and accurate as they analyze increasing amounts of data.

Before the pandemic, about 15 percent of U.S. auto claims were settled using photos rather than in-person visits by adjusters. Industry analysts estimate that by 2025, roughly 80 percent of claims will be settled using digital photos and machine learning systems.

Some foreign insurers have deployed a completely automated process for virtual estimates, at least for some kinds of damage. The Spanish insurer Admiral Seguro, for example, has begun using a machine learning system to resolve auto claims within minutes after policyholders upload photos of the damage.

As another example, in March 2021, Israeli smart-dashcam company Nexar began working with Japan's Mitsui Sumitomo Insurance to translate the high-definition video footage and acceleration and GPS data captured by its cameras into scripts, like subtitles on a foreign movie. Adjusters can use the machine-generated scripts to resolve claims. The technology learns as adjusters translate those scripts into line items on estimates.

It is interesting that despite the greater efficiencies generated by the machine learning systems, some body shop owners still prefer that the appraisers visit their shops. This process enables the owners to develop a relationship with the appraisers and to discuss the cost of repairs in person. In addition, many shop owners assert that the vast majority of virtual estimates are too low. One owner argued that adjusters cannot diagnose suspension damage or a bent wheel or frame misalignment from a photograph.

Further, the owners contend that they are spending more time arguing with insurance companies to determine the correct price for a repair—time for which they are not compensated. In some cases, this process results in damaged vehicles remaining in the shop longer than usual.

During the pandemic, insurers used estimates produced from customers' photos for all types of collisions, even severe ones. Insurance companies sometimes consider these estimates "starting places" for in-person repairers. Body shop owners, however, contend that customers become frustrated with them when the insurer's initial estimate is lower than the repairer's quote. As a result, repair shops are stuck in the middle. The shops do not know when artificial intelligence has been applied to the estimates they receive. According to the shop owners, whatever is happening in the process is not consistent.

The automobile repair industry illustrates the impacts of technology replacing in-person interactions. Insurance companies hope that their algorithms can evolve into agreed-upon standards that reduce disagreements between insurers and repairers.

Questions

1. Among the four entities in the car repair business, who would be the "winner" as the industry implements machine learning solutions to the claims adjustment process? That is, which of the four entities would realize the most benefits? Support your answer with examples.

2. Among the four entities in the car repair business, who would be the "loser" as the industry implements machine learning solutions to the claims adjustment process? That is, which of the four entities would realize the fewest benefits? Support your answer with examples.

Sources: Compiled from T. Laurinavicius, "How AI Is Transforming the Insurance Industry," v7labs.com, July 19, 2022; M. Thomas, "25 AI Insurance Examples to Know," Builtin.com, July 11, 2022; N. Shevchuk, "Digital Transformation in Car Insurance Industry: Streamline Recognition of Car Damage Assessment," Altamira.ai, April 7, 2022; M. Ksycinski, "How AI Is Transforming Automotive and Car Insurance," *Grape Up*, 2022; "Embracing AI in the World of Auto Insurance," *Inside Big Data*, October 10, 2021; L. Tucker, "Car Repair Claims See Increased Use of AI," iot techtrends, April 16, 2021; A. Marshall, "AI Comes to Car Repair, and Body Shop Owners Are Not Happy," *Wired*, April 13, 2021; R. Balasubramanian et al., "Insurance 2030—The Impact of AI on the Future of Insurance," McKinsey & Company, March 12, 2021; A. Linn, "Less Stress, Less Time: How a Brazilian Startup Is Using Azure AI to Make Car Repairs Easier," Microsoft.com, November 8, 2019; T. Keller, "Embracing Artificial Intelligence in Auto Repair Shops," *Shop Owner*, July 23, 2019; and T. Kwartler, "How AI Is Changing the Way We Assess Vehicle Repair," *Venture Beat*, February 4, 2017.

Hardware

TECHNOLOGY GUIDE OUTLINE	LEARNING OBJECTIVES
TG 1.1 Introduction to Hardware	**TG 1.1 Identify** the major hardware components of a computer system.
TG 1.2 Strategic Hardware Issues	**TG 1.2 Discuss** strategic issues that link hardware design to business strategy.
TG 1.3 Computer Hierarchy	**TG 1.3 Describe** the various types of computers in the computer hierarchy.
TG 1.4 Input and Output Technologies	**TG 1.4 Differentiate** the various types of input and output technologies and their uses.
TG 1.5 The Central Processing Unit	**TG 1.5 Describe** the design and functioning of the central processing unit.

Introduction

As you begin this Technology Guide, you might be wondering, "Why do I have to know anything about hardware?" There are several reasons why you will benefit from understanding the basics of hardware. First, regardless of your major (and future functional area in an organization), you will be using different types of hardware throughout your career. Second, you will have input concerning the hardware that you will use. In this capacity, you will be required to answer many questions, such as these:

- Is my hardware performing adequately for my needs? If not, what types of problems am I experiencing?
- Do I need more functionality in my hardware, and if so, what functionality would be most helpful to me?

Third, you will have input into decisions when your functional area or organization upgrades or replaces its hardware. Some organizations will allocate the hardware budget to functional areas or departments. In such cases, you might be responsible for making hardware decisions (at least locally) yourself. MIS employees will act as advisors, but you will provide important input into such decisions.

TG 1.1 Introduction to Hardware

LEARNING OBJECTIVE

Identify the major hardware components of a computer system.

Recall from Chapter 1 that the term *hardware* refers to the physical equipment used for the input, processing, output, and storage activities of a computer system. Decisions about hardware focus on three interrelated factors: appropriateness for the task, speed, and cost. The incredibly rapid rate of innovation in the computer industry complicates hardware decisions because computer technologies become obsolete more quickly than other organizational technologies.

The overall trends in hardware are that it becomes smaller, faster, cheaper, and more powerful over time. In fact, these trends are so rapid that they make it difficult to know when to purchase (or upgrade) hardware. This difficulty lies in the fact that companies that delay hardware purchases will, more than likely, be able to buy more powerful hardware for the same amount of money in the future. It is important to note that this is a trade-off. An organization that delays purchasing computer hardware gives up the benefits of whatever it could buy today until the future purchase date arrives.

Hardware consists of the following:

- *Central processing unit (CPU):* Manipulates the data and controls the tasks performed by the other components
- *Primary storage:* Temporarily stores data and program instructions during processing
- *Secondary storage:* Stores data and programs for future use
- *Input technologies:* Accept data and instructions and convert them to a form that the computer can understand
- *Output technologies:* Present data and information in a form people can understand
- *Communication technologies:* Provide for the flow of data from external computer networks (e.g., the Internet and intranets) to the CPU, and from the CPU to computer networks

TG 1.2 Strategic Hardware Issues

LEARNING OBJECTIVE

Discuss strategic issues that link hardware design to business strategy.

For most businesspeople, the most important issues are what the hardware enables, how it is advancing, and how rapidly it is advancing. In many industries, exploiting computer hardware is a key to achieving competitive advantage. Successful hardware exploitation comes from thoughtful consideration of the following questions.

- How do organizations keep up with the rapid price reductions and performance advancements in hardware? For example, how often should an organization upgrade its computers and storage systems? Will upgrades increase personal and organizational productivity? How can organizations measure such increases?
- How should organizations determine the need for the new hardware infrastructures, such as cloud computing? (We discuss cloud computing in Technology Guide 3.)
- Portable computers and advanced communications technologies have enabled employees to work from home or from anywhere. Will these new work styles benefit employees and the organization? How do organizations manage such new work styles?

- How do organizations manage employees who use their own portable devices (e.g., tablets and smartphones) for both personal and work purposes? That is, how do organizations handle the bring-your-own-device (BYOD) phenomenon?

- How should organizations make use of Device-as-a-Service (DaaS)? DaaS allows organizations to outsource the purchase and maintenance of hardware to the service provider. DaaS allows for more flexibility to meet the needs of users as their needs and responsibilities change.

TG 1.3 Computer Hierarchy

LEARNING OBJECTIVE

Describe the various types of computers in the computer hierarchy.

The traditional standard for comparing classes of computers is their processing power. This section presents each class of computers from the most powerful to the least powerful. It describes both the computers and their roles in modern organizations.

Supercomputers

The term *supercomputer* does not refer to a specific technology. Rather, it indicates the fastest computers available at any given time. In mid-2017, the fastest supercomputers had speeds approaching 100 petaflops (1 petaflop is 1,000 trillion floating-point operations per second). A floating-point operation is an arithmetic operation that involves decimals.

Large organizations use supercomputers to execute computationally demanding tasks involving very large data sets, such as for military and scientific applications. In the business environment, for example, large banks use supercomputers to calculate the risks and returns of various investment strategies, and health-care organizations use them to analyze giant databases of patient data to determine optimal treatments for various diseases.

An emerging form of supercomputing is called exascale computing. It is difficult to understand the power of exascale supercomputing, but imagine this: Exascale supercomputing can process one quintillion operations per second. In comparison, if all 7.7 billion people on earth completed one calculation per second, it would take over 6 years to do what exascale supercomputing systems can do in 1 second. This type of computing power will change weather forecasting, electricity distribution, complex engineering designs, and much more.

Mainframe Computers

Mainframes remain popular in large enterprises for extensive computing applications that are accessed by thousands of users at one time. Examples of mainframe applications are airline reservation systems, corporate payroll programs, website transaction processing systems (e.g., Amazon and eBay), and student grade calculation and reporting.

Today's mainframes perform at teraflop (trillions of floating-point operations per second) speeds and can handle millions of transactions per day. Mainframes can also provide a secure, robust environment in which to run strategic, mission-critical applications.

In 2021, IBM released version 2.5 of its z/OS mainframe operating system. This update will upgrade mainframes to incorporate AI capabilities as well as support hybrid cloud operations. Since many organizations have a significant investment in their on-premise mainframe computers, this will allow those organizations to utilize their existing technology in more modern ways.

mainframes Relatively large computers used in large enterprises for extensive computing applications that are accessed by thousands of users.

microcomputers The smallest and least expensive category or general-purpose computers, also called micros, personal computers, or PCs.

laptop computers (notebook computers) Small, easily transportable, lightweight microcomputers.

notebook computer See **laptop computers**.

thin client A computer that does not offer the full functionality of a fat client.

fat clients Computers that offer full functionality without having to connect to a network.

server Computers that support networks, enabling users to share files, software, and other network devices.

Microcomputers

Microcomputers—also called *personal computers*, or *PCs*—are the smallest and least expensive category of general-purpose computers. It is important to point out that people frequently define a PC as a computer that uses the Microsoft Windows operating system. In fact, a variety of PCs are available, and many of them do not use Windows. One well-known example is the Apple Mac, which uses the Mac OS operating system.

Laptop and Notebook Computers

Laptop computers (or **notebook computers**) are small, easily transportable, lightweight microcomputers that fit comfortably into a briefcase (**Figure TG 1.1**). They provide users with access to processing power and data outside an office environment.

For example, the Google Chromebook is a thin client laptop that runs Google's Chrome operating system. A **thin client** is a computer that does not offer the full functionality of a PC. A **fat client** is a computer that has the ability to perform many functions without a network connection. Thin clients are less complex than fat clients because they do not have locally installed software. When thin clients need to run an application, they access it from a **server** over a network rather than from a local disk drive.

A thin client would not have Microsoft Office installed on it. Thus, thin clients are easier and less expensive to operate and support than fat clients. The benefits of thin clients include fast application deployment; centralized management; lower cost of ownership; and easier installation, management, maintenance, and support. The main disadvantage of thin clients is that if the network fails, users can do very little on their computers. In contrast, if users have fat clients and the network fails, they can still perform some functions because they have software, such as Microsoft Office, installed on their computers.

UmbertoPantalone/Getty Images

FIGURE TG 1.1 **Laptop computers are lightweight and easily portable.**

Tablet Computers

A *tablet computer* (or *tablet*) is a complete computer contained entirely in a flat touch screen that users operate with a stylus, digital pen, fingertip, or soft (virtual) keyboard, instead of a physical keyboard or mouse. Examples of tablets include the Apple iPad Pro (shown here in **figure TG 1.2**) and the Microsoft Surface Pro 7.

Sasin Paraksa/Shutterstock

FIGURE TG 1.2 **The iPad is a popular tablet option.**

Handheld Computers

Handheld computers are mobile devices that are typically flat touch screen devices with which users interact using their voice or touch. These devices typically have multiple network antennas, allowing for satellite, cellular, Wi-Fi, Bluetooth, and near field communication (NFC) connections. Most handheld computers unify several devices in one. They operate as a camera, GPS, computer (with near-desktop–type experiences), mobile phone, music player, and much more. They operate through applications (apps) that provide endless possibilities for these devices. They connect to wearable computers (discussed in the next topic) to create personal area networks around users. Handheld computers can connect watches, headphones, car radios, pens, scanners, medical devices, weight scales, and much more. Often, we refer to these handheld computers as smartphones.

Wearable Computers

Wearable computers are miniature computers that people wear under, with, or on top of their clothing. Key features of wearable computers are that there is constant interaction between the computer and the users and that the users can multitask, meaning they do not have to stop what they are doing to use the device. Examples of wearable computers are the Apple Watch (**www.apple.com/watch**), the Sony SmartWatch, Bose Frames (**www.bose. com/en_us/products/frames.html**), Amazon Echo Frames, and the Fitbit and the Fitbit (**www.fitbit.com**) activity tracker.

wearable computer
A miniature computer worn by a person allowing the users to multitask.

TG 1.4 | Input and Output Technologies

WILEY PLUS

**Author Lecture Videos are available exclusively in *WileyPLUS*.
Apply the Concept activities are available in the Appendix and in *WileyPLUS*.**

LEARNING OBJECTIVE

Differentiate the various types of input and output technologies and their uses.

Input Technologies

Input technologies allow people and other technologies to enter data into a computer. The two main types of input devices are human data-entry devices and source-data automation devices. As their name implies, *human data-entry* devices require a certain amount of human effort to input data. Examples are keyboard, mouse, pointing stick, trackball, joystick, touchscreen, stylus, and voice recognition.

In contrast, *source-data automation* devices input data with minimal human intervention. These technologies speed up data collection, reduce errors, and gather data at the source of a transaction or other event. Bar code readers are an example of source-data automation.

An interesting type of human input is gesture-based input. **Gesture recognition** refers to technologies that enable computers to interpret human gestures. These technologies are an initial step in designing computers that can understand human body language. This process creates a richer interaction between machines and humans than has been possible with other input devices.

Gesture recognition enables humans to interact naturally with a computer without any intervening mechanical devices. With gesture-based technologies, the user can move the cursor by pointing a finger at a computer screen. These technologies could make conventional input devices (the mouse, keyboards, and touchscreens) redundant. Examples of gesture-based input devices are the Microsoft Kinect (**www.xbox.com/kinect**) and the Leap Motion Controller (**www.ultraleap.com**).

Zoom (**www.zoom.us/**) added gesture recognition to its platform to allow more natural engagement in online meetings. For example, if a participant physically raises their hand, the gesture will be recognized and trigger the virtual hand raise for the other meeting participants.

gesture recognition An input method that interprets human gestures, in an attempt for computers to begin to understand human body language.

Common source-data automation input devices include magnetic stripe readers, point-of-sale terminals, bar code scanners, QR code readers, optical mark readers, magnetic ink character readers, sensors (see the **Internet of Things** in Chapter 8), and cameras.

Output Technologies

The output generated by a computer can be transmitted to the user through several output devices and media. These devices include monitors, printers, plotters, and voice.

Current output technologies include retinal scanning displays and heads-up displays. Retinal scanning displays project images directly onto a viewer's retina and are used in medicine, air traffic control, and controlling industrial machines. Heads-up displays are transparent and present data without requiring the user to look away from his or her usual viewpoint.

Augmented Reality, Virtual Reality, and Mixed Reality

augmented reality (AR)
A live, direct or indirect, view of a physical, real-world environment whose elements are enhanced by computer-generated sensory input such as sound, video, graphics, or GPS data.

virtual reality (VR) A term that describes a realistic, three-dimensional, computer generated environment that replicates sight, touch, hearing, and in some cases, smell.

Augmented reality (AR) is a live, direct, or indirect, view of a physical, real-world environment whose elements are augmented, or enhanced, by computer-generated sensory input such as sound, video, graphics, or GPS data via smartphones, tablets, heads-up displays, or smart glasses. Smart glasses include Google Glass Enterprise Edition 2 and Vuzix Blade (**www.vuzix.com**). A very popular form of augmented reality is the filters on Snapchat that allow users to add apparel, change hair styles, have animals crawl on them, or change their face completely.

Virtual reality (VR) is a fully immersive experience that provides a realistic, three-dimensional, computer-generated environment replicating sight, touch, hearing, and in some cases, smell. Virtual reality brings the user into the virtual environment by removing outside stimuli via VR headsets.

VR is designed to reproduce a real environment or create an imaginary environment in which users can explore and interact. The user becomes a part of the virtual world and, while there, can manipulate objects or perform a series of actions. VR devices include Meta's Oculus Quest 2 (**www.oculus.com**), Sony's Playstation VR (**www.playstation.com**), Magic Leap One (**www.magicleap.com**), and HTC's Vive Cosmos (**www.vive.com**).

Mixed reality (MR) is an extension of augmented reality that allows physical and virtual elements to interact with one another in an environment. Because MR maintains a connection to the real world, it is not considered a fully immersive experience. In a MR environment, wherever users go and whatever they see wearing MR technology, the three-dimensional content that they encounter will react to them the same way as it would in the real world. For example, an object will move closer to users when they move closer to it. Also, users can turn an object using gestures.

Mixed reality technology integrates the virtual and physical worlds into one connected experience with the help of eye tracking, gesture recognition, and voice recognition technology through a headset or a pair of smart glasses and a pair of motion controllers. MR devices include Microsoft HoloLens 2 (**www.microsoft.com**), Lenovo Explorer (**www.lenovo.com**), Samsung Odyssey (**www.samsung.com**), Acer Windows Mixed Reality (**www.acer.com**), and Google Cardboard (**www.arvr.google.com/cardboard**).

In a look into the near future, Mojo Vision (**www.mojo.vision**) is a startup company that is developing the Mojo Lens. These smart contact lenses are essentially flexible displays which feature AR. The prototype, first demonstrated in January 2020, includes a 14,000 pixel-per-inch display with eye tracking, image stabilization, and a custom wireless radio. An external battery pack provides power to the contact lens and handles sensor data sent to the display. By 2022, the hardware was ready but the software was still under development and will require FDA approval before going to market.

Augmented Reality Examples

POM **Transportation**

- The Skully AR-1 motorcycle helmet (**www.facebook.com/skullytechnologies**) provides a heads-up display on the front face shield of the helmet. This shield displays basic information such as temperature, driving directions, and a real time 180-degree rear view to riders. By using Bluetooth connectivity, riders can make calls, send texts, and play music by giving voice commands.

POM Manufacturing

- For simulation purposes, Airbus (www.airbus.com) deployed an AR model of a new aircraft, allowing designers and engineers to view various components, potential upgrades, and sensors, before going into production. With the AR model, Airbus gave its employees the opportunity to make important design changes before beginning production.

- BMW (www.bmw.com) is speeding up its vehicle concept and prototype engineering processes by as much as 12 months using a new AR application. Engineers and designers use AR goggles that allow the real-world, physical vehicle body to be overlaid with true-to-scale holographic 3D models. This process helps in assessing different concept variations and assembly procedures for future vehicles without the need for many test models. People at different locations around the world can use multi-user mode to review designs and concepts together.

POM Cargo Management

- The International Air Transport Association (IATA; www.iata.org), whose 290 airlines supply 82 percent of the world's air traffic, deployed industrial technology company Atheer's AR headsets to employees working in cargo management. The system allowed air cargo employees to have instant access to clear and consistent working instructions for key tasks, such as accepting cargo as ready for air carriage. The instructions are delivered directly into the field of view of warehouse cargo handlers and updated wirelessly. The IATA reported a 30 percent improvement in cargo handling speed and a 90 percent reduction in errors.

HRM POM Training

- In Porsche's (www.porsche.com) assembly plant in Leipzig, Germany, equipment experts guide employees through their AR glasses and teach them on the job.

POM MKT Customer Service

- Vuforia Chalk (www.ptc.com/en/products/vuforia/vuforia-chalk) is an AR tool that helps customers repair appliances with real-time virtual assistance. Users point their smartphone cameras toward the appliance and remote tech support workers draw on customers' screens to guide them through the repair steps.

MKT Grocery Shopping

- Hyperar (www.hyperar.com) provides an in-store app that provides directions to customers so that they can locate any product. As customers use this app, store employees can focus on other tasks rather than directing or taking customers to products.

MKT Advertising

- AR in marketing and advertising creates a better buying experience for customers and increases their level of engagement. Many advertising campaigns use AR technologies. Consider the Starbucks AR campaign called "Everylove on Every Cup." Using AR, the retailer turned every Starbucks cup into a Valentine's Day card. By using a dedicated Starbucks AR app to scan their cups, users could watch the design come to life.

- At Universal Studios Orlando (www.universalorlando.com), park visitors can engage directly with the dinosaurs of the Jurassic Park franchise by using a mobile app. Visitors stand on a Hollywood star to trigger the app and a variety of dinosaurs come up to investigate them.

- With the AMC app (**www.amctheatres.com/mobile/app**), movie posters can do more than just basic advertising. Posters have an AR symbol at the top to indicate that the poster is scannable. Once the poster is recognized by the app, moviegoers can either watch the film's trailer or buy tickets to see the movie. The app also works on images in magazines and news articles.

MKT **Retail**   Retailers are using AR to improve the buyer's experience by bridging the gap between the perception of a product and the actual product. For instance, with AR buyers can know the size and look of the product in a realistic way.

- Augment (**www.augment.com**) is a SaaS platform where users can visualize their products in 3D in a real environment using mobile phones and tablets.
- Yihaodian (owned by Walmart) is the largest Chinese online grocery store. The grocer has placed physical images of stocked grocery shelves on walls and other surfaces in urban public areas in China. Passersby can scan codes under the images with a mobile device to purchase corresponding groceries online.
- NexTech AR Solutions (**www.nextechar.com**) provides a try-it-on feature that can be added to existing digital storefronts. The feature uses the camera on a customer's smartphone or desktop device to enable shoppers to digitally put on eyewear, jewelry, and clothing to see how these items look.
- Warby Parker (**www.warbyparker.com**) has a proprietary try-it-on feature in its app so customers can see how different styles of eyewear will look on them.
- Sephora (**www.sephora.com**) allows customers to try on makeup with its Virtual Artist 3D live experience.
- Google Lens (**https://lens.google/**) allows users to scan QR codes and objects through their smartphone cameras. Google Lens's Style Match feature provides consumers the capability to identify pieces of clothing or furniture and view similar designs available online and through e-commerce platforms.
- Walmart provides an AR price checking tool for customers that allows them to scan physical products to display up-to-date information that includes the product name, how much the item costs, customer reviews from Walmart.com, and other valuable information.
- Living Wine Labels (**www.tweglobal.com/living-wine-labels**) offers a unique experience for their customers. Under 11 brands, they provide an augmented version of reality ranging from criminal confessions to a more colorful living space to the Walking Dead "breaking" your phone screen!

Entertainment

- Dance Reality (**www.dancerealityapp.com**) guides users through detailed steps and timing of countless dance styles by placing virtual footprints on the floor in front of them.

Education

- Textbooks are being printed on clickable paper, which is an interactive print solution that bridges the traditional offline–online gap. Pages contain multiple hotspots; each hotspot links to one or multiple sources, instantly taking readers from two-dimensional printed content to online, multichannel content.
- Magic Leap's (**www.magicleap.com**) Lumin operating system allows multiple wearers to share in a digital experience, such as a dissection or historical map or event. Also, students can use Magic Leap's computer-aided design application to collaborate on 3D designs.
- Numerous AR apps can identify objects in a user's sight, instantaneously presenting relevant information. For instance, if you walk past an old building, you might effortlessly learn about its history and appearance, dating back to its first construction. Imagine if you were looking at the White House, the Louvre, Westminster Abbey, and many other historical sites.

- BBC's Civilisations (www.bbc.co.uk) lets users hold, spin, and view X-rays of ancient artifacts while listening to historical narrations.
- The World Wildlife Fund's (www.worldwildlife.org) Free Rivers app transforms users' tabletops into natural landscapes, allowing users to digitally manipulate entire ecosystems to better understand how water flow impacts habitats.

Travel

- If someone is looking to explore a destination without traveling to the city, he or she could use an Oculus Quest Virtual Reality headset and an app called Wander. This combination accesses Google Streetview maps and allows users to see streets, inside museums, at special landmarks, without leaving their home!
- Translation between languages is particularly important in travel. For example, if a traveler takes an image of any foreign street sign, menu, or label, Google Translate provides an instantaneous translation. Travelers can also access subtitles while conversing across a language barrier.

Healthcare

- AccuVein (www.accuvein.com) helps doctors and nurses locate patients' veins more easily.
- Philips's Azurion (www.usa.philips.com) image-guided therapy platform, built specifically for the HoloLens 2, provides surgeons with real-time patient data and 3D imagery as they operate.
- SyncThink (www.syncthink.com) has developed eye-tracking technology to diagnose concussions and balance disorders.
- New developments in AR are helping the more than 3.4 million visually impaired individuals in the United States. For example, the OrCam (www.orcam.com) MyEye allows the user to be able to read text without asking others for help. The device snaps a picture of any text from any surface and relays the information to the user via a small earpiece.
- Smart glasses such as the Solos (www.solos-wearables.com) and Everysight Raptor (www.everysight.com) provide cyclists with data on speed, power, and heart rate, along with navigation instructions.

Virtual Reality Examples

HRM Training

- One increasingly common area of potential for VR is training. Traditional flight simulators, which physically duplicate the cockpits of various types of aircraft, have been used to train pilots for more than 80 years. The simulator is mounted on a platform that allows the cockpit to move as an airplane would. The model uses video displays that allows pilots to look out over a landscape or runway and other technologies that closely mimic actual flight with respect to motion, visualizations, communications, and air traffic. Pilots use simulators for initial pilot training (e.g., converting to a new type of aircraft) and recurrent commercial pilot training.

    Flight simulators enable students to interact with an aircraft cockpit, save fuel and wear-and-tear on the aircraft and engines, and can replicate hazardous conditions and system failures without putting any real-life passengers or crew at risk. However, they can cost over $12 million each.

    VR is changing the way that pilots are trained. In April 2019, the U.S. Air Force launched a pilot training class with 30 students using VR headsets and biometric sensors instead of traditional flight simulators. Thirteen students were certified in four months, where the usual pilot training system takes about one year. Students fully immersed themselves in a cockpit using an HTC Vive VR headset while sensors monitored heart rate and pupil measurement. The sensors gave flight instructors an accurate reading of how immersed students actually were in the learning experience. These readings were not available in traditional flight simulators.

The VR system significantly lowered costs. Another advantage was that VR enabled the flight program to change one cockpit for another, taking just 10 seconds for a student to transition from one type of aircraft to another. Students could also analyze each of their flights because they had been captured and uploaded into the VR simulator. The VR flight training cost $1,000 per unit (headset and AI software) in contrast to the multi-million-dollar cost of a traditional flight simulator.

- **HRM** Walmart (www.walmart.com) is using more than 17,000 Oculus Go headsets in stores to train staff on new technology, customer service, and regulatory compliance. The retailer also uses VR to test whether workers have the skills for middle management.

- **HRM** Farmers Insurance (www.farmers.com) has developed a VR training program that uses AI-powered skills. The insurer also has a VR tool with 500 simulated damage combinations and scenarios to help staff practice home damage assessments.

- **HRM** Walmart's VR training includes the "Avoid, Deny, Defend" method developed at Texas State University, which outlines actions to take such as escaping, protecting yourself, or preparing to fight in response to an active shooter. Following the shooting at a Walmart in El Paso, Texas, Walmart got feedback from employees at the store about the VR training. The associates asserted that the training saved lives. Significantly, the employee feedback was unsolicited.

- **HRM** Firefighters can combat virtual wildfires with VR platforms such as FLAIM Trainer (www.flaimsystems.com) or TargetSolutions (www.targetsolutions.com).

- **HRM** Fidelity Investments (www.fidelity.com) is using VR to build workplace relationships among new employees who are working remotely as a result of the COVID-19 pandemic. Fidelity has also created a VR conference room to foster collaboration among its remote employees.

MKT Retail

- Macy's (www.macys.com) is offering a VR experience across 90 of its stores where customers provide the dimensions of a room and the retailer lays out the virtual space. Customers can then pick their pieces, design the room, including wall color and flooring, and put on the VR goggles to see how the room would appear.

  Macy's noted that in three pilot stores, VR-influenced furniture sales increased by more than 60 percent versus non-VR furniture sales, while returns decreased to less than two percent. Macy's VR service also enables the retailer to offer a full range of furniture in a much smaller space.

POM Engineering

- Engineers use VR in three-dimensional computer-aided design. For example, the automotive, aerospace, and ground transportation industries use VR in their product development, engineering, and manufacturing processes.

Architectural design

- Architects use VR during the design process to actually "see" the projects before they are built, thereby giving the architect a sense of scale and proportion. VR models also eliminate the need to make physical miniatures of projects and enable clients to experience the project before and during construction.

MKT Entertainment

- Disney released a VR experience titled Disney Movies VR (www.disneymoviesvr.com), free for download. The experience allows users to interact with the characters and worlds from the Disney, Marvel, and Lucasfilm universes.

- Many companies use omnidirectional cameras (also known as 360-degree or VR cameras) by GoPro, Nokia, Samsung, Ricoh, and Nikon. These cameras record in all directions, a process called VR photography. Films produced by VR cameras permit the audience to view an entire environment in every scene. In a notable example, Hyundai used VR cameras in its 2017 Super Bowl commercial, which virtually reunited service members overseas with their families at the game.

- Video games are rapidly incorporating VR, particularly with the emergence of VR headsets. In August 2020, *PC Magazine* picked the top VR video games of 2020, which included *Astro Bot Rescue Mission*, *Beat Saber*, *Budget Cuts*, *Danger Goat*, *Everybody's Golf*, *Far Point*, and others.

- In 2016, *Pokémon Go* placed virtual creatures all over the world for players to view through their smartphone screens, as if the creatures were standing in front of them in the real world. The game has been downloaded over 1 billion times and has generated billions in revenue for the developers.

Education

- In a collaboration with IBM Research, Rensselaer Polytechnic Institute offers students studying Chinese an interesting option: a 360-degree virtual environment that teleports them to the busy streets of Beijing or a crowded Chinese restaurant. Students can haggle with street vendors or order food. The environment is equipped with different capabilities to respond to the students in real time.

- Many K-12 programs are using headsets from Oculus, HTC, and Google Cardboard to send students on virtual field trips, tour the solar system, and walk through the Jurassic period.

MKT Real Estate

- The real estate industry relies heavily on customers visualizing themselves in a new home. Customers can take virtual tours of properties thanks to companies such as Matterport (www.matterport.com).

MKT Travel

- Companies in the retail travel industry such as CruiseAbout (www.cruiseabout.com) and Flight Centre (www.flightcentre.com.au) use VR to enable customers to view cruise ship cabins and hotel rooms before booking their trips.

- The Oculus Quest 2 offers an app called Wander where users can virtually wander around the world. Search by text or by a map and see Google Street View images. Since Street View images are captured with a 360 degree camera, users can turn in any direction from any location and experience the area.

Healthcare

- Virtually Better (www.virtuallybetter.com) has developed Bravemind in collaboration with the University of Southern California's Institute of Creative Technologies. Bravemind provides two virtual environments: Iraq and Afghanistan.

  Therapists can recreate difficult memories at a pace that patients can handle. They customize the experience based on the patient's history to include explosions, firefights, insurgent attacks, and roadside bombs. The virtual experience includes sound effects such as weapon discharges and radio chatter, as well as vibrations designed to mimic engine rumbling and explosions. Bravemind also uses a scent machine to create smells appropriate to the experience such as diesel fuel, garbage, and gunpowder.

- HRM Medical Realities (www.medicalrealities.com) uses VR modules to help train health-care practitioners. The firm's platform covers a variety of training scenarios, including a physician's office and the operating room, as well as medical school education such as dissecting VR cadavers.

- Microsoft's Hololense 2 (www.microsoft.com/en-us/hololens/buy) was used in late 2020 by three surgeons to collaborate in real time with data in a 10-hour spinal surgery. But, only one was actually performing the surgery. The others were consulting as they all worked together to make decisions on behalf of the patient.

Mixed Reality Examples

Health Care

- A research project at Imperial College Healthcare Trust in London is using Microsoft's mixed-reality headset, HoloLens, to plan plastic surgery. The system can identify which tissue and veins can be used in reconstructive operations.
- Medical services such as 3D4Medical (**www.3d4medical.com**) and Echopixel (**www.echopixel.com**) use existing medical image datasets to create mixed-reality environments of patient-specific anatomy, allowing students and physicians to view and dissect images just as they would a real-world, physical object. These services also help physicians explain medical conditions to patients.

Entertainment

- Monster Park brings Jurassic Park dinosaurs into any landscape you desire.

MKT Retail

- Lowe's (**www.lowes.com**), IKEA (**www.ikea.com**), Wayfair (**www.wayfair.com**), Sotheby's (**www.sothebys.com**), and other home-product retailers use MR that allows customers to see how their products will look like in their homes and whether the products will fit into specific rooms and spaces.

HRM Training

- Honeywell has developed a mixed-reality simulation tool to train its industrial employees using Microsoft HoloLens.
- Organizations can use headsets to help guide staff through complicated tasks such as fixing a particular piece of machinery or diagnosing and repairing an automobile.

Holograms

- Startup 8i (**www.8i.com**) has created a lifelike hologram of John Hamm for the Sundance Film Festival and a Buzz Aldrin hologram for the South by Southwest (SXSW) Conference. Analysts anticipate that the company's Holo app will have many more applications for musicians, brands, and celebrities. The public can download the Holo app to their phones to create their own 3D animations.

WILEY PLUS

Author Lecture Videos are available exclusively in *WileyPLUS.*
Apply the Concept activities are available in the Appendix and in *WileyPLUS.*

central processing unit (CPU) Hardware that performs the actual computation or "number crunching" inside any computer.

microprocessor The CPU, made up of millions of transistors embedded in a circuit on a silicon wafer or chip.

control unit Portion of the CPU that controls the flow of information.

TG 1.5   The Central Processing Unit

LEARNING OBJECTIVE

Describe the design and functioning of the central processing unit.

The **central processing unit (CPU)** performs the actual computation or "number crunching" inside any computer. The CPU is a **microprocessor** (e.g., Intel's Core i3, i5, and i7 chips with more to come) made up of millions of microscopic transistors embedded in a circuit on a silicon wafer, or *chip*. For this reason, microprocessors are commonly referred to as chips.

As shown in **Figure TG 1.3**, the microprocessor has different parts, which perform different functions. The **control unit** sequentially accesses program instructions, decodes them, and controls the flow of data to and from the arithmetic logic unit, the registers, the caches,

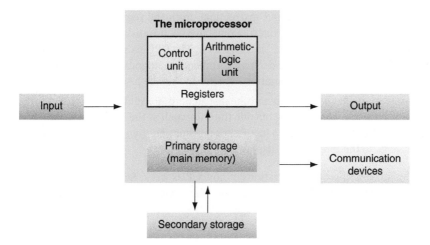

FIGURE TG 1.3 Parts of a microprocessor.

primary storage, secondary storage, and various output devices. The **arithmetic logic unit (ALU)** performs the mathematical calculations and makes logical comparisons. The registers are high-speed storage areas that store very small amounts of data and instructions for short periods.

arithmetic logic unit (ALU) Portion of the CPU that performs the mathematical calculations and makes logical comparisons.

How the CPU Works

In the CPU, inputs enter and are stored until they are needed. At that point, they are retrieved and processed, and the output is stored and then delivered somewhere. **Figure TG 1.4** illustrates this process, which works as follows:

- The inputs consist of data and brief instructions about what to do with the data. These instructions come into the CPU from random access memory (RAM). Data might be entered by the user through the keyboard, for example, or read from a data file in another part of the computer. The inputs are stored in registers until they are sent to the next step in the processing.

- Data and instructions travel in the chip through electrical pathways called *buses*. The size of the bus—analogous to the width of a highway—determines how much information can flow at any time.

- The control unit directs the flow of data and instructions within the chip.

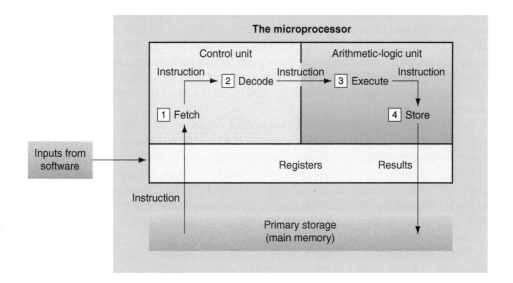

FIGURE TG 1.4 How the CPU works.

binary form The form in which data and instructions can be read by the CPU—only 0s and 1s.

- The ALU receives the data and instructions from the registers and makes the desired computation. These data and instructions have been translated into **binary form**—that is, only 0s and 1s. A "0" or a "1" is called a bit. The CPU can process only binary data. All types of data, such as letters, decimal numbers, photographs, music, and so on, can be converted to a binary representation, which can then be processed by the CPU.
- The data in their original form and the instructions are sent to storage registers and then are sent back to a storage place outside the chip, such as the computer's hard drive. Meanwhile, the transformed data go to another register and then on to other parts of the computer (e.g., to the monitor for display or to storage).

Intel offers excellent demonstrations of how CPUs work. Search the Web for "Intel" with "Explore the Curriculum" to find their demos. This cycle of processing, known as a *machine instruction cycle*, occurs billions of times per second.

Advances in Microprocessor Design

Moore's law Prediction by Gordon Moore, an Intel cofounder, that microprocessor complexity would double approximately every two years.

Historically, improvements in chip designs occurred at an increasing rate, as described by **Moore's law**. In 1965, Gordon Moore, a cofounder of Intel Corporation, predicted that microprocessor complexity would double approximately every 18 months. His prediction was amazingly accurate for some 45 years. The advances predicted from Moore's law arose mainly from the following innovations:

- Producing increasingly miniaturized transistors. For example, the Intel i9 chip has approximately 50 billion transistors.
- Placing multiple processors on a single chip. Chips with more than one processor are called *multicore* chips. For example, the most powerful Intel i9 chip contains 10 cores.
- Three-dimensional (3D) chips require less power than two-dimensional chips while improving performance. These chips are particularly valuable in handheld devices because they extend the device's battery life.

Moore's law has been slowing down because it is becoming increasing difficult to place transistors even more close together on chips. As a result, chip manufacturing plants (called fabrication plants, or *fabs*) have taken longer to build and have become much more expensive. Intel's newest fab, designed to build 10-nanometer chips, was delayed. The fab began delivering chips in 2019, five years after the previous generation of chips. (A *nanometer* is one-billionth of a meter. Ten nanometers represents the distance between transistors on a chip.) In addition to the delay, the cost of a fab is expected to reach $16 billion or more by 2022. Not coincidentally, only three companies are planning to manufacture the next generation of chips, down from eight in 2010 and 25 in 2002.

While Moore's law might be slowing down, it is not dead. In 2022, Apple released the M1 Ultra. This chip has an amazing 114 billion transistors in over a hundred processing cores dedicated to logic, graphics, and artificial intelligence. The most significant innovation was the use of a bridge to connect multiple chips to create one high-performance chip. Chip production had almost reached the limit of being able to add more processors, and this technique (the bridge) will allow Moore's law, and the subsequent hardware improvements, to continue to progress.

In addition to increased speed and performance, Moore's law has had an impact on cost. For example, in 1997, a desktop computer with a Pentium II microprocessor, 64 megabytes of random access memory (RAM), a 4-gigabyte hard drive, and a 17-inch monitor cost $4,000. In late 2022, a computer with a twelfth generation Intel i7 processor, 32 gigabytes of RAM, and a 1-terabyte solid-state drive, all packed into an all-in-one 27-inch touchscreen, cost approximately $1,700. It is significant to note that the 2022 desktop is far faster, has 500 times more RAM, and has 500 times more hard drive storage (without counting the solid-state storage) than the 1997 desktop, for 42.5 percent of the cost.

Two developments are making the slowing of Moore's law less problematic: graphics processing units and quantum computing. *Graphics processing units* (GPUs) were invented by

NVIDIA (www.nvidia.com) in 1999. Traditional CPUs are composed of a limited number of cores with a large amount of cache memory. As a result, CPUs can manage a few tasks at one time and are effective at serial processing (one task at a time).

In contrast, GPUs consist of hundreds of cores and can manage thousands of tasks simultaneously. Therefore, GPUs are effective at parallel processing (many tasks at once), meaning that they break down complex problems into thousands or millions of separate tasks and work them out at once. GPUs are particularly suited for computer graphics, image processing, and artificial intelligence applications.

A new computing paradigm has emerged, called *quantum computing*. Classical computers manipulate bits (0s and 1s) to perform operations. In contrast, quantum computers use quantum bits, or qubits. Quantum computers also use 0s and 1s, but qubits have a third state called *superposition*. That is, superposition allows qubits to represent a one or a zero, or any linear combination of a one and a zero, at the same time. Superposition enables quantum computers to process exponentially more data than classical computers.

For example, let's say we want to search for a particular name in a telephone book. With one classical computer, we would start at the beginning and search the phone book sequentially until we found the name we wanted. With two classical computers, we could search the phone book twice as fast because one computer would start at the beginning and one would start at the end until one or the other found the correct name. With three classical computers, we would search the phone book three times as fast, and so on. If we search the phone book with a quantum computer, it would examine all the names in the book simultaneously, finding the correct name instantaneously.

Quantum computers are an emerging technology and the race is on to develop these machines. For example, on September 29, 2020, D-Wave (www.dwavesys.com) launched its 5,000-qubit quantum computing platform that purportedly handles 1 million variables. D-Wave calls the new system Advantage and is making it available to business customers over the Internet via the company's quantum cloud service. Since its launch, customers are using D-Wave in amazing ways. For example, a grocery retailer in Western Canada has used the product to reduce an optimization analysis from 25 hours to 2 minutes.

Computer Memory

The amount and type of memory that a computer possesses has a great deal to do with its general utility. A computer's memory also determines the types of programs that the computer can run, the work it can perform, its speed, and its cost. There are two basic categories of computer memory. The first is *primary storage*. It is called "primary" because it stores small amounts of data and information that the CPU will use immediately. The second category is *secondary storage*, which stores much larger amounts of data and information (e.g., an entire software program) for extended periods.

Memory Capacity   As you have seen, CPUs process only binary units—0s and 1s— which are translated through computer languages into bits. A particular combination of bits represents a certain alphanumeric character or a simple mathematical operation. Eight bits are needed to represent any one of these characters. This eight-bit string is known as a byte. The storage capacity of a computer is measured in bytes. Bits typically are used as units of measure only for telecommunications capacity, as in how many million bits per second can be sent through a particular medium.

The hierarchy of terms used to describe memory capacity is as follows:

- *Kilobyte.* Kilo means "one thousand," so a kilobyte (KB) is approximately 1,000 bytes. To be more precise, a kilobyte is 1,024 bytes. Computer designers find it convenient to work with powers of 2: 1,024 is 2 to the 10th power, and 1,024 is close enough to 1,000 that for *kilobyte* people use the standard prefix *kilo*, which means exactly 1,000 in familiar units such as the kilogram or kilometer.

- *Megabyte.* Mega means "one million," so a megabyte (MB) is approximately 1 million bytes. Most personal computers have hundreds of megabytes of RAM.

- *Gigabyte.* Giga means "one billion," so a gigabyte (GB) is approximately 1 billion bytes.
- *Terabyte.* A terabyte is approximately 1 trillion bytes. The storage capacity of modern personal computers can be several terabytes.
- *Petabyte.* A petabyte is approximately 1,000 terabytes.
- *Exabyte.* An exabyte is approximately 1,000 petabytes.
- *Zettabyte.* A zettabyte is approximately 1,000 exabytes.

To get a feel for these amounts, consider the following example: If your computer has one terabyte of storage capacity on its hard drive (a type of secondary storage), it can store approximately 1 trillion bytes of data. If the average page of text contains about 2,000 bytes, then your hard drive could store approximately 10 percent of all the print collections of the Library of Congress. That same terabyte can store 70 hours of standard-definition compressed video.

Primary Storage

primary storage (also called main memory) High-speed storage located directly on the motherboard that stores data to be processed by the CPU, instructions telling the CPU how to process the data, and operating system programs.

Primary storage, or main memory, as it is sometimes called, stores three types of information for very brief periods of time: (1) data to be processed by the CPU, (2) instructions for the CPU as to how to process the data, and (3) operating system programs that manage various aspects of the computer's operation. Primary storage takes place in chips mounted on the computer's main circuit board, called the *motherboard*. These chips are located as close as physically possible to the CPU chip. As with the CPU, all the data and instructions in primary storage have been translated into binary code.

The four main types of primary storage are (1) register, (2) cache memory, (3) random access memory (RAM), and (4) read-only memory (ROM).

registers High-speed storage areas in the CPU that store very small amounts of data and instructions for short periods.

Registers are part of the CPU. They have the least capacity, storing extremely limited amounts of instructions and data only immediately before and after processing.

cache memory A type of high-speed memory that enables the computer to temporarily store blocks of data that are used more often and that a processor can access more rapidly than main memory (RAM).

Cache memory is a type of high-speed memory that enables the computer to temporarily store blocks of data that are used more often and that a processor can access more rapidly than main memory (RAM). Cache memory is physically located closer to the CPU than RAM. Blocks that are used less often remain in RAM until they are transferred to cache; blocks used infrequently remain in secondary storage. Cache memory is faster than RAM because the instructions travel a shorter distance to the CPU.

random access memory (RAM) The part of primary storage that holds a software program and small amounts of data when they are brought from secondary storage.

Random access memory (RAM) is the part of primary storage that holds a software program and small amounts of data for processing. Compared with the registers, RAM stores more information and is located farther away from the CPU. However, compared with secondary storage, RAM stores less information and is much closer to the CPU.

RAM is temporary and, in most cases, *volatile*—that is, RAM chips lose their contents if the current is lost or turned off, as from a power surge, brownout, or electrical noise generated by lightning or nearby machines.

Most of us have lost data at one time or another because of a computer crash or a power failure. What is usually lost is whatever is in RAM, the cache, or the registers at the time, because these types of memory are volatile. Therefore, you need greater security when you are storing certain types of critical data or instructions. Cautious computer users frequently save data to nonvolatile memory (secondary storage). Most modern software applications also have autosave functions.

read-only memory (ROM) Type of primary storage in which certain critical instructions are safeguarded; the storage is nonvolatile and retains the instructions when the power to the computer is turned off.

Read-only memory is the place—actually, a type of chip—where certain critical instructions are safeguarded. ROM is nonvolatile, so it retains these instructions when the power to the computer is turned off. The read-only designation means that these instructions can only be read by the computer and cannot be changed by the user. An example of ROM is the instructions needed to start or boot the computer after it has been shut off.

Secondary Storage

secondary storage Technology that can store very large amounts of data for extended periods.

Secondary storage is designed to store very large amounts of data for extended periods. Secondary storage has the following characteristics:

- It is nonvolatile.
- It takes more time to retrieve data from it than from RAM.
- It is cheaper than primary storage (see **Figure TG 1.5**).
- It can use a variety of media, each with its own technology.

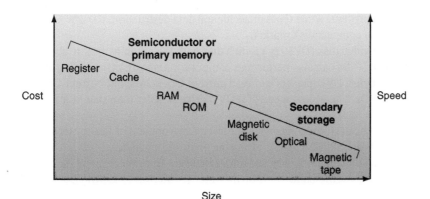

FIGURE TG 1.5 Primary memory compared with secondary storage.

One secondary storage medium, **magnetic tape**, is kept on a large open reel or in a smaller cartridge or cassette. Although this is an old technology, it remains popular because it is the cheapest storage medium, and it can handle enormous amounts of data. As a result, many organizations (e.g., the U.S. Government Social Security Administration) use magnetic tape for archival storage. The downside is that it is the slowest method for retrieving data because all the data are placed on the tape sequentially. This process means that the system might have to run through the majority of the tape before it comes to the desired piece of data.

Magnetic disks (or hard drives or fixed disk drives) are the most commonly used mass storage devices because of their low cost, high speed, and large storage capacity. Hard disk drives read from, and write to, stacks of rotating (at up to 15,000 rpm) magnetic disk platters mounted in rigid enclosures and sealed against environmental and atmospheric contamination (see **Figure TG 1.6**). These disks are permanently mounted in a unit that may be internal or external to the computer.

Solid-state drives (SSDs) are data storage devices that serve the same purpose as a hard drive and store data in memory chips. Whereas hard drives have moving parts, SSDs do not. SSDs use the same interface with the computer's CPU as hard drives and are therefore a seamless replacement for hard drives. SSDs offer many advantages over hard drives. They use less power, are silent and faster, and produce about one-third the heat of a hard drive. The major disadvantage of SSDs is that they cost more than hard drives.

Unlike magnetic media, **optical storage devices** do not store data through magnetism. Rather, a laser reads the surface of a reflective plastic platter. Optical disk drives are slower than magnetic hard drives, but they are less fragile and less susceptible to damage from contamination.

Optical disks can also store a great deal of information, both on a routine basis and when combined into storage systems. Types of optical disks include compact disk read-only memory and digital video disk.

Compact disk read-only memory (CD-ROM) storage devices have high capacity, low cost, and high durability. However, because a CD-ROM is a read-only medium, it cannot be written on. *CD-R* can be written to, but once this is done, what was written on it cannot be changed later. That is, CD-R is writable, which CD-ROM is not, but it is not rewritable, which *CD-RW* (compact disk, rewritable) is. There are applications about which not being rewritable is a

magnetic tape A secondary storage medium on a large open reel or in a smaller cartridge or cassette.

magnetic disks (or hard drives or fixed disk drives) A form of secondary storage on a magnetized disk divided into tracks and sectors that provide addresses for various pieces of data.

solid-state drives (SSDs) Data storage devices that serve the same purpose as a hard drive and store data in memory chips.

optical storage devices A form of secondary storage in which a laser reads the surface of a reflective plastic platter.

FIGURE TG 1.6 Traditional hard drives are less expensive, but solid-state drives are faster and are more reliable.

plus, because it prevents some types of accidental data destruction. CD-RW adds rewritability to the recordable compact disk market.

The digital video disk *(DVD)* is a 5-inch disk with the capacity to store about 135 minutes of digital video. DVDs can also perform as computer storage disks, providing storage capabilities of 17 gigabytes. DVD players can read current CD-ROMs, but current CD-ROM players cannot read DVDs. The access speed of a DVD drive is faster than that of a typical CD-ROM drive.

Blu-ray disks can store 50 gigabytes per layer. Development of Blu-ray technology is ongoing, with multilayered disks capable of storing up to 100 gigabytes.

The various disk technologies are under pressure from on-demand, streaming services over the Internet. As the bandwidth of the Internet increases, so will the pressure on disk technologies.

Flash memory devices (or *memory cards*) are nonvolatile electronic storage devices that contain no moving parts and use 30 times less battery power than hard drives. Flash devices are also smaller and more durable than hard drives. The trade-offs are that flash devices store less data than hard drives. Flash devices are used with digital cameras, handheld and laptop computers, telephones, music players, and video game consoles.

One popular flash memory device is the **thumb drive** (also called *memory stick, jump drive,* or *flash drive*). These devices fit into Universal Serial Bus (USB) ports on personal computers and other devices, and they can store many gigabytes. Thumb drives have replaced magnetic floppy disks for portable storage.

flash memory devices
Nonvolatile electronic storage devices that are compact, are portable, require little power, and contain no moving parts.

thumb drive   Storage device that fits into the USB port of a personal computer and is used for portable storage.

Before you go on...

1. Decisions about hardware focus on what three factors?
2. What are the overall trends in hardware?
3. Define hardware and list the major hardware components.
4. Describe the different types of computers.
5. Distinguish between human data-input devices and source-data automation.
6. Briefly describe how a microprocessor functions.
7. Distinguish between primary storage and secondary storage.

What's in IT for Me?

For All Business Majors

The design of computer hardware has profound impacts for business-people. Personal and organizational success can depend on an understanding of hardware design and a commitment to knowing where it is going and what opportunities and challenges hardware innovations will bring. Because these innovations are occurring so rapidly, hardware decisions both at the individual level and at the organizational level are difficult.

At the *individual level*, most people who have a home or office computer system and want to upgrade it, or people who are

contemplating their first computer purchase, are faced with the decision of *when* to buy as much as *what* to buy and at what cost. At the *organizational level*, these same issues plague IS professionals. However, they are more complex and costly. Most organizations have many different computer systems in place at the same time. Innovations may come to different classes of computers at different times or rates. Therefore, managers must decide when old hardware *legacy systems* still have a productive role in the organization and when they should be replaced. A legacy system is an old computer system or application that continues to be used, typically because it still functions for the users' needs, even though newer technology is available.

Summary

TG 1.1   Identify the major hardware components of a computer system.

Modern computer systems have six major components: the central processing unit (CPU), primary storage, secondary storage, input technologies, output technologies, and communications technologies.

TG 1.2   Discuss strategic issues that link hardware design to business strategy.

Strategic issues linking hardware design to business strategy include the following: How do organizations keep up with the rapid price/performance advancements in hardware? How often should an organization upgrade its computers and storage systems? How can organizations measure benefits gained from price/performance improvements in hardware?

TG 1.3   Describe the various types of computers in the computer hierarchy.

Supercomputers are the most powerful computers, designed to handle intensive computational demands. Organizations use mainframes for centralized data processing and managing large databases. Microcomputers are small, complete, and general purpose computers. Laptop or notebook computers are small, easily transportable computers.

Tablet computers are complete computers contained entirely in a flat touchscreen that uses a stylus, digital pen, fingertip, or soft (virtual) keyboards as input devices. Wearable computers are miniature computers that people wear under, with, or on top of their clothing.

TG 1.4   Differentiate the various types of input and output technologies and their uses.

The two main types of input devices are human data-entry devices and source-data automation devices. *Human data-entry* devices require a certain amount of human effort to input data. Examples are keyboard, mouse, pointing stick, trackball, joystick, touchscreen, stylus, and voice recognition. *Source-data automation* devices input data with minimal human intervention. These technologies gather data at the source of a transaction or other event. Bar code readers are an example of source-data automation.

TG 1.5   Describe the design and functioning of the central processing unit.

The CPU consists of the arithmetic logic unit, which performs the calculations; the registers, which store minute amounts of data and instructions immediately before and after processing; and the control unit, which controls the flow of information on the microprocessor chip. After processing, the data in their original form and the instructions are sent back to a storage location outside the chip.

Key Terms

arithmetic logic unit (ALU)   481
augmented reality (AR)   474
binary form   482
cache memory   484
central processing unit (CPU)   480
control unit   480
fat clients   472
flash memory devices   486
gesture recognition   473
laptop computers (notebook
   computers)   472

magnetic disks (or hard drives or
   fixed disk drives)   485
magnetic tape   485
mainframes   471
microcomputers   472
microprocessor   480
Moore's law   482
notebook computer   472
optical storage devices   485
primary storage (also called main
   memory)   484

random access memory (RAM)   484
read-only memory (ROM)   484
registers   484
secondary storage   484
server   472
solid-state drives (SSDs)   485
thin client   472
thumb drive   486
virtual reality (VR)   474
wearable computer   473

Discussion Questions

1. What factors affect the speed of a microprocessor?

2. If you were the CIO of a firm, what factors would you consider when selecting secondary storage media for your company's records (files)?

3. Given that Moore's law has proved itself over the past two decades, speculate on what chip capabilities will be in 10 years. What might your desktop PC be able to do?

4. If you were the CIO of a firm, how would you explain the workings, benefits, and limitations of using thin clients as opposed to fat clients?

5. Where might you find embedded computers at home, at school, or at work?

6. You are the CIO of your company, and you have to develop an application of strategic importance to your firm. What are the advantages and disadvantages of using open-source software?

7. What does the statement "hardware is useless without software" mean?

Problem-Solving Activities

1. Access the websites of the major chip manufacturers—for example, Intel (www.intel.com) and Advanced Micro Devices (www.amd.com)—and obtain the latest information regarding new and planned chips. Compare performance and costs across these vendors. Be sure to take a close look at the various multicore chips.

2. Compare the Apple ipad (www.apple.com/ipad) to the Samsung galaxy tablet (www.www.samsung.com/us/tablets). How would these tablets help you in class? Which of the two would you prefer and why?

3. Choose one of the examples of augmented reality mentioned in this tech guide and discuss how you see it implementing your future career.

Software

TECHNOLOGY GUIDE OUTLINE	LEARNING OBJECTIVES
TG 2.1 **Software Issues**	TG 2.1 **Discuss** the major software issues that confront modern organizations.
TG 2.2 **Systems Software**	TG 2.2 **Describe** the general functions of the operating system.
TG 2.3 **Application Software**	TG 2.3 **Identify** the major types of application software.

Introduction

As you begin this Technology Guide, you might be wondering, "Why do I have to know anything about software?" There are several reasons why you will benefit from understanding the basics of software. First, regardless of your major (and future functional area in an organization), you will be using different types of software throughout your career. Second, you will have input concerning the software that you will use. In this capacity, you will be required to answer many questions, such as:

- Does my software help me do my job?
- Is this software easy to use?
- Do I need more functionality in my hardware or software, and if so, what functionality would be most helpful to me?

Third, you will have input into decisions when your functional area or organization upgrades or replaces its software. Some organizations will allocate the software budget to functional areas or departments. In such cases, you might be responsible for making software decisions (at least locally) yourself. MIS employees will act as advisors, but you will provide important input into such decisions.

Computer hardware is only as effective as the instructions you give it. Those instructions are contained in **software**. The importance of computer software cannot be overestimated. The first software applications for computers in business were developed in the early 1950s. At that time, software was less costly. Today, software comprises a much larger percentage of the cost of modern computer systems; the price of hardware has dramatically decreased while both the complexity and the price of software have dramatically increased.

software A set of computer programs that enable the hardware to process data.

The ever-increasing complexity of software has also increased the potential for errors, or *bugs*. Large applications today may contain millions of lines of computer code, written by hundreds of people over the course of several years. Thus, the potential for errors is huge, and testing and debugging software is expensive and time consuming.

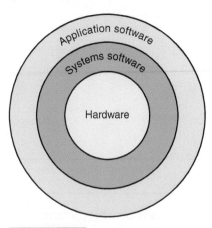

In spite of these overall trends—increasing complexity, cost, and numbers of defects—software has become an everyday feature of our business and personal lives. Your examination of software begins with definitions of some fundamental concepts. Software consists of **computer programs**, which are sequences of instructions for the computer. The process of writing, or coding, programs is called programming. Individuals who perform this task are called *programmers*.

Computer programs include **documentation**, which is a written description of the program's functions. Documentation helps the user operate the computer system, and it helps other programmers understand what the program does and how it accomplishes its purpose. Documentation is vital to a business organization. Without it, the departure of a key programmer or user could deprive the organization of the knowledge of how the program is designed and functions.

The computer can do nothing until it is instructed by software. Computer hardware, by design, is general purpose. Software enables the user to instruct the hardware to perform specific functions that provide business value. There are two major types of software: systems software and application software. **Figure TG 2.1** illustrates the relationship among hardware, systems software, and application software.

computer programs The sequences of instructions for the computer, which comprise software.

documentation Written description of the functions of a software program.

WILEY PLUS

Author Lecture Videos are available exclusively in *WileyPLUS.*
Apply the Concept activities are available in the Appendix and in *WileyPLUS.*

| TG 2.1 | # Software Issues |

LEARNING OBJECTIVE

Discuss the major software issues that confront modern organizations.

The importance of software in computer systems has brought new issues to the forefront for organizational managers. These issues include software defects (bugs), licensing, updates and agility, open systems, and open-source software.

Software Defects

All too often, computer program code is inefficient, poorly designed, and riddled with errors. The Software Engineering Institute (SEI) at Carnegie Mellon University in Pittsburgh defines good software as usable, reliable, defect-free, cost-effective, and maintainable. As our dependence on computers and networks increases, the risks associated with software defects are becoming more serious.

The SEI maintains that, on average, professional programmers make between 100 and 150 errors in every 1,000 lines of code they write. Fortunately, the software industry recognizes this problem. Unfortunately, however, the problem is enormous, and the industry is taking only initial steps to resolve it. One critical step is better design and planning at the beginning of the development process (discussed in Chapter 13).

Software Licensing

Many people routinely copy proprietary software. However, making copies without the manufacturer's explicit permission—a practice known as *piracy*—is illegal. The Business Software Alliance (BSA; www.bsa.org), a nonprofit trade association dedicated to promoting a safe and legal digital world, collects, investigates, and acts on software piracy tips. The BSA has calculated that piracy costs software vendors around the world billions of dollars annually. Most of the tips the BSA receives come from current and past employees of offending companies.

To protect their investment, software vendors must prevent their products from being copied and distributed by individuals and other software companies. A company can copyright its software, which means that the U.S. Copyright Office grants the company the exclusive legal right to reproduce, publish, and sell that software.

The number of computing devices in organizations continues to grow, and businesses continue to decentralize, so IS managers are finding it increasingly difficult to supervise their software assets. In fact, the majority of chief information officers (CIOs) are not confident that their companies are in compliance with software licensing agreements. For example, one medium-sized company was fined $10,000 for unknowingly using Microsoft Exchange mailbox licenses that had not been purchased. Worse, the company was also fined $100,000 for not having the necessary licenses for Autodesk, Inc.'s AutoCAD design software.

To help companies manage their software licenses, new firms have arisen that specialize in tracking software licenses for a fee. For example, Ivanti (**www.ivanti.com**) will track and manage a company's software licenses to ensure that a client company is in compliance with U.S. copyright laws.

Software Updates and Agility

Organizations are in constant need of changes and updates to their software applications. As the number of applications and users has grown over the years, the need for updates and changes has grown as well. Not only has the volume grown, but the speed at which these changes are needed also has accelerated. Many IT Departments now cannot keep up with the volume or speed of change requests. As such, many organizations are making use of software development strategies that involve users in the development and maintenance of the software.

DevOps, defined in Chapter 13 as combination of "development" and "operations," includes users in the entire process. The goal is to reduce the time to deployment, increase the usability of the finished product, and lower the cost of new app development. DevOps often makes use of Low-Code/No-Code development tools (Chapter 13) that do not require any coding skills, but allow the users to work alongside the development team to visually create the software as they want it. Updates and ongoing modifications can be handled in the same way. While IT departments will maintain control over security, data access, and style guidelines, users can modify the look, feel, and function of the application as they and their customers need it.

Open Systems

The **open systems** concept refers to a group of computing products that work together. In an open system, the same operating system with compatible software is installed on all computers that interact within an organization. An example would be an organization that installed Microsoft Windows on every PC in the organization and made this standard so that everyone understood the compatibility requirements.

A complementary approach is to employ application software that will run across all computer platforms. Through the use of open (also referred to as public) application programming interfaces (API), companies can easily share their data with each other and their customers. An open or public API is made available to everyone and allows third parties to develop apps that interact with other applications and software based on the same architecture. Where hardware, operating systems, and application software are all designed as open systems, users can purchase the best software, called *best of breed*, for a job without worrying whether it will run on particular hardware. Some refer to this model as "composable" architecture (see Chapter 10 Opening Case).

open systems Computing products that work together by using the same operating system with compatible software on all the computers that interact in an organization.

Open-Source Software

Organizations today are increasingly selecting open-source software rather than proprietary software. **Proprietary software** is purchased software that has restrictions on its use, copying, and modification. Companies that develop proprietary software spend money and time developing their products, which they then sell in the marketplace. This software is labeled *proprietary* because the developer keeps the source code—the actual computer

proprietary software Software that has been developed by a company and has restrictions on its use, copying, and modification.

instructions—private (just as Coca-Cola does with its soft drink formula). Therefore, companies that purchase the software can use it in their operations, but they cannot change the source code themselves.

In contrast, the source code for open-source software is available at no cost to both developers and users. This software is distributed with license terms that ensure that its source code will always be available for all users.

Open-source software is produced by worldwide "communities" of developers who write and maintain the code. Inside each community, however, only a small group of developers, called *core developers*, is allowed to modify the code directly. All the other developers must submit their suggested changes to the core developers.

There are advantages to implementing open-source software in an organization. According to OpenSource (www.opensource.org), open-source development produces high-quality, reliable, low-cost software. This software is also flexible, meaning that the code can be changed to meet users' needs. In many cases, open-source software can be more reliable than proprietary software. Because the code is available to many developers, more bugs are discovered early and quickly, and they are fixed immediately. Technical support for open-source software is also available from firms that offer products derived from the software. An example is Red Hat (www.redhat.com), a major Linux vendor that supplies solutions to problems associated with open-source technology. Specifically, Red Hat provides education, training, and technical support for a fee.

Open-source software, however, has disadvantages. The major drawback is that companies that use open-source software depend on the continued goodwill of an army of volunteers for enhancements, bug fixes, and so on, even if they have signed a contract that includes support. Some companies will not accept this risk, although as a practical matter the support community for Linux, Apache, and Firefox is not likely to disappear. Furthermore, organizations that do not have in-house technical experts will have to purchase maintenance-support contracts from a third party. Open-source software also poses questions concerning ease of use, the time and expense needed to train users, and compatibility with existing systems either within or outside the organization.

There are many examples of open-source software, including the GNU (GNU's Not UNIX) suite of software (www.gnu.org) developed by the Free Software Foundation (www.fsf.org), the Linux operating system (www.linux.com), Apache web server (www.apache.org), sendmail SMTP (Send Mail Transport Protocol) e-mail server, the Perl programming language (www.perl.org), and the Firefox browser from Mozilla (www.mozilla.com). In fact, more than 150,000 open-source projects are under way at SourceForge (www.sourceforge.net), the popular open-source hosting site.

Open-source software is moving to the mainstream, as you see by the many major companies that use this type of software. For example, Japan's Shinsei Bank (www.shinseibank.com/english/) uses Linux on its servers, SugarCRM (www.sugarcrm.com) for certain customer relationship management tasks, and MySQL (www.mysql.com) open-source database management software. Furthermore, the *Los Angeles Times* uses Alfresco (www.alfresco.com) to manage some of the images and video for its website.

open-source software Software made available in source-code form at no cost to developers.

WILEY PLUS

Author Lecture Videos are available exclusively in *WileyPLUS.*
Apply the Concept activities are available in the Appendix and in *WileyPLUS.*

TG 2.2 Systems Software

LEARNING OBJECTIVE

Describe the general functions of the operating system.

systems software The class of computer instructions that serve primarily as an intermediary between computer hardware and application programs; provides important self-regulatory functions for computer systems.

Systems software is a set of instructions that serves primarily as an intermediary between computer hardware and application programs. Systems software performs many functions.

- It controls and supports the computer system and its information-processing activities.
- It enables computer systems to perform self-regulatory functions by loading itself when the computer is first turned on.

- It provides commonly used sets of instructions for all applications.
- It helps users and IT personnel program, test, and debug their own computer programs.
- It supports application software by directing the computer's basic functions.

The major type of systems software with which we are concerned is the operating system. The **operating system (OS)** is the "director" of your computer system's operations. It supervises the overall operation of the computer by monitoring the computer's status, scheduling operations, and managing input and output processes. Well-known desktop operating systems include Microsoft Windows (**www.microsoft.com**), Apple Mac OS X (**www.apple. com**), and Linux (**www.linux.com**). When a new version with new features is released, the developers often give the new version a new designation. For example, in mid-2020, the current version of Windows was Windows 10, and the latest version of the MacOS was Catalina.

The operating system also provides an interface between the user and the hardware. This user interface hides the complexity of the hardware from the user. That is, you do not have to know how the hardware actually operates; you simply have to know what the hardware will do and what you need to do to obtain the desired results.

The ease or difficulty of the interaction between the user and the computer is determined to a large extent by the **graphical user interface (GUI)**. The GUI allows users to directly control the hardware by manipulating visible objects (such as icons) and actions that replace complex commands. Microsoft Windows provides a widely recognized GUI.

GUI technology incorporates features such as virtual reality, head-mounted displays, speech input (user commands) and output, pen and gesture recognition, animation, multimedia, artificial intelligence, and cellular/wireless communication capabilities. These new interfaces, called *natural user interfaces* (NUIs), will combine social, haptic, and touch-enabled gesture-control interfaces. (A *haptic interface* provides tactile feedback through the sense of touch by applying forces, vibrations, or motions to the user.)

A **social interface** guides the user through computer applications by using cartoon-like characters, graphics, animation, and voice commands. The cartoon-like characters can be puppets, narrators, guides, inhabitants, or *avatars* (computer-generated human-like figures). Social interfaces are hard to create without being corny. For example, the assistant "Clippy" was so annoying to users of Microsoft Office 97 that it was eliminated from Office 2003 and all subsequent versions.

- *Motion control gaming consoles* are another type of interface. In November 2020, Microsoft released its Xbox Series X and Sony released its PlayStation 5. These consoles track your movements without a physical controller, offer voice recognition, and accommodate multiple players.
- The Leap Motion Controller is a motion-sensing, matchbox-sized device placed on a physical desktop. Using two cameras, the device "observes" an area up to a distance of about three feet. It precisely tracks fingers or items such as a pen that cross into the observed area. The Leap can perform tasks such as navigating a website, using pinch-to-zoom gestures on maps, performing high-precision drawing, and manipulating complex three-dimensional visualizations. The smaller observation area and higher resolution of the device differentiates it from the Microsoft Kinect, which is more suitable for whole-body tracking in a space the size of a living room.

Touch-enabled gesture-control interfaces enable users to browse through photos, "toss" objects around a screen, "flick" to turn the pages of a book, play video games, and watch movies. Examples of this type of interface are Microsoft Surface and the Apple iPhone.

The operating system and the interfaces combine to create the **User Experience** (UX), sometimes called the customer experience (CX) if the user is a customer. UX simply refers to how people interact with a system or an application. It is crucial to design for UX today so that users do not push back on adopting or using a system. Within an organization, employers might be able to tell employees what systems they will use, but if your customers do not enjoy CX with your app, they will leave and find another app that fits their needs. According to a 2022 study published by TechJury.com, over 70 percent of users will abandon an app if it takes more than 3 seconds to load, And while many users download an average of 40 apps on their phones, less than half are regularly used. The UX/CX is crucial to keeping users/customers in the app.

operating system (OS)   The main system control program, which supervises the overall operations of the computer, allocates CPU time and main memory to programs, and provides an interface between the user and the hardware.

graphical user interface (GUI)   Systems software that allows users to have direct control of the hardware by manipulating visible objects (such as icons) and actions, which replace command syntax.

social interface   A user interface that guides the user through computer applications by using cartoon-like characters, graphics, animation, and voice commands.

user experience or customer experience   The way people interact with a system or application.

application software The class of computer instructions that directs a computer system to perform specific processing activities and provide functionality for users.

package Common term for an integrated group of computer programs developed by a vendor and available for purchase in prepackaged form.

software suite See **package**.

personal application software General-purpose, off-the-shelf application programs that support general types of processing, rather than being linked to any specific business function.

speech-recognition software Software that recognizes and interprets human speech, either one word at a time (discrete speech) or in a stream (continuous speech).

TG 2.3 | Application Software

LEARNING OBJECTIVE

Identify the major types of application software.

Application software is a set of computer instructions that provide specific functionality to a user. This functionality may be broad, such as general word processing, or narrow, such as an organization's payroll program. Essentially, an application program applies a computer to a certain need. As you will see, modern organizations use many different software applications.

Application software may be developed in-house by the organization's information systems personnel, or it may be commissioned from a software vendor. Alternatively, the software can be purchased, leased, or rented from a vendor that develops applications and sells them to many organizations. This "off-the-shelf" software may be a standard package, or it may be customizable. Special-purpose programs or "packages" can be tailored for a specific purpose, such as inventory control and payroll. A **package**, or **software suite**, is a group of programs with integrated functions that have been developed by a vendor and is available for purchase in a prepackaged form. Microsoft Office is a well-known example of a package or software suite.

General-purpose, off-the-shelf application programs designed to help individual users increase their productivity are referred to as **personal application software**. Table TG 2.1 lists some of the major types of personal application software.

Speech-recognition software, also called *voice recognition*, is an input technology, rather than strictly an application, that enables users to provide input to systems software and application software. As the name suggests, this software recognizes and interprets human speech, either one word at a time (*discrete speech*) or in a conversational stream (*continuous speech*). Advances in processing power, new software algorithms, and better microphones have enabled developers to design extremely accurate speech-recognition software. Experts predict that, in the near future, voice recognition systems will be built into almost every device, appliance, and machine that people use. Applications for voice recognition technology abound.

TABLE TG 2.1 Personal Application Software

Category of Personal Application Software	Major Functions	Examples
Spreadsheets	Use rows and columns to manipulate primarily numerical data; useful for analyzing financial information and for what-if and goal-seeking analyses	Microsoft Excel Quattro Pro- Word Perfect Apple iWork Numbers
Word processing	Allow users to manipulate primarily text with many writing and editing features	Microsoft Word Apple iWork Pages
Desktop publishing	Extend word processing software to allow production of finished, camera-ready documents, which may contain photographs, diagrams, and other images combined with text in different fonts	Microsoft Publisher QuarkXPress Adobe
Data management	Allow users to store, retrieve, and manipulate related data	Microsoft Access FileMaker Pro
Presentation	Allow users to create and edit graphically rich information to appear on electronic slides	Microsoft PowerPoint Apple iWork Keynote
Graphics	Allow users to create, store, and display or print charts, graphs, maps, and drawings	Adobe PhotoShop Corel DRAW
Personal information management	Allow users to create and maintain calendars, appointments, to-do lists, and business contacts	Google Calendar Microsoft Outlook

(continued)

TABLE TG 2.1   Personal Application Software *(continued)*

Category of Personal Application Software	Major Functions	Examples
Personal finance	Allow users to maintain checkbooks, track investments, monitor credit cards, and bank and pay bills electronically	Quicken Microsoft Money
Web authoring	Allow users to design websites and publish them on the Web	Microsoft FrontPage Adobe Dreamweaver
Communications	Allow users to communicate with other people over any distance	Micro Focus GroupWise Slack Zoom Google Meets

Before you go on...

1. What does the statement "hardware is useless without software" mean?
2. What are the differences between systems software and application software?
3. What is open-source software, and what are its advantages? Can you think of any disadvantages?
4. Describe the functions of the operating system.

What's in IT for Me?

ACCT For the Accounting Major

Accounting application software performs the organization's accounting functions, which are repetitive and performed in high volumes. Each business transaction (e.g., a person hired, a paycheck processed, an item sold) produces data that must be captured. Accounting applications capture these data and then manipulate them as necessary. Accounting applications adhere to relatively standardized procedures, handle detailed data, and have a historical focus (i.e., what happened in the past).

FIN For the Finance Major

Financial application software provides information about the firm's financial status to persons and groups inside and outside the firm. Financial applications include forecasting, funds management, and control applications. Forecasting applications predict and project the firm's future activity in the economic environment. Funds management applications use cash flow models to analyze expected cash flows. Control applications enable managers to monitor their financial performance, typically by providing information about the budgeting process and performance ratios.

MKT For the Marketing Major

Marketing application software helps management solve problems that involve marketing the firm's products. Marketing software includes marketing research and marketing intelligence applications. Marketing applications provide information about the firm's products and competitors, its distribution system, its advertising and personal selling activities, and its pricing strategies. Overall, marketing applications help managers develop strategies that combine the four major elements of marketing: product, promotion, place, and price.

POM For the Production/Operations Management Major

Managers use production/operations management (POM) application software for production planning and as part of the physical production system. POM applications include production, inventory, quality, and cost software. These applications help management operate manufacturing facilities and logistics. Materials requirements planning (MRP) software is also widely used in manufacturing. This software identifies which materials will be needed, how much will be needed, and the dates on which they will be needed. This information enables managers to be proactive.

HRM For the Human Resources Management Major

Human resources management application software provides information concerning recruiting and hiring, education and training, maintaining the employee database, termination, and administering benefits. HRM applications include workforce planning, recruiting, workforce management, compensation, benefits, and environmental reporting subsystems (e.g., equal employment opportunity records and analysis, union enrollment, toxic substances, and grievances).

MIS For the MIS Major

If your company decides to develop its own software, the MIS function is responsible for managing this activity. If the company decides to buy software, the MIS function deals with software vendors in analyzing their products. The MIS function is also responsible for upgrading software as vendors release new versions.

Summary

TG 2.1 Discuss the major software issues that confront modern organizations.

Computer program code often contains errors. The industry recognizes the enormous problem of software defects, and steps are being taken to resolve this issue. Software licensing is another issue for organizations and individuals. Copying proprietary software is illegal. Software vendors copyright their software to protect it from being copied. As a result, companies must license vendor-developed software to be able to use it. Organizations must also decide between open-source software and proprietary software. Each type of software has its pros and cons that must be carefully considered.

TG 2.2 Describe the general functions of the operating system.

Operating systems manage the actual computer resources (i.e., the hardware). They schedule and process applications; manage and protect memory; manage the input and output functions and hardware; manage data and files; and provide security, fault tolerance, graphical user interfaces, and windowing.

TG 2.3 Identify the major types of application software.

The major types of application software are spreadsheet, data management, word processing, desktop publishing, graphics, multimedia, communications, speech recognition, and groupware. Software suites combine several types of application software (e.g., word processing, spreadsheet, and data management) into an integrated package.

Key Terms

application software 494
computer programs 490
customer experience 493
documentation 490
graphical user interface (GUI) 493
open-source software 492

open systems 491
operating system (OS) 493
package 494
personal application software 494
proprietary software 491
social interface 493

software 489
software suite 494
speech-recognition software 494
systems software 492
user experience 493

Discussion Questions

1. You are the CIO of your company, and you have to develop an application of strategic importance to your firm. What are the advantages and disadvantages of using open-source software?

2. Describe how hardware and software are synergistic.

3. If you are a CIO, what is more important to you—the number of downloads or the number of active users? Why?

Problem-Solving Activities

1. A great deal of free software is available over the Internet. Go to www.100-downloads.com/programs/internet, and observe all the software available for free. Would you feel safe downloading a software program from this site onto your computer? Why or why not?

2. Enter the IBM website (www.ibm.com) and perform a search on the term "software." Click on the drop box for Products and notice how many software products IBM produces. Is IBM only a hardware company?

3. Visit your mobile device's app store. Select an app that has been available for at least 12 months and read the user reviews over time. Describe the comments on the experience (UX) people have interacting. Would you use this app? Why or why not?

4. Compare Microsoft Windows to Apple's Mac OS. What are the similarities between the two operating systems? What are the differences? Which operating system do you prefer and why?

Cloud Computing

We devote this Technology Guide to a vital topic: cloud computing. A working knowledge of cloud computing will enhance your appreciation of what technology can and cannot do for a business. It will also enable you to make an immediate contribution by analyzing how your organization manages its IT assets. Going further, you will be using these computing resources in your career, and you will have input into decisions about how your department and organization can best use them. Cloud computing can also be extremely valuable if you decide to start your own business.

We present many examples of how the cloud can be used for business purposes. The cloud can also provide you with personal applications. Therefore, this guide can help you plan for your own use of the cloud. For a more detailed discussion of how you can use the cloud, see the section titled IT's Personal: "The Cloud."

TG 3.1 | Introduction

LEARNING OBJECTIVE

Describe the problems that modern information technology departments face.

You were introduced to the concept of IT infrastructure in Chapter 1. Recall that an organization's *IT infrastructure* consists of IT components–hardware, software, networks, and databases–and IT services–developing information systems, managing security and risk, and managing data. (It is helpful to review Figure 1.3 of Chapter 1 here.) The organization's IT infrastructure is the foundation for all of the information systems that the organization uses.

The Evolution of Modern Information Technology Infrastructure

Modern IT infrastructure has evolved through several stages since the early 1950s, when firms first began to apply information technology to business applications. These stages are as follows:

- *Stand-alone mainframes:* Organizations initially used mainframe computers in their engineering and accounting departments. The mainframe was typically housed in a secure area, and only MIS personnel had access to it.

- *Mainframe and dumb terminals:* Forcing users to go to wherever the mainframe was located was time consuming and inefficient. As a result, firms began placing so-called dumb terminals–essentially electronic typewriters with limited processing power–in user departments. This arrangement enabled users to input computer programs into the mainframe from their departments, a process called *remote job entry*.

- *Stand-alone personal computers:* In the late 1970s, the first personal computers appeared. The IBM PC's debut in 1981 legitimized the entire personal computer market. Users began bringing personal computers to the workplace to improve their productivity–for example, by using spreadsheet and word processing applications. These computers were not initially supported by the firm's MIS department. However, as the number of personal computers increased dramatically, organizations decided to support these devices, and they established policies as to which PCs and software they would support.

- *Local area networks (client/server computing):* When personal computers are networked, individual productivity increases. For this reason, organizations began to connect personal computers to local area networks (LANs) and then connected these LANs to the mainframe, a type of processing known as *client/server computing*.

- *Enterprise computing:* In the early 1990s, organizations began to use networking standards to integrate different kinds of networks throughout the firm, thereby creating enterprise computing. As the Internet became widespread after 1995, organizations began using the TCP/IP networking protocol to integrate different types of networks. All types of hardware were networked, including mainframes, personal computers, smartphones, printers, and many others. Software applications and data now flow seamlessly throughout the enterprise and between organizations.

- *Cloud computing and mobile computing:* Today, organizations and individuals can use the power of cloud computing. As you will see in this Technology Guide, cloud computing provides access to a shared pool of computing resources, including computers, storage, applications, and services, over a network, typically the Internet.

Keep in mind that the computing resources in each stage can be cumulative. For example, most large firms still use mainframe computers (in addition to all the other types of computing resources) as large servers to manage operations that involve millions of transactions per day.

On-Premise Computing

To appreciate the impacts of cloud computing, you first need to understand traditional IT departments in organizations and the challenges they face. Traditionally, organizations have used **on-premise computing**. That is, they own their IT infrastructure (their software, hardware, networks, and data management) and maintain it in their data centers.

On-premise computing incurs expenses for IT infrastructure, the expert staffs needed to build and maintain complex IT systems, physical facilities, software licenses, hardware, and staff training and salaries. Despite all of this spending, organizations, however, typically do not use their infrastructure to its full capacity. The majority of these expenses are typically applied to maintaining the existing IT infrastructure, with the remainder being allocated to developing new systems. As a result, on-premise computing can actually inhibit an organization's ability to respond quickly and appropriately to today's rapidly changing business environments.

As you will see in the next section, cloud computing can help organizations manage the problems that traditional IT departments face with on-premise computing. In the next section we define cloud computing and describe its essential characteristics.

on-premise computing A model of IT management in which companies own their IT infrastructure (their software, hardware, networks, and data management) and maintain it in their data centers.

> ### Before you go on...
>
> 1. Describe the stages in the evolution of today's IT infrastructure.
> 2. Describe the challenges that traditional IT departments face.

TG 3.2 The Basics of Cloud Computing

LEARNING OBJECTIVE

Describe the key characteristics and advantages of cloud computing.

Information technology departments have always been tasked to deliver useful IT applications to business users. For a variety of reasons, today's IT departments are facing increased challenges in delivering useful applications. As you study cloud computing, you will learn how it can help organizations manage the problems that occur in traditional IT departments. You will also discover why so many organizations are using cloud computing.

What Is Cloud Computing?

We define **cloud computing** as a type of computing that delivers convenient, on-demand, pay-as-you-go access for multiple customers to a shared pool of configurable computing resources (e.g., servers, networks, storage, applications, and services) that can be rapidly and easily accessed over the Internet. Cloud computing allows customers to acquire resources at any time and then delete them the instant they are no longer needed.

Cloud native is the name of an approach to building applications and services specifically for a cloud computing environment. The term also refers to the characteristics of those apps and services. Cloud-native applications tend to be developed to operate in containers and are deployed as a collection of microservices. See Chapter 13 and recall that microservices are the individual functions within an application.

With cloud computing, setting up and maintaining an IT infrastructure need no longer be a challenge for an organization. Businesses do not have to scramble to meet the evolving needs of developing applications. Cloud computing also reduces upfront capital expenses and

cloud computing A technology in which tasks are performed by computers physically removed from the user and accessed over a network, in particular the Internet.

operational costs, and it enables businesses to better use their infrastructure and to share it from one project to the next. In general, cloud computing eases the difficult tasks of procuring, configuring, and maintaining hardware and software environments. It allows enterprises to get their applications up and running faster, with easier manageability and less maintenance. It also enables IT to adjust IT resources (e.g., servers, storage, and networking) more rapidly to meet fluctuating and unpredictable business demand.

Significantly, cloud computing is often a key ingredient in an organization's digital transformation. Let's take a look at Guinness World Records.

People from anywhere on the globe can apply online for a record attempt at Guinness World Records (GWR; **www.guinnessworldrecords.com**). Any attempt must be measurable and repeatable. Would-be record breakers must provide evidence, which usually includes video, photos, and witness statements.

In 2019, the volume of the data coming in from the public has increased from 500 megabytes per month to 4 terabytes. The organization receives some 50,000 applications per year.

The organization has changed from being a publishing house that produces its iconic book of feats to a creative consultancy that works with brands on marketing campaigns. The book remains the core of GWR's business and it allows the organization to engage in marketing efforts.

When working with brands, GWR helps create records-based marketing initiatives. For example, LG Electronics came to Guinness with what it believed was the most stable washing machine on the market. LG needed proof of reduced vibrations and noise levels.

GWR created an attempt for the tallest house of cards built in 12 hours. Professional card stacker Bryan Berg subsequently built a 3.3-meter-high tower of cards, consisting of 48 levels, on an LG washing machine spinning at 1,000 revolutions per minute. GWR and LG felt that the record attempt successfully demonstrated the stability of the washing machine.

GWR's move from publishing house to creative consultancy was supported by its digital transformation program. In its transformation, GWR migrated its IT infrastructure to an Amazon Web Services cloud-computing platform. AWS enabled GWR to introduce a standard records management platform, which integrates all the records from GWR's global business units. Further, AWS enabled GWR to deploy a digital asset management system that controls all the evidence relating to record attempts as well as the videos that GWR produces for its marketing clients.

Cloud Computing Characteristics

The cloud computing phenomenon has several important characteristics. We take a closer look at them in this section.

Cloud Computing Provides On-Demand Self-Service

A customer can access needed computing resources automatically. This characteristic gives customers *elasticity* and *flexibility*. That is, customers can increase (scale up) or decrease (scale down) the amount of computing they need.

For example, during the Christmas buying season retailers need much more computational capacity than at other times of the year. By using cloud computing, they can scale up before Thanksgiving (and Black Friday) and scale down after New Year's. That is, they scale up during peak periods of business activity and scale down at other times.

Consider Canadian video game and entertainment software retailer EB Games (**www.ebgames.ca**), which opened its first store in Australia in 1997. By 2020, the retailer operated over 550 brick-and-mortar stores across Australia and New Zealand. After a lengthy merger with GameStop, in 2021 all locations began operating under the GameStop brand.

In 2010, EB began online operations, which grew rapidly. Initially, the firm purchased its own hardware to manage the increasing demand for its online offerings. However, the hardware was unable to scale up to meet the demand. Accordingly, EB shifted its online operations to Amazon Web Services.

By using cloud computing, the retailer was able to move faster with new projects, reduce its IT infrastructure costs, improve its user experience, and manage peak demand as well as daily operations. EB was also able to move to a continuous delivery model for new IT services. The firm went from deploying new features about once per month to multiple deployments per week.

Cloud Computing Encompasses the Characteristics of Grid Computing

Grid computing pools various hardware and software components to create a single IT environment with shared resources. Grid computing shares the processing resources of many geographically dispersed computers across a network.

- Grid computing enables organizations to use their computing resources more efficiently.
- Grid computing provides fault tolerance and redundancy, meaning that there is no single point of failure, so the failure of one computer will not stop an application from executing.
- Grid computing makes it easy to *scale up*–that is, to access increased computing resources (i.e., add more servers)–to meet the processing demands of complex applications.
- Grid computing makes it easy to *scale down* (remove computers) if extensive processing is not needed.

Consider Oxford (United Kingdom) University's Digital Mammogram National Database project. The project aims to improve breast cancer screening and reduce the rate of erroneous diagnoses. The users of the system are radiologists, doctors, and technicians who want to query, retrieve, process, and store patients' breast images and diagnostic reports. These images tend to be large, requiring fast access, high quality, and rigid privacy.

The system uses a large distributed database that runs on a grid computing system. The grid is formed in a collaborative way, by sharing resources (CPU cycles and data) among different organizations. The database contains digital mammographies with explanatory notes and comments about each image. Because medical and university sites have different equipment, the images and reports are standardized before they are stored in the database.

The system enables individual medical sites to store, process, and manage mammograms as digital images and to enable their use through data mining and sharing of these mammography archives. Radiologists can collaborate on diagnoses without being in the same physical location.

With this system in place, the institutions involved have improved their collaboration, resulting in quicker and more accurate diagnoses. By pooling their resources, each institution gained access to a much larger and more sophisticated set of resources, without increasing their costs proportionately.

Cloud Computing Encompasses the Characteristics of Utility Computing

In **utility computing**, a service provider makes computing resources and infrastructure management available to a customer as needed. The provider then charges the customer for its specific usage rather than a flat rate. Utility computing enables companies to efficiently meet fluctuating demands for computing power by lowering the costs of owning the hardware infrastructure.

Cloud Computing Uses Broad Network Access

The cloud provider's computing resources are available over a network, accessed with a Web browser, and they are configured so that they can be used with any computing device.

Cloud Computing Pools Computing Resources

The provider's computing resources are available to serve multiple customers. These resources are dynamically assigned and reassigned according to customer demand.

Cloud Computing Often Occurs on Virtualized Servers

Cloud computing providers have placed hundreds or thousands of networked servers inside massive data centers called **server farms** (see **Figure TG 3.1**). Recall that a *server* is a computer that supports networks, thus enabling users to share files, software, and other network devices. Server farms require massive amounts of electrical power, air-conditioning, backup

grid computing A technology that applies the unused processing resources of many geographically dispersed computers in a network to form a virtual supercomputer.

utility computing A technology whereby a service provider makes computing resources and infrastructure management available to a customer as needed.

server farms Massive data centers, which may contain hundreds of thousands of networked computer servers.

FIGURE TG 3.1 **A server farm. Notice the ventilation in the racks and ceiling.**

F64/DigitalVision/Getty Images

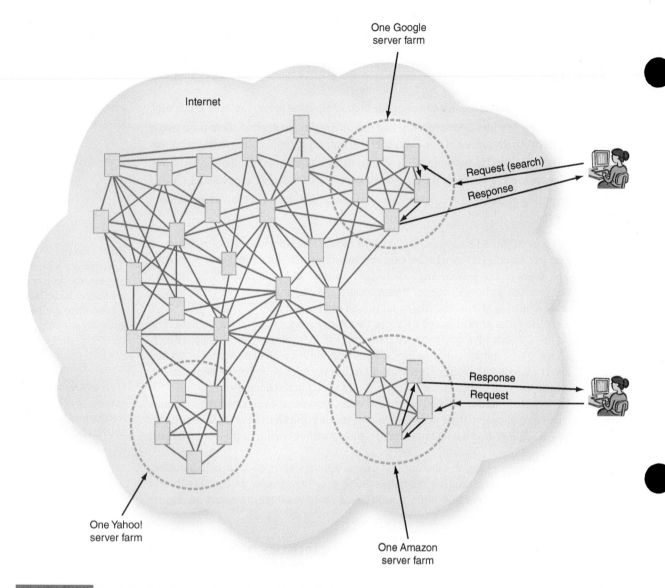

FIGURE TG 3.2 Organizational server farms in relation to the Internet.

generators, and security. They also need to be located fairly close to fiber-optic communications links (**Figure TG 3.2**).

Going further, Gartner estimates that typical usage rates on servers are very low, generally from 5 to 10 percent. That is, most of the time, organizations are using only a small percentage of their total computing capacity. Chief information officers (CIOs) tolerate this inefficiency to make certain that they can supply sufficient computing resources to users in case demand should spike. To alleviate this problem, companies and cloud computing providers are turning to virtualization.

server virtualization A technology that uses software-based partitions to create multiple virtual servers (called *virtual machines*) on a single physical server.

Server virtualization uses software-based partitions to create multiple virtual servers—called *virtual machines*—on a single physical server. The major benefit of this system is that each server no longer has to be dedicated to a particular task. Multiple applications can run instead on a single physical server, with each application running within its own software environment. As a result, virtualization enables companies to increase server usage. Companies can also realize cost savings in two areas. First, they do not have to buy additional servers to meet peak demand. Second, they reduce their utility costs because they are using less energy. The following example illustrates the benefits of virtualization for the city of Yawata in Kyoto, Japan.

The city of Yawata in Kyoto Prefecture, Japan, is very active in developing its networked city government. Deployed in 2002, the city's information system was designed to support the daily operations of the city. Since that time, the system has functioned as an IT service for city employees and members of the public.

Over a decade later, the city's continuing efforts to develop a more advanced digital community resulted in an increasing number of physical servers, with accompanying increases in power consumption. The rise in power usage was a particular problem as the city has a strong commitment to eco-friendliness.

To reduce hardware expenses, the city was running multiple applications on a single physical server, an approach that sometimes caused server availability issues. To make the system more secure and stable, the city wanted to have an individual dedicated server for each application.

The city decided to implement a server virtualization solution and realized a number of benefits. First, the city reduced its number of physical servers from 12 to 4. This reduction led to decreases in power consumption, which has helped the city reduce its environmental impact. Second, each application now runs on a single virtual machine. This means that server availability has markedly increased, each app runs more efficiently, and the entire system is more stable. Third, by virtualizing its data center, the city is able to address future server resource needs without having to add additional physical servers.

In the next section, you learn about the various ways in which customers (individuals and organizations) can implement cloud computing. Specifically, you read about public clouds, private clouds, hybrid clouds, and vertical clouds.

Before you go on...

1. Describe the characteristics of cloud computing.
2. Define server virtualization.

TG 3.3 | Different Types of Clouds

LEARNING OBJECTIVE

Describe each of the four types of clouds.

There are three major types of cloud computing that companies provide to customers or groups of customers: public clouds, private clouds, and hybrid clouds. A fourth type of cloud computing is called vertical clouds (**Figure TG 3.3**).

Public Cloud

Public clouds are shared, easily accessible, multicustomer IT infrastructures that are available nonexclusively to any entity in the general public (individuals, groups, and organizations). Public cloud vendors provide applications, storage, and other computing resources as services over the Internet. These services may be free or offered on a pay-per-usage model. Sambatech is an example of a young company using the public cloud.

International media companies such as Paramount (**www.paramount.com**), Bloomberg (**www.bloomberg.com**), and ESPN (**www.espn.com**) rely on Sambatech to deliver video content to online viewers across Latin America. As a result of its rapid growth, Samba decided to use cloud computing. The firm's chief technology officer noted that buying and managing complex IT (i.e., on-premise computing) was never part of the company's strategy.

public clouds Shared, easily accessible, multicustomer IT infrastructures that are available nonexclusively to any entity in the general public (individuals, groups, and organizations).

FIGURE TG 3.3 Public clouds, private clouds, and hybrid clouds.

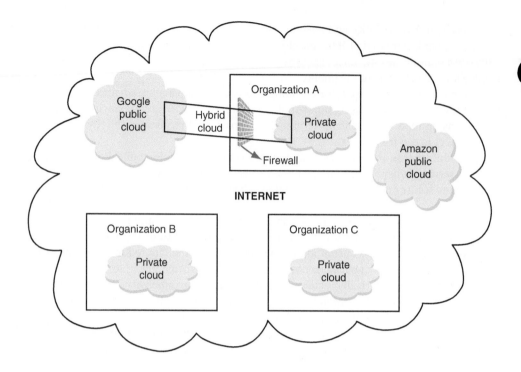

Samba turned to Rackspace (www.rackspace.com), a public cloud provider, to help it with its huge IT capacity demands. In 2009, Samba needed Rackspace to host about 1 terabyte of data. In 2015, Rackspace hosted over 100 terabytes of Samba's data. Furthermore, when Samba needs additional processing power–to deliver videos for a new marketing campaign, or to coincide with a large sporting event–Rackspace provides that power quickly and affordably.

Private Cloud

private clouds (also known as *internal clouds* **or** *corporate clouds*) IT infrastructures that are accessible only by a single entity or by an exclusive group of related entities that share the same purpose and requirements, such as all the business units within a single organization.

Private clouds (also known as *internal clouds* or *corporate clouds*) are IT infrastructures that can be accessed only by a single entity or by an exclusive group of related entities that share the same purpose and requirements, such as all of the business units within a single organization. Private clouds provide IT activities and applications as a service over an intranet within an enterprise. Enterprises adopt private clouds to ensure system and data security. For this reason, these systems are implemented behind the corporate firewall. As an example of a private cloud, let's take a look at the National Security Agency (NSA; www.nsa.gov).

The NSA was running out of storage space for hundreds of different databases that contain information needed to run the agency as well as to produce intelligence on foreign matters. As a result, NSA analysts had to access many different databases to do their jobs. Questions that spanned more than one database had to be manually integrated by the analyst. The agency had to consolidate its databases to make its analysts more efficient and effective.

At first, the NSA decided to simply add more storage capacity. However, this approach actually added to the problem, so the agency decided to implement a private cloud. By putting all its different databases into one private cloud, analysts had to interface with only one system, making their jobs much easier.

The private cloud contains data that the agency acquires and uses for its missions. The cloud has strict security protocols and strong encryption, as well as a distributed architecture across multiple geographic areas. The cloud also provides a way to track every instance of every individual accessing data as specific as a single word or name in a file. This tracking includes when the data arrived, who can access them, who did access them, who downloaded them, copied them, printed them, forwarded them, modified them, or deleted them. Furthermore, if the data have legal requirements, such as they must be purged after five years, a notice will automatically tell NSA staff that the data need to be purged. One agency staff member noted that if the NSA had had this ability at the time, it is unlikely that U.S. soldier Bradley Manning would have succeeded in obtaining classified documents in 2010.

After implementation of the private cloud, analysts can perform tasks in minutes that once took days, overall data management costs have decreased, and the security of the data has been greatly enhanced.

Hybrid Cloud

Hybrid clouds are composed of public and private clouds that remain unique entities but are nevertheless tightly integrated. This arrangement offers users the benefits of multiple deployment models. Hybrid clouds deliver services based on security requirements, the mission-critical nature of the applications, and other company-established policies. For example, customers may need to maintain some of their data in a private cloud for security, privacy, and regulatory reasons while storing other, less-sensitive data in a public cloud because it is less expensive. Let's examine Amazon's deployment of hybrid cloud computing.

For decades, Amazon maintained that renting computing power and storage space through its Amazon Web Services (AWS) cloud was more cost effective and advantageous than buying the servers themselves. In December 2019, Amazon began selling hybrid cloud computing systems, including servers. Amazon's service, called Outposts, competes with IBM, Hewlett Packard Enterprise, Dell Technologies, and Microsoft.

With Outposts, Amazon customers purchase its servers, plus software that integrates those servers with Amazon's machines in its cloud. Outposts is a *hybrid cloud*, which is the ability to use cloud services for some applications, on-site servers for mission-critical applications, and a common interface to integrate all these applications.

Amazon entered this market because approximately 80 percent of organizations operate their software applications in corporate data centers (called on-premise computing) for security, regulatory, or practical reasons. For instance, Disney (**www.disney.com**) hosts video streaming and animation software on AWS. For Disney animators working in the Los Angeles area, a delay of more than 10 milliseconds between touching a stylus to the screen and seeing the mark itself made the rendering software useless. *Rendering* is an extremely computer-intensive process of generating a digital image from a physical picture of model. Amazon's main West Coast data center, more than 1,000 miles to the north in Oregon, could not resolve the problem due to speed-of-light considerations. As a result, Disney's use of AWS hybrid cloud computing provided the solution.

There are many other examples of organizations using Outposts. For example, Verizon Communications is testing Outposts to manage a new service designed to enable faster 5G browsing speeds, starting with customers in Chicago. Fox Corporation is using Outposts to help power its production facilities and modernize its video systems.

All firms in the hybrid cloud computing space offer specially assigned teams that deliver their products directly to customers' data centers. There, the customers' IT personnel can just plug the servers in, link them to a cloud vendor account, download software updates, and begin operations. If a server fails, the cloud vendor will mail the customer a new server and a return box for the defective one.

Multiple Clouds (Multiclouds)

Multicloud environments are the most common approach to cloud computing. Global security firm McAfee's (**www.mcafee.com**) 2019 Cloud Adoption and Risk Report had a surprising finding. The firm asked 1,400 IT professionals in 11 countries to estimate the total number of cloud services in use in their organization. Respondents came up with an average of 31 cloud services. When McAfee investigated further, the actual average figure was almost 2,000 services.

Let's distinguish between hybrid clouds and multiclouds. *Hybrid cloud* has traditionally meant the combination of private (either on-premise or hosted in a colocation facility) and

hybrid clouds Clouds composed of public and private clouds that remain unique entities but are bound together, offering the benefits of multiple deployment models.

public cloud infrastructure, with orchestration tools used to deploy workloads and manage the balance between the two. *Colocation* means that a cloud vendor either rents out an entire facility to a customer or when the vendor rents out servers within a data center to a customer. For instance, a customer employs public cloud resources for regular or episodic increases of computing and/or storage requirements.

In contrast, multicloud describes how organizations use multiple cloud providers to meet different technical or business requirements. With multicloud environments, customers use cloud-native applications built from containers and microservices using component services from different cloud providers.

There are several reasons for using multiclouds. One of the most common reasons is the desire to avoid being locked into a particular cloud vendor's infrastructure, add-on services, and pricing model. Cloud-native applications based on containers and microservices are designed to be portable between clouds, but providers will generally try to make their platforms difficult to leave with specific functions and services that differentiate them from their competitors. Another reason for avoiding vendor lock-in is so that organizations can take advantage of best-of-breed solutions.

Organizations can also minimize latency by choosing a cloud provider with data centers that are geographically close to their customers. The reason is that network performance degrades as the number of network transmissions between servers increases.

Data governance requirements, such as the European Union's General Data Protection Regulation, will often require customer data to be held in particular locations. Unless organizations are willing to deploy and operate their own on-premise data centers, these firms will have to take a multicloud approach.

All cloud vendors suffer outages. Therefore, organizations are reluctant to run their entire workloads in one vendor's cloud because they run the risk of a mission-critical application becoming unavailable. Multiclouds provide better security, failover, and disaster recovery; that is, resilience. *Failover* occurs when standby servers automatically take over when a server fails.

Vertical Clouds

vertical cloud A set of cloud computing services optimized for use in a particular industry.

A **vertical cloud** is a set of cloud computing services optimized for use in a particular industry. Unlike organizations that can use general-purpose cloud computing services, those within certain industries often have more specific information technology requirements involving security, compliance, and other issues. Vertical cloud computing vendors offer services that help their customers meet those unique requirements.

Many industries use vertical cloud computing services, such as healthcare, financial services, manufacturing, government, utilities, oil and gas, and others. For example, healthcare organizations must ensure data privacy in accordance with the Health Insurance Portability and Accountability Act (HIPAA). Therefore, these organizations might prefer a cloud provider that offers HIPAA-compliant services, as well as services for electronic medical records and other applications unique to the healthcare industry. See CareCloud Corporation (**www.care cloud.com**) for example. There are a number of specialized vertical cloud vendors. In addition, some of the major public cloud vendors also offer industry-specific services. For example, Amazon Web Services provides AWS GovCloud (**www.aws.amazon.com/govcloud-us/**), a service tailored specifically for U.S. government agencies that have sensitive operations and strict regulatory requirements.

Before you go on...

1. What is a public cloud?
2. What is a private cloud?
3. What is a hybrid cloud?
4. What is a vertical cloud?

TG 3.4   Cloud Computing Services

WILEY PLUS

Author Lecture Videos are available exclusively in *WileyPLUS*.

Apply the Concept activities are available in the Appendix and in *WileyPLUS*.

LEARNING OBJECTIVE

Explain the operational model of each of the three types of cloud services.

Cloud computing services are based on three models: infrastructure-as-a-service (IaaS), platform-as-a-service (PaaS), and software-as-a-service (SaaS). These models represent the three types of computing generally required by consumers: infrastructure to run software and store data (IaaS), platforms to develop applications (PaaS), and software applications to process their data (SaaS). **Figure TG 3.4** illustrates the differences among the three models.

As you examine the figure from left to right, note that the customer manages the service less and less, and the vendor manages it more and more.

Although each model has its distinctive features, all three share certain characteristics. First, customers rent them instead of buying them. This arrangement shifts IT from a capital expense to an operating expense. Second, vendors are responsible for maintenance, administration, capacity planning, troubleshooting, and backups. Finally, obtaining additional computing resources–that is, scale from the cloud–is usually fast and easy. Examples are more storage from an IaaS vendor, the ability to handle more PaaS projects, and more users of a SaaS application.

Infrastructure as a Service

With the **infrastructure-as-a-service (IaaS)** model, cloud computing providers offer remotely accessible servers, networks, and storage capacity. They supply these resources on demand from their large resource pools, which are located in their data centers. We can think of IaaS as a domain for systems administrators, as IaaS allows clients to migrate their physical or hardware infrastructure to the cloud. Examples include Amazon Elastic Compute Cloud, Google Compute Engine, Rackspace, and many others.

IaaS customers are often technology companies with IT expertise. These companies want access to computing power, but they do not want to be responsible for installing or maintaining it. Companies use the infrastructure to run software or simply to store data.

infrastructure-as-a-service (IaaS)   A model with which cloud computing providers offer remotely accessible servers, networks, and storage capacity.

ON-PREMISE SOFTWARE	INFRASTRUCTURE-AS-A-SERVICE	PLATFORM-AS-A-SERVICE	SOFTWARE-AS-A-SERVICE
CUSTOMER MANAGES Applications / Data / Operating system / Servers / Virtualization / Storage / Networking	**CUSTOMER MANAGES** Applications / Data / Operating system **VENDOR MANAGES** Servers / Virtualization / Storage / Networking	**CUSTOMER MANAGES** Applications / Data **VENDOR MANAGES** Operating system / Servers / Virtualization / Storage / Networking	**VENDOR MANAGES** Applications / Data / Operating system / Servers / Virtualization / Storage / Networking
Examples	Amazon, IBM, Google, Microsoft, Rackspace	Microsoft Windows Azure, Google App Engine	Salesforce.com, Google Apps, Dropbox, Apple iCloud, Box.net

FIGURE TG 3.4 Comparison of on-premise software, infrastructure-as-a-service, platform-as-a-service, and software-as-a-service.

To deploy their applications, IaaS users install their operating system and their application software on the cloud computing provider's computers. They can deploy any software on this infrastructure, including different operating systems, applications, and development platforms. Each user is responsible for maintaining their operating system and application software. Cloud providers typically bill IaaS services on a utility computing basis–that is, the cost reflects the amount of resources the user consumes.

Cloud data management is an important application of IaaS. *Cloud data management* is the practice of storing a company's data on an offsite server that is typically owned by a vendor who specializes in cloud data hosting. Cloud data management offers many benefits to clients, which include:

- *Improved security.* Improved security results first from reduced risk of data loss due to device damage or hardware failure. Second, cloud vendors typically employ very advanced security measures and practices.

- *Scalability and savings.* Cloud vendors allow users to add and subtract storage and computing power as needed, which results in cost savings.

- *Governed access.* Cloud vendors enable all authorized users to access the data they need from wherever they are, a process called *data democratization*. Such access supports a collaborative work culture.

- *Automated backups, disaster recovery, and updates.* Cloud vendors provide automated data backups that speed up the process of disaster recovery after emergencies. For example, if a ransomware attack encrypted a firm's data, the cloud vendor would enable the client to restore data and continue business operations. In addition, cloud vendors update applications automatically, ensuring that the client does not have to pause work while the in-house IT group updates applications.

- *Improved data quality.* Cloud data management solutions help companies remove data silos and create a single source of truth for every data point. Data remains clean, consistent, and current. *Single source of truth* is a concept ensuring that everyone in an organization bases business decisions on the same data.

- *Sustainability.* Cloud data management enables organizations to reduce the carbon footprint created by their own IT facilities and to provide telecommuting options to their employees.

Let's look at an example. Southern Water (www.southernwater.co.uk) is a utility that used cloud data management to remove data silos. The utility manages the supply of water and waste management to 4.5 million people in southeastern England. The utility's assets include 83 water treatment plants, 8,700 miles of water mains, 2,375 pumping stations, and approximately 2,500 miles of sewers. The utility employs 3,000 people and 1,500 contractors.

The utility's data are varied and complex, with some of the data concerning assets that are 200 years old (i.e., some of the water mains in the area date back to the early 19th century). The company has 80,000 sensors that gather data every 15 minutes. Its call center staff deal with thousands of customer calls, generating audio data that is analyzed to provide better customer service.

In the past, Southern Water had groups of people in individual departments managing data. The data from many of the utility's essential business processes were isolated in departmental spreadsheets and Microsoft Access databases. If the utility had ignored this problem, it would have caused additional costs and difficulties in the future, a situation called technical debt. *Technical debt* refers to the implied cost of additional rework caused by choosing an easy solution now instead of using a better approach that would take longer.

Southern Water transformed its approach to data management to improve decision making. This process involved transitioning to a Microsoft Azure cloud-based data management solution and placing all its data workers into a centralized team. With the transition, the utility gained access to a cloud-based analytics solution that delivered significant savings. In just one instance, Southern Water was able to integrate pump data to assess pump efficiency when many pumps are named differently. Also, the team gained a better understanding of the entire organization's data, which helped to improve data literacy throughout the organization.

Platform as-a-Service

In the **platform-as-a-service (PaaS)** model, customers rent servers, operating systems, storage, a database, software development technologies such as Java and .NET, and network capacity over the Internet. We can think of PaaS as a domain for software developers. PaaS helps software developers build, test, deploy, maintain, and manage every step of the development lifecycle of applications. Examples include Amazon Web Services Elastic Beanstalk, Microsoft Azure, Cloud Foundry, and many others.

The PaaS model allows the customer to both run existing applications and to develop and test new applications. PaaS offers customers several advantages, including the following.

- Application developers can develop and run their software solutions on a cloud platform without the cost and complexity of buying and managing the underlying hardware and software layers.

- Underlying computing and storage resources automatically scale to match application demand.

- Operating system features can be upgraded frequently.

- Geographically distributed development teams can work together on software development projects.

- PaaS services can be provided by diverse sources located throughout the world.

- Initial and ongoing costs can be reduced by the use of infrastructure services from a single vendor rather than maintaining multiple hardware facilities that often perform duplicate functions or suffer from incompatibility problems.

Novartis International AG (**www.novartis.com**), a pharmaceutical company based in Basel, Switzerland, has used PaaS to improve its performance. The company employs approximately 100,000 people in 140 countries and has core businesses in pharmaceuticals, vaccines and diagnostics, and consumer health.

Novartis needed an alternative to its systems development process. The process was inflexible, expensive, and delivered new functionality much too slowly. These problems meant that the company was limited in the number of new development projects it could undertake. Novartis needed to reduce its systems development effort and cost while delivering systems with the required functionality more quickly.

As a result, Novartis turned to Dell Boomi AtomSphere (**www.boomi.com**). Using this PaaS product, Novartis was able to reduce development efforts and deliver twice the amount of new functionality in one-sixth the time than was possible earlier.

platform-as-a-service (PaaS) A model in which customers rent servers, operating systems, storage, a database, software development technologies such as Java and .NET, and network capacity over the Internet.

Software-as-a-Service

With the software-as-a-service (SaaS) delivery model, cloud computing vendors provide software that is specific to their customers' requirements. We can think of SaaS as a domain for end users or business clients. That is, users and clients can run SaaS programs on their own data. Examples include Google Apps, Salesforce, Dropbox, and numerous others.

SaaS is the most widely used service model, and it provides a broad range of software applications. SaaS providers typically charge their customers a monthly or yearly subscription fee.

SaaS applications reside in the cloud instead of on a user's hard drive or in a data center. The host manages the software and the infrastructure that runs this software and stores the customer's data. The customers do not control either the software, beyond the usual configuration settings, or the infrastructure, beyond changing the resources they use, such as the amount of disk space required for their data. This process eliminates the need to install and run the application on the user's computers, thereby simplifying maintenance and support.

What differentiates SaaS applications from other applications is their ability to scale. As a result, applications can run on as many servers as is necessary to meet changing demands. This process is transparent to the user.

To reduce the risk of an infrastructure outage, SaaS providers regularly back up all of their customers' data. Customers can also back up their data on their own storage hardware.

To understand how SaaS operates, consider Mary Kay (www.marykay.com). The cosmetics giant implemented Oracle's Taleo cloud-based recruitment software in the United States, China, and Brazil. Before 2014, Mary Kay did not have an applicant tracking system. The company's recruiting process was performed with Microsoft Excel spreadsheets and Access databases. Recruiters at Mary Kay lacked visibility on the manual system. If someone applied for a job in two different departments, a recruiter from each department would often call the applicant without realizing that the other recruiter had also contacted the applicant.

Taleo provides Mary Kay with a centralized repository for tracking internal and external job candidates. The software also automated processes such as job applications, onboarding, and forms. Taleo also integrates with LinkedIn, providing instant access to LinkedIn profiles and candidate records with a single click. Furthermore, Taleo can fill in forms with LinkedIn credentials.

A subset of SaaS is the *desktop-as-a-service* (DaaS) model, also known as a *cloud desktop* or *desktop in the cloud*. In this model, a SaaS provider hosts a software environment for a desktop personal computer, including productivity and collaboration software–spreadsheets, word processing programs, and so on–such as Google Apps, Microsoft 365, and other products. The DaaS model can be financially advantageous for consumers because they do not need to purchase a fully configured personal computer, or fat client. This model also makes the PC environment simpler to deploy and administer.

Functions-as-a-Service

functions-as-a-Service (XaaS) A category of cloud computing services that provides a platform allowing customers to develop, run, and manage applications functions without the complexity of building and maintaining the infrastructure typically associated with developing and deploying an app.

Functions-as-a-service (FaaS or XaaS) is a category of cloud computing services that provides a platform allowing customers to develop, run, and manage applications' functions without the complexity of building and maintaining the infrastructure typically associated with developing and deploying an app. These functions are triggered by a given event.

Functions-as-a-service are a good choice for real-time (event-driven) actions. Suppose an organization needs daily sales data to help manage inventory. Every time a customer buys an item, that transaction is added to a database table. An FaaS function would trigger a function within that database table, process the data from the transaction, and either display it to a manager or even trigger another function to order more of that product.

There can be confusion between FaaS and serverless computing. *Serverless computing* is a cloud computing execution model in which the cloud vendor runs the server and dynamically manages the allocation of machine resources. That is, customers do not need to be concerned with a server configuration when deploying an application. With this model, customers shift more of the responsibilities for running an application.

For example, suppose an organization needed to deploy an e-commerce application. It would be easier to build and deploy just one application that did all the work of presenting products, managing the shopping cart, and configuring the payment system. If the firm deployed such a complex system with so many embedded functions, it would be much more manageable to keep all the business logic within one single cloud platform.

In this case, serverless computing would be the best way to go. Even if the company's e-commerce store grows, the serverless computing service will scale the application to meet the demand. Further, the application will always be running and ready to process new orders. Another example would be if an organization needed to run a mission-critical database.

Security-as-a-Service

Security-as-a-service (SECaaS) A delivery model in which cloud computing vendors provide software that is specific to their customers' requirements.

Security-as-a-service (SECaaS) is a category of cloud services where an external provider handles and manages cybersecurity for an organization. Outsourced security solutions cover services like data loss prevention, antivirus management, and intrusion detection, among others. SECaaS provides the latest security advancements and a dedicated, 24/7 security team to focus on managing your resources. It is also much easier and faster to scale security operations

---

IT's Personal: "The Cloud"

This Technology Guide defines the cloud as distributed computing services, and it presents many examples of how the cloud can be used for both personal and business purposes. This IT's Personal is intended to help you differentiate between the business and personal applications of the cloud and to help you plan for your own use of the cloud.

First, you need to understand that there is no single "cloud." Rather, almost all businesses refer to their Internet-based services as "cloud services." Basically, anything you do over the Internet that you used to do on a local computer is a form of cloud computing. When you store files on Dropbox, create a document using Google Docs, or use iCloud to store purchases or sync documents, you are using cloud-based services that are intended for personal use.

Infrastructure-as-a-service is an important application of the cloud for personal purposes. Dropbox is one of the most prominent companies in this area. In the past, users had to carry around a USB drive, a CD, an external hard drive, or (back in the day) floppy disks to store their personal information. Today, users can employ Dropbox for this purpose. At the time of this writing, a free Dropbox account offered 2 GB of online storage. Not only does Dropbox offer you a place to store your files (eliminating the need for a personal infrastructure of removable storage), but it also provides synchronization across computers and access from mobile devices.

Software-as-a-service has been a popular option for quite some time. For example, Google Docs offers Internet-based word processing, spreadsheet, presentation, forms, and drawing tools. Microsoft's Office 365 product also offers these services and allows you to use a computer program without having to install it on your computer or mobile device. You simply access the entire program (and your saved files) over the Internet.

Google has combined a couple of these cloud services with Google Drive, a service that offers the same services as Dropbox in addition to Google Docs' online editing and file-sharing capabilities. Google Drive encompasses SaaS because of the added benefit of Google Docs. It is very likely that one day Google will merge virtualization, infrastructure, and software into a single cloud-based service. If this technology becomes available, then all you will need as a consumer is an Internet-connected device, and you will be able to store, access, edit, and share your files from the cloud. You will also be able to choose apps to run on your "virtual machine" much the way you currently purchase applications for your mobile devices from a vendor-approved store.

So, what is the point? Simply, cloud-based services are here to stay. The rise of ubiquitous Internet access has engendered a new world of possibilities.

A word of caution, however. Along with its seemingly endless possibilities, cloud computing raises many critical security and privacy issues. Because your files, apps, and editing capability will no longer be stored on a local machine, they are only as safe as the company to which you have entrusted them makes them. So, when you select a cloud provider, make sure you choose wisely!

---

when the third party focuses solely on this aspect of your technology. SECaaS also provides guidance, support, and protection during data migrations, when organizations are especially vulnerable to attack.

Low-code and no-code cloud services

Low-code and no-code tools (see Technology Guide 2) allow anybody, regardless of their programming knowledge, to create applications and to use data to solve problems. Many of these tools are now available in the cloud, and they require little more than a subscription to the service for employees to begin design and building applications. This category of low-code and no-code solutions includes tools for building websites, Web applications, and designing just about any kind of digital solutions that companies may need. Low-code and no-code solutions are even becoming available for creating AI-powered applications, drastically lowering the barriers to entry for companies that want to leverage AI and ML. Tools like Figma (www.figma.com), Airtable (www.airtable.com), and Zoho (www.zoho.com) allow users to carry out tasks that previously would have required coding experience. Cloud-based programming tools further remove barriers to end-user development.

Before you go on...

1. Describe infrastructure-as-a-service.
2. Describe platform-as-a-service.
3. Describe software-as-a-service.
4. Describe function-as-a-service.

| TG 3.5 | # The Benefits of Cloud Computing |

LEARNING OBJECTIVE

Identify the key benefits of cloud computing.

Cloud computing offers benefits for both individuals and organizations. It allows companies to increase the scale and power of their IT and the speed at which it can be deployed and accessed. It eliminates administrative problems and it operates across locations, devices, and organizational boundaries.

Nearly half of the respondents in a recent CIO economic impact survey indicated that they evaluate cloud computing options first–before traditional IT approaches–before making any new IT investments. IBM predicts that the global cloud computing market will grow 22 percent annually to $241 billion by 2020. Next we examine three major benefits that cloud computing provides to individuals and organizations.

Benefit 1: Cloud Computing Has a Positive Impact on Employees

Cloud computing enables companies to provide their employees with access to all the information they need no matter where they are, what device they are using, or with whom they are working. Consider this example.

The attorneys of one multistate law firm needed to access documents and data on a constant basis. Since 2000, the firm's data volume had expanded from 30 gigabytes to more than 40 terabytes. Moreover, all of these data have to be stored and accessed securely. In the past, attorneys often had to manually copy case-relevant data onto external hard drives and USB devices, and then ship these devices back and forth among themselves and the firm's headquarters. These processes were nonsecure, time-consuming, and expensive.

To address these needs, the law firm turned to cloud computing for data storage, offsite disaster recovery, and multisite access within a highly secure public cloud. Rather than maintaining a massive inventory of extra storage as required by its old IT infrastructure, the firm can now increase storage capacity on demand. The cloud provides attorneys with constant access through encrypted communication channels. Furthermore, the cloud facilitates collaboration among distributed teams of attorneys, thereby increasing their overall productivity. The cloud environment has made the firm's attorneys much more efficient and the firm's IT expenses have declined by 60 percent.

Benefit 2: Cloud Computing Can Save Money

Over time, the cost of building and operating an on-premise IT infrastructure will typically be more expensive than adopting the cloud computing model. Cloud providers purchase massive amounts of IT infrastructure (e.g., hardware and bandwidth) and gain cost savings by buying in large quantity. As a result, these providers continually take advantage of Moore's law (discussed in Technology Guide 1). For example, the Amazon cloud, known as Amazon Web Services, has reduced its prices many times over the last 10 years.

As a result, cloud computing can reduce or eliminate the need to purchase hardware, build and install software, and pay software licensing fees. The organization pays only for the computing resources it needs, and then only when it needs them. This pay-for-use model provides greater flexibility and it eliminates or reduces the need for significant capital expenditures.

Let's consider the United States General Services Administration (GSA; www.gsa.gov). In 2010, the agency began a multiyear strategy to migrate core agency information systems to the cloud. In the first phase of the strategy, the GSA migrated 17,000 employees to Google

Apps, making it the first federal agency to move basic e-mail and collaboration services entirely into a cloud environment. The GSA notes that the migration saves the agency approximately $3 million per year.

In the second phase of the strategy, the GSA worked with **Salesforce.com** (**www.salesforce.com**) to implement cloud-based software that made it easier for GSA employees to collaborate on projects, share and manage case files, find internal subject-matter experts, and capture new ideas. In one instance, employees used the software to generate 640 ideas in 30 days to streamline GSA business processes, an initiative that eventually saved the agency $5 million per year.

The GSA also established a rapid application development platform (discussed in Chapter 13) in the cloud. Within six months, GSA's IT department developed and delivered more than 100 enterprise applications that replaced more than 1,700 legacy applications. The new applications lowered the total cost of ownership by 92 percent.

And the bottom line? The GSA spent $593 million on IT in fiscal year 2014, nearly $100 million less than it spent the previous year.

Benefit 3: Cloud Computing Can Improve Organizational Flexibility and Competitiveness

Cloud computing allows organizations to use only the amount of computing resources they need at a given time. Therefore, companies can efficiently scale their operations up or down as needed to meet rapidly changing business conditions. Cloud computing is also able to deliver computing services faster than the on-premise computing can. Let's take a closer look at cloud gaming.

With 2.4 billion online gamers worldwide, the online-gaming industry is network- and data-intensive. Network traffic from online gaming is forecast to grow 900 percent by 2022, and gaming-related data reached 568 petabytes in 2020. To put that number in context, 1 petabyte is equal to 3.4 years of 24/7 high-definition video recording.

The gaming industry must manage enormous amounts of computational capacity and storage. Further, the industry must manage new technologies such as augmented reality, virtual reality, and multiplayer gaming that require even more computation and storage. As a result, online gaming has moved to the cloud and is now referred to as cloud gaming, or gaming-as-a-service (GaaS). Many vendors offer cloud gaming, including Microsoft xCloud (**www.xbox.com/en-US/xbox-game-pass/cloud-gaming**), Apple Arcade (**www.apple.com/apple-arcade**), and Amazon's Prime Gaming (**www.gaming.amazon.com**).

Gaming providers process gaming data in two ways: cloud processing and edge computing. With cloud processing, vendors send gaming data for processing in the cloud and the results are sent back to the gamer's device for play. This process does eliminate the need for intensive computing that would normally occur on the gamer's desktop, laptop, smartphone, or tablet, but data transmission can cause delays while playing the game.

As a result, some providers employ edge computing. With *edge computing*, providers group individual gamers according to location and process data in servers close to the gamers' locations, thus routing traffic over shorter distances. The benefit is reduced network latency (delay), which improves the user experience.

Most gaming accounts contain personally identifiable information such as the player's name, birthday, address, mobile number, e-mail address, and a linked credit card. As a result, cloud computing enables providers to enforce two-factor authentication, requiring users to verify their identity before logging on via a time-sensitive code sent to a mobile number or e-mail. For even greater security, some providers use an authentication app that generates a QR code that can be scanned within the game. Gamers' user names are stored in the app and a new code is generated for each login.

And the bottom line? Cloud gaming is growing rapidly, valued at $1.1 billion in 2019 and expected to grow to $7 billion by 2025. The use of cloud computing has transformed the user experience largely because cloud-gaming vendors can embrace new technologies such as augmented reality and virtual reality.

1. Describe how cloud computing can help organizations expand the scope of their business operations.
2. Describe how cloud computing can help organizations respond quickly to market changes.

TG 3.6   Concerns and Risks with Cloud Computing

LEARNING OBJECTIVE

Discuss the concerns and risks associated with cloud computing.

Gartner predicted that cloud computing would grow at an annual rate of 19 percent through the year 2016. Even if this prediction was accurate, however, cloud computing would still account for less than 5 percent of total worldwide IT spending that year. Why is this percentage so low? The reason is that there are serious concerns with cloud computing. These concerns fall into six categories: legacy IT systems, reliability, privacy, security, the legal and regulatory environment, and criminal use of cloud computing.

Concern 1: Legacy IT Systems

Historically, organizational IT systems have accumulated a diversity of hardware, operating systems, and applications. When bundled together, these systems are called "legacy spaghetti." These systems cannot easily be transferred to the cloud because they must first be untangled and simplified. Furthermore, many IT professionals have vested interests in various legacy systems, and they resist efforts to exchange these systems for cloud computing.

Concern 2: Reliability

Many skeptics contend that cloud computing is not as reliable as a well-managed, on-premise IT infrastructure. Although cloud providers are improving the redundancy and reliability of their offerings, outages still occur. Consider the examples of Google and CenturyLink.

In June 2019, a Google Cloud outage caused portions of the Internet to go offline. The outage also blocked access to the tools that Google needed to fix the problem, which occurred when Google began what should have been a routine configuration change. These changes are maintenance events intended for a few servers in one geographic region. When such an event happens, Google routinely reroutes jobs that those servers are running to other machines or just pauses those jobs until the maintenance is finished. Unfortunately, Google's software cancelled network control jobs in multiple locations, leading to the outage.

Google engineers were aware of the problem within two minutes. However, they were not able to diagnose the problem for hours because the outage prevented them from accessing the necessary tools.

In August 2020, U.S. Internet service provider CenturyLink (www.centurylink.com) suffered a major technical outage after a misconfiguration in one of its data centers. The outage was serious enough to cause an overall 3.5 percent drop in global Internet traffic. CenturyLink engineers took seven hours to fix the problem.

Concern 3: Privacy

Privacy advocates have criticized cloud computing for posing a major threat to privacy because the providers control, and thus lawfully or unlawfully monitor, the data and communication stored between the user and the host company. For example, AT&T and Verizon collaborated with the NSA to use cloud computing to record more than 10 million phone calls between American citizens. Providers could also accidentally or deliberately alter or even delete some of that information.

Using a cloud computing provider also complicates data privacy because of the extent to which cloud processing and cloud storage are used to implement cloud services. The point is that customer data may not remain on the same system or in the same data center. This situation can lead to legal concerns over jurisdiction.

There have been efforts to address this problem by integrating the legal environment. One example is the U.S.–EU Safe Harbor, a streamlined process for U.S. companies to comply with the European Union directive on the protection of personal data.

Concern 4: Security

Critics also question how secure cloud computing really is. Because the characteristics of cloud computing can differ widely from those of traditional IT architectures, providers need to reconsider the effectiveness and efficiency of traditional security mechanisms. Security issues include access to sensitive data, data segregation (among customers), privacy, error exploitation, recovery, accountability, malicious insiders, and account control.

The security of cloud computing services is a contentious issue that may be delaying the adoption of this technology. Security issues arise primarily from the unease of both the private and public sectors with the external management of security-based services. The fact that providers manage these services provides great incentive for them to prioritize building and maintaining strong security services.

Another security issue involves the control over who is able to access and use the information stored in the cloud. (Recall our discussion of least privilege in Chapter 4.) Many organizations exercise least-privilege controls effectively with their on-premise IT infrastructures. Some cloud computing environments, in contrast, cannot exercise least-privilege controls effectively. This problem occurs because cloud computing environments were originally designed for individuals or groups, not for hierarchical organizations in which some people have both the right and the responsibility to exercise control over other people's private information. To address this problem, cloud computing vendors are working to incorporate administrative, least-privilege functionality into their products. In fact, many have already done so.

Consider Panama City, Florida, as an example. Panama City was one of the first cities in the United States to adopt Google Apps for Government. The city was searching for a way to gain visibility into who was using Google Apps and how users were collaborating both inside and outside the city's IT domain. Furthermore, the city had to have the ability to control and enforce data-sharing policies where necessary. The city decided to adopt Cisco CloudLock (**www.cisco.com/c/en/us/products/security/cloudlock/index.html**).

CloudLock provides a security system to protect its clients' information assets located in public cloud applications like Google Apps. CloudLock provides key data management issues such as the following:

- Data inventory: How many information assets exist and what are their types?
- Which information assets are shared with the public or over the Internet?
- Who has access to what information asset and what information asset is accessible to whom?

Using CloudLock, Panama City was able to notify data owners of policy violations or exposed documents containing potentially sensitive information, change or revoke excessive privilege, and audit permissions changes. Furthermore, the city's IT manager was able to designate department leaders to manage their respective organizational unit's data policies and usage by giving them access to the CloudLock application.

Concern 5: The Regulatory and Legal Environment

There are numerous legal and regulatory barriers to cloud computing, many of which involve data access and transport. For example, the European Union prohibits consumer data from being transferred to nonmember countries without the consumers' prior consent and approval. Companies located outside the European Union can overcome this restriction by demonstrating that they provide a "safe harbor" for the data. Some countries, such as Germany, have enacted even more restrictive data export laws. Cloud computing vendors are aware of these regulations and laws, and they are working to modify their offerings so that they can assure customers and regulators that data entrusted to them are secure enough to meet all of these requirements.

To obtain compliance with regulations such as the Federal Information Security Management Act (FISMA), the Health Insurance Portability and Accountability Act (HIPAA), and the Sarbanes–Oxley Act in the United States; the Data Protection Directive in the European Union; and the credit card industry's Payment Card Industry's Data Security Standard (PCI DSS), cloud computing customers may have to adopt hybrid deployment modes that are typically more expensive and may offer restricted benefits. This process is how, for example, Google is able to "manage and meet additional government policy requirements beyond FISMA," and Rackspace (**www.rackspace.com**) is able to claim PCI compliance. FISMA requires each federal agency to develop, document, and implement a program to provide information security for the information and information systems that support the operations of the agency, including those provided by contractors. PCI DSS is a set of requirements designed to ensure that all companies that process, store, or transmit credit card information maintain a secure environment.

Concern 6: Criminal Use of Cloud Computing

Cloud computing makes available a well-managed, generally reliable, scalable global infrastructure that is, unfortunately, as well suited to illegal computing activities as it is to legitimate business activities. We look here at a number of possible illegal activities.

The huge amount of information stored in the cloud makes it an attractive target for data thieves. Also, the distributed nature of cloud computing makes it very difficult to catch criminals.

Cloud computing makes immense processing power available to anyone. Criminals using cloud computing have access to encryption technology and anonymous communication channels that make it difficult for authorities to detect their activities. When law enforcement pursues criminals, the wrongdoers can rapidly shut down computing resources in the cloud, thus greatly decreasing the chances that there will be any clues left for forensic analysis. When criminals no longer need a machine and shut it down, other clients of cloud vendors immediately reuse the storage and computational capacity allocated to that machine. Therefore, the criminal information is overwritten by data from legitimate customers. It is nearly impossible to recover any data after the machine has been *de-provisioned*.

Criminals are registering for an account (with assumed names and stolen credit cards, of course) with a cloud vendor and "legitimately" using services for illegal purposes. For example, criminals use Gmail or the text-sharing website Pastebin (**www.pastebin.com**) to plan crimes and share stolen information. Another example is that criminals use cloud computing in brute-force password cracking (see Chapter 4). Although such uses are prohibited by most company's terms-of-service agreements, policing the cloud is expensive and not very rewarding for cloud providers.

Many cloud vendors offer geographical diversity–that is, virtual machines that are located in different physical locations around the world. Criminals can use this feature in transnational attacks. Such attacks place political and technical obstacles in the way of authorities seeking to trace a cyberattack back to its source.

Another weakness exploited by criminals arises from the Web-based applications, or SaaS offerings, provided by cloud vendors. With millions of users commingling on tens of thousands of servers, a criminal can easily mix in among legitimate users.

Even more complicated for authorities and victims, cyberattacks can originate within cloud programs that we use and trust. For example, researchers at the security firm F-Secure reported that they had detected several phishing sites hosted within Google Docs. What made the attacks possible is a feature within Google's spreadsheet system that lets users create Web-based forms, with titles such as "Webmail Account Upgrade" and "Report a Bug." These forms, located on a Google server, were authenticated with Google's encryption certificate. Significantly, they requested sensitive information such as the user's full name, username, Google password, and so on, according to the F-Secure researchers.

Before you go on...

1. Discuss the various risks of cloud computing.
2. In your opinion, which risk is the greatest? Support your answer.

TG 3.7 The "Big Three" Cloud Computing Vendors

LEARNING OBJECTIVE

Describe the pros and cons for each of the Big Three cloud computing vendors.

WILEY PLUS

Author Lecture Videos are available exclusively in *WileyPLUS.*
Apply the Concept activities are available in the Appendix and in *WileyPLUS.*

The "Big Three" public IaaS and PaaS cloud vendors are Amazon Web Services (AWS), Microsoft Azure, and Google Cloud Platform. According to Synergy Research Group (www. srgresearch.com), AWS is the global market leader for public IaaS and PaaS with 33 percent of this market, followed by Azure at 18 percent, Google at 9 percent, and Alibaba at 5 percent. Other leading public cloud vendors include VMware Cloud, IBM Cloud, and Oracle Cloud. Let's take a closer look at the Big Three cloud vendors.

All of the Big Three American cloud vendors offer largely similar services. For example, all three offer managed services around popular container services such as Kubernetes and all three offer excellent networking capabilities with automated server load balancing and connectivity to on-premise systems.

All three support relational databases, NoSQL databases, and data warehouses. Specifically, Amazon offers its Relational Database Service, DynamoDB (NoSQL), as well as Redshift, the firm's data warehouse product. Microsoft offers its Azure SQL Database, DocumentDB (NoSQL), and Azure Data Warehouse. For relational database support, Google offers Cloud SQL and Cloud Spanner. For NoSQL database support, Google offers Cloud Bigtable, Cloud Firestore, Firebase Realtime Database, and Cloud Memorystore. For data warehouse support, Google offers Cloud Bigtable.

All three vendors support serverless computing. AWS Lambda, Azure serverless computing, and Google Cloud serverless computing are event-driven, serverless computing platforms that run code in response to events and automatically manage the computing resources required by that code.

Prices for the three vendors are roughly comparable, particularly because AWS shifted from by-the-hour to by-the-second pricing in 2017, bringing it into line with Azure and Google. Overall, prices have been decreasing as the three compete with each other.

The three vendors offer slightly different pricing models, discounts, and make frequent price cuts. Not all customers pay the sticker price, especially at the enterprise level, where volume discounts can be negotiated. All three vendors offer free introductory tiers, allowing customers to try their services before they buy.

The key question is: What differentiates each of these cloud providers? Selecting one cloud vendor over the others depends on the individual customer and the workloads that the customer operates. Often, organizations use multiple cloud providers within different parts of their operations or for different use cases.

Amazon Web Services

Strengths   The key strength for AWS is the breadth and depth of its services, offering more than 175 services across compute, storage, database, analytics, networking, mobile, developer tools, management tools, the Internet of Things, security, and others.

Compute   AWS's main offering is its Elastic Compute Cloud (EC2), which can be customized with a large number of options. Amazon also provides related services such as Elastic Beanstalk for app deployment, the EC2 Container service, and AWS Lambda.

Storage   AWS storage includes its Simple Storage Service (S3), Elastic Block Storage, Elastic File System, and Import/Export large volume data transfer service. AWS also offers Glacier archive backup and Storage Gateway, which integrates with on-premise computing environments.

Hybrid options   AWS Outposts is Amazon's hybrid cloud computing product. As noted in Section TG 3.3, Outposts is a fully managed service where the vendor delivers pre-configured servers to a client's premises, and the client can run AWS services in its data center.

Machine Learning   Amazon deployed SageMaker to simplify the adoption of machine learning. SageMaker is a fully managed service that enables developers and data scientists to quickly build, train, and deploy machine learning models. AWS offers a broad set of off-the-shelf machine-learning services for use cases such as image recognition (AWS Rekognition), text-to-speech deep learning models (Polly), and the engine that powers Alexa (Lex).

Customer base   High-profile customers are a strong point of AWS. Major customers include Netflix, which decided to close all of its data centers in a final transition to the cloud in 2016; AstraZeneca; Airbnb; Financial Times; Dow Jones; Nasdaq; Nike; Pfizer; and others.

Pros and cons   Amazon ranks highly on platform configuration options, monitoring and policy features, security, and reliability. Its partner ecosystem and general product strategy are market leading and its AWS Marketplace has a large number of third-party software services.

In the past, Amazon has been dismissive of the benefits of hybrid cloud computing. As noted in Section TG 3.3, though, the company is now competing in this area with its product, Outposts. Another problem is that certain organizations may not want to contribute to Amazon's revenue and profits, as the giant company continues to expand and compete in a growing number of industries, such as health care and finance. In fact, some boards of directors in potentially threatened industry verticals have directed their IT groups to avoid the use of AWS where possible.

Microsoft Azure

Strengths   Azure is popular with executives who have long-standing relationships with Microsoft. Microsoft also seamlessly integrates Azure with Office 365 and Teams.

Compute   Azure's offering is centered around its Virtual Machines, with other tools such as Cloud Services and Resource Manager to help deploy applications in the cloud.

Storage   Microsoft offers its Azure Storage service, Azure Blob (binary large object) block storage, as well as Table, Queue, and File storage. Azure also offers Site Recovery, Import Export, and Azure Backup. A *binary large object (blob)* is a collection of binary data stored as a single entity in a database management system. Blobs are typically images, audio, or other multimedia objects.

Hybrid options   Microsoft is an established vendor for hybrid deployments with Azure. Azure provides customers with the hardware and software required to deploy Azure public cloud services from a customer's data center with a shared management portal.

Machine Learning   Microsoft's Azure Machine Learning enables developers to write, test, and deploy machine learning algorithms.

Customer base   Microsoft customers include Ford, NBC News, Easyjet, and others. One of Microsoft's highest-profile customer wins occurred in late 2019, when it signed the $10 billion U.S. Department of Defense Joint Enterprise Defense Infrastructure (JEDI) contract. In February 2020, a federal judge ordered a temporary block on the JEDI cloud contract in response to a suit filed by Amazon. Despite the Department of Defense reaffirming Microsoft as the winner of the JEDI contract in September 2020, Amazon's lawsuit continued.

Pros and cons   The biggest attraction for Azure is if Microsoft already has a strong presence within an organization and can easily play a role in helping these companies transition to the cloud. Azure integrates well with key Microsoft on-premise systems such as Windows Server, System Center, and Active Directory.

One of Azure's problems, though, has been a series of outages over the years, including a major global outage in May 2019. Zeus Kerravala (**www.zkresearch.com**) found that, through 2018 to May 2019, AWS and Google had comparable levels of IaaS downtime. During that same period of time, Azure had five times the outage rate of its two major competitors. Gartner analyst Lydia Leong recommended consider disaster recovery capabilities other than Azure for critical applications hosted in the cloud.

Google Cloud Platform

Strengths   Although all three vendors are strong in machine learning, Google excels in this area. Google also has expertise with open-source technologies, particularly with containers. The reason is that Google played a leading role in the development of Kubernetes for orchestration and the Istio service mesh, which are becoming industry standard technologies.

Kubernetes orchestration allows organizations to build application services that span multiple containers, schedule containers across a cluster, and scale those containers. Kubernetes orchestration eliminates many of the manual processes involved in deploying and scaling containerized applications.

Istio is an open-source, independent service mesh that provides the fundamentals for an organization to operate a distributed microservice architecture. Istio reduces the complexity of managing microservice deployments by providing a uniform method to secure, connect, and monitor microservices, as well as a method to control how microservices share data with one another.

Compute   Google's scalable Compute Engine delivers virtual machines in the company's data centers. The virtual machines are quick to start up, come with persistent disk storage, offer consistent performance, and are highly customizable depending on the needs of the customer.

Storage   Google offers Cloud Storage for objects and blobs as well as for archival storage. Its Persistent Disk and Local SSD provides storage for virtual machines and containers. Firestore offers scalable file storage and Cloud Storage for Firebase provides scalable storage for user-generated content from apps. Google Data Transfer Services for fast offline, online, or cloud-to-cloud data transfer.

Hybrid options   Google's hybrid offering Anthos, enables customers to build and manage hybrid applications in customers' data centers or in Google's cloud. Built on open-source technologies including Kubernetes, Istio, and Knative, Anthos provides consistency between on-premise and cloud environment. Knative is an open-source community project that adds components for deploying, operating, and managing serverless, cloud-native applications on Kubernetes.

Significantly, Anthos not only allows organizations to run applications on-premise and in Google's public cloud but also to manage workloads running on third-party clouds such as

AWS and Azure. This feature gives customers the freedom to deploy, run, and manage their applications on the cloud(s) of their choice, without requiring administrators and developers to learn new and different environments.

Machine Learning   Google offers a one-stop-shop AI platform, which enables machine learning developers and data scientists to build and deploy models based on the firm's open source TensorFlow deep learning library.

Customer base   Google has not had quite the same level of enterprise success as its two main competitors but does have notable customers. Spotify completed its migration to Google Cloud Platform in 2018, and United Kingdom bank HSBC has also chosen Google for its analytics and machine learning capabilities. Note that HSBC is also taking a multi-cloud approach, partnering with all three cloud vendors for different tasks.

Pros and cons   Google has a good track record with innovative cloud-native companies and a solid standing in the open-source community. The company has strengths in Big Data and analytics applications, machine learning, and cloud-native applications. Google's market strategy has focused on smaller, innovative projects at large organizations, rather than becoming a strategic cloud partner.

Google has struggled to break into the enterprise market. In addition, Google has the smallest footprint of global instances of the big three and has no presence in China, one of the world's largest markets. AWS and Azure have regions in mainland China that are owned and operated by Chinese third-party partners. AWS's partners are Beijing Sinnet Technology and Ningxia Western Cloud Data Technology, and Azure has partnered with 21Vianet.

Before you go on...

1. Describe the similarities among the Big Three cloud computing vendors.
2. What is the single biggest advantage for each of the Big Three cloud computing vendors? Support your choice.
3. What is the single biggest disadvantage for each of the Big Three cloud computing vendors? Support your choice.

TG 3.8 | Web Services and Service-Oriented Architecture

LEARNING OBJECTIVE

Explain the role of web services in building a firm's IT applications, providing examples.

Web services Applications delivered over the Internet that IT developers can select and combine through almost any device, from personal computers to mobile phones.

Thus far, we have explained how cloud computing can deliver a variety of functionality to users in the form of services (think IaaS, PaaS, and SaaS). We conclude by examining Web services and service-oriented architecture.

Web services are applications delivered over the Internet (the cloud) that MIS professionals can select and combine through almost any device, from personal computers to mobile phones. By using a set of shared standards, or protocols, these applications permit different systems to "talk" with one another–that is, to share data and services–without requiring human beings to translate the conversations. Web services have enormous potential because they can be employed in a variety of environments: over the Internet, on an intranet inside a corporate firewall, or on an extranet set up by business partners. They can also perform a wide variety of tasks, from automating business processes to integrating components of an enterprisewide system to streamlining online buying and selling.

Web services provide numerous benefits for organizations:

- The organization can use the existing Internet infrastructure without having to implement any new technologies.
- Organizational personnel can access remote or local data without having to understand the complexities of this process.
- The organization can create new applications quickly and easily.

The collection of Web services that are used to build a firm's IT applications constitutes a **service-oriented architecture**. Businesses accomplish their processes by executing a series of these services. One of the major benefits of Web services is that they can be reused across an organization in other applications. For example, a Web service that checks a consumer's credit could be used with a service that processes a mortgage application or a credit card application.

Web services are based on four key protocols: XML, SOAP, WSDL, and UDDI. **Extensible markup language (XML)** is a computer language that makes it easier to exchange data among a variety of applications and to validate and interpret these data. XML is a more powerful and flexible markup language than **hypertext markup language (HTML)**. HTML is a page-description language for specifying how text, graphics, video, and sound are placed on a web page document. HTML was originally designed to create and link static documents composed primarily of text (**Figure TG 3.5**). Today, however, the Web is much more social and interactive, and many web pages have multimedia elements, such as images, audio, and video. To integrate these rich media into web pages, users had to rely on third-party plug-in

service-oriented architecture An IT architecture that makes it possible to construct business applications using Web services.

extensible markup language (XML) A computer language that makes it easier to exchange data among a variety of applications and to validate and interpret these data.

hypertext markup language (HTML) A page-description language for specifying how text, graphics, video, and sound are placed on a web page document.

(a) html

```
<!DOCTYPE HTML PUBLIC "-//W3C//DTD XHTML 1.0 Transitional//EN" http://www.wiley.com/college/gisslen/0470179961/video/
video111
<html xmlns="http://www.wiley.com/college/rainer/0470179061/video/video111.html"><head>
<meta http-equiv="content-Type" content="text/html; charset=ISO-8859-1">
<title>CSS Text Wrapper</title>
<link type="text/css" rel="stylesheet" href="css/stylesheet.css">
</head><body id="examples">

<div id="container">
        <div class="wrapper">
                <div class="ex">
                        <script type="text/javascript">shapewrapp
er("15","7.5,141,145|22.5,89,89|37.5,68,69|52.5,46,50|67.5,3
height: 15px; width: 39px;"></div><div style="float: left; clear: left; height: 15px; width: 27px;"></div><div style="float:
15px; width: 4px;"></div><div style="float: left; clear: left; height: 15px; width: 6px;"></div><div style="float:
right; cle
width: 43px;"></div><div style="float: left; clear: left; height: 15px; width: 57px;"></div><div style="float: right; clear:
                        <span style="font-size: 13px;" class=c">
```

(b) XML

```
<feature numbered="no" xml:id="c08-fea-0001">
    <titleGroup>
        <title type="featureName">OPENING CASE</title>
        <title type="main">Tiger Tans and Gifts</title>
    </titleGroup>
    <section xml:id="c08-sec-0002">
        <p>
            <blockFixed onlyChannels="print" type="graphic">
                <mediaResource alt="p0310" copyright="John Wiley &amp; Sons, Inc." eRights="yes"
                    href="urn:x-wiley:9781118443590:media:rainer9781118443590c08:p0310" pRights="yes"/>
            </blockFixed>
            Lisa Keiling owns & tanning salon in Wedowee, Alabama, that does very well from January to May....
        </p>
    </section>
</feature>
```

FIGURE TG 3.5 **(a) Screenshot of an HTML wrapper. This wrapper gives instructions on how to open a video associated with this book. (b) Example of XML tagging.**

HTML5 A page-description language that makes it possible to embed images, audio, and video directly into a document without add-ons. Also makes it easier for web pages to function across different display devices, including mobile devices as well as desktops. It supports the storage of data offline.

applications such as Flash, Silverlight, and Java. Unfortunately for users, these add-ons require both additional programming and extensive computer processing.

The next evolution of HTML, called **HTML5**, solves this problem by enabling users to embed images, audio, and video directly into a document without the add-ons. HTML5 also makes it easier for web pages to function across different display devices, including mobile devices and desktops. HTML5 supports offline data storage for apps that run over the Web. Web pages will execute more quickly, and they will resemble smartphone apps. HTML5 is used in a number of Internet platforms, including Apple's Safari browser, Google Chrome, and Mozilla Firefox. Google's Gmail and Google Reader also use HTML5. Websites listed as "iPad ready" are using HTML5 extensively. Examples of such sites are CNN, the *New York Times*, and CBS.

Where HTML is limited to describing how data should be presented in the form of web pages, XML can present, communicate, and store data. For example, in XML a number is not simply a number. The XML tag also specifies whether the number represents a price, a date, or a ZIP code. Consider this example of XML, which identifies the contact information for Jane Smith.

```
<contact-info>
<name>Jane Smith</name>
<company>AT&T</company>
<phone>(212) 555-4567</phone>
</contact-info>
```

Simple object access protocol (SOAP) is a set of rules that define how messages can be exchanged among different network systems and applications through the use of XML. These rules essentially establish a common protocol that allows different Web services to interoperate. For example, Visual Basic clients can use SOAP to access a Java server. SOAP runs on all hardware and software systems.

The *Web services description language (WSDL)* is used to create the XML document that describes the tasks performed by the various Web services. Tools such as VisualStudio.Net automate the process of accessing the WSDL, reading it, and coding the application to reference the specific Web service.

Universal description, discovery, and integration (UDDI) allows MIS professionals to search for needed Web services by creating public or private searchable directories of these services. In other words, UDDI is the registry of descriptions of Web services.

Examples of Web services abound. As one example, the Food and Nutrition Service (FNS) within the U.S. Department of Agriculture (USDA) uses Amazon Web Services successfully. The FNS administers the department's nutrition assistance programs. Its mission is to provide children and families in need with improved access to food and a healthier diet through its food assistance programs and comprehensive nutrition education efforts.

The Supplemental Nutrition Assistance Program, or SNAP, is the cornerstone of the USDA's nutrition assistance mission. More than 47 million people–most of them children–receive SNAP benefits each month. To help recipients, in 2010 the FNS created a Web application called the SNAP Retail Locator. Faced with limited budget and time to implement the solution, the FNS selected Amazon Web Services to host the application. As its name suggests, the SNAP Retail Locator, which receives 30,000 visitors each month, helps SNAP recipients find the closest SNAP-authorized store and also provides driving directions to the store. The application has been available 100 percent of the time since it was launched. By employing Amazon, the FNS also saved 90 percent of the cost it would have incurred had it hosted the application on-premises.

Before you go on...

1. What are Web services?
2. What is a service-oriented architecture?

What's in IT for Me?

For All Business Majors

As with hardware (see Technology Guide 1), the design of enterprise IT architectures has profound impacts for businesspeople. Personal and organizational success can depend on an understanding of cloud computing and a commitment to knowing the opportunities and challenges they will bring.

At the organizational level, cloud computing has the potential to make the organization function more efficiently and effectively, while saving the organization money. Web services and SOA make the organization more flexible when deploying new IT applications.

At the individual level, you might use cloud computing yourself if you start your own business. Remember that cloud computing provides startup companies with world-class IT capabilities at a very low cost.

Summary

TG 3.1 Describe the evolution of the information technology function.

- Stand-alone mainframes: Organizations initially used mainframe computers in their engineering and accounting departments. The mainframe was typically housed in a secure area and only MIS personnel had access to it.

- Mainframe and dumb terminals: Firms placed dumb terminals in user departments. This arrangement enabled users to input computer programs into the mainframe from their departments.

- Stand-alone personal computers: In the late 1970s, users began bringing personal computers to the workplace to improve their productivity. These computers were not initially supported by the MIS department, but organizations eventually decided to support the computers.

- Local area networks (client/server computing): Organizations began to connect personal computers to local area networks (LANs) and then connected these LANs to the mainframe, a type of processing known as *client/server computing*.

- Enterprise computing: In the early 1990s, organizations began to use networking standards to integrate different kinds of networks throughout the firm, thereby creating enterprise computing. As the Internet became widespread after 1995, organizations began using the TCP/IP networking protocol to integrate different types of networks. All types of hardware were networked, including mainframes, personal computers, smartphones, printers, and many others. Software applications and data now flow seamlessly throughout the enterprise and between organizations.

- Cloud computing and mobile computing: Today, organizations and individuals can use the power of cloud computing. Cloud computing provides access to a shared pool of computing resources, including computers, storage, applications, and services, over a network, typically the Internet.

TG 3.2 Define cloud computing and its key characteristics.

Cloud computing is a type of computing that delivers convenient, on-demand, pay-as-you-go access for multiple customers to a shared pool of configurable computing resources (e.g., servers, networks, storage, applications, and services) that can be rapidly and easily accessed over the Internet.

The essential *characteristics* of cloud computing include the following:

- Cloud computing provides on-demand self-service.
- Cloud computing includes the characteristics of grid computing.
- Cloud computing includes the characteristics of utility computing.
- Cloud computing uses broad network access.
- Cloud computing pools computing resources.
- Cloud computing typically occurs on virtualized servers.

TG 3.3 Describe each of the four types of clouds.

Public clouds are shared, easily accessible, multicustomer IT infrastructures that are available nonexclusively to any entity in the public (individuals, groups, and organizations). *Private clouds* (also known as *internal clouds* or *corporate clouds*) are IT infrastructures that are accessible only by a single entity, or by an exclusive group of related entities that share the same purpose and requirements, such as all the business units within a single organization. *Hybrid clouds* are composed of public and private clouds that remain unique entities but are bound together, offering the benefits of multiple deployment models. *Vertical clouds* serve specific industries.

TG 3.4 Explain the operational model of each of the three types of cloud services.

With the *infrastructure-as-a-service* model, cloud computing providers offer remotely accessible servers, networks, and storage capacity. In the *platform-as-a-service* model, customers rent servers, operating systems, storage, a database, software development technologies such as Java and .NET, and network capacity over the Internet. With the *software-as-a-service* delivery model, cloud computing vendors provide software that is specific to their customers' requirements.

TG 3.5 Identify the key benefits of cloud computing.

The benefits of cloud computing include making individuals more productive, facilitating collaboration, mining insights from data, developing and hosting applications, cost flexibility, business scalability, improved usage of hardware, market adaptability, and product and service customization.

TG 3.6   Discuss the concerns and risks associated with cloud computing.

Cloud computing does raise concerns and have risks, which include "legacy spaghetti," cost, reliability, privacy, security, and the regulatory and legal environment.

TG 3.7   Describe the pros and cons for each of the Big Three cloud computing vendors.

Amazon. Amazon ranks highly on platform configuration options, monitoring and policy features, security, and reliability. Its partner ecosystem and general product strategy are market leading, and its AWS Marketplace has a large number of third-party software services.

In the past, Amazon has been dismissive of the benefits of hybrid cloud computing. As noted in Section TG 3.3, though, the company is now competing in this area with its product Outposts. Another problem is that certain organizations may not want to contribute to Amazon revenue and profits, as the giant company continues to expand and compete in a growing number of industries, such as health care and finance. In fact, some boards of directors in potentially threatened industry verticals have directed their IT groups to avoid the use of AWS where possible.

Microsoft. The biggest attraction for Azure is if Microsoft already has a strong presence within an organization and therefore can easily play a role in helping these companies transition to the cloud. Azure integrates well with key Microsoft on-premise systems such as Windows Server, System Center, and Active Directory.

One of Azure's problems, though, has been a series of outages over the years, including a major global outage in May 2019. Gartner analyst Lydia Leong recommended consider disaster recovery capabilities other than Azure for critical applications hosted in the cloud. Note: AWS had its last major outage in 2017 and Google Cloud last had a major outage of its own in November 2019.

Google. Google has a good track record with innovative cloud-native companies and a solid standing in the open-source community. The company has strengths in Big Data and analytics applications, machine learning, and cloud-native applications. Google's market strategy has focused on smaller, innovative projects at large organizations, rather than becoming a strategic cloud partner.

Google has struggled to break into the enterprise market. In addition, Google has the smallest footprint of global instances of the big three and has no presence in China, one of the world's largest markets. AWS and Azure have regions in mainland China which are owned and operated by Chinese third-party partners. AWS's partners are Beijing Sinnet Technology and Ningxia Western Cloud Data Technology, and Azure has partnered with 21Vianet.

TG 3.8   Explain the role of Web services in building a firm's IT applications, providing examples.

Web services are applications delivered over the Internet that MIS professionals can select and combine through almost any device, from personal computers to mobile phones. A *service-oriented architecture* makes it possible for MIS professionals to construct business applications using Web services.

Key Terms

cloud computing 499	infrastructure-as-a-service (IaaS) 507	server virtualization 502
extensible markup language (XML) 521	on-premise computing 499	service-oriented architecture 521
functions-as-a-Service (XaaS) 510	platform-as-a-service (PaaS) 509	utility computing 501
grid computing 501	private clouds 504	vertical cloud 506
HTML5 522	public clouds 503	Web services 520
hybrid clouds 505	Security-as-a-service (SECaaS) 510	
hypertext markup language (HTML) 521	server farms 501	

Discussion Questions

1. What is the value of server farms and virtualization to any large organization?

2. If you were the chief information officer of a firm, how would you explain the workings, benefits, and limitations of cloud computing?

3. What is the value of cloud computing to a small organization?

4. What is the value of cloud computing to an entrepreneur who is starting a business?

Problem-Solving Activities

1. Investigate the status of cloud computing by researching the offerings of the following vendors: Dell (www.dell.com), Oracle (www.oracle.com), IBM (www.ibm.com), Alibaba (www.alibaba.com), and Tencent (www.tencent.com). Compare Alibaba and Tencent with American cloud vendors.

2. Visit www.morpheusdata.com and watch the demo. Summarize the platform's benefits in hybrid cloud computing.

3. Compare www.dropbox.com and google drive. Which service would you prefer to use during your next group project and why?

Apply the Concept Activities

Apply the Concept 1.1

LEARNING OBJECTIVE 1.1

Identify the reasons why being an informed user of information systems is important in today's world.

STEP 1: Background (Here is what you are learning.)

Section 1.1 discussed how businesses are utilizing modern technologies to become more productive by connecting to their customers, suppliers, partners, and other parties. Those connections, however, do not exist simply to support the businesses. Do you realize how connected you are? Computers and information systems have become an essential feature of our everyday lives. Most of you have a cell phone within reach and have looked at it within the past 5 minutes. No longer is a phone just a phone; rather, it is your connection to family, friends, shopping, driving directions, entertainment (games, movies, music, etc.), and much more.

When you embark on your career, you likely will have to interface with information systems to post transactions and search for or record information. Accomplishing these tasks will require you to work effectively with computers, regardless of the industry in which you find yourself employed.

STEP 2: Activity (Here is what you do.)

Visit the websites of three local businesses: a bank, a dentist, and a retail shop. Examine their information to see if you can determine what types of information systems they use to support their operations. It is likely that you will find some similarities and differences among the three. Also, see if they have any open positions. If they do, what technical skills do these positions require? Summarize your findings in a paragraph or two.

STEP 3: Deliverable (Here is what you turn in.)

Based on your research, identify five reasons why it is important for you to be an informed user of information technology. Reference your summarized findings to support your reasoning. Submit this list to your instructor, but also keep it in mind. You have just looked into the real world (your local world, in fact) and identified a reason for taking this course!

Apply the Concept 1.2

LEARNING OBJECTIVE 1.2

Classify the activities supported by various types of computer-based information systems in an organization.

STEP 1: Background

Section 1.2 discussed the various functional areas in which you most likely will be employed and the different IS that support them. It should be no surprise that these are the majors from which you can choose in most colleges of business. The four major functional areas are marketing and sales, finance and accounting, manufacturing, and human resources. Often, these areas will use the same database and networks within a company, but they will use them to support their specific needs. This activity will help you develop a solid understanding of the role of IS within the different functional areas.

STEP 2: Activity

Review the section material that describes the major functions of the four major functional areas. Then, review the basic functions of the following types of information systems: transaction processing, management information, and decision support.

After you have acquired a solid understanding of the functional areas and information systems that support them, you are ready to move forward with the activity!

STEP 3: Deliverable

Create a table like the one shown below, and classify the activities supported by various types of computer-based information systems. To assist you, we have prefilled one item in each type of system. After you complete your chart, submit it to your professor.

	Transaction Processing	Management Information System	Decision Support System
Marketing and Sales	Enter Sales Data		
Accounting and Finance			
Human Resources			Comply with EEOC
Manufacturing		Inventory Reporting	

Apply the Concept 1.3

LEARNING OBJECTIVE 1.3

Discuss ways in which information technology can affect managers and nonmanagerial workers.

STEP 1: Background

Section 1.3 demonstrated that the essential reason businesses use information systems is to add value to their daily activities. In fact, IS have radically transformed the nature of both managerial and nonmanagerial work. Managers employ IT to instantly track information that previously was available only in monthly reports. Support staff can view calendars and schedules for all employees and can schedule meetings more easily. Sales representatives can view current product information while visiting with clients. This list does not even scratch the surface of the countless ways technology has added value to modern businesses.

STEP 2: Activity

Consider the restaurant industry. You have probably visited some "old-school" restaurants where your order is written down on a piece of paper and never entered into a computer system for preparation. You have most likely also been to a very modern restaurant where you enter your own order with a tablet, smartphone, or other piece of technology. Visit the link associated with this activity and and learn about the Ziosk system and how it affects restaurants.

STEP 3: Deliverable

Imagine you are a restaurant manager considering whether or not to adopt the Ziosk system. Write a report for your boss outlining the systems benefits and how it could help your restaurant stay competitive.

Apply the Concept 1.4

LEARNING OBJECTIVE 1.4

Identify positive and negative societal effects of the increased use of information technology.

WILEY PLUS

This activity requires visiting an external url link. Url links are available within *WileyPLUS*. If you do not have *WileyPLUS*, ask your instructor to provide the link.

STEP 1: Background

As you have just read, the increased use of IS has had a significant impact on society. Section 1.4 focused on three areas—quality-of-life improvements, robotics, and health care—to spark your interest in the ways our lives are being touched. Unfortunately, the technologies that provide quality-of-life improvements can also create economic and political problems. For example, robots that help streamline production also eliminate jobs. Similarly, health care improvements raise concerns regarding shared data and privacy violations.

STEP 2: Activity

Visit the link associated with this activity and learn about the ways robots are expanding opportunities by providing safer, cleaner, more cost effective ways for people around the globe to work.

STEP 3: Deliverable

Write a summary of the impact of Universal Robots. Select one project mentioned in the video and detail its benefits and future potential.

Apply the Concept 2.1

LEARNING OBJECTIVE 2.1

Discuss ways in which information systems enable cross-functional business processes and business processes for a single functional area.

STEP 1: Background

This chapter defines a business process as an ongoing collection of related activities that create a product or a service of value to the organization, its business partners, and/or its customers. Normally, we do not see everything that goes into a process; rather, we observe only the results of the process. For example, when you shop at a grocery store, you see stocked shelves. However, the inventory-management processes that operate to keep the shelves stocked—as well as the information systems that support those processes—remain essentially invisible.

STEP 2: Activity

Visit the link provided for this activity and watch the video that demonstrates how ZOHO Inventory supports data flow across several business processes.

STEP 3: Deliverable

Based on the video from Step 2, write a brief description of how the ZOHO Inventory system enables multi-channel selling. Submit your description to your instructor.

Apply the Concept 2.2

LEARNING OBJECTIVE 2.2

Compare and contrast business process reengineering (BPR) and business process management (BPM) to determine the advantages and disadvantages of each.

STEP 1: Background

One of the most difficult decisions related to business processes is whether they need to be reengineered or simply managed. Reengineering business processes is a "clean-slate" approach in which you build completely new processes to accomplish current tasks. In contrast, managing these processes involves making current processes more efficient. Put simply, reengineering is radical, whereas management is incremental.

STEP 2: Activity

Consider the many processes involved in getting you (as a student) accepted, enrolled, registered, housed, fed, and, ultimately, educated. Do you recall the processes you went through to accomplish these tasks? Did any of these processes strike you as inefficient?

STEP 3: Deliverable

Imagine that you are a student representative on a committee whose task is to consider reengineering or modifying (managing) these business processes. Prepare a written statement for the committee that will compare and contrast BPR and BPM to determine the advantages and disadvantages of each strategy. Make a recommendation as to which one your university should follow, and present your recommendation to your instructor.

Apply the Concept 2.3

LEARNING OBJECTIVE 2.3

Identify effective IT responses to different kinds of business pressures.

STEP 1: Background

Businesses face immense pressures today from every angle imaginable. The market is constantly shifting, technology becomes obsolete almost as quickly as it is implemented, society expects businesses to take more responsibility for the communities their work impacts, and legal compliance is required. Businesses increasingly employ cutting-edge technologies to navigate these difficult waters.

STEP 2: Activity

Pick one business pressure from each of the three broad categories presented in the chapter: Market, Technology, and Societal/Political/Legal. Now search for a real-world business story related to each of the pressures you have chosen.

STEP 3: Deliverable

After you have selected your three examples, identify an effective IT response to each one. Feel free to use the responses listed in the chapter. For each example, explain why you feel this is an appropriate response to the business pressure you have identified.

Perhaps there is a response outlined in the story you found. If so, determine whether the response was truly effective in dealing with the business pressure. Your submission should follow the outline below:

Broad Category: _____

Business Pressure: _____

IT Response: _____

Description: _____

Apply the Concept 2.4

LEARNING OBJECTIVE 2.4

Describe the strategies that organizations typically adopt to counter Porter's five competitive forces.

STEP 1: Background

This section has exposed you to Porter's five forces model, which explains how various forces can affect an organization. The threat of entry of new competitors, bargaining power of suppliers, bargaining power of customers, threat of substitute products or services, and rivalry among existing firms in the industry all have an impact on the organization's success. Based on this model, the chapter presents five strategies for competitive advantage: cost leadership, differentiation, innovation, operational effectiveness, and customer orientation.

Walmart is a worldwide company that focuses on a cost-leadership strategy. Review the ways Walmart uses the five forces (or controls them) to maintain their position as a global cost leader. Although it may be somewhat easy to perform this exercise with a global giant like Walmart, it is very difficult to apply these concepts to small businesses.

STEP 2: Activity

Visit your favorite restaurant and ask to speak to the manager. Asking only a few questions, evaluate whether the manager has a grasp of the five forces model. Do not ask anything specifically about Porter. Rather, inquire about rivals, substitutes, customers' bargaining power, suppliers' power, and so on. A good manager should be familiar with these concepts regardless of whether he or she uses the term *Porter's five forces*. Finally, ask the manager what strategy he or she uses. Then, try to classify that strategy as a cost leadership, differentiation, innovation, operational effectiveness, or customer orientation strategy.

STEP 3: Deliverable

Identify which of the five forces are at work based on the manager's feedback. Then, describe the strategies that *could* help deal with these particular forces, and explain *if* this is what the restaurant is currently attempting to do. If it is not, then explain what they should do differently. Your submission will have two parts: (1) a definition of the forces and (2) a description of the strategies at play in response to those forces.

Apply the Concept 3.1

LEARNING OBJECTIVE 3.1

Describe ethics, its three fundamental tenets, and the four categories of ethical issues related to information technology.

STEP 1: Background

As you begin your career, you need to be aware of the current trends affecting the four areas of concern presented in Section 3.1. Privacy (what people know about you), property (who owns the data about you), accuracy (are the data about you accurate), and accessibility (who can access your data) are major topics in today's high-tech world. They are especially important in the migration to electronic health records, mobile wallets, social media, and government-run databases, to name a few.

STEP 2: Activity

Visit the link associated with this activity and read the article posted from Forbes magazine that was posted in November 2013. The article describes an unusual (or not-so-unusual) action on the part of Goldman Sachs. It seems they decided that their junior bankers should have weekends off!

Understand that it isn't illegal to require your employees to work weekends, nor is it illegal to give them time off. It also isn't illegal to work people 75 hours a week. Many of the talking points in this article focus expressly on ethics. An employer is trying to do the "right" thing, and they have used a new standard to define "right."

STEP 3: Deliverable

Summarize the article for your professor. In your summary, make certain to define ethics and to describe how the three fundamental tenets of ethics (responsibility, liability, and accountability) played a role in Goldman Sachs' decision. Finally (not from the article), discuss how these same bankers deal with the four areas of ethical concern with regard to your financial information.

Apply the Concept 3.2

WILEY PLUS

This activity requires visiting an external url links. Url links are available within *WileyPLUS*. If you do not have *WileyPLUS*, ask your instructor to provide the link.

LEARNING OBJECTIVE 3.2

Discuss at least one potential threat to the privacy of the data stored in each of three places that store personal data.

STEP 1: Background

Section 3.2 defines privacy as the right to be left alone and free of unreasonable personal intrusions. Information privacy is the right to determine when and to what extent information about you can be gathered and/or communicated to others. And, where our data are concerned, we are in control, right? If so, why do people always fear that "Big Brother" is spying on us and violating our privacy? The law generally assigns a higher priority to society's right to access information than an individual's right to privacy.

STEP 2: Activity

Visit the link associated with this activity and and watch the video where author, Amy Gajda, discusses a recent book about privacy and the public's right to know. As you watch, consider whether privacy is more objective (clear-cut and easy to understand) or subjective (dependent on situations, persons, ethics, etc.).

STEP 3: Deliverable

Considering the dynamics presented in the chapter and the video, now imagine that your boss has tasked you with researching a customer list to see what you can find out about them on Facebook. It feels a little creepy because their information was not shared on Facebook for what your boss is asking you to use it for. It feels like an invasion of their privacy. Is it? Prepare a response for your boss that addresses whether you will or will not comply with this task.

Apply the Concept 4.1

LEARNING OBJECTIVE 4.1

Identify the five factors that contribute to the increasing vulnerability of information resources and specific examples of each factor.

STEP 1: Background

Section 4.1 has taught you about the importance of information security, particularly when you are conducting business over the Web. It is important to note that a chain is only as strong as its weakest link. Therefore, although you may have been careful to maintain security across your network, if your business partners have not done so as well, then as your information passes over their networks it will be at risk.

STEP 2: Activity

Visit VeriSign's website. As you read this page, keep in mind that VeriSign is in the business of protecting websites and Web users, which is something we all appreciate. In fact, it is likely that you feel some level of comfort when you see the VeriSign symbol on an e-commerce site.

STEP 3: Deliverable

Compose a brief memo from VeriSign to a potential client. Identify the five factors that contribute to the increasing vulnerability of information resources and provide examples of how VeriSign can help protect the client's digital assets against these threats. Submit your memo to your instructor.

Apply the Concept 4.2

LEARNING OBJECTIVE 4.2

Compare and contrast human mistakes and social engineering, along with specific examples of each one.

STEP 1: Background

Sensitive information is generally stored in a safe location, both physically and digitally. However, as you have just read, this information is often vulnerable to unintentional threats that result from careless mistakes. As one example, employees frequently use USB (flash) drives to take information home. Although these actions are perfectly legal, the USB drive makes it easy to lose the information or to copy it onto unauthorized machines. In fact, any device that stores information can become a threat to information security—backup drives, CDs, DVDs, and even printers! Printers? Because people can "copy" information? Not quite. Continue the activity to find out more.

STEP 2: Activity

Visit the link associated with this activity. You will find an article about how the hard drive in a printer sometimes stores images of all the documents that have been copied. In the past, when these printers were discarded, their hard drives were not erased, leaving medical records, police reports, and other private information in a vulnerable state.

STEP 3: Deliverable

Compare and contrast human mistakes and social engineering using the example above. How might someone make a mistake with a printer? How might someone use social engineering to access or create copies of personal information? Put your thoughts into a report and submit it to your instructor.

Apply the Concept 4.3

WILEY PLUS

This activity requires visiting an external url links. Url links are available within *WileyPLUS*. If you do not have *WileyPLUS*, ask your instructor to provide the link.

LEARNING OBJECTIVE 4.3

Discuss the 10 types of deliberate attacks.

STEP 1: Background

Unfortunately there are many people who take advantage of others. Fraud, espionage, information extortion, identity theft, cyberterrorism, spamming, phishing, and many other deliberate acts have created a world where we must always confirm the identity of the people with whom we share information.

STEP 2: Activity

Visit www.consumer.ftc.gov/features/imposter-scams and review at least three of the videos that provide information on how to spot a scam. What do you notice that is similar across the scams?

STEP 3: Deliverable

Prepare a table that includes a title and description of each recommendation on how to spot a scam. Add a statement under your table that discusses the similar methods for spotting a scam.

Apply the Concept 4.4

LEARNING OBJECTIVE 4.4

Describe the three risk mitigation strategies and provide examples of each one in the context of owning a home.

STEP 1: Background

Section 4.4 discussed at length the ways businesses deal with risk. Risk management is so important that companies frequently assign an entire department to oversee risk analysis and mitigation. When companies address risk, they have three basic methods from which to choose: risk acceptance, risk limitation, and risk transference. Significantly, we do the same thing when it comes to our personal assets.

Like businesses, homeowners face intentional and unintentional threats. To mitigate against these threats, almost all homeowners take certain actions. These actions reflect, among other things, where your home is located. For example, a home on the beach is much more susceptible to hurricanes than is a home in Nebraska. However, the home in Nebraska is (perhaps) more susceptible to tornadoes than is the home on the beach.

STEP 2: Activity

Imagine that you own your home. What risks do you need to manage? What property do you need to assess? What is the probability that any asset will be compromised? (*Note:* You will need to assess the risk to each asset.) What are the costs associated with each asset being compromised?

STEP 3: Deliverable

In a document, define the three risk management strategies and provide an example of each one in the context of owning a home. Submit your document to your instructor.

Apply the Concept 4.5

LEARNING OBJECTIVE 4.5

Identify the three major types of controls that organizations can use to protect their information resources and provide an example of each one.

STEP 1: Background

Security controls are designed to protect all components of an information system, including data, software, hardware, and networks. Because there are so many diverse threats, organizations utilize layers of controls. One security feature discussed in this chapter is public key encryption. This feature requires a public key and a private key. The public key is shared and is used to encrypt a message that only the individual's private key can decrypt.

STEP 2: Activity

Visit the link associated with this activity. The link will take you to an article about the 2004 movie *National Treasure*. Watching the actual film is preferable, but you may not have access to it. For this activity, reading about it will suffice. In this movie, Ben Gates (played by Nicholas Cage) steals one of our nation's most sacred documents—the Declaration of Independence. In the process, you see how the thief breaches all three of the major types of controls.

STEP 3: Deliverable

Identify the three major types of controls that the National Archives employs—and that Gates ultimately penetrates—and provide examples of them from the movie. Prepare a document with the three types of controls and examples from the movie and submit it to your instructor.

Apply the Concept 5.1

LEARNING OBJECTIVE 5.1

Discuss ways that common challenges in managing data can be addressed using data governance.

STEP 1: Background

Data governance is of key importance today. Many companies compile data from multiple datasets for the purpose of adding value to the business through data analytics and business intelligence. However, the source of the data is critical.

STEP 2: Activity

Visit https://enterprisetalk.com/featured/data-governance/ and read this short article about the use of AI and how data governance plays a key role in the reliability of the suggestions AI provides to users.

STEP 3: Deliverable

Write a short summary that describes at least three ways data governance can help create more effective use of AI.

Apply the Concept 5.2

LEARNING OBJECTIVE 5.2

Discuss the advantages and disadvantages of relational databases.

STEP 1: Background

This section has introduced you to the advantages and disadvantages of using a relational database. This is one of those concepts that cannot really be appreciated until you work through the process of designing a database. Even though very few people go on to become database administrators, it is still valuable to have some understanding of how a database is built and administered. In this activity, you will be presented with a scenario, and you will then apply the concepts you have just read about. In the process, you will develop a solid foundation to discuss the advantages and disadvantages of relational databases.

STEP 2: Activity

You are employed as the coordinator of multiple ongoing projects within a company. Your responsibilities include keeping track of the company's commercial projects, its employees, and the employees' participation in each project. Usually, a project will have multiple team members, but some projects have not been assigned to any team members. For each project, the company must keep track of the project's title, description, location, estimated budget, and due date.

Each employee can be assigned to one or more projects. Some employees can also be on leave and therefore will not be working on any assignments. Project leaders usually need to know the following information about their team members: name, address, phone number, Social Security number, highest degree attained, and expertise (for example, IS, accounting, marketing, finance).

Your manager has instructed you to present an overview of the advantages and disadvantages of a database that would support the company's efforts to manage the data described in this scenario. At a minimum, you should define the tables and the relationships among the key variables to provide structure to the information that would be included in the database.

STEP 3: Deliverable

Using the relational database design you created in Step 2, prepare a discussion of the advantages and disadvantages of this database. How will it benefit the company? What additional challenges might it create?

Submit your design and your discussion to your instructor.

Apply the Concept 5.3

LEARNING OBJECTIVE 5.3

Define Big Data and its basic characteristics.

STEP 1: Background

This section describes Big Data as an ongoing phenomenon that is providing businesses with access to vast amounts of information. The key "ingredients" that make the Big Data phenomenon a reality are volume, velocity, and variety.

STEP 2: Activity

Precision medicine is a relatively new approach to healthcare that aims to provide custom recommendations to patients dealing with chronic disease. Many doctors specialize through years of study and experience, but precision medicine attempts to offer this level of specialization by analyzing data – BIG data. Visit the link associated with this activity and read about the impact of big data on precision medicine.

STEP 3: Deliverable

Write a summary describing how volume, velocity, and variety affect precision medicine and what you think the future holds. will support

Apply the Concept 5.4

LEARNING OBJECTIVE 5.4

Explain the elements necessary to successfully implement and maintain data warehouses.

STEP 1: Background

A set of general ingredients is required for organizations to effectively utilize the power of data marts and data warehouses. Figure 5.4 presents this information. Health care as an industry has not been centralized for many business, legal, and ethical reasons. However, the overall health implications of a centralized data warehouse are unimaginable.

STEP 2: Activity

Visit the link associated with this activity and read the article in *HealthTech* magazine from July 11, 2018, titled "Fitbit Pushes into the Clinical Space to Make Medicine More Personal." As you read the article, think about how Fitbit and Google are using data warehouses. (The term *warehouse* is not used, but the concept is applicable.)

STEP 3: Deliverable

To demonstrate that you recognize the environmental factors necessary to implement and maintain a data warehouse, imagine that the date is exactly five years in the future. Write a blog post titled "Data from Gadgets Like Fitbit Changed How Medical Data Was Used."

In your article, imagine that all of the ingredients necessary in the environment have come together. Discuss what the environment was like in 2018 and how things have changed today with devices like the Apple Watch and Fitbit.

Be aware that there is no right or wrong answer to this exercise. The objective is for you to recognize the necessary environment for a successful data warehouse implementation. The health care–related example simply provides a platform to accomplish this task.

Apply the Concept 5.5

LEARNING OBJECTIVE 5.5

Describe the benefits and challenges of implementing knowledge management systems in organizations.

WILEY PLUS

This activity requires visiting an external url links. Url links are available within *WileyPLUS*. If you do not have *WileyPLUS*, ask your instructor to provide the link.

STEP 1: Background

As you have learned in this text, data are captured, stored, analyzed, and shared to create knowledge within organizations. This knowledge is exposed in meetings when colleagues are interpreting the information they received from the latest report, in employee presentations, in e-mail among coworkers, and in numerous other scenarios. The problem many organizations face is that there are massive amounts of knowledge that are created and shared, but this information is not stored in a centralized, searchable format.

STEP 2: Activity

Visit the links associated with this activity. They will take you to two YouTube videos: *Discover What You Know* by user Ken Porter and *Lee Bryant—Knowledge Management* by user UsNow-Film. Both videos illustrate the importance of capturing knowledge within an organization so it can be shared with the right person at the right time to support effective decision making.

STEP 3: Deliverable

Write a short paragraph or two to discuss the benefits and challenges faced by companies when they attempt to implement a knowledge management system. How many of these elements are technical and how many are social? Also, discuss the ways that companies can use technologies to help capture and share knowledge.

Submit this essay to your instructor.

Apply the Concept 5.6

LEARNING OBJECTIVE 5.6

Understand the processes of querying a relational database, entity-relationship modeling, and normalization and joins.

STEP 1: Background

It is very important that you understand the connections among entities, attributes, and relationships. This section has defined each of these terms for you. Typically, entities are described by their attributes, and they are related to other entities. For example, if "student name" is the entity, then age, gender, country of origin, marital status, and other demographic data are the attributes (characteristics) of that particular student. That student is also related to other entities such as financial information, major, and course information.

STEP 2: Activity

An entity–relationship model is one of the most challenging aspects of designing a database because you have to (1) understand the rules that govern how processes work and (2) be able to define and describe these rules in a picture. This section has provided you with the necessary tools to draw a basic ER model.

Imagine the following scenario. You are designing a database for your local police department to keep track of traffic violations. The department has provided you with the following rules:

- Each officer can write multiple tickets.
- Each ticket will list only one officer.
- Each ticket will list only one driver.
- Drivers can receive multiple tickets.

STEP 3: Deliverable

Using the tools described in this section, demonstrate that you understand the process of ER modeling by drawing and submitting an ER model for the scenario provided in Step 2.

Apply the Concept 6.1

LEARNING OBJECTIVE 6.1

Compare and contrast the major types of networks.

STEP 1: Background

Section 6.1 has introduced you to the different types of networks that connect businesses around the world. These networking capabilities enable modern organizations to operate over many geographic locations. Frequently, a company's headquarters are located in one city with various branches in other countries. In addition, employees often work from home rather than commute to a physical office. The computer network is the technology that allows all of this to happen. For a network to function, a few components are required. In this activity, you will place these components in the appropriate places to create a computer network.

STEP 2: Activity

Consider the following company, called JLB TechWizards, and the following potential network components:

1. Headquarters: JLB TechWizards manufactures, sells, and services computer equipment. The company's headquarters, located in Chicago, house several key functions, including marketing, accounting, HR, and manufacturing. Each office has a number of PCs that connect to the main server. All offices share data and printers.

2. Salesforce: The company has technicians who service equipment sold within the United States. Each technician has a laptop that must connect to the database at headquarters about three hours each day to check inventory, enter repairs, and place orders. Technicians are constantly on the road and they need to be able to check inventory whether they are in a hotel or at a customer site. In addition, each evening the technicians must log on to check for updates and to post their daily activities.

3. Employees from home: JLB TechWizards has a number of employees who work from home part-time on flex time. These employees must have a fast, secure connection because some of them are dealing with financial data stored in the main computer and its databases at headquarters. They all live within 20 miles of their workplace.

STEP 3: Deliverable

Use the description of JLB TechWizards presented above to compare and contrast the types of networks discussed in this section. Explain how these networks will or will not meet the needs of each situation. A table may be useful to present this information, but it is not required. Create a Word document with your description and explanations and submit it to your instructor.

Apply the Concept 6.2

LEARNING OBJECTIVE 6.2

Describe the wireline communications media and transmission technologies.

STEP 1: Background

Section 6.2 covers network channels, protocols, and other network fundamentals. These computer networks enable businesses to receive and share information with customers, suppliers, and employees. Made up of several possible cable types and protocols, they are quite literally the backbone of modern businesses.

STEP 2: Activity

Imagine that you work in the billing department of a midsized hospital. Recently, your supervisor stated that team effectiveness had not declined at all due to COVID and that they had decided to repurpose the billing department office space. You would now begin to work from home permanently and would be reimbursed for setting up your home office and for your home Internet connection. The only requirement is that you finalize the same number of bills each day from home as you did in the office. You can schedule your own time as long as your work gets done.

Visit the links associated with this activity to watch a few videos about telecommuting.

STEP 3: Deliverable

Describe the wireline communication media and the transmission technologies (protocols) that you will need to be able to telecommute. Your description should (at a minimum) include the home Internet connection, use of the Web, and connections within the office. It should also describe the protocols that operate to support these connections. Submit your description to your instructor.

Apply the Concept 6.3

LEARNING OBJECTIVE 6.3

Describe the most common methods for accessing the Internet.

STEP 1: Background

Section 6.3 has explained the difference between the Internet and the World Wide Web. Although many people use these terms interchangeably, they are very different. Most computers today are continuously connected to the Internet, though they are not always accessing the Web. Offices and other places of employment typically set up an Internet connection via a local area network (LAN). However, at home you have several options to consider.

STEP 2: Activity

Visit the links associated with this activity and watch the YouTube videos listed there. These videos go into a little more detail about the types of connections mentioned in Table 6.2. You will learn about advantages, disadvantages, and things to consider for the different methods of connecting to the Internet.

STEP 3: Deliverable

Imagine that your parents are "technologically challenged" (some of you may not have to imagine). They have just bought a house at the beach and they are getting ready to set up an Internet connection. At home, there is only one provider, so DSL versus cable versus cellular versus satellite is not an issue. However, there are several options at the beach and your parents do not know where to begin.

Compose an e-mail to your parents that describes the most common methods for accessing the Internet to help them develop criteria for making their choice.

Apply the Concept 6.4

LEARNING OBJECTIVE 6.4

Explain the impact that discovery network applications have had on business and everyday life.

STEP 1: Background

Section 6.4 has introduced you to the discovery aspect of networks, specifically the Web. Search engines (of all kinds) open up doors of knowledge for anyone with a question. Translation tools allow you to even discover your answer from other languages. These, however, are very broad tools. Portals help by focusing your search within a narrow realm of information. They also push very specific information to you rather than waiting on you to request everything.

STEP 2: Activity

Before there were online search tools, there was the library card catalog. It was a method of organizing information in a library so that you could easily retrieve the information you needed. Today, research is handled very differently. Access the link associated with this activity to watch a video about the use of the "old-school" library card catalog.

STEP 3: Deliverable

Search the Web for the book referenced in the YouTube video linked above. Use multiple search engines (such as google.com, yahoo.com, or bing.com), some meta search engines (such as dogpile.com or excite.com), and your school's library system. Make note of the amount of and type of information you are able to find in just a few minutes about the book referenced in the YouTube video above. Write a paragraph that compares your experience to the card catalog system.

Now think even bigger. If discovery applications have made this much impact on something as simple as finding a book (or information on the book), how much bigger is the impact on business and everyday life? Prepare a second paragraph that discusses the latter question.

Submit both paragraphs to your instructor.

Apply the Concept 6.5

LEARNING OBJECTIVE 6.5

Explain the impact that communication network applications have had on business and everyday life.

WILEY PLUS

This activity requires visiting an external url links. Url links are available within *WileyPLUS*. If you do not have *WileyPLUS*, ask your instructor to provide the link.

STEP 1: Background

Section 6.5 has introduced you to the communication aspect of networks that have radically changed the way humans interact with each other. Most of these methods of communication are even available on our mobile devices now via a cellular connection. Such drastic changes have brought about many struggles and possibilities for businesses.

STEP 2: Activity

The methods that we use to communicate today vary greatly from just 50 years ago. Accessthe link associated with this activity to watch a YouTube video about how communication has changed. While it only goes up to 1965, you will still recognize the situations and the uses of improved communications.

STEP 3: Deliverable

Consider the various uses of communications in the video (work, personal, military, emergency, etc.). How do our modern technologies such as Internet, video, mobile, and text impact what is possible on these types of communication? Create a list of the ways that the technologies discussed in this section have changed the way we communicate on a personal level, at work, in emergencies, and in military situations and give a brief explanation of each. Discuss at least three changes for each area of communication. Submit your answers to your professor.

Apply the Concept 6.6

WILEY PLUS

This activity requires visiting an external url link. Url links are available within *WileyPLUS*. If you do not have *WileyPLUS*, ask your instructor to provide the link.

LEARNING OBJECTIVE 6.6

Explain the impact that collaboration network applications have had on business and everyday life.

STEP 1: Background

As you have seen, collaboration tools impact people inside and outside the organization. Some collaboration tools allow geographically separated employees to work together, while some allow those across the hall to work more effectively. Other tools just allow larger groups to brainstorm and be creative. The big idea here is that there is synergy created when people are able to work together via digital tools that overcome time and space.

STEP 2: Activity

Brightidea provides a suite of products that touches on many of the topics in the chapter. Access the link associated with this activity and watch the YouTube video that introduces the company. Then click the second link to visit the Brightidea website. There are several case studies, videos, and product explanations that will help you understand what this product offers.

STEP 3: Deliverable

As you peruse Brightidea's website, look for evidence that the software supports the topics discussed in this section: workflow, virtual collaboration, crowdsourcing, and teleconferencing. Prepare a set of presentation slides (use any tool at your disposal or at your instructor's request) that discusses the impact that collaboration network applications (such as Brightidea's products) have had on businesses. Present your slides to your class and professor.

Apply the Concept 6.7

WILEY PLUS

This activity requires visiting an external url link. Url links are available within *WileyPLUS*. If you do not have *WileyPLUS*, ask your instructor to provide the link.

LEARNING OBJECTIVE 6.7

Explain the impact that educational network applications have had on business and everyday life.

STEP 1: Background

Imagine that you are an expert in math. Someone hands you a piece of chalk and a small chalkboard and gives you a task of creating an educational experience to share your knowledge with other people. You would probably create a traditional classroom. Now imagine that you are not handed chalk, but are given the Internet, video capabilities, file sharing, collaboration, tools, and more! Imagine the possibilities!

STEP 2: Activity

Access the link associated with this activity and view the first video, and then visit the website about Brightspace. Be sure to look at the video about how technology has changed education.

Brightspace (you may have heard it called by its former name, Desire2Learn) is a learning management system that several schools use as a platform to offer educational activities using the digital tools available today. This platform can be used to offer e-learning experiences, distance learning opportunities, or fully virtual classrooms.

There are many discussions about how these educational network applications impact an individual's everyday life. Single parents are able to go to school using educational network applications. Working professionals are able to pursue graduate degrees online. But what about the impact on businesses?

STEP 3: Deliverable

Many organizations use these tools to facilitate mandatory training or for onboarding new employees. Visit the secondlink associated with this activity and view the another video about Brightspace's enterprise offerings. Research their site to create and discuss a list of five ways that educational network applications impact businesses.

Apply the Concept 7.1

LEARNING OBJECTIVE 7.1

Describe the six common types of electronic commerce.

STEP 1: Background

Today, there are many companies that specialize in making e-commerce a reality for small businesses. Amazon, Yahoo!, PayPal, and other entities offer services that provide everything a small business needs to sell products and accept payment over the Internet. In fact, many consumers prefer that their transactions go through these larger global companies because they trust these companies' security.

STEP 2: Activity

Visit PayPal's website (www.paypal.com). Click on the business link at the top of the page. You will find that PayPal offers easy solutions for both businesses and customers.

STEP 3: Deliverable

Create and submit a table that lists and describes the six common types of e-commerce. Which ones are supported by PayPal and which are not? For the second group, can you explain why they are not supported? Should PayPal move into these areas of e-commerce as well?

Apply the Concept 7.2

LEARNING OBJECTIVE 7.2

Describe the various online services of business-to-consumer (B2C) commerce, along with specific examples of each.

STEP 1: Background

At this point in your "buying" career, you have probably purchased something online, visited an auction site (and possibly won a bid), and engaged in some form of online banking. Your generation is very comfortable with the retail side of e-commerce. While you were engaging in B2C e-commerce, you probably created an account with a few vendors and received some e-mail advertisements. No doubt you have also received some pop-up ads promoting products during your Internet searches. Another aspect of modern business that has changed is that companies now want you to do their advertising for them. The text refers to this development as viral marketing.

STEP 2: Activity

Imagine that you and some friends decide to start a new online thrift store. To become a member, an individual has to donate to the thrift. For every 10 items a person donates, he or she is awarded a two-month membership. However, you have no IT platform for e-commerce. After some research, you determine that Shopify is your best provider. Shopify is an e-commerce platform that enables individuals and businesses to create online stores.

Visit Shopify's website. Near the top of the page, you will see a link to "Examples" of other providers. Look through the examples to identify ideas you would like to incorporate into your store.

STEP 3: Deliverable

After reviewing the Shopify site, prepare a presentation or a document that describes the various online services of B2C commerce provided by Shopify. Provide specific examples of services that attracted your attention and discuss how you would apply these services to your store.

Apply the Concept 7.3

LEARNING OBJECTIVE 7.3

Describe the three business models for business-to-business electronic commerce.

STEP 1: Background

Section 7.3 describes forward auctions, reverse auctions, and exchanges. Forward auctions are used when a seller is trying to reach several buyers, and reverse auctions are used when a buyer is soliciting from several sellers. In an exchange, both buyers and sellers come to a central website to quickly and easily establish a B2B relationship. Some of these websites or exchanges are for materials involved in manufacturing a product; others involve materials that help run the business.

STEP 2: Activity

Visit the link associated with this activity. This link will take you to one of the horizontal exchanges (an exchange for many buyers and sellers across industries) listed in the section. As you examine the available products, you should get a better understanding of the breadth of a horizontal exchange.

STEP 3: Deliverable

Describe the three business models for B2B e-commerce by comparing and contrasting them to Globalsource. Submit your description to your professor.

Apply the Concept 7.4

LEARNING OBJECTIVE 7.4

Discuss the ethical and legal issues related to electronic commerce, along with examples.

STEP 1: Background

Amazon.com is the world's largest online retailer. In fact, it is one of a kind in many ways. It competes with Apple, Google, Microsoft, and Walmart, some of the biggest names in the tech and retail universe (online and in-store).

However, for many years there was a huge controversy surrounding Amazon. Specifically, the retailer did not collect sales tax in all states. A recent Supreme Court decision in 2017 has changed that.

STEP 2: Activity

Read the article in the *Los Angeles Times* titled "Small retailers who sold through Amazon are facing a tax time bomb" from May 1, 2019. What do you think about the Supreme Court decision and California's subsequent actions?

STEP 3: Deliverable

Take a little time to consider this controversy. Then, create a list of arguments for and against California's new requirements. Make certain your argument identifies both the ethical and legal aspects of this issue.

Apply the Concept 8.1

LEARNING OBJECTIVE 8.1

Identify advantages and disadvantages of each of the four main types of wireless transmission media.

WILEY PLUS

This activity requires visiting an external url link. Url links are available within *WileyPLUS*. If you do not have *WileyPLUS*, ask your instructor to provide the link.

STEP 1: Background

As stated in this section, mobile communication has changed our world more rapidly and dramatically than any other technology. Although several wireless transmission media are available, rarely will one technology meet all of a business's needs by itself. For example, several industrial sites are too large for Wi-Fi but are not conducive for LTE or 5G cellular connections. Rajant (www.rajant.com) mesh networks provide access through mobile nodes or "breadcrumbs" to provide reliable network speeds in a cost effective manner.

STEP 2: Activity

Visit the link associated with this activity and watch the video where Rajant demonstrates how their technology can overcome the limitations of cellular and Wi-Fi wireless connections.

STEP 3: Deliverable

As you watch the video, pay attention to the industrial illustrations depicted. Write a summary of the usefulness of mesh networks in these environments. Also, come up with and discuss at least one additional environment where a mesh network would be beneficial.

Apply the Concept 8.2

LEARNING OBJECTIVE 8.2

Explain how businesses can use technology employed by short-range, medium-range, and long-range networks, respectively.

STEP 1: Background

Many cellular phones today, including both Apple and Android devices, contain multiple radios. These include cellular, Bluetooth, Wi-Fi, infrared, GPS, and NFC chips. With all of these radios embedded in a small mobile device, the possibilities of connectivity are nearly endless because one device can utilize short-range, mid-range, and wide-range connectivity.

STEP 2: Activity

Visit the link associated with this activity and view the video demonstration by Serial IO. There is also a link to their website, where you will find several examples of wireless products intended for business use. Although most of these products are short-range devices, you must assume they will be connected to some mid-range and/or wide-range wireless network. In fact, these devices support Windows, Mac, Android, iOS, BlackBerry, and other platforms.

STEP 3: Deliverable

Based on the video and the Serial IO website, create and submit a table to explain how businesses can use the technologies employed by short-range, medium-range, and long-range networks to achieve their business purposes.

Apply the Concept 8.3

LEARNING OBJECTIVE 8.3

Provide a specific example of how each of the five major m-commerce applications can benefit a business.

STEP 1: Background

Section 8.3 introduced you to five of the most popular mobile commerce applications. These applications are location-based applications, financial services, intrabusiness applications, accessing information, and telemetry. Although you may not have had experience with each of these, it is likely that you have experienced some.

STEP 2: Activity

Read (or reread) the section and consider the following questions related to your personal experiences with mobile commerce: Do you use a mobile wallet? Has using a mobile wallet replaced your traditional wallet? What location-based services do you allow on your mobile device? Do you freely share your location, or are you more private? What type of intrabusiness applications do you utilize as an employee or customer of an organization? What type of information do you access on a regular basis? Do you utilize any telemetry information (such as a wireless connection to your vehicle computer to record information on your mobile phone)?

STEP 3: Deliverable

Based on your answers to the questions in Step 2, build a table that provides a brief discussion of how each of the five major m-commerce applications benefit businesses and provide your personal experiences with each.

Apply the Concept 8.4

LEARNING OBJECTIVE 8.4

Describe the Internet of Things, along with examples of how organizations can utilize the Internet of Things.

WILEY PLUS

This activity requires visiting an external url link. Url links are available within *WileyPLUS*. If you do not have *WileyPLUS*, ask your instructor to provide the link.

STEP 1: Background

Section 8.4 has introduced the concept of the Internet of Things (IoT) and provided several examples. There is no doubt that the IoT will continue to grow and shape our lives. Many industries will change from reactive (correcting problems after they happen) to proactive (acting to prevent problems before they happen based on IoT data).

STEP 2: Activity

Visit the link associated with this activity and watch the YouTube video. It describes examples of personal applications of IoT and professional uses of IoT. After watching the video, let your mind wander into the future to a time when everything is connected via the IoT—not just the devices mentioned in the video (like your car) but also your coffee pot, bed, clothes, closet door, front door, toothbrush, and so much more.

STEP 3: Deliverable

Write a paragraph or two to first describe the IoT, and then provide current examples of how it has impacted your life and is currently making a difference for businesses and industries. Finally, provide a few ideas of how the IoT will shape the future.

Apply the Concept 9.1

LEARNING OBJECTIVE 9.1

Describe five Web 2.0 tools and the two major types of Web 2.0 sites.

STEP 1: Background

This section differentiates Web 1.0, which consists of places to visit, from Web 2.0, where users interact and share information. Whether or not you have thought of these media in these terms, you are familiar with these differences. No doubt you are much more accustomed to Web 2.0, and businesses have begun to integrate information sharing into their public sites.

STEP 2: Activity

Visit the link associated with this activity. This video provides a valuable overview of Web 2.0 technologies. Take notes of the various features that Web 2.0 makes available, and then click on the second link. This link will take you to a CNN Money Web page that provides a rank-order list of the Fortune 500 companies. Visit the websites of the top 10 firms and identify the Web 2.0 technologies they employ on their site.

STEP 3: Deliverable

Create a table that displays the following information about 5 of the top 10 companies on the CNN Money rankings:

- The company's name
- The company's rank
- The industry (e.g., retail, consulting services, communications)
- A description of the Web 2.0 technologies/applications that each company uses
- A description of the Web 2.0 tools the company does not use

Submit your table to your professor.

Apply the Concept 9.2

LEARNING OBJECTIVE 9.2

Describe the benefits and risks of social commerce to companies.

STEP 1: Background

Collaborative consumption has been fueled by social networks because it allows owners to share their goods with those who would rather rent something than permanently own it. Sharing also makes items cheaper to own because the cost of ownership is spread across many users. The sharing economy has changed drastically in recent years as companies like Uber and Airbnb continue to gain in popularity, and social media has driven this rise.

STEP 2: Activity

Visit https://davidbuckingham.net/ and read his 2017 critique, "Media and the Sharing Economy." Now think about how you can apply these lessons to bike sharing. Look up a company called Citi Bike.

STEP 3: Deliverable

Many of these companies, including Citi Bike, got their start in big cities. Why do you think they started in such heavily populated areas? What advantages would a collaborative consumption business model have in a heavily populated area? What disadvantages would they face? In what ways might a college campus be a prime location to introduce users to collaborative consumption services? Create a table that compares the advantages and disadvantages of collaborative consumption for the biking industry. Submit your table to your instructor.

Apply the Concept 9.3

LEARNING OBJECTIVE 9.3

Identify the methods used for shopping socially.

STEP 1: Background

Section 9.3 defines shopping socially as taking the key aspects of social networks (e.g., groups, reviews, discussions) and applying them to shopping. This phenomenon is not new. People have shopped socially for years, through general conversation.

Today, most consumers conduct a lot of research before they make a purchase by reading reviews posted by other customers. Recently, however, the validity of these reviews has been questioned. As you learn about social shopping, you should also become aware of the potential fraud that takes place online.

STEP 2: Activity

Visit www.wired.com/story/how-to-spot-fake-reviews-amazon/ and read this article about how to spot falsified recommendations and ratings. Talk to some of your classmates about this topic and record their feedback. How did they respond to the fact that product ratings may not be legitimate? Ask them the following questions:

- What star rating do you rely on when you are considering a product?
- Do you read reviews or simply notice the number of stars?
- If you read reviews, do you read only the good ones, only the bad ones, or a mixture of both?
- Do you rely on reviews more than a third-party organization such as Consumer Reports?

STEP 3: Deliverable

Considering the material you have read and your conversations with your classmates, identify various methods of shopping socially and discuss the role that trust plays in each method. Prepare a paper or presentation for your professor documenting what you have learned.

Apply the Concept 9.4

WILEY PLUS

This activity requires visiting an external url link. Url links are available within *WileyPLUS*. If you do not have *WileyPLUS*, ask your instructor to provide the link.

LEARNING OBJECTIVE 9.4

Discuss innovative ways to use social networking sites for advertising and market research.

STEP 1: Background

Section 9.4 presented the major uses of social computing in advertising and market research. Social advertising is simply a way of presenting information to potential customers via a social platform. Social market research makes use of these same social platforms to examine the ongoing communication between the company and its customer community for information that the company can use to improve products or services.

STEP 2: Activity

Access the links associated with this activity. First, read the article called "20 Companies You Should Be Following on Social Media." Some of these companies are not specifically related to advertising or market research, but you will still enjoy learning about them. Next, read the article on Digimind.com about the innovative ways people are using social media as a rich pool of information.

STEP 3: Deliverable

After reviewing the examples in the articles linked in Step 2, prepare a discussion of the top three innovative ways that these companies are using social networking for advertising and the top three innovative ways that companies are using the information available on social networks as a mechanism for learning about their customers. Submit your discussion to your instructor.

Apply the Concept 9.5

LEARNING OBJECTIVE 9.5

Describe how social computing improves customer service.

STEP 1: Background

Social customer relationship management involves using social networks to maintain customer loyalty. One company that employs this strategy quite skillfully is ZAGG (Zealous About Great Gadgets; www.zagg.com). ZAGG makes and sells accessories for mobile devices such as smartphones and tablets. To help sell its products, the company has developed one of the best social customer relationship management plans around.

When ZAGG develops a new product, it not only posts notes about the product on its social networking page, but it also involves customers in the process. For example, when ZAGG was releasing its ZAGGFolio for the iPad, the company allowed fans to vote on the colors of the new product.

ZAGG is also proficient at monitoring the social network for product-related issues. It is not uncommon for a customer to complain and then receive feedback from a ZAGG employee. Not only does the company retain that individual customer, but it also develops a sense of trust with all of its customers, who are confident they would receive the same treatment.

STEP 2: Activity

Visit ZAGG's website. At the bottom of the page you will find a link to all of the company's social networks. Visit their Facebook page and review their timeline. Search for customer complaints and for how the company deals with them. Did you find a customer representative present on the social networking site? Does the site offer any competitions? Polls? Give-aways? Can you reverse-engineer the company's social customer relationship management methodology?

STEP 3: Deliverable

Imagine that you are a marketing manager, and you have been selected to present a report to the president to describe how social computing improves customer service. Create the outline that you would use to make your points and present it to the class and to your instructor.

Apply the Concept 9.6

LEARNING OBJECTIVE 9.6

Discuss different ways in which human resource managers make use of social computing.

STEP 1: Background

Social human resource management is redefining the ways we search and apply for jobs and make hiring decisions. Going digital was a natural step, but it was also an awkward one. When position announcements went from the bulletin board and local newspaper to Monster.com, the number of positions and applicants exploded. We are so connected today that it is impossible to go back. After you graduate, you will no doubt use social networks to find and apply for jobs.

STEP 2: Activity

Visit LinkedIn, a professional social network. Create a profile that includes the college you currently attend. Connect to your classmates as they also complete this activity. You never know when you will need to call on one of these individuals.

Next, search the Web for "job search websites," and see which ones will allow you to connect with your LinkedIn profile. As you connect with these professional sites, consider the differences between a professional and a personal social network.

STEP 3: Deliverable

In a paper, discuss the various ways in which human resources managers can make use of social computing and how you can best present yourself online. Present your paper to your instructor.

Apply the Concept 10.1

LEARNING OBJECTIVE 10.1

Explain the purpose of transaction processing systems.

STEP 1: Background

Section 10.1 has explained that transaction processing systems (TPS) capture data and then automatically transmit those data to the various functional area systems. Most TPS are designed based on an organization's existing processes. To better understand how a TPS operates, you should consider the flow of data through the student application process.

STEP 2: Activity

Access the link associated with this activity. This link will take you to a Web page that describes the process of creating data flow diagrams (DFDs). The page uses the example of a college student application to demonstrate the flow of data through a university. Review this description and identify the transactions that take place throughout the process.

STEP 3: Deliverable

Consider your student application process. Are there any pieces of your application that you feel were handled differently than the example described? Prepare a short description of the application process described in the video and discuss the purpose of the TPS for this process.

Apply the Concept 10.2

LEARNING OBJECTIVE 10.2

Explain the types of support that information systems can provide for each functional area of the organization.

STEP 1: Background

Section 10.2 introduced you to the concept of functional area information systems (FAIS). As you can see, every area of business has processes in place that define how data are stored, analyzed, applied, and distributed across the area. For example, inventory management is easy to manage with a computer system because it involves simply keeping track of your materials and products. However, when you integrate inventory management with production and operations management (POM), you have a very effective functional system that supports the internal production line.

STEP 2: Activity

Access the links associated with this activity. You will be directed to four websites that present real-world examples of the information systems discussed in this section. Read over them, and look for any specific material that you can tie back into the concepts covered in the chapter.

STEP 3: Deliverable

Prepare a report that explains the types of support the IS reviewed in Step 2 can provide for each functional area within an organization. Submit your report to your instructor.

Apply the Concept 10.3

LEARNING OBJECTIVE 10.3

Identify advantages and drawbacks to businesses implementing an enterprise resource planning system.

STEP 1: Background

Section 10.3 explained that enterprise resource planning (ERP) works toward removing information silos within an organization by implementing a single system to support all of the functional areas. One example of an ERP system is SAP Business One. SAP is an industry-leading ERP company. In this activity, you will consider the advantages and drawbacks of using an ERP such as SAP.

STEP 2: Activity

Access the link associated with this activity. This link will take you to a YouTube video titled *SAP-Business-One*. As you watch the video, consider how many departments the representative would have to contact to find the information that SAP Business One can present in just a few moments. If this organization operated out of silos, the representative would have to take extensive notes, visit multiple departments, and call the customer back at a later time with the answers.

STEP 3: Deliverable

After considering how complicated it would be for OEC to handle the customer's requests without an ERP, identify the advantages and drawbacks to OEC of using the SAP Business One ERP. Submit your thoughts to your professor.

Apply the Concept 10.4

LEARNING OBJECTIVE 10.4

Describe the three main business processes supported by ERP systems.

STEP 1: Background

We have discussed reports that you can receive from TPS, FAIS, and ERP systems earlier in this chapter. In particular, these reports truly are the power of an ERP. Getting the right information to the right person at the right time to make the right decision is the underlying purpose for installing and utilizing an ERP. Recall from earlier in the text that managers need IT decision-support tools because decisions are becoming more complex, there is less time to make decisions, there are more options, and the costs of making incorrect decisions are increasing.

STEP 2: Activity

Access the link associated with this activity. This link will take you to a YouTube video titled Phoebus *ERP—Customized Dashboard*. This video will introduce you to the dashboard tool provided by Phoebus, which individual users can customize to provide the specific information they need. This type of dashboard pulls together the many reports you have learned about in this chapter. As you watch the video, look for examples of the three major types of processes (procurement, fulfillment, and production) that are supported by ERP systems as discussed in this section.

STEP 3: Deliverable

Discuss the three major types of processes and the ways that an ERP can support them. Use what you learned in the dashboard video to discuss the types of information that could be presented in a dashboard to support these processes.

Apply the Concept 11.1

LEARNING OBJECTIVE 11.1

Identify the primary functions of both customer relationship management (CRM) and collaborative CRM strategies.

STEP 1: Background

Section 11.1 introduced the concept of a CRM system, and it suggested that it is better to focus on relationships than on transactions. The idea is that relationships create transactions, so if you grow the relationship, you keep the customers (and the transactions)!

STEP 2: Activity

Access the link associated with this activity. This link will take you to a YouTube video that illustrates how Recreational Equipment Incorporated (REI) uses CRM to service their customers.

STEP 3: Deliverable

In a report, identify the primary functions of both customer relationship management (CRM) and collaborative CRM strategies. What are REI's approaches to CRM? Can you make any suggestions to help them improve? Submit your report to your professor.

Apply the Concept 11.2

LEARNING OBJECTIVE 11.2

Describe how businesses might utilize applications of each of the two major components of operational CRM systems.

STEP 1: Background

Section 11.2 introduced you to the concept of customer-facing and customer-touching CRM applications, the two major components of operational CRM systems. Many organizations use a combination of both types of systems to establish, develop, and maintain relationships with consumers. This activity will help you to see these systems in action when you do business on a website or in a brick-and-mortar business.

STEP 2: Activity

Visit a physical store where you like to shop (or recall a recent visit and discuss it with some friends), and visit the store's website. Make certain to select a company that has both an Internet site and a physical store so you can compare the two channels.

As you walked through the store, did you notice any cues that could tie a customer to a CRM? Did the business have a customer loyalty program? Are there any significant advantages to joining the program? Is the in-store membership tied to anything online? If so, how? Or, does the store seem to have separate in-store and online memberships?

STEP 3: Deliverable

After considering the points mentioned in Step 2, describe how businesses might utilize both the customer-facing and customer-touching applications of a CRM to integrate the online and traditional shopping experiences. Prepare a report and submit it to your instructor.

Apply the Concept 11.3

LEARNING OBJECTIVE 11.3

Explain the advantages and disadvantages of mobile CRM systems, on-demand CRM systems, open-source CRM systems, social CRM systems, and real-time CRM systems.

WILEY PLUS

This activity requires visiting an external url link. Url links are available within *WileyPLUS*. If you do not have *WileyPLUS*, ask your instructor to provide the link.

STEP 1: Background

Section 11.3 has outlined different CRM systems—not operational or analytical, but, instead, the different ways you can actually implement a CRM system. For example, you can run mobile CRM, open-source CRM, on-demand CRM (cloud), and more. You will have most—if not all—of these options with any system you plan to implement!

STEP 2: Activity

Access the links associated with this activity. One link will take you to a YouTube video that describes an on-demand CRM system (Salesforce). Another will take you to a video that highlights an open-source CRM (Sugar CRM). The final link will illustrate a hybrid approach, Sales Cloud (mobile-cloud CRM). Watch these videos, paying special attention to the advantages and disadvantages of each approach. The advantages will be easy to spot (these are promotional videos). The disadvantages of each one will become obvious as you compare the advantages of the others because you may notice particular functions that system one cannot perform but the others can.

STEP 3: Deliverable

Build a table that highlights the advantages and disadvantages of each approach. Do the differences reside in the capabilities of the software or in the user experience? Submit your table to your instructor.

Apply the Concept 11.4

LEARNING OBJECTIVE 11.4

Describe the three components and the three flows of a supply chain.

STEP 1: Background

Section 11.4 focused on supply chain flows, materials, and "positions" (upstream, internal, and downstream). It is important to understand how products move in the supply chain because data move along with them every step of the way. In fact, the data that travel with materials and products are more important to the efficiency of the operation than the products themselves!

STEP 2: Activity

Visit http://www.wiley.com/go/rainer/IS9e/applytheconcept and click on the link provided for Apply the Concept 11.4 Access the link associated with this activity. This link will take you to a YouTube video titled *What Is Supply Chain Management?* As you watch the video, consider the data that would be transferred with each product movement within the bottled water supply chain. Certain types of data, such as inventory updates, shipment information, quality checks, and supplier information, would deal just with the bottled water itself. In addition, there will be HR information, employee data, and machine data from the internal organization as well as from all of the suppliers!

STEP 3: Deliverable

Using the example you learned about in Step 2, describe the three components and the three flows of a water bottle supply chain in a report. Submit your report to your instructor.

Apply the Concept 11.5

LEARNING OBJECTIVE 11.5

Identify popular strategies to solving different challenges of supply chains.

STEP 1: Background

Section 11.5 explained that managing a supply chain is not a simple task because consumer demand is so uncertain. Although organizations can forecast demand with some accuracy, actual demand almost inevitably will differ from the organizations' predictions. To manage demand fluctuations, organizations are moving toward JIT (just-in-time) inventory models. These data must be shared in a timely fashion if organizations are to remain flexible and capable of adapting to consumer demand.

STEP 2: Activity

Access the links associated with this activity. The first link will take you to an article that examines how the bullwhip effect wreaks havoc on the supply chain, and the second will take you to an activity in which you will manage a supply chain for beer. This latter task might not sound difficult until you consider that there are serious timing issues due to the perishable nature of the product. The simulation begins with your supply chain in equilibrium, but it then suddenly shifts. Your job is to put things back in order!

As you work through the simulation, pay attention to how much information needs to be shared across the supply chain to make the entire operation function smoothly.

STEP 3: Deliverable

Based on your experience, discuss how the popular strategies for dealing with supply chain challenges (building inventory, JIT inventory, vendor-managed inventory) would or would not work for this product. Write a report and submit it to your instructor.

Apply the Concept 11.6

LEARNING OBJECTIVE 11.6

Explain the utility of each of the three major technologies that support supply chain management.

STEP 1: Background

Electronic data interchange (EDI) is defined in this section as a communication standard that enables business partners to exchange routine documents, such as purchasing orders, electronically. You should understand the need for electronic sharing of information if you completed the activity in Apply the Concept 11.6. That activity required you to manage a supply chain on your own. Imagine the challenge of performing this function without being able to share data electronically!

STEP 2: Activity

Access the link associated with this activity. The link will take you to a YouTube video titled *What is EDI*. You will also link to an article that defines EDI and discusses some of its standards.

As you watch the video, pay attention to the important components that are necessary to share information between two organizations. Then, consider the fact that suppliers rarely operate in only a single supply chain. In fact, suppliers typically have multiple customers, which means they are sharing information with many organizations via EDI.

STEP 3: Deliverable

Based on the content of this section and the video you watched in Step 2, explain the utility of each of the three major technologies (EDI, extranets, and corporate portals) that support supply chain management. In other words, how might these technologies interact to enable the participating parties to exchange data? Put your explanation in a report and submit it to your instructor.

Apply the Concept 12.1

LEARNING OBJECTIVE 12.1

Use a decision support framework to demonstrate how technology supports managerial decision making at each phase of the decision-making process.

STEP 1: Background

If you look back through this section, you will see that Henry Mintzberg's 1973 book, *The Nature of Managerial Work*, was referenced when the three basic roles of a manager were presented. This text focuses on the decisional role because that is the one that is most supported by information systems. However, Mintzberg's work goes well beyond the decisional role.

STEP 2: Activity

Access the link associated with this activity. The link will take you to a YouTube video titled *Data-Driven Decision Making*. This video mentions a strategic plan, operational control, and decisional control. As you view the video, make certain to watch for these key points, and pay special attention to how they are supported by data.

STEP 3: Deliverable

Write a short paper (a couple of paragraphs is plenty) for your professor that will identify the phases in the decision-making process for Minnetonka Schools. Be sure to demonstrate how technology supports their decision making in each phase.

Apply the Concept 12.2

LEARNING OBJECTIVE 12.2

Describe each phase of the business analytics process.

STEP 1: Background

In this section you learned that BA is a concept that encompasses everything from the collection, analysis, and dissemination of data to the technology tools that enable this process to take place. In particular, organizations use BA to support the following:

- Specific departmental needs
- Organizational change

STEP 2: Activity

There are several companies that provide data management and BA tools to help make decisions. Two of these companies are Avitas and Intricity. Access the link associated withthis activity to watch a short YouTube video about BA by each of these companies. While you watch, look for examples of how their tools support departments, enterprises, and/or organizational change.

STEP 3: Deliverable

Write a short description of how Avitas and Intricity help users work through the BA process (see Figure 12.3). Try to show how the process is supported, but also be aware that there might be gaps. Make note of any areas for improvement as well, if you find any.

Apply the Concept 12.3

LEARNING OBJECTIVE 12.3

Describe each of the various analytics tools and examples of their uses.

STEP 1: Background

This section explained that data are more abundant today than ever before. One thing we are learning is that there is much we can know that we do not know. In fact, there are many questions we are not even aware we should be asking! For such questions, we use multidimensional analysis and data-mining tools to extract valuable insights from the data. When we know the questions, we frequently employ decision support systems to run sensitivity, what-if, or goal-seeking analysis.

STEP 2: Activity

Consider your university. Various departments focus on teaching, student academic support, financial aid, admissions, recruitment, administration, and much more. Each of these departments has its special purpose, but overall the enterprise exists to support student learning.

Visit your university's website, and look for these various functions. What can you learn about their purpose? Based on this knowledge, what can you imply about the types of BA applications they might use?

STEP 3: Deliverable

Within the context of higher education, describe the various tools and provide an example of how each could be used to support your campus. Submit your response to your instructor.

Apply the Concept 12.4

LEARNING OBJECTIVE 12.4

Provide a definition and a use case example for predictive analytics.

STEP 1: Background

According to the text, predictive analytics attempts to detect patterns that can be used to predict, or forecast, future events. While trends change, when you look at them over time, they can show periods of growth and decline. This information is invaluable to managers who are required to make decisions about resource allocation to prepare for the future.

STEP 2: Activity

Imagine that you work for a fast-food restaurant. You have been there for a long time, but the new boss is just figuring things out. Last week, your boss stopped you and asked for some help planning labor for various times of the day and days of the week. Obviously, once the crowd arrives it is too late to bring in more labor. But the restaurant cannot afford to keep a full staff all of the time. What kind of analytics could help?

STEP 3: Deliverable

Put together a short report for your boss that defines predictive analytics and explains how you intend to use them in the restaurant. Use the example above to give context to the solution. Discuss ways that data from past weeks, months, and years can help inform patterns that can be used to determine labor needs for the future.

Apply the Concept 12.5

LEARNING OBJECTIVE 12.5

Provide a definition and a use case example for descriptive analytics, predictive analytics, and prescriptive analytics.

STEP 1: Background

Section 12.5 discusses descriptive, predictive, and prescriptive analytics. Descriptive analytics describe what has happened, predictive analytics predict what might happen, and prescriptive analytics prescribe probabilities to future outcomes based on future activities.

STEP 2: Activity

Access the link associated with this activity. This link will take you to a video that describes prescriptive analytics to help a rock climber determine the best path to the top based on certain decisions. While this is a simple example, it illustrates the need to think past the next choice and to see how this choice will impact the overall probability of reaching the desired outcome.

STEP 3: Deliverable

Based on the video and any of your own Web research, describe and give examples of how a rock climber might use descriptive analytics, predictive analytics, and prescriptive analytics to determine the best path to the goal.

Apply the Concept 12.6

LEARNING OBJECTIVE 12.6

Identify and discuss two examples of presentation tools.

STEP 1: Background

Visual aids have been around for a long time. In fact, most of our communication is through visual aids. Letters represent sounds and from them, we can put together words and meaning. Additionally, today a growing number of messages are sent primarily using emojis! Liking pictures and images on Instagram or similar platform is a regular activity for many people. Sharing data is no different. Graphs and charts have been used for years to help viewers quickly grasp the meaning of data.

STEP 2: Activity

Imagine that you manage a children's clothing store. Each month you make decisions on products, quantities, prices, timing of sales, and much more. What kind of information do you think you would you like to see? Sales by department? Sales over time? Product line comparisons? What else?

STEP 3: Deliverable

Sketch an example of a dashboard that would provide at least six visual aids to understand the data you might want to see as a clothing store manager.

Apply the Concept 13.1

LEARNING OBJECTIVE 13.1

Discuss the different cost–benefit analyses that companies must take into account when formulating an IT strategic plan.

WILEY PLUS

This activity requires visiting an external url links. Url links are available within *WileyPLUS*. If you do not have *WileyPLUS*, ask your instructor to provide the link.

STEP 1: Background

You may not realize it, but you perform cost–benefit analyses all the time. Imagine that you want to go to the beach for the weekend, but you decide not to because you would have to drive eight hours each way and therefore would not get to spend much time there. In this case, the costs outweigh the benefits. However, if you could extend your stay another day, then the benefits might outweigh the costs. The difficulty in this example is that the benefits are difficult to measure. A cost–benefit analysis is designed to quantify all of the key elements, and sometimes there are subjective benefits for which there are no clear-cut numerical values.

STEP 2: Activity

Acess the links associated with this activity. You will watch three short videos that offer a financial explanation for net present value (NPV), return on investment (ROI), and break-even analysis. The business case approach is not a financial approach, and it does not require further explanation.

STEP 3: Deliverable

Imagine you are creating a website to sell promotional items. You have no experience developing a site, so you will have to pay someone to do this for you. You research this service and discover that the site you have in mind will cost $3,500. (For this example, assume there are no monthly hosting fees.) This design will last five years, after which you will need to update it. You anticipate that you can make $500 in year 1, $750 in year 2, $750 in year 3, $1,000 in year 4, and $1,500 in year 5 from the site. Calculate the NPV, ROI, and break-even analysis for this case, and discuss which metric is most helpful. Also, explain how a business case analysis would be helpful beyond what the numbers provide. Prepare a document with your figures and present it to your instructor.

Apply the Concept 13.2

LEARNING OBJECTIVE 13.2

Discuss the four business decisions that companies must make when they acquire new applications.

STEP 1: Background

Section 13.2 discusses the many options available to acquire information systems. One of the more popular methods is software-as-a-service (SaaS). SaaS is popular because it eliminates the need for the company purchasing the software to maintain the hardware on which the software will run. They simply need an Internet connection to access the software from the host company.

STEP 2: Activity

Access the links associated with this activity. There are two videos linked there that illustrate SaaS. As you watch these videos, consider the types of hardware that are required on both sides of the relationship. Also, give some thought to the legal nature of the relationship, given that the data will likely reside with the service provider.

STEP 3: Deliverable

Imagine that a company has decided to use an SaaS model to acquire a new piece of software. Prepare a paper discussing the four business decisions they have made in light of this type of acquisition. Submit your paper to your instructor.

Apply the Concept 13.3

LEARNING OBJECTIVE 13.3

Enumerate the primary tasks and the importance of each of the six processes involved in the systems development life cycle.

STEP 1: Background

The systems development life cycle uses a very systematic approach in which each stage builds on work completed at an earlier stage. It is an excellent model to follow, assuming that the right decisions are made at each stage of the SDLC and are appropriately communicated to the next stage of the SDLC.

STEP 2: Activity

Access the link associated with this activity and watch the video titled *Software Development Life Cycle*. The video conveys a realistic (though perhaps a bit pessimistic) view of how poor communication can severely damage the software-development process.

STEP 3: Deliverable

After watching the video, build an outline that specifies the primary tasks and the importance of each of the six processes involved in the SDLC. Make certain to discuss the importance of communication from one step to the next.

Apply the Concept 13.4

LEARNING OBJECTIVE 13.4

Describe alternative development methods and the tools that augment development methods.

STEP 1: Background

The systems development life cycle is a very thorough method of development. However, it is also very time consuming and expensive. Section 13.4 discusses several alternative methods. Joint application design, rapid application development, and agile development are used in conjunction with several tools for systems development.

STEP 2: Activity

Access the link associated with this activity. This link will take you to a Vimeo about prototyping. Imagine that you are a developer of iPhone apps. At lunch the other day, someone mentioned a very cool idea for a new camera app that would enable users to take pictures simply by opening the app and saying "click" rather than having to push a button.

Describe the idea to a couple of friends to develop a list of user needs and preferences. From this list, make a sketch of the app. Then let the same people review your design and make suggestions. Use the second set of suggestions to create your "final" drawings of the app.

STEP 3: Deliverable

Write a short report documenting the alternative development methods you have used and how the tools discussed in this section might help you to actually develop your app. Be sure to mention how you might use different tools at different stages of development.

Apply the Concept 14.1

LEARNING OBJECTIVE 14.1

Explain the potential value and the potential limitations of artificial intelligence.

STEP 1: Background

This section introduced you to several applications of artificial intelligence. One of these applications was the Google self-driving car. This innovation presents a scenario in which technology could potentially greatly enhance the safety of motorists, pedestrians, and passengers. However, there are also significant risks posed by turning over the keys to the computer.

STEP 2: Activity

Visit YouTube and watch the video titled *Self-Driving Car Test: Steve Mahan* that introduces the Google self-driving car. Although this innovation is very exciting, it can also be very scary! While you are watching the video, imagine the advantages and disadvantages of this type of intelligent system. Would it function best as a "pilot" or a very helpful "copilot"?

STEP 3: Deliverable

Build a table that displays both the potential value (advantages) and the potential limitations (disadvantages) of artificial intelligence for different scenarios illustrated in the example below.

	Advantages	Disadvantages
Tired driver		
Distracted driver (texting)		
Sick/stressed driver		
Ambulance driver		
School bus driver		
Soccer mom, minivan driver		

Apply the Concept 14.2

LEARNING OBJECTIVE 14.2

Provide use case examples of expert systems, machine learning systems, deep learning systems, and neural networks.

STEP 1: Background

Throughout much of human history, expertise was transferred from a master to an apprentice through years of training. Only after the apprentice had mastered all of the "tricks of the trade" was he or she considered ready to perform on his or her own. We still employ a similar system for doctors, who must participate in a residency program under the guidance of the resident doctor before they can begin their own practice. This approach is not appropriate, however, for many non–life-threatening situations. In some cases, being able to make an expert decision is simply a matter of having access to the experts' knowledge and experiences. If this knowledge can be captured in a computer-based information system, then it can be distributed for other people to use in similar scenarios. Although this sounds great, there are many challenges to developing this type of system.

STEP 2: Activity

Acces the link associated with this activity. This video will show you a short demonstration of an expert cooking system. The video mentions that you are responsible for building and testing an expert system, but that is not part of this activity. As you watch the video, pay particular attention to the miscommunication between the cook and the computer. You will find this interaction to be quite comical.

STEP 3: Deliverable

Based on the video and material in this section, provide examples of the benefits, applications, and limitations of using artificial intelligence in the world of cooking. Create a Word document to submit to your instructor.

Apply the Concept 14.3

LEARNING OBJECTIVE 14.3

Describe the structure of a neural network and discuss how that structure contributes to the purpose of neural networks in machine learning.

STEP 1: Background

This section describes the structure of a neural network using terms such as nodes, synapses, weights, biases, and functions. This structure parallels the structure of the human brain, allowing computer systems to recognize patterns and create a means for identifying and predicting the future.

STEP 2: Activity

Reread the section examples about the convolutional neural networks. Pay special attention to the portion regarding the mistakes the system made. The system appeared to be learning and doing a good job identifying wolves and huskies. But in the end, it was not accurate at all.

STEP 3: Deliverable

Imagine a scenario where artificial intelligence is used to identify potential thieves. The system is given a series of videos, some of which include theft and some of which do not. What kind of potential problems do you anticipate? What limitations could exist in the outcomes? Answer these questions in an email to your instructor.

Apply the Concept 14.4

LEARNING OBJECTIVE 14.4

Provide use case examples (other than the ones in the text) of computer vision, natural language processing, robotics, image recognition, and intelligent agents.

STEP 1: Background

This section presented many interesting examples of AI. However, there are new technologies being developed each day. As hard as authors try, the time it takes to print a textbook always leaves us a few months behind the latest and greatest examples of technology.

STEP 2: Activity

Use your favorite search engine and look up each of the use cases presented in the text (computer vision, natural language processing, robotics, speech recognition, and intelligent agents) and see what companies are making headlines in these areas.

STEP 3: Deliverable

Build a table like the one below and include the new examples you have discovered.

Technology	Company	Product/Progress
Computer Vision		
Natural Language Processing		
Robotics		
Speech Recognition		
Intelligent Agents		

Apply the Concept 14.5

LEARNING OBJECTIVE 14.5

Provide use case examples (other than the ones in the text) of artificial intelligence applications in accounting, finance, marketing, production and operations management, human resource management, and management information systems.

STEP 1: Background

This section presented many interesting examples of the functional use of artificial intelligence. However, as is stated in Apply the Concept from Section 14.4, new technologies are being developed each day. As hard as authors try, the time it takes to print a textbook always leaves us a few months behind the latest and greatest examples of technology.

STEP 2: Activity

Use your favorite search engine and look up each of the use cases presented in the text (accounting, finance, marketing, production and operations management, human resource management, and management information systems) and see what companies are making headlines in these areas.

STEP 3: Deliverable

Build a table like the one below and include the new examples you have discovered.

Technology	Company	Product/Progress
Accounting		
Finance		
Marketing		
Production and Operations Management		
Human Resource Management		
Management Information Systems		

Apply the Concept Technology Guide 1.1

LEARNING OBJECTIVE TG 1.1

Identify the major hardware components of a computer system.

STEP 1: Background

At a basic level, a computer is a computer, just like an automobile is an automobile. The purpose of the automobile drives its size, design, build, price, and much more. Similarly, the purpose of a computer dictates its build requirements, storage capability, and price.

STEP 2: Activity

Imagine a colleague has been asked to create high-quality training videos for internal purposes. The project will take six months to complete and she has been given a $1,500 budget for purchasing any needed equipment. After searching, she finds out that a 4K webcam will cost $150 and a high-quality USB microphone will cost $125. This leaves $1,225 for a new computer. Think of which features will be most important for your colleague's uses and how they will function in conjunction with the webcam and microphone.

STEP 3: Deliverable

Review the definitions of central processing and primary and secondary storage that are detailed in this tech guide. Then visit Dell's website and customize a computer that would meet your friend's needs and stay within the budget. Write a memo to your professor describing your selection with a justification for the choices.

Apply the Concept Technology Guide 1.2

LEARNING OBJECTIVE TG 1.2

Discuss strategic issues that link hardware design to business strategy.

STEP 1: Background

In the modern business environment, computer hardware components are inextricably linked to business strategy. Put simply, computers are tools that allow businesses to automate some transactions and make others more efficient. As technology evolves, businesses need to evolve the ways they use that technology to execute their business strategies. The generally accepted rule is that technology should *not* drive business strategy, but business strategy *must* consider how the organization can implement new types of hardware to achieve its goals.

STEP 2: Activity

This technology guide presented augmented reality as an emerging solution to helping customers visualize what a product would look like in their space, or on them.

Visit https://www.computerweekly.com/feature/Augmented-reality-in-retail-the-second-coming and read about the current and potential applications of augmented reality.

STEP 3: Deliverable

After considering the examples in the article and the technology guide, prepare a table that lists 5 applications of augmented reality that you anticipate will become part of your life. Describe how you would use them for each example.

Apply the Concept Technology Guide 1.3

LEARNING OBJECTIVE TG 1.3

Describe the various types of computers in the computer hierarchy.

STEP 1: Background

All computers require processing power and storage capability. But as you move along the computer hierarchy, that processing and storage can sometimes be distributed to another location. We refer to this as fat and thin clients.

STEP 2: Activity

You are an inventory manager for a local tire shop. You have well over 2,000 SKUs that you are responsible for. Inventory management has been managed on paper by keeping up with invoices for items in stock and receipts of items sold. Monthly reconciliation has been sufficient, but now upper management is seeking daily clarity on inventory and there is a need for an up-to-date system.

STEP 3: Deliverable

Search the Web for inventory management software and review the type of computers that are used in the specific inventory management system. It is likely that it will have some type of server, desktop PC, and mobile devices. Prepare a list of those and describe each one relative to the computer hierarchy.

Apply the Concept Technology Guide 1.4

LEARNING OBJECTIVE TG 1.4

Differentiate the various types of input and output technologies and their uses.

STEP 1: Background

Computers in and of themselves are not very useful to us. They are usually boxes that make some noise and create some heat. However, it is our ability to interact with their power that makes them invaluable to us. Input and output technologies allow us to engage with the processing power of the computer and all the "knowledge" of the Internet to be able to make decisions.

STEP 2: Activity

Traditional input and output technologies have relied heavily on keyboards, mice, and flat displays. However, this is changing rapidly. New technologies are allowing for more virtual interaction that is changing what is possible with computers.

STEP 3: Deliverable

Search the Web for virtual and augmented reality. As you read about them, consider the different forms of input and output technologies. Prepare a table that describes these innovative tools for interacting with a computer.

Apply the Concept Technology Guide 2.1

LEARNING OBJECTIVE TG 2.1

Discuss the major software issues that confront modern organizations.

STEP 1: Background

Today's organizations deal with many decisions when it comes to technology. Will it meet our needs? Will it be flexible enough to meet our needs in the future? Will there be support for problems? Will it be user-friendly? Can we afford it? Will the licensing change in the future? Is there some technology that will make this useless in the next three to five years? These are just a few of the questions that will be considered when looking at software.

STEP 2: Activity

Imagine that you are meeting with your boss about a new software package for the human resources department of your organization. A focus group has created a list of user requirements for the new system to be functional and supportive, and your boss is meeting with them next week.

STEP 3: Deliverable

Help prepare a list of questions that the boss should discuss concerning the software from an administrative perspective. Remember, the group has focused on what they "want and need," not necessarily what is best for the organization (or what is feasible).

Apply the Concept Technology Guide 2.2

LEARNING OBJECTIVE TG 2.2

Describe the general functions of the operating system.

STEP 1: Background

There are a lot of computing terms that are commonly used in the wrong way. For example, most of the time when people say they have a "PC," they are referring to a computer that runs some version of the Microsoft Windows OS. This was even used in the Mac versus PC commercials that Apple ran a few years ago. In reality, though, a PC is just a personal computer and could run any operating system.

STEP 2: Activity

Operating systems are a necessary part of the computer. Without them, the computer will not function. Imagine that you are helping your friend pick out a computer. He just wants to pick out the color, shape, and size of the computer, but you are trying to help him understand the differences in computers.

STEP 3: Deliverable

One major difference is the type of operating system. Write a paragraph that describes what an operating system does and why it is important to be careful about your selection.

Apply the Concept Technology Guide 2.3

LEARNING OBJECTIVE TG 2.3

Differentiate between the two major types of software.

STEP 1: Background

There are two types of software (systems and application), two general ways of obtaining software licenses (proprietary versus open-source), and two general types of uses (traditional versus mobile). You should be sufficiently familiar with software to be able to categorize programs that you use.

STEP 2: Activity

Visit www.download.cnet.com At this website, you should immediately notice one of the categories mentioned above. At the time of this writing, the site automatically recognized the type of computer operating system on the user's computer. For example, this author is writing on a Mac, and the system recognized the Mac OS and defaulted to the Mac software page. Review the available software and differentiate between the operating systems and the applications. Within applications, differentiate by method of obtaining a license—some you have to pay for, and some are available by open-source or freeware licensing.

STEP 3: Deliverable

Build a table that differentiates between the two major types of software. To complete this task, list 10 applications you reviewed on the website mentioned in Step 2. Use the template provided below. Turn your completed table in to your instructor.

Application	Operating System	Licensing

Apply the Concept Technology Guide 3.1

LEARNING OBJECTIVE TG 3.1

Describe the problems that modern information technology departments face.

STEP 1: Background

This section discussed the evolution of computer infrastructure over time. Early computing models were called "terminal to host." Today we have "cloud," or "distributed computing," models available. A knowledge of how infrastructure models have changed can help you understand the challenges confronting modern IT departments.

STEP 2: Activity

Review the evolution of IT infrastructure as presented in this section. It is likely that all businesses today have some form of a local area network (LAN) in the client/server model of computing. Beginning with that stage, consider the problems that modern IT departments face as their systems evolve.

Imagine that your boss has asked your advice on moving from traditional LAN computing, in which each department operates a separate network, toward enterprise or cloud computing. What type of challenges could you help your boss anticipate?

STEP 3: Deliverable

Write a letter to your boss (your instructor) that describes the problems that modern IT departments must address as they evolve toward enterprise and cloud computing.

Apply the Concept Technology Guide 3.2

LEARNING OBJECTIVE TG 3.2

Describe the key characteristics and advantages of cloud computing.

STEP 1: Background

One of the more popular virtual servers is a virtual Web server offered by Web hosting companies. Historically, someone would simply purchase and share space on a server that would host his or her files. However, many people today need dedicated servers that guarantee performance for their consumers.

STEP 2: Activity

Access the link associated with this activity. This link will take you to a case study on an offshore drilling company, Seadrill, that migrated from in-house data centers to a virtual private cloud data center. As you review the site, focus carefully on the advantages and concerns mentioned in the case study.

STEP 3: Deliverable

In a Word document, describe the key characteristics and advantages of cloud computing for Seadrill. Submit your document to your instructor.

WILEY PLUS

This activity requires visiting an external url links. Url links are available within *WileyPLUS*. If you do not have *WileyPLUS*, ask your instructor to provide the link.

Apply the Concept Technology Guide 3.3

LEARNING OBJECTIVE TG 3.3

Identify a use case scenario for each of the four types of clouds.

STEP 1: Background

This section describes four types of clouds: public, private, hybrid, and vertical. The common feature among all four types is that resources are hosted remotely and made available to a wide range of devices over high-speed Internet connections. All four types display the basic features of the cloud that were presented in earlier sections. However, the applications of these features differ for each type.

STEP 2: Activity

Visit https://builtin.com/cloud-computing/hybrid-cloud-data-management and read over the 15 examples of hybrid clouds. Look for commonalities in why they are used.

STEP 3: Deliverable

Select three of the examples from the link above and write a summary on how these three applications of hybrid cloud use are similar.

Apply the Concept Technology Guide 3.4

LEARNING OBJECTIVE TG 3.4

Explain the operational model of each of the three types of cloud services.

STEP 1: Background

Infrastructure-as-a-service, platform-as-a-service, and software-as-a-service are relatively new processing models made available by the rise in dependable, high-speed Internet access and powerful "host-computer" processing capabilities. The three cloud models are differentiated by how users employ them and which services providers offer with each one.

STEP 2: Activity

Review the material in this section. For each operational model, consider who owns the infrastructure, the operating systems, and the applications.

STEP 3: Deliverable

In a Word document, explain the operational model for each of the three types of cloud services by highlighting the differences in who is responsible for the infrastructure, the operating systems, and the applications for each model. Submit your document to your instructor.

Apply the Concept Technology Guide 3.5

LEARNING OBJECTIVE TG 3.5

Identify the key benefits of cloud computing.

STEP 1: Background

This section has outlined the benefits that are driving many organizations to transition to cloud computing. Productivity, cost reductions, collaboration, more robust data mining, flexibility, and scope expansion are just the beginning. Cloud computing is a powerful tool that is changing the ways we do business.

STEP 2: Activity

Visit the Amazon Web Services (AWS) site (www.aws.amazon.com) and learn about the variety of cloud computing services Amazon provides. This site contains video of several customer testimonials. As you watch them, look for common benefits the various customers receive from cloud computing.

STEP 3: Deliverable

Based on the video and the material in this section, identify the key benefits of cloud computing that Amazon offers its business customers. Detail these benefits in a memo to your boss (instructor).

Apply the Concept Technology Guide 3.6

LEARNING OBJECTIVE TG 3.6

Discuss the concerns and risks associated with cloud computing.

WILEY PLUS

This activity requires visiting an external url links. Url links are available within *WileyPLUS*. If you do not have *WileyPLUS*, ask your instructor to provide the link.

STEP 1: Background

This section discussed why the risks associated with cloud computing outweigh the benefits for some organizations. The statistics provided early on that cloud computing will remain a small portion of IT spending reflect concerns regarding these risks.

STEP 2: Activity

Access the lik associated with this activity. This link will take you to an article that addresses some of the risks of cloud computing that senior managers need to consider. As you read the article, try to organize the managers' thoughts according to the concerns presented in this section: legacy systems, costs, reliability, security, privacy, and regulatory and legal environment. Imagine you have just overheard a conversation about how wonderful cloud computing is that mentioned all of the positives and none of the negatives. How would you respond?

STEP 3: Deliverable

Based on the material contained in this section and the information conveyed in the article, write a response to the above scenario that discusses the concerns and risks associated with cloud computing.

Apply the Concept Technology Guide 3.7

LEARNING OBJECTIVE TG 3.7

Explain the role of Web services in building a firm's IT applications and provide examples.

STEP 1: Background

Web services allow companies to increase functionality with minimal effort by using standard protocols to access and share data. The advantage of using Web services is that they standardize the Web platform. Using the same Web protocols that allow you to access any website makes sharing data much easier.

STEP 2: Activity

Imagine you work for a bank and you want to display some financial data on your intranet to keep your employees up to date on major market trends. One option is to gather data, perform an analysis, build and share charts and graphs, and then keep everything current. This probably sounds like a lot of work. But, suppose someone else had done all of the work for you?

Access the link associated with this activity. This link will take you to a website that discusses the available "widgets" (another name for an embeddable Web service) that businesses can select to display on their sites. Review the available information and consider how it would help you add content to your bank's intranet with minimal effort.

STEP 3: Deliverable

Write a summary that explains the role of Web services in building a firm's IT applications. Include a few examples based on the options you viewed in Step 2.

A

access controls   Controls that restrict unauthorized individuals from using information resources and are concerned with user identification.

accountability   A tenet of ethics that refers to determining who is responsible for actions that were taken.

ad hoc (on-demand) reports   Nonroutine reports that often contain special information that is not included in routine reports.

adware   Alien software designed to help pop-up advertisements appear on your screen.

affinity portal   A website that offers a single point of entry to an entire community of affiliated interests.

agile development   A software development methodology that delivers functionality in rapid iterations, measured in weeks, requiring frequent communication, development, testing, and delivery.

algorithm   A problem-solving method expressed as a finite sequence of steps.

alien software   Clandestine software that is installed on your computer through duplicitous methods.

analytical CRM system   CRM system that analyzes customer behavior and perceptions in order to provide actionable business intelligence.

anti-malware systems (antivirus software)   Software packages that attempt to identify and eliminate viruses, worms, and other malicious software.

application (or app)   A computer program designed to support a specific task or business process.

application portfolio   The set of recommended applications resulting from the planning and justification process in application development.

application service provider (ASP)   An agent or vendor who assembles the software needed by enterprises and packages them with outsourced development, operations, maintenance, and other services.

application software   The class of computer instructions that directs a computer system to perform specific processing activities and provide functionality for users.

arithmetic logic unit (ALU)   Portion of the CPU that performs the mathematical calculations and makes logical comparisons.

artificial intelligence (AI)   A subfield of computer science concerned with studying the thought processes of humans and recreating the effects of those processes with machines such as computers.

attribute   Each characteristic or quality of a particular entity.

auction   A competitive process in which either a seller solicits consecutive bids from buyers or a buyer solicits bids from sellers, and prices are determined dynamically by competitive bidding.

audit   An examination of information systems, their inputs, outputs, and processing.

augmented analytics   A type of analytics platform that integrates artificial intelligence (AI) and machine learning (ML) into the traditional analytics process to automate the selection and preparation of data, the generation of insights, and the communication of those insights.

augmented reality (AR)   A live, direct or indirect, view of a physical, real-world environment whose elements are enhanced by computer-generated sensory input such as sound, video, graphics, or GPS data.

authentication   A process that determines the identity of the person requiring access.

authorization   A process that determines which actions, rights, or privileges the person has, based on verified identity.

B

backbone networks   High-speed central networks to which multiple smaller networks (e.g., LANs and smaller WANs) connect.

bandwidth   The transmission capacity of a network, stated in bits per second.

batch processing   Transaction processing system (TPS) that processes data in batches at fixed periodic intervals.

Big Data   A collection of data so large and complex that it is difficult to manage using traditional database management systems.

binary form   The form in which data and instructions can be read by the CPU—only 0s and 1s.

biometrics   The science and technology of authentication (i.e., establishing the identity of an individual) by measuring the subject's physiological or behavioral characteristics.

bit   Short for *binary digit* (0s and 1s), the only data that a CPU can process.

blacklisting   A process in which a company identifies certain types of software that are not allowed to run in the company environment.

blogosphere   The term for the millions of blogs on the Web.

blog (weblog)   A personal website, open to the public, in which the site creator expresses his or her feelings or opinions with a series of chronological entries.

Bluetooth   Chip technology that enables short-range connection (data and voice) between wireless devices.

bot   A computer that has been compromised by, and under the control of, a hacker.

botnet   A network of computers that have been compromised by, and under control of, a hacker, who is called the botmaster.

brick-and-mortar organizations   Organizations in which the product, the process, and the delivery agent are all physical.

broadband   The transmission capacity of a communications medium that is faster than 25 Mbps.

broadcast media (also called wireless media)   Communications channels that use electromagnetic media (the "airwaves") to transmit data.

browsers   Software applications through which users primarily access the Web.

bullwhip effect   Erratic shifts in orders up and down the supply chain.

business analytics (BA) systems   See **business intelligence systems**.

business analytics (BA)   The process of developing actionable decisions or recommendations for actions based on insights generated from historical data.

business continuity   The chain of events linking planning to protection and to recovery.

business environment   The combination of social, legal, economic, physical, and political factors in which businesses conduct their operations.

business–information technology alignment   The tight integration of the IT function with the strategy, mission, and goals of the organization.

business intelligence (BI)   A broad category of applications, technologies, and processes for gathering, storing, accessing, and analyzing data to help business users make more informed decisions.

business intelligence (BI) systems   Systems that provide computer-based support for complex, nonroutine decisions, primarily for middle managers and knowledge workers.

business model   The method by which a company generates revenue to sustain itself.

business process   A collection of related activities that create a product or a service of value to the organization, its business partners, and its customers.

business process management   A management technique that includes methods and tools to support the design, analysis, implementation, management, and optimization of business processes.

business process reengineering (BPR) A radical redesign of a business process that improves its efficiency and effectiveness, often by beginning with a "clean sheet" (i.e., from scratch).

business rules Precise descriptions of policies, procedures, or principles in any organization that stores and uses data to generate information.

buy-side marketplace B2B model in which organizations buy needed products or services from other organizations electronically, often through a reverse auction.

byte A group of eight bits that represents a single character.

C

cable media (also called wireline media) Communications channels that use physical wires or cables to transmit data and information.

cache memory A type of high-speed memory that enables the computer to temporarily store blocks of data that are used more often and that a processor can access more rapidly than main memory (RAM).

cellular telephones (cell phones) Phones that provide two-way radio communications over a cellular network of base stations with seamless handoffs.

central processing unit (CPU) Hardware that performs the actual computation or "number crunching" inside any computer.

certificate authority A third party that acts as a trusted intermediary between computers (and companies) by issuing digital certificates and verifying the worth and integrity of the certificates.

channel conflict The alienation of existing distributors when a company decides to sell to customers directly online.

chatbot A computer program that uses artificial intelligence and natural language processing to simulate human conversation, either by voice or text communication.

clicks-and-mortar organizations Organizations that do business in both the physical and digital dimensions.

clients Computers, such as users' personal computers, that use any of the services provided by servers.

client/server computing Form of distributed processing in which some machines (servers) perform computing functions for end-user PCs (clients).

cloud computing A technology in which tasks are performed by computers physically removed from the user and accessed over a network, in particular the Internet.

coaxial cable Insulated copper wire; used to carry high-speed data traffic and television signals.

code of ethics A collection of principles intended to guide decision making by members of an organization.

collaboration Mutual efforts by two or more individuals who perform activities to accomplish certain tasks.

collaborative consumption An economic model based on sharing, swapping, trading, or renting products and services, enabling access over ownership.

collaborative CRM system A CRM system in which communications between the organization and its customers are integrated across all aspects of marketing, sales, and customer support processes.

commercial (public) portal A website that offers fairly routine content for diverse audiences. It offers customization only at the user interface.

communications channel Pathway for communicating data from one location to another.

communications controls (also network controls) Controls that deal with the movement of data across networks.

comparative reports Reports that compare performances of different business units or times.

competitive advantage An advantage over competitors in some measure such as cost, quality, or speed; leads to control of a market and to larger-than-average profits.

competitive forces model A business framework devised by Michael Porter that analyzes competitiveness by recognizing five major forces that could endanger a company's position.

component-based development A software development methodology that uses standard components to build applications.

computer-aided software engineering (CASE) Development approach that uses specialized tools to automate many of the tasks in the SDLC. Upper CASE tools automate the early stages of the SDLC and lower CASE tools automate the later stages.

computer-based information system (CBIS) An information system that uses computer technology to perform some or all of its intended tasks.

computer-integrated manufacturing (CIM) An information system that integrates various automated factory systems; also called *digital manufacturing*.

computer network A system that connects computers and other devices through communications media so that data and information can be transmitted among them.

computer programs The sequences of instructions for the computer, which comprise software.

computer vision The ability of information systems to identify objects, scenes, and activities in images.

containers A method of developing applications that run independently of the base operating system of the server.

continuous application development The process of steadily adding new computer code to a software project when the new computer code is written and tested.

controls Defense mechanisms (also called *countermeasures*).

control unit Portion of the CPU that controls the flow of information.

convolutional neural network A type of neural network designed to separate areas of image inputs by extracting features to identify edges, curves, and color density and then recombine these inputs for classification and prediction.

cookies Small amounts of information that websites store on your computer, temporarily or more or less permanently.

copyright A grant from a governmental authority that provides the creator of intellectual property with ownership of it for a specified period of time, currently the life of the creator plus 70 years.

corporate portal A website that provides a single point of access to critical business information located both inside and outside an organization.

cross-departmental process A business process that originates in one department and ends in another department or originates and ends in the same department while involving other departments.

cross-functional processes No single functional area is responsible for a process's execution.

crowdsourcing A process in which an organization outsources a task to an undefined, generally large group of people in the form of an open call.

customer-facing CRM applications Areas in which customers directly interact with the organization, including customer service and support, sales force automation, marketing, and campaign management.

customer identity management A marketing technology intended to complete a 360° view of a customer across an organization.

customer interaction center (CIC) A CRM operation in which organizational representatives use multiple communication channels to interact with customers in functions such as inbound teleservice and outbound telesales.

customer relationship management (CRM) A customer-focused and customer-driven organizational strategy that concentrates on addressing customers' requirements for products and services, and then providing high-quality, responsive services.

customer-touching CRM applications (also called electronic CRM or e-CRM) Applications and technologies with which customers interact and typically help themselves.

customer touch point Any interaction between a customer and an organization.

cybercrime Illegal activities executed on the Internet.

cyberterrorism A premeditated, politically motivated attack against information, computer systems, computer programs, and data that results in violence against noncombatant targets by subnational groups or clandestine agents.

cyberwarfare War in which a country's information systems could be paralyzed from a massive attack by destructive software.

D

dashboard A business analytics presentation tool that provides rapid access to timely information and direct access to management reports.

database A collection of related files or tables containing data.

database management system (DBMS) The software program (or group of programs) that provide access to a database.

data dictionary A collection of definitions of data elements; data characteristics that use the data elements; and the individuals, business functions, applications, and reports that use these data elements.

data file (also table) A collection of logically related records.

data governance An approach to managing information across an entire organization.

Data items An elementary description of things, events, activities, and transactions that are recorded, classified, and stored but are not organized to convey any specific meaning.

data lake A central repository that stores all of an organization's data, regardless of their source or format.

data mart A low-cost, scaled-down version of a data warehouse that is designed for the end-user needs in a strategic business unit (SBU) or a department.

data mining The process of searching for valuable business information in a large database, data warehouse, or data mart.

data model A diagram that represents entities in the database and their relationships.

data silo A collection of data held by one group that is not easily accessible by other groups.

data warehouse A repository of historical data that are organized by subject to support decision makers in the organization.

decision A choice that individuals and groups make among two or more alternatives.

decision-support systems (DSSs) Business intelligence systems that combine models and data in an attempt to solve semistructured and some unstructured problems with extensive user involvement.

deep learning A subset of machine learning where artificial neural networks learn from large amounts of data.

demilitarized zone (DMZ) A separate organizational local area network that is located between an organization's internal network and an external network, usually the Internet.

departmental/functional information system ISs that support a particular functional area within the organization.

descriptive analytics A type of business analytics that summarize what has happened in the past and allow decision makers to learn from past behaviors.

digital certificate An electronic document attached to a file certifying that the file is from the organization it claims to be from and has not been modified from its original format or content.

digital divide The gap between those who have access to information and communications technology and those who do not.

digital dossier An electronic description of an individual and his or her habits.

digital transformation The business strategy that leverages IT to dramatically improve employee, customer, and business partner relationships; support continuous improvement in business operations and business processes; and develop new business models and businesses.

direct conversion Implementation process in which the old system is cut off and the new system is turned on at a certain point in time.

disintermediation Elimination of intermediaries in electronic commerce.

distance learning (DL) Learning situations in which teachers and students do not meet face-to-face.

distributed denial of service (DDoS) attack A denial of service attack that sends a flood of data packets from many compromised computers simultaneously.

distributed processing Network architecture that divides processing work between or among two or more computers that are linked together in a network.

distribution portals Corporate portals that automate the business processes involved in selling or distributing products from a single supplier to multiple buyers.

documentation Written description of the functions of a software program.

domain names The name assigned to an Internet site, which consists of multiple parts, separated by dots, that are translated from right to left.

domain name system (DNS) The system administered by the Internet Corporation for Assigned Names (ICANN) that assigns names to each site on the Internet.

drill-down reports Reports that show a greater level of details than is included in routine reports.

E

e-learning Learning supported by the Web; can be performed inside traditional classrooms or in virtual classrooms.

electronic business (e-business) A broader definition of electronic commerce, including buying and selling of goods and services, and servicing customers, collaborating with business partners, conducting e-learning, and conducting electronic transactions within an organization.

electronic commerce (e-commerce) systems A type of interorganizational information system that enables organizations to conduct transactions, called business-to-business (B2B) electronic commerce, and customers to conduct transactions with businesses, called business-to-consumer (B2C) electronic commerce.

electronic commerce (EC or e-commerce) The process of buying, selling, transferring, or exchanging products, services, or information through computer networks, including the Internet.

electronic CRM (e-CRM) See **customer-touching CRM applications**.

electronic data interchange (EDI) A communication standard that enables business partners to transfer routine documents electronically.

electronic mall A collection of individual shops under one Internet address; also known as a *cybermall* or an *e-mall*.

electronic marketplace A virtual market space on the Web where many buyers and many sellers conduct electronic business activities.

electronic payment mechanisms Computer-based systems that allow customers to pay for goods and services electronically, rather than writing a check or using cash.

electronic retailing (e-tailing) The direct sale of products and services through storefronts or electronic malls, usually designed around an electronic catalog format and auctions.

electronic storefront The website of a single company, with its own Internet address, at which orders can be placed.

electronic surveillance Tracking people's activities with the aid of computers.

employee monitoring systems Systems that monitor employees' computers, e-mail activities, and Internet surfing activities.

encryption The process of converting an original message into a form that cannot be read by anyone except the intended recipient.

end-user development Approach in which the organization's end users develop their own applications with little or no formal assistance from the IT department.

enterprise application integration (EAI) system A system that integrates existing systems by providing layers of software that connect applications together.

enterprise network An organization's network, which is composed of interconnected multiple LANs and WANs.

enterprise resource planning (ERP) systems Information systems that take a business process view of the overall organization to integrate the planning, management, and use of all of an organization's resources, employing a common software platform and database.

entity Any person, place, thing, or event of interest to a user.

entity–relationship (ER) diagram Document that shows data entities and attributes and relationships among them.

entity–relationship (ER) modeling The process of designing a database by organizing data entities to be used and identifying the relationships among them.

entry barrier Product or service feature that customers expect from organizations in a certain industry; an organization trying to enter this market must provide this product or service at a minimum to be able to compete.

e-procurement. Purchasing by using electronic support.

ERP II systems Interorganizational ERP systems that provide Web-enabled links among key business systems (e.g., inventory and production) of a company and its customers, suppliers, distributors, and others.

ethernet A common local area network protocol.

ethics The principles of right and wrong that individuals use to make choices to guide their behaviors.

exception reports Reports that include only information that exceeds certain threshold standards.

exchanges See **public exchanges.**

expert systems (ES) An attempt to duplicate the work of human experts by applying reasoning capabilities, knowledge, and expertise within a specific domain.

explicit knowledge The more objective, rational, and technical types of knowledge.

exposure The harm, loss, or damage that can result if a threat compromises an information resource.

extensible markup language (XML) A computer language that makes it easier to exchange data among a variety of applications and to validate and interpret these data.

extranet A network that connects parts of the intranets of different organizations.

extranets Networks that link business partners over the Internet by providing them access to certain areas of each other's corporate intranets.

F

fat clients Computers that offer full functionality without having to connect to a network.

feasibility study Investigation that gauges the probability of success of a proposed project and provides a rough assessment of the project's feasibility.

fiber-optic cable A communications medium consisting of thousands of very thin filaments of glass fibers, surrounded by cladding, that transmit information through pulses of light generated by lasers.

field A characteristic of interest that describes an entity.

file server (also called network server) A computer that contains various software and data files for a local area network as well as the network operating system.

Fintech An industry composed of companies that use technology to compete in the marketplace with traditional financial institutions and intermediaries in the delivery of financial services, which include banking, insurance, real estate, and investing.

firewall A system (either hardware, software, or a combination of both) that prevents a specific type of information from moving between untrusted networks, such as the Internet, and private networks, such as your company's network.

flash memory devices Nonvolatile electronic storage devices that are compact, are portable, require little power, and contain no moving parts.

foreign key A field (or group of fields) in one table that uniquely identifies a row (or record) of another table.

forward auctions Auctions that sellers use as a selling channel to many potential buyers; the highest bidder wins the items.

front-office processes Those processes that directly interact with customers; that is, sales, marketing, and service.

functional area information systems (FAIS) Systems that provide information to managers (usually mid-level) in the functional areas to better support managerial tasks of planning, organizing, and controlling operations.

functional dependency A means of expressing that the value of one particular attribute is associated with, or determines, a specific single value of another attribute.

functions-as-a-Service (XaaS) A category of cloud computing services that provides a platform allowing customers to develop, run, and manage applications functions without the complexity of building and maintaining the infrastructure typically associated with developing and deploying an app.

G

geographic information system (GIS) A computer-based system for capturing, integrating, manipulating, and displaying data using digitized maps.

gesture recognition An input method that interprets human gestures, in an attempt for computers to begin to understand human body language.

globalization The integration and interdependence of economic, social, cultural, and ecological facets of life, enabled by rapid advances in information technology.

global positioning system (GPS) A wireless system that uses satellites to enable users to determine their position anywhere on Earth.

graphical user interface (GUI) Systems software that allows users to have direct control of the hardware by manipulating visible objects (such as icons) and actions, which replace command syntax.

grid computing A technology that applies the unused processing resources of many geographically dispersed computers in a network to form a virtual supercomputer.

group purchasing The aggregation of purchasing orders from many buyers so that a volume discount can be obtained.

H

hardware A device such as a processor, monitor, keyboard, or printer. Together, these devices accept, process, and display data and information.

hotspot A small geographical perimeter within which a wireless access point provides service to a number of users.

HTML5 A page-description language that makes it possible to embed images, audio, and video directly into a document without add-ons. Also makes it easier for web pages to function across different display devices, including mobile devices as well as desktops. It supports the storage of data offline.

hybrid clouds Clouds composed of public and private clouds that remain unique entities but are bound together, offering the benefits of multiple deployment models.

hyperlink A connection from a hypertext file or document to another location or file, typically activated by clicking on a highlighted word or image on the screen or by touching the screen.

hypertext markup language (HTML) A page-description language for specifying how text, graphics, video, and sound are placed on a web page document.

hypertext Text displayed on a computer display with references, called hyperlinks, to other text that the reader can immediately access.

Hypertext Transfer Protocol (HTTP) The communications standard used to transfer pages across the www portion of the Internet; it defines how messages are formulated and transmitted.

I

identity theft Crime in which someone uses the personal information of others to create a false identity and then uses it fraudulently.

implementation The process of converting from an old computer system to a new one.

individual social responsibility See **organizational social responsibility**.

industrywide portal A Web-based gateway to information and knowledge for an entire industry.

information Data that have been organized so that they have meaning and value to the recipient.

information privacy The right to determine when, and to what extent, personal information can be gathered by or communicated to others.

information security Protecting an organization's information and information systems from unauthorized access, use, disclosure, disruption, modification, or destruction.

information system (IS) A system that collects, processes, stores, analyzes, and disseminates information for a specific purpose.

information technology components Hardware, software, databases, and networks.

information technology infrastructure IT components plus IT services.

information technology (IT) Any computer-based tool that people use to work with information and support the information and information-processing needs of an organization.

information technology platform The name given to the combination of the IT components of hardware, software, networks (wireline and wireless), and databases.

information technology services Activities performed by IT personnel using IT components; specifically,

developing information systems, overseeing security and risk, and managing data.

informed user A person who is knowledgeable about information systems and information technology.

infrastructure-as-a-service (IaaS) A model with which cloud computing providers offer remotely accessible servers, networks, and storage capacity.

instance Each row in a relational table, which is a specific, unique representation of the entity.

integrated CASE (ICASE) tools CASE tools that provide links between upper CASE and lower CASE tools.

intellectual capital (or intellectual assets) Other terms for knowledge.

intellectual property The intangible property created by individuals or corporations, which is protected under trade secret, patent, and copyright laws.

Internet2 A new, faster telecommunications network that deploys advanced network applications such as remote medical diagnosis, digital libraries, distance education, online simulation, and virtual laboratories.

Internet backbone The primary network connections and telecommunications lines that link the computers and organizational nodes of the Internet.

Internet of Things (IoT) A scenario in which objects, animals, and people are provided with unique identifiers and the ability to automatically transfer data over a network without requiring human-to-human or human-to-computer interaction.

Internet Protocol (IP) address An assigned address that uniquely identifies a computer on the Internet.

Internet Protocol (IP) A set of rules responsible for disassembling, delivering, and reassembling packets over the Internet.

Internet service provider (ISP) A company that provides Internet connections for a fee.

Internet telephony (Voice-over-Internet Protocol, or VoIP) The use of the Internet as the transmission medium for telephone calls.

Internet (the Net) A massive global WAN that connects approximately 1 million organizational computer networks in more than 200 countries on all continents.

interorganizational information system (IOS) An information system that supports information flow among two or more organizations.

interorganizational information systems (IOSs) Information systems that connect two or more organizations.

intranet A private network that uses Internet software and TCP/IP protocols.

IS operational plan Consists of a clear set of projects that the IS department and the functional area managers will execute in support of the IT strategic plan.

IT steering committee A committee composed of a group of managers and staff representing various organizational units that is set up to establish IT priorities and to ensure that the MIS function is meeting the needs of the enterprise.

IT strategic plan A set of long-range goals that describe the IT infrastructure and major IT initiatives needed to achieve the goals of the organization.

J

join operation A database operation that combines records from two or more tables in a database.

joint application design (JAD) A group-based tool for collecting user requirements and creating system designs.

just-in-time (JIT) An inventory system in which a supplier delivers the precise number of parts to be assembled into a finished product at precisely the right time.

K

key indicator reports Reports that summarize the performance of critical activities.

knowledge Data and/or information that have been organized and processed to convey understanding, experience, accumulated learning, and expertise as they apply to a current problem or activity.

knowledge management (KM) A process that helps organizations identify, select, organize, disseminate, transfer, and apply information and expertise that are part of the organization's memory and that typically reside within the organization in an unstructured manner.

knowledge management systems (KMSs) Information technologies used to systematize, enhance, and expedite intra-and interfirm knowledge management.

knowledge workers Professional employees such as financial and marketing analysts, engineers, lawyers, and accountants, who are experts in a particular subject area and who create information and knowledge, which they integrate into the business.

L

laptop computers (notebook computers) Small, easily transportable, lightweight microcomputers.

least privilege A principle that users be granted the privilege for some activity only if there is a justifiable need to grant this authorization.

liability A legal concept that gives individuals the right to recover the damages done to them by other individuals, organizations, or systems.

local area network (LAN)   A network that connects communications devices in a limited geographic region, such as a building, so that every user device on the network can communicate with every other device.

location-based commerce (L-commerce)   Mobile commerce transactions targeted to individuals in specific locations, at specific times.

logic bombs   Segments of computer code embedded within an organization's existing computer programs.

lower CASE tools   Tools used to automate later stages in the SDLC (programming, testing, operation, and maintenance).

loyalty program   Programs that offer rewards to customers to influence future behavior.

M

machine learning systems   The ability of information systems to accurately perform new, unseen tasks, built on known properties learned from training or historical data that are labeled.

magnetic disks (or hard drives or fixed disk drives)   A form of secondary storage on a magnetized disk divided into tracks and sectors that provide addresses for various pieces of data.

magnetic tape   A secondary storage medium on a large open reel or in a smaller cartridge or cassette.

mainframes   Relatively large computers used in large enterprises for extensive computing applications that are accessed by thousands of users.

make-to-order   The strategy of producing customized products and services.

malware   Malicious software such as viruses and worms.

management   A process by which organizational goals are achieved through the use of resources.

mashup   A website that takes different content from a number of other websites and mixes them together to create a new kind of content.

mass customization   A production process in which items are produced in large quantities but are customized to fit the desires of each customer.

master data   A set of core data, such as customer, product, employee, vendor, geographic location, and so on, that spans an enterprise's information systems.

master data management   A process that provides companies with the ability to store, maintain, exchange, and synchronize a consistent, accurate, and timely "single version of the truth" for the company's core master data.

metasearch engine   A computer program that searches several engines at once and integrates the findings of the various search engines to answer queries posted by users.

microblogging   A form of blogging that allows users to write short messages (or capture an image or embedded video) and publish them.

microcomputers   The smallest and least expensive category or general-purpose computers, also called micros, personal computers, or PCs.

microprocessor   The CPU, made up of millions of transistors embedded in a circuit on a silicon wafer or chip.

microwave transmission   A wireless system that uses microwaves for high-volume, long-distance, point-to-point communication.

mobile commerce (or m-commerce)   Electronic commerce transactions that are conducted with a mobile device.

mobile computing   A real-time connection between a mobile device and other computing environments, such as the Internet or an intranet.

mobile CRM system   An interactive CRM system in which communications related to sales, marketing, and customer service activities are conducted through a mobile medium for the purpose of building and maintaining customer relationships between an organization and its customers.

mobile portal   A portal that aggregates and provides content and services for mobile users.

mobile wallet (m-wallet)   A technology that allows users to make purchases with a single click from their mobile devices.

Moore's law   Prediction by Gordon Moore, an Intel cofounder, that microprocessor complexity would double approximately every two years.

multichanneling   A process in which a company integrates its online and offline channels.

multidimensional data analysis   See **online analytical processing (OLAP)**.

multidimensional structure   Storage of data in more than two dimensions; a common representation is the data cube.

N

natural language processing   The ability of information systems to work with text the way that humans do.

near-field communication (NFC)   The smallest of the short-range wireless networks that is designed to be embedded in mobile devices like cell phones and credit cards.

network access points (NAPs)   Computers that act as exchange points for Internet traffic and determine how traffic is routed.

network   A connecting system (wireline or wireless) that enables multiple computers to share resources.

network controls   See **communications controls.**

network server   See **file server**.

neural network   A set of virtual neurons, placed in layers, which work in parallel in an attempt to simulate the way the human brain works, although in a greatly simplified form.

node   Software unit in a neural network that has one or more weighted connections, a transfer function that combines the inputs in some way, and an output connection.

normalization   A method for analyzing and reducing a relational database to its most streamlined form to ensure minimum redundancy, maximum data integrity, and optimal processing performance.

notebook computer   See **laptop computers**.

O

object-oriented development   A systems development methodology that begins with aspects of the real world that must be modeled to perform a task.

on-demand CRM system   A CRM system that is hosted by an external vendor in the vendor's data center.

online analytical processing (OLAP) (or multidimensional data analysis)   A set of capabilities for "slicing and dicing" data using dimensions and measures associated with the data.

online transaction processing (OLTP)   Transaction processing system (TPS) that processes data after transactions occur, frequently in real time.

on-premise computing   A model of IT management in which companies own their IT infrastructure (their software, hardware, networks, and data management) and maintain it in their data centers.

open-source CRM system   CRM software whose source code is available to developers and users.

open-source software   Software made available in source-code form at no cost to developers.

open systems   Computing products that work together by using the same operating system with compatible software on all the computers that interact in an organization.

operating system (OS)   The main system control program, which supervises the overall operations of the computer, allocates CPU time and main memory to programs, and provides an interface between the user and the hardware.

operational CRM system   The component of CRM that supports the front-office business processes that directly interact with customers (i.e., sales, marketing, and service).

optical storage devices   A form of secondary storage in which a laser reads the surface of a reflective plastic platter.

opt-in model   A model of informed consent in which a business is prohibited from collecting any personal information unless the customer specifically authorizes it.

opt-out model   A model of informed consent that permits a company to collect personal information until the customer specifically requests that the data not be collected.

order fulfillment process   A cross-functional business process that originates when the company receives a customer order, and it concludes when it receives a payment from the customer.

organizational social responsibility (also individual social responsibility)   Efforts by organizations to solve various social problems.

outsourcing   Use of outside contractors or external organizations to acquire IT services.

P

package   Common term for an integrated group of computer programs developed by a vendor and available for purchase in prepackaged form.

packet switching   The transmission technology that divides blocks of text into packets.

passphrase   A series of characters that is longer than a password but is still easy to memorize.

password   A private combination of characters that only the user should know.

patent   A document that grants the holder exclusive rights on an invention or process for a specified period of time, currently 20 years.

peer-to-peer (P2P) processing   A type of client/server distributed processing that allows two or more computers to pool their resources, making each computer both a client and a server.

personal application software   General-purpose, off-the-shelf application programs that support general types of processing, rather than being linked to any specific business function.

personal area network   A computer network used for communication among computer devices close to one person.

personalized pricing   Personalized pricing is the practice of pricing items at a point determined by a particular customer's perceived ability to pay

phased conversion   Implementation process that introduces components of the new system in stages, until the entire new system is operational.

phishing attack   An e-mail attack that uses deception to fraudulently acquire sensitive personal information by masquerading as an official looking e-mail.

physical controls   Controls that restrict unauthorized individuals from gaining access to a company's computer facilities.

pilot conversion   Implementation process that introduces the new system in one part of the organization on a trial basis. When the new system is working properly, it is introduced in other parts of the organization.

piracy   Copying a software program (other than freeware, demo software, etc.) without making payment to the owner.

platform-as-a-service (PaaS)   A model in which customers rent servers, operating systems, storage, a database, software development technologies such as Java and .NET, and network capacity over the Internet.

portal   A Web-based personalized gateway to information and knowledge that provides information from disparate information systems and the Internet, using advanced searching and indexing techniques.

predictive analytics   A type of business analytics that examines recent and historical data in order to detect patterns and predict future outcomes and trends.

prescriptive analytics   A type of business analytics that recommends one or more courses of action, showing the likely outcome of each decision.

primary activities   Those business activities related to the production and distribution of the firm's products and services, thus creating value.

primary key   A field (or attribute) of a record that uniquely identifies that record so that it can be retrieved, updated, and sorted.

primary storage (also called main memory)   High-speed storage located directly on the motherboard that stores data to be processed by the CPU, instructions telling the CPU how to process the data, and operating system programs.

privacy codes   See **privacy policies**.

privacy policies (or privacy codes)   An organization's guidelines for protecting the privacy of customers, clients, and employees.

privacy   The right to be left alone and to be free of unreasonable personal intrusions.

private clouds (also known as *internal clouds* **or** *corporate clouds***)**   IT infrastructures that are accessible only by a single entity or by an exclusive group of related entities that share the same purpose and requirements, such as all the business units within a single organization.

privilege   A collection of related computer system operations that can be performed by users of the system.

Procedures   The set of instructions for combining hardware, software, database, and network components in order to process information and generate the desired output.

procurement portals   Corporate portals that automate the business processes involved in purchasing or procuring products between a single buyer and multiple suppliers.

procurement process   A cross-functional business process that originates when a company needs to acquire goods or services from external sources, and it concludes when the company receives and pays for them.

production process   A cross-functional business process in which a company produces physical goods.

productivity   The ratio between the inputs to a process and the outputs from that process.

profiling   The process of forming a digital dossier.

programmers   IS professionals who modify existing computer programs or write new computer programs to satisfy user requirements.

programming   The process of writing or coding software programs.

propagation delay   Any delay in communications from signal transmission time through a physical medium.

proprietary software   Software that has been developed by a company and has restrictions on its use, copying, and modification.

protocol   The set of rules and procedures that govern transmission across a network.

prototype   A small-scale working model of an entire system or a model that contains only the components of the new system that are of most interest to the users.

prototyping   An approach that defines an initial list of user requirements, builds a prototype system, and then improves the system in several iterations based on users' feedback.

public clouds   Shared, easily accessible, multicustomer IT infrastructures that are available nonexclusively to any entity in the general public (individuals, groups, and organizations).

public exchanges (or exchanges)   Electronic marketplaces in which there are many sellers and many buyers, and entry is open to all; frequently owned and operated by a third party.

public-key encryption   (also called *asymmetric encryption*) A type of encryption that uses two different keys: a public key and a private key.

pull model   A business model in which the production process begins with a customer order and companies make only what customers want, a process closely aligned with mass customization.

push model   A business model in which the production process begins with a forecast, which predicts the products that customers will want as well as the quantity of each product. The company then produces the amount of products in the forecast, typically by using mass production, and sells, or "pushes," those products to consumers.

Q

query by example   To obtain information from a relational database, a user fills out a grid or template—also known as a *form*—to construct a sample or a description of the data desired.

R

radio-frequency identification (RFID) technology A wireless technology that allows manufacturers to attach tags with antennae and computer chips on goods and then track their movement through radio signals.

radio transmission Uses radio-wave frequencies to send data directly between transmitters and receivers.

random access memory (RAM) The part of primary storage that holds a software program and small amounts of data when they are brought from secondary storage.

ransomware (or digital extortion) Malicious software that blocks access to a computer system or encrypts an organization's data until the organization pays a sum of money.

rapid application development (RAD) A development method that uses special tools and an iterative approach to rapidly produce a high-quality system.

read-only memory (ROM) Type of primary storage in which certain critical instructions are safeguarded; the storage is nonvolatile and retains the instructions when the power to the computer is turned off.

Really Simple Syndication (RSS) A technology that allows users to receive the information they want, when they want it, without having to surf thousands of websites.

real-time CRM system A CRM system enabling organizations to respond to customer product searches, requests, complaints, comments, ratings, reviews, and recommendations in near real time, 24/7/365.

record A grouping of logically related fields.

registers High-speed storage areas in the CPU that store very small amounts of data and instructions for short periods.

reinforcement learning A type of machine learning where the system learns to achieve a goal in an uncertain, potentially complex environment.

relational database model Data model based on the simple concept of tables in order to capitalize on characteristics of rows and columns of data.

relationships Operators that illustrate an association between two entities.

responsibility A tenet of ethics in which you accept the consequences of your decisions and actions.

reverse auctions Auctions in which one buyer, usually an organization, seeks to buy a product or a service, and suppliers submit bids; the lowest bidder wins.

risk management A process that identifies, controls, and minimizes the impact of threats, in an effort to reduce risk to manageable levels.

risk The likelihood that a threat will occur.

router A communications processor that routes messages from a LAN to the Internet,
across several connected LANs, or across a wide area network such as the Internet.

routine reports Reports produced at scheduled intervals.

S

sales force automation (SFA) The component of an operational CRM system that automatically records all the aspects in a sales transaction process.

satellite radio (or digital radio) A wireless system that offers uninterrupted, near CD-quality sound that is beamed to your radio from satellites.

satellite transmission A wireless transmission system that uses satellites for broadcast communications.

scope creep Adding functions to an information system after the project has begun.

search engine A computer program that searches for specific information by keywords and reports the results.

secondary key A field that has some identifying information, but typically does not uniquely identify a record with complete accuracy.

secondary storage Technology that can store very large amounts of data for extended periods.

secure socket layer (SSL) See **transport layer security**.

Security-as-a-service (SECaaS) A delivery model in which cloud computing vendors provide software that is specific to their customers' requirements.

security The degree of protection against criminal activity, danger, damage, or loss.

sell-side marketplace B2B model in which organizations sell to other organizations from their own private e-marketplace or from a third-party site.

semi-supervised learning A type of machine learning that combines a small amount of labeled data with a large amount of unlabeled data during training.

server Computers that support networks, enabling users to share files, software, and other network devices.

server farms Massive data centers, which may contain hundreds of thousands of networked computer servers.

servers Computers that provide access to various network services, such as printing, data, and communications.

server virtualization A technology that uses software-based partitions to create multiple virtual servers (called *virtual machines*) on a single physical server.

service-oriented architecture An IT architecture that makes it possible to construct business applications using Web services.

shadow IT Technology implemented by end-users without receiving proper approvals from the organizational IT department.

social advertising Advertising formats that make use of the social context of the user viewing the ad.

social capital The number of connections a person has within and between social networks.

social commerce The delivery of electronic commerce activities and transactions through social computing.

social computing A type of information technology that combines social behavior and information systems to create value.

social CRM The use of social media technology and services to enable organizations to engage their customers in a collaborative conversation in order to provide mutually beneficial value in a trusted and transparent manner.

social engineering Getting around security systems by tricking computer users inside a company into revealing sensitive information or gaining unauthorized access privileges.

social graph A map of all relevant links or connections for one member of a social network.

social intelligence The monitoring, collection, and analysis of socially generated data and the resultant strategic decisions.

social interface A user interface that guides the user through computer applications by using cartoon-like characters, graphics, animation, and voice commands.

social marketplaces Websites that act as online intermediaries that harness the power of social networks for introducing, buying, and selling products and services.

social network A social structure composed of individuals, groups, or organizations linked by values, visions, ideas, financial exchange, friendship, kinship, conflict, or trade.

social networking Activities performed using social software tools (e.g., blogging) or social networking features (e.g., media sharing).

social shopping A method of electronic commerce that takes all of the key aspects of social networks (friends, groups, voting, comments, discussions, reviews, etc.) and focuses them on shopping.

software A program or collection of programs that enable the hardware to process data.

software-as-a-service (SaaS) A method of delivering software in which a vendor hosts the applications and provides them as a service to customers over a network, typically the Internet.

software A set of computer programs that enable the hardware to process data.

software suite See **package**.

solid-state drives (SSDs) Data storage devices that serve the same purpose as a hard drive and store data in memory chips.

spamming   Indiscriminate distribution of e-mail without the recipient's permission.

spam   Unsolicited e-mail.

spamware   Alien software that uses your computer as a launch platform for spammers.

spear phishing   An attack in which the perpetrators find out as much information about an individual as possible to improve their chances that phishing techniques will obtain sensitive, personal information.

speech-recognition software   Software that recognizes and interprets human speech, either one word at a time (discrete speech) or in a stream (continuous speech).

speech recognition   The ability of information systems to automatically and accurately transcribe human speech.

spyware   Alien software that can record your keystrokes or capture your passwords.

Strategic information systems (SISs) Systems that help an organization gain a competitive advantage by supporting its strategic goals and increasing performance and productivity.

strong AI   Hypothetical artificial intelligence that matches or exceeds human intelligence and could perform any intellectual task that humans can.

structured data   Highly organized data in fixed fields in a data repository such as a relational database that must be defined in terms of field name and type (e.g., alphanumeric, numeric, and currency).

structured query language   The most popular query language for requesting information from a relational database.

supervised learning   A type of machine learning where the system is given labeled input data and the expected output results.

supply chain management (SCM) An activity in which the leadership of an organization provides extensive oversight for the partnerships and processes that compose the supply chain and leverages these relationships to provide an operational advantage.

supply chain   The flow of materials, information, money, and services from suppliers of raw materials through factories and warehouses to the end customers.

supply chain visibility   The ability of all organizations in a supply chain to access or view relevant data on purchased materials as these materials move through their suppliers' production processes.

support activities   Business activities that do not add value directly to a firm's product or service under consideration but support the primary activities that do add value.

systems analysis   The examination of the business problem that the organization plans to solve with an information system.

systems analysts   IS professionals who specialize in analyzing and designing information systems.

systems design   Describes how the new system will resolve the business problem.

systems development life cycle (SDLC) Traditional structured framework, used for large IT projects, that consists of sequential processes by which information systems are developed.

systems investigation   The initial stage in the traditional SDLC that addresses the business problem (or business opportunity) by means of the feasibility study.

systems software   The class of computer instructions that serve primarily as an intermediary between computer hardware and application programs; provides important self-regulatory functions for computer systems.

systems stakeholders   All people who are affected by changes in information systems.

T

table   A grouping of logically related records.

tacit knowledge   The cumulative store of subjective or experiential learning, which is highly personal and hard to formalize.

tag   A keyword or term that describes a piece of information.

technical specialists   Experts on a certain type of technology, such as databases or telecommunications.

telecommuting   A work arrangement whereby employees work at home, at the customer's premises, in special workplaces, or while traveling, usually using a computer linked to their place of employment.

teleconferencing   The use of electronic communication that allows two or more people at different locations to have a simultaneous conference.

telemetry   The wireless transmission and receipt of data gathered from remote sensors.

thin client   A computer that does not offer the full functionality of a fat client.

threat   Any danger to which an information resource may be exposed.

thumb drive   Storage device that fits into the USB port of a personal computer and is used for portable storage.

trade secret   Intellectual work, such as a business plan, that is a company secret and is not based on public information.

transactional data   Data generated and captured by operational systems that describe the business's activities, or transactions.

transaction   Any business event that generates data worth capturing and storing in a database.

transaction processing system (TPS)   Information system that supports the monitoring, collection, storage, and processing of data from the organization's basic business transactions, each of which generates data.

Transmission Control Protocol/Internet Protocol (TCP/IP)   A file transfer protocol that can send large files of information across sometimes unreliable networks with the assurance that the data will arrive uncorrupted.

transport layer security (TLS) An encryption standard used for secure transactions such as credit card purchases and online banking.

Trojan horse   A software program containing a hidden function that presents a security risk.

tunneling   A process that encrypts each data packet to be sent and places each encrypted packet inside another packet.

tweet   Messages and updates posted by users on Twitter.

twisted-pair wire   A communications medium consisting of strands of copper wire twisted together in pairs.

Twitter   A free microblogging service that allows its users to send messages and read other users' messages and updates.

U

ultra-wideband (UWB)   A high-bandwidth wireless technology with transmission speeds in excess of 100 Mbps that can be used for applications such as streaming multimedia from, say, a personal computer to a television.

unified communications   Common hardware and software platform that simplifies and integrates all forms of communications—voice, e-mail, instant messaging, location, and videoconferencing—across an organization.

uniform resource locator (URL)   The set of letters that identifies the address of a specific resource on the Web.

unstructured data   Data that do not reside in a traditional relational database.

unsupervised learning   A type of machine learning that looks for previously undetected patterns in a dataset with no pre-existing labels and with a minimum of human supervision.

upper CASE tools   Tools that are used to automate the early stages of the SDLC (systems investigation, analysis, and design).

user experience or customer experience The way people interact with a system or application.

utility computing   A technology whereby a service provider makes computing resources and infrastructure management available to a customer as needed.

V

value chain   A sequence of activities through which the organization's inputs, whatever they are, are transformed into more valuable outputs, whatever they are.

value chain model   Model that shows the primary activities that sequentially add value to the profit margin; also shows the support activities.

value system   A stream of activities that includes the producers, suppliers, distributors, and buyers, all of whom have their own value chains.

vendor-managed inventory (VMI)   An inventory strategy where the supplier monitors a vendor's inventory for a product or group of products and replenishes products when needed.

vertical cloud   A set of cloud computing services optimized for use in a particular industry.

vertical integration   Strategy of integrating the upstream part of the supply chain with the internal part, typically by purchasing upstream suppliers, so as to ensure timely availability of supplies.

videoconference   A virtual meeting in which participants in one location can see and hear participants at other locations and can share data and graphics by electronic means.

virtual collaboration   The use of digital technologies that enable organizations or individuals to collaboratively plan, design, develop, manage, and research products, services, and innovative information systems and electronic commerce applications.

virtual group (team)   A workgroup whose members are in different locations and who meet electronically.

virtual (or pure play) organizations   Organizations in which the product, the process, and the delivery agent are all digital.

virtual private network (VPN)   A private network that uses a public network (usually the Internet) to securely connect users by using encryption.

virtual reality (VR)   A term that describes a realistic, three-dimensional, computer generated environment that replicates sight, touch, hearing, and in some cases, smell.

virtual universities   Online universities in which students take classes on the Internet at home or at an offsite location.

virus   Malicious software that can attach itself to (or "infect") other computer programs without the owner of the program being aware of the infection.

voice portal   A website with an audio interface.

vulnerability   The possibility that an information resource will be harmed by a threat.

W

weak AI   (also called **narrow AI**) Performs a useful and specific function that once required human intelligence to perform and does so at human levels or better.

wearable computer   A miniature computer worn by a person allowing the users to multitask.

Web 2.0   Websites that emphasize user-generated content, ease of use, participatory culture, and compatibility with other products, systems, and devices for end users.

Web services   Applications delivered over the Internet that IT developers can select and combine through almost any device, from personal computers to mobile phones.

website   Collectively, all the Web pages of a particular company or individual.

whitelisting   A process in which a company identifies acceptable software and permits it to run, and either prevents anything else from running or lets new software run in a quarantine environment until the company can verify its validity.

wide area network (WAN)   A network, generally provided by common carriers, that covers a wide geographical area.

wiki   A website on which anyone can post material and make changes to other material.

wireless access point   An antenna connecting a mobile device to a wired local area network.

Wireless Fidelity (Wi-Fi)   A set of standards for wireless local area networks based on the IEEE 802.11 standard.

wireless local area network (WLAN)   A computer network in a limited geographical area that uses wireless transmission for communication.

wireless media   See **broadcast media**.

wireless sensor   An autonomous device that monitors its own condition as well as physical and environmental conditions around it, such as temperature, sound, pressure, vibration, and movement.

wireless   Telecommunications in which electromagnetic waves carry the signal between communicating devices.

wireline media   See **cable media**.

workflow   The movement of information as it flows through the sequence of steps that make up an organization's work procedures.

World Wide Web (the Web or www)   A system of universally accepted standards for storing, retrieving, formatting, and displaying information through a client/server architecture; it uses the transport functions of the Internet.

worm   Destructive programs that replicate themselves without requiring another program to provide a safe environment for replication.